The **Rough Guide** to

Kenya

written and researched by

Richard Trillo

with additional research by

Daniel Jacobs and Nana Luckham

and an additional contribution by

Doug Paterson

NEW YORK · LONDON · DELHI

www.roughguides.com

Contents

Crafts and shopping
insert following p.128

Traditional dress
insert following p.512

◄◄ Giraffes, Maasai Mara ◄ Elephants, Tsavo National Park

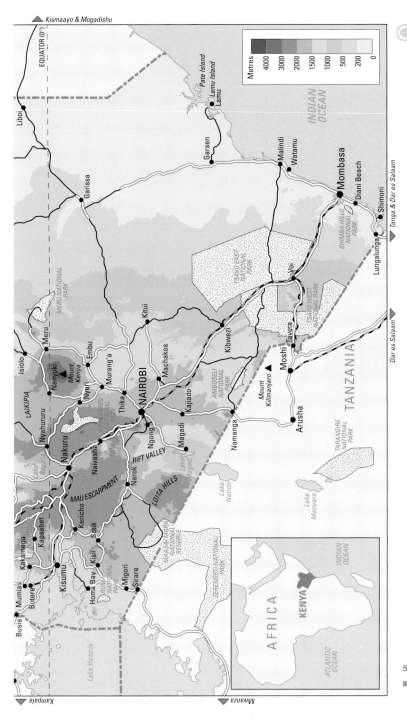

Introduction to
Kenya

Stretched across the equator, with the peaks of Mount Kenya – the second highest mountain in Africa – rising out of a natural environment of exceptional beauty, Kenya is a hugely rewarding place to travel. The country's dramatically diverse geography has resulted in a great range of natural habitats, harbouring a stunning variety of mammals and birds, while its history of migration and conquest has brought about a complex social panorama, which includes the Swahili city-states of the coast and the nomadic pastoralists of the Rift Valley. The world-famous national parks, unselfconsciously colourful peoples and superb beaches lend the country a genuinely exotic image with magnetic appeal.

But treating Kenya as a succession of tourist sights isn't the most stimulating way of experiencing the country. Travelling with your eyes open, you can enter the very different world inhabited by most Kenyans: a ceaselessly active landscape of farm and field, of streams and bush paths, of wooden and corrugated-iron shacks, tea shops and lodging houses, of crammed buses and pick-up vans, of overloaded bicycles, and of streets wandered by goats, chickens and toddlers. Off the more heavily trodden tourist routes, you'll find real warmth, openness and curiosity towards visitors. And out in the wilds, there is an abundance of superb scenery – vistas of rolling savanna dotted with Maasai and their herds, high Kikuyu moorlands, dense forests

▲ A matatu, or minibus taxi, in downtown Nairobi

bursting with bird song and insect noise, and stony, shimmering desert – all of which comes crisply into focus when experienced in the context of an economically beleaguered African nation riven by deep social tensions.

Where to go

The **coast** and major **game parks** are the most obvious targets, and if you come to Kenya on an inclusive tour you're likely to have your time divided between these two attractions. Despite the impact of human population pressures, the country's **wildlife spectacle** remains a fascinating and addictive experience. Kenya's million-odd annual visitors are easily absorbed in such a large country, and there's nothing to prevent you escaping the predictable tourist bottlenecks: even on an organized tour, you should not feel constrained to follow the prescribed plan.

The vast majority of the population live in the rugged **highland areas** in the **southwest** quarter of the country, where the ridges are a mix of *shamba* smallholdings and plantations. Through the heart of these highlands sprawls the **Great Rift Valley**, an archetypal East African scene of dry, thorn tree savanna, splashed with lakes and studded by volcanoes. It's great walking country, as are the high forests and moors of the **Central Highlands** and **Mount Kenya** itself – a major target and a feasible climb for

7

Fact file

• With an **area** of 582,000 square kilometres, Kenya is about two and a half times the size of Britain and nearly one and a half times the size of California. The **population**, which for many years had a growth rate higher than that of any other country, has now started to stabilize at a little over 30 million.

• Kenya regained **independence** in 1963 after nearly eighty years of British occupation and colonial rule. The republic is a multiparty democracy, but the opposition is hamstrung by internal divisions and by the ruling party's ruthless hunger for power.

• Kenya has a huge **debt burden**, currently (2006) running at more than $7billion, or roughly $240 for every man, woman and child. Every month, Kenya spends as much on servicing this debt as it does on health care for the whole year.

• With no oil or natural gas and few mineral resources, most of the foreign currency Kenya needs for vital imports is earned from coffee and tea exports, and tourism. Most Kenyans scrape a living by subsistence **agriculture**.

• Kenyan society consists of a huge, impoverished underclass, a small but growing middle class and a tiny, rich elite whose success often owes much to nepotism and graft. **Corruption** still percolates every corner of the country, especially in business dealings, despite the promises of the Kibaki government to clean up public life, and some reform of the police and civil service.

most people. **Nairobi**, the capital, on the highlands' southern edge, is generally used only as a gateway to Kenya, but has plenty of diversions to occupy your time while arranging an onward trip. The **national parks and reserves**, watered by seasonal streams, are mostly located in savanna country on the highland fringes.

Further west, towards **Lake Victoria**, lies gentler countryside, where you can travel for days without seeing another foreign visitor and get perhaps the best immersion in Kenyan life and culture. Beyond the rolling tea plantations of Kericho and the hot plains around the port of Kisumu lies the steep volcanic massif of **Mount Elgon**, astride the Ugandan border. The little-known **Kakamega Forest** rainforest reserve, with its unique wildlife, is here too, and more than enough reason to strike out west.

In the north, the land is **desert** or semi-desert, broken only by the highlight of **Lake Turkana** in the northwest, almost unnaturally blue and gigantic in the wilderness. Although northeast Kenya, towards the Somalian border, is currently unsafe for travellers, the routes up to Turkana are still open, and you can even get there by public transport. For serious adventure, it is one of the most spectacular and memorable of all African regions.

Separating Kenya's interior – or "upcountry" – from the Indian Ocean, the arid Maungu Plains form a barrier which accounts in

large part for the separate history and culture of the **coast**. Here, a distinct Islamic **Swahili** civilization exists with a long historical record in its mosques and tombs and the ruins of several ancient towns cut from the jungle, while along the length of the coast, beyond the white sandy beaches – invariably shaded by coconut palms or casuarina trees – runs an almost continuous coral reef, protecting a shallow, safe lagoon from the Indian Ocean.

When to go

Kenya has complicated and rather unpredictable **climatic shifts**. Broadly, the pattern is that January to March is hot and dry, while from April to June it is hot and wet, a period known as the "long rains". From July until October the weather is very warm and dry, and then come the "short rains", making November and December warm and wet. At high altitudes, however, it may rain at almost any time. Western Kenya has a scattered rainfall pattern influenced by Lake Victoria, while the eastern half of the country, and especially the coast itself, are largely controlled by the Indian Ocean's monsoon winds – the dry northeast monsoon

"Kenya" or "Keenya"?

Although you'll hear "Kenya" most of the time, the second pronunciation is still used, and not exclusively by the old settler set. The colonial pronunciation was closer to the original name of Mount Kenya, Kirinyaga. This was abbreviated to "Ki-nya", spelt Kenya, which came to be pronounced with a short "e", and when Jomo Kenyatta became president after independence, the pure coincidence of his surname was exploited.

Kenya's peoples

Certain language groups remain easily identifiable through dress and lifestyle, although urban growth and intermarriage are blurring distinctions. The brilliantly beaded and closely related Maasai and Samburu peoples are associated with the parks named after them, but they herd their animals across vast reaches of savanna and, when access to water demands it, even into the big towns. Many Turkana and members of some of the other remote northern groups also retain their traditional garb and rather tooled-up appearance, with spears much in evidence.

Kenya's biggest language groups, namely the Kikuyu in the highlands, the Akamba east of Nairobi, and the Luo in the west, have had a largely Westernized orientation for three generations, and their economic, if not political, influence is notable. There's more on language and ethnicity on p.85; for more on traditional dress, see the second colour insert.

▼ Kisumu, Western Kenya

(*kaskazi*) blowing from December to March and the moist southeast monsoon (*kusi*) from April to November, which normally brings the heaviest rain in May. **Temperatures** are determined largely by altitude: you can reckon on a drop of 6°C (or 11°F) for every 1000m you climb from sea level. Nairobi, for example, (at 1600m, higher than the Cairngorms or the Appalachians) has a moderate climate, and can get down to 5°C (41°F) at night.

The main **tourist seasons** tie in with the rainfall patterns: the biggest influxes are in December and January and, to a lesser extent, July and August. **Dry-season** travel has a number of advantages, not least of which is the greater visibility of wildlife as animals are concentrated along the diminishing watercourses. July

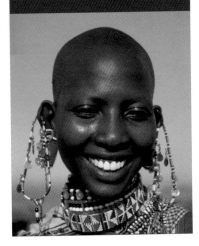

Kenya's climate

		Jan	Feb	Mar	Apr	May	June	July	Aug	Sept	Oct	Nov	Dec
Nairobi (Alt 1661m/5449ft)													
Av day temp	(°C)	25	26	25	24	22	21	21	21	24	24	23	23
	(°F)	77	79	77	75	72	70	70	70	75	75	73	73
Av night temp	(°C)	12	13	14	14	13	12	11	11	11	13	13	13
	(°F)	54	55	57	57	55	54	52	52	52	55	55	55
Rainfall	(mm)	38	64	125	211	158	46	15	23	31	53	109	86
	(in)	1.5	2.5	4.9	8.3	6.2	1.8	0.6	0.9	1.2	2.1	4.3	3.4
Days with rainfall		5	6	11	16	17	9	6	7	6	8	15	11
Mombasa (sea level)													
Av day temp	(°C)	31	31	31	30	28	28	27	27	28	29	29	30
	(°F)	88	88	88	86	82	82	81	81	82	84	84	86
Av night temp	(°C)	24	24	25	24	24	23	22	22	22	23	24	24
	(°F)	75	75	77	75	75	73	72	72	72	73	75	75
Rainfall	(mm)	25	18	64	196	320	119	89	66	63	86	97	61
	(in)	1	0.7	2.5	7.7	12.6	4.7	3.5	2.6	2.5	3.4	3.8	2.4
Days with rainfall		6	3	7	15	20	15	14	16	14	10	10	9
Kisumu (Alt 1135m/3724ft)													
Av day temp	(°C)	29	29	28	28	27	27	27	27	28	29	29	29
	(°F)	84	84	82	82	81	81	81	81	82	84	84	84
Av night temp	(°C)	18	19	19	18	18	17	17	17	17	18	18	18
	(°F)	64	66	66	64	64	63	63	63	63	64	64	64
Rainfall	(mm)	48	81	140	191	155	84	58	76	64	56	86	102
	(in)	1.9	3.2	5.5	7.5	6.1	3.3	2.3	3	2.5	2.2	3.4	4
Days with rainfall		6	8	12	14	14	9	8	10	8	7	9	8

and August are probably the best months, overall, for **game-viewing**. October to January are the months with the clearest seas for **snorkelling** and **diving** – especially November. In the long rains, the mountain parks are sometimes closed, as the muddy tracks are undriveable. But the **rainy seasons** shouldn't deter travel unduly: the rains usually come only in short afternoon or evening cloudbursts, and the landscape is strikingly green and fresh even if the skies may be cloudy. There are bonuses, too, in the lack of tourists: hotel and other prices are reduced and people generally have more time for you.

23

things not to miss

It's not possible to see everything Kenya has to offer in one trip – and we don't suggest you try. What follows is a taste of the country's highlights, ranging from remarkable events to compelling sights and activities. They're all arranged in five colour-coded categories, to help you find the very best things to see, do and experience. All highlights have a page reference to take you straight into the guide, where you can find out more.

01 Climbing Mount Kenya Page **180** • Africa's second highest peak, glacier-topped Mount Kenya is an extinct volcano straddling the equator. You can hike the lower slopes at will, but if you attempt the 5200-metre summit you need to go slowly enough to acclimatize to the altitude.

02 Turkana overland safaris
Page **558** • Remote Turkana is most easily visited on a camping safari from Nairobi, involving days of bumping through arid wilderness; encounters with local people, wildlife and swollen rivers are all on the cards.

04 Rhino sanctuaries Page **215**
• Kenya has several of these, such as the Solio Game Ranch, close to the Aberdares, which offers the chance to see both black and white rhino.

06 Balloon safaris Page **407** •
Not a real safari, these are an unforgettable experience, almost worth every cent of the US$400 or so you'll pay to be aloft over the plains at dawn (that's around five bucks a minute).

03 Kakamega Forest
Page **339** • An isolated patch of the equatorial forest that once girdled the breadth of Africa, Kakamega is a haven for hundreds of species that exist nowhere else in Kenya.

05 Eco lodges Page **228** •
Kenya boasts some superb, if pricey, accommodation in pristine parks and reserves, such as at Shompole Conservancy.

07 Cave of skulls Page **368**
• The Taita keep the exhumed skulls of their deceased in concealed rock niches – an example of traditional religious practice that is becoming increasingly rare.

08 Dhow trips Page **543** • Play Sinbad the sailor for a day on a tranquil dhow cruise around Lamu.

11 Birdwatching Page **637** • Kenya's diversity of habitats explains its extraordinary 1070 species of birds, including this Von der Decken's hornbill. Even the uninitiated are soon converted, so take a pair of binoculars.

13 Diving and snorkelling Page **75** • Kenya's coral reef has superb underwater opportunities, with diving schools in all the main centres, and snorkelling equipment widely available to rent for a couple of hours. Wasini, Watamu and Kiwaiyu are outstanding sites.

09 The tea country Page **314** • Kericho, Kenya's tea capital and the most important centre for the bush in the whole of Africa, is surrounded by an endless rolling sea of brilliant green plantations.

10 Lamu Page **528** • Lamu is a welcoming island getaway with no shortage of things to do. It also has some of Africa's best preserved ancient town architecture, many of the houses dating back hundreds of years.

12 Crafts See *Crafts and shopping colour section* • Wooden carvings are the stock-in-trade of Kenya's curio-sellers, but there's a huge range of other crafts to be tempted by, from gorgeous cloth wrap garments to musical instruments.

14 Maasai Mara wildebeest migration Page **406** • Observing the cacophonous herds from the banks of the flood-swollen Mara River – especially at one of the deadly, crocodile-infested crossing points – is one of nature's most awe-inspiring experiences. The migration takes place between July and October.

15 Nyama choma Page **65** • Kenya's most popular big meal out is *nyama choma* or roast meat – goat, mutton or beef – and lots of beer. Nyama choma bars are to be found throughout the country.

17 The David Sheldrick Trust Page **161** • This superb Nairobi sanctuary plays an instrumental role in the rehabilitation of orphaned young elephants and rhino.

16 Live music Page **145** • Any weekend it's easy to find live music in the towns. Nairobi is the biggest focus, with dozens of clubs and bands, but wherever you are, taxi drivers or hotel staff can help point you in the right direction.

18 **Bush walks** Page **402** • Immerse yourself in the bush experience by getting out there on foot; bush walks are on offer at game lodges in and around a number of parks and reserves, such as the Maasai Mara.

20 **Gedi ruins** Page **501** • Eerily atmospheric ruins of a Swahili town abandoned in the seventeenth century – take time to wander the jungle-shaded lanes away from the main site.

22 **Mzima Springs** Page **377** • A remarkable oasis in Tsavo West National Park, bubbling with crystal-clear water and inhabited by hippos, crocodiles and a diversity of smaller species.

19 **Fort Jesus, Mombasa** Page **437** • The site of gruesome battles between Portuguese and Arab colonizers and local people; today, the fort's spacious leafy interior houses an excellent historical museum.

21 **Tiwi Beach** Page **473** • Simply one of the nicest beaches in Kenya, easily accessed from Mombasa, and less crowded than Diani Beach, further south.

23 **Maulidi** Page **530** • The annual Muslim celebrations to mark the Prophet's birthday are an important event on the coast, best witnessed in Lamu.

The mammals of East Africa

This field guide provides a quick reference to help you identify the larger mammals likely to be encountered in East Africa, together with their Swahili names. Straightforward photos show easily identified markings and features. The notes give you clear pointers about the kinds of habitat in which you are most likely to see each mammal; its daily rhythm (usually either nocturnal or diurnal); the kind of social groups it usually forms; and general tips about sighting it on safari, its rarity and its relations with humans. For further details and background, see p.625.

For further details and background, see p.625.

✸ HABITAT   ◑ DAILY RHYTHM   ⚲ SOCIAL LIFE   ✓ SIGHTING TIPS

Yellow Baboon
Papio cynocephalus (Nyani)

 open country with trees and cliffs; adaptable, but always near water

🌓 diurnal

troops led by a dominant male

✓ common throughout East Africa; two species, *P. cynocephalus* (illustrated) and *P. anubis* (Olive); both species adapt quickly to humans, are frequently a nuisance and occasionally dangerous

Black-and-White Colobus Monkey
Colobus guereza (Mbega)

🌼 thick forest, both in highlands and along water courses in otherwise arid savanna; almost entirely arboreal

🌓 diurnal

small troops

✓ two species of black and whites, *C. angolensis* on the Indian Ocean coast and in northern Tanzania, and the much larger *C. guereza*, in up-country Kenya; troops maintain a limited home territory, so easily located, but can be hard to see at a great height

Red Colobus Monkey
Procolobus badius (Kima punju)

🌼 thick forest, both in highlands and along water courses in otherwise arid savanna; almost entirely arboreal

🌓 diurnal

troops of several dozen individuals

✓ limited distribution and highly endangered; most common in Jozani Forest on Zanzibar (*P. b. kirkii*), Tanzania's Udzungwa Mountains (*P. b. gordonorum*) and the Tana River Primate National Park in Kenya (*P. b. tephrosceles*)

Patas Monkey
Erythrocebus patas (Ngedere)

🌼 savanna and forest margins; tolerates some aridity; terrestrial except for sleeping and lookouts

🌓 diurnal

small troops

✓ endangered and infrequently seen; can run at high speed and stand on hind feet supported by tail

🌼 HABITAT   🌓 DAILY RHYTHM   SOCIAL LIFE   ✓ SIGHTING TIPS

Vervet Monkey

Cercopithecus aethiops or C. pygerythrus (Tumbili)

🌸 most habitats except rainforest and arid lands; arboreal and terrestrial

🌓 diurnal

💭 troops

✓ widespread and common; occasionally a nuisance where used to humans (will steal food and anything else to hand)

Blue or Sykes' Monkey

Cercopithecus mitis (Nyabu)

🌸 forests; arboreal and occasionally terrestrial

🌓 diurnal

💭 families or small troops

✓ widespread; shyer and less easily habituated to humans than the Vervet; can be a pest for farmers

Lesser Bushbaby or Galago

Galago senegalensis (Komba)

🌸 woodland; arboreal

🌓 nocturnal

💭 solitary or in small family groups

✓ unfazed by humans, these small foragers often frequent lodge restaurants; call is a distinctive wail like a baby's; huge eyes, inquisitive fingers, fondness for bananas

Aardvark

Orycteropus afer (Mhanga)

🌸 open or wooded termite country; softer soil preferred

🌓 nocturnal

💭 solitary

✓ rarely seen animal, the size of a small pig; old burrows are common and often used by warthogs

🌸 HABITAT   🌓 DAILY RHYTHM   💭 SOCIAL LIFE   ✓ SIGHTING TIPS

Pangolin or Scaly Anteater
Manis temminckii (Kakakuona)

 termite savanna and woodland; terrestrial

nocturnal

solitary or in pairs; baby carried on mother's back

✓ armoured ant and termite eater resembling an armadillo; when frightened, they secrete a smelly liquid from anal glands and roll into a ball with their scales erect (*pangolin* is Malay for "rolling over")

Spring Hare or Cape Jumping Hare
Pedetes capensis (Kamendegere)

savanna; softer soil areas preferred

nocturnal

burrows, usually with a pair and their young; often linked into a network, almost like a colony

✓ fairly widespread rabbit-sized rodent; impressive and unmistakable kangaroo-like leaper

Crested Porcupine
Hystrix cristata (Nungu or Nungunungu)

adaptable to a wide range of habitats, often in caves

nocturnal and sometimes active at dusk

family groups

✓ large rodent (up to 90cm in length), rarely seen, but common away from croplands, where it's hunted as a pest, or for its quills

Bat-eared Fox or Cape Fox
Otocyon megalotis (Mbweha masikio)

open country

mainly nocturnal; diurnal activity increases in cooler months

monogamous pairs

✓ distribution coincides with termites, their favoured diet; they spend many hours foraging using sensitive hearing to pinpoint their underground prey

HABITAT   DAILY RHYTHM   SOCIAL LIFE   ✓ SIGHTING TIPS

Black-backed Jackal

Canis mesomeles (Bweha)

🌺 broad range from moist mountain regions to desert, but drier areas preferred

◑ normally nocturnal, but diurnal in the safety of game reserves

🔲 mostly monogamous pairs; sometimes family groups

✓ a common, bold scavenger the size of a mid-sized dog that steals even from lions; three species in East Africa: black-backed with a "saddle" (illustrated); the shy side-striped (*C. adustus*); and golden (*C. aureus*) – the commonest species in Tanzania, restricted in Kenya to the Rift Valley and Laikipia

African Hunting Dog or Wild Dog

Lycaon pictus (Mbwa mwitu)

🌺 open savanna in the vicinity of grazing herds

◑ diurnal

🔲 nomadic packs

✓ extremely rare and rarely seen, but widely noted when in the area; the size of a large dog, with distinctively rounded ears and blotchy orange and brown fur

Honey Badger or Ratel

Mellivora capensis (Nyegere)

🌺 very broad range of habitats

◑ mainly nocturnal

🔲 usually solitary, but also found in pairs

✓ widespread, omnivorous, badger-sized animal; nowhere common; extremely aggressive

African Civet

Civettictis civetta (Fungo)

🌺 prefers woodland and dense vegetation

◑ mainly nocturnal

🔲 solitary

✓ omnivorous, medium-dog-sized, short-legged prowler; not to be confused with the smaller genet

---

🌺 HABITAT   ◑ DAILY RHYTHM   🔲 SOCIAL LIFE   ✓ SIGHTING TIPS

Genet
Genetta genetta (Kanu)

🌸 light bush country, even arid areas; partly arboreal

◐ nocturnal, but becomes active at dusk

🔲 solitary

✓ quite common, slender, cat-sized omnivore, often seen at game lodges, where it easily becomes habituated to humans

Banded Mongoose
Mungos mungo (Nguchiro)

🌸 thick bush and dry forest

◐ diurnal

🔲 lives in burrow colonies of up to thirty animals

✓ widespread and quite common, the size of a small cat; often seen in a group, hurriedly foraging through the undergrowth. The main East African species are the banded (illustrated); dwarf (*Helogale parvula*); and black-tipped or slender (*Galerella sanguinea*)

Spotted Hyena
Crocuta crocuta (Fisi madoa)

🌸 tolerates a wide variety of habitat, with the exception of dense forest

◐ nocturnal but also active at dusk; also diurnal in many parks

🔲 highly social, usually living in extended family groups

✓ the size of a large dog with a distinctive loping gait, quite common in parks, especially early in the morning; carnivorous scavenger and cooperative hunter; dangerous; not to be confused with the shy, solitary and rarely seen striped hyena (*Hyaena hyaena*; Fisi miraba)

Caracal
Caracal caracal (Simba mangu)

🌸 open bush and plains; occasionally arboreal

◐ mostly nocturnal

🔲 solitary

✓ lynx-like wild cat; rather uncommon and rarely seen

🌸 HABITAT ◐ DAILY RHYTHM 🔲 SOCIAL LIFE ✓ SIGHTING TIPS

Cheetah
Acinonyx jubatus (Duma)

🐾 savanna, in the vicinity of plains grazers

🌓 diurnal

💭 solitary or temporary nuclear family groups

✓ widespread but low population; much slighter build than the leopard, and distinguished from it by a small head, square snout and dark "tear mark" running from eye to jowl

Leopard
Panthera pardus (Chui)

🐾 highly adaptable; frequently arboreal

🌓 nocturnal; also cooler daylight hours

💭 solitary

✓ the size of a very large dog; not uncommon, but shy and infrequently seen; rests in thick undergrowth or up trees; very dangerous

Lion
Panthera leo (Simba)

🐾 all habitats except desert and thick forest

🌓 nocturnal and diurnal

💭 prides of three to forty; more usually six to twelve

✓ commonly seen resting in shade; dangerous

Serval
Felis serval (Mondo)

🐾 reed beds or tall grassland near water

🌓 normally nocturnal but more diurnal than most cats

💭 usually solitary

✓ some resemblance to the cheetah but far smaller; most likely to be seen on roadsides or at water margins at dawn or dusk

🐾 HABITAT   🌓 DAILY RHYTHM   💭 SOCIAL LIFE   ✓ SIGHTING TIPS   23

Rock Hyrax
Procavia capensis (Pimbi or Wibari)

🐾 rocky areas, from mountains to isolated outcrops

◐ diurnal

👁 colonies consisting of a territorial male with as many as thirty related females

✓ rabbit-sized; very common; often seen sunning themselves in the early morning on rocks

---

African Elephant
Loxodonta africana (Tembo or Ndovu)

🐾 wide range of habitats, wherever there are trees and water

◐ nocturnal and diurnal; sleeps as little as four hours a day

👁 almost human in its complexity; cows and offspring in herds headed by a matriarch; bulls solitary or in bachelor herds

✓ look out for fresh dung (football-sized) and recently damaged trees; frequently seen at waterholes from late afternoon; dangerous

---

Black Rhinoceros
Diceros bicornis (Faru/Kifaru)

🐾 usually thick bush, altitudes up to 3500m

◐ active day and night, resting between periods of activity

👁 solitary

✓ extremely rare and in critical danger of extinction; largely confined to parks and heavily protected wildlife reserves; distinctive hooked lip for browsing; bad eyesight; very dangerous

---

White Rhinoceros
Ceratotherium simum (Faru/Kifaru)

🐾 savanna

◐ active day and night, resting between periods of activity

👁 males solitary, otherwise small same-sex herd or nursery group

✓ Not found in Tanzania; confined to protected reserves; distinctive wide mouth (hence "white" from Afrikaans *wijd*) for grazing; docile

🐾 HABITAT   ◐ DAILY RHYTHM   👁 SOCIAL LIFE   ✓ SIGHTING TIPS

Burchell's Zebra

Equus burchelli (Punda milia)

🌸 savanna, with or without trees, up to 4500m

🌑 active day and night, resting intermittently

💭 harems of several mares and foals led by a dominant stallion are usually grouped together, in herds of up to several thousand

✓ widespread and common inside and outside the parks

Grevy's Zebra

Equus grevyi (Punda milia)

🌸 arid regions

🌑 largely diurnal

💭 mares with foals and stallions generally keep to separate troops; stallions sometimes solitary and territorial

✓ easily distinguished from smaller Burchell's Zebra by narrow stripes and very large ears; rare and localized but easily seen; not found in Tanzania

Bush Pig

Potamochoerus porcus (Nguruwe mwitu)

🌸 forest and dense thickets close to water

🌑 nocturnal

💭 groups (sounders) of up to twenty animals

✓ resembles a long-haired domestic pig with tasselled hair on its ears and white-crested back

Warthog

Phacochoerus aethiopicus (Ngiri or Gwasi)

🌸 savanna, up to an altitude of over 2000m

🌑 diurnal

💭 family groups, usually of a female and her litter

✓ common; boars are distinguishable from sows by their prominent facial "warts"

Hippopotamus

Hippopotamus amphibius (Kiboko)

✿ slow-flowing rivers, dams and lakes

◖ principally nocturnal, leaving the water to graze

♡ bulls are solitary, but other animals live in family groups headed by a matriarch

✓ usually seen by day in water, with top of head and ears breaking the surface; frequently aggressive and very dangerous when threatened or when retreat to water is blocked

Giraffe

Giraffa camelopardalis (Twiga)

✿ wooded savanna and thorn country

◖ diurnal

♡ loose, non-territorial, leaderless herds

✓ common; many subspecies, of which Maasai (*G. c. tippelskirchi*, left), Reticulated (*G. c. reticulata*, bottom l.) and Rothschild's (*G. c. rothschildi*, below) are East African

African or Cape Buffalo

Syncerus caffer (Nyati or Mbogo)

✿ wide range of habitats, always near water, up to altitudes of 4000m

◖ nocturnal and diurnal, but inactive during the heat of the day

♡ gregarious, with cows and calves in huge herds; young bulls often form small bachelor herds; old bulls are usually solitary

✓ very common; scent much more acute than other senses; very dangerous, old bulls especially so

Red Hartebeest
Alcelaphus buselaphus (Kongoni)

🏵 wide range of grassy habitats

◖ diurnal

♀ females and calves in small, wandering herds; territorial males solitary

✓ hard to confuse with any other antelope except the topi; many varieties, distinguishable by horn shape; most common is the Red or Cape (illustrated); others include Coke's (*A. cokei*), Lichtenstein's (*A. lichtensteinii*), and Jackson's (*A. jacksoni*), found only in Kenya

Topi or Sassaby
Damaliscus lunatus (Nyamera)

🏵 grasslands, showing a marked preference for moist savanna, near water

◖ diurnal

♀ females and young form herds with an old male

✓ widespread, very fast runners; male often stands sentry on an abandoned termite hill, actually marking the territory against rivals, rather than defending against predators

Blue Wildebeest or Brindled Gnu
Connochaetes taurinus (Nyumbu)

🏵 grasslands

◖ diurnal, occasionally also nocturnal

♀ intensely gregarious; wide variety of associations within mega-herds which may number over one million animals

✓ unmistakable, nomadic grazer; long tail, mane and beard

Gerenuk
Litocranius walleri (Swala twiga)

🏵 arid thorn country and semi-desert

◖ diurnal

♀ solitary or in small, territorial harems

✓ not uncommon; unmistakable, its name is Somali for "giraffe-necked"; often browses standing upright on hind legs; the female is hornless

🏵 HABITAT   ◖ DAILY RHYTHM   ♀ SOCIAL LIFE   ✓ SIGHTING TIPS

Grant's Gazelle
Gazella granti (Swala granti)

✿ wide grassy plains with good visibility, sometimes far from water

◗ diurnal

▽ small, territorial harems

✓ larger than the similar Thomson's Gazelle, distinguished from it by the white rump patch which extends onto the back; the female has smaller horns than the male

Thomson's Gazelle
Gazella thomsoni (Swala tomi)

✿ flat, short-grass savanna, near water

◗ diurnal

▽ gregarious, in a wide variety of social structures, often massing in the hundreds with other grazing species

✓ smaller than the similar Grant's Gazelle, distinguished from it by the black band on flank; the female has tiny horns

Impala
Aepyceros melampus (Swala pala)

✿ open savanna near light woodland cover

◗ diurnal

▽ large herds of females overlap with several male territories; males highly territorial during the rut when they separate out breeding harems of up to twenty females

✓ common, medium-sized, no close relatives; distinctive high leaps when fleeing; the only antelope with a black tuft above the hooves; males have long, lyre-shaped horns

Common (or Southern) Reedbuck
Redunca arundinum (Tohe)

✿ reedbeds and tall grass near water

◗ nocturnal and diurnal

▽ monogamous pairs or family groups in territory defended by the male

✓ medium-sized antelope, with a plant diet unpalatable to other herbivores; only males have horns

Common Waterbuck
Kobus ellipsiprymnus (Kuro)

🌸 open woodland and savanna, near water

🌓 nocturnal and diurnal

🛡 territorial herds of females and young, led by dominant male, or territorial males visited by wandering female herds

✓ common, rather tame, large antelope; plant diet unpalatable to other herbivores; shaggy coat; only males have horns

Kirk's Dikdik
Madoqua kirkii (Digidigi or Dika)

🌸 scrub and thornbush, often far from water

🌓 nocturnal and diurnal, most active morning and evening

🛡 monogamous pairs for life, often accompanied by current and previous young

✓ tiny, hare-sized antelope, named after its alarm cry; males are horned, females slightly larger; found next to or in bushes, and almost always in pairs; territory marked by piles of droppings and black secretions deposited on grass stems

Common Duiker
Sylvicapra grimmia (Nysa)

🌸 adaptable; prefers dense scrub and woodland, some subspecies prefer mountainous forests

🌓 nocturnal and diurnal

🛡 most commonly solitary; sometimes in pairs; occasionally monogamous

✓ widespread and common small antelope with a rounded back, up to 70cm tall; seen close to cover; rams have short straight horns.

Suni *Neotragus moschatus* (Suni)

🌸 forest, or dense, dry bush

🌓 nocturnal and crepuscular

🛡 monogamous pairs, sometimes with additional non-breeding females

✓ even smaller than dikdiks, no higher than 32cm; extremely isolated populations scattered throughout East Africa including Zanzibar, particularly forested coastal hills; hide in shade by day; freeze when threatened before darting into undergrowth

🌸 HABITAT 🌓 DAILY RHYTHM 🛡 SOCIAL LIFE ✓ SIGHTING TIPS

Sitatunga

Tragelaphus spekei (Nzohe)

🌸 swamps

◑ nocturnal and sometimes diurnal

🔲 territorial and mostly solitary or in pairs

✓ very localized and not likely to be mistaken for anything else; usually seen half submerged; females have no horns

Bushbuck

Tragelaphus scriptus (Kulungu or Mbawala)

🌸 thick bush and woodland close to water

◑ principally nocturnal, but also active during the day when cool

🔲 solitary, but casually sociable; sometimes grazes in small groups

✓ medium-sized antelope with white stripes and spots; often seen in thickets, or heard crashing through them; the male has shortish straight, spiralled horns

Eland

Taurotragus oryx (Mpofu or Mbungu)

🌸 highly adaptable; semi-desert to mountains, but prefers scrubby plains

◑ nocturnal and diurnal

🔲 non-territorial herds of up to sixty with temporary gatherings of as many as a thousand

✓ common but shy; the largest and most powerful African antelope; both sexes have straight horns with a slight spiral

Greater Kudu

Tragelaphus strepsiceros (Tandala mkubwa)

🌸 semi-arid, hilly or undulating bush country; tolerant of drought

◑ diurnal when secure; otherwise nocturnal

🔲 territorial; males usually solitary; females in small troops with young

✓ impressively big antelope (up to 1.5m at shoulder) with very long, spiral horns in the male; very localized; shy of humans and not often seen

🌸 HABITAT   ◑ DAILY RHYTHM   🔲 SOCIAL LIFE   ✓ SIGHTING TIPS

Lesser Kudu

Tragelaphus imberbis (Tandala mdogo)

🏵 semi-arid, hilly or undulating bush country; tolerant of drought

🌓 diurnal when secure; otherwise nocturnal

🛡 territorial; males usually solitary; females in small troops with young

✓ smaller than the Greater Kudu; only the male has horns; extremely shy and usually seen only as it disappears

Fringe-eared Oryx

Oryx gazella callotis (Choroa)

🏵 open grasslands; also waterless wastelands; tolerant of prolonged drought

🌓 nocturnal and diurnal

🛡 highly hierarchical mixed herds of up to fifteen, led by a dominant bull

✓ the *callotis* subspecies is one of two found in East Africa, the other, in northeastern Kenya, being the Beisa Oryx (*Oryx g. beisa*)

Sable Antelope

Hippotragus niger (Palahala)

🏵 open woodland with medium to tall grassland near water

🌓 nocturnal and diurnal

🛡 territorial; bulls divide into sub-territories, through which cows and young roam; herds of immature males; sometimes pairs in season

✓ large antelope; upper body dark brown to black; mask-like markings on the face; both sexes have huge curved horns

Roan Antelope

Hippotragus equinus (Kirongo)

🏵 tall grassland near water

🌓 nocturnal and diurnal; peak afternoon feeding

🛡 small herds led by a dominant bull; herds of immature males; sometimes pairs in season

✓ large antelope, distinguished from the Sable by lighter, greyish colour, shorter horns (both sexes) and narrow, tufted ears

🏵 HABITAT   🌓 DAILY RHYTHM   🛡 SOCIAL LIFE   ✓ SIGHTING TIPS   31

Steinbok
Raphicerus campestris (Dondoo or Dondoro)

❀ dry savanna

◐ nocturnal and diurnal

♈ solitary or (less often) in pairs

✓ widespread small antelope, surprisingly aggressive towards attackers but shy with humans; males have horns

Grysbok
Raphicerus melanotis sharpei (Dondoo or Dondoro)

❀ thicket adjacent to open grassland

◐ nocturnal

♈ rams territorial; loose pairings

✓ small, rarely seen antelope; the East African subspecies is Sharpe's (illustrated); distinguished from more slender Steinbok by light underparts; rams have short horns

Oribi
Ourebia ourebia (Kasia)

❀ open grassland

◐ diurnal

♈ territorial harems consisting of male and one to four females

✓ localized small antelope, but not hard to see where common; only males have horns; the Oribi is distinguished from the smaller Grysbok and Steinbok by a black tail and dark skin patch below the eye

Klipspringer
Oreotragus oreotragus (Mbuzi mawe)

❀ rocky country; cliffs and *kopjes*

◐ diurnal

♈ territorial ram with mate or small family group; often restricted to small long-term territories

✓ small antelope; horns normally only on male; extremely agile on rocky terrain; unusually high hooves, giving the impression of walking on tiptoe

❀ HABITAT   ◐ DAILY RHYTHM   ♈ SOCIAL LIFE   ✓ SIGHTING TIPS

Basics

Basics

Getting there

Flying is really the only practicable way of getting to Kenya, apart from taking overland routes – currently only really feasible from southern Africa. Flights to Kenya are generally most expensive from late June to mid-August, and from mid-December to mid-January.

Round-trip tickets are generally of three types – short excursions (usually up to one month), three-month excursions and one year. The cheaper tickets generally have fixed dates that you won't be able to change without paying a penalty fee.

Charter flights from Britain or Europe are often cheaper than scheduled flights, but there's usually a maximum stay of four or six weeks. The fare will depend on the number of days you stay, and you won't be able to change your dates.

Some airlines grant various **restricted eligibility fares** which students and under-26s can take advantage of. The advantage of some of these fares may lie more in the length of stay they offer and an easing of booking regulations than in the price.

If you want to see Kenya as part of a much longer journey, consider a **round-the-world (RTW) ticket** (Nairobi is on several RTW itineraries). You set a date for the first outbound flight in advance, and then reserve the others (the ticket entitles you to touch down in around half a dozen cities) as you go, completing the entire journey within either six months or a year. Figure on £1200–1700/$2200–3000 for a RTW ticket including Kenya.

Book as far **in advance** as you can if you want to travel in high season (airlines can be full at peak periods, especially Christmas), and to get the cheapest scheduled tickets before they sell out. On the other hand, if you find early on that flights seem to be "full", check the same outlets again nearer your departure date – assuming you haven't got something by then – for reservations not taken up.

An inclusive **package holiday** to Kenya can make a lot of sense as some, based around mid-range coast hotels, are inexpensive, and if you choose carefully, you shouldn't feel too packaged. Packages – comprising a flight and two weeks' half board (dinner and bed and breakfast) in a beach hotel can cost as little as £550 from the UK, or $2200 from the US. Beach hotels vary greatly in price, atmosphere and amenities, so choose carefully, though note that you aren't obliged to stay at your hotel all the time – you can simply use it as a base to make independent trips around the country.

A **safari** component in a package tour will knock up the price to around £1000 or $3000. While you'll pay more at home for a safari package than in Kenya, the convenience of booking in your home country is well worth it on a short trip. If booking in Kenya, see pp.148–152 for safaris from Nairobi, p.446 from Mombasa, and the section on pp.81–82. If you're looking for a package, see p.36 or p.42. Even on a tour devoted to safari activities, you may well have the option of a hotel-based beach holiday extension.

Many airlines offer the opportunity to book flights **on line**, cutting costs associated with middlemen and agents. An Internet search will also turn up good deals on Kenya flights and packages from a large number of discount travel websites.

From Britain and Ireland

London Heathrow is the only British airport with **direct flights** to **Nairobi**, operated by both Kenya Airways and British Airways, taking around nine hours. **Fares** start at around £550 return in low season, £800 in high season. It may well be cheaper to take an **indirect flight**, changing planes in the airline's hub city in Europe, Africa or the Middle East.

There are also several **charter operators** with whom you can get seats to Mombasa, out of London or Manchester, from around

£500. These normally come with accommodation, which at the budget end doesn't affect the price much, but you can also get "seat only" deals. The main operators are Somak and Thomson (see opposite for contact details).

Flying from Ireland, your easiest bet is to take Aer Lingus to Heathrow, connecting there for a British Airways or Kenya Airways flight, though you can also fly via Europe or Africa. A return flight will cost between €650 and €900, depending on the season.

Airlines

African Safari Airways UK ☎ 0845/345 0014, ⓦ www.africansafariclub.com. Flights from London Gatwick and other European airports to Mombasa, mostly filled by package tourists though a few standby seats are available.
Air Mauritius UK ☎ 020/7434 4375–7, ⓦ www .airmauritius.com. Heathrow to Nairobi en route to Mauritius, a couple of times a week.
British Airways UK ☎ 0870/850 9850, Ireland ☎ 1890/626 747, ⓦ www.ba.com. London Heathrow direct to Nairobi, with connecting flights from most UK airports, and connecting Aer Lingus flights from Ireland.
Condor ⓦ www.condor.com. Flights from Frankfurt to Mombasa, which can be booked through offices of the German airline Lufthansa.
Egyptair UK ☎ 020/7734 2395, ⓦ www.egyptair .com.eg. Heathrow to Nairobi via Cairo.
Emirates UK ☎ 0870/243 2222, ⓦ www.emirates .com. London, Birmingham, Glasgow and Manchester to Nairobi via Dubai.
Ethiopian Airlines UK ☎ 020/8987 7000, ⓦ www .flyethiopian.com. London to Nairobi via Addis Ababa.
Kenya Airways UK ☎ 01784/888222, ⓦ www .kenya-airways.com. London Heathrow direct to Nairobi.
KLM UK ☎ 0870/507 4074, Ireland ☎ 1850/747 400, ⓦ www.klmuk.com. From London and Dublin, plus a large number of UK regional airports, to Nairobi via Amsterdam.
Lufthansa UK ☎ 0870/837 7747, Ireland ☎ 01/844 5544, ⓦ www.lufthansa.com. London, Dublin, Birmingham, Edinburgh and Manchester to Nairobi, via Frankfurt.
Qatar Airways UK ☎ 020/7896 3636, ⓦ www .qatarairways.com. London and Manchester to Nairobi via Doha.
Saudia UK ☎ 020/7798 9898, ⓦ www .saudiairlines.com. Heathrow to Nairobi via Jeddah.
SN Brussels Airlines UK ☎ 0870/735 2345, ⓦ www.flysn.com. London, Bristol, Glasgow and Manchester to Nairobi via Brussels.

Swiss UK ☎ 1890/200 515, ⓦ www.swiss.com. London, Dublin, Birmingham and Manchester to Nairobi via Zürich.

Discount agents in Britain and Ireland

Africa Travel Centre UK ☎ 0845/450 1541, ⓦ www.africatravel.co.uk. Helpful and resourceful.
Co-op Travel Care UK ☎ 0870/112 0085, ⓦ www .travelcare.com. Scheduled flights to Nairobi, or packages based on charter flights to Mombasa.
Flight Centre UK ☎ 0870/499 0040, ⓦ www .flightcentre.co.uk. Flights and safari packages.
Flights4Less UK ☎ 0871/222 3432, ⓦ www .flights4less.co.uk. Good price deals on scheduled flights to Nairobi and Mombasa.
Joe Walsh Tours Ireland ☎ 01/241 0800, ⓦ www .joewalshtours.ie. Budget fares from Ireland to Kenya.
North South Travel UK ☎ 01245/608291, ⓦ www .northsouthtravel.co.uk. Discounted fares, with profits used to support projects in the developing world.
Soliman Travel UK ☎ 020/7244 6855, ⓦ www .solimantravel.co.uk. Deals on flights to Kenya with British Airways or Egyptair.
STA Travel UK ☎ 0870/160 0599, ⓦ www .statravel.co.uk. Specialists in low-cost flights and tours for students and under-26s, though other customers are welcome.
Trailfinders UK ☎ 0845/058 5858, ⓦ www .trailfinders.com, Ireland ☎ 01/677 7888, ⓦ www .trailfinders.ie. One of the best-informed and most efficient agents for independent travellers, with cheap flights to Kenya, and some package deals.
Travel Bag UK ☎ 0800/082 5000, ⓦ www .travelbag.co.uk. Discount flight deals.
USIT Ireland ☎ 01/602 1904, Northern Ireland ☎ 028/9032 7111, ⓦ www.usit.ie. Student and youth specialists, offering cheap flights, and Nairobi city breaks.
World Express Travel UK ☎ 020/7434 1654, Ⓔ worldexpresstvl@btconnect.com. Consolidators for Kenya Airways, SN Brussels and Ethiopian Airlines.
World Travel Centre Ireland ☎ 01/416 7007, ⓦ www.worldtravel.ie. Cheap flight deals from Ireland to Kenya.

UK specialist tour operators and agents

Abercrombie and Kent ☎ 0845/070 0611, ⓦ www.abercrombiekent.com. Upmarket long-haul specialists, offering safaris, beach holidays, even camel treks, with a wide knowledge of Kenya, where the company originated.
Africa Archipelago ☎ 020/7471 8780, ⓦ www .africaarchipelago.com. Packages and tailor-made tours featuring safaris, beach holidays, and small lodges off the beaten track.

Exodus ☎0870/240 5550, ⓦwww.exodus.co.uk.
Long-established outfit, with an interesting selection
of Kenya tours, including six days learning bush
survival skills, a thirteen-day camel trek in the northern
desert, safaris in Kenya alone or in combination with
neighbouring countries.

Explore Worldwide ☎0870/333 4001, ⓦwww
.explore.co.uk. Highly respected small-groups
operator that runs a small selection of two-week
Kenya or Kenya-with-Tanzania safaris, including one
with some photographic tuition thrown in.

Footloose Adventure Travel ☎01943/604030,
ⓦwww.footlooseadventure.co.uk. Enthusiastic
independent outfit offering a selection of treks and
safaris; they'll tailor-make a safari to fit your budget
and interests, offer advice on overland travel and track
down good-value flights.

Gane & Marshall ☎020/8441 9592 ⓦwww
.ganeandmarshall.co.uk. African tourism specialists,
with responsible travel credentials and a good Kenya
programme.

Guerba Expeditions ☎01373/826611, ⓦwww
.guerba.co.uk. The acknowledged African experts,
running a string of Kenya trips, including an eight-day
camping safari, or a more expensive eight-day lodge
safari, plus longer East African trips.

Hayes & Jarvis ☎0870/366 1636, ⓦwww
.hayes-jarvis.com. Long-established, experienced
operator, originally from Kenya, offering a range of
beach holidays and luxury safaris.

The Imaginative Traveller ☎0800/316 2717,
ⓦwww.imaginative-traveller.com. Offers an eight-
day camping safari to Mount Kenya, Samburu, Lake
Nakuru and Maasai Mara, plus packages combining
Kenya with neighbouring countries.

IntoAfrica ☎0114/255 5610, ⓦwww.intoafrica
.co.uk. Eco-minded firm whose safaris, treks and
cultural trips aim to give a genuine insight into the
country while having "minimum impact" on its people
and environment.

Kuoni ☎01306/747731, ⓦwww.kuoni.co.uk.
Long-haul holiday operator with a flexible approach
and lots of experience. Good choice of safaris and
coastal destinations.

Responsible Travel ⓦwww.responsibletravel
.com. Online travel agent, marketing pre-screened
holidays from over 270 companies that aim to benefit
the environment and local people.

Safari Consultants ☎01787/228494,
ⓦwww.safari-consultants.co.uk. Tailor-made
itineraries including less usual destinations and
arrangements.

Somak Holidays ☎020/8423 3000, ⓦwww
.somak.co.uk. Well-established company offering a
wide selection of safaris, including tailor-mades, and
charter flights. Recommended.

Steppes Travel ☎01285/650011, ⓦwww
.steppestravel.co.uk. Innovative travel stylists with a
personal approach, specializing in tailor-made trips,
based in luxury lodges and hotels at safari parks, or
by the Indian Ocean, Lake Naivasha or Lake Victoria.

The Ultimate Travel Company ☎020/7386
4646, ⓦwww.theultimatetravelcompany.com.
Tailor-made trips with unusual emphases, including
"homestead" safaris, staying on private estates as the
guests of experienced guides and wildlife experts.

Thomson ☎0870/160 7430, ⓦwww.thomson
-holidays.com. Large, mass-market tour firm with
an assortment of beach and safari options in their
Faraway Shores and *Worldwide* brochures. Also runs
charter flights from London to Mombasa.

Wildlife Worldwide ☎020/8667 9158, ⓦwww
.wildlifeworldwide.com. Packages and tailor-made
trips for wildlife and wilderness enthusiasts, offering a
"big cat weekend", and migration specials at Maasai
Mara, a Rift Valley special based at Mara and Lake
Naivasha, and the option of an Amboseli add-on.

Flights from the USA and Canada

There are no direct flights from the USA or
Canada to East Africa. The fastest routes
to Nairobi are usually **via London**, either on
British Airways or a combination of Virgin
Atlantic and Kenya Airways. Air Canada can
also connect in London for an onward BA
flight to Nairobi. Another good option is **via
Amsterdam** with KLM.

Fares from the US extend upwards from
$1100 for a two-week round trip out of New
York in low season, $1850 in high season,
or out of Los Angeles, from $1250 or $2250
respectively. From **Canada**, Toronto–Nairobi
fares start at around Can$1630 in low
season, Can$3150 in summer and at Christ-
mas. Note that package prices you see
advertised tend to exclude the cost of the
flight to Kenya.

Airlines

British Airways ☎1-800/AIRWAYS, ⓦwww
.ba.com. From several US and Canadian airports to
Nairobi via London.

EgyptAir US ☎1-800/334 6787 or 212/315 0900,
Canada ☎416/960 0009, ⓦwww.egyptair.com.eg.
New York to Nairobi via Cairo.

Emirates ☎1-800/777 3999, ⓦwww.emirates
.com. New York and Houston to Nairobi via Dubai.

Ethiopian Airlines ☎1-800/445 2733, ⓦwww
.flyethiopian.com. Washington DC to Nairobi via Addis

Ababa (but requiring an overnight stay at Addis on the way out).

KLM/Northwest ☎1-800/4474747 ⓦwww.klm .com. From several US and Canadian cities to Nairobi via Amsterdam, sometimes in conjunction with Kenya Airways.

Saudia ☎1-800/4-SAUDIA, ⓦwww.saudiairlines .com. New York and Washington DC to Nairobi via Jeddah.

SN Brussels Airlines US ☎516/622 2248, Canada ☎1-866/308 2230, ⓦwww.flysn.com. Chicago and Toronto to Nairobi via Brussels.

Swiss ☎1-877/FLY-SWISS, ⓦwww.swiss.com. Boston, Chicago, Los Angeles, Miami, Montreal and New York to Nairobi, via Zürich.

Virgin Atlantic ☎1-800/862 8621, ⓦwww .virgin-atlantic.com. Through tickets from several US cities to Nairobi via London, in conjunction with Kenya Airways.

Discount agents

Air Brokers International ☎1-800/883 3273, ⓦwww.airbrokers.com. Consolidator and RTW specialist.

Airtech ☎212/219 7000, ⓦwww.airtech.com. Standby seat broker; also deals in consolidator fares.

Airtreks ☎1-877/AIRTREKS, ⓦwww.airtreks.com. Specialist in RTW tickets.

Educational Travel Center ☎1-800/747 5551 or 608/256 5551, ⓦwww.edtrav.com. Student/youth discount agent.

Flight Centre US ☎1-866/WORLD-51 ⓦwww .flightcentre.us, Canada ☎1-877/WORLD-02, ⓦwww.flightcentre.ca. Low airfares to Kenya.

Flytime ☎212/760 3737, ⓦwww.flytimetravel .com. Discounted fares on Emirates, KLM and Northwest.

STA Travel US ☎1-800/781 4040, ⓦwww.sta -travel.com, Canada ☎1-888/427 5639, ⓦwww .sta-travel.ca. Independent travel specialists, geared up to students and under-26s, though not exclusively.

TFI Tours ☎1-800/7458000 or 212/7361140, ⓦwww.lowestairprice.com. Well-established consolidator.

Travel Cuts US ☎1-800/592-CUTS, Canada ☎1-888/246 9762, ⓦwww.travelcuts.com. Popular, well-established student travel organization.

Travelosophy ☎1-800/332 2687, ⓦwww .itravelosophy.com. Discounted and student fares.

Specialist operators and agents

US

Abercrombie & Kent ☎1-800/554 7016, ⓦwww .abercrombiekent.com. Upscale operator with over

thirty years of experience organizing African safaris, with options in Kenya alone, or Kenya and Tanzania combined.

Absolute Africa ☎1-800/736 8187, ⓦwww .absoluteafrica.net. A nice handful of safari packages, including a ten-day Safari and Sand tour that ends up in Lamu, and the option of a three-day Lake Victoria extension.

Africa Tours ☎1-800/235 3692 or 631/264 2800, ⓦwww.africasafaris.com. A choice of two off-the-peg safaris in Kenya, or one in Kenya and Tanzania, or a customized safari, with the option of a three-day beach holiday extension.

African Adventure Company ☎1-800/8829453 or 954/4918877, ⓦwww.africa-adventure.com. One of the best agencies in the business, offering six safari options in Kenya, and another six in Kenya and Tanzania.

Eco-Adventure International ☎888-710-WILD, ⓦwww.eaiadventure.com. Small-group, eco-friendly safaris, with coast and specific park add-ons available.

David Anderson Safari Consultants ☎1-800/927 4647, ⓦwww.davidanderson.com. No expense spared here: escorted wildlife safaris and first-class accommodation.

Geographic Expeditions ☎1-800/777 8183 or 415/922 0448, ⓦwww.geoex.com. Fifteen-day off-the-shelf Kenya safaris, private deluxe safaris, and combination Kenya/Tanzania safaris.

Fly less – stay longer! Travel and climate change

Climate change is a serious threat to the ecosystems that humans rely upon, and travel and transport – after industry – is the most significant contributor to the problem. Rough Guides regard travel, overall, as a global benefit, and feel strongly that the economic advantages to developing economies are important, as is the opportunity of greater contact and awareness among peoples. But we all have a responsibility to limit our personal impact on global warming, and that means giving thought to how we travel, and how we can redress the harm caused to the environment by flights, in particular.

Flying and climate change

Pretty much every form of motorized travel generates CO_2 (the main cause of human-induced climate change) but planes are far and away the worst offenders, on average generating – per person, per mile – about 25 percent more CO_2 than cars. Furthermore, aircraft emit not only CO_2 but also oxides of nitrogen and sulphur, which compound the greenhouse effect (and also damage the ozone layer).

Fuel-cell and other less harmful types of plane may emerge eventually. But until then, there are really just two options for concerned travellers: to reduce the amount you travel by air (take fewer trips – stay for longer!), and to make your journeys "carbon neutral" via a carbon offset scheme.

Carbon offset schemes

Offset schemes allow you to make up for some or all of the greenhouse gases that you are responsible for releasing. To do this, they provide "carbon calculators" that allow you to work out the global-warming contribution of a specific flight and then let you contribute an appropriate amount of money to fund offsetting measures. These include the planting of trees to soak up CO_2 or other initiatives to reduce future energy demand, such as distributing low-energy long-life light bulbs in developing countries. Rough Guides, together with Lonely Planet and other concerned partners in the travel industry, are supporting a **carbon offset scheme** run by climatecare.org.

Please take the time to view the climate change section of our website, where you can enter details of your intended trip, and see how you can help make your travel carbon neutral.

www.roughguides.com/climatechange **www.climatecare.org**

Also check out TIST (The International Small Group Tree-Planting Programme; Ⓦ www.tist.org) whose Kenyan project has seen nearly 400,000 trees planted and greenhouse gas credits – a virtual cash crop – channelled into local hands.

Holbrook Travel ☏ 1-800/451 7111, Ⓦ www .holbrooktravel.com. Top-quality natural history tours and safaris led by experts, and an Elderhostel programme in Kenya for older travellers.
Journeys International ☏ 1-800/255 8735 or 734/665 4407, Ⓦ www.journeys-intl.com. Prestigious, award-winning operator focusing on ecotourism and small-group trips, including an eight- or a sixteen-day safari trip in Kenya.
Ker & Downey ☏ 1-800/423 4236 or 281/371 2500, Ⓦ www.kerdowney.com. Renowned upmarket safaris with an "Edwardian feel", including Kenya under canvas, and one that bills itself as "Kenya off the beaten path", though the reference is to the accommodation rather than the places visited.
Micato Safaris ☏ 212/545 7111, Ⓦ www.micato.com. Very highly regarded and

long-established tour operator with a variety of Kenya offerings.
Mountain Travel Sobek ☏ 1-888/MTSOBAK or 510/594 6000, Ⓦ www.mtsobek.com. Walking safaris, hiking and trekking, even a camel trek.
Nature Expeditions International ☏ 1-800/869 0639 or 954/693 8852, Ⓦ www.naturexp.com. A twelve-day educational tour with optional lectures on wildlife, natural history and culture, or a fifteen-day Kenya and Tanzania tour, both with the option of beach holiday extensions.
Somak Safaris ☏ 1-800/757 6625, Ⓦ www .somaksafaris.com. A wide range of safaris to Kenya and all of Africa with frequent cost-cutting special promotions, and low-priced flight-only deals.
Tamsin & Cooke ☏ 828/697 0588, Ⓦ www.tamsinandcooke.com. Customized

itineraries based on thirty years' residence in Africa, with emphasis on luxury, away-from-it-all accommodation, as well as mobile and walking safaris.

Wilderness Travel ☎1-800/368 2794, @www .wildernesstravel.com. Small-group expeditions to the great game parks.

Canada

Adventure Center ☎1-800/2288747 or 403/439 9118, @www.adventure-center.com. Hiking and "soft adventure" specialists, with a very wide range of tours covering Kenya alone, or in combination with other countries.

Trek Holidays ☎1-800/661 7265, @www .trekholidays.com. Agents for a number of safari holidays run by Imaginative Traveller (see p.37) and Peregrine (see opposite), as well as two or three safari deals of their own.

Worldwide Quest Adventures ☎1-800/387 1483, @www.worldwidequest.com. Natural history safaris combining Kenya with Tanzania.

From Australia and New Zealand

There are no direct flights to Kenya from Australia or New Zealand – all require a

change of plane in southern Africa, the Indian Ocean, Asia or the Middle East. Flying via Europe is also possible in theory, but it's a very long way round, and will cost rather more.

From Australia, South African Airways (SAA) has some good connections to Nairobi, via Johannesburg, while Emirates also offer good connections and fares. **From New Zealand**, Emirates via Dubai is your most obvious bet, but Air New Zealand and Qantas can get you to Kenya in combination with other airlines, such as SAA from Johannesburg.

Except for the Christmas period, when you will probably have to pay around Aus\$200/ NZ\$200 more, **fares** to Kenya are not generally seasonal. The lowest-priced return tickets bought from a discount agent or direct from the airline cost around Aus\$1850–3000 including tax from Australia, NZ\$2750–3200 from New Zealand.

Airlines

Air Mauritius Australia ☎02/9262 2477, @www .airmauritius.com. Perth to Nairobi via Mauritius. Also connections from Melbourne and Sydney, requiring you to overnight before catching your Kenya flight.

Air New Zealand New Zealand ☎0800/737 000, @www.airnewzealand.co.nz. To Nairobi from most NZ airports in conjunction with another carrier.

Emirates Australia ☎02/9290 9700, New Zealand ☎09/968 2200, @www.emirates.com. Sydney, Melbourne, Perth and Auckland to Nairobi via Dubai.

Qantas Australia ☎13/1313, New Zealand ☎0800/808 767 or 09/357 8900, @www.qantas .com. To Nairobi from most Australian and New Zealand airports in conjunction with another carrier.

South African Airways Australia ☎1800/221 699, New Zealand ☎09/977 2237, @www.flysaa .com. From Sydney, Melbourne and Perth to Nairobi and Mombasa. Connections are complex though – you may need to overnight or even fly via Hong Kong.

Travel agents

Flight Centre Australia ☎13 31 33, @www .flightcentre.com.au, New Zealand ☎0800/243 544, @www.flightcentre.co.nz. Some of the best Nairobi fare deals.

Holiday Shoppe New Zealand ☎0800/808 480, @www.holidayshoppe.co.nz. Good prices on flights.

OTC Australia ☎1300/855 118, @www.onlinetravel .com.au. Reasonably priced flights to Kenya.

STA Travel Australia ☎1300/733 035, ⓦwww
.statravel.com.au, New Zealand ☎0508/782 872,
ⓦwww.statravel.co.nz. Specialists in low-cost
flights, overland and holiday deals. Good discounts for
students and under-26s.
Trailfinders Australia ☎1300/780 212, ⓦwww
.trailfinders.com.au. One of the best-informed agents
for independent travellers.

Tour operators and agents

Many of these firms are representatives not
only for Australian and New Zealand companies but also for adventure travel operators
whose head offices are in Britain (see p.42).
Note that the package prices they quote
tend to exclude Kenya flights.
Abercrombie & Kent Australia ☎1300/851 800,
New Zealand ☎0800/441 638, ⓦwww
.abercrombiekent.com.au. Classy operator with a
strong reputation, offering a ten-day air safari (using
flights to get around) with an optional three-day
beach extension, or a twelve-day safari in Kenya and
Tanzania.
Adventure Travel New Zealand ☎03/364
3400, ⓦwww.adventuretravel.co.nz. Agents for a
number of package holiday and overland adventure
companies, including Peregrine.
Adventure World Australia ☎02/8913 0755,
ⓦwww.adventureworld.com.au, New Zealand
☎09/524 5118, ⓦwww.adventureworld.co.nz.
A varied selection of tours, from city mini-stays in
Nairobi and on the coast to safaris at the Maasai
Mara, Amboseli, Samburu and elsewhere.
African Wildlife Safaris Australia
☎1300/363 302 or 03/9696 2899, ⓦwww
.africanwildlifesafaris.com.au. Upmarket camping
and lodge-based safaris.
Africa Travel Centre Australia ☎02/9327 0671,
ⓦwww.africatravelcentre.com.au. Agents for a
number of overland operators.
Classic Safari Company Australia
☎1300/130 218 or 02/9327 0666, ⓦwww
.classicsafaricompany.com.au. Deluxe safaris
including a nine-day jaunt around Samburu, Laikipia,
Lake Nakuru and Maasai Mara.
Peregrine Australia ☎03/9663 8611, ⓦwww
.peregrine.net.au. A number of safari options in
Kenya alone, or in combination with Uganda and/or
Tanzania. Their budget brand, Gecko's (ⓦwww
.geckosadventures.com), also offers a variety of
adventure tours.

Flights from South Africa

There are daily **direct flights** to Nairobi from
Johannesburg on South African Airways

(☎0861/359722, ⓦwww.flysaa.com) and
Kenya Airways (☎011/8819795, ⓦwww
.kenya-airways.com). Fares start at around
R4000 for a fixed-date one-month trip
booked at least five days in advance; open
yearly returns go from around R7400.

Tour operators and travel agents

African Safari Shop ☎011/8886364, ⓦwww
.safarishop.co.za. A range of options for many
budgets.
Free Spirit Adventures ☎011/6622057, ⓦwww
.freespiritadventures.co.za. Exclusive package tours.
STA Travel ☎0861/781781, ⓦwww.statravel
.co.za. Good youth and student fares.
Wild Frontiers ☎011/7022035, ⓦwww
.wildfrontiers.com. An excellent range of mid-priced
tours to Amboseli, Maasai Mara, Mombasa, Lamu and
other popular Kenyan destinations.

Overlanding to Kenya

With unlimited time and a sense of adventure, **travelling overland** can be an exciting and rewarding way of getting to Kenya.
However, conflicts have effectively closed
routes from West Africa for the time being,
and while it is possible to get to Kenya from
Egypt – taking a boat from Aswan to Wadi
Halfa in Sudan, crossing into Ethiopia at
Humera or Metema, and entering Kenya at
Moyale, this route is not an easy one. With
the settlement in southern Sudan, it may
soon be possible to travel via Juba, entering
Kenya at Lokichokio.

Currently the only advisable route is from
southern Africa. From **Harare**, you can take
the train through Zambia and Tanzania, go
overland by local transport, or hook up with
any number of foreign-operated overland
trips from Harare, Cape Town or Johannesburg to Nairobi, most of which are very good
value for money and take a month or two for
the trip.

Most of the following operators offer five- to
eight-week Nairobi–Cape Town runs, which
are usually possible in the other direction too,
and most also offer shorter trips covering
Kenya and either Uganda, Tanzania or both
(game parks in Kenya and gorillas in Uganda
is a favourite). Most of these companies are
based in the UK, but wherever they're based,
firms often sell their trips internationally (see
their websites for their agents).

Most overland operators run occasional slide and video sessions, when you can decide if a packaged adventure is for you. Otherwise, scrutinizing their literature gives an indication of their preparedness and know-how; if the blurb looks cheap or hasty, you should probably give them a wide berth.

Overland operators

Absolute Africa UK ☎020/8742 0226, ⓦwww .absoluteafrica.com. A variety of overland trips in Kenya and neighbouring countries, including Nairobi–Cape Town journeys taking six to eleven weeks.
African Routes South Africa ☎031/563 5080, ⓦwww.africanroutes.co.za. Overland operator and agent for northbound trips from South Africa.
African Trails UK ☎0870/777 6344, ⓦwww .africantrails.co.uk. Various trips from eight days in Kenya, or two weeks in Kenya and Tanzania to a ten-week Nairobi–Cape Town trip.
Bukima UK ☎0870/757 2230, ⓦwww.bukima .com. Long-established overlanders, pricier than most.

Dragoman UK ☎01728/86113, ⓦwww .dragoman.com. Personal and creative with notably good trucks and competitive prices. Trips covering Kenya range from fourteen days in Kenya and Uganda to a forty-week combination overlander all the way from Hong Kong to Cape Town.
Drifters South Africa ☎011/8881160, ⓦwww .drifters.com. Fortnightly overland departures from Cape Town to Nairobi (thirty days on the road), or a twelve-day overland safari just in Kenya.
Exodus UK ☎0870/240 5550, ⓦwww.exodus .co.uk. Besides a wide range of Kenya tours, they also offer an eleven-week Nairobi–Cape Town overlander.
Kumuka Expeditions UK ☎0800/389 2328, ⓦwww.kumuka.com. An assortment of trips including Kenya and other countries in East and southern Africa, from eighteen days in Kenya and Uganda for around £750 to a nine-week Nairobi–Cape Town overlander for around £2350.
Phoenix Expeditions UK ☎01509/881818, ⓦwww.phoenixexpeditions.co.uk. Well-equipped outfit offering three weeks in Kenya, Uganda and Tanzania, or eight- to eleven-week trips from Kenya to the Cape.

Visas and red tape

Nationals of the UK, USA, Canada, Australia, New Zealand, South Africa, all EU countries and Japan need visas to visit Kenya. Requirements change however, and you should always check in advance with a Kenyan embassy, consulate or high commission to confirm the current situation. Check also that your passport will remain valid for at least six months beyond the end of your projected stay in Kenya, and ensure it has plenty of spare pages for stamps if you're travelling further afield in Africa.

Visas and visitor's passes

Visas can be obtained in advance from any Kenyan embassy, consulate or high commission (see the "Missions" section of ⓦwww.statehousekenya.go.ke for a full list). Applications normally take two to four working days to process, and require one or two passport-size photos. You may be asked to produce an **air ticket** out of the region

(not just to Uganda or Tanzania) or proof of sufficient funds for your trip, but this is less common these days. A single-entry tourist visa costs £30/$50 and is valid for three months, and allows re-entry to Kenya after a visit to Uganda or Tanzania. Multiple-entry visas cost roughly £60/$100. Seven-day transit visas are also available for about half the price of a single-entry tourist visa. Remember that Kenyan diplomatic missions are closed on Kenyan public holidays (see p.71 for a list of holidays). Visas are normally valid for entry within three months of the date of issue.

If you only need a single-entry tourist or transit visa, you can **buy it on arrival** in Kenya at the airport. This costs the same as getting a visa in advance, and the fee is payable in dollars or, usually, in major hard currencies such as sterling or euros (cash only).

If you have got a visa in advance, upon your arrival in Kenya your passport will be stamped with a **visitor's pass** usually allowing for a stay equal to that specified on your visa. However, various factors may influence the length of time actually granted, including your stated address or itinerary, your appearance, how much money you have and how long a stay you ask for.

A single-entry visa allows **re-entry** to Kenya after visits to Uganda or Tanzania. For other trips outside Kenya, unless you have a multiple-entry visa, you'll need to reapply for a visa to get back in, or else obtain a re-entry permit from an immigration office (see below).

Kenyan embassies, consulates and high commissions

Australia 33–35 Ainslie Ave, Canberra ☎02/6247 4788, ✉kenrep@dynamite.com.au.
Canada 415 Laurier Ave East, Ottawa, Ontario K1N 6R4 ☎613/563 1773, ⊛www .kenyahighcommission.ca.
Ethiopia Hiher 16, Kebele 01, Fikre Mariam Rd; PO Box 3301 Addis Ababa ☎01/610303, ✉kenya .embassy@telecom.net.et.
Ireland Contact Kenyan representation in the UK.
New Zealand Contact Kenyan representation in Australia.
South Africa 302 Brooks St, Menlo Park, Pretoria 0081 ☎012/3622249, ✉kenp@pta.lia.net.
Sudan Street 3, Amarat; PO Box 8242 Khartoum ☎011/40386.
Tanzania Plot #14, Ursino Kawawa Rd; PO Box 5231 Dar es Salaam ☎022/2701747–9, ✉khc@raha.com.

Uganda Plot #41, Nakasero Rd; PO Box 5220 Kampala ☎041/258235.
UK 45 Portland Place, London W1N 4AS ☎020/7636 2371, ⊛www.kenyahighcommission. com.
USA 2249 R St NW, Washington, DC 20008 ☎202/387 6101, ⊛www.kenyaembassy.com; Park Mile Plaza, Mezzanine Floor, 4801 Wilshire Boulevard, Los Angeles, CA 90010 ☎323/939 2408, ✉losangeles@kenyaembassy.com.

Extending your stay

If you intend to stay beyond the validity period of your visa, it's important to **renew** the visa well in advance of the expiry date. You can only renew your pass for a further three months (giving a six-month maximum stay in all), after which you'll have to leave East Africa.

Confusion over expiry dates can arise if, for example, you can't decipher KVP5W/H ("Kenya Visitor's Pass 5-Week Holiday") – if in doubt, ask. There have been a number of cases of travellers overstaying their visa validity period by a few days and finding themselves invited to spend the night behind bars while a suitable fine was discussed.

Visa renewals can be done at the **immigration offices** in Nairobi, Mombasa, Malindi or Kisumu. Addresses for these are given in the relevant "Listings" sections in the guide.

Customs

The **duty-free allowance** on entering Kenya is one bottle of spirits or wine, and one carton of 200 cigarettes or 50 cigars or 225g of tobacco. If you're stopped at Customs, you will normally be asked if you have any photographic equipment, camcorders, audio players and so on. Unless you're a professional with mountains of specialist gear, there shouldn't be any question of paying duty on personal equipment, though some customs officers like to make notes of it in your passport to ensure it is re-exported. If you have friends in Kenya, however, and are taking presents for them, you are likely to have to pay duty if you declare the items.

Information and maps

The Kenya Tourist Board (KTB; ⓦ www.magicalkenya.com) no longer runs walk-in offices abroad, but has franchised its operations to local PR companies, who can answer queries, and will send information packs out on request. The best map available of the country is the Rough Guide Map: Kenya & Northern Tanzania (1:950,000) printed on rip-proof, waterproof plastic paper, which should work well alongside this guide. The Survey of Kenya (PO Box 30046; their Public Map Office in Nairobi is on the Thika road – see map, pp.106–107) and Macmillan have published a number of maps of parks and reserves – helpful for getting around but variable in quality and mostly out of date. For details of Kenya Wildlife Service park maps, see p.77.

KTB representatives abroad

Canada Discover the World, ☏ 1-866/891 3909, Ⓔ contact@kenyatourism.ca.
France Interface Tourism, ☏ 01/5325 1207, Ⓔ kenya@interfacetourism.com.
Germany Travel Marketing Romberg, ☏ 02104/832 919, Ⓔ kenia@travelmarketing.de.
Italy Adam & Partner Italia, ☏ 02/4810 2361, Ⓔ kenya@adams.it.
Netherlands TMC, ☏ 020/421 2668, Ⓔ kenia@travelmc.com.
Spain CS Développement, ☏ 93/292 0655, Ⓕ 93/415 4577, Ⓔ kenya@ketal.com.
UK Hills Balfour, ☏ 020/7202 6384, Ⓔ kenya@hillsbalfour.com.
USA Carlson Destination Marketing Services, ☏ 1-866/44-KENYA, Ⓔ infousa@magicalkenya.com.

Useful magazines

Africa Confidential ⓦ www.africa-confidential.com. Fortnightly eight-page newsletter with solid inside info on politics and other matters. Subscription only, but you can subscribe online.
African Business ⓦ www.africasia.com/africanbusiness. Good general coverage, issued monthly, available worldwide.
BBC Focus on Africa ⓦ www.bbc.co.uk/worldservice/africa/features/focus_magazine. News, general-interest features, and information from the BBC World Service.
New African ⓦ www.africasia.com/newafrican. A monthly news and lifestyle magazine after the style of the French Jeune Afrique, with quarterly special supplements. Available internationally.
Travel Africa ⓦ www.travelafricamag.com. Excellent quarterly magazine with high-quality articles and practical information of the kind often unavailable elsewhere.

Insurance

You'd do well to take out an insurance policy prior to travelling to cover against theft, loss and illness or injury. Before paying for a new policy, however, it's worth checking that you won't duplicate the coverage of any existing plans which you may have. For example, many private medical schemes include cover when abroad.

A typical travel insurance policy usually provides cover for the loss of baggage, tickets and – up to a certain limit – cash or cheques, as well as cancellation or curtailment

Rough Guides travel insurance

Rough Guides has teamed up with Columbus Direct to offer you travel insurance that can be tailored to suit your needs. Readers can choose from many different travel insurance products, including a low-cost backpacker option for long stays; a short break option for city getaways; a typical holiday package option; and many others. There are also annual multi-trip policies for those who travel regularly, with variable levels of cover available. Different sports and activities (trekking, skiing, etc) can be covered if required on most policies.

Rough Guides travel insurance is available to the residents of 36 different countries with different language options to choose from via our website – ⓦ www .roughguidesinsurance.com – where you can also purchase the insurance. Alternatively, UK residents should call ☎ 0800 083 9507; US citizens should call ☎ 1-800 749-4922; Australians should call ☎ 1 300 669 999. All other nationalities should call ☎ +44 870 890 2843.

of your journey. Most of them exclude so-called dangerous sports unless an extra premium is paid: in Kenya these could mean scuba-diving, windsurfing and climbing, though not safaris. If you do take medical coverage, ascertain whether benefits will be paid as treatment proceeds or only after return home, and whether there is a 24-hour

medical emergency number. When securing baggage cover, make sure that the per-article limit – typically under £600/$1000 – will cover your most valuable possession. If you need to make a claim, you should keep receipts for medicines and medical treatment, and in the event you have anything stolen, you must obtain an official statement from the police.

Health

Disease is an ever-present threat to people in Kenya, most of whom have no access to clean water, and not enough money to afford a doctor if they do fall ill. Malaria is endemic to the country, as are other diseases such as bilharzia, and rates of HIV infection are high. As a visitor it's wise to take precautions – wash and dress all cuts, and avoid food that has been left lying around after cooking.

If you're going to be on the road for a long time, it may be worth considering taking some vitamin tablets with you, though these are no substitute for a balanced diet with plenty of fresh fruit and vegetables. One of the biggest hazards, though, is the fierce heat of the tropical sun.

Get a thorough **dental checkup** before leaving home. A freshly cut "toothbrush twig" (*msuake*) is a useful supplement – some varieties contain a plaque-destroying enzyme; you can buy them at markets.

Sexually transmitted diseases (STDs), including **HIV/AIDS**, are rife in Kenya. Four out of five deaths among 25- to 35-year-olds are AIDS-related. Using a condom will help to protect you from this and other sexually transmitted diseases, including **hepatitis B**, which is quite widespread in Kenya. Though rarely fatal if treated, hepatitis B can lead to chronic liver disease and is something you really want to avoid catching.

Condoms are available from town pharmacies and supermarkets, and are often dispensed free in hotels, especially cheap ones. Family planning clinics in most main towns are helpful (see Nairobi "Listings", p.153) and will sometimes provide them and – with a prescription – oral contraceptives, free or for a small charge. But it's far wiser to bring all you'll need. Be aware that oral contraceptives may be rendered ineffective if you go down with a dose of diarrhoea.

For a useful account of the health problems which travellers encounter worldwide, consult the *Rough Guide to Travel Health* by Dr Nick Jones.

Medical resources for travellers

Your doctor is your best first source of advice and probable supplier of jabs and prescriptions. For yellow fever and other exotic shots you'll normally have to visit a specialist clinic.

Websites

Ⓦ **www.cdc.gov/travel** The US government's official site for travel health, including a page of information specific to East Africa (to find it, click on "Destinations").

Ⓦ **www.fitfortravel.scot.nhs.uk** Scottish NHS website on travellers' health, with a page on travel to Kenya (click on "Africa" in the left-hand bar, then on Kenya on the map).

Ⓦ **www.tmvc.com.au** Lists information for travellers to Kenya (click on "Travel Health Advisory Reports").

Ⓦ **www.tripprep.com** Provides destination information on Kenya (you have to log in to use this), and a list of travel medicine providers in the US and elsewhere.

Britain and Ireland

British Airways Travel Clinic 213 Piccadilly, London W1J 9HQ ☏0845/600 2236. Vaccinations, tailored advice from an online database and a complete range of travel healthcare products. No appointment necessary, but get there 1hr before closing time. Mon–Fri 9.30am–5.30pm, Sat 10am–3.30pm.

Communicable Diseases Unit Brownlee Centre, Glasgow G12 0YN ☏0141/211 1074. Travel vaccinations including yellow fever.

Hospital for Tropical Diseases Travel Clinic 2nd floor, Mortimer Market Centre, off Capper St, London WC1E 6AU ☏020/7388 9600, Ⓦwww .thehtd.org. A consultation costs £15, which is waived

if you have your injections or buy your malaria pills here. Mon–Fri 9am–5pm by appointment.

Liverpool School of Tropical Medicine Pembroke Place, Liverpool L3 5QA ☏0151/708 9393, Ⓦwww.liv.ac.uk/lstm. Appointment not required for jabs other than for yellow fever. Walk-in clinic Mon–Fri 9am–noon.

MASTA (Medical Advisory Service for Travellers Abroad) ☏0870/606 2782, Ⓦwww .masta.org. Contact them for the location of their travel clinic nearest you. For a small fee they can supply a health brief tailored to the country you are visiting.

Nomad Pharmacy Ⓦwww.nomadtravel.co.uk. Locations in London, Bristol and Southampton, for travel advice (free if you go in person), vaccinations (by appointment or walk-in) and health/medical supplies for travellers.

Travel Health Centre Department of International Health and Tropical Medicine, Royal College of Surgeons in Ireland, Mercers Medical Centre, Stephen's St Lower, Dublin 2 ☏01/402 2337. Expert pre-trip advice and inoculations.

Travel Medicine Services 16 College St, Belfast BT1 6BT ☏028/9031 5220. Medical advice before a trip and help afterwards in the event of a tropical disease.

Tropical Medical Bureau Grafton Buildings, 34 Grafton St, Dublin 2 ☏1850/487 674, Ⓦwww.tmb .ie. Also more than a dozen other centres across the Republic of Ireland.

USA and Canada

Canadian Society for International Health Ⓦwww.csih.org. The website has an extensive list of travel health centres across Canada.

International Association for Medical Assistance to Travelers (IAMAT) ☏716/754 4883, Ⓦwww.iamat.org. A membership organization that can provide members with a list of approved participating doctors in Kenya who will charge a set fee for a member's first visit; also has climate charts and information on various diseases and inoculations.

International SOS Assistance ☏1-800/523 8930, Ⓦwww.intsos.com. Members receive pre-trip medical referral info, as well as emergency services including, if necessary, emergency evacuation and repatriation.

MEDJET Assistance ☏1-800/9633538 or 205/5956626, Ⓦwww.medjetassistance.com. Annual membership programme for travellers that will, in the event of illness or injury, fly members home or to the hospital of their choice in a medically equipped and staffed jet.

Australia, New Zealand and South Africa

Inoculations

For arrivals **by air** from Europe, Australia, New Zealand and North America, Kenya has no required inoculations. Entering **overland**, though, you may well be required to show an International Vaccination Certificate for **yellow fever**, and it is just possible that you may be asked for a **cholera** certificate too (Western vaccination centres will usually provide a "cholera vaccination not required" stamp in your certificate for just such an eventuality). If you intend to enter Kenya by land or to break your journey to Kenya elsewhere in Africa, plan ahead and start organizing your jabs at least six weeks before departure. Remember that a yellow fever certificate only becomes valid ten days after you've had the jab.

Tetanus and **polio** boosters are necessary and doctors usually recommend **typhoid** jabs. For **hepatitis A**, Havrix is now commonly prescribed, and needs a booster after six months to knock up your immunity to ten years. Gamma-globulin (or immunoglobulin) shots are much cheaper though only effective for a few months. To reduce the risk of contracting hepatitis, be extra careful about cleanliness and in particular about contamination of water – a problem wherever a single cistern holds the whole water supply in a cockroach-infested toilet/bathroom, as often happens in Lamu.

Malaria

Malaria is endemic in tropical Africa and has a variable **incubation period** of a few days to several weeks, meaning you can get it long after being bitten. It's caused by a parasite carried in the saliva of female Anopheles mosquitoes. Anopheles mosquitoes prefer to **bite** in the evening, and can be distinguished by their eager, head-down position as they settle to bite. Though not infectious, the disease can be very dangerous and

sometimes fatal if not treated quickly. The destruction of red blood cells by the falciparum type of malaria parasite can lead to **cerebral malaria** (blocking of the brain capillaries) and is the cause of a nasty complication called **blackwater fever** in which the urine is stained by excreted blood cells.

Though the **malaria** risk is low in Nairobi and the highlands, mosquito bites are almost a certainty and protection against the disease is essential. The best and most obvious method is to **avoid being bitten**. Keep arms, legs and feet covered as much as possible after dusk (long, light-coloured sleeves and trousers are best), and cover exposed parts with a strong repellent. **Deet** (the insecticide diethyltoluamide) is best; citronella oil is considered much less effective, and has the disadvantage that elephants are attracted to the smell, and have been known to break into cars and tents to get at it. Sleep under a **mosquito net** (if you're using your own, you might want to impregnate it with Deet) and burn **mosquito coils**, readily available in Kenya. Electronic buzzers don't work.

It's also normally considered vital to take **anti-malaria tablets**. The old anti-malaria drug combination of Nivaquin (chloroquine) and Paludrine (proguanil) is now considered next-to-useless in East Africa; the commonly recommended preventatives are Lariam (mefloquine, which has a poor record for side effects), the antibiotic doxycycline and Malarone (which, while expensive, appears to have few, if any, side effects). Your doctor will advise which pills to take and what the various side effects can be. It's important to maintain a careful routine and cover the period **before and after** your trip with doses.

Going down with malaria

If you do contract malaria, you'll soon know about it: the fever, shivering and headaches are something like severe flu and come in waves. if you suspect anything, go to a hospital or clinic immediately. If you can't get to a doctor and need a **cure**, take three Fansidar tablets (available at most pharmacies and supermarkets). It is also possible to cure malaria using mefloquine (20–25mg per kilo of body weight in one or two doses), Malarone (four tablets daily for three days), or doxycycline (200mg daily for a week – always finish the course). However, none of these drugs should be used if you are pregnant, in which case you will have to fall back on quinine – 600mg twice a day for five days. Both mefloquine and quinine are widely available in Kenya.

Water-borne diseases

Serious stomach upsets don't afflict a large proportion of travellers. That said, Kenya's once fairly safe **tap water** is increasingly unfit to drink and the supply can be particularly suspect during periods of drought or heavy flooding. Where there is no mains supply, be very cautious of rain- or well-water. To purify water intended for drinking, use purifying tablets or, better, iodine (six drops per litre of water, then wait for half an hour), or boil it (if at high altitude, for thirty minutes).

If your stay is brief, you might as well stick to **bottled water**, which is widely available. For longer stays, think of **re-educating your stomach**; it's virtually impossible to travel around the country without exposing yourself to strange bugs from time to time. Take it easy at first, don't overdo the fruit (and wash it in clean water), don't keep food too long, and be very wary of salads served in cheap restaurants. It is also wise to eat food that is freshly cooked and piping hot, rather than things that have been lying around for hours hatching germs.

Should you go down with **diarrhoea**, it will probably pass of its own accord in 24–48 hours without treatment. In the meantime, and especially with children, for whom it may be more serious, it's essential to replace the fluids and salts lost, so drink lots of water with oral rehydration salts (if you can't get them from pharmacies, use half a teaspoon of salt plus eight of sugar in a litre of water). It's a good idea to avoid greasy food, heavy spices, caffeine and most fruit and dairy products. Plain rice or *ugali* with boiled vegetables is the best diet. Drugs like Lomotil and Imodium simply plug you up – undermining the body's efforts to rid itself of infection – though they can be useful if you have to travel. Stay away from the popular Kaomycin, which isn't particularly safe to use and can even encourage diarrhoea. Avoid jumping for antibiotics at the first sign of trouble:

they annihilate what's nicely known as your "gut flora" and will not work on viruses. If you continue to feel bad, seek medical help. Also note that having diarrhoea can make oral medication less effective, as they can pass straight through your system without being absorbed – this can apply to malaria pills for example, and the contraceptive pill.

Bilharzia (medical name schistosomiasis) is a dangerous disease. It comes from tiny flukes (the schistosomes) that live in freshwater snails and which burrow into animal (or human) skin to multiply in the bloodstream. The snails only favour stagnant water and the chances of picking up bilharzia are small. The usual recommendation is never to swim in, wash with, or even touch, lake water that can't be vouched for. The stagnant and weed-infested parts of most Kenyan lakes and rivers harbour bilharzia, to some extent, but the possible danger of crocodile attack means you are unlikely to want any close contact with inland waters. If you feel major fatigue and pass blood – the first symptoms of bilharzia – see a doctor: it's curable.

Heat and altitude

It's important not to underestimate the power of the **equatorial sun**: a hat and sunglasses are strongly recommended at all times to combat the heat and bright light. The sun can quickly burn, or even cause **sunstroke**, so a high-factor sunblock is vital on exposed skin, especially when you first arrive. Be aware that overheating can cause **heatstroke**, which is potentially fatal. Signs are a very high body temperature, without a feeling of fever but accompanied by headaches and disorientation. Lowering body temperature (by taking a tepid shower for example) and resting in a cool place is the first step in treatment.

The sun's radiation is stronger at higher altitudes, but the biggest risk if you climb to over 2500m above sea level is **altitude sickness**, which may affect climbers on Mount Kenya, and even walkers in the Cherangani Hills. For further advice on altitude sickness, see p.184.

Many people get occasional **heat rashes**, especially at first on the coast. A warm shower, to open the pores, and loose cotton clothes should help, as can zinc oxide powder. **Dehydration** is another possible problem, so make sure you are drinking enough fluids (but not alcohol or caffeine), especially when hot or tired. The main danger sign is irregular urination. Dark urine definitely means you should drink more.

Cuts and bites

Take more care than usual over minor **cuts and scrapes**. In the tropics, the most trivial scratch can quickly become a throbbing infection if you ignore it. Take a small tube of antiseptic with you, or apply alcohol or iodine.

Dogs are usually sad and skulking, posing little threat, but rabies does exist in Kenya, and can be transmitted by a bite or even a lick, so it's best to avoid playing with pets unless you know the owner and are sure they are safe. **Scorpions and spiders** abound, but are hardly ever seen unless you deliberately turn over rocks or logs: scorpion stings are painful but almost never fatal, while spiders are mostly quite harmless, even the really big ones. **Snakes** are common but, again, the vast majority are harmless. To see one at all, you'd need to search stealthily; walk heavily and they obligingly disappear. For more on other, potentially dangerous, animals, see p.64.

Medical treatment in Kenya

For serious treatment there's a frightening lack of well-equipped hospitals and drugs,

and in most hospitals you're routinely expected to pay for treatment, syringes, plastic gloves, cotton wool, drugs and other medical equipment. The Consolata Sisters' hospitals – the Nazareth Hospital on Riara Ridge, outside Nairobi (⊕020/342185), and another in Nyeri (⊕061/31010) – are well run and modestly priced, as is Kijabe Hospital on the east side of the Rift Valley near Naivasha (⊕020/32046500). We've mentioned the best local hospitals throughout the text in the "Listings" sections.

Kenya's flying doctor **Air Ambulance service** (which also operates in Tanzania) offers free evacuation by air to a medical centre – very reassuring if you'll be spending time out in the wilds. Tourist membership costs $15 per person for two weeks, $25 for two months for cover up to 500km from Nairobi, $30/$50 for up to 1000km. The income goes back into the outreach programme and the African Medical Research Foundation (AMREF) behind it. You can contact AMREF in advance (Langata Rd; PO Box 27691–00506 Nairobi ⊕020/6993000, ⊛www.amref.org) or buy their insurance on arrival; they have an office at Wilson Airport, from where most of their rescue missions set out. Similar services are offered by AAR Health Services, also based in Nairobi (⊕020/271 5319, ⊛www.aarhealth.com).

Medicine bag

Various items worth taking on a trip include:

☐ **Alcohol swabs** Invaluable for cleaning minor wounds or insect bites.

☐ **Antihistamine cream** Apply immediately after insect bites to reduce itchiness.

☐ **Anti-malaria tablets** Enough for prevention, plus extra for a cure if necessary.

☐ **Antibiotics** If you are likely to be far from medical help for any length of time, your doctor should be able to prescribe you suitable antibiotics in case you need to treat a serious lower bowel crisis or dysentery.

☐ **Antiseptic cream**.

☐ **Aspirin or paracetamol** for pain or fever relief.

☐ **Iodine tincture, with dropper, or water purifying tablets** If you can't get clean water, these will do the trick.

☐ **Lens solution/eye drops** If you wear contacts, take a good supply.

☐ **Lip-salve/chapstick**

☐ **Thermometer** Get a plastic one that sticks on your forehead.

☐ **Zinc oxide powder** Useful anti-fungal powder for sweaty crevices.

Costs, money and banks

Kenya's currency, the Kenyan shilling (Ksh), is a colonial legacy based on the old British currency. Like people in pre-decimal Britain, Kenyans often refer to shillings as "bob", and they occasionally use "pound" to mean Ksh20 (you'll also hear "quids" for pounds). There are Ksh1000, 500, 200, 100 and 50 notes, and coins of Ksh20, 10, 5, 1 and 50 cents (half a shilling). Some foreign banks stock shillings should you wish to buy some before you leave, but at rates about ten percent less than what you might find in Kenya, and it's illegal to import more than Ksh100,000. You are allowed to take up to Ksh100,000 out of the country so long as you've kept the exchange receipts.

At the time of writing, the **rates of exchange** were approximately Ksh120 to £1, Ksh70 to $1, Ksh90 to €1. Street money changers in Nairobi and Mombasa may offer slightly better rates, but the black market is illegal, and most of them (certainly in Nairobi) are just muggers aiming to lure you into an alley and rob you, so you're strongly advised not to change money on the street. An exception to this rule is when entering Kenya by land from Uganda, where moneychangers in the border towns of Busia and Malaba will give Kenyan shillings for Ugandan or for cash dollars; always count the shillings very carefully before handing over your bucks.

Costs

Kenya can be **expensive** if you want to rent a car or go on organized safaris, especially in high season (see p.60). But by staying in the more economical hotels, eating in local places and using public transport, you can get by easily enough on £15/$25 a day. On a daily average budget of £25/$40, you would be living very well most of the time, even occasionally staying in the more luxurious tourist hotel.

Getting around by bus and matatu is very cheap (rarely more than £6/$10 for the longest journey), but the main disadvantage is that they can't drive you around the game parks. **Renting a vehicle** – and paying for fuel – will add at least £50/$80 a day to your costs; see "Car rental and driving" on p.56. You can also find all-inclusive **camping safaris** from around £40/$70 a day, sometimes even less, but some of the very cheap ones are organized by disreputable companies and undermine legitimate operators and the preservation of wildlife – for more information see the "Safaris" section on p.81.

Bargaining

Bargaining is an important skill to acquire, and you'll need to get into it quickly; once you do, you'll rarely end up paying more than the going rate for food, transport or accommodation. If you do pay an unreasonable price for goods or services, you contribute to local inflation, so be cautious over your purchases until you've established the value of things.

It's surprising how little is sold at a fixed price – it's nearly always worth making an offer. You're expected to knock most negotiable prices down by at least half. Souvenirs are sometimes offered at first prices ten times what the vendor is prepared to accept. You can avoid the silly asking prices by having a chat and establishing your streetwise credentials. The bluffing on both sides is part of the fun; don't be shy of making a big scene. Where prices are marked, they are generally fixed – which you'll quickly discover if you walk away and aren't called back.

Most **prices** in this guide are given in Kenyan shillings. However, we've given prices in US dollars for those establishments – especially **tourist services** such as safaris and car rental – which quote their rates in dollars. Almost all the more expensive hotels and lodges also charge non-Kenyans in dollars, though you are legally entitled to pay in Ksh, usually at inferior rates of exchange.

Banks and exchange

You can **exchange** hard currency in cash or traveller's cheques (passport and sometimes receipt required) at banks and foreign exchange bureaux ("forex") all over the country, and at most large hotels for a substantially poorer rate. US dollars, pounds sterling and euros are always the most acceptable; always ask first what commission and charges will be deducted, as they vary mysteriously even within branches of the same bank (it shouldn't be more than one percent, sometimes with a small charge per cheque). Cash invariably attracts better rates than traveller's cheques. Comparative tables of bank and forex bureau rates are published daily (except Sun) in the *Nation*, *Standard* and *People* newspapers.

Credit cards and cash machines

The best way to carry your money is in the form of **plastic**. This is not so much because you can use credit or debit cards to buy things, but because they are more secure than cash, and you can use them to obtain cash from ATMs. Obviously, ATMs present their own security concerns (you're a tempting target with your back turned to the street), so if you're wary, get a friend to come along and look out for you. Some branches have machines inside the building or armed guards on the street.

Larger branches of Barclays Bank, Standard Chartered, Kenya Commercial Bank (KCB) and other banks have 24-hour **ATM cash machines**, where you can use your PIN (make sure that it can be used outside the country where the card was issued) to withdraw cash. The machines accept cards with Visa, Visa Electron, MasterCard, Plus or Cirrus symbols. Before leaving home, you might want to check with your bank or card issuer about any charges for cash withdrawals. Most branches of Barclays and Standard Chartered also give **cash advances** in shillings (no charge), US dollars or sterling (one percent charge) on Visa and MasterCard. The maximum amount you can withdraw per day is usually Ksh40,000 from an ATM, or Ksh50,000 over the counter.

Visa and American Express are widely accepted for tourist services such as upmarket hotels and restaurants, flights, safaris, and car rental; MasterCard and Diners Card are more limited. There's usually a two- to five-percent mark-up on top of the price for the cost of the transaction to the company. A credit card can be very useful for leaving a deposit for car rental.

Abuse of credit cards is not uncommon in Kenya. If you're paying a sum in shillings by credit card, make sure that the voucher specifies the currency before you sign. If it doesn't, it's all too easy for the vendor to fill in a dollar sign in front of the total after you've left. Also fill in the leading digits with zeros. If in doubt, be careful not to let the card out of your sight, to ensure that only one slip is filled in.

Cash and traveller's cheques

It's wise to carry **hard currency**, as well as passport and air ticket, in a very safe place. You could use a leather pouch or money belt under your belt or waistband, but do wrap your things in a plastic bag to avoid damage by sweat. Pouches hanging around your neck are easy targets for grab-and-run robberies and ordinary wallets are an invitation to pickpockets. Similarly, the voluminous "bum bags" worn back to front by many tourists over their clothing invite a slash-and-grab mugging.

As for Kenyan shillings, you'll be carrying around large quantities of coins and paper money. Be aware that, except in the towns, Ksh1000 bills can be hard to change – so make sure you have a safe purse or secure zip pocket to stuff all the small denominations in.

Traveller's cheques can be worth carrying as a backup to plastic, and have a major advantage over **cash** in that they are replaceable if lost or stolen. In theory you should keep the receipt separate from the cheques themselves, but in practice banks and forex bureaux may demand to see it when changing cheques, so keep an extra record of the serial numbers separately, too. If your cheques are lost or stolen, the issuing company will expect you to report the loss immediately; most companies claim to replace them within 24 hours.

Banks

Banks are usually open Monday to Friday from 9am to 3pm, and may be open some or all Saturdays, from 9am to 11am.

Branches of Barclays and the Commercial Bank of Africa, as well as forex bureaux (which are open longer hours), are normally fastest, and Standard Chartered is also reasonable. The KCB is ubiquitous but usually slow and in places charges outrageous commission. In out-of-the-way places, you may have to wait until 10am to change money, as the rates take ages being sent up from Nairobi. Lastly, if a clerk is being unhelpful or otherwise difficult, a polite but firm demand to see the manager can work miracles.

Wiring money

Having **money wired** from home is not cheap, but it is relatively easy. You can have it sent with Western Union to branches of PostBank and KCB, or with MoneyGram to branches of the Co-op Bank and some forex bureaux. The transfer is instantaneous, and fees depend on the amount being transferred but, as an example, wiring £1000/$1000 will cost around £47/$65. From some parts of the world, MoneyGram offer a cheaper economy service, taking three working days and costing around half as much.

Money-wiring companies

MoneyGram UK ℡0800/018 0104; Ireland ℡1800/205800; US ℡1-800/926 9400; Canada ℡1-800/933 3278; Australia ℡1800/230 100; New Zealand ℡0800/262 263 or ℡09/379 8243; ⓦwww.moneygram.com (money can be sent online).

Western Union UK ℡0800/833 833, Ireland ℡1800/395 395, US & Canada ℡1-800/325 6000, Australia ℡1800/173 833, New Zealand ℡0800/005 253, ⓦwww.westernunion.com (customers in the US, Canada, the UK, Ireland and Australia can send money online).

Getting around

There's a wide range of public transport vehicles on Kenya's roads. Alongside the flashy air-conditioned coaches tearing up one or two of the main highways, you'll find smaller "country bus" companies operating a single battered Leyland. In towns of any size, a whole crowd of Nissan minibuses and pick-ups (both referred to as matatus) and Peugeot taxis hustle for business constantly.

Kenya has a number of reasonably priced **internal flights**, and is well worth seeing from the air at least once; the flight from Malindi to Lamu is an especially exotic and exhilarating one over reefs and jungle.

Trains nearly always leave right on time; buses often have punctual departures as well. In more remote areas though, if a driver tells you he's going somewhere "today", it doesn't necessarily mean he expects to arrive today.

A quick roundup of regional **travel details** is given at the end of each chapter. Transport booking numbers are given in the "Practicalities", "Moving on" or "Listings" sections for each town.

Buses, matatus and taxis

Matatus, and to a lesser extent buses, have had a bad **safety record**, and although new rules governing matatus have reduced road accident fatalities considerably, they aren't always respected. The most dangerous matatus are those billed as "express" (they mean it). Don't hesitate to ask to get out of the vehicle if you feel unsafe, and to demand a partial refund – which will usually be forthcoming. If you're driving yourself, beware of buses and matatus and keep your distance from them.

On road transport, it's worth considering your general direction through the trip and which side of the vehicle will be **shadier**. This is especially important on dirt roads when the combination of a slow, bumpy ride, dust and fierce sun through closed windows can be horrible.

Buses

Ordinary **buses** cover the whole country, getting you close to almost everywhere.

Some, on the main runs between Nairobi and Mombasa, and to a lesser extent the west, are fast, comfortable and keep to schedules; you generally need to **reserve** seats on these a day in advance. The large companies – in particular Akamba Public Road Services – have ticket offices near the bus stations in most towns, where they list their routes and prices, but their parking bays are rarely marked and there are no published timetables. The easiest procedure is to mention your destination to a few people at the bus park and then check out the torrent of offers. Keep asking – it's virtually impossible to get on the wrong bus. Once you've acquired a seat, the wait can be almost a pleasure if you're in no hurry, as you watch the throng outside and field a continuous stream of vendors proffering wares through the window. Aside from Akamba (which has the best safety record; ℡020/553000, ℂakamba@skynet.co.ke), the best-known and generally safest bus companies are Coastline (℡020/217592), Scandinavian Express (℡020/242523) and Kenya Bus (℡020/229707, ⊛www.kenyabus.com).

Matatus and shared taxis

Matatus are usually white Nissan minibuses along main routes, or pick-up trucks fitted with wooden benches and a canvas roof for rural trips. The Nissans are especially dangerous: try to sit at the back (to avoid too graphic a view of blind overtaking), and it's a good idea to avoid sitting near a front window – they can shatter in the event of an accident.

New **regulations** governing matatus were introduced in 2003, but although the more trivial of these are followed (drivers have to wear uniforms and badges, for example), others seem to go by the board. All seats are supposed to be fitted with seat belts, but these are often broken; loud music is banned but often still played (which, really, is part of the matatus' charm); **speed governors** are supposed to prevent the vehicle travelling above 80kph, but do not always work. Passenger loads are limited to a stipulated number, but on many routes, especially off the main roads, the old maxim of "always room for one more" still applies. A "little something" for police officers on the road ensures blind eyes are turned towards minor infringements.

Nonetheless, matatus can on occasions be an enjoyable way of getting about, giving you close contact (literally) with local people, and some hilarious encounters. They are also often the most convenient and sometimes only means of transport to smaller places off the main roads.

Peugeot taxis, faster and more expensive than minivans, operate mainly from Nairobi to the highlands and the west. They usually drive directly from one point to another with a full complement of passengers – one person in the front (who sometimes pays a supplement), four in the middle and three in the back, which is marginally less uncomfortable than a matatu.

Always choose a vehicle that's full or you'll have to wait inside until they are ready to go – sometimes for hours. Beware of being used as bait by the driver to encourage passengers to choose his car, and equally of a driver filling his car with young touts pretending to be passengers (spot them by the newspapers and lack of luggage), who disappear when you've bought a ticket. Competition is intense and people will lie unashamedly to persuade you the vehicle is going "just now".

Try not to hand over any money before you set off and, when the taxi does get going, wait until you've left town. This isn't a question of being ripped off, but too often the first departure is just a cruise around town rounding up passengers and buying petrol, and then back to square one.

If your destination doesn't lie on a standard shared-taxi route, or if you don't want to wait for a car to fill up (or, indeed, if you just want to travel in style), drivers will happily negotiate a price for the rental of the whole car. The amount will normally be the same as all the fares they would receive from the passengers in a full taxi over an equivalent distance.

Lastly, some matatu terminology: **stage** or **stand** is the matatu yard; *manamba* or turnboy is the one whose job it is to tout for business, take the fares and hang on dramatically; **dropping** is what you do when you're getting off, as in "I'm dropping here".

Fares

Bus and matatu **fares** are typically around Ksh1.50–3 per kilometre. Even the longest journey by matatu (Nairobi to Kisumu, for example, a six-hour journey of around 300km), should not cost you more than Ksh800. Rarely does anyone attempt to

Place names

Place names not just in Kenya but all over Africa are remarkably confusing to outsiders. In some parts, every town or village seems to have a name starting with the same syllable. In the Kenya highlands, you'll find Kiambu, Kikuyu, Kiganjo, Kinangop and so on. Further west you confront Kaptagat, Kapsabet, Kabarnet and Kapsowar. As soon as you detect a problem like this, just get into the habit of "de-stressing" the first syllable and remember the second.

A more practical problem all over rural Kenya is the vague use of names to denote a whole district and, at the same time, its nucleus, be it a small town, a village, or just a cluster of corrugated-iron shops and bars. Sometimes there'll be two such focuses. They often move in a matter of a few years, so what looks like a junction town on the map turns out to be away from the road, or in a different place altogether. Ask for the "shopping centre" and you'll usually find the local hive of activity and the place with the name you were looking for.

charge more than the going rate. Baggage charges should not normally be levied unless you're transporting a huge load. If you think you're being overcharged, check with other passengers.

Taxis around town (even smallish towns have them) usually cost Ksh100–200, though drivers may try to overcharge you – haggle hard, and if you get nowhere, try another driver. Always settle on a fare before getting in, because the meters hardly ever work.

For journeys around small towns, particularly in the west of the country, there are also bicycle taxis known as **boda-bodas**, consisting of a bicycle with a padded seat on the back. These are very cheap and often the easiest way to get around, but they can be tricky if you're heavily laden with baggage.

The latest addition to Kenya's urban transport scene is an import from Asia, the **tuk-tuk**. This is a three-wheeled vehicle consisting of two seats mounted on the back of a motor-scooter, and should cost around half the price of an ordinary taxi.

Nairobi is the only Kenyan city with a metro **bus** service, and only Nairobi, Mombasa and Kisumu have **matatu** services within town. A bus or matatu ride about town rarely costs more than Ksh30.

Trains

Kenya's **railways** had been underfunded (or funds for it had been siphoned off) for years, with the result that all passenger trains were halted in 2001, with the exception of the Nairobi–Mombasa service. Services have since been restored between Nairobi and Kisumu (three trains weekly, via Naivasha and Nakuru), and between Kisumu and Butere, near Mumias (three weekly). The service between Voi and Taveta had been suspended at the time of writing. By the time you read this, further changes may have occurred with the takeover of Kenya's railways by a consortium led by the South African company Sheltam, who in 2005 won the tender to operate rail services in Kenya and Uganda until 2030.

The main draw for travellers is the overnight **Nairobi–Mombasa** run, which leaves in either direction at 7pm, to arrive any time between 8.30 and 10am the following morning. Frustrating though the (almost routine) delays are, they at least mean you are likely to have a couple of hours of morning light to watch the passing scene: approaching Nairobi, the animals on the Athi Plains; approaching Mombasa, the sultry crawl down from the Maungu Plains to the ocean. The **Nairobi–Kisumu** train follows a similar timetable, departing thrice weekly at 6.30pm, with arrival at 8.30am or so the next day. The **Butere–Kisumu** train connects with the Nairobi service only once a week.

The Nairobi–Mombasa and Nairobi–Kisumu services have three **seat classes**, while Kisumu–Butere is third class only. Only first and second offer any kind of comfort. In first class, you get a private, two-berth compartment; second class has four-berth compartments, which are usually single-sex, though this may be disregarded, for example if all four people are travelling together; third class has seats only and is packed. Meals and bedding, available in first and second class only, cost a little extra, and must be paid for when you buy your ticket (on the Nairobi–Mombasa service it's normally assumed you will take them).

Planes

The main operators for **internal flights** are Kenya Airways (⊛www.kenya-airways.com), Airkenya (⊛www.airkenya.com) and SafariLink (⊛www.safarilink.co.ke). One or two routes are operated by smaller local firms. The destinations served include big cities (Nairobi, Mombasa, Kisumu and Eldoret), coastal resorts (Malindi, Lamu and Kiwaiyu), the Sudan aid centre at Lokichokio, the air force base at Nanyuki, and several national parks and reserves (such as Amboseli, Maasai Mara, Samburu).

Baggage allowances on internal flights, apart from Kenya Airways, are usually under 20kg and may be as little as 10kg. Fortunately, the excess baggage charges are nominal. There is an airport tax of Ksh900 on domestic flights, which is included in the fare.

It's worth bearing in mind that ordinary **connecting times** shouldn't be relied on if you're flying to catch an international departure. Many of the cheaper flight tickets to Europe cannot be endorsed to another

Fare comparisons

The prices given below are one-way fares. The first- and second-class rail fares include bedding and meals.

	Bus	Matatu	Rail (first, second and third class)	Air
Nairobi–Kisumu (307km)	Ksh400–500 (up to Ksh800 deluxe)	Ksh400 (Nissan microbus); Ksh600 (Peugeot)	Ksh2140 Ksh1445 Ksh300	Ksh6500
Nairobi–Mombasa (520km)	Ksh750–900 (Ksh1600 deluxe overnight)	–	Ksh3160 Ksh2275 Ksh400	Ksh6300

airline if you miss your flight, and domestic services are often delayed.

Chartering a small plane for trips to safari parks and remote airstrips is an option worth considering if time is more important to you than money. Costs are typically around $800–1200 for a flight, which isn't unthinkable if split between several people. The place to ask is at Nairobi's Wilson airport (see p.148), but some of the safari operators listed on pp.149–152 can also arrange things.

Ferries

There are no regular ferries up and down the coast, other than those connecting the islands of the Lamu archipelago, but dhow journeys can be negotiated, in particular between Shimoni and Pemba (Tanzania). On Lake Victoria, the network of steamer routes was suspended when the lake became clogged up with water hyacinth, and has now been suspended again due to falling water levels.

Hitchhiking

Hitching is how the majority of rural people get around, in the sense that they wait by the roadside for whatever comes, and will pay for a ride in a passing lorry or a private vehicle – the cost is as it would be in a matatu. Except on the main Kisumu–Nairobi–Mombasa artery, and along the coast, private vehicles driven by Kenyans are comparatively rare and often full, but getting a lift when there is space is not difficult. Hitching rides with other tourists at the gates of national parks and reserves is also sometimes possible.

Hitching techniques need to be fairly exuberant; a thumb is more likely to be interpreted as a friendly, or even rude, gesture than a request for a lift. Beckon the driver to stop with your palm and be quite open in enquiring how much the ride will cost.

Car rental and driving

Renting a car has advantages which makes it seriously worth considering for a week or two. All the parks and reserves are open to private vehicles, and there's a lot to be said for the freedom of choice that having your own wheels gives you. Unless there are more than two of you, though, it won't save you money over one of the cheaper camping safaris. If you're going to be in Kenya for some time, or you're planning to travel more widely, buying a **secondhand** vehicle in Nairobi is a realistic possibility, though prices are inflated, and you need to be confident about engines. The *Nation* and *Standard* carry lots of ads.

Car rental **tariffs** vary greatly, with some quoted in Kenyan shillings, though most are in dollars. It's cheaper to rent by the week than the day if you do enough kilometres – reckon on driving an average of 1000km per week (around 600–700 miles). The minimum age to rent a car is usually 23, sometimes 25.

Shop around for the best deals (making sure the price you're quoted includes the minimum daily mileage and VAT at sixteen percent) and try to negotiate as you might with any purchase, bearing in mind the season (July, August and Christmas are busy, so you might want to book ahead) and how long you're renting. This is easier with independent companies than the big-name franchises. Check the insurance details and always pay the daily **collision damage waiver (CDW)** premium, sometimes included in the price; even a small bump could be very costly otherwise. **Theft protection waiver (TPW)** should also be taken. However, even with these, you'll still be liable for an **excess**, usually $500–1000. You're also required to leave a hefty deposit, roughly equivalent to the anticipated bill – credit cards are useful for this.

If stopped at a police checkpoint, you may be asked to produce evidence that the rental car has a **PSV (**passenger service vehicle) **licence**. You should have a windscreen sticker for this as well as the letters "PSV" written somewhere on the body; if in doubt, check this out out with the rental company before you leave.

Choosing a vehicle

Four-wheel drive (4WD) is always useful, but, except in mountainous areas and on some marginal dirt roads during periods of heavy rain, is not essential. **High clearance**, however, is, thanks to the dire state of many roads. However, few, if any, agencies will rent out non-4WD vehicles for use in the parks, and most park rangers will turn away such cars at the gate. Maasai Mara and the mountain parks (Mount Elgon, Mount Kenya and the Aberdares) are the most safety-minded.

Four-wheel drive **Suzuki jeeps** are the most widely available vehicles, but ensure you get a long wheelbase model with rear seats, room for four people (or five at a pinch) and luggage space at the back. These are more stable than the stumpy short wheelbase versions. Don't expect a Suzuki to do much above 80kph (50mph) even on a good road, and beware their notorious tendency to topple on bends or on the dangerously sloping gravel hard shoulders that line so many roads. Warnings aside, Suzukis are light and dependable, capable of great feats in negoti-

ating rough terrain, and can nearly always be fixed by a local repair shop.

That said, don't automatically assume the vehicle is roadworthy before you set off. Have a good look at the engine and tyres, and don't set off without checking the spare (preferably two) and making sure you have a few vital tools. Ideally, always carry a tow rope, spare water and fuel. You might also take a spare fan belt, brake pads, and brake fluid. Check that your vehicle's PSV status (see opposite) is displayed. You are, of course, responsible for any **repair** and **maintenance work** that needs doing while you're renting the vehicle, but keep any receipts as the company should reimburse you. Try to get a list of recommended service stations from the rental company; to avoid bogus repairs some will insist you use certain garages. Always bargain hard before work begins.

Driving in Kenya

You can drive in Kenya with either a valid driving licence from your home country, or an international one. In theory you **drive on the left**, though in reality vehicles keep to the best part of the road until they have to pass each other.

At the time of writing, **petrol** (gasoline) costs about Ksh75 per litre, which is about $4 per US gallon. Keep an eye on the fuel gauge and top up whenever possible. Towns and villages (except the very smallest) have petrol for sale, but you should carry spare fuel in cans if you're intending to do a lot of driving in a remote area. When refilling, check the pump gauge is set to zero and anticipate how many litres your tank will need – fixing the pumps is not unknown. If you plan to pay by credit card, note that some places only accept Kenyan-issued cards.

On most of the main paved highways you can make good time, but as soon as you leave them, **journey times** are very unpredictable. We've tried to give some idea of road conditions in various places throughout the book, but they can change radically in half a year. The north and highland regions are the most unpredictable, particularly during periods of heavy rain when districts may become virtually cut off.

Signposting in Kenya, while generally useful, is haphazard – especially on dirt

Driving on mud tracks

A low-clearance, **2WD** car limits your driving, especially in safari parks, to fairly solid roads. In a **4WD**, your options are wider, but you still have to be an experienced rough-road driver to get much further than usual 2WD territory. Good *murram* (earth) roads are usually fine, but the surface can wear away if it isn't maintained. Take local advice if attempting unsurfaced roads in the rainy season, when **mud pits** with a smooth and apparently firm surface can disguise deep traps from which you can only hope to get towed out. A covering of vegetation usually means a relatively solid surface.

If you have to negotiate a large puddle of muddy water, first kick off your shoes and wade through the entire length to check its depth and subsurface (better getting muddy than bogged down). If it's less than a foot deep, and the subsurface relatively firm (ie your feet only sink in a few inches), you should be able to drive across: engage 4WD, slip into first gear, and drive slowly (without decelerating) straight through the middle. Alternatively, if there's a sufficiently hard shoulder on one side, you could try driving across at speed with one wheel on it (beware of toppling over in a Suzuki) – you need good control for this. For smaller pools, gathering up speed on the approach and then barrelling across in second gear usually works, but at the risk of clogging up the carburettor.

Approaching **deep mud** is really touch and go – drive as fast as you dare, never over-steer when skidding (it'll send you into a spin and may get you bogged down), keep the accelerator pressed, and pray.

On a swampy **"black cotton" soil** surface, especially during or after rain, you'll need all your wits about you, as even the sturdiest 4WDs have little or no grip on this. The usual way involves a mixture of high-rev driving and luck, which leaves you open to hair-raising spins and sudden, crunching jolts, as well as the possibility of getting bogged down when you lose control. Much better might be to keep in second gear as much as possible, and keep your speed down. Try to keep at least one wheel within a well-defined rut or on vegetation-covered ground.

If you do **get stuck**, stop immediately (spinning the wheels gets you even more stuck) and try reversing once (rev the engine as far as it will go before engaging the gear). If this doesn't work, you'll just have to wait for another vehicle to pull you out.

roads. If a junction appears to lack a sign, it's assumed you'll keep to the busiest track. Beware of **speed bumps**, found both in rural areas, wherever a busy road has been built through a village, and on the roads in and out of nearly every large town. Although occasionally you'll see a sign like "Rumble strips ahead", usually the first you'll know of them is when your head hits the roof.

A handheld **GPS** navigational device is very useful on safari. A basic model with a screen that draws your route as you go enables you at a glance to see your distance covered, your speed and altitude and, most significantly, the way back to where you came from. With a GPS you can drive confidently in the parks and never lose your bearings (and they work just as well when hiking).

Try to **avoid driving at night**, and be careful when passing heavy vehicles, especially

if they are groaning uphill in the opposite direction. A line of lorries churning out diesel fumes can cut off your visibility without warning – extremely dangerous on a narrow mountain road. If you're driving in a city at night (especially Nairobi and Mombasa), keep your doors locked and windows rolled up to avoid grab-and-run incidents. Incidentally, **carjackings** are not uncommon in Nairobi and the northeast. However, tourists and rental cars are generally not a target, at least not unless you're in a flashy, high-powered cruiser. The puny Suzuki jeeps are the safest in this respect.

Finding somewhere to **park** is rarely a problem, even in Nairobi or Mombasa. There are parking meters in Mombasa and over-eager traffic wardens in Nairobi from whom you can buy a ticket for the day (Ksh50–100). If you don't, your car will either be clamped or towed away (in Nairobi, find it at City Hall – the fines are around Ksh1000). Never leave your vehicle with anything of value in it.

Driving etiquette

Beware of unexpected rocks, ditches and potholes – and animals and people – on the road. It's accepted practice to honk your horn stridently to warn pedestrians.

It's **common practice** to flash oncoming vehicles (especially if they're leaving you little room or the headlights are blinding you) and to signal right to indicate your width and deter drivers behind you from overtaking. You may find both practices disconcerting at first. Left-hand signals are used to say "Please overtake me", but you shouldn't assume the driver in front of you can really see that it is safe for you to pass. In fact, never assume anything about other drivers.

Accidents and the police

Kenya's **accident** statistics are horrifying. Police records suggest that an average of eight to nine people die on Kenya's roads every day – an annual death toll of nearly 3000, extremely high considering the relatively small number of vehicles on the road.

Should you have the misfortune to have an **accident** or a **breakdown**, the first thing to do is pile bundles of sticks or foliage 50m or so behind and in front of the car. These are the universally recognized "red warning triangles" of Africa, and their placing is always scrupulously observed (as is the wedging of a stone behind at least one wheel). When you get a flat tyre, as you will, get it mended straight away – it costs very little (Ksh50–100) and can be done almost anywhere there are vehicles. Local mechanics are usually very good and can apply ingenuity to the most disastrous situations. But spare parts, tools and proper equipment are rare off the main routes. Always settle on a price before the work begins. And beware of scams and con-artists; the "oil leak" under your parked car catches many people out.

Being **stopped by the police** is a common occurrence (one or two regular checkpoints are mentioned in the text). Checkpoints are generally marked by low strips of spikes across the road with just enough room to slalom round. Always stop, greet the officer and wait to be waved through. If they accuse you of breaking any law, then politely accept what you are told, including the possibility of a court appearance (highly unlikely). Being set up for a bribe used to be fairly common, but the police have cleaned up their act and will normally wave visitors on their way with a warning.

Cycling

Kenya's climate and varied terrain make it challenging **cycling** country. With a bike, given time and average determination, you can get to parts of the country that would be hard to visit except perhaps on foot. Cycling is also one way you will get to see wildlife outside the confines of the game parks (and several of the smaller game parks allow bikes – including Hell's Gate at Naivasha, Lake Bogoria Reserve and Kakamega Forest). You need to consider the **seasons**, however, as you won't make much progress on dirt roads during the rains. On **main roads**, a mirror is essential and, if the road surface is broken at the edge, give yourself plenty of space and be ready to leave the road if necessary. That said, cycle tourists are still a novelty in Kenya – drivers often slow down to look and you'll rarely be run off the road.

The energetic might like to try an organized **bicycle tour** of Kenya. In North America, try Bicycle Africa of Seattle (☎206/767 0848, ⓦwww.ibike.org/bikeafrica), which offers mountain-bike trips with a pioneering spirit and a wide variety of accommodation. You can fix up similar arrangements in Kenya through a number of agents and operators (see p.148) and book short jaunts to Hell's Gate and lakes Naivasha, Nakuru, Baringo and Bogoria.

Practical considerations

Most towns have bicycle shops which sell both mountain bikes and the trusty Indian three-speed roadsters (the cheapest bikes start at Ksh8500) – we've mentioned some outlets in the Mombasa and Nairobi "Listings" sections. Whatever you take – and a mountain bike is certainly best – it will need low gears and strongly built wheels, and you should have some essential spare parts.

If you're taking a bike with you, then you'll probably want to carry your gear in

panniers. These are fiendishly inconvenient when not attached to the bike, however, and you might instead consider a backpack you can lash down on the rear carrier. An arrangement like this is probably what you'll have to do if you buy a bike in Kenya. With light wood, or the kind of cane used to make cane furniture, plus lashings of inner tube rubber strips, you can create your own highly unaerodynamic carrier, with room for a box of food and a gallon of water underneath.

With a bike from home, take a battery **lighting system** – it's surprising how often you'll need it. The front light doubles as a torch, and getting the large-sized U2 batteries is no problem. Also take a **U-bolt cycle lock**. In situations where you have to lock the bike, you'll always find something to lock it to. Out in the bush it's less important. Local bikes can be locked with a padlock and chain passed through a length of hosepipe, which you can buy and fix up in any market.

Buses and matatus with **roof racks** will always carry bicycles for about half-fare – even if flagged down at the roadside – and trucks will often give a lift. The trains take bikes, too, at a low fixed fare.

Accommodation

Accommodation in Kenya exhibits a fine diversity, ranging from campsites and local lodging houses for $4–6 a night to genuinely excellent, luxury hotels costing fifty or a hundred times as much. Beds can also be found in "tented camps" and "tree hotels" at the expensive end of the spectrum, and bandas and a clutch of youth hostels at the budget end.

If you're planning a trip to Kenya using moderate or expensive accommodation, it's useful to know that a lot of money can be saved by not going in the **high season**. Resort hotels and safari lodges have separate low-, mid- and high-season rates (this pattern applies much less to town hotels). Low-season rates can be anything from a third to a half of the high-season tariff. The seasons of many of the coastal, cottage-type establishments are tied closely to the school year, with the Easter and Christmas holidays, plus July and August, being considered "high". Otherwise, the following seasons apply:

Low season: After Easter to end June or mid-July (coinciding with the "Long Rains").

Mid-season: July to November or mid-December (coinciding with the "Short Rains").

High season: December to Easter (hot and sunny weather until March).

Boarding and Lodgings

In any town you'll find **Boarding & Lodgings** (for which we've coined the abbreviation "B&Ls"). These can vary from a mud shack with water from the well, to a little multistorey building of self-contained rooms with washing facilities, a bar and restaurant. B&Ls tend to be noisy; they're sometimes rather airless and often double unofficially as brothels, but the better ones are clean and comfortable.

Prices of rooms aren't always a good indication of the standard, though you should rarely have to pay more than Ksh800 for a double or Ksh600 for a single, often much less. You can often bargain for a good price. It's worth checking several places, testing the hot water (if any) as well as cold (buckets in the bathrooms mean it has to be carried up and chances are it'll be cloudy) and asking to see the toilets; you won't cause offence by saying no thanks. Bringing toilet paper, a towel and soap is a good idea, though in

Accommodation price codes

Most accommodation rates in this guide have been price-coded according to the categories below. The prices indicated are non-resident (tourist) rates for standard **double** or **twin** rooms. For dormitory accommodation, hostels and campsites (which charge per person), and cottages sleeping more than two, exact prices have been given where possible. Where there are **seasonal differences**, as in some park lodges and in all tourist- or luxury-class accommodation on the coast, the high- and low-season price codes may be given. All Nairobi hotels, most up-country hotels and most places in the cheapest three categories have non-seasonal tariffs.

Cheap hotels quote their rates in **Kenyan shillings**, while hotels in categories ⑦ and above tend to quote their rates in **dollars**. You should still be able to pay at these establishments in Ksh, although often at an inferior rate of exchange. Special rates for **Kenya residents** (typically discounts of fifteen to thirty percent, sometimes much greater) are offered at some establishments in category ⑦ and above. The facilities you can expect in each category are as follows, unless otherwise specified in the guide's reviews. The rates of exchange used in the following conversions is approximately Ksh75 to $1.

① Under Ksh500: very basic B&L with shared facilities.
② Ksh500–1000: B&L with elementary comforts (s/c) or cheap hotel; B&B basis.
③ Ksh1000–1600: adequate hotel with s/c rooms; B&B.
④ Ksh1600–2500: mid-range local hotel or modest tourist-class hotel; B&B.
⑤ Ksh2500–4000: tourist-class hotel; B&B or HB.
⑥ Ksh4000–6000: tourist-class hotel or cheap lodge; HB or FB.
⑦ Ksh6000–8,000/$80–105: luxury hotels and lodges; FB.
⑧ Ksh8,000–12,000/$105–160: luxury hotels and lodges with special facilities; FB.
⑨ Over Ksh12,000/$160: as preceding category.

fact even the cheapest places usually supply all those. If your lodging seems noisy in the afternoon, it will probably become cacophonous during the night, so you may want to ask for a room away from the source of the din. This applies especially to Wednesday, Friday and Saturday nights, when most discos operate.

Security is also an important factor. Obviously, the more the establishment relies on its bar for income, the less guarantees you have. You can leave valuables with the owner, though you'll need to use your judgement. Leaving valuables in rooms is usually safe enough, especially if things are not left lying around – better still, if they allow you, would be to take your key with you.

Some lodgings have lock-up yards where you can park – helpful in avoiding mysteriously deflated tyres and lost wing-mirrors and wipers. Obviously, don't leave anything inside an unattended car at any time.

Hotels and lodges

Hotels are a variable commodity. At the **top end** of the range are the big tourist establishments, many in one of the country's handful of small chains. In the game parks, they are known as **lodges**. Some establishments are extremely good value – a night in a good hotel can be tremendously fortifying if you're usually on a tight budget. Others are shabby and overpriced, so check carefully before splurging. If possible, you should try to reserve the more popular establishments in advance, especially for the busiest season in December and January.

At the level of the **medium-priced** places, some were once slightly grand, while others are old settlers' haunts that don't fit modern Kenya, and some newer ones cater for the black middle class. A few are fine – delightfully decrepit or bristlingly smart and efficient. Most are boozy and uninteresting, and it adds more colour to your travels to mix the cheapest B&Ls with the occasional night of luxury.

Accommodation terms and abbreviations

a/c air-conditioned (usually only on the coast).

banda thatched cottage or chalet, sometimes round and dubbed "rondavel", generally cheap, occasionally converted into upmarket "bush" accommodation for tourists.

B&B bed and breakfast.

B&L "Boarding and Lodging" house.

cube sometimes used to refer to a small room in a B&L.

FB full board, meaning all meals included.

HB half board – dinner, bed & breakfast.

hoteli or sometimes just "hotel", a cheap restaurant or diner; rarely with accommodation.

lodge designer hotel or country house, usually in the game parks.

long-drop self-explanatory; the kind of non-flushing toilet found in some B&Ls, and in most *bandas* and campsites.

s/c "self-contained", with private shower and toilet.

tented camp lodge in the bush, or in a game park, using large tents and *bandas*, often with all the usual hotel facilities plumbed into a solid bathroom at the back.

tree hotel an animal-viewing hotel in the trees, or on stilts, after the style of *Treetops*.

As a rule, expect to pay anything from Ksh800–3000 for a decent double or twin room in a town hotel, with attached bathroom, electricity, hot water and breakfast included. Singles usually cost around seventy percent of a double. Out of the towns and on the

Unique,
Comfortable,
Authentic...

...your best friends in Africa!

www.mbwehacamp.com
www.africansafarisinstyle.com

coast, hotels and lodges in the top price brackets are normally quoted in dollars and on a half- or full-board basis, and prices can go right into orbit ($100–350 is common, with some super-deluxe places far above this level). Most of these hotels cut their prices in the low season, and many have much lower rates for Kenyan residents (sometimes citizens only).

Addresses and telephone numbers for most hotels are included in the guide. Many are part of chains or management groups and rooms can be reserved by contacting the head offices. A good range of upmarket hotels and lodges can also be booked through ⓦ www.lets-go-travel.net.

Hotel chains and groups

Alliance Hotels ☎020/4443357–8, ⓦwww .alliancehotels.com. Small, highly rated group with very pleasant package-tour hotels, noted for their good food and experienced management.
Block Hotels ☎020/650500 or 651991, ⓦwww .blockhotelske.com. Generally good, sometimes excellent, package-tour establishments, popular with Kenya residents too.
Bush Homes of East Africa ☎020/600457 or 605108, ⓦwww.bush-homes.co.ke. The marketing company for over a dozen small, very exclusive privately owned tented camps and ranch houses in less accessible corners of Kenya (guests usually arrive by air).
Governors' Camps ☎020/2734000, ⓦwww .governorscamp.com. Expensive, and not as exclusive as they claim.
Heritage Hotels ☎020/4442115 or 6651, ⓦwww.heritage-eastafrica.com. A range of hotels and lodges from deluxe "Explorer" establishments to adventurous "Safari Clubs".
Kenya Safari Lodges & Hotels Kenya ☎041/447 1861–5; US & Canada ☎1-888/790 5264, ⓦwww .kenya-safari.co.ke. Three properties – one in Mombasa and two in Tsavo – originally built in the 1970s, but well maintained and superbly positioned.
Lonrho Hotels Kenya ☎020/216940, US ☎1-800/845 3692 or 941/951 1155, ⓦwww .lonrhohotels.com. Busy upmarket package-tour refuges, with excellent standards across the board.
Msafiri Inns ☎020/229752–4. A group formed to look after some of the Kenya Tourist Development Corporation's less successful lodges and town hotels, some of which (such as the *Tea Hotel* in Kericho and *Mount Elgon Lodge*) are quite rundown.
Sarova Hotels Kenya ☎020/2713333; UK c/o Market Places ☎01305/751510; US c/o Kartagener

Associates ☎1-800/5247979 or 631/8581270, ⓦwww.sarovahotels.com. Mostly high quality; good service at competitive prices for the level of comfort.
Serena Hotels ☎020/2842000 or 2333, ⓦwww.serenahotels.com. Some of Kenya's most comfortable and well-managed hotels, combining strong architectural themes with harmonious local blending. Mostly recommended.

Cottages, villas and homestays

Increasingly, it's possible to book **self-catering apartments**, **villas** or **cottages**, especially on the coast. Home from Home (☎020/891314, ⓦwww.kenyasafarihomes. com) and Holiday Homes Ltd (☎020/444 4051–3), are agents for a wide range of holiday homes. Also on the increase are **homestays** – inclusive accommodation in a (usually Anglo-Kenyan) household in the countryside. Meals and drinks are generally part of the package, and excursions and safaris with generous helpings of local insight, or occasionally prejudice, are optional. Let's Go Travel (ⓦwww.lets-go -travel.net) have details of some.

Youth hostels

Only four Kenyan **youth hostels** are affiliated to Hostelling International (HI) – Nairobi (see p.119), Naro Moru (Mount Kenya, see p.180), Embu Scouts Center (see p.200) and Thomson's Falls Sports Camp (see p.219). Non-members normally have to join the association first (Ksh700), though this can be done by buying Ksh120 "stamps" on each of your first six overnights, which then qualifies you for international membership. The hostels can be booked from outside Kenya through HI, or in Kenya through the Kenyan Youth Hostelling Association at the *Nairobi Youth Hostel*. There's also an unaffiliated hostel in Nanyuki.

There are **YMCAs and YWCAs** in Kisumu, Naivasha, Nairobi, Likoni and Mombasa, and **church-run hostels** and dormitories in a number of small towns in which the atmosphere can be a stark contrast to the sleazier lodging-houses.

Camping

There are enough campsites in Kenya to make it worthwhile carrying a tent, and camping wild is sometimes a viable option, too. Bring the lightest tent you can afford and remember the main point of a tent is to keep insects out. You might consider making your own tent: nylon netting with a sewn-in groundsheet is the basic tent. A rip-stop nylon fly sheet adds privacy. Outside poles back and front can be used for guys and tension, but you'll probably resort to trees if there are any. A tube of **ant-killer** comes in handy if you're camping, particularly on the coast.

Campsites in the parks are usually very cheap and basic, though a handful of privately owned sites have more in the way of facilities. In rural areas, hotels are often amenable if you ask to camp discreetly in their grounds.

The mysterious **special campsites** in a number of parks are, in reality, simply restricted sites which you can reserve on an exclusive basis for private use. They cost more than standard campsites, but are still cheap compared to lodges. Some of them are especially attractive – so they draw film crews and the like – but they are all quite devoid of facilities. To **book** them, either write to the warden in question or to Special Campsite Reservations, Kenya Wildlife Service, Langata Rd; PO Box 40241 Nairobi ⊤020/600800, ⓕ505866, ⓔtourism@kws .org. You can also visit this KWS office, which is one of those right by Nairobi National Park main gate. On top of the flat booking fee of Ksh5000, you have to pay daily camping charges at the prevailing rates (see p.77).

Camping wild depends on whether you can find a suitable space. In the more heavily populated and farmed highland districts, you should ask someone before pitching in an empty spot. Out in the wilds, hard or thorny ground is likely to be the only obstacle (a foam sleeping-mat is a good idea if you don't mind the bulk). During the dry seasons, you'll rarely have trouble finding wood for a fire so a stove is optional, but don't burn more fuel than you need. You're not allowed to collect firewood in the mountain parks. Camping gas cartridges and packaged, dried food is available in variety in Nairobi, but the easiest and cheapest camping food is *ugali* (see p.694), flavoured with curry powder or sauce mixes if you like.

Safety

Camping is generally pretty **safe**, although in populated areas you should ask beforehand. An important caveat applies to the coast: almost anywhere between Malindi and the Tanzanian border, sleeping out on the **beaches** should be counted as an invitation to robbery.

Be aware of areas where there are ethnic tensions (these are mentioned in the text), or where cattle-rustling is prevalent. A fire may worry local people and delegations armed with *pangas* sometimes turn up to see who you are, and might want to stay and chat. Camping right by the road, in dried-out river beds, or on trails used by animals going to water, however, would be unwise.

On the subject of **animals**, lions and hyenas, which are occasionally curious of campfires, rarely attack unprovoked. More dangerous are buffaloes: steer well clear of solitary bulls. In the vicinity of lakes and slow-moving rivers you should watch out for hippos, which will attack if you're blocking their route back to water, and crocodiles, which can be found in most inland waters and occasionally attack swimmers. Lake and river-swimming is not advised.

Eating and drinking

Not surprisingly, perhaps, Kenya has no great national dishes. The living standards of the majority of people don't allow for frills, food is generally plain and filling, and eating out is not a Kenyan tradition. For culinary culture, it's only the coast, with its long association with Indian Ocean trade, that has produced distinctive regional cooking, where rice and fish, flavoured with coconut, tamarind and exotic spices, are the dominant ingredients. For food terms and help translating Swahili menus, see pp.694–695.

In the most basic local restaurant, decent meals can be had for less than Ksh100, slightly more in Nairobi. Fancier meals in touristy places rarely cost more than Ksh1000 a head, though there's a handful of classy establishments in Nairobi and on the coast which take delight in charging, for Kenya, outrageous prices for lavish meals – up to Ksh4000 – generally with some justification.

Home-style fare and nyama choma

If meals are unlikely to be a lasting memory, at least you'll never go hungry. In any **hoteli** (small restaurant) there's always a number of predictable dishes intended to fill you up at the least cost. Potatoes, rice and especially **ugali** (a stiff, cornmeal porridge) are the national staples, eaten with chicken, goat, beef, or vegetable stew, various kinds of spinach, beans and sometimes fish. Portions are usually gigantic; half-portions (ask for *nusu*) aren't much smaller. But even in small towns, more and more cafés are appearing where most of the menu is fried – eggs, sausages, chips, fish, chicken and burgers. The standard blow-out feast for most Kenyans is a huge pile of **nyama choma** (roast meat). *Nyama choma* is usually eaten at a purpose-built *nyama choma* bar, with beer and music (live or on a jukebox) the standard accompaniment, and *ugali* and greens optional. You go to the kitchen and order by weight (half a kilo is plenty) direct from the butcher's hook or out of the fridge. There's usually a choice of goat, beef or mutton. After roasting, the meat is brought to your table on a wooden platter and chopped

to bite-size with a sharp knife. *Kuku choma* is roast chicken.

Snacks and breakfast

Snacks – which can easily become meals – include samosas, chapatis, paratha, miniature kebabs, roasted corncobs, *mandaazi* (sweet, puffy, deep-fried dough cakes) and "egg-bread". *Mandaazi* are made before breakfast and served until evening time, when they've become cold and solid. Egg-bread (misleadingly translated from the Swahili *mkate mayai*) is a light wheat-flour "pancake" wrapped around fried eggs and minced meat, usually cooked on a huge griddle. While you won't find it everywhere, it's a delicious Kenyan response to the creeping burger menace. Snacks sold on the street include cassava chips and, if you're very lucky, termites (which go well as a bar snack with beer).

Breakfast varies widely. Standard fare in a *hoteli* consists of a cup of sweet tea and a chapati or a doorstep of white bread thickly spread with margarine (on both sides, and often the edges too). At the other extreme, if you're staying in a luxury hotel or lodge, breakfast is usually a lavish acreage of hot and cold buffets that you can't possibly do justice to. In the average mid-priced hotel, you'll get "full breakfast", like something from an English B&B – greasy sausage, bacon and eggs (look for Swahili menus saying something like *mayai kukaanga*), with tea or instant coffee (in a pot) and soggy "toast" (which is rarely in fact toasted).

Restaurant meals

Kenya's seafood and meat are renowned and they are the basis of most serious

Special diets

If you're a **vegetarian** staying in tourist-class hotels, you should have no problems, as there's usually a meat-free pasta dish, or else the usual omelettes. Vegetarians on a strict budget don't have an easy time because meat is the conventional focus of any meal not eaten at home – and *hotelis* seldom have much else to accompany the starch. Even vegetable stew is normally cooked in meat gravy. Nor are salads and green vegetables served much in the cheaper *hotelis*. Eggs, at least, can be had almost anywhere, and milk is distributed widely. With bread and tinned margarine, two more staples available everywhere, you won't starve. Look out for Indian vegetarian restaurants where you can often eat remarkably well at a very low cost.

Many restaurants on the coast serve **halal fare**, while in areas without a sizeable Muslim population, you'll usually be able to find a Somali-run *hoteli* that has halal meat.

meals. **Game meat** is a bit of a Kenyan speciality, most of it farmed on ranches. Giraffe, zebra, impala, crocodile and ostrich all regularly appear at various restaurants, and often on a weekly basis in hotel buffets. Gazelle and impala is especially good, as is zebra – not the horse meat you might imagine. *Carnivore* in Nairobi (see p.141) is one of the best places to try game.

Indian restaurants in the larger towns, notably Nairobi and Mombasa, are generally excellent (locally, there's often a strong Indian influence in *hoteli* food as well), with *dal* lunches a good stand-by and much fancier regional dishes widely available too. When you splurge, apart from eating Indian, it will usually be in **hotel restaurants**, with food often very similar to what you might be served in a restaurant at home. The **lodges** usually have buffet lunches at about Ksh800–1000, which can be great value if you're really hungry, with table-loads of salads and cold meat. Among Kenya's exotic cuisines, you'll find Italian restaurants and pizzerias, various Chinese options, and French, Japanese, Thai, and even Korean food.

Phone numbers are given in the guide for those restaurants where it's advisable to make reservations.

Fruit

Fruit is a major delight. Bananas, avocados, pawpaws and pineapples are in the markets all year, mangoes and citrus fruits more seasonally. Look out for passion fruit (the familiar shrivelled brown variety, and the sweeter and less acidic smooth yellow ones),

cape gooseberries (physalis), custard apples and guavas – all highly distinctive and delicious. On the coast, roasted cashew **nuts** are cheap, especially at Kilifi where they're grown and processed (never buy any with dark marks on them), while coconuts are filling and nutritious, going through several satisfying changes of condition (all edible) before becoming the familiar hard brown nuts.

Drinking

The national beverage is **chai** – tea. Universally drunk at breakfast and as a pick-me-up at any time, it's a weird variant on the classic British brew: milk, water, lots of sugar and tea leaves, brought to the boil in a kettle and served scalding hot. It must eventually do diabolical dental damage, but it's addictive and very reviving. The main tea-producing region is around Kericho in the west, but the best tea is made on the coast. Upcountry it's all too often a tea bag in a cup of vaguely warm water or milk. Instant **coffee** – fresh is rare – is normally available in *hotelis* as well, but it's expensive (ironically, as the country is a large coffee producer), so not as popular as tea.

Soft drinks (sodas) are usually very cheap, and crates of Coke, Fanta and Sprite find their way to the wildest corners of the country. Krest, a bitter lemon, is a lot more pleasant. Krest also makes a ginger ale, but it's watery and insipid; instead go for Stoney (ginger beer) which has more of a punch. Sometimes you can get Vimto (a mixed-fruit concoction), and occasionally plain soda water.

Fresh fruit **juices** are available in the towns, especially on the coast (Lamu is fruit juice heaven). Passion fruit, the cheapest, is excellent, though nowadays it's likely to be watered-down concentrate. Some places serve a variety: you'll sometimes find carrot juice and even tiger milk – made from tiger nuts (a tuber, the same as the Spanish *chufa*). Bottled Picana mango juice is also available at some shops that sell sodas.

Bottled **mineral or spring water** is relatively expensive but widely available. Mains water may be drinkable, but it's safer to stick with bottled (see p.48 for more).

Beer

Kenyan **lager beer** is generally good, costing from Ksh70 in local dives up to Ksh150 in posher establishments. Of the conventional beers, Tusker, White Cap, Pilsner (a little stronger) and the South African Castle Lager are the main brands, sold in half-litre bottles, or in one-third-litre sizes at fancier places and hotel bars. White Cap and Pilsner are the oldest brands, and Tusker is the biggest seller. Most Kenyan lagers are made with cornstarch and sugar as well as the traditional water, malt and hops; the exception is Tusker Malt, which is pricier (you get a smaller bottle for the same price), but has a finer flavour. There are also two **stouts**: a head-thumping version of Guinness at over seven percent, and Castle Milk Stout, a milder competitor.

There are two points of beer **etiquette** worth remembering. First, never take your bottle out of the bar (bottles carry deposits and this is considered theft – surprisingly ugly misunderstandings can ensue). Secondly, in small places out of the cities (especially in western Kenya), men buy each other beers and accumulate them on the table in a display of mutual generosity. When he's drunk enough, each customer takes his unopened presents back to the bar and stores them for the next day.

Other alcoholic drinks

Several quite drinkable **white wines** made from Kenyan grapes are available – notably the products of Naivasha Wineries – as is reasonably priced South African wine. A whole range of fruity wines has recently appeared, including passion and mango. **Papaya wine** is Kenya's desperate solution to its shortage of vineyards. This – ostensibly in medium or dry, white and rosé – is certainly an acquired taste, but one you might acquire quickly. The stuff is potent and much cheaper than imported wine. **Kenya Cane** (white rum) and **Kenya Gold** (a gooey, coffee-flavoured liqueur) deserve a try perhaps, but they are expensive and nothing special.

You won't often find **cocktails** except in expensive hotels and restaurants. One popular Kenyan mix to try is a **dawa** ("medicine") – vodka, white rum, honey and lime juice.

There's a battery of laws against **home brewing** and distilling – perhaps because of the loss of tax revenue on legal booze – but these are central aspects of Kenyan culture and they go on. You can sample *pombe* (bush brews) of different sorts all over the country. It's as varied in taste, colour and consistency as its ingredients: basically fermented sugar and millet or banana, with herbs and roots for flavouring. The results are frothy and deceptively strong.

On the coast, where the coconuts grow, merely lopping off the growing shoot produces a naturally fermented **palm wine** (*mnazi*), which is indisputably Kenya's finest contribution to the art of self-intoxication. There's another variety of palm wine, tapped from the doum palm, called *mukoma*. Though there's usually a furtive discretion about *pombe* or *tembo* sessions, consumers rarely get busted.

Not so with spirits: think twice before accepting a mug of **chang'aa**. It's treacherous firewater, and is also frequently contaminated, regularly killing drinking parties en masse, and filling a niche in the Kenyan press. Sentences for distilling and possessing *chang'aa* are harsh, and police (or vigilante) raids common.

Communications

Keeping in touch by post, telephone and email is generally easy, but not fantastically reliable. Mail takes a few days to Europe and around ten days to North America, Australia and New Zealand; times from these places to Kenya are slightly longer, and things go missing frequently enough – keep photocopies of letters you don't want to lose, and don't send valuables. If you want speedy delivery, pay a little extra for express. The internal service, like the international one, is not entirely reliable.

Prepaid **aerogrammes** are the cheapest way of writing home, but tend to sell out quickly. **Stamps** can be bought only at post offices and large hotels. There are main post offices in all the towns and, except in the far north, sub-post offices throughout the rural areas. **Post offices** are usually open Monday to Friday 8am to 5pm, Sat 9am to noon.

Poste restante (general delivery) is free, and fairly reliable in Nairobi, Mombasa, Malindi and Lamu. Have your family name marked clearly, but look under any combination of initials and be ready to show your passport. Smaller post offices will also hold mail but your correspondent should mark the letter "To Be Collected". Parcels can be received, too, but expect to haggle over import duty when they're opened. Ask the sender to mark packages "Contents To Be Re-exported From Kenya".

It's expensive to send airmail **packages** from Kenya, but surface mail (up to a maximum of 20kg) is good value and reliable. Parcels must be no more than 105cm long and the sum of the three sides less than 200cm, and must be wrapped in brown paper or a plain carton. They are usually examined in advance, so everything has to be checked, in the post office, before you wrap it. Cheaper for large consignments (over 10kg) is to get yourself and the parcel to the British Airways cargo counter at JKI Airport in Nairobi. BA can send it to any airport they serve – delivery is rapid to London, but can take weeks to anywhere else.

Note that there's no mail delivery service to homes and offices. All **postal addresses** in Kenya therefore comprise a post office box number and the name of a town or city, except out in the sticks where some are just given as "Private Bag", or "PO", followed by the location of the post office. In this book, the city or town where the PO Box is located is omitted unless it's different to the place where the addressee is based.

Telephones

To make **local calls** from a call box you need a good handful of Ksh5 and 10 coins. When you pick up any pay phone you'll hear

> To call Kenya from abroad, dial your international access code followed by 254 for Kenya, the area code (omitting the initial 0), and then the number itself. For calls out of Kenya, the international access code is 000. The following **country codes** may come in handy:
> Australia 61
> Canada 1
> Ireland 353
> Netherlands 31
> New Zealand 64
> South Africa 27
> UK 44
> USA 1
> The following numbers are useful in Kenya:
> International directory enquiries/
>   operator ☏0195 or 0196
> Local operator ☏900
> Local directory enquiries ☏991 or 992
> Emergency (fire, police, ambulance)
>   ☏999

a sustained tone and, in the background, a series of beeps. After five beeps you dial (you can dial before that, but you might lose your money). Use the area code or dial 900 for the operator.

Conventional phonecards have been phased out in favour of Telekom Kenya's prepaid **VoIP Calling Cards**, available in denominations of Ksh100, Ksh200 (valid 30 days), Ksh500 (valid 60 days), and Ksh1000 or Ksh2000 (valid 120 days). On these, you scratch off a panel on the back, revealing the card's number and a "password" number, which you have to tap in every time you make a call. The cards can be used from any landline phone with tone dialling, including call boxes, for both local and international calls. When using them for international calls, having keyed in your card number and password, you dial 888 for international access, followed by the country code, area code and number. Although international calls are relatively cheap using calling cards (usually Ksh15–20 a minute), local calls are relatively expensive, at Ksh10 a minute.

Collect calls can be made, but not from call boxes. Three minutes' worth costs about Ksh1500. It works out cheaper overall if you call your correspondent briefly and ask them to call you back at a hotel.

In 2003, there was a massive overhaul of Kenyan telephone numbers, almost all of which have now been changed. If you have an old number and need to find out what it is now, you will find a list of the changes at ⓦwww.wtng.info/ccod-2.html. Note that not all numbers changed exactly as listed, and that an increasing number of places are abandoning their unreliable land lines in favour of mobile phones. A few more recent number alterations appear on ⓦwww.telkom.co.ke.

Some hotels and offices have several land lines, numbered consecutively; these appear in this book as, for example, ☎213456–8, indicating ☎213456, 213457 and 213458.

Cell phones

More people in Kenya have cell phones than land lines, and most of the country has coverage. The main exception is the far north, but reception can also be very patchy in rural areas close to the Tanzanian border.

If you want to use a mobile phone brought from abroad in Kenya, you'll need to check with the phone provider as to whether they have a roaming agreement with a Kenyan provider, and what the call charges are. If your phone is American or Canadian, it will have to be tri-band to work in Kenya.

You may wish to use a **SIM card**, costing around Ksh200, from either of the two Kenyan providers, Celtel (numbers beginning ☎073) and Safaricom (☎072); your handset may need to be unlocked for this to work. With a Kenyan SIM card, you get a Kenyan number and pay Kenyan local and international call charges, which works out rather cheaper per call than using your SIM card from home with global roaming. SIM cards and airtime can be bought throughout the country.

Internet access

Internet offices are reasonably widespread in Kenya, but they can be thin on the ground in small places. It's worth knowing, however, that many post offices have Internet facilities – you have to buy Ksh100 of time on a prepaid card to use these, but the card is valid in any post office. The **charge** for using the Internet is Ksh1 per minute almost everywhere, though occasionally you will find cheaper places in big cities, and conversely in a few small places, you may pay more. Note that connections in Kenya can be painfully slow; mornings are the best time to get a fast connection.

The media

The press in Kenya is pretty lively and provides reasonable coverage of international news, while CNN, the BBC and European sports stations are available on satellite TV. Although most Kenyan television is in Swahili, most newspapers are in English, as are most radio stations. English tends to predominate over Swahili in public life; higher education and parliament get by almost exclusively on it.

Radio and TV

KBC **radio** has three services, broadcasting in English, Swahili and local languages, as well as a Nairobi station, Metropolitan (101.9FM), competing with the independent Capital FM (98.4Mhz). Better for music is another independent station, Kiss 100 (actually 100.3FM). *The Nation* newspaper runs a news station, Nation Radio (96.4FM). The BBC World Service can be picked up on FM in Nairobi (93.7MHz), Mombasa (93.9MHz) and Kisumu (88.2MHz).

Kenyan **television**, much of it imported, carries a mix of English and Swahili programmes. There are three main channels: the stuffy and hesitant state-run KBC, which carries BBC World for most of the morning; the upbeat, mainly urban KTN, which carries CNN during the night and much of the morning; and *The Nation* newspaper's channel, Nation TV, which also sometimes carries CNN. In addition to these, KBC operates a pay channel, KBC2, which is run in conjunction with South Africa's M-NET, and there is also a Christian Channel called Family TV. An increasing number of homes, and certainly bars and hotels, now have **satellite dishes**, giving access to Britain's Sky TV, Eurosport and other foreign channels. Kenya's Super-Sport 3 pay-channel shows a lot of English premiership football.

The press

Kenya is a nation absorbed in its press, which is often quite outspoken. At one time, the mainstream press was joined by a gaggle of unofficial scandal sheets, which were even more outspoken, but early in 2004, the government banned all of them and made it a criminal offence to sell unregistered newspapers. Since then, a number of the scandal sheets have registered as newspapers and returned to the streets.

The leading mainstream daily is the *Daily Nation* and *Sunday Nation* (@www.nation media.com), part-owned by the Aga Khan, which has meaty news coverage (international, too, as well as European football results), a forthright editorial line, and a letters page full of insights into Kenyan life. Its main competitor, *The Standard* (@www .eastandard.net) is somewhat lightweight in comparison. *The People*, whose logo "Fair, Frank and Fearless" is about right, and which verges on the scurrilous, looks a lot scrappier and arrives later on the newsstands than *The Nation* and *The Standard*. Less worthwhile is the *Kenya Times* (@www .kenyatimes.com), a stodgy government organ. The Nation Group also publishes the excellent and highly recommended *The East African* (@www.nationmedia.com/ eastafrican/current) on Mondays, a relatively weighty, conservatively styled roundup of the week's news in Kenya, Uganda and Tanzania, shot through with an admirable measure of justified cynicism. Its own reporting is consistently incisive, intelligent and thought-provoking, and it also carries the cream of the foreign press news features.

Of the other papers, *Taifa Leo* is the most important Swahili daily. The *Weekly Review* is always worth picking up, as is the business newsmagazine *Finance*.

Of the **foreign press**, weekly editions of the UK's *Daily Telegraph* and the *Daily Express* often reach areas with substantial white populations, mostly Nairobi and the west and central highlands. Other British papers and the *International Herald Tribune* can usually be found in Nairobi or, a few days old, at one or two stores around the country. *Time* and *Newsweek* are hawked widely and, together with old *National Geographics* and copies of *The Economist*, filter through many hands before reaching the second-hand booksellers.

Opening hours, public holidays and festivals

Standard opening hours, where there are any, follow familiar patterns. In larger towns, the major stores and tourist services will be open Monday to Saturday from 8am to 5 or 6pm, often with a break for lunch. Offices and museums open at similar times, though offices will usually be closed on Saturdays. In rural areas and out in the bush, small shops can be open at almost any hour, and may double as hotelis or chai kiosks.

The main Christian religious holidays and the Muslim festival of Id ul Fitr are observed, as well as secular national holidays. Other Muslim festivals are not public holidays but are observed in Muslim areas. Local seasonal and cyclical events, peculiar to particular ethnic groups, are less well advertised.

Public holidays and Muslim festivals

Note that if a public holiday falls on a Sunday, the following Monday is usually declared a public holiday.

1 Jan	New Year's Day
March/April	Good Friday
March/April	Easter Monday
1 May	Labour Day
1 June	Madaraka Day (celebrating 1960 granting of self-government)
10 Oct	Moi Day (this may be abolished in the future)
20 Oct	Kenyatta Day (anniversary of his imprisonment)
1 Shawwal	Id ul Fitr
12 Dec	Jamhuri (Independence) Day
25 Dec	Christmas Day
26 Dec	Boxing Day

Islamic festivals: approximate dates

	2006	2007	2008	2009
Beginning of Ramadan (1st Ramadan)	Sept 24	Sept 13	Sept 2	Aug 22
Id ul Fitr/Id al-Saghir (1st Shawwal)	Oct 24	Oct 13	Oct 2	Sept 21
Tabaski/Id al-Kabir (10th Dhu'l Hijja)	Jan 10, Dec 31	Dec 20	Dec 8	Nov 28
Muslim New Year (1st Moharem)	Jan 31	Jan 20	Jan 10 & Dec 31	Dec 20
Ashoura (10th Moharem)	Feb 9	Jan 30	Jan 20	Dec 30
Maulidi/Mouloud (12th Rabia I)	April 11	March 31	March 20	March 9

On the coast, throughout the northeast, and in Muslim communities everywhere, the lunar **Islamic calendar** is used for religious purposes. The Muslim year has 354 days, so dates recede against the Western calendar by an average of eleven days each year. Only the month of fasting called **Ramadan**, and Id ul Fitr – the feast at the end of it which begins on the first sighting of the new moon – will have much effect on your travels. During Ramadan, most stores and *hotelis* are closed through the daylight hours in smaller towns in Islamic districts, while shops and businesses will close in time for sunset, to break the daily fast. Public transport and official business continue as usual. **Maulidi**, the celebration of the prophet's birthday, is worth catching if you're on the coast at the right time, especially if you'll be in Lamu.

Agricultural shows

The Agricultural Society of Kenya (ASK) puts on a series of annual **agricultural shows** – featuring livestock and produce competitions,

ASK show dates	
Eldoret	Early March
Kakamega	Mid-May
Meru	Early June
Nanyuki	Mid-June
Embu	Late June
Nakuru	Mid-July
Kisii	Early August
Kisumu	Mid-August
Garissa	Late August
Mombasa	End of August
Nyeri	Mid-September
Nairobi	Early October
Kabarnet	Mid-October
Kitale	End of October/early November

beer and snack tents, as well as some less expected booths, concerned with family planning or herbalism. These can be lively, revealing events, borrowing a lot from the British farming show tradition, but infused with Kenyan style.

Entertainment and sport

Kenya's espousal of Western values has belittled much traditional culture, so only in remote areas are you likely to come across traditional dancing and drumming which doesn't somehow involve you as a paying audience. If you're patient and reasonably adventurous in your travels, however, you'll be able to witness something more authentic sooner or later – though most likely only by accident or if you stay somewhere off the beaten track long enough to make friends. Kenyan popular music, gospel, and spectator sports are much more accessible.

Dance

The hypnotic swaying and displays of effortless leaping found in **Maasai and Samburu dancing** are the best known forms of Kenyan dance. Similar dance forms occur widely among other non-agricultural peoples. **Mijikenda dance troupes** (notably from the Giriama people) perform up and down the coast at tourist venues. As with

the Maasai dancing, it's better to ignore any purist misgivings you might have about the authenticity of such performances and enjoy them as distinctive and exuberant entertainments in their own right.

Music

As for **popular music**, apart from what your ears pick up on the street and in buses (often amazingly loud), the live spectacle is limited to Nairobi, coastal entertainment spots, and a fair scattering of upcountry **discos** and "**country clubs**". The indigenous music scene seems overshadowed by foreign influences: American soul and hip-hop, Jamaican reggae (especially in the sacred image of Bob Marley) and a vigorous contribution from Congo predominating on radio and in record shops. The guide to the Nairobi club and music scene (see pp.142–147) includes a detailed rundown on where to hear the home-grown product. See pp.645–659 for a condensed history of music in Kenya and a discography.

If you're lucky enough to be invited to a coastal Swahili wedding with all the trimmings, a **taarab** band may be playing. *Taarab* music, especially the older music (modern *taarab* relies heavily on synthesizers) is hauntingly beautiful, an effervescent blend of African, Arabic and Indian musical influences. Steady drumbeats, tambourines, accordions, an instrument called the *udi* – basically a lute – and plaintive Swahili lyrics are the traditional components, while electric guitars, fiddles and microphones are modern additions.

Theatre and film

Theatrical performances are effectively limited to one or two semi-professional clubs in Nairobi and Mombasa and a handful of upcountry amateur dramatic groups. African actors and scripts tend to be rare but things are improving, at least in Nairobi, where there are a number of groups performing in English.

Cinema in Kenya revolves almost entirely around imports. The big towns have cinemas and a few drive-ins, while smaller towns may have one cinema with the occasional screening. American and Indian box-office hits are the staple fodder.

Sports

Sports received encouragement from Kenya's much-vaunted – if financially disastrous – hosting of the 1987 All Africa Games. The country's Olympic successes are indisputable, with a regular clutch of gold and silver in the **track events**. Kenya's athletes are among the continent's leaders and the country's long-distance runners are some of the best in the world. It has even been suggested that certain Kalenjin communities may have a genetic make-up which makes them more likely to be strong athletes, but Kalenjins as much as anyone else have played down this idea. Kenya has possibly the most successful athletics training school in the world in St Patrick's High School, Iten, in the Rift Valley. You'll also find evidence of keen amateur involvement – joggers, martial arts enthusiasts and road cyclists in training.

Football is wildly popular. A lot of people, in fact, support English Premiership teams, and there are even matatus decorated with the colours of teams such as Arsenal and Manchester United. Kenya's national team, known as the Harambee Stars, frequently wins the East and Central African CECAFA Championship, most recently in 2002, but it has never qualified for the World Cup finals, nor done especially well in the African Nations Cup. In the Premier League, Nairobi's AFC Leopards and Gor Mahia rank with the best clubs on the continent, alongside Tusker FC and, champions in 2003, 2004 and 2005, **Ulinzi Stars**. The last time a Kenyan club won an African competition, however, was in 1987 when Gor Mahia took the Cup Winner's Cup. Crowds are pretty well behaved, perhaps because forking out for the modest gate fee precludes getting drunk as well.

Kenyan **cricket** received a boost when Kenya beat the West Indies at the World Cup in 1996 and came third overall in 2003. Most matches are played in the Nairobi area. Check out Ⓦwww.frendsofkenyacricket.org.uk for news.

Racing at the racecourse in Nairobi (see p.154) goes back to colonial times. But an unsuspected sport for which Kenya is achieving international recognition is **camel-racing**. Since 1990, there's been an annnual international camel derby in Maralal (see p.572), now co-promoted with some serious international **mountain-bike racing** at the same event.

Car rallies

The **Equator Rally**, held in July, is Kenya's main rally event, and is part of the African Rally Championship, run by FIA (the International Automobile Federation). In December, the three-day **East African Safari Rally** blazes a trail across Kenya, Uganda and Tanzania. For information on both these events, contact the Automobile Association of Kenya at AA House, North Airport Rd, Embakasi, Nairobi PO Box 40087 (℡020/825060, ✉aakenya@wananchi.com).

Another annual event is the **Rhino Charge** motor race, which takes place at different places around Kenya, attracting adventurers from across the globe. Funds raised from the race go to the Rhino Ark fencing project (℡020/604246, ⊛www.rhinoark.org) taking place in the Aberdares – the 2005 event raised over Ksh 53 million. Anyone with a car can take part in this test of endurance, engineering and navigational skills across Kenya's rugged and beautiful terrain but, for environmental reasons, numbers are limited to a maximum of fifty vehicles and a strict policy of first-come first-allowed-to-drive is observed. The challenge is to reach ten control posts in remote locations, whose whereabouts are revealed to the entrants only the night before the event. The teams of up to six people set off at dawn with ten arduous hours of driving ahead of them. Speed is not the objective, the winner being the team that completes the course with the least distance recorded.

Outdoor activities

Kenya is a country with huge untapped potential for outdoor activities. The following brief notes suggest the possibilities for walking, riding, fishing, golf, diving, wind- and kite-surfing, climbing and rafting. Elsewhere in Basics are sections on cycling (see p.59) and safaris (see p.81).

It's worth seeking advice from the Mountain Club of Kenya (see below), not just on climbing but on outdoor pursuits in general. For detailed descriptions of various climbing, hiking and caving locations in Kenya, see the "East Africa Mountain Guide" section of ⊛www.kilimanjaro.cc.

Walking

If you have plenty of time and a suitable map, **walking** is highly recommended and gives you unparalleled contact with local people. In isolated parts, it's often preferable to waiting for a lift, while in the Aberdares, Mau and Cherangani ranges, and on mounts Kenya and Elgon, it's the only practical way of moving away from the main tracks. You will sometimes come across animals out in the bush, but buffaloes and elephants (the most likely dangers), unless solitary or with young, usually move off. Don't ignore the dangers, however, and stay alert. You'll need to carry several litres of water much of the time, especially in lower, drier regions.

You might prefer to go on an organized **walking safari**, at least as a starter. Such trips are offered by a number of companies in Nairobi (see p.151).

Climbing

Apart from Mount Kenya, there are **climbing** opportunities at all grades in the Aberdares, Cheranganis, Mathews Range, Hell's Gate and Rift Valley volcanoes – including Longonot and Suswa. The Mountain Club of Kenya (PO Box 45741 Nairobi; ℡020/602330, ⊛www.mck.or.ke; clubhouse at Wilson Airport) is a good source of advice and contacts. If you intend to do any serious climbing in the country, you should make early contact. Don't expect them to answer detailed route questions, however; leave that until you arrive. Safari companies in Nairobi offer everything from a simple hike to technical ascents of Mount Kenya.

Caving

Kenya's big attractions for caving buffs are its unusual **lava tube caves**, created when molten lava flowing downhill solidified on the surface while still flowing beneath. Holes in the surface layer allowed air to enter behind the lava flow, forming the caves.

Lava tubes in Kenya include the Suswa caves near Narok, and Leviathan cave in the Chyulu Hills. Leviathan is the world's second-biggest lava tube system, with over 11km of underground passages. Caving should, of course, not be undertaken without the right equipment, training and safety precautions. For more information, contact Cave Exploration Group of East Africa, PO Box 47583 Nairobi (℡020/520883, Ⓔfajo@kenyaweb.com).

Riding

There are good opportunities for **horseback riding** in the Central Highlands and an active equestrian community in Nairobi. Safaris Unlimited (see p.151) offers riding safaris near the Maasai Mara National Reserve. **Camel safaris** are popular too, though the best operators to contact tend to change from year to year. Contact any of the addresses under "Special activity safaris" on p.151.

Fishing

Some of the highlands' streams are well stocked with **trout**, which were imported early in the last century by British settlers. A few local fishing associations are still active and the usual rules about seasons and licences apply. Tackle can be rented from tourist accommodation in the highlands. The Fisheries Department, next to the National Museum in Nairobi (PO Box 58177 Nairobi 00100; ℡020/3742320) can supply more details and various permits (including trout-fishing licences from Ksh200 for two weeks, up to Ksh500 for twelve months). Sirikwa Safaris (see p.327) can arrange trout-fishing expeditions. For **lake fishing**, it's possible to rent rods and boats at lakes Baringo, Naivasha and Turkana, and there are luxury fishing lodges on Rusinga, Mfangano and Takawiri islands on Lake Victoria.

Kenya's superb stretch of offshore coral reef, with its deepwater drop-offs and predictable northerly currents, is ideal for **near-shore angling**. Watamu, Malindi and the resorts around Mombasa are the most popular centres for **ocean fishing**.

Diving and snorkelling

Kenya's coastal waters are warm all year round so it's possible to **dive** without a wetsuit and have a rewarding dip under the waves almost anywhere.

Most of the diving bases are located at Malindi, Watamu or on the coast south of Mombasa; Diani Beach is probably the most popular area. There are centres here which will provide training to PADI leader level. For underwater photographers, in particular, the immense coral reef is a major draw – the landscape is spectacularly varied, with shallow coral gardens and blue-water drop-offs sinking as deep as 200m and, as there are few rivers to bring down sediment, visibility is generally excellent. *The Dive Sites of Kenya and Tanzania*, by Anton Koornhof (New Holland, London 1997) is highly recommended, and also covers sites suitable for snorkelling. For fish identification, *A Guide to Common Reef Fishes of the Western Indian Ocean and Kenyan Coast* by Kenneth Bock (Macmillan, London 1992; out of print, but available secondhand) or *Coral Reef Fishes – Indo-Pacific & Caribbean* by Ewald Lieske and Robert Myers (Collins, London 1994) are the obvious choices.

If you plan to do a fair bit of **snorkelling**, it makes sense to bring your own mask and snorkel, though they can always be rented.

Wind- and kite-surfing

Windsurfing has been a feature of the Kenya coast since the 1970s. **Kitesurfing**, however, is a fast-growing new sport and Diani Beach (see p.481) is making a name for itself among enthusiasts. Kitesurfers use a large inflatable kite to harness the wind, and ride on a board not dissimilar to a wakeboard or snowboard. The coast has excellent kitesurfing condtions from December to February, with the northeast monsoon tending to get up in the afternoon, blowing between 16 and 22 knots (Force 4 to 5 Beaufort), which is ideal for both beginners and experienced riders. While the southeast monsoon, blowing from June through to September, isn't as reliable as the northeasterly, it can offer some exceptional conditions.

Rafting

Both the Tana and Athi rivers have sections which can be **rafted** when they're in spate. Approximate dates are early November to mid-March, and mid-April to the end of August. Savage Wilderness Safaris is the main operator (see p.151), and most trips are for one day only.

Golf

Kenya has almost forty **golf clubs**, mostly patronized by the European and Asian communities, notably around the old colonial centres of Nairobi, Naivasha, Thika, Nanyuki and Nyeri in the Central Highlands, and Kisumu and Kitale in the west. There are also a number on the coast, and – incontestably the most bizarre – on the scorched moonscape shore of Lake Magadi. Green fees vary widely, usually from about $30 per person per day. Details for all of these from the Kenya Golf Union, PO Box 49609 Nairobi (☏020/3763898, ✆www.kgu.or.ke). For organized upmarket **golfing safaris**, contact Tobs Golf Safaris Ltd, PO Box 20146 Nairobi (☏020/271 0825 or 6, ✆www.kenya-golf -safaris.com).

National parks and reserves

The national parks are administered by the Kenya Wildlife Service (KWS; ✆www .kws.org) as total sanctuaries where human habitation (apart from the tourist lodges) is prohibited. Things seem to be gradually changing, however, as the benefits of readmitting traditional pastoralists begin to be appreciated (humans and wildlife lived in equilibrium before the British arrived). National reserves, run by local councils, tend to be less strict on the question of human encroachment.

Parks and reserves are not fenced in (except for Nakuru National Park, parts of the Aberdares and the north side of Nairobi National Park). Animals are thus free to come and go, though they do tend to stay within the boundaries, especially in the dry seasons when cattle outside compete for water.

Most parks and reserves are open to **private visits** (though foreign-registered commercial overland vehicles are not allowed in). A few parks have been heavily developed for tourism with graded tracks, signposts, lodges and the rest, but none has any kind of bus service at the gate for people without their own transport. You may be able to hitch a lift at the park gate with visitors in a private vehicle, but in general, without your own transport, you'll have to go on an organized safari. The largest and most frequently visited parks are covered in depth in chapter 5. An introduction to the main game parks, giving you some idea of what to expect from

them and the best times to visit, is given in the table on pp.78–79. Details about smaller and lesser-known parks and reserves, some of which can be visited on foot, are included in the rest of the guide.

Entry fees

Park entry fees, payable in dollars or Ksh, are charged per person per 24-hour visit. Entry to certain parks is by smartcard only. You can buy smartcards and load them with credit at **points of issue** (POI) – the main gates at Nairobi National Park, Nakuru NP, Tsavo East NP and the KWS office in Mombasa. You can add further credit at POI and also at points of sale – the KWS headquarters at Mweiga (near the Aberdares NP), Tsavo West NP main gate at Mtito Andei, Amboseli NP Meshanani gate (on the route from Namanga) and Malindi Marine Park. As long as you have sufficient credit, your smartcard is good for entry by any entrance to any smartcard park. Unused credit is non-refundable, and the card is retained as soon as credit runs out – meaning you have to go to a POI to get a new one if you want to make further visits to smartcard parks. If you're visiting the relevant parks independently, all this requires some planning and makes last-minute changes of itinerary problematic.

Fees vary according to the popularity of the park; the marine parks, such as those at Watumu and Malindi, are very cheap ($5, or $2 children). Children's rates apply to anyone under 18; students under 23, in a group of at least ten, can claim student rates if they have valid student IDs and contact the KWS in advance. **Kenyan citizens** and **residents** are eligible for massively reduced rates (not exceeding Ksh500). If you qualify, you must have ID to prove it. For **Kenyan** residents only, there's an **Annual Pass** (Ksh7000 per adult; Ksh5000 per child under 18) allowing a year's unlimited access to national parks, though not national reserves.

Vehicles with fewer than six seats are charged Ksh200 per day (6–12 seats Ksh500, 13–24 seats Ksh1000). A **guide service** costs, per guide, Ksh1000 for a day, Ksh500 for half a day (4hr). If you want to **camp**, you have to stay in a recognized campsite and pay a fee ($8–15, depending on the park and whether it's a "special" campsite). Prices, gate opening times, regulations and information on maps are given at the start of the relevant sections in the guide.

Practical considerations

The parks usually get two **rainy seasons** – brief rains in November or December, more earnest in April and May – but these can vary widely. As a general rule, you'll see more animals during the dry season when they are concentrated near water and the grasses are low. After the rains break and fill the seasonal watering places, the game tends to disperse deep into the bush. Moreover, if your visit coincides with the rains, you may have to put up with some frustrating game drives, with mud and stranded vehicles. The effects of climate have led to several temporary closures over recent years and impressions

one season may be quite different the next. By way of compensation, if your plans include luxury accommodation, you'll save a fortune at lodges and tented camps in the low season. Most places reduce their tariffs by anything from a third to a half between April and June, with savings particularly spectacular for singles.

Security is also a consideration, especially in Meru, Samburu, Shaba and Buffalo Springs, where banditry from the northeast and Somalia occasionally spills over. You'd be advised to check up on the latest situation with a reputable travel agent in Mombasa or Nairobi before visiting these parks independently.

More of a persistent problem than the occasional robbery in the parks is the continued, unstoppable damage done by those loutish hooligans, **baboons**. A locked vehicle might be safe; an unwatched tent certainly isn't. Insurance companies don't cover such contingencies.

If you want to get as much as possible out of your visit, you need to have detailed **maps** of the parks. The best map for each park is mentioned in the brief details at the start of each park section. KWS maps are available at the parks' main gates, at the KWS shop by the entrance to Nairobi National Park, and (sometimes at slightly inflated prices) in some lodges. These maps number road junctions in the parks, corresponding to signage on the ground. However, bear in mind that information on campsites and lodgings in any of the maps isn't always up to date. Accommodation options change frequently in most of the parks.

It's important to bear in mind some simple facts to ensure you leave the park and the animals as you found them, for others to enjoy. **Harassment** of animals disturbs feeding, breeding and reproductive cycles, and too many vehicles surrounding wildlife is not only unpleasant for you, but also distresses the animals. Take only photographs and memories, leave nothing behind. Collecting **firewood** (for camping) is strictly prohibited, as is picking wild flowers. If you **smoke** while on your visit, tip all ash in an ashtray. Carelessly discarded cigarettes start numerous bush fires every year, which cause great damage to vegetation and wildlife.

National Park/ National Reserve	Description	Main attractions	Accommodation
*(Non-resident entry fee; * indicates payment by Smartcard)*			
Aberdares NP * $30 (child $10) See p.208	forest and montane grassland, access by 4WD only	plentiful elephants and buffaloes, plus black rhino, bongo antelope and giant forest hog	*Treetops* and *The Ark* tree hotels, limited budget accommodation and camping
Amboseli NP * $30 (child $10) See p.384	small and busy, in the shadow of Kilimanjaro	elephants, hyenas, buffalo, zebras, hippos, giraffes	lodges, *bandas*, one campsite outside the park
Arabuko-Sokoke NP $10 (child $5) See p.499	coastal forest, home to pioneering community conservation projects	Aders' duiker, golden-rumped elephant shrew, birds and butterflies	camping in the park, hotels in Watamu
Buffalo Springs NR $15 (child $5) See p.407	smallish reserve adjacent to Samburu but with more varied terrain	lions, elephants, reticulated giraffe, Somali ostrich, gerenuk, crocodiles	two lodges, four public campsites
Lake Nakuru NP * $30 (child $10) See p.253	soda lake surrounded by a variety of vegetation, accessible by taxi	flamingos, pelicans, vervet monkeys, baboons, lions leopards	stylish lodges, camping, B&Ls, or stay in town
Lewa Conservancy $35 See p.204	privately owned former cattle ranch with fenced rhino sanctuary	white rhino, elephants, Grevy's zebra	one lodge, one tented camp, eight cottages
Maasai Mara NR $15 (child $5) See p.392	best reserve in Kenya for spotting animals, but also the most heavily touristed	wildebeest migration (Aug–Sept), balloon trips, big variety of wildlife including all the "Big Five" (elephant, rhino, buffalo, lion, leopard), plus hippos, giraffes and zebras	large number of upmarket camps and lodges, but little budget accommodation
Meru NP $27 (child $10) See p.412	lots of bush cover, not many tourists, despite being the *Born Free* park	lions, elephants, buffaloes, reticulated giraffe, Grevy's zebra, white rhino	two lodges, plus bandas, a public campsite and "special" campsites
Mount Elgon NP $15 (child $5) See p.330	Kenyan half of the caldera of an extinct volcano on the Ugandan border	elephants, salt-lick caves, hot springs, scenery	campsites, *bandas*, one rather down-at-heel lodge outside the park

National Park/ National Reserve	Description	Main attractions	Accommodation
*(Non-resident entry fee; * indicates payment by Smartcard)*			
Mount Kenya NP $15 (child $8) See p.180		climbing the mountain; high-altitude flora	hiking huts, hotels at the base
Nairobi NP * $23 (child $10) See p.156	small park in a handy location right by Nairobi, with a surprising variety of wildlife (but no elephants)	giraffes, lions, cheetahs, zebras, wildebeest, black rhino	none in the park, plenty in town
Saiwa Swamp NP $15 (child $5) See p.327	the smallest park in Kenya, access on foot only, mainly marshland	sitatunga antelope	none in the park, *Sirikwa Safaris* homestay 11km away
Samburu NR $15 (child $5) See p.407	peaceful and beautiful park in arid lowlands north of Mount Kenya	leopards, elephants (especially drinking at the river), reticulated giraffe, Grevy's zebra, Somali ostrich, gerenuk, cheetah, Beisa oryx, crocodiles	four lodges
Shaba NR $15 (child $5) See p.412	near Samburu and Buffalo Springs, but better watered and less visited	elephants, jackals, lions, Grevy's zebra, reticulated giraffe	one lodge and two campsites (not always open)
Shimba Hills NP $23 (child $10) See p.470	hilly terrain near the coast, with scattered jungle and grassland	elephants, sable antelope, bushbabies, leopards, great views	tree lodge, campsites, *bandas*
Tsavo East NP * $27 (child $10) See p.378	biggest national park in Kenya, popular for budget camping safaris, with Yatta plateau lava flow on west side, popular for budget camping safaris	elephants, black rhinos, Mudanda Rock, Aruba Dam, Lugard's Falls	four public campsites, one lodge, plenty of tented camps
Tsavo West NP * $27 (child $10) See p.374	large park around smaller "developed area"	lava flows, Mzima Springs with underwater hippo-watching, Ngulia Rhino Sanctuary, elephants, zebras, giraffes, lions, buffaloes, lesser kudu antelope	lodges, *bandas*, campsites and tented camps in the park, budget accommodation in Mtito Andei

Driving

If you're driving during the rains, remember that none of the park roads are paved and unless you're content to keep to the main graded tracks, you will need a 4WD vehicle to venture down the smaller ones. A night spent stuck in the mud in Maasai Mara (a likely enough occurrence if you only have 2WD) isn't recommended, nor is trying to reverse down a boulder-strewn slope in Tsavo West. In any case, a normal saloon will be shaken to bits on the average park road, and most car-rental companies will insist you have 4WD.

Be sensitive to the great damage that can be done to delicate ecosystems by **driving off marked roads**. Even apparently innocent diversions can scour fragile, root-connected grasslands for years, spreading dust, destroying the integrity of the lowest levels of vegetation, and hindering the life cycles and movements of insects and smaller animals, with consequent disruption to the lives of their predators. (The effects of this are especially visible in Amboseli and Maasai Mara, both of which are now ecologically at risk.) So use only signposted roads and tracks, or ones marked on official maps (admittedly, it can sometimes be hard to judge whether you're following an agreed route, or the tracks of others who broke the rule), and if you have a driver, ask him to do the same. Safari minibuses which do go off-road are operating illegally and should be reported to the rangers. If this all means being denied the opportunity to see one of the "Big Five", consider the fact that cheetahs, which hunt by day, are very sensitive to noise and interference by vehicles – when surrounded by minibuses, they may offer great photo-ops, but are unable to hunt.

Stick to the official maximum **speed limit** posted at the gates, usually 30kph. This avoids accidents and prevents too much dust being kicked up. **Night driving** (usually 7pm–6am) is illegal in all Kenyan parks and reserves without express permission from the warden. For advice on coping with mud tracks, see p.58.

Accommodation

If you're visiting independently, with or without a vehicle, it may well be worth bringing a **tent** (consider renting or buying one in Nairobi – see p.153). If you don't have one, parks such as Amboseli, Maasai Mara and Samburu can be very limiting, as there is no cheap *banda* accommodation at any of them. In any case, camping out adds to the adventure. If you're visiting the parks on a more comfortable basis and staying in lodges or tented camps, it would be wise to make advance reservations as there's heavy pressure on beds during the peak seasons. Note that if you book via a travel agent, you may be given discounts on official "rack rates", sometimes up to ten percent off.

Besides campsites, KWS has a limited range of lodges and *bandas* at some parks, listed under the "Where to stay" section of ⓦ www.kws.org; these can be booked through the park itself or KWS in Nairobi (ⓣ 020/600800, ⓔ tourism@kws.org).

Game-viewing

Most of the lodges and tented camps have their own 4WD vehicles and run regular **game drives**. These can be very worthwhile because the drivers usually know the animals and the area. Expect to pay around $50 per person for scheduled departures and around $150 for exclusive use of the vehicle for two to three hours. The usual pattern is two (or sometimes three) game drives a day: at dawn, mid-morning and late afternoon (though if you keep this up for more than a day or two you'll be exhausted). In the middle of the day, the parks are usually left to the animals; you'll be told it's because they are all hiding. A more likely reason is that the midday hours are a lousy time to take pictures. The animals are around, if sleepy, and if you can put up with the heat while most people are safely in the lodges, it can be a tranquil and satisfying time.

Rangers can usually be hired for the day (KWS rates are Ksh500 per day, or Ksh300 for four hours, with a tip usually expected) and, if you have room, someone with intimate local knowledge and a trained eye is a good companion (knowing some Swahili animal names is a help – see pp.695–696).

Be quiet when viewing, switch off your engine, and never, under any circumstance, get out of your vehicle, and don't feed animals as it upsets their diet and leads to dependence on humans. Habituated baboons, especially, can become violent if refused handouts. Animals have **right of way**, and are not to be disturbed (even if sitting across the track). This means keeping a minimum distance of 20m, having no more than five vehicles viewing an animal at any one time (wait your turn if necessary), no loud noises or flashed headlights, and not following the animals if they start to move away.

To see as much as possible, stop frequently to scan with binoculars, watch what the herds of antelope and other grazers are doing (a predator will usually be watched intently by them all), and talk to anyone you meet on your way. The best time of day is sunrise, when nocturnal animals are often still out and about and you might see that weird dictionary leader, the aardvark.

Safaris

Before arranging a safari, think about whether you want comfort or a more authentic experience, and whether you want the convenience of having it prebooked as part of a package holiday, or the independence of picking and choosing once in Kenya itself. Remember, too, that the parks and reserves can also be visited privately, allowing you to set your own itinerary – sometimes an attractive alternative to an organized trip.

Types of safari

Air safaris, using internal flights to get around, will add enormously to the cost and comfort of your trip and give you spectacular views but a much less intimate feel of Africa. On the other hand, long bumpy **drives** to meet the demands of an itinerary can be exhausting (and impossible for the physically infirm) while hours of your time are eaten away in a cloud of dust.

Many safaris take you from one game park hotel (known as a **lodge**) to another, using **minibuses** with lift-up roofs for taking pictures. Make sure you have a window seat and ask about the number of passengers and whether the vehicle is shared by several operators or is for your group only.

The alternative to a standard lodge safari is a **camping safari**, usually in a minibus, where the crew – or you, if it's a budget trip – pitch your tents each day. With this kind of trip you have to be prepared for a degree of discomfort along with the self-sufficiency: insects can occasionally be a menace, you may not get a shower every night, the food won't be so lavish and the beer not so cold.

It's common on camping safaris to spend the hot part of the day at the campsite. Some

campsites are shady and pleasant, but that's not always the case and, where there are lodges with swimming pools, cold beer and other amenities nearby, it's worth paying to spend a few hours in comfort. Similarly, if you want to go on an early game drive, don't be afraid to suggest to the tour operator that you skip breakfast, or take sandwiches. Too often, the itinerary is a product of what tour operators think customers want, that's passed from management to drivers and cooks.

On the best camping safaris, you travel in a fairly **rugged vehicle** – a four-wheel-drive land cruiser or even an open-sided lorry – giving more flexibility about where you go and how long you stay. The more expensive camping safaris come very expensive indeed and tend to model their style on images culled from *Out of Africa*; they can easily cost over £200/\$350 a day.

Note that the "**balloon safaris**" you see advertised are short balloon flights, not complete tours. They take place at dawn and last a couple of hours at most. They can be done in several parks, most popularly in the Maasai Mara, and the bill is a big one – around £250/\$400 per person. There are more details on p.407.

Booking at home

Most travel agents can fix you up with brochures for the more **mainstream tour operators** whose packages generally fall into the more expensive lodge and minibus category. For more **offbeat adventure trips**, or a better selection of camping safaris, you should contact the operator directly. Note that the **single-person supplement** tends to be high on conventional beach-and-safari packages and somewhat less (or you can share) on the more adventure-spirited trips, where prices are per person, but depend also on the size of the group, which can make things extremely expensive if there are only two or three people.

The minibus safaris fitted into most of the inexpensive Mombasa-based charter packages venture no further afield than the three national parks easily accessible from the coast – Tsavo East, Tsavo West and Amboseli. Trips up to Samburu or west to Maasai Mara are more expensive, and therefore cheaper if arranged from Nairobi.

Booking in Kenya

Independently choosing a **safari company** to spend your money on can be fairly hit or miss. Unless you have the luxury of a long stay, your choice will probably be limited by the time available. If you're booking at the last minute, many companies are willing to offer a discount in order to fill unsold seats. Some outfits will also give student discounts if you ask. In fact, you should use any angle you can employ to get a good deal.

This is not to recommend the very cheapest outfits. Some camping operators, not all of them licensed, sell safaris at the very bottom of the market in a price war which completely undercuts the legitimate firms. Any safari which is offered at less than £50/$80 per day is likely to be cutting corners. The easiest way for disreputable operators to cut costs is to avoid paying park entry fees, which threatens the preservation of wildlife in Kenya. Give these fly-by-night companies a miss.

A number of **recommended operators** are given in the Nairobi account on pp.148–152, but it's difficult to find a company that's absolutely consistent. Give them a try unless an alternative sounds especially good and reliable; the Nairobi grapevine is probably your best guide on this. If the company is a member of the Kenya Association of Tour Operators (KATO; PO Box 48461, Kato Place, Longonot Rd, Upper Hill, Nairobi ☎020/2713348, ⓦwww.katokenya .org), that's a good sign.

Unpredictables such as weather, illness and visibility of animals all contribute to the degree of success of the trip; group relations among the passengers can assume surprising significance in a very short time. More controllable factors like breakdowns, food, equipment and competence of the drivers and tour leaders, really determine reputations. If anything **goes wrong**, reputable companies will do their best to compensate on the spot (an extra day if you broke down, a night in a lodge if you didn't make it to a campsite, partial refunds without demur). If your grievance is unresolved, you might want to contact KATO, who can intercede with its members.

Staff relations

When on your trip, it's important not to take a passive attitude. Although some of the **itinerary** may be fixed, it's not all cast in stone, and daily routines may be altered to suit the clients easily enough if you ask – though going over-budget on fuel is likely to be an issue.

As long as they know there will be reasonable **tips** at the end of the trip, most staff will go out of their way to help. Tipping on budget trips, however, can often cause lengthy misunderstandings between the clients, who are usually expected to organize themselves to give collective gratuities on the last day. Good companies make suggestions in their briefing packs. Around $5 per member of staff per day from each client is about right, slightly more for a small group (of two or three), and less for a very large group, or one that includes children, or where service has been poor. If this sounds like a lot in Kenyan terms, bear in mind that such gratuities form the bulk of the income of staff who spend many weeks each year not on safari.

Photography

Kenya is immensely photogenic and with any kind of camera you'll get beautiful pictures. Except in the game parks (where some kind of telephoto is essential if you want pictures of animals rather than savanna), you don't really need cumbersome lenses. Animal photography is a question of patience and not taking endless pictures of nothing happening. While taking photos, try keeping both eyes open and, in a vehicle, always turn off the engine.

Whatever kind of camera you take, make sure you have a dust-proof bag to keep it in. If your camera uses non-rechargeable or unusual batteries, take spares – they can be outrageously expensive or hard to find in Nairobi. If you intend to email digital pictures home, note that cybercafés outside Nairobi and Mombasa rarely have USB-capable computers, and that it would probably take ages to email even a few photos at the bandwidth of the average Kenyan Internet connection. The lack of USB also means you may have difficulty archiving your photos to CD, so it pays to take enough memory cards with you to last the duration of your trip.

Film is not especially expensive in Kenya, but can be hard to find outside of sizeable towns, so try to bring all you'll need. Try to keep it cool by stuffing it inside a sleeping bag, or wrapping it in newspaper. If you're away for some time, posting film home seems a good idea but is still risky, even if registered – better to leave it with a reliable hotel or friend in Nairobi or Mombasa. Machine developing and processing can be quick (four-hour service is not uncommon) and is not particularly expensive. A few places in Nairobi have a decent enough reputation (see p.155).

The question of **photographing local people** can be prickly, but you should always ask permission first. If you won't accept that some kind of interaction and exchange are warranted, you won't get many pictures. Blithely aiming at strangers won't make you any friends and it may well get you into trouble. The Maasai and Samburu – Kenya's most colourful and photographed people – are usually prepared to do a deal (at monopoly prices, but bargain), and in some places you'll even find professional posers making a living at the roadside. Other people may be happy to let you take their picture for free, but will certainly appreciate it if you take their name and address, and send a print when you get home. Even better, and a way of achieving instant popularity, is to take a Polaroid camera – many people in rural areas don't possess a single photo of themselves.

Though most people are amazingly tolerant of the camera, sensitivity on your part is essential. The superstition that pictures capture part of the soul is still prevalent in some rural areas, and some Maasai and Samburu people in particular may object strongly to you snapping their children or animals, whose souls are weaker than those of human adults. It's also a bad idea to take pictures of anything that could be construed as strategic, including any military or police building, prisons, airports, harbours, bridges and the President of the Republic.

The environment and responsible tourism

Tourism's growth in Kenya has been spectacular, from 36,000 visitors in 1955 to over a million in 2000, since when it has remained roughly stable. It has been a boon for the economy, but with serious and potentially disruptive effects environmentally, socially, culturally and economically. Environmental and land degradation as a direct consequence of tourists is evident in Maasai Mara, Samburu and Amboseli, as well as on the beaches.

Local issues have been covered throughout this book. If you're at all concerned about the impact of tourism or environmental matters, get in touch with the organizations mentioned in the text, or the ones listed below. See also the box "Responsible snorkelling, diving and fishing" (p.421).

Forests and land-grabbing

The rate of clearance of Kenya's remaining areas of indigenous **forest** is alarming, worsening the problem of soil erosion, and consequently the siltation of lakes, rivers and estuaries. Illegal "land grabbing" made headlines in the late 1990s and sparked off countless demonstrations, legal moves and protests. The government responded with the 1999 Environment Conservation Management Act, which protects forest areas that are officially gazetted, and allows members of the public to oppose degazettement. This did not stop the government from announcing, in early 2001, the excision of 6700 square kilometres from gazetted forests for development, resulting in widespread protests by environmentalists, and attempts in the High Court to halt the move. Some of the land was eventually regazetted. The area most affected on that occasion was the Mau Forest in the Rift Valley (see p.260), but areas threatened by land grabbing and illegal logging also include Kakamega Forest (pp.339–348), parts of Mount Kenya Forest with its near extinct camphor plant, the coastal mangroves, and Arabuko-Sokoke Forest (pp.499–501).

Contacts

African Wildlife Foundation Kenya: Britak Centre, Mara Ragati Rd; PO Box 48177 Nairobi ☏ 020/2710367; USA ☏ 202/939 3333, ⊛ www .awf.org. They run an African Heartlands programme in eight key conservation areas including Kenya's Samburu, involving species conservation (particularly elephants and rhinos) and wildlife management.
East African Wildlife Society PO Box 20110; Nairobi ☏ 020/3874145, ⊛ www.eawildlife.org. Influential Kenya-based group, strongly involved in the movement to ban the ivory trade (achieved 1989), and remaining active in other areas, recently raising awareness about forest and mangrove protection.
Ecotourism Society of Kenya PO Box 10146 Nairobi ☏ 020/2724755, ⊛ www.esok.org. A Kenyan organization working to promote sustainable tourism that contributes to rather than destroys local communities and the environment.
Friends of Conservation Kenya: Great Jubilee Centre, Langata Rd; PO Box 74901 Nairobi ☏ 020/890143, ⓔ info@fockenya.org; UK ☏ 020/7603 5024, ⊛ www.foc-uk.com; USA ☏ 630/954 3388, ⊛ www.friendsofconservation .org. Concerns itself with raising awareness of the detrimental consequences of tourism in eastern and southern Africa.
Friends of Nairobi National Park (FoNNaP) PO Box 42976 Nairobi 00100 ☏ 020/607974, ⓔ fonnap@africaonline.co.ke. Strives to keep the migratory routes to the park open, and to raise awareness among Nairobi citizens about the park.
Green Belt Movement Kilimani Lane (off Elgeyo Marakwet Rd) Adams Arcade; PO Box 67545 Nairobi ☏ 020/573057 ⊛ www.greenbeltmovement .org. Grassroots conservation movement founded by Nobel Peace Prize winner Wangari Maathai (see p.623) to stop the illegal expropriation of public land, now with wider community-based conservation aims.
Kenya Forests Working Group (KFWG) ☏ 020/571335, ⊛ www.kenyaforests.org.

Concerned with conserving and managing Kenya's forests, and has a "Forest Hotline" for up-to-date information on current issues.
Kenya Tourism Concern PO Box 22449 Nairobi

☏ 020/535850. Kenyan sister organization to the UK's Tourism Concern, a campaigning organization that works with local communities to reduce social and environmental problems connected with tourism.

Peoples, languages and religions

Whether called peoples, ethnic groups or tribes (the term still used officially and in casual conversation), Kenyans have a multiplicity of racial and cultural origins. Distinctions would be simple if similarities in physical appearance were shared by those who speak the same language and share a common culture. But "tribes" have never been closed units, and appearance, speech and culture have always overlapped. Families, for instance, often contain members of different tribes. Tradition still dictates whether an individual's "tribe" is determined through their father's line, or through their mother's brother's line.

In the last fifty years, **ethnic identities** have broken down as broader class, political and national ones have emerged. However, political parties still tend to be ethnically rather than ideologically based, and casual inter-ethnic prejudice is still commonplace, much as the intelligentsia may decry it.

Languages

The most enduring ethnic distinction is **language**. A person's "mother tongue" is still important as an index of social identity, and a tribe is best defined as people sharing a common first language. However, in the towns and among affluent families, language is increasingly unimportant. Many people speak three languages (their own, Swahili and English) or even four if they have mixed parentage. And for a few, English has become a first language (and is, alongside Swahili – or **Kiswahili** as it's correctly known – the offical language of the country).

The history and culture of the main language groups in each region are covered throughout the book.

African language groups in kenya

What follows is, broadly speaking, the breakdown of Kenya's language groups into separate ethnic identities. You'll find variations on these spellings, and inconsistencies in the use of prefixes (ie Kamba instead of Akamba, Agikuyu instead of Kikuyu, and so on).

Bantu-speaking

Western Bantu Luhya, Gusii, Kuria.
Central Bantu Akamba, Kikuyu, Embu, Meru, Mbere, Tharaka.
Coastal Bantu Swahili, Mijikenda, Segeju, Pokomo, Taita, Taveta.

Nilotic-speaking

Lake-River Nilotic Luo.
Plains Nilotic Maasai and Samburu (Maa-speakers), Turkana, Teso, Njemps, Elmolo.
Highland Nilotic Kalenjin group (Nandi and its dialects), Marakwet, Pokot, Tugen, Kipsigis, Elkony.

Cushitic-speaking

Southern Cushitic Boni.
Eastern Cushitic Somali, Rendille, Orma, Boran, Gabbra ("Oromo" is often used to describe all these language groups except the Somali).

Names and groups

Books and the media continue to use various unwieldy terms. **Bantu** and **Nilotic** are language groups (like Indo-European or

85

Semitic) and, restricted to their linguistic sense, are fair enough. "Hamitic", which still pops up occasionally, is an almost meaningless term of biblical origin, with racist overtones that reflect the early European presumption that lighter-skinned people with thinner lips and straighter noses were more intelligent than other Africans. The origins of these people in northeast Africa and their implied association with the wellsprings of Mediterranean civilization were further "evidence" of this. The term "Nilo-hamitic" (used to refer to the Maasai and other pastoralists admired by the Europeans) confuses the issue further.

In terms of appearance, members of some ethnic groups have more "Negroid" (wider, flatter) features, while members of others have more "Caucasoid" (sharper, thinner) ones. Such variations obviously indicate different ancestry, but have little to do with people's language or culture.

Indigenous ethnic groups make up about 99 percent of the population. The largest ethnic group are the **Kikuyu**, based in the central region, who make up about 20 percent of the population, followed by the **Luo** from the Nyanza region around Kisumu, who comprise around 14 percent. The **Luhya** of western Kenya form 13 percent, followed by the **Akamba** from the eastern region around Machakos who comprise 11 percent of the population, and the Kalenjin from the Rift Valley, also 11 percent. Many tourists are surprised that only about 1.4 percent of the population are **Maasai**.

Kenya also has a considerable and diverse **Asian** population (perhaps over 100,000), predominantly Punjabi and Gujarati speakers from northwest India and Pakistan. Most of them live in Nairobi, Mombasa, Kisumu and Nakuru. Descendants in part of the labourers brought over to build the railway, they also number many whose parents and grandparents came in its wake, to trade and set up businesses, and they are still overwhelmingly dominant in commerce. Some of these families, notably on the coast, have lived in Kenya for centuries. There's a dispersed Christian Goan community, too, identified by their Portuguese surnames, who tend to have less formalized relations with other Kenyans. A diminishing Arab-speaking community remains on the coast.

Lastly, there are still an estimated 34,000 **European** residents – a surprisingly motley crew from British ex-servicemen to Italian aristocrats – scattered through the highlands and the rest of the country, some four thousand of whom hold Kenyan citizenship. Some maintain a scaled-down version of the old planter's life, and a few still hold senior civil service positions. Increasingly, though, the community is turning to the tourist industry for a more secure future.

Religion

Varieties of **Catholicism** and **Protestantism** are dominant in the highlands and westwards, and are increasingly pervasive elsewhere. In the Rift Valley and the far west, especially towards Lake Victoria, there are many minor Christian sects and churches – over a thousand denominations – often based around the teachings of local prophets and preachers.

Broad-based, non-fundamentalist **Sunni Islam** dominates the coast and the northeast, and is the fastest growing religion in the country. Many towns have several mosques (or dozens on the coast), but one usually serves as the focal Friday mosque for the whole community. The Aga Khan's **Ismaili** sect is an influential Asian constituency with powerful business interests. Politically, Kenyan Muslims tend towards moderation, but the likes of Osama Bin Laden do command a certain following among disaffected youth on the coast, and Kenyan Muslims were involved in bomb attacks on American and Israeli targets in Kenya in 1998 and 2002.

Hindu and **Sikh** temples are found in most large towns, and there are adherents of **Jainism** and the **Bahai** faith, too. **Indigenous religion** (mostly based around the idea of a supreme god and intercession between the living and the spirit worlds by deceased ancestors) survives as an inclusive belief system only in the remotest areas of northern Kenya, among the remaining Okiek (or Ndorobo) hunter-gatherers in a very few forests, and among pastoralists like the Maasai. While it is continually under threat from Christian missionaries, its influence over the lives of many nominally Christian or Muslim Kenyans remains powerful.

Culture and etiquette

Every contact between people in Kenya starts with a greeting. This means a handshake followed by polite enquiries, even as you enter a shop. Traditionally, such exchanges can last a minute or two, and you'll often hear them performed in a formal manner between two men, especially in rural areas. Long greetings help subsequent negotiations. In English or Swahili you can exchange something like "How are you?" "Fine, how's the day?" "Fine, how's business?" "Fine, how's the family?", "Fine, thank God". It's usually considered polite, while someone is speaking to you at length, to grunt in the affirmative, or say thank you at short intervals. Breaks in conversation are filled with more greetings.

Hissing ("Tsss!") is an ordinary way to attract a stranger's attention, though less common in more sophisticated urban situations. You may get a fair bit of it yourself, and it's quite in order to hiss at the waiter in a restaurant.

Answering anything in the negative is often considered impolite. If you're asking questions, don't ask yes/no ones. And try not to phrase things in the negative ("Isn't the bus leaving?") because the answer will often be "Yes" (it isn't leaving).

Body language and dress

Shaking hands upon meeting and departure is normal between all men present. Women shake hands with each other, but with men only in more sophisticated milieux. Soul brother handshakes and other exotic variations are popular among young men, while a common, very respectful handshake involves clutching your right arm with your left hand as you shake or, in Muslim areas, touching your left hand to your chest when shaking hands.

You are likely to notice a widespread and unselfconscious ease with close physical contact, especially on the coast. Male visitors may need to get used to holding hands with strangers as they're shown around the guesthouse, or guided down the street, and, on public transport, to strangers' hands and limbs draped naturally wherever is most comfortable — which can include your legs or shoulders.

Be aware of the **left hand rule**: traditionally the left hand is reserved for unhygienic acts and the right for eating and touching, or passing things to others. Like many "rules" it's very often broken, at which times you have to avoid thinking about it.

Unless you want a serious confrontation, never point with your finger. It's equivalent to an obscene gesture. For similar reasons, beckoning is done with the palm down, not up.

Don't be put off by apparent shiftiness in **eye contact**, especially if you're talking to someone much younger than you. It's normal for those deferring to others to avoid direct looks.

On the coast, it's always best to **dress** in loose-fitting long sleeves and skirts or trousers in the towns, but shorts and T-shirts won't get you into trouble; people are far too polite to admonish strangers. Lamu calls more for *kikoi* and *kanga* wraps for both sexes and, because it's so small, more consideration for local feelings. For more on suitable dress for women, see p.88. You'll also need to be suitably attired to enter **mosques**. Few are very grand, however, and you rarely miss much by staying outside.

Sexual attitudes

Although there is a certain amount of ethnic and religious variation in attitudes, sexual mores in Kenya are generally hedonistic and uncluttered. Expressive sexuality is a very obvious part of the social fabric in most communities, and in Muslim areas Islamic moral strictures tend to be generously interpreted. The age of consent is 16.

Female prostitution flourishes almost everywhere, with a remarkable number of cheaper hotels doubling as informal brothels. There are no signs of any organized sex trade and such prostitution appears to merge seamlessly into casual promiscuity. If you're a man, you're likely to find flirtatious pestering a constant part of the scene, especially if you visit bars and clubs. With HIV infection rates extremely high, even protected sex is extremely inadvisable.

Women travellers

Women travellers will be glad to find that machismo, in its fully fledged Latin varieties, is rare in Kenya and male egos are usually softened by reserves of humour. Whether travelling alone or together, women may come across occasional **persistent hasslers**, but seldom much worse. **Drinking** in bars unaccompanied by men, you can expect a lot of male attention, as you can in many other situations. Universal rules apply: if you suspect ulterior motives, turn down all offers and stonily refuse to converse, though you needn't fear expressing your anger if that's how you feel. You will, eventually, be left alone. Really obnoxious individuals are usually on their own, fortunately. These tactics are hardly necessary except on the coast, and then particularly in Lamu.

Travelling on your own, you'll usually be welcomed with generous hospitality. On **public transport** a single woman traveller causes quite a stir and fellow passengers don't want to see you badly treated. Women get offers of **accommodation** in people's homes more often than male travellers. And, if you're staying in less reputable hotels, there'll often be female company – employees, family, residents – to look after you.

The way you look and behave get noticed by everyone and they're more important if you don't appear to have a male escort. Your **head** and everything from **waist to ankles** are the sensitive zones, particularly in Islamic regions. Long, loose hair is seen as extraordinarily provocative; doubly so if blonde. Pay attention to these areas by keeping your hair fairly short or tied up (or by wearing a scarf) and wearing long skirts or, at a pinch, very baggy long pants. If you find it's too hot to wear a **bra**, it's unlikely to bother people. If you'll be travelling much on rough roads,

Women's rights in Kenya

Women's groups flourish across the country, but are concerned more with improvement of incomes, education, health and nutrition than social or political emancipation, though this is changing. The government-sponsored Maendeleo ya Wanawake Organization (MYWO) started to help women at a very basic level in the 1950s. It now encourages economic independence and, with a nominal annual membership fee, almost every woman in Kenya can belong. The umbrella group teaches basic literacy, family planning and nutrition and is also working hard to abolish the practice of ritual **female genital mutilation**, "female circumcision". This is carried out as a rite of passage on an estimated fifty percent of Kenyan girls, and is more prevalent in some ethnic groups (the Gusii and the Maasai for example) than others. Unsurprisingly, it is more common in rural areas and among uneducated people than in cities and among those with schooling. Kenya is a signatory to the UN's Human Rights Convention, which proscribes genital mutilation, and the government promised in 1990 to ban the practice, but a motion calling for its prohibition was heavily defeated in parliament in 1996, and it remains legal. Womens' groups are meanwhile trying to persuade rural communities to accept a mutilation-free "alternative rite of passage", with some limited success.

Kenya is still used as something of a contraceptive testing ground, with less stringent rules on over-the-counter drugs than many countries. Depo-provera, high-level oestrogen pills and the Dalkon shield have all been foisted on Kenyan women.

For more information and contacts, get in touch with MYWO (Maendeleo House, Monrovia St, PO Box 44412; Nairobi ☎02/222095, ⓦwww.maendeleo-ya-wanawake .org), or the much more independent National Council of Women of Kenya (PO Box 43741 Nairobi ☎02/603416).

however, you'll need a bra for support. Seriously.

Tampons are available in town chemists but expensive, so bring your own supplies.

Gay and lesbian travellers

Sex between men is illegal in Kenya, and homosexuality is still largely a taboo subject, lesbianism doubly so; many Kenyans take the attitude that it's a foreign, un-African practice. While there is no gay scene as such, male homosexuality is an accepted undercurrent on the coast, where it finds most room for expression in Lamu and Malindi, and to a small extent in Nairobi. The Lake Victoria region has a fairly relaxed attitude, too. *Msenge* is the Swahili for "gay man".

You'll find a small amount of information on the male gay scene in Kenya in the *Spartacus Gay Guide*. The US website Purple Roofs (⊛www.purpleroofs.com) maintains a list of gay-owned and gay-friendly accommodation and tour companies in Kenya, while Promote Kenya in Malindi (☎042/31951 or 21232, ⊛www.kenya-travel.com) is a gay-friendly company offering tailor-made safaris and beach holidays.

Crime and personal safety

Though things seem to have improved since the change of government in 2002, there's no denying that petty crime is a problem in Kenya, and you have a far higher chance of being a victim in touristy areas, where pickings are richer. It's important to bear in mind, however, that most of the large number of tourists who visit the country each year experience no difficulties.

For up-to-date safety warnings, check the travel advisories on the websites of the UK Foreign Office (⊛www.fco.gov.uk/travel) or the US State Department (⊛travel.state.gov), or the security section of KATO's website (⊛www.katokenya.org). For advice on wildlife safety, see p.64.

Avoiding trouble

After **arriving** by air for the first time, a fair few people get robbed during their first day or two in Nairobi, before they've had chance to get used to the pace and dangers of the place. Try to be acutely conscious of your belongings: never leave anything unguarded even for five seconds, never take out cameras or other valuables unless absolutely necessary, and be careful of where you walk, at least until you've dropped off your luggage and you're settled in somewhere. It's hard not to look like a tourist, but try to **dress** like a local – short-sleeved shirt, slacks or skirt and sunglasses – and try not to wear anything brand new. **Sunglasses** make avoiding unwanted eye contact easier. Most importantly, don't carry a **bag**, particularly not the little day-pack over your shoulder which will virtually identify you as a tourist.

The only substantial risks outside Nairobi are down at the coast (where valuables often disappear from the beach or occasionally get grabbed), in the other big towns (Nakuru and, to a lesser extent, Kisumu), and in some of the game parks – Samburu and Maasai Mara have had a number of incidents in recent years.

If you're **driving**, it's never a good idea to leave even a locked car unguarded if it has anything of value in it. In towns, there's usually someone who will volunteer to guard it for you for a tip (Ksh20–50 is enough).

All of this isn't meant to induce paranoia, but if you flaunt the trappings of wealth where there's urban poverty, somebody will want to remove them. There's always less risk in leaving your valuables in a locked hotel room or – judiciously – with the management, than in taking them with you. Don't wear dangling earrings or any kind of chain or necklace, and even a cheap wrist watch is tempting. If you clearly have nothing on you, you're unlikely to feel, or be, threatened. In Nairobi, the rush hour at dusk is probably the worst time, but it's a good idea to be alert getting off a night bus early in the morning, too. There are always more pickpockets about at the end of the month too, when people are carrying their pay packet.

When you have to **carry money**, put it in several places if possible. A money belt tucked into your trousers or skirt is invisible and thus usually secure for traveller's cheques, passport and large amounts of cash. Put the rest – what you'll need for your day/walk/night out – in a pocket or somewhere more accessible. You're safer with at least some money to hand, as few muggers will believe you have nothing on you.

Cons and scams

Doping scams are an occasional problem, with individuals on different public transport routes managing to drug tourists and relieve them of their belongings. Don't accept any food or drink on public transport, even at the risk of causing offence.

Approaches in the street from "schoolboys" with sponsorship forms (only primary education is free, and even then, books, uniforms, even furniture have to be bought) and from "refugees" with long stories are not uncommon and probably best shrugged off,

even though some, unfortunately, may be genuine.

One scam, almost "traditional" by now, and surprisingly successful to judge by the number of tourists who fall for it, relies entirely on people's belief in the paranoid republic. It involves an approach by a "student", followed by a request for a small sum of money, or sometimes just someone who engages you for a chat and claims to be a Sudanese or Somali refugee. Shortly after you part company, a group of heavies surround you and claim to be undercover police, interested in the discussion you've been having with that "terrorist", or whatever, and a large fine is demanded, or they may want to "arrest" you and then demand money with menaces. You can ask to see ID, or just tell them to go to hell – such aggressions are never the real thing. Also beware of people offering to change money on the street, especially in Nairobi – it's usually a trick to get you down an alley where you can be relieved of your cash.

A treat for Nairobi motorists is a small boy popping up and slapping you in the face as you get out after parking. As you make to go after him in outrage, his friends grab what they can from the car. Other car tricks are described in the section on Nakuru (p.248).

Muggings

If you get mugged, **don't resist**, as knives and guns are occasionally carried. It will be over in an instant and you're unlikely to be hurt. But the hassles, and worse, that gather when you try to do anything about it

Would-be helpers

It's very easy to fall prey to **misunderstandings** in your relations with people (usually boys and young men) who offer their services as guides, helpers or "facilitators" of any kind. You should absolutely never assume anything is being done out of simple kindness. It may well be but, if it isn't, you must expect to pay something. If you have any suspicion, it's best to confront the matter head on at an early stage and either apologize for the offence caused by the suggestion, or agree a price. What you must never do, as when bargaining, is enter into an unspoken contract and then break it by refusing to pay for the service. If you're being bugged by someone whose help you don't need, just let them know you can't pay anything for their trouble. It may not make you a friend, but it always works and it's better than a row and recriminations.

make it imperative not to let it happen in the first place. Thieves caught red-handed are usually mobbed – often killed – so avoid the usual Kenyan response of shouting "Thief!" ("*Mwizi!*" in Swahili), unless you're ready to intercede instantly once you've retrieved your belongings.

Usually you'll have no chance to catch the thief, and the first reaction is to go to the **police** (recognizable by their blue uniforms). Unless you've lost a lot of money (and cash is virtually irretrievable) or irreplaceable property, however, think twice about doing this. They rarely do something for nothing – even stamping an **insurance form** will probably cost you, though you will need it to claim – and secondly, you should consider the ramifications of trying to catch the culprits (with you in the back of a police car expected to point out the thief in the crowds – a complete waste of time). Never agree to act as a decoy in the hope that the same thing will happen again in front of a police ambush. Police shootings take place all the time and you may prefer not to be the cause of a cold-blooded murder.

If you have to visit the police in Nairobi, go to the main police station, rather than the smaller posts and offices.

The police

If you have official business with the police, then politeness, smiles and handshakes always help. If you're expected to give a **bribe** – *chai* (the usual word, actually meaning "tea") or *kitu kidogo* ("something small") – wait for it to be hinted at and haggle over it as you would any payment; the equivalent of a dollar or so is often enough to oil small wheels. Be aware, of course, that bribery is illegal. If you know you've done nothing wrong and are not in a rush, refusing a bribe will only cost a short delay until the policeman gives up on you and tries another potential source of income.

In **unofficial dealings**, the police, especially in remote outposts, can go out of their way to help you with food, transport or accommodation. Try to reciprocate. Police salaries are low – no more than a few thousand shillings a month – and they rely on unofficial income to get by. Only a brand new police force and realistic salaries could alter a situation which is now entrenched.

Drug and other offences

Though **illegal**, marijuana (*bhang* or *bangi*) is widely cultivated and smoked, and is remarkably cheap. However, with the authorities making efforts to control it and penalties of up to ten years for possession (life and a million-shilling fine for trafficking), its use is not advisable. Official busts result in a heavy fine and deportation at the very least, and quite often a prison sentence, with little sympathy from your embassy. Heroin is becoming a major problem on the coast, and possession of that, or of anything harder than marijuana will get you in a lot worse trouble if you're caught. *Miraa* (or *qat*; see p.197), a herbal stimulant, is legal and widely available, especially in Meru, Nairobi, Mombasa and in the north, but local police chiefs sometimes order crackdowns on its transport.

Besides drug possession, common ways of exciting police interest are staggering around a city late at night – which needs lots of humble pie and nothing more – and **driving offences**. On the road, you may sometimes be stopped with the sole purpose of finding fault to elicit a bribe. In such cases, you could insist on a receipt before handing over any money (if it's refused, you can probably talk yourself out of it). It's worth knowing that some forces have speed-trap radar equipment which they set up outside towns; drive with caution as speed limits are often vague.

Be warned that failure to observe the following points of **behaviour** can get you arrested. Stand in cinemas and on other occasions when the national anthem is playing. Stand still when the national flag is being raised or lowered in your field of view. Don't take photos of the flag or the president (often seen on state occasions in Nairobi). If the presidential motorcade appears, pull off the road to let it pass. It's also a criminal offence to tear or deface a banknote of any denomination, and, officially, to urinate in a public place.

Travelling with children

Wherever you go, the reaction of local people to families and their children is exceptionally welcoming. However, if you're considering taking very young kids, ask yourself if you can really be bothered with all the hassle. It's a good start if they're already enchanted with the idea of Africa and its wildlife.

The following is aimed principally at families with babies and under-fives. For the under-fives, Kenya is a mixture of fun – in the pool, on the beach, with other kids – and tedium – in the car or plane, on a game drive, in a restaurant.

Children's health

Health issues figure most prominently in most people's minds. With the exception of malaria, however, you can discount fears about your children getting tropical diseases in Kenya. Remember how many healthy second-generation expatriate children have been brought up there (the biggest health problem for Kenyan children is poverty).

It can, however, be very difficult to persuade small children to take **malaria pills**, under any guise. Breast-feeding babies will be as protected as their mother. With toddlers you may have to choose between ramming pills down their throats or giving in and risking it. In the latter case, up-country Kenya is much safer territory than the coast, but you should be extremely careful to cover them with Deet repellent early each evening and be sure they sleep under secure nets (take a small net for babies). For more on malaria, see p.47.

You can buy **nappies/diapers** in Kenya, but they are expensive (around Ksh600 for 36), so bring your own supply for a short stay. **Baby foods** are also available in large supermarkets, but here you'll have few problems if you're staying in hotels as there's usually a good variety of fresh food and staff who, given some warning, are happy to prepare it to infants' tastes.

Unless your time is to be spent exclusively on the coast, bring some **warm clothing** for upcountry mornings and evenings. Temperatures in some parts drop low and hotels are not heated.

Probably the most important health concern is the **sun**. On the equator, even when the altitude keeps temperatures down, the effect of thirty minutes' ultra-violet on delicate skin can be severe. Keep them thoroughly smothered in factor 40 and insist they wear hats. Children should also wear T-shirts when swimming, and especially if snorkelling. Sunglasses, too, are a good idea, even for babies, to reduce the intense glare – you can always find little novelty ones that will fit. And of course, make sure they drink plenty of clean **water**.

Travelling

Air travel with under-twos (who get no seat for their ten percent fares) can be a nightmare. Make every possible effort to get bulkhead seats and a bassinet (hanging cradle) for a baby. These requests should be a priority in your plans. When you reconfirm 48 hours before flying, double-check you still have them. If you have lively children who won't easily settle, consider the simple drugging method: trimeprazine can be obtained on prescription and they'll sleep right through the flight and wake up refreshed.

For a young family, going on a group safari (whether organized from home as part of a package or booked in Kenya) is probably not on. **Renting a car** is quite feasible, however, and gives you the flexibility and privacy you need for changing nappies, toilet stops and so on. For babies and children too small for seat belts, you'll need a car seat which, if you have the right model, also works as an all-purpose carrier, pool-side recliner and picnic throne.

If you have a light, easily collapsible **buggy**, bring it. Many hotels and lodges have long paths from the central public areas to the rooms or cottages. A **child-carrier** backpack is another very useful accessory.

For flying with all this baggage, remember you have a full luggage allowance for each passenger with a seat. Children aged 2 to 12 get their own seat and a reduced fare.

Safaris and hotels

On **safari** with young children, your driving time is more likely to be spent in getting from one lodge to the next than in purposeful game drives, but if the children are old enough to enjoy spotting the animals, make sure they have their own **binoculars**. Some **parks** are more child-friendly than others. Nairobi National Park is great (if you can divert their attention from the planes landing at the airport) and Lake Nakuru is a hit as well, as distances are small and the animals close. Equally, Amboseli's small size and the presence of large numbers of elephants make it popular with younger children.

Most **hotels**, lodges and tented camps do not specifically exclude children of any age, but a number of organized tours have a minimum age of 7, while several of the more exclusive tented camps and all four of the "tree hotels" have minimum ages (restrictions are noted in our reviews). The **coast hotels** are on sandy beaches facing a warm sea, safely protected by the reef, and particularly suitable family hotels are mentioned in the text.

Very few places make provision for **babysitters**. The management can usually find a local woman to come in, given a few hours' notice, but they tend to leave the question of payment up to you – Ksh500 for a full evening is the most you should need to pay. Alternatively, if the children are asleep, speak to the restaurant manager and arrange for an *askari* (night watch) to sit outside.

Swimming pools, focus of attention for most children, are only sure to be warm on the coast. In the higher, upcountry regions, including Nairobi, the invariably unheated pools are always chilly, which can be a big disappointment for keen splashers.

Travellers with disabilities

Although by no means easy for people with disabilities, Kenya does not pose insurmountable problems. While there is little government involvement in improving access, tourist industry staff – not to mention passers-by – are usually prepared to help whenever necessary. For wheelchair-users and those who find stairs hard to manage, many hotels have ground-floor rooms; a number on the coast have ramped access walks to public areas and adapted rooms; and larger hotels in Nairobi have elevators. Safari vehicles can usually manage wheelchair-users.

If you're flying from London, you can avoid a change of plane by going with BA or Kenya Airways to Nairobi. Mombasa airport, on the other hand, is easier than Nairobi as it has no steps (other than those coming off the plane) or long distances to negotiate.

In Kenya

Getting around Nairobi is difficult in a wheelchair. While distances are short, there is little ramping of pedestrian areas and drivers are not used to wheelchairs crossing the road. The capacious London-style taxi cabs, however, are a boon.

Safari vehicles have superb springing, but taking a pressure cushion is a wise precaution. Even then, off-road trips can be very arduous, especially on the awful roads in and around Maasai Mara, where flying in is recommended. It's perhaps better to use

Nairobi as a base, and go on one of the many one-day excursions, to Nakuru, Naivasha or the Outspan near Mount Kenya for example. If you are determined, however, any of the luxury lodges and tented camps should be accessible, with help, making a proper safari quite feasible, especially if you fly. One or two places even have baths (as well as showers). Only on the most adventurous trips, with temporary camps set up in the bush, and long-drop toilets, would wheelchair-users really have problems.

The all-night Nairobi–Mombasa **sleeper train** sounds improbable but, again, is possible. On this, though, if completely wheelchair-dependent, you would have to be carried – with some difficulty – from your cabin to the toilets and dining car, as the corridors are very narrow. Your wheelchair would go in the luggage van, too, so expect a delay in retrieving it on arrival. With the exception of the "luxury" coaches plying between Nairobi and Mombasa, other public transport in Kenya is not at all wheelchair-friendly.

Contacts for travellers with disabilities

If you're looking for an all-in **tour**, contact the upmarket Abercrombie & Kent, which has offices in the UK, USA and Australia (see the listings in the relevant section of "Getting there"), who have some experience in carrying disabled passengers on their regular itineraries, as do Southern Cross Safaris (see p.446).

Access-Able Ⓦ www.access-able.com. US online resource for travellers with disabilities, with a small amount of information on Kenya.

Society for the Advancement of Travelers with Handicaps (SATH) US ☎ 212/447 7284, Ⓦ www.sath.org. Non-profit educational organization which can offer general advice on travelling with specific disabilities.

Tripscope UK ☎ 0845/758 5641, Ⓦ www.tripscope.org.uk. Registered charity offering free advice on travel logistics, and connections to sources of specific information on travel in Kenya.

Work

Unless you've lined up a job or voluntary work before leaving for Kenya, you have little chance of getting employment. Wages are extremely low – for school teachers, for example, they start at the equivalent of just £100/$170 per month – and there's serious unemployment in the towns. Particular skills are sometimes in demand – mechanics at game park lodges, for example – but the employer will need good connections to arrange the required papers. It's illegal to obtain income in Kenya while staying on a visitor's pass.

An international **work camp** is no holiday, and conditions are usually primitive, but it can be a lot of fun, too, and is undoubtedly worthwhile. One group to contact is the **Kenya Voluntary Development Association** (PO Box 48902, 00100 Nairobi; ☎ 020/225379, Ⓦ www.kvdakenya.com), a locally inspired organization bringing Kenyans and foreigners together digging irrigation trenches, making roads, building schools, or just producing as many mud bricks as possible. There's no upper age limit (but volunteers older than 25 are unusual) and the minimum age is 18. The groups are very mixed in terms of nationality. The registration fee is $200 or, if you're very energetic, $350 for two consecutive work camps (they last about three or four weeks).

Another group that employs volunteers in community projects is **Inter-Community Development Involvement** (ICODEI; Ⓦ www.volunteerkenya.org), whose main focus is on AIDS awareness, education and women's income generation. Volunteers can join several programmes, some of which require specific training, such as taking a Red Cross AIDS instructor course. The programme fee for volunteers is quite steep, currently $1175 per month. You need to apply well in advance.

Volunteer programmes in wildlife monitoring and conservation as well as education and community development are offered by the **Taita Discovery Centre** (Ⓦwww.savannahcamps.com/tdc; see p.95 and p.366), close to Tsavo East National Park. Community programmes include language and IT teaching, or even building schoolrooms; wildlife conservation here generally involves quantifying numbers of animals or plants in a given area. The cost is $1100 for the first month, and $230 a week after that.

Directory

Beggars In central Nairobi and Mombasa beggars are fairly common; most are visibly destitute, and many are disabled, lepers or homeless mothers with children. While some have regular pitches, others keep on the move, and all are harassed by the police. Kenyans often give to the same beggar on a regular basis and, of course, to the many Kenyans who are Muslim, alms-giving is a religious requirement, believed to benefit the donor. Alms-giving is also an important safety net for the destitute in a country with no social security system.

Bookshops Literacy has massively improved in Kenya over the last couple of decades (85 percent of the population can now read, a high score for Africa), and books have a high profile. Bookstores in Nairobi, Mombasa and in the tourist hotels have imported paperback selections. Locally printed books are sometimes very cheap, and provide insights into Kenyan life you wouldn't otherwise find. Secondhand book stalls are often worth looking at, too. Books by Kenyan and other African authors are much cheaper in Kenya than they would be at home, and Kenya has some fine authors writing in English (see pp.664–666).

Departure tax $20 on international flights, Ksh895 for domestic, both of which should be included in the price of your ticket.

Electricity Kenya's electricity supply is less and less reliable. As in Britain, it uses square, three-pin plugs on 220–240V. Only fancier hotels have outlets or shaver points in the rooms. Australian, New Zealand and European appliances will need an adaptor to fit Kenyan sockets (available in Nairobi from major supermarkets), while North American appliances that work on 110V will also need a transformer.

Emergencies For police, fire and ambulance dial ℡999. They take ages to arrive.

Gifts Ballpoint pens and postcards are about the only small items worth taking and can always be given to children, but they encourage begging if just handed out of a truck or minibus window. These gifts will be appreciated by many adults, too. If you'll be travelling or staying for some time and really want to prepare, get a large batch of photos of you and your family with your address on the back. You'll get lots of mail.

Laundry There are virtually no launderettes in Kenya, but hotels, even cheap ones, often run a laundry service for guests, and you'll easily find people offering the same service (*dobi* in Swahili) in most towns. As *dobis* on street stalls and in cheap hotels do not usually accept underwear however, you may have to wash at least some of your own clothes. Washing powder is easy to buy in small packets, and things dry fast in the sun. Don't spread clothes on the ground to dry: they might be infested by the *tumbu* fly,

Things to take

❑ **Sunglasses** are a necessary health precaution, and they're expensive to buy in Kenya.

❑ A **multipurpose penknife** is handy for cutting food and all sorts of things.

❑ A **torch** (flashlight) can help you navigate unlit roads at night, and is also good to have in case of power cuts.

❑ An **alarm clock** is handy for pre-dawn starts.

❑ A **padlock** can be useful in lodgings where doors don't lock.

❑ **Binoculars** (the small, fold-up ones) are invaluable for game watching. Without them you'll miss half the action. Take a pair for each person.

❑ **Plastic bags** are invaluable: large bin-liner bags to keep dust off clothes, small resealable ones to protect cameras and film.

❑ On the coast, **plastic sandals** are best for walking on the reef; they can be bought cheaply in Kenya.

❑ **Flip-flops** for casual wear and for bathrooms in cheap hotels.

❑ A **sheet sleeping bag** (sew up a sheet) is essential if you intend staying in the very cheapest accommodation.

❑ A **GPS** is immensely useful when hiking, or driving round the parks.

❑ A **stove** is worth considering, even if you're not camping, to boil water or for simple cooking. Camping gas canisters can be bought in Nairobi and a few other places, or take a Trangia stove that works on methylated spirit (easily available in any town), though this is less reliable at altitude.

❑ **Earplugs** are a help in some lodgings if you're a light sleeper.

❑ Loose cotton **clothes** are best, comfortable sandals (or suede shoes or boots for the highlands), plus at least one really warm sweater or, better still, a soft-lined jacket with pockets. (See the "Mount Kenya" section, pp.183–184, for advice on what you need at high altitudes.) Also, some nicer clothes to wear in lodges, as access is often difficult for the ragged.

---

which lays its eggs in them for the larvae to hatch and burrow into your skin.

Receipts Petty bureaucracy is deeply engrained in Kenya and you will often be given a hand-written receipt after making the most elementary purchase. If you have cause to doubt that the sum you're being asked to pay is officially sanctioned, however – for example, an obscure entrance fee, or a fee for a guide, or in cases where police try to impose an on-the-spot fine – just ask for a receipt and this will often clarify matters.

Time Kenya is three hours ahead of Greenwich Mean Time (UTC) all year round. It's eight hours ahead of North American Eastern Standard Time, and eleven hours ahead of Pacific Standard Time. Take off an hour from these during summer daylight saving time. Kenya is seven hours behind Sydney and nine behind New Zealand; add an hour to these during summer daylight saving time. With slight variations east and west, it gets light at 6am and dark at 6pm. If you're learning Swahili, remember that "Swahili time" runs from dawn to dusk to dawn rather than midnight to midday to midnight: 7am and 7pm are both *saa moja* (one o'clock) while midnight and midday are *saa sita* (six o'clock). It's not as confusing as it first sounds – just add or subtract six hours to work out Swahili time (or read the opposite side of your watch).

Tipping If you're staying in tourist-class establishments, you will be expected to tip staff. In expensive hotels, Ksh100 wouldn't be out of place for portering a lot of luggage, but coins are usually adequate, or small notes at most. For most small services, Ksh20 is fine (euphemisms for a tip include a *chai* or a soda – an indication of how much is expected; the price of a beer would be generous). Many mid-range hotels have a gratuities box, where you can leave a single tip for all the staff when you leave. However, in the very humblest establishments, tipping is not the custom. Note that on safaris, tips are considered almost part of the pay and you're expected to shell out at the end of the trip (see p.82).

Toilets Carry toilet paper – which you can buy in most places – as few cheap hotels provide it. Town public toilets (*Wanawake* for Women; *Wanaume* for Men) are invariably disgusting, as are those in cheaper B&Ls. Public buildings and hotels are unlikely to turn you away if you ask.

Weddings Many of the coastal hotels and a few game lodges will lay it on thick if that's what you really want – garlands of flowers, gospel choirs, "complimentary" cakes and tributes, tree-planting ceremonies and so on. The whole experience can feel rather conveyor-belt-driven (you may be just one of half a dozen happy couples getting hitched on the same day at your dream resort hotel), and you might find that being gawped at by holidaymakers in swimming togs as you say "I do" doesn't do much for the solemnity of the occasion. Choose your venue carefully.

Guide

Guide

Nairobi and around

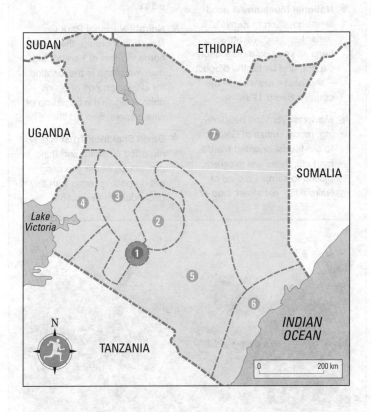

CHAPTER 1 # Highlights

✳ **The Thorn Tree** The original acacia has gone, but its recently planted successor continues the tradition of pinning up notices for fellow travellers. See p.122

✳ **National Museum** As good an introduction to Kenya's natural and cultural attractions as you could reasonably expect, and by far the biggest – and best – museum in the country. See p.128

✳ **Markets** From the bewildering, muddy maze of Gikomba to the tourist oriented Maasai markets, these are excellent places to sample a slice of Nairobi life, eat street food or pick up trinkets at a fraction of the prices charged by curio shops. See p.131

✳ **Carnivore** Tacky, touristy but fun temple to meat-eating, on the outskirts of town. See p.141

✳ **Nairobi National Park** On Nairobi's doorstep, the park is home to most of Kenya's big mammals, and is the location for classic photos of plains animals against a backdrop of skyscrapers. See p.156

✳ **David Sheldrick Trust** Highly regarded elephant and rhino orphanage where you can get on petting terms with tiny pachyderms. See p.161

△ David Sheldrick Trust

Nairobi and around

E asily the largest city in East Africa, **NAIROBI** is also the youngest, the most modern, the fastest growing, the largest and, at 1700m, the highest. The superlatives could go on forever. "Green City in the Sun", runs one tour brochure sobriquet, "City of flowers", another. Less enchanted visitors growl "Nairobbery". The city catches your attention at least; this is no tropical backwater. Most roads, particularly paved ones, lead to Nairobi and, like it or not, you're bound to spend some time here. But walking down Kenyatta Avenue at rush hour, or up Tom Mboya Street after dark, when the security men armed with whips and clubs cluster around their fires on the pavement, it's perhaps easy to forget how quickly you can leave the city and be in the bush.

Apart from being the **safari** capital of the world, Nairobi is an excellent **base for travel**. It's just nine hours by road or an overnight train journey to the coast; about the same time to the far west; and just a couple of hours northwest to the great trough of the Rift Valley or north to the slopes of Mount Kenya. A great **day-trip**, and one literally on the city's doorstep, is **Nairobi National Park**, a wild attraction where you'd expect to find suburbs.

Nairobi

NAIROBI is one of Africa's major cities: the UN's fourth "World Centre", East Africa's commercial and aid hub, and a significant capital in its own right, with a population of between a million and a half and three million, depending on how big an area you include. As a traveller, your first impressions are likely to depend on how – and where – you arrive. If you've come here overland, some time resting up among the fleshpots can seem a pleasant proposition. Newly arrived by air from Europe, though, you may wonder – amid the rash of signs for *Nandos*, *Wimpy* and *Oriental Massage* – just how far you've travelled. Nairobi, just over a century old, has real claims to Western-style sophistication but, as you'll soon find, it lacks a convincing heart. Apart from some lively musical attractions – some of East Africa's busiest **clubs** and best **bands** – there's little here of magnetic appeal, and most travellers stay long enough only to take

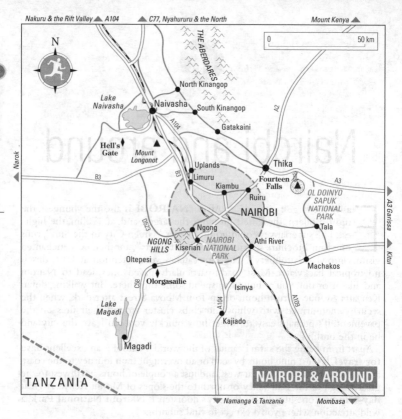

THE ABERDARES

North Kinangop

Lake Naivasha

Naivasha

South Kinangop

Gatakaini

A2

Hell's Gate

Mount Longonot

Uplands

Limuru

Kiambu

Thika

Fourteen Falls

A3

OL DOINYO SAPUK NATIONAL PARK

Ruiru

NAIROBI

Tala

Ngong

NAIROBI NATIONAL PARK

Athi River

NGONG HILLS

Kiserian

Oltepesi

Machakos

Olorgasailie

Isinya

Lake Magadi

Kajiado

Magadi

NAIROBI & AROUND

TANZANIA

A3 Garissa ▶

Kitui ▶

A104

A109

Mombasa ▼

▼ Namanga & Tanzania

Narok ◀

B3

B3

A104

D523

C58

0   50 km

N

stock, make some travel arrangements and maybe visit the **National Museum**, before moving on.

If you're interested in getting to know the real Kenya, though, Nairobi is as compelling a place as any and displays enormous vitality and buzz. The controlling ethos is commerce rather than community, and there's an almost wilful superficiality in the free-for-all of commuters, shoppers, police, hustlers and tourists. It's hard to imagine a city with a more fascinating variety of people, mostly immigrants from rural areas, drawn to the presence and opportunities of money. Nairobi, on the surface at least, seems to accept everyone with complete tolerance. On any downtown pavement you can see a complete cross section of Kenyans, plus every variety of tourist and refugees from many African countries.

Nairobi's rapid growth inevitably has a downside however (read any newspaper or talk to any resident and you'll hear some jaw-dropping stories of crime and police shootings), and, although the city has become safer over the past few years, you should certainly be aware of its reputation for **bag-snatching** and **robbery**, frequently directed at new tourist arrivals (see the box on security on p.108). If you plan to stay for any length of time, learn the art of survival; with the right attitude, you're unlikely to have problems. For the few days that most people spend in Nairobi – if initial misgivings can be overcome – it's a stimulating city.

Some history

Nairobi came into being in May 1899, an artificial settlement created by Europeans at Mile 327 of the East African railway line, then being systematically forged from Mombasa on the coast to Kampala, now the Ugandan capital. It was initially a supply depot, switching yard and campsite for the thousands of Indian labourers employed by the British. The site, bleak and swampy, was simply the spot where operations came to a halt while the engineers figured out their next move – getting the line up the steep slopes that lay ahead. The name came from the local Maasai word for the area, *enkare nyarobi*, "the place of cold water", though the spot itself was originally called Nakusontelon, "Beginning of all Beauty".

Surprisingly, the unplanned settlement took root. A few years later it was totally rebuilt after an outbreak of plague and the burning of the original town compound. By 1907, it was so firmly established that the colonists took it as the capital of the newly formed "British East Africa" (BEA). Europeans, encouraged by the authorities, settled in large numbers, while Africans were forced into employment by tax demands (without representation) or onto specially created **reserves** – the Maasai to the Southern Reserve and the Kikuyu to their own reserve in the highlands.

The capital, lacking development from any established community, was somewhat characterless – and remains so. The **original centre** retains an Asian influence in its older buildings, but today it's shot through with glassy, high-rise blocks. Surrounding the commercial hub is a vast area of **suburbs**: wealthiest in the west and north, increasingly poor to the south and especially the east, where they become, in part, out-and-out slums.

Names of these suburbs – Parklands, Lavington, Eastleigh, Kibera, among others – reflect the jumble of African, Asian and European elements in Nairobi's population, none of whom was local. The term "Nairobian" is a new one that still applies mostly to the younger generation. Although it has a predominance of Kikuyu, the city is not the preserve of a single ethnic group, standing as it does at the meeting point of Maasai, Kikuyu and Kamba territories, nor is it built on any distinctively tribal land. Its choice as capital, accidental though it may have been (Kikuyu Limuru and Kamba Machakos were also considered), was a fortunate one for the future of the country.

△ Nairobi taxi driver

Orientation and arrival

Nairobi has widespread suburbs but its inner area is relatively small: a triangle of stores, offices and public buildings, with the train station on the southern flank and the main bus stations to the east. The triangle of **central Nairobi** divides into three principal districts bisected by the main thoroughfares of **Kenyatta**

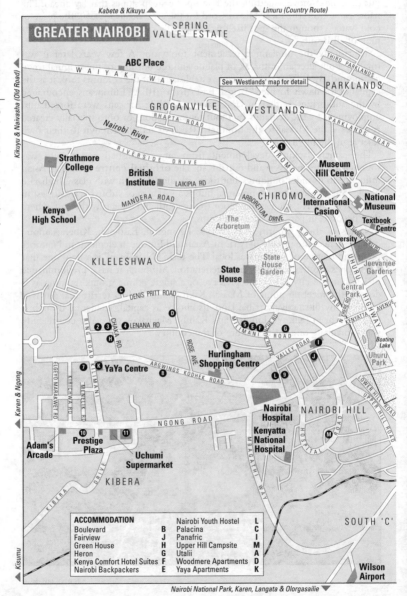

GREATER NAIROBI

Kabete & Kikuyu ▲　　　　　　　▲ Limuru (Country Route)

SPRING VALLEY ESTATE

THIRD PARKLANDS

ABC Place

WAIYAKI WAY

See 'Westlands' map for detail

PARKLANDS

GROGANVILLE　WESTLANDS

RHAPTA ROAD

PARKLANDS ROAD

Kikuyu & Naivasha (Old Road) ◀

Nairobi River

RIVERSIDE DRIVE

Strathmore College

British Institute　LAIKIPIA RD

Museum Hill Centre

CHIROMO

National Museum

Kenya High School

MANDERA ROAD

ARBORETUM DRIVE

The Arboretum

International Casino

Textbook Centre ❸

University

KILELESHWA

STATE HOUSE ROAD

State House Garden

State House

Jeevanjee Gardens

MAMLAKA ROAD

Central Park

UHURU HIGHWAY

DENIS PRITT ROAD ❸

❹ ❹ LENANA RD

CHAKA RD

❹

MILIMANI ROAD

❺ ❻ ❼

❻

KENYATTA AVENUE

Boating Lake

Karen & Ngong ◀

RING ROAD KILIMANI

ROSE AVE

ARGWINGS KODHEK ROAD

Hurlingham Shopping Centre ❻

VALLEY ROAD

❾ ❾

Uhuru Park

YaYa Centre

ELGEYO MARAKWET RD

KIRICHWA RD

MENELIK RD

❼

❽

NAIROBI HILL

Adam's Arcade

Prestige Plaza ❿

Uchumi Supermarket ⓫

NGONG ROAD

Nairobi Hospital

Kenyatta National Hospital

UPPER HILL ROAD

HOSPITAL ROAD

⓭

LOWER HILL ROAD

MBAGATHI WAY

KIBERA

KIBERA DRIVE

SOUTH 'C'

Kisumu ◀

Wilson Airport

ACCOMMODATION		Nairobi Youth Hostel	L
Boulevard	B	Palacina	C
Fairview	J	Panafric	I
Green House	H	Upper Hill Campsite	M
Heron	G	Utalii	A
Kenya Comfort Hotel Suites	F	Woodmere Apartments	D
Nairobi Backpackers	E	Yaya Apartments	K

Nairobi National Park, Karen, Langata & Olorgasailie ▼

Avenue and **Moi Avenue**. The grandest and most formal part of town is the area around **City Square**, in the southwest. This square kilometre is Nairobi's heart: government buildings, banks and offices merge to the north and east with upmarket shopping streets and luxury hotels. The area's big landmarks are the extraordinary **Kenyatta International Conference Centre**, with its huge cylindrical tower and artichoke-shaped conference centre, the blue-glass

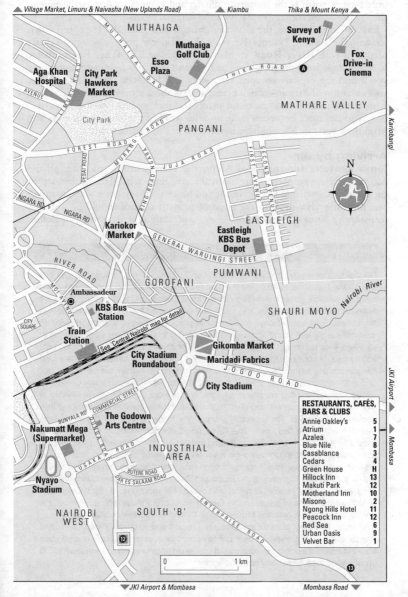

RESTAURANTS, CAFÉS, BARS & CLUBS

Annie Oakley's	5
Atrium	1
Azalea	7
Blue Nile	8
Casablanca	3
Cedars	4
Green House	H
Hillock Inn	13
Makuti Park	12
Motherland Inn	10
Misono	2
Ngong Hills Hotel	11
Peacock Inn	12
Red Sea	6
Urban Oasis	9
Velvet Bar	1

skyscraper of **Lonrho House**, and the bizarre zebra-striped "legs" of the **Nation Centre**, all visible from miles outside the city. To the south of this area, towards the train station, stands the **Memorial Park** on the site of the bombed Cooperative Bank Building (see the box on p.123).

North of Kenyatta Avenue, there's a shift to smaller scale and lesser finance. The **City Market** is here, surrounded by a denser district of shops, restaurants and hotels. The **Jeevanjee Gardens** are a welcome patch of greenery, and a little further north is the university district and Nairobi's oldest establishment, the *Norfolk Hotel*, contemporary with the original rebuilding of the city.

East of Moi Avenue, the character changes more radically. Here, and down towards the reeking Nairobi River, is the relatively poor, inner-city district identified with **River Road**, its main thoroughfare. The River Road quarter is where most long-distance buses and matatus start and terminate, and where you'll find the capital's cheapest restaurants and hotels, as well as the highest concentration of African-owned businesses. It's also a somewhat notorious area, with a traditional concentration of sharks and pickpockets (see the "Security" box). You can meet European residents who work five minutes' walk away and in all their years in Nairobi have never been to this part of town.

Arriving by air

Jomo Kenyatta International Airport is 15km southeast of town, off the Mombasa highway. Arrivals are normally straightforward, but do beware of **pickpockets**, even inside customs. If you haven't already got a visa, obtaining one from the **visa desk** to the right of passport control should be a simple formality (£30 or $50 in cash only, and with only pounds sterling or dollars

---

Security

Nairobi isn't nearly as bad as its "Nairobbery" reputation would suggest. The city has cleaned up considerably over the past few years, mostly due to measures taken by Mwai Kibaki's government. The city centre is cleaner and less chaotic; there are fewer street children, beggars and touts, and a dedicated tourist police force patrols the streets. That said, it pays to take some precautions against crime. It helps to memorize any route you're walking, as lost-looking tourists are the easiest target of all. Keep your hands out of reach and be – rationally – suspicious of everyone until you've caught your breath. It doesn't take long to get a little streetwise. Every rural Kenyan coming to the city for the first time goes through exactly the same process, and many are considerably greener than you, having never been in a city before.

Most areas of the city are fine in daylight, but be extra vigilant if you're walking at night within the city centre and don't wander outside the commercial district unless you're really clued in. Be especially wary in the following parts of the city, where tourist pickings are fairly rich. The **River Road district**, which in practical terms means anything east of Moi Avenue, and indeed sometimes including the avenue, has become something of a **no-go area for tourists** at night. Even locals avoid walking there and taxi drivers are quite often reluctant to venture into certain parts of the district. **Uhuru Highway** plus **Uhuru** and **Central parks** are fine during the day but prime muggers' territory at night, with occasional shootings. At night, the stretch of Valley Road west of between the *Serena Hotel* and the *Nairobi Youth Hostel* is unsafe, and the area near the **Museum** and **Casino** is extremely dangerous.

All main **bus** and **matatu stations** are chaotic and ideal for pickpockets and snatch-and-run robberies; it's best not to accept food, drinks, sweets or cigarettes from strangers, as doping is common. If you're **driving**, keeping the windows rolled up is a good idea, especially at traffic lights.

accepted; two passport photos may be asked for as well). Once through passport control, check your **luggage** is intact as soon as you get it off the carousel; if anything appears to be missing, go straight to the "Lost Luggage" desk before passing through customs. If at any stage someone asks you for a **bribe**, refuse tactfully, pointing out the many signs on the walls concerning the heavy penalties for attempted bribery and corruption. If you really get stuck, kicking up a loud fuss and demanding to see the airport manager usually works. While still in baggage reclaim, take the time to get your luggage in order, hiding cameras, small handbags and other valuables – you'll have rather less privacy to do so in the main arrivals hall.

There's a **bank** (open 24hr in theory) inside customs and an exchange bureau in the main hall, both with ATM machines and both refusing traveller's cheques from time to time. If changing money, examine the receipt and your money carefully – there have been reports of rip-offs. Also inside customs is a **duty-free shop**. The airport has an office of the **Flying Doctors** organization, where you can buy their special brand of life-saving insurance (see p.49). The restaurant at the top of the arrivals building is surprisingly good and reasonably priced and there is also a branch of the popular *Java House* coffee shop near Gate 14.

Invariably, hordes of **taxi** touts assail you once you're through customs. Ignore them and walk straight to the waiting cabs lined up outside, or else to the Kenatco office – but if you'd prefer to be met, try contacting Let's Go Travel (address on p.150). For the London-style cabs there's a fixed price to the city centre, currently around Ksh1500, depending on which hotel you want to go to. Other taxis to the city centre should be less than this – they don't have meters, so bargain hard and don't be afraid to ask several drivers their price.

If your plane arrives **late at night**, you may well feel intimidated by a nighttime first contact with central Nairobi and you'll find many of the cheapest hotels are already closed before midnight. Curling up in a corner of the arrivals hall until dawn is to be considered only as a last resort – comforts and even basic facilities are limited.

The local Bustrack **bus #34** leaves from outside the arrivals hall roughly every twenty minutes (daily 6am–8pm; Ksh30), entering the city through the eastern suburbs (rather than running straight up Uhuru Highway) and stopping at the central KBS bus station on Mfangano Street before continuing to the youth hostel on Nairobi Hill. People have been known to be robbed on this bus, so be on your guard if you take it.

Arriving by train

The **train station** is virtually in the city centre, with one of Nairobi's biggest matatu stages right in front. You can just walk straight out through the station concourse and follow Moi Avenue into town. Watch out for taxi drivers and porters who will more or less kidnap your luggage if you let them. The only real attention you'll attract is from **safari touts** – they're persistent, but friendly enough, and useful if you need an escort to one of the cheaper River Road addresses; a small tip (say Ksh50) would be appreciated. There is a **left luggage** facility at the station.

Arriving by bus and matatu

Most **bus companies** have their booking offices or parking areas in the River Road district, and many of the matatu stages are here, too. All the bus company terminals are marked on the map on pp.114–115, and the main bus and matatu routes and their terminals are listed in the box on pp.112–113. On the way into town, you can generally ask to be dropped off anywhere along the route.

Information and city transport

Nairobi has no official **tourist information** service – a lamentable state of affairs. The *Standard* and *Nation* newspapers are useful sources of current information and special offers, and the free and widely circulated monthly *Going Out* is always worth a glance; if you can't find a copy, ask at the Nation Centre building, Kimathi Street. If you need a detailed **map** of the city, buy the *A–Z of Nairobi*, available from bookshops.

Getting around central Nairobi is straightforward. By day, most visitors walk; by night, when certain parts of the city are definitely not recommended for pedestrians, they take a taxi. Unless you're only here for a day or two, though, it's certainly worth getting to know the city's public transport systems.

Taxis

Nairobi's **taxis** are overpriced by Kenyan standards. Grey, **London-style** taxi cabs, operated by the Kenya Taxi Cabs Association (℡020/222953), crowd around key spots in the city – notably outside the *Hilton Hotel*, the *680* and the *Meridian Court Hotel* – and have pretty fixed prices, with the current bottom-line fare for any trip in the city centre well known by all (the cheapest ride isn't likely to be less than around Ksh250; Ngong Rd to the centre costs Ksh400). Another reliable company is Kenatco, who have a central office at Uchumi House on Aga Khan Walk (24hr; ℡020/225123 or 338611), and a branch at Jomo Kenyatta International Airport (℡020/824248 or 822356).

It's possible to bargain only with the private drivers, who drive sometimes astonishingly battered cars. You'll find them angling for business on Mama Ngina Street, Kimathi Street outside the *Oakwood Hotel*, and at the junction of Standard Street and Muindi Mbingu Street, by the *680 Hotel*.

Tuk-tuks, motorized rickshaws, are also now available, mostly at the corner of Kenyatta Avenue and Kimathi Street. They cost a little less than regular taxis, though bargain hard. Note that all registered taxis and tuk-tuks must now bear a **yellow stripe**.

Buses and matatus

Buses and matatus save you money on getting around, certainly for longer trips out of the city centre, but take some figuring out. The Bustrack and Citi Hoppa buses which roar around Nairobi all day are cheap (Ksh10–30; pay the conductor) and very unpredictable: buses are numbered, but bus stops aren't and routes

---

Driving in Nairobi

Driving in **Nairobi** can be a nerve-wracking experience for inexperienced or nervous drivers, though you will get used to it after a few days. The main things to watch out for are matatus, which stop as suddenly as they lurch back into the fray, and roundabouts or traffic circles. These labour under "priority traffic" regulations, which in theory means cars already on the roundabout have priority, but in practice means chaos as no one is keen to cede right of way. Always stay in lane. If you're worried, you should pick up the car at the airport, which gives you time to get used to the car and the traffic before joining the city-centre fray.

Parking in central Nairobi can be difficult during business hours, though there's usually space at the Loita Street Car Park, next to Barclays Plaza (Ksh70/day) or at the Kenyatta International Conference Centre (entrance off City Hall Way).

change frequently. Nairobi's **matatus** – which, like the city's taxis, must bear a yellow stripe – tend to take the same routes as buses and often display the same route numbers. They're generally faster, more dangerous and packed, though bad accidents rarely happen in the city. Matatu stages are scattered throughout River Road district.

Accommodation

Finding **accommodation** in Nairobi isn't difficult. There's loads of choice, and hotels are rarely full even during the peak season. The main question is which area fits your needs; travellers end up congregating at a number of different spots. If you're arriving in town very early, beware that most places won't allow you to take a room before 10am.

If you're travelling by rented car and concerned about safe parking, don't panic – the city council and most hotels employ *askaris* (security guards), who can be persuaded to up their workload for a modest tip. Most top-of-the-range places have guarded or enclosed parking anyway. Naturally, leave nothing in, or attached to, the vehicle. If you're making an early getaway, note that rush-hour cross-city traffic can be slow moving (see p.165), so stay in an appropriate part of town.

To help you aim straight for the best places, the ones in the following short-list meet with near-universal approval: *Iqbal* and *Primetime Safaris* (low-budget, popular with travellers, River Road district); *Nairobi Backpackers* and the *YMCA* (out-of-centre meeting places, popular with travellers); *Fairview* (peaceful mid-range out-of-centre hotel, great for families); *Boulevard* (reliable mid-range out-of-centre base); *680* (reliable mid-range city-centre base); the *Stanley* and the *Serena* (excellent value in the luxury range); and *Safari Park* (totally Kenya-proof luxury resort out of town).

River Road area

The very cheapest lodgings are around **River Road**, the main drag through the city centre's poorest quarter – although in recent years, a number of more expensive hotels have been built here. Despite the constant worry about safety, River Road is the city's most stimulating and animated area, and offers a plunge into a world which would pass you by if you stayed elsewhere in the city centre or out in the suburbs.

The cheapest places generally double as rowdy bars and nightclubs (not for lone women), and are neither terribly clean nor secure. Should a modicum of hygiene and perhaps self-contained facilities be important to you, you're looking at Ksh1000–1400 for a double room. If you're genuinely broke, try the welcoming **Sikh Temple** on Gaberone Road: overnights and meals are free, though you're expected to leave a donation. All places below are shown on the "Commercial Centre and River Road Area" map, pp.114–115.

Inexpensive

Abbey Hotel Gaberone Rd; PO Box 75260 ☎020/243256 or 241562. A noisy, boozy place, rather pricey for what it offers, but the rooms have nets and are mostly clean and fresh, with tiled bathrooms (hot showers). Unlovely but adequate. ❸

Cana Lodge Hotel Duruma Rd; PO Box 41237

☎020/217254 or 223284. Small box-like rooms with phones and hot water available mornings and evenings. A good first base in Nairobi, with clean sheets daily and good breakfasts. ❷

Danika Lodge Dubois Rd; PO Box 12840 ☎020/230687. Very secure (the gate is locked at all times), friendly and quieter than most, with

Nairobi bus and matatu routes

Local buses are run by Citi Hoppa and KBS Bustrack, which have their main bus stations in the eastern corner of River Road district, between Ronald Ngala, Mfangano and Uyoma streets, beside the bizarre-looking Siri Guru Singh Sabha Temple. This is also a major stage for matatus. Other bus and matatu stops include: outside the **Ambassadeur** hotel on Moi Avenue (mainly eastbound); outside the **Kencom** building facing the *Hilton* on City Hall Way and also outside the **GPO** tower on Kenyatta Avenue (mainly westbound); the **train station** end of Moi Avenue (west and southwest); and **Latema Road** (north and northeast). For national bus, matatu and train services, see pp.165–168.

1 (bus) Ngong Road, Dagoretti Corner; from GPO.

2 (bus) Ngong Road, Dagoretti Corner, Kikuyu town; from KBS bus station or GPO.

3 (bus/matatu) Ngong Road, Adam's Arcade, Dagoretti Corner; from GPO.

4 (bus) Ngong Road, Adam's Arcade, Dagoretti Corner; from Kencom or GPO.

4 (bus) Kariokor market, General Waruinge Road, Eastleigh; from *Ambassadeur*.

6 (bus) Kariokor market and Eastleigh; from Accra Road or Tom Mboya Street; from GPO.

7c (bus) Nairobi Hospital; from Kencom.

8 (matatu) Kenyatta National Hospital, Kibera; from railway stage.

9 (matatu) Eastleigh; from corner Accra Road/Tom Mboya Street.

11 (matatu) South B; from railway stage.

15 (matatu) Langata Road (National Park, Wilson Airport); Otiende Town; from Mfangano Street/Ronald Ngala Street.

17B (matatu) Thika Road, Kasarani; from KBS bus station.

18 (bus) Kenyatta National Hospital; from GPO.

20 (bus) Kenyatta National Hospital; from GPO.

21 (bus) National Museum, Westlands; from Kencom.

21 (bus) City Stadium roundabout, Jogoo Road; from *Ambassadeur*.

23 (matatu) National Museum; Westlands; Kangemi; from Latema Road.

24 (bus/matatu) Langata Road, Bogoni Road, Karen; from Mfangano Street/Hakati Road.

25 (matatu) Murang'a Road, Thika Road; from Odeon Cinema Latema Road, or Koinange Street.

28 (bus) Eastleigh, Kariobangi; from *Ambassadeur*.

30 (matatu) Murang'a Road, Westlands; from KBS bus station.

31 (bus) Kariobangi; from *Ambassadeur*.

32 (matatu) Kariokor market; Eastleigh; from Tom Mboya Street.

32c (bus) Kibera; Ayang; from Kencom.

33 (matatu) Kenyatta Hospital; Ngummo; from railway stage.

34 (bus) Jogoo Road, Jomo Kenyatta International Airport; from *Ambassadeur* and KBS bus station.

36 (bus) Jogoo Road, Kariobangi South; from *Ambassadeur* and KBS bus station.

37 (bus) Jogoo Road, Kariobangi South; from *Ambassadeur*.

38 (matatu) Jogoo Road, Kariobangi South; from KBS bus station.

39 (matatu) Jogoo Road, Kariobangi South; from KBS bus station.

---

breezy s/c rooms, 24hr hot water, and the rare luxury of mosquito nets. Good laundry service. Recommended. ❷

Destiny Hotel Duruma Rd; PO Box 72780 ☎ 020/253123–6. This four-storey block offers good value and is conscientiously run, with airy s/c

40c (matatu) Ngummo City; from railway stage.

41 (bus) Valley Road (*Youth Hostel*), Argwings Kodhek Road; from GPO.

42 (matatu) Kariokor market, Eastleigh; from corner Accra Road/Tsavo Road.

42 (bus) Kibera; from Kencom or KBS bus station.

44A (matatu) Ngumba Estate, Thika Road; from Muraga Road.

45 (bus) Thika Road (Moi Sports Centre); from Kencom.

46 (matatu) Valley Road, Youth Hostel; Argwings Kodhek Road; from railway stage and GPO.

46 or **46B** (bus) Valley Road, Yaya Centre; Kawangwere; from Kencom.

48 (matatu) Arboretum; from Odeon cinema, Latema Road.

49a Hurlingham; Yaya; Congo; Kanengaga; from Kencom.

58 (matatu) Maringo, Buru Buru; from *Ambassadeur*.

61B (bus) Kenyatta National Hospital; from GPO.

71 (matatu) Likoni Rd, Lunga Lunga Rd, Industrial Area; from Temple Road.

100 (matatu) Kiambu Road, Kiambu; from KBS bus station.

102 (bus/matatu) Ngong Road, Dagoretti Corner, Kikuyu town; from KBS bus station.

103 (bus) Ngong Road, Dagoretti Corner, Kikuyu town; from KBS bus station.

104 (matatu) Westlands; from KBS bus station.

105 (matatu) Westlands; Kanoo; Kikuyu; from railway station.

108 (bus) Murang'a Road; Muthaiga Road; Limuru Road (for Village Market mall); from KBS bus station.

110 (matatu) Kitengela, Athi River; from KBS bus station.

111 (bus) Ngong Road, Dagoretti Corner, Karen, Ngong, Kiserian; from Kencom.

114 (matatu) Limuru; from Jamia Mosque (Kigali Road) or Tom Mboya Street.

115 (matatu) Kikuyu town; from railway stage.

118 (matatu) Westlands; from Latema Road.

119 (bus) National Museum, Westlands, Peponi Road, Wangige; from KBS bus station.

123 (matatu) Thika, from MP station on Ronald Ngala Street.

125 (matatu) Langata Road, Magadi Road, Kiserian; from railway stage.

126 (bus) Langata Road, then either to Karen or Kiserian along Magadi Road; from outside Kencom.

137 (matatu) Thika Road; from Koinange Street.

145 (bus) Thika Road (Moi Sports Centre); from Kencom.

237 (matatu) Thika; from Kencom. Other Thika matatus from corner BP station on Ronald Ngala Street.

Un-numbered
Marked "Industrial Area/Hillock" To Enterprise Road; from Afya Centre, Tom Mboya Street.

Marked "Parklands/Aga Khan" To Parklands; from Latema Road, facing *Iqbal Hotel*, or from along Tom Mboya Street.

rooms and hot showers. There is a payphone in the corridor and a laundry service. ❸
Eureka Highrise Hotel Tom Mboya St; PO Box

28229 ☎020/247459. Three floors up, with large s/c rooms, each with desk and hot shower. Security is good, and there's a nice pub/restaurant. ❸

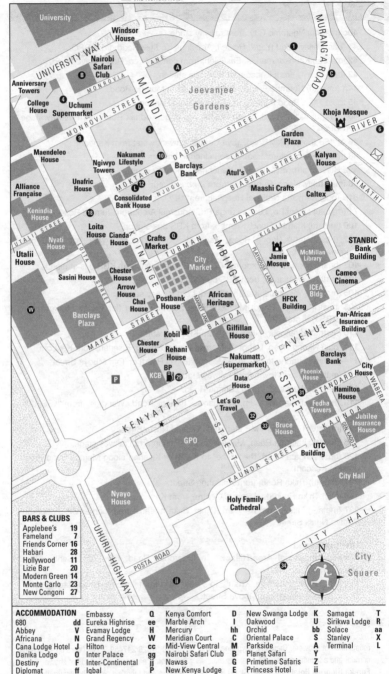

▲ The Norfolk Hotel ▲ Parklands

University

Windsor House

MURANG'A ROAD

UNIVERSITY WAY

LANE

MUINDI

Nairobi Safari Club **B**

A

MONROVIA

Anniversary Towers

College House **4**

Uchumi Supermarket

MONROVIA STREET

9

D

5

Jeevanjee Gardens

STREET

DADDAH

LANE

BIASHARA STREET

River

Khoja Mosque

C

3

1

6

Garden Plaza

Kalyan House

Maendeleo House

Nakumatt Lifestyle

Ngiwyo Towers

10

Barclays Bank

Atul's

Maashi Crafts

Caltex

Alliance Française

Unafric House

MOKTAR

11

12

Consolidated Bank House

NJUGU

ROAD

KIGALI ROAD

KIMATHI

Kenindia House

18

Loita House

Cianda House

Crafts Market **Q**

TUBMAN

MBINGU

PLAYHOUSE LANE

Jamia Mosque

McMillan Library

STANBIC Bank Building

Nyati House

UTALII STREET

LOITA

City Market

Cameo Cinema

Utalii House

Sasini House

STREET

KOINANGE

Chester House

Arrow House

Chai House

Postbank House

MARKET LANE

BANDA

African Heritage

STREET

ICEA Bldg

HFCK Building

Pan-African Insurance Building

W

Barclays Plaza

MARKET

STREET

Kobil

Gilfillan House

AVENUE

Barclays Bank

City House

WABERA

Chester House

Rehani House

KCB

BP

29

P

Nakumatt (supermarket)

Data House

Phoenix House

STANDARD

Hamilton House

Fedha Towers

KAUNDA

Jubilee Insurance House

Let's Go Travel

dd

31

32

33

Bruce House

BEN KIAROGO ST

KENYATTA

★

GPO

STREET

KAUNDA STREET

UTC Building

City Hall

Nyayo House

UHURU HIGHWAY

Holy Family Cathedral

CITY

HALL

N

City Square

POSTA ROAD

34

jj

BARS & CLUBS

Applebee's	19
Fameland	7
Friends Corner	16
Habari	28
Hollywood	11
Lizie Bar	20
Modern Green	14
Monte Carlo	23
New Congoni	27

ACCOMMODATION

680	dd	Embassy	Q	Kenya Comfort	D	New Swanga Lodge	K
Abbey	V	Eureka Highrise	ee	Marble Arch	I	Oakwood	U
Africana	N	Evamay Lodge	H	Mercury	hh	Orchid	bb
Cana Lodge Hotel	J	Grand Regency	W	Meridian Court	C	Oriental Palace	S
Danika Lodge	O	Hilton	cc	Mid-View Central	M	Parkside	A
Destiny	F	Inter Palace	gg	Nairobi Safari Club	B	Planet Safari	Y
Diplomat	ff	Iqbal	P	Nawas	jj	Primetime Safaris	Z
		Inter-Continental		New Kenya Lodge	E	Princess Hotel	ii
						Samagat	T
						Sirikwa Lodge	R
						Solace	aa
						Stanley	X
						Terminal	L

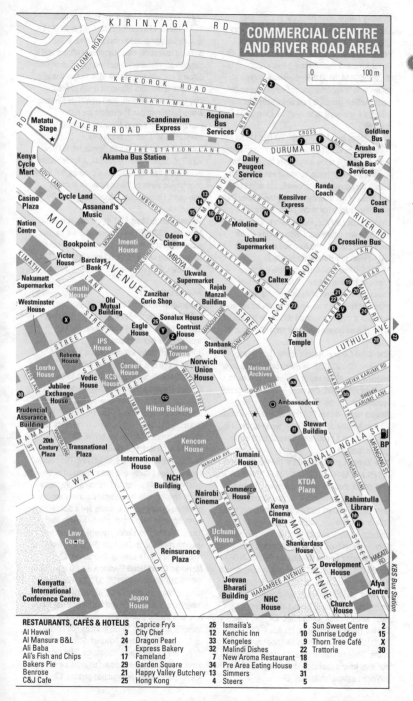

COMMERCIAL CENTRE AND RIVER ROAD AREA

0   100 m

KIRINYAGA RD

KILOME ROAD

KEEKOROK ROAD

NGARIAMA LANE

RIVER ROAD

Matatu Stage ★

Kenya Cycle Mart

Casino Plaza

Nation Centre

Cycle Land

Assanand's Music

GOVI LANE

MOI

Bookpoint

Victor House

Nakumatt Supermarket

Westminster House

Imenti House

Barclays Bank

Kimathi House

Old Mutual Building

Eagle House

TOM MBOYA AVENUE

KIMATHI STREET

Zanzibar Curio Shop

Sonalux House

Contrust House

Union Towers

Norwich Union House

Stanbank House

Scandinavian Express

Regional Bus Services

FIRE STATION LANE

Akamba Bus Station

LAGOS ROAD

TIMBORDA ROAD

MONDLANE ST

CABRA STREET

GOVERNMENT LANE

MARARA LANE

Daily Peugeot Service

DURUMA RD

CROSS LANE

Goldline Bus

Arusha Express

Mash Bus Services

Randa Coach

Coast Bus

Kensilver Express ★

Crossline Bus

RIVER RD

Mololine

Uchumi Supermarket

Odeon Cinema

Ukwala Supermarket

Rajab Manzal Building

Caltex

Sikh Temple

National Archives

Ambassadeur

ACCRA ROAD

LUTHULI AVE

SHEIKH KARUME RD

SHEIKH KARUME LANE

GABERONE RD

MUNYU RD

Thorn Tree Café

IPS House

Rehema House

Lonrho House

Vedic House

KCS House

Corner House

Jubilee Exchange House

Prudential Assurance Building

Hilton Building

20th Century Plaza

Transnational Plaza

International House

NCH Building

Nairobi Cinema

Kencom House

Tumaini House

Commerce House

Stewart Building

RONALD NGALA ST

KTDA Plaza

Rahimtulla Library

Kenya Cinema Plaza

Shankardass House

Development House

Afya Centre

BP

KBS Bus Station

MEANGANO STREET

TOM MBOYA AVENUE

MOI AVENUE

Law Courts

Reinsurance Plaza

Uchumi House

Kenyatta International Conference Centre

Jogoo House

Jeevan Bharati Building

NHC House

HARAMBEE AVENUE

Church House

HAKATII RD

SHORT STREET

WATUU STREET

BANK STREET

SIMBA STREET

AGA KHAN WALK

NKRUMAH AVE

KRUMAH WALK

WABERA LANE

TAIFA ROAD

NGINA STREET

MAMA NGINA

MAMA ST

WABERA LANE

PRESS LANE

TSAVO LANE

DUBOIS ROAD

JATEMA ROAD

SAVO LANE

TAVETA ROAD

TIMBORDA LANE

GABERONE RD

VOI RD

NGARIAMA ROAD

RESTAURANTS, CAFÉS & HOTELIS			
Al Hawal	3	Caprice Fry's	
Al Mansura B&L	24	City Chef	12
Ali Baba	1	Dragon Pearl	33
Ali's Fish and Chips	17	Express Bakery	32
Bakers Pie	29	Fameland	7
Benrose	21	Garden Square	34
C&J Cafe	25	Happy Valley Butchery	13
		Hong Kong	4
Ismailia's	26	Sun Sweet Centre	2
Kenchic Inn	10	Sunrise Lodge	15
Kengeles	9	Thorn Tree Café	X
Malindi Dishes	22	Trattoria	30
New Aroma Restaurant	18		
Pre Area Eating House	8		
Simmers	31		
Steers	5		

Evamay Lodge River Rd at the junction with Duruma Rd; PO Box 16000 ⓣ 020/216218. Very good value for the price, the s/c rooms have phones and mosquito nets, and good security. ❸

Hotel Africana Dubois Rd; PO Box 47827 ⓣ 020/220654, ⓕ 331886. Linoleum-floored s/c rooms with telephones and hot water. The single beds are tiny. There's a café downstairs. Recommended if you want to be near the Latema Rd area. ❷

Iqbal Hotel Latema Rd; PO Box 11256 ⓣ 020/220914. A very friendly place whose main advantage is the opportunity to meet other travellers. Though basic, rooms are cleanish and secure (no "guests" are allowed), but aren't s/c, and those at the front overlooking the matatu stand are noisy. There's hot water in the mornings, a cheap laundry service, lock-up store, safari booking office and noticeboard. Renovations should have taken place by the time you read this. ❷

Mercury Hotel Tom Mboya St ⓣ 020/212504. Comfortable carpeted rooms with perks like small dining tables and chairs and free mineral water. Doubles have a proper bath. There's also a nice courtyard restaurant with a bizarre miniature rockery in the corner, and a *nyama choma* bar. A cut above others in its class. ❸

Mid-View Central Hotel Latema Rd; PO Box 64678, ⓣ 020/223351, ⓦ www.realty-kenya.com/ midview. One of the newer and better options in the River Rd district, this large hotel has spotless, spacious s/c rooms. ❸

Nawas Hotel Nawas Building, Latema/River roads; PO Box 248000 ⓣ 020/243158. Small rooms with hot water, and a good, friendly restaurant on the ground floor. ❷

New Kenya Lodge River Rd at the top of Latema Rd; PO Box 43444 ⓣ 020/222202 or 248225. A long-established dorm-only place, very much a backpackers' haunt, with a popular communal area, but be warned that it's also unhygienic, with little or no hot water, and uncertain security. They organize reasonable safaris for around $50 per day. There's also a book exchange. Dorms Ksh350.

New Swanga Lodge Duruma Rd; PO Box 46387 ⓣ 020/213777 or 213827. The rooms here, though not large, are comfortable, s/c, have telephones and nets, and are secured behind spectacular, time-consuming, triple locks. Clean sheets daily. Good value, though hardly quiet. ❸

Orchid Hotel Mfangano St; PO Box 45613 ⓣ 020/222797. Confusingly this still has its old name, *Dolat*, written outside. It's rather dilapidated but does have a safe lock-up for luggage when you're on safari (Ksh30/day). ❷

Primetime Safaris 9th Floor, Contrust House, Moi Ave ⓣ 020/215773 or 217136, ⓦ www.primetime.co.ke. This place has a few dorms, a reasonably clean communal kitchen and a convivial atmosphere. You get two nights' accommodation if you take one of their trips. Dorms Ksh350.

Princess Hotel Tom Mboya St ⓣ 020/214640. Very busy establishment, used mainly by Kenyans, with a restaurant/bar. The rooms are rather cramped but have good showers. Basic but adequate, and it fills up quickly. ❷

Samagat Hotel Park House, Taveta Rd; PO Box 10027 ⓣ 020/217668, ⓕ 220604. A former apartment block, this has spacious s/c rooms, the upper ones having views of the commercial district's high-rises. There's a ninth-floor dining room/TV lounge. ❸

Sirikwa Lodge Munyu Rd, at the corner with Accra Rd ⓣ 020/221359. Reasonable s/c rooms accessed over a *miraa* shop, and great for observing the chaos at the Accra Rd matatu stages. Hot water 24hr. ❸

Moderate

Diplomat Hotel Tom Mboya St; PO Box 30777 ⓣ 020/245050 or 246114, ⓕ 220475. Fifty large, well-kept s/c rooms with telephone, shower, lift access and a swanky lobby. ❹

Inter Palace Hotel Interfina House, corner of Ronald Ngala and Tom Mboya streets ⓣ 020/241501, ⓔ intpalacehotel@yahoo.com. Above a shopping centre, this large hotel has over one hundred s/c rooms, while the so-called "executive" rooms have TV, too. No rooms have a/c, and a big drawback is the excruciating noise, into the early hours, from the bar below. ❹

Marble Arch Hotel Lagos Rd; PO Box 12224 ⓣ 020/240940 or 245656, ⓕ 245724. The polished marble, brass fixtures and tacky fountains of this hotel's coffee shop, bar and restaurant are totally out of keeping with the generally slummy accommodation in the area. The rooms are a disappointment, however, with rather grubby looking tiled floors, TVs that don't work properly and seriously uncomfortable beds. There are proper big baths though, and secure parking. Overpriced. ❻

Meridian Court Hotel Murang'a Rd; PO Box 30278 ⓣ 020/313283 or 313991, ⓕ 333658. In a grim position hemmed in by traffic, all rooms have bath, fridge, a safe, satellite TV and kitchenette (equipped only with toaster oven and fridge), and most have separate living areas. These facilities don't make up for their shabby state, however. Still, amenities do include a rooftop pool, bar, sauna, 24hr room service, and there is a good Indian restaurant, the *Khyber* (see p.140). Underground parking. ❻

Oriental Palace Hotel Taveta Rd; PO Box 72237 ℡020/217600, ℻212335. One of the best-appointed hotels in the district, although rather overpriced. All 106 rooms have TV (with in-house video), direct-dial phone and – fortunately – ceiling fans (no a/c), which help dispel smells from the *Little India* restaurant on the ground floor. ④

Solace Hotel Tom Mboya St; PO Box 48867 ℡020/331277. The corridors and stairs here are tatty, but the rooms themselves are very decent, with telephones and nets, and reliable hot water to fill the baths. One of the better mid-range choices. ④

West of Moi Avenue

The following listings cover the more monied parts of the city, roughly north as far as the museum and west as far as Central and Uhuru parks. There are a number of mid-priced places on the west side of Moi Avenue up near Jeevanjee Gardens and City Market. For the faint-hearted, this may be a better prospect than the River Road area – quieter and more salubrious. Most of the places reviewed appear on the "Commercial Centre and River Road Area" map, though a few are shown on the "Central Nairobi" map (pp.124–125) or the "Greater Nairobi" map (pp.106–107).

Inexpensive

Hotel Embassy Tubman Rd, right behind the City Market; PO Box 47247 ℡020/224087, ℻224534. Scruffy but quite decent, with ancient telephones lovingly preserved in some rooms (they don't all work) and a nice restaurant. Discounts for group bookings, and a pretty inexpensive breakfast is available. ③

Central YMCA State House Rd, 300m from Uhuru Highway; PO Box 30330 ℡020/2724116–7, ℻2728825, ⓦwww .kenya-ymca.org; see "Central Nairobi" map. Popular with travellers not quite on a shoestring budget,

the *YMCA* is well equipped, with a choice of dorms and s/c rooms, and isn't markedly different from a modest hotel. There's well-priced if average food, and a guarded parking lot, but the clincher is the excellent facilities – pool, tennis courts, aerobics studio and massage services. And no, you don't have to be Christian or male. Open 24hr; no alcohol allowed. B&B: dorm beds Ksh640. ③

Planet Safari Ninth floor, Sonalux House, Moi Ave; PO Box 79347 ℡020/229799, ℻211899, ⓔplanet@africaonline.co.ke. Dorm-only, very popular backpacker place; reach it by taking the lift to the fifth floor, then the stairs. There's a safari

△ Norfolk Hotel

booking office for its captive market (you can stay free for up to three days if you take them up on a trip). Security is reasonable, despite some off-putting hangers-on. Dorms Ksh300.

Moderate

680 (Six-Eighty) Hotel Corner of Kenyatta Ave and Muindi Mbingu St; PO Box 43436 Ⓣ020/315371 or 344000, Ⓕ218314, Ⓦwww.680-hotel.co.ke. Somewhat soulless but much better value than most of the other central hotels. Rooms have a bath and satellite TV and there is safe underground parking. Make sure to ask for a room at the back unless you want to be kept awake by the nightly live music from *Simmers* restaurant opposite. (6)

Hotel County County Lane, off Haile Selassie Ave; PO Box 41924 Ⓣ020/226190 or 220390, Ⓕ213889, Ⓔaladins@africaonline.co.ke; see "Central Nairobi" map. A very reasonable, functional block, quieter than most and popular with African businessmen. It's close to the railway museum, but relatively far from the main shopping streets. Internet access available. Good value. (5)

Hotel Terminal Moktar Daddah St Ⓣ020/228817–8, Ⓕ220075. A long-time backpackers' favourite, with large, well-kept rooms, all with nets, telephone and sporadic hot water. No guests after 7pm. Good value, but bring some earplugs to counter the noise from the *Dove Cage* bar and restaurant below. (3)

Kenya Comfort Hotel Corner of Muindi Mbingu and Monrovia streets Ⓣ020/317605, Ⓦwww.kenyacomfort.com. This large hotel is popular with tour groups and has decent en-suite rooms with satellite TV. Breakfast is included but best avoided. (4)

Parkside Hotel Monrovia St; PO Box 53104 Ⓣ020/214154–6, Ⓕ310435. Facing Jeevanjee Gardens, the *Parkside* is large, secure, reasonably quiet and has airy, pleasant s/c rooms, hot water and telephones. It is slightly overpriced though, and not as slick as its brochures make out. The restaurant is nothing special. (4)

YWCA Mamlaka Rd, off Nyerere Ave, just west of Central Park; PO Box 40710 Ⓣ020/2724789, Ⓕ2710519, Ⓦwww.kenyaywca.org; see "Central Nairobi" map. Best value for men as well as women (and couples can share). Contact them well in advance to reserve. Monthly rates are available: a double room with washbasin costs around $100. Dorms Ksh800. (4)

Expensive

Grand Regency Off Loita St; PO Box 57549 Ⓣ020/211199, Ⓕ217120, Ⓦwww.grandregency.co.ke. A successful example of modern technology melded to architectural ambition, with a cool marble-clad atrium. Three glass and gold-lacquer lifts glide up and down one side to the rooms (starting at around $350), the more expensive among which have balconies opening onto the atrium. Service is efficient, the clientele mostly businessmen. There's also an expensive pool and health club. (9)

Hotel Inter-Continental City Hall Way; PO Box 30533 Ⓣ020/261000, Ⓕ210675, Ⓦwww.ichotelsgroup.com. Some 30 years old and not as good value as its competitors, but still fairly palatial. It has some surprisingly secluded corners in the grounds, many amenities (including a heated pool, health club, casino and a good Mediterranean restaurant, *Le Mistral*) and disabled facilities. They can pick you up or drop you at the airport. Rates start at $200 excluding breakfast. (9)

Hilton Hotel Mama Ngina St; PO Box 30624, Ⓣ020/250000, Ⓕ226477, Ⓦwww.hilton.com. The cylindrical tower is unmistakable, and the lobby impressive, but this is somewhat impersonal and caters mainly for expense accounts. Rooms get better the higher you go. The "rooftop pool" is down at second-floor level and rather overshadowed. Also offers a health club, Jacuzzi, sauna and steam bath, as well as four restaurants, but is nonetheless overpriced compared to the *Stanley*. Rooms from $250. (9)

Nairobi Safari Club University Way; PO Box 43564 Ⓣ020/251333, Ⓕ224625, Ⓦwww.nairobisafariclub.com. Not as exclusive as you might imagine, despite the copy of the club's bylaws issued to you at reception and the steep rates. It's a twelve-storey block, ill-placed on the loud and fume-filled University Way, but has good service and seems to be moving away from its pompous club atmosphere. Rooms are well-equipped suites, though rates are too high for what you get – you're even charged to use the small pool and health club. From $250 a night, excluding breakfast. (9)

Norfolk Hotel Harry Thuku Rd; PO Box 58581 Ⓣ020/216940, Ⓕ2167962, Ⓦwww.lonrhohotels.com; see "Central Nairobi" map. Nairobi's oldest and most historic lodgings, built in mock-Edwardian style. It's much too pricey for the facilities on offer, limited to a pool, expensive shop, health club and sauna, but it remains the haunt of visiting celebrities. Doubles from $300. (9)

Oakwood Hotel Kimathi St; PO Box 40683 Ⓣ020/220592, Ⓕ332170, Ⓦwww.madahotels.com. An endearing oddity lost amid the skyscrapers rising all around, this older two-storey hotel has wood panelling, very basic telephones and TVs, and a great antique lift. The location is very convenient, with good rooms and excellent bathrooms (hot water and actual baths), and there's good security. It also has a first-floor bar overlooking the touristy *Thorn Tree Café*: **❼**

🏃 **Serena Hotel** Nyerere Rd, off Kenyatta Ave; PO Box 46302 ☎020/725111, 📠718103, 🌐www.serenahotels .com; see "Central Nairobi" map. Impeccable hotel done out in a Pan-African style, replete with sculptures and wall hangings. Rooms are excellent, many having been refurbished, and feature intricately carved wooden furniture and wardrobes, marble bathrooms, and African artworks. All rooms have Internet access. Amenities include a health club, pool and shops. Unfortunately, the location, fronting onto Central Park, is dangerous at night. From $340 excluding breakfast. **❾**

Stanley Hotel Corner of Kimathi St and Kenyatta Ave; PO Box 30680 ☎020/228830, 📠229388, 🌐www.sarovahotels.com. Complete with its famous *Thorn Tree Café* rendezvous, this is as central as you can get, and is a popular base for tourists and businessmen alike. It was originally an Edwardian structure, with touches of Art Deco, though the period decor isn't overdone. The rooms are equipped with satellite TV, mini-bar and noise-excluding double glazing, and rooms designed for disabled guests are available. Facilities include a modern gym, sauna and a pleasant heated rooftop pool and bar. From $220 excluding breakfast. **❾**

Out of the centre

Most of Nairobi's better value mid- and upper-range hotels are located out of the city centre, in the relatively affluent **suburbs** of Westlands and Parklands (also the main focus for more sophisticated night-time bars and clubs), and along the main roads radiating out of the city. Buses/matatus #21, #23, #30, #104 and #119 go to Westlands; for Parklands, catch a matatu on Latema Road. Both areas are relatively safe for walking around with luggage during the day. Two of the main focuses for budget travellers, the youth hostel and *Nairobi Backpackers*, are a short journey away from the city centre in the suburbs. Unless otherwise noted, the places listed below appear on the "Greater Nairobi" map, pp.106–107, or, in the case of Westlands and Parklands hotels, on the "Westlands" map, p.120.

Camping and hostels

🏃 **Nairobi Backpackers** Milimani Rd; PO Box 9545 ☎020/2724827, 🌐www .nairobibackpackers.com. Cleaner and friendlier than the youth hostel, with Internet access, hot showers and a self-service bar. Breakfast is included in the rates, good evening meals are provided for those who want them, and safaris can be organized. A good place to meet other travellers. Recommended. Dorms Ksh550, **❸**.

Nairobi Youth Hostel Ralphe Bunche Rd, near Nairobi Hospital; PO Box 48661 ☎020/723012, 📠724862, 📧kyha@africaonline.co.ke. Once one of the better budget places in Nairobi, but these days the dorms are rundown, the bathrooms are dirty (several of them lack hot water) and the management unhelpful. Still, there is Internet access and a passable café, and it's a good place to meet Kenyan students. Dorms Ksh600 per night, an extra Ksh120 a night for those without YHA cards; s/c one-bedroom apartments from Ksh2000 per night.

🏃 **Upper Hill Campsite** Menengai Rd, off Hospital Rd ☎020/720290, 📠719662, 📧campsite@thorntree.com. A small, relaxed campsite, very popular with overlanders. There are dorms and double rooms, hot showers, a kitchen, a bar and a restaurant. Tent rental is inexpensive and security is good. Take bus #7C or #34 to Kenyatta National hospital; the campsite is a 500m walk from the top of Hospital Rd. Dorms Ksh250, **❷**.

Hotels and apartments

Westlands and Parklands

Holiday Inn Parklands Rd; PO Box 66807 00623 ☎020/3740920–1, 📠3748823, 🌐www.holiday -inn.com/nairobikenya. Classy, well-maintained modern establishment in pastiche Edwardian and Art Nouveau styles (the original structure was a 1930s hotel), with small tropical gardens and a bar. It's rather business-oriented, but efficiently run and has good disabled access, with some specially designed rooms. There's also a pool, the obligatory fitness centre and sauna, and the Mayfair Casino next door. Excellent value. B&B from $250. **❾**

Impala Hotel Parklands Rd, Parklands; PO Box 14144 ☎020/3742346–7, 📠743258. Not at all touristy, with reasonably priced rooms, good parking and a shaded, leafy bar. **❺**

Jacaranda Hotel Just off Waiyaki Way, Westlands; PO Box 14287 ☎020/4448713, 📠4448977,

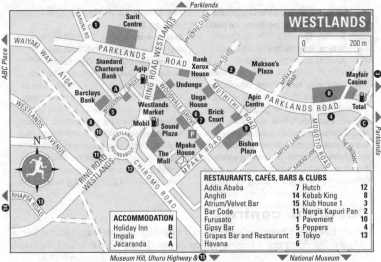

▲ Parklands

WESTLANDS

0 — 200 m

RESTAURANTS, CAFÉS, BARS & CLUBS

Addis Ababa	7	Hutch	12
Anghiti	14	Kebab King	8
Atrium/Velvet Bar	15	Klub House 1	3
Bar Code	11	Nargis Kapuri Pan	2
Furusato	1	Pavement	10
Gipsy Bar	5	Peppers	4
Grapes Bar and Restaurant	9	Tokyo	13
Havana	6		

ACCOMMODATION

Holiday Inn	B
Impala	C
Jacaranda	A

Museum Hill, Uhuru Highway & ⑮ ▼   ▼ National Museum

Ⓦ www.jacarandahotels.com. Rooms here are a bit small, but have satellite TV and fan. Service varies between middling and excellent, and there's a nice pizza garden with live music every night. Be careful when walking in the vicinity at night. B&B ⑧

Elsewhere in Greater Nairobi

Boulevard Hotel Harry Thuku Rd; PO Box 42831 ☏020/227567, Ⓕ334071, Ⓦwww .hotelboulevardkenya.com. Functional rather than extravagant, this well-cared-for hotel has a pleasant garden setting, a good pool (unfortunately on the traffic side of the building), tennis court, TV in all rooms and ample parking. To overcome Uhuru Highway's noise, get a room at the back in the middle, overlooking the garden. Buses #21, #23 and #119, matatu #104. Rate excludes breakfast. ⑦

Fairview Hotel Bishops Rd; PO Box 40842 ☏020/2711321–2, Ⓕ721320, Ⓦwww .fairviewkenya.com. A peaceful, rambling country-style place with pleasant grounds (great for bird-watching), a wide variety of accommodation and excellent security. All rooms have nets and TVs, some have bath. Family rooms have bunk beds for kids, and the deluxe doubles are excellent, but some of the standard rooms are not much better than a decent B&L. Meals are good though, and it's popular with families, so reserve ahead. Bus/matatu #1, #2, #3, #4, #41, #46 or #111 to 3rd Ngong Ave, then a 3min walk. ⑧

Heron Hotel Milimani Rd; PO Box 41848 ☏02/2720740–3, Ⓕ2721698, Ⓦwww.heronhotel .com. The exterior has been impressively

renovated but the improvements don't quite stretch to the collection of studio, one- and two-bed apartments which, while adequate, are hardly luxurious. Still, staff are helpful, and there's a decent restaurant with a large balcony overlooking Milimani Rd. Bus/matatu #1, #2, #3, #4, #34, #41, #46 or #111 to *Panafric*, then a 5min walk up Milimani Road. ⑤

Kenya Comfort Hotel Suites Decent serviced apartments with secure parking; see p.122 for address and more details. ⑤

Palacina Hotel and Suites Kitale Lane, off Dennis Pritt Rd, ☏020/2715517, Ⓦwww.palacina.com. A wonderful boutique hotel tucked away in the suburbs, offering suites and long-stay apartments that manage to be both luxuriously stylish and homely. The service is efficient and very friendly and there is a top-class restaurant attached. If you've got the cash, this is great place to spend it. B&B from $380. ⑨

Panafric Hotel Kenyatta Ave, Nairobi Hill; PO Box 30486 ☏020/2714444, Ⓕ2721878, Ⓦwww .sarovahotels.com. A good uptown option, 500m up the hill west of Uhuru Park, this has views over the city and good service. Its *Flame Tree Restaurant* is deservedly popular. Bus/matatu #1 to #4, #34, #41, #46 or #111. ⑧

Utalii Hotel Thika Rd, 6km from town; PO Box 31067 ☏020/802540/1–7, Ⓕ860514, Ⓦwww .utalii.co.ke. Run by the Utalii College, Kenya's tourism institute, hence you get impeccable, if slightly hesitant, service. Amenities include a

120

large outdoor heated pool, tennis courts and an astonishingly good restaurant (Tues Kenyan buffet lunch, Sat eve poolside BBQ, Sun buffet lunch). The slum facing it, across the banana tops, is Mathare Valley, one of Nairobi's worst. Courtesy bus to city centre, or bus/matatu #45, #137, #145, #160 or #237. B&B ⑦

The outskirts

The places reviewed below appear on the map on pp.158–159. Where public transport isn't suggested, take a taxi to reach the establishment.

Giraffe Manor Koitobos Rd, adjacent to the AFEW Giraffe Centre, Langata ☏020/891078, ⒻFax 890949, ⓦwww.giraffemanor.com. Neck and shoulders above the rest is this wonderfully eccentric Scottish-style manor house in the grounds of AFEW Giraffe Centre, to which profits go, and whose inhabitants like to share your breakfast through the first-floor dining room windows. It's extremely exclusive and astoundingly expensive. Reservations are compulsory. Closed April. HB from $525. ⑨

House of Waine Masai Lane/Bogani Rd, Karen; PO Box 25035, ☏020/891920/891553, Ⓕ892091, ⓦwww.houseofwaine.co.ke. Eleven luxurious individually themed rooms set in peaceful gardens in the suburbs of Karen. Take a taxi. From $220 a night. ⑨

Karen Camp Marula Lane, Karen ☏020/883475, ⓦwww.karencamp.com. B&B-cum-overlander's camp with pleasant s/c rooms, permanent tents, dorm beds ($5) and a big lawn for camping in your own tent ($3 per person) as well as good food and a bar. Quiet and peaceful, but a long way from town. Rate excludes breakfast. Dorms $5. ❸

Kentmere Club Limuru Rd, Tigoni; PO Box 39508 ☏0154/41053, Ⓕ40692, Ⓔkentclub@net2000ke.com. Situated 16km north of Nairobi amid the tea and coffee plantations of the Tigoni highlands, *Kentmere* is a small and friendly country inn, pretty much what you might find in the Cotswolds in England, all wooden beams and wooden "slate" roofs. It has sixteen s/c rooms in cottages with beautiful gardens and cosy fireplaces, and a good restaurant using mostly locally grown ingredients. Ten minutes' drive away is the Limuru Country Club with its golf course and swimming pool. Matatu #114. HB $120. ❽

Nairobi Park Services Campsite Magadi Rd, off Langata Rd just past Langata Gate; PO Box 54867 ☏020/890661, Ⓔnps@swiftkenya.com. The campsite is one of the best equipped in Nairobi, popular with overlanders, with single and double rooms and some dorm beds. The site is secure, and the bar is a good place to talk to staff from a number of safari operators. There's food available, a cybercafé and cable TV. Matatu #125 or bus #126. Camping Ksh250 per person (tent hire Ksh60 per person/night), Ksh200 per vehicle; dorm beds Ksh300. ❸

Panari Hotel Mombasa Rd; PO Box 4372 ☏020/6946000, Ⓕ828985, Ⓔinfo@panarihotel.com. New, ultramodern five-star establishment on the way into town from the airport. Rooms from $180. ⑨

Safari Park Hotel Thika Rd, 14km from town; PO Box 45038 ☏02/3633000, Ⓕ3633919, ⓦwww.safaripark-hotel.com. A huge, purpose-built "inland resort" offering a wholly sanitized vision of "Real Africa". Nonetheless it's an attractive base for an upmarket stay, with faultless service, landscaped gardens, a massive swimming pool, health club, tennis courts, horse-riding, four-poster beds in all rooms, seven excellent and remarkably affordable restaurants, and a casino, should you have any money left over. There's a regular shuttle bus, or you could use bus/matatu #45, #137, #145, #160 or #237. From $220 excluding breakfast. ⑨

Windsor Golf & Country Club Off Kigwa Rd, Ridgeways, 15km north of the city; PO Box 45587 ☏020/862300, Ⓕ860160, ⓦwww.windsorgolfresort.com. Situated on an old coffee plantation, this golfers' resort has been styled in mock-Victorian and Georgian style, complete with landscaped gardens, copper-plate clock tower, gazebos, and even designer creaking floorboards. It's rather absurd but also superbly run, with services and amenities second to none. Facilities include an outdoor heated pool, health club with steam room and massage, tennis and squash courts, a croquet lawn, fishing and riding, and there's a resident ornithologist. Accommodation ranges from rooms and suites to some lovely twin cottages (570). Rooms from $370. ⑨

Long stays

For long stays in Nairobi, cheap **flats**, **rooms** and **studios** are advertised in the classified columns of the *Nation* and the *Standard*. Otherwise, contact an apartment agency (Westlands is probably the most promising area), or there's a very useful noticeboard at the supermarket in Karen. For a stay of a month or two, the *YWCA* is your best bet (see p.118). Note that if the place you're considering has no *askari*, the danger of burglary is very real. The establishments below are on the Greater Nairobi map, pp.106–107.

Fairview Bishops Rd (same management and details as *Fairview Hotel*, p.120). Three-room flats available for three-month stays or longer at Ksh72,000 per flat per month.

Kenya Comfort Hotel Suites Junction Milimani and Ralph Bunche roads; PO Box 30425, ☏020/2719060–1, ℻2727989, ℗www.kenya comfort.com. The building is an ugly concrete structure but the apartments, from studios to three-bedroom affairs, are pretty nice and there is a swimming pool, daily maid service and 24hr reception and parking. Studios from $500 a month.

Woodmere Apartments Rose Ave, off Lenana Rd, three blocks from the Yaya Centre; PO Box 74381 ☏020/2712511, ℻2720721, ℗www .woodmerenairobi.com. Well-guarded premises with

a small pool, sauna, garden and space for kids. Accommodation ranges from fully furnished, small, serviced studios with tiny kitchen and loft sleeping to spacious, tasteful apartments in various sizes. From $685 a month for a budget studio to $3000 a month for a palatial four-bedroom apartment with fireplace.

Yaya Apartments Yaya Centre, Argwings Kodhek Rd; PO Box 76377 ☏020/2713360/1, ℗561902, ℗www.yaya-apartments.com. The top luxury option for long stays, with fully furnished and serviced apartments (with up to four bedrooms) including kitchen and satellite TV. There's an Olympic-sized pool, two floodlit tennis courts, an Internet cafe and safe parking. One-bedroom apartments from around Ksh160,000 per month.

Central Nairobi

Kenyatta Avenue is the obvious place to start looking around Central Nairobi. A good initial overview of it can be had from the vertigo-inducing, glass-walled lifts in the **ICEA building**, on the northwest corner of Wabera Street. If the guards at the bottom need an excuse, tell them you're visiting the Japanese Embassy on the fifteenth floor; they may even be persuaded to escort you onto the roof. Tipping (Ksh20–50) might be helpful.

The avenue was originally designed to allow a twelve-oxen team to make a full turn, though livestock is nowadays no longer permitted within the city limits. Broad, multi-laned and planted with flowering trees and shrubs, it remains (along with the Kenyatta Conference Centre) the capital's favourite tourist image. The avenue is smartest – and most touristy – on its south side, with would-be moneychangers, itinerant souvenir hawkers and safari touts assailing you from every direction, and wily shoeshiners inspecting each passing pair of feet from their stands (who, given half a chance, will throw some wax on your shoes and then insist on having to clean it off).

The focus of the avenue's eastern end is the *Stanley Hotel*'s **Thorn Tree Café**, diagonally opposite Nakumatt supermarket on the corner of Kimathi Street. Nairobi's one proper pavement café, the *Thorn Tree* is an enduring meeting place despite its prices and largely *wazungu* and rich businessman clientele. The thorn tree in question was cut down in 1997 and replaced with a new sapling in December 1998 and a smaller message board.

Still on Kenyatta Avenue, close to Uhuru Highway, is the skyscraper of the **General Post Office** (GPO) and, just before it, **Koinange Street**, named after the Kikuyu Senior Chief Koinange of the colonial era. The peculiar caged **Galton–Fenzi Memorial**, just here on the left, is a monument to the man who founded, of all things, the Nairobi branch of the Automobile Association. Fenzi was also the first motorist to drive from Nairobi to Mombasa, back in 1926 when there was only a dirt track.

City Square and Parliament

Heading south down Koinange Street and on to Kaunda Street, passing the *Inter-Continental* on your right and Holy Family Cathedral on your left, you cross City Hall Way and enter **City Square**. Jomo Kenyatta's statue sits benevolently, mace in hand, on the far side of the wide, flagstoned court; his mausoleum, with flickering eternal flames, is on the right as you approach the Parliament building further on. When the flags are out for a conference it all looks very bright and confident.

The legend over the main doors of Kenya's **Parliament** reads: "For a Just Society and the Fair Government of Men". The motto seems finally to be losing its edge of irony, the government having been forced by both national and international pressures to allow greater democracy and accountability in its business. A host of contentious motions are openly debated here, concerning corruption and ethnic violence, and there's even the occasional vote of no-confidence in the government.

To sit in the **public gallery** you must first register for a visitors permit at the gatehouse on the corner of Parliament Road and Harambee Avenue, leaving all your belongings with the attendant outside. The gallery tends to be full of schoolchildren who are very well-behaved – which of course is more than can be said of the members of parliament. Try to get hold of a copy of the Orders of the Day – there may be a juicy question or two worth anticipating. The guards at the gate can tell you when the next parliamentary session is taking place (usually Wed & Thurs at 2.30pm; Parliament is in recess mid-July to mid-October) or, when it's not in session, how to get a tour of the building. If you're assigned a guide, make sure both parties are clear about how much you'll pay.

Kenyatta Conference Centre

From Parliament, walking down Harambee Avenue along the shady pavement, you come to Nairobi's pride and joy – the **Kenyatta International Conference Centre** (KICC) and its tall brother, "KANU tower", the ruling party headquarters. This, for a long time the tallest building in Kenya, is capped by a mile-high (a mile above sea level that is) formerly revolving restaurant. The restaurant has closed, but it's worth making an effort to get as high as possible. If you talk to the security staff in the foyer, assent is usually given for ascent, partly because it has become accepted practice to tip the guards who come with you (a mean Ksh200 is the going rate, though

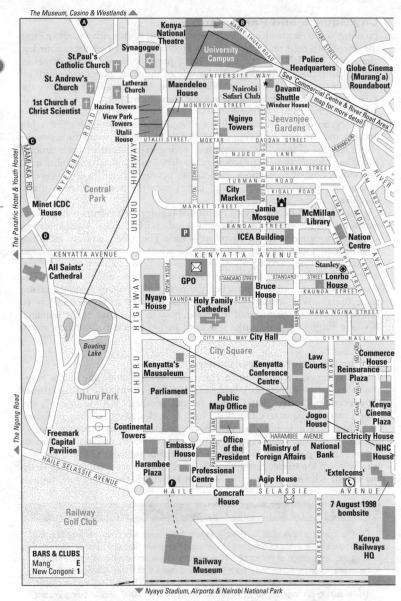

The Museum, Casino & Westlands ▲

St. Paul's Catholic Church †
St. Andrew's Church †
1st Church of Christ Scientist †
Synagogue ✡
Lutheran Church †
Maendeleo House
Kenya National Theatre
University Campus
HARRY THUKU ROAD
Police Headquarters
Globe Cinema (Murang'a) Roundabout
KIJABE STREET

UNIVERSITY WAY
See 'Commercial Centre & River Road Area' map for more detail
Hazina Towers
View Park Towers
Utalii House
Nairobi Safari Club
Davanu Shuttle (Windsor House)
Nginyo Towers
MONROVIA STREET
Jeevanjee Gardens
MURANGA ROAD

Central Park

Minet ICDC House
UTALII STREET
MOKTAR
NJUGU LANE
DAADDAH STREET
BIASHARA STREET
TUBMAN ROAD
KIGALI ROAD
City Market
Jamia Mosque
McMillan Library
MARKET STREET
BANDA STREET
ICEA Building
Nation Centre

KENYATTA AVENUE
All Saints' Cathedral
GPO
POSTA ROAD
STANDARD STREET
Bruce House
KAUNDA STREET
Stanley ●
Lonrho House
Nyayo House
Holy Family Cathedral
MAMA NGINA STREET
WABERA ST

CITY HALL WAY
City Hall
City Square
CITY HALL WAY
Kenyatta's Mausoleum
Kenyatta Conference Centre
Law Courts
Commerce House
Reinsurance Plaza
Parliament
Public Map Office
Kenya Cinema Plaza
Jogoo House
Electricity House
Boating Lake
Uhuru Park
Freemark Capital Pavilion
Continental Towers
Embassy House
Office of the President
Ministry of Foreign Affairs
National Bank
NHC House
HARAMBEE AVENUE
HAILE SELASSIE AVENUE
Harambee Plaza
Professional Centre
Agip House
'Extelcoms'
Comcraft House
7 August 1998 bombsite
Railway Golf Club
WORKSHOPS ROAD
Kenya Railways HQ

BARS & CLUBS
Mang'   E
New Congoni 1

Railway Museum

▼ Nyayo Stadium, Airports & Nairobi National Park

nothing's fixed). The view of Nairobi is without equal and a firm reminder of the vastness of Africa. Just 4km to the south, the Mombasa road can be seen leaving the suburbs behind and taking off across the yellow plains; northwards, hills of coffee – and, at higher altitudes, tea – roll into the distance. On a good day you really can see Mount Kenya in one direction and Kilimanjaro in the other. Immediately below, the traffic swarms – and

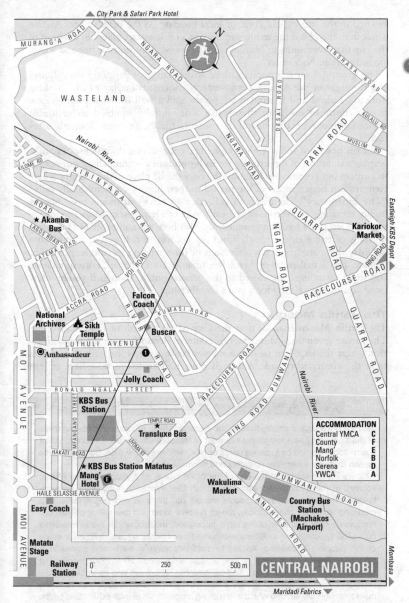

City Park & Safari Park Hotel

Jogoo House (containing government offices) is suddenly seen to be built remarkably like a Roman villa.

National Archives

Straight down Harambee Avenue, cut across Moi Avenue and up to the **National Archives** (Mon–Fri 8am–5pm, Sat 8.30am–1pm; Ⓦ www.kenyarchives.go.ke).

Housed in the striking old Bank of India building on the bend of Moi Avenue across from the *Hilton*, the archives amount to a museum/art gallery in the heart of the city that few visitors to Nairobi seem to know about; entry is free and a look around takes an hour or so.

The ground floor is a public gallery with a range of paintings from Kenya and throughout the African continent; an enormous display of Maasai, Luo, Turkana, Luhiya and Ethiopian weaponry; and a wall of tribal photographs. In the centre of the floor there's also a delightfully jumbled collection of African ethnographia – musical instruments, masks, weapons, domestic artefacts.

Past the first floor and its photograph library, the second floor houses a photographic exhibition of the struggle for **independence** – compelling not just for its content but because this is almost the only public place in the country where Kenyans can be reminded of the period in their history euphemistically called "The Emergency". There's also a collection of black-and-white press photos, highly revealing as a record of the early part of Daniel Arap Moi's presidency, with foreign tours figuring prominently. Also here are a number of fascinating portraits of tribal elders, mostly from the colonial era. If you're around on a Saturday, there are free 10am screenings of films relating to culture, politics or wildlife. The actual archives themselves (mainly books, papers, correspondence and some recordings) are closed to the general public, though if you're interested you can pay Ksh50 for a year's membership.

The Jamia Mosque

The **Jamia Mosque** stands near the City Market, north of Kenyatta Avenue. The ornate green-and-white exterior contrasts strikingly with the simple interior, where the large central dome appears far larger from beneath than it does from the courtyard outside. Although most Kenyan towns now have at least

Kibera

Said to be the largest shanty town in sub-Saharan Africa, Kibera is a sprawling mass of slum housing just a few kilometres west of Nairobi's city centre. It's safe to visit if you're accompanied by local residents or NGO workers in the area, but there's little reason to do so – there are no sights and nowhere special to hang out.

Kibera initially started at the end of the World War II, as a village housing African soldiers of the demobilized armies of British East Africa. Subsequently, as rural-to-urban migration increased, people moved into the area and began putting up mud-and-wattle structures. Today, Kibera is home to around one million of Nairobi's residents – over a quarter of the city's population, most of whom live in makeshift huts. The typical home in Kibera measures three metres square, with an average of five people per dwelling. Access to electricity, running water and sanitation is minimal – there's an average of one pit latrine for every 50 to 500 people. The streets are a mass of seemingly endless trenches, alleyways and open sewers; the Nairobi–Nakuru rail line that snakes through the shanty town actually serves as the main thoroughfare, around which enterprising residents set up makeshift stalls selling everything from charcoal to plastic bags and shoelaces.

In addition to lacking even the most basic amenities, Kibera has an HIV infection rate of over twenty percent. Four-fifths of Kibera youths are unemployed and the number of orphans rises daily; yet the social services needed to look after them are absent as are urban development policies that would begin to tackle the many issues facing Kibera, let alone Nairobi in general.

one mosque, often financed by Saudi Arabia, few are as large or as beautiful as the Jamia. It's unlikely that non-Muslims will be allowed in, although polite requests, a genuine interest in Islam and the usual modesty of attire may help. For a bird's-eye view of the mosque, the top of the ICEA building is (again) a good vantage point.

The museums and parks

Covered here are the handful of **parks** and **museums** in Nairobi itself. Nairobi National Park gets separate coverage in the "Nairobi Province" section later in this chapter (see p.156), as do the Bomas of Kenya, the Karen Blixen Museum and the Langata Giraffe Centre. Unless you have your own wheels you may be better off joining a tour for them. The following sites, however, are all easily walkable within Nairobi.

To keep up with developments in Kenya's museums, contact the Kenya Museum Society (PO Box 40658; ℡020/3743808, ⓦwww.kenyamuseum society.org). As well as publishing the excellent annual journal *Kenya Past and Present*, they organize a two-week "Know Kenya Course" (Ksh4500) in October or November every year, featuring behind-the-scenes access to museums, visits to places of historical or environmental interest and lectures by well-known Kenyan writers and academics.

The Railway Museum

Nairobi's **Railway Museum** (daily 8.15am–4.45pm; Ksh200, children Ksh100; camera Ksh100, camcorder Ksh200; free guides) is a natural draw for rail fans and of more than passing interest for anyone else. Privately run, it's a signposted ten-minute walk from the train station, but be careful, as there was a rash of grab-and-run robberies down here a few years back.

△ Nairobi matatu

The main hall contains a mass of memorabilia: photos of early stations, of the "Lunatic Express" East African Railway from Mombasa to Kampala being built, and the engineering feats involved in getting the carriages up and down the escarpment, and strange pieces of hardware, such as the game-viewing seat mounted at the front of the train. Passengers who risked this perch were reminded that "The High Commissioner will not be liable for personal injury (fatal or otherwise)". In the museum annexe, the motorized bicycle inspection trolley is quite a sight but, as the write-up explains, the experiment in the 1950s "was not really successful", as the wheels kept slipping off the rail.

Outside, exposed to the elements, is the museum's collection of old **locomotives**, most of them built in Britain. You can clamber inside any of the cabs to play with the massive levers and switches. The restriction on forward visibility in some of the engines seems incredible; the driver of the *Karamoja Express* couldn't have had any idea what was in front of him while steaming down a straight line. If it all fills you with nostalgic delight, you should also note that Nairobi and Mombasa stations both have locomotive graveyards which, with persistence, you should be able to look around.

Lions figure prominently in the early history of the railway. Look in the shed for first-class coach no. 12 to learn the story of Superintendent C. H. Ryall. During the hunt for the "Maneaters of Tsavo" in 1898, Ryall had readied his gun one evening, settled down in the carriage and offered himself as bait. Unfortunately, he nodded off and was dragged from this carriage and devoured while colleagues sat frozen in horror. The coach, together with the repainted loco no. 301, took part in the filming of *Out of Africa* at Kajiado.

The National Museum

At the time of writing, the **National Museum** is undergoing its first major facelift since its opening, the Ksh760million "Museum in Change" project, slated to end in mid-2007. A new administration block will be built and the main building expanded to create additional gallery space. The museum is expected to remain closed for the duration of the project, and when it re-opens (call ☏020/742878 or see ⓦwww.museums.or.ke for details of times and prices) it will once again be Nairobi's prime sight, the best possible prelude to any tour around the country. In the past surprisingly few travellers have made the small effort to get to the museum, which is only about a thirty-minute walk from Kenyatta Avenue – or a few minutes by taxi or buses #21, #23 or #119. The account below assumes that the renovations will not involve the layout being significantly reorganized; check with museum staff for the latest details.

Opposite the museum and going downhill (in both senses of the word) is the **Snake Park** (daily 9.30am–6pm; Ksh200, children/students Ksh100). It's only fair to say that you'd have to be very enthusiastic about reptiles to find this interesting; there are much better (and cheaper) snake parks on the coast. Exhibits take in East African snakes, a crocodile or two, some murky terrapins, monitor lizards and fish tanks. The **gardens** around the museum offer interesting opportunities for bird-watching (see box opposite).

Natural history and geology

The museum's most extensive collections are **ornithological**, with most of Kenya's thousand-plus species of birds represented. Kenya's birdlife usually makes a strong impression, even on non-bird-watchers. Look out for the various species of hornbills, turacos and rollers, and for the extraordinary standard-wing nightjar, which is frequently seen fluttering low over a swimming pool at

Crafts and shopping

Kenya is a good place to buy carvings and textiles in particular, the former usually made specifically for the tourist market. Beadwork and traditional utensils made from gourds are also popular, but Kenya's most important artisanal traditions are ironwork and metal jewellery, and basketware, both of which go back centuries in some communities. What you take home will depend, to some extent, on what you can carry. Big city dealers will ship items for you, but it's easy, when bargaining on the beach or at the roadside, to get carried away: some carvings and soapstone are extremely heavy as well as fragile, and can be hard to cart home.

Souvenirs on sale, Diani Beach

Whatever you're buying, bargaining is almost always the order of the day, although there are fixed-price shops in Nairobi and Mombasa, and most hotel boutiques are fixed-price, too (and not always as expensive as you might imagine). There are three cardinal rules for bargaining: firstly, don't begin if you're not in the mood or in a hurry; secondly, don't show interest ("just looking") if you're not actually looking to buy; and finally, never offer a price you won't pay.

If you can, try to buy from cooperatives and development organizations. Places such as Kazuri in Nairobi (see p.133), the Makindu Handicrafts Cooperative (see p.362) and Bombolulu (see p.454) all provide their staff and members with above-average rewards.

Carving giraffes

Carvings

Kenya is one of the world's biggest manufacturers of wooden carvings. From the ubiquitous animals of doubtful appearance to finely chiselled bowls and plates, carvings are created here in the millions, mostly by Akamba (see p.358), specifically for the local tourist market and for export.

The most striking carvings are in the dramatically vertical and delicate makonde style (after the Makonde people of Mozambique and Tanzania, a group of whom live west of the Taita Hills). Makonde carvings are ostensibly done in ebony, but most are blackened rosewood or something similar, a fact which shouldn't deter you from buying – this conserves ebony forest stocks and the result looks just as wonderful on your mantelpiece.

The other very popular carving material is soapstone – a soft, heavy, lustrous mineral also known as steatite, mined from one locality, Tabaka (see p.311), near Kisii. Apart from having a tendency to snap when carved too thin (which makes soapstone hippos more popular than giraffes), soapstone is one of the most versatile materials, and the industry has sprouted in the last few decades to encompass a wide variety of plates, bowls, boxes and utensils, as well as decorative items such as chess sets and candlesticks.

Basket weavers using sisal

Baskets

The Akamba are, again, big in basketware (see p.356): the familiar sisal baskets (*chondo*, or *vyondo* in the plural) come in a huge variety of patterns and can be made from cheap nylon string as well as sisal and, much more rarely, baobab bark twine, with beads woven in. They're all light and functional and, since they achieved some status as fashion accessories in the West a few years back, are now much more expensive than they were: buying direct from weavers, especially when leather straps and other decorations have still to be added, can be an excellent deal for all.

Beadwork and tribal items

Beadwork (*ushanga*, *mkufu*) and tribal regalia – weapons such as bows, arrows, spears and clubs, shields, drums (*ngoma*), carved stools and headrests, traditional utensils made from gourds (sometimes beaded), cowhorn keepsafes and tobacco pouches and metal jewellery – are fairly common as well, but much more expensive when they're the genuine article rather than made for the tourist industry. The best region in which to buy metal goods is the north: Turkana-land can yield some fairly spectacular

Turkana wrist-knives (*aberait*)

examples of lethal weaponry, crafted indiscriminately for murderous assault or living room wall. The bracelet-like wrist knives used to slash an enemy are particularly impressive souvenirs.

Masks are mostly imported from west and central Africa (they do not figure in traditional Kenyan art) and are by no means sure to be old or "authentic" no matter how much congealed cow dung appears to fill the crevices. In fact you can be well nigh certain of the fact – and a good thing too if some original pieces are going to remain in the communities which hold them in esteem.

Textiles and footwear

Textiles, although always imported, bear a certain stamp of authenticity in that they are worn locally and make good-value, and practical, souvenirs. The printed women's wraps – kanga – in cotton, and the heavier-weave men's sarongs – kikoi – are really good buys on the coast, and older ones represent collectable items worth seeking out. Kangas are always sold in pairs and are printed with intriguing Swahili proverbs. Local tailors will make them into garments for you at very reasonable prices. Footwear can be really good value. The widespread Bata chain has great deals on basic sandals, beach thongs and trainers, but you can get much

Maasai bead necklaces

more interesting sandals from tourist stalls, including pretty but touristy beaded leather sandals, and the much tougher and more local sandals made from discarded car and truck tyres – "five-thousand-mile shoes".

Toys

Whether or not you have children or are buying presents for kids, the **toys** you'll come across from time to time are highly recommended souvenirs. Most worthwhile are the beautifully fashioned, and sometimes big and intricate, push-along wire buses, cars and lorries. These used to be fitted with disproportionately large stick-up steering wheels, and would be given to lucky boys in rural areas by older brothers and uncles. Today, they're vastly outnumbered by hand-mass-produced wire vehicle toys, specifically made as tourist souvenirs. Also widely available are various push-along men-on-bikes, birds and monkeys, which include a little crank to emulate cycling legs or bobbing feet.

Although you will rarely be offered it, be aware that **ivory**, carved or otherwise, is strictly illegal; most countries have banned all ivory imports. Any ivory that's found by customs will be seized and, in many countries, the carrier will be subject to a heavy fine. You may also wish to avoid buying things made of woods such as **ebony** and **mahogany**, whose existence is threatened by logging. Carvings made of neem and acacia are more environmentally friendly.

Music and musical instruments

Other good buys include **music** (on cassette as well as CD, though try to listen before buying), and **musical instruments** – for example the *nyatiti*, a Luo lyre – though it's very hard to get quality instruments if you're serious about your sounds. Drums can be bulky and some people even buy them to use as tables, but beware if the skins look poorly cured. Those designed to be held under one arm, more common on the coast, are the most practical as souvenirs. Lamu has its own wind instrument called a *siwa*, a huge side-blown thing traditionally made from an elephant tusk, but these days from hardwood.

Homemade wire truck toy

Bird-watching in Nairobi

Bird-watching need not be exclusively a bush pursuit. For any visitor staying in central Nairobi, an impressive sight during the early morning and late evening is groups of **black kites** circling as they move between feeding and roosting sites; among these are **pied crows**, readily identified black-and-white birds. **Marabou storks**, **sacred ibises** and **silvery-cheeked hornbills** can sometimes be seen flying over the city (dramatically large marabous may also be seen in the thorn trees on Uhuru Highway, near Nyayo Stadium), while flocks of **red-winged starlings** call noisily from office buildings. The leafier areas of the city are likely to produce even more birds.

The gardens adjacent to the National Museum are an interesting and relatively safe area to start bird-watching. Here, keen bird-watchers may encounter the **cinnamon-chested bee eater**, a common, small, green bee eater found in open areas with scattered bushes. The plants and flowering shrubs outside the front steps of the museum provide excellent opportunities to observe **sunbirds**; several species, including variable and Hunter's sunbirds, can be seen here. Another bird of the gardens is the **African paradise monarch**, a species of flycatcher. In breeding plumage, the rufous males have long tail streamers, which trail behind them like ribbons as they flit from tree to tree.

Nature Kenya organizes bird walks from the National Museum every Wednesday morning at 8.45am for Ksh100. They usually proceed to another part of Nairobi. Longer trips are also held at least once a month. For more information, contact Nature Kenya at the museum (PO Box 44486; ☎020/3749957, ☺www.naturekenya .org).

dusk, hunting for insects. There are also dioramas of Kenyan mammals in the large mammal room, casts of fish, even a whale skeleton, as well as the skeleton and a fibreglass replica of Ahmed, the famous elephant from Marsabit, to whom Kenyatta accorded protection.

Quite useful if you're going anywhere near the Rift Valley, the **Geology Gallery** is a mine of information on plate tectonics and the life-cycle of volcanoes, with a good collection of rocks and minerals which you may see on your travels.

Gallery of Contemporary East African Art

On the second floor, next to the birds, the **Gallery of Contemporary East African Art** is an exhibition space and **showroom** for principally Kenyan, Tanzanian and Ugandan artists to display their work and wares. Everything is for sale and the gallery, although non-profit-making, takes a commission from what's sold and ploughs this back into running the place, and into acquiring work for the museum's own, long-planned Modern Art Gallery. It's also become an increasingly popular venue for foreign embassies in Nairobi to mount exhibitions from their own countries.

Human prehistory

The special interest of Nairobi's museum lies in the cultural, human and proto-human exhibits. The **Prehistory Gallery**, where the paleontology exhibits are housed, is entered through a room whose walls are disguised with stunning reproductions of Tanzanian rock paintings. Ahead, in a hall named rather incongruously after Mahatma Gandhi, casts from the skulls of ancient ape ancestors and hominids are displayed along the right-hand wall, and include a number of australopithecine remains, as well as skull 1470, whose discovery debunked the idea that the australopithecines were our direct ancestors (see p.603). Ahead, on the floor, is a cast of wide-splayed, human-looking footprints which belonged to australopithecines and which were squeezed into the mud about three and a half million years ago. Standing next to them, an almost complete *Homo erectus* skeleton guards the doorway to a tableau (rather like a scene from *Planet of the Apes*) featuring eerily lifelike reconstructions of *Australopithecus africanus*, *Australopithecus boisei* and, most striking of all, a family of *Homo erectus* wolfing down an antelope carcass. There's a separate display, to the right of the Prehistory Gallery entrance, telling the story of the Koobi Fora excavations at Lake Turkana.

Ethnography and history

In contrast, the rather dry second-floor cases of **ethnographic** exhibits aren't particularly illuminating, though you can piece a lot of information together if you've the time. However, they contain some fascinating odds and ends – don't miss the Maasai ear-stretching devices, and the "divining sandals" made of elephant hide tanned in dung and urine. If you're planning on travelling through any of the areas inhabited by pastoral peoples (especially Pokot, Samburu, Maasai or Turkana), then seeing some old and authentic handicrafts beforehand is a good idea. This will also be a big help when you find yourself faced with, for example, an urgent vendor offering you a dozen different carved headrests – not an uncommon experience. The collections indicate the tremendous diversity of Kenya's cultures, a quality impressively evoked by Joy Adamson's series of ethnic portraits mounted on the walls, commissioned by the colonial government and now an impressive record of, in many cases, already vanished cultures. Her beautiful **botanical paintings** are displayed downstairs by the main entrance.

Finally, in the **Lamu Gallery** on the main floor, the first-rate exhibition "The Kenya Coast 9th–19th Century", provides an excellent introduction to Swahili culture and society.

The city's parks

The **Arboretum** (gates close at dusk), northwest of Uhuru Park on Arboretum Drive (matatu #48), is a lovely place to wander or picnic and, of course, a must if you're botanically inclined. Somewhat overgrown, almost jungly in parts, it boasts over two hundred varieties of tree, even the odd monkey. There are security notices everywhere, so don't take any valuables. You may be reassured – or unnerved – by the officious plain-clothes policemen who stalk the glades (it backs onto State House). On the last Monday of each month there is a guided walk; be at the gate by 9.30am if you're interested.

Otherwise, Nairobi's **parks** aren't always very inviting, but several are pleasant places to retreat to for a while. Biggest and best is **City Park** in the north, a half-hour stroll from the National Museum down Forest Road and Limuru Road, or by matatu #11. City Park has a wealth of tropical trees and birdlife, several troops of vervet monkeys, a small stream with wooden bridges, gravel paths, shady lawns and, on weekends, families everywhere. During the week it's delightful, though not for women alone.

Uhuru and **Central** parks, on the western side of Uhuru Highway, are unfenced and never closed, but they have the city's worst reputation for muggings, particularly after dark. There are rowing boats for rent in the small murky lake in Uhuru Park, which are very popular at weekends and holidays.

In a more reputable part of the city (though a night walk even here would be foolish), try **Jeevanjee Gardens**, especially during a weekday lunchtime when you can picnic on a bench and chat with the office workers not thronging the

Saba Saba and the Trees of Peace

The months preceding the December 1997 **general election** were fraught with violence. It all began on July 7, already nicknamed Saba Saba Day ("seven-seven day", from the anniversary of a brutal crackdown on a pro-democracy demonstration on July 7, 1990), when history repeated itself. A rally in central Nairobi degenerated into running battles with police, whose brutality was widely reported on Kenyan and international TV. This in turn led to nationwide riots in which thirteen people were killed. Police, chanting *Uua! Uua!* (Kiswahili for "kill") stormed an examination room at Nairobi University and beat up students; others stormed the Anglican Cathedral – a focal point of the pro-reform movement – where many people had taken refuge, while on the streets police dragged passengers out of taxis and beat them up, and TV news bulletins carried pictures of women with their babies strapped to their backs being attacked by policemen.

The effect of all this, together with the spiralling violence of the following months, was to shatter Kenya's previously peaceful international image, and indirectly led to the suspension of an IMF loan to the country, as well as the virtual collapse of Kenya's tourist industry. Hemmed in on all sides, President Moi finally acceded to the demonstrators' demands and promised to institute a set of reformist measures, including the unbanning of Richard Leakey's Safina party, just before the election. A poignant **memorial** to the many lives lost in political violence over the past decade, can be seen at the roadside verge of **Uhuru Park** at Kenyatta Avenue ("Freedom Corner"), where the Green Belt Movement (see p.84) planted a dozen saplings (themselves destroyed and replanted several times) as "Trees of Peace", each bearing a simple wooden cross with the name of a victim and the words "Saba Saba".

nearby restaurants. You can listen, too, to the preachers who have made Jeevanjee their church and the bemused picnickers their congregation. The park contains a curiously small statue, just about recognizable, of Queen Victoria, presented to Nairobi by nineteenth-century business tycoon A. M. Jeevanjee, founder of the *Standard* newspaper.

A colour map of Nairobi suggests a multitude of cool green spaces around the city. However, the two remaining **forests** – Ngong Road in the west and Karura in the north – have been fierce battlegrounds between environmentalists and those who have illegally expropriated these public lands for development amid a morass of corruption and government inaction. Unless you're accompanied by someone who knows the area well, a visit is inadvisable as illegal activity persists in both forests, including game trapping and the collection of forest produce.

Markets and shopping

It doesn't take long to realize that commerce is Nairobi's *raison d'être*. Disappointingly perhaps, the form which trade takes here is not always very exotic. But Nairobi is the best place in East Africa to buy **handicrafts**, with the widest (if not the cheapest) selection and the best facilities for posting the stuff home. The city also has some lavish **produce markets**, enjoyable even if you only want to browse. The upper part of Moi Avenue is Nairobi's busiest ordinary shopping street, all colonnaded shop-fronts and antiquated name-boards, fun to wander past.

Bargaining is expected at all Nairobi's markets and most shops, with the exception of supermarkets and stores selling imported goods. Be aware, however, that the "last price" varies seasonally and can skyrocket when a major conference hits town.

Produce markets and food

Though it doesn't offer the city's lowest prices, for a colourful and high-quality range of fruit and vegetables, the **City Market** (Mon–Fri 7.30am–6.30pm, Sat 7.30am–3pm, Sun 8.30am–noon) is the obvious target (beware of bag-snatching in the area). The best-value stalls are in the outside aisle flanking the main hall on the right. Fish and meat are on either side of the main building, and the supermarket at the entrance has a good variety of Kenyan cheeses. The other large produce markets are the **Wakulima** (farmers) market, also known simply as Marikiti, a cavernous and dank hall at the bottom of River Road, just before the Country Bus Station, and the excellent, if totally chaotic, open-air **Kariokor market** at the north end of Racecourse Road at the junction with General Waruingi Street. Also good for fruit and vegetables is the **Forest Road Open-Air market** on Limuru Road in Parklands, opposite the Aga Khan Primary School (daily 6am–6pm).

Supermarkets and grocery stores can be found all over the city. Branches of Chum (Agar Khan Walk; Kamahi House, Kamahi St; Market St; Nkrumah Ave; Caveat Lane) and Manumit (Kenyatta Ave at Kimathi St; Moktar Daddah St) are open Monday to Saturday from 8.30am to 8.30pm and on Sunday from 10am to 7pm. They're also good for camping supplies, sleeping bags, and have general household goods and stationery. Samaki & Tilley, on Kaunda Street, are first-class **butchers** and **fishmongers**. You can get good wines at Wines of the World, Mandera Road (west of the Arboretum), or at the Continental Supermarket at ABC Place on Waiyaki Way (the northwestern extension of the Uhuru Highway). The Cocoa Bean at the Village Market mall sells excellent handmade **chocolates**. There are a number of excellent **delicatessens** in Lenana Forest Centre on Ngong Road, and in Westlands' many malls (see "Shopping malls" on p.136). An excellent **bakery**, with daily supplies of fresh rye and wholemeal bread, is Oscarsson's in 20th Century Plaza, Mama Ngina Street (there's another branch at Rank Xerox House in Westlands). For **health foods**, try Healthier Options, Soin Arcade, Westlands.

Crafts

For the exhausting business of buying **crafts and curios**, it's advisable to decide what you want before stepping into a shop or looking at a stall. At some of the more pretentious places you can browse for ages undisturbed, but at the cheaper outlets dilly-dallying is not encouraged and the pressure may be on to part with your money. To browse and to establish comparative values, pay a visit to the excellent Zanzibar Curio Shop on Moi Avenue, which has a huge range of stuff at fixed and very reasonable prices. Unless you're after certain antique sculptures, masks and xylophones, you'd be hard-pressed to match its prices by bargaining anywhere else.

Curio shops and hawkers

There are dozens of **curio shops** in Nairobi and you might get a good deal at almost any of them. Never accept their first price, and bargain hard. The upmarket places are clustered on Standard, Kaunda and Mama Ngina streets.

If you are in no hurry and are after something unique, but not necessarily Kenyan, the warehouse-like Zebra Crafts Centre at the bottom of Koinange Street, near Kenyatta Avenue, is worth a visit, with a great selection of carvings, masks and jewellery from across the continent at very reasonable prices, as is Batik Heritage on Muindi Mbingu Street. African Heritage, in Libra House on the Mombasa road, on the way to JKI Airport, has some beautiful items including great musical instruments such as thumb pianos and lyres. Its newest branch is at *Carnivore* (see p.141).

You'll find lots more curio shops in the streets around the **City Market**, mostly overpriced and unresponsive to substantial bargaining. Usually cheaper are places where they don't have to pay a shop rent – **street stands** and **market booths** – though these are an almost extinct species, constantly being harassed and demolished by the city council. The more permanent booths in the enclosure at the back of the City Market off Koinange Street are an obvious choice, especially for soapstone, batiks and basketwork, but the whole area is something of a tourist trap and, while you'll probably find what you're looking for, you're unlikely to knock it down to a good price.

For **traditional fabrics and clothes** such as *kikois* and *kangas*, there are around a dozen shops to browse through along Biashara Street. Of these, Haria's Stamp Shop has an excellent and very reasonably priced range (KSh200–600 per metre). The **traditional masks** you'll see everywhere are imported from elsewhere. Only a handful of Kenyan tribes make masks, the Kikuyu being the best known, and these are exceedingly rare. Mount Kenya Sundries, Vedic House, Mama Ngina Street, has is one of the best selections from West and Central Africa, albeit mostly reproductions, and is knowledgeable about their varied significance and use in ritual. For more masks, batiks and outstanding **beads**, a wonderful if expensive place is Kenafro Antiques & Crafts, Olympic House, at the corner of Tubman and Koinange streets, but you'll need to have honed your haggling skills to ruthless perfection.

Community craft centres

Nairobi has a number of craft shops with charitable status, or associated with development or self-help projects. Although sometimes a little expensive – and bargaining isn't possible – they often have unusual and well-made stock (some of which finds its way into the Christmas charity catalogues overseas). A few are a little way out of town, but well worth making special journeys to visit – good tonics if you're suffering from curio shop fatigue.

Bega Kwa Bega Korogocho Projects; PO Box 64533, ☎020/2791734, ⊛www.begakwabega .com. Federation of small handicrafts producers from the Korogocho slum area of eastern Nairobi, offering sisal bags, necklaces, batiks, furniture and cloth puppets. Take a taxi.

Kamili Designs Langata Rd, Karen ☎020/883640. This textile workshop sells locally designed, hand-printed fabrics. The designs are typically bold and colourful, available both by the metre and as cushions, bedspreads and the like. Buses/matatus #24, #111 or #126. Mon–Fri 9am–4.30pm.

Kazuri Beads & Pottery Centre Mbagathi Ridge, Karen ☎020/883500, ⊛www.kazuri .com. Kazuri, which means "small and beautiful", employs nearly a hundred formerly destitute women, who make an extraordinary variety of handmade jewellery and beads, principally ceramic. You can watch the whole process from shaping and

colouring to firing, and there's also a pottery show-room. It's expensive, but the stuff is lovely. They also have retail outlets at Village Market, Limuru Rd, Westlands, and the Junction Shopping Centre, Ngong Rd. Buses/matatus #24, #111 or #126. Workshops Mon–Fri 9am–4.30pm, Sat 8am–noon; shop Mon–Sat 8am–4.30pm, Sun 11am–4.30pm.

Maridadi Fabrics City Stadium roundabout, Landhies/Jogoo Rd, 2km east of the train station ☎020/554250. Church-based Maridadi was created in 1966 as an income-generating community project for women in one of Nairobi's oldest slum areas – Pumwani and Shauri Moyo. The main workshop is a delight if you're into making your own clothes. A large screen-printing workshop (on view from the visitors' gallery) produces the wide range of prints for sale in the shop. Especially appealing are the bark cloth prints – a natural weave used for clothing by many East African peoples until the end of the nineteenth century. Buses #21, #34 or #36. Mon–Fri 8am–5pm.

Mikono Craft Shop Opposite Ratna Fitness Studio, Gitanga Rd, Kawangware, just north of Dagoretti Corner ☏ 02/577498. The outlet of the Jesuit Refugee Service, with well-made work (especially beautiful patchwork textiles) from refugees, and superb Mozambican carvings. Bus #46 or #46B.

Spinner's Web Second floor, Viking House, Waiyaki Way, Westlands ☏ 020/4440882. A large shop selling a lot of good stuff – crafts, textiles, woollen goods and jewellery, much of it made by self-help groups and individuals, including Meru's Makena Textile Workshop. Any Westlands bus/matatu.

Terra Pottery Centre Opposite the War Cemetery, Ngong Rd ☏ 02/567636. A pottery shop with a difference: they encourage you to try your hand at casting and turning. Any Ngong Rd bus.

Undugu Woodvale Grove, opposite Westlands produce market ☏ 020/4443525, ⊛ www.undugukenya.org. With its roots in the church, Undugu ("fraternity") is the most vigorous society of its kind in the country and organizes regular guided visits to their slum projects. The shop sells a good selection of well-priced, high-quality crafts with some more unusual items, such as Ethiopian jewellery, basketwork, and crafts from Congo, Somalia, Tanzania and Uganda. You may be able to have a look around the workshops. Any Westlands bus/matatu. Mon–Fri 8.30am–5pm.

Utamaduni Crafts Centre Bogoni East Rd, between the Ostrich Park and Giraffe Sanctuary, Langata ☏ 020/891798, ⊛ www.utamadunicrafts .com. Eighteen individual craft shops in one large house, opened by Richard Leakey in 1991 (a portion of the profits go to the Kenya Wildlife Service). It has everything you might want, much of it made on site or from street-kid projects; quality and prices are high. The attached *Verandah* restaurant is excellent. Bus/matatu #24. Daily 9am–6pm.

Woodley Weavers Joseph Kag'ethe Rd, Karen (behind Adam's Arcade) ☏ 020/577620, ⊛ www .woodleyweavers.com. Often referred to as the "rug gallery", this place has a variety of rugs made by local women, often single mothers from the Kibera slum, using local wool, cotton and plant dyes. Any bus or matatu to Ngong Rd.

The Maasai markets

If you're after Maasai traditional and tourist gear, the **Maasai Market** (Tues 9am–3pm) is recommended. Here Maasai and other women from upcountry areas display their wares on waste ground beside the Globe Cinema (Murang'a) roundabout. You'll find prices here well below those in any tourist mart, with especially good deals on the simpler designs of beaded jewellery, and also on baskets and gourds. You can bargain down to as little as ten percent of the sort of prices marked in fancy curio stores, if you've the time and energy. However, the market now also attracts more aggressive male vendors, which can make for an unpleasant shock early on in a trip.

The market also convenes on Saturday, in the car park by the *Hilton Hotel*, and there's a much smaller, "civilized" Maasai crafts market held every Friday at the village market, Limuru Road, and every Sunday outside the Yaya Centre, Hurlingham.

Kariokor Market

Between Racecourse Road and Ring Road, **Kariokor Market** (named after the despised wartime "Carrier Corps"; bus/matatu #4, #6, #7, #14, #30, #32, #40, #42, or #46/46B) is closer to an oriental bazaar than most markets in Kenya, with permanent booths for the traders. Note that you may sometimes be mobbed by kids and touts here. Inside, there's as much manufacture and finishing going on as selling – you'll find sisal weavers, leather workers, makers of tyre-rubber sandals ("5000-mile shoes", about Ksh100 a pair and surprisingly comfortable), carpenters, toy-makers, tailors, hairdressers, and a row of good, very cheap, amazingly clean eating places, popular at lunchtime with local workers.

Kariokor is without question *the* place in Nairobi to buy **baskets** (*vyondo*), made with sisal, coloured with natural or artificial dyes; with garish plastic; or with cord manufactured from the bark of the baobab tree. The cord baskets can be truly exquisite, with tiny beads included in the tight weave. A number of booths sell vaguely pharmaceutical oddities – snuff, remedies, charms, amulets and so on – where you can pick up anything from feathers to snakeskin. Outside you'll find the odd African literary gem on the secondhand bookstalls.

Embakasi Village Crafts Market

This market, located on the Mombasa road on the way to the airport (second turning on the left just after *City Cabanas Restaurant*; bus #34B), is perhaps one of the most organized in Kenya; there's definitely less hassle here. Apart from the occasional collection of Central African carvings, Ethiopian and West African beads, you'll find most of what is sold here at much higher prices in the other markets in Nairobi. There is an area where you can watch the carvers in progress (commissioning the individual carvers is allowed). On Monday, Wednesday and Friday there's an open-air market with traders from the Maasai Market and craft centres from further afield turning up. If you want to see traditional dancers, call ☏020/247039 to find out when the next performance will be.

General merchandise, clothes, shoes and toys

The largest market in Nairobi is **Gikomba Market**, off Landhies Road, past the Country Bus Station (to get there by public transport, take any bus or matatu for Jogoo Road and get off at Gikomba). This is a spot that few tourists ever see, a labyrinth of muddy alleyways, courtyards, and open sewers. It's also a place to experience an exhilarating slice of Nairobi life, and just about anything can be found on sale, from school uniforms and electronic equipment to industrial-size ovens. There are also tailors, shoe repair shops, hairdressers and numerous little bars and food stalls. Come with someone who knows the place though; it's very easy to get lost and Gikomba can be unsafe.

For everyday **general merchandise stores**, the eastern part of the City Market district is the most worthwhile area. **Biashara Street** (*biashara* means commerce) is the street for fabrics and the best place to buy tents and mosquito nets (see "Listings" on p.153). For cheap and not-so-cheap imports, the hangar-like Freemark Pavilion in south **Uhuru Park** has hundreds of stalls.

You'll find **clothes** shops all over, with high-fashion outlets on Standard and Kaunda streets, and more down-to-earth gear on Kenyatta Avenue, Moi Avenue and Kimathi Street. Abdulla Fazal in the Jubilee Exchange House on Mama Ngina Street has a good selection of locally made clothes. Good-value **footwear** is available from the African Boot Co, on Moi Avenue opposite Bookpoint, and Bata, which has numerous branches around the city including Moi Avenue, next to Sonalux House, the corner of Banda St and Koinange St and the Yaya Centre. Even cheaper footwear can be found at Miniprice Footwear Supermarket on River Road.

If you're buying **toys**, the best items are locally made wire-and-fabric contraptions – cars, bicycles, flapping birds – which are sometimes beautiful works of art. Scouring the out-of-centre markets will find you some, but the better ones are usually made at home for sons and nephews and not for sale. The best general toy shop, full of standard imports, is Hobby Centre on Kaunda Street (☏020/222765 or 229081) in the Jubilee Insurance House.

Cassettes and CDs

Pirated cassettes – identifiable by the lack of labels on the cassettes themselves – may seem a good deal at under Ksh100 (originals cost Ksh200) but quality and durability are so bad they're practically worthless. For CDs and tapes, try Assanand's and Musikland on Moi Avenue, Melodica on Tom Mboya or, better still, any of a host of shops and stalls on and around River Road and Accra Road.

Shopping malls

Nairobi now has the dubious distinction of having more **shopping malls** – over twenty – than any other African city barring those in South Africa, providing a hassle-free environment for getting on with ordinary shopping and office business. You'll find most of them stuffed into more affluent suburbs like Westlands and Parklands. They cater to the expatriate and middle-class Kenyan markets, and many include banks, travel agents, specialist food suppliers and an assortment of cafés and restaurants.

The Mall Westlands. Shops and offices including a branch of Let's Go Travel, a sports shop, a French bakery, ice-cream parlour, a 7-11-style convenience store and numerous fashion and clothing stores. Buses #21, #25, #29, #30 and many others.
Prestige Plaza Ngong Rd. Features a large supermarket, coffee shop and brand new cinema showing the latest Hollywood blockbusters.
Sarit Centre Westlands. A big, established complex, with over sixty shops and offices, including a dry-cleaner, a health-food shop, a watch repairer, a post office, a multiplex cinema, an Uchumi Hypermarket, the Areana Health Club and a large branch of the Textbook Centre. Buses as for The Mall.

Village Market Limuru Rd Ⓦ www.village market-kenya.com. Upmarket shopping centre that looks more like something out of California than Nairobi, complete with miniature waterfall. It has over 125 shops, a cinema, a Nakumatt hypermarket, a bowling alley and an excellent food court with great German, Thai and African outlets. Bus/matatu #106 and #108 come here.
Yaya Centre Argwings Kodhek Rd, Hurlingham. There's a good deli here, a useful newsagent with a wide selection of mainly British magazines, a bookshop, supermarket, health-food shop, French bakery, post office, chemist, and a useful "for sale" noticeboard. Bus/matatu #41, #46/46B or #56.

Eating

Nairobi has no shortage of **eating places**. Their diversity is one of the city's best points, and eating out is an evening pastime which never dulls. Admittedly, African food is generally not highlighted in the more expensive restaurants, which offer a range of Asian and European food, and spectacular quantities of meat. You can save money *and* eat African and Asian food in hundreds of unpretentious places, and if you want a burger, pizza, a huge steak or totally vegetarian salad, it's all available. With some exceptions, the following listings are restricted to the city centre. Elsewhere, **Westlands** in particular is a culinary growth area (reachable on bus or matatu #21, #23, #30, #104 or #119), with every street and shopping mall containing a handful (we've mentioned a few of the best) and *Vasili & Sons*, on Mpaka Road, an extremely good **bakery**.

You can get an excellent **breakfast** at the *Java House* or *Dormans* (see p.138). For something heartier, most of the *hotelis* around River Road serve up stacks of well-prepared eggs, sausages, beans and toast. The big hotels do lavish breakfast

> ### Drinking water
>
> Nairobi's tap water is unfit to drink. Most people boil their water, even those on very low incomes, and the more affluent drink only bottled water. If in any doubt, or if eating in hotels where bottled water is not offered, stick to sodas.

△ The *Thorn Tree Café*

buffets, of which the *Hilton Hotel*'s is highly rated. Alternatively, both the *Meridian Court*'s and the *Ambassadeur*'s are also good, and cheaper (around Ksh500). For something simpler, all the cafés and snack bars listed below cater for early-birds, as do *Pasara* and *Berber's Oasis*.

To avoid cluttering up the "Commercial Centre and River Road Area" map on pp.114–115, we've omitted marking those restaurants located in commercial buildings which are already on the map. Restaurants located out of the centre on other maps are noted accordingly, together with directions on how to get there by bus or matatu.

Hotelis and other cheap eating places

The **River Road area** has one *hoteli* after another on most streets, generally dishing up standard fare of chips or *ugali* with fish or fried chicken. Most of the places reviewed below are in this area (see the Commercial Centre and River Road map, p.114; for Westlands places, see the map on p.120).

Kariokor Market has an enclosure containing dozens of *chai*, *ugali* and *nyama choma* joints vying for business. The meat and fish is very fresh and sizzling outside on charcoal grills, as reggae music blares. Prime rump steak, brains or sweetmeats, it's all there, and if you're thirsty, several dodgy bars oblige. Other very cheap places to eat include the shacks near the country bus station, where you can fill up on tea and *mandaazi* for next to nothing, and the stretch of Haile Selassie Avenue by the Agip Garage, where women cook up *githeri,* which you eat squatting down on the pavement. Otherwise, street food in Nairobi is limited to roasted corncobs (which are so tough and take so long to eat you'll feel you've had a whole meal), sausages, *mandaazi* and fruit.

Al Mansura B&L Munyu Rd. Good for *mandaazi* and *chai* breakfasts. Open from 6am.

Ali Baba Murang'a Rd, opposite *Meridian Court Hotel.* Superficially Lebanese (some kebabs, falafel and kibbe), but popular mainly for its filling lunch-time mini-buffets (Ksh280) and simple but tasty standard Kenyan fare at other times (*ugali*, stews and goat *nyama choma*).

Ali's Fish and Chips Tsavo Rd. Cheap, greasy and satisfying.

Benrose Gaberone Rd. Bustling, with reasonable *chai* and samosas.

Caprice Fry's Moi Ave. Busy fast-food joint doing fried chicken and fish and chips; popular with the local office crowd.

C&J Cafe Gaberone Rd. Cheerful and well-run café/diner serving good fish curries and meat stews served with a choice of rice, *ugali* or chapatti.

Fameland Duruma Rd. Good solid meals (notably *nyama choma* with *ugali*) with excellent music, sometimes live, in this unusually good "day and night club".

Happy Valley Butchery Latema Rd. Cheap *nyama choma* and fried meat. Order in the butchery downstairs, then sit upstairs and wait for your meat to arrive.

Ismailia's River Rd. Very inexpensive, welcoming and comfortable, with a good vegetarian selection.

🏃 **Kebab King** Waiyaki Way, Westlands. Permanent kebab stand serving fantastic shawarmas and shish kebabs. A great place to fill up after a few too many at the nearby *Gipsy* bar.

Kenchic Inn Corner of Moktar Daddah and Muindi Mbingu streets. No-frills halal fish and chicken bar, busier than most and therefore fresher.

Malindi Dishes Gaberone Rd. Self-service cafeteria with good cheap Swahili dishes.

Pre Area Eating House Duruma Rd. Snacks, stews and booze – great for breakfast after a long night out.

Sunrise Lodge Latema Rd, across from the *Iqbal Hotel*. Standard *hoteli* fare in a reasonably bright, workaday atmosphere. Take a table at the front and watch street life on Latema Rd.

Swara Imenti House, Tom Mboya St. Cheap and reliable for proper meals (steaks, fish, stews; meals around Ksh200), with good service in a slightly tattered dining room full of velvet-upholstered chairs and dusty textile lampshades. Popular with office workers. Daily 7.30am–10pm.

🏃 **Wheels Restaurant** Second floor, The Mall, Westlands. Primarily an inexpensive *nyama choma* joint (but you can order other local dishes too) with a pleasant veranda overlooking the area, and attracting local business types at lunchtimes during the week.

Cafés, fast-food joints and ice-cream parlours

You'll find most cafés and snack bars as well as a rash of Western-style fast-food joints (at Stateside prices) situated in the upmarket business district **north of City Hall Square**. Most are closed on Sundays after lunch.

Commercial Centre and River Road Area

Bakers Pie The best and cleanest branch is on Kenyatta Ave, near the BP petrol station between Koinange and Loita streets. They make excellent spicy meat pies.

City Chef Moktar Daddah St. Fresh passion-fruit juice and quality baked goods, especially the doughnuts.

Creamy Inn Union Towers, Moi Ave/Mama Ngina St. Serves great ice creams in a variety of tempting forms, including a spectacular honey crunch waffle sundae.

Dormans the Coffee Experts Jubilee Exchange Building, Mama Ngina St ☎0724/238976. Among the best of Nairobi's many coffee shops, *Dormans* is full of glamorous young Nairobi residents and business people. Serving an excellent range of flavoured coffees and home-made cakes, it also has branches in the Sarit Centre, Village Market and Dagoretti Corner.

Express Bakery Standard St, next to Let's Go Travel. Always crowded at lunchtime, but otherwise a good place to sit and recoup your energy.

Fridays Restaurant Unafric House, corner of Koinange and Moktar Daddah streets. A lively place, popular with the lunch and post-work crowd, serving cheap burgers, cocktails and grills.

Gawa Foods Utalii House, Utalii St. Pies, burgers, cheap breakfasts and cakes.

Hooters Hamilton House, Kaunda St. American-style sports bar and fast-food joint (milkshakes, burgers, pizzas), with music videos on the monitors. Prices are bearable, and the service is good.

La Scala Pizzeria Phoenix House Arcade, Standard St/Kenyatta Ave. Inexpensive place serving mix of Italian and Kenyan food. Pizzas and pastas are inexpensive (under Ksh300), and decent enough, if inauthentic. Good service, and the lunchtime specials are a bargain. Daily until midnight.

🏃 **Nairobi Java House** Transnational Plaza, Mama Ngina St ☎020/313564. This hugely popular coffee shop has some of the best breakfasts in Nairobi, as well as a great variety of coffees and coffee-based drinks. Also has branches at ABC Place, Westlands, Nakumatt Junction and Jomo Kenyatta airport.

Kahawa Coffee House Fedha Towers, Kaunda St. An elegant, crowded and notably upmarket setting, filled with delicious smells. Great for breakfast – fried eggs, milkshakes, excellent samosas and iced tea.

Kengeles Koinange St. One of a chain of fast-food joints serving cheap burgers, steaks, toasted sandwiches and Kenyan dishes. There is a pleasant balcony overlooking Koinange St and permanent loud music blares. Branches include one at Yaya Centre, Hurlingham.

Mandy's Restaurant and Take Away Rehani House, Koinange St. Burgers, hot dogs, ice creams and decent pizzas.

Nando's Union Towers, corner of Mama Ngina St and Moi Ave. Three fast-food emporia in one, serving pizzas, Portuguese snacks and fried chicken, with a large and spotless dining room upstairs overlooking the busy junction. Same prices as European equivalents, but still busy. Free drinking water.

Pasara Second mezzanine floor, Lonrho House, Standard St. At the front is the coffee shop, decorated with old black and white movie posters; at the back are the restaurant and bar, with a vaulted ceiling. Excellent cooked breakfasts and cakes.

Steers Locations include Muindi Mbingu St (opposite Jeevanjee Gardens); at the junction of Tom Mboya and Ronald Ngala streets. The Islamic South African fast-food chain's venture into Kenya offers the usual junk food, plus toasted sandwiches, salads, milk shakes, juices and great toffee ice cream. Also at the Apic Centre in Westlands and Village Market, Limuru Rd.

Thorn Tree Café *Stanley Hotel*, Kimathi St. Hard to avoid as it's in the thick of the worst zone for tourist hustling, so a welcome refuge, and a handy meeting place. Snacks are average and way overpriced. There's a cheesy band in the evenings. Closes around 11pm.

Greater Nairobi

Grapes Bar and Restaurant Corner of Mpaka and Muthithi roads, Westlands. Okay African food and a good selection of beers.

Hidden Agenda Second Floor, Sarit Centre, Westlands. Upmarket café and bar, with smart leather decor and outdoor tables, popular with Westlands teenagers. Serves yummy pancakes at breakfast.

Urban Oasis Café & Wine Bar Upper Hill Medical Centre, Ralph Bunche Rd ☎ 020/2721622. Good place for lunch, serving pasta, Thai, and burgers. Handy if you're staying at the *YHA* opposite.

Restaurants

The following listings are mostly for more **upmarket** eating houses, where it's often a good idea to reserve a table. Many are closed one day a week, often Tuesday or Sunday, and most are closed between 3pm and 6pm. The city has famously good beef and other fleshy delights so, if you enjoy it, indulge while you're here, as the rest of the country is much less well endowed.

Prices, without drinks, should normally work out at around Ksh600 a head, though you can certainly eat more cheaply at several of the curry houses. In the more international league, specializing mainly in meat, prices are a little higher, and you can pay up to Ksh3000 at fancy establishments.

River Road area

Al Hawal Twiga Towers, Murang'a Rd ☎ 020/253702. Very clean and quiet, serving African as well as Lebanese food.

Cheers Bhajia Hotel Under the *New Kenya Lodge*. Popular, inexpensive south Indian vegetarian.

Sun Sweet Centre Ngariama Rd. Vegetarian Indian place, large sparse and slightly lacking in atmosphere, but excellent veg food, with tempting sweets and open till late.

West of Moi Avenue

Alan Bobbe's Bistro Cianda House, Koinange St ☎ 020/224945. One of the oldest restaurants in the city (since 1962); still devoutly French and devotedly patronized. The manicured poodle logo is a welcome touch of humorous absurdity, though your first impression of high camp pretentiousness is soon belied by their genuine interest in seriously good food. Around Ksh3500 for dinner with wine is normal. Closed Sat lunchtime and all day Sun. *Stop Press*: moved to 24 Riverside Drive, Westlands.

Le Belvedere Thirteenth Floor, *Grand Regency Hotel*, Loita Street/Uhuru Highway ☎ 020/211199. High-class French cuisine served in glamorous surroundings. Daily noon–3pm & 7–10pm.

Berber's Oasis Mezzanine Floor, NHC Building, Aga Khan Walk. Good, filling African food – kisamvu na karanga (cassava leaves with peanuts), githeri – served in a quirky dining room with rather overbearing palm tree wallpaper. The attached terrace bar is decent apart from the dreadful country music.

Dragon Pearl Standard St, opposite the *680 Hotel* ☏020/338863. Average Chinese food, but relatively cheap, with sizeable portions.

Fiesta Third floor, Chester House, Koinange St. Despite the name and the hacienda-gone-wrong interior, this is not a Mexican restaurant; it serves pasta, fish and grilled meat.

Five Star Chinese Restaurant First floor, Loita House, Loita St ☏020/244286. Friendly, serving very tasty food and cheaper than most other Chinese restaurants in the vicinity.

Garden Square Restaurant Garden Square, City Hall Way ☏020/226474. Relaxed, spacious place, occasionally with live Kenyan bands. Cheap African buffets at lunchtime, occasionally in the evenings too. Safe parking.

Hong Kong Ground floor, Kenya House, Koinange St ☏020/228612. Excellent Cantonese place – try the excellent "steam boat", a communal fondue – you cook meat and seafood slices in bubbling stock at the table. Closed Mon.

Khyber *Meridian Court Hotel*. Excellent and very reasonably priced Mughlai cuisine, with a good lunchtime set menu (around Ksh700).

Kowloon Restaurant Nginyo Towers, Koinange St ☏020/318885. Large, well-stocked bar and an extensive menu, with lots of vegetarian dishes. Has excellent-value Ksh250 lunch specials.

Panda First floor, Fedha Towers, Kaunda St ☏020/213018. One of the best Chinese restaurants in the city, with an elegant dining room, wood lattice screens, flowers and Chinese pottery. Staff are extremely efficient and friendly.

Red Bull First floor, Transnational Plaza, Mama Ngina St ☏020/223332. Old fashioned steak house with a Swiss chalet interior. They also do game and seafood – the *impala chasseur* is particularly good. Sat & Sun closed lunchtime.

Seasons Restaurant Uchumi House, Aga Khan Walk. A variety of Kenyan dishes, with an evening African buffet at a very reasonable Ksh300. Extremely popular with locals at the weekend. Breakfast is Ksh100, the same price as a beer.

Simmers Corner of Muindi Mbingu St and Standard St ☏020/217659. Large and laid-back, central Nairobi's only *nyama choma*-style joint (and thus very popular), with an "African lunchtime buffet" for Ksh500. There are live bands nearly every night of the week. Daily 7am–midnight.

Stavrose Mezzanine floor, Postbank House, Market St ☏020/2728157. A posh fish restaurant, famed for its tilapia, cooked any way you want it. They also do good salads. Expensive.

Swahili Corner Nginyo Towers, Koinange St ☏020/316854. Superb Kenyan restaurant serving Swahili food, including such delights as coconut chicken curry, kingfish marinated in coriander and chilli, and freshly squeezed juices. Ksh250–300 per head for a main course including salad, rice and assorted condiments. Recommended.

Tamarind National Bank Building, Harambee Ave ☏020/251811, ⓦwww.tamarind.co.ke. Nairobi's largest, best and most expensive seafood restaurant. Highly rated. Reservations essential. Open Mon–Sat for lunch & dinner, Sun dinner only.

Trattoria Corner of Wabera and Kaunda streets ☏020/340855. This still gets enthusiastic notices from budget travellers having a splurge. The pasta dishes and pizzas are the real thing and the cakes and ice cream magnificent.

Zanze Bar Fifth floor, Kenya Cinema Plaza, Moi Ave ☏020/222568. Quiet lunchtime getaway with an economical salad buffet, KTN television and soft rock in the background. Famous for its "twelve-inch hot dogs". Lively bar in the evening and sometimes live bands. Wed, Fri, Sat are disco nights. Open daily.

Greater Nairobi

Westlands and Parklands

Addis Ababa Ethiopian Restaurant Woodvale Place, Woodvale Grove ☏020/447321. Upmarket Ethiopian, with beautiful decor, attentive service, fantastic food, and regular live music and dancing (patrons are encouraged to participate).

Anghiti New Rehema House, Rhapta Rd ☏020/4441258. The decor is a bit stark, but this is, along with the *Haandi*, Westland's leading Indian gastronomic experience. The speciality, *raan anghiti*, is whole mutton leg marinated overnight in garlic, ginger, vinegar and chillies before being baked. No beef or pork.

The Atrium Chiromo Rd, Westlands ☏0724/600031. In a white Cape Dutch-style house off Chiromo Rd, this airy restaurant has wood floors, wicker furniture and a patio garden. They serve excellent French and Italian fare (the ravioli is particularly good), beautifully presented. Buffet lunch (Ksh1000) on weekdays.

China Jiangsu Soin Arcade, Westlands Rd ☏020/4446700. Authentic dishes including jellyfish, green onion pancakes as well as the old sweet-and-sour favourites. Reasonably priced.

Furusato Karuna Rd ⊕020/4442508. Japanese food, rather expensive, though the restaurant has the benefit of a fantastically elegant dining room and large garden terrace.

Haandi The Mall, Westlands ⊕02/4448294/5. Generally considered Nairobi's best (north) Indian restaurant, if a little expensive (Ksh1000 per head), specializing in masalas. Skip breakfast to make room.

Nargis Kapuri Pan Next to Global Museum Yoga Centre, Parklands Rd. Small inexpensive meals of the likes of chicken tikka and kebabs. Pleasant tables outside, and some colourful child-sized tables and chairs. Safe parking. Daily 1–3pm & 6–10pm.

Peppers Parklands Rd, opposite *Holiday Inn* ⊕020/3755267, ©peppersrestaurant@kenyaweb.com. Great steaks, grilled chicken and fish as well as a nice line in cocktails served with style by the very knowledgeable barman. There's a huge garden as well as an indoor and outdoor kids' play area. Popular with families.

Siam Thai First floor, Unga House, Muthithi Rd ⊕02/3751727. Run by an Indian family in love with Thai food, and it shows – it's probably the best Thai restaurant in town, despite the uninspired decor. The use of herbs and spices is subtle and sometimes unusual. Try the tangy *tom yam goong* soup, spare ribs, or *larb gai* – spiced minced chicken with onions, mint leaves and lemon grass. Food around Ksh850, with cheaper lunchtime set menus, often under Ksh600. Licensed and open daily.

🏃 **Tamambo Bar and Grill** Second floor, The Mall, Westlands ⊕020/4448064, ⊛www.tamarind.co.ke. Modern African brasserie serving delicious African and European food (try the crab cigars or the Kachos – Kenyan nachos made with cassava). The dining room is appealingly understated, decked out with plants and African artefacts. There's an attached bar serving excellent frozen *dawas*, live jazz every Fri eve and Sun lunch, and a disco Sat night.

Tokyo Rhapta Rd, Westlands ⊕020/4444651; and at the Village Market, Limuru Rd. Tasty Japanese cuisine, especially the sushi. Sun lunch features an excellent Japanese/Korean barbecue.

Elsewhere in Greater Nairobi

Azalea Bar and Restaurant Komo Lane ⊕0722/411843. Brand new restaurant in the Lavington suburbs (best reached by taxi) serving Continental food. There's a nice terrace and Italian country-style decor. The mains are decent but nothing special, though the desserts are excellent – try the Kenya green tea parfait.

🏃 **Blue Nile Ethiopian Restaurant** Argwings Kodhek Rd, Hurlingham ⊕020/2728709. Very pleasant, laid-back place, with a "mix dish" where you can try a bit of everything for Ksh375. Wash it down with *tej*, a mead-like Ethiopian honey beer. Steer clear if you don't like chilli. Buses #41, #46/46B or #56.

Cedars Lenana Rd ⊕020/2710399. Excellent Lebanese food, if a little pricey. The dining room is charming, with understated Middle Eastern decor and a roaring fire for the cold July evenings.

Makuti Park South "B" Shopping Centre, Mchumbi Rd, South "B" ⊕020/531835. Mellow and entirely free of touristy panderings, this famous music venue has recently started concentrating on Kenyan food – simple, cheap and very traditional, including dried meat (*aliya*), fire-dried meat (*athola*), liver, *kienyeji* and coastal Swahili dishes. There's also a children's "fun corner". Matatus from railway stage.

Misono Lenana Rd, next to South African High Commission, Hurlingham ⊕020/568959. Japanese venue, popular at lunchtime with those working nearby. Good set menus, lunchtime specials and bento boxes served in a large and lovely tree-filled garden. Recommended.

Moonflower Restaurant *Palacina Hotel*, Kitale Lane ⊕020/2715517. Stylish and expensive restaurant where grills, lobster and Asian are on the menu. The outdoor tented setting is neat, and there's live jazz at weekends.

Red Sea Lenana Rd ⊕020/2712531. Top quality, beautifully presented Ethiopian fare in a peaceful garden setting.

Toona Tree At the International Casino, Westlands Rd, off Museum Hill ⊕020/3740820. Very pleasant, open-air place, set among the boughs of the eponymous tree, and majoring on seafood. There's a playground for kids and live jazz or African music every evening and all day Sun. The food is average though. Buses #21, #23 or #119 come here.

Nairobi outskirts

🏃 **Carnivore** Langata Rd, towards the National Park entrance ⊕020/605933–7, ⊛www.tamarind.co.ke. Nairobi's most famous restaurant had ceased serving plains game meat at the time of writing, but a meal here is still part of every package itinerary, and very few people seem to dislike it. The all-you-can-eat menu (lunch Ksh1200, dinner Ksh1500) includes camel, ostrich and crocodile; less exotic meat is served first to lessen your appetite. There's a good vegetarian selection, too. On Sat afternoons kids can disappear to their Funland, with a fairground, donkey and camel rides, magic shows and face-painting.

Discos Wed–Sun in the adjoining *Simba Saloon*. See also "Live-music venues", p.145. Buses/matatus #15, #24, #31, #34, #125, #126 all pass the entrance road, from where it's a 1km walk – much easier by taxi.

Horseman Restaurant Karen Shopping Centre, Karen ☎020/882782. Comprises different dining rooms serving a variety of food (including Chinese and Indian) and a wide choice of game. The food is fresh and imaginative, and they have the best steaks in Nairobi, as well as real Italian ice cream. Daily 11.30am–11pm.

The Lord Erroll Gourmet Restaurant Ruaka Rd, Runda Estate, behind Village Market ☎020/7122433, ✪www.lord-erroll.com. A colonial-style house containing an old fashioned,

mahogany-panelled bar, the *Highlander*, and three dining rooms. The best of these is the Claremont: its food and service are excellent, and there's a fine selection of imported wines to go with the classic French menu (including snails and rock lobster, cooked with wine, mushrooms, mustard and cream, and served in the shell). The bill, presented on a silver platter, is bound to be hefty, in the order of Ksh2000–5000 per person, including wine.

Nyama Choma Ranch *Safari Park Hotel* ☎02/802561. At once classy and tacky, with perfectly grilled food served by an assortment of dancers, and wildlife videos to keep you entertained. Better value than *Carnivore*, but you'll need a taxi to get back at night.

Drinking, nightlife and entertainment

Drinking and dancing are what a night out in Nairobi is usually about. Entrance fees are low by international standards and prices for drinks are much the same as you'll pay in similar establishments elsewhere in the country. Be warned however that, male or female, if you're not accompanied by a partner of the opposite sex, you soon will be. As with restaurants, the bars and clubs within the area shown by the "Commercial Centre and River Road Area" map are omitted from the map if they lie within buildings that appear on the map

Nairobi has seen an encouraging proliferation of **artistic activities** in the last few years. Though the arts scene is still modest by international standards, it is infectiously energetic and well worth discovering. As with restaurants, the bars and clubs within the area shown by the "Commercial Centre and River Road Area" map are omitted from the map if they lie witin buildings that appear on the map.

Bars and local dives

Central Nairobi is still a bit of a dead loss at night if you just want a **drink**, as most people tend to head off towards **Westlands** for its sleeker, more upmarket bars, or else pack into a number of sweaty discos. The great exception for city-centre revelling is the **River Road area** where, suitably stripped down (to the clothes on your back and a little cash), you can venture out to the land of "**day and night clubs**". The district vibrates from dawn to dusk and back to dawn again with the sound of beery mayhem and jukeboxes. If you like the sound of it, you might consider taking a room nearby to avoid the hassle of getting back.

Bars

Commercial Centre and River Road area

Applebee's Pub/Restaurant Gaberonne Rd. A congenial spot for a drink. Cheap beers, friendly staff, slightly kitsch decor, and a lively soundtrack of mostly Lingala music, sometimes live.

Lord Delamere Terrace Bar *Norfolk Hotel*; see "Central Nairobi" map. Sooner or later a people-watching drink or a snack here is a must,

though at times it can feel a bit stuffy. It does, however, offer the full range of Tusker beers, and the snacks aren't as expensive as you might expect.

Tacos Eagle House, Kimathi St. An exuberant, energetic young crowd pack this bar, spilling out onto the balcony overlooking the street. There's an infectious mix of Kenyan and international hip-hop and pop, and as the night wears on, tables and chairs are pushed aside and the bar becomes an impromptu dancefloor.

Zanze Bar Fifth floor, Kenya Cinema Plaza, Moi Ave. A pleasant place to down beers or cocktails in the afternoons or evenings, before it gets disco-feverish.

Greater Nairobi

Annie Oakley's Milimani Rd, behind *Nairobi Backpackers*. Very friendly bar with a mixed crowd of locals, expats, backpackers and working girls. It has several pool tables, a big-screen TV for sporting events, and good, cheap food. Tues is country night, Wed rock, there's a pool comp on Sat.

Casablanca Lenana Rd, attached to the *Osteria Del Chianti* restaurant. Stylish Moroccan-themed bar with a wonderful oasis-style garden, complete with sand, baby palms, outdoor fireplaces and bright blue deck chairs. The cocktails are expensive, but delicious and very potent.

Westlands

BarCode Ground floor, Westview Centre ☎0723/743714. A trendy lounge specializing in shooters and cocktails.

Gipsy Bar (aka *Tropicanna*) Woodvale Grove ☎020/4440836. Near the *Jacaranda Hotel*, this is a popular upmarket choice, with a gay-friendly reputation. It serves tapas, remains open to the early hours and has daily deals on alcohol; Mon is fifty percent off rum.

Havana Woodvale Grove. Dark and smoky Latin restaurant and bar attracting a chic young crowd. Good Cuban snacks and cheap pitchers of cocktails.

Hutch Bar Grill and Carwash Chiromo Rd. Large, boisterous, loud and very local open-air bar, playing jazz and Kenyan pop. There's a good *nyama choma* bar, and cheap beer.

Mercury Lounge ABC Place, off Waiyaki Way ☎020/4450364. Nairobi's coolest designer watering hole has a curved wooden bar and dark green and purple leather furniture. In keeping with the retro feel, the DJ spins Seventies funk and soul.

Velvet Bar Chiromo Rd ☎0724/600031. Joined with the *Atrium* restaurant, this is small, cosy and cheaper than most of the bars in the vicinity. The dodgy rock music doesn't quite go with the slick interior, however. There's a DJ Fri and Sat nights, and the bar stools are cleared away for dancing.

Nairobi outskirts

Bedouin Lounge *Horseman Restaurant*, Karen Shopping Centre, Karen. New cocktail bar with a stunning interior – tented ceiling, lanterns, Persian rugs and cushion-strewn four-poster beds, all perfect for lounging. Shame about the dodgy Europop, which is completely at odds with the decor.

Local dives – city centre

On **Latema Road**, people contort themselves just to get into the *Modern Green Day and Night Club*. With the usual arguments and hustle going on in the doorway, it might appear a place to avoid, but squeeze inside, drink a beer or two, and soak up the elevated (and very relaxed) atmosphere. People make friends quickly here, though having a conversation over the racket of the throng and the din of the jukebox is exhausting. Entrance is free, cold beer is not the fashion – though you can get it, from the barman in his security cage – and the floor show is you and the rest of the customers. Just why the place is so popular is hard to say. For the girls, it's partly because of the steady trickle of potential customers from the lodgings nearby; for some of the men, it's a place to chew *miraa* all night for the price of a soda.

If you can't take the pace, try the *New Congoni Day and Night Club* on Luthuli Avenue (see "reggae discos", p.144), and the excellent *Fameland* on Duruma Road (great music and food). *Habari Day & Night Club*, on Luthuli Avenue, and *Lizie Bar* at the corner of Gaberone Lane and Munyu Road, are both raucous and cheap like the *Modern Green*, but minus the hustling young women. The tiny *Madhuka*, in the Casino Plaza, Moi Avenue, is friendly and plays nonstop reggae music, while *Friends Corner*, on the corner of Latema and Tsavo roads, is also a favourite spot for a drink, though the toilets are horrible. There's nothing to keep you from checking out dozens of other places – plenty of people do; for starters, try **Munyu Road**, off Accra Road and just south of River Road, which has more bars and clubs per hundred metres than any other place in Kenya.

Local dives: Dagoretti Corner and Ngong Road

Aside from the city-centre clubs and the fairly touristy places which draw their custom from a wide area, there are plenty of other nightspots catering for a more local clientele. Reputations change depending on the state of the neighbourhood and the security situation – asking around River Road's clubs will fill you in pretty quickly about what's in (and safe) and what's not. Currently one of the livelier of such communities, musically or otherwise, is **Dagoretti Corner**, at the junction of Ngong Road and Naivasha Road (see the "Nairobi outskirts" map). Although only a fifteen-minute bus ride from town (bus/matatu #1, #2, #3, #4, #102, #103 or #111), it has a completely different look and feel from the modern centre. Quite a number of bars in and around Dagoretti Corner feature **live music** (another reason to think of staying out there), if not necessarily on a regular schedule. Check out the four-storey *Matigari Bar* (hard to miss as it's painted top to toe with a Guinness ad) between Ngong and Naivasha roads, which sometimes features bands and is an interesting enough place the rest of the time.

The best disco at Dagoretti Corner is the so-called *Holiday Inn* on Ngong Road, past the junction with Naivasha Road, which is wildly packed at weekends. Elsewhere along Ngong Road, on the way to Dagoretti Corner, choices include the *Motherland Inn* and *Ngong Hills Hotel* (covered on p.146), both of which feature fairly regular live music, are less boisterous and attract an older crowd than many of the bars in the city centre or Westlands.

Discos and clubs

Reggae is the popular staple sound of the **cheap discos**, often not much more than "day and night clubs". Nairobi also has a scattering of **nightclubs** complete with flashy interiors and the latest dance hits from Europe and America, as well as more danceable tunes from Congo. If this appeals, try one of the established places below (or *Simba Saloon* at *Carnivore*, see p.146). The big nightclubs all put on floor shows for those who stay late enough – gyrating trios, limbo dancing and all – but except for the once-weekly "African Nites", don't come expecting any startling African musical revelations. In the glitzy places, men usually pay more than women, around Ksh100–300 as against Ksh50–100. Rootsier discos have free or very cheap entrance.

Commercial centre and River Road area

Reggae discos

Hollywood Moktar Daddah St. Mostly a drinking club, with dancing and regular fights – something the regulars do to keep from falling asleep – though the action finishes early. Wed–Sun, live reggae on Sun; Ksh50 entry fee.

Monte Carlo Club Accra Rd ☏020/223181. A cavernous place with a good atmosphere and music. "No weapons or *miraa*", say the signs – a necessary notice, judging from the few unsavoury types. Daily till dawn; reggae disco Wed from 8pm, Sat from 4pm, Sun from 2pm; Ksh100.

New Congoni Day & Night Club Luthuli Ave, off River Rd. Unpredictable live music, predictably smelly toilets. Reggae discos Sun afternoons.

Nightclubs

Club Sound Second floor, Hamilton House, Kaunda St. Upmarket place featuring live bands and poetry readings. On Sundays there are salsa lessons in the afternoon, followed by a salsa club night.

Dolce Club Cianda House, Koinange St ☏020/218275. Slick and smooth *soukous* and soul for a glitzy crowd; deafening sound system. Daily.

Florida 2000 First floor, Commerce House, Moi Ave, near the Kenya Cinema ☏020/229036. *New Florida's* sister, attracting similar clients and offering equally unambiguous entertainment, pumped up with what they call "most exotic floor shows" (nightly 1am). For the local ladies, this means grabbing drunken *wazungu* on the razzle. The Sun afternoon disco is *the* place to keep on swinging if sleep has somehow eluded you. It's a wildly popular venue. Daily.

New Florida Chai House, Koinange St ℡020/334870. Irresistible for its tackiness (with matching floorshows), this big red and white mushroom of a building above the Total filling station is always full of hookers and rather desperate-looking business types, but the atmosphere is merely steamy, not heavy. To go with the beer, there's a traditional English restaurant (ie Chinese). Reggae on Wed. Tacky floorshows at 1am.

Westlands and Parklands

Klub House 1 Ojijo Rd ℡020/541608. Nightclub with a sports bar, restaurant and a pool room upstairs. The beer garden is pleasant and popular during happy hour (5–8pm).
Pavement Westview Centre, Ring Rd ℡020/441711. In-place for the young and funky, but a sizeable crowd of the not-so-youthful and trendy hang on with a vengeance.

Nairobi outskirts

Black Cotton Langata Rd, Karen. Large and very popular open-air disco attracting clubbers from far and wide. First Fri of the month.
Club Sikiliza Village Market, Limuru Rd ℡020/7120903. Live Kenyan pop music and jazz Thurs & Sun. Also features theme nights (rock, hip-hop) and has monthly Yellow and Red parties, when the club and the clientele are decked out in said colour.
Sahara City Mombasa Highway ℡02/822933. Arguably Nairobi's top disco with the best sound system – an excellent place for dance freaks, and popular with young, affluent Asians. Matatu #110.
Swamp Village Park Inn Kikuyu Rd, Siruta ℡020/571361. A thorough convert to the Congolese *ndombolo* invasion, which is featured Sat & Sun, together with tempting extras like beer-drinking competitions, dance contests and hair beauty shows. Occasional live acts. Matatus #2 or #102.

Live-music venues

Although there are a few downtown music places, much of Nairobi's live music action takes place on the perimeter of the city. Given the volatile nature of the music business in Kenya, venues and bands change at a moment's notice; the following listings include all the places that have been around for some time, plus a few new ones. In addition, you might check out Friday's and Saturday's *Daily Nation* for one-off gigs. **Starting times** vary considerably for all the clubs. On weekdays, 7.30 or 8pm wouldn't be too early, while weekend warm-ups usually begin around 9–10pm, and some may not get really rolling until midnight. Don't judge any band by their first hour: many run through some pretty dreadful warm-up material.

Many clubs have Sunday afternoon **"jam sessions"** that can be just as lively as the evening shows, and often include acrobats, jugglers, magicians or comedians as well – excellent for families and convenient if you don't want to be

Nairobi bands

Some of the big names to watch out for include Super Mazembe (see p.652), Kayamba Africa (six-piece vocal harmony, at the *Panafric* hotel most Sundays) and Achieng Abura (Afro-Jazz sung in French, Kiswahili and Luo). There are also a number of popular younger musicians who blend traditional sounds with Western music and can be found playing some of Nairobi's larger venues. Look out for Harry Kimani (Kenyan R&B and hip-hop), Eric Wainaina (blends *benga* rhythm and East African guitar styles with Western harmony), Mercy Myra (R&B, ragga, Congolese dance) and Nazizi (a pioneering female MC with amazing lyrical delivery).

Also look out for number-one female *benga* singers Queen Jane and Princess Jully. Special shows may take place at *Safari Park Hotel* and *Carnivore*. The *Panafric Hotel* offers regular cultural theme nights showcasing a variety of Kenyan music including Luo, Maasai and Kalenjin. Possibly less interesting sounds come from the voices and instruments of a clutch of touristy and international-style pop and rock bands – the Pressmen and Big Matata Band, to name two.

taxiing around the city late at night. Every September the Alliance Française puts on an event called "Spotlight on Kenyan Music", a good opportunity to see the newest talents on the scene.

Central Nairobi

The following are on the "Commercial Centre and River Road Area" map unless otherwise stated.

Arturo's Tumaini House, Moi Ave. The first-floor veranda has live music (could be anything – Congolese, Kikuyu, Luo) on Wed, Fri & Sat nights. Very danceable, very local, and entrance is free.

Fameland Club Duruma Rd ☏020/2248000. Live bands and good DJs weekends in this elegant and cosy joint. Thurs is African disco night, with plenty of hip-gyrating rhythms to grind to. Don't walk around here unaccompanied.

Green Corner Restaurant Tumaini House, Nkrumah Rd. The *Cactus Bar* here is handy to fill a

dull night but nothing special in itself. There's the obligatory Wed ladies' night, a busy "Friday Jam" (DJs), and live music from the Hot Rod Band, an Afro-jazz/rap outfit, on Thurs & Sat.

Mang' Hotel Haile Selassie Ave; see "Central Nairobi" map. An exuberant local venue where Congolese *soukous* and Lingala still reign. There's a disco most nights and live *soukous* after midnight.

Simmers Kenyatta Ave ☏020/217659. Locals and tourists gather here to listen to live Kenyan and Congolese music nightly.

Suburban and out of town

Almost all of the following double as *nyama choma* joints.

Greater Nairobi

The Green House Nyangumi Rd, Hurlingham ☏0735/543095. This outdoor bar and restaurant, serving Kenyan food, has an excellent reputation for live music, with a variety of well-known Kenyan bands playing on Fri & Sat night.

Hillock Inn Enterprise Rd ☏020/544819 or 545668. In the unlovely Industrial Area, this is a long-established venue, with several bars, tacky fountains and the Intelligent Band resident Wed, Fri & Sat (6pm to past midnight), and Sun afternoons. They have inexpensive s/c rooms available if you feel less than clever for the taxi ride back (Ksh800). Get there on a matatu for "Industrial area/Hillock" from outside the Afya Centre, junction of Tom Mboya St and Hakati Rd.

Motherland Inn Ngong Rd, opposite Menelik Rd. Lively bar serving good Ethiopian food. Slightly more subdued than central venues, it has live music – Frantal Tabu play here regularly. Buses/matatus #1, #2, #3, #4, #102, #103 and #111.

Ngong Hills Hotel Ngong Rd ☏02/567137. One of the best venues, not at all intimidating and with uniformly excellent acts, including Super Mazembe resident on Fri & Sat nights (8pm–3am). Sun afternoons host a very laid-back jam session, complete with dancers, acrobats, tight-rope walkers and *nyama choma* by the green pool to drown your hangover in. Ideal for kids. Staying the night here is in principle convenient, but the rooms are in pretty poor shape for a mid-priced place. Ample parking. Bus/matatu #1, #2, #3, #4, #102, #103 or #111.

Peacock Inn Dai Dai Rd, Nairobi South "B" Shopping Centre ☏020/552639. Occasional visits by Tanzanian bands on Fri nights.

Toona Tree International Casino, Westlands Rd. The Nairobi Jazz Trio plays here Mon, Tues & Thurs night; the Weavers, a four-piece specializing in Lingala and *benga* tunes, on Wed & Sat, and there's African jazz every Sun from 2pm.

The outskirts

Calabash Bezique Thika Rd at Kahawa Sukari, opposite Kenyatta University ☏020/811084. A large 24hr *nyama choma* place with studenty discos Thurs–Sat and occasional live bands – phone in advance for details. Bus/matatu #137 or #237.

City Cabanas Mombasa Highway, 3km before the airport turning ☏020/820549 or 820992. A massive entertainments complex, one of the prime venues for visiting international stars, as well as a lot of home-grown talent – look in the press for details. Big-name tickets around Ksh1000. Matatu #110.

Roasters Inn Garden Estate Rd, opposite Kenya Breweries ☏020/861000. The resident Forvics Band plays classic Kenyan pop, and there's cabaret as well. Wed, Fri & Sat are the main nights. Bus/matatu #45, #137, #145, #160 or #237.

Simba Saloon Carnivore Restaurant ☏020/602764, ⊛www.tamarind.co.ke. A successful melding of live music and disco in a pleasant outdoor environment. Wed nights are rock (till 2am; free before 9pm); Fri is "Africa Nite" (Ksh300 from 6pm); Sat is "Saturday Night Fever" (mix of music from hip-hop to bhangra; 6pm till dawn, Ksh300); and Sun is for soul (6pm till 2am; free till 9pm, Ksh200 thereafter) There's more live music, both Kenyan and international – big names such as Manu Dibango and Youssou N'dour have played here. The adjacent *Carnivore Gardens* is a concert venue holding up to 15,000 people.

Wida Highway Motel Naivasha Rd, Kikuyu ☎0154/32813. Part beer garden, part *nyama choma* with live music (especially Fri), part disco (*Groove Syde*; soul and R&B Sat). The live music is mainly local bands with the odd rowdy beauty contest thrown in for fun. Sat & Sun afternoons have family-oriented shows, with R&B disco, some gospel, acrobats and comedy. Bus/matatu #2 or #102.

The performing arts

After years of stagnation, the Nairobi **arts scene** seems to be finally finding a rhythm of its own, independent of the tourist market which had previously driven much of it. Besides checking out the theatres and multidisciplinary arts centres listed below, you might want to see if the **Sarakasi Players** are doing anything in the basement of the conference centre; look into the productions of the **Miujiza Players** at the Rahimtulla Trust Library Theatre in Mfangano Street, off Ronald Ngala Street (☎020/212660); and enquire about the **Tamduni Players**, a long-established group run by a Gambian woman, Janet Young, who do occasional productions. It's also worth investigating the African and Caribbean theatre performances at the Education Department Lecture Theatre of Nairobi University. For more details of the above, and current happenings, check the theatre pages in the Thursday's *Standard* and the Friday and Saturday *Nation*.

If you're around at the beginning of November, check out the **Kenya Music Festival** at the Kenyatta International Conference Centre, heavy on choirs but with a lot of other fascinating song and dance.

Venues and arts centres

GoDown Arts Centre Dunga Rd, Industrial Area ☎020/5575785. A not-for-profit entity where creative ideas can be mingled. It features an art gallery, a dance studio with performance space, a painters' studio and hi-tech recording facilities with a theatre and a puppet workshop planned. An art market takes place here on the last Saturday of the month. Also based at the GoDown are the Kuona and Sarakasi Trusts, whose mandate is to promote contemporary
African art, music and dance to local and international audiences.

Kenya National Theatre Opposite the *Norfolk Hotel*, Harry Thuku Rd ☎020/225174. They give considerable emphasis to Kenyan drama and African theatre in general – though with a less hectic schedule than the Phoenix Players. To mark a new era of liberalization, the Kibaki government and the private sector together raised $150,000 to refurbish the theatre, which was built in 1952; it's now been restored to its Art Deco grandeur.

Mzizi Creative Centre Mzizi House, Mumias South Rd, Buru Buru ☎020/785086. A self-supporting initiative with a dedicated nucleus of writers, artists and musicians staging exhibitions, concerts, and innovative theatrical productions, often by young Kenyan playwrights. The centre organizes highly recommended performances of *sigana* – an art form combining acting, narration, music and other expressive techniques. An offshoot of the Mzizi group is the Museum Performing Arts Program, housed at the Museum Studio and Arts Centre, Museum Hill (☎02/751049, ✉aghano@yahoo.com).

Paa Ya Paa Arts Centre Ridgeways Rd, off Kiambu Rd, Ridgeways ☎020/512421. An artistic space where performers, artists and poets work, exhibit, and live.

Professional Centre At the southern end of Parliament Rd ☎020/241230. The small theatre here has assumed the mantle of Nairobi's leading playhouse, and is highly recommended. Its energetic repertory company, the Phoenix Players (formed in 1948), stages contemporary works by Kenyan or foreign playwrights, or sometimes performs classics adapted for Kenya. Their productions, especially following the reduction in self-censorship over the past decade, have always been worth catching and are sometimes excellent.

Cinema

The Sarit Centre, Village Market, Prestige Plaza and Nakumatt Junction all have modern **multiplexes** showing recent mainstream movies. In the **city centre**, the 20th Century on Mama Ngina Street (℡02/338070) and the Kenya Cinema on Moi Avenue (℡020/226982) show fairly recent mainstream releases – usually blockbusters or award winners – when they can get them. Other movie theatres tend to show kung fu, vintage James Bond, old Westerns and, of course, Hindi and Punjabi movies, which you don't need to understand to enjoy. Seats cost up to Ksh200 in the mainstream cinemas, and around Ksh60 in the dives. Daily programmes can be found in the *Nation* and the *Standard* newspapers.

Casinos and bingo halls

There are more than enough places in Nairobi in which to unburden yourself of your money. One place that draws a fair number of tourists is the **International Casino** (℡020/742600; buses #21, #23 or #119) on Westlands Road off Museum Hill, close to the *Boulevard Hotel* and museum. The complex consists of the main gaming room itself (main entrance off Chiromo Rd; Mon–Fri from 9pm, Sat & Sun from 4pm; smart casual dress code; nominal entrance fee), a couple of restaurants (including *Toona Tree*, see p.141), a slot machine hall, and a private member's club (*Galileo's*, basically a disco). The whole area around the casino is dodgy – and extremely unsafe after dark. Other options include the classy Casino Paradise at the *Safari Park Hotel*, sumptuous in every respect (no minimum bet, and it stays open, obligingly, until the last bankruptcy), but rather too far to walk back from if you're penniless.

Lower down the social gambler's scale are a number of **bingo halls**, complete with nasally intoning callers and slot machines (usual prices are around Ksh500 for five bingo cards, entrance is free); try Joker Wild under the *Oakwood Hotel* in Kimathi Street.

Safari transport and operators

Nairobi is the travel hub of Africa, with a mass of opportunities for **safaris** around Kenya and literally hundreds of safari operators, car-rental outlets and travel agents to provide you with everything you need for your trip. If you're organizing your own safari, see the list of **car rental** companies on p.153. One possibility not often considered is **cycling**: Hell's Gate at Naivasha, Lake Bogoria Reserve and Kakamega Forest allow bikes, and there's a lot of wonderful cycling country besides. For listings of bike shops, see p.153; for bicycle rental, contact Bike Treks (Ksh1800 per day; see "Special activity safaris", p.151), though note that they prefer you to cycle out of town as there's a risk of theft in Nairobi.

The opportunities for photography and seeing the country are without equal if you **charter a plane**. A few small operators, mostly based at Wilson Airport, will oblige; see "Airlines, internal", p.152, for details. The current standard rate for a Cessna 182 (two passengers) is around $2 per mile (1.6km). Minimum mileage is usually 500 miles (800km or three hours' flying – which takes you a very long way; $1000). You shouldn't be charged for *démarrage* (the plane being parked on the ground) if you're coming back the same day.

Safari operators

You can pick up plenty of leaflets about safaris from touts, or at any travel agent or ticket-booking company. Anxious to take you to operators' offices, **touts** are by no means a bad thing, as they often work for several companies and their commission is never added to the price you pay. Indeed, some are quite knowledgeable and will be able to advise you relatively truthfully about which companies are good for what. Bear in mind, however, that because relatively few companies with established reputations give them commission, they are unlikely to take you to them.

The best of the **travel agents** are reputable, but it's always a good idea to meet the company you're travelling with in advance and to try to ensure that it is that company and not you who is paying the agent their commission. You should also check whether the advertised safari is actually run by the company in question, as the practice of one company subcontracting a safari to another is quite common, especially in low season, and gives you less redress if things go wrong. This is especially important for safaris to **Tanzania** and **Uganda** – ensure that the company has at least an office in the relevant country.

The **Kenya Association of Tour Operators (KATO)**, (Longonot Rd, off Kilimanjaro Ave, Upper Hill; PO Box 48461 ⓣ020/713348, ⓕ719226, ⓦwww.katokenya.org), should also be able to advise you on the reputation of a company you're considering going with. They can also give you a list of companies which adhere to their code of conduct. If you do decide to choose a cheaper company which is not a member of KATO, you'll not necessarily be ripped off. Take your time, ask to see the vehicles, demand everything in writing including a breakdown of the costs, and don't be pressured into making any decisions until you are ready. In the unfortunate circumstance that you have been duped, KATO may be able to help.

The following listings are subdivided broadly – several operators could be put into more than one bracket. All except those marked with an asterisk are **members of KATO**.

Camping safaris

Every other shop seems to belong to a safari outfit and it's obviously impossible to mention more than a few. With so much to go wrong, spotless reputations are hard to maintain, but the following, who run most of their **camping trips** by truck or minibus, are good value and only rarely come in for criticism.

Amicabre Travel Services* Mezzanine floor, office no. 6, Avenue House, Kenyatta Ave ⓣ020/318233, ⓕ318235, ⓦwww.amicabretravel.com. A wide variety of excellent lodge and camping safaris as well as a programme called "Meet the Kenyans", combining a safari holiday with a week or two living with a Kenyan family and work in the local community.

Gametrackers Fifth floor, Ninyo Towers, Koinange/Moktar Daddah St; PO Box 62042 ⓣ020/251771, ⓦwww.gametrackersafaris.com. Popular and consistently good operator with some twenty tours, featuring – apart from game safaris – cycling, camel treks, Aberdares walking and Mount Kenya climbs, as well as trips further afield (they have branches in Tanzania and Uganda). Around $60 per day and up. They run an excellent eight-day Turkana safari via Samburu National Reserve, Marsabit National Park and the Chalbi Desert, which is highly recommended ($440).

Guerba Kenya First floor, International House, Mama Ngina St, PO Box 43935 ⓣ & ⓕ020/543244, ⓦwww.guerba.co.uk. The Kenyan arm of the respected Africa overland specialists, offering safaris to walk-in customers, usually on a small commission.

Habib's Tours & Travel First floor, Horton Court Building, Lenana Rd ⓣ020/578096, ⓕ576812, ⓦwww.habibtours.com. Pricier than most, but reliable and long-established, specializing in tailor-made safaris and packages to suit most price ranges (aided by discount deals with many hotels). From $75 per day for safaris involving camping, $110 upwards if staying in lodges or hotels.

Ice Rock Mountain Treks and Safaris* Fourth floor, NCM Building, Tom Mboya St; PO Box 50155 ⊕020/244608, ⓦwww.climbingclimbingafrica .com. A small professional setup with knowledge-able guides, mainly dealing with safaris to Mount Kenya, Kilimanjaro and Hell's Gate. The owner, who used to be a member of the Mount Kenya rescue team, organizes and leads every expedition. Prices for the four-day Sirimon route up Mount Kenya start from $400 per person.

Jocky Tours ⊕0722/782256, ⓦwww.jockytours .com. New company dealing mainly in camping safaris and Mount Kenya excursions.

Kenia Tours and Safaris Fourth floor, Jubilee Insurance House, Kaunda/Wabera streets; PO Box 19730 ⊕020/223699, ⓦwww.keniatours.com. Proficient Kenya camping safaris specialist, keenly priced: $70–80 per day for camping safaris, $95–100 for lodge safaris, discounts in low season.

Nguruman Safaris PO Box 20253, Lavington ⊕020/574434, ⓦwww.ngurumansafaris.com.

Specializes in camping safaris in Land Cruisers and overland trucks. Trips include the usual safaris, as well as trips to the Chalbi desert. They offer good meals, knowledgeable guides and well-maintained vehicles.

Primetime Safaris* Contrust House, ninth floor, Moi Ave; PO Box 56591, ⊕020/215773, ⓕ217136, ⓦwww.primetime.co.ke. A wide range of tours, particularly aimed at backpackers; good camping safaris and Mount Kenya excursions.

Savuka Tours & Safaris* Fourth floor, Panafric House, Kenyatta Ave; PO Box 20433 ⊕02/215256, ⓕ215016, ⓦwww.savuka-travels.com. Good-value camping safaris and climbing packages. They get favourable recommendations from budget travellers and the food is surprisingly good.

Spirit of Africa Safaris* Seventh floor, Sonolux House, Moi Ave ⊕020/215309. Good budget safaris aimed at the backpacker market. As well as the usual camping safaris, they specialize in more unusual tours such as visits to see a witchdoctor in Eastern Kenya.

Lodge and homestay safaris

The following are all conscientious and helpful operators and agents, catering for those who appreciate their wildlife taken with more than a modicum of luxury. Most have discounted deals with hotel chains, which means that their more popular trips are generally better value than less frequently run ones. All also run half- and full-day trips in and around Nairobi for $40–80. Note that renting a car and booking accommodation yourself shouldn't work out much more expensive than buying a comparable upmarket package.

Let's Go Travel Caxton House, Standard St; PO Box 60342 ⊕02/340331, ⓕ336890, ⓦwww.lets-go-travel.net. Also has branches in Karen shopping centre (⊕020/882505), while its head office is at ABC Place, Westlands (⊕020/4447151). Apart from acting as agents for a large number of homestay and ranch-house sites throughout Kenya (and offering some specially negotiated deals on the more expensive hotels), Let's Go also runs its own well-organized budget camping safaris, from $60 per day. Lodge safaris are $130–170 per day, depending on season and group size. One of the few companies to have offices in both Tanzania and Uganda and run trips there.

Pollman's Tours & Safaris Pollman's House, Mombasa Rd; PO Box 84198 ⊕02/533140, ⓕ544544. ⓦwww.pollmans.com. One of the largest operators, running to all the major parks, though decidedly package-tour in feel (travelling in "convoy" with four or five other Pollman's mini-buses isn't unusual). Around $450 for three nights. Popular with German visitors.

Rhino Safaris Rhino Safaris Building, opposite the Baptist Church, Ngong Rd; PO Box 48023

⊕020/720610, ⓕ720624, ⓔrhinosafarisnbo @kenayweb.com. Highly regarded firm, founded in 1970, specializing in scheduled lodge, homestay and flying safaris. Customer service is second to none, and they're happy to tailor itineraries to individual needs. Prices start from around $390 for a three-day/two-night Mara trip, to over $1000 for a six-night tour covering Samburu, the Aberdares, Lake Nakuru, and Maasai Mara or Amboseli. They have offices in Mombasa and Arusha in Tanzania.

Somak Travel Mombasa Rd; PO Box 48495 ⊕020/535508/9, ⓕ535172, ⓦwww.somak-nairobi.com. Well regarded, offering a range of scheduled departures to all the main parks. Prices start at around $120 per person per day.

Suntrek Tours & Travel Safari Centre, Waiyaki Way, Westlands; PO Box 48146 ⊕020/4442982, ⓕ4448351, ⓦwww.suntreksafaris.com. Long-established quality outfit happy to tailor itineraries and accommodation to your needs. Standard trips cover all the major game parks and use reliable lodges. Recommended, if you're short on time, are their five- or six-night trips which cover a combina-tion of different parks and scenery, for example

Tsavo West, Amboseli, the Aberdares, Lake Nakuru and Maasai Mara national parks. Lack of regularly scheduled departures means you're unlikely to have other tourists on the same safari, although this makes things more expensive if there are only two of you. They also run trips into Tanzania. From $165 per night.

Tour Africa Safaris Dennis Pritt Rd, off State House Rd; PO Box 34187 ☎020/2729333, ⓕ723513, ⓦwww.tourafrica-safaris.com. Well-run travel agency with its own tailor-made lodge safaris (its camping safaris are arranged through other companies). A seven-day jaunt in high-class lodges costs $1000.

Special activity safaris

The following are recommended because they offer unusual, normally much more expensive, trips – notably safaris on foot (sometimes using pack animals), by bicycle (usually with vehicle backup), on horseback or camel. Those that don't have walk-in addresses are usually small companies: enquire and book with a large agent like Let's Go Travel (see opposite).

For a unique cultural experience, contact Green Belt Safaris, Kilimani Lane, off Elgeo Marakwet Road (PO Box 67545; ☎020/573057, ⓦwww.greenbelt movement.org/green_safari.php). They offer community **homestays**, the guests participating in field activities (seed collection, nursery preparation, tree planting, community projects, harvesting, meal preparation, etc) for up to a week. This is followed by a few days of conventional tourism, such as a spell hiking in the Aberdares.

Bateleur Safaris Ndorobo Rd, Langata; PO Box 42562 ☎020/890454, ⓕ891007, ⓦwww.bate-leursafaris.com. Walking safaris for ornithologists.

Bike Treks Kabete Gardens, behind Sarit Centre, off Karuna Rd, Westlands; PO Box 14237 ☎ & ⓕ020/446371, ⓦwww.biketreks.co.ke. Truly adventurous, tailor-made trips, with vehicle back-up, led by a veteran mountain-bike enthusiast; the trans-Mara ride during the wildebeest migration is quite something. Minimum three people for guaranteed departures. They can also arrange trekking and mountain-climbing trips. Around $100 per day.

Desert Rose Camels ☎020/5677251, ⓕ564945, ⓦwww.desertrosekenya.com. Expertly guided and flexible camel (or horseback) expeditions in and around the Mathews, Ndoto and Nyiru mountain ranges of Samburu district – a wonderful experience, with plenty of contact with local people. Reckon on $170–210 per person per day. Don't come expecting total comfort. They also run the exquisite *Desert Rose Lodge*, between Baragoi and South Horr (see p.580).

Ewaso Nyiro River Camel Hikes Book through Bookings Ltd, Standard St ☎02/220365. Based near Loisaba, 2hr northeast from Rumuruti in Laikipia on the Ewaso Nyiro River. Camel-assisted walks at $205 per person, while camel hire costs $35 per beast, if you've got your own wheels to get there (the nearby *Colcheccio Lodge*, see p.571, is one of Kenya's priciest).

Naturetrek Adventure Safaris* Sixth floor, Vedic House, Mama Ngina St; PO Box 34817

☎020/341188, ⓕ243572, ⓦwww.naturetrek safaris.com. Specialists in walking safaris, notably a seven-day walk in the Rift Valley and Loita Hills on the Tanzanian border, and a thirteen-day jaunt in Tanzania itself. Reckon on $150–250 per day.

Origins Safaris No walk-in address ☎020/229009, ⓕ216528, ⓦwww.originsafaris .info. Excellent bird-watching trips as well as trout fishing safaris on the slopes of Mount Kenya and "origins of man" safaris. Not cheap though – in the range of $300–500 a day all in, with accommodation at well-selected lodges and tented camps.

Safaris Unlimited 328 Langata Rd; PO Box 24181 ☎020/890435, ⓕ891113, ⓦwww .safarisunlimited.com. Specialists in horseback safaris, for confident riders only, covering the Maasai Mara, Chyulu Hills and other wilderness areas, and their own Longonot Ranch House at Naivasha. Exclusive and expensive: trips cost $300–500 per person per day.

Savage Wilderness Safaris* Thigiri Rd; PO Box 44827 ☎020/521590, ⓦwww.whitewaterkenya .com. Excellent programme of technical climbing and walking trips on Mount Kenya, "white-water" rafting, and walking safaris in the Chyulu and Loita hills. One-day rafting from $95; other trips $100 per day and up.

Tropical Ice* Suite 8, first floor, Muthaiga Shopping Centre, Muthaiga Rd; PO Box 57341 ☎ & ⓕ020/884652, ⓦwww.tropical-ice.com. Upmarket walking safaris along the Galana river for $160 per day.

Yare Safaris Union Towers, Moi Ave; PO Box 63006 ⊕020/559313, ⓕ214099. One of the leaders in North Kenyan safaris, offering various offbeat tours and camel treks in the Samburu district from

their base in Maralal (see p.575). A seven-day camel safari, with transfer from Nairobi, costs $495 per person.

Upmarket safaris

Expensive safari outfits are mostly operated to very high standards. The following firms will give good return for your money if you are in the $300–1000 per day league and want something special. At this level, what you do is entirely "tailor-made" – in other words, it's largely up to you. Transport is usually by Land Cruiser, accommodation is in luxury lodges or pre-set private campsites, and leader/tour guides tend to be white-hunter types who know the ground well and their clients' requirements even better.

Abercrombie & Kent Bruce House, Standard St; PO Box 59749 ⊕020/334955, ⓕ215752, ⓦwww.abercrombiekent.com.
Cheli & Peacock PO Box 39806 ⊕020/603090, ⓕ0154/22553, ⓦwww.chelipeacock.com.
Glen Cottar Safaris 60 Forest Lane, Karen; PO Box 44191 ⊕020/882408, ⓕ882234, ⓔcottars@form-net.com.

Ker & Downey Safaris Langata Link, off Langata South Rd, Karen; PO Box 86 ⊕020/890754, ⓕ891903, ⓦwww.kerdowneysafaris.com.
Richard Bonham Safaris Nandi Rd, Karen; PO Box 24133 ⊕020/600457, ⓕ605008, ⓦwww.richardbonhamsafaris.com.
Tor Allan Safaris 80 Bogani East Rd; PO Box 15114 ⊕020/891190, ⓕ890142, ⓔtorallan@africaonline.co.ke.

Listings

Airlines, internal AeroKenya ⊕020/601001–2; Aircraft Leasing Services ⊕020/608362; Airkenya Aviation Ltd ⊕020/601727, ⓦwww.airkenya.com; Blue Bird Aviation ⊕020/602338; Boskovic Air Charters Ltd ⊕020/606364, ⓕ609619, ⓔboskyops@swiftkenya.com; East African Air Charters ⊕020/603859, ⓕ502358, ⓦwww.eaaircharters.co.ke; Safarilink ⊕020/600777, ⓦwww.safarilink.co.ke. Most airline offices are open Mon–Fri 8am or 8.30am–1pm & 2–4.30pm or 5pm, Sat 8.30am–1pm.
Airlines, International Aero Zambia, ground floor, International House, Mama Ngina St ⊕020/246519; Air India, first floor, Jeevan Bharati Building, Harambee Ave ⊕020/313300; Air Madagascar, first floor, Hilton Building, City Hall Way ⊕020/225286; Air Malawi, International House, Mama Ngina St ⊕020/317113; Air Mauritius, mezzanine, International House, Mama Ngina St ⊕020/229166; Air Tanzania, mezzanine floor, International Life House, Mana Ngina St ⊕020/227486; Air Zimbabwe, first floor, Sasini House, Loita St ⊕020/253029 British Airways, International House, Mama Ngina St ⊕020/3277000; Cameroon Airlines, ninth floor, Rehani House, Kenyatta Ave ⊕020/224743; Egyptair, Hilton Building, City Hall Way ⊕020/226821; El Al, ninth floor, KCS

House, Mama Ngina St ⊕020/228123; Emirates, twentieth floor, View Park Towers, Loita St ⊕020/3290000; Ethiopian Airlines, Bruce House, Muindi Mbingu St ⊕020/217558; Gulf Air, eighth floor, International House, Mama Ngina St ⊕020/214441; Kenya Airways, fifth floor, Barclays Plaza, Loita St ⊕020/3274100; KLM, Barclays Plaza, Loita St ⊕020/32074747; Royal Swazi National Airways, fourth floor, KCS House, Mama Ngina St ⊕020/210670; Saudi Arabian Airlines, mezzanine II, Anniversary Towers, University Way ⊕020/312431; South African Airways, mezzanine floor, International Life House ⊕02/229663; Swiss Airlines, first floor, Caltex Plaza, Limuru Rd ⊕020/3744045.
American Express Hilton Hotel, Mama Ngina St ⊕020/222906.
Art galleries Gallery Watatu, Lonrho House, Standard St (⊕020/228737) promotes contemporary African art, as does the Rahimtulla Museum of Modern Art (RAMOMA), Rahimtulla Tower, Upper Hill (⊕020/2729181).
Banks and exchange There are branches of Barclays, Standard Chartered and Stanbic banks everywhere, most with ATMs. Many of the exchange bureaux are little more than a desk and armed askari; some don't accept traveller's

cheques and almost all require your proof of purchase, while others refuse plastic. There are no banks open on Sun except at the airport, though the larger hotels may oblige with their facilities. Western Union transfers are received by Postbank, Postbank House, Market Lane (☏020/651696, 🖷 210593; Mon–Fri 8.30am–4pm, Sat 8.30–11am).

Bike shops Kenya Cycle Mart, the best parts, repair and sales shop, is in Butere Road, Industrial Area. Also try Cycleland, lower ground floor, Sarit Centre, Westlands.

Books Good bookshops include: Textbook Centre, Kijabe St ☏020/330340; Nation Bookshop, Kenyatta Ave (entrance also from the *Stanley Hotel*); Bookpoint, Loans House, Moi Ave; Premier Bookshop, corner of Tom Mboya St and Ronald Ngala St; Prestige, Prudential Assurance Building, Mama Ngina St; and the Textbook Centre, at the Sarit Centre, Westlands. For a good secondhand selection, try Prestige or Book Stop, Yaya Centre, Hurlingham.

Bus companies Akamba Bus, Lagos Rd ☏020/222027 or 225488, Wabera St office, ☏020/223304; Arusha Express, Cross Rd/River Rd ☏02/212083 or 338322; Busscar, Duruma Rd/Kumasi Rd ☏020/227650; Coastline, Accra Rd/Duruma Rd ☏020/217592; Colobus Shuttle, Village Market, Limuru Rd ☏020/581726, 🖂 sales@colobusenroute.com; Cross Road Travellers, Cross Rd ☏020/331531; Daily Peugeot Service (DPS), Dubois Rd ☏020/242824; Davanu Shuttle, Fourth floor, Windsor House, University Way ☏020/217178; East Africa Shuttles, Portal Place, Muindi Mbingu St ☏020/248453, 🖳www .eastafricashuttles.com; Goldline, top of Accra Rd/Cross Rd ☏020/225279 or 221963; Impala Shuttle (for Arusha and Moshi in Tanzania; pick up from city-centre hotels) ☏020/2730953, 🖳www .impalashuttle.com; Kensilver Express, Dubois Rd ☏020/221839 or 240218; Mwingi Coach, opposite Eastleigh KBS depot, General Waruinge St ☏02/765763; Riverside Shuttle, fifth floor, Consolidated Bank House, Koinange St ☏020/335561; Scandinavian Express, River Rd ☏020/242523; Transluxe, opposite OTC (behind the KBS bus station), Temple Rd ☏020/220059. The following have no phone: Easy Coach, from Haile Selassie Ave. Falcon Coach, from River R Kumasi Rd; Jolly Coach, from Sheikh Karume Rd, off Munyu Rd; MASH Bus Services from Accra Rd/Duruma Rd; Randa Coach Services, River Rd; Regional Coach Services, River Rd. Eastern Express (no phone) and other companies not listed above operate from the Country Bus Station (aka "Machakos Airport").

Camping equipment Try Atul's, Biashara St (Mon–Fri 9am–1pm & 2.30–5.30pm, Sat 9am–3pm;

☏020/225935), or Kenya Canvas Ltd (Mon–Fri 8am–5pm, Sat 8am–1pm; ☏020/343262).

Car rental Avis, College House, University Way ☏020/244977; Budget, Mombasa Rd ☏020/652144–50, airport ☏020/822370; 🛪 Central Rent-A-Car, *680 Hotel*, Muindi Mbingu St ☏020/222888; 🛪 Concorde, Shell Petrol Station, Ring Rd, Westlands ☏020/4448953; Crossways, Banda St ☏020/220848; Hertz, ground floor, *Stanley Hotel*, Standard St ☏020/311143; Platinum Tours and Car Hire, opposite MP Shah Hospital ☏020/4445439; Rasuls, Butere Rd, Industrial Area ☏020/558234; Suntrek Tours & Travel, Safari Centre, Wayaki Way, Westlands ☏020/4442982.

Car repairs Kwik Fit Tyres & Auto Care, Ring Rd, is reliable (☏020/3740215).

Contraceptives Oral contraceptives are available from the Family Planning Association of Kenya, fifth floor, Phoenix House, Kenyatta Ave (☏020/342323).

Courier and freight services DHL, DHL House, Witu Rd, PO Box 67577 ☏020/6925120, 🖷536803; Federal Express, Bruce House, Standard St, PO Box 49707 ☏020/240106, 🖷211307; TMX Express Worldwide, Vision Plaza, Mombasa Rd, PO Box 4630 ☏020/828054–7; UPS, Fedha Towers, Kaunda St, PO Box 45422 ☏020/252200.

Cultural Centres British Council, Upper Hill Rd ☏020/2836000, 🖳www.britishcouncil.org/kenya; Alliance Française, Maison Française, Loila St ☏020/340054; Goethe-Institut, Maendeleo House, corner of Loita and Monrovia streets ☏020/224640, 🖂info@nairobi.goethe.org; the Italian Cultural Institute, Ex-Agip House, fifth & sixth floors, Woodvale Grove ☏020/4451266, 🖳www.iicnairobi.org; Japan African Culture Interchange Institute (known as Jacii), Kamburu Dr ☏020/566262.

Dentist Dr Peter Griffiths, Kolloh Rd, Lavington ☏020/4348211 or 0722 736439.

Doctors Ask your embassy for a list. For blood tests, Alliance Health Services, Pioneer House, fifth floor, Moi Ave ☏020/313339.

Embassies, high commissions and consulates Australia, ICIPE House, Riverside Dr, off Chiromo Rd, PO Box 47718 ☏020/4445034; Austria, second floor, City House, Standard/Wabera streets, PO Box 30560 ☏020/228281; Belgium, Limuru Rd, Muthaiga, PO Box 30461 ☏020/522166; Burundi, fourteenth floor, Development House, Moi Ave, PO Box 44439 ☏020/575249; Canada, Limuru Rd, Gigiri, PO Box 1013 ☏020/3663000; China, Woodlands Rd, off State House Rd, Hurlingham, PO Box 30508 ☏020/2726851; Cyprus, fifth floor, Eagle House, Kimathi St, PO Box 30739 ☏020/220881; Czech Republic, Embassy House,

Harambee Ave, PO Box 30204 ⊕020/210494 or 223448; **Democratic Republic of the Congo**, twelfth floor, Electricity House, Harambee Ave, PO Box 48106 ⊕020/3754253; **Denmark**, eleventh floor, HFCK Building, Kenyatta Ave/Koinange St, PO Box 40412 ⊕020/4451460; **Egypt**, seventh floor, Harambee Plaza, Uhuru Highway/Haile Selassie Ave, PO Box 30285 ⊕020/570360; **Eritrea**, second floor, New Rehema House, Rhapta Rd, PO Box 38651 ⊕020/4443163; **Ethiopia**, State House Ave, Nairobi Hill, PO Box 45198 ⊕020/2732050; **Finland**, second floor, International House, Mama Ngina St, PO Box 30379 ⊕020/318575; **France**, ninth floor, Barclays Plaza, Loita St, PO Box 41784 ⊕020/316363; **Germany**, eighth floor, Williamson House, Fourth Ngong Ave, PO Box 30180 ⊕020/2712527; **Greece**, thirteenth B floor, Nation Centre, Kimathi St, PO Box 30543 ⊕020/340722; **Hungary**, Ole Odume Rd, off Argwings Kodhek Rd, PO Box 61146 ⊕020/560060; **Iceland**, Bendera Lane, off Spring Valley Rd, PO Box 45000 ⊕020/521487; **India**, second floor, Jeevan Bharati Building, Harambee Ave, PO Box 30074 ⊕020/222566–7; **Ireland**, Dante Diesel Workshop Building, Masai Rd, PO Box 30659, ⊕020/556647; **Israel**, Bishops Rd, PO Box 30354 ⊕02/724021–2; **Italy**, ninth floor, International House, Mama Ngina St, PO Box 30107 ⊕020/247750; **Japan**, fifteenth floor, ICEA Building, Kenyatta Ave, PO Box 60202 ⊕020/315852; **Luxembourg**, eighth floor, International House, Mama Ngina St, PO Box 30610 ⊕020/224318; **Madagascar**, first floor, Hilton Building, Mama Ngina St, PO Box 41723 ⊕020/225286; **Malawi**, Mvuli Rd/Church Rd, off Waiyaki Way, Westlands, PO Box 30453 ⊕020/4440569; **Mozambique**, third floor, Bruce House, Standard St ⊕020/221979; **Netherlands**, Riverside Lane, off Riverside Dr, PO Box 41537 ⊕020/4447412; **New Zealand**, Wajiiri House, Argwings Kodhek Rd, PO Box 43811, ⊕020/2712466; **Nigeria**, Lenana Rd, Hurlingham, PO Box 30516 ⊕020/570226; **Norway**, Lion Place, Waiyaki Way, Westlands, PO Box 46363 ⊕020/4451510–6; **Pakistan**, Church Rd, off Rhapta Rd, Westlands, PO Box 30045 ⊕020/4443911–2; **Poland**, Kabarnet Rd, off Ngong Rd, Woodley, PO Box 30086 ⊕020/566288; **Portugal**, tenth floor, Reinsurance Plaza, Taifa Rd, PO Box 34020 ⊕020/251879; **Russia**, next to Army HQ, Lenana Rd, PO Box 30049 ⊕020/2722462; **Rwanda**, twelfth floor, International House, Mama Ngina St, PO Box 48579 ⊕020/317400; **Seychelles**, 114 James Gichuru Rd, PO Box 20400 ⊕020/580500; **Slovakia**, Milimani Rd ⊕020/721896–7; **Somalia**, fifth floor, International House, Mama Ngina St, PO Box 30769 ⊕020/580165; **South Africa**, third floor, Roshanmaer Place, Lenana Rd, PO Box 42441 ⊕020/2827100; **Spain**, third floor, International House, Mama Ngina, PO Box 45503 ⊕020/226568; **Sudan**, seventh floor, Minet ICDC House, Mamlaka Rd, PO Box 74059 ⊕020/2720883; **Sweden**, third floor, Lion Place, Waiyaki Way, Westlands, PO Box 30600 ⊕020/4234000; **Switzerland**, seventh floor, International House, Mama Ngina St, PO Box 30752 ⊕020/228735; **Tanzania**, ninth floor, Reinsurance Plaza, Taifa Rd, PO Box 47790 ⊕020/311948; **Uganda**, first floor, Uganda House, Kenyatta Ave, PO Box 60853 ⊕020/311814; **United Kingdom**, Upper Hill Rd, off Haile Selassie Ave, PO Box 30465 ⊕020/2844000; **USA**, United Nations Ave, Gigiri, PO Box 30137 ⊕020/3636000; **Zambia**, Nyerere Rd, PO Box 48741 ⊕020/2724796; **Zimbabwe**, 2 Westlands Close, Westlands Rd, PO Box 30806 ⊕020/3744052.

Football (soccer) Nyayo Stadium, at the junction of Uhuru Highway and Langata Rd. Seats cost Ksh100–150.

Golf Tobs Golf Safaris Ltd, PO Box 20146 (⊕020/2721722 ⓔtobsgolf@form-net.com), organizes golfing excursions around the country. Courses in Nairobi itself include: Windsor Golf & Country Club, Kigwa Rd, 5km north of the city (⊕020/862300); Nairobi Golf Club, Mucai Dr (off Ngong Rd; ⊕020/725769); Muthaiga Golf Club on Muthaiga Rd (⊕020/3761280); Karen Golf & Country Club, Karen Rd (⊕020/884089).

Guides Guides for almost anywhere in Kenya can be arranged through Utalii College, Kenya's college for tourist-oriented trades, though it would be advisable to contact them well in advance (PO Box 31052 ⊕020/212372).

Horse racing The race course is on Ngong Rd; frequent buses head out there on race days from the KBS bus station.

Horse-riding Karen Riding School ⊕020/88415; Nkudzi Riding School ⊕020/882745.

Hospitals Aga Khan Hospital, Third Parklands Ave ⊕020/3662020; Kenyatta National Hospital, Hospital Rd ⊕020/2726300; Nairobi Hospital, Argwings Kodkek Rd ⊕020/2722160; Nazareth Hospital, Riara Ridge, outside Nairobi ⊕020/342185.

Internet access Good places to surf include Lazards, which has a branch on the third floor of Data House, Kenyatta Ave; and another on the corner of Moi and Harambee avenues; and Agx the Internet Café, in the basement of Barclays Plaza.

Language schools Trans Africa Language Services, Joseph Kangethe Rd, Adam's Arcade, off Ngong Rd ⊕020/566971; Makioki Language Services, Kijabi St ⊕020/242330; Nairobi Cultural Institute, Ngong Rd ⊕020/340310.

Laundry Tintoria Ltd Laundry and Dry Cleaners, Koinange St, next to Cianda House (also has a branch at Village Market); Mbuni Dry Cleaners, corner of Chiromo and Mpaka roads, Westlands; Niki's, Hurlingham Plaza, Argwings Kodhek Rd, Hurlingham.

Left luggage Bags can be left safely at either of the two left-luggage offices at the train station. There are lockers at the side of the first/second class entrance (daily except Sun 6.30am–noon & 2–6.30pm; Ksh150 per item), while larger bags can be left at the third-class hall (daily 7.30am–7.30pm; Ksh300 per item). There is no left-luggage facility at the airport.

Libraries The British Council, Upper Hill Rd (Tues–Fri 10am–5pm, Sat 9am–noon; ☏020/2844000); the McMillan Memorial Library, Banda St (Mon–Fri 9am–5pm, Sat 9.30am–1pm; free; ☏020/224281 ext 2253); the British Institute in Eastern Africa, 3km northwest of town at Laikipia Rd (off Arboretum Dr), Kileleshwa (☏020/4343330). Also good for research is the reading room in the National Archives, Moi Ave (see p.125).

Newspapers and magazines Foreign papers are available from several newsstands around Kenyatta Ave.

Notice boards The *Thorn Tree Café* at the *Stanley Hotel*, the *Iqbal, the Upper Hill Campsite* and the *Fairview Hotel* all have useful noticeboards for travellers seeking travelling companions, accommodation to rent and so forth.

Opticians Eye Modes Ltd, Kenya Cinema Plaza, Moi Ave ☏020/222601 (Mon–Fri 7.30am–6pm, Sat 9am–2pm); Family Eye Care Centre, Princely House, Moi Ave ☏020/312426 (Mon–Sat 8.30am–5pm, Sun 9am–noon).

Passport photos Five-minute passport photo service at Studio One, corner of Moi/Nkrumah avenues, and at Custom Color, Kaunda St. There's a Colour Studio at Vedic House on Mama Ngina St.

Pharmacies AAA Pharmaceuticals, Sarit Centre, Westlands ☏020/4451091; Acacia Pharmacy, ICEA Building, Kenyatta Ave (☏020/212175) and on Ralph Bunche Rd ☏020/2711611.

Photocopying MBIM, bottom of Consolidated Bank House, corner of Loita and Koinange streets; Xerox, right by the entrance to the *Hilton.*

Photography For camera repairs, try Camera Clinic, Biashara St (☏020/222492). For batteries and to rent cameras and binoculars, the main outlet is Elite Camera House, Kimathi St, south of Kenyatta. Try any branch of Colorama for prints and slides.

Post The GPO (Mon–Fri 8am–6pm, Sat 9am–noon) on Kenyatta Ave has *poste restante.* There are smaller branch offices on Moi Ave opposite Tubman Rd, and another nearby on Tom Mboya St.

Sports and health clubs The *Norfolk Hotel* sells one-month membership for its health club (under $50), which includes use of its heated pool and gym, and aerobics. The *Serena Hotel* has a similar deal, which includes its unheated pool and multi-gym. The *Nairobi Safari Club's* facilities are ridiculously expensive, as are the *Grand Regency's.* Much more fun than any of these is Grand-Prix Karting, next to *Carnivore,* with its 500m circuit (Wed–Sun; ☏020/501758). There's indoor bowling at the Cosmic Bowling & Pool Centre in Sound Plaza, Woodvale Grove, Westlands. For golf, see opposite.

Swimming pools Pools open to the public include those at the *Hotel Boulevard,* the YMCA, the *Panafric,* and the modern sports complex behind the Aga Khan Hospital. For real water-babies, the waterslides and fountains at the Splash! water park of the *Carnivore* restaurant (see p.141) are a must.

Taxis Kentaco ☏020/225123 (and at JKI airport; ☏020/824248); Kenya Taxi Cabs Association ☏020/222953.

Telephone and faxes The main place is the official Extelcoms on Haile Selassie Ave. Calls are made through an operator – you fill in a form stating how many minutes you'd like. Outside the building are blue IDD card phones (also found in the Kenyatta International Conference Centre; note that card phones elsewhere in the city are for national calls only. Most Internet cafés have phone services – Lazards charges Ksh15/min for most international calls. Faxes can also be sent and received from most cybercafés.

Travel agents and airline bookings Bankco Tours & Travel, first floor, Mulji Jetha Mansion, Latema Rd/Lagos Rd, PO Box 11536 ☏02/336144, ☏331874; Crocodile Travel, Stewart Building, Tom Mboya St, PO Box 20380 ☏02/335250; Haidery Tours & Travel, first floor, Impala House, Tom Mboya St, PO Box 45728 ☏02/335256, ☏211949; Hanzuwan El-Kindy Tours & Travel, Dubois Rd, PO Box 49266 ☏02/227387; Kambo Travel, Tom Mboya St, opposite Latema Rd, PO Box 41819 ☏02/228131, ☏228734; Prince Safaris, ground floor, Kenyatta International Conference Centre, PO Box 51096 ☏02/219499, ☏217692; Tour Africa Safaris, seventh floor, Rehani House, corner Kenyatta Ave and Koinange St, PO Box 34187 ☏020/336767, ☏338271, ☏www.tourafrica-safaris.com; Trade & Travel Ltd, Monrovia St, opposite Jeevanjee Gardens, PO Box 11392 ☏02/227575, ☏228710; Travel Service, Pan Africa House, Standard St, PO Box 45456 ☏02/3221992, ☏214120, ☏info@bunsontravel.co.ke.

Vaccinations Cholera, yellow fever, typhoid and hepatitis jabs can be obtained from City Hall, City Hall Way.

Visitor's passes/visas Visitor's pass extensions can be obtained at Nyayo House, Posta Rd, behind the GPO (Mon–Fri 8.30am–12.30pm & 2–3.30pm; ☎020/332022).

Worship As well as many mosques and temples, Nairobi has a number of churches, two cathedrals,

and a synagogue. The four main churches and synagogue are located in the northwest of the city centre. All Saints' Cathedral, a beautiful church behind Uhuru Park, has often been a gathering point for peaceful opposition protest to the government.

Nairobi Province

NAIROBI PROVINCE stretches way beyond the city suburbs, taking in an area of some 690 square kilometres (270 square miles) and ranging from agricultural and ranching land to jungle and national park. For visitors, most of the interest lies to the **south**, in the predominantly Maasai land that begins with **Nairobi National Park**, and includes the watershed ridge of the **Ngong Hills**. It's a striking landscape, vividly described in Karen Blixen's *Out of Africa* (see "Books", p.663). **North** of the city, the land is also distinctive, narrow valleys twisting down from the Kinangop plateau, some still filled with jungle and, it's said, leopards. In spite of that, the steep slopes here are high-value real estate, still being developed as exclusive suburbs, planted with shady gardens and festooned with security signs. To the **west** lies largely Kikuyu farmland, densely cultivated with corn, bananas and the cash crop insecticide plant, pyrethrum. **East**, beyond the shanty suburb of Dandora, are the wide Athi plains, which are mostly ranching country.

Nairobi National Park and around

Daily 6am–7pm, no entry after 6.15pm; $20, children $5; Smartcard entry; 30kph speed limit. Warden PO Box 42076 ☎020/500622, ☏ 505866. Maps: the best is the KWS one usually sold at the Main Gate (1997); otherwise, Survey of Kenya SK71 (1990) has loads of detail, but is a little out of date.

Despite the hype, it really is remarkable that the 113-square-kilometre patch of plains and woodland making up **Nairobi National Park** should exist almost uncorrupted within earshot of the downtown traffic, complete with more than eighty species of large mammals and the second-largest herbivore migration after that of the Mara/Serengeti. Spending at least a morning or afternoon in the park gives you the chance to see some species which might elude you in the bigger Kenyan reserves. There are no elephants, but this is a small deficiency among a surprisingly high concentration of animals. For all the low-flying planes and lines of tourist minibuses, you have a greater chance of witnessing a kill here than in any of the other parks. Kenya residents use the park as a route from Karen and Langata to Jomo Kenyatta International airport – it does make a pleasant way of leaving the country if you can work it into your flight times.

Access to the park

Without your own transport, the cheapest and most adventurous way in is to **hitch a ride** at the main gate. This is probably easiest on a Saturday or Sunday morning, when Kenyans are most likely to visit. The weekends are also by far the busiest time; during the week you'll find it very quiet. Early birds can get the bus #125 or matatu #126 (at around 5.40am) from Nairobi's KBS bus station to the main gate; after that time you can use any bus or matatu which goes down Langata Road.

Alternatively, you should be able to swing a good deal on a **rental car** for a day – you won't need anything more than a saloon car and kilometre charges won't amount to much. If you charter a **taxi** for a few hours, check if fuel is included in the price.

Most of the safari shops in town sell three- to four-hour **trips around the park** for $45–90. An operator with regular scheduled trips is East Africa Shuttles, Portal Place, Muindi Mbingu St (PO Box 42196; ⊕020/248453, ⊛www .eastafricashuttles.com), charging $60, excluding lunch. The problem with organized tours is that they normally leave at 10am and 2pm, which are not ideal times – though late afternoon is better than midday. A trip like this doesn't guarantee anything, but your chances of sighting most of the animals are high. Note that open-topped minibuses provide better vantage points than cars.

The park

The first hours of the day are always best for **game-watching**. Ask any ranger on arrival and you'll get the day's results: "Number 13 for a cheetah; two rhinos at 6; lions at number 4 . . .", the numbers referring to the road junctions, marked on every map of the park. Alternatively, just follow your nose. If you're driving around independently, go to the western end, near the main entrance, where most of the woodland is concentrated. This is where you are most likely to see giraffe and, just after dawn, if you're very lucky, a leopard – back perhaps from a nocturnal foray into Langata, hunting for guard dogs (apparently quite a problem). The highest point here, known as **Impala Hill**, is also a **picnic site** (with toilets) and a good spot from which to scan the park with binoculars, but **lions**, usually found in more open country, are better located by checking with the rangers at the gate. There are a few families of **cheetahs** in the park, though you have to be lucky, and seasonal long grass will make seeing them very difficult. It's not so difficult to see some of the park's fifty-odd **rhinos**, however, most often found in the forest glades in the west. This is the largest population anywhere in Kenya, attesting in part to the perseverance of the David Sheldrick Trust.

The Mbagathi/Athi forms the **southern boundary** of the park and is its only permanent river. It's fringed with the yellow acacias that early explorers and settlers dubbed "fever trees" because they seemed to grow in the areas where fever (malaria) was most common. Several of the park's seasonal streams are dammed to regulate the water supply; in the dry season, these **dams** – all located on the northern side of the park where the streams come down off the Embakasi plain – draw the heaviest concentrations of animals. Many of the herds cross the Mbagathi every year and disperse across the Athi plains as the rains improve the pasture, returning to the park during the drought. Before 1946, when the park was opened, only the physical barrier of Nairobi itself diverted the northward migration. The erection of fences along the park's northern perimeter has changed that, but the occasional lion still finds its way up as far as the suburb of Karen.

Birdlife in the park is staggering – a count of more than four hundred species. Enthusiasts won't need priming, and will see rarities from European latitudes as well as the exotics. Even if you're fresh off the plane and ornithologically

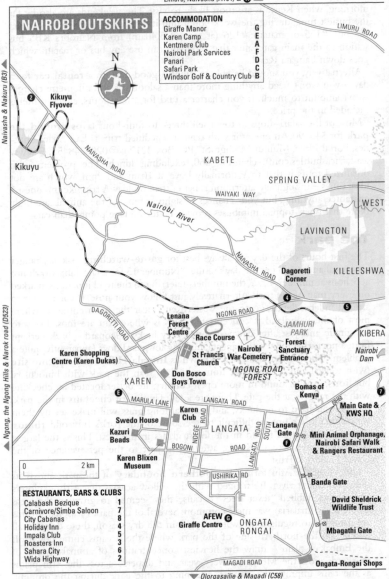

NAIROBI OUTSKIRTS

ACCOMMODATION

Giraffe Manor	G
Karen Camp	E
Kentmere Club	A
Nairobi Park Services	F
Panari	D
Safari Park	C
Windsor Golf & Country Club	B

RESTAURANTS, BARS & CLUBS

Calabash Bezique	1
Carnivore/Simba Saloon	7
City Cabanas	8
Holiday Inn	4
Impala Club	5
Roasters Inn	3
Sahara City	6
Wida Highway	2

illiterate, the first glimpses of ostrich, secretary bird, crowned crane and the outlandishly hideous marabou stork never fail to impress.

If you're looking for a spot to **picnic**, go a couple of kilometres from the main gate, to the first fork. There's a shady site on the left, beside a raised mound of elephant-tusk ash, publicly burned in 1989 by President Moi to mark the start of a major (and astonishingly successful) offensive on ivory poaching and

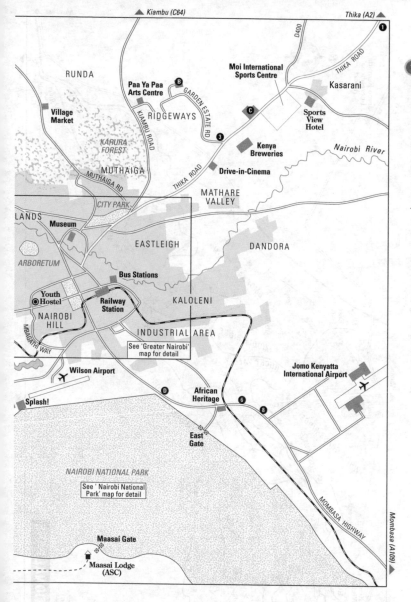

smuggling, led by the then director of the Kenya Wildlife Service, Dr Richard Leakey.

There are two gates out onto the Mombasa road in the east, so you don't have to retrace your route from the park's western end. En route to Cheetah Gate near the town of Athi River is the lovely **Mokoyeti picnic site** (junction 14B), near the "Leopard Cliffs" (junction 15). This route gives you a chance to drive

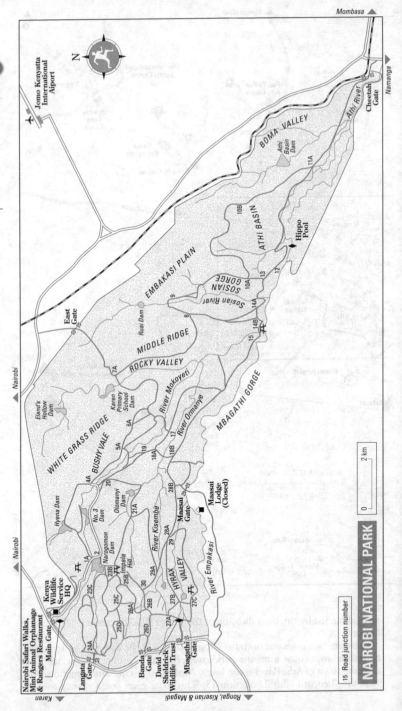

NAIROBI NATIONAL PARK

0   2 km

15 Road junction number

through the open savanna country favoured by **zebra** and **antelope**. There are large herds of introduced **buffalo**, which you can see out here and almost anywhere in the park. **Hippos** can usually be viewed at a pretty pool at the confluence of the Mbagathi and Athi rivers (junction 12), beyond the Leopard Cliffs, which has the added attraction of a **nature trail** and **picnic site** where you can leave the car and disappear into the thickets for closer communion with nature (there's an armed ranger on guard until around 5.30pm). As you're wandering, look out for crocodiles in the river (to an untrained eye little different from submerged logs), and monkeys in the bushes.

The Mini Animal Orphanage and Nairobi Safari Walk

Mainly intended for children, the **Mini Animal Orphanage** (daily 8am–6.30pm; $5) by the park's Main Gate is moderately interesting if you're fed up with seeing animals only from a distance. Here, a motley and shifting collection of waifs and strays, protected from nature, have for some years been allowed to regain strength before being released. That anyway was the idea, though many of the inmates seem to be established residents and it appears doubtful whether "this orphanage is not a zoo", as the sign claims. At least it's a zoo with a difference; there are as many wild monkeys outside the cages as in them.

A better alternative is the **Nairobi Safari Walk**, on the right of the Main Gate before entering the park. It's a showcase of Kenya's vast ecological diversity – the wetlands, the savanna and the woodland/forest found across the country are simulated behind concealed safety barriers to create an intimate environment which is both captivating and informative. This is the closest you come to seeing captive animals behaving as they would in their natural habitat. The boardwalks to the open-air pens, observation points and platforms are clearly signposted and full of useful information about the animals. Also accessible through the walk is **Rangers Restaurant**, recommendable if only because of its comfortable veranda, which is partly in the national park and overlooks a floodlit water hole. There is an extensive menu consisting of African, continental and vegetarian dishes here, and the food is usually good.

The David Sheldrick Wildlife Trust elephant and rhino orphanage

Off the Magadi road, the **David Sheldrick Wildlife Trust** elephant and rhino orphanage (daily 11am–noon; ☎020/891996, ⊛www.sheldrickwildlifetrust .org) offers a chance to see baby elephants, and sometimes baby rhino, that have been orphaned by poachers, lost or abandoned for natural reasons, being cared for. To get there, head south out of town on the Magadi road, and you'll pass the Nairobi National Park's Banda gate on the left; the next gate on the left, some 4.5km from the start of the Magadi road, is the entrance to the Kenya Wildlife Service central workshop. Once through this gate, follow signs for "Sheldrick" to reach the orphanage, which is run by Daphne Sheldrick in memory of her husband, the founding warden of Tsavo National Park; entrance is by donation (Ksh500 is appropriate). During the hour-long open house, the elephant keepers bring their juvenile charges up to an informal rope barrier where you can easily touch them and take photos.

After many years of trial and error, Sheldrick and her staff have become the world's experts on hand-rearing baby elephants, sometimes from birth, using a special milk formula for the youngest infants and assigning keepers to individual 24-hour guardianship of their charges, a responsibility that includes sleeping in their stables. Without the love of a surrogate family and plenty of stimulation, orphaned baby elephants fail to thrive: they can succumb to fatal infections when teething, and, even if they survive, can grow up unhappy and badly prepared for reintroduction to the wild.

Rehabilitation is one of the Sheldrick Trust's major preoccupations. For rhinos, which mature at twice the speed of elephants, this involves a year or more of walks with their keeper, introducing the orphan's scent, via habitual dung middens and "urinal" bushes, to the wild population. Many of Nairobi National Park's rhinos grew up in the Sheldrick nursery; the last surviving member of Amboseli's famous long-horned rhino herd was rescued by the Trust in 1987 and is now a successful breeding female, having been released in Tsavo East. In the case of elephants, which mature at about the same rate as humans, the process of reintroduction is more attuned to the individual: outgoing animals are encouraged while young to meet wild friends and potential adoptive mothers, again through walks with their keepers, most often in Tsavo National Park. More traumatized elephants take longer to find their feet: matriarchs who were Sheldrick orphans themselves, such as Eleanor at Tsavo East, have been responsible for adopting many returnees.

The Bomas of Kenya

Forest Edge Road, at the junction with Langata and Magadi roads, 1km past National Park Main Gate; from city centre, bus/matatu #15, #125 or #126; performances Mon–Fri 2.30–4pm, Sat, Sun & holidays 3.30–5.15pm; Ksh600, students/children Ksh30; ⊕020/891801–2.

The **Bomas of Kenya** were originally an attempt to create a living museum of indigenous Kenyan life, with a display of eleven traditional homesteads (*bomas*) and an emphasis on regional dances. Unfortunately, the place has always had a heavily touristy feel, not helped by its huge indoor amphitheatre where the dances are performed. Its vitality is channelled mainly into souvenir-selling. The homesteads (a guided tour is included in the price), representing the architectural styles of Kenya's people, are for the most part sadly unkempt. Even so, if you're looking to fill an afternoon, or you want a change from the national park, they can be enjoyable enough, particularly on weekends when they're crowded and a disco follows the dance show.

Surprisingly, perhaps, the dances are not performed by the appropriate Kenyan nationalities; instead, the **Harambee Dancers** do fast costume changes between acts and present the nation's traditional repertoire as professionals rather than participants. If the sound system were good, the acoustics bearable and the whole place less of an amphitheatre, the impression would undoubtedly be better, but at least you do get a very comprehensive taste of Kenyan dance styles, from the mesmeric jumps and sinuous movements of the Maa-speaking peoples to the wild acrobatics of some of the Mijikenda dances.

AFEW Giraffe Centre

Although promoted as a children's outing, the **AFEW Giraffe Centre** (daily 9am–5.30pm; Ksh500, children Ksh250; ⊕020/891658) on Koitobos Road, 3km off Langata Road (signposted), has serious intentions. Run by the African Fund for Endangered Wildlife, it has successfully boosted the population of the rare Rothschild's giraffe from the original nucleus of animals which came from the wild herd near Soy (see p.322), and educates children about conservation. You'll get some great mug shots from the giraffe-level observation tower, where the giraffes push their huge heads through to be fed by pellets offered by the

△ The Giraffe Centre

visitors. There are various other animals around, including a number of tame warthogs and a fine new wooden "Safari Walk". If you really like it here, and have money to burn, stay overnight at the wonderful, Scottish-style **Giraffe Manor** (p.121).

Karen

Until recently, **KAREN** was the quintessential white suburb – five-acre plots spaciously set on eucalyptus-lined avenues amid fields grazed by ponies. But the number of African homes is steadily increasing. Still separated from Nairobi by a dwindling patch of dense, bird-filled woodland, the Ngong Road Forest, Karen is a reminder of how completely the settlers visualized and created little Europes for themselves. In Karen you could almost be in the English shires – or, for that matter, northern California.

If you're driving the more direct way to Karen from the city, along Ngong Road, you pass **Jamhuri Park** (the Agricultural Society of Kenya showground, see p.72), the **Nairobi War Cemetery** and the **racecourse**. The World War II cemetery is a peaceful and dignified place, set far back from the busy road among shady trees, with pink stone and carefully tended lawns. Buses to Karen include the #111 (fast) from the KBS bus station and the interminable bus or matatu #24.

The Karen **shopping centre** (aka Karen *dukas*), at the crossroads of Langata and Ngong roads, includes the mock-Tudor *Horseman Restaurant* (see p.142), branches of Barclays and Standard Chartered banks, both with ATMs, a forex bureau, and an arty riding-tack and gift shop.

Karen Blixen Museum and Swedo House

Bus #24 can drop you at the **Karen Blixen National Museum**, Karen Road (daily 9.30am–6pm; Ksh200, children Ksh100; ☎020/882779), the house where much of the action of Karen Blixen's *Out of Africa* took place. The epitome of colonial Africa, it was presented to Kenya by the Danish government as an Uhuru gift, along with the agricultural college built in the grounds. It's a beautiful, well-proportioned house with square, wood-panelled rooms; the restoration of its original appearance and furnishings has evidently been very thorough. The gardens, laid out as in former times, are delightful. A guided tour is included in the price but can be somewhat rushed, especially at weekends, and there's no guarantee that they'll let you wander around on your own. On weekends, too, you may be suffocated by Mozart and tour groups complaining about how little Denys Finch Hatton resembles Robert Redford. An organized tour from town, which may include the AFEW Giraffe Centre, costs anything from $45 to $70.

The fake-1920s Nairobi that was built nearby for the shooting of *Out of Africa* would have been a more magnetic attraction than the museum house. The dictates of licensing agreements ensured its demolition once the film crews left. Just up the road towards Karen shopping centre is **Swedo House**, an old Swedish coffee plantation manager's residence, built in 1912. It's stuffed with archetypal colonial memorabilia and fittings, but is usually closed to the public, though the grounds are delightful. There's a bar and restaurant here, the *Karen Blixen Coffee Garden* (daily 9.30am–11pm), with tables in the gardens under the trees; the food is variable, but the Sunday buffet lunch (Ksh700) remains popular. There's also a craft shop, although much better local handicrafts can be bought at the nearby **Kazuri Bead Centre**, behind Hillcrest School (see p.133 for more details). Incidentally, the suburb was not named after Karen Blixen (who went by the name Tania von Blixen when in Kenya) as is popularly supposed, but her cousin, Karen Melchior, whose father was the chairman of the Karen Coffee Company Ltd.

The Ngong Hills

Ngong village, the jumping-off point for the **Ngong Hills** ahead, is 8km past Karen shopping centre (bus #111 every 30min, every 20min at weekends; sometimes bus #126, but you might have to change at Kiserian); turn right after the police station in Ngong. If you have the chance, stop on the way at **Bulbul** and take a look at the pretty mosque of this largely Muslim village. Islam spread here through the settlement of discharged troops from other British-ruled territories (in this case Sudanese Nubia), as often happened in Kenya. Ngong itself is basically just a small junction town with limited shops and services and the rough D523 road trailing out to the right towards the Maasai Mara.

The hills are revered by the Maasai, who have several traditional explanations of how they were formed. The best known says that a giant, stumbling north with his head in the clouds, tripped on Kilimanjaro. Thundering to the ground, his hand squeezed the earth into the Ngongs' familiar, knuckled outline. An even more momentous story explains the Ngongs as the bits of earth left under God's fingernails after he'd finished creating.

The walk along their sharp spine was once a popular day's hike and picnic outing. The views, of Nairobi on one side and the Rift Valley on the other, are magnificent, and the forested slopes are still inhabited by buffalo and antelope. Unfortunately, the number of attacks and robberies of unwary walkers has discouraged people, Kenyans included, and the north side is considered especially dangerous. The Kenya Wildlife Service will provide a wildlife ranger as an escort (Ksh500 for 3hr). Women travelling without men are, as usual, at a disadvantage. With a car (4WD if it's been raining), you can get to the summit, **Point Lamwia** (2459m), which offers a 360-degree view. Down on the lower ridges on privately owned land, almost due east of the highest point, is the **Finch Memorial** (Ksh100 entrance fee), Karen Blixen's tribute to the man who took her flying.

Moving on from Nairobi

Getting out of Nairobi by public transport is normally a fairly haphazard business. The following is intended to lend a degree of structure to a chaotic scene. If in doubt, ask: you'll always get where you want to, somehow.

Matatus for different destinations congregate in different areas of town, the most useful of which are listed in "Travel details" below, with reference to chapters in this book. Be warned, however, that the locations change fairly frequently – ask around, and remember, the suicidal reputation attached to matatus is by no means entirely the result of paranoia. Matatus to Nakuru, Naivasha and Thika have a particularly bad reputation.

Slower, cheaper and generally safer than matatus are the **bus services** which cover almost all of Kenya. The smaller companies operate out of the **Country Bus Station** (aka "Machakos Airport"), 1500m east of the city centre just past Wakulima market, between Pumwani Road and Landhies Road (buses #4, #18 or #28 from the *Ambassadeur*). The larger companies have booking offices in various locations around River Road (see p.153), from where most of their services operate. Most services will sell seats to towns on the way, when space permits. Seats should, if possible, be reserved in advance at the bus offices. A couple of **warnings** about buses and bus stations. Drugging of food, drink, cigarettes and chewing gum has been reported – do not accept such gifts, even at the risk of giving offence, nor leave your own stuff unattended. Secondly, as the most useful services often leave at night, take a taxi to the bus station or hire an *askari* from your hotel rather than walk unaccompanied with your luggage.

Shared taxis, usually Peugeot station wagons displaying destination boards, are faster, cost roughly twice as much and cover all the main towns in the centre and west of the country (chapters 2–4). They're best caught around 8am on Accra Road or Ronald Ngala Street.

With overnight services to Mombasa and to Kisumu, the **train station** (☎020/221211 ext 2700 or 2701) is at the south end of Moi Avenue, beyond the bustle and confusion of the railway matatu stage. It's important to make **reservations**, especially if you want a first-class compartment. While it may be fine to leave this until a couple of hours before departure during the low season, it's advisable to reserve well in advance during the busy Christmas and New Year period when trains are often full.

Driving out of Nairobi, allow plenty of time to get clear of the city traffic. Nairobi has no ring road or bypass – all vehicles, including trans-continental trucks, go through the city centre. If you make an early start from Westlands or Karen, for example, bound for the coast or Mount Kenya, you're often bumper to bumper for more than an hour before getting under way. A small accident can cause huge problems for the whole day.

By air

International flights and **internal Kenya Airways** services leave from Jomo Kenyatta International Airport (☎020/822111 or 822206, ⓦwww.kenya airports.co.ke). Remember to **reconfirm** flight reservations and also try to check that the plane is scheduled to arrive on time (see "Listings", p.152, for airline details). To get to the airport, take the KBS Stagecoach #34 bus (Ksh20 from the *Ambassadeur Hotel*, Ksh30 from the *Youth Hostel*; 6am–8pm every 20min) or, after 8pm, a taxi, costing around Ksh1000 if you pick one up on the street. All hotels can arrange a taxi, or contact one of the travel agents listed on p.155. Always check in with time to spare – overbookings are commonplace.

Wilson Airport (☎020/501941–3) has regular scheduled services within Kenya (and to the Kilimanjaro region in Tanzania), and unscheduled flights into Somalia and the Democratic Republic of Congo. Get to the airport on bus or matatu #15, #24, #31, #34, #125 or #126, alighting at the BP station (it's on your left). Note that several internal operators here have a 10kg baggage allowance ($1 per kilo above this limit is the usual surcharge), although a blind eye is sometimes turned. If you're in the market for **chartering a plane**, see the "airlines, internal" listing on p.152. There are also about a dozen commercial and NGO aviation companies who may take passengers, all with offices at Wilson Airport. Some flights are advertised in the *Nation* and *The People*. Among these are Eagle Aviation (for Lamu, Mombasa, Malindi and Zanzibar), East African Air Charters (Tsavo West) and Trackmark (Lokichokio).

Bunson Travel Group (☎020/221992, ⓦwww.bunson.co.ke) publishes a free comprehensive **timetable** of all scheduled national and international flights from Nairobi, while Let's Go Travel (see p.150) has a handy list of flights within Kenya and for Zanzibar. The *Nation* publishes a timetable of flights in and out of JKI every Friday.

Travel details

Trains

Nairobi to: Kisumu (3 weekly; 14hr); Mombasa (3 weekly; 14hr); Naivasha (3 weekly; 2hr 30 min); Nakuru (3 weekly; 7hr); Voi (3 weekly; 9hr).

Buses

Most of the services below operate from the Country Bus Station – or "Machakos Airport". For bus company booking offices, see "Listings", p.153.

Chapter 2: The Central Highlands

A continual stream of buses leaves for Thika (45min) and destinations in Kiambu district. The most frequent runs are provided by Sunbird Services, with almost hourly departures to Maua via Embu (2hr 30min), Chogoria (3hr 30min) and Meru (4–5hr). Kensilver runs comfortable 25-seater minibuses to Meru via Chogoria. Akamba covers all the main destinations, usually only once or twice a day. Smaller companies operate to Nanyuki (3hr 30min) and Nyeri (2hr 30min). Services to Nyahururu are relatively infrequent, usually via Gilgil (chapter 3).

Chapter 3: The Rift Valley

There are a couple of daily buses to Magadi and Olorgasailie. Many buses call at Naivasha (1hr 30min) en route for points west, including Nakuru. Mololine and Easy Coach services, both departing from the depot on Haile Selassie Ave, go to Nakuru (frequent; 2–3hr). Nakuru is also covered by most westbound (chapter 4) services.

Chapter 4: Western Kenya

Akamba and Easy Coach are the main companies, with several daily and overnight departures to most locations. Other buses run to Kakamega (several daily; 7–9hr), Kericho (several daily; 5hr) and Kisumu (several daily; 6hr). Eldoret Express have frequent runs to Eldoret (5hr) and Kitale (7–9hr).

Chapter 5: The Mombasa Road and major game parks

There are a few services daily to Machakos (1hr), Kitui (2hr), Namanga (2hr), Narok (5hr) and Isiolo (5hr).

Chapter 6: The coast

Competition is fierce over the Nairobi–Mombasa route, with reputations tarnished all round and accidents not uncommon. Safest of the lot is

Akamba. Other companies include Coast Bus, MASH, Randa Coach, Busscar and Falcon Coach. Most companies run at least two buses a day and one at night (Nairobi–Mombasa takes around 9hr). It's hard to decide which is worse – arriving after dark or driving all night.

Chapter 7: The north

With the dangers inherent in travel there, the north sees only a few matatus; some people hitch rides on cattle tracks.

Tanzania

Apart from regular public buses run by Akamba to Arusha (4hr 30min) and Dar es Salaam (13hr), more comfortable (and expensive, around Ksh1000–2000) coaches to Arusha and Moshi are operated twice daily by Davanu Shuttle, Riverside, Scandinavian Express and the very plush (you can even choose your seat online) Impala Shuttle. Pick-ups are from the *Norfolk* and *Stanley*, and occasionally other hotels.

Uganda

Malaba is served by buses from the Country Bus Station (Ksh550). Akamba runs both day and night services via Busia to Kampala (12hr; tickets from Ksh1000), as do Regional Bus Services, Falcon Coach and Scandinavian Express.

Matatus and shared taxis

Chapter 2: The Central Highlands

Accra Rd between River Rd and Duruma Rd to: Embu (2hr–2hr 30min).
Accra Rd/River Rd to: Karatina (2hr); Nyeri (3hr).
Accra Rd between River Rd and Tsavo Rd to: Meru (4hr 30min); Mwea (5hr 30min); Nanyuki (4hr).
Latema Rd to: Nyahururu (3hr).
Ronald Ngala St (by the BP station) to: Thika (40min).

Chapter 3: The Rift Valley

Duruma Rd (*Nyamakima Bar*) to: Gilgil (1hr 30min); Naivasha (1hr); Nakuru (2hr).
Train station stage to: Magadi (2hr).

Chapter 4: Western Kenya

Accra Rd/Dubois Rd (Peugeot shared taxis) to: Bungoma(6hr); Busia (7hr); Eldoret (5hr); Kakamega (7hr); Kericho (6hr); Kisii (7–9hr); Kisumu (5–6hr); Kitale (5hr).

Accra Rd/River Rd to: Eldoret (4hr).
Duruma Rd (*Nyamakima Bar*) to: Eldoret (4hr);
Kitale (5–7hr).

Chapter 5: The Mombasa Road and major game parks

Country bus station (from car park just to the north) to: Machakos (1hr).
Duruma Rd (*Nyamakima Bar*) to: Narok (2hr 30min).
Ronald Ngala St to: Kajiado (1hr); Namanga (3hr).

Chapter 6: The coast

There are no direct matatus to the coast.

Chapter 7: The north

Accra Rd between River Rd and Duruma Rd to: Isiolo (4hr 30min–6hr).
Accra Rd/River Rd to: Archers Post (6hr).
Duruma Rd (*Nyamakima Bar*) to: Maralal (6hr).

Flights

JKI airport (Kenya Airways only) to: Kisumu (1 or 2 daily; 1hr); Lamu (1 daily; 1hr 45min); Malindi (1 daily; 1hr 10min); Mombasa (at least 6 daily; 1hr–1hr 15min).

Wilson Airport to: Amboseli lodges (Airkenya and SafariLink; 2 daily; roughly 45min); Eldoret (AeroKenya; 1–2 daily; 1hr) ; Kilimanjaro (Tanzania; Airkenya and SafariLink; 2 daily; 1hr 25min); Kiwaiyu (Airkenya and SafariLink; daily; 1hr 45min); Lamu (Manda Island; Airkenya and SafariLink; 2 daily; 1hr 45min); Lewa Downs (Airkenya and SafariLink; 3 daily; 1hr); Lokichokio (Aircraft Leasing Services; 4 weekly); Maasai Mara lodges (Airkenya and SafariLink; 4 daily; roughly 45min depending on lodge); Malindi (Airkenya; 3 weekly; 1hr 15min); Meru (Airkenya; 3 weekly; 50 min; $190); Naivasha (SafariLink; 1 daily; 30min); Nanyuki (Airkenya and SafariLink; 3 daily); Samburu (Airkenya and SafarLink; and 3 daily; 1hr 35min); Tsavo lodges (SafariLink; 1 daily; 50 min).

The Central Highlands

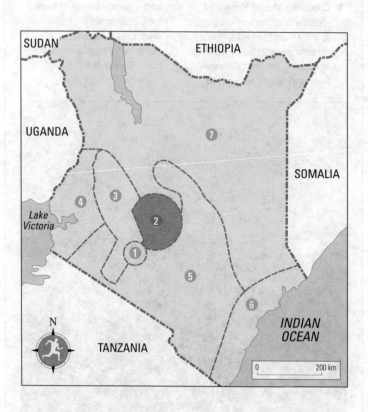

CHAPTER 2 Highlights

* **Tree-hotels** Three to choose from – the original *Treetops*, its upstart competitor *The Ark*, and the less vaunted, more spacious *Mountain Lodge*, which also has some of the best wildlife. See p.178 & p.210

* **Climbing Mount Kenya** Africa's second-highest mountain is a memorable and highly recommended climb, with various routes and diverse flora and fauna. See p.180

* **Laikipia eco-lodges** Visiting one of the private game sanctuaries in this high plains region is highly recommended for seeing rhinos, even introduced chimpanzees. See p.205

* **Aberdares** Sensational views and a good chance of seeing large mammals (including elephants and lions) in a compelling, highland environment. See p.206

△ Mount Kenya, seen from Laikipia

2

The Central Highlands

As the political and economic heartland of the country, the **Central Highlands** stand at the focal point of Kenyan history. Mount Kenya, Africa's second-highest peak, gave the colonial nation its name, and the majority of British and European settlers carved their farms from the countryside around it. Later, and as a direct consequence, it was this region which saw the development of organized anti-colonial resistance culminating in Mau Mau.

Until independence, the fertile highland soils ("A more charming region is not to be found in all Africa," thought Joseph Thomson, exploring in the 1880s) were reserved largely for Europeans and considered, in Governor Eliot's breathtaking phrase, "White Man's Country". The **Kikuyu peoples** were skilled farmers and herders who had held the land for centuries before the Europeans arrived. They were at first mystified to find themselves "squatters" on land whose ownership, in the sense of exclusive right, had never been an issue in traditional society. They were certainly not alone in losing land but, by supplying most of the fighters for the Land and Freedom Army (see Contexts, p.612), they were placed squarely in the political limelight. In return, they have received a large proportion of what Kenyans call the "Fruits of Independence". Today, most of the land is in African hands again, and it supports the country's largest rural population. There's intensive farming on almost all the lower slopes, as well as much of the higher ground, beneath the **national parks** of **Mount Kenya** and the **Aberdares**.

There are considerable rewards in travel through the Highlands. Above all, if you're into hiking, there's the ascent of Mount Kenya. And, while hikes lower down and in the Aberdare range are easier, they are scarcely less dramatic, with the bonus of a chance to see some of the highland **wildlife**. The mountain streams are full of the trout that were introduced early last century, and most tourist lodges will rent out **fishing** tackle. Another great draw is the **Laikipia plateau**, spanning eight thousand square kilometres of wild savanna in the shadow of Mount Kenya. Second in wildlife density only to Maasai Mara, it boasts more endangered species than anywhere else in Kenya.

Nor is travel itself ever dull in the Highlands, where the range of scenery is a spectacular draw in its own right: primary-coloured **jungle** and **shambas**, pale, windswept **moors** and dense **conifer plantations**, all with a mountain backdrop. People everywhere are friendly and quick to strike up a conversation, the

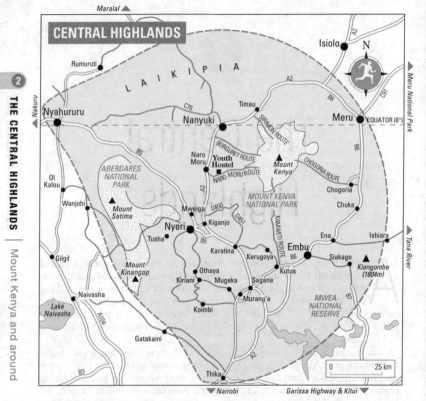

CENTRAL HIGHLANDS

Maralal

Isiolo

N

Meru National Park

Rumuruti

L A I K I P I A

Nakuru

Nyahururu

Timau

A2

C76

Nanyuki

Meru

EQUATOR (0°)

B6

B6

Meru National Park

SIRIMON ROUTE

Naro Moru
Youth Hostel

BURGURET ROUTE

Mount Kenya

CHOGORIA ROUTE

NARO MORU ROUTE

ABERDARES NATIONAL PARK

MOUNT KENYA NATIONAL PARK

Chogoria

Chuka

Tana River

Ol Kalou

Wanjohi

Mount Satima

Mweiga

Kiganjo

D450

D451

KAMWETI ROUTE

Ena

Ishiara

Nyeri

B5

Tusha

Karatina

Kerugoya

Embu

Siakago

Kiangombe (1804m)

Gilgil

Mount Kinangop

Othaya

Mugeka

Kutus

Kiriani

Sagana

MWEA NATIONAL RESERVE

Naivasha

Koimbi

Murang'a

Lake Naivasha

A104

B3

Gatakaini

0   25 km

Nairobi

Garissa Highway & Kitui

towns are animated and markets colourfully chaotic. **Public transport** is good, too, and bus journeys invariably packed with interest and amusement. There's a wide range of reasonably priced **accommodation**, and a handful of tourist hotels and lodges – including the famous *Treetops* – that will give fair return for your cash if you're in the mood to splurge.

Mount Kenya and around

After the main game-viewing areas and the coast, the circuit provided by the **Kirinyaga ring road** is one of the most travelled in Kenya. While it's not overcrowded or really touristy, there are always a few safari minibuses to be seen somewhere on the road and other signs that the tourist industry up here is growing. Apart from the high forests, moors and peaks, little of this remains wild country, with *shambas* steadily encroaching the ridges and the burgeoning

Ancestors of the **Kikuyu** migrated to the Central Highlands between the sixteenth and eighteenth centuries, from northeast of Mount Kenya. Stories describe how they found various hunter-gatherer peoples already in the region (the **Gumba** on the plains and the **Athi** in the forests), and a great deal of intermarriage, trade and adoption took place. The newcomers cleared the forests and planted crops, giving the hunters gifts of livestock, honey, or wives in return for using the land. As this Bantu-speaking, cultivating, livestock-keeping culture expanded, the indigenous peoples gradually lost their old identities.

Likewise there was trade and intermarriage between the Kikuyu and the **Maasai**, though relations between these two peoples were less easy. They both placed (and still place) high value on the ownership of cattle, the Maasai depending entirely on livestock. During bad droughts, Maasai might raid their Kikuyu neighbours' herds, with retaliation at a later date being almost inevitable. But such **intertribal warfare** often had long-term benefits, as ancient debts were forever being renegotiated and paid off by both sides, thus sustaining the relationship. Married Kikuyu women enjoyed a special immunity enabling them to organize trading expeditions deep into Maasai-land, often with the help of a *hinga*, a middleman, to oil the wheels. As well as economic and social relations, the Kikuyu had close **cultural affinities** with the Maasai. Like them, the Kikuyu advanced in status as they grew older, through named age-sets and rituals still important today. A Kikuyu who discovers you're both the same age is likely to say, "We're age mates then!"

Circumcision still marks the important transition into adulthood for most Kikuyu males. Men who haven't been circumcised are not accorded the same respect as those who have, and can be denied the right to marry or to be included in social gatherings. Female circumcision (clitoridectomy) is illegal and performed less and less, though reluctance to talk about it makes estimating just how widespread it still is difficult. In the past, the operations were accompanied by changes in dress and ornament. Boys grew their hair and dyed it with ochre in the style of Maasai warriors (in fact, the Maasai got their ochre from the Kikuyu, so it may really be the other way around). They also wore glass beads around their necks, metal rings on their legs and arms, and pulled their ear lobes out with ear plugs. Women wore a similar collection of ornaments and, between initiation and marriage, a headband of beads and discs, still worn today by most Maasai women.

Traditionally, the Kikuyu had no centralized **authority**, no tribal or clan leaders; "chiefs" were only installed by the colonial administration. When disputes had to be settled or far-reaching decisions made, the elders of a district would meet as a council and the matter would be cleared up in public, with a party to follow. After their deaths, elders – as ancestors – continued to be respected and consulted.

The Kikuyu traditionally believed that the most likely abode of Ngai or Mwininyaga (God), or at least his frequent resting place, was **Kirinyaga** (Place of Brightness), Mount Kenya. Accordingly, they used to build their houses with the door always looking out towards the mountain – hence the title of Jomo Kenyatta's book, *Facing Mount Kenya*. Christianity has altered beliefs in the last few decades, though many church-goers still believe strongly in an **ancestor world** where the dead have powers for good and bad over their living descendants because of their closeness to Ngai.

Today, the Kikuyu remain in the forefront of Kenyan development. Despite sometimes being associated with nepotism, they are accorded respect as successful business people and formidable politicians, especially with the election of Mwai Kibaki, who hails from Nyeri, as president in December 2002.

of small towns into larger ones, but the Kikuyu, Meru and Embu have created an extraordinary spectacle of cultivation on the steep slopes, gashed by the road to reveal brilliant red earth.

As you travel, you're also aware of the looming presence of the mountain. With a base 80km across, **Mount Kenya** is one of the largest free-standing volcanic cones in the world. The twin peaks – always distant when visible from the road – are normally obscured by clouds, but early in the morning and just before sunset, the shroud can vanish suddenly, leaving them magically exposed for a few minutes. To the east and south, the mountain slopes steeply away to the broad expanse of Ukambani (Akambaland) and the Tana River basin. Westward, and to the north, it drops more gently to the rolling uplands of Laikipia, drier than the east and for the most part treeless.

Getting here is an easy trip from Nairobi up a busy road. If you're not driving, you could buy a bus ticket from Nairobi direct to any of the towns in this section, or make **Thika** or **Murang'a** a first destination before heading around the mountain. **Naro Moru**, the usual base for climbing Mount Kenya, lies on the west side some 25km south of **Nanyuki**, an alternative base for a climb from the north. On the eastern slopes, **Chogoria**, between **Meru** and **Embu**, offers arguably the finest route up the mountain.

Thika and around

Despite the literary connection – Elspeth Huxley's *The Flame Trees of Thika* – and being the first major town on the way from Nairobi to Mount Kenya, **THIKA** is a dull little place, not even redeemed by the profusion of flame trees you might expect. These days, it's essentially a satellite of Nairobi. Pineapples, introduced in 1905, are Thika's contemporary claim to fame. Thousands of acres flourish here, easily confused with the sisal also grown in the area. Until 1968, most of the valuable export crop was produced on *shambas*; since then Del Monte has held the lion's share of the plantations.

A laid-back, friendly sort of place, Thika is off the tourist route – or at least the main road to Mount Kenya. You can get here using matatu #237 from the Kencom Building in Nairobi, and there are also Thika matatus from the BP station on Ronald Ngala Street. Thika has Barclays and Standard Chartered **banks** with ATMs, and **Internet access** at Mbambu Cyber Café on Uhuru Street. There are Mathai **supermarkets** in Thika Arcade and a couple of streets west of Kwame Nkrumah Street; the **market** is east of town, past the thriving street stalls at the stadium roundabout.

The best-value **accommodation** is *New Fulia Hotel*, Uhuru Street (PO Box 1161; ℡067/21840; ❷) which has s/c rooms; also good is its sister hotel the *New Fulia 1987* on Kwame Nkrumah Street. Other slightly more expensive possibilities include *December Hotel*, Commercial Street (PO Box 156; ℡067/22140; ❸), whose enormous rooms have telephones (ask for s/c), and *White Line Hotel*, Stadium Road (PO Box 290; ℡067/22857; ❷), which is acceptable and has a lively bar, though the single rooms are non-s/c. The upmarket choice, out of town on the Nairobi–Murang'a road, is ⚲ *Blue Posts Hotel* (PO Box 42; ℡ & ℻067/22241 or 21086; ❺), which is older than the town itself, dating from 1908. The old place has been refurbished and rooms in the Chania wing are excellent, en suite and with balconies overlooking lush gardens. The grounds contain both the Chania Falls and the Thika Falls – with a five-minute walk between the two.

The *Blue Posts'* **restaurant** has a sweeping view of the Chania Falls and good lunchtime buffets for Ksh600. Restaurants in town include the relatively swish (and expensive) *Prismos Hotel*, MTC Building, Uhuru Street; the *New Fulia's* bar-restaurant, which is a deal cheaper; *New Fish World*, which has great fresh tilapia and squeezed juices; and good local eats at *Golden Plate* and *Porkies Garden*. For a decent cup of **coffee** (the plantations around Thika are the nearest to Nairobi), the *December Hotel* has a great Parisian-style pavement café which was opened by Kenyatta himself in December 1970.

Foot-tappers should try out *NK Bar* on Kwame Nkrumah Street, which plays **Congolese music** and **reggae**, sometimes live. Otherwise, the *Cascades Disco* at the *Blue Posts* entertains Nairobi clubbers, while heavy-duty drinkers can fade away at *Sky Motel Day & Night Club* or the less-than-sparkling *Brilliant Bar*, another good place to meet inebriated locals. More dignified clubbing can be had at Thika Sports Club, Bendor Road, which has a **golf course** set amid the pineapple and coffee plantations. The clubhouse is unusually rustic, with a large fireplace and wooden beams running along the ceiling.

The Fourteen Falls and Ol Doinyo Sapuk National Park

From Thika, the trip out to tiny **Ol Doinyo Sapuk National Park** and **Fourteen Falls** on the Athi River is a popular one with motorized travellers and Nairobi weekenders. For either site, head for Kilima Mbogo village, some 22km down the Garissa road. There are matatus here from Thika's "U Shops" stage by the stadium. If you're lucky, the matatu might carry on to Ol Doinyo Sapuk village ("Doinyo"), 2.5km off to the right down a dirt track, which passes close to the entrance to the falls and is some 2km from the national park gate. Doinyo village, itself, is surprisingly busy, with dozens of *dukas*, bars and lodges.

Ten minutes' walk from Doinyo village down a very dusty track, **Fourteen Falls** (daily 9am–5pm; Ksh150, children Ksh100, vehicles Ksh200, cameras Ksh150) is a broad cascade of white water which plunges 30m over a precipice with many lips, hence the name. The falls are especially spectacular after rain, when they flood into a single, thundering red cataract, though a vague, obnoxious smell hangs in the air, presumably caused by effluent from Thika's emerging industries. There are no hotels hereabouts, but you can **camp** or stay in spartan but dirt-cheap *bandas* at the council-run *Fourteen Falls Campsite* on the Athi River, for which you theoretically need YHA membership (camping Ksh50 per person; *bandas* Ksh100 per person).

Ol Doinyo Sapuk National Park

Daily 6am–6pm; $15, children $5; vehicle entry Ksh200; camping from $5. Warden: PO Box 1514, Thika. Map: Survey of Kenya SK113, 1990.

Seen from a distance, **Ol Doinyo Sapuk** (Maasai for Big Mountain), or Kilima Mbogo (Kikuyu for Buffalo Mountain), is not the most inspiring of hulks, nor is it high in Kenyan terms, rising to 2146m. Its attractions only become apparent when you approach the gate, as the dry scrubland gives way to redder soil, forest and cooler air. The national park encloses the entirety of the mountain, and surrounding the summit is a primal forest with some of the giant plants, notably the lobelia *giberroa*, associated with the Afro-alpine zones of mounts Kenya, Elgon and Kilimanjaro. Birdlife is diverse, though the mammals – a few leopards, buffaloes, sykes' and colobus monkeys and porcupines – make themselves scarce in the thick vegetation. Watch out for snakes, too.

The **national park gate** is reached by crossing the Athi river, then taking a (signposted) right turn at the end of Kilima Mbogo village. The gate is 3km further on, and is the only place where you're allowed to camp (park fees are payable). At the seven-kilometre mark, you come to the grave of Sir William Northrup MacMillan, the fattest of famous settlers, whose intended burial place on the summit had to be abandoned when the modified tractor-hearse's clutch burned out. He rests here with his wife, maid and dog. Views from the spot are tremendous and you're not likely to get further in a vehicle, even with four-wheel drive, because the final couple of kilometres of track is particularly bad.

Between the MacMillans' graves and just below the summit, the track winds through dense forest cover. If you make it to the top, the 360-degree panorama over a huge oxbow in the Athi River, Thika's pineapple fields and mounts Kenya and Kilimanjaro can be wonderful in December and January, when the air is really clear. **Walking** the 9km to the summit, long prohibited for security reasons (large numbers of buffalo, and sporadic incidents of banditry up to 1997), requires that you take an armed ranger with you (Ksh300 per person for half a day, Ksh500 per person for a whole day).

Murang'a

Established as the administrative outpost of **Fort Hall** in 1900, **MURANG'A** has since come to be thought of as the "Kikuyu Homeland" because of its proximity to Mukuruwe wa Nyagathanga, the "Garden of Eden of the Kikuyu". Here, in Kikuyu mythology, God made husbands for the nine daughters of Gikuyu and Mumbi, spiritual ancestors of all the Kikuyu people. The husbands, who became the ancestors of the nine Kikuyu clans, were found by Gikuyu under a large fig tree. Take a matatu to **Mugeka** and walk from there to Gakuyu village if you'd like to see the site. The original *mukuruwe* (fig tree) disappeared long ago. Colonel Richard Meinertzhagen, an officer in the King's African Rifles, posted here in 1902, found time (when not shooting animals – or people) to write, "If white settlement really takes hold in this country it

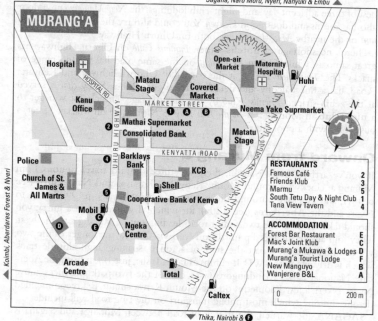

MURANG'A

Hospital ✚

Open-air Market

Maternity Hospital ✚

Huhi

Matatu Stage

Covered Market

HOSPITAL RD

Kanu Office

MARKET STREET

❶ Ⓐ Ⓑ

Neema Yake Suprmarket

UHURU HIGHWAY

❷

Mathai Supermarket

Consolidated Bank

❸

Matatu Stage

Barklays Bank

KENYATTA ROAD

❹

KCB

N

Police

Church of St. James & All Martrs ✝

❺

Shell

Cooperative Bank of Kenya

C71

Mobil

Ⓒ

Ⓔ

Ngeka Centre

Ⓓ

Arcade Centre

Total

Caltex

RESTAURANTS	
Famous Café	2
Friends Klub	3
Marmu	5
South Tetu Day & Night Club	1
Tana View Tavern	4

ACCOMMODATION	
Forest Bar Restaurant	E
Mac's Joint Klub	C
Murang'a Mukawa & Lodges	D
Murang'a Tourist Lodge	F
New Manguyo	B
Wanjerere B&L	A

0   200 m

▼ Thika, Nairobi & Ⓕ

is bound to do so at the expense of the Kikuyu who own the best land, and I foresee much trouble." That said, Meinertzhagen helped put down some of this trouble, launching "punitive expeditions" from Fort Hall with his African troops.

At the beginning of the twentieth century, Fort Hall consisted of "two grass huts within a stone wall and a ditch". Fort Hall itself was never a settlers' town: the district was outside the zone earmarked for white colonization and most of it comprised the "Kikuyu reserve". Present-day Murang'a, perched above the busy main road, remains a small but expanding commercial centre, strewn with litter – a happy enough place, bustling energetically. In the **CPK Cathedral** (formerly the Church of St James and All Martyrs) hangs an unusual *Life of Christ* mural sequence, depicting the Nativity, Baptism, Last Supper, Gethsemane and Crucifixion of an African Christ in an African landscape. The murals were painted by the Tanzanian artist Elimo Njau in 1955 – the year the church was founded by the Archbishop of Canterbury – as a memorial to the thousands of Kikuyu victims of Mau Mau attacks.

Practicalities

Co-operative Bank has an ATM, and there is an **Internet café** in the Arcade Centre on Uhuru Highway. The western end of Market Street has a Mathai **supermarket**. Recommended **lodgings** include *Murang'a Mukawa & Lodges* on Uhuru Highway (PO Box 207; ☎060/30778; B&B ❷), with nets in the bedrooms and a great terrace bar with views over the hills; and *Murang'a Tourist Lodge*, 2km down the Thika road (PO Box 552; ☎060/30307; ❷), with airier rooms and nets, but breakfast costs extra. *Wanjerere B&L* on Market Street (PO Box 243 ☎062/22527; ❷) is very basic but has a pleasant courtyard, and is the best of three adjacent day-and-night-club lodgings; the *New Manguyo* next door also has rooms and does good *kienyeji*. You could also try the *Forest Bar Restaurant* or the nearby *Mac's Joint Klub*, both on Uhuru Highway.

There's no shortage of **hotelis** either. *Famous Café* on Uhuru Highway has great samosas, while *Marmu Restaurant* on the same road has a good range of snacks. The *Tana View Tavern*, at the corner of Uhuru Highway and Kenyatta Road, has a fine balcony and decent curried goat dishes. Spicy *chai* is served at the zebra-striped *Friends' Klub* by the matatu stage. The closest you get to a **nightclub** in Murang'a is *South Tetu Day & Night Club* on Market Street, a busy joint with a pool table.

Onward from Murang'a

If you've arrived from Nairobi, there are three onward travel options from Murang'a: clockwise around Mount Kenya via Karatina and Naro Moru (see below); anti-clockwise around the mountain via Embu (see p.199); or up to Nyeri and the **Aberdares** (see p.206), for which, if you're not in a hurry, you should take either of the two minor roads leading out of Murang'a to the west. They join at Kiriani and dip north to Nyeri via Othaya; the longer of the two, via Koimbi, takes you past the start of a rough, snaking, high-altitude track which is drivable with 4WD. It climbs as far as Tusha, just 10km from the Aberdare National Park's Kiandongoro Gate, one of the two park entrances above Nyeri. Nyeri, a few kilometres off the Mount Kenya circuit, is a recommended detour and one which most public transport on the ring road will include.

SAGANA (be warned, the stretch of road between Muranga and Sagana is full of potholes) is a district dotted with rice fields and a place to which you'll be glad you brought your mosquito repellent. It lies at the junction for Thika, Nyeri and Embu, but has little to recommend it apart from some basic accommodation options. The pleasant, thatched roof *Roots Motel* (PO Box 25 Sagana ☎060/46229; ②), on the Nairobi road 500m before the junction, has singles and doubles, good solid meals, a bar and tables outside under some trees. In town itself, try *Hotel Chakaka* at the western (Murang'a) end; decent eats can be had at the *Savannah Cafeteria*. You can **camp** for free at the **river-rafting** base run by Savage Wilderness (see p.151); if you're coming from Nairobi, it's a few kilometres before Sagana and signposted on the left.

Karatina

If you pass through the feverish commercial centre of **KARATINA** on a Tuesday, Wednesday, Thursday or Saturday, stop to have a look around the market; it's one of East Africa's biggest cattle and produce sales. There are several **lodgings** in town, including the reasonable *Karatina Tourist Lodge* (Private Bag, Karatina ☎061/533968; ③), which has safe parking. Cheaper options include the more lively *Three-in-One Hotel* (PO Box 768; ☎061/72710; ②), and *Ibis Hotel* (PO Box 240; ☎061/72777, ℱ72777; ②) opposite Agip petrol station. For the *Wajee* **campsite** (PO Box 148, Nyeri; ☎061/60359), turn off the main road 2km north of town onto the Gakonya road (it's about 20km). There's good, filling **food** at *Karatina Express Café* by the railway, with a shaded terrace and smooth service. The main **nightspot** in town is *Galaxy Club*.

Mountain Lodge

Further up the A2, **KIGANJO** is the base for 🦌 **Serena Mountain Lodge** (PO Box 123 Kiganjo; ☎061/2030785; ⓦwww.serenahotels.com; ⑨, HB $260), the most accessible of Kenya's three highland tree-hotels, and the only one on the slopes of Mount Kenya. It's set at an altitude of 2200m, about 20km from Kiganjo; take the turning on the right 4km north of Kiganjo (there's an access road from Karatina but this is in far worse condition). Less cramped than either of its competitors, the lodge has en-suite rooms, balconies which face the floodlit water hole, and consistently good **game-viewing**. You can stay up all night or be picky about your animal-watching, in which case you tick off what you're interested in being woken to see (they wake you at 6am in any case). You have to be quick to see the shyer animals such as rhinos, as they vanish at the first click of a camera.

Castle Forest Lodge

Castle Forest Lodge, nestling in the forest on the southern slopes of the mountain (PO Box 29886, Kimunye Kirinyaga district, Kerugoya; ☎0721/422908, ⓦwww.oja-services.nl/kenya; HB ❻), is a private home reputedly built for British royalty before World War I. There are large, comfortable rooms and several cottages in the grounds, as well as camping ($8 per person). Meals are available to order, there's a well-stocked bar and, in between sleeping and eating, you can walk in the woods, sit by the waterfalls of the Karute stream, or fish in it for trout. The lodge is about 50km from Murang'a, via Sagana and then **Kutus** on the C73. From Kutus, head east on the C73 for 400m, then turn left on the tarmac D458 and, after about 6km, at Rukenya, turn left onto a *murram* track. Fifteen kilometres up here (an extremely slippery and slow-going drive when wet) you reach the Mount Kenya forest boundary gate, *Thiba Fishing Camp*, and, 5km further, the house.

If you're keen to try an unusual approach to the summit of Mount Kenya, the seldom-used **Kamweti route** begins at the roadhead, a steep 8km north of *Castle Forest*. The managers at the lodge can arrange a climbing package for you from $60 a day.

Naro Moru

Heading north up the A2 towards Naro Moru from Kiganjo, you emerge from the folded landscape of Kikuyu cultivation onto a high, windswept plain. Here, you're crossing one of the great animal migration routes, severed by human population pressure. Until 1948, when the two mountain parks were created, every few years used to see the mass migration of **elephants** from one side to the other. When the parks were opened, it was decided to keep the elephants away from the crowded farmlands in between, so an eight-kilometre ditch was dug across their route.

The road climbs gently and steadily to nondescript **NARO MORU**, which stands on the watershed between the Tana and the Ewaso Nyiro river basins. Built around its now disused train station, Naro Moru is the most straightforward **base** for climbing **Mount Kenya**, or simply exploring the mountain forests lower down. The town has a post office but no banks, the nearest being in Nyeri or Nanyuki. There's not a lot in the **food** department either; the centre's offerings are strictly in the bread and milk, *karanga na chapati*, line. If you want to eat in style, head to the *Naro Moru River Lodge* (see overleaf), which does excellent buffets, or the *Trout Tree Restaurant* (see p.193) 9km north of town.

Accommodation

Naro Moru offers several cheap **accommodation** options. Besides the ominous-sounding *Silent Lodge* (❷), there's the *'82 Lodge* (❷), with s/c rooms, and *Mountain*

View Hotel (☎062/62088; ❷) also with a balcony. Out of town, the cheapest and closest place to stay is the rather exposed **campsite** (Ksh200 per person), with its freezing showers and pretty expensive firewood, which is to be found at *Naro Moru River Lodge* (about 1500m west of town and signposted). Naro Moru has an excellent **youth hostel** (PO Box 274, Naro Moru; ☎062/62412, ℱ62078; dorms Ksh250) about 9km up the well-signposted track to Mount Kenya's Naro Moru Gate. You might get a lift up from the main road; otherwise break your walk with a *chai* at the *Kariaku Restaurant*. Housed in a rebuilt farmhouse, the hostel is a popular travellers' meeting place; dorms are comfortable if basic, camping is welcomed in the grounds, and there are hot showers and a well-equipped kitchen. For a quick taste of Mount Kenya, you can fix up a **day-hike** to *Mackinder's Camp*, inclusive of lifts up to the gate and back down again, for around $50 (plus park fees), through one of the caretakers of the youth hostel. They also have equipment for rent, at prices a good deal cheaper than at the *Naro Moru River Lodge*. Three little *dukas* up the track, 1km or so beyond the youth hostel, sell one or two vital commodities, but they're very basic indeed.

There are two more expensive accommodation options. ⚑ *Naro Moru River Lodge* itself (PO Box 18 Naro Moru; ☎062/62023, ℱ62211, ⓦwww.alliance-hotels.com; HB ❺) is very good value, with a welcoming atmosphere, pretty gardens and superb bird-watching. While birds and butterflies in the grounds are a naturalist's delight, don't count on any rewards from the uninformative "nature walk". And if you want to fish for trout, the stream here barely has any these days. Still, most of the rooms have fireplaces and balconies, and a sauna, squash and tennis courts, a pool facing the mountain, horseback rides and a great ski-lodge-style bar with a huge fireplace complete the picture. It tends to be full of upmarket mountain-climbing package clients and has an expensive but well-stocked equipment-rental shop. Kids' rates are, for a change, substantially cheaper. Here you can also purchase a packaged Mount Kenya climb, all inclusive. The *Mountain Rock Lodge*, about 8km north of Naro Moru (PO Box 333, Nanyuki; ☎062/62625, ℱ62051, ⓦwww.mountainrockkenya.com; B&B ❼), is an good alternative west-side base. The entrance can't be missed, as it's marked by two enormous Kikuyu figures carved out of tree trunks and flamboyantly painted. They have fairly decent **rooms** with log fire, and a restaurant and bar. You can **camp** in the grounds ($6 per person; tent rental from $44 for two people, including bedding). There's **horse-riding** too and you can do escorted walks through the forest in the vicinity of the lodge.

Mount Kenya National Park

$15 per person daily, camping $10 per night. Porters pay the residents' rate. Entry allowed on foot; minimum group two people (lone travellers can hire a guide to make up the number); vehicle Ksh250 a day. Warden: PO Box 753 Nyeri; ☎061/55201.

An extinct volcano some three-and-a-half million years old, **Mount Kenya** is Africa's second-highest mountain, with two jagged peaks. Its heart is actually the remains of a gigantic volcanic plug – the mountain stood at over 7200m above sea level about a million years ago – from which most of the outpourings of lava and ash have been eroded by glacial action to create the distinctive silhouette. The peaks are permanently iced with snow and glaciers, the latter retreating due to climate change. On the upper slopes, the combination of altitude and a position astride the equator results in forms of **vegetation** that exist only here and at a few other lofty points in East Africa. It's hard to believe

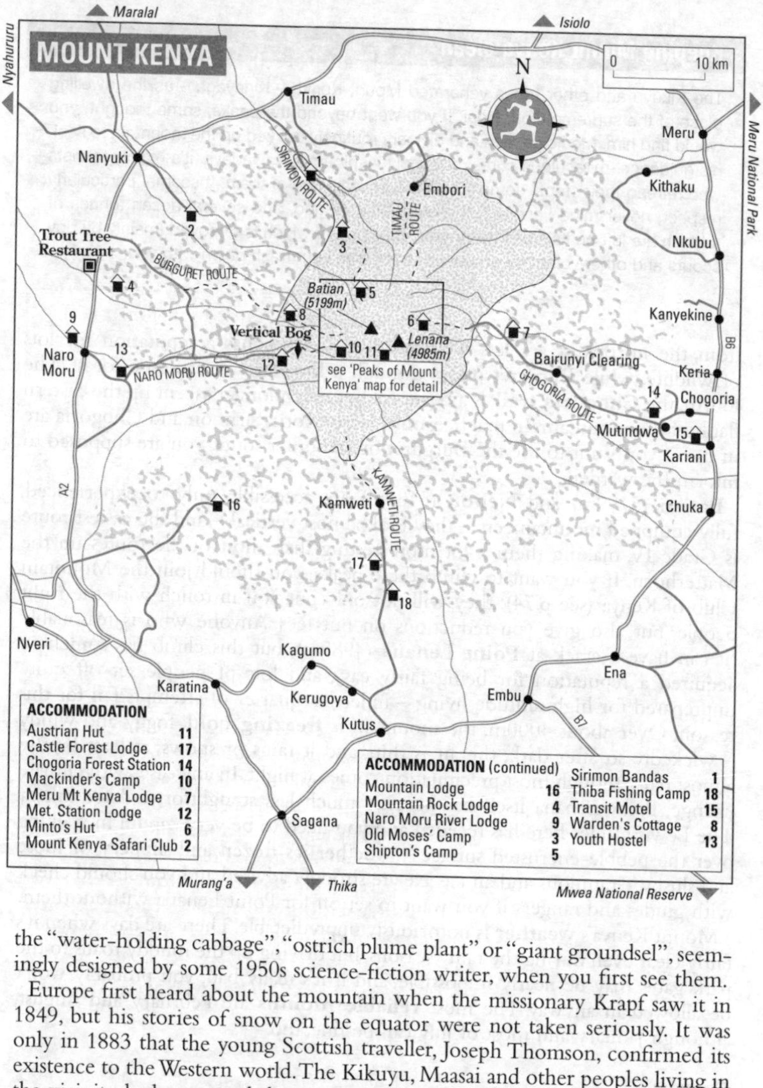
MOUNT KENYA
Maralal
Isiolo
Nyahururu
Meru National Park
N
0
10 km
Timau
Meru
Nanyuki
Kithaku
SIRIMON ROUTE
Embori
TIMAU ROUTE
Nkubu
Trout Tree Restaurant
BURGURET ROUTE
Batian (5199m)
Kanyekine
Vertical Bog
Lenana (4985m)
Naro Moru
NARO MORU ROUTE
see 'Peaks of Mount Kenya' map for detail
Bairunyi Clearing
Keria
CHOGORIA ROUTE
Chogoria
Mutindwa
Kariani
B6
A2
Kamweti
KAMWETI ROUTE
Chuka
Nyeri
Kagumo
Ena
Karatina
Kerugoya
Embu
B7
Kutus
Sagana
ACCOMMODATION
Austrian Hut 11
Castle Forest Lodge 17
Chogoria Forest Station 14
Mackinder's Camp 10
Meru Mt Kenya Lodge 7
Met. Station Lodge 12
Minto's Hut 6
Mount Kenya Safari Club 2
ACCOMMODATION (continued)
Mountain Lodge 16
Mountain Rock Lodge 4
Naro Moru River Lodge 9
Old Moses' Camp 3
Shipton's Camp 5
Sirimon Bandas 1
Thiba Fishing Camp 18
Transit Motel 15
Warden's Cottage 8
Youth Hostel 13
Murang'a
Thika
Mwea National Reserve

the "water-holding cabbage", "ostrich plume plant" or "giant groundsel", seemingly designed by some 1950s science-fiction writer, when you first see them.

Europe first heard about the mountain when the missionary Krapf saw it in 1849, but his stories of snow on the equator were not taken seriously. It was only in 1883 that the young Scottish traveller, Joseph Thomson, confirmed its existence to the Western world. The Kikuyu, Maasai and other peoples living in the vicinity had venerated the mountain for centuries. Park rangers still occasionally report finding elderly Kikuyu high up on the moorlands, drawn by the presence of Ngai, whose dwelling place this is. It's not known, however, whether anyone had actually scaled the peaks before Sir Halford Mackinder reached the higher of the two, **Batian**, in 1899. Another thirty years passed before **Nelion**, a tougher climb, was conquered. Both are named after nineteenth-century Maasai *laibon* or ritual leaders.

Climbing Mount Kenya: practicalities

There are **four main routes** up Mount Kenya. The **Naro Moru trail** provides the shortest and steepest way to the top. The **Burguret** and **Sirimon trails**

Keeping Mount Kenya clean

The Kikuyu and other tribes venerated Mount Kenya – Kirinyaga – as the dwelling place of the supreme God, Ngai. If you went beyond the peaks, some thought, you would find him. Medicine men and diviners routinely trekked up the mountain to seek his guidance, miraculous cures, or simply inspiration. Nowadays, it's mainly tourists who retread their steps: some 15,000 each year. Few of them, it seems, particularly respect, never mind venerate, the old mountain god, and several dozen tonnes of rubbish are left on its sides every year, only part of which is removed (mainly by boy scouts and other voluntary groups). Please take your trash down with you.

from the northwest are less well trodden; Sirimon has a reputation for lots of wildlife, while Burguret passes through a long stretch of dense forest. The fourth, the **Chogoria trail**, is a beautiful but much longer ascent up the eastern flank of the mountain. In practice, only Naro Moru, Sirimon and Chogoria are in use; if you want to use the Burguret or any other route, you are supposed to inform the warden.

Batian (5199m) and **Nelion** (5189m) are accessible only to experienced, fully equipped mountaineers – they look almost vertical – and the easiest route is Grade IV, making them a lot more testing than most of the routes up the Matterhorn. If you want to climb these peaks, you should join the Mountain Club of Kenya (see p.74); they will not only put you in touch with the right people, but also give you reductions on hut fees. Anyone who is reasonably fit can have a crack at **Point Lenana** (4985m), but this climb has somehow acquired a reputation for being fairly easy, and lots of people set off quite unprepared for high-altitude living – indeed, a quarter of attempts fail for this reason. Over about 4000m, the mountain is **freezing cold**, foggy and windy – wickedly so after dark; the air is thin, and it rains or snows, at least briefly, almost daily, though most precipitation comes at night. In any case, with climate change, Point Lenana itself has become much less straightforward for hikers. The Lewis glacier here has receded and you need to be very careful in walking over the pebble-encrusted surface – whether it's frozen and slippery or loose and slushy. Crampons and an ice axe are strongly advised and you should check with guides and rangers if you want to set off for Point Lenana without them.

Mount Kenya's **weather** is notoriously unpredictable. There are days when it's fairly clear even during the rainy seasons, but driving up the muddy roads to the park gates may be nearly impossible, and if it's really bad, you probably won't be allowed in anyway. The most **reliable months** are February and August, although January and most of July can be fine, too.

Costs

Climbing Mount Kenya is a fairly expensive business. A DIY four-day trek for two people, excluding guides or porters, costs Ksh10,000–15,000 per person (including park fees, overnights, food and transport to the roadhead, not including any equipment and tent rental). Expect to pay, per day, up to Ksh1000 for a guide, Ksh500 for a porter, Ksh600 for a cook (plus their park and camping fees – Ksh250 per person per day). An organized trek costs well over $100 a day.

The park, which encloses all parts of the mountain above 3200m, plus salients down the Naro Moru and Sirimon streams, operates a sign-in/sign-out system, and you pay **fees** on entry for your anticipated stay (don't overestimate, as there are no refunds). It's a bad idea to try to evade the exit gate on departure if you've stayed longer than intended: they will go looking for you and eventually organize an air search if you don't show up. Stories circulate of people being pursued to Nairobi and beyond for non-payment of huge rescue service bills. If you need to **change money**, do so in Nairobi or in the ring-road towns of Nyeri, Nanyuki, Meru, Embu, Chuka or Karatina.

Guides and porters

It's possible to hire a **guide** or **porter** near Naro Moru at the *Naro Moru River Lodge* and *Mountain Rock Lodge* (see p.180); at the youth hostel up the Naro Moru route (the best place to find someone much more cheaply; see p.180), at the *Cousin Café* and *Nanyuki River Lodge* in Nanyuki (see p.195), and at the *Transit Motel* in Chogoria (see p.189). You're not likely to find a guide up at the park gates themselves.

Insist on a written agreement showing the wages, the number of days, who's providing the food – everything. You shouldn't pay the full fee until the trip is finished, nor should you entirely rely on your guide to make every necessary preparation. Incidentally, any guide needs to possess an **official KWS guiding permit** – ask to see it, and don't be fobbed off with local guiding association cards.

What to bring

Above all, it's essential to have a really **warm sleeping bag**, four-season at the very least, ideally with an additional liner and/or Gore-tex bivouac bag. Taking a **tent** is almost essential because the only other accommodation on the mountain is a handful of very basic cabins and mountain huts, which can become so cold at night as to threaten hypothermia and rob you of much-needed sleep.

One **thick sweater** at the very least (better still, several thinner ones) and either a **windproof jacket** or a down- or fibre-filled one are absolutely

△ Peaks of Mount Kenya

necessary. A **change of footwear** is pretty much essential, too, as you're bound to have wet feet by the end of each day. **Gloves** and a **balaclava** or **woolly hat** are also handy. A light cagoule or anorak is good to have, as is a set or two of thermal underwear for the often shivering nights. Out of season (that is, most of the year), an **emergency foil blanket** is advisable and weighs and packs down to next to nothing. Another prerequisite is a **stove**, as you'll be miserable without regular hot fluids. Firewood is not available and cannot be collected once you enter the park. For **food**, dehydrated soup and chocolate are perhaps the most useful.

The *Naro Moru River Lodge* (see p.180) has a **rental** shop where you can get just about anything, at prices that may make you wish you'd simply bought it in Nairobi (see under "Camping equipment" in the Nairobi listings, p.153); the youth hostel has a limited range of items for rent. **Excess baggage** can be left for about Ksh80 a day at the *River Lodge*.

Coping with altitude

The various ascents themselves are mostly just steep hikes, if rough underfoot in parts. It's the altitude rather than the climb that may prevent you from reaching the top. Much more relevant than the training programmes that some people embark on is giving yourself enough time to acclimatize, so your body has a chance to produce extra oxygen-carrying red blood cells.

Above 4000m, you are likely to notice the **effects of altitude**. Symptoms vary between individuals, and appear unrelated to how fit you are – indeed, fit young males often suffer the most acute symptoms. Breathlessness, nausea, disorientation and even slurred speech are all possible, and headaches are fairly normal at first, especially at night. You may find Ibuprofen works against headaches and that Diamox is helpful against the general effects of altitude.

All this can be largely avoided by taking your time over the trek, as minor symptoms gradually disappear. You may consider bringing a tent for this reason, to avoid the sometimes rapid climbs between huts. Do not attempt to climb from the base of the mountain (that is, from the ring road) to Point Lenana in less than 72 hours; if you've just arrived in Kenya, allow five days for the ascent. Giving yourself a week for the whole trip is a good idea. Keeping your **fluid intake** as high as possible will also help (three to five litres a day is recommended) and it's best to avoid alcohol. If someone in your group shows signs of being seriously tired and weak, stay at that altitude. Should the symptoms develop into unsteadiness on the feet and drowsiness, **descend immediately**, whatever the circumstances. The effects of altitude are remarkable – especially on bodies tuned only to sea level – and can quickly become very dangerous, even fatal. Every year, dozens of climbers are struck by pulmonary oedema (when water collects in the lungs), accounting for almost half the cases worldwide.

Accommodation on the mountain

With a tent, you can **camp** anywhere in the park, the only practical advantage of the campsites at the Met Station (3048m) and *Mackinder's* (4200m), and various other designated campsites on the mountain, being water pipes and "long drop" toilets. Most water on the mountain is reckoned to be safe to drink (exceptions are noted) and you're never far from it.

The small, bare **huts** built by the Mountain Club of Kenya are located near the peaks, a fact that would make it possible to spend a day or two around the high tarns and glaciers – were the huts not in a deplorable state. The huts, most of which are free to use, have four walls, a roof, bunks, and nothing else

Guidebooks and maps

The **topographical map** *Mount Kenya 1:50,000 Map and Guide* by Andrew Wielochowski and Mark Savage covers just the mountain itself, and includes a detailed rundown on the huts (now somewhat out of date) and technical information for scalers of Nelion and Batian. If you're a climbing enthusiast, you'll want to get hold of the Mountain Club of Kenya's *Guide Book to Mount Kenya and Kilimanjaro*, which is adequate on the technical ascents.

The *Tourist Map of Mount Kenya National Park and Environs* (Ordnance Survey, through regular stockists) is an updated version of an excellent Survey of Kenya map. At 1:125,000 it provides a very useful – and visually pleasing – overview of the whole district, showing all the routes, the region around the base and most of the ring road. It's frankly not much use for the final ascent, however. There's also a quite user-friendly, small Survey of Kenya topographical map of the **peak area** at 1:25,000 that's worth getting hold of in Nairobi if you're intending to walk around the peaks. Don't expect to find any maps in the Naro Moru area or at any of the park gates.

– in many cases you're better off sticking to your tent. *Austrian Hut*, near Point Lenana, costs Ksh1000 per person, payable at the park gate; *Top Hut*, next to *Austrian Hut*, is reserved for MCK members.

Mountain accommodation options are covered in more detailed in the following accounts of the routes up Mount Kenya.

The Naro Moru route

The driveable earth road between Naro Moru town and the Meteorological Station is a 26-kilometre haul; even from the youth hostel (see p.180) it's at least a five-hour walk. *Naro Moru River Lodge* will taxi you up here – for an extortionate price – or you may be lucky and get a lift, but a completely free ride would be a miracle. Some 9km from the youth hostel, you come to the airstrip, the **national park gate** and **park HQ**, and usually a few gigantic buffalo chewing the cud on the lawn.

From the park gate, you leave the conifer plantations and occasional *shambas* behind as the road twists and climbs through shaggy forest into a zone of colossal **bamboo**. Look out for elephant and particularly **buffalo** if you walk this stretch, though you'll more often see their droppings and footprints. If you find buffalo on the path, you're supposed to lob stones at them – and they're supposed to move out of the way. Much safer is the tried and trusted retreat-steadily-without-taking-your-eyes-off-them-until-they've-gone approach: more people are killed by buffalo than by any other wild animal in Kenya.

The final 3km to the Met Station are a series of steep hairpins usually driveable only in a 4WD (and often not at all when wet). You start to get some magnificent views out over the plains from up here, while right under your nose you may find a three-horned **chameleon**, stalking cautiously through the foliage like a miniature dinosaur. The high forest is its favourite habitat. **Black panthers** – the melanistic form of the leopard found at high altitudes – can also be seen in this habitat, as, sometimes, can lions.

With an early start, it's quite possible to reach *Mackinder's* (at 4200m) in one day, but unless you're already acclimatized, you'll probably feel well below par by the time you get there. It's far better to take it easy and get used to the Met Station's 3050-metre altitude; perhaps stroll a little higher before returning for the night or, if you have a tent, climb an hour or so up to the tree line and camp there. The mountain's weather is another good reason to stop here. After

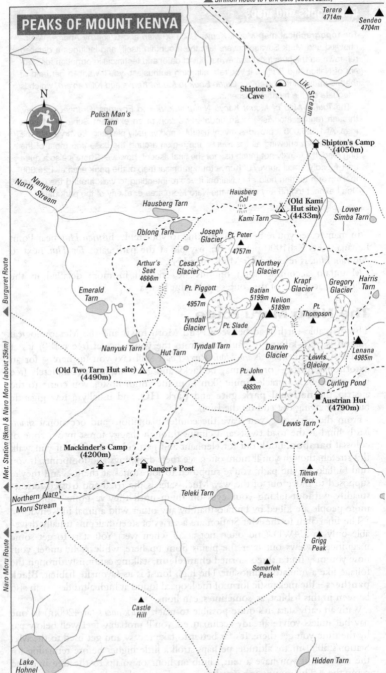

PEAKS OF MOUNT KENYA

N

▲ Sirimon Route to Park Gate (about 22km)

Terere 4714m

Sendeo 4704m

Shipton's Cave

Liki Stream

Shipton's Camp (4050m)

Polish Man's Tarn

Nanyuki North Stream

Hausberg Tarn

Oblong Tarn

Hausberg Col

Kami Tarn

(Old Kami Hut site) (4433m)

Lower Simba Tarn

Joseph Glacier

Pt. Peter 4757m

Arthur's Seat 4666m

Cesar Glacier

Northey Glacier

Krapf Glacier

Gregory Glacier

Harris Tarn

Emerald Tarn

Pt. Piggott 4957m

Batian 5199m

Nelion 5189m

Pt. Thompson

◄ Burguret Route

Tyndall Glacier

Pt. Slade

Darwin Glacier

Lewis Glacier

Lenana 4985m

Nanyuki Tarn

Hut Tarn

Tyndall Tarn

(Old Two Tarn Hut site) (4490m)

Pt. John 4883m

Curling Pond

Austrian Hut (4790m)

◄ Met. Station (9km) & Naro Moru (about 35km)

Lewis Tarn

Mackinder's Camp (4200m)

Ranger's Post

Tilman Peak

Northern Naro Moru Stream

Teleki Tarn

◄ Naro Moru Route

Grigg Peak

Somerfelt Peak

Castle Hill

Lake Hohnel

Hidden Tarn

▼ Kamweti Route to Castle Forest Lodge (about 25km)

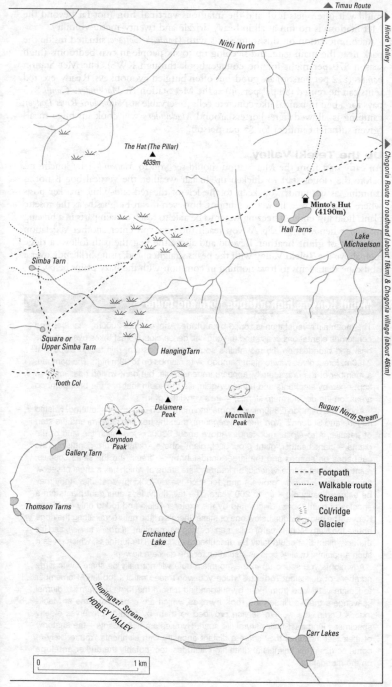

Nithi North

The Hat (The Pillar)
▲
4639m

🏠 Minto's Hut
(4190m)

Hall Tarns

Lake
Michaelson

Simba Tarn

Square or
Upper Simba Tarn

Hanging Tarn

Tooth Col

Ruguti North Stream

Delamere
Peak

Macmillan
Peak
▲

Coryndon
Peak
▲

Gallery Tarn

Thomson Tarns

Enchanted
Lake

--- Footpath
······ Walkable route
— Stream
⌒ Col/ridge
⬭ Glacier

Rupingazi Stream

HOBLEY VALLEY

Carr Lakes

0 ———————— 1 km

midday, it often gets foul, and the infamous **vertical bog** (not far beyond the Met Station) is no fun at all in heavy drizzle and twenty-metre visibility.

Accommodation on this route starts with *Warden's Cottage*, situated inside the park near the main gate, and sleeping up to six people in two bedrooms (high season \$70 per night for the cottage; book through KWS). The Met Station *bandas* (\$12 per person) are good, but often burgled by monkeys. Ready-erected tents can be rented (\$8 per person) at the Met Station. At *Mackinder's Camp*, \$15 pays for a bed in bandas like concrete cells (reservable at *Naro Moru River Lodge*); camping is allowed here. Porters around *Mackinder's* will cook up huge meals (given sufficient notice) for \$5 per person.

Up the Teleki Valley

An early start from the Met Station should see you to *Mackinder's* by lunchtime, before the clouds start to thicken up. In fair weather, the vertical bog is not as daunting as it sounds: you keep to the left of the red-and-white marker posts where it isn't as wet. In wet conditions, however, it can be ghastly, as the rosette plants hold just enough freezing water to be able to reach certain parts in a bracing manner whenever you slip. As you reach the bog, you enter another vegetation zone, that of **giant heather**. Beyond and above the bog, the path follows a ridge high above the **Teleki Valley** with the peaks straight ahead, rising brilliantly over a landscape that seems to have nothing in common with the hazy plains below.

Mount Kenya's high-altitude flora and fauna

The mountain's vegetation is zoned by **altitude**. Above about 2000m, *shambas* and coniferous plantations cease and the original, dense cloud forest takes over, with the best and broadest on the mountain's southern and eastern, rain-facing slopes. At 2400m, forest gives way to giant bamboo, with clumps up to 20m high. The bamboo, a member of the grass family, appears impenetrable, but dark-walled passages are kept open by elephants and buffalo. Again, it's the south that has the best bamboo areas; on the dry, northern slopes, there's very little of it.

Above the bamboo (2800m) you come into more open country of scattered, twisted *hagena* and St John's Wort trees (*hypericum*), then the tree line (3000m) and the start of peculiar, Afro-Alpine moorlands. Above about 3300m, you reach the land of the giants – giant heather, giant groundsel, giant lobelia. Identities are confusing: the cabbages on stumps and the larger candelabra-like "trees" are the same species, giant groundsel or tree senecio, an intermediate stage of which has a sheaf of yellow flowers. They are slow growers and, for such weedy-looking vegetables, they may be extraordinarily old – up to 200 years. The tall, fluffy, less abundant plants are a species of giant lobelia discovered by the explorer Teleki and found only on Mount Kenya. The name plaque below one of these (there's a little nature trail along the ridge above the Naro Moru stream) calls it an "ostrich plume plant" (*Lobelia telekii*), and it's the only plant that could fairly be described as cuddly. The furriness, which gives it such an animal quality, acts as insulation for the delicate flowers.

Any nights you spend up in the mountain huts will normally be shared with large numbers of persistent **rodents**, which you won't see until it's too late. Remember to isolate your food from them by suspending it from the roof. The familiar diurnal scavengers that you'll see are **rock hyraxes**, which are especially tame at Mackinder's Camp; the welfare service provided to them by tourists preserves elderly specimens long past their natural life span. Hyraxes are not rodents – the anatomy of their feet indicates they share a distant ancestry with elephants. You're likely to come across other animals at quite high altitudes, too, notably the **duiker antelope** on the moorlands.

For **Mackinder's Camp**, you follow the contours across the valley side and jump, or cross by stepping stones, over the snowmelt Northern Naro Moru stream. The camp, virtually at the head of Teleki Valley, is a long stone and concrete bunkhouse with dishevelled tents tacked into the icy ground around it. Certainly no hotel, it does at least provide some warmth and the company of others: climbers, Kikuyu guides and porters. **Batian** and **Nelion** tower magnificently over the valley, with a third pinnacle, **Point John**, even closer. There's usually a fresh icing of snow every morning, but early sunlight melts most of it by midday.

If you want to climb straight to **Point Lenana**, you're likely to find at least one group leaving early the following morning (around 3am) with a guide, though it's not that difficult to find your own way up, especially if there's a moon. It's probably safest to scramble straight up the ridge to Point Lenana from *Austrian Hut* rather than cross the unpredictable vestiges of the Lewis glacier without proper equipment. Leaving this early allows you to get to the top by dawn for a fabulous view (sometimes) from northern Kenya on one side to Kilimanjaro on the other. It's not advisable to rush into this final ascent, however. For most people, day three is better spent getting acclimatized in the Teleki Valley, making the climb to Point Lenana the next morning. And note, spending your third night on the mountain at *Austrian Hut*, just below Point Lenana, is a bad idea. Not only is *Austrian* uninviting (it's in constant use), but sleeping unacclimatized at high altitude is literally a nightmare. For more on treks around the peaks, see p.192.

The **descent** doesn't take long. You can do it in one day, right down to Naro Moru or further, assuming you've left your vehicle at the *Met Station*, or else manage to find a lift. Rather than retrace your steps to Naro Moru, a more exhilarating and less frequently used alternative is to descend by one of the other routes: the Chogoria trail, for example. This would mean taking all your gear up with you, as well as extra food.

The Chogoria route

The **Chogoria trail** is scenically far superior to any of the others, and it's become more popular now that the road around the east side of the mountain has been paved. It's also the longest route, requiring good shoes and probably a plentiful supply of blister pads. From the eastern side, the hike to the top can be done in three days, but it's easier to allow four or five if you're setting out from Nairobi. Note that the Chogoria route is a camping-only climb: you have to show you have a tent when passing through the park gate.

Up to the park entrance

The not especially friendly village of **CHOGORIA** is your first target. Akamba have regular buses from Nairobi which pass the Chogoria turn-off en route to Meru, leaving you with a three-kilometre walk. The *Transit Motel*, 3km south of Chogoria centre at Karaa Market (PO Box 190 Chogoria; ☏064/22096; B&B ❷) is by far the best of several **lodgings**, with reasonable self-contained rooms, most with a balcony but no nets, and a restaurant of sorts. Alight at Kariani stage a few kilometres before the Chogoria turn-off, which leaves you with a 1500-metre walk.

There are a number of **porter/guide** associations in Chogoria, most of whose members are extremely pushy. The most reliable (also the most expensive) is the Mount Kenya Chogoria Guides Association based at the *Joywood Hotel Marima* (PO Box 107 Marima; ☏064/22266 or 0733/262448). Their usual (bargainable) rates are $10 a day for a guide, $60 for four-wheel drive transport to the park gate for three to five people.

From the hamlet of **Mutindwa**, 4km up the mountain, it's about 26km to the park gate. On weekends, you may stand a better-than-average chance of getting a lift. Transport can be chartered at the *Transit Motel* or elsewhere in Chogoria. There are a number of options from Chogoria, prices varying with the state of the track: halfway to the park gate (15km drive, 15km walk; up to Ksh1500); two-thirds (20km drive to Bairunyi Clearing, 10km walk; up to Ksh2000); to the park gate (Ksh3000–4000); or to the roadhead, some 7km further (Ksh4000). It's a good idea not to pay (at least not everything) until reaching the destination – a feat that for most of the year is by no means guaranteed because of the weather. You may prefer to walk up in any case, because it gives you a chance to acclimatize. If you get a lift up early in the day, avoid climbing any higher before stopping for the night.

There's a good **campsite** just a couple of kilometres from Mutindwa, with firewood available. Exciting, dense rainforest follows, where you're likely to see colobus monkeys, spotted hyena, buffalo and numerous elephant droppings. Before, during and after the rains, though, you'll probably be more occupied with fending off swarms of hungry **tsetse** fly, which isn't much fun and carries the (slight) risk of sleeping sickness. The next available campsite is the only clearing in the forest, at a place called **Bairunyi Clearing**, 15km further up the track (no water). The national park's **Chogoria Gate** is 9km further up the increasingly steep and rough track (4WD vital, and not always enough), flanked by giant, creaking bamboo forest. If you arrive late in the day and are not going beyond the roadhead (the actual boundary of the national park), the rangers may waive park fees for that day, but keep receipts for the fees you pay to satisfy the rangers at whichever gate you exit from.

The park entrance and roadhead

The very good and wonderfully sited *bandas* of the *Meru Mount Kenya Lodge* (from Ksh1050 per person), run by the district council, are just before the gate. They have a spartan shop that sells beer, and wood fires in each *banda*. They're often visited by buffaloes, and you can sometimes see elephants at the nearby water holes, visible from the ridge of the hill behind the *bandas*. It may be worth booking in advance through Let's Go Travel in Nairobi (see p.150).

If you're not staying in the *bandas*, but it's time to stop for the day, you might as well stay put by the gate with your tent; alternatively follow the main track up from the park gate and you'll come to a "special campsite" with running water and toilet. This is a beautiful place to camp (reservable through the warden; $10 per person).

Both the main track and the side branch, via the site of the old *Urumandi* hut, eventually meet up at the **roadhead**, 7km further on. The side branch is the more interesting walk, but tougher on vehicles. The roadhead, with a small parking area, is on the north side of the Nithi stream and there's a very pleasant **campsite** here, with good stream water.

There are good walks round about, useful for acclimatizing to the 3000-metre-plus altitude. Short scrambles from the roadhead take you to the four sets of **Nithi Falls**, while longer walks (3–6hr round trip) take you north to **Mugi Hill**, **Lake Ellis** and the flat-topped peak Kilingo – the **Giant's Billiard Table**.

On the mountain

From the roadhead, all wheels are abandoned as you slog on foot up towards *Minto's Hut*, a six-hour (9hr from *Meru Mount Kenya Lodge*) stint away in the high moorlands. The route tracks along the axis of an ascending ridge, then flattens onto the rim of the spectacular **Gorges Valley**, carved deep by glaciation. There are unobstructed and encouraging views up to the peaks as you hug the contours of the valley wall.

Minto's Hut, like *Mackinder's* on the west side of the mountain, is three to five hours from Point Lenana. Situated by the four small Hall Tarns, it's perched above the larger Lake Michaelson at the head of the valley below – a very beautiful place, inspiringly set off by giant groundsel, lobelia plants and weird volcanic formations inhabited by rock hyraxes. You will have to camp here as the hut is reserved for porters only. Be aware that the tarn water is not pure, and boiling it at this altitude will not kill all the bugs, so you should use purifying tablets or iodine.

In the morning you have two options. The first is to head up to the ridge west of *Minto's* and follow it, through pretty scenery, to **Simba Tarn**, below Simba Col. From there, head due south around the peaks and past little **Square Tarn** before turning right to follow the contours for a tough kilometre to the so-called **Curling Pond** (matches have been held on the ice here) and *Austrian Hut*. If you're thinking of a short cut straight up to Square Tarn, note that it's very steep. Alternatively, from *Minto's* make for the base of the ridge extending east from Point Lenana, then tackle the cruel scree slope to the south for a ninety-minute scramble up to a saddle, followed by a straight drop to the head of the **Hobley Valley** with its two tarns. From here, it's just an hour across to the base of Lenana Ridge, behind which, again, is *Austrian Hut*. Mercifully, whichever route you choose, this day's hike is a short one and at this altitude (over 4000m), you'll be glad to spend the rest of the day at one of the huts, recuperating for the final ascent. Considering the altitude, a safer and probably more comfortable option would be to spend a second night, acclimatizing at the base of Simba Tarn (tent only), followed by a pre-dawn assault on Point Lenana.

After the climb to Lenana, you have a ninety-minute **descent** from *Austrian Hut*, tracking back and forth over miserable scree, to the Teleki Tarn at the head of the Naro Moru stream. *Mackinder's*, and the scent of civilization, is just an hour away down the valley. But if you can resist that lure, and it is still early in the day, *and* if you have enough food and water, you can continue around the west side of the peaks to Hut Tarn, then up and down over the ridges to the old site of *Kami Hut*, at the head of the Sirimon route on the north side. If you want to do it, and you feel acclimatized, there's no problem making it from *Minto's* to Point Lenana and on down to the Met Station in one day.

The Sirimon route

The **Sirimon route** leads up from the Mount Kenya ring road some 14km east of Nanyuki. The route climbs over the northern moorlands, giving superb views on the way of the main peaks as well as the twin "lesser" peaks of Terere (4714m) and Sendeyo (4704m), which have small glaciers of their own.

There are certain advantages in using this route: it's the driest, the scenery is more open, and it's renowned for wildlife. The *Mountain Rock Lodge* (see p.180) offers inclusive three- or four-day **guided tours** up to Point Lenana using this route (the *Naro Moru River Lodge*, p.180, also offers trips up this way); prices are around $450 per person for a four-day trip, including transport to and from the base of the trail, all food and equipment, and a last night at *Mountain Rock Lodge*, but excluding park fees. Much cheaper, if you're just looking for a guide, is to enquire at the *Cousin Café* or *Nanyuki River Lodge* (see p.195).

Unpackaged walking on this route is fine if you're in a small group, but you're much less likely to find company up here than on the Chogoria or very busy

Naro Moru routes, as there isn't any real base to start from, excepting a huddle of *dukas* on the ring road, 9km from the park gate.

Mountain accommodation on the route consists of two self-contained *bandas* by Sirimon gate, sleeping four ($70 per *banda*; bedding provided; book through KWS); *Old Moses Camp* (at the roadhead, 3300m up and accessible by 4WD only; $10 per person, students/children $8); and *Shipton's Camp* **bunkhouses** (4200m; $12 per person, students/children $10). The last two are not in great condition, but can be booked through *Mountain Rock Lodge*, though you can also simply pay on arrival for a nominal surcharge.

The Burguret route

Mountain Rock Lodge's preferred route used to follow the **Burguret River** up from the hotel through thick bamboo forest and moorland, but this is now mostly overgrown and hard to follow without a guide (available at *Mountain Rock* for Ksh1200 per day, excluding the guide's park fees). A 4WD vehicle can drive as far as an elevation of 3000m on this route, which terminates at *Two Tarn Hut's* old site, behind Teleki Valley. En route, it passes a clutch of caves described as a "Mau Mau conference centre". *Mountain Rock Lodge* still offers four-hour trips to the caves, including some waterfall hiking, for around $7 per person, depending on group size, or the same on mountain bikes (from $20 per person). You're required to notify the warden if you intend to use this route.

Treks around the peaks

Though most people head straight up to Point Lenana, trekking round the peaks is a far more exhilarating experience, with the added chance to explore some of the tarns and glacial valleys on the north side. It's supposed to be easier to do this anti-clockwise in two or three days. If you want to do it in one, however, set off clockwise from *Mackinder's* via *Two Tarn Hut's* old site by **Hut Tarn**, set in a glorious and eerily silent col beneath the glaciers and scree. The walk from here round to Point Lenana is very much a switchback affair but, as long as the mists stay away, the scenery is fairy-tale. If you're fairly fit and acclimatized, it should take eight to ten hours. Both *Two Tarn* and *Kami Hut*, on the north side of the peaks, have been demolished, but you can still camp at both sites. *Austrian Hut* is the most suitable, though not the most inviting, night stop, but again you may not get much sleep at this altitude.

Other routes

The trails described above represent only the most obvious and well-trodden of the mountain's hiking possibilities. All ground above 3200m is within the boundaries of the national park and, with time and proper equipment, you could hike the moors and highland zone for weeks. Note, however, that you must be fully self-sufficient and that you must inform the warden. On the north side, a very rarely used route leads up from **Timau** (see p.195) through dense forest, for which a guide, a good map and accurate navigation skills are essential. The southern flanks of the mountain seem to have largely escaped the notice of hikers, but there are several forest stations in the vicinity of Embu and plenty of scope for exploration – the **Kamweti route** is a possibility (see p.179). Most of the southern slopes were a designated "Kikuyu reserve" during the colonial period, so few European climbers created routes up here. A **warning**: hiking in the forests, though feasible, is absolutely not advised unless you're with a guide;

it's easy to get hopelessly lost, as a number of apocryphal tales circulating tell. Hyena and other hungry or bad-tempered beasts abound, and without serious jungle or rainforest experience, you're asking for trouble.

Nanyuki and on to Meru

North of Naro Moru, the A2 runs along smoothly across the yellow-and-grey downs, scattered with stands of tall gum trees, roamed by cattle and overflown by brilliant blue roller birds, before dropping to the equator and **Nanyuki**. You might be forgiven for expecting something momentous to take place at the **equator**. There's a sprouting of several signs – "This sign is on the Equator" – outside curio shops, offering the usual beadwork, carvings, soapstone and bangles at the prices you'd expect. There's even an "Equator Professor" who claims to demonstrate the Coriolis effect of the earth's rotation using a bucket of water and a match-stick (aided by sleight of hand). In the northern hemisphere water should gurgle through a plug hole anticlockwise, whereas in the southern hemisphere it should flow clockwise – though in practice the direction of flow is random because the Coriolis effect is too tiny to have an impact. The demonstration is free, the "certificate" comes for a fee. The town centre is just 1500m down the road, so you could reasonably ask to be dropped at the equator and then walk in.

An excellent stop on the A2, especially for lunch, is the ⚲ *Trout Tree Restaurant* (☎062/62053; daily 11am–4pm), about 9km north of Naro Moru and 15km south of Nanyuki. Look out for their huge fish-skeleton-shaped sign, on the left if you're travelling north. Based at a working fish farm, and built on wooden platforms among giant fig trees, overlooking the trout ponds, the restaurant serves wonderfully fresh trout in a variety of ways – barbecued whole, as salmon trout sashimi and even trout masala.

The Town

NANYUKI has the dual distinction of being Kenya's air force town as well as playing host to the British Army's training and operations centre. Once an affluent place, Nanyuki saw an influx of refugees fleeing the **ethnic violence** between Kalenjin and Kikuyu in the 1990s. Most of them were housed in the slum camps to the west of town and have remained there ever since, despite the decline in violence. Nevertheless, Nanyuki remains in atmosphere very much a country town, and is oddly charming despite its poverty. A wide, tree-lined main street and the mild climate lent by its two-thousand-metre altitude bestow an unfamiliar, cool spaciousness that seems to reinforce its colonial character. Shops lining the main road include the Settlers Store ("since 1938") and the Modern Sanitary Stores (which sells camping gas).

The first party of settlers arrived in the district in 1907 to find "several old Maasai *manyattas*, a great deal of game and nothing else". Nanyuki is still some-thing of a settlers' town and European locals are always around. The animals, sadly, are not. Although you may see a few grazers on the plains, the vast herds of zebra that once roamed the banks of the Ngare Nanyuki (Maasai for Red River) were decimated by hunters seeking hides, by others seeking meat (particularly during World War II, when eighty thousand Italian prisoners of war were fed a pound each day), but most of all by ranchers protecting their pastures. As the zebra herds dwindled, so lions became a greater threat to live-stock; they retreated – under fire – to the mountain forests and moors. And the rhinos just disappeared, almost to the brink of extinction.

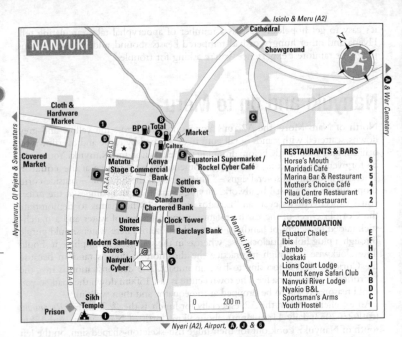

▲ Isiolo and Meru (A2)

▲ & War Cemetery

RESTAURANTS & BARS

Horse's Mouth	6
Maradadi Café	3
Marina Bar & Restaurant	5
Mother's Choice Café	4
Pilau Centre Restaurant	1
Sparkles Restaurant	2

ACCOMMODATION

Equator Chalet	E
Ibis	F
Jambo	H
Joskaki	G
Lions Court Lodge	J
Mount Kenya Safari Club	A
Nanyuki River Lodge	B
Nyakio B&L	D
Sportsman's Arms	C
Youth Hostel	I

▼ Nyeri (A2), Airport, **A**, **J** & **G**

If you have time, pay a visit to the 🖈 **Nanyuki Spinners and Weavers** workshop (closed Sun), located about 1km down the Nyahururu road, on the left opposite the District Hospital. This women's group provides the Spinners' Web shop in Nairobi with rugs and other articles woven on hand looms, which you can buy here at reduced prices. There's also astonishingly ambrosial **wild honey** from the *dukas* a kilometre or so east of the last police barrier, on the road to Meru.

Practicalities

Nanyuki's **airstrip** is 5km south of town on the A2 (take a taxi) and has flights to Nairobi and Maasai Mara. For **money-changing**, the best bet is the KCB (bureau de change open Mon–Fri 9am–3pm, Sat 9–11am). Standard Chartered and Barclays have an ATM. If you're looking for a **guide** for the Sirimon route up Mount Kenya, try the *Cousin Café* next to *Marina Bar & Restaurant*, or else the boys down at *Nanyuki River Lodge*. **Emails** can be sent from Nanyuki Cyber or the Rockel Cyber Café, in the same building as the Equatorial Supermarket.

Accommodation

For **overnight stays**, you have a number of options, the best of which are listed below; **camping** is available at the *Sportsman's Arms*. Nanyuki does have a very cheap, friendly **youth hostel** on Market Road (PO Box 1427; ☎062/22112; not HI-affiliated), but it is spartan and the toilets are a hazard.

🖈 **Equator Chalet** PO Box 1147
☎062/3148011. The best value in town: comfortable rooms with satellite TV, hot showers and mosquito nets, grouped round a pleasant courtyard with a balcony overlooking the street. ❸

Ibis Hotel Bazaar Rd; PO Box 209 ☎062/31536. Rooms are sparsely decorated, but come complete with slippers and Afro combs. ❸
Jambo Hotel PO Box 245 ☎062/31894. Opposite the park, reasonably clean and quiet, with

hot water and secure parking. Based here is one company organizing Mount Kenya tours, Montana Treks. ❷

Joskaki Hotel Lumumba Rd; PO Box 101 ☏062/22820, ℱ32912. Good s/c rooms, generally excellent food and rooftop views of the town and Mount Kenya. Unfortunately, it's a vast, corridor-riddled warren and can be indescribably noisy when the bar is open all night, or there's a disco. ❷

Lions Court Lodge About 1km south of the Market Rd junction; PO Box 371 ☏062/31639, ℮lionscourtlodge@yahoo.com. Pleasant resort set on acres of land, with views of Mount Kenya. The *bandas* are rather dark and gloomy, but have nice balconies; the newly built deluxe en-suite cottages are good value, with satellite TV and small terraces looking onto the gardens. There's also a playground and a great "beach bar" in the middle of small man-made lake. You can also camp in the grounds. ❹

Mount Kenya Safari Club 8km southeast of Nanyuki; PO Box 58581 ☏062/216940, ℱ216796, ⓦwww.lonrhohotels.com. Founded by Hollywood star William Holden, this reaches the heights of equatorial comfort with magnificent meals, slick service and kinky round baths in the cottages. A range of activities and facilities in and around the hotel – including tennis, riding, fishing, gyms, a bowling green, heated pool and an animal orphan-age – fill the day very pleasantly. If you ever dreamed of golf on the equator, what they term a "brutal" nine-hole course obliges. For all this, however, it's massively overpriced. Day membership costs Ksh500, including use of the pool; doubles $270 low season, $390 high season; ❾

Nanyuki River Lodge PO Box 101 ☏062/32523. This would be good value if it wasn't for the hustley touts and curio pedlars at the entrance, and the uncertain security. Rooms are reasonable, and there's a pool. The lodge can arrange Mount Kenya treks at reasonable rates (porter-guides Ksh1000 per day) for tackling the Sirimon route. Their all-in package prices are as expensive as any ($450 per person for a four-day jaunt). ❸

Nyakio B&L Bazaar Rd; PO Box 179 ☏062/22505. Good s/c rooms and a lively atmosphere thanks to the busy terrace restaurant/bar. ❸

Sportsman's Arms PO Box 3 ☏062/31448, ℱ31826, ⓦwww.sportsmansarms.com. An old establishment, the walls smothered by letters and photos, reminders of the good old days. There's a wide choice of accommodation: s/c rooms in a new wing, and even newer cottages. The rooms and newer cottages are better equipped, and there's a pool (Ksh200 for non-residents), Jacuzzi and sauna (ksh 200, residents only). The disco and *nyama choma* joint at weekends make sleeping difficult. B&B ❻

Eating and drinking

The best place to **eat** and **drink** in Nanyuki is the 🍴 *Horse's Mouth* pub, housed in a small wooden colonial-style house on Haile Selassie Road, 1km south of town. A great spot for a quiet pint with the locals, it has an indoor area with pool table and fireplace and a charmingly ramshackle outdoor restaurant and bar. The friendly owner dishes out great advice about the area. Wholesome food is available at the *Maridadi Café*, while you can get good snacks and great curries at *Pilau Centre Restaurant*. *Mother's Choice Café*, on Main Street, has cheap snacks and cakes. For a lively drink, try the *Marina Bar & Restaurant* opposite the post office, a popular hangout for tourists and soldiers, although steer clear of the food. The *Sparkles Restaurant* is a glitzy place by the Total petrol station with a lively **disco** at the weekends.

Timau and east to Meru

Leaving Nanyuki eastwards, the ring road skirts closer to the mountain than at any other point in its circumference. The land here, extremely fertile, is owned for the most part by large commercial estates; you'll see *wananchi* (peasants) cultivating the verges between the road and the estate fences to eke out a living.

After 14km you come to the high–altitude village of **TIMAU**, unremarkable but for two outstanding stopover possibilities with accommodation. Rates at both are per person, good value if you're on your own. *Kentrout trout farm*, 3km to the right down a rough, signposted track from the village (4WD in rainy weather; PO Box 14 Timau; ☏ & ℱ062/41016; B&B $55 per person), is a delightful retreat, the gardens, river and indigenous forest teeming with birdlife and colobus monkeys. They have delicious lunchtime alfresco buffets (Ksh1000), the ingredients for which are grown or bred on the farm; you can catch your own trout in the local fish ponds and have it prepared by the chef. They also have two wonderful, huge stone cottages for rent (all s/c), three rooms in a rambling old ranch house and a number of self-contained *bandas* (reservations can also be made through Let's Go Travel in Nairobi, see p.150). **Camping** is possible on request.

The other great draw is *Timau River Lodge*, 2km east from Timau and 1km off to the right (PO Box 212 Timau; ☎062/41230; B&B Ksh1400 per person). The dream of a charming Afghan couple, the "lodge" (actually a varied collection of s/c log, mud and "underground" houses) was built to run on ecological principles, though a generator has replaced the idealistic but inefficient method of powering the lighting by sunlight and water-turbine. The accommodation is wonderful: every *banda* has its own small kitchen (there's also a communal cooking area with ancient Scottish cast-iron ovens) and kids will adore the loft bedrooms in the largest *bandas*. You can **camp** anywhere you like or in the campsite (Ksh300 per person including hot showers and other facilities; tent rental Ksh600). Trout fishing, mountain climbing, camel- and horse-riding are on offer, and there are secluded waterfalls and river pools for bathing in, and a huge expanse of forest to get lost in.

After Timau, the scenery acquires a real grandeur as you pass through the Lewa Wildlife Conservancy (see p.204). The 70km from Timau to Meru couldn't illustrate better the amazing variety of climate and landscape in Kenya. The road climbs steeply to almost 3000m, passing alternative routes to the peaks and giving unparalleled views of them in the early morning. A spectacle you might not have guessed at is the panorama that spreads out to the north as the road drops once again – on a really clear day, after rain has settled the dust, this is devastatingly beautiful. Even on an average day, you can see as far as the dramatic mesa of **Ol Olokwe**, nearly 100km north in the desert. Isiolo (p.588) lies out there, too, first stop on the way to the northern wilderness. Beyond the Isiolo turn-off, the road to Meru suddenly plunges through verdant jungle, with glimpses through the trees of the Nyambeni Hills and the volcanic pimples dotting the plain.

Meru

The moist, jungly atmosphere around Meru, with wood smoke curling up against a background of dark forest, is very reminiscent of parts of West Africa (and the local Meru inhabitants are much darker-skinned than their neighbours) – a total change of mood after the dryish grasslands on the northwest side of the mountain. **Meru oak** is the commercial prize of this forested eastern side of the mountain, though judging by the number of active sawmills at the upper end of the town, supplies won't last much longer. The forest still comes almost to the town's edge, however, and paths lead off to cleared *shambas* where, for a year or two, just about anything will grow.

MERU town, the base for visits to Meru National Park (see p.412), is strung out over 2–3km. It's an unusual place in an interesting location – there are great views from the upper (**Makutano**) half of town over the densely settled slopes – and well worth a stay. The municipal **market** is a large one, selling a wide range of goods – baskets, clothes, domestic utensils – as well as

Miraa

Throughout Kenya, and especially in the Central Highlands and on the coast, you'll often see people selling and chewing what looks like a bunch of twigs wrapped in a banana leaf. This is in fact **miraa**, more commonly known abroad by its Somali name **qat**, a natural stimulant that is particularly popular among Somalians, Somali Kenyans and Yemenis. The shrub (*Catha edulis*) grows in the hills around Meru (the world centre for its production), and the red-green young bark from the shrub's new shoots is washed, stripped with the teeth and chewed, with the bitter result being something of an acquired taste (it's usually taken with bubble gum to sweeten it). *Miraa* contains an alkaloid called cathinone, a distant relative of amphetamine, with similar **effects**, though you have to chew it for some time before you'll feel them. When they do kick in, they include a feeling of alertness, ease of conversation and loss of appetite. Long-term daily use can lead to addiction. It's not always looked upon favourably, with signs prohibiting the chewing of it in many hotels and bars.

Miraa comes in bundles of a hundred sticks called "kilos" (not a reference to their weight) and various **qualities**, from long, twiggy *kangeta*, which is the ordinary, bog-standard version, to short, fat *gisa kolombo*, which is the strongest. As it loses its potency within 48 hours of picking, it's wrapped in banana leaves and transported at speed. Street stalls selling it often display the banana leaves to show that they have it, and the best place to buy *miraa* in many towns is where the express matatus arrive from Meru. The use of *miraa* by bus, truck and matatu drivers goes a long way towards explaining why they have so many accidents.

There are no **legal restrictions** on the use of *miraa* in Kenya, although imams have issued a *fatwa* (legal judgement) condemning it as an intoxicant, like alcohol, which means that it is forbidden to true believers. In fact, in many countries, including neighbouring Tanzania, as well as the US, Canada, Ireland and most EU countries (but not the UK), *miraa* is a controlled narcotic, the possession of which is a criminal offence. In the UAE, supplying any amount of it to anyone carries the death penalty, and several Kenyans are serving long sentences in Tanzanian prisons for carrying *miraa* across the border with intent to supply it.

the excellent agricultural produce of the district. They grow the best **custard apples** in Kenya here, and you won't find cheaper, bigger or better bunches of *miraa* anywhere (see box, above).

The tiny but fascinating **Meru Museum** (PO Box 597; ☏064/20482; ✉nmkmeru@africaonline.co.ke; Mon–Fri 9.30am–5.30pm, Sat 9.30am–2pm; Ksh200) is also a treat. It occupies the oldest stone building in town, a former District Commissioner's office, where you're likely to be the only visitor. Emphasis is on the traditional culture of the Meru people: small ethnographic exhibits, pick-up-and-feel blocks of fossilized wood, stone tools from the Lewa Downs prehistoric site and some woefully stuffed animals. The museum's Meru homestead is well presented and feels authentic. There's a particularly good **herbal pharmacopoeia** – a collection of traditional medicinal plants growing in the garden, where you can see what a *miraa* bush looks like, among others. Nearby, a pool contains a mean-looking Nile crocodile, turtles and tortoises.

If you're really interested in the Meru people, ask at the museum about the **Njuri–Ncheke traditional courthouse**, approximately 9km north of Meru on the road to Maua. The Njuri–Ncheke are a semi-secret society of elders sworn to preserve and uphold traditional cultural structures and religion, mainly through creating and enforcing traditional law and presiding over ceremonies and the administration of oaths.

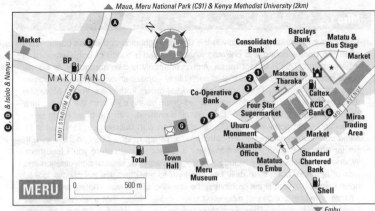

Maua, Meru National Park (C91) & Kenya Methodist University (2km)

MERU 0 — 500 m

ACCOMMODATION				RESTAURANTS, BARS & CLUBS			
Meru County	G	Three Steers	D	Bubbles Café	1	Keen Restaurant	2
Meru Safari	F	White Star	A	Candy Café	3	Millie 2000	7
Nanyuki Guesthouse	B			Clouds	6		
New Milimani	E			Hunter's Makuti Village	5		
Rocky Hill Inn	C			Ivory Springs Café	4		

Practicalities

Meru is a hub for transport south, west and east. Numerous **bus** companies have their offices between the mosque and *miraa* trading area. The safest companies are Akamba (☎064/20151) and Kensilver (☎064/30659); they have almost a dozen daily runs to the capital via Embu, and also run to Maua for Meru National Park. As for **matatus**, most major destinations are served from the main stage, with the exception of Embu (at the western end of Moi Avenue).

Among the **banks**, Standard Chartered and Barclays both have ATMs. **Emails** can be sent from *Candy Café*, on the main road by *Meru Safari Hotel*.

Accommodation

In keeping with its market-town functions, Meru has no shortage of **accommodation**, including one place out of town, the *Rocky Hill Inn*, 8km out on the Nanyuki road (☎064/41321; ❷). An ornate construction with chalets among pseudo-Japanese gardens, it has an unreliable water supply and is perhaps more a weekend *nyama choma* bar than anything else, but for all that, it's endearingly weird.

Hotel Three Steers 2km along the Nanyuki road; PO Box 155 ☎064/30467, ☞20634. This large motel-type complex has good rooms (s/c with hot water and telephones), a *nyama choma* joint, two bars and a cheap Indian-influenced restaurant. There's a loud disco (sometimes with guest bands) Fri & Sat. Enclosed parking. B&B ❸
Meru County Hotel PO Box 1386 ☎064/20432, ☞31264. A central option and fairly upmarket, with large, bright and breezy s/c balconied rooms (choice of bath or shower), a video lounge and reasonable restaurant. Well run and good value. B&B ❸

Meru Safari Hotel Tom Mboya St; PO Box 6 ☎064/31500, ☞20050, ✉union@mcfcu.co.ke. A large hotel with rather small rooms, satellite TV, room service and a nice terrace bar/restaurant. B&B ❸
Nanyuki Guest House Maua Rd; PO Box 211 ☎064/20677. A very acceptable B&L on the outskirts. ❷
New Milimani Hotel Moi Stadium Rd; PO Box 9 ☎064/20224. Rooms here are decent and s/c, and the menu long. It's also the cheapest place with safe parking in town. Lively and noisy Wed & nonstop Fri–Sun, when it hosts the *Club Dimples* disco – but deserted during the week. ❷

White Star Hotel Moi Stadium Rd; PO Box 259 ☎ 064/20247 or 20989. Meru's newest and nicest hotel features large, airy rooms decorated with Kenyan batiks, and a great leafy terrace for relaxing. Deluxe rooms have four-poster beds and a separate shower and bath. The restaurant is alcohol-free, but there are plenty of boozers to chose from down the road. B&B ❹

Eating and drinking

For **eating**, Meru will treat you well, at little expense. The most upmarket place, which isn't saying all that much, is the *Meru County Hotel*, serving curries and *nyama choma*, with set lunches at Ksh500. *Ivory Springs Café* is the friendliest place, and its samosas are satisfyingly tasty. Recommended for *nyama choma* is the zebra-striped *Keen Restaurant* on Moi Avenue, which is busier than most, while for chicken the place to head for is *Bubbles Café*, next to Consolidated Bank. The *Candy Café* and *Millie 2000* do good snacks. There's a fresh milk bar next to the KCB bank, and a **supermarket** – the Self-Choice – 2km up the Nanyuki road at the upper end of town.

Makutano district is the centre for **nightlife**. Try the sweaty *Club Dimples* disco at the *New Milimani hotel* (Wednesday is ladies' night, Thursday studenty, Friday and Saturday hip-hop and soul, Sunday jams; food available); the barn-like *Hunter's Makuti Village* dance hall, nearly opposite, which sometimes also has live bands; or weekend nights at the classier *Three Steers*. In the centre, try *Clouds* on Moi Avenue, with the usual Saturday night disco mayhem and a marathon Sunday dance which starts at 3pm.

Embu and around

The fast (and dangerous if going by matatu) road from Meru to Embu swoops around the eastern slopes of Mount Kenya through vibrant scenery. Five kilometres south of Meru, you cross the **equator**. Hundreds of streams – run-off from luxuriant rainfall blown in by the southeast monsoon – cut deeply into the volcanic soil of this eastern flank. As a result, this side of the mountain has a much broader covering of jungle, which extends, *shambas* permitting, down to the level of the road and beyond. You plunge from one green and tan gorge to the next; if you take an early-morning bus (slow, and considered safe), you can relax and admire. Sit on the right side for glimpses of snow-capped peaks, normally visible at this time of day.

Most public transport between Meru and Embu stops at **Chogoria**, a base for the eastern Mount Kenya ascent (see p.189), although if you're staying overnight you might consider continuing to the livelier (and friendlier) market town of **CHUKA**. Chuka has a bank with exchange facilities and accommodation at the *Kimwa Farmer's Hotel* (PO Box 794 ☎ 064/630570; ❸), with *nyama choma*, a busy disco, live music at the weekends and a life-size model elephant and a fibreglass replica of Mount Kenya in its car park.

If you head west from Embu, you begin to leave the red earth and lush vegetation of Mount Kenya behind as the land levels out into a series of intricately irrigated **rice paddies**, part of the Mwea rice scheme, originally a resettlement area for landless farmers supported by Japanese NGOs. South of Embu, a more leisurely alternative to the main Nairobi road is to head southeast along the tarmacked but rarely driven B7, skirting the intriguing Kiangombe Hills (see p.201), then past Mwea National Reserve and the huge Tana reservoirs, before reaching the fork at Kangonde. Here there are roads west to Thika (see p.174), east to Garissa (too dangerous to be a recommended route at the time of writing) or south along good *murram* to Kitui in Akambaland (see p.355).

2

Embu town

EMBU, like Meru, is situated at the bottom of a hill. At any rate, the town begins high and descends, with your expectations, to the centre. There's very little to get excited about here, and it's not obvious why it was chosen as the capital of Eastern Province. Certainly, without the apparatus of a provincial headquarters, Embu would amount to little. The extremely persistent street kids can also make it an unpleasant place for a stroll.

Most **public transport** from Embu along the Kangonde route goes to Thika, with only a few matatus bound for Kitui. The two-hour trip to Nairobi via Sagana is covered by dozens of buses and matatus; Akamba and Kensilver's services are the best. In order to climb Mount Kenya from Embu, get yourself over to *Castle Forest Lodge* and the Kamweti route (see p.179).

Embu has a number of decent **hotelis**: *Morning Glory Hotel,* right opposite the Exhibition Centre, which does chicken and chips and other inexpensive fare; *Rehana's Café,* a little way up the hill near the post office, busy and well known for excellent spicy samosas; and the spotless *Roska Café,* with good curries. The Somali-run *Zamzam Hotel* serves sweetly spiced pilau and *mataha* (rice, maize, beans, vegetables and potatoes all mashed together and eaten with beef). E–Touch, close to EMCO House and adjacent to a Catholic bookshop, has **Internet access**.

Accommodation

Highway Court 20298 By the BP station in the centre; PO Box 354 ℡ 068/20046, ℻ 30659. Newish four-storey block with s/c rooms, all with nets, good security and safe parking, but not especially clean. It also has a rowdy first-floor disco and bar, so get a room at the top. ②

Izaac Walton Inn At the top end of town on the way in from Meru, and 1500m from the centre; PO Box 1 ℡ 068/20128–9, ℻ 30135. Originally a colonial farmhouse, this is by far the best option, with pleasant, shaded gardens and a welcoming atmosphere. Rooms have bath or shower, and there's a guarded car park. A very satisfying buffet break-

fast here costs Ksh300 (lunches and dinner Ksh600). ⑤

Kenya Scouts Hotel A few hundred metres further north of *Izaac Walton's*; PO Box 1859 ℡ 068/30459. A welcoming place with rooms and dorms. Dorms Ksh 300; ②

Kubu Kubu Along the Kitui road, above the Mugo Shopping Centre; PO Box 180 ℡ 068/20191. Small, comfortable rooms. ②

New White Rembo Guesthouse PO Box 1241 ℡ 068/30692. The best of the cheap options in the town centre. Rooms are fresh and s/c, with nets and hot water. Besides safe parking, there's also a quiet bar with pool table, and good *nyama choma*. ②

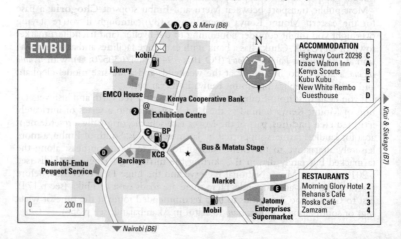

EMBU

Kobil

Library

EMCO House

Kenya Cooperative Bank

Exhibition Centre

BP

Bus & Matatu Stage

KCB

Nairobi–Embu Peugeot Service

Barclays

Market

Jatomy Enterprises Supermarket

Mobil

▲ Ⓐ, Ⓑ & Meru (B6)

▼ Nairobi (B6)

► Kitui & Siakago (B7)

N

0   200 m

ACCOMMODATION
Highway Court 20298 ... C
Izaac Walton Inn ... A
Kenya Scouts ... B
Kubu Kubu ... E
New White Rembo Guesthouse ... D

RESTAURANTS
Morning Glory Hotel ... 2
Rehana's Café ... 1
Roska Café ... 3
Zamzam ... 4

The Kiangombe Hills and the Mwea Reserve

The relatively modest altitudes of the **Kiangombe Hills** (Kiangombe peak is 1804m) aren't enough to lure climbers, but the unspoilt hills, upstaged by Mount Kenya and ignored by tourists and travellers, are worth a visit if you have an interest in the region's mysterious folklore. The hills are the home of the **Mbere**, who are related to the Kikuyu, Embu and Meru, and have a reputation in Kenya as possessors of magical powers. Some villages have elderly sages, **Arogi**, credited with terrifying abilities, though others – the **Ago** – have more beneficent gifts like the ability to foretell the future or find missing goats. The identity of these "witches" – at best a hazy and mysterious one which people aren't in any hurry to talk about – is further confused by the supposed existence in the hills of a race of "**little red men**" whose diminutive size (estimated at 1.2m) and fleeting appearance and disappearance in the bush have led the odd scientist to suppose that they might be australopithecine – ape-men hanging on into the twenty-first century. They and the Ago-Arogi may be just part of the "old people" mytho-history of central Kenya, which is at least partially based on the real, ancient and probably Cushitic-speaking peoples of two thousand or more years ago. Such, anyway, are the stories that might draw you from Embu. If you've ever entertained thoughts of seeing a bigfoot or a yeti – and if you kept an eye open for Nandi bears near Eldoret (see p.318) – it's an interesting trip.

Siakago

The main centre of the Kiangombe Hills, **SIAKAGO**, can be reached from Embu by matatu five or six times daily, in all conditions except the worst rains. Driving, take the B7 road from Embu, turning off at Musonoke or further down at Kiritiri.

Siakago isn't a ki-Mbere word and its derivation is uncertain. It may well have derived from "Chicago", along with the group of American anthropologists who based themselves here in the 1930s and started the ape-men stories. Siakago is an unusually pleasant and relaxed one-street town, all deep-red earth, green vegetation and colourfully painted shop fronts. There's a scattering of *hotelis* (usually combined with butcheries), a petrol station, two B&Ls, a noisy little market (main days Tues & Fri), which mostly sells livestock at extortionate prices, and several mission churches set amid the huts and *shambas* on the outskirts. The very cheap *Check Inn Bar*, 300m down the Embu road (PO Box 157; ●) has basic **accommodation** and is a good base for hiking. Out of Siakago, *dukas* are few and poorly stocked, and there's no accommodation.

The Kiangombe Hills

The Kiangombes rise behind Siakago and look deceptively easy to **climb**. In fact, it's a stiff hike to the top, better as a two-day trip; there's a self-contained overnight camp in the hills. The main route approaches the summit area from the huts of the **forest rangers' station** beyond the village of **Kune**, 10km north of Siakago. You should pick up a **guide** at the forestry station, which usually has to be arranged the day before you set out.

There's no transport between Siakago and Kune; the walk should take about three hours. Once at the forestry station (thirty minutes' hike beyond Kune), ignore the disused vehicle track which winds into the hills; it soon becomes difficult to follow. Instead, use the **footpath** leading straight up from behind the huts. At any time but the end of the dry season, much of your way is likely to be impeded by thick vegetation. If you're alert to every photographic possibility, you'll find that concentrating on following the overgrown trail is tiresome – especially without a *panga* to trail-blaze with. As you climb, human population quickly thins out; this is red-people territory and traditionally feared by the Mbere. The peaks area is about four hours' hike from the forest station.

The Mwea National Reserve

Daily fees $10, students/children $5; $8 to camp; PO Box 8-60116 Kiritiri.

The **Mwea National Reserve** is well worth the effort if you're looking for solitude and want to avoid the touristy atmosphere of most other parks and reserves. It's a beautiful area with a wealth of ornithological interest and wildlife – though hard to see – including giraffes, buffaloes, antelopes, crocs and elephants. With your own tent you can camp either by the main gate or on the sloping site near the shore of the reservoir here, though swimming is at your own risk – the crocs have a mean reputation.

The easiest way to get to the reserve is via the B7 Embu–Kangonde road; there is no public transport. Some 15km south of Embu, the signposted *murram* road off the B7 to the reserve is passable all year round. Further along the B7, on the south side of the hydro-electric Kamburu dam, another signposted road heads in via Masinga Dam from just before the village of Kaewa: the first 11km are tarmac, the remaining 12km *murram*, liable to be impassable in wet weather. One kilometre to the left, at the end of the tarmac, is the hilltop *Masinga Resort* (bookings through KWS), overlooking the reservoir and Mount Kenya, which has a choice of rooms (prefab or stone-and-tile with better views), and the benefit of a pool and the off-chance of lifts with workers at the hydro-electric dam. You can have lunch or dinner here for under Ksh500.

Laikipia

Northwest of Mount Kenya, **Laikipia District** is a vast plateau about the size of Wales, encompassing much of the transitional lands between the well-watered central highlands to the south and the semi-desert grazing steppe of the Samburu in the north. On the face of it, Laikipia is not an obvious destination and the few roads that cross it are uniformly awful, often impassable in the rains. It also straddles the disputed division between the Kikuyu people in the east and the Kalenjin to the west, and became notorious in the run-up to the 1997 elections, when **ethnic violence** swept the district, leaving several hundred dead and tens of thousands homeless. More recently, a century-old dispute between the Laikipiak Maasai and ranchers (mostly white) has escalated at times into land invasions and skirmishes, with the army brought in to police the fences. At the same time, in several areas, cooperation between local people and ranchers has resulted in some of Kenya's most encouraging conservation success stories, where community land is being managed in ways that respect traditional pastoral lifestyles while meeting the needs of wildlife and producing revenues from tourism. And group ranches are themselves beginning to work independently to achieve the same ends.

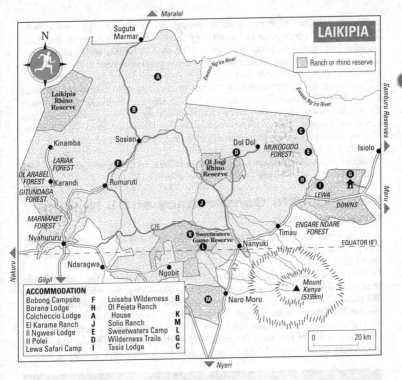

Laikipia is one of the best regions to see **wildlife** outside the national parks. Thanks mainly to its isolation, the district contains a wealth of endangered species, including **black rhinos**, whose world population today is barely two thousand, five hundred of them in Kenya. They are grouped in five heavily-guarded sanctuaries (Solio, Lewa, Ol Jogi, Ol Pejeta and Ol Ari Nyiro) set up by cattle farmers as part of ongoing experiments in integrated ranching, and latterly also for tourism. As browsers, black rhinos don't interfere with cattle pasture, and do well in the same environment so long as the bush isn't cleared. Apart from the rhinos, several **elephants** still undertake a seasonal migration from Laikipia north into the Samburu rangelands during the long rains, and the district also supports an estimated 25 percent of the world's remaining population of **Grevy's zebra**, a species fast disappearing in its other habitats in Ethiopia and Somalia, and several, very elusive packs of **African wild dogs**. For further information, check out the excellent website of the Laikipia Wildlife Forum (Ⓦ www.laikipia.org), the body that coordinates the region's various interest groups.

Ol Pejeta Ranch

For **day-trips** from Nanyuki under your own steam, **Ol Pejeta Ranch** (Ⓦ www.olpejetaconservancy.org) is the place to aim for, as it contains one of Laikipia's biggest concentrations of wildlife, including black rhinos. The ranch covers some 400 square kilometres, nearly a quarter of which is given over to a rhino sanctuary, **Sweetwaters Game Reserve** (entry $20 per person), one inmate of which, "Morani", is tame enough to be approached very closely. There's also a **chimpanzee sanctuary** here, with animals from the Jane Goodall Institute in Burundi (chimps aren't found in Kenya) and orphans from the bushmeat trade and former pets from other parts of central and west Africa, now numbering more than forty apes.

Unless you fly in, the only way to get to the area is to take the **C76** road to Nyahururu (all-weather in theory), which starts at Nanyuki. This is good for wildlife-spotting: you've every chance of seeing giraffes, gazelles and even elephants if you set off early. There's little or no public transport along this route, so your own 4WD is essential, though you might be lucky and catch a lift with a rancher in Nanyuki.

For the more adventurous, luxury **camel safaris** in the district are offered by Ewaso River Camel Hikes (p.151), among others.

Lewa Wildlife Conservancy and Il Ngwesi Group Ranch

Lewa daily fees $50 per adult, $20 per child; entry by 4WD only; Il Ngwesi daily fees $20 per adult, $10 per child; excellent map of both areas available at Lewa headquarters (Ksh1500).

In the east of Laikipia, the Matunda gate on the north side of the Timau–Isiolo road, 4km from the Meru junction, takes you 8km along dirt track to the **Lewa Wildlife Conservancy** (Ⓦwww.lewa.org). Formerly a cattle ranch, it incorporates the former Ngare Sergoi Rhino Sanctuary, currently containing around 40 black rhinos and 36 white, and some five hundred **Grevy's zebra**, accounting for a tenth of the world's remaining wild population. During the 1980s, **elephants** flooded into Lewa seeking safety from the heavy poaching further

△ Il Ngwesi Lodge

north, but as security in the north improved, they returned to their former range. However, there are always some on Lewa, and their numbers increase in the dry season, or whenever there is a fresh outbreak of poaching.

Lewa is conservation as a business: as well as the high fees, the revenue from the gift shop and expensive accommodation all help to support the **Northern Rangelands Trust**, partnering Lewa with local communities, foremost among which is the six-thousand-strong Laikipiak Maasai community of **Il Ngwesi Group Ranch**. Il Ngwesi, a 145-square-kilometre slab of wilderness, adjoins Lewa to the north and is bounded by the Ngare Ndare and Tinga rivers to the east and north, and by the dramatic hills of the Mukogodo Forest to the west. Most people staying at the only accommodation, the small and exclusive *Il Ngwesi Lodge* (see below), fly in, either to the Lewa HQ airstrip, or to Il Ngwesi's own airstrip. If you drive up, ensure you leave a clear ninety minutes to two hours to get from Lewa HQ to *Il Ngwesi Lodge*. The tracks are rough in parts and hard to follow: GPS, or better still a guide, is very useful.

Accommodation

Many **game ranches** have opened their doors to guests, and combine a quasi-colonial welcome and atmosphere with all-inclusive game drives and visits to the rhino sanctuaries. Other options are *Solio Game Ranch* near Nyeri (p.215) and several exclusive places near Rumuruti (see p.571). You can book most of the following at Let's Go Travel in Nairobi (see p.150).

With few exceptions, accommodation in Laikipia is for the well-heeled and requires your own transport, although all places can arrange for you to be picked up from Nanyuki (at additional cost). Most guests fly in; Airkenya and SafariLink have scheduled services to Nanyuki and Lewa, while Tropic Air Ltd (PO Box 161 Nanyuki; ☎062/32890–1, ℻32787, ✉tropic@africaonline.co.ke) can arrange air charters.

Borana Lodge Between the Mokogodo and Engare Ndare forests; PO Box 56923 Nairobi ☎020/600457/609699, ℻605008, ⊛www.borana.co.ke. Surrounded by a private commercial "conservation" ranch, this has six cedar, thatch and stone cottages and offers day and night game drives, visits to a rhino reserve, entertainment at a nearby water hole and horse riding, all for a gigantic $860 per double in high season. ❾

El Karama Ranch 42km northwest of Nanyuki off the track to Maralal; PO Box 172 Nanyuki; reservations through Let's Go Travel (see p.150). From Nanyuki, fork right after 9km, continue for 23km, then turn left at the signboard "Ol Jogi – No Shooting" for 10km. An exceptionally nice set-up on the banks of the Ewaso Nyiro River, with some cheap farmhouse and self-service *banda* accommodation (bring food and drinking water); otherwise, you're welcome to pitch your tent here. Ksh500 per person per night.

Il Ngwesi Lodge Il Ngwesi Group Ranch; bookings through Let's Go Travel (see p.150). A much lauded eco-lodge. Accommodation consists of six double thatched *bandas*, remarkable open-plan structures on stilts, incorporating huge branches and open-air bathrooms. Two (nos. 1 and 5) have "star beds" which can be pulled onto their decks under the night sky. There's a delightful swimming pool and wonderful views, with guaranteed wildlife, including elephants. Options included in the price are night drives, bush walks, riverside breakfasts and climbing the Mukogodo escarpment that faces the lodge; also included are visits to Il Ngwesi's heavily guarded rhino sanctuary, where the first transplant from Lewa, a male called Omni, is tame enough for very close encounters through the wire. Extras include a goat dinner at the "cultural village" and, more uncertainly, tracking wild dog packs in the area. FB $220 per person; ❾

Il Polei Campsite Part of the Il Polei Group Ranch, an hour's drive from Nanyuki along the Doldol road ☎062/31650, ℻31744. This campsite can only be rented out as a whole and can cater for three families. Elephants, leopards, greater kudu, gerunuk and Grevy's zebra are some of the animals you may see in the 20 square kilometres put aside by the Mokogodo Maasai for wildlife conservation. Ksh2300 per night for the whole unit.

Lewa Safari Camp Lewa ⊛www.lewasafaricamp.com. In Lewa's rhino sanctuary itself, the main lodge building is a thatched cedarwood cottage, with a lounge overlooking a floodlit waterhole where rhino, elephant and other animals come to drink. Accommodation is in eleven well-spaced luxury tents raised on lava-rock platforms stilts, and there are optional horseback safaris ($15/hr). FB $490; ⑨

Ol Pejeta House PO Box 763 Nanyuki ☎0176/23414, ⓦwww.serenahotels.com. Seven kilometres beyond (and more expensive than) *Sweetwaters*, this has long been a hideaway for the rich and famous, and is a genuinely classy option. There are only six bedrooms, lots of semi-tame giraffe poking around the gardens, two swimming pools, a resident naturalist, and the same activities as for *Sweetwaters*. FB $650; ⑨

Sweetwaters Tented Camp Ol Pejeta Ranch; PO Box 763 Nanyuki ☎ & ⓕ0176/32409, ⓦwww.serenahotels.com. Upmarket but good value when compared with similar setups in the national parks and reserves, this is a well-laid-out tented camp popular with Kenya residents, especially families,

with high-quality food and service, and a pool. The lower tents are probably preferable to the ones set on stilts. It specializes in night game drives, and camel- and walking safaris are also offered. FB $180 low, $310 high; ⑨

Tassia Lodge PO Box 137 Nanyuki, ⓦwww.tassiakenya.com. Owned by the Lekurruki Community Conservation Ranch, this place overlooks a small scenic valley where you have a good chance of spotting elephants. Accommodation comprises five self-contained doubles and one twin with a shower room; activities include game drives, walking safaris and paragliding. From $450 per person per night; ⑨

Wilderness Trails Lewa ⓦwww.bush-homes.co.ke. All-inclusive accommodation in eight cottages and an atmosphere reminiscent of a comfortable 1930s English country house. The welcome is congenial, the cooking excellent, and the price includes game drives to Lewa swamp in an antiquated Land Rover to see the rare sitatunga water antelope. Closed April, May & Nov. Doubles FB $690; ⑨

Around the Aberdares

The **Aberdare range**, which peaks at 4001m, is less well known than Mount Kenya. The lower, eastern slopes have long been farmed by the Kikuyu (more recently by European tea and coffee planters), and the dense mountain forests covering the middle reaches are the habitat of leopard, bongo antelope, buffalo and some six thousand elephants. Above about 3500m, lions and other open-country animals roam the cloudy moorlands. Melanistic forms – especially of leopard, but also of serval cat and even bushbuck – are also present.

The Kikuyu called these mountains Nyandarua ("drying hide", for their silhouette) long before Thomson in 1884 named them after Lord Aberdare, president of the Royal Geographical Society. In their bamboo thickets and tangled forests, **Kikuyu guerrillas** hid out for years in the 1950s, living off the jungle and surviving thanks to techniques learned under British officers during the Burma campaign in World War II, in which many of them had fought. Despite the manhunts through the forests and the bombing of hideouts, little damage was done to the natural habitat, and Aberdares National Park remains one of Kenya's most pristine forest reserves.

On the western side, the range drops away steeply to the Rift. It was here, in the high **Wanjohi Valley**, that a concentration of settlers in the 1920s and 1930s created the myth of **Happy Valley** out of their obsessive – and unsettled – lives. There's not much to see (or hear) these days. The old wheat and pyrethrum farms were subdivided after independence and the valley's new settlers are more concerned with making their market gardens pay. The memories live on only among veteran *wazungu*.

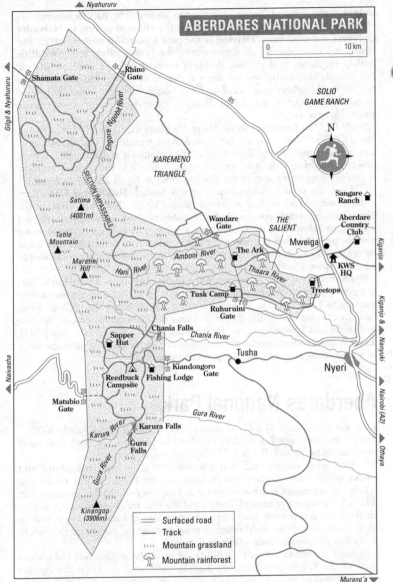

Map labels:

Nyahururu

Shamata Gate

Rhino Gate

Giligil & Nyahururu

B5

SOLIO GAME RANCH

N

Engare Ngobit River

KAREMENO TRIANGLE

Satima (4001m)

Table Mountain

Sangare Ranch

Wandare Gate

THE SALIENT

Aberdare Country Club

Maratini Hill

Hani River

Amboni River

The Ark

Mweiga

KWS HQ

Kiganjo

Tusk Camp

Thaara River

Treetops

Ruhuruini Gate

Kiganjo & Nanyuki

Chania Falls

Naivasha

Sapper Hut

Chania River

Tusha

Nyeri

Reedbuck Campsite

Fishing Lodge

Kiandongoro Gate

Gura River

Kiganjo & Nanyuki

Nairobi (A2)

Matubio Gate

Karura River

Othaya

Karura Falls

Gura Falls

Gura River

Kinangop (3906m)

| Surfaced road |
| Track |
| Mountain grassland |
| Mountain rainforest |

Murang'a

0   10 km

The Kinangop plateau (p.243) was settled by Europeans, too, but in 1950 the high forest and moorland here was declared **Aberdares National Park**. The park stretches 60km along the length of the peaks, with the Salient on the lower slopes reaching out east. Like Mount Kenya National Park, it includes the worst of the weather: rainfall up here is high, often closing the Aberdares to vehicles in the wet season, although in the Salient the "tree-hotel" **game**

lodges – the *Ark* and *Treetops* – stay open all year. The park is nevertheless close enough to Nairobi to be well worth the effort of getting to **Naivasha** or **Nyeri**, the usual bases. **Driving** in the park is beautiful, with waterfalls and sensational views more than compensating for comparatively scarce **wildlife**: buffalo, elephants (and colobus monkeys lower down) are most often seen. For animals in quantity, and for any real chance of seeing rhinos, giant forest hog, or the Aberdares' prize inhabitant, the bongo antelope, you really have to spend a night at either the *Ark* or *Treetops* – expensive, but not an experience you're likely to forget.

You'll find less **transport** in the lower Aberdares than around Mount Kenya, but it's still relatively easy to get around, with regular bus and matatu services between the villages. To head over the mountains and through the park, however, **hitching** is the sole, very uncertain, option if you don't have a vehicle. If you're going to try, stop at the *Outspan Hotel* in Nyeri and try to arrange a lift. If you tire of this, matatu-hop your way towards **Ruhuruini Gate**, deep in the forest, and try waiting at the gate itself. This, like **Matubio Gate** on the Naivasha side (which you could also probably reach in a half-day of lifts and walking) is helpful and would certainly allow you to camp. If you're **driving** into the park (which is the only really practicable way to do it, other than going by organized safari), you need four-wheel drive; it's also a very sensible idea to have two spare wheels.

Nyahururu, the other important town in the region, has **Thomson's Falls** as a postcard attraction, and is also the setting-off point for a wild cross-country journey to Lake Bogoria in the Rift Valley, 1500m below (see p.264). From here, too, begins one of the four routes into the northern deserts, in this case to Maralal and Loiyangalani on the eastern shore of Lake Turkana (see p.571). Though independent travel is still an option on this route, going up in the safety of a safari company's organized trip is recommended.

Aberdares National Park

Daily fees $30, children $10; $10 to camp, $15 in "special" campsites; vehicles Ksh200. Nearest Smartcard outlet is at the KWS HQ in Mweiga (see p.215). Entry on foot with permission of the warden: PO Box 753 Nyeri ☎ 061/55645.

The park splits into two different environments – the **high moorland and peaks** which form the park's main body, and the lower **Salient** to the east where the vegetation is dense rainforest and there is considerably more wildlife. The Salient slopes (location of *Treetops* and the *Ark*) are closed to casual visitors; all the earth access roads have locked barriers. You can arrange to get keys to these from the warden in Mweiga, or possibly from the rangers at the eastern gates (but not from Matubio Gate in the west).

In order to protect the park's **wildlife,** in particular its fifty-odd black rhino (one of the largest populations in Kenya), but mainly to arrest the conflict between wildlife and humans, which most visibly manifested itself in the trashing of crops and homes fringing the park by "rogue" or "rampaging" elephants, the KWS is building an electrified fence to encircle both the Aberdares National Park and the demarcated forestry areas which make up the Aberdares Conservation Area. To this end, the rangers are busy clearing a path on which to erect some 350km of electrified fence, a project known as the **Rhino Ark** (ⓦ www.rhinoark.org) – partly funded by the exciting Rhino Charge **motor race** (see p.74).

The high park

The high moorlands have some exceptional **walking** and include **three peaks**, Satima (the highest) in the north, Kinangop in the south, and Kipipiri, an isolated cone outside the park above the Wanjohi Valley in the west. They can be climbed relatively easily, given good weather conditions: ask the Mountain Club of Kenya in Nairobi for details (see p.74). Hiking in the park is allowed only with the approval of the warden, so apply in good time. You may be offered, or be required to take, a guide (whom you'll have to pay).

Unless you're planning several days of walking, fishing or camping, the most straightforward visit to the moorlands is to spend a day driving through from one side to the other between the **main gates**, Matubio and Ruhuruini. There are two other eastern gates further from Nyeri (Wandere and Kiandongoro) and two at the remote north end of the park (Shamata, accessible from Nyahururu, and Rhino Gate, from the B5 Nyeri–Nyahururu road), but there's no reliable route through the park from south to north, and the small circuit of tracks in the north is very rough. Driving via the park from Naivasha to Nyeri (or vice versa) is easy enough in good weather with 4WD. If conditions are less than ideal, however, and you get stuck, you could be in for a long day – or a rather miserable night. You really need to check **road conditions** with the rangers at the park gates. Surfaces are mostly red *murram*, though there are a few, very steep, rocky sections. It's usually permissible to wander a short distance from your car, though the situation changes from time to time – over the years there have been a number of near-misses with several apparently human-hungry lions.

Naivasha to Matubio Gate

From Naivasha, follow the signs for the park via the Uplands road as if going to Nairobi, as far as the junction for Kinangop on the north side of town. From here, you climb about 14km, on reasonably intact tarmac, to another junction where the bad road begins. Go easy if you're driving – the cambered, rock-built surface is perfect for punctures. After another 5km or so, you reach Kipipiri junction and, seasonally, a strange egret nesting colony in eleven conifers along the roadside.

At **Ndunyu Njeru** centre, you pass the last chance of a puncture repair or petrol (fuel isn't always available) and the final stop of matatus up from Naivasha, before a few more kilometres of very bad surface. Finally, the road runs out of reasons to continue except to the national park itself – becoming a narrow, quite acceptable, tarmac switchback – and climbs through the vegetation zones, with increasing evidence of elephants (dung everywhere), to pitch out finally through the highest extent of the forest at Matubio Gate, right on the threshold of the moorland. Along the last 7km there are some excellent views back over the climb and down to Lake Naivasha. Allow two to three hours to get this far.

Matubio Gate to Ruhuruini Gate

Allowing four hours from Matubio Gate to Ruhuruini Gate gives time enough, in good weather, for visits to the Chania Falls and the Karura Giant Falls. Proper access to the top of the **Karura Falls** (there's no way down to the bottom) was built only in 1992, by the British Army's Royal Engineers. They've created two superb, dizzy, timber viewpoints, one on each side, from which you can look across through dripping, Afro-Alpine vegetation to the babbling, four-metre-wide Karura stream as it plunges over the abyss, dropping nearly 300m in three stages. To the south, the distant veil of the **Gura Falls**, a kilometre or two across the yawning canyon, seems to make for a surfeit of dramatic beauty.

The much lower, sheer drop of the **Chania Falls** has rickety access walks and platforms (be careful) and you can gaze from the top, or the bottom, and even contemplate a swim in the pool. It was in this vicinity, in 1984, that an American tourist was badly mauled by a lion, an incident that so unnerved the park's authorities that for many years there were tough rules on unaccompanied walking. This followed a controlled lion cull, aimed as much at public relations as at giving various herbivores (such as giant forest hog and bongo) a chance to rebuild their endangered populations. A cautionary sign by the path still warns about "wild animals", though there seems no reason to believe they favour this spot over any other.

The 15km east to **Ruhuruini Gate** descends in a breathtaking helter-skelter through the cloud forest, with stunning views across jungle-cloaked valleys. The road down to Nyeri from the gate is in good condition and you soon reach tarmac.

Accommodation

There are several accommodation options in the **high park**, including **camping** at the basic *Reedbuck Campsite* near the *Fishing Lodge*.

Fishing Lodge Barely 2km inside the Kiandongoro Gate, and located on open moors above the Magura River, are these two stone-built, tin-roofed cottages, each with three bedrooms sleeping a total of seven. Book through KWS (or take a chance and pay at the park gate), and share the central open-fire cooking and eating area with other guests. You need to take food, warm sleeping bags and firewood; wood-fired boiler tanks outside produce hot water. $200 per night for the whole lodge.

Sapper Hut Some 10km further west from the *Fishing Lodge*, on a little tributary of the Chania river; reservations through KWS. At an altitude of around 3000m, this is a wooden *banda* with a living room, double bedroom,

fireplace, veranda, wood-fired boiler and external bathroom. Lamps (bring paraffin), bedsheets, firewood and basic cooking facilities are provided. Take bedding, towels, food and drinking water. Collect the key from the *Fishing Lodge*. 30 for the hut.

Tusk Camp 2km in from Ruhuruini Gate; reservations through KWS. At 2300m, tucked into a glade surrounded by forest. There are several wooden *bandas* here (sleeping eight in total), an ill-equipped kitchen (bring pots, pans and cutlery), a pit latrine with one of Kenya's most regal views, and a caretaker to help you out. Visits from here to the Salient should be possible if you enquire first with the rangers at the gate. $100 per night for the whole lodge.

The tree-hotels

For many visitors, a night in one of the two Aberdare tree-hotels, the *Treetops* and the *Ark* – both located in the **Salient**, with guests arriving on the lodges' own transport – is the stuff of dreams. Yet both tree-hotels can at first be a disappointment. Having invested heavily for a night, you find yourself confined to the interior of a wooden building with a hundred or more fellow tourists, are shown to your tiny bedroom, and are then briefed on the animals you can hope to see and the things you're not allowed to do. It can all feel somewhat contrived.

But when the sun goes down and the floodlights come on, it's strange how quickly this is forgotten. The wildlife below draws everyone's attention and the cameras start clicking in earnest. Herds of heavyweights – elephant and buffalo especially – can be taken for granted, and the prospect of a night's sleepless vigil becomes magical, as even your cramped confines acquire a certain charm.

Treetops

PO Box 24 Nyeri, ☎ 061/55030, F2286; reservations also through Let's Go Travel, p.150. Minimum age 7 years (no child rates, except on occasional "children's nights");

FB $185 low, $250 high, including lunch at the Outspan Hotel *(see p.214). Park fees extra.*

Perhaps Kenya's most famous hotel, **Treetops** was where Princess Elizabeth became Queen Elizabeth II on the death of her father George VI, while she was staying in the original *Treetops* on the other side of the water hole. The original tree house was burned down in 1955 by Mau Mau freedom-fighters; the present, much larger construction is built on stilts among the trees. Intentionally like an officers' mess, it has something of the creaking atmosphere of a wooden ship, and the bedrooms and facilities (shared) are cramped.

During daylight hours, reality is never far below the surface. Through the forest, Kikuyu *shambas* and homesteads are visible in every direction and the main Nyeri road passes by just 3km away. The lodge is no longer *in* the forest, either. Down by the **water hole**, a large area is now virtually bare, red dust and dead wood – the result of foliage destruction by elephants. The problem, as always, is balancing tourist receipts with the needs of wildlife – which themselves conflict with those of farmers on the slopes nearby. Many of the animals which come to *Treetops* are lured by the **salt** spread beneath the viewing platform every afternoon before the visitors arrive. This draws large herds of elephant and buffalo, but very few rhino, and in the long term it would seem to ensure the ruination of the environment around the lodge. It certainly discourages those animals that need plenty of cover. The curious **giant forest hog** sometimes turns up, but **leopards** are rarely seen and the large, shy **bongo** antelope hasn't put in an appearance for many years – understandably.

△ Treetops

Ⓦ *www.lonrhohotels.com. Minimum age 7 years; FB $150 low, $250 high, including lunch at* Aberdare Country Club *(see opposite). Park fees extra.*

For better game-viewing, the **Ark**, *Treetops'* upstart competitor, is set at a higher altitude, actually in the mountain forest. Here, they do on occasion see leopards (and, perhaps once a year, bongos), and there are almost guaranteed nightly sightings of elephant, rhino and buffalo. Transport from the *Aberdare Country Club* leaves daily at 2.30 and 5pm, returning at 8am. You should try to get an afternoon nap as buzzers through the night announce the arrival of one of the "big five". The attraction for wildlife is the muddy pool and salt lick at the "prow" of the hotel, under the viewing terraces and next to a ground-level photographic hide. There's usually an animated scene here as the animals jostle for salt, and fights sometimes break out, especially when newborn calves are around. Accommodation is better than at *Treetops*, with en-suite rooms, though don't expect luxury; the rooms are still poky and dark.

Nyeri and around

Self-styled capital of Kikuyuland – a title the Kikuyu of Kiambu might dispute – **NYERI** is, more prosaically, the administrative headquarters of Central Province and one of the liveliest, most chaotic and friendly highland towns. An attractive trading centre despite its fantastically broken-up streets, Nyeri nestles in the green hills where the broad vale between Mount Kenya and the Aberdares drops towards Nairobi. Tumultuous markets, scores of *dukas*, even a few street entertainers, lend it an air of irrepressible commercialism.

Another former British military camp, Nyeri emerged as a market town for European coffee growers in the hills and for settlers on the ranching and wheat farms further north. Of more specialist interest, Nyeri was also the last home of Robert **Baden-Powell**, founder of the worldwide scouting movement, whose cryptically named Paxtu cottage, now a small museum (Ksh250), stands in the grounds of the *Outspan Hotel* and whose grave and memorial are to be found on the north side of town.

The extraordinary density of **cultivation** in the tightly spaced *shambas* around Nyeri (crops include maize, cassava, sugar cane, millet, squash, citrus fruit, as well as tea, coffee and macadamia nuts) is partly a hangover from white settlerdom, when a rapidly growing population was deprived of huge tracts of land and forced to cultivate intensively. Partly, too, it's the result of land consolidation, the "rationalization" of fragmented land holdings into unitary *shambas* that took place in the 1950s, turning people who had held traditional rights into deed-holding property owners. And partly, it's the simple consequence of an excellent climate and soil, plus a birth rate reckoned (like Kisii's, see p.307) to be one of the highest in the world.

There's no doubt that the changes which have taken place in Nyeri District have been some of the most profound and rapid anywhere in the country. Even the villages of Kikuyuland are nearly all innovations of the last fifty years, the irreversible effects of the Emergency. Until then, the Kikuyu had mostly lived in scattered homesteads among their crops and herds. British security forces, unable to contain open revolt in the countryside, began the systematic intern-ment of the whole Kikuyu population into fenced and guarded villages, forcing the guerrillas into the high forests, and the villages of today have mostly grown from such places.

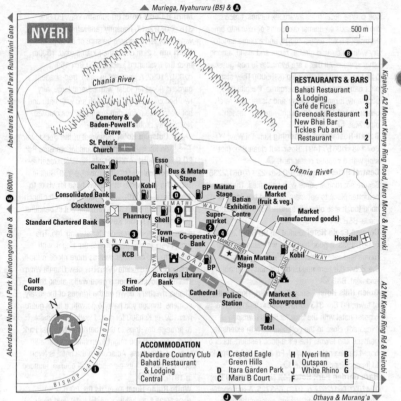

NYERI

0   500 m

Ⓑ

RESTAURANTS & BARS

Bahati Restaurant & Lodging	D
Café de Ficus	3
Greenoak Restaurant	1
New Bhai Bar	4
Tickles Pub and Restaurant	2

Chania River

Aberdares National Park Ruhuruini Gate

Cemetery & Baden-Powell's Grave

St. Peter's Church

Caltex

Cenotaph

Kobil

Esso

Bus & Matatu Stage

BP

Matatu Stage

Batian Exhibition Centre

Chania River

Covered Market (fruit & veg.)

Market (manufactured goods)

Consolidated Bank

Clocktower

KIMATHI WAY

Super-market

Standard Chartered Bank

Pharmacy

Shell

Town Hall

Co-operative Bank

KIMATHI WAY

Hospital

KENYATTA WAY

KCB

MOI NYATO WAY

NYATO ROAD

Main Matatu Stage

Kobil

TEMPLE ROAD

Golf Course

Fire Station

Barclays Bank

Library

Cathedral

Police Station

Market & Showground

BISHOP GATIMU ROAD

N

Total

ACCOMMODATION

Aberdare Country Club	A	Crested Eagle	H	Nyeri Inn	B
Bahati Restaurant & Lodging	D	Green Hills	I	Outspan	E
Central	C	Itara Garden Park	J	White Rhino	G
		Maru B Court	F		

Kiganjo, A2 Mount Kenya Ring Road, Naro Moru & Nanyuki

A2 Mt Kenya Ring Rd & Nairobi

Ⓐ (600m)

Aberdares National Park Kiandongoro Gate ▲

Ⓙ ▼

Othaya & Murang'a ▼

Nyeri was on the front line – as much as there was one – during the war for independence. On the main street, Kimathi Way, is a **cenotaph**, unusual in the frankness of its inscription: "To the Memory of the Members of the Kikuyu Tribe who Died in the Fight for Freedom 1951–1957".

Practicalities

Both the bus stage and main matatu stage are on Kimathi Way. The town has several **banks**, including branches of Barclays, a KCB, a Co-operative and a Standard Chartered, all with ATMs. **Email** facilities are available at Kanjo Cyber Café and Jaydee Systems, both in the Batian Exhibition Centre on Market Street.

Accommodation

Nyeri's role as rural business centre and major transport crossroads means there are plenty of cheap places to stay in town, as well as the historic and upmarket *Outspan Hotel* and, much further out, the atmospheric *Aberdare Country Club*.

Aberdare Country Club 11km out on the Nyahururu road near Mweiga, then 3km along a passable *murram* road (signposted); PO Box 449 Nyeri ☎061/55620, ℱ55224,

ⓦ www.lonrhohotels.com. The base for the *Ark* (see opposite), this luxuriously rural affairs dates from 1938, and has rooms in stone cottages (nos. 28–31 have the best views). There's a pool, nine-hole golf course (local rules award six inches' grace if the ball lands on animal droppings or rolls into an aardvark's hole), tennis courts, and a game sanctuary with reticulated giraffe, zebra and eland, among other species. All these are available to non-guests on a temporary membership (Ksh500). They also offer game drives in the Aberdares. Despite its popularity, it remains classy, and visitors are rarely disappointed. Prices rise slightly in high season, otherwise ❽

Bahati Restaurant & Lodging Kimathi Way; PO Box 148 ☎061/71491. Basic but clean B&L (not s/c), with a popular restaurant. ❷

Central Hotel Kanisa Rd; PO Box 229 ☎061/2235. Secure s/c rooms, some with balconies. There's no better place to eat *kienyenji*, and breakfast is good too. It also offers live music Fri & Sat. Good value. B&B ❷

Crested Eagle Hotel Market St; PO Box 12465 ☎061/4933. A good high-rise with standard s/c rooms and safe parking, but it's expensive and the *Zebra Bar* here makes things noisy up until midnight. B&B ❹

Green Hills Hotel Bishop Gatimu Rd, 1km south of town; PO Box 313 ☎061/30604, ℉ 2199. The biggest hotel with the best facilities (*Outspan* excepted), close to the golf course, with extensive gardens and lawns. There's a pool, restaurants and bar; it can be noisy on Wed, Fri & Sat nights thanks to its popular discos. B&B ❺

Itara Garden Park Hotel Moi Nyayo Way; PO Box 12470 ☎061/2537 or 0721/653725. A reasonable hotel if you don't mind staying outside the town centre, with decent s/c rooms and hot water. The live music nights showcase Congolese Lingala oldies and acrobatic shows. B&B ❺

Maru B Court Hotel Off Kimathi Way; PO Box 316 ☎061/2817. Recently renovated and with hot water. Get there early to be sure of a room. ❷

Nyeri Inn 3.2km down the Kiganjo road, 1500m from the Nyahururu junction; PO Box 159 ☎061/31092. A gem, set in calm, tree-shaded gardens (ideal for kids), with several large, airy two-bed cottages for rent, each s/c with bath and hot water. The restaurant mainly serves chicken. No security problems. B&B ❸

Outspan Hotel 2km west of the clocktower on Kanisa Rd, off the Kiandongoro Gate Rd; PO Box 24 Nyeri ☎061/24245, ℉ 2286; reservations also through Let's Go Travel, p.150. Built in 1927, the *Outspan* is the stately base for visits to *Treetops* (see p.210), where you check in for lunch and are driven up in the afternoon. Set in beautiful gardens, with Mount Kenya rising behind, it offers more than enough reasons for staying, too. The rooms vary in size (larger ones are huge), with wonderful old baths, as well as more modern facilities (including satellite TV) in the new Chania Wing. There's a pool, and some good walks along the Chania riverbank down on the fringes of the lovely gardens, though you have to go with a hotel guard (Ksh150, or Ksh300 for a bird walk). It's possible to arrange day-trips to the Aberdares National Park from here, and you might even find yourself a lift over the Aberdares. Adjacent to the hotel is Nyeri Sports Club, with its nine-hole golf course, founded in 1910. B&B ❽

White Rhino Hotel Kenyatta Rd; PO Box 30 ☎061/4384. A shabby colonial hotel, laid-back, with reasonable rooms and a *nyama choma* bar. It's *the* place for conscientious boozing, and there are disco and jam sessions Sun. B&B ❸

Eating, drinking and nightlife

Nyeri has a number of interesting **eating** options. It also has a **cheese** factory – lots of its produce is available locally. There are discos at the *Green Hills Hotel*, where Sunday afternoons feature traditional dances. The *White Rhino Hotel* is a popular place for whiling away an afternoon with a bottle or five, while the busy *Zebra Bar* at the *Crested Eagle Hotel* is open till midnight.

Bahati Restaurant & Lodging Kimathi Way. Known for its chicken cooked any way you want it, so long as it's fried or stewed.

Café de Ficus Kenyatta Rd. A bar with conspicuous booths and *nyama choma*.

Greenoak Restaurant Surprisingly good, dishing up great trout and *nyama choma*. If the weather's okay, the first-floor terrace-bar, overlooking the commotion below, is fun too.

New Bhai Bar Market St. Lively little place serving good samosas and *mandaazi*, as well as beer.

Outspan Hotel See above. This atmospheric pile welcomes day-visitors for its excellent buffet lunches (Ksh1200), or for tea on the lawn and a swim in the pool (Ksh500). The hotel's *Kirinyaga Bar* is pleasant enough for a beer in the evening in civilized surroundings.

Tickles Pub and Restaurant Next to the Mathai Supermarket is this balcony bar serving good burgers and *nyama choma*.

Mweiga and routes out of Nyeri

A signposted route leads **west**, past the *Outspan*, up into the Aberdares and the park's Kiandongoro gate in the high moorland. In the other direction, the road splits out of town, forking **south** to Murang'a via Othaya, or continuing **east** to the A2 Mount Kenya ring road and the quickest return route to Nairobi (also via Murang'a).

A fourth route takes you in a northwest direction heading out of town, splitting in two after 2km. Take the right fork if you want the A2 Mount Kenya ring road for Naro Moru and Nanyuki via Kiganjo. Fork left and you're on the B5, which sweeps past the road for the Ruhuruini Gate in the forest of the Salient, then the unmarked tracks for *Treetops* and the *Ark* – with the turning for the *Aberdare Country Club* between them, just before the hilltop centre of **Mweiga**, 8km from Nyeri. A kilometre or so south of Mweiga, on the east side of the road, is the Aberdares National Park headquarters, the park's only Smartcard point of sale.

The highway, in pretty good condition, continues across lonely, forested ridges and wide savanna to Nyahururu (Thomson's Falls), on the northern fringes of the Highlands.

Sangare Ranch

Near Mweiga, you'll find Kenya's possibly most charming luxury tented camp, 🏕 **Sangare Ranch** (reservations through Let's Go Travel, p.150; FB $520, ❾), located some 5km north of the *Aberdare Country Club*; the ranch will pick you up in their own 4WD from the club, while a matatu to the signboard near Mweiga will leave you with a three-kilometre walk to the ranch). The landscape and atmosphere at the ranch could hardly be more different from the club: the track winds up and down precarious forested ravines before emerging onto a fresh high plateau of scrub and meadow, with a good view of Mount Kenya when the air is clear. There are only six tents, each with wood-heated showers and solar-powered lighting, sited on the east side of a small freshwater lake. The style is refreshingly informal: the superb farmhouse meals are eaten in a small dining room in the company of the manager.

The **birdlife** is the main draw, with black-headed herons squawking loudly in the trees over the tents, some migratory pelicans, and glimpses of crowned eagles, accompanied by a fantastic chorus of frogs and toads throughout the night. There are usually some elephants and buffalo in the vicinity, as well as zebra, gazelle, hyena, colobus and sykes' monkeys, and the occasional leopard. **Horse-riding** is possible, as are guided night walks in search of bats, bushbabies, and the beautiful maned rat.

Solio Game Ranch

Northwards along the B5 from Mweiga, the **Solio Game Ranch** (PO Box 2 Naro Moru; ☎020/249177 or 061/55271–3, Ⓕ55235; single entry fee of Ksh1600, under 12s free; open all year unless very wet) lies a few kilometres further on, off to the right. Privately run, Solio more or less single-handedly saved the Kenyan rhino population from extinction, breeding them here for subsequent translocation into the national parks and other Kenyan reserves. From an original population of 23 black rhino, there are now over 50; of the original 16 white rhino, imported from South Africa, the population now stands at over 70; and all of the relocated black rhinos, and most of the white, at Nakuru National Park's Rhino Sanctuary were bred here. Without a 4WD, you can visit the ranch by hiring a vehicle and driver or by joining a trip from the *Aberdare Country Club*. If you have your own wheels, the ranch provides maps, and a free guide if there's one available. They have four basic campsites (water and firewood provided; Ksh400 per person).

Nyahururu (Thomson's Falls)

Like Nanyuki, **NYAHURURU** is almost on the equator, and it shares much of Nanyuki's character. It's high up (at 2360m, Kenya's highest town), cool (in fact, very cold on January and February mornings), and set on open savanna lands with patches of indigenous forest and plenty of coniferous plantation. Since the B5 road to Nyeri was completed, Nyahururu has been less cut off, but it's still

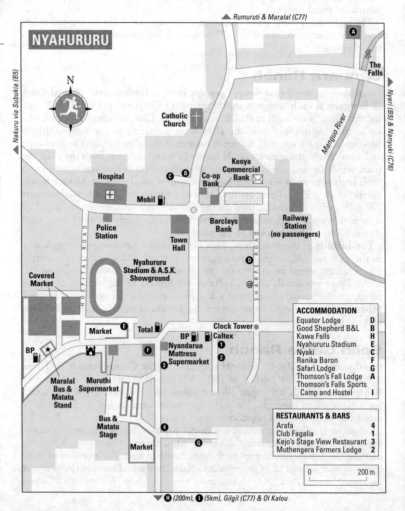

NYAHURURU

▲ *Rumuruti & Maralal (C77)*

◄ *Nakuru via Subukia (B5)*

► *Nyeri (B5) & Nanyuki (C76)*

N

The Falls

Manguo River

Catholic Church

Kenya Commercial Bank ⊠

Hospital ✚

Co-op Bank

Ⓒ Ⓑ

Mobil 🅿

Barclays Bank

Railway Station (no passengers)

Police Station

Town Hall

Nyahururu Stadium & A.S.K. Showground

Ⓓ

SHARPE ROAD

HOSPITAL ROAD

Covered Market

Market Ⓔ

Total 🅿

Clock Tower ●

BP 🅿 Caltex

ACCOMMODATION

Equator Lodge	D
Good Shepherd B&L	B
Kawa Falls	H
Nyahururu Stadium	E
Nyaki	C
Ranika Baron	F
Safari Lodge	G
Thomson's Fall Lodge	A
Thomson's Falls Sports Camp and Hostel	I

BP 🅿 ★

Ⓕ

Nyandarua Mattress Supermarket ❸

Maralal Bus & Matatu Stand

Muruthi Supermarket

Bus & Matatu Stage

Market

★

RESTAURANTS & BARS

Arafa	4
Club Fagalia	1
Kejo's Stage View Restaurant	3
Muthengera Farmers Lodge	2

0   200 m

▼ Ⓗ *(200m),* ❶ *(5km), Gilgil (C77) & Ol Kalou*

something of a frontier town for routes north to Lake Turkana and the desert – a tarred road goes out as far as Rumuruti and then the fun begins (see p.571).

Joseph Thomson gave the town its original name when he named the nearby waterfall after his father in 1883. Many still call it "T Falls" – and not just the old settlers you might expect. Thomson's Falls was one of the last settler towns to be established. The first sign of urbanization was a hut built by the Narok Angling Club in the early 1920s to allow its members to fish for the newly introduced trout in the Ewaso Narok, Pesi and Equator rivers. In 1929, when the railway branch line arrived, the town began to take shape. The line has closed now, but the hotel built in 1931, *Thomson's Falls Lodge*, is still going strong, and Nyahururu remains an important market town – and not really a tourist centre. The **market** is well worth a browse, especially on Saturdays. Find it anywhere west of the stadium – it sprawls out over most of the district, an indication of the town's rapid growth over the last decade or so.

The falls, and other excursions around Nyahururu

On the northeast outskirts of town, **Thomson's Falls** are pretty rather than spectacular – though they can be dramatic after heavy rain. They're a popular stop-off

△ Thomson's Falls

for tourists travelling between Samburu and Maasai Mara game reserves (fourteen minibuses at one time is nothing), and the lawns above the falls get crowded with picnickers from town at weekends. The path leading down to the bottom of the 75-metre falls is somewhat dangerous, especially when wet. Don't attempt to climb up again by any other route, because the cliffs are extremely unstable.

With more time to spare, you can search for a longer walk down into the forested valley, following the **Ewaso Narok River**. If you want to try this, cross the bridge first, then look for a way downstream. The spray-laden trees are shaken periodically by troops of colobus monkeys and, as on Mount Kenya, three-horned chameleons are always around. The area is also fruitful for ornithologists. A much shorter stroll also takes you over the bridge and past the electricity substation, beyond which the first trail you come to leads to the top of a hill with a communications tower and a skeletal lookout post. Excellent views from here stretch south towards Ol Kalou and the marshy trough of Lake Ol' Bolossat.

A longer excursion, for which you might want transport, takes you in quest of the highest **hippos** in Kenya. A kilometre from the turning off to *Thomson's Falls Lodge* on the Nyeri road, you come to a small cluster of *dukas* on the right. Walk down towards the houses closest to town and, about 300m from the road, you emerge by a swampy area fed by Lake Ol Bolossat. The area immediately by the access path is thick with reeds, but walk round the lake to the clump of trees and you can shin up one of these and select a natural observation platform. Sit and watch and you may see as many as half a dozen or so hippos. If you don't find them here, then they're likely to be in Lake Ol Bolossat itself, which has its north shore some 15km south of Nyahururu on the road to Aberdare National Park's Shamata gate.

Practicalities

There are several buses and matatus each day down the B5 to Nyeri, or you could hitch from outside *Thomson's Falls Lodge*. This road was built, for most of its length, along a new route, so villages are few; for the most part it either bucks up and down across forested valleys or soars across immense plains of swaying grass. It's not much used by heavy transport and still in relatively good condition. The mostly unsurfaced C76 road to Nanyuki can be treacherous in wet weather and it can be hard to locate the turning off from the B5, around 10km outside town. For a spectacular change of scene, take the road down the **scarp** to Nakuru, via the Subukia valley, following the route to Lake Bogoria described in chapter 3. Lastly, a straightforward and reasonably quiet road to Gilgil and the Rift Valley heads south out of town, crossing the Equator, with the usual smattering of souvenir stalls and eager demonstrators of the "Coriolis effect" (see p.193).

There is **Internet** access at Heri General Merchants, on Sharpe road, halfway between Barclays Bank and the clock tower. For **meals**, *Kejo's Stage View Restaurant* has a lively atmosphere and cheap Swahili food; *Muthengera Farmers Lodge* is recommended for chicken; while *Arafa* at the Cyrus Lodging, opposite the market, does good veggie curries. For action after dark, check out *Club Fagalia*, which has reggae, soukous and one-man guitar shows.

Accommodation

For accommodation, most people head out to the touristy *Thomson's Falls Lodge*. This is also the place to **camp** in Nyahururu, but there are plenty of cheap B&Ls in town.

Equator Lodge PO Box 678 ☏ 065/32748, ℱ 22250. Nice treehouse-style terrace restaurant with basic rooms attached. ❷

Good Shepherd B&L In a traditional compound by the Nyaki Hotel, with basic singles only and limited hot water. ❶

Kawa Falls Hotel PO Box 985 ☏ 065/32295, ℱ 32256. A friendly five-storey block away from the noise of the centre. Rooms are basic, slightly damp and poky, though they are s/c, and there's safe parking and an airy first-floor bar. ❷

Nyahururu Stadium Hotel PO Box 152 ☏ 065/32773. Above the Karabui Gospel Music Store; cheap, secure and a good deal if you don't mind the deeply religious atmosphere. ❷

Nyaki Hotel PO Box 214 ☏ 065/22313. Rooms are s/c with hot water, but are rather dark and small, and in need of renovation. ❷

Ranika Baron Hotel In the centre at the start of the Ol Kalou road; PO Box 423 ☏ 065/32056. Slightly better than average, but it suffers greatly from the loud Equatorial Hotel over the road and the matatu stage next door,

the former jumping till 4am, the latter honking from 6am. ❸

Safari Lodge Hotel PO Box 678 ☏ 065/32748. Pastel green six-storey building with good s/c rooms and hot water. Alcohol is banned. ❸

Thomson's Fall Lodge PO Box 38 ☏ 065/22006, ℱ 32170; reservations in Nairobi on ☏ 020/340311, ℱ 340311. A highlands farmhouse atmosphere and log fires in the rooms. Some rooms have big old-fashioned baths, others rather more basic showers – ask to see a selection. The campsite (tents not available to rent) is popular with budget safari groups; the price includes showers and ample firewood. Alternatively, you can camp in the grounds within earshot of the falls. Campsite Ksh400 per person, B&B ❺

Thomson's Falls Sports Camp and Hostel 5km south of town on the Gilgil road; PO Box 3171; ☏ 0722/635149, ℮ thomsonfalls20@yahoo. co.uk. Dorm accommodation (including one dorm in an old London bus), plus a large campsite. Activities include cycling, bird- and hippo-watching, horse-riding and trekking. Dorms Ksh400.

Travel details

Trains

Nakuru to: Kisumu (3 weekly; 7hr); Nairobi (3 weekly; 7hr); Naivasha (3 weekly; 4hr 30 min).

Buses

Chorogia to: Embu (several daily; 1hr 30min); Meru (several daily; 1hr); Nairobi (several daily; 4hr).

Embu to: Meru (several daily; 2hr); Nairobi (several daily; 2hr 30min); Sagana (several daily; 40min); Thika (several daily; 30min).

Meru to: Embu (several daily; 2hr); Maua (3 daily; 1hr); Mombasa (4 weekly; 10hr); Nairobi (several daily; 5hr); Nanyuki (2–3 daily; 1hr 30min); Thika (several daily; 4hr).

Nanyuki to: Meru (2–3 daily; 1hr 30min); Nairobi (2–3 daily; 3hr 30min); Nakuru (1 daily; 3hr); Naro Moru (2–3 daily; 30min); Nyahururu (1 daily; 3hr); Nyeri (2–3 daily; 1hr 30min).

Nyahururu to: Nairobi (1 daily; 3–4hr); Nakuru (1 daily; 1hr); Nanyuki (1 daily; 2hr); Nyeri (1 daily; 1hr 30min).

Nyeri to: Eldoret (1 daily; 5hr); Nairobi (2–3 daily; 2hr 30min); Nanyuki (2–3 daily; 1hr 30min); Sagana (2–3 daily; 40min).

Matatus

Frequencies are given only where there are relatively few services.

Embu to: Isiolo (3hr 30min); Meru (2hr 30min); Nairobi (2hr 30min); Sagana (40min); Siakago (several daily; 30min).

Meru to: Embu (2hr 30min); Isiolo (1hr); Maua (several daily; 1hr); Nairobi (5hr); Nanyuki (1hr 30min).

Nanyuki to: Isiolo (several daily; 1hr 30min); Meru (1hr 30min); Nakuru (several daily; 5hr); Nairobi (several daily; 3hr 30min); Nyeri (1hr 30min); Nyahururu (3hr).

Nyahururu to: Maralal (several daily; 4hr); Naivasha (several daily; 1hr 30min); Nakuru (several daily; 1hr 30min); Nanyuki (3hr); Nyeri (1hr 30min).

Nyeri to: Eldoret (4 daily; 4hr); Kisumu (6hr); Nairobi (2hr); Nakuru (2hr 30min); Nanyuki (1hr 30min); Nyahururu (1hr 30min).

Flights

Lewa to: Maasai Mara (1 daily; 1hr 45min); Nairobi (2 daily; 1hr).

Nanyuki to: Maasai Mara (2 daily; 1hr 30min); Nairobi (2 daily; 50min); Nyeri (1 daily; 10min).

3

The Rift Valley

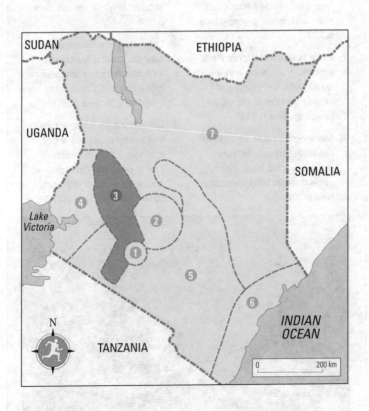

CHAPTER 3 # Highlights

* **Olorgasailie prehistoric site** Stark site in the southern Rift Valley, with fossil evidence of one of our ancestors preserved in situ. See p.225

* **Lake Naivasha & Hell's Gate National Park** Hauntingly atmospheric freshwater lake near Hell's Gate's sheer, red cliffs and winding gorge. See p.229

* **Lake Nakuru National Park** Woods, grasslands and lakeshore, with the chance of seeing flamingos, rhinos and leopards. See p.253

* **Menengai crater** This colossal crater outside Nakuru makes a good hike, with superb views on a clear day. See p.256

* **Hyrax Hill** If you don't visit any other Stone-Age sites in Kenya, try to take an hour out for a wander around Hyrax Hill, east of Nakuru. See p.258

* **Kipkelion Monastery** This multinational Cistercian outpost is a fine retreat. See p.260

* **Lake Bogoria** Steaming hot springs, greater kudu antelope and remote campsites make this a highly recommended visit. See p.261

* **Lake Baringo** A beautiful freshwater oasis in the dry northern Rift, with hippos, crocs, over 400 bird species and several good accommodation options. See p.267

△ Njemps people, Lake Baringo

3

The Rift Valley

K enya's **Rift Valley** is only part of a continental fault system that runs 6000km from Jordan clean across Africa to Mozambique. Perhaps Kenya's most important topographical feature, it is certainly one of the country's great distinguishing marks, acting as both a human and natural divide. As such, it has come to be seen as a monumental valley of teeming game and Maasai herders, a trough of grasslands older than humanity. This image is not entirely borne out by reality. The valley certainly is spectacular, a literal rift across the country, with all the stunning panoramas and gaunt escarpment backdrops you could wish for, and the plains animals are still abundant in places. Nevertheless, much of the game has been dispersed by human population pressure onto the higher plateaus to the southwest, and most of the Maasai nowadays live further south.

At least the Rift Valley's **historical influence** cannot be diluted. People have trekked down it, generation after generation, over perhaps the last two or three thousand years, from the wetlands of southern Sudan and the Ethiopian highlands. Some of these immigrants were the ancestors of the **Maasai**, who dominated much of the valley and its surroundings for several centuries before the Europeans arrived. Until the beginning of the twentieth century, they lived on both sides, and the northern **Ilaikipiak** group were a constant threat to caravans coming up from the coast. With European settlement, they were forced from their former grazing grounds in the valley's turbulent bottleneck and confined to the "Southern Reserve" for much of the colonial era. Although many have now returned to the valley, and many towns retain their ancient Maa names, the Maasai are at their most conservative and traditional in southern Kenya, for more on which see p.404.

In practical terms, the parts of the Rift Valley covered in this chapter offer several exceptional **lakes**, lots of spectacular twisting tracks, and some of the wildest country in central Kenya. If you're at all interested in wildlife, especially **birds**, you'll find this area a source of endless fascination, with wonderful nature reserves at lakes **Nakuru** and **Bogoria**, freshwater ecosystems at lakes **Naivasha** and **Baringo**, and a soda lake at **Magadi** supporting flamingos. In addition, there's a handful of interesting **prehistoric sites** with a refreshing rawness about them.

Apart from **Naivasha**, **Nakuru** and the string of towns up the western escarpment (**Njoro**, **Elburgon** and **Molo**), the area covered in this chapter contains few places larger than a village, and lodgings, strictly speaking, are scarce. Though there is usually somewhere to lay your head, this is a region where a **tent** will be worth its extra weight, and good walking shoes are a definite advantage. **Transport** in the higher, agricultural parts of the south is

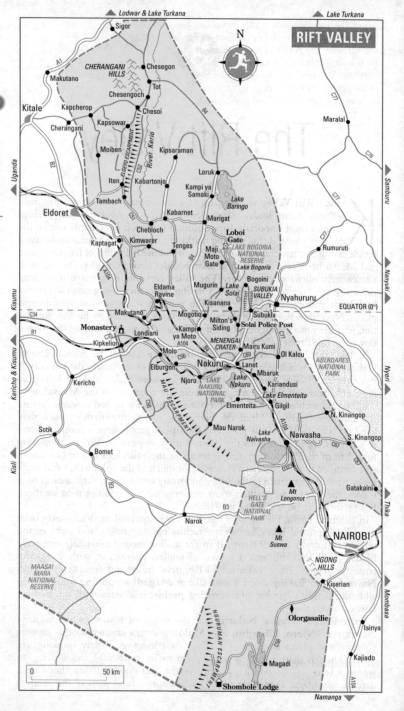

RIFT VALLEY

0   50 km

generally fine, but northwards, or off the main Nakuru–Baringo–Kabarnet axis, you can expect long waits, next-to-no buses and infrequent matatus. **Roads** are variable; the **A104** between Naivasha and Nakuru is very rough and prone to flooding during the rains. Both Naivasha and Nakuru are served by **trains** between Nairobi and Kisumu. Note that the northern Rift is lower – and consequently hotter – than most upcountry regions, so be prepared for some very high temperatures and don't underestimate your **water** requirements.

The Southern Rift

The journey south from Nairobi down into the hot, sparsely inhabited southern districts of the Rift Valley takes you first to the prehistoric site at **Olorgasailie**, then on to the dramatic salt lake of **Magadi**, and finally to the **Nguruman Escarpment** and the remote nature conservancy at **Shompole**. There should be two matatus from Nairobi to Olorgasailie and Magadi leaving in the early afternoon; there are also two daily buses, one in the morning and one in the afternoon, leaving from Nairobi's Country Bus Station. The scenery opens out dramatically as you skirt the southern flank of the Ngong Hills and descend steeply down the escarpment; travelling by public transport, try to get a front seat as giraffe and other animals are often seen.

KISERIAN, 15km from Nairobi National Park's main gate, is your chance to buy last-minute provisions, as there's almost no food available further south. *Kituo Bar* is a basic **B&L** at the eastern end of the market square, with good *nyama choma* and a first-floor balcony overlooking the wonderful bustle of the market. There is also a **restaurant** serving good barbecued food, the *Greengos Inn*, a couple of minutes' drive down the Isinya road. Bang in the centre of Kiserian, the *Eureka Hotel* (☎020/522346; ❷) has a lively restaurant and bar with occasional live music, as well as decent s/c rooms.

Accommodation in a different class altogether can be found at *Whistling Thorns*, 13km east of Kiserian on the rather potholed Isinya road (PO Box 51512 Nairobi; ☎ & ⊕020/350720, ⊛www.whistlingthorns.com; ❻). Overlooking the Ngong Hills and the plains south of Nairobi National Park, this offers one and two-bedroomed cottages in rather uninspiring concrete blocks, and you can camp here too. There's a swimming pool, decent food – including excellent pizzas, grilled game and game liver paté – and opportunities for walks, cycling and horse-riding.

There's a pleasant picnic site at *Olepolos Country Club*, 12km southwest of Kiserian. At **Olepolos** itself, there are a number of *nyama choma* joints, a good bar with chairs on the roadside under some trees, and entirely Maasai clientele.

Olorgasailie

Olorgasailie Prehistoric Site (1500m from the main road; daily dawn–dusk; Ksh200) is signposted 3km after **Oltepesi**. The site is endowed with numerous pathways, catwalks and informative signs, and is a peaceful place to stay, while the **guided tour** around the excavations (included in the entrance charge) is not to be missed.

The accommodation and **museum** are just above the excavations on a ridge overlooking what was once a wide, shallow lake. Between 400,000 and 500,000 years ago, the lakeshore was inhabited by a species of hominid, probably by *Homo erectus* of the **Acheulian culture** (after St Acheul in France, where it was first discovered). They made a range of identifiable stone tools: cleavers for skinning animals; round balls for crushing bones, perhaps for hurling or possibly tied to vines to be used, à la gaucho, as *bolas*; and heavy hand axes, for which the culture is best known, but for which, as Richard Leakey writes, "embarrassingly, no one can think of a good use". The guides tell you they were used for chopping meat and digging. This seems reasonable, but some are very large, while hundreds of others (particularly at the so-called factory site) seem far too small, the theory being that they were made by children practising.

Mary and Louis Leakey's team did most of the unearthing here in the 1940s. Thousands of the stone tools they found have been left undisturbed, *in situ*, under protective roofs. Perhaps the most impressive find is the fossilized leg bone of a gigantic, extinct elephant, dwarfing a similar bone from a modern elephant placed next to it. It was long hoped that human remains would also be uncovered at Olorgasailie, but despite extensive digging none have been found – more scope for speculation.

Practicalities

It only takes a couple of hours to look around the site, and most visitors choose not to spend the night. If you don't have your own transport, make sure you find out exactly when the next bus or matatu will be passing by, as they are few and far between.

There are double **bandas** on site, which can be booked through the public relations office at the National Museum in Nairobi (☎020/741424; ❷), though it's rarely necessary – or you can **camp**; in either case, bring food and bedding. Do-it-yourself showers and free firewood are available. Sitting in the shade of the open-sided picnic *bandas* with a pair of binoculars and looking out over what used to be the lake can yield some rewarding animal-watching, especially in the brief dusk. Go for a walk out past the excavations towards the gorge and you'll see more: gerenuk, duiker, giraffe, eland and baboons. Contacts with Maasai are good here, too and there's usually some jewellery for sale. You can cultivate further friendships – and collect some scant **provisions** – at the cluster of desolate *dukas* at Oltepesi, 3km back along the Nairobi road, where they also have warm beer and soft drinks.

Lake Magadi

Lying in a Rift Valley depression, 1000m below Nairobi, **Lake Magadi** is a vast shallow pool of soda (sodium carbonate), a sludge of alkaline water and crystal trona deposits, and one of the hottest places in the country. Magadi is also the second largest source of soda in the world, after the Salton Sea in the USA.

The Magadi Soda Company, until 1991 an ICI interest, has built the very model of a company town, on a barren spit of land jutting out across the multicoloured soda. The company's investment here is guaranteed – hot springs gush out of the earth's crust to provide an inexhaustible supply of briney water for evaporation. Everything you see, apart from the homes of a few Maasai on

△ Lake Magadi

the shore and a few *dukas* and places to eat in town, is owned and run by the corporation. You pass a company police barrier where you sign in and enter over a causeway, past surreal pink salt ponds. On company territory, a sign advises visitors that "it is dangerous to walk across the lake surface", just in case you were wondering. Note that some of the company police are touchy about you taking photos of the factory installations. Despite this, the atmosphere here, somewhat surprisingly because of the nature of the work and harshness of the environment, is relaxed and welcoming. By comparison with the rest of Kenya, the company pays high wages; people tend to get drunk a lot, and accommodation and services are free.

Many visitors come to Magadi specifically for its **birdlife**. There's a wealth of avifauna here including, usually, large numbers of flamingos at the southern end of the lake. At this end, there are also freshwater swamps which attract many species.

The lake

Lake Magadi is fascinating to walk across (on the causeways: in practice only the inlet between Magadi and the eastern shore). On the eastern side, where you first arrive, you can watch the sweepers in rubber boots shovelling the by-product, sodium chloride (common salt), into ridges on the technicolour "fields". Common salt crystallizes on top of the sodium carbonate and is loaded on to tractor-drawn trailers and taken away to be purified for human and animal consumption. Magadi soda, used principally for glass-making, is Kenya's most valuable mineral resource. The dried soda is exported, first by rail to Mombasa via Kajiado and Konza, thence, much of it, to Japan. But, despite the "high" wages, you wonder how anyone can be persuaded to work in this lurid inferno: the first rains here are usually "phantom rain", the ground so hot that the raindrops evaporate before hitting the surface. It's important to wear sunglasses and a hat while out in the sun, and bring plenty of water.

Practicalities

Behind the police station, which stands on the highest point of the peninsula, is the lake. If you look the other way (to the west), the road to the left leads to the "European" end of town, where a dozen or so managers live and where there's a strange, barren golf course; to the right, the town slopes gently down to a crusty shore where most of the Kenyan employees live. There's a Co-operative Bank here (daily 9.30am–3pm) in the building behind the Total Petrol station, but it has no ATM.

Magadi has a thriving daily market and two **places to stay**, with good doubles and hot showers: the *Lower Guesthouse*, opposite the hospital (PO Box 8; ℡020/330008 ext 278 or 33278 out of hours; ❸) and the slightly more upmarket *Sportsclub Hotel* (℡020/6999265; ❸). You can pitch a tent almost anywhere south of the township – though the bizarre golf course has two equally bizarre "Keep Off" signs. Anywhere here is baking hot during the day and a favourite haunt for baboons – but it's likely you'll be invited home by employees, anyway.

The company has built blocks of apartments, a church, a mosque and schools and, with a touch of inspiration, a glittering **swimming pool** which is "for residents only", although you can use the poolside bar and *nyama choma* kiosk. For a drink and cheap **meals**, try the *Flamingo*, a club for staff, though it accepts guests. Also good is the unnamed **bar** opposite the petrol station off Duka Hill Road, which is full of friendly Maasai. Across from the town, on the western shore, Maasai will sell you *pombe* made from a base of roots and herbs, and fermented with honey. It's a lot cheaper than beer, and stronger, too.

The matatu **to Nairobi** leaves at 5am and the **buses** have one morning and one afternoon departure, or you could ask about hitching a ride on the soda **train** to Kajiado (on the main Kenya–Tanzania highway) or to Konza and Mombasa if you're headed that way.

The Nguruman Escarpment and Shompole

With your own vehicle you can drive on from Magadi, across the lake to the **hot springs** on the western side; check the map in the police station first (in any case, you're bound to find a local in town who'll offer to guide you there). From the hot springs, you can drive to the Ewaso Ngiro River at the foot of the Ol Choroi plateau, also known as the **Nguruman Escarpment**. By the river is the Olkiramatian **campsite** run by the Maasai Olkiramatian Group Ranch. Forget about trying to four-wheel-drive it up the rough track beyond the river, over the escarpment and on to the Mara. People have done that in the past, but the whole area is privately owned Maasai land and, for the moment at least, not accessible.

Further south, along the escarpment, is the 142-square-kilometre **Shompole Conservancy**, home to lion, buffalo, elephant, zebra and wildebeest, among others. An ecotourism venture involving the Maasai Shompole Group Ranch, Shompole can be reached by chartered plane, as it has its own private **airstrip**. The only **accommodation** is at the super-expensive *Shompole Lodge* (🌐www .shompole.com; reservations through Art of Ventures, PO Box 10665 Nairobi;

ⓣ020/883280, ⓔreservations@theartofventures.com; FB from $580, plus conservation fee $20 per day; ⓞ), constructed from natural materials and featuring the area's abundant natural water supply all around the lodge in the form of streams and pools. There are eight tented rooms in the main lodge, each with a small private pool, sitting area and stunning views. Away from the main lodge are two luxury suites – referred to as "Little Shompole" – sharing a lounge and dining area, with their own staff, guide and butler service. Guests can also elect to spend a night or two in Shompole's rustic *Bush Camp*, equipped with canvas tents, camp beds, bucket showers and flush toilets, and offering excellent game viewing and bird-watching in the surrounding grasslands. Other activities include game drives, canoeing, bush dinners and sundowner visits to Lake Natron to see the flamingos.

The central Rift Valley

Many travellers' first view of the Rift Valley is from the souvenir-draped **A104 Uplands road**. This barrels through the forests north of Nairobi, crosses a broad, bleak plateau, then flirts with the precipice before following the contours of the slopes above Naivasha and dropping into the Rift. They sell rhubarb up here, as well as plums, carrots and potatoes. In the wet season, you can find yourself driving over a thick, white carpet of hailstones between gloomy conifer plantations. All this contrasts dramatically with the endless, dusty plains below. With binoculars, you can pick out herds of gazelle, Maasai with their cattle and, bizarrely, a satellite-tracking station near the grey cone of Mount Longonot.

The Uplands road is a good one to hitch on, and buses and matatus often use it; heading north, sit on the left for the best views. If you have a car of your own, you can stop at some of the stands on the roadside. Small sheepskins are often excellent value, but check they have been properly cured; the big woven grass baskets are also worthwhile and surprisingly cheap. Note that the last set of stands in the best location is also the most expensive. More seriously, if you are driving, treat this road as a continuous **black spot** – overtaking can be lethal.

The "**old road**", built by Italian POWs during World War II, runs parallel to and lower than the Uplands road; it's insanely bumpy and narrow and is only used by heavy goods vehicles which in theory are banned from the top road. Corresponding to the lower altitude, vegetation down here takes on a more Mediterranean aspect, candelabra euphorbia and spikey agave predominating. The little **chapel** before the Mai Mahiu junction for Narok, also Italian-built, seems fitting in this scene, though it's more often used as a pit-stop picnic site.

Lake Naivasha and around

Naivasha, like so many Kenyan place names, is a corruption of a local (Maasai) name *E-na-iposha* (heaving waters), a pronunciation still used by Maa speakers you'll meet in the vicinity. The grassy shores of the lake were traditional Maasai grazing land for centuries, prior to its "discovery" by Joseph Thomson in 1884.

The Kalenjin peoples

The **Kalenjin** form the majority of the population in the central part of the Rift Valley. Their name, actually a recent adoption by a number of peoples speaking dialects of Nandi, means "I tell you" in all of them. The principal Kalenjin are the Nandi, Terik, Tugen, Elgeyo, Elkony, Sabaot, Marakwet and Kipsigis, and more contentiously the Pokot. They were some of the earliest inhabitants of Kenya and probably absorbed the early bushmen or pygmy peoples who were here for hundreds of thousands of years before.

Primarily **farmers**, the Kalenjin have often adapted their economies to local circumstances; it's supposed that the first Kalenjin were herdsmen whose lifestyle has changed over the centuries. The pastoral **Pokot** group, who still spurn all kinds of cultivation and despise peoples who rely on anything but livestock, call the **Marakwet**, living against the western Rift escarpment, *Cheblong* (the Poor), for their lack of cattle.

The **Okiek** (Ndorobo) are another interesting clue to the past. Hunter-gatherers, they live in scattered groups in the forests of the high slopes flanking the Rift, but unlike most hunter-gatherers, they do very little gathering. Meat, and honey from their hives, are the traditional staples. They consider wild fruits and vegetables barely palatable, though cornmeal and gardening have been introduced, and they now keep some domestic animals too. They may be the descendants of Kalenjin forebears who lost (or ate) their herds. There are other groups in Kenya who live mostly by hunting – Ndorobo or Wanderoo – for whom such a background is very likely, and who are all gradually abandoning their old lifestyles and dislikes to the inexorable advance of "civilization".

Many of the mainstream Kalenjin played key roles in the founding of the Kenya African Democratic Union (KADU – now disbanded), but the most famous of their number in recent years was President Moi, a **Tugen** from Baringo District. As he was from a small ethnic group, his presidency for years avoided the accusations of tribalism levelled so bitterly against Kenyatta. But in the run-up to the 1992 elections, it became increasingly obvious that the country was not being run for the benefit of all. The president's firm grip on the reins of power was being exercised through the Kalenjin-dominated civil service, rather than the more ethnically mixed cabinet. This fact, coupled with the "ethnic cleansing" in the Rift Valley of non-Kalenjin by groups of surprisingly well-organized young men (widespread evictions from Rift Valley villages, the burning of compounds and several hundred people killed) fulfilled President Moi's prophecy that multi-partyism would do nothing to harmonize tribal relations in the country. The same story repeated itself in the run-up to the 1997 elections, with Kikuyu the main victims. The tables were turned in 2002, when the Kalenjin lost power. At the time of writing, many Kalenjin feel marginalized by Mwai Kibaki's government, and believe they are being targeted by anti-corruption sweeps and resettlement campaigns.

Before the nineteenth century was out, however, the "glimmering many-isled expanse" had seen the arrival, with the railway, of the first European settlers. Soon after, the *laibon* Ole Gilisho, whom the British had appointed chief of the Naivasha Maasai, was persuaded to sign an agreement ceding his people's grazing rights all around the lake – and the country houses and ranches went up. Today the Maasai are back, though very much as outsiders, either disputing grazing rights with the many European landowners still left here, or as workers on the vast horticultural farms which export the bulk of fresh flowers sold in the UK.

The **lake**, slightly forbidding but picturesque with its purple mountain backdrop and floating islands of papyrus and water hyacinth, has some curious characteristics. It is fresh water – Lake Baringo is the only other example in the Rift – and the water level has always been prone to mysterious fluctuations. It dropped massively in the 1980s (partly the unmysterious result of farmers to the north taking off some of the Thurusha River's inflow), though the shore did not recede enough to regain the areas that were cultivated in the 1950s, when the lake was half its present size. Even though the lake level rose in 1998 following the El Niño floods, the shoreline the settlers knew is still marked by the outer edge of the fringing band of papyrus, and you can still see fence posts sticking up.

Perhaps of more immediate and visible interest is the lake's **wildlife**, especially its protected **hippo** population. Despite their bulk, hippos seem remarkably sensitive creatures, and they must be able to see in the dark, too, for nary a camper's guy-line is twanged. By day, you can occasionally see **giraffes**, floating blithely through the trees, taking barbed wire and gates in their stride. Naivasha has extraordinary **birdlife** too: all kinds, from the grotesque marabou storks to pet shop lovebirds in pairs (which are illegal to buy or sell), doves cooing in the woods and splendid fish eagles, whose mournful cries fill the air like seagulls. Southwest of the lake, **Hell's Gate National Park** boasts the best expedition in the area – the hike through the Njorowa gorge. Not far away, **Mount Longonot**, also a national park, is worth climbing for the fabulous views in every direction as you circle the rim. All these attractions, and the area's climate, with a light breeze always drifting through the acacias, make Naivasha hard to beat as a first stop out from Nairobi.

Besides good train, bus and matatu services from Nairobi and Nakuru, Naivasha has an airstrip for daily SafariLink flights from the capital, and there are also buses to Naivasha from western Kenya and the central highlands.

Naivasha town

All told, **NAIVASHA** town has little to offer as a place to stay. Unless you arrive late in the day, you may as well head straight down to the lake. Coming from Nairobi on the old road, you could ask to be dropped off at the lake road turning. If you're hitching or coming by bus or matatu, you may arrive on the **A104 Uplands road** and might be dropped inconveniently at the top junction, 1500m uphill behind the town. The **airstrip** is just off Moi South Lake Road; arriving here to stay at one of the luxury lodges, you can ask to be picked up from there.

If you plan to spend any time in the area, you may want to go into Naivasha town to stock up on essentials. For **food supplies**, try *La Belle Inn*, which has choice picnic fare, including honey and capers, and the Happy Valley Supermarket at the upper end of Biashara Road. Good lake fish can be bought at the kiosk opposite *La Belle Inn* and super-fresh milk and yoghurts at Delamere Dairies, 3km north on the Nakuru road. There's a **post office** on Moi Avenue (Mon–Fri 8am–1pm & 2–5pm, Sat 9am–noon) and two **banks** with ATMs, namely Barclays and KCB on Moi Avenue. The Sera Centre on Kenyatta Avenue has an **Internet** cafe.

Accommodation

If you do stay in town, the *La Belle Inn* and the *Ken-Vash* are your best bets.

Heshima B&L Kariuki Chotara Rd; PO Box 1141 ☎050/2020631. Rooms at the top are nice and the café is popular with Congolese music fans. ❷

Ken-Vash Hotel Posta Lane; PO Box 211 ☎050/2021503, ⓕ2030084. Though lacking in atmosphere, Naivasha's biggest hotel has excellent rooms for the price, with wall-to wall carpeting and

NAIVASHA

ACCOMMODATION

Heshima B&L	C
Ken-Vash	B
La Belle Inn	E
Lakeside Tourist Lodge	G
Naivasha Guest Inn	H
Naivasha Silver	F
Othaya Annexe B&L	D
Wambuku	A

RESTAURANTS, BARS & CLUBS

Back to Eden	3
Beano Bar and Pool Hall	6
Bright Moon Chinese	7
Diplomat Hotel	4
Golf Club	8
Kiwa Highway Motel	9
Railway Club	2
Super Highway Hotel	5
Sweet Banana Lodge	1

& Nakuru (A104)

North Kinangop & Aberdares National Park ▶

▼ *Nairobi (Old Road) & Lake Naivasha Road*   ▼ *Nairobi (A104 Uplands Road)*

---

satelite TV. The service is good and there is safe parking. ④

La Belle Inn Moi Ave; PO 532 ☎050/2021007, ⓕ2021119. A popular old staging post on the main street through town, with a variety of pleasant if overpriced rooms, set around a central courtyard. The terrace restaurant serves great fried breakfasts and is a good place to while away a few hours. There's a good bar, too. B&B ⑤

Lakeside Tourist Lodge Moi Ave; PO Box 894 ☎050/2030267 or 2020856, ⓕ2030268. A spacious construction just off the Nairobi–Nakuru road, playing frequent host to Methodist church groups from the US. Rooms are good and service is efficient. At the time of writing the place was

undergoing renovations which will make it the largest hotel in town. B&B ③

Naivasha Guest Inn Kenyatta Ave; PO Box 491 ☎050/2021227. Two kilometres from the town centre, this is a well-kept joint to collapse into if you've just been dropped at the junction. Rooms (all s/c) are reasonable, and there's a nice terrace bar-restaurant. Secure parking. B&B ③

Naivasha Silver Hotel Kenyatta Ave; PO Box 989 ☎050/2022580. A bright fuchsia building, the pink theme continuing inside. A step up from a regular B&L. ③

Othaya Annexe B&L Kariuki Chotara Rd; PO Box 651 ☎050/2020770. Cheap and cheerful, but not too clean; the s/c rooms have a large bed and a set price for a single or a couple. There's a good *hoteli* downstairs and a bakery on the premises. ❶

Wambuku Hotel Moi Ave next to the post office; PO Box 1141 ☎050/ 2020117. Big and impersonal, the *Wambuku* has decent if rather small s/c rooms. B&B ❸

Eating and drinking

There's a whole clutch of cheap, local **places to eat** at on Moi Avenue around the Caltex and Total gas stations. Among the better places here is *Sweet Banana Lodge*, which serves great *nyama choma* and features one-man guitar shows at the weekend.

Back to Eden Corner of Mama Ngina Rd and Biashara Rd. Wonderful little juice bar with freshly squeezed juices and fruit salads to take away.

Diplomat Hotel Mama Ngina Rd. Small, friendly café dishing up excellent, spicy curries and samosas.

Bright Moon Chinese Restaurant Moi Ave. Average but inexpensive food.

Kiwa Highway Motel A104 Highway, near the top junction. A windblown *nyama choma* joint, fairly expensive except for beef at Ksh150 a kilo. There's also a bar and disco.

La Belle Inn Moi Ave. Serves up a mix of Kenyan and European fare, with a good selection for vegetarians (easily the best in town) and a nice line in steak and chicken dishes. Fish is particularly recommended – barbecued tilapia, spiced Louisiana crayfish, Naivasha bisque (lakefish soup) and the like.

Super Highway Hotel Moi Ave. Inexpensive fish and chips and amazingly filling *mandaazi*.

Nightlife

Music is inescapable in Naivasha, as almost all the B&Ls double as café-bars which bounce along on the infectious rhythms of Congolese and South African sounds. Venues tend to have a short lifespan, so ask around for the latest. The *Railway Club* by the station has live bands Thursday to Sunday evenings (closing time 3am). Also good for a night's entertainment are the *Sweet Banana Lodge* and – for a game of pool and a few beers with locals – the *Beano Bar & Pool Hall*. The *Golf Club* (north up Moi Ave) is an almost exclusively white meat market, its "members only" rule not applied to out-of-towners with a bit of cash to spend.

Lake Naivasha

The fast lakeside road has brought thousands of migrant workers to the **farming estates**, where they grow string beans, mangetout and flowers, all exported by air to European supermarkets. Great stretches of acacia scrub have been cleared since the late 1980s for the expansion of the farms and the ugly lines of squalid field-hand housing, still sprouting in the dust between the plantations. As you pass through this scene of ragged-clothed backs stooping between the rows, with rambling country houses in the background, it's difficult to ignore the images of American slavery that spring to mind. There are always people out of work and looking for work, and in recent years the lakeshore homesteads have been hit by a number of high-profile armed robberies and murders. And while there are a fair few Europeans of more modest means around the lake, the contrasts between rich and poor, black and white, are stark and undeniable. Sadly, too, the lakeshore environment has altered hugely over the last two decades, and the small patches of relatively undisturbed bush that remain are no longer adequate for most of the larger mammals. To see the giraffe that used to take fences in their stride, you need to go to Hell's Gate.

Travel practicalities

To get to the lake from Naivasha town, there's easily hitchable traffic, a regular shuttle of matatus, and a bus every hour or so. The Sulmac estate is the main

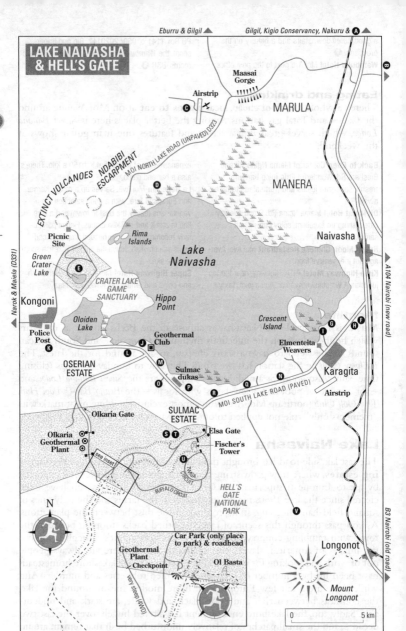

LAKE NAIVASHA & HELL'S GATE

Eburru & Gilgil ▲

Gilgil, Kigio Conservancy, Nakuru & Ⓐ ▲

Ⓑ ▶

Maasai Gorge

Airstrip Ⓒ

MARULA

MANERA

MOI NORTH LAKE ROAD (UNPAVED) D323

NDABIBI ESCARPMENT

EXTINCT VOLCANOES

Ⓓ

Rima Islands

Lake Naivasha

Naivasha

A104 Nairobi (new road) ▶

Ⓕ ▶

Picnic Site

Green Crater Lake

Ⓔ

CRATER LAKE GAME SANCTUARY

Hippo Point

Crescent Island

Ⓖ Ⓘ

Ⓗ

Kongoni

Oloiden Lake

Geothermal Club Ⓙ

Elmenteita Weavers

Police Post Ⓚ

OSERIAN ESTATE

Ⓛ

Ⓜ

Sulmac dukas

Karagita

Airstrip

B3 Nairobi (old road) ▶

Ⓞ

Ⓟ Ⓡ Ⓠ

Ⓝ

MOI SOUTH LAKE ROAD (PAVED)

Olkaria Gate

SULMAC ESTATE

Ⓢ Ⓣ

Elsa Gate

Olkaria Geothermal Plant

Fischer's Tower

Ⓤ

NABA CIRCUIT

BUFFALO CIRCUIT

see inset

HELL'S GATE NATIONAL PARK

Ⓥ

Longonot

Mount Longonot

Geothermal Plant Checkpoint

Car Park (only place to park) & roadhead

Ol Basta

very steep (4WD)

0   5 km

Narok & Maiela (D331) ◀

Narok & Maiela (D331) ◀

Narok Road & Suswa ▼

ACCOMMODATION

Crater Lake Camp	E	Fish Eagle Inn	M	Lake Naivasha Simba	
Crayfish Campsite	P	Fisherman's Camp	O	Lodge	Q
Eburru Guest		Kiangazi	L	Lake Naivasha Sopa	
Cottage	C	Kongoni Game Valley	K	Lodge	N
Elsamere	J	Lake Naivasha Country		Longonot Ranch	
Endachata Campsite	S	Club	I	House	V
Fischers Tower Hotel	H	Lake Naivasha Lodge	G	Malewa River Lodge	A

Malu Farm	B
Nairburta	
Campsite	T
Ol Dubai Campsite	U
Olerai House	D
Yelo Green Hotel	F
YMCA	R

Lake dangers

Beware out on Naivasha. The possibility that underground springs may feed the lake, its location on the floor of the Rift Valley, and its shallowness all combine to produce notoriously fast changes of mood and weather: grey and placid one minute, suddenly green and choppy with whitecaps the next. Boating mishaps are all too common. Watch out, too, for hippos, which can overturn a small boat easily enough if frightened or harassed. Although there's no bilharzia in Naivasha, the hippos, the dense weeds, and the reported recent sighting of a crocodile, combine to offset any enthusiasm you might have had for a swim.

south lake transport focus, though there is a bus that goes beyond it, as far as *Fisherman's Camp*, returning from here to Naivasha town at around 8am and 1pm every day.

Circumnavigating the lake in a vehicle, you soon reach the 30km mark on the **Moi South Lake Road** and hit the dust and potholes of **Moi North Lake Road**, which represented the condition of the whole lake road until a few years back; there's 35km of this (between an hour and two hours' worth) before you reach the Naivasha–Nakuru highway at a point 9km north of Naivasha. If you're hitching or using public transport, you'll find very few vehicles have reason to go beyond Kongoni Village, and it's not really worth trying to go the whole way.

Bicycles are a good way of exploring the lakeshore, and particularly for getting around Hell's Gate National Park: *Fisherman's Camp* rents out bikes, and has good photocopied sketch maps of the lake and Hell's Gate. Great Rift Lakes Bikes and Tents, 3.5km along the Moi South Lake Road (℡050/2020514, ℱ2021116) and opposite the turning for *Lake Naivasha Lodge*, rents out not only bicycles (Ksh500 per day) but also a variety of modern tents (Ksh500–800 for 24hr). They also offer biking trips to Crescent Island, along a narrow cause-way from private farmland. Other bike rental places include *Fish Eagle Inn* and *Lake Naivasha Country Club*. Incidentally, by all means give lifts if you're cycling – it's a great way of making friends on equal terms.

It's possible to go out in a **boat** at many of the lakeshore establishments. *Fisherman's Camp*, for example, has a fast motorboat at about Ksh1750 per hour and a half-speed one for Ksh1000 (both take up to eight passengers), and charges elsewhere aren't markedly different. You need an hour in the fast boat to get over to the main concentration of hippos and back. **Exploring on foot** can also be very pleasant. From *Fisherman's Camp*, it's worth walking up to the superb viewpoint, and visiting *Elsamere* (see p.237).

Accommodation

There's a wide variety of accommodation along Moi South Lake Road – every-thing from frugal *bandas* and camping to stately hotels and homestays. The distances mentioned in the reviews below refer to the distance from the lake road junction with the main Nairobi road (which is 3km from Naivasha town itself). Places to stay off Moi North Lake Road are generally more difficult to get to given the condition of the road; directions are given in the listings where appropriate. A number of extremely luxurious ranch and farmhouses also lie dotted around the lake, as well as the idyllically situated *Eburru Guest Cottage*, well within the reach of even the lowliest budget.

Note that both *Fisherman's Camp* and *Fish Eagle Inn* receive occasional noctur-nal visits from **hippos**, of which you should be very wary.

Budget and mid-range

Crayfish Campsite 17km; PO Box 176
☎050/2020239. A 10min walk from the lake, this is little more than a small field and bar, which can get noisy and is frequented by "better-paid locals", according to the manager. The docile guard dogs don't give much of an impression of security, either. There's hot water, tent rental (Ksh300), and the usual boat rides. If you order food, be prepared for a long wait. Ksh250 per person.

Eburru Guest Cottage Bookings through Let's Go Travel (see p.150). In beautiful walking country (beware of buffalo), the cottage has gorgeous views over the lake and Mount Longonot. It's basic but fully s/c, and has two double bedrooms. Bring your own food (a kitchen/lounge is at your disposal); water is provided. Part of its charm is its inaccessibility. Matatus run twice daily (once on Sun) from Moi Ave in Naivasha, leaving you with a 2km walk from Green Park Development gate; taxis Ksh700–1000. Hitching a ride on a *shamba* vehicle is also possible: ask at *La Belle Inn*. ❸

Fisherman's Camp 19.3km; PO Box 79
☎050/2030088 or 2030276; reservations also through Let's Go Travel (see p.150). This favourite budget hideaway has the best situation in Naivasha, right by the water's edge, and is shaded by tall, beautiful fever trees. Besides camping (tent rental Ksh200 per person), there's a choice of s/c, if rather dingy *bandas* and a "youth hostel" consisting of seven very basic dormitories, each with four narrow bunk beds. The bar has limited food. Some people find the sometimes beery white Kenyan atmosphere at *Bottom Camp* off-putting; others love it. Activities include parascending and water-skiing. Camping Ksh200 per person; dorms Ksh400; *bandas* ❷

Fischers Tower Hotel 800m; PO Box 436
☎050/2020062. Next to the *Yelo Green Hotel*, right by the main road and rather far from the lake, though it does have a nice garden setting with a large bar and *nyama choma* joint. A friendly place, mainly frequented by Kenyans, with live bands at the weekend. Rooms are reasonable, if a bit tatty, with hot showers and comfy sofas. B&B ❹

Fish Eagle Inn 19.3km, entrance beside *Fisherman's Camp*; PO Box 1554 ☎050/2030306, ℻2021158, ⊛www.fisheagleinn.com. You can camp here (tent rental Ksh450 for a two-person tent), sleep in a dorm or stay in a variety of dull if well-equipped *bandas* (with nets, hot water and spotless toilets); doubles are tiny, but the more expensive "suites" are cosier. It's pleasant and calmer than *Fisherman's Camp*, if overpriced. The restaurant is good, and there's a gym (as well as sauna, steam room and outdoor pool; around Ksh700 per day for their use). Mountain bikes for rent. Camping Ksh200; dorms Ksh500; B&B ❺

Yelo Green Hotel 800m; PO Box 561 ☎ & ℻050/2030269. Far from the lake itself, and a little tatty, but with acceptable chalet-style *bandas* (all s/c with hot water), set in lovely bougainvillea-filled gardens, plus a campsite. The owners are charming and helpful, and there's a restaurant and bar, popular with locals at weekends. However, room prices are a little over the odds. B&B ❹

YMCA 15.1km; PO Box 1006 ☎050/2030396. Still one of the lake's cheapest (and friendliest) places to stay, a 10min walk from the shore itself – and certainly the easiest base if you're planning an early-morning hike into Hell's Gate National Park, as the Elsa Gate is just up the road. You can camp in what's left of the acacia grove (tent rental Ksh200), stay in the dorm (you need bedding), or rent one of the spartan *bandas*. Firewood, eggs, lake fish and milk are sporadically available, but the shop has almost nothing. There's hot water, boat rental and food can be cooked to order. Camping Ksh200 per person; ❷

Expensive

Crater Lake Camp Green Crater Lake (see p.239) ☎050/2020613, ℻050/2021372, ⊛www.mericagrouphotels.com. Luxury tented camp with superb views from ten secluded, yellow-acacia-shaded *bandas* (or from a specially built "raft" for bird-watching), and nice touches like china dinner service and silverware. You can also just drop in for lunch ($20). The price includes night game drives and escorted walks. No disabled access. FB $225; ❾

Elsamere 22.1km; PO Box 1497 ☎050/2021055, ℻2021074, ℮elsa@africaonline.co.ke. Joy Adamson's former home, open to the public as a conservation centre (see opposite), offers comfortable and very peaceful rooms in cottages, each with verandas facing towards the lake. The grounds are beautiful, too, but they don't put up children under 7 years old unless by prior arrangement, and they don't like the house to be treated as a hotel, preferring guests to have a measure of enthusiasm for the lady and her works, or at least for natural history. Reservations advisable. FB ❽

Kiangazi 25.5km; PO Box 719 ☎050/2021052, ℻2021059. A very personable family-run guesthouse with a large veranda overlooking the valley. Three artificial pools (two for buffalo, zebra and antelope, the other for you to swim in) provide entertainment, and game drives (both day and night) are included in the price. The food is superb and served with excellent wines. FB $200; ❾

Kongoni Game Valley 28.5km; PO Box 15026 Nairobi ☎02/882439, ⓦwww.kgvalley.com. The plushest homestay in Naivasha, though not exactly the most tasteful – an enormous, overly modernized ranch house built by the Count and Countess de Perigny at the turn of the last century. FB $200 per person per day; ⑨

Lake Naivasha Country Club 3.8km; PO Box 15 ☎050/2021004, ⓕ2021161, ⓦwww.blockhotelske.com. The best hotel on the lake (still usually known as the *Lake Hotel*), with magnificent gardens and a lounge evocative of the old colonial days between 1937 and 1950, when the clientele included passengers in the flying-boats which landed on the lake. Rooms are generally old-fashioned but range from adequate to luxurious. It's suitable for children (small adventure playground and huge lawns) and visitors with disabilities (all ground-floor rooms; a few steps up to the dining room). Casual visitors (Ksh1000) are usually attracted by the sumptuous lunchtime buffets in the garden (Ksh900). There are bicycles for rent (Ksh200/hr, Ksh800/day), massages, bird walks (with fish-eagle-eyed guides; Ksh500), boat rides (Ksh3500/hr for a seven-seat boat) and waterskiing (Ksh1700/30min). FB $170 in low season, a third higher otherwise; ⑨

Lake Naivasha Lodge 3.5km; PO Box 685 ☎050/2020611, ⓕ2021156, ⓦwww.lakenakurulodge.com (check website for Nairobi and Mombasa offices). Twelve spacious double rooms, s/c and spotless, some with a private veranda and overlooking the enormous gardens. It's a 10min walk to the lakeshore through pleasant grounds. Boat trips offered. Secure parking. FB ⑥

Lake Naivasha Simba Lodge 12.2km; ☎050/2050305–8, ⓕ050/2050042, ⓦwww.marasimba.com. One of Naivasha's newest lodges, with villas built of ugly concrete blocks. Still, the service is good and It features nice little touches such as bush dinners in the gardens with traditional Kenyan music. Activities Include the usual boat rides and nature walks. All rooms are doubles, with sunken TV lounges; the downstairs rooms have balconies – ask for one with an enclosed outdoor shower. They charge Ksh200 entry for non-guests (though getting in can be like entering Fort Knox) and additional charges to use the facilities. FB $280; ⑨

Lake Naivasha Sopa Lodge 8.6km; PO Box 1008 ☎050/2050398. The newest and most luxurious lodge on the lake has beautiful gardens strewn with baobab, cacti and roaming ostrich. Rooms are in groups of four in cottages spaced throughout the grounds, boasting large entrance halls, sunken bathtubs, Kenyan art on the walls and private balconies with stunning lake views. There's also a beautiful circular lounge bar with a vaulted ceiling, picture windows and a huge fireplace. Activities include horse-riding, lakeside nature walks, bike rides and visits to Crescent Island. FB $250; ⑨

Longonot Ranch House 10.5km, then left 8km up a rough track signposted "Kedong Ranch"; reservations through Safaris Unlimited (see p.151). A traditional long ranch house (six double en-suite bedrooms), atop a hillock under the shadow of Mount Longonot, and fully staffed; it was built by Martha Gellhorn, journalist and one-time wife of Ernest Hemingway. The attractions are manifold: stunning scenery, lots of wildlife (escorted game walks and night game drives available), stables and horse-riding ($15/hr). Reservations essential. FB $370; ⑨

Malu Farm PO Box 536 ☎050/2021200 or 2030181, ⓕ2020272, ⓦwww.webvivant.com/malu. If you head towards Nakuru from Naivasha, Malu is off a terrible *murram* road on the right leading to Gilgil and Nyahururu. Getting here is a drag, but the reward is exquisite – Malu nestles up in an ancient cedar forest, with breathtaking views of the Great Rift Valley, Lake Naivasha and Longonot. You stay in one of the tastefully decorated private cottages or one of the large family villas; all have cedar-encased tubs in en-suite bathrooms, four-poster beds and a fireplace. The home-made Italian food is excellent. Activities include fishing along the banks of the nearby Malewa River, horse-riding and mountain biking. FB 220; ⑨

Olerai House Moi North Lake Road; bookings through Let's Go (see p.150). The former home of Iain and Oria Douglas-Hamilton, who were involved in the struggle to ban the ivory trade (they still live on the estate), this has six s/c double bedrooms in guesthouses surrounding the main, flower-covered house. Breakfast and lunch are served under fever trees from a long dug-out boat. Excursions, walks and boat rides are included in the price – hugely expensive at $540 a double, full board. ⑨

Elsamere

Twenty-two kilometres down Moi South Lake Road is **Elsamere** (daily 3–6pm; Ksh350; ☎050/2021055, ⓦwww.elsatrust.org), former home of the naturalist and painter Joy Adamson. Together with the neighbouring

The thorns of the rose

Cynics among environmentalists were unimpressed when, in 1995, the Lake Naivasha Riparian Association (LNRA) and Earthwatch succeeded in getting Naivasha listed as a Ramsar site, a wetland of internationally recognized ecological importance whose status, in theory, obliges both government and local inhabitants to preserve the lake. The ecological consequences of Naivasha's multimillion-dollar **horticultural industry** was the primary cause for concern among the sceptics, who worried about the farmers' continuing use of **pesticides**.

In 1999, the LNRA won the Ramsar Wetland Award and was commended as an inspiring example of community leadership, demonstrating that conservation and the wise use of wetlands could be achieved in Africa. However, it's become increasingly apparent that the survival of the lake and its wildlife depends on a multitude of other factors ultimately linked to Kenya's **growing population**. Since 1977 the number of people living within 5km of the lake has risen at least fivefold, and human waste has become a major problem because of inadequate sewage treatment facilities, with the result that some partially treated effluent is finding its way into the lake. Recently, the flow of the rivers Malewa and Gilgil, from which Lake Naivasha has been feeding, have been diverted by a **dam**, in order to provide for domestic use in Naivasha, Nakuru and the surrounding townships – which has made the lake even more vulnerable.

All these problems mean that the lake's wildlife has been seriously damaged, too. Until the exceptional 1997 rains raised the lake levels, thereby diluting the pollutants, the **fish eagle** had been especially badly affected, though its numbers now appear to be stable. The birds were not getting enough to eat and **Louisiana crayfish**, introduced in the Seventies for commercial fishing, were largely to blame. By eating their way through the lake's flora (which as well as acting as a soak for excess nutrients and a sediment trap, is food and cover for some fish species and birds such as the coot), the crayfish caused the water to become murkier. This in turn meant that the fish eagle, unable to see its prey in the lake and unable to find any coots left in the area to feed on, became too undernourished to breed. Torrential rains in 2000 washed huge amounts of agrochemicals into the lake, killing fish and other aquatic life, prompting the government to impose a ban on fishing. The ban has since been lifted but fishermen complain that tilapia and blackbass species have sharply declined, and many are losing their livelihood.

At the same time, many **companies** finally appear to be waking up to their responsibilities. Oserian, a huge Dutch-owned flower exporter, has developed a new way of fighting fungal diseases without resorting to chemicals by using geothermal steam in the greenhouse to get rid of diseases. Other flower companies are adopting technology such as computerized drip-irrigation to ensure that very little water is used. In addition, the Kenya Flower Council has initiated a code of practice requiring protective clothing for workers, safer pesticides and the careful use of water.

In spite of these optimistic signs, Lake Naivasha's **future** is still uncertain. Some of the area's 350 types of bird, hippopotamus and other wildlife are still threatened with extinction, and already the lily-trotter, the great crested grebe and the crested helmet shrike have all but disappeared.

Environmental Education Centre, it's the focus for the Naivasha region's environmental issues, with regular seminars involving scientists and researchers, plus local schools and universities. For visitors, there's a video (which you don't have to watch) followed by a copious and civilized afternoon tea on the lawn (Ksh400). You can take lunch (Ksh800) or dinner (Ksh1200) here if you book ahead. It's unlicensed, but you can bring your own wine for dinner. If the house is somewhat shrine-like, the garden is a fine place to while away a couple of hours with a pair of binoculars: a troop of colobus monkeys (normally found only in moist forests) can be seen in the acacias around the grounds. There's also **accommodation** available (see p.236).

Crescent Island Game Sanctuary

A very popular short trip is a visit to the **Crescent Island Game Sanctuary**. The "crescent" is the outer rim of a volcanic crater which forms a deep bay, the deepest part of the lake. The island, barely two square kilometres in size, is attached to the shore by a narrow causeway on the private land of Sanctuary Farm (about 6km from the lake road junction), but don't try to enter there; go instead to Lake Naivasha Country Club and ask at the reception desk about a **boat** (Ksh1500 per person including the entrance fee). You have to state the time you wish to be picked up – if you miss the boat, you'll be charged for the cost of a search party.

The boatmen can detour en route to show you hippos and giant kingfisher. Once on the island, you're free to wander at will. At first you may think there's nothing there, but the island is home to hundreds of species of birds as well as gazelle, giraffe, waterbuck (caution – they can be dangerous) and some startlingly large, though harmless, pythons. **Horse-riding** is available at Sanctuary Farm, at about Ksh1000 per hour (Ⓣ050/2021324).

Green Crater Lake

Green Crater Lake is a straightforward target for a short trip – preferably with a vehicle, as it's 17km past *Fisherman's Camp* and 6km beyond the end of the tarmac and reliable transport. There is one matatu daily, leaving Crater Lake at 9am, returning towards 4pm (it leaves Naivasha at 3pm). A proper **game sanctuary** has been set up all round the crater (Ksh200, plus Ksh50 if you bring a car), with various tracks you can take, though the one to the crater rim is only for hikers or 4WD vehicles. You'll see a fair amount of plains game if you follow the perimeter fence; there are plenty of buffalo in the sanctuary, so exercise caution. There's also an exclusive tented lodge in the crater itself (see p.236). The brilliant, jade lake is quite breathtaking, in a small way: the Maasai consider its deep alkaline waters good for sick cattle, but it's also a favourite place for them, with sacred associations. From the main viewpoint on the west rim, it's possible to scramble up for ten minutes to the highest point. There are not many places where you can get down to the crater floor – the easiest are on the south side.

Eating and drinking

You can drop in for meals and drinks at *Fish Eagle Inn*, *Fisherman's Camp*, *Lake Naivasha Country Club*, *Lake Naivasha Lodge*, and the *Yelo Green Hotel*. *Crayfish Campsite* has a bar. *Geothermal Club* (21.8km along Moi South Lake Rd) is a gem of a place owned by *La Belle Inn*, with some of the best views over the lake, excellent English breakfasts, gastronomic African dishes for lunch and dinner, and cheap drink.

Shopping

There are a number of decent shopping options around the lake. As in the accommodation reviews, the number of kilometres in the reviews refers to the distance along Moi South Lake Road from the junction with the main Nairobi road.

Elmenteita Weavers 4.3km, and 800m along the signposted track; PO Box 85 Ⓣ050/203011. A very friendly weaving shop, its looms behind the showroom. Carpets and rugs, sweaters (some superb), *kangas* and *kikois* compete with various other bought-in crafts. Justifiably expensive;

credit cards accepted. Mon–Sat 9am–5.30pm, Sun 9am–5pm.

Heidi Lange's At the junction of the Nairobi road and Moi South Lake Road (there's a small sign), this is where German-born artist Heidi Lange sells her batik seconds (very slight flaws; Ksh100–1000).

"Sulmac" dukas 17.6km. Near *Fisherman's*

Camp, Sulmac is one of the biggest flower plantations in the area, employing over 4000 people. Near the main entrance is a small shopping centre where you can eat for next to nothing. Newspapers are on sale in the morning by the farm gate and, 500m further west, you'll usually find a gathering of ladies selling produce from their small vegetable plots.

Hell's Gate National Park

Daily dawn–dusk; $15, children $5; $8 to camp, $10 at the "special" campsite. Warden: PO Box 234 Naivasha ☎ 050/2020284, Map: Survey of Kenya "Hell's Gate National Park" at 10cm:1.25km (1993). The road to the park at Olkaria Gate, 21.5km from the lake road junction, is tarred all the way (5km) through the geothermal area, but there's a very steep descent to the gorge and roadhead at the end.

Hell's Gate was the outlet for the prehistoric freshwater lake that stretched from here to Nakuru and which, it's believed, would have supported early human communities on its shores. Today it's a spectacular and exciting area, the Njorowa gorge's red cliffs and undulating expanse of grassland providing one of the few remaining places in Kenya where you can walk among herds of **plains game** without having to go a long way off the beaten track. Buffalo, zebra, eland, hartebeest, Thomson's gazelle and baboons are all usually seen, lions and leopards hardly ever, but you might just see a cheetah, and you'll certainly come across their footprints if you scan the trail. There are servals – one of the most delicate cats – and, high on the cliffs, small numbers of klipspringer ("cliffjumper") antelope. That said, the gorge is occasionally rather empty of animals, as the quantity of wildlife varies seasonally.

The main entrance road to Hell's Gate is just south of the *YMCA*, with the Elsa Gate a further 1500m along this track. If you're driving a small vehicle, be aware of the low clearance on

240

△ Hell's Gate

some of the tracks. **Cycling** through Hell's Gate, you're better off entering by Olkaria Gate, which makes for an easier downhill ride to Elsa Gate. It's about 25km to the roadhead and back and, if you need a lift, note that while a fair number of vehicles visit at weekends, there are far fewer during the week. The best time to arrive is dawn, in any case, when most animals are about. Try at any cost to avoid the midday hours, as the heat away from the lake is intense. You'll need to carry plenty of water and some food (the only place to buy anything in the park is a simple staff kiosk in the Olkaria Geothermal Area).

There are several **campsites** in the park, with picnic benches, shower stands, taps and pit latrines. The nicest camping is at the shady and superbly sited *Ol Dubai* campsite on the clifftop south of Fischer's Tower. *Nairburta* and *Endachata* campsites (the latter a more expensive "special campsite") are across the gorge on the northern cliffs.

The upper gorge

From Elsa Gate, take a look first at the rock known as **Fischer's Tower**, after the German explorer who arrived at Lake Naivasha via Hell's Gate. The rock is a volcanic plug, the hard lava remaining from an ancient volcano after the cone itself has been eroded. It's now the home of a colony of very astute rock hyraxes ("dassies"), which look like large, shaggy guinea pigs and expect to be fed.

Through the gorge along the main track, you'll find more and more animals visible on the slopes leading up to the sheer cliffs. Secretary birds are always sighted, mincing carefully through the grass at a safe distance. At least one pair of rare **lammergeier eagles** used to nest on the cliffs, but they are rarely seen – report any sightings to a ranger.

If you're driving or on a mountain bike, you can take the longer Twiga and Buffalo Circuits. Twiga climbs up to the left from just inside Elsa Gate before you reach Fischer's Tower. Off Twiga is Buffalo Circuit, which ploughs through thick bush (don't go anywhere near the buffaloes, though, as they can be extremely unpredictable and dangerous). Both tracks are insanely dusty but, when the dust clears, the views out over Hell's Gate and across to the Aberdares range are magnificent.

The lower gorge

At the southern end of the gorge (12km from the entrance), a second rock tower – **Ol Basta** – marks its transition into tangled ravine. There's a car park here but nowhere to park on the narrow, rocky track that follows the gorge to the south for a short distance. The nearby "Interpretation Centre" is now a **viewpoint**, a good place to picnic and to shelter from rain or sun. The best move you can make from this roadhead is to cross the gorge and follow the "Nature Trail" round the north side of Ol Basta. There's nothing nature trail about it, but it's easy enough to follow as far as the rock tower, where most people turn back.

Hiking in the ravine is tough but exhilarating. Note that the trail from Ol Basta – the only realistic route – becomes more indistinct as you go, and it's quite easy to lose your way until you turn down into the head of the ravine itself. Beware of suggestions that there's a path around the south side of Ol Basta, directly above the eastern branch of the ravine: there isn't, and trying to prove otherwise is dangerous. Equally dodgy is the very steep way down into the ravine just south of the gorge crossing, near the car park. You need tough walking shoes for this and shouldn't attempt it alone.

Once down on the ravine floor, you've a one-hour walk southwards to the point where you can climb up to the road on the west side. Watch out for unexpected slippery surfaces and seek advice if it's been raining, as flash floods sometimes rip through the ravine.

If you've come equipped for a night out, you can press on, to emerge after a further (and difficult) 12km at the end of the canyon – still 15km short of the Narok road. For orientation, aim for **Mount Suswa** – itself an area of great exploring interest, only properly documented in the last few years. Otherwise, either turn back and retrace your path to Elsa Gate, or else climb up towards the noise and steam of Olkaria geothermal station. On the clifftop you can look out over the gorge and a Maasai village below, with your back to the first productive **geothermal installation** in Africa. The underground temperature of the super-heated, pressurized water is up to 304°C, one of the hottest sources in the world, and the station is expected to supply half of Kenya's energy requirements eventually. Although the whole complex is working at full tilt, the impact on the local environment appears to be small, and it certainly doesn't spoil the landscape.

Heading for the main buildings through the scrub, and the maze of pipes and hissing steam jets, you meet a perfect **tarmac road**. From here, you shouldn't have any problem getting a ride with plant workers down to the lake road at a point 2km past *Fisherman's Camp*. The road emerges near the Oserian farm where they produce carnations. If you hike it, allow about three hours to complete this section, which has fine views of Oloiden and Green Crater lakes.

Mount Longonot National Park

Daily dawn–dusk; $15, children $5; $8 to camp. Contact details as for Hell's Gate.

Don't try to make the ascent of **Mount Longonot** from the lake road or Hell's Gate – it's further and steeper than it looks, and the north slopes are covered in dense bush, frequented by buffalo. Instead, head for Longonot village on the old Nairobi road. A road leads 6–7km from just southeast of the level crossing by the main road to the base of the mountain, and you can leave your car there safely and get a drink (even for a day's climb, remember to take an ample quantity of water with you). The village itself has a couple of cheap, basic B&Ls.

Up the mountain

Longonot's name comes from the Maasai *oloonong'ot*, "mountain of many spurs" or "steep ridges", and you soon find out why. The cone is composed of very soft volcanic deposits that have eroded into deep gulches and narrow ridges.

There's only one straightforward route up to the crater rim, and you may be escorted by Kenya Wildlife Service rangers. The hike to the rim takes about an hour. At the top you can collapse (the last section is rather steep) and look back over the Rift Valley on one side and the enormous, silent crater on the other. Joseph Thomson, the first *mzungu* up here in 1884, was overcome:

The scene was of such an astounding character that I was completely fascinated, and felt under an almost irresistible impulse madly to plunge into the fearful chasm. So overpowering was this feeling that I had to withdraw myself from the side of the pit.

Avoiding the same urge, you can now scramble down a steep **crater path**; you turn left from the gravelly landing on the rim and find the path after about ten minutes' walk. Exciting encounters with buffalo on the crater floor aren't uncommon: a 1937 guidebook observes that "any attempt to descend into the crater is accompanied by hazard".

The walk around the **crater rim** is what most climbers do. The anticlockwise route is easier because the climb to the summit on the western side is quicker and steep sections more negotiable. It doesn't look far, but allow two to three hours. Much of the path is over crumbly volcanic tufa and has been worn, by a combination of walkers and rain, into a channel so deep and narrow that it's almost impossible to put one foot in front of the other.

Until recently, Longonot's crater was famous for its steam jets (the volcano is classed as "senile", not "extinct"). Although their vents, like pockmarks, are still visible in several places around the rim and on the crater walls, emissions of steam have decreased since the Olkaria plant went on line, though the hot-air thermals are said to be still sufficient to deflect light aircraft.

For **overnight stays** on the mountain, you need a tent (there are no official campsites) and possibly special permission from the Hell's Gate warden.

Naivasha to Thika via Kinangop

If you're serious about hiking, mountain biking, or fairly adventurous expeditionary driving, a route to take to **Thika** (see p.174) is the dramatic one from **North Kinangop**. It cuts up from the Rift Valley and right over the southern flank of the Nyandarua (Aberdare) range – still, in large part, virgin mountain rainforest. The approach **from Naivasha** is quite straightforward, as frequent matatus make the journey up to North Kinangop. Routine though it may be, this part of the journey is still spectacular. The road climbs constantly towards the **Kinangop Plateau**, with the Rift Valley and Lake Naivasha way below. The land hereabouts is Kikuyu farming country, once widely settled by Europeans, who were lured by the wide open moors, rocky outcrops and gushing streams; sheep and cattle graze everywhere.

NORTH KINANGOP is nowadays a rather isolated rural community, a village of big rubber boots and raggy sweaters (it can freeze here at night), whose road becomes nearly impassable during the long rains. Transport onwards is usually little problem outside the rainy season – at least as far as South Kinangop. Tractors will pick you up and there are a few old lorries, too, trundling around. **SOUTH KINANGOP** (also known as **Njabini**) is livelier than its northern counterpart, a small trading centre with a paved road (and matatus) straight from Naivasha (look out for the quaint, red-tiled colonial buildings which are now a Caltex station). If you get stuck in South Kinangop, give the *Gimwa Rest Lodge* (☎050/3032447; ❷) a try at the Thika end of town; it has s/c rooms and good hot showers.

South Kinangop to Gatakaini is a thirty-kilometre stretch, taking seven to eight hours on foot, and a great mountain-bike trip. A *murram* road (the C67) does continue, but there's very little traffic as it switchbacks in descent, across a series of streams flowing south from the Aberdares to the Chania River. The road follows the river, with tremendous scenic variation, though almost always through forest – sometimes wild, sometimes conifer plantation. But after the turn-off (left) for **South Kinangop forest station**, the occasional *shambas* and all signs of habitation stop completely. From here down, the forest is untouched mountain jungle – trees with huge dark green leaves, birds shrieking in alarm, the crashing of colobus monkeys, chameleons wobbling across the road and even tell-tale elephant dung. In the wrong season, the road becomes an appalling quagmire, really just for tractors. On foot or mountain bike, there's no danger of getting stuck.

You reach tarmac and human population again at **GATAKAINI**. Just before you do, there's the very pleasant *Kimakia Fishing Camp* (*bandas*, toilets and running water), unsupervised but a good place to spend the night with your own tent. The camp is run by the Fisheries Department (contact the Naivasha Senior Fisheries Officer on ℡050/2020505). At Gatakaini you can find matatus and buses to get you down to Thika. Towards evening public transport thins out and the country bus may leave you stranded at **Gatura**. If you have no luck hitching, give the excellent, but no longer appropriately named, *Tarmac End Inn* a try – it's a clean B&L with hot water (❶).

Kigio, Gilgil and around

Leaving or passing Naivasha, you continue northwest on Kenya's contribution to the Trans-African Highway (a projected paved ribbon joining Lagos with Mombasa) into the central Rift Valley – and the area around lakes Elmenteita and Nakuru.

Some 15km from Naivasha, on the north side of the road, lies the **Kigio Wildlife Conservancy**, a former cattle ranch rolling from the scrubby plains near the road and railway down through lightly wooded hills to the lush valley of the **Malewa River**. Established in 1997, Kigio already has an impressive conservation record, with the herd of **Rothschild's giraffe** relocated here in 2002 now breeding, and a pair of **white rhinos** relocated here in 2005 settling in well, though harder to find than the unmissable giraffes. Both relocations were filmed by the BBC. Although the conservancy (Ksh200) rarely contains any large predators (it's entirely fenced except along its riverbank side), the park's count of large animal species is very healthy, and includes hippo, buffalo, impala, Thomson's gazelle, waterbuck, zebra, warthog and ostrich.

△ Malewa River Lodge

The reserve is a great place to visit for a few hours or as an alternative Naivasha base. As well as wildlife-viewing (by car, on foot or with rented mountain bikes) and riverside bird-watching, Kigio offers abseiling, horse-riding, hikes up the densely wooded Kasuki gorge, and river swims (and rock-jumping) just 1500m downstream from the 🛩**Malewa River Lodge** (PO Box 446 Naivasha; ☎050/2030312, ⓕ2050063, ⓦwww.malewariverlodge.com; from $210; ◎). The lodge serves good food and the best coffee in the area, and offers delightfully eccentric accommodation, based around reclaimed timber, mud walls and thatched roofs. Besides a main lodge with public lounge, open fire and dining terrace, there are also six private cottages in the grounds, and the new, more luxurious *Malewa Ranch House* 3km upstream. There's also good camping (Ksh200).

Gilgil

GILGIL – pronounced "Girgir" by many Kenyans – is as dull a town as you could expect to find anywhere, with fragile-looking *dukas* and dusty streets with scavenging goats. On the outskirts lie the serried, pastel-coloured ranks of new housing for the hi-tech Gilgil Telecomms Industries workers, who assemble Zebra-brand computers among other things.

You may well find yourself hitching or changing buses or matatus in Gilgil. There are cheap rooms at the *Gilgil Makutano Hotel* (PO Box 255; ☎049/2079). Water supplies seem problematic, but in Gilgil maybe you should just count your blessings. The town has a Gilgil Mattresses supermarket, a bank next door, a post office and several car mechanics and petrol stations, but not much else. For details of a wonderful cycling or driving route around the area, see the box on p.247.

Gilgil War Cemetery

If you have a couple of hours to spare, walk 2–3km north out of town into the quiet, breezy savanna and have a look at the **Gilgil Commonwealth War Cemetery**. Of more than forty cemeteries in Kenya tended by the Commonwealth War Graves Commission, this is one of the most meticulously kept, and a good place to stop for a picnic and some moments of contemplation. There are about two hundred graves here from the East African campaign of World War II and from the war for independence – "the Emergency" – in the 1950s. Whether by accident (which doesn't seem credible) or design, the African graves are all at the bottom of the slope, and record no personal details apart from name and rank. The graves of British soldiers are higher up, the stones inscribed with family messages. As well as World War II graves, there are also poignant reminders of lives lost between 1959 and 1962, after the British government's futile attempt to prevent the inevitable.

Beyond, the C77 climbs past *Gilgil Country Club* on through moorland and conifer plantations around the resettlement zone of Ol Kalou, where some of the most violent Mau Mau attacks took place, and over the equator to Nyahururu (see p.216), Kenya's highest town.

Lake Elmenteita

Beyond the turn for Gilgil, the fast A2 road sweeps the eastern wall of the Rift Valley and pushes up high above **Lake Elmenteita**. This shallow soda lake, which has been known to shrivel to a huge white salt pond, is a good site for flamingos when Lake Nakuru is out of favour, and always good for pelicans; there are an estimated three hundred bird species in all. Like Lake Nakuru, Elmenteita has no outflow, and its accumulated alkaline salts make it uninhabitable for all but one species of fish, *Tilapia grahami*.

The setting is spectacular and primeval, framed by the broken caldera walls of several extinct volcanoes, which resemble a reclining human figure. The Maasai know these peaks as Elngiragata Olmorani (Sleeping Warrior) – a name which is ironically fitting, since the lake and its lands were expropriated from the Maasai at the start of the colonial period by Lord Delamere (the caldera is now also known as "Delamere's Nose"). You can get a good view from the big "parking lane" viewpoint – if you survive the rather desperate assaults from the curio sellers.

One top-notch establishment offers lakeshore **accommodation**, *Lake Elmenteita Lodge* (PO Box 561 Nakuru; reservations through Lake Nakuru Lodges, second floor, Arrow House, Koinange St; PO Box 70559 Nairobi ☎020/212405, ℱ227062, ⓦwww.lakenakurulodge.com; FB ⑤). Built around the 1930s brick homestead of the cattle farmer Lord Cole, this ranch-style lodge has jaw-dropping views, but is some distance above the lake (a track leads down to it). This is one place it may be advisable to visit when it has been raining, to avoid the persistent breeze which is practically brown with dust in the dry season. There's a resident naturalist, a pool and a very good restaurant. A hundred metres down the driveway from the main road is the **Ostrich Park Farm** (Ksh250), which provides amusing entertainment for kids.

Nearly all the land around the lake is, in theory, part of the private (and fenced-in) **Soysambu Wildlife Sanctuary**. In practice, the eastern shoreline is accessible if you're staying at the ⚑*Flamingo Camp* (PO Box 12957 Nakuru; ☎051/212382; ⓦwww.flamingocamp.com; ❸). Reached down a track signposted near the rocky pass on the highway 8km west of Gilgil, this offers cottages and camping (with your own equipment or in their safari-style tents) with plumbed-in toilets and showers. Go Ballooning Kenya (☎020/2717373 or 0723/702181, ⓦwww .goballooningkenya.com), based out of the Soysambu Ranch, runs one-hour **balloon flights** over the lake for $325 per person. The price includes a champagne breakfast and transfers to and from accommodation in the Nakuru area.

Back on terra firma, a number of prehistoric sites are scattered around the lake's once-lush shores, of which **Gambles Cave**, 10km southwest of Elmenteita village at Eburru, is the most famous. It can be visited by making arrangements ahead of time – ask at the National Museum in Nairobi.

Kariandusi

For an easier shot of prehistory, try a visit to **Kariandusi**, with a surprising sideshow in the shape of a neighbouring diatomite mine. Kariandusi (signposted off the A104 highway, 1500m to the east or a 20min walk; daily 8am–6pm; Ksh200, children Ksh100) is an **Acheulian site** characterized, like Olorgasailie (see p.225), by heavy hand-axes and cleavers. The site is very small, consisting of just two excavated areas cleared by Louis Leakey in 1928–31 and 1947, each displaying a scattered assortment of stone tools, many of them made of the black glassy volcanic rock, obsidian. There's a small **museum** too, which explains the formation of the Rift Valley, and has comparative skull specimens of our various distant ancestors.

Neither Kariandusi nor Olorgasailie have any signs of permanent habitation. This, and the fact that some 120,000 years ago Lake Elmenteita came right up to here, some 180m higher than its present level, and contained fresh water, suggests that it attracted hunter-gatherers who would wait to catch animals coming to drink. Tools were made on the spot and simply left for the next occasion, as the Acheulians had yet to invent receptacles to carry them in. As the lake level fluctuated, many tools were covered by it, and as the waters receded again, were carried by streams to their present clusters. Nothing much is known about

Between Gilgil and Nakuru, if you're hiking – or driving or cycling with a few hours to spare – give the fast (but by no means smooth and occasionally unnerving) main A104 a miss and follow the tarmac **former route** which mostly runs parallel to the new road a few hundred metres off on the right-hand side. The old road is potholed but quite negotiable and far from busy, serving as a rural footpath for people carrying firewood or cycling to the next hamlet.

You can join the old road at Gilgil by turning off the main highway at the junction 26.5km from Naivasha (Gilgil itself isn't signposted, though Gilgil Telecomms Industries and a host of schools and other places are). Go right through Gilgil and you arrive, 4km to the north of the town, at a fine viewpoint over Lake Elmenteita. Shortly after, on the right, you pass the obscure little **Church of Goodwill** – a settler's sentimental folly – still used on Sundays, in whose small graveyard rest the remains of a few old colonials and military men.

Shortly after the church, you pass Kariandusi and, rounding a bend, the diatomite mine (both left). Between the two, by the crash barriers to the right, a pale-coloured, rocky, 4WD track leads, after 3km, up over the raily line to a stream. Here you can leave your vehicle and climb (guided by the usual retinue of boys) to a crystal-clear, **warm-water source** in the woods – known, blandly enough, as *maji moto* (meaning "hot water"). You can swim in the natural swimming pool – there are usually people about, washing clothes or bathing. Beyond the Kariandusi junction, the old road dries up and you have to rejoin the highway. You can get onto the quiet road again at the turning to "Mbaruk", 3km further on, then follow the railway to Lanet, a suburb of Nakuru.

If you want to take further time out and see a remote part of the Central Province highlands, take a right turn off the old road, 4km after the "Mbaruk" turning, and follow the steep dirt road under the railway bridge and steeply up to the **Mbaruk Valley**. This is a beautiful road, rugged in parts (again, you're best off with 4WD) but with splendid compensation in the lush, forested cliffs across its far side. There's even a little **waterfall** 3km along the way, easy to miss unless it's in spate. Turn left at the Ngorika crossroads (tasty chapatis are provided at the *hoteli* on the corner) and you hit the tarmac C69 after 6km, where, turning left again, you start to make a fine, looping descent to the Rift Valley floor, with distinctive flat-topped acacias between the sloping *shambas* and the glint of Lake Nakuru down in the distance.

To follow this route in the other direction, Nairobi-bound, take the left turning for the C69 immediately before the Lanet Esso petrol station, before you reach the railway bridge bend.

the tool-makers themselves, apart from the fact that they obviously had a formidable grip. The most likely candidate is *Homo erectus*, an early hominid whose remains have been found at Olduvai Gorge in Tanzania alongside Acheulian artefacts, but Kariandusi bears no evidence of fire, nor of combination tools (for example stone axes with wooden handles) or carrying receptacles, which *Homo erectus* is generally known for. This would suggest that the tool-makers were a primitive form of *Homo erectus*.

The diatomite mine

A fascinating complement to the prehistoric site is a **diatomite mine** just 800m from the highway. Diatomite is a light, white, crumbly rock composed of the compressed silica skeletons of microscopic sea organisms (diatoms). The Kikuyu used it as body paint (*karia andus*), and a "clean" variety of it is still eaten by pregnant women and sick children (it's full of calcium).

The manager will gladly tell you more about diatomite (they're happy to receive visitors), but the real excitement comes when you walk down into the mine itself: a track spirals down the inside of a giant bowl, scooped out of the ground by pick and shovel over the last sixty years, to a level about 50m down where high-grade, brilliant white diatomite is found. Here, a dozen or more **tunnels** dive into the cliffs to form a maze of ghostly subterranean passages, home to thousands of fluttering fruit **bats**. The tunnels are wonderfully cool and vents keep the air circulating. You'll be assured that the structure of diatomite makes rock falls extremely unlikely, but a number of shored-up passageways may leave you glad to have an accounts clerk – or some other conscripted employee – to guide you. You need a torch even though the light goes in a surprisingly long way, but you can't really get lost.

Nakuru

As you approach **Nakuru** along the main highway from Nairobi, the *shamba*- and conifer-cloaked mound directly ahead is the southern flank of the vast **Menengai crater**, while to the left are the scrub-covered eastern heights of the **Nakuru National Park**. A noisy, dusty and hustly town, Nakuru is also close to the prehistoric settlement site at **Hyrax Hill**, and is the jumping-off point for trips into the **northern Rift Valley**.

Nakuru came into existence on the thrust of the Uganda railway and owed its early growth, at least in part, to **Lord Delamere**, the colony's most famous figure. In 1903 he acquired four hundred square kilometres of land on the lower slopes of the Mau escarpment, followed by two hundred more at Soysambu, on the other side of the lake. Eager to share the empty vistas with compatriots – though preferably with other Cheshire or Lancashire men – he promoted in England the mile-square plots being offered free by the Foreign Office. Eventually, some two hundred new settler families arrived and Nakuru – a name which as usual could mean various things, including "Place of the Waterbuck" (Swahili) and "Swirling Dust" or "Little Soda Lake" (Maasai) – became their country capital. It lies on the unprepossessing steppe between the lake and the flanks of Menengai crater. This desolate shelf has a nickname: "the place where the cows won't eat grass" (the pasture was found to be iron-deficient). Farmers near the town turned to pyrethrum, the plant used to make insecticide, as a cash crop.

Roadside rip-offs

If you're driving, beware of anyone around Nakuru telling you there's anything wrong with your car – this is the con-mechanic capital of Kenya. **Tricksters** hang around along the roadside either between Lanet and the town centre or between the town centre and the national park main gate, and have also been seen along the road to Eldoret. They work in teams, pointing one after another at your wheels as you drive past or, if you stop anywhere, "discovering" oil dripping from your engine – anything to get you into their garage for a bogus repair job. Gangs have recently taken to placing large rocks across already badly pot-holed stretches of highway (especially between Nakuru and Eldoret), forcing you to slow right down: ignore their demands to stop.

The Town

NAKURU is Kenya's fourth largest city (though it projects a noticeably busier and more energetic image than Kisumu, the third), and capital of the enormous, sprawling Rift Valley Province that stretches from the Sudanese border to the slopes of Kilimanjaro. Still largely a workaday farmers' town, with unadorned old seed shops and veterinary paraphernalia much in evidence on the main street, Nakuru is a little Nairobi without the flashy veneer, its streets frequently undergoing ear-shattering repairs. Ongoing outbursts of ethnic violence in the Rift Valley have resulted in an influx of Kikuyu refugees from outlying parts of the province; it is, in many ways, more of a social barometer than Nairobi.

The town can appear intimidating at first, and most of the tourists on their way to the national park stay in one of the lodges there. Still, Nakuru has some positive aspects: the **market** is animated and a pleasure to look around (though it has its fair share of hassle), and there's a glimmer of charm remaining in the colonnaded old streets and the jacaranda-lined avenues at the edge of town.

Practicalities

The **train** and **bus/matatu stations** are packed together at the east end of town, with **lodgings** all around. If entering Nakuru bus station from the train station side, go in via "Exit" to avoid the bevy of enthusiastic touts who hang around at "Entrance".

Accommodation

You're spoilt for choice for **cheap rooms**, with plenty of other places apart from the following found in the centre, though few of them stand out. A number of **mid-range hotels** are dotted about the western avenues, and are amazingly good value if you've just come from Nairobi. However, the sewers there can turn even the hardiest stomachs, and the distantly throbbing noise from the *Millennium Hotel* nightclub is also a nuisance. The only hotel at the luxury end is the *Merica*, although it's not as classy as it likes to think. If you're **camping**, go to the national park.

Amoodi's B&L Nehru Rd; PO Box 1731 ☏051/41939. A no-frills B&L with excellent security, plenty of hot water, clean toilets and the cheapest twin beds in town, in shoe-box rooms. ❷

Carnation Hotel Mosque Rd, first floor; PO Box 1620 ☏051/43522. A large, well-run and attentive establishment – the best in the town centre and very fair value, and with a good

Moving on from Nakuru

Heading away from Nairobi, the **bus** lines all run regular and frequent services to Eldoret, Kisumu, Kitale, Kisii and other points west (Akamba Bus is safest; ☏051/213775–6). Alternatively, you can take the quieter road west, through the high-land towns of Njoro, Elburgon and Molo, a route covered on p.259. Southwards, you can get to Narok (for the Maasai Mara) by **matatu** up the fantastic Mau escarpment (allow a day to arrive; see p.394). At least one bus heads daily to Marigat at Lake Baringo, and matatus make the run to Kabarnet in the hills to the west. There are also **trains** to Nairobi and to Kisumu.

There's a lavishly scenic route to Nyahururu through the Subukia Valley, an ascent of the Rift that, for sheer grandeur, comes close to the Naivasha escarpment (daily bus and matatu runs). If you're driving, note that the turn-off 2.5km down the Nairobi road is not signposted – turn left at the Shell petrol station opposite *Kunste hotel*.

NAKURU

0 — 200 m

F, G, Hyrax Hill & ▲ Nairobi (A104) ▲ Lanet & Nairobi

Menengai Crater ▲

Hospital, Baringo & Bogoria (B4) ▲

Eldoret (A104) and Njoro & Elburgon (C56) ▼

Nakuru National Park (3km) & ⑩ ▼

MENENGAI DRIVE

SHOWGROUND ROAD

Train Station

Covered Market

See inset below

Covered Market

MBARU GICHUA ROAD

NEHRU ROAD

MOSQUE ROAD

GUSII ROAD

OGINGA ODINGA AVENUE

Uchumi Supermarket

Esso

KENYATTA LANE

BANK LANE

Odeon Cinema

Bressalex Centre

Caltex

Nakuru Patisserie

Crater Travel Agency

Rift Valley Sports Club

Barclays Bank

CLUB LANE

CLUB ROAD

Standard Chartered Bank

GK KAMAU HIGHWAY

KENYATTA AVENUE

Clock Tower

KCB

Gilani's Supermarket

COURT ROAD

Gilani's Butchery

Police Station

MOI ROAD

Kobil

Mobil

MUDAVADI ROAD

MOSES MUDAVADI ROAD

Nakuru Players' Theatre

Barclays Bank

KENYATTA ROAD

TOM MBOYA ROAD

GOVERNMENT AVENUE

KIPCHOGE AVENUE

OGINGA ODINGA AVENUE

RONALD NGALA AVENUE

Cathedral of Christ the King

Afraha Stadium

STADIUM ROAD / LAKE ROAD

KARIBA AVENUE

WEST ROAD

KUFANYA ROAD

TOWER FACT ROAD

KCB 'Bureau de Change'

ACCOMMODATION

Amigo's B&L J
Amoodi's B&L I
Carnation K
Gitwamba B
Hotel Waterbuck E
Kunste F
Merica D
Midland A
Pivot H
Shik Parkview C
Stem G

RESTAURANTS, CAFÉS, BARS & CLUBS

Café Lemon Tart 1
Club Coco Savannah 11
Club Dimples 3
Courtyard 8
Golden Spoon/Club Utugi 4
Millennium Hotel 10
Nakuru Coffee House 2
Nakuru Sweet Mart 7 & 12
Planet Kitchen 9
Ribbons Café 6
Summit 14
Tipsy Restaurant 13
XTC Discotheque 5

TRANSPORT

c Big Buses to: Nairobi, Kisumu, Kakamega, Kisii, Eldoret, Kitale & Baringo District

e Town service, matatus & minibuses

d Peugeot Express taxis

b Nissans to Nairobi; 504s to Nyeri & Eldoret; pick-ups to Kericho & Eldoret

a Matatus to Molo, Elburgon, Njoro, Narok, Subukia, Siria & Nyahururu restaurant. The waiters are keen to persuade you to go on a park trip. ❸

Gitwamba Hotel Gusii Rd; PO Box 586 ☎051/40754. One of the best joints in this quarter of town, with light and spacious rooms (though only one s/c), good cheap breakfasts and a matatu stage opposite. It's raucous on disco nights – Wed & Fri–Sun. ❷

Kunste Hotel 2.5km down the Nairobi road; PO Box 1369 ☎051/212140. A good hotel with sensibly priced rooms, but sometimes near deserted, which may explain why the service is so rusty. They sometimes allow camping. B&B Ksh2000.

Merica Hotel Corner of Court Rd and Kenyatta Ave; PO Box 560 ☎051/214232, ⓦwww .mericagrouphotels.com. Large, plush rooms (although some are starting to look a bit shabby for what is supposed to be a luxury hotel), an excellent restaurant, a swimming pool and live music at the weekends. ❺

Midland Hotel GK Kamau Highway; PO Box 908 ☎051/212125, ⓕ44517, ⓔenquiries@midland .co.ke. Long-established and good-value s/c rooms with thick carpeting, wood panelling and decent bathrooms. A new wing is under construction. The attached bar-restaurant is lively, but the food isn't great. B&B Ksh2300.

Pivot Hotel Lower Factory Rd; PO Box 1369 ☎051/210226. Despite resembling a military hospital in every aspect, this is recommended: the rooms are shiny clean and have new mosquito nets. Staying in any of rooms 1–15 will help you avoid the deafening disco din on some weekend nights. ❹

Shik Parkview Hotel Kenyatta Ave; PO Box 614 ☎051/212345 or 212346. Airy rooms, on the small side, in a medium-sized establishment with a separate bar and restaurant. ❷

Stem Hotel Nairobi road, close to the Nakuru National Park Lanet Gate, 8km from the town centre; PO Box 1076 ☎051/350135, ⓕ51273. Pleasant (in a functional, motel manner), with a small pool, gym, steam room and sauna (Ksh80– 200/hr), acceptable s/c rooms, and good Indian Mughlai food. They also provide transport into the National Park (Ksh5000 per minibus), and normally allow camping. B&B ❻

Waterbuck Hotel West Rd; PO Box 3327 ☎051/2215672, ⓕ214163. Large doubles with orange walls, animal print rugs and cable TV. The showers leave a lot to be desired, however, and the ground floor singles are dingy and cramped. On the plus side, there's a lively swimming pool and friendly bar area which is full of Kenyan families at the weekends. Also has safe parking. ❹

Eating and drinking

Finding good **meals** isn't that easy in Nakuru. As a guide, the older, more down-at-heel establishments are bunched towards the east end of town near the train station, while the west end, especially along Kenyatta Avenue, tends to be more upmarket.

For provisions, the best **supermarkets** in town are the main Uchumi on Kenyatta Lane, just off GK Kamau Highway (Mon–Sat 9.30am–8pm, Sun 9.30am–2pm) and the Ukwala on Kenyatta Avenue (same hours). If you're driving through, check out the Sita Supermarket, at the Sita Shopping Centre a few kilometres east of the town centre on the Nairobi road, or the shopping centre 4km west of town on the Kisumu road. A smaller grocery is Gilani's on Club Road, while Gilani's Butchery on Moi Road has a good **cheese** counter. Nakuru Patisserie on Club Lane has a wholesome selection of **bread** and baked bites, as does the Nakuru Sweet Mart French Bakery and Café on Moi Road. The main **produce market**, near the transport parks and railway station, has the full display of fruit and vegetables, but watch out for pickpockets and petty thieves.

For a **drink**, the *Millenium Hotel* is actually quite a pleasant beer garden with thatched huts, wicker chairs and a wicked sound system, and on Saturday nights the bar at the *Waterbuck Hotel* is a lively place to be.

Restaurants, cafés and snack bars

Café Lemon Tart Moi Rd. Cheap and cheerful little place serving good coffees, snacks and breakfasts.
The Courtyard Government Ave. Very relaxing

place for a substantial feed – mainly grills, Indian and local fare, and seafood – at around Ksh500. Steer clear of the pizzas though.
Golden Spoon/Club Utugi Kenyatta Lane. Pleasant pavement café with a zebra-striped

awning, serving the usual grills, burgers and curries. At night it turns into a mellow live music joint.

Millennium Hotel Government Ave. Besides being a beer garden, this is also a reasonable *nyama choma* joint.

Nakuru Coffee House Moi Rd. A reliable venue for real coffee and tasty pastries.

Nakuru Sweet Mart Gusii Rd. A long-established Indian place which does an excellent and massive vegetarian *thali*, great *bhajhias, masala tea* and a good range of breads. Very cheap, but avoid if you're on an oil-free diet. They also own the *Nakuru Sweet Mart* French bakery and café on Moi Rd, opposote Gilani's butchery.

Planet Kitchen Government Ave. Laid-back and friendly bar/café with outdoor seating, serving good curries, steaks and grilled fish.

Ribbons Cafe Gusii Rd. Good first-floor terrace snack bar, with a stripey pink and white exterior, overlooking the commotion below.

The Summit By the Lake Nakuru park gates, Lake Rd. A few minutes' drive from town, this is a large, mostly open-air complex, with a dance floor and a pool area. There are several different dining areas, serving excellent *nyama choma* and grills. Very friendly.

Tipsy Restaurant Gusii Rd. Next door and similar to, but cheaper than, *Nakuru Sweet Mart*, and for the less hungry. The place looks clean, but there is no running water.

Waterbuck Hotel West Rd. A good all-day snack menu – samosas, burgers and soups.

Nightlife and entertainment

Surprisingly, Nakuru is jumping when it comes to **nightlife**. Try *Club Dimples* or *Club Coco Savana* on Club Road, (the latter open nightly, with a jam session on Sundays and a good restaurant next door). One of best places is the *Summit*, packed out at the weekends with patrons of all ages getting down to Western and Kenyan pop and golden oldies. Also worth investigating is the glitzy *XTC Discotheque* and, for live jazz, the *Golden Spoon/Club Utugi*.

If you're in town for more than a day, you may get the chance to see the Nakuru Players in action at their dour-looking **theatre** (⊕051/40805) on Kipchoge Avenue. Of the two main **cinemas**, the Odeon and the Eros, both on GK Kamau Highway, the latter is smaller and more inviting (screenings daily 6 & 9pm, plus Saturday 3pm).

Listings

Banks Scattered all over the town: there's a KCB with a "Bureau de Change" flagged on the western outskirts. Both Standard Chartered at Moi Rd and Barclays on Kenyatta Ave have ATMs.

Books Ereto Bookshop, Kenyatta Lane; and the Flamingo Bookshop, Kenyatta Ave. Both specialize in school textbooks and religious volumes.

Car repairs There are myriad workshops at the western ends of Government and Kipchoge avenues. Get quotes from several places before bringing your vehicle down. Hertz recommend CMC Motors Group (⊕051/211875–7) or D.T. Dobie (⊕051/211775–7), both on George Morara Ave.

Clinic Nakuru Medical Clinics, by Barclays on Kenyatta Ave (⊕051/214655), has a range of specialists.

Internet access There are two Internet cafes in the Bressalex Centre on Kenyatta Ave (both closed Sun). Telephone and fax facilities available also.

Pharmacy Medika Chemists, first floor, Equator House, Kenyatta Lane, next door to Uchumi (⊕051/214847).

Post office At Moi Rd/Kenyatta Ave, with good telephone and fax facilities, and an EMS counter round the back.

Travel agents Crater Travel, Inder Singh Building, just off Kenyatta Ave (PO Box 2631; ⊕ & ℱ051/2215019), offers a full service for air ticketing, plus the usual range of (expensive) tour deals. For general local arrangements, especially Nakuru National Park visits and other safaris, Blackbird Tours at Caleb's Arcade in the *Carnation* hotel (⊕051/45383) is friendly and competent. The going rate for the use of a four-seater Suzuki, including the driver-guide but excluding park fees, is at least Ksh4000 for 5–6hr. They're happy to pick you up from your hotel.

Around Nakuru

Though not large, **Lake Nakuru** is a beautiful park, the terra firma mostly under light acacia forest, well provided with tracks to a variety of hides and lookouts. It's also one of the easiest parks to visit, with or without a vehicle, and the contrast and apparent dislocation between the shallow soda lake – with its primeval birds – and the animated woodlands all around give it a very distinctive appeal. The easy-to-follow topography (it's a pleasure to drive around, which takes around 3hr) means you really can't get lost.

Rising directly behind Nakuru town is the extinct volcanic giant **Menengai**, its sloping mass somehow not especially noticeable from the town. Another easy target is **Hyrax Hill**, a settlement site for at least three thousand years, with finds dating from the Neolithic period.

Lake Nakuru National Park

Admission $30, children $10 (Smartcard only); $8 to camp, $15 in a "special" campsite. No entry on foot. Warden: PO Box 439 Nakuru ☎ 051/44069. Maps: Tourist Maps of Kenya, Lake Nakuru National Park 1:50,000 (2003).

The mystery of the vanishing flamingos

Despite their more or less continual absence since 1995, Lake Nakuru has always been considered a flamingo lake par excellence. At one time, it was believed that up to two million **lesser flamingos** (perhaps one third of the world's population) were massing in the warm alkaline water to feed on the abundant blue-green algae cultivated by their own droppings. In addition, the lake was also home to a small population of the much rarer **greater flamingo** which have less hooked beaks used to sift for small crustaceans and plankton with the birds' heads underwater.

Like Lake Elmenteita, Nakuru has no outlet, meaning that its level fluctuates wildly. In 1962, it dried up almost completely, and in the late 1970s, a combination of increased rainfall and decreased evaporation lowered the lake's salinity and raised the water level. The flamingos began to disperse, some to lakes Elmenteita, Magadi and Natron (the latter in Tanzania), some up to Turkana, the majority to Lake Bogoria. Since then, flamingos have been sporadically seen again in the surreal pink flocks that have become a photographic cliché, but the situation has become increasingly unpredictable. They were absent in late 1995, when the lake started drying up. Water levels increased greatly due to the 1997–98 El Niño rains, with the result that the lake again became too fresh for the flamingos. From 2000 they began to return, but their numbers aren't what they once were and they are still under threat from occasional droughts and water pollution.

A great debate has raged in the Kenyan press about the causes of their disappearance and its detrimental effect on the tourist trade. Over the last twenty years, large areas of forest in the lake's catchment area have been converted to small farms, and Nakuru town has undergone rapid growth and industrialization. Pollution from the town's sewer effluent and industries is believed to be a major factor behind the flamingos' decline here, as are water diversion, soil erosion (leading to siltation) and even sand-harvesting along the Njoro River. The introduction in the Sixties of a hardy species of fish, *tilapia grahami* – partly to control mosquitoes – has encouraged large flocks of **white pelicans** in recent years and it's likely that their presence is another disruptive element (on Elmenteita a breeding colony of greater flamingos was forced off by the pelicans). The Nakuru Wildlife Trust has been studying the ecology of Rift Valley lakes since 1971 in an effort to find some of the answers, and the WWF now organizes educational trips to the park for local kids, as well as running a scheme to monitor pollution from individual industries.

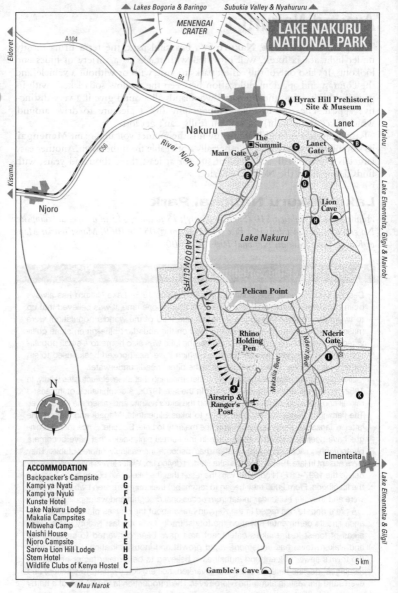

▲ Lakes Bogoria & Baringo   Subukia Valley & Nyahururu ▲

MENENGAI
CRATER

LAKE NAKURU
NATIONAL PARK

A104

B4

Eldoret ▲

◉ A Hyrax Hill Prehistoric
Site & Museum

Lanet

Nakuru

River Njoro

The
Summit   Lanet
Main Gate   ◉ C   Gate

◉ B   Ol Kalou ▲

C56

◉ D
◉ E

◉ F
◉ G

Lion
Cave

Kisumu ◀

Njoro

Lake Nakuru

◉ H

BABOON CLIFFS

Pelican Point

Nderit Gate

Nderit River

◉ I

Rhino
Holding
Pen

Makalia River

◉ K

◉ J

Airstrip &
Ranger's
Post

◉ L

Elmenteita

Lake Elmenteita, Gilgil & Nairobi ▶

Lake Elmenteita & Gilgil ▶

ACCOMMODATION
Backpacker's Campsite	D
Kampi ya Nyati	G
Kampi ya Nyuki	F
Kunste Hotel	A
Lake Nakuru Lodge	I
Makalia Campsites	K
Mbweha Camp	L
Naishi House	J
Njoro Campsite	E
Sarova Lion Hill Lodge	H
Stem Hotel	B
Wildlife Clubs of Kenya Hostel	C

N

0   5 km

Gamble's Cave ⌂

▼ Mau Narok

The park has three gates. **Main Gate** (the point of issue for Smartcards), at the
edge of Nakuru town, is also the park headquarters and has the main campsites
nearby, plus a good, hand-painted map showing the most recent circuits, most
of which are in fair condition. Entering through **Lanet Gate** gives the most
direct access from Naivasha or Nairobi to the park's two **lodges**, and avoids the

congestion of Nakuru town. The 1500-metre track to the gate, not properly signposted, starts opposite the *Stem Hotel*; if you're heading towards Nakuru and you cross the railway bridge, you've overshot. **Nderit Gate**, in the southeast corner, is useful only if you're coming cross-country from Lake Naivasha or over the Mau escarpment from Narok.

The most straightforward way to see the park if you don't have a vehicle is **by taxi**, especially as some of the taxi drivers around Nakuru town know the park well. The *Midland Hotel* is as good a place as any to track one down. This naturally works out cheaper for a group, but you'll probably want to reach an agreement with the driver before you're all present. Reckon on some stiff bargaining, then three hours at about $15 an hour, with park fees on top. Alternatively, contact Blackbird Tours (see p.252).

An alternative – though not always a very practical one – is to **hitch** at the Main Gate, about an hour's walk from the town centre. The rangers are usually sympathetic: they may help by asking drivers on your behalf, and they won't ask you to pay park fees unless you get a lift (if you don't, you can camp at the backpackers' campsite). Expect to spend the night in the park once you get a ride, so be prepared for this. If you don't have a tent either, you could always stay the night at the cheap and cheerful *Florida Day & Night Club B&L* (❶) right on the boundary between park and town. This won't give you a restful night, but you'll want to be up bright and early waiting for a lift in any case; there's the added bonus that you're bound to meet park staff here.

Accommodation

The park has two expensive lodges, a hostel and a few campsites; southeast of the park is an excellent alternative to all of these, the *Mbweha Camp*.

Lake Nakuru Lodge PO Box 561 Nakuru ☏051/850228, ☎216250, ☜www.lakenakuru-lodge.com. Established lodge based around an old Delamere Estate house in shady gardens, with a pool ($5 for visitors) and uninterrupted views of the lake, though several kilometres from it. The *banda*-style rooms are on the small side and rather dark, though the newer and much more expensive chalet suites, down a viewing platform/walkway, are first-class. The food is nothing special. FB ❽ low season, ❾ high

🏃 **Mbweha Camp** Just outside the park, a 15min drive from the Nderit Gate; PO Box 7112, ☏051/210943 or 0722/677449; bookings also through their Nairobi office ☏020/574395, ☜www.mbwehacamp.com. Nestled among euphorbia trees, the camp has nine private cottages, all made from local materials and with private verandas and views of the Eburu and Mau ranges. There's also a sunken lounge and bar area looking out onto a small watering hole, and a fantastic restaurant. A range of activities are on offer including bike rides, game drives, bush dinners and sundowners. Camping is available, with hot showers and bush toilets. Conservation fees Ksh100 a day. HB ❽

Naishi House Bookings through KWS (see p.64). A peaceful place commanding a wonderful view of Nakuru Park, with a fully furnished kitchen and four bedrooms to suit a group of eight. There's a cleaner, and firewood is provided. Game drives in the company of a ranger can be arranged. 200 for the whole house.

Sarova Lion Hill Lodge 12km from the city centre; PO Box 7094 Nakuru ☏051/850235, ☎210836, ☜www.sarovahotels.com. Extremely comfortable, with a low-key atmosphere, helped along by friendly staff. There are good views from the very pleasant, chalet-style rooms stacked high above the main parts of the lodge, and the meals are excellent and slightly cheaper than at *Lake Nakuru Lodge*. Pool and sauna (small fee for visitors); game drives and bush lunches are available. FB $205–235 depending on season; ❾

Wildlife Clubs of Kenya Hostel On the northern side of the park; PO Box 33 Nakuru ☏051/850929. Offering dorms only, this is the only reasonably priced accommodation here, but is somewhat rundown. The dorms and do-it-yourself catering arrangements seem just about adequate; the kitchen is well equipped. Dorm beds Ksh300.

Camping

There's a **backpackers' campsite** (cold showers, toilets, communal tap) on a pleasant grassy site under fine old yellow acacias, but beware the audacious vervet monkeys and baboons, who've taken to attacking campers and wrecking their tents. Other possibilities include the **Njoro campsite** on the northwestern shore and the somewhat elusive **Makalia campsites**, in a wonderful location at the southern tip of the park, on either side of the stream of the same name and close to the waterfall. Very few organized tours come down this way, but should you feel isolated, you may be reassured to know there's a ranger station fairly close by.

There are also a couple of "**special campsites**" in the northeast part of the park **Kampi ya Nyati** (Buffalo Camp) and **Kampi ya Nyuki** (Bee Camp, the nicer of the two). They're both located in clearings among the trees between the road and the open shore, and have splendid "private" access to quiet vantage points on the shore through driveable tunnels of undergrowth.

Around the park

The **northern shores** of the lake are the most opened-up, with a busy route between the Main Gate and *Sarova Lion Hill Lodge*; the southern parts are usually empty. The vegetation in the north is mostly lightly wooded acacia forest and this is the least interesting area for wildlife, close to Nakuru town.

Taken clockwise, the main track runs through the woods, past the *Sarova Lion Hill Lodge* and into an exotic-looking forest of candelabra **euphorbia** – great cactus-like trees up to 15m high. At the southern end of this zone you come into a spell of more open country, past the turning (left) up to *Lake Nakuru Lodge*, and one or two side tracks down to the mud and the lakeshore (right); then the road turns west into the southern park's dense acacia jungle. This is where you may see a **leopard** and – if they overcome their shyness – one of the park's thirty-odd **black rhino**. Several kilometres further, the road opens again onto wider horizons with plenty of buffalo, waterbuck, impala and eland all around. This is also the most likely area for seeing the park's introduced **Rothschild's giraffe** herd.

Down in this **southern part** of the park, take a northerly side track and you can circle around the savanna; opt for a southerly side track and you plunge into deep scrub and thicket – perfect rhino country. Eventually, heading south, you reach the electric boundary fence and the perimeter patrol track, which you can follow, east or west, back to the main circuit route.

The **west shore**, especially "pelican point", has the best opportunities for seeing the **flamingos**, if they've returned. In places, the road runs on what is virtually a causeway, past the lake's edge, with high cliffs rearing up behind. Finally, the main route leaves the shore and ploughs north, through thick forest with many tall trees and dense undergrowth, back to the Main Gate.

Good **vantage points** around the lake include the northern **mud flats** (follow established tracks across the dry surface); the dead tree **watchtower** (northeast); *Kampi ya Nyuki* and *Kampi ya Nyati* campsites; *Lake Nakuru Lodge*, for a general view across unobstructed savanna; and the high "**baboon cliffs**" in the west.

Menengai crater

Containing an enormous caldera, **Menengai crater** is 12km across and nearly 500m deep in places. From Nakuru town centre, it's about an eight-kilometre (3hr) hike to the crater rim; on weekends, you might be lucky and get a lift, but there's no public transport other than taxis.

Lake Nakuru's wildlife

Fortunately, in view of the flamingos' here-today-gone-tomorrow caprice, there's a lot more to the lake's spectacle than the pink flocks. Its shores and surrounding woodlands are home to some four hundred other species of **birds** including, during the northern winter, many migratory European species. Towards the end of the dry season in March, the lake is often much smaller than the maps suggest and, consequently, water birds are a greater distance from the park roads.

There's a good number of **mammals** here as well. The lake isn't too briny for **hippos** – a herd of a dozen or more snort and splash by day and graze by night at the northern end. Nakuru has also become a popular venue for introduced species: there are **Rothschild's giraffe** from the wild herd near Kitale, and **lion** and secretive **leopard** from wherever they're causing a nuisance.

In the early 1990s, a number of **black rhinos** were relocated from Solio Game Ranch (see p.215), and ten **white rhinos** were donated by South Africa in 1994; the park now has one of the highest concentrations of rhino in the country. Electric fencing has been installed around the entire perimeter of the park – the only park in the country to be so enclosed – with the intention of maintaining a viable number of rhinos in a zone secure from poachers.

Nakuru is possibly Swahili for "place of the waterbuck", and the park is **waterbuck** heaven. With only a handful of lions and small numbers of leopards to check their population, the shaggy, red-deer-size beasts number several thousand, and the herds (either bachelor groups or a buck and his harem) are large and exceptionally tame. **Impala**, too, are very numerous, though their lack of fear means you rarely witness the graceful flight of a herd vaulting through the bush.

The two other most often seen mammals are **buffalo** – which you'll repeatedly mistake for rhinos until you get a look through binoculars – and **warthog**, scuttling nervously in singles and family parties everywhere you look. Elephants are absent, but you're likely to see **zebra**, **dik-dik**, **ostrich** and **jackals** and, in the southern part of the park, **eland** and **Thomson's and Grant's gazelles**. More rarely you can encounter the odd **striped hyena** loping along the road in the eastern euphorbia forest at dawn, **reedbuck** down by the shore and **bushbuck** dashing briskly through the herbage. Along the eastern road, near *Lake Nakuru Lodge*, are several over-tame **baboon troops** to be wary of. The park is also renowned for its very large **pythons** – the patches of dense **woodland** in the southwest, between the lakeshore and the steep cliffs, are a favourite habitat.

Lastly, if you tire of the living spectacle, go looking for the **Lion Cave**, beneath Lion Hill ridge in the northeast; it's an excavated prehistoric rock shelter and rarely contains lions.

If you walk, you're best advised to go up in company as muggings are a possibility. To reach the crater, head up Menengai Drive and take the fourth left turn (Crater Climb) through the modestly affluent suburbs above the town. Some 4.5km up the hill is a telecommunications tower: head for this, then turn right, following the path through a fragrant forest of gum trees for twenty minutes, to a fire lookout tower on the bare cliff. From the top of this, the massive crater spreads out beneath you, a spectacular sea of bush-covered lava, its black waves frozen solid.

The crater was the site of a battle around 1854 in which the Ilpurko Maasai defeated the Ilaikipiak, whom they considered upstarts disrespectful to Batian, the *laibon* (paramount chief) of the time, after whom the highest peak of Mount Kenya was named. At intervals throughout the nineteenth century, these **Maasai civil wars** flared up over the issue of true Maasai identity. In this case, it was not simply a matter of honour but also of grazing rights in the Rift Valley, especially around Lake Naivasha and on the scarp slopes. The Ilpurko were herders, while the Ilaikipiak from the north grew crops as well. Both had been preparing for battle for some time and it is said that hundreds of Ilaikipiak *morani* were hurled over the crater rim to their deaths. The place retains a sinister reputation – even the normally fearless Maasai traditionally have it as the dwelling place of devils and other evil – and local people prefer not to go near the edge.

A century later, at the highest point of this windy crest, the Rotary Club erected a signpost. Apart from informing you that Nairobi is 140km away and Rome 2997km in the opposite direction, it also points out that the crater wall is 2272m above sea level and its area covers some 90 square kilometres – the whole dramatic extent of which you can see. You'll get fantastic views over Lake Nakuru if you walk down the dirt road along the south side of the gum-tree plantation.

Hyrax Hill

Named for the hyraxes which once scampered over it, **Hyrax Hill** (daily 9.30am–6pm; Ksh200) is an easy target, 3.5km out of town, just to the left (north) of the Nairobi road. Matatus bound for Lanet and Gilgil will drop you at the turn, then it's a two-kilometre walk to the small museum where you pay the fee. If you're driving, don't be misled by the sign next to the *Kunste Hotel* which appears to indicate a left turn here (the Subukia/Nyahururu road): it's about a kilometre further to the entrance track.

The settlement site here was discovered by Louis Leakey in 1926, excavated by Mary Leakey in 1937–38 and by others in 1965, 1973 and 1987. An excellent guide booklet (1983) is on sale in the museum. You can normally **camp** here, free or for a small fee (staff facilities only).

The Northeast Village

The path leading out to the right of the museum winds its way around the north side of the hill to an excavated pit dwelling, or at any rate a "sunken enclosure", with baulks left in place to show the depth of material that was removed during the digging. There are thirteen similar depressions in this "**Northeast Village**" (curiously named, as it is in the northwest), but it's uncertain exactly how they were used. They have yielded a tremendous quantity of pottery shards, tools made from flakes of obsidian and animal-bone fragments. The absence of post-holes normally needed to support a roof suggests they may have been shelters for livestock, but just as plausibly, a roof might have been added whenever needed, leaving no trace, and animals and people may have shared the shelters.

It's believed the inhabitants would have been semi-nomadic Sirikwa- or Nandi-speaking (Kalenjin) herders. Today, the Kalenjin mostly live further west, but they're associated with so-called pit-dwellings elsewhere (see p.276) and, in the case of Hyrax Hill, they may have been forced to flee by an expanding Maasai population from the north.

The fort and burial sites

Following the path towards the top of the hill, you come to an exposed "**fort**" facing out towards Nakuru, which consists of a circle of hefty boulders enclosing a flattened area. It's said to have been an Iron-Age lookout post, but there's no way of being certain what this actually was, nor even how old it might be, since no artefacts have been found. From here, you can scramble over the volcanic boulders – the whole hill is a tongue of lava – to the summit, where you get a good view of the southern part of the site and the lake. Now several kilometres away, the lake once extended, probably as fresh water, right to the base of the hill and across much of the Rift Valley, turning Hyrax Hill into a peninsula or even an island.

A hundred metres down the hillside in a fenced-in shelter, the massive stone slab which sealed a **Neolithic burial mound** has been removed to display part of a skull and some limb bones. The remains of a further nineteen Neolithic skeletons were discovered north of this, beneath a more recent Iron Age occupation area marked by the two stone circles (which were hut foundations). Nineteen Iron Age skeletons were also discovered, overlying the Neolithic graves, mostly of young men, possibly slain warriors, apparently buried unceremoniously or in a hurry, their skulls and limbs in tangled heaps. The coincidence of nineteen skeletons at each level may be just that – coincidence. Or perhaps the Iron Age survivors who buried their young men knew about the ancient Neolithic graves beneath.

Neolithic recreation

For a less dramatic, but more accessible, impression of life at Hyrax Hill, the **Bau game**, cut into the rock just before you get back to the museum, is a delightfully fresh record. *Bau* is the Bantu name for a game of skill and – depending on the rules used – amazing complexity that has been played all over Africa for a very long time. Two people play, moving pieces (cowries, seeds or pebbles) from one hole to another to win. There are a number of these "boards" around the hill; the one near the museum is a particularly good example.

West of Nakuru: out of the Rift Valley

West of Nakuru, the **A104** is a fast, busy, single-lane road, along which long-distance lorries and buses thunder by at top speed. It's hair-raising if you're driving yourself, and even more wearing on the nerves if you're travelling by matatu. The surface varies but is generally good, the worst stretch running from Timboroa, some 90km west of Nakuru, for about twenty hilly, winding kilometres to Nabkoi. Beyond there it's mostly excellent.

To head into Western Kenya, the **C56** is a scenic and much quieter alternative to the main highway. It climbs gently up to Njoro, Elburgon and Molo – in ascending order of altitude and size – before rejoining the Kisumu-bound fork of the main road (the A104). If you're heading towards **Lake Baringo** in your own vehicle, you can avoid doubling back to Nakuru by heading north to the A104 from Molo and turning west towards Eldoret. After 5km, when you reach Makutano, take the surfaced road to the right, which goes through some wonderful mountain scenery via Eldama Ravine and Tenges, up to the C51 where you can turn right and join the B4 to the lake.

Njoro

The turn-off (left) to Njoro and the Mau escarpment is 5km west of Nakuru, usually marked by the presence of a police roadblock. Along with Laikipia District north of Nanyuki and Nyahururu, the Njoro and Molo areas were those worst affected by the inter-tribal clashes that rocked the Rift Valley through the 1990s.

NJORO is the home town of **Egerton University** (main campus 5km out of town on the main road to Narok), which has several other campuses scattered through the highlands. The jacaranda-fringed main road runs straight past the "centre" of town – a great acreage of mud (or, at best, dust), backed by a humble row of *dukas* and *hotelis*. Beyond the Narok junction, there's another and more soulful Njoro of wooden-colonnaded, tin-roofed, one-storey *dukas*. Here you'll also find a KCB bank and the Njoro Farmer's Petrol Station, a Shell garage. On the other side of town, past timber yards, is flat cereal country, with herds of dairy cattle and racehorses between the lines of gum trees and copses of acacia. Some 8km further along the C56 to Elburgon, past the junction for Menengai road, is the excellent **Kembu Campsite and Cottages** (PO Box 23 Njoro; ☎051/343203 or 0722/361102, ✉kembu@africaonline .co.ke; Ksh300 per person camping, cottages from \$30), signposted on the left. Run by the Nightingale family, it also has farm produce for sale and mountain bikes for rent.

Elburgon, Molo and the Mau Forest

ELBURGON is a good deal bigger than Njoro, and higher up. You're into seriously muddy, conifer country up here, the buildings, characteristically chalet-style, built of dark, weathered planks. It's timber money that gives Elburgon a degree of commercial prosperity and can be the only reason for the massive investment in the *Hotel Eel* (PO Box 36 Elburgon; ☎051/31271 or 31471, ⨍31477; ❺). On offer here are comfortable rooms and cottages, secure parking, a disco at weekends and an adventure playground set in well-landscaped grounds.

West of Elburgon, the road winds and dips through the thick Mau forest for several kilometres, with glimpses of railway viaducts across the valleys, until it emerges, still higher up, among the cereals and pyrethrum fields at **MOLO**. Molo straggles for several kilometres down into a broad valley across the rail tracks and up the other side on to Mau Summit Road, where you find a post office, banks and several petrol stations with carefully tended floral forecourts. The *Highlands Hotel* (PO Box 142 Molo; ☎051/721036; ❺) is tremendous value for its huge, wood-floored rooms with log fires, and its lamb with baked potatoes speciality (Ksh200). It's extremely quiet, the misty gardens are pleasant, and they have riding stables.

South of Molo, up into the **Mau forest**, a graded road runs to **Keringet** (where the huge old estate, once owned by Italians and exhibiting all the most ostentatious trappings of colonial wealth, is gradually crumbling) and on to **Olenguerone**. From here, the road tunnels eerily through a forest of huge gum trees, traipsed by elephant and even rhino, to Bomet (see p.397). There are several daily matatu runs along this route from Molo. The Kenya Wildlife Service has been trying for years to open up the mountain forest, like the Aberdares Park, but there is some stubborn resistance, not least from the forest's indigenous Okiek (Dorobo) hunter-gatherers, as well as from the loggers. There's more background on this area, and details of the Mau route to the Maasai Mara, on p.394.

Kipkelion Monastery

The **Our Lady of Victoria Abbey** is a Cistercian monastery between Londiani and **Kipkelion**, in an area formerly known by the Maasai as "Lumbwa", though Kipkelion ("Kif-*kel*-ion") is the original and much-preferred Kipsigis name. Founded in 1956, this is the only Cistercian monastery in Africa and, deep in this rural hill country, the tall cement-block church is a remarkable sight. The monks make a living from their dairy herd and chickens, and run the only hospital in the area and an important school.

Our Lady of Victoria began as a Trappist monastery, with the silence the reformist order stipulates, but later reverted to the rather less stringent code of the older Cistercian order. The brothers still talk only when necessary, but they are happy to receive visitors. If you like the idea of silence and contemplation in a harmonious rural setting, write to let them know you're coming (PO Box 40 Kipkelion). You should obviously leave an appropriate donation.

The monastery is 11km up a rough track – signposted "Monastery Hospital" – from the small centre of **Baisheli** on the C35 (15km west of Londiani), and the track is rough, narrow and steep in parts, winding through intensively cultivated Kipsigis *shambas*. A few **matatus** service this road, but to get up to the monastery without your own vehicle you need luck in scoring a lift or several hours to walk it. If you're approaching from the west, the easiest route to the monastery is via **Kipkelion station**, signposted off the main B1 highway, 25km east of Kericho. The road to the station, 10km of good tarmac, gives out at the valley-floor station itself; to continue to the monastery you have a rocky, three-kilometre climb then, turning right onto the C35, 6km to the track (left) up to the abbey. There's a "short cut" up to the monastery which is signposted ("Trappist", overwritten with "*Cistercian* Monastery 6km") just after you get onto the C35 – this track is often impassable.

The Northern Rift

North of Nakuru, the Rift Valley drops away gently and, as the road descends, so temperatures rise, the landscape dries and human population becomes sparser. Not far from Nakuru or Nairobi, and not necessarily a difficult journey, this region has a bright, harsh beauty, quite different from the central Rift. Its **lakes**, Bogoria and Baringo, both make alluring targets. This region also offers three possible routes up to Lake Turkana (see p.558), two of them joining with the Kitale–Lodwar road west of the lake, the third curving up to Maralal for the east side. Although public transport is virtually nonexistent and the roads pretty rough, the **Kerio Valley** route (see p.271) deserves a special recommendation if you're visiting the west side of Turkana.

Lake Bogoria National Reserve and around

Daily 6am–7pm; daily fees: Ksh1500, children Ksh100, cars Ksh100, camping Ksh500 per person; access usually permitted on foot or bicycle. Warden: PO Box 64 Marigat ☎ 051/2211987.

One of the least-visited lakes in the Rift Valley, **Lake Bogoria** is a sliver of saline water – unbelievably foul-tasting – entrenched beneath towering hills,

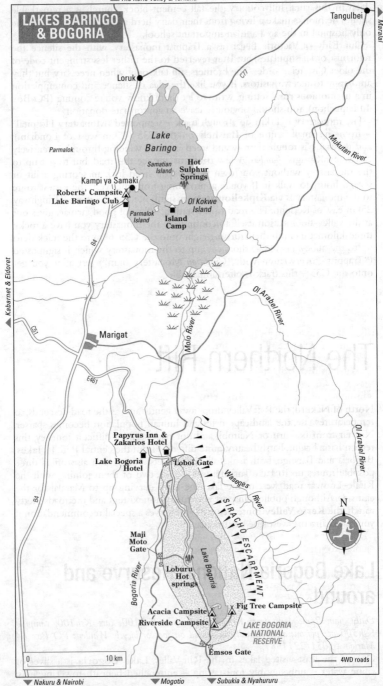

LAKES BARINGO & BOGORIA

The Kerio Valley & Turkana

Tangulbei

Maralal

Loruk

C77

Parmalok

Mukutan River

Lake Baringo

Samatian Island

Hot Sulphur Springs

Kampi ya Samaki

Roberts' Campsite

Lake Baringo Club

Ol Kokwe Island

Parmalok Island

Island Camp

Ol Arabel River

Kabarnet & Eldoret

C51

B4

Molo River

Ol Arabel River

Marigat

E461

Papyrus Inn & Zakarios Hotel

Lake Bogoria Hotel

Loboi Gate

Waseges River

SIRACHO ESCARPMENT

Maji Moto Gate

Loburu Hot springs

Lake Bogoria

Bogoria River

Fig Tree Campsite

Acacia Campsite

Riverside Campsite

LAKE BOGORIA NATIONAL RESERVE

N

Emsos Gate

0   10 km

4WD roads

Nakuru & Nairobi

Mogotio

Subukia & Nyahururu

60km north of Nakuru. With the increasing pollution of Lake Nakuru, Lake Bogoria has become the adopted feeding ground of tens (at times hundreds) of thousands of **lesser flamingos**. The lakeshore itself is one of the few places where **greater kudu** antelope can easily be seen. But the reserve is worth visiting as much for its physical spectacle as for the wildlife. It's largely a barren, baking wilderness of scrub and rocks, from which a series of furious **hot springs** erupts on the western shore, and the bleak walls of the Siracho range rise sheer from the east. Even in the far north of the country, there are few places so unremittingly severe.

Fortunately, the rigour of the landscape is relieved by three superb, shady **campsites** at the southern end of the lake, though they're difficult to get to unless you have 4WD. There are also a few **accommodation** options just outside the reserve's main Loboi Gate in the north. The **warden** here, William Kimosop, is quite an authority on **birds** and, if he's free, will happily take you around or accompany you in your vehicle (it's a good idea to try to arrange this in advance). While you are allowed into the reserve on foot or by bicycle, in theory this is only permitted from Loboi as far as the Loburu hot springs, but exceptions may be made (and perhaps a ranger provided, for a fee) if you're heading for one of the three campsites.

Further background information on the lake can be found in *A Guide to Lake Baringo and Lake Bogoria* by Marguerita North Lewis (Horizon Books, 1998), which is available in several of the Nairobi bookshops listed on p.153, priced Ksh600.

Routes to the lake

The **B4** road north from Nakuru skirts to the west of Lake Bogoria by a margin of 20km and carries little traffic; tortoises in the road present the greatest hazard to motorists. The reserve is signposted (right) 36km from Nakuru at **Mogotio** (fill up on petrol here), from where a good *murram* road, easily motorable in the dry season, cuts across to the lake. Some 23km from this junction, shortly after **Mugurin**, you fork left for the western **Maji Moto Gate** (an incredibly rough 17km further, bringing you to the hot springs and tarmacked lakeshore road), or right/straight ahead for the southern **Emsos Gate** (an equally rough 13km, which brings you to the wooded part of the reserve from where a further rough track leads to the springs, though a ranger will probably be needed for this last section; see p.266). You'll need 4WD beyond Mugurin; there's no public transport.

It's easier and quicker, however, to continue on up the B4 to the signposted junction a few kilometres before **Marigat**. From here, a fast tarmac road, the E461, takes you straight to the **Loboi Gate**, some 20km further on. There are infrequent matatus from Marigat to Loboi Gate (most leave Marigat around 3–5pm), but you could negotiate a taxi fare, or simply wait for a lift at the junction – it's a safe bet something suitable will pass within the hour. Those staying at Lake Baringo often try to arrange lifts with fellow tourists from there; most vehicles visiting Bogoria come from Lake Baringo rather than Nakuru. Returning to Marigat, matatus leave early, at around 6–8am. For more on Marigat, see p.268.

On the E461, 3km before the Loboi Gate, is the *Lake Bogoria Hotel* (PO Box 208 Menengai West; ☏051/221 6441 or 6351, ⓦwww.bogoriasparesort.com; ⑤). A large stuffed lion dominates the lobby, but even this does little to alleviate the blandness of what is really a town hotel in the bush; rooms and cottages are functional and taste-free, and way overpriced for non-Kenyans. The best feature is a sanitized **thermal pool**. The friendly but rundown *Papyrus Inn* (PO Box 186 Marigat; ☎051/221 6980; ❷), right by Loboi Gate, has shared toilets and showers (hot water in buckets), and an area set aside for **camping** (Ksh300 per tent). A better budget choice is *Zakarios Hotel* in Loboi village, about 500m from the gate (PO Box 12 Marigat; ☎053/51045; ❶), which has small but decent s/c rooms, mosquito nets, a small restaurant, and a bar serving *nyama choma*. Alternatively, you could camp at Loboi Gate, just outside the reserve – there's usually water here but you'll need your own stove or firewood and supplies.

The cross-country route to Lake Bogoria

If you have a 4WD vehicle or are into hiking or mountain biking, you might like to approach the Emsos Gate from the southeast, initially using the B5 tarmac route between Nakuru and Nyahururu. Along the way there are several turnings northwest towards the lake. The tarmac portions of this trip can be made by country bus or matatu (there are several daily runs between Nyahururu and Nakuru via Subukia), but without your own transport, you should be prepared to **hike** the rest of the way down to Bogoria if necessary – a good two days. Aside from the pleasure of tackling roads used by very few tourists, this route gives you a special feel for the Rift Valley's striking topography as it drops from one monumental block of land to another, with dramatic changes of climate and scenery. When you reach the plain at the bottom, you've an indelible impression of the way the earth has split apart and sunk to form the Rift over the last twenty million years.

From Nakuru, it's a fourteen-kilometre trip past Menengai crater to **Mairu Kumi**, where the road divides. The left fork (unsignposted) leads, after 14km of rough *murram*, to the **police post** at Solai (see opposite), while the right fork continues on tarmac to Subukia and Nyahururu. Beyond the fork, you enter a steep, hilly landscape of Kikuyu *shambas*, increasingly interspersed with plots of tea bushes and pyrethrum.

From Nyahururu, the target is also the Solai police post. The early part of the route is particularly stimulating as it falls in a series of breathtaking steps over the fault lines until it reaches a high scarp above Subukia, where it hairpins its way steeply down to the valley. Descending from the cool highlands around Nyahururu, you start to feel the heat building up. Fields of sugar cane and bananas seem to grow before your eyes in the hothouse atmosphere and the earth takes on a rich, redolent smell.

The police post at **Solai** is served rather infrequently by direct matatu from Nakuru, but a better bet for getting there from Nakuru (or indeed from Nyahururu or Subukia) is to take a matatu to Mairu Kumi and another one from there.

The Subukia Valley and Lake Solai

The **Subukia Valley** was the Maasai's "Beautiful Place" (Ol Momoi Sidai) and its lush pastures their insurance against the failure of the grass up on the Laikipia plateau. But they were evicted in 1911 to the "Maasai Reserve" and the way was clear for the **settler families**. It's easy to see why they chose this high valley because, despite its isolation, it has a soft, arcadian beauty far removed from the windy plateaus above or the austere furnace of the Rift Valley floor below.

The village of **SUBUKIA** has a scattering of *hotelis* and *dukas*, and a Fuelex filling station. Simple lodgings are available at the friendly *Malindi Hotel* at the southern end of the village (PO Box 15901 Nakuru; ☎0734/980423; ❶), as well as food and, at *Uncle's Pub* next door, beer and *nyama choma*. Buses and matatus stop near the T-junction where the Subukia Valley road meets the B5, and there's regular transport to Nakuru and Nyahururu. The equator is just

4km south of Subukia, confusingly marked by signs in two different places (the northernmost is the genuine one, the other having been put up to attract punters to a curio shop).

If you have transport of your own and two or three hours to spare, or a couple of days to walk it, you can take a major **diversion** up the Subukia Valley, then turn west and cut back south again, past small Lake Solai. From the grubby junction at Subukia village where the main road passes, head north about 700m to an old T-junction, with roads to Nakuru (left) and Lower Subukia (right); take the latter. The track, consisting of rough dirt and rocks, is easy to follow, but will clock up some 45km. Sources of food along the way are negligible, so you must be self-sufficient, and, although the road is being "improved" (made broader and more bone-shaking), transport is sparse, with only four matatus daily between Subukia and Bogoini. Matatus between Bogoini and Mairu Kumi via Solai are slightly more frequent, but you may still have to wait a few hours for one. Travel between Subukia and Bogoini is also possible by *boda-boda*.

Lake Solai is a curiously isolated soda lake with a reedy shoreline grazed by cattle and a scattering of sisal plots. For many years it was seasonal lake, but has been a permanent feature since the early 1980s. South of Lake Solai, the road climbs through scattered euphorbia and acacias to the junction (hard right) at **Solai police post**. Lines of jacaranda streak the scenery at intervals all over this district, bordering old driveways – evidence of the erstwhile community of white settlers.

Down to the Emsos Gate and Bogoria

The most **direct route** from Subukia village to Bogoria begins by climbing 4km out of the valley on the tarmac to Nakuru. An unsignposted right turn (or left if you've just come from Nakuru) goes over the hill past the curious **St Peter's** – a quaint Anglican church that looks as if it just flew in from England – and then 15km down to the Solai police post. From here, the 50km to Bogoria is rough in many places, though normally negotiable in a 4WD vehicle (allow 3hr). Hitching varies from slow to impossible from this point on, and matatus are sparse, though they do run. If you're on foot or bicycle and still want to do it, check your emergency water and food supplies, tighten your bootlaces – or check your brakes – and set off west.

The road descends steeply to the Solai Valley with its disused railway line, which you cross at a place called **Milton's Siding**. When you reach the tracks, follow the road, parallel to the right and which runs for a kilometre, and then turn sharp left to cross them. The road descends in a series of steps to a broad, flat valley with a sharp, right-hand bend up the hill on the far side, which it crosses to reach **Kisanana** – life-saving *chai* and a place to stop for the night if necessary, though there's no formal accommodation.

From Kisanana, you turn left at the old signpost and follow decent *murram* tracks for some 5km to a fork around some buildings. Here you head left and are soon pitching up a diabolical slope – rarely used by motor vehicles and by all appearances dynamited out of solid bedrock – which winds up and over a scrub-covered **hog's back ridge** for some 7km, eventually twisting north and dropping to better red *murram*, interspersed, strata-wise, with white, rocky stretches. You come to a crossroads (turn left), then after a few hundred metres a T-junction at a place of a few huts named **Mugurin** (turn right), where you may find a solitary *hoteli* open. From here, you're within the compass of the lake, some 25km away. The road descends steadily now as you travel north – there's only the odd signpost but no danger of taking a wrong turn: if in doubt, head right.

The reserve

Hidden in its deep bowl, **Lake Bogoria** – when approached from Mugurin – is only visible when you're almost on top of it. The final stretch of the track leading down to the Emsos Gate is steep and rocky as well as being savagely beautiful, the landscape transformed into a strident dazzle of red and blue and splashes of green. The lake itself, a glistening pool of soapy blue and white, has a mirage of pink flamingos tinting its shores.

While the Bogoria Reserve **paved road** between the Loboi Gate and the Loburu hot springs is in good condition, the **east shore road** has been quite impassable for years (a huge rock fall coupled with higher water levels), so there is no circuit round the lake. If you're driving up from the Emsos Gate, there's a river bed to negotiate before you reach the tarmac, for which 4WD is essential, and with the high lake level is not advisable unless you're with a ranger who knows the road.

At the southern end of the lake are the three public campsites, *Acacia*, *Riverside* and *Fig Tree*, which are accessible only by 4WD or, with permission, on foot. The furthest, **Fig Tree Campsite** (a 40min walk from Emsos Gate), is an absolute delight, unless your visit coincides with a fresh covering of vegetation after the rains, when squads of determined tsetse flies can ruin what is otherwise an unusually verdant and picturesque scene. Enquire with the rangers about heading down further to the thickly wooded shore at the south end (they might provide an escort, for a fee), and also check with them about **food**; a few basics are usually available just outside Emsos Gate to eke out your rations. **Water** is not a problem – a permanent, miniature brook, clear and sweet, runs right through the campsite and provides a natural Jacuzzi. Less delightfully, the magnificent glade of giant fig trees that bathe the site in shade is a favourite haunt of baboons who gorge themselves day and night. In the fruiting season (Dec–Feb), be wary of camping directly beneath any concentrations of figs, for reasons which need no elaboration. Buffalo also graze near here and are not to be trifled with.

The *Fig Tree Campsite* is something of a dead end and, if you're down here and don't have your own vehicle, you may be in for a long wait before someone turns up to give you a lift out. Your only option is to walk the 15km around to the hot springs on the western shore, passing *Riverside* and *Acacia Tree* campsites. The *Riverside* is the most basic of the three campsites, without even a source of water.

Wildlife, with the exception of the flamingos at the springs, makes itself scarce, most animals preferring the remote and inaccessible eastern shore: buffalo, hyenas, klipspringer, impala, dik-dik, zebra, warthog and Grant's gazelle. The mild and nervous **greater kudu** formerly lived predominantly in the northeastern part of the reserve, but they have spread and multiplied in recent years and are now frequently seen in the more exposed western parts of the reserve. Once widespread, the kudu is a splendidly unmistakable, striped antelope; the bulls have long, spiral horns, shaggy dewlaps and enormous, spoon-like ears. The great rinderpest epidemics of the nineteenth century, which took such a toll on cattle, wiped out much of the kudu population too, leaving pockets only in the least favourable cattle country. Today, Bogoria is the most southerly part of the greater kudu's range in Kenya. The Bogoria **fish eagles**, incidentally, have made a gruesome adjustment to their fierce, fishless environment: they prey on flamingos. Other birds to look out for include avocets, transitory pelicans and migratory steppe eagles.

The Loburu hot springs

However you enter the reserve, you're bound to want to see the **hot springs**, a series of boiling water spouts on the shore. Although they hardly touch Yellowstone or Rotorua standards, "hot springs" is a tame appellation for this very impressive, terrifying and photogenic phenomenon. At the time of writing the lake level was high, and so only one of the springs broke the surface – the others signal led their presence by the agitated green water above them, some steam and a strong smell. With normal water levels, they burst up from huge natural cauldrons of super-heated water not far below the surface and drain into steaming rivulets that cut through the crusty ground, continuously collapsing and reforming their courses down to the lake. Even at midday, when the sun glares like a furnace, clouds of steam drift across this infernal scene.

The **flamingos**, for some curious reason – possibly chemical – tend to flock in their greatest numbers to the shallows opposite the hot streams' debouch-ment (they appear immune to the heat). Tufts of grass tempt you to sit down and reward you with vicious spines while, closer to the lakeshore, the macabre bleached skeletons of flamingos lie strewn in the sand and, in the background, the dull thundering of the springs fills the air. It's like some water garden in Hell.

There's a drinks kiosk at the springs, but no food. Picnickers sometimes think it's fun to boil eggs and heat tins of food in the pools, but the consequences of a fall can be messy and even fatal: over the years a number of people have slipped and died as a result. An *askari* has now been posted to watch out for visitors, but if you scald yourself, help might still be a long time coming.

Lake Baringo

Roadblock operates 7am–7pm; adults Ksh200, children Ksh50, vehicles Ksh100. Office: PO Box 79 Marigat ☎ 053/51453.

At one time a barely accessible retreat favoured by just a few weekenders, **Lake Baringo** (see map, p.262) now has a highway from Nakuru, and another from Eldoret. The lake remains a peaceful oasis in the dry-thorn country, rich in **birdlife** and with a captivating character entirely its own. The waters are heavily silted with the red topsoil of the region, and they run through a whole range of colours every day from yellow to coral to purple, according to the sun's position and the state of the sky. On the lakeshore are villages inhabited by the **Il Chamus** (Njemps) people, who live by an unusual mixture of fishing and livestock herding, breaking the taboo on the eating of fish, which is the norm among pastoralists. Speaking a dialect of Maa – the Maasai language – these fishermen paddle out in half-submerged dinghies made from saplings of the fibrous *ambatch* tree that grows in profusion at the southern end of the lake.

Practicalities

Most matatus from Nakuru come up only as far as Marigat, though around 1pm daily there's a vehicle from Nakuru all the way to the lakeside **KAMPI YA SAMAKI** village, via Marigat. From Marigat you can hitch or get a local matatu to the lake. Kampi ya Samaki is 2km from the main road, beyond the council-run roadblock where you pay your **admission fee** (make sure you get a receipt). From Eldoret, you can catch a bus at 10am for Kabarnet, and go by matatu from there to Marigat. Kabarnet is also accessible by matatu from Eldoret, changing vehicles at Iten.

If you're moving on **via Marigat**, get up early for the matatu into town, from where there are plenty of onward vehicles to Nakuru or Kabarnet. A matatu direct to Nakuru leaves Kampa ya Samaki around 6am.

Travelling **north of Baringo** is a hit-or-miss affair without your own wheels, so try to arrange something with mobile tourists. Otherwise, you'll have to hitch: there's no public transport either to Maralal or to Tot and Lodwar from here. If you're driving, there's the highly recommended and not too rough road from north of Lake Baringo towards Maralal (one day) or Samburu National Reserve (best done over two days). This route swings north from the lakeshore, leaving tarmac and tourism behind, and takes you into the rugged country of the Lerochi plateau, dotted with Tugen and Pokot settlements. With the right conditions, there are stunning views back over Baringo. You join the Rumuruti–Maralal *murram* road as far as Kisima, where you choose between a short journey to Maralal or some inspiring but wheel-shattering driving along the C78/79 to Samburu (see p.572). There's **fuel** at Marigat and at *Lake Baringo Club*, but none after that until Maralal or Archer's Post.

MARIGAT itself ought to be the hub of the Baringo–Bogoria tourist circuit, but it's a bland, dust-blown little place. Among the tin shacks stands an impressive bright green and white **mosque** – apparently funded by some wealthy Saudi Arabian – with two tiers of large windows and a capacity that obviously exceeds the area's Muslim population. There are a couple of B&Ls on the main road near the junction with the B4, of which *Dadina Lodge* (PO Box 99; ☏0735/359351; ①) is reasonably well-kept, with s/c singles or non-s/c doubles. A little better is *Marigat Inn* (PO Box 22; ☏0735/354743; ②), 1500m east of the junction in the village itself, just beyond the end of the tarmac. The s/c rooms are small but pleasant, set in a small jungly garden, but the location is less handy for transport connections and food than the junction.

Lake accommodation

Accommodation by Lake Baringo is sharply divided between budget and deluxe, with not much in between, though if you do need something in the mid-range, the cottages at *Roberts Camp* might well fit the bill. Aside from the campsite at *Roberts Camp*, the only budget options are some basic B&Ls in Kampi ya Samaki. At the luxury end, on the other hand, you're spoilt for choice. Even if none of these establishments is within your budget, it's still worth splashing out for cold drinks and a swim on a casual visit.

Kampi ya Samaki doesn't offer a lot to do other than check out the lakeside scenery and wildlife, but it does have a small **reptile park** (daily 8am–6pm; Ksh200), east of the village by the *Island Camp* boat stage, where you can see mambas, adders, and other slithery, scaly denizens of the region at close range.

Bahari Hotel Lodge PO Box 3 Kampi ya Samaki ☏053/51408. By far the best of the village B&Ls, warm and welcoming, with good food and decent, non-s/c rooms (upstairs ones are best). ①

Hippo Lodge Kampi ya Samaki ☏0724/472785. Rundown B&L with slummy non-s/c single rooms at rock-bottom prices and bucket showers (warm water on request). Food can be ordered. A fallback. ①

🏃 **Island Camp** On the southern tip of Ol Kokwe Island in the middle of the lake; PO Box 1141 Nakuru ☏051/850858 or 0735/939878, ✉islandcamp@africaonline.co.ke; reservations also through Let's Go Travel, p.150. Not as luxurious as some of Kenya's "tented camps", but who cares – the location is idyllic, dense with birdlife, as well as numerous varieties of lizard. The 23 tents each have expansive views over the lake, and there's a good-sized pool and a poolside cocktail bar. As well as boat trips, water-skiing and guided walks on the island are on offer. The stepped nature of the site makes disabled access impossible. The price includes boat transfer from their jetty just east of Kampi ya Samaki. FB $315; **❾**

Lake Baringo Club PO Box 23 Kampi ya Samaki ⊕053/51401–2, ⓔblockbaringo@africaonline.co.ke; reservations also through Kenya Hotels ⊕020/445 0635–9. A sumptuous and unpretentious hotel, this is a regular stop on ornithological tours of Kenya, and there are regular wildlife films and nightly audio-visuals to introduce guests to the local bird species. Children are made very welcome and will be round-eyed at the experience of encountering lake hippos at close range, coming to graze the well-watered lawns after dark (guards keep a careful watch). The meals are generally excellent (lunch Ksh950, supper Ksh1460 excluding drinks). For casual visitors, it's Ksh200 to use the small but irresistible swimming pool, and kids have badminton and table tennis to keep them amused. FB $180; **❾**

Roberts Camp PO Box 2 Kampi ya Samaki ⊕051/851879 or 0721/307033, ⓔrobertscamp @africaonline.co.ke. Lovely campsite in a large, acacia-shaded garden on the lakeside south of the village, with lots of space, good facilities and great bird-watching. Most visitors camp (Ksh350 per person), but there are also three good non-s/c *bandas* with electricity and bedding (Ksh1000 per person), and three very nice cottages with two double bedrooms and a sitting room (Ksh5000 for up to four people, Ksh500 each for up to two additional people). They have a very good, reasonably priced restaurant-bar, the *Thirsty Goat*. If you want a *banda* or a cottage, it's worth booking ahead. **❹**

Samatian Island ⊕0722/207772, ⓦsamatianislandlodge.com; reservations through Bush and Beyond ⊕020/600457. Upmarket but rustic, a new place with staffed cottages, the choice of full-board or self-catering (they provide the cook, you provide the food, but you must rent the whole place if self-catering), and a boat which can be chartered (Ksh2000/hr). $400 per night for up to ten people if self-catering, FB $740 per cottage per night; **❾**

Soi Safari Lodge PO Box 45 Kampi ya Samaki ⊕053/51242, ⓦwww.soisafarilodge.com; reservations via Jubilee Place, fourth floor; PO Box 3170 Nairobi ⊕020/318774. The newest place in town, conveniently located on the lakeshore but also right in the village, it's airy and bright with a/c rooms, a big pool (Ksh200 for non-guests) and cool furnishings. **❼** or FB **❾**

Weavers Lodge PO Box 10 Kampi ya Samaki ⊕0723/923143. Quite large s/c rooms, but not as homely as the *Bahari*, and well overpriced for what you get. **❸**

The lake

Lake Baringo is freshwater (Naivasha is the only other Rift Valley lake that's not saline), so its fish support **birds** less often seen – fish eagles, pelicans, cormorants and herons, for example – as well as quite a sizeable **crocodile** population. **Hippos** are common, too. Though you rarely see much more than ears and snout by day, they come ashore after dark, and on a moonlit night their presence can be unnervingly obvious; even in pitch darkness, they're too noisy to be ignored.

Activities tend to centre around *Lake Baringo Club* or *Island Camp*, and include boat trips around the shores (Ksh5000 per hour for up to seven people), water-skiing (at *Island Camp*; Ksh850 for 15min), and visits to a nearby Il Chamus *enkang* (from *Lake Baringo Club*; Ksh400). The headman here is paid a retainer and in return allows visitors to look around his compound and freely photograph his wives and children. The visit isn't a particularly comfortable one – you may feel obliged to buy some of the decorated gourds inscribed with planes and ostriches (among other motifs) that the women lay out – but your presence isn't resented.

Motor boats to **Ol Kokwe Island** (Ksh600) leave on request from *Island Camp*'s jetty on the north side of Kampi ya Samaki. Community Boats and Excursions (⊕0720/523874) opposite *Roberts' Camp* charges the same, though you may find it harder to organize the return trip. A Ksh200 landing fee is payable if you are neither staying nor eating at *Island Camp*. *Roberts Camp* also runs boat trips for Ksh2400 an hour for up to seven people. Community Boats and Excursions have boats at pretty much the same prices, but if you charter

Bird-watching at Lake Baringo

Baringo's 448 species of **birds** are one of its biggest draws, and even if you don't know a superb starling from an ordinary one, the enthusiasm of others tends to be infectious, especially at *Lake Baringo Club*. The bird population rises and falls with the seasons (the dry season is the leanest time for bird-watching), but the lakeshore resounds with birdsong (and frogs) at most times of year. It's surprisingly easy to get within close range of the birds – some species, such as the starlings and the white-bellied go-away bird, are positively brazen – so you'll find rapt amateur photographers lurking behind practically every bush. There's some interesting bush just beyond the *Club* to the south (accessible by walking back along the road), where you should see some unusual species such as the white phase of the paradise flycatcher, grey-headed bush shrike, violet wood hoopoe and various kingfishers. Hippos commonly graze here, too, even in daylight hours.

Lake Baringo Club offers short, informal lecture **tours** (7am or 5pm; Ksh1100) with its resident ornithologist. Bird-watching by boat along the lake's reedy shore is best done in the morning, in combination with a visit to **Goliath Heronry** (known locally as Gibraltar), a rocky islet near Ol Kokwe Island where the birds breed. Afternoons can profitably be taken up on a trip out near the main road under some striking red cliffs, an utterly different habitat where, apart from hyraxes and baboons, you can see several species of hornbill, sometimes the massive nest of a hammerkop (wonderful-looking birds in flight, resembling miniature pterodactyls with their strange crests) and, with luck, the rare Verraux's eagle. Marabou storks are fed from the kitchens. You'll have a few dozen species pointed out to you in an hour. The world record "bird-watch" for 24 hours is 342 species – held by former Baringo ornithologist Terry Stevenson.

one, make sure that you are insured, that lifejackets are provided, and that no more than seven passengers are carried – should those conditions not be met, it's best not to take the excursion. Most of the village boatmen are practised at luring fish eagles by tossing them fresh fish; take your camera for spectacular close-ups as the birds swoop down for the bait. On dry land meanwhile, *Roberts Camp* offers walking safaris at Ksh250 per person.

There are, of course, cheaper ways of arranging excursions in the vicinity of the lake. A retinue of pushy young touts will try to get you onto a boat at prices that need to be haggled down, but it's worth avoiding these – they aren't insured, don't provide lifejackets and may well overload the boat. In 2004, a number of people drowned when their boat capsized on the lake.

Although some reports claim Baringo **crocodiles** are too small to be a threat to swimmers, what constitutes a dangerous size in a Nile crocodile is debatable, and reliable sources suggest that some of the Baringo crocs are potentially dangerous (an alleged man-eater was shot in 1981). Swimming in the lake is inadvisable.

Kabarnet and the Kerio Valley

The journey between Lake Baringo and Kabarnet mirrors the trip to Lake Bogoria down the eastern side of the Rift from the B5 Nakuru–Nyahururu road, covered on p.264. Frequent matatus from Marigat climb the first stage to **Kabarnet**, the road soaring and plunging through at times almost alpine scenery. From Kabarnet, you should be able to matatu-hop all the way to **Eldoret** across the hot and fascinating **Kerio Valley** (you should only need to change vehicles once, at Iten). Leave early, as services tend to fill up towards afternoon, and you'd be lucky indeed to cadge a lift at night.

KABARNET has a superb setting on the **Kamasia massif** – the slab of rift country, also known as the Tugen Hills, that remained upstanding on the brink of the Kerio Valley when the rest of the rift sank – and the road up the escarpment offers breathtaking views over the Rift Valley floor to Lake Baringo. But the town itself could hardly be more dull. From a small nucleus of *dukas* on the hillside, it has been considerably expanded in every direction in accordance with its designated function as capital of Baringo District. This was undoubtedly related to Kabarnet's status as President Moi's home town (he was born in Sacho, 30km away), but the result is a motley scattering of offices and civil servants' housing interspersed with wasteland. Apart from its **post office**, KCB and Standard Chartered **banks** with ATMs, a **supermarket** and a covered **market**, Kabarnet's only point of interest is a small **museum** (daily 9.30am–6pm; Ksh100) featuring exhibits on human evolution, headdresses from around the country, and artefacts and homesteads of the Tugen, Pokot and Il Chamus peoples who inhabit the region, plus a small snake farm.

Standing above the town, the *Kabarnet Hotel* (PO Box 109; ☎0328/22150; B&B ❹) is quiet and a bit tatty in places, but is worth a visit for its mountain views (better on the Kerio Valley side) and above-average food. There's also a swimming pool. Just across the road, *Lelian B Hotel* (PO Box 125; ☎053/21458; ❶) offers simple s/c rooms and the best value in town. *New Hotel Sinkoro*, by the matatu stage (PO Box 256; ☎0733/785745, ✉sinkoro2004@yahoo.com; ❷), has safe parking, a bar and a passable restaurant, but it's not cheap for what you get.

Moving on from Kabarnet, you'll find buses to Nakuru, and to Eldoret, but none after 9am. Matatus serve Nakuru and Eldoret, and also Iten, Marigat, Tenges and occasionally even Loruk.

Kipsaraman

From Kabarnet a paved road runs 38km north to **KIPSARAMAN** in the Tugen Hills, which you can reach by matatu, changing vehicles halfway at Kabartonjo. Past the village of Kipsaraman itself, and just before the end of the tarmac, a rough and rather steep track to the right leads down 2.5km to a small **museum** (daily 9am–6pm; Ksh200), which, if you have an interest in human evolution, is worth going out of your way to see. Its exhibits, mostly fossils of extinct mammals dating back some four to six million years, include the remains of *Chemositia tugenensis*, a creature related to modern-day horses and hippos, though it looks more like an ape. The survival of this beast into modern times has been suggested as a possible explanation for the legend of the Nandi bear (see p.318). Pride of place, however, goes to the remains of *Orrorin tugenensis*, the earliest known bipedal hominid, and possibly the first creature on our side of the evolutionary divide between humans and chimpanzees. *Orrorin*'s few surviving bones, unearthed in 2000, may not look like much, but from them scientists have been able to determine that our ancestor walked on two legs, was similar in size to a modern chimp, and ate mostly grains and nuts, with some meat. And from such humble beginnings, right here in the Rift Valley, emerged the human race.

Across the Kerio Valley to Iten

The quickest and easiest route across the valley is the paved **C51**. The excitement of this route builds only after you leave Kabarnet and plunge into the

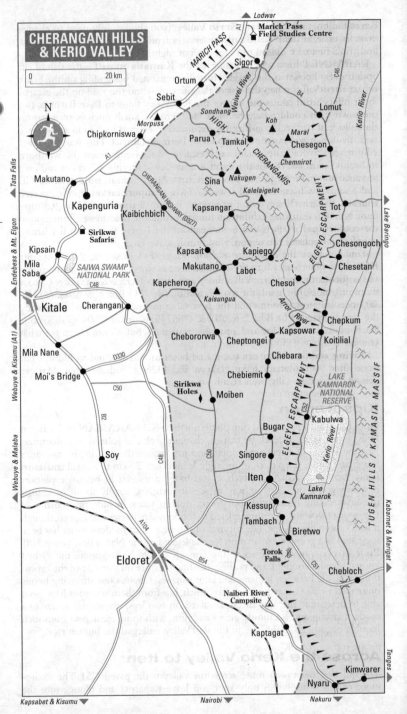

CHERANGANI HILLS & KERIO VALLEY

0   20 km

N

Tata Falls
Endebess & Mt. Elgon
Webuye & Kisumu (A1)
Webuye & Malaba

Marich Pass Field Studies Centre

Lodwar

A1

MARICH PASS

Sigor

Ortum

Sebit

Sondhang

Weiwei River

HIGH

Chipkorniswa

Morpuss

Parua   Tamkal

CHERANGANIS

Koh

Maral

Lomut

B4

C46

Kerio River

Chesegon

Chemnirot

Makutano

Kapenguria

Kaibichbich

CHERANGANI HIGHWAY (D327)

Sina   *Nakugen*

Kalelaigelat

Tot

ELGEYO ESCARPMENT

Kapsangar

Kipsain

Mila Saba

Sirikwa Safaris

SAIWA SWAMP NATIONAL PARK

Kapsait   Kapiego

Makutano   Labot

Chesoi

Chesongoch

Chesetan

Lake Baringo

Kitale   Cherangani

C48

Kapcherop

Kaisungua

Mila Nane

Moi's Bridge

Z3

D330

C50

Chebororwa   Cheptongei

Chebara

Chebiemit

Arror River

Kapsowar

Chepkum

Koitilial

LAKE KAMNAROK NATIONAL RESERVE

Sirikwa Holes

Moiben

Kabulwa

Kerio River

TUGEN HILLS / KAMASIA MASSIF

Bugar

Singore

C50

C48

Soy

Iten

Kessup

Lake Kamnarok

Kabarnet & Marigat

Tambach   Biretwo

Eldoret

A104

B54

Torok Falls

C52

C51

Chebloch

A1

Naiberi River Campsite

Kaptagat

Kimwarer

Nyaru

Kapsabet & Kisumu   *Nairobi*   *Nakuru*   *Tenges*

Kerio Valley, a drop of 1000m in not much more than the same distance. You'll find pretty constant matatu traffic across the valley (and two morning buses from Kabarnet to Eldoret).

There are magnificent views as the road rolls through **Chebloch**, with its old bridge over the Kerio River. The road then turns sharply up the **Tambach escarpment** on the western side of the Kerio Valley. A turn right just before the hamlet of Biretwo is the start of the lonely trans-valley route north to Tot (see p.274). Also before Biretwo, look out for the **Torok Falls**, looming high above to your left at the top of the Tambach escarpment, which are worth a visit if you like waterfalls; count on a good half-day if you're hiking up.

After a few more hairpins and a spectacular viewpoint (with obligatory curio and drinks stall), the road finally levels out at **ITEN**, a tiny grass-verged market town on the rim of the escarpment. Iten is the main centre this side of the Kerio Valley, with petrol, a KCB bank and a small market (handy for leather goods). Iten is also home to the remarkable **St Patrick's High School**, which must be the world's top school for runners, having produced middle-distance stars such as Peter Rono, Wilson Kipketer and Ibrahim Hussein, while its associated athletics camps have produced female runners such as Lydia Cheromei and Susan Chepkemei. The phenomenon is one that sports scientists have yet to explain fully, but has a lot to do with climate, altitude and physiological factors, and seems particularly to involve the Nandi. The school is just after the main shops of Iten, on the road north to Kapsowar.

It's possible to stay in town at the *Jumbo Hotel and Restaurant* (PO Box 425; ☏053/42265; ❷), which has a good bar and restaurant, but a better option lies 6km out on the Kabarnet road, just south of **Kessup**. Here you'll find the *Lelin Overland Campsite* (PO Box 589 Iten; no phone), a friendly place with magnificent views and the choice of camping (Ksh600 per person) or *bandas* (❸) with wood-fired hot showers. It has its own nature trail down to a waterfall with cave behind, or a longer (5hr) walk to a more spectacular waterfall. Food is available, though the menu isn't large.

To Iten via Tenges and Kimwarer

An **alternative** to the C51 is the turn-off from the C51 east of Kabarnet, taking you south to **Tenges** on a surfaced road that twists spectacularly along the spine of the Tugen Hills, with lovely views across the valley. You'll find some public transport to Tenges from Kabarnet, but very little when you turn right (west) for Kimwarer down in the valley over very bad *murram*. Kimwarer is more easily reached via a better road that meets the C51 just west of Chebloch at the bottom of the valley. Whichever way you're heading in this region, if you have a **tent**, use it. There are loads of potential camping spots in spectacular countryside, and the locals are a pretty trustworthy lot. As ever, ask permission from the village headman if you plan to stay near a settlement or on cultivated land.

KIMWARER, known locally as Fluorspar, is a company town for the **fluorspar mine** at the head of the Kerio River (fluorspar – calcium fluoride – is used in the manufacture of steel, aluminium and cement). With nothing but bush, Kalenjin herders and the occasional party of honey-hunters round about, Kimwarer's tidy managerial villas and staff quarters come as a surprise, and "Fluorspar Primary School" looks positively progressive with its brilliant paint job and playground trees all neatly labelled with their Latin names. The only public transport to Kimwarer is a once-daily matatu that comes from Eldoret every evening and returns in the morning, plus a very occasional vehicle from Iten or Kabarnet. Most people take a matatu from Eldoret to Nyaru, at the top of the road down the escarpment, and hitch a paying ride on one of the lorries travelling to or from the mine. The nearest **accommodation** is 8km up the road to Chebloch, at the *Sego Club* (℡053/21399 or 0722/007470; or book through the *Wagon Hotel* in Eldoret, p.319; B&B ❹), which has s/c cottages, food and views of the escarpment.

North up the Kerio Valley

There's a dearth of public transport through the **Kerio Valley** off the main Kabarnet–Iten C51 road. The route north from Chebloch along the east side of Lake Kamnarok National Reserve is passable only by 4WD (forget it when it rains). The road from **Biretwo to Chesongoch** on the west side of the reserve has a good *murram* surface passable in an ordinary car; north of Chesongoch, it's very rough as far as Tot, but improves thereafter.

It's possible to **hitch** this road north to Tot, Lomut and Marich, especially in mango season (Nov–Jan), when lorries come down as far as Tot and Chesongoch for fruit. Otherwise, transport is sparse until you reach Lomut, where there are regular matatus to Sigor, Marich and Makutano (near Kapenguria), especially on Lomut's market day (Saturday). Otherwise, between Biretwo and Tot, you may well end up "footing" or waiting by the side of the road; no matter (as long as you have several days), for this road, following one of Kenya's most beautiful valleys, is worth a few blisters. Note, however, that the villages along the way have no facilities for travellers, and only limited supplies. For most of the year the valley, wooded and not much cultivated in the south, resonates with dry heat and the rattle of cicadas and crickets. Climatic conditions are best in the few months of vivid greenery after the April to June long rains – and fiercest in February and March, just before they break. The section from Tot to the Marich Pass is covered below.

The Elgeyo Escarpment and Cherangani Hills

You can head **north from Iten** along a good *murram* road to Kapsowar, passing the villages of Singore and Bugar; frequent matatus do the run from Eldoret. Some 4km after Bugar, the road branches right to continue north via Chebiemit, Chebara and Cheptongei, where bearing right will bring you to Kapsowar. The road from Kapsowar to **Chesengoch** and thence to **Tot** along the **Elgeyo Escarpment** is in pretty bad shape, despite having been upgraded. Most easily approached on the returning leg of a trip to Turkana (make sure you've enough petrol as there's no fuel along the way), the road is diabolical, too rocky for any kind of ordinary car and too steep for any but the most steel-nerved of drivers. It's a thrilling, gut-wrenching trip in a Land Rover – someone else's preferably – but think twice before driving *up* this road yourself. It is very steep and there's no fuel.

North of Tot, the B4 road continues through the villages of Chesegon, Lomut and Sigor to meet the A1 at the Marich Pass (see p.329). Between Tot and Sigor, there are very occasional matatus – one or two a day if you're lucky, but transport opportunities improve if you can coincide with weekly markets at Chesegon (Wednesdays), Lomut (Saturdays) and Sigor (Thursdays). The market at Lomut is particularly worth a visit. Matatus operate between Lomut and Makutano near Kapenguria on the A1 (see p.329). Accommodation is available in Lomut at **PoViLo** (Pokot Village Lomut), a compound in the style of a Pokot homestead, associated with local self-sufficiency projects such as bee-keeping (no phone; bookings through Let's Go Travel, or c/o ⓔrolf@skyfile .com, making sure you put "rgloor" in the subject line; B&B ⓖ).

The Marakwet canals and Chesoi

From Kapsowar, **CHESOI** is only 8km away as the crow flies, but 20km by road, a hike around the highland spurs which is much more easily accomplished in the other direction, a fine and easy, mostly downhill walk. The land here buckles like a patchwork quilt, with the Cherangani Hills stretching west. The area up near Chesoi is the best place to see the area's irrigation system – undeniably impressive in scope, if not especially in appearance. From Chesoi, you can walk or hitch (but don't count on seeing a vehicle, much less on its having space) the 25 breathtaking kilometres down to **Tot**, turning left halfway at **Chesengoch**.

The rocky, almost perpendicular slopes around Chesoi are dotted with **Marakwet** homesteads, the huts unusual in being built of stone (there's a limitless supply up here), which gives them an ancient-looking permanence rarely seen in Kenyan rural architecture. A thousand metres below, spreading like a grey-green carpet into the haze, are the scrubby, bush-covered plains of Pokot and south Turkana. Dozens of tiny wisps of smoke from charcoal burners combine to smudge out the distant peaks of Mount Kenya to the southeast. Places where the trees grow thicker mark the passage of seasonal streams which flood and dry up with the rains; Pokot gold-panners still find enough gold in them to trade with anyone passing through.

To add to this distinctive sense of place, the escarpment itself is the location of an ancient **irrigation system**, stretching north–south for over 40km to divert water from the Cherangani Hills' gushing streams into a branching layout of furrows and aqueducts. Complex, unwritten laws ensure that each Marakwet sub-clan is fairly provided for by the system, which is without parallel anywhere else in the country; the results, as you'll see along the base of the scarp, are spectacular. Indeed, for a considerable distance up the Kerio Valley, there's a band of intensive, luxuriant gardening: tiny *shambas* slotted back-to-back between the spurs and down towards the main river. Magnificent, richly flavoured bananas are on sale everywhere. Many of the irrigation channels now pass under the road, but a few still flow over it and a great deal of ongoing repair work is obviously needed to keep the streams flowing in the right direction.

The Marakwet irrigation system

The Marakwet – part of the broadly related Kalenjin group of peoples – may have arrived on these slopes as far back as a thousand years ago. They say the **irrigation** channels were there long before their own forefathers arrived, and it is possible the original irrigators were a mysterious group called the **Sirikwa**. These people have disappeared, or more likely been absorbed, and the only reminders of them are their name and a lot of curious **holes**, earthworks and cairns (see p.276) noticed by archeologists around the Kerio Valley and in other parts of western Kenya.

Marakwet elders still remember stories of a small people called the **Terngeng**, who may have lived in pits in the ground something like those at Hyrax Hill and Moiben. Other stories refer to tall, long-haired, bearded men who roamed the Rift Valley. Either or both of these groups might have been responsible for the building of the irrigation system, but neither sounds very agricultural; perhaps the Marakwet's claim to have inherited the system but not built it is just a way of saying how old it really is.

"Chesoi canal" is a major water supply a couple of kilometres behind Chesoi centre, a metre-wide channel clinging to the hillside (ask someone to show you). In other places, the irrigation system has become almost a piped water supply, with hollow logs used as aqueducts, but this channel has been built with cement. Unfortunately, the water round about, diverted from the Arror River, tastes disgusting, even when boiled; it's a problem you encounter often in the Cheranganis.

There's nothing in Chesoi village itself – no water, no *hotelis* and certainly nowhere to stay – so stop down at the junction if you plan to overnight here. At least the people up here at the edge of the Cheranganis are delighted to meet strangers. You could also **camp** easily, just about anywhere, if you can find a flat space – ask the landowner.

The Sirikwa holes

Near **Moiben**, the **Sirikwa holes** are a collection of depressions, some circular, about 10m across and a few metres deep, others a longer oval shape, all ringed by large stones. To seek out the holes purely for their own sake would require a certain degree of scholarly dedication, but makes an interesting diversion if you're approaching the Cherangani Hills from the Iten–Eldoret road, or following the route out of the northern Kerio Valley from Kapsowar. Matatus run daily from Eldoret or Iten to Moiben (continuing on to Chebororwa on the edge of the Cheranganis); you might have to change at the junction where the *murram* road to Moiben leaves the paved C51. Occasional farm vehicles pass this way, but you could be in for a long wait.

The holes are some 6km west of Moiben. From the crossroads by the upper primary school and chief's office, follow the dirt track past another school on the left and out into farmland. You may need to ask directions, first for Rany Moi Farm and then for the holes themselves – known locally as "Maasai holes" or "Maasai homes". (Don't ask for "Sirikwa Holes", as Moiben is the main location of Sirikwa District and you'd probably be directed to the district offices.) Some holes are alone, others are joined by passages dug a metre or so into the ground. They are thought to have been cattle pens rather than dwellings, but would each have had a small hut by the entrance. The site is relatively undisturbed, but as the pressure from local farms increases, it seems likely that these enigmatic remains will eventually be demolished and ploughed over. You'll find more, though less well preserved, holes at the *Naiberi River Campsite* near Kaptagat (see p.322), and there are others scattered around the district.

Walking in the Cheranganis

If you have the time and inclination, **walking in the Cheranganis** is exhilarating. The thickly forested hills are wild, hardly explored, and still home to bongo antelope. Higher up (Kamelogon peak on Mount Chemnirot is 3581m), they give onto mountain moorland and giant Afro-alpine vegetation, some superb hiking country where you're very unlikely to meet any others doing the same. A couple of days will see you over the southern ridges to Kapcherop, where you'll have no difficulty picking up transport west to Kitale or Eldoret.

For this route, you first climb through Chesoi village and past the mission for about ninety minutes through *shambas*; then there's an hour's walk through forest, mostly flat; ninety minutes of climbing through bamboo forest; and a further two hours though hilly pasturelands and woods before you reach **Kapiego**. If you're driving, note that the Kapiego–Chesoi part of this route is non-motorable and that you can only drive to Kapiego from the south or west.

Kapiego is a crossroads centre, a suitable stop for the night with a few *hotelis* and a morning and/or evening matatu run to Eldoret. From Kapiego, routes lead northwest to Kalelaigelat summit (motorable to the base in a couple of hours, but with no matatus and no water); north to the main Cherangani peaks (again motorable in 2–3hr or a day's walk); and west on a little-used road to **Labot** and – 5km further – **Makutano** (not the Makutano near Kapenguria). Labot has some *hotelis*; Makutano has one, with no refreshments beyond *chai* and chapatis, though it is on another significant crossroads. One or two matatus pass through Makutano most days on their way between Kapcherop and Kapsait, and there's one to Kapiego. There's usually one matatu a day between Labot (leaving around 7am) and the other Makutano near Kapenguria (leaving there at lunchtime). South of the Makutano near Kapsait, a quiet road leads down through grassland, then forest to **Kapcherop** (home of Kenya's former international athletics champion Moses Kiptanui) – about a three-hour walk. From there you'll find matatus to Cherangani, and thence to Eldoret and Kitale.

If your hiking plans are more ambitious, get hold of the relevant Survey of Kenya 1:50m-scale maps and set off, suitably equipped, over the high central districts of the massif. There are several, relatively easily scaled peaks up here. *Mountain Walking in Kenya* by David Else (Robertson McCarta, UK) provides detailed guidance on certain routes. The best base for exploring this area is *Sirikwa Guesthouse* (see p.327), with *Marich Field Studies Centre* (see p.330) as a lower-budget alternative. You'll be able to find local guides at both.

The Cherangani Highway circuit

The scenic D327 road from Makutano through **Kapsait** and **Kaibichbich** is known as the "Cherangani Highway", and the northern stretch forms part of a popular driving circuit. The road does however suffer landfalls, and you should check on the current state of it before setting out (the *Sirikwa Guesthouse* should be able to advise).

If you start at the junction on the A1 near Kapenguria, you can drive down through Kaibichbich to a junction north of Kapsait, where you take a left, passing through Kapsangar towards the peak of Kalelaigelat. Another left turn takes you northwest through **Sina** and back to meet the A1 at Chipkorniswa. The hills between Sina and the villages of Parua and Tamkal to its north are popular for hiking, with footpaths connecting the three villages, although you'll need a guide to follow them. All three villages are connected to the A1 by *murram* roads. If you are going to Tamkal, it's worth trying to coincide with market day, which is Tuesday.

Travel details

Trains

Nakuru to: Nairobi (3 weekly; 7hr); Naivasha (3 weekly; 2hr 30min); Kisumu (3 weekly; 6hr 45min).

Buses

Kabarnet to: Eldoret (2 daily; 1hr 30min); Nakuru (3 daily; 2hr).
Magadi to: Nairobi (2 daily; 2hr).

Naivasha to: Nairobi (several daily; 1hr 30min); Nakuru (several daily; 1hr).
Nakuru to: Eldoret (3 daily; 4hr); Kabarnet (1 daily; 2hr 30min); Kericho (1–2 daily; 2hr); Kisii (1–2 daily; 5hr); Kisumu (7 daily; 4hr 30min); Kitale (3 daily; 3hr); Marigat (1 daily; 1hr 30min); Nairobi (16 daily; 3hr); Nanyuki (1 daily; 5hr); Nyahururu (daily; 2hr).

Matatus

Frequencies are only given below if services are relatively few.

Kabarnet to: Eldoret (several daily; 1hr 30min); Iten (40min); Kabartonjo (change for Kipsaraman; 30min); Marigat (30min); Naivasha (several daily; 2hr); Nakuru (daily; 2hr 30min); Tenges (occasional; 1hr).

Magadi to: Nairobi (2 daily; 2hr); Olorgasailie (2 daily; 1hr).

Marigat to: Kabarnet (30 min); Kampi ya Samaki (15min); Nakuru (several daily; 1hr 30min).

Naivasha to: Eldoret (several daily; 2hr); Kabarnet (several daily; 2hr); Kericho (several daily; 2hr).

Nakuru to: Eldoret (several daily; 2hr); Kabarnet (daily; 2hr 30min); Kericho (several daily; 2hr); Kisumu (several daily; 4hr); Kitale (several daily; 5hr); Marigat (several daily; 1hr 30min); Nairobi (2hr 30min); Narok (daily; 5hr); Nyahururu (several daily; 1hr 30min); Subukia (1hr).

Flights

Naivasha to: Nairobi (SafariLink; 1 daily; 30min).

Western Kenya

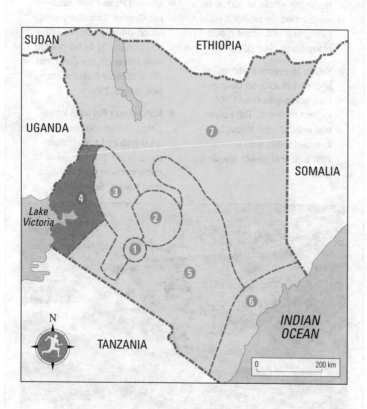

CHAPTER 4

Highlights

✳ **Mfangano Island** Vehicle-less, remote and rarely visited, Mfangano Island, in Lake Victoria, is famous among archeologists for its rock art. See p.303

✳ **Tea country** Kericho, the most important centre for tea in the whole of Africa, is surrounded by an endless rolling sea of brilliant green plantations. See p.312

✳ **Kitale Museum** Fascinating and well-displayed collection where you would not expect to find it. The nature trail behind runs through a forested valley and teems with bird and insect life. See p.324

✳ **Saiwa Swamp National Park** Home to the unusual sitatunga antelope, several species of monkey and a variety of birds, Saiwa Swamp also offers peaceful camping and the chance to explore on foot. See p.327

✳ **Marich Pass Field Studies Centre** Beautifully sited, much-praised centre, where you can easily fix up guided walks through the bush and visits to local Pokot communities. See p.330

✳ **Kakamega Forest** Unique patch of lowland rainforest, off the tourist trail, preserving a fauna that has more in common with central Africa than Kenya. See p.342

△ Fishing boats at Dunga, near Kisumu

4

Western Kenya

ike the tiers of a great amphitheatre, **western Kenya** slopes away from Nairobi, the major game parks and the coast, down to face the stage of Lake Victoria. Cut off by the high Rift wall of the **Mau and Elgeyo escarpments**, the western region of dense agriculture, rolling green valleys and pockets of thick jungle is one of the least-known parts of the country to travellers. Although more accessible than the far north, or even some of the big parks, it has been neglected by the safari operators – and that's all to the good. You can travel for days through lush landscapes from one busy market town to the next and rarely, if ever, meet other tourists or travellers.

It's not easy to see why it has been so ignored. Granted, the disastrous history of Uganda up until the late 1980s discouraged the through traffic that might otherwise have thrived. But there's a great deal more of intrinsic interest than the tourist literature's sparse coverage would suggest. What the west undeniably lacks are teeming herds of antelope and zebra, lions at the side of the road and narcissistic warriors in full regalia. What it does offer is a series of delightfully low-key, easily visited attractions. There are **national parks** at **Kakamega Forest**, a magnificent tract of equatorial rainforest bursting with species found nowhere else in Kenya; **Saiwa Swamp**, where pedestrians, for once, have the upper hand; and **Mount Elgon**, a volcano to rival Mount Kenya in everything but crowds. **Lake Victoria**, with the region's major town, **Kisumu**, on its shores, is a draw in its own right, dotted with out-of-the-way islands and populated by exceptionally friendly people.

Travel is generally easy. The region has a high population and many well-paved roads, so you'll rarely have long to wait for a bus or matatu, and driving is often a pleasure. If you're inclined to plan ahead, there *is* a vague circuit that begins in Kisumu (as this chapter does) and runs through **Kisii** (of Kisii-stone fame), Kericho, Eldoret, Kitale and Kakamega. You could easily do this in a couple of weeks – or a couple of months. But it's often more rewarding to let events dictate your next move: this area will repay your interest repeatedly if you take time to look around. Much of it, even the areas of intensive farming, is ravishingly beautiful: densely animated jungle near **Kakamega** and **Kitale**, regimented landscapes of tea bushes at **Kericho**, highland pastures and forests in the **Cherangani Hills**, and dank swamp and grasslands alive with birds by the lake.

There's almost no tourist infrastructure – the west has only a handful of hotels that could, by a long stretch of the imagination, be described as luxurious – but there's no lack of good, modest **lodgings**. **Food** is as cheap as anywhere and generally excellent; most of Kenya's tea and sugar comes from the west, and agricultural concerns are paramount.

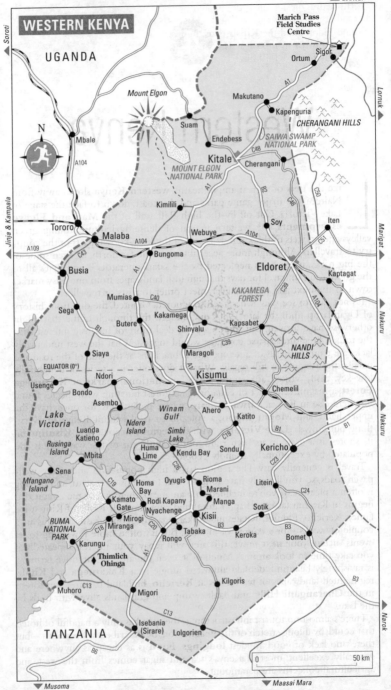

Ethnically, the region is dominated by the **Luo** on the lakeshore lowlands, but other important groups speak dialects of Nandi (principally the **Nandi** around Eldoret and the **Kipsigis** in the Kericho district) and there are Bantu-speaking **Luhya** in the sugar lands north of Kisumu along with **Gusii** in the formidably fertile Kisii Hills.

Around Lake Victoria: Luoland

Lake Victoria is the obvious place to make for in the west, but frustratingly few main roads get close to its shores. Most travellers arrive in Kisumu, which used to have ferries linking it with Kendu Bay, Homa Bay and Mbita, and even with Tanzania and Uganda, but all services are currently suspended because low water levels prevent navigation on parts of the route, though they may resume in the future if levels rise again. Meantime, the only way of getting from Kisumu to other lakeshore towns is by road, though there is a ferry service in operation across the mouth of the Winam Gulf between Luanda Katieno and Mbita.

Kisumu itself, while it's a pleasantly relaxing town, offers only incidental lake views. In order to get a good look at the lake, take the short trip out of town to **Hippo Point** and the fishing village of **Dunga**, or ask around at the port for matatu-boat services to nearby fishing villages and islands. If you really must mess about in a boat, the best place to head for is **Mbita**, which has regular matatu-boats (called "engine boats" by locals) to Mfangano Island, one of the least-visited corners of Kenya, with the added attraction of some wonderful prehistoric **rock art**.

Kisumu

In the still, sultry atmosphere of **KISUMU**, the regional capital and Kenya's third largest town, a distinctive smell off the lake – not unpleasant – blows in on a vague breeze from central Africa, but the layout of the town turns its back on the water, focusing instead on its commercial centre and land links to the rest of Kenya. In the well-to-do residential district, guarded mansions are discreetly spaced along quiet, fragrant avenues and occasional expensive cars cruise the broad, colonnaded commercial streets. Even in the poorer quarters, Kisumu retains a great deal of tattered charm.

Kisumu's fortunes were founded on the lucrative lake shipping business, funnelling goods between Kenya, Uganda and Tanzania, and the town suffered badly following the East African Community's break-up. During the 1980s and early 1990s, the port was practically dormant, with little or no merchandise passing through and signs of dereliction everywhere – empty warehouses, broken windows, deserted dockworkers' houses. Commercial shipping services

▲ **5**, **6**, Kiboso, Nakuru, Nairobi, Kisii & Homa Bay

KISUMU

ACCOMMODATION
Imperial	N
Joy Guesthouse	U
Kimwa Grand	Q
Kisumu	A
Lake View	M
Lodgers Palace	I
Guesthouse	R
Milimani Resort	E
Miruka's Lodge	O
Museum View	P
Natasha	K
New East View	D
New Victoria	H
Palmers	B
Perch	J
Razbi's Guesthouse	C
River Sand	S
Saint Anna Guesthouse	V
Sooper Guesthouse	T
Sunset	F
Tot Coffee House	L
Western Lodge	G
YWCA	

BANKS
Barclays Bank	③
Central Bank	⑥
Co-op Bank	②
Kenya Commercial Bank	⑤
Postbank	④
Standard Chartered Bank	①

RESTAURANTS, BARS & CLUBS
Apoc Complex	5
Expresso Coffee House	12
Gatiba Bar	10
Grill House	8
Hunter's Café	7
Kenshop Cyberstation	11
Kimwa Annex	13
Kisumu Social Club	3
Lakers Inn	6
Mon Ami	15
Octopus/Bottoms Up Night Club	4
Oriental	14
Señorita	9
Show Breeze Club	1
Simba Club	2
Somi Snacks	16

▲ Kondele suburb, Kakamega, Kitale, Malaba, **A** & **1**

Museum

Library

Market

Buses & Matatus

Esso

Police

Law Courts

KNA House

Nyanza Provincial HQ

Mayfair Bakery

Yatin Supermarket

SomKen

Al-Imran Plaza

Alpha House

Mega Plaza

Craft Stalls

Akamba Bus Office

Ukwala Supermarket

Jamia Mosque

Total

Esso

Clocktower

Swan Centre

Train Station

Hotelis

Ferry Dock

▲ Kisumu Airport & Busia

▲ **S**, **T**, **U**, Hippo Point, Dunga & Impala Sanctuary

NAIROBI ROAD
OMINO CRESCENT
GUMBI ROAD
BUSIA ROAD
BULERE ROAD
NZOIA ROAD
LOOWAR STREET
ORE ROAD
OKORE ROAD
AGAM ROAD
OTIENDE ROAD
HUMA ROAD
CHURCH ROAD
ADALA OTUKO ROAD
ODINGA ROAD
AWUOR ROAD
NEW ROAD
OMOLO ROAD
JOMO ROAD
KENYATTA AVENUE
OGINGA ODINGA ROAD
ANGAWA AVENUE
APINDI STREET
ACCRA STREET
OPERA STREET
MBUTA STREET
MARIA STREET
OYOO STREET
MOSQUE ROAD
OTIENO ROAD
PAUL MBOYA ROAD
MARK ASEMBO ROAD
GOR ROAD
OBOTE ROAD
OGINGA LANE
KENDU LANE
ALEGO STREET
KAMPALA STREET
NEW STATION ROAD
BANK STREET
MARINA DRIVE

0 500 m

N

have now resumed on a modest scale and the port sporadically buzzes with activity, but it will take a long stretch of sustained growth to restore Kisumu to its former affluence.

Some history

The **railway line** from Mombasa had reached the lake by 1901, reassuring the British public who were having serious doubts that the "Lunatic Line", as it was dubbed, would ever reach completion, but the first train only chugged into the station at **Port Florence** (as Kisumu was originally known) in 1903 when the Mau Escarpment viaducts were completed. By then, European transport had already arrived at the lake in the form of a steamship brought up from Mombasa

The Luo

The **Luo** are the second largest ethnic group and one of the most cohesive "tribes" in Kenya. Their language, Dholuo, is distinctive and closely resembles the Nuer and Dinka languages of southern Sudan, from where their ancestors migrated south at the end of the fifteenth century. They found the shore and hinterland of Lake Victoria only sparsely populated by hunter-gatherers, scattered with occasional clearings where Bantu-speaking farmers had settled over the previous centuries. Otherwise, the region was wild: untouched grassland and tropical forest, dense with heavy concentrations of wildlife.

The Luo were swift invaders, driving their herds before them, always on the move, restless and acquisitive. They raided other groups' cattle incessantly and, within a few decades, had forced the Bantu-speakers away from the lakeshore. Nevertheless, over the generations, **intermarriage** (essentially the buying of wives) was common and the pastoral nomads were greatly influenced by their Bantu-speaking in-laws and neighbours, ancestors of the present-day Luhya and Gusii.

Early in the **colonial period**, the Luo benefited from some inspired, if dictatorial, leadership. They had inherited the institution of the *ruoth* (king or chief) from the original immigrants from Sudan. The *ruoth* of Gem, a location northwest of Kisumu, was Odera Akang'o, an ambitious and perceptive young man with an almost puritanical attitude to his duties. He had a private police force to inspect farms and report any idleness to him, and he regularly had his subjects beaten or fined for "unprogressive" behaviour. He introduced new crops and, under British protection, made himself quite a sizeable fortune. He was widely feared.

In 1915, the colonial government sent him, with two other chiefs, to Kampala. He returned full of admiration for the European education and health standards there, and ashamed of Gem and Luoland in general. Fired with enthusiasm, he applied his style of schooling and hygiene, bullying his subjects into sending their children to classes and keeping their shirts clean, while the British turned a blind eye. The results were rapid educational advances in Gem, which is still considered a progressive district today. Odera, unfortunately for him, was employed by the British to use his methods on the Teso people in Uganda, where they singularly failed. He was accused of corruption and sent into internal exile, where he died.

The Luo today are best known as fishermen, but they also cultivate widely and still keep livestock. Culturally, they have remained surprisingly independent, and are one of the few Kenyan peoples who don't practise circumcision. Traditionally, children had six teeth knocked out from the lower jaw to mark their initiation into adulthood, but the operation is rarely carried out these days. **Christianity** has made spectacular inroads among the Luo, with an estimated ninety percent being believers, but doesn't so far seem to have destroyed the traditional culture quite as thoroughly as it has elsewhere. Despite the ubiquity of Gospel, **traditional music**, especially the playing of the *nyatiti* lyre, is still very much alive and well worth seeking out.

The westward view from Kisumu gives you little sense of the vastness of **Victoria Nyanza (Lake Victoria)**. The shores of the relatively narrow Winam Gulf curve gently to left and right, and it's difficult to grasp the fact that there's another 300km of water between the horizon and the opposite (Ugandan) shore, and an even greater distance south to Mwanza, the main Tanzanian port. Victoria, the second largest freshwater lake in the world (after Lake Superior), covers a total **area** of close on 70,000 square kilometres – almost the size of Scotland or Nebraska – of which only a fraction belongs to Kenya.

It was barely five centuries ago that the **Luo** first settled beside the vast equatorial lake they called **Ukerewe**, and the lake remained uncharted and virtually unknown outside Africa until well into the second half of the nineteenth century. Then, in the midst of the scramble to pinpoint the **source of the Nile**, the lake suddenly became a focus of attention.

To the nineteenth-century explorers, the search for the source of Africa's longest river was something of a Holy Grail. When English adventurer **John Hanning Speke** set eyes upon Ukerewe in 1858, he was convinced that the long search was over, and promptly renamed the lake in tribute to Queen Victoria. In 1862, he became the first person to sail the Nile all the way from Lake Victoria to Cairo, and triumphantly cabled the Royal Geographical Society in London with the words "The Nile is settled", but sceptics continued to counter that Lake Tanganyika was the true source, and it took a daring circumnavigation of Victoria, led by Stanley in 1875, to prove Speke right. Sadly, Speke did not live to glory in the vindication – he was killed in a shooting accident in 1874.

Lake Victoria was of great strategic significance to the explorers, but it was no paradise. **Bilharzia-carrying snails** flourished in the reeds around the lake's fringes, and the steamy shore was a fertile breeding ground for **malarial mosquitoes**. These hazards persist today. Though the Luo wash, swim and sail their vividly painted, dhow-like, mahogany canoes in and on Victoria Nyanza, the danger of bilharzia is all too real. Instances of the disease are rare after brief contact with infected water, but for the visitor it's not worth the risk: take care if you're going fishing or boating on the lake, and don't even think about going swimming.

Lake ecology

Lake Victoria fills a shallow depression (no deeper than 80m) between the Western and Eastern Rift valleys, yet is not part of the Rift system. Until the 1960s, it was home to around 500 different species of brilliantly coloured tropical **fish**, known as haplochromines or **cichlids** – all of them unique to the lake. Scientists, puzzling over how such a dazzling variety of species came to evolve in this largely uniform environment in the space of no more than a million years, have suggested that, at some stage in its history, the lake must have dried into a series of small lakes in which the

piece by portered piece, having steamed out from Scotland in 1895. Many of the ship's parts were evidently seized en route from the coast and recycled into Nandi ornamentation and weaponry, and it was five years before a complete vessel could be assembled and launched on its maiden voyage across the lake to Port Bell in Uganda.

Kisumu was, by all accounts, a pretty disagreeable place in the early years. Apart from the endemic sleeping sickness, bilharzia, malaria and the nasty malarial complication known as "blackwater fever", the climate was sweltering and municipal hygiene primitive. But it quickly grew into an important administrative and military base and, with the consolidation of the colonies in the 1930s and 1940s, became a leading East African entrepôt and transport fish evolved separately. Lake Victoria's cichlids are popular aquarium fish, and one of the commonest larger species, the tilapia, is a regional speciality, grilled or fried and served whole.

In the early 1960s, a voracious carnivore, the **Nile Perch**, was introduced to the lake, and proceeded to eat its way through the cichlid population, driving most of the species to extinction. For the lake peoples the perch were a boon: they can grow to weigh as much as 250kg, and are both consumed locally and sold for export (in France, Nile perch steaks are sold as *capitaine*). But traditional fish mongering and processing suffered as modern vessels and factories moved in, their products mainly destined for European tables, and the voraciousness of the perch themselves began to send shock waves through the lake ecosystem, with ecologists thrown into a panic by the prospect of the perch eating their way through the entire cichlid population and ultimately starving to death themselves. This has not happened because the demise of the cichlids (and some put this down to over-fishing with fine-mesh nets rather than to predation) caused a proliferation of lake prawns which served as an alternative source of food for the perch. Meanwhile, some species of cichlids held on in parts of the lake which were free of perch, such as where the water was too shallow for them to reach, as well as in smaller lakes around the main one.

The lake has other problems however. Due to deforestation around the shore, plus industrial pollution and human sewage, the algae has proliferated, depriving the lake of oxygen. The link to human population growth is a direct one – over three million litres of human waste drain into the lake every day, and the Swedish development agency, SIDA, estimates that Kenya, with the smallest share of the lake's shoreline, is its main polluter. As well as suffering a dramatic fall in oxygen levels, the lake is becoming so murky that the remaining cichlids are unable to identify their correct mates and hybridization is occurring. Meanwhile, the building of the causeway from Mbita to Rusinga Island turned the Winam Gulf into a pond with only one outlet, inhibiting currents, with serious consequences for the local lake environment.

Another threat comes from the **water hyacinth**, originally native to Brazil. This floating weed grows quickly around the lakeshore and spreads like a carpet across the surface, blocking out the light and slowly choking the lake to death, as well as snaring up vessels. Since 1997, the ports of Homa Bay and Kendu Bay, and even Kisumu, have been at times strangled by a mile-wide cordon of the weed, which has inhibited passage to all but the smallest canoes, with disastrous results for the local economy. Solutions have included the promotion of products (furniture, paper, even building materials) made from the hyacinth. Finally, in 2001, mechanical clearance enabled passenger ferries to start functioning again, only for falling water levels to reduce the depth so much that most ferries could not operate, and in 2004 the Kisumu–Homa Bay service ceased running again.

hub, attracting Asian investment on top of the businesses that had been set up at the railway terminus when the Indian labourers were laid off. Kisumu's rise seemed unstoppable until 1977, when the sudden **collapse of the East African Community**, more or less overnight, robbed the town of its *raison d'être*. The partial reformation of the community in 1996 brightened prospects again, and by 1999, the port was relatively busy, thanks largely to UN World Food Programme transit goods destined for war-torn Rwanda and Congo.

Since then however, Kisumu has again seen a downturn in its fortunes, due to the decline of the local sugar industry, sugar cane being the surrounding region's main cash crop. Dumping of subsidized sugar by the EU led to a worldwide crash in prices, and this in turn forced the closure of sugar refineries at nearby

Muhroni and Miwani, which were the mainstays of the local economy. The good news is that a long-promised molasses plant north of town has finally opened, and may help to reverse the decline. On the other hand, traffic across Lake Victoria has dried up, due in part to a fall in the water level of as much as two metres, which has made this end of the lake all but unnavigable to commercial shipping.

But the picture isn't entirely bleak. Kisumu does have considerable charm, and it's no small advantage to be one of the few upcountry towns with real character (though the slightly time-warped atmosphere of a place that's been treading water for over two decades may not be much comfort to its inhabitants). In many ways, Kisumu seems to have more in common with neighbouring Uganda than with the rest of Kenya. It's a distinctly tranquil, easy-going town, the *manambas* in the bus station are unusually laid-back, and any anticipation of claustrophobia is quickly soothed by the spacious, shady layout. The contrast with Nakuru, if you've just come from there, is striking.

Arrival and accommodation

Kisumu is a natural base, excellently located for exploring western Kenya; half a day's travelling should get you to any of the centres detailed in this chapter. The **bus** and **train stations** are on opposite sides of town: the former is sited by the big junction of the Nairobi and Kakamega roads, the latter at the bottom of New Station Road, down the hill in the port area. It's a good idea to install yourself soon after arriving, before starting any energetic wanderings, as it gets tremendously hot here. Sundays are very quiet in Kisumu – more than most towns, on the "day of rest" the majority of places, including restaurants, shut down.

Moving on from Kisumu

Kisumu is very well connected to the rest of the country by **bus** and **matatu**. The bus and matatu stage is on Gumbi Road, behind the SonKen station at the intersection of Kenyatta Avenue and Otieno Oyoo Street. They run to more or less anywhere in western Kenya, and to cities further afield like Nakuru and Mombasa. Eldoret Express buses run pretty much hourly to Nairobi, but not in fact from Kisumu to Eldoret. Coast Bus (℡057/2024141) has an overnight run to Mombasa at 6pm, taking fifteen hours, and a service to Nairobi at 9.30pm, arriving inconveniently at 3 or 4am. Departures, along with those of cheaper firms, are from the main stand, though tickets can be bought at its office on Alego Street. Akamba has its office further east on Alego Street (℡057/23554, ℮aprsksm@africaonline.co.ke), with four buses daily to Nairobi (9am, 11am, 1pm & 9pm), and one for **Kampala** (1pm). If you're aiming for **Kakamega Forest**, buses and matatus run from the main stage to Khayega and Kakamega town, from where it's possible to find transport to the forest (for details see p.345).

There are currently three weekly overnight passenger **rail** services, with first- and second-class sleepers and third-class seats, to Nairobi leaving at 6.30pm (Tues, Thurs & Sun), scheduled to arrive at 8.30am next morning, and a third-class-only service to Butere at 8.45am (Tues, Thurs & Sun), taking just over three hours. Call the station for latest details (℡057/43591).

Ferry services on Lake Victoria, run by Kenya Railways, are currently suspended due to low water levels. Should they resume, there should be boats to Kendu Bay, Kowuor, Homa Bay, Mbita and Asembo.

Kisumu **airport** (℡057/2020667), 5km up the Busia road, is served by Peugeots from the main stage. Kenya Airways runs one or two daily flights to Nairobi from here; East African Safari Air runs two or three.

Accommodation

There's a wide choice of **places to stay**, with a good number of modest, mid-range hotels, though prices tend to be higher than usual. At the lower end, some of the B&Ls are pretty basic, even verging on squalid. Temperature, humidity and mosquitoes will conspire to give you an uncomfortable night if you don't have a net or a fan (preferably both), so it's worth paying a little more for the few nights you may be in town. Unless you want to leave early, try not to stay near the mosque – the morning call to prayer is loud-speakered at 5.30am, and note that most hotels in Kisumu have a 9.30am checkout time.

Boarding & lodgings

Joy Guesthouse Dunga, on the road to Hippo Point; PO Box 9105 ⊕0720/98388, ⓦwww.joyguesthouse.com. A small (four rooms, all with nets), clean, family-run guesthouse, almost like a European *pension*, in Dunga village. ❷

Lodgers Palace Guesthouse Paul Mbuya Rd; PO Box 6234 ⊕0735/961208. Breezy but basic non-s/c rooms with nets, and friendly people. ❷

Miruka's Lodge Apindi St; PO Box 1717 ⊕0721/765844. The best of three low-cost hotels in the same block, with s/c singles that are decent enough, but have only cold water. ❶

Razbi's Guesthouse Oginga Odinga Rd; PO Box 1418 ⊕057/2025488. Clean, reasonably well-kept rooms, though some are a bit poky. Non-s/c doubles and singles, and a few pricier s/c singles (Ksh 600). ❶

Sooper Guesthouse Oginga Odinga Rd, next door to *Razbi's*; PO Box 1729 ⊕0733/622099. Spanking new and gleaming bright, this place tries to live up to its name. Some of the s/c rooms share a balcony, and there's a nice roof terrace, with restaurant facilities about to open. ❷

Tot Coffee House Paul Mbuya Rd; PO Box 649 ⊕057/2024713. Large, good-value but not entirely spotless rooms, s/c with bathtubs and running hot water, with a bar and restaurant downstairs. B&B ❷

YWCA off Ang'awa Ave; PO Box 1618 ⊕057/2024788. Friendly, cheap but rather bland, with a canteen, camping facilities – largely unused – and few double rooms (❷). Ksh300 per person in three- or four-bed dorms. B&B.

Cheap hotels

Kimwa Grand Hotel Kondele suburb, 3km along the Kakamega road; PO Box 2226 ⊕0720/740718. Sixty-one good s/c rooms with fans and nets, plus a good restaurant and safe parking. Rooms on the top floors have excellent views of the Nandi Hills. The main attraction is the music in the attached club (see p.293), though this makes it rather noisy. Catch a matatu from Oginga Odinga Rd. B&B ❸

Lake View Alego St; PO Box 9833 ⊕057/2020982. No exceptional views, though with its corner position, it does offer some breeze and it also boasts a very congenial bar. Rooms have nets and hot water but no fans, and may sometimes be shared by more than two people. B&B ❸

Natasha Otuona Rd; PO Box 1247 ⊕057/2020189. Decent s/c rooms with hot water and fans, good value and well located for the town centre. ❷

New East View Omolo Agar Rd; PO Box 2634 ⊕0722/556721. A quieter alternative to the nearby *Palmers*, well kept and scrupulously clean with safe parking. B&B ❹

New Victoria Gor Mahia St; PO Box 276 ⊕057/2020413 or 2021067. This well-maintained and efficiently run hotel is bright and cheerful inside and out. Rooms 206–9 have good lake views. B&B ❸

Palmers Omolo Agar Rd; PO Box 1434 ⊕057/2024867. Handy for the bus and matatu stand, and with parking space if you're in a car, this friendly place has a relaxed bar and *nyama choma* joint in the back yard. B&B ❸

Perch corner of Mark Asembo Rd and Obote Rd; PO Box 1224 ⊕0721/523617. A sweeping wooden staircase leads you up to the safari-lodge-style lobby. There's lots of wood panelling in the public areas, comfortable, carpeted rooms (all with TV, most with a lake view), and a good bar and restaurant. B&B ❸

River Sand Accra Rd; PO Box 807 ⊕057/2025672. Gloomy corridors but bright, clean, airy s/c rooms, some with balcony access and lake views. B&B ❸

Western Lodge Kendu Lane; PO Box 1519 ⊕057/2023707. Relatively clean and secure (with a large locking cupboard in every room) and some lake views. Unfortunately, there's no food and, when the nearby goods yard and port road are busy and the bar opposite turns the music up, it's noisy. ❷

Mid-range hotels

Imperial Jomo Kenyatta Ave; PO Box 1866 ⊕057/2022661–7, ⓦwww.imperialkisumu.com. The first choice for wealthy Kenyans. All rooms are a/c, "deluxe" ones with satellite TV and mini-bars. The cocktail lounge has views over the lake, as do some rooms. Outdoor café and covered pool, and forex for guests. Prices fall by $15 at weekends. B&B ❼

Kisumu Hotel Jomo Kenyatta Ave; PO Box 1690 ☎057/2024155 or 7, ✉hotel@maseno.ac.ke. Once Kisumu's top hotel, now making a comeback after years of decline, refurbished with comfortable, carpeted though not huge a/c rooms; facilities include three bars, a restaurant and a decent-sized pool. B&B ❻

Milimani Resort off Got Huma Rd; PO Box 2652 ☎057/2023245, ✉info@milimaniresort.com. Cosy rooms, all with satellite TV, some with stereo, in a secure compound in Kisumu's quiet residential district, with good views from the upper floors. The staff are friendly and gracious, and facilities include a restaurant and lounge (no alcohol served), and a pool. B&B ❺

Museum View near the museum; PO Box 544 ☎057/2021538, ☎2024808. A friendly place in a quiet location, with large, bright, though slightly bare s/c rooms with mosquito nets (check for holes). B&B ❸

Saint Anna Guesthouse 3km south at Milimani; PO Box 19100 ☎057/2024792, ✉stanna@swiftkisumu.com. In a posh residential area (follow the signposts from the Central Bank building on Jomo Kenyatta Ave), a modest Catholic-run two-storey hotel, with good large rooms and hot showers. Safe parking. B&B ❹

Sunset Aput Lane, 2.5km out of town to the south; PO Box 215 ☎057/2020464–6, ✉hotelsunset1977@yahoo.co.uk. Fronting on to the Impala Sanctuary (see below) and with a whiff of plasticky highlife, this five-storey complex is fraying around the edges, but offers great lake views and beautiful sunsets from every room above the first floor (all have balconies), plus well-tended gardens complete with a swimming pool, and ramps and lift access for disabled guests. A taxi from town costs around Ksh250. Prices drop by Ksh800 at weekends. B&B ❻

The Town

The **market** by the bus station is the biggest and best in western Kenya, and an absorbing place to wander, crammed with fruit and vegetables (including some oddities like breadfruit) and all the usual household paraphernalia – pots and plates, reed brushes, wickerwork and wooden spoons. The market is such a success that it has mushroomed out into the adjacent municipal park, much to the consternation of the local authorities.

The row of craft stalls opposite the *Hotel Royale* is one of the region's best hunting grounds for **souvenirs**. The things to buy here (if you have space) are the heavy, three-legged Luo stools, the best of which are intricately inlaid with beads, and dark brown from repeated oiling. Also on offer are bangles, wooden carvings and row upon row of soapstone knick-knacks. Soapstone (or Kisii-stone) is more expensive to buy in Kisumu than at source (Tabaka, near Kisii), but it's cheaper than in most places, and the craftsmen will carve designs to order.

Another worthwhile visit for crafts, just out of town, is **Pendeza Weaving** (PO Box 1786 ☎0735/229904, ✉pendezawp@yahoo.com), about 3km down the Nairobi road, past the chief's camp (on the right in the large field) and indicated by a small white sign on the right. Handwoven *kikois* here are as cheap as you'll find; they turn up later at Spinner's Web in Nairobi.

The prayer calls from Kisumu's pastel green-and-white **Jamia mosque**, on Otieno Oyoo Street, sound odd in this town, but Islam is well established here and in Mumias (see p.348), and is an important regional influence dating from well back into the nineteenth century. The orthodox Shafi'ite mosque was built in 1919, though the women's section on the right was only finished in 1984. The beautiful long mats inside are from Saudi Arabia.

Kisumu Museum

Foremost among the town's sights is the engaging and ambitious **Kisumu Museum** (daily 8.30am–6pm; Ksh200), just a short walk east from the market. Set in a large garden with carefully labelled trees, the single-roomed main gallery happily mingles **zoological** exhibits with ethnographic displays. Apart from the row of trophy-style game heads around the walls, the stuffed animals and preserved insects and crustaceans are displayed with considerable flair and imagination. Particularly good use has been made of old and moth-eaten exhibits from Nairobi's National Museum. A free-swinging vulture, for example, spins like a model aircraft overhead while, centre stage, a lion is caught in full, savage pounce, leaping onto the back of a hysterical wildebeest in the most action-packed piece of taxidermy you're ever likely to see.

The **ethnographic** exhibits are uncommonly illuminating, too. The Maasai aren't the only people who take blood from their cattle for food: Kalenjin peoples like the Nandi and the Kipsigis once did the same, and even the Luo lived mostly on cow's blood mixed with milk before they arrived at Lake Victoria and began to cultivate and fish. There's a good selection of **musical instruments**, including a fine *nyatiti* (a Luo lyre, the East-African equivalent of the *kora*); it's the kind of thing crudely reproduced in a hundred curio shops and now occasionally heard at African concerts abroad. And look out for the disembodied hands pumping the bellows in the metal-working display.

In separate halls from the main gallery are a disappointing **aquarium**, where you can see what your curried tilapia looked like before it left the lake, and a **snake house** with a fairly comprehensive collection of Kenyan species. Among them are venomous snakes from the Kakamega Forest and some unnervingly lethal-looking black mambas and forest cobras from the Kisumu area. Outside, a tortoise pen, a snake pit – one of the pythons was rescued from a hole beneath the tea counter at the bus station – and a croc pond are rather pointless extras. The crocodiles are fed on Mondays around 5pm.

In the "**Traditional Luo Homestead**" recorded voices in English and Swahili recount how people used to live in the region. Until relatively recently, an elderly Luo man actually occupied the "First Wife's house", and would tell you in slow Swahili that this is how he himself was brought up.

The Impala Sanctuary, Hippo point and Dunga

For a pleasant walk out of town, you could head for Hippo Point and the Luo fishing village of **DUNGA**. From the vicinity of the *Sunset Hotel* you follow the main road – or the shoreline – south. Close by is the small **Impala Sanctuary** (daily 6am–6pm; $5), which has a herd of 24 very tame impala and some vervet monkeys, plus a few distressingly small cages, due for an upgrade when funds allow – animal-loving donors sought – containing a couple of bored leopards, some baboons and jackals, a lion and a hyena (not laughing). It's more like a city park than a nature reserve, but worth a visit just for the chance to stretch your legs in the shade (accompanied by a warden, to protect not against wild beasts but "bad people").

Five hundred metres further on you come to **Hippo Point**, where you can watch often riotous sunsets from the rock-strewn shore while being bitten senseless by clouds of merciless mosquitoes. Hippos are still seen here, and boatmen will offer to take you out to view them (around Ksh1500 for a round trip). There's a strong, warm breeze at dusk, and it's a curiously stifling sensation to sit by this giant body of water without a whiff of ozone in the air. Around the lake, Luo fishermen cast their lines from the shallows.

Dunga village itself is some 2km further, on the headland, a picturesque settlement with Dunga Fishermen's Co-operative Society the main feature on the shore. If you'd like to spend a night with the **fishermen** on their boats, the co-op is the first place to ask, though you should expect some good-natured negotiations first.

Eating and drinking

Kisumu has a number of reasonable **places to eat**, but dine early as many places close shortly after dusk. Fish is the commonest dish, but there are some tasty curries around, too. There are **supermarkets** at Mega Plaza (Nakumatt; where the post office is on Oginga Odinga Road), in the Swan Centre (Raiya), and on Kenyatta Avenue (Yatin). Good **bakeries** in town include Victoria by the *New Victoria Hotel* in Gor Mahia Street, Kenshop by the *Mona Lisa* in Oginga Odinga Road, Bhavniks up the street in Mega Plaza, and Mayfair on Ang'awa Avenue just off Kenyatta Avenue. *Nyama choma* can be had in shack-type "**kiosks**" at the top of Omolo Agar Road, by the market, but the best deal in town is **fresh fried tilapia** in a series of *hotelis* down by the lakeside at the far northern end of Oginga Odinga Road, served with a choice of *ugali* or chapatis.

Expresso Coffee House Otuona Rd. A long and decent menu of fry-ups, but the coffee is instant, despite the name, and the "juice" isn't fresh-pressed either. Not bad for breakfast or lunch nonetheless, but closes at 6pm.

Grill House Swan Centre, Accra Rd. The expats' favourite and a great spot for breakfasts, snacks and moderately priced meals, with good steaks, chicken and lamb dishes, a selection of vegetarian options and – the speciality – mixed grills. Beer is served, so you can have a drink with your meal.

Hunter's Café Paul Mbuya Rd. In the same building as the *Lodgers Palace Guesthouse*, and run by the same management, this good-value little diner has great *githeri* (Kikuyu bean and maize stew – the "special" version is with meat and veg) and other Kenyan dishes, most at under Ksh100.

Imperial Hotel Jomo Kenyatta Ave. The *Florence* restaurant (evenings only, 7.30–10.30pm) offers Kisumu's poshest nosh, with starters like shash-lik (beef kebabs), or tilapia fingers with tartare sauce, a small selection of vegetarian dishes, mostly pasta-based, and a range of steaks and international or local main courses such as prawn tempura or *kuku na ndizi* (chicken with tomato and banana). Alternatively, there's a barbecue terrace with good *nyama choma*.

Kenshop Cyberstation Oginga Odinga Rd. An excellent locale for breakfast or tea, with real espresso coffee, fresh juices (the cane juice with ginger is heavenly), plus pies,

sandwiches, burgers and snacks. Tasty and spotless.

Kimwa Annex Otuona Rd. A bright, clattery, self-catering canteen/bar open 24hr, good for cheap, filling plates of *kima* (mince) with rice or *githeri*, and *nyama* or chicken *choma*.

Mona Lisa Restaurant Oginga Odinga Rd. Does a good breakfast, but the food (inexpensive café fare – mostly meat stews with rice or *ugali*) is otherwise variable. Closes 7pm.

Oriental upstairs at al-Imran Plaza, Oginga Odinga Rd. All the usual Chinese favourites, including soya chicken and squid in white sauce, plus some Thai starters; good but quite pricey.

Señorita Oginga Odinga Rd. A long and varied menu of Indian and African dishes, spaghetti even, but nothing Latin American or Spanish, despite the name. Closes 6.30pm.

Simba Club Jomo Kenyatta Ave. The restaurant here is open to non-members (11am–3pm for lunch, 7pm–midnight for supper), with an excellent menu of tandoori dishes and curries. Specialities such as Amritsari fish (in a tandoori-style marinade, but fried rather than baked) and fish à la Simba (marinaded in coriander and green chilli) make good use of Lake Victoria tilapia, but prices are high by local standards.

Somi Snacks Mega Plaza, Oginga Odinga Rd. South Indian vegetarian dishes including *masala dosa* and *idli sambar*, plus vegetarian pizzas, falafel and vegetarian Mughlai dishes such as *malai kofta*. Open daily 8.30am–10pm.

Bars and nightlife

If you make the effort, Kisumu more than rewards the enthusiastic, with ample opportunities for catching **live bands**, and sometimes even big-name stars. More run-of-the-mill **discos** are plentiful, too. The regional music speciality is *ohangala*, based on Luo folk music, which is just as danceable as the Lingala (Congolese *soukous*) alternative, or the old standby, *benga*, which is also largely Luo in origin (see p.650).

Apoc Complex Nyamasaria, 4km from town on the Nairobi road. Live bands, mainly Lingala, Wed–Sun 6pm–midnight, in what is essentially a lively beer hall and *nyama choma* joint. Reached by matatu or *boda-boda* from the main stage.

Gatiba Bar Kendu Lane. A pleasantly seedy little bar with a vintage jukebox, open daily till midnight.

Kimwa Grand Hotel Kondele suburb, 4km out on the Kakamega road. Excellent live music Wed–Sun from Congolese bands and resident group the Malo Malo Kings.

Kisumu Social Club Off Gumbi Rd, by the library. Live bands 6pm–midnight daily, a hub of *ohangala*.

Mon Ami Mega Plaza, Oginga Odinga Rd. Cold beer, pub-like atmosphere, and CNN or English Premiership football on the TV, plus English and Indian food, and dancing in the evenings. A favourite hangout with expats and Kenyans alike. Open till 3am daily.

Lakers Inn On the Kiboso road, 4km from town (☎057/44897) – get a taxi or a *boda-boda*. Big-name Congolese bands and others, with Sunday family day. Also has food and accommodation.

Octopus/Bottoms Up Night Club Ogada St. A pick-up joint of the first order – but for an enjoyable night out, this is relaxed enough if you just want to mingle over a beer or two. The restaurant is often empty, but the disco is always lively, and the *Pirate's Den* roof terrace (with barbecue and dartboard) is a popular, breezy rendezvous point, albeit with dire service. In theory open 24hr, but pretty much dead in the daytime.

Show Breeze Club Mamboleo, near Kondele. Live *ohangala*, some *benga*, in fierce below-the-belt competition with *Lakers* for the big stars.

Listings

Airlines Kenya Airways, Alpha House, Oginga Odinga Rd, PO Box 1427 ☎057/2020081–2, ℻2020241; airport ☎057/2020667; East African Safari Air, upper ground floor, block B, Mega Plaza ☎057/2024929.

Banks Standard Chartered, Barclays and KCB all have ATMs. Victoria Forex near Barclays and PEL Forex in al-Imran Plaza charge no commission for changing cash or traveller's cheques, with only slightly lower rates for the latter.

Boat trips From Hippo Point, or from behind the *hotelis* at the northern end of Oginga Odinga Rd. Bargain hard to get a good price, but expect to pay Ksh1000–1800 for a trip to see the hippos, or out to some of the offshore islands.

Books Sarit Bookshop, Oginga Odinga Rd on the corner of New Station Road; F.K. Shah, Oginga Odinga Rd by *Señorita* restaurant. Street stalls selling used books are concentrated on the north side of Ang'awa Ave at the junction with Jomo Kenyatta Ave.

Car rental Pieper, Swan Centre, Accra St ☎057/2024249, ℮piepercaps@yahoo.com; Kisumu Tours & Travel near Barclays Bank, PO Box 764 ☎057/20785; check cars carefully before taking them.

Courier services DHL, c/o Securicor, Obote St ☎057/22022; FedEx, first floor, Jubilee Insurance House, Ang'awa Ave at the clocktower square ☎057/2024778; EMS, Mega Plaza, ☎057/2024516.

Hospitals The main place is Nyanza Provincial General Hospital ☎057/2020801; Aga Khan Hospital (☎057/2020005) is the best private hospital. You can call an ambulance on ☎057/44897.

Immigration The Immigration Department, first floor, Reinsurance Plaza, behind Alpha House on Oginga Odinga Rd (PO Box 1178; ☎057/2024935), is generally helpful, stamping visa and visitor's pass extensions on the spot without objection. If you need a photo, there's a shop down the east side of Alpha House that does them while you wait.

Internet access There are several places along Oginga Odinga Rd: in Mega Plaza and the Swan Centre, and on the block between Otuona Rd and New Station Rd. The cheapest at time of writing (Ksh0.50 per min) was Global Computer Solutions, third floor, block C, Mega Plaza (Mon–Sat 7.30am–7.30pm).

Kisumu ASK Show Held in the first week of August, 6km north of town on the Miwani road.

Library Off Gumbi Rd, behind the bus and matatu station; Mon–Thurs 8am–6.30pm, Fri & Sat 8am–4pm.

Pharmacies Open late and on Sundays: Sunchem, Nzoia Rd, just south of Butere Rd (Mon–Sat 9am–9.30pm); Miriu Chemist, Kondele suburb, opposite MTC (daily 7.30am–8pm; ☎057/2020788); Dosefield, Mega Plaza, Oginga Odinga St (daily 9am–9pm); Winam, Ang'awa Ave, 100m from the clock tower (daily 7am–7.30pm).

Police Olmolo Agar Rd ☎057/2024719.

Post office Mon–Fri 8am–5.30pm, Sat 9am–noon. Poste restante available.

Swimming pools A swim at the *Sunset Hotel* is always a pleasure – non-residents pay Ksh120. You might also take a dip in the *Kisumu Hotel*'s pool (Ksh150). The *Imperial* has a less enticing, semi-indoor pool, surrounded by a very plain concrete terrace (Ksh120).

Siaya District and the road to Uganda

Heading northwest out of Kisumu, down a broad avenue of flame trees, you pass first the Sunni Muslim, Ismailia and Hindu cemeteries, then the golf club and emerge into the wide plains of **Siaya District**. Transport to the border town of Busia is fairly constant. The region is pleasantly rural but unremarkable. One possible place to stay, just off the road at **Siaya**, is the *Mwalimu Hotel* (PO Box 605; ☎057/321105; ❹) offering good-value rooms with breakfast.

USENGE (or Usengi), a short bus ride from Kisumu, is something of a diversion if you're en route to Uganda, and a useful target if you're planning an exploration of the district, but it's also a town of precolonial historical significance in its own right. The nearby hill, Got Ramogi, is by tradition the site where the first Luo arrived at the lake from further north. It's not a hard climb to the top for a satisfying view over the island-dotted lake, the lagoon below (Lake Saru), and the land which the Luo fought for and eventually won from the Bantu-speakers at the end of the fifteenth century. Usenge itself is a pretty town with a causeway over the lake that connects with the Uganda road. Lodgings there are cheap.

Busia

BUSIA, on the Uganda border, is a surprisingly nice little town and a better place to cross than Malaba, the frontier post on the railway line further north. If you're staying the night, the *Emmanuel Hotel*, on the north side of the main drag, 300m from the border post (PO Box 885; ☎0724/958158; ❶), is the best budget option – try for room no 1, with windows on two sides; some of the other rooms are rather stuffy. Similar places on the Ugandan side cost more. Of a much better standard are *Blue York Hotel*, south of the main drag on Bulanda Road (PO Box 511; ☎055/22081, ✉consitawa@yahoo.com; ❸), and *Farm View Hotel* on Hospital Road, a kilometre south of the main drag (PO Box 141; ☎055/23036; ❸), with good s/c rooms with nets, kids' play area, and "traditional" dancers and discos at weekends; both places offer B&B.

There are several daily **buses** from Busia to Nairobi (8hr) via Kisumu (2hr 30min). Most companies run one morning and one evening service; Akamba's (☎055/22069) leave at 10am and 8pm. **Matatus** serve Kisumu, Malaba and Bungoma, with morning departures to Kitale and Nairobi. On the Ugandan side, there are matatus to Jinja and Kampala. **Money changers** on both sides of the border will change Ugandan and Kenyan shillings, or give either for dollars or sterling, but check the current rates in advance. There is also a Kenya National Bank on the Kenyan side (just east of *Emmanuel Hotel*) with an ATM.

From Kisumu to Kisii

If you want it to be, the ride **from Kisumu to Kisii** can be a rapid transition along the main A1 highway from dusty or flooded plain (depending on the season) up into the ample, fecund hills of the Gusii. But there are various ornithological diversions along the way, if you're independently mobile or enthusiastic enough to make the effort with public transport and your own feet.

There's also a fine **alternative route** from Kisumu to Kisii, using the **lakeshore road** from Katito (south of Ahero) to Kendu Bay (see p.296), and then taking the road to Oyugis back on the A1, just a short journey from Kisii. Except when the Kendu Bay–Oyugis road is in very bad condition after heavy rain, the route takes barely longer than the direct approach.

Kisumu bird sanctuary

The swampland beyond Kisumu to the southeast is very rich in birdlife, and the first place worth investigating off the main A1 road is the **heronry** (Kisumu Bird Sanctuary; information from Lake Victoria Sunset Birders; PO Box 4201 Kisumu; ℡057/2024162, ⓦwww.lvsb.50megs.com) on the way to **Ahero**. From April to May, especially, this is the nesting site of hundreds of pairs of not just herons, but ibises, cormorants, egrets and storks, the dark and curiously scruffy open-bill stork included. Ornithologically world famous, the sanctuary is a must if you're interested in birds.

To get there, take a right turn (south, towards the lake) around 7–8km from Kisumu (about 16km west of Ahero), to the school at **Orongo**, and from there branch left and follow the track for another 2–3km. Ask local people's advice, as the best vantage points and the easiest access to the colony move each year. The site is usually a good place to camp. This low-lying region between Kisumu and the Western Highlands is known as the **Kano plains** – disablingly hot, humid flatlands, swaying with sugar cane and rice fields, fertilized by occasional disastrous flooding.

There are a number of other breeding sites for herons and ibises beyond the sanctuary, some 20km from Kisumu, again to the right of the road in the marshy district southwest of Ahero.

South Nyanza

The territory south of Kisumu is interesting to explore – it's fairly easy to get around, if you're willing to go by matatu, and includes a number of small towns, the Lake Victoria islands, a national park and even an archeological site. This section covers the agreeable little town of **Kendu Bay**, the main town of **Homa Bay**, **Ruma National Park**, the intriguing ruins of **Thimlich Ohinga**, the islands of **Rusinga and Mfangano** (perch fishing for the rich; walking and hanging out for the poor) and, down near the Tanzanian border, the one-street town of **Migori**.

The **lakeshore** west of Migori is remote and, in parts, beautiful, with **Karungu Bay** a rewarding side trip. In the other direction, **Kihancha**, on the south bank of the Migori River, on another back-country route to Maasai Mara, is a pretty area.

South Nyanza is largely Luo country, but there are also scattered, rural communities of **Kuria** people down here. The Kuria have an interesting, quasi-matriarchal system found in various parts of Africa, which essentially allows women of means to "marry" younger women in order to have children without the need to live with a man. In practice, it's often a married woman who can't have children who invites a younger woman into her home. The young "bride", in turn, chooses a male partner, often in secret, to father (biologically speaking) her children, who are brought up by the two women without the involvement of the father or the older woman's husband. The older woman is sometimes a widow, sometimes simply a single woman. In any case, she lives like a male elder – attending to light business affairs but essentially waited upon hand and foot from dawn to dusk. It's a system with much to recommend it, especially when it takes care of unmarried mothers (who are barred from marrying men), who come into the family as "wives" – surrogate mothers – and whose children are automatically adopted. Ironically, despite these apparently female-controlled arrangements, it's male children that women-families want – and men who inherit land.

Kendu Bay

KENDU BAY has a good deal of intrinsic charm, though next to nothing to offer the casual visitor. The one-street old town is 500m off the Kisumu–Homa Bay main road, turning off just before the tarmac ends. One notable building in the old town is the gorgeous **Masjid Tawakal** mosque. You can look around it – though there's not much to see – and climb on the roof. The smaller **Masjid Jamia**, built in 1902, is older, but not as ornate.

Kendu Bay's local fame comes from the curiosity of **Simbi Lake**, about 4km (45 minutes' walk) west of the village: head out of the village on the Homa Bay road and pass the left turn to Oyugis/Kisii. Just over 2km further on, over the river bridge, turn right down the path and walk for another fifteen minutes. Alternatively, just take a *boda-boda*.

The lake, and the nearby Ondago Swamp, have been adopted as feeding grounds (in June and July) by a couple of thousand **flamingos**, refugees from Lake Nakuru (see p.253). It has in the past been suggested that Homa Bay County Council should fence off Simbi Lake, impose admission charges, and make provision for local traders to set up stalls, but as yet they have not done so, and the lake remains a tranquil beauty spot where the only commerce is the odd local resident selling sugar cane.

Even without the flamingos, the lake is unquestionably weird: several bright green but changeable acres of opaque water sunk 20–30m below the surrounding land and only a few kilometres from Lake Victoria itself. It has no apparent source and its origins are somewhat mysterious. It looks like a huge meteorite crater with a footpath around the rim.

The **story** goes that an old wandering woman was refused hospitality one rainy night at the village that once occupied the site of the lake. A big beer party was going on and she was ignored. Only one woman would allow her to warm

△ Masjid Tawakal, Kendu Bay

herself and the old woman insisted she and her family leave the village with her. The young woman tried in vain to persuade her husband to come with them, fearing the old lady's revenge for her ill-treatment. So the two women left alone. Later that night there was a tremendous cloudburst and the rain came down so hard that the village was swamped to become Simbi Lake. Further variations on the story (there are many) improve on the theme of drunkenness and debauchery to give a Sodom and Gomorrah ring to the tale. Other lakes in Kenya have similar tales of origin.

The little lake's shores are almost devoid of vegetation. Nobody goes out on it in boats and it doesn't look as if they fish there either. It's usually described with the catch-all term "volcanic" and is apparently extraordinarily deep. According to one local belief, visitors should throw money in to avoid bad luck. Whatever the natural explanation, it seems plausible that the area was inhabited when the lake was formed, the disaster accounting for the legends. Similar, though smaller, lakes can be seen east of Kendu Bay along the road to Kisumu.

If you're heading on to Homa Bay, you might like to see the **Oriang Pottery Centre** in the village of the same name, 2km past the Simbi Lake turning. It's a UNDEP-funded programme, relying on clay from the local river bed.

Practicalities

The Total petrol station is on the main road by its junction with the road to Oyugis, the post office about 100m west. There are no banks. The ferry **dock** (a pier partly made of concrete-filled barges) is about a kilometre from the old town, with no boat services at the time of writing due to low water levels in the lake.

There's one **B&L** in the old town: *Milimani Bar & Restaurant* (PO Box 77; ☏0735/861614; ❶) has eight basic non-s/c singles, bucket showers and solar-powered electric lights. Handier for transport, the *Hotel Big Five* at the Total station (PO Box 218; ☏0724/157955; ❷) is decorated with Disneyesque concrete trees and animals, with rooms set apart from its **restaurant**, which serves excellent fish, and its **nightclub**, which plays music every night, but is only really lively on Saturdays. A few doors east, the *New Wedewo*, a shacky *hoteli* that's not much to look at, serves unbeatable *mandaazi*, and pretty good meals too.

Leaving Kendu Bay, the *murram* road up to **Oyugis** (on the main A1 highway between Kisii and Kisumu) is generally firm, but it sometimes takes a beating in wet weather and becomes, on occasions, impassable. Normally, though, you'll have no difficulty getting a matatu up to Oyugis or west to Homa Bay. The obvious alternative escape route is the tarred **lakeshore road** from Kendu Bay to Katito, where it meets the A1 on to Kisumu. An excellent, fast highway when it was built, it has quickly become very rough, but resurfacing is now in progress, so it should soon be restored to its former smooth condition. There's a wealth of interest in the surrounding Luo countryside, most of it so recently a rural backwater, with scenes of fishing boats and compounds of square, mud-brick-built, thatched houses (a fairly recent change; traditionally they were round).

Homa Bay

At first glance a scruffy and unremarkable place, the small port town of **Homa Bay**, the region's main centre and also a good base for visits to Ruma National Park, Rusinga Island and Simbi Lake, is in fact one of the friendliest towns in Kenya. The town admittedly has nothing much of interest, just a few dirty,

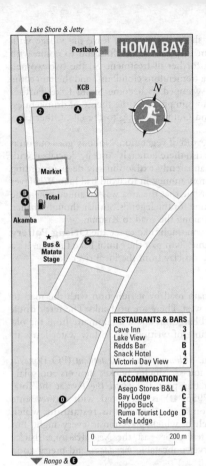

Lake Shore & Jetty

HOMA BAY

Postbank

KCB

N

Market

Total

Akamba

★ Bus & Matatu Stage

RESTAURANTS & BARS

Cave Inn	3
Lake View	1
Redds Bar	B
Snack Hotel	4
Victoria Day View	2

ACCOMMODATION

Asego Stores B&L	A
Bay Lodge	C
Hippo Buck	E
Ruma Tourist Lodge	D
Safe Lodge	B

0   200 m

Rongo & E

pot-holed streets and an unusual straw-hat-shaped **Catholic cathedral** atop a low hill behind town, with an open-air central altar and great views. However, if you're into **traditional Luo music**, Homa Bay is the place to track down tapes of *nyatiti* (lyre), *orutu* (single-stringed bow fiddle) and *onand* (accordion) music, as well as the ubiquitous gospel pop.

Homa Bay used to have a busy port, but in 1997 this, and much of the shoreline, became hemmed in by over a kilometre of **water hyacinth**. The weed infestation happened quickly, trapping some boats. Six people actually walked 4km over the weed to safety, and one woman gave birth on a trapped vessel. Ferries were suspended, and people sold off their boats. The hyacinth was eventually cleared mechanically, and fishermen keep the remainder at bay by hand, but the port is a shadow of its former self.

A **hike** up **Got Asego**, the impressive conical hill on the east side of town, is recommended. The hill is the highest of dozens of volcanic plugs (cores of old volcanoes) across the plain; from its table-sized summit, you'll have a 360-degree panorama of lake-shore and surrounding plains. It is remarkable how little of the land is not used – Luo thatched huts are interspersed with tin-roofed homesteads, a patchwork of small plots and agave hedges. Take binoculars and you can see more: clumps of papyrus drifting across the lake, and traffic along the road where it snakes east to Kendu Bay.

It takes about an hour to reach the top from the centre of town (actual ascent 30–45min), an easy climb but best tackled late in the afternoon (early morning ascents, though cooler, can be treacherous thanks to dew on the rocks). Head up the Rongo road, turn left 500m south of the Total petrol station and turn right up the *murram* road after Homa Bay School. The hill itself is best approached up the northwest ridge, where there's a well-defined footpath. Beware of columns of ants.

Practicalities

Most of the town is strung out along the main street, which starts at the jetty and runs uphill towards Rongo. On its way, it passes a turn-off for Kendu Bay (passing the Co-op Bank), a street that leads to the Kenya Commercial Bank (with ATM), and another leading to the post office, then the matatu stage, with buses parked up in front. The market is between the street with the KCB and the street with the post office.

Matatus leave Homa Bay from the stage on the main road, serving Kendu Bay, Kisii, Kisumu, Mbita and Migori. If you don't find a direct vehicle to Kisii, the best way to head eastward is by taking a Migori matatu, which drops you at Rongo on the A1 highway, where you can soon find a Kisii-bound vehicle coming up from the south. Northbound, the road to Kendu Bay looks short on the map, but matatus take a good hour to bump along its rough surface. The road is then paved from Kendu Bay to Kisumu. **Bus** companies operating to Nairobi include Linear, with no offices, and Akamba, which has an office 100m down from the matatu stage, opposite the Total petrol station (℡059/22578), and runs a day service at 7am and a night service at 7.30pm.

Accommodation

There isn't much in the way of upmarket accommodation in Homa Bay (the *Hippo Buck* the closest you'll get), but there are plenty of good budget choices.

Asego Stores B&L (Summer Bay Hotel) next to the mosque opposite KCB bank; PO Box 856; no phone. Clean but basic rooms set around a patio café-restaurant; hot water mornings only. The best room here is the large triple – worth the extra if you like a bit of space. B&B ❷
Bay Lodge above the matatu stage; PO Box 96 ℡0724/325729. Nothing fancy, and no hot water, but cheap, bright and breezy, with secure parking and friendly staff. Some rooms are s/c. ❶
Hippo Buck 2km up Rongo road; PO Box 274 ℡059/22032 or 22132. Homa Bay's top offering: functional s/c rooms including

spotless bathrooms with hot water, a nice garden and good restaurant (especially fried fish). Live *orutu* and *onand* music on Fri and Sat evenings. B&B ❸
Ruma Tourist Lodge PO Box 17040 Nairobi ℡0736/226653. Small but clean and pleasant s/c rooms set apart from a very congenial outdoor bar-restaurant in a garden, with safe parking. ❷
Safe Lodge opposite the Total station; PO Box 60 ℡0724/912315. Poky but decent non-s/c rooms behind *The Redds Bar*, but no hot water and often full come evening time. ❶

Eating and drinking

For **food**, there are lots of inexpensive *hotelis* almost everywhere. One of the best is *Snack Hotel* opposite the Total station and next to *The Redds Bar*.

Homa Bay is not especially hot on **nightlife**, but it does have a few bars worth checking out of an evening, most notably the *Cave Inn* on the main road, which has a disco playing *benga* and other local sounds, *The Redds Bar*, the *Lake View* on the same road as the KCB bank, and the *Victoria Day View* opposite, which has live bands at weekends.

Ruma National Park

Daily 6am–6pm; $15, children $5, camping $8 per person. Warden: PO Box 420 Homa Bay; phone enquiries to Homa Bay on ℡059/22544.

Ruma National Park (previously known as Lambwe Valley Nature Reserve) can be a little tricky to reach – the nearest matatu route (Homa Bay to Mbita) skirts the reserve by 11km – but if you're independently mobile and self-sufficient the effort of getting there is usually repaid by animal-watching undisturbed by the presence of other visitors; you're virtually guaranteed the place to yourself. Four-wheel drive is best for seeing the park, and in the rainy season – around April and October – essential.

The Lambwe Valley's 194 square kilometres of tsetse-fly-ridden bush is one of the few places in Kenya where you can see **Jackson's hartebeest** and two opposite extremes of antelope: the enormous, horse-like **roan** and the miniature **oribi**. There are about seventy of the beautiful **Rothschild's giraffe** and they're not hard to see above the tall grass. You'll have more difficulty spotting **leopard**.

Practicalities

To get there, head south out of Homa Bay along the main road to Rongo and turn off after 3km onto the Mbita road leading southwest. From this (signposted) turning, an eight-kilometre drive along the rough *murram* brings you to a signposted turning to the left, where another *murram* road runs for 11km to the gate and the reserve. If you're coming from Kisii or Kisumu, rather than Homa Bay, use the C18 road towards Karungu. A signposted *murram* road leads straight to the main entrance. You are likely to be greeted by surprised rangers – they get few visitors. There are two campsites in the park, but you'll need to bring your own equipment, food and water.

Work is in progress to make Ruma National Park more accessible to visitors, in order to safeguard its future, but for the present it isn't practical without your own transport. If you're dedicated, your best hope is to talk to the park warden in Homa Bay, whose office is in the District Commissioner's compound.

Thimlich Ohinga

Thimlich Ohinga (daily 8.30am–6pm; Ksh200) is an archeological site of potentially huge significance – "the greatest stone enclosures in East Africa", as the Kisumu Museum bumper stickers declare. The site is the most striking example of an architecture whose remnants are scattered across South Nyanza. Similar to the drystone enclosures of Zimbabwe (of which Great Zimbabwe is the classic example), its main structure consists of a compound about 150m in diameter, inside which are five smaller enclosures – probably used as cattle pens – and at least six house pits, the sites of former dwellings. The walls range in height from 2.5m to 3.5m – higher than those of the seventeenth- and eighteenth-century stone ruins in the Inyanga Highlands in Zimbabwe. Outside the main compound wall on the southeast side, evidence of iron-working has been discovered.

Thimlich Ohinga in Luo means "thick bush with stone enclosures". It's estimated they were built around the fifteenth century by a people whose history has been forgotten. But successive generations of various communities have used stone enclosures and, in some places, modern Luo families have their homesteads inside such walls. It's certainly an unusual and worthwhile site. In up-country Kenya it rates as the equal of Hyrax Hill (see p.258) and is quite absorbing compared to Chetambe's Fort (p.338), but if your interest in ruins is limited, pass on.

Arrival

You really need your own transport to get to Thimlich. **From Kisii** (105km) or **Homa Bay** (60km), head for Rodi Kapany on the C20 between Homa Bay and Rongo, where you take the C18 southwest, through Mirogi and Ndhiwa to Miranga. Just beyond Miranga's shops, a signpost shows the direction of Thimlich Ohinga down a rough *murram* track that can take an ordinary car when dry, but requires 4WD in the wet. After about 25km, on an area of flat land before the road begins its descent from the plateau, there's a crossroads, where a signpost formerly pointed the way east (left). Unfortunately, the signpost has now gone, as has the next one, 3km down the road, where you turn left again by the *Ohinga Hotel* (a basic café that will stretch to a tea and chapati if you're lucky) and neighbouring primary school, heading towards a small hill. A right turn after another kilometre or so will take you to the ruins. If you are very determined, and very intrepid, it is just about possible to do this **by public transport**, but there's nowhere to stay, barely anywhere to eat, and if you can't get there and back in a day, you'll need a tent and supplies. One way to do it is by matatu from Homa Bay (via Rodi Kapany and Ndhiwa) down the *murram* road to Mnhoro. There are one or two matatus on this route most days, but some days there are none, and there's precious little other traffic. Assuming the matatu driver knows which crossroads is for Thimlich Ohinga, he will drop you there to walk the remaining 4km; it's a good idea to check when he's likely to do the return run. Alternatively, negotiate a ride by *boda-boda* from Miranga, which should cost around Ksh500 for the round trip.

If you're approaching **from Migori**, take the Isebania/Tanzania road, and after 4km turn off right onto rough *murram*, at the junction for Muhoro Bay, where there is a National Cereals and Produce Board depot. A couple of kilo-metres from the depot you reach another junction where you take a right and drive straight on through Suna and Macalder. The journey is about 55km from the Cereals Board Depot. All these roads necessitate 4WD in wet weather.

Rusinga Island

Far more practical than Ruma National Park or Thimlich Ohinga is a trip to **Rusinga Island**. The narrow channel between Mbita and the island was bridged by a **causeway** in 1984, whatever your map may show, so driving around Rusinga is quite feasible, as long as the rains aren't too heavy. The road from Homa Bay is unsurfaced, tough on suspensions and often tricky in the rains. There is a steady stream of matatus (Ksh150) from Homa Bay to Mbita through-out the day, but they're often packed. From Kisumu, it's quicker to get a matatu to Luanda Katieno, from where there are ferries over to Mbita at 8am, 11am, 3pm and 6pm (matatus leave Kisumu three to four hours earlier to connect).

Mbita, straddled on either side of the causeway, is very unprepossessing indeed, but things improve once you get on to the island. The building of the causeway – partly over two dumper trucks which fell into the lake during the opera-tion and couldn't be recovered – has had some unwanted side effects. Vervet monkeys now move onto the island to raid crops, and fish have become scarce on the Kisumu side of Rusinga because the causeway blocks the current, turn-ing the water there into a stagnant pond. A bridge to replace the old chain ferry would have been the best solution to the island's access problem. As it is, the single bit of civil engineering represented by the causeway has ended Rusinga's slight isolation at what many local people feel is an unacceptable cost.

Mbita and around

Excepting one matatu which runs around Rusinga Island, **MBITA** is as far as you can go by public road transport. The last matatu returns to Homa Bay around 3pm. There are, however, some wooden **engine boats** which connect Mbita daily (until around 2pm) with various ports on Mfangano Island, Takawiri Island, and a **car ferry** to Luanda Katieno on the opposite side of Rusinga Channel, which provides road access northeast via Asembo and Ndori to Kisumu. The car ferry runs four times daily, currently leaving Mbita at 7am, 10am, 2pm and 5pm, returning an hour later. Matatus complete the run from Luanda Katieno to Kisumu.

Accommodation in the village itself is decent but basic. *Elk Lodge*, across the square from the matatu stand (PO Box 12; ☏0720/716665, ◍www.safarikenya .net/Elk.htm; ❷), has clean s/c rooms around a patio garden with flowers and pawpaw trees, but no hot water, though they may provide some in a bucket if you ask. The same landlady also runs the cheaper *Viking Rest House*, just 20m away (PO Box 12; ☎0720/716665, ⓦwww.safarikenya.net/Viking.htm; ❶), with smaller, non s/c rooms, but reasonable enough for the price. *Patroba Ogweno Lodge*, behind the *Elk* (PO Box 315; ☎0733/731638; ❷), is also very good value, especially if you get a s/c room (which costs the same as non-s/c). There's hot water on tap and the downstairs rooms are nice and cool.

Just outside the village, in the ISIPE compound (run by an NGO specializing in insect study), which is at the beginning of the Sindo road, *ISIPE Guesthouse* (PO Box 30; ☎059/22212, ⓔmgh@mbita.mimcom.net; ❶) is where politicians and diplomats stay when they happen to be in town – even the president has been known to stay here. The rooms are comfortable, with hot water, TV and a fan, but they're a bit institutional, and pricey for what you get. Compensations include a bar to buy a beer and a lakeside garden to drink it in. Three kilometres further down the road, ⚜ *Lake Victoria Safari Village* (PO Box 12; ☎0721/912120, ⓦwww.safarikenya.net; B&B ❺), run by the Norwegian husband of the *Elk's* landlady, is an excellent place to stay, with spacious s/c rooms in thatched huts overlooking a lakeside beach, and a magnificent honeymoon suite in a mock-lighthouse. Breakfast is included, but half- or full-board are available, and they'll usually charge non-resident rates for backpackers. It's also a great location for bird-watching (the former British High Commissioner helped draw up its 157-species birdlist), and the website has handy information on transport links, among other things.

If you've an afternoon to while away, there's flourishing birdlife in the vicinity, and doubtless a lot more to be uncovered by adventurous travellers. **Sindo**, 10km south of Mbita, and inside the crater of an ancient volcano – as satellite photos reveal – is reckoned a good place to go out in fishing boats, while from the top of **Gemba Hill**, just a few kilometres from the Mbita–Sindo road, there's a superb view across to Homa Bay and down towards Tanzania.

The island

RUSINGA is small and austerely pretty, high crags dominating the desolate, goat-grazed centre, and a single dirt road running around the circumference. Life here is difficult, drought commonplace, and high winds a frequent torment. The occasional heavy rain either washes away the soil or sinks into the porous rock, emerging lower down where it creates swamps. Ecologically, the island is in very dire straits: almost all its trees have been cut down for cooking fuel or to be converted into lucrative charcoal. These conditions make harvests highly unpredictable and most people fish to make ends meet, either selling the catch on to refrigerated lorries or bartering directly with traders from Kisii. The causeway has forced them to make longer fishing trips. Yet the islanders, in common with their mainland cousins, remain an unfailingly friendly and cheerful bunch, who are more than happy to make contact with wayward travellers.

The island is rich in **fossils**, and was the site of Mary Leakey's discovery of a skull of *Proconsul africanus* (a primitive anthropoid ape), which can be seen in the National Museum. It was also the birthplace of **Tom Mboya** (see Contexts, p.616), civil rights champion, trade unionist and charismatic young Luo politician who was gunned down in Nairobi in 1969, sparking off a crisis that led to over forty deaths in widespread rioting and demonstrations, and was a turning point for the worse in Kenya's post-Independence history.

Tom Mboya's mausoleum lies on family land at **Kasawanga** on the north side of the island, about 7km by the dirt road from Mbita, or roughly 5km directly across the island. There's one matatu that does the round of the island most days, and the lorries that travel round the island collecting fish from local communities for sale inland will take paying passengers in the driver's cab if they have room, but otherwise you'll need to walk the whole way there and back if necessary (allow 4hr and take some water). Local residents will no doubt show you the way, but Rusinga is so small you're unlikely to get lost. Aim for the crags in the centre (if you're feeling energetic, you could climb the tallest to get a view of the whole island), skirt them to the right and then walk down to rejoin the road on the other side of the Tom Mboya Memorial Health Centre. There's a little *hoteli* here with cold sodas. From here, it's less than 2km to Mboya's mausoleum, the conical silver roof clearly visible just off the road. The mausoleum was built in the shape of a bullet to recall the manner of his death, and contains various mementoes and gifts Mboya received during his life, plus the briefcase he was carrying when murdered. The inscription on the grave reads:

THOMAS JOSEPH MBOYA
August 15th 1930 – July 5th 1969
Go and fight like this man
Who fought for mankind's cause
Who died because he fought
Whose battles are still unwon!

You don't have to know anything about the man to be impressed. In any other surroundings his memorial might seem relatively modest, but on this barren, windswept shore, it stands out like a beacon. Members of Mboya's family live right next door, and are usually on hand to open the gates. They are happy to see foreign visitors, who rarely come here, and they maintain the mausoleum themselves, so they always appreciate donations, though these are not obligatory.

Fifty metres past the Tom Mboya Secondary School, the path to the right takes you through *shambas* of millet and corn to a seasonally grassy lakeside called Hippo Bay. Here you can watch nesting fish eagles as well as, usually, hippos. If you're lucky, you may see the pretty and little-known spotted-necked otters that live around Lake Victoria and nowhere else in Kenya.

Also on this side of the island is the amazingly expensive ($350 per person) *Rusinga Island Club* (ⓦ www.rusinga.com; reservations through Private Wilderness at PO Box 6648 Nairobi 00100; ⓣ 020/882170, ⓦ www.privatewilderness .com; all-inclusive $700; ◎), the sort of rustic-luxury retreat you would expect, with a high proportion of its clients flying in from a Maasai Mara safari to the nearby airstrip. Attractions here include sport fishing – Rusinga holds the record for the heaviest Nile perch ever landed – as well as water-skiing, windsurfing, bird-watching and guided sightseeing. There are excursions to islands inhabited only by birds, fossil walks including a short one to the cave where Mary Leakey discovered *Proconsul africanus*, and visits to see the rock paintings on Mfangano (see p.306). A lot of people fly in for a day-trip from Maasai Mara (bookable there through any lodge), which offers a chance to spot wildlife from the air, but it's possible (and a joy) to stay overnight – the club sleeps ten in thatched cottages. Boat excursions (watch the fish eagles for how to catch tilapia in style), activities, meals and drinks are all included in the price.

Mfangano Island

Said to have been inhabited for centuries, enigmatic **Mfangano Island** is out of range of the smallest fishing boats, and entirely without vehicles. The island is

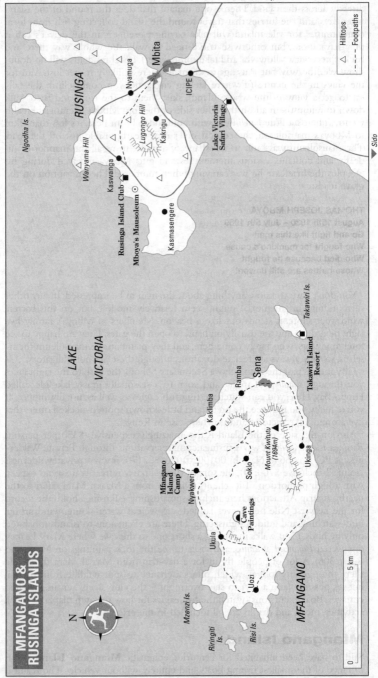

MFANGANO &
RUSINGA ISLANDS

LAKE
VICTORIA

RUSINGA

Ngodha Is.

Wanyama Hill

Kaswanga

Nyamuga

Mbita

ICIPE

Lugongo Hill

Kakrigu

Lake Victoria
Safari Village

Rusinga Island Club

Mboya's Mausoleum

Kasmasengere

Sido

Takawiri Is.

Sena

Ramba

Takawiri Island Resort

Kaklimba

Mfangano Island Camp

Sokio

Nyakweri

Mount Kwitutu
(1694m)

Ukinga

Cave
Paintings

Ukula

MFANGANO

Uozi

Mzenzi Is.

Riringiti
Is.

Risi Is.

N

△ Hilltops
--- Footpaths

0   5 km

4

populated by a curious mixture of immigrants from all over Kenya, administered by a chief and three sub-chiefs with help from a trio of policemen. Monitor lizards swarm on the sandy shores and **hippos** are much in evidence out in the water.

Larger and more populous than Rusinga, with a similarly rugged landscape but better vegetation cover, Mfangano's greatest economic resource is still the lake itself. Local **fishing techniques** are unusual: the islanders fish with floating kerosene lamps hauled shorewards, or towards a boat, to draw in the schools to be netted. Of more immediate interest, however, are the island's **rock paintings**, certainly worth the trip if you're into such things, and a good excuse to get to know the island in any case. The rock paintings are thought to be at least a thousand and maybe as much as 4000 years old, and were painted by the island's original inhabitants, Batwa Pygmies, like those who live today in parts of Rwanda and the Congo. They were displaced around the sixteenth century by Luo incomers, who were themselves displaced a couple of centuries ago by a Bantu people called the Abasuba. Local residents rely on a network of temporary **footpaths** which are constantly changing course. If you arrive at Sena by boat, you can walk all over the island, though it's always easier if you have a guide – Ksh500 per day is considered a fair fee.

Practicalities

Unless you're rich enough to fly in, the only means of access to the island is on the large wooden boats with outboard motors ("matatu boats") which run a service shuttling local people and their produce between Mbita and the surrounding islands and peninsulas. Most stop at Takawiri then head around Mfangano in an anti-clockwise direction, calling at Sena, Nyakweri and Ukula, though others go around clockwise. The first boat leaves Mbita around 8.30am (the last around 3pm), with the last boat back from Sena at around 2.30pm, so a day-trip isn't really a practical proposition unless you have enough money (around Ksh2500) to hire a boat plus skipper for the day.

It's a ninety-minute crossing to **SENA** – the chief's camp and also the capital of Mfangano. Sena has a couple of small *dukas* and *hotelis* and a post office, and is home to the **Abusuba Community Peace Museum** (Mon–Sat 9am–5pm; Ksh200), which displays cultural artefacts such as traditional cooking pots and farming implements, but is most of interest because it allows camping in its grounds, either in tents, its or yours (Ksh300 per person), or in traditional Abasuba huts (Ksh500 per person), with drinking and washing water, but no showers. More importantly, the museum can organize guided excursions to the island's main sights, and can even arrange transport from Mbita. For further information, contact the museum's director, Jack Obonyo, on ℡0723/898406. The museum can also organize food if you don't want to eat at Sena's *hotelis*. There is no other accommodation as such in Sena, though local people may be prepared to put you up at B&L-type rates. Don't forget in such cases that Mfangano is desperately poor, without mains electricity or piped water, and you should bring anything you think you might need.

The alternative accommodation-wise, if you have money to burn, is the exclusive and expensive **Mfangano Island Camp**, a fishing lodge similar to Rusinga's (see p.303). Most of the camp's visitors fly in from the Maasai Mara on a day-trip (fishing and bird-watching in the morning, lunching and lounging in the afternoon), but some stay on to enjoy the beautiful setting, gourmet food and punctilious service. The price includes all meals, and a boat with driver at your disposal. The camp, a huddle of clay-and-thatch buildings laid out in the shape of a Luo homestead, but fitted out in deluxe style, overlooks a private bay and sleeps twelve (reservations through Governor's Camps, p.63; FB $500, plus around $810 for a return flight from Maasai Mara for up to four people). There's a similar, though less expensive place on **Takawiri Island**, off Mfangano: the *Takawiri Island Resort*, which offers windsurfing, snorkelling and sailing, as well as fishing and bird-watching. Like *Mfangano Island Camp*, it faces west, for unforgettable sunsets, and you can get there on a matatu-boat from Mbita, or else by light aircraft or on the resort's own cruiser from Kisumu. However, it was closed and up for sale on our last check, and it is not certain when it will again be back in operation.

The rock paintings

The Peace Museum can arrange trips to three sites featuring prehistoric **rock paintings** in the form of reddish spirals and whorls, some with rays, up to 50cm across, that could come from any Von Daniken paperback. The main sites (at Kwitone and Mawanga) are close to Ukula on the north coast. You pay a Ksh500 guiding fee to be taken to them from Sena, and a Ksh200 entry fee at each site. The paintings were probably used for rainmaking ceremonies, and all kinds of rituals and taboos are still supposed to apply to people visiting them – a period of sexual abstinence, for example, and not telling anybody that you are coming to the site before you actually do so.

If you're still really into rock art, the Odengere Hills, also on Mfangano, are unique among Lake Victoria's prehistoric sites in that they have depictions of insects, some of them so fine that even the species can be identified. Experts are at a loss as to their significance. Site-by-site descriptions of Lake Victoria's rock art can be found in the 1994 (vol.9) issue of the academic journal *Azania* (copies at the British Institute in Nairobi; see "Libraries" p.155). The Peace Museum also publishes a pamphlet explaining local rock art.

Migori

MIGORI is a border town spread out along 4km of the A1 highway. Market days are interesting for the variety of peoples and for traditional activities untainted by tourism. The Maasai here are less calculating and aloof than many of those further to the east whose lives have been invaded by cameras and minibuses, but you're still likely to be the object of some curiosity. There are two good places to **stay**, but water supplies are sporadic, and even cold water may not be available on tap. Turn eastward just north of the bridge for *Gilly Hotel* (PO Box 831 Suna-Migori; ☎059/20523, ☏20556; B&B ❷). Ignore the bland concrete exterior, as the welcome is warm, and rooms are very reasonable s/c with nets, the better ones with distant views of the river, and with good breakfasts, but try to get a room with an outside window, and don't believe tales of 24-hour hot water. *Girango Hotel*, at the south end of town (PO Box 1019 Suna-Migori; ☎059/20014; B&B ❹), is friendly, quiet and peaceful, with rooms in a number of outhouses scattered in pleasant gardens (guarded parking). There's a choice of different rooms, and the better ones are definitely worth the extra hundred bob they cost. Hot water is provided in buckets, and there are tubs rather than showers. There's a popular bar, and a licence for weekend discos has been applied for. If you need something cheaper, there are a few B&Ls around the matatu stand and north of the bridge. For **food**, the *Exile Chis Palace* is the best of the *hotelis* just north of the post office, serving good, wholesome Kenyan staples.

If you've just arrived **from Tanzania**, there are **buses to Nairobi and Mombasa** leaving between 6 and 8am, or in the evening, going via Kisii, Kericho and Nakuru. There are also morning buses to Eldoret, and matatus to Kisumu, Kisii and Homa Bay. Heading down **to Tanzania**, there are direct buses to Mwanza mornings and evenings, but otherwise you'll have to take a matatu to the border post at Isebania (also called Sirare, and served by direct matatus from Kisumu), or at Kianja, cross on foot and take an onward vehicle from the other side. The road east to **Maasai Mara** (p.396) is in a pretty dreadful state, and should only be attempted by 4WD and in dry conditions.

The Western Highlands

The Western Highlands rise all around Lake Victoria in a great bowl. There's superb walking country throughout, in the **Nandi Hills**, for example, or in the little-known **Mau Massif**, east of Kericho. But the undoubted highlights are **Saiwa Swamp National Park** and the **Kakamega Forest**, recently accorded national park status of its own. For serious, sensibly equipped hikers, **Mount Elgon** must also be a major temptation, sharing much of Mount Kenya's flora and fauna, but none of its popularity. Also wonderful walking country are the high hills of the **Cheranganis**, though, like Elgon, they take some getting to. The highland towns are, on the whole, not arresting. **Kisii** is lively and perhaps worth a visit, but **Kericho** ("tea capital of Kenya"), **Eldoret** and **Kitale** are best thought of simply as bases for getting to the real attractions.

Kisii and around

Headquarters of the **Gusii** (or Kisii or Kosova) people, and district town of a region vying with Nyeri in having the fastest-growing population in the country, **KISII** is a bustling, rubbish-strewn trading centre in the hills, prosperous and hard-working with a muddy main street (officially called Moi Highway) which has pretty much turned into a giant bus and matatu stage. The surrounding region, lavishly fertile, gets rain all year, in remarkable contrast to the semiarid lowlands of the lakeshore just a few kilometres away. One thing you may notice is the occasional **earth tremor** – Kisii lies on a fault line and minor earthquakes are not uncommon, only a slight worry if you're asleep at the top of *Sakawa Towers* hotel at the time. Wildlife enthusiasts will want to check out the tree full of **giant bats** in the government compound between Moi Highway and Kisii Sports Club at the southern end of town. **Getting around** is on foot or by taxi, as Kisii is too hilly for *boda-bodas*.

Kisii is also famous for its fine **soapstone**. Surprisingly, there's little of this to be seen in the town itself, though *Kwanji's Café* has some for sale. The best locality for watching the carvers and making on-the-spot purchases is Tabaka, some way south (see p.311). In Kisii itself, a large open-air **market** spreads itself along the main road north of the *Kisii Hotel* on Mondays and Thursdays.

Accommodation

You'll find plenty of **places to stay**, although a lot of them are pretty awful, and most are noisy, especially on Wednesdays and weekends when bars and discos (their own or some nearby) are at their loudest, and women travelling alone will want to avoid most of the cheaper places (the *Whitestone* is a possible exception). You should be prepared for power fluctuations during heavy rain – have some candles handy – and water supplies are uniformly erratic. It's worth staying the night, though, as, once you've settled in, there are several rewarding local **excursions**, and the town itself buzzes day and night with a slightly hassly energy.

Highway Lodge Moi Highway; PO Box 910 ☎0722/555574. Pretty basic, but dirt cheap and not outrageously filthy, with quite large non-s/c rooms and hot water. ❶

Kisii Hotel PO Box 26 ☎058/30134 or 30254. On the road out to Kisumu, this ramshackle but quiet place has an agreeable creaking colonial atmosphere, large s/c rooms, and hot water round the clock, and there's guarded parking and a huge and beautiful bird-filled garden, great for relaxing in with a cold beer, though the food in the restaurant isn't great. B&B ❷

Kisii Sports Club PO Box 103 ☎058/30169. You have to take out temporary membership to stay here, but rates are very reasonable (Ksh2000 for a month), and as well as the rooms, which are spacious if a little worn round the edges, you can use the pool, bar and other facilities (see p.310). All in all, this beats the other mid-range options in town. ❸

Metro Highway Hotel Moi Highway; PO Box 1295 ☎0735/717234. Reasonable s/c rooms above a rowdy bar, a step up from the *Highway Lodge* next door. ❷

Mwalimu Hotel PO Box 1335 ☎058/30357. This 1979 concrete block at the southern end of town was once a teachers' hostel and is still run by the teachers' union, with parking facilities and a bar. The rooms are comfortable and carpeted, all s/c with nets and hot water, and some with nice views, but they do rather feel like offices that have been converted into bedrooms. ❷

Sakawa Towers Hospital Rd; PO Box 81 ☎058/30477. Named after a Gusii medicine man and prophet, this six-storey block, with great town views from the roof and upper floors, has been taken over by new management who are gradually getting it in order. All the rooms are s/c with nets and balconies, but some are small and cramped, so be choosy. The

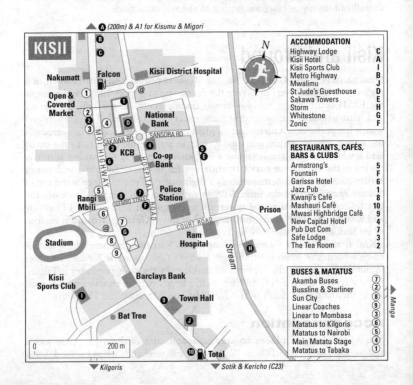

A (200m) & A1 for Kisumu & Migori

KISII

N

ACCOMMODATION

Highway Lodge	C
Kisii Hotel	A
Kisii Sports Club	I
Metro Highway	B
Mwalimu	J
St Jude's Guesthouse	D
Sakawa Towers	E
Storm	H
Whitestone	G
Zonic	F

RESTAURANTS, CAFÉS, BARS & CLUBS

Armstrong's	5
Fountain	F
Garissa Hotel	6
Jazz Pub	1
Kwanji's Café	8
Mashauri Café	10
Mwasi Highbridge Café	9
New Capital Hotel	4
Pub Dot Com	7
Safe Lodge	3
The Tea Room	2

BUSES & MATATUS

Akamba Buses	7
Bussline & Starliner	2
Sun City	8
Linear Coaches	9
Linear to Mombasa	3
Matatus to Kilgoris	6
Matatus to Nairobi	5
Main Matatu Stage	4
Matatus to Tabaka	1

Nakumatt — Falcon — Kisii District Hospital — Open & Covered Market — National Bank — SAKAWA RD — SANSORA RD — KCB — Co-op Bank — Rangi Mbili — OGEMBO STREET — Police Station — Prison — COURT ROAD — Ram Hospital — Stream — Stadium — Kisii Sports Club — Barclays Bank — Town Hall — Bat Tree — Total — MOI HIGHWAY — HOSPITAL ROAD

0 — 200 m

▼ Kilgoris

▼ Sotik & Kericho (C23)

► Manga

Some Gusii history

The Bantu-speaking **Gusii** (after whom the town is named) were only awakened to the brutal realities of British conquest in 1905, when they rebelled – pitching themselves with spears against a machine gun. It was "not so much a battle as a massacre", one of the participants recalled, leaving "several hundred dead and wounded spearsmen heaped up outside the square of bayonets". In 1908, after the District Commissioner was speared in a personal attack, the same thing happened again, only this time the Gusii were trying to escape, not attacking. Crops were burned and whole villages razed to the ground. Churchill telegraphed from the Colonial Office: "Surely it cannot be necessary to go on killing these defenceless people on such an enormous scale."

The Gusii were totally demoralized. In a few brief years, the fabric of their communities had been torn apart, hut taxes imposed, and cattle confiscated to be returned only in exchange for labour. And then came World War I. Kisii was the site of the first Anglo-German engagements in East Africa, and thousands of men were recruited into the hated Carrier Corps by trickery or press gang.

It seems extraordinary that the exceptionally friendly people of Kisii are the grandchildren of the conscripts. The powerful, millennial religious movements which burst among them during the colonial period under the name **Mumboism** may partly account for the very strong ties of community they've maintained against all odds. Prophets and medicine men have always been important here, and even in today's superficially Christianized society, the Gusii have solidly kept their cultural identity. **Witchcraft** and **sorcery** still play important roles in the life of the town and its district. The practice of **trepanning**, for example, which involves tapping a small hole in the skull to relieve headache or mental illness, seems to be as old as the Gusii themselves. It has received the ironic laureate of medical journal credibility and the attentions of a German film crew. "Brain operations" are still performed, clandestinely, but apparently quite successfully. However, the rising influence of Christianity, as well as occasional abuses of power by witches, has led to spates of **lynchings** of suspected witches and sorcerers (the last in September 1998, when ten people were killed). Residents were reticent to divulge the names of the lynchers to the authorities, which prompted the local police chief to say: "We hope we can get them [the witches] and if possible charge them in court. This way we shall save their lives."

---

one suite comes complete with a bathtub and a huge animal-skin drum doubling as a table. Hot water still comes in buckets, but the management are hoping to sort that. The restaurant isn't bad either. B&B ❷

St Jude's Guesthouse PO Box 2653 ☏ 058/21189. Spacious, fresh s/c rooms with hot water and mostly with balconies. Rooms 11–19 have good views over the countryside, but it's worth paying a little bit extra for room 10, which has a large balcony with a quite magnificent view. B&B ❶/❷

Storm Hotel Court Rd; PO Box 973 ☏ 058/30649. The quietest hotel in Kisii offers a choice of adequate rooms, all s/c with nets, plus some more expensive suites, and an outside bar and *nyama choma* joint. Coming here at night, it's best to take a taxi (Ksh100)

as there have been robberies on the approach road (which passes the police station). B&B ❸

Whitestone Hotel Moi Highway; PO Box 401 ☏ 058/300014. Excellent-value cheapie, secure and clean with s/c doubles downstairs, and s/c or non-s/c singles upstairs, hot water, a cramped little bar called the *Macho Pub*, that lives up to its name, and a good cheap restaurant. ❶

Zonic Hotel PO Box 541 ☏ 058/30298. The top hotel in town, five storeys high with balconies for most rooms, and a restaurant, a rather quiet bar, and a rooftop pool and terrace with a café and great views. On the minus side, there are no mosquito nets or parking, and the single rooms are a bit poky, though the doubles are fine. ❸

Eating and drinking

Despite the noxious drain smells, the overflowing **market** is the first base for hungry travellers. The lodgings mostly have **dining rooms** or **restaurants** of their own, of which the *Fountain*, belonging to and underneath the *Zonic* hotel, is the best, offering the usual tilapia and *nyama choma* as well as more exotic delights such as "tamu tamu veggie" (honey-grilled vegetables in garlic sauce) or Malaysian lamb (cooked in coconut cream). *Sakawa Towers* has a few Indian dishes, including three sorts of chicken curry. The *Whitestone*'s restaurant is also recommended, especially for stewed fish. Reliable places for a shot of cholesterol include *The Tea Room* on Moi Highway, which, true to its name, does a gorgeous cup of Indian-style *chai*. *Garissa Hotel*, just up the street, is tawdry and grubby, but open 24/7. Slightly better are *Kwanji's Café*, with a pleasant atmosphere and wooden tables, and two places at the southern end of town, the *Mwasi Highbridge Café* and *Mashauri Café*, all offering the usual choice of stewed or fried meat with *ugali*, chips or rice, but in bright, clean surroundings.

Kisii has some excellent **drinking** holes. The happening bar these days is the *Jazz Pub* on Hospital Road, a relaxed venue open till midnight, with waiter service to the tables and an eclectic mix of sounds, despite the name; Wednesdays are dedicated to African music. *Armstrong's*, on the ground floor of the same building as *St Jude's Guesthouse*, is a long bar also with a congenial atmosphere, plus several screens of sport (usually English Premiership football), and good music, but it closes at 10pm. If you don't want football, music or crowds, try the bar at the *Zonic*: it's very quiet – some would call it dead – but you might just find that's what you need. For somewhere less refined (and women probably won't want to brave these places on their own), try the *New Capital Hotel* at the corner of Hospital Road and Sansora Road, a lively upstairs bar overlooking the street. *Pub Dot Com*, opposite the *Zonic*, is a small and sweaty drinking den with good but loud music. Finally, with its own very rough and ready charm, the *Safe Lodge* on Sakawa Road has three pool tables (called Arsenal, Chelsea and Manchester United), plays reggae music, and is open round the clock.

Listings

Banks Barclays and the National Bank have ATMs. Don't go near the KCB – they charge outrageous commission.

Football Kisii stadium is the home ground of Shabana FC, in Kenya's First Division.

Garage Rangi Mbili ☎ 058/30204. A very helpful parts store/workshop if your car is in trouble. Helpful anyway, for that matter – they're eager to meet travellers.

Hospital The main one is Kisii District Hospital, Hospital Rd (☎ 058/20471); a private option (and not expensive – Ksh200 to see a doctor) is Ram Hospital, Court Rd (☎ 058/30236).

Internet access Cyber, opposite the hospital, Pemo on Hospital Rd, and Sciencenet near the stadium all close early (6 or 6.30pm) and all day Sat, but are open on Sun.

Kisii Show Held annually in July.

Police On the road to the *Storm Hotel* ☎ 058/30023.

Post office Mon–Fri 8am–5pm, Sat 9am–noon. The entrance is round the side and the counters upstairs. Phones outside.

Sports club The friendly Kisii Sports Club, PO Box 103 (☎ 058/30169), has a swimming pool, golf, squash, darts, bingo and a bar, with temporary membership required (Ksh2000 for a month).

Moving on

Kisii is something of a route focus, with both regional and national bus and matatu services passing through. There are plenty of **matatus** leaving throughout the day. Most leave from the main stage in front of the market. The exceptions are matatus for Nyachenge and Tabaka, which leave from opposite the Falcon station at the north end of town; and for Kericho and Kilgoris, which go from the bus park beside Rangi Mbili. There are also useful early-morning departures for Narok via the B3, passing the junctions for the C12 and C13

Maasai Mara access roads. **Bus services** are also numerous: Akamba, with its office by the *Whitestone Hotel* (☎058/30137) for Nairobi (9am & 9pm), Homa Bay (4pm), and Mwanza in Tanzania (3am); Linear Coach (☎0381/31322), with an office opposite Akamba for Nairobi (hourly all day until midnight, then two-hourly till 6am), and one a day to Mombasa. All Nairobi buses call at Nakuru and Naivasha. Locations of the bus company ticket offices and matatu stages are marked on our map.

If you have your own wheels and are headed along the minor but increasingly popular route to **Maasai Mara** via Kilgoris and Lolgorien, note that beyond **Kilgoris**, the road to the Mara is difficult, even with 4WD, and the section down the Oloololo Escarpment can be impossible after rain. Heading for the east end of the reserve, the fastest route is via Sotik and the new road to Bomet and Amala River (see p.397).

Tanzania is accessible by services to the **border crossing**, variously known as Isebania or Nyabikaye on the Kenyan side, and Serira, Sirare or Siria on the Tanzanian, as well as by a daily Akamba bus service to Mwanza (on Lake Victoria).

Lastly, if you fancy **cycling**, you can buy an Indian-made bicycle at the supermarkets in Kisii for as little as Ksh3000.

Tabaka

TABAKA is one of the most important centres in the world for **soapstone** (steatite) production. Most of the carvings are bought up by buyers from the curio shops in Nairobi and elsewhere, but shops selling the carvings now line the road through the town, and they are happy to sell direct to visitors.

The turn-off for Tabaka is at **Nyachenge**, 18km west of Kisii on the A1 Migori road. A sign to the left, if coming from Kisii, points to the St Amillus Tabaka Mission Hospital and Kisii Soapstone Carvers Co-operative Society. From here it's 5km into the village (6km to the Co-operative Society) on a rough dirt road that's treacherous (and requires 4WD) in wet weather, though an ordinary car can traverse it if dry. Coming by matatu from Kisii, it's best to get one that goes direct, even if this means waiting. The alternative is hanging around just as long at the halfway point, or a long walk from Nyachenge. The last matatus from Tabaka back to Kisii leave around 5 or 6pm.

The soapstone quarries and carvers

Beyond Tabaka are the four **quarries**, with two main ones, the first on the left, and the other further down on the right. There must, however, be vast reserves of stone under the ground all over the district, which provides a large proportion of the world supply of soapstone. It emerges in a variety of colours and densities: white is easiest to work, shades of orange and pink harder, and rosy-red the hardest and heaviest. A number of families have become full-time carvers, but for most people it's simply a spare-time occupation after agriculture, a way of making a few shillings. You'll even see children walking home from school carving little animals from chips of stone. The professional carvers often specialize in a variety of designs from chess sets and traditional animals, to vases, cups and, more recently, human figures. The stone is dampened to bring up the colour and make it easier to work, then waxed to retain the lustre.

Manga Ridge

This dramatic escarpment **cliff** is two or three hours' walk north of Kisii, wonderful in the early morning – or the late afternoon, as long as you can arrange a ride back again.

Leaving Kisii on the Kericho road, turn left into Manga Road at the bottom of the hill, 500m after Barclays, and follow the road as it sweeps you towards and then alongside the ridge. After about 5km you can cut down one of the tracks across the lush valley to your left and continue straight up the escarpment (several hundred metres high). Beware of snakes lurking among the rocks and grass on the upward scramble. Alternatively, you can continue along the road for a further 5km to come up behind the ridge; from here it's a ten-minute hike up to the edge, where a path follows the cliff for a kilometre or two. Magnificent views out over Kisii and down to Lake Victoria are your reward. It's possible to get matatus to Manga from Kisii (in front of *St Jude's Guesthouse*), but make it clear you want to get off at the ridge.

Kericho and the tea country

KERICHO, named after the early English tea planter John Kerich, is Kenya's **tea capital**, a fact that – with much hype from the tourism machine embellished by the presence of the *Tea Hotel* – is not likely to escape you. Its equable climate and famously reliable, year-round afternoon rain showers make it the most important tea-growing area in Africa. While many of the European estates have been divided and reallocated to small farmers since independence, the area is still dominated by giant tea plantations. Compact Kericho itself seems as neat as the serried rows of bushes that surround it. The central square has shady trees and flowering bushes – a bandstand would make it complete – and even the matatu park has lawns around it. It's a gentle, hassle-free place to wander, the people mild-mannered. Clipped, clean and functional, there's little of the shambolic appearance of most upcountry towns. And, in many ways, it's an oddity. With so many people earning some sort of salary on the tea plantations or in connection with them, and so

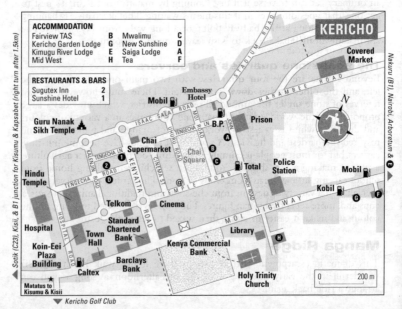

△ Harvesting tea

few acres under food or market crops, the patterns of small-town life are changed here. Most workers live out on the estates, their families often left behind in the home villages. Kericho is above all an administrative and shopping centre, and a relay point for the needs of the estates. The produce market is small and trading limited. Everything seems to close at 5pm.

In town, there's a substantial Asian population. Many of the streets have a strikingly oriental feel – single-storey *dukas* fronted by colonnaded walkways where the plantation "memsahibs" of forty or fifty years ago presumably did their shopping. This curious, composite picture is completed by the grey stone **Holy Trinity Church**, with its small assembly of deceased planters in a miniature cemetery. Straight out of the English shires and entwined with creepers, it tries so hard to be Norman that it's a pity to point out that it was only built in 1952.

Accommodation

Kericho has a decent number of **places to stay** and you should find something to suit, though prices seem high in comparison with hotels of similar standards elsewhere in the country. A couple of the best options are out along the Nairobi road, Moi Highway. You can **camp** at the *Tea Hotel* and *Kericho Garden Lodge* (both Ksh300 per person).

Fairview TAS Hotel Moi Rd; PO Box 1260 ☏052/21507. The entrance is down the side of a busy and characterful *hoteli*-cum-bar. The rooms (s/c with hot water) are a bit grubby, but adequate if you aren't too fussy. ❶

Kericho Garden Lodge Moi Highway; PO Box 2026 ☏052/32021. The non-s/c singles are rather poky, but the newer s/c singles and doubles are quite acceptable and clean with hot water mornings and evenings, and some look out over the pleasant gardens, where you can camp (Ksh300 per person, same as the non-s/c singles – the *Tea Hotel* is better value). The beer garden is pleasant, but the food isn't great, and women may find the atmosphere in the restaurant/bar/TV room off-putting. ❷

Kimugu River Lodge off Moi Highway; PO Box 25 ☏0733/504942, ✉ kimuguriverlodge@yahoo.com.

Take the signposted turning opposite the BP station, 700m northeast of the town centre, and follow this track for 600m to this rather downmarket alpine-chalet-like place, with a great location above a weir in the Kimugu River. The rooms are simple but very comfortable with hot water, but the concrete cottages (some with fireplaces) are somewhat better than the newer wooden shacks. There's also a decent bar and good restaurant. B&B ❸

Mid West Hotel PO Box 1175 ☏052/30196, ✉ midwesthotelkenya@yahoo.com. A large, soulless place and popular conference venue. Nothing special to recommend it, but usually a safe bet if you want a proper hotel room. There's a health club with a gym, sauna and steam room (all Ksh150 per day), and a dartboard in the bar. B&B ❹

Mwalimu Hotel Moi Rd; PO Box 834 ☎052/30656. Adequate and relatively large s/c rooms, kept separate from its bar-restaurant. On the downside, there's hot water in the morning only, and no mosquito nets, and the price is high for what you get. **②**

New Sunshine Hotel Tengecha Rd; PO Box 1910 ☎052/30037. Spotless rooms, with hot water round the clock, but the cheaper ones are rudimentary, with inward-facing windows only, though the pricier rooms, with TV, are bigger and brighter. **②**

Saiga Lodge John Kerich Rd; PO Box 1159 ☎0733/377416. A surprisingly large establishment hidden away behind the shops, with a selection of very cheap s/c and non-s/c rooms, hot water, and parking in the yard. Most of the rooms have inward-facing windows, so they're a bit dark, but not at all bad value for the price. **①**

Tea Hotel Moi Highway; PO Box 75 ☎052/30004–5, ✉teahotel@africaonline.co.ke (reservations made through Msafiri, p.63). The best hotel in town, built in 1952 for the tea corporation Brooke Bond, it fell on hard times with the collapse of subsequent owners Africa Tours and Hotels, and has been in slow decline ever since, though it retains a faded charm. The rooms are large and comfortable, and the cottages, which cost the same, are even more spacious, but they are all somewhat overpriced. The gardens are beautiful and well kept, and you can still walk through them to the tea fields beyond. You can also camp (Ksh300 per person) and use the pool and attached washing facilities. B&B **⑦**

Eating

Kericho has its fair share of cheap and fairly ungastronomic *hotelis*, heavy on the chips and *ugali*. The busiest of the *hotelis* is the *Fairview TAS Hotel*, packed at lunchtimes with workers, but the best is the *Sunshine Hotel* on Kenyatta Road – the *pilau*, for example, is massive. Of the upmarket hotels, the *Mid Western* offers better eating than the *Tea Hotel*, but the best food in town (and not expensive) is at the ✴ *Kimugu River Lodge*, which has an extensive menu of mainly Indian food, including chicken *methi*, *malai kofta* and, when they have it, a wonderful crayfish *masala*.

Those in need of a **bar** might try the *Sugutex Inn* on Tengecha Road, a typical rowdy tavern, mainly for men. The *Kericho Garden Lodge* has a good bar and beer garden, and the bar at the *Kimugu River Lodge* is quiet and civilized. For a nice cup of **tea**, you can't beat the terrace of the *Tea Hotel*, overlooking the gardens and tea fields – worth sixty bob of anybody's money.

Listings

Banks Barclays, Standard Chartered and the KCB, all with ATMs, are on Moi Highway at the Kisumu end of town.

Car repair There are a few places at the western end of Isaac Salat Rd, near the Sikh temple.

Golf The Kericho Club (PO Box 82 Kericho ☎052/20086) has a nine-hole course.

Hospital Kericho District Hospital, Hospital Rd (☎052/31192), isn't very clean; Central Hospital, on the Unilever tea estate, 1km past the *Tea Hotel* (☎052/30028 or 31381), is much better.

Internet access Try Chemtech, Temple Rd, on the corner of Uhuru Rd, Cyber Haven on Temple Rd opposite Telecom, and Twins next to the post office.

Library By the *Mid West Hotel*. Not bad at all, though it goes for quantity rather than diversity, with about ten copies of each title. Open Mon–Thurs 8am–6.30pm, Fri 8am–4pm, Sat 8.30am–5pm.

Market Much better at weekends than weekdays, when there's a variety of fruit and vegetables, snacks and spices, at lower-than-expected prices.

Post office Mon–Fri 8am–5pm, Sat 9am–noon.

Swimming pool Clean but chilly, at the *Tea Hotel* (Ksh100).

Taxis A bit of a problem in Kericho: there are very few apart from matatus, and no *boda-bodas*. After dark it's hard to get out much if you don't have your own vehicle or aren't prepared to walk.

Around Kericho

The area around Kericho is **tea country**. Kenya is the world's third largest producer after India and Sri Lanka, and the biggest exporter to Britain. As you gaze across the dark green hills, you might pause to consider that the land, which you now see covered in vast regimented swathes of tea bush, was only, a century ago virgin rainforest, only a tiny part of which – Kakamega Forest (p.342) – still survives. The estates were first set up after World War I with tea bushes imported from India and China. Big business as it is – and despite the relative prosperity of Kericho – you can't help feeling that the local population would be better served if this fertile land were given over instead to intensive cultivation of food.

It is possible to **visit the tea estates** on a guided tour from the *Tea Hotel* (see opposite). The factories operate every day except Monday, the day after the pickers' day off. If you want to visit a tea factory and see the whole process, you can book a tour (usually about 2hr) for two or more people, two weeks in advance (maybe one week at a pinch), costing Ksh200 per person plus Ksh500 for transport per group, unless you have your own. If you are alone, or if you cannot give the required notice, you may be able to tag along with a group that has already booked. Alternatively, you can just take a tour of the tea fields combined with a nature walk (Ksh200 per person). The hotel's guide, Watson Byegon, can also be hired for **bird-watching** tours in the immediate vicinity, or at the Chagaik Dam

Tea

Tea (*Camellia sinensis*) is a psychoactive shrub originally native to China. Its effects are said to have been discovered by legendary third millennium BC Chinese emperor Shen Nung, who was apparently taking a cup of hot water in the shade of a shrub when one of the buds fell into it, making him an invigorating drink. For centuries the Chinese had a monopoly on tea, but with its rise in popularity at home, the British were keen for an independent source of supply, and eventually managed to smuggle some cuttings to India. The first tea was grown in Kenya in 1903, though it was nearly twenty years before commercial production got under way here. Kenyan teas are known for their strength and full flavour, and are a major component of most commercial blends sold in the UK and Ireland. Kenya's other main customers are Egypt, Pakistan and Afghanistan.

Tea production, though not complicated, is very labour-intensive. Picking continues throughout the year, and you'll see the pickers moving through the bushes in their brilliant yellow-and-green (KETEPA) plastic smocks, nipping off the top two leaves and bud of each bush (nothing more is taken) and tossing them into baskets. Working fast, a picker can collect up to seventy kilos in a day, though half that is a more typical figure; the piece-rate is set at less than three shillings per kilo picked. After withering, mashing, a couple of hours' fermentation and a final drying in hot air, the tea leaves are ready for packing and export. The whole process can take as little as 24 hours.

Tea can be harvested three years after planting, and in the first year of production it must be picked every eight days, then every fourteen days in the second year and every seventeen in the fourth, after which the bush must be pruned to keep it at the right height for picking, which can begin again after three months. Weeding is not necessary as the foliage is sufficiently dense to prevent other plants from growing under it.

The stimulating **effects** of tea are due to the presence of caffeine, and a cup of strong tea can contain as much caffeine as a cup of medium-strength coffee. The effect feels different because it is moderated by other alkaloids such as thebaine, which is a relaxant. Because the human body requires fluid to process caffeine and thebaine, tea depletes the body of water, even though it appears to quench a thirst. Like beer, therefore, strong tea should not be taken as a fluid against dehydration.

and Arboretum (see below), and excursions to **Lelartet Cliff**, which is home to a large number of red, and black and white colobus monkeys.

Kimugu Valley and Chagaik Dam

Down in the **Kimugu Valley**, behind the *Tea Hotel* and *Kimugu River Lodge*, you can get some idea of what the land was like before the settlers arrived. The valley is a deep, tangled channel of sprawling trees and undergrowth, with shafts of sunlight picking out clouds of butterflies. The cold brown waters of the Kimugu flow down from Chagaik Dam and allegedly harbour **trout**.

To get to **Chagaik Dam** and the graceful **arboretum** nearby, you'll need a lift in the Nairobi direction, past the KETEPA buildings to the turn marked "Chagaik", about 8km east of town. From there, turn right, then immediately left; it's a five-minute walk to the arboretum – "Founded by Tom Grumbley, Tea Planter 1946–75". Acres of beautiful trees from all over the tropical and subtropical world lead steeply down through well-tended lawns to a lily-covered lake. There are magnificent stands of bamboo on the banks. Entry to this haven of landscaped tranquility is unrestricted and you can picnic or rest up as long as you like, though there are gardeners around who won't let you camp.

Across the lake, thick **jungle** drops to the water's edge. Mysterious splashes and rustles, prolific bird and insect life, and at least one troop of colobus monkeys are a surprising testament to the tenacity of wildlife in an environment hemmed in on all sides by the alien ranks of the tea bushes.

Moving on

Kericho has hassle-free travel options in every direction: **southwest** to Kisii and Migori (near the Tanzanian border), **east** over the Mau Escarpment to Nakuru (route covered in Chapter 3, pp.259–260), or **northwest** to Kisumu on Lake Victoria and Kapsabet in the Nandi Hills. Heading **south to Maasai Mara** is more problematic, though the first part of the route, from Litein (30km or so from Kericho) to Bomet, follows a good road through splendid farming country (see p.397). If you're going **east**, Nairobi and Nakuru buses generally originate in Kisii and pass through Kericho throughout the day (and night); you should have time for a leisurely morning.

Matatus leave for most destinations from the BP station, but for Kisumu, Migori and Kisii you'll find more departures on Moi Highway, opposite the Caltex garage, which is also the place to catch westbound **buses**. Kenya Bus has its ticket office here. The Akamba office (☎052/20221) is on the Caltex forecourt, and that is where to board all Akamba services, and all Nairobi-bound buses.

Eldoret and around

The journey from Kericho to Eldoret through the **Nandi Hills** is one of the most varied and spectacular in the west, through country often far wilder than you'd expect – bleak mountainous scrublands and jungle-packed ravines. Midway, you cross the Kano Plains and you may have to change transport at **Chemelil**, a major crossroads on the flat sugar lands. Beyond, the road zigzags into high tea country again, the homeland of the **Nandi**, the fiercest early opponents of the British, and the haunt of a crypto-zoological mystery known as the **Nandi bear** (see box on p.318). The only town of any size before Eldoret is **Kapsabet**, which has a couple of banks, a market, and a trio of reasonable lodgings, but nothing to warrant a stopover unless, again, you need to change matatus there.

Although more bustling with trade than Kericho, and somewhat healthier and pleasanter than Nakuru, **ELDORET** has, in all honesty, hardly anything to do or see that couldn't be done or seen in dozens of other highland centres. At first glance, life here seems pleasantly humdrum, at least on the outside: ordinary occupations and careers are actively pursued; the **Uasin Gishu Plateau** all around is reliably fertile cereal, vegetable and stock-raising country; wattle plantations provide the tannin for the town's leather industry; the Raymond textile factory – one of the country's biggest – provides employment, as does a new armaments factory (with a ready market in neighbouring countries); and a centre of higher education, Moi University, has proved a shot in the arm for local schools. The town is also the terminus for the oil pipeline from Mombasa, which Uganda would like to extend to Kampala, and it also has one of the best hospitals in Kenya. Eldoret's prosperity is shown clearly enough by the windows of the Eldoret Jewellers on the main road.

Eldoret doesn't have any sights to keep you for very long, but you may well find it a useful stopover, and it's refreshingly unthreatening and friendly despite its size. The town's affluence is reflected by a wide variety of places to stay, eat and drink – and enough nightlife to see you through an evening or two.

Though places of interest are limited, you may wish to visit the **Kip Keino sports and book shop** in Oginga Odinga Street, set up by athlete and Christian philanthropist Kepchugi Keino. Keino's double gold at the 1964 Olympics blazed a trail that has since been followed by other Kenyan runners, mainly from this region of the country. Since retiring from sport, he has used his name and earnings to sponsor children's homes and other good causes.

Some history

Eldoret was a backwoods post office on Farm 64, later chosen in 1912 as an administrative centre because the farm's soil was poor and the deeds were never taken up by the owner. The name started as Eldare (a river), was then Nandi-ized to Eldaret, and finally misprinted in the *Official Gazette* as Eldoret. Pronunciation is fluid.

Before the town existed, the area was settled by **Afrikaners**. They gave it much of the dour worthiness that seems to have characterized its first half-century and which is perceptible even today, though most of the Boers trekked on after Independence. Modern inhabitants are mainly Kalenjin (Elgeyo and Nandi) but there's also a long-established and respected Asian community (Juma Hajee's supermarket, now a shopping arcade, was the oldest business in the town); in addition there are Somali-speakers, the remnants of a European community, and immigrants from the rest of Kenya. Under Daniel Arap Moi's presidency, Eldoret's status as capital of the Kalenjin homelands made it the choice for location of what was billed as an "international" **airport**, though in fact the only scheduled flights it receives are a couple a day from Nairobi.

Arrival and accommodation

The main **matatu** enclosure is at the east end of Arap Moi Street. Eldoret International **Airport** (℡053/206 3377) is 16km out of town on the Kapsabet road; matatus bound for Kapsabet or Kisumu will drop you there.

Eldoret has no shortage of **accommodation**. Cheap places tend to be grubby or clearly intended for "short-term guests". There are also one or two quaint

At the end of the nineteenth century, the **Nandi** (dialects of whose language is spoken by all the Kalenjin peoples) were probably in the strongest position in their history. Their warriors had drummed up a reputation for such ferocity and daring that much of western Kenya lived in fear of them. Even the Maasai – at a low point in their own fortunes – suffered repeated losses of livestock to Nandi spearsmen, whose prestige accumulated with every herd of cattle driven back to their stockades. The Nandi even crossed the Rift Valley to raid Subukia and the Laikipia plateau. They were intensely protective of their own territory, relentlessly xenophobic and fearful of any adulteration of their way of life. Foreigners of any kind were welcome only with express permission.

With the killing of a British traveller, Peter West, who tried to cross their country in 1895, the Nandi opened a decade of guerrilla warfare against the British. Above all, they repeatedly frustrated attempts to lay the railway line and keep communications open with Uganda. They dismantled the "iron snake", transformed the copper telegraph wires into jewellery, and took whatever livestock and provisions they could find. Despite increased security, the establishment of forts, and some efforts to reach agreements with Nandi elders, the raiding went on, often costing the lives of African soldiers and policemen under the British. In retaliation, **punitive expeditions** shot more than a thousand Nandi warriors (about one young man in ten), captured tens of thousands of head of livestock, and torched scores of villages. The war was ended by the killing of Koitalel, the *Orkoiyot* or spiritual head of the Nandi who, having agreed to a temporary truce, was then murdered at a meeting with the British. As expected, resistance collapsed (his people had believed Koitalel to be unassailable); the Nandi were hounded into a reserve and their lands opened to settlers.

Traditionally keepers of livestock, the Nandi have turned to agriculture with little enthusiasm and focus instead on their district's milk production, the highest in Kenya. *Shambas*, however, are widespread enough to make your chances of seeing a **Nandi bear** – the source of scores of Yeti-type rumours – remote. Variously said to resemble a bear, a big wild dog or a very large ape, the Nandi bear is believed to have been exterminated in most areas. But in the less accessible regions, on the way up to Kapsabet, many locals believe it still exists – they call it *chemoset*. Exactly what it is is another matter, but it doesn't seem to inspire quite the terror you might expect; the occasional savagely mutilated sheep and cattle reported in the press are probably attributable to leopards. As for the *chemoset*, a giant anthropoid ape, perhaps a gorilla, seems the most likely candidate, and the proximity of the Kakamega Forest may account for the stories. This is a surviving tract of the rainforest that once stretched in a continuous belt across equatorial Africa and is still home to many western and central African species of wildlife (though not, as far as is known, giant apes). The *chemoset* possibly survived up until the early twentieth century in isolated valleys, even if it no longer survives. A presumed-extinct mammal by the name of *Chemositia tugenensis* (see p.271) has been suggested as a candidate. Whatever the truth, if you camp out in the Nandi Hills, you won't need reminding to zip your fly sheet.

old haunts from way back. The Reformed Church Centre should allow **camping** in the field.

Cheap hotels and lodgings

Aya Inn Oginga Odinga St; PO Box 401 ☏ 053/2062259. A friendly place with large rooms, a couple of rowdy but good-natured

and fun bars and a *nyama choma* restaurant. B&B ❷

Eldoret Valley Hotel Uganda Rd; PO Box 734 ☏ 053/2032314. An excellent-value little place: the rooms are smallish but s/c and scrupulously clean, with hot water in the mornings, and the restaurant serves decent Kenyan fare and good tea. The nearby *Places* disco makes rooms at the back noisy. ❶

Eldoret New Lincoln Hotel Oloo Rd; PO Box 551 ☏ 0721/466162. With original fixtures and fittings, and a creaking charm that seems to augur imminent collapse, this is Eldoret's most interesting hotel. It's close to the transport park and top-volume nightclubs, and it can be noisy but not excessively so. There's a pleasant bar and decent food, but beware of leaving valuables in rooms. ❷

Moons Lodge Arap Moi St; PO Box 1996 ☏ 0721/463020. A simple, clean B&L in a Somali area, situated over a very male-dominated bar. The rooms are non-s/c but have TVs. Handy for buses (Akamba and a slew of other firms have offices close by), with good views from the roof and good food to be had nearby. ❶

Reformed Church of East Africa Conference and Training Centre 2km out of town on the Kapsabet road; PO Box 746 ☏ 053/62497. Secure accommodation with a minimum of stimulation. The old wing has dorms (Ksh100) and non-s/c

rooms, while rooms in the new wing are all s/c. Take a matatu from the junction of Nandi Rd with Oginga Odinga St, and ask for "Conference". ❷

Sosiana View Hotel Arap Moi St; PO Box 840, no phone. Situated by the transport terminus, this five-storey block has good views – the best from the fifth floor, which is also the quietest, though more of a climb. The first-floor bar is a good place to down a beer or two. ❷

Moderate to expensive hotels

Eldoret Wagon Hotel Elgeyo Rd; PO Box 2408 ☏ 053/62270–1, ⊛ www.eldoretwagonhotel.co.ke. Sunny, and with quiet, comfortable rooms, *nyama choma* bar and safe parking, this gets quite lively at weekends. Much more intimate than the *Sirikwa* opposite. B&B ❹

Sirikwa Hotel Elgeyo Rd; PO Box 3361 ☏ 0321/63433, ⓔ hotelsirikwa@multitechweb.com (reservations through *Magret International*, Phoenix House, third floor, Kenyatta Ave; PO Box 67440 Nairobi ☏ & ℻ 020/224925). The town's "premier" hotel, this is a monolithic and faintly pompous pile,

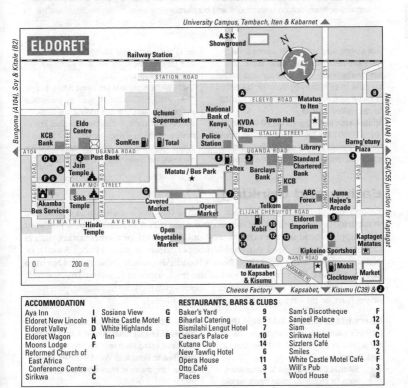

University Campus, Tambach, Iten & Kabarnet ▲

ELDORET

Bungoma (A104), Soy & Kitale (B2)

Nairobi (A104) & C54/C55 junction for Kaptagat

Cheese Factory ▼   Kapsabet, ▼ Kisumu (C39) & ⓙ

A.S.K. Showground

Railway Station

STATION ROAD

ELGEYO ROAD **Matatus to Iten**

National Bank of Kenya

Uchumi Supermarket

KVDA Plaza **Town Hall** ★

UTALII STREET

KCB Bank

Eldo Centre

SomKen Total

Police Station

Library

Barng'etuny Plaza

UGANDA ROAD

Post Bank

Jain Temple

ARAP MOI STREET

Matatu / Bus Park ★

Caltex

Barclays Bank

Standard Chartered Bank

KCB

Akamba Bus Services

Sikh Temple

Covered Market

Open Market

Telkom

ABC Forex

Juma Hajee's Arcade

KIMATHI   AVENUE

Hindu Temple

Open Vegetable Market

ELIJAH CHERUIYOT ROAD

Eldoret Emporium

Kobil

Kipkeino Sportshop ★

Kaptaget Matatus ★

NANDI ROAD

0   200 m

Matatus to Kapsabet & Kisumu

HARAMBEE RD

Mobil

Clocktower

Market

ACCOMMODATION

Aya Inn	I	Sosiana View	G
Eldoret New Lincoln	H	White Castle Motel	E
Eldoret Valley	D	White Highlands	
Eldoret Wagon	A	Inn	B
Moons Lodge	F		
Reformed Church of			
East Africa			
Conference Centre	J		
Sirikwa	C		

RESTAURANTS, BARS & CLUBS

Baker's Yard	9	Sam's Discotheque	F
Biharlal Catering	5	Sanjeel Palace	12
Bismilahi Lengut Hotel	7	Siam	4
Caesar's Palace	10	Sirikwa Hotel	C
Kutana Club	14	Sizzlers Café	13
New Tawfiq Hotel	6	Smiles	2
Opera House	11	White Castle Motel Café	F
Otto Café	3	Will's Pub	3
Places	1	Wood House	8

Moving on from Eldoret

At the time of writing, there are no passenger train services from Eldoret, though there are AeroKenya **flights** (two daily, but only one on Sundays) to Nairobi.

Matatus from the main enclosure run to Kabarnet and Kakamega, as well as main road services for Kisumu, Kitale and further afield. Eldoret Express buses (for Kitale and Nairobi) also stop there, as do Linear Buses (for Kisumu and Kericho) and the one daily bus (10am) for Kabarnet. Matatus for Iten leave from the stage in Utalii Street on the corner of Oginga Odinga Street, while services for Kapsabet and some for Kisumu go from the corner of Oginga Odinga Street and Nandi Road. For Kaptagat they leave a block east on the corner of Nyala Road. The Akamba bus office (℡053/206 1047) is on Arap Moi Street, opposite *New Tawfiq Hotel*.

For **Kakamega Forest** (see p.342), if you don't want to go all the way round to the other side and approach it from Kakamega town, you can take a bus or matatu going to Kisumu via Kapsabet, and get off at the D267 turning about 20km after Kapsabet (signposted "Kisieni 12km"), from where it's a walk of about three hours to the *Rest House* (see p.346).

If you intend to cross the Rift Valley to Lake Baringo, you'll find a fair number of matatus bound for Kabarnet, and two daily buses, using the tarmacked **Tambach Escarpment** route. This is a spectacular journey: from the high pastures and wheat fields of the plateau, the valley suddenly yawns out beneath, some 1500m below.

Heading directly towards the **Ugandan border**, there's little to delay your progress to Malaba, two or three hours away. Webuye, en route, is covered on p.337. The busy **A104** road from Eldoret east to **Nakuru**, uphill and then down again, is a fast one, the sombre scenery dotted with moors and conifers.

---

with a whole wing just for VIPs. Rooms are very good, with real baths – the "senior suites" bizarrely have two bathrooms, the "junior suites" are exactly the same as an ordinary double room, but located in the VIP wing – and it has a large pool (Ksh150 for day visitors). B&B ➏

White Castle Motel Uganda Rd; PO Box 566 ℡053/2062773 or 2061362, ℻2062209. Although first impressions are very unpromising – a bland modern building on a noisy road – the rooms turn

out to be far better than average, and there's a lift after the initial two steps. The hotel even has a sauna and health club. ➌

White Highlands Inn Elgeyo Rd; PO Box 2189 ℡053/2061541. Spacious, presentable and normally quiet, with safe parking, and baths and TVs in all rooms. Outside there's a small kids' playground and an alfresco bar/restaurant serving *nyama choma* and other standards, and another bar and restaurant inside. Very good value. B&B ➍

Eating and drinking

Eldoret has plenty of good places to grab a bite, with a clutch of established snack bars, several options for dinner, and one or two evening haunts. For your own supplies, head for the markets west of Oloo Road, or a supermarket such as Uchumi behind the Total station, Eldo Supermarket at Juma Hajee's Arcade, or Naivasha opposite the market on Nandi Road. Also worth a visit is the **Dorinyo Lessos Cheese Factory** at the end of the track south of Kenyatta Street, where you can buy various European-style cheeses (quarter kilo minimum purchase), or yoghurt or ice cream (smaller quantities available).

Baker's Yard Juma Hajee's Arcade, Elijah Cheruiyot Rd. Excellent place with biscuits, pies, cakes and pastries as well as bread, and also good for a quick filter coffee.

 Biharlal Catering Kago St. An excellent place for vegetarian Indian meals, snacks

and sweets; good for lunch but closes at 6.30pm.

Bismilahi Lengut Hotel Oloo Rd. A large, bright and cheap eating place near the market.

New Tawfiq Hotel Arap Moi St. Standard, cheap Kenyan fare; mainly of interest because it's open 24/7.

Otto Café Uganda Rd. Popular *hoteli* with a long and well-priced menu and excellent *mandaazi*. The downstairs seating area is one of the few upcountry places with real atmosphere, but closes at 7pm, so you'll have to make your evening meal tea rather than supper if you want to eat it here.

Siam Nyala Rd, corner of Uganda Rd. A Chinese posing as a Thai. The Chinese dishes, with the accent on chilli, are not bad, though overpriced, but the "Thai" dishes aren't even a vague approximation. What makes this place worthwhile, however, are the great-value Ksh200–300 lunchtime specials.

Sirikwa Hotel Huge barbecue buffet lunches for Ksh550 – worth it if you've just spent three days in the Kakamega Forest or up Mount Elgon.

Sizzlers Café Kenyatta St. A popular American-style joint, offering speedy, high-quality burgers plus ice cream and other desserts.

Sanjeel Palace Kenyatta St. This is where Eldoret's Asian community come when they want to eat out, with fine curries (veg and non-veg), plus good *naan*, and a selection of Indian, European and African dishes at moderate prices.

White Castle Motel Café Uganda Rd. Burger and chips, sausage and chips, pie and chips, fish (tilapia) and chips . . . and possibly chicken with *ugali* if you don't like chips.

Will's Pub Uganda Rd. A good place for a beer, but also for solid Kenyan food and snacks, including tasty meat samosas.

Nightlife

Most of these places charge a small entry fee at weekends but, with the exception of *Caesar's Palace*, are free midweek.

Caesar's Palace Kenyatta St. A revamped disco, loud and enjoyable, with ladies' night on Wed, generally packed at weekends when they play soul, ragga and hip-hop, with live English and European football on screen.

Kutana Club Oloo Rd, next to the *New Lincoln*. Rustic African atmosphere and beery bonhomie, with a live visiting band at weekends. Music is mostly African, especially Congolese.

Opera House (Club Santa Cruz) Oloo Rd. Very firmly established nightspot, playing mainly reggae Fri and Sat nights until dawn; the rest of the week it's basically just a bar. Pronounced "O-pair-a" rather than "Oprah" if you're asking people about it.

Places Uganda Rd. Sophisticated decor, a sunken dance floor, and a well-mannered clientele, with snacks available and good DJs. Music is mainly Western disco

Sam's Discotheque Uganda Rd, under the *White Castle Motel*. Middle-of-the-road nightspot with a mixed clientele, always busy but, aside from the odd live gig, open only weekends (Fri & Sat all night, Sun daytime).

Smiles Uganda Rd. A sweaty den of iniquity and outrageous pick-up joint, but fun in a sleazy kind of way. Music is mostly Congolese or reggae.

Wood House Kenyatta St. An ordinary bar midweek, but a lively nightspot on Fri and Sat with a mix of soul and reggae.

Listings

Airlines AeroKenya, at the airport ☎053/2060237.
Banks Barclays, Standard Chartered and KCB (two branches) all have ATMs. Wall Street Forex in Barng'etuny Plaza on Uganda St and Safari Forex in KVDA Plaza give similar rates for cash (but not small bills), and slightly lower rates for traveller's cheques, with no commission on either.
Books Eldoret Emporium on the corner of Elijah Cheruiyot St and Oginga Odinga St has a good selection of Kenyan books, as does Student's Choice on Oginga Odinga St, which is easier to browse and also carries foreign titles plus magazines such as *Time* and *Newsweek*. Uchumi supermarket stocks quite a lot of American pulps,

and a huge range of British, American and Indian magazines, as well as UK tabloids. The library on Utalii St has a good African history section.
Golf Eldoret Club; PO Box 78 ☎053/31395. Eighteen holes.
Hospitals Eldoret Hospital, Mark Asembo Rd ☎053/2062000–1.
Internet access Numerous Internet offices include Internet4Less In Juma Hajee's Arcade in Elijah Cheruiyot Rd, Cyber World by *Otto Café* in Uganda Rd, Alice Cyber Café near *Sosiana View Hotel* In Arap Moi St, and a trio of places in Utamaduni House behind Barclays Bank in Kenyatta St.
Pharmacies Several on Kenyatta and Oginga

Odinga streets; out of hours try Asisco Pharmacy, Bandaptai House, off Nandi Rd, one block east of Nyala Rd (☎053/2062496; daily 8am–midnight).
Police Uganda Rd, opposite Caltex ☎053/2032222–3.
Post office Mon–Fri 8am–5.30pm, Sat 9am–noon. Phones outside, but more outside Telkom in Elijah Cheruiyot Rd.

Swimming pool The *Sirikwa Hotel* has a pool (non-residents Ksh150) in its large, dull, grassy gardens. At weekends it's overrun with Kenyans in holiday mood.
Tourist office second floor, KVDA PLaza; PO Box 4286 ☎053/2032086. Doesn't have much in the way of handouts, but very helpful with information on local attractions.

Around Eldoret

If you arrived in Eldoret early enough in the day, there are a couple of worthwhile bases outside town to head to for a night or longer.

Near **Kaptagat**, 20km from Eldoret on the well-surfaced C54/C55 road, en route to the Kerio Valley, are two very pleasant places to stay. ☀ **Naiberi River Campsite** (PO Box 142 Eldoret; ☎053/2062916, ⊛www.naiberi .com) has a wonderful scenic location on the Naiberi River, with cosy, fully equipped s/c rooms and *bandas* (❹), as well as dorm accommodation (Ksh600) and camping facilities (Ksh300 per person), hot showers and a great pub-restaurant with waterfalls and a big central fireplace. Also within the site are a number of Sirikwa holes (see p.276), but you may not be too keen on the almost exclusive company of Brits and Aussies (it's popular with overland groups) if you're looking for "the real Kenya", though Kenyans do come for a drink in the evenings. It's off the main road, 7km before the Kaptagat village turn-off, and matatus will happily drop you at the junction, but be sure they deposit you at the new site, not the old one (which is 5km further on, and no longer in use). Alternatively, call the owner (Mon–Fri 10am–5pm; ☎053/203 2644) or email him (⊜factory@kenknit.com) to arrange a free lift from Eldoret.

More sedate, but also rather special, the **Kaptagat Hotel**, 500m off the main road a couple of kilometres further on (PO Box 2900 Eldoret; ☎0722/778654), was an erstwhile colonial hangout which had rather gone to seed, but has now been renovated. Set in extensive and beautifully kept grounds, including lawns, woodland and a river, it offers a choice of s/c rooms off a common lounge (❸), or cottage rooms with fireplaces and a slightly higher standard of comfort (❹), and also allows camping (Ksh250 per person). Alternatively, you can just pop in for a meal or a drink, or picnic in the grounds (Ksh100 per person to enter).

Beyond Kaptagat, the unpaved route from Nyaru down to the fluorspar mine at Kimwarer (see p.273) – which, believe it or not, used to be the main way across the valley – no longer sees much traffic, though you can usually hitch a ride with a lorry travelling to or from the mine. It's an incredible hairpin descent that seems to go on forever. Kerio Valley route details continue on p.273.

In the other direction (west) out of Eldoret, there's transport towards Kitale by bus, minibus or Peugeot throughout the day, but the **Soy Safari Resort**, a third of the way there, is nice enough to break your journey for (PO Box 457 Eldoret; ☎0722/350343; B&B ❸). A very pukka country retreat, this is a peaceful place to stay, with single-storey wings laid out in classic colonial style, complete with wood-tiled roofs, brick chimneys and a formal garden. The rooms are comfortably homely, and there's a swimming pool (non-residents Ksh100), a bar, and a restaurant with a short menu of Indian vegetarian and Kenyan non-veg dishes. Most of the rooms are triple, and cost the same for one, two or three people, but it's only ever busy at weekends.

Kitale and northward

KITALE is smaller than Eldoret, and not much more exciting, but it has more going for it from a traveller's point of view, primarily because it is the base for visits to **Mount Elgon** and the superb, very underrated, hiking country around Kenya's second giant volcanic cone. It's also an obvious base for the **Cherangani Hills**, and a straightforward departure point for trips to the west side of **Lake Turkana**. There's a **national park** nearby – the little-known but easily accessible **Saiwa Swamp**, where for once the tables are turned on drivers: you can explore on foot only. The town itself boasts a good **regional museum**, one excellent restaurant, and a few good nightlife possibilities.

A lot of travellers only pass through here on the way to Lake Turkana, which is a shame. Unless you're on a tight schedule, the museums, Mount Elgon and Saiwa Swamp, as well Kitale's friendly people (even the streetkids, once you get to know them) add up to a good reason to delay a day or three. The town itself is calm and unprepossessing, with smooth tarmac streets planted with trees, and a lively northern district around and beyond the market, almost a slum in parts, where visitors rarely wander, but shouldn't encounter serious problems if they do.

Some history

Originally Quitale, a relay station on the old slave route between Uganda and Bagamoyo in Tanzania, the modern town was founded only in 1920, as the capital of Trans-Nzoia District. When the first white settlers arrived (mostly after World War I), this vale of rich grasslands between Mount Elgon and the Cherangani Hills was apparently almost uninhabited. But just a few years earlier it had been a Maasai grazing area, and a group of people who consider themselves Maasai still live on the eastern slopes of Elgon. With the arrival of the railway in 1925, the town and the region around it began to flourish, with a fantastic array of fruit, cereals, vegetables and livestock, and all the attendant settler paraphernalia of agricultural and flower shows, church fetes and gymkhanas. This heady era lasted barely forty years, but the region's **agriculture** is still famous; almost anything, including such exotic fruit as apples and pears, can be grown here. The Kitale Show happens each year at the end of October or beginning of November.

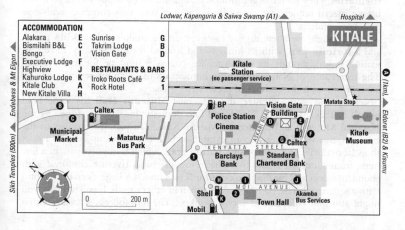

The town's present population is a mix of several tribes, including Nandi, Pokot, Marakwet, Sabaot and Sengwer, as well as a few Luhya, Kisii, Kikuyu and Asians. As a result, at the end of the 1990s it became a focus for people fleeing ethnic violence and bloody cattle-rustling raids in the surrounding region, especially along the Trans-Nzoia/West Pokot border area, to the northeast of Kitale, and was the venue for **peace talks** held during 1998–99, after which the ethnic violence declined markedly, and has now completely subsided.

Kitale Museum and the VI Agroforestry Project

Given its location, **Kitale Museum** (daily 8am–6pm; Ksh200) is remarkably successful. Originally the "Stoneham Museum", a collection opened to the public by a lieutenant colonel on his Cherangani farm in 1927, it was transferred here in 1972. For the most part, Stoneham's curious collections are just that: collected curiosities in striking contrast to the recent, more educationally motivated, Kenyan additions.

In the main hall, the **ethnographic displays** on Pokot, Elkony (Elgon), Luhya, Maasai, Turkana and Luo are interesting, though perhaps more so if you've seen the stuff in real life and now have a chance to return and see it again. The reconstructed landscape featuring members of the extinct hominid species *Australopithecus boisei* is almost comical. Among the artefacts are Kamba carvings – skin-covered animals and smooth polished abstracts; a Pokot goat bell made from a tortoise shell; Pokot bowls used for collecting blood from cattle; and intricate Turkana belts and beadwork. In the small room to the right of the entrance in the main building is a collection of traditional musical instruments (as well as an old piano and accordion), which really are becoming museum pieces as younger generations embrace more cosmopolitan musical genres (though you can buy cassettes of traditional Luhya music in town). In the room to the left of the entrance, the collection of British African war medals will interest enthusiasts, but nobody else.

The motley wildlife collection on the walls and downstairs is perhaps best ignored, but the entomology is more interesting – a very fine collection of butterflies and bugs collected in the region in recent years, which are upstairs, to the right as you enter. Incidentally, if you're fed up with the diet of KTN and KBC TV, the museum occasionally screens real celluloid **wildlife documentaries**. They prefer larger groups, though they'd be happy to oblige if you have a special request, are especially keen, or if your visit coincides with one by schoolchildren.

Outside, there are a few display cases containing **snakes**, a **crocodile pond**, and a **tortoise pen**, with its hinged- and leopard-tortoise inmates. Except in mating season, though, it's as boring for you as it must be for the tortoises. The recreations of Nandi and Luhya homesteads make an interesting point of comparison with the realities of present-day villages.

Next to the main entrance, the octagonal **Museum Hall** has some bold murals of Turkana, Maasai, Nandi and Luo domestic life, commissioned by the National Museum and painted by Maggie Kukler. In planned changes to the museum, this should become an exhibition hall. The museum also has a craft shop, laboratories and a surprising **nature trail**, which transports you, in a few steps, from suburban Kitale to a chattering, dripping, riverine rainforest with abundant insect and birdlife; look out for Ross's turaco, a large, deep purple bird with a square red crest, commoner here than in other forests. If you're lucky, you might also spot colobus and vervet monkeys. The trail follows a stream with a muddy path and rickety footbridges (unsuitable for anyone with mobility problems), but the forest itself is natural and some of the trees stately. The picnic site, near the end of the trail, is a wonderful place if you can cope with the bugs.

Next door to the Kitale Museum, though its entrance is 300m further east, the Swedish-backed **VI Agroforestry Project** (daily 8am–5pm; free; PO Box 2006; ℡054/31498) was set up to educate cultivators in Trans-Nzoia and West Pokot about the basics of tree planting. This accomplished, it has now progressed to concerning itself with the problems of soil erosion and over-grazing, and offers practical advice to farmers on the selection of plant and tree species best adapted to local conditions. There's a small gallery here with well-captioned photographs explaining their work and, outside, a "demonstration *shamba*" which showcases environmentally sound techniques to increase crop yield.

The most interesting of Kitale's museums is the **Treasures of Africa Museum** (Mon–Sat 9am–noon & 2–5.30pm; Ksh250; ℡054/30867, Ⓔtoam@multitechweb.com), northeast of the main road, out past the Kitale Club (Ksh30 by *boda-boda* from town). Run by John Wilson, a retired former colonial administrator in Uganda, the museum displays cultural artefacts, mainly from the Karamojong, a pastoral Nilotic people of northern Uganda. The exhibits are arranged to illustrate the proprietor's case – based on linguisitic parallels between Karamojong and supposedly unrelated languages, such as Scottish Gaelic – that a single worldwide farming culture existed in the ice age, long before agriculture is thought to have developed anywhere in the world.

Moving on from Kitale

Matatus spill out from the stage near the municipal market onto the adjoining main road, and there's a smaller gathering opposite Kitale Museum on the corner of the Lodwar road of Nissans bound for Eldoret, Kakamega and Kisumu, but if in doubt, go to the main matatu stage.

Heading west, if you're interested in exploring **Mount Elgon** (full details start on p.330), matatus leave daily around 3–5pm for *Mount Elgon Lodge* near the park's Chorlim Gate. If you don't coincide with these, the next closest destination is Endebess, reached quickly enough by regular matatus (which continue to the Ugandan border at **Suam**). **Southwards**, Kakamega and Kisumu are, with luck, no more than two or three hours away down the A1, a very busy road. As ever, Akamba **buses** (℡054/31732) are the best bet for long hauls back to Nakuru and Nairobi, though with only two buses daily (9am & 9pm), you may find Eldoret Express's frequent departures more useful: they leave when full, which is approximately hourly.

Passenger train services haven't run from Kitale for a long time, but it is still possible that they may resume in the future.

Most people setting off from Kitale are **heading north** (route details in chapter 7, p.561). The road to Lodwar and Kalokol near Lake Turkana is in such an appalling condition beyond Marich that it may as well not be paved at all. A 2WD car could just about manage it, in the absence of flash floods (which can bar the way for a few hours, occasionally washing away a short stretch). There are several buses a day – best caught early, from around 8am – and enough traffic to make hitching a practical option. Remember to take water, and also to stock up on provisions, as you'll only find more basic stuff on sale further north (fresh fruit and veg is expensive and of low quality in Lodwar). If you're driving yourself, note that there is nowhere to get fuel between Ortum and Lodwar. It may be more fun to spend the night before at Saiwa Swamp National Park (see p.327), Sirikwa Safaris (p.327), or Marich Pass Field Studies Centre (p.330) rather than in Kitale itself.

The proprietor himself is usually on hand to explain all this in person, but if you want to be sure of a guided tour, it's best to call or email him in advance of your visit.

Practicalities

Barclays and SCB both have ATMs, and will change cash and traveller's cheques. Soy Supermarket in Kenyatta Street sells weekly editions of some UK newspapers, but for provisions, there's a wider choice at the Transmatt Supermarket across the street. Internet access is available at Multitech on the first floor of the Vision Gate Building at the eastern end of Askari Road, at the Silver Springs Centre next door, and at On The Web Cybercafé in room 64 of the *Sunrise Hotel*.

Accommodation

If you're heading north out of town anyway, you may want to stay at **Sirikwa Guesthouse Safaris** (*Barnley's Guesthouse*; opposite). If you don't have your own vehicle, allow an hour to get there. In Kitale itself, there are a number of **cheap lodgings**, down to the usual standard, the most economical found at the grubby north end of town, past the market. As to **mid-range hotels**, you're spoilt for choice. Note that Kitale suffers from sporadic cuts in its water supply, which affect even the better hotels. The Kitale Museum intends to open a **campsite** in its grounds, and even *bandas*, and should allow camping in the meantime (around Ksh250 per person, but without shower facilities) if you ask the curator first.

Alakara Hotel Kenyatta St; PO Box 1984 ☎054/20395. A large, bright place with surprisingly good beds, baths in most rooms (cheaper non-s/c rooms available) and 24hr hot water. The restaurant is good too. B&B ❷

Bismilahi B&L PO Box 1191 ☎0721/794826. A very basic Somali-run place, fronted by a *miraa* shop, not for women, with only cold water (and that just in the evenings only), but it's not insalubrious and extremely cheap. ❶

Bongo Hotel Moi Ave; PO Box 530 ☎0325/20593. Decent, properly furnished s/c rooms with good breakfasts and (barring the odd hiccup in the supply) hot showers. Slightly cheaper than the *Highview*, *Sunrise* and *Alakara*, but not quite as good. B&B ❷

Executive Lodge Kenyatta St; PO Box 3570 ☎0723/882421. Secure, but off-puttingly dark, with small and tatty rooms, some s/c. There's a TV room and a reasonable restaurant attached, but at the same price you'd be much better off at the *Alakara* opposite. B&B ❷

Highview Hotel Moi Ave; PO Box 2925 ☎0325/31570. A friendly high-rise with good, breezy and relatively clean s/c rooms with nets; the luxury rooms, which cost slightly more than the ordinary ones, are much bigger, with a sitting area, and there's also one cheaper room, actually a suite of sorts, with a box-like bedroom and separate sitting room. B&B ❷/❸

Kahuroko Lodge Moi Ave, behind the SomKen garage; PO Box 2290; no phone. Basic lodgings fronted by a rather noisy bar-restaurant. Some single rooms are s/c, but the doubles aren't. ❶

Kitale Club PO Box 30 ☎054/31330 or 31338, ☏30924. This place, 1km out on the road towards Eldoret, has older cottages with cement floors, a new block whose rooms are larger with wooden floors, and new cottages with wooden floors, TVs and fireplaces. Prices include temporary membership and access to club facilities including the golf course (Ksh800) and pool (Ksh200). ❺

New Kitale Villa Moi Ave; PO Box 4240 ☎0735/405800. Above a day and night club, with simple but clean non-s/c rooms, very friendly and good for a night out – the club plays upbeat sounds day and night. Women on their own might prefer to look elsewhere. ❶

Sunrise Kenyatta St; PO Box 337 ☎054/31841. Behind its uninviting entrance are the best lodgings in town: calm, clean and welcoming, with parquet floors and proper baths and nets in all rooms. The more expensive "deluxe" doubles are huge and have balconies fronting onto the street. ❷

Takrim Lodge on the main road at the northern end of town ☎0725/496394. Basic but neat and clean, Somali-run and by a mosque, with quite a Middle-Eastern feel, s/c rooms and cold showers but hot water in a bucket on request. ❶

Vision Gate third floor, Vision Gate Building, Askari Rd; PO Box 1829 ⊤054/31547, ⨍31250. A new hotel, with lots of shiny tiles and polished floors in the public areas, and a decent restaurant downstairs, but rather plain rooms and nothing really to justify the price differential over its competitors. B&B ❸

Eating and drinking

The best **food** in Kitale is to be found at *The Lantern* in the *Sunrise Hotel* on Kenyatta Street, which has a large menu, including Chinese and Indian dishes suitable for vegetarians, as well as meats and French-style cuisine, red wine and Irish coffees too. Service is professional, the surroundings pleasant, and the food is great if you've been living on a diet of *ugali* and *irio* for a few weeks. Other dependable options include the *Alakara* and *Highview* hotels, and the *Kitale Club*, if you don't mind paying for temporary membership (Ksh500) on top of the price of a set meal (Ksh350) to eat at the latter. ⚘*Iroko Roots Café* on Moi Avenue is a good place for cheap but good Kenyan fare including stews, curries and *pilau*. As elsewhere, many restaurants are closed on Sundays.

After dark, there are a number of places providing drink and lively conversation. The bars at the *Bongo*, the *Alakara* and the *Highview* are quiet but congenial. Of the more energetic nightspots (women should go accompanied), the best is *New Kitale Villa* on Moi Avenue, a cheerful and friendly dive with upbeat music 24/7, and a live band every evening. The *Rock Hotel* disco, at the north end of Kenyatta Street is more rough and ready, with less inspiring musical sounds, but still quite fun.

Sirikwa Safaris - Barnley's Guesthouse

You could also stop off for a day – or quite happily for a week – at the homely ⚘**Sirikwa Safaris**, aka **Barnley's Guesthouse** (PO Box 332 Kitale; ⊤0733/793524, ✉sirikwabarnley@swiftkenya.com), signposted off to the right precisely 23.6km north of Kitale on the A1. Situated on a tree-covered hill, there are superb gardens to camp in (Ksh450 per person including firewood and use of bathroom facilities), three furnished tents with electricity (❹; may be replaced by *bandas* in future) and the Barnley family's fine old house (❻), which provides excellent meals to order. Laundry can be arranged most days. Another great draw here are the **guides** (Ksh600/day; Ksh300/day for a porter; Ksh1800/day for the ornithologist), who can take you on some exceptional walking and bird-watching trips into the Cherangani Hills, from day-walks to week-long hikes. Three- to four-day trips to Marich Pass (p.330) are recommended, or you can visit Kongolai escarpment (more bird-watching), Tartar falls (local beauty spot), or the Turkwel Dam (see p.562). This is also an excellent base for visiting Saiwa Swamp and Mount Elgon, and it is even possible to arrange trout-fishing trips given sufficient advance notice, and a permit (see p.75).

Saiwa Swamp National Park

Open daily 7am–7pm; $15, children $5, Ksh200 for vehicle; car park; entry on foot. Warden: PO Box 4506 Kitale 30200; ⊤054/55022.

Specially created for the protection of the **sitatunga**, a rare and vulnerable semi-aquatic antelope, **Saiwa Swamp National Park** is the country's smallest park. Despite its accessibility – 11km from *Barnley's House*, and easy by matatu from there or from Kitale – it is rarely visited, which is a pity. The requirement that you walk (rather than drive) around the two square kilometres of jungle and swamp, plus the chance of seeing the antelope as well as various monkeys and birds, make it an exciting and interesting goal for a day. If you're staying at *Barnley's*, think about hiring a guide there for the trip – not at all expensive, and really worthwhile.

Game-watching

The **sitatunga** (pronounced "statunga") is an unusual antelope with strange splayed and elongated hooves, which you probably won't see because the animal lives most of its life partly submerged in water and weed. It's hard to see quite how the hooves help it "to move freely on the surface of boggy swamps": the theory makes sense, but the design needs more work – the warden may be able to show you a sitatunga hoof if you are interested. Otherwise, the sitatunga is reddish-brown with a moth-eaten look, very large ears and, on the males, horns. Due to poaching, numbers in the park were down from over 70 when it opened to fewer than 20 at the last count and, unfortunately, the park is inadequately fenced and protected.

Sitatunga can be found in scattered locations throughout western and central Africa, but only at Saiwa Swamp have they grown really used to humans. They can be watched from the **observation platforms** which have been built in the trees at the side of the swamp – one on the east side, three on the west. The best times are early morning and, to a lesser extent, late afternoon, and the furthest platform is less than a kilometre from the campsites (see below). These lookouts are unmaintained, Tarzan-esque structures enabling you to spy down on the life among the reeds. The park also shelters plenty of **bushbuck**, easily distinguished from the sitatunga by their terrified, crashing escape through the undergrowth as you approach. The sitatunga evidently have steadier nerves, as they pick their way through the morass of waterweed regardless of human attention.

A delightful, simple to follow, **early-morning walk** takes you across the rickety duckboards over the swamp and down a jungle path on the eastern shore. Here you're almost bound to see the park's four species of **monkey**: colobus, vervet, blue, and the distinctively white-bearded de Brazza monkey.

Saiwa Swamp is also a great draw for ornithologists, with a number of untypical Kenyan **bird species**, including several turacos, many kingfishers, and the splendid black-and-white casqued hornbill. Most conspicuous of all are the **crowned cranes**, whose lurching flight is almost as risible as their ghastly honking call.

Practicalities

The park lies to the east of the main Kitale–Lodwar road, near the village of **Kipsain** (also known as Kipsoen). Matatus call at the village, which is some 18km from Kitale. From here, it's Ksh50 each way by *boda-boda*, or a poorly signposted five-kilometre walk to the park gates. You can pitch a tent in the park ($8), but there are no facilities, nor any water supply, though you'll find plenty of firewood, and there are *hotelis* (but no accommodation) in the village. You'll need to make a fire, as the swamp mist makes it very chilly up here at night. Otherwise, the best base is at Sirikwa Safaris, just up the road (see p.327), where the Barnleys are a mine of information about the park, and also keep maps of it.

Kapenguria, Ortum and the Marich Pass

KAPENGURIA, off the highway north, is surprisingly small given its status as the capital of West Pokot, and notable only for its role of minor notoriety in colonial history. If you turn off the main road to visit, you'll find an immaculately tarred main street leading incongruously up through the hovels of "old Kapenguria" to the smarter new town on higher ground, with its hospital, large police station, huge, red, octagonal Catholic church (stained-glass windows and a spire), and the West Pokot District headquarters.

Also here is the excellent **Kapenguria Museum** (daily 8am–6pm; Ksh200; PO Box 383; ☎054/62050), occupying the prison where Kenyatta and his colleagues were detained during their parody of a trial. Their individually named cells have been "restored", and contain copies of contemporary press reports, photographs, depositions and the charges laid against each of the men (some almost laughably nebulous). Largely inaccessible during the colonial period, the town was deliberately chosen to hinder the work of the defence lawyers – "a maze of rascalities", one of them called it. All six defendants were found guilty of belonging to Mau Mau and sentenced to seven years in jail with hard labour. Much more visually interesting are the ethnographic displays of Pokot and Cherangani cultures, including well-described photographs of traditional ceremonies (circumcision dances and initiatory groups), musical instruments, and a telling series on the changes wrought by "modern" life. Look out for the chisel for removing teeth, and the small Cherangani horn "for sucking after making incisions on both sides of the head if one has a headache" – both are in the Cherangani Gallery, showcase #3. In the museum grounds are three reconstructed Pokot and Cherangani family compounds, which the museum caretaker will be happy to explain to you. Oddly prescient, given the recent flare-up of ethnic violence and cattle-raiding in West Pokot, is the pastoralist Pokot compound, featuring solid mud roofs which were designed to deflect firebrands flung by raiders.

Matatus from Kitale will drop you on the main road (A1) at **Makutano**, the service town for the western Cherangani Hills, from where you'll have to hire a taxi, squeeze into a shared one, or take a *boda-boda* for the last few kilometres to Kapenguria town itself (the turn-off is just north of Makutano). Makutano is also where you'll find **accommodation** and **food**, and there's also a KCB **bank** with an ATM (opposite the Caltex filling station). The *Sebit Hotel*, west of the main road, north of Caltex (PO Box 409 Kapenguria 30600; ☎0734/406521; ❶), is clean and well kept, with s/c rooms (singles, but they'll sleep a couple) and parking facilities, as well as *nyama choma*, stews and snacks. Just next to Caltex, *Perkau Princess Lodge* (PO Box 160 Kapenguria 30600 ☎054/62405; ❶) is owned by the Olympic marathon runner Tegla Loroupe and offers decent s/c single rooms (again, suitable for one person or a couple), those with a hot water supply costing very slightly more than those with only cold. It is also possible to stay in Kapenguria itself, at the *White House Resort Club*, on the right 400m before the museum (PO Box 1; ❷), a bar and nightspot with live music on Saturdays, and s/c double rooms with hot water.

North of Makutano, the road enters the truly spectacular countryside of West Pokot proper, winding up the western ridge of Lenan forest, then plunging steeply to the Marun (or Moruny) river. After some 45km you reach **ORTUM**, beautifully positioned beneath the heights of the Cheranganis, close to the **Marich Pass**, and a good locale to start hiking in the hills. If you're heading north by car, Ortum has the last petrol before Lodwar, though it's better to fill up at Makutano to be on the safe side. There are two cheap and basic **B&Ls** in the village, just off the main square: *Sondany Lodge* (PO Box 40; no phone; ❶), which is the better of the two, and *Simotwo Hotel* (PO Box 55; no phone; ❶), which is slightly cheaper. Of a large number of *hotelis*, the winner is *Rafikis' Hotel* on the main square, which serves tasty meals and manages cold sodas despite the absence of electricity. You can do a short **hike to a waterfall**, three hours' walk up from Ortum. From the post office, head across the main road, where the first dirt track takes you straight there.

Matatus plying between Kitale and Lodwar will drop you off anywhere on the main road. Otherwise, you can take a matatu from Kitale to Makutano, and pick up an onward vehicle there. Heading into the Kerio Valley (p.273) on the other side of the Cheranganis, you'll find plenty of matatus between Makutano and Lomut, especially on Sigor's market day (Thursday) or Lomut's (Saturday), with fewer onward to Tot, unless you can coincide with the weekly market at Chesegon (Wednesdays).

An excellent base to make for in this district is the ⚡ **Marich Pass Field Studies Centre** (PO Box 564 Kapenguria 30600; no phone), beautifully sited on the banks of the Marun River, just north of the small shopping centre of **Marich**, at the junction of the A1 Lodwar and B4 Kerio Valley roads: the centre (signposted) is 1km off the Lodwar road. There is a short cut on foot from just north of the B4 turn-off, by a signpost that reads "Marich Mixed Boarding Primary School", but the path (at twenty rather than ninety degrees to the right) is not easy to follow, and it's worth enlisting local help. The centre has a lovely shaded campsite (Ksh300 per person; one tent available for rent at Ksh150), some good *bandas* with mosquito nets (s/c ❸, non s/c ❷), including two s/c *bandas* adapted for wheelchair use, and a dorm block (Ksh350 per person). Firewood, stoves and lamps are available for a small fee. The food is basic but impressively plentiful – order well in advance – and drinking water comes pure from the well. Even if you're not staying, it's well worth dropping in for a picnic (daily admission Ksh100), as the centre is surrounded by dense bush, quivering with bird and animal life, and there are guides to help you on excursions around the hills, to Pokot homesteads and local markets if you have the energy (fixed rates: Ksh400 for 5hr, Ksh550 for 10hr). **Mount Sekerr** (Mtelo) is the peak that looms to the northwest – it's a three-day hike to the top (3354m) and back. It's possible to stay overnight at the *Mount Mtelo View Campsite*, either camping (Ksh250 per person), or in traditional thatched round huts (❶). Nearer Marich, 3206-metre **Mount Koh** to the southeast is a one-day hike if you've got 4WD to get halfway up; two full days otherwise.

Mount Elgon

Straddling the Kenya-Uganda border, **Mount Elgon** is hidden in clouds most of the time, its precise outline hard to discern. The name comes from the Maasai **Ol Doinyo Ilgoon**, meaning "Breast Mountain", and like Mount Kenya, it's an extinct volcano, around whose jagged and much-eroded crater rim the flat-topped peaks crop up like stumpy fingers of an upturned hand. The two mountains are comparable in bulk, but Elgon is lower (below the snowline) and less precipitous – an encouragement, perhaps, if the thought of tackling the "loneliest park in Kenya" was putting you off.

Part of the east side of the mountain is enclosed within the confines of **Mount Elgon National Park**. Outside this zone is a forest reserve, with some restrictions on movement at present due to the presence of cattle rustlers from across the Ugandan border. Despite this, it is now possible to visit the national parks on **both sides of the border** together (see p.334).

The smoothing effects of erosion make hiking relatively easy within the park, and there's invigorating walking country up near the peaks. The highest of these, **Wagagai** (4321m; there's also another Wagagai nearby, at 4298m), is

MOUNT ELGON

UGANDA

THE CALDERA

Mubiyi ▲

Jackson's Tarn

Jackson's Summit

Wagagai 4321m ▲

Little Wagagai 4298m ▲

Sacred Lake (Lower Elgon Tarn)

Lower Elgon Tarn ▲

Hot Springs

Sudek 4176m ▲

Suam Gorge

Suam River

Koitoboss 4187m ▲

Kubaror ▲

MOUNT ELGON NATIONAL PARK

Koitcut 3302m ▲

Suam Saw Mill

Masara ▲

Kiptogot River

Mbere River

Khybe River

Koitoboss River

Elephant Platform

Chepnyalil Cave

Mackingeny Cave

Salt Lake Campsite

Kitum Cave

Mount Elgon Lodge

Kapkuro Campsite

Chorlim Gate

Nyati Campsite

Rongai Campsite

Kossowai Gate (closed)

Kimothon Gate (closed)

Kimothon River

Kassowai River

Kiboiwan River

Sosio River

Elgon (Austrian) Hut (disused) 3353m ■

Kibusi River

Kaptit River

Terim River

Malikisi River

Malikisi River

Sit River

N

0 2 km

▲ Endebess, Kitale & Suam Bridge   Endebess & Kitale ▲

▶ Chepkitale Forest Station & Kimilili (30km)

▲ Bumagabula (6km)

across the caldera in Uganda, but the most evocatively shaped peaks (Sudek, 4176m; Lower Elgon, 4301m; Koitoboss, 4187m; and Endebess Bluff, 2563m) belong to Kenya. The mountain has good rock-climbing but you must be properly equipped; the best is on the cliffs of Lower Elgon, Sudek and the nearby pinnacles. Again, you'll need clearance from someone in authority. Actually up in the caldera (technically in Uganda), the **warm springs** by the Suam River provide a tempting bath.

In the 1980s, Elgon was the scene of a number of **violent confrontations** between elephant poachers and armed park rangers. The last serious outbreak was in 1988 and resulted in several deaths. For some time, Kenyan officials were turning back non-4WD vehicles, even outside the park, and preventing hikers on foot from climbing. In 1992, **ethnic strife** swept the communities of Elgon's eastern slopes as the democracy movement gained momentum. The people of Kimilili, Endebess and Kolongolo towns were victims of arson, sporadic violence and furious bouts of intimidation directed against non-Kalenjin by gangs of youths of uncertain identity. Fortunately, violence and poaching have since abated, and should not affect your visit to the park as a tourist.

Practicalities

In most respects, you should treat a trip up Mount Elgon much as you would one to Mount Kenya (see p.180). However, **altitude** is less of a problem on Elgon and, given several days to climb it, few people will be badly affected by the ascent, except perhaps near the summits. Access to the national park is easy, with two or three matatus most days from Kitale, and **hiking within the park** is now permitted if you take a **ranger** as a chaperone/guide (Ksh1000 per day, or Ksh500 for half a day). It is possible to reach the peak from within the national park on foot or with a vehicle, but the vehicle would have to be an extremely sturdy, high-slung 4WD, and you'd need steely nerves, as it's a steep, rocky and extremely muddy ride up to the start of the trail to Koitoboss Peak. Indeed, the route is often completely impassable (January and February are the best months), and at other times of the year even the area west of Chorlim Gate can be extremely treacherous, with plenty of mud, slippery tyre-ruts and ample opportunities to bog down or even roll your vehicle. Without a car, you would need to bring supplies for your party, including ranger, for all the time you are likely to spend in the park.

Timing and guides

Elgon is best from December to March and rather less good in June and July, with the heaviest rains falling during the April to May and August to September periods. This is a lonely mountain, and while there are no specific permanent restrictions on hiking outside the park boundaries (which enclose less than a quarter of the Kenyan slopes), it's probably better not to go up alone. You aren't likely to see anyone else for a day or two, and if something were to happen to you on the heights you can forget about rescue. Finding **guide-porters** is easy enough in villages around the base. Just ask around, and expect to pay up to Ksh1000 per day, plus park entrance fees if necessary. As usual, women travelling alone should try and hitch along with a group.

Maps

If you plan more than a look into the park by vehicle, it's useful to have the *Mount Elgon Map & Guide* by Andrew Wielochowski, obtainable from Executive Wilderness Programmes, Haulfryn, Cilycwm, Llandovery

SA20 0SP (☎01550/721319, ⓦwww.ewpnet.com; £7 including postage within the UK, $18 from elsewhere), and sometimes available at bookshops such as Prestige and Primrose Sundries in Nairobi or in the UK. Survey of Kenya maps are also available, and the 1:125,000 map can be obtained without clearance, though border sensitivity means some other sheets may be restricted at times.

Equipment

Take a **compass** or GPS and supplies for at least two to three days of self-sufficiency. Suggestions on clothing and equipment can be found in the Mount Kenya section (p.180). A **tent** will enable you to stay up in the peaks area, and a **torch** is required if you fancy poking about the caves. If you have a vehicle (4WD essential in the rainy season), you can adjust these requirements. The park rangers are often willing to accompany drivers for a fee (Ksh1000 per day, or Ksh500 for half a day).

Accommodation

Inside the park itself, and on the slopes of the mountain, **camping** is the most obvious way to stay ($8 per person per night), and for hiking deep within the park, it's your only choice. You should try, if at all possible, to **camp** at one of the sites in the lower half of the park – they're highly recommended as some of the most beautiful in the country – and visit the caves. There are four campsites within a kilometre of the Chorlim Gate, of which *Kapkuro* (or *Kuro*), the nearest to the gate, has four good *bandas* available (❹), with showers, but bring food and drinking water.

   Mount Elgon Lodge (PO Box 7 Endebess; ☎0722/572452; reservations also through *Msafiri Inns*, p.63; B&B ❺), is located 1km outside the park on the track leading to Chorlim Gate (no park fees payable), and will appeal to those with money to splash who are partial to faded remnants of the British empire. It's an atmospheric retreat, despite the emptiness, if rather run-down. The manorial reception rooms have lovingly polished wood-block floors and quintessentially English garden views, and the bedrooms are comfortable enough (no nets, but the few mosquitoes here aren't malarial). You can choose between one of three original rooms up a creaking flight of stairs ("Cherangani" is the best), or a more modern cottage room overlooking the lawns. **Camping** in the grounds is an accepted, and very acceptable, alternative to taking a room (Ksh600 per person, including use of bathroom and showers).

   An alternative base is **Delta Cresent Farm** (aka "Captain Davies'", after its owner, who's also the local MP). It's on the way to Chorlim Gate from Endebess (6km from the former, 5km from the latter; PO Box 126 Endebess; ☎054/31462, ⓦwww.deltacrescentcamps.com), where you can camp in your own tent (Ksh200 per person), rent a small tent (Ksh600), or sleep on a bed in a large tent or *banda* (Ksh2000). The campsite is beautifully kept, next to a game sanctuary with Rothschild's giraffes (which can be hand-fed), white rhino, zebras, elands and gazelles. Horses are available for riding, and there are cooking facilities, a lounge, and food and drinks available. Although the farm is accessible from Endebess by *boda-boda*, it's a six-kilometre hike from the park.

Routes to Elgon

There are three **routes** up the Kenyan side of Elgon: one directly into the park and two hikes around either side, but only the former is open to the public at present.

Direct to the park

Daily fees $15, children $5; camping $8 per person; vehicle carrying up to five people Ksh200, six or more people Ksh500. Warden: PO Box 753 Kitale; ☏ 054/31456 or 31457.

The only currently allowed entrance into the **national park** (unless you have permission to enter from the Ugandan side) is through **Chorlim Gate**, which lies some 12km beyond Endebess. Kimothon and Kossowai gates have been closed and unstaffed for some time – using them risks landing you in a lot of trouble, as you will be assumed to be evading park fees. To reach Chorlim Gate, stock up on petrol at Kitale, and head northwest towards Endebess along the tarmac road. There's a brown Kenya Wildlife Service signpost marking the left-hand turning to the national park, 500m after the Kenya Seed Company and ADC compounds. From here, a mostly decent *murram* road heads straight to *Mount Elgon Lodge* and Chorlim Gate (passable with 2WD in dry seasons). If you miss the turning, there's another left turn signposted at Endebess, leading to the same *murram* road (this route is boggier and not for 2WD). Matatus usually run three times a day to *Mount Elgon Lodge* from Kitale (leaving around 3–5pm, depending on passenger numbers), and there are frequent services to Endebess, leaving you with a pleasant two-hour walk, of which you can take a *boda-boda* for the first couple of kilometres. Hoping to find a spare seat in a tourist vehicle isn't really an option: with barely a handful of visitors per month you might be in for a long wait.

Once inside the park, the fine (signposted) campsites a few kilometres from the gate are a good target. They are also the best base for visiting the **Elkony Caves** (see p.336). For **Koitoboss Peak** (4187m), follow the driveable track into the moorlands to the trailhead outside the park (allow 3–4hr to cover the 30km; a ranger should accompany you in your vehicle; 4WD only, and then only safely Jan–Feb). From here it's a three-hour hike to the pass at the southern base of the peak, where there are flat (but cold and windy) places where you can camp. You can then make the one-hour scramble to the top, or take a two- to three-hour diversion to the Suam Springs in the crater.

Crossing into Uganda

If you want to cross the mountain **into Uganda**, you will need to make arrangements in advance with the senior warden (PO Box 753 Kitale; ☏054/31308, ✉menp@swiftkenya.com), who will coordinate with the Ugandan parks authorities on the west side of the mountain. You will also need to stay on the mountain overnight, which means bringing enough food and shelter. You will need to hire a Kenyan ranger to accompany you as far as the hot springs on the border, where you are handed over to the care of a Ugandan ranger (or vice versa if coming the other way), and you will also have to visit Suam to complete border formalities

The **Suam border post** is easily reached by road, and a lot more easy-going than those further south at Malaba and Busia, which are used by commercial traffic. Suam is accessible by regular matatus from Kitale and Endebess. On the other side, there are matatus to Kapchorwa and thence to Mbale, where you'll find onward transport to the rest of Uganda.

The Kimilili and Kimothon routes (currently closed)

The other two routes up the mountain lie outside the national park, but both are within a forest reserve and were closed to the public at last check due to the Ugandan cattle rustlers who operate in the area. However, they may reopen in the future, so it's worth enquiring with the rangers if you would like to try either of them.

Elija Masinde's Dini: the cult of the ancestors

In the 1940s and 1950s, there was a resurgence of **Bukusu resistance** and national-ism in the *Dini ya Msambwa* (Cult of the Ancestors) movement, spearheaded by the charismatic prophet-rebel, **Elija Masinde**. The heart of the movement was in the Elgon foothills between Kimilili and the Ugandan border. It called for the eviction of all *wazungu* and the transfer of their property to Africans. As the *Dini* spread, there were violent confrontations with colonial forces, and a number of deaths. Masinde was sent into internal exile but, by now a folk hero, his followers kept the sparks of resistance alive throughout the more organized uprising of Mau Mau in the Central Highlands, until Independence was finally obtained. The movement collapsed in the early years of *uhuru*, when Masinde was allowed home to Kimilili and his continued denouncements of all authority and claims to divine inspiration began to lose their coherence. Until his death in the 1990s, he could still be seen on the streets of Kimilili – a rather terrifying figure shouting at the wind.

The **western route** begins in **KIMILILI**, a village between Kitale and Bungoma. Matatus between Kitale and Webuye will drop you off at the turn-off for Kimilili, where onward transport is available, and there are a couple of cheap lodges in the village. Kimilili is most lively on a Thursday, when the **market** attracts rural dwellers from a wide radius. From Kimilili it's a seven-kilometre morning matatu ride to **Kapsakwony**, followed by a two-kilometre walk (bear left at the fork above the village) to the Forest Reserve gate, currently closed. When access reopens, you can follow a trail from the gate to the disused Elgon Hut (or Austrian Hut), where you can camp. The trail takes you through the last village, **Kaberua**, 2.5km past the gate, and after a further 8km gets notice-ably worse as it plunges into the cathedral gloom of tsetse-fly-infested bamboo forest. An hour of this and you break into open stands of moss-enveloped giant podocarpus trees ("podos") with spiralling trunks. The **Elgon Hut** is 28km above Kaberua, with a stream nearby but little firewood, so remember to collect some on the way. A brisk three to four hours the following morning should see you to **Lower Elgon Tarn**, from where it's another hour to the top of Lower Elgon.

Alternatively, you could make the five-hour trek from the hut to **Koitoboss Peak** and the **Suam hot springs**, inside the national park (you would need to clear it with the rangers if you intend to do this).

The **third route**, on the north side of the park, which obviates some of the lengthy foot-slogging of the trail from Kimilili, is also currently out of action. It would involve entering the park at the Kimothon Gate, which has been closed for some years now, and where entry remains illegal. The route starts in Endebess and leads west about 12km up to the village of **Masara** and thence to **Kimothon Forest Station**. After spending the night in the station, continue the next day across the park on the well-marked trail to Koitoboss and the Elgon (Austrian) Hut. Downhill from here, you can follow the Kimilili trail (about 40km, as described above) in reverse. Once you reach Kapsakwony there are matatus for the last 7km to Kimilili; it's a ten-hour knee-wobbler of a hike if you want to walk the whole way.

Wildlife

Vegetation on Mount Elgon is similar to Mount Kenya's, and equally impressive, with bamboo and podocarpus forests (the latter more accessible than Mount Kenya's) giving way to open moorland inhabited by the strange statues of giant groundsel and lobelia. **Wildlife** isn't easily seen until you get onto the moors, but some elephant and a fair few buffalo do roam the woods (be extremely wary of both). The best place to see elephants used to be the **Elephant Platform** – herds would congregate here to feed on the acacias – but large numbers were wiped out by Ugandan poachers in the turbulent 1980s, and the remainder became somewhat more reclusive. While the Kenya Wildlife Service is confident that poaching is now under control, and estimates that the elephant population in the park is approaching 200, in a single group, it remains to be seen how long they will remain under effective protection. The lions have long gone and, though there are still leopards and servals, you're not likely to see one. The primates are more conspicuous: blue monkeys (found only in western Kenya) and black and white colobus crash through the forested areas, troops of olive baboons patrol the scrub, and along the Kimothon River there's a scattering of rare de Brazza's monkeys.

The Elkony Caves

Elgon's most captivating attraction is the honeycomb of caves on the lower slopes, inside the national park boundaries. Some of these were long inhabited by one of the loosely related Kalenjin groups, the **Elkony** (whose name, in corrupted form, was given to the mountain), and used both as living quarters and as stock pens at night. There is evidence that the caves may have had a ritual function as well – **Chepnyalil Cave** contains a structure that might have served as an altar or shrine, and its walls are painted with a red-and-white frieze of cattle. To find the cave from the park gate, head north for 2km to the signposted junction for the Caves (south), Park Gate (east) and Koitoboss Peak (north), and turn right 2.5km towards Endebess Bluff, taking the narrow and overgrown track on the left just before the waterfall. Male circumcision ceremonies among the Luhya people are also linked with the caves (as well as others in the region), where boys spent their month-long initiation period, before returning home as

△ Kitum Cave

men, covered head-to-toe in the white diatomite powder found nearby (especially visible at Kitum). The Elkony were officially evicted from the caves by the colonial government, who insisted that they live in the open "where they could be counted for tax", but caves with ceilings as high as two-storey buildings were still occupied by extended families within living memory.

Some of the caves are so large and labyrinthine that deep exploration is only possible with navigational aids and breathing apparatus. It is rumoured that there is a route that leads far into the mountain and emerges in Uganda, a secret passage known only to coffee smugglers. The largest and most spectacular cave is **Makingeny**, marked by a cascade falling over the entrance.

Early explorers believed that some of the caves were man-made, and one report referred to "thousands of chisel and axe marks on the walls". If you actually visit the caves, you'll realize very quickly (from the stench and football-sized droppings, among other clues) that generations of elephants were responsible: the well-signposted **Kitum Cave** achieved TV fame as the salt fix of local elephants, which still walk into the cave at night on occasion to gouge the salty rock from the walls with their tusks. There have even been cases of elephants falling into crevasses or dying under rock falls caused by their over-eager salt-mining. If you're exceptionally lucky, a night vigil at Kitum Cave may be repaid by a visit from the elephants; the bats and the forest are compensation if you're not.

Kitum Cave earned a certain notoriety in 1994 when it featured as the opening and closing location of *The Hot Zone*, a "true-life thriller" about the deadly Ebola virus written by American journalist Richard Preston. In the book, Preston points out that two victims of Ebola had visited Kitum Cave shortly before they became ill. However, a comprehensive examination of the cave by the US Army's Infectious Diseases Unit, in conjunction with the Kenya Medical Research Unit, found absolutely nothing to link it with the deaths. Preston's book hangs a question mark over the conclusiveness of these findings, but those who know the Elgon area well unanimously wrote off his claims as irresponsible scaremongering. Assuming that it hasn't put you off (and it shouldn't), you'll need permission from the rangers and a good torch to visit the caves, but be warned that it is a potentially dangerous exercise: plan your escape route well.

The Uganda road: Webuye and Malaba

Though it's the least interesting part of western Kenya to look at mostly undulating grasslands and Kenya's largest sugarcanefields, the route through Malaba is a good alternative to that via Busia (see p.294) for travellers passing between Kenya and Uganda. Should passenger rail services resume, it will undoubtedly become the main border crossing point, as indeed it once was.

If you're making your way to the south from this district down towards Kakamega and Kisumu, the busy A1 will take you through some fine strands of forest and tropical woodland, heralding the Kakamega Forest zone (see p.342) to the southeast.

Webuye and around

WEBUYE is the site of the giant Panafrican (abbreviated as "Pan") Paper Mills, which dominate the countryside around. The explanation for the factory's siting is **Webuye Falls**, gushing through rock clefts behind and above the mills, about 5km from the main road. Formerly known as Broderick Falls, they are hardly spectacular but make a nice spot for a picnic. To reach them by car or on foot (a long walk), turn off the main road at the factory and climb northwards between housing developments and mills. Alternatively, take a *boda-boda*.

Chetambe's Fort

A few kilometres away, on top of the steep scarp that rears up beyond the Kitale road, lies a different kind of monument, the remains of **Chetambe's Fort**. This was the site, in 1895, of a last-ditch stand by the Bukusu group of the Luhya tribe against the motley line-up of a British punitive expedition, which had enrolled Ugandan, Sudanese, Maasai and even other Luhya troops. A predictable – Hotchkiss gun – massacre took place, with negligible losses on the attackers' side, and equally few survivors among the defenders. How the British managed to storm the scarp in the first place, however, is a mystery: presumably the Bukusu were all inside their walled fort at the top.

The "Fort" itself is quite unimpressive, and in fact not easy to make out: all that remains these days is a circular field covering a couple of hectares, surrounded by a ditch, and next to an old water tower. The spot where the British placed their deadly gun is just west of the water tower, but you'd need to know where to look, and not all local residents will be able to tell you, though some of the people who live nearby are glad to show visitors the site, and can even tell you stories of finding bones in the compound area, of women coming here to weep in the evenings, and even of animal sacrifices to the dead warriors.

A roundabout alternative to the steep climb up the cliffs, if you feel like a hike, is to take the road that leads to Webuye Falls, taking a left at *Wembuye Falls (Nabuyole) Lodge* – a basic **B&L** (❶), with a bar. Continue for about 8km, past a KBC satellite transmitter, to the water tower, and be aware that if you ask local people for directions en route, they may simply assume, whatever you say, that it's the falls you're looking for.

The road to Uganda

The only town of any size between Wembuye and the Ugandan border is **BUNGOMA**, an unremittingly dull place, which has the first ATM you'll find if coming from Uganda (at the local branch of Barclays), but doesn't otherwise merit a visit. West of Bungoma, the tarmac is smooth and the scenery unexciting until you reach the border crossing at Malaba.

Malaba: the Ugandan border

MALABA is less used by passenger road traffic than Busia, but it's where most freight, as well as the (presently freight-only) railway line, crosses the border with **Uganda**. While there are usually endless lines of lorries waiting on both sides, pedestrians can cross without difficulty. Formalities are relatively simple, and Irish citizens do not currently need a Ugandan visa, although Brits, North Americans, Australians and New Zealanders do. Money changers are on hand both sides of the border. Try to find out the current rates in advance (around Ush1700 for $1 or Ush25 for Ksh1 in late 2005) and watch out for scams (such as trying to pass off Ush105,000 as Ush150,000): count the currency you're buying carefully before handing yours over.

Arriving in Kenya, note that there are currently no passenger train services, but several bus companies do the run to Nairobi via Eldoret, of which Akamba (☎055/54232; departures at 11am & 8pm) has the safest reputation. Matatus serve Bungoma, Kisumu, Kitale and Eldoret; on the Ugandan side, they run to Tororo, Jinja and Kampala. Few people hang around here, but if you do need to stay, *Jaki Guesthouse*, on the south side of the main drag about 500m from the border post (PO Box 20; ☎055/54004; ❷), is your best bet, with cheap, plain and simple s/c singles and doubles, or pricier and fancier doubles in the main block. While near the border, especially if distracted by the formalities of crossing, don't make the mistake of relaxing your security routines – people are sometimes robbed soon after arrival here.

Kakamega and Kakamega Forest

KAKAMEGA is the headquarters of the **Luhya**, a loosely defined group of peoples whose only clear common denominator is a **Bantu language**, spoken in more than a score of vernaculars, that distinguishes them from the Luo to the south and the Kalenjin to the east. Numerically, the Luhya (Abaluhya/Luyia) are Kenya's second largest ethnic group, and most are settled farmers.

Kakamega's only sight as such, and some 5km south of town at that, is a landmark known as the **crying stone**, a tooth-like pillar of rock to the east of the A1 road between Kakamega and Khayega, just north of the hamlet of Ilesi. A boulder sits on top of the rock in a shallow indentation, and when it rains, water seeps out under the boulder, running down the pillar of rock and leaving what looks like a tear stain. Keep an eye out for it if you're travelling along the main road.

Kakamega itself was founded as a buying station on the ox trail known as Sclater's Road, which reached here from the coast in 1896. Historically, its only fame came in the 1930s, when gold was discovered nearby and more than a thousand prospectors came to the region. Very few fortunes were made. In the early 1990s, Kakamega became the first town in Kenya to use the bicycle taxis known as *boda-bodas*, now almost a nationwide institution. Today, it's a lively town, but with little to detain casual visitors.

Conversely, the nearby **Kakamega Forest** is one of western Kenya's star attractions; if you have any interest at all in the natural world, it's worth going far out of your way to see. Fortunately, it's fairly easy to get to from Kisumu or, if you've been in the Mount Elgon region, from Webuye along a very scenic stretch of the A1.

Practicalities

If you arrive late in the day (or after around 2.30pm in 2WD, when the rain starts to fall), you may want to **stay in town** rather than arrive in the forest after dark. There are several decent lodgings and places to eat.

Akamba buses (☎056/30517) run daily to Nairobi via Kisumu at 8.30am and 8pm. Coast Buses has a service to Nairobi and Mombasa at 5.30pm, and to Mumias and Bungoma at 4.30pm. All depart from opposite the Hindu Temple, just off the main roundabout. Alternative services are run by Easy Coach (to Kisumu, Kericho, Nairobi and Mumias) and Star Liner (to Mombasa) from offices close by. Most matatus leave from the main stand on the Sudi Road, but those for Mumias have their own stand on the Mumias Road.

Accommodation

Ambwere Alliance Hotel Sudi Rd, nearly opposite the Total station; PO Box 423 ☎0721/646948. A hotel rather than a B&L, at the lower end of mid-range but decent enough, with clean but plain rooms, hot water, mosquito nets and parking. B&B ❸

KAKAMEGA

ASK Showground, Kakamega Forest National Reserve & Webuye (A1)

Mumias (C40)

Mumias Road

Kisumu & Kakamega Forest National Reserve (A1)

KHASAKHALA ROAD

KENYATTA AVENUE

CANNON AWORI STREET

SUDI ROAD

N

0   100 m

Mumias Matatus
Mobil
Deep Supermarket
Vaghela Bookshop
Coastline Buses
Easy Coach
Akamba Buses
Hindu Temple
Library
Barclays Bank
Caltex
Kakamega Sports Club
SomKen
Standard Chartered Bank
KCB (bank)
Mama Watoto Supermarket
Town Hall
Muliro Garden
Taxis
Kenol
SomKen
Market
Matatu & Bus Park
Total

RESTAURANTS, BARS & CLUBS

Lawino 2000	4
Merry Eating House	2
Msafari Bar	5
Musera Bar & Restaurant	3
Pizza Hut Café	6
Salama	10
Snack Stop Café	D
Stardom	1
Umoja Bar	8
Western Hotel	9
Western Region Bar	7

ACCOMMODATION

Ambwere Alliance	G
Franka	B
Golf	F
Jionee Guesthouse	D
Premier	E
Vike Guesthouse	A
Voi Guesthouse	C

Franka Hotel PO Box 621 ☏ 0734/929787. Secure parking, plenty of clean s/c rooms, some with good views, erratic hot water, a good bar, reasonable breakfasts, and *nyama choma* in the evenings. All in all, a good choice. ❶

Golf Hotel Khasakhala Rd; PO Box 118 ☏ 056/30150–1, ✉ golfhotelkak@africaonline .co.ke (reservations via Msafiri Inns, p.63). A relatively luxurious hotel with its pretensions comically clipped by the vultures hopping over the lawns. There's a pool and gift shop, but non-Kenya resident rates are high. B&B ❻

🏃 **Jionee Guesthouse** Cannon Awori St; PO Box 2249 ☏ 056/30840. A friendly little place above the *Snack Stop Café*, the plain but spick-and-span rooms have nets, though bathroom facilities are shared. ❷

Premier Hotel Cannon Awori St; PO Box 1961 ☏ 0331/30134. Once you get past the rather kitsch lobby, it looks like they started building this hotel and gave up halfway, but the rooms are s/c, large and comfortable, some with balconies, and a choice of baths or showers, and the bar has Congolese and Luhya *isukuti* music Fridays and Sundays (so those in need of quiet should ask for a room away from it on those days). ❷

Vike Guesthouse PO Box 1649 ☏ 056/30314. Balconied rooms, all s/c with spotless squat toilets, nets and hot water. It can get loud at night, though, thanks to its ground-floor bar-restaurant and echoing acoustics. ❶

Voi Guesthouse PO Box 2413 ☏ 0722/967290. A couple of doors from the *Vike*, and a reasonable alternative, with metal-doored, concrete-floored single or double s/c rooms, hot water, and good views over town from the top floors. ❷

Eating and drinking

In addition to the hotel restaurants, there are some great cheap **eats** in Kakamega, and plenty of places to drink and listen to music, too. One good cheap eatery is the *Merry Eating House* – don't be put off by its dingy exterior or tumbledown interior: the fried tilapia is excellent. Cannon Awori Street has a few good eating places: the Somali-run *Salama Hotel* serves cheap and copious meals, there's a long list of Kenyan standards at the *Western Hotel*, and a shorter list of plain but decent Kenyan fare at *Snack Stop Café*. Across the street, *Pizza Hut Café* is a bright little place that only actually has one variety of pizza on the menu, and fairly awful at that, but it offers plenty of other choices. Quite an interesting option is 🏃 *Lawino 2000* ("our mission – West Kenya cuisine becomes global"), which has a variety of local dishes, such as *alya* (smoked beef), with a wide choice of staples to accompany, plus real coffee, low prices, and even wine. For **drinking places** with character, you're spoilt for choice: the bar at the *Franka* is one of the liveliest drinking holes; *Musera Bar and Restaurant* is very mellow, as is *Msafari Bar*. *Umoja Bar* and *Western Region Bar* (the latter with pool tables) are for more hardened boozers. The town's only **nightclub**, 🏃 *Stardom*, has a good bar with forest-style decor, and opens up its dancefloor on Wednesdays, Fridays and Saturdays for a mix of reggae, rumba and soul sounds.

Listings

Books Vaghela Bookshop by the Akamba bus office has a reasonable selection of Kenyan and other English-language fiction. The local library is open Mon–Thurs 8am–6.30pm, Fri 8am–4pm, Sat 8am–5pm.

Initiation ceremonies In August every year, Kakamega hosts a mass circumcision and initiation ceremony for boys from all the Luhya-speaking communities in the district. It's not certain how much you can get involved, but the party atmosphere should be unmistakeable. Ask locally.

Internet access A few places in the complex in front of the *Ambwere Alliance Hotel* offer Internet access. There's also a place by the SomKen station on Sudi Rd, but it costs twice as much.

Kakamega Show End of November for three days at the ASK Showground.

Kenya Wildlife Service To reach the KWS office, go past the *Golf Hotel*, turn right at the roundabout, follow the road past the District Commissioner's office (which it's behind) to the next junction, where you turn left and it's on the left after 50m (☏ 056/30603).

Market There's a very lively one next to the bus station. Among the local produce on offer you'll find natural remedies and medicines made from forest plants. Main market days are Wed and Sat.

Supermarkets Mama Watoto on Cannon Awori St, and Deep Supermarket next to Agip.
Swimming pool A small one at the *Golf Hotel* (Ksh100 if you aren't a guest).

The Kakamega Forest

Some four hundred years ago, the tract of rainforest now called **Kakamega Forest** would have been at the eastern end of a broad expanse of forest stretching west, clear across the continent, virtually unbroken as far as the Atlantic. Three hundred years later, after the advent of the human population explosion and widescale cultivation, the forests everywhere had receded, and had reduced Kakamega to an island of some 2400 square kilometres, cut off from the rest of the Guineo-Congolan rainforest. Today, with an area not surpassing 230 square kilometres, it's a tiny patch of relict equatorial jungle, famous among zoologists and botanists around the world as an example of how an isolated environment can survive cut off from its larger body. The Kakamega Forest is a haven of shadowy gloom for over 300 species of birds, 45 percent of all recorded butterflies in Kenya, seven species of primates and other mammals, as well as snakes, various other reptiles and untold varieties of insects. Many of these animals are found nowhere else in East Africa because similar habitats no longer exist. The very real fear among environmentalists now is that even this tiny surviving remnant of rainforest, unique in Kenya, is itself in grave danger of complete elimination.

Despite a laudable scheme aiming to educate the local population about the forest (see box, p.346), the lack of any coherent backing or action from the authorities means that the long-term future of the forest isn't looking bright. Pressure from the local people who need grazing for their livestock, land to cultivate, and firewood, amounts to a significant threat. The present area is less than a tenth of what it was in 1900, and its closed canopy cover (which indicates the forest's health and maturity) has dropped from ninety to fifty percent. This has led to the inevitable degradation of the local natural habitat, which in turn has led to some species being threatened, and some – like leopard, which was last seen in 1992 – becoming extinct (the year coincided with an attack by Nandi villagers on the forest cats which, they claimed, had been killing their livestock). Much of the wardens' time is spent patrolling the forest or observing it from lookout points on nearby hilltops, although some newspaper reports in 1998 accused the wardens themselves of adding to the forest's destruction by illegally selling off plots for cultivation. The way things stand, the survival of this unique habitat depends to a considerable degree on the continued support and concern of visitors to the region.

The forest is fragmented, interspersed with open fields of grassland, cultivated stream margins, small settlements and even tea plantations, though the latter have in part been planted by the government in order to provide a natural protective barrier, as well as to give the locals an alternative source of income to plundering the forest. **Two main areas** can be visited. The first, which has been accessible for many years, is the central **Kakamega Forest Reserve**, lying east of Kakamega town and somewhat off the beaten track. It is to a part of one of the densest stands in this area that most visitors come, to the **Forest Rest House** in the glade at its edge. The second section, the **Kakamega Forest National Reserve**, is northeast of the town and very easy to get to.

The central district: Kakamega Forest Reserve

On arriving at *Forest Rest House* (see below), visitors are greeted by an official guide (a member of Kakamega Biodiversity Conservation Tour Operators,

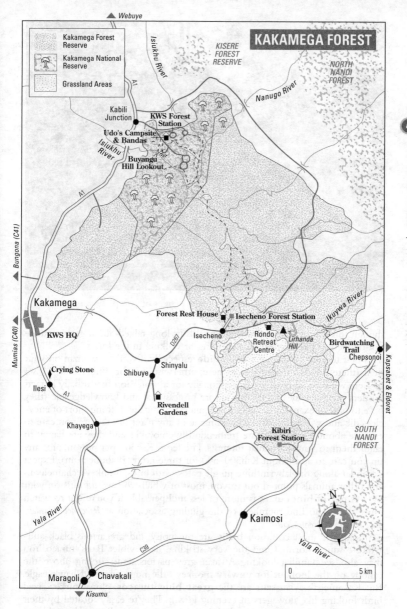

KaBiCoTOa for short), whose name should be on the board outside the hut on the path up to the house. You will be given a brief introduction to the region and the conservation work being done by KEEP (see box on p.346; all guides should have a KEEP identity card), which is attempting to educate villagers and schoolchildren on the outskirts of the forest on the importance of preserving it. You may be asked to make a contribution to the effort (Ksh100 minimum),

△ Kakamega Forest

though this is optional – until KWS installs its long-talked-about gates, you are not obliged to pay anything for entering or walking in the forest.

It's best to take up the offer of a **guide**, especially if you're a woman on your own (there are five female guides here; otherwise, ask for Wilberforce, Moses or Ben, who are all reliable). Exceptionally for a profession that usually attracts hustlers out for easy money, this lot are professional and knowledgeable (they have to pass an exam before becoming guides). Some are nothing short of encyclopedic and will rattle off the Latin name of any plant or creature you care to enquire about. Their walks are tremendously enjoyable, and they are happy to tailor them to your particular interests. The fee is Ksh300 per person, plus any tip you care to add (about Ksh300–500 for three hours is about right). Expect a wander along the labyrinthine jungle paths, with birds, monkeys, chameleons and other animals pointed out to you, most of which you would miss on your own. A pair of **binoculars** is more or less indispensable if you're out to watch birds. You'll also find members of the guiding association at *Rivendell Gardens* and *Rondo Retreat Centre*.

Among the most common **birds** are the noisy and gregarious black-and-white-casqued hornbill and the very striking, deep violet Ross' turaco. You may also see familiar-looking African grey parrots and, circling above the canopy on the lookout for unwary monkeys, the huge crowned hawk eagle. But Kakamega's avian stars are the **great blue turacos**, glossy, turkey-sized birds looking like dowagers in evening gowns. They're easily located by their raucous calls; a favourite spot at dusk is the grove of very tall trees down by the pumphouse. They arrive each evening to crash and lurch among the branches as they select roosting sites.

The forest draws mammal-watchers as well, particularly for the **monkeys**. Troops are often seen at dusk, foraging through the trees directly opposite the *Rest House* veranda. Apart from the ubiquitous colobus, you can see blue monkeys and the much slimmer black-cheeked white-nosed monkey (most easily recognized by its red tail). They're often seen milling around with the hornbills. You may also see pairs of giant forest squirrels capering in the treetops; the deep booming call you sometimes hear in the morning is theirs.

At **night**, armed with a powerful torch, you might catch a glimpse of bush-babies, palm civets, genets or a potto, a slow-moving, lemur-like animal whose name aptly conveys its appearance and demeanour. The forest is also home to several species of fruit bat, of which the hammer-headed fruit bat (*Hypsignathus monstrosus*) is the largest in Africa, with a wingspan of a metre and an enormous head. Other nocturnal Kakamega specialities are the otter shrew, which lives in some of the forest streams, the tree pangolin (a kind of arboreal scaly anteater) and the flying squirrel.

The forest's **reptile life** is legendary, but few people seem to actually see any **snakes** (you're much more likely to come across **chameleons**). Reptiles spend a good deal of time motionless, especially when frightened, and to see any in the dense foliage you have to be well tuned in. Visible or not, however, snakes are abundant and you certainly shouldn't walk in the forest in bare feet or sandals: the gaboon viper, growing to a metre or more in length, and fatter than your arm, is a dangerous denizen of the forest floor. To avoid an encounter, simply walk heavily – they're highly sensitive to vibration and will flee at your seismic approach.

If you have time for more than one daylight walk, you could ask a guide to show you the way to **Lirhanda Hill**, via a trail rich in medicinal plants. You will be shown which leaves, berries and saps the forest dwellers chew, swallow or anoint themselves with to treat various ailments. Lirhanda Hill itself is a lookout point, offering fine views over the whole expanse of forest, with the sombre bulk of Mount Elgon glowering in the distance. Cutting into the hillside near the top is a gold-mining shaft, long disused and now home to a large colony of bats. With a powerful torch and a steely nerve you can grope your way along the tunnel to meet them at close quarters.

Arrival

There are several ways of **getting to** the *Forest Rest House* (beware that maps of Kenya sometimes locate the forest incorrectly). If you're **driving**, the easiest road is from **Khayega**, some 10km south of Kakamega on the A1. From here, an earth road leads 7km to Shinyalu. The junction is marked by signposts for the Arap Moi Girls' School and the Office of the President. Keep right at Shinyalu and continue for another 5km, and turn left just after the barrier and a signposted arrow. From here, it's less than a kilometre up the trail to the *Rest House*. An alternative route from Kakamega turns off to the left at the southern edge of Kakamega town, past the KWS offices, up to Shinyalu, whilst there's a more direct route from Eldoret and Kapsabet starting at Chepsonoi on the C39 (signposted "Kisieni 12km D267"). The direct road from Kakamega is in a worse condition than the Khayega road, but note that whichever approach you're taking, the surfaces get treacherously slippery in wet weather (especially for low-clearance 2WDs). Given the relatively metronomic afternoon rains, this limits you to getting there between 10am and 2pm, when the road is at its driest. Even so, 4WD is advisable.

If you're using **public transport**, the best way is to catch a matatu from Kakamega **SHINYALU**; there are very occasional matatus from Khayega too, or you could take a *boda-boda* from there. From Shinyalu, it's a lovely hour-long walk to Isecheno, along the road heading left. If you don't want to walk, you'll have to hitch a lift with a passing vehicle, or else hire a *boda-boda* (baggage permitting; Ksh50). Shinyalu itself often has a cattle auction and a major market on Saturdays, when it's worth pausing an hour to soak up the atmosphere of cowboys and corrals in the jungle. It's perfectly possible, of course, to hire a private **taxi** for the trip from Kakamega to the *Rest House* (Ksh600–800), but beware that both taxi drivers and matatu touts sometimes overcharge tourists for the run to the forest (especially if it's raining). **From Eldoret**, any bus or matatu heading towards Kisumu via Kapsabet, Chavakali and Maragoli will pass the turning for Isecheno at **Chepsonoi**, signposted "Kisieni 12km D267". From the junction it takes about three hours to walk through the gorgeous forest scenery to the *Rest House*.

Accommodation

If you're not fussed about luxury, the wooden ⚘ **Forest Rest House** is a delight. Someone writing in the visitor's book calls it a "budget *Treetops*", a description that scarcely does it justice. Ringed by forest, the *Rest House* has just four first-floor two-bed rooms, with a long veranda facing onto the wall of tropical greenery a few metres away. There are blankets, pillows and sheets, but you might bring an extra blanket or sleeping bag as it can get decidedly chilly early in the morning. Water supplies are somewhat erratic: when the pump is working, each room has a functioning bathroom and toilet, otherwise you have to fetch water from the pumphouse. There's no electricity and the closest reliable *dukas* are about 3km away on the road to Shinyalu, so it's best to bring your own supplies. For candles and simple staples – bananas, *chai*, mineral water, biscuits, sodas and occasional beers – there's a small *duka*/canteen on the way to the pumphouse, which is open daily. Here hot meals are cooked to order (given a few hours' notice); apart from breakfast, the food is generous, reliable and very fresh, and a much better bet than struggling to build your own cooking fire in the campsite or underneath the *Rest House* itself (during the wet season it can rain for days on end).

To be sure of a room – especially at weekends – you can **reserve in advance** (write to: The Forester; PO Box 1233 Kakamega, Western Province; rates are very economical, at around Ksh385 per person). It is also possible to **camp** by

---

"Keep our forest"

Building on groundwork laid by the Kenya Indigenous Forest Conservation Project, the **Kakamega Environmental Education Programme** (KEEP) was set up by the guides at *Forest Rest House* to coordinate environmental educational programmes to primary and secondary school children from the local area. This combines lessons with visits to the forest, and it is hoped that by convincing the children of the importance of protecting and preserving the forest, the message will be passed to their parents and other family members. They've started a tree nursery to demonstrate basic tree-planting techniques to children, as well as giving information on waste recycling and more efficient use of firewood. A butterfly farm has also been set up, with the aim of breeding local butterflies to mount, frame and sell as souvenirs or to collectors, thus generating income for the local community from the forest itself. Other projects in the pipeline with similar aims include bee-keeping and snake farming, all sustainable sources of income dependent on forest conservation.

They're especially keen to involve environmentalists and other experts in their effort: "to give us ideas, material and mental assistance for our project". You can also become a "Friend of KEEP" for a subscription of Ksh1500 per year. If you're interested in joining, or can offer any other help, contact KEEP at Kakamega Forest Station; PO Box 11, 50107 Shinyalu; ☏0722/619150, ✉keeporg@yahoo.com, or meet up with Wilberforce Okeka at the KEEP office.

the *Rest House*, or even underneath it (Ksh225 per person, but don't leave tents unattended), or to sleep on the veranda, or use one of two empty *bandas* for the same price.

Alternatively, KEEP's own **Isecheno Bandas** are located right next door to the *Rest House*. At $10 per person, they are more expensive, but the money is used locally for KEEP's ongoing community conservation projects. There are five *bandas*, with beds, blankets, sheets and pillows, and a separate shower and toilet block. They can be booked through KEEP, or via Let's Go Travel in Nairobi (see p.150). As at the *Forest Rest House*, you can either bring food and firewood to self-cater, or make arrangements locally to have meals provided.

For those who require a higher level of comfort, the upmarket option is the ⚘ **Rondo Retreat Centre**, a fine old 1928 sawmiller's house (location for much of the filming of Harry Hook's *The Kitchen Toto*) about 4km east of the *Rest House* turning (no phone at the centre, reservations c/o Trinity Fellowship; PO Box 2153 Kakamega; ☎056/30268, ⓦwww.rondoretreat.com; FB ❺). This is a comfortable base: very fresh and elegant, furnished like an English country house with just enough clutter to make it feel homely, and wonderful bright four-poster bedrooms, set among cool lawns. The dining room is open to non-residents, but the Christian management does not serve alcohol. It's highly advisable to reserve well in advance, as it is often booked up, and arrangements can be made to collect guests from Kakamega town or even Kisumu. Again, the way to get here without your own transport is by matatu to Shinyalu and *boda-boda* or on foot from there.

If on the other hand you want to stay somewhere with beer and music, and to socialize with ordinary local residents, the **Camiha Café** at the start of the Isecheno road in Shinyalu itself (PO Box 297 Shinyalu; ☎0724/142645; ❶) might fit the bill. It's really just a café and bar, with four basic rooms (singles, but can fit a couple) and bucket showers (hot water on request); food is available, and there's music till late. The disadvantage is that it isn't actually in the forest.

Also outside the forest and 2km to the south (1.5km down a track leading off the Khayega road from the village of Shibuye), **St Gonzaga Rivendell Gardens** (PO Box 249 Khayega ☎0735/214644; ❸) is a quieter and more sober retreat with a wooden ranch house and five guest *bandas* (not s/c) in the gardens. Camping is allowed (Ksh400 per person), and food can be arranged. Again, you'll have to make do with bucket showers, but hot water is available.

Kakamega Forest National Reserve

Kenya Wildlife Service District Warden; PO Box 879 Kakamega; ☎056/30603, Ⓔwarden@africaonline.co.ke; $10 per day/overnight; children $5; private vehicle Ksh200.

Some 20km north of Kakamega town, there are two turnings off to the right: one is signposted to the Kakamega Forest National Reserve; the other, 50m further on, is signposted "Kenya Wildlife Service Kisere Nature Reserve 6km" and "Kambiri 7km D267". It's the first track you want – if heading north from Kakamega on an Eldoret-bound vehicle, ask for Kabili Junction. The Kakamega Forest National Reserve Forest Station is 2–3km along the way and you can pick up a KaBiCoTOa guide to help you orientate yourself if you wish, though they have in the past been prone to overcharging (see overleaf). Women on their own might prefer to take a guide from the *Forest Rest House* anyway.

For visitors with their own vehicles, it's easier to get around this part of Kakamega Forest than the central zone. The forest proper is, in fact, a fair walk from the base of the KWS-run *Udo's Bandas and Campsite* ($10 per person), named after the ornithologist Udo Savalli. Here there are seven thatched *rondavels* (due to be upgraded), six with two beds and one with four beds, and a stream for fresh water, but no food (book through the KWS District Warden; see above). You can also camp ($8 per person). Entrance to the reserve costs $10; in the past unscrupulous guides have been known to claim there was a Ksh100 fee for all forest walks, guided or not – this is not the case, and if in doubt about the authenticity of any charges, you should ask for a receipt.

A number of driveable – and walkable – tracks through the coolness of the forest begin just beyond the forest station. The main trail is well signposted and there are numerous branches and "exit" trails that allow for a relatively quick return when you've had enough of the deep forest. It's not a place you're likely to get lost in, despite its remoteness.

The significant difference between the reserve here and the forest further south is the age of the growth in the reserve. Many of the **trees** are colossal (indeed some have plaques inviting you to guess the girth – answers round the back). The climate is generally drier and there's a greater diversity of habitat, including areas of scrub, young forest and ancient forest. It's an impressive area and, as in the southern forest, there's a huge variety of birdlife and many monkeys.

An easy excursion from the forest station is to the **Isiukhu Falls**, a rather feeble waterfall 1.5km away along a rocky path. **Buyangu Hill viewpoint**, a four-kilometre drive or walk from the forest station, is much more worthwhile – a precipice with a spectacular vista east across the forest to the Nandi Escarpment.

The **Kisere Forest Reserve** (as signposted at the turn-off) is a separate area, a small outlying part of the main reserve and home to de Brazza's monkeys among others, with some superb examples of the prized timber tree, the Elgon olive.

Onwards from Kakamega

The obvious routes out of the area lie along the A1 to Kitale or Kisumu. The road **down to Kisumu** is a real roller coaster, though in relatively good condition (occasional patches of potholes), with a final eight-kilometre descent over the picturesque, boulder-strewn Nyando Escarpment, which brings Lake Victoria into view. In clear weather, it allows fantastic panoramas across the sugar fields of the Kano plains towards the massif of the Mau and the Kisii hills. Look out for the florid **church** on the left, the headquarters of a local denomination that models itself on the Coptic church, founded in Egypt in the early years of Christianity.

Alternatively, there's a beautiful road **east to Kapsabet** in the Nandi Hills, starting at the bustling rural centre of Maragoli/Chavakali (also spelled Chyvakali and Kyavakali), along the Kisumu road. Note that Maragoli is the "shopping centre" on the A1, while Chavakali, effectively part of the same community, is a kilometre or so off to the east.

Lastly, if you have time and inclination for a diversion far off any beaten track, you could visit the small town of **Mumias**, the sugar belt's biggest processing centre and also one of western Kenya's Muslim strongholds. The road from Kakamega is paved and there's regular transport.

Mumias

MUMIAS was originally *Mumia's*, capital of the Luhya-speaking mini-state of **Wanga**, and well established by the middle of the nineteenth century at the head of an important caravan route to the coast. **Mumia**, who came to power in 1880, was its last king. His 10,000-strong army – half of them dispossessed Maasai from the Uasin Gishu Plateaum – was largely responsible for smashing Bukusu resistance at Chetambe's Fort fifteen years later (see p.338).

Even at the beginning of Mumia's reign, Europeans were beginning to arrive in the wake of Arab and Swahili slave-traders, who in turn had been settling in since the 1850s with the full accord of the Wanga royal family. By 1894 there was a permanent British sub-commissioner or collector of taxes posted here. Mumia had always welcomed strangers, and he allowed the slavers to continue their work on other Luhya groups (notably the Bukusu), but he was unprepared for the swift usurpation of his authority by the British, whom he'd assumed were also there to trade. He was appointed "Paramount Chief" of a gradually diminishing state and then, as an old man, was retired without his real knowledge. He died in 1949, aged 100, and with him expired Kenya's first (and only) indigenous, upcountry state, almost without notice.

The town's present **mosque** (just by the junction of the Bungoma and Kakamega roads) was built in King Mumia's honour and its Koran school is just one of about 25 around the town. Mumias has long been a centre of Islam, famous for its coastal ways, but today women in *buibuis* – the long, black coverall of the coast – are rarely seen, and Islam is losing ground to Catholicism. The Catholic church (2km down the Kakamega road) is also reasonably impressive, though neither of the two houses of worship are worth going out of the way for. They do however supply a good excuse for visiting what is a charming and lively little market town.

Mumias has a CKB **bank** with an ATM, and a couple of **places to stay**, of which the best is *Jamaii Yako Guesthouse*, by the supermarket of the same name behind the matatu stand (PO Box 112; no phone; ❶), with basic s/c rooms, nets, and hot water in the mornings. For **food**, *Crossroads Café* opposite the matatu stand on Bungoma Street does breakfasts and snacks, *nyama choma*, and even chicken tikka and chips. **Buses** serve Kakamega, Kisumu and Nairobi, and there's even one a day direct to Mombasa. **Matatus** run to Kakamega, Kisumu, Bungoma and Busia.

The Butere–Kisumu train

Leaving Mumias, a paved road leads directly to Kisumu. Three days a week (Tues, Thurs & Sun at 1pm), there is an alternative in the form of a **train from Butere**, 12km down the road. This branch line was intended to reach Mumias, but never did. Though diesel-hauled since 1988, the train is little faster than it was under steam, taking three hours to cover barely 60km, but it's a boon to rural dwellers with more time than money, as a ticket (third-class only) costs Ksh115, while by matatu you'd have to change vehicles at Mumias, paying a total of Ksh230.

Travel details

Kisumu is the west's transport centre. Buses and matatus run from there to most major centres in this chapter within half a day.

Buses

Eldoret to: Kampala (1 daily; 6hr); Kabernet (1 daily; 2hr); Kericho (4 daily; 5hr); Kisumu (13 daily; 3hr); Kitale (approximately hourly; 1hr 30min); Malaba (2 daily; 3hr); Nakuru (approximately hourly; 2hr 30min); Nairobi (approximately hourly; 5hr).

Kakamega to: Mombasa (1 daily; 14hr); Nairobi (10 daily; 7–9hr) via Kisumu and Kericho, or via Kapsabet and Nandi Hills.

Kericho to: Kisii (1–2 hourly; 3hr); Kisumu (frequent daily; 2hr); Nairobi (1–2 hourly; 6hr).

Kisii to: Homa Bay (4 daily; 2hr); Kisumu (3 daily; 2hr); Migori (5 daily; 2hr); Mombasa (2 daily; 14hr); Nairobi (1–2 hourly; 7–9hr) via Kericho (2hr 30min).

Kisumu to: Eldoret (13 daily; 2hr) via Kapsabet (1hr 15min); Kampala (1 daily; 6hr); Mombasa (5 daily; 14hr); Nairobi (frequent daily; 8hr) via Kericho (2hr) and Nakuru (4–5hr).

Kitale to: Lodwar (6 daily; 7hr); Nairobi (several services daily and overnight; 8–11hr) via Eldoret (1hr 30min) and Nakuru (4hr).

Matatus

With nearly half the population of Kenya living in this region, matatus are widespread and most minor roads have services. Many also run on bus routes at approximately the same fare, but to even less predictable schedules. As usual, Peugeots move faster than Nissan minibuses, which are faster than vans. Slower vehicles are safer.

Eldoret to: Cherangani (1hr); Iten (30min); Kabarnet (1hr 30min); Kakamega (2hr); Kaptagat (20min); Kericho (2hr 30min); Kisumu (2hr); Kitale (1hr); Malaba (2hr 30min); Mumias (2hr 30min); Nairobi (4–6hr); Nakuru (3hr).

Homa Bay to: Kendu Bay (1hr); Kisii (1hr 30min); Kisumu (3hr); Mbita (1hr 30min); Migori (1hr 30min); Rongo (1hr); Sirare (1hr 45min).

Kakamega to: Kericho (2hr 30min); Kisumu (1hr); Mumias (40min); Webuye (1hr).

Kisii to: Eldoret (3hr 30min); Homa Bay (1hr 30min); Kericho (2hr); Kisumu (2hr); Migori (1hr 30min); Nairobi (5hr); Naivasha (3hr); Rongo (30min).

Kisumu to: Busia (2hr 30min); Eldoret (2hr); Homa Bay (3hr); Kakamega (1hr); Kendu Bay (2hr); Kericho (1hr 30min); Kisii (2hr); Kitale (3hr); Luanda Kotieno (2hr 30min); Mbita (4hr 30min); Nairobi (5–6 hr); Nakuru (3hr); Sirare (3hr).

Kitale to: Busia (3hr); Cherangani (30min); Eldoret (1hr); Endebess (30min); Kakamega (3hr); Kisumu (3hr); Makutano (for Kapenguria) (30min); Malaba (2hr 30min); Nairobi (5–7hr); Suam (45min).

Trains

Kisumu to: Butere (3 weekly; 3hr 10min); Nairobi (3 weekly; 14hr).

There are currently no passenger services from Eldoret, Kitale or Malaba, though it is possible that these may resume in the future.

Ferries

Mbita to: Luanda Katieno (4 daily; 45min); Sena (matatu-boat service; 2–5 daily; 1hr) via Takawiri (45min).

The Kisumu–Kendu Bay–Kuwuor–Homa Bay–Mbita–Asembo service is currently suspended.

Flights

Eldoret to: Nairobi (AeroKenya; 1–2 daily; 1hr).

Kisumu to: Nairobi (Kenya Airways and East African Safari Air; 3–5 daily; 40min).

5

The Mombasa road and major game parks

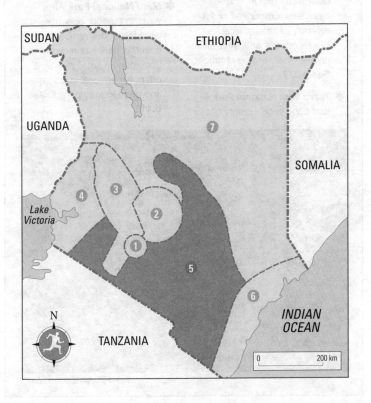

CHAPTER 5 # Highlights

✳ The Taita Hills Steep and densely cultivated, the untouristy Taita Hills are like an outcrop of upcountry highland Kenya, peaking out of the dry plains. Visit the skull caves, rock niches where the heads of Taita ancestors are interred. See p.367

✳ Mzima Springs A remarkable oasis, bubbling with crystal-clear water and inhabited by hippos, crocodiles and a diversity of smaller species. Check out the walkways and under-water viewing chamber. See p.377

✳ Tsavo East National Park A vast park, largely empty but for the plentiful elephants, offering spectacular vistas and relatively easy access. See p.378

✳ Maasai Mara National Reserve At any time of the year, Kenya's most famous park yields an extraordinary diversity of wildlife, and a visit during the annual wildebeest migration can be truly awesome. See p.392

✳ Meru National Park After years in the tour operators' wilderness, this remote and beautiful park has recently undergone a small revival; it offers exceptional landscapes and great lodge options. See p.412

△ A lurking hippo at Mzima Springs

5

The Mombasa road and major game parks

This chapter covers the well-travelled **route** from **Nairobi to Mombasa** and a number of detours off it, along with six of the country's **major game parks**, most within reasonably easy reach of the capital: Amboseli, Maasai Mara, Meru, Samburu-Buffalo Springs-Shaba, and Tsavo East and West.

The **Mombasa Highway** is Kenya's most important thoroughfare. Three-quarters of it has been upgraded, between Sultan Hamud and Katolani, 60km from Mombasa, but the remainder is in a dismal state, ragged-edged, potholed and deeply rutted. With scenic interest marginal for much of the journey, the temptation is to head straight for the coast, stopping only at the **Amboseli** or **Tsavo game parks**. But there are some rewarding diversions, not greatly explored, off the main road (a rental car is helpful for this): east into **Akamba country** and the towns of **Machakos** and **Kitui**, or south towards the base of **Kilimanjaro** (the mass of the mountain lies across the border in Tanzania) and the **Taita Hills**.

The **game parks** in this chapter are, together with the coast, the most visited parts of Kenya – and the archetypal image. This is not to take anything away from their appeal, for the experience is genuinely fabulous. In the 24,000 square kilometres covered by the six parks, animals, not humans, hold sway. Their seasonal movements, most spectacularly in **Maasai Mara**'s wildebeest migration, are the dominant plots in the drama going on all around. Seeing the wildlife isn't difficult, but does require patience and an element of luck that makes it exciting – and addictive.

Most visitors will either already be on a safari, or will book one once in Kenya – either from the coast or from Nairobi. The increasingly popular alternative is to **rent a vehicle**, a sensible if quite expensive option if you want to have more than a few days of wildlife-viewing, and the freedom of choosing your own route. With a limited budget, a no-frills camping safari is about the only practical way; there are details on the ins and outs in Basics, pp.76–82, and plenty of

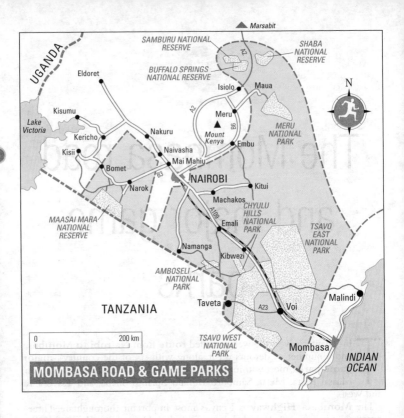

Marsabit

SAMBURU NATIONAL
RESERVE

SHABA
NATIONAL
RESERVE

UGANDA

Eldoret

BUFFALO SPRINGS
NATIONAL RESERVE

Isiolo   Maua

Kisumu

A2

Meru

MERU
NATIONAL
PARK

Lake
Victoria

Nakuru

Mount
Kenya

B6

Kericho

Naivasha

Embu

Kisii

Mai Mahiu

Bomet

B3

NAIROBI

Narok

Kitui

Machakos

CHYULU
HILLS
NATIONAL
PARK

A109

TSAVO
EAST
NATIONAL
PARK

MAASAI MARA
NATIONAL
RESERVE

Emali

Namanga

Kibwezi

AMBOSELI
NATIONAL
PARK

TANZANIA

Taveta

A23

Voi

Malindi

0   200 km

TSAVO WEST
NATIONAL
PARK

Mombasa

INDIAN
OCEAN

N

MOMBASA ROAD & GAME PARKS

operators listed in Nairobi (see pp.149–152) and Mombasa (see pp.446–447).
It remains possible, though by no means easy, to explore the parks by **hitch-ing around** with whoever you meet and **camping** at designated sites. More
specific details are included in the sections on each park. Summaries of the
game parks' individual attractions are given in the introduction on p.272.

Between Nairobi and the
coast

If you take one of the **express buses** from Nairobi to Mombasa, you might
well end up believing that there's nothing worth stopping for along the way
and, if you take the **train**, you won't see anything anyway as it travels in both
directions at night. On the other hand, with a touch of imagination and, ideally,

the luxury of a vehicle, this stretch of the country has a great deal to offer. And any detour into the less well-known parts of **Akamba territory** or down to **Taveta** and the foothills of **Kilimanjaro** should prove a worthwhile antidote to the more purple-rinse excesses of safari-land. There were trains between Voi and Taveta, third-class only and painfully slow; the service was suspended at the time of writing but might be worth considering if it resumes, as it did offer a very cheap three-hour journey through Tsavo West national park with no park fees to pay.

Machakos and Kitui – "Ukambani"

One very good way to start a trip heading towards the coast, if you're in no particular hurry, is to take an excursion right into the heart of **Ukambani**, the land of the Akamba people (adjective and language: Kamba). Buses, matatus and Peugeot taxis leave from Nairobi's Country Bus Station (aka "Machakos Airport") for Machakos all the time. In addition, there's also at least one company that runs a daily Nairobi–Mombasa service by way of the town. From Machakos, frequent buses and matatus continue to Kitui, from where you could catch transport to Kibwezi, back on the Mombasa road.

Akamba men who served in World War I were introduced to the techniques of **wood sculpture** by the Makonde ebony carvers on the Tanganyikan coast. Today, the vast majority of carvings in Kenya are produced by Akamba artists, often in workshops far from Ukambani. The main problem appears to be the middlemen, who take much of the profits; if you're after woodcarvings, try to buy direct from the people who make them, such as in Wamunyu, en route from Machakos to Kitui.

Machakos

The Imperial British East African Company's first upcountry post, established in 1889, **MACHAKOS** is ten years older than Nairobi (and therefore the first

The Machakos miracle

The whole of Ukambani is prone to **drought** and, according to conventional environmental wisdom, its farms and plots should have blown to dust long ago, especially under ever-increasing population pressure. In the 1930s, when the population was five times smaller than now, a British Colonial soil inspector condemned the Ukambani hills as "an appalling example" of environmental degradation in which "the inhabitants are rapidly shifting to a state of hopelessness and miserable poverty and their land to a parched desert of rocks, stones and sand."

Seventy years later, it would be unfair to paint the same picture. Instead of relying on cattle herding, as they did in the past, many Akamba have shifted into small-scale agriculture as a means of survival, with surprising results. You even find apples offered for sale by the roadside, an "exotic" fruit otherwise confined to the perennially rain-soaked orchards of Kisii near Lake Victoria. The trick has been the clever use of the little rain which does fall, through small-scale **terracing** and **irrigation techniques** (such as using roads for catchments) learned by Akamba soldiers while serving in India during World War II. So much for the hopelessness of the 1930s; the situation has been turned around so successfully that some have begun calling this "The Machakos Miracle".

The largely dry stretch of central Kenya from Nairobi to Tsavo park and north as far as Embu has been the traditional homeland of the Akamba people for at least the last five centuries. They moved here from the regions to the south in a series of vague migrations, in search, according to legend, of the life-saving **baobab** tree whose fruit staved off the worst famines, and whose trunks held vast quantities of water.

With a diverse economy in better years, including mixed farming and herding as well as hunting and gathering, the Akamba slowly coalesced into a distinct tribe with one Bantu language. As they settled in the hilly parts, the population increased. But drier areas at lower altitudes couldn't sustain the expansion, so **trade** for food with the Kikuyu peoples in the fatter Highlands region became a solution to the vagaries of their generally implacable environment.

In return for farm produce, the Akamba **bartered** their own manufactured goods: medicinal charms, extra-strong beer, honey, iron tools, arrowheads and a lethal and much-sought-after hunting poison. In the eighteenth and nineteenth centuries, as the Swahili on the coast strengthened their ties inland, **ivory** became the most important commodity in the trade network. With it, the Akamba obtained goods from overseas to exchange for food stocks with the highlands tribes.

Long the **intermediaries** between coast and upcountry, the Akamba acted as guides to Swahili and Arab caravans, and led their own expeditions. Settling in small numbers in many parts of what is now Kenya, they were naturally enlisted by early European arrivals in East Africa. Their broad cultural base and lack of provincialism made them confident travellers and employees, and willing soldiers and porters. Even today, the Kenyan army has a disproportionately high Akamba contingent, while many others work as policemen and private *askaris*.

In the early years of **colonialism**, the Akamba were involved in occasional bloody incidents, but these seem to have been more often the result of misunderstandings than anything concerted. The most famous of these blew up after an ignorant official at Machakos cut down a sacred *ithembo* tree to use as a flagpole. On the whole, the Akamba's old trade links helped to ease their relations with the British. Living – and dying – with British soldiers during **World War I** gave them insights into the ways of the Europeans who now ruled them. Together with the Luo and Kikuyu, the Akamba suffered tens of thousands of casualties in white men's wars.

Akamba **resistance to colonialism** was widespread but mostly non-violent. As early as 1911, however, a movement of total European rejection had emerged. Led by a widow named Siotune wa Kathake, it channelled opposition to colonialism into frenetic dancing, during which teenage girls became "possessed" by an anti-European spirit and preached radical messages of non-compliance with the government. Later, in the 1930s, the Ukamba Members Association (one of whose leaders was **Muindi Mbingu**) was formed in order to pre-empt efforts to settle Europeans in Ukambani and reduce Akamba cattle herds by compulsory purchase. Five thousand Akamba marched in peaceful protest to Kariokor market in Nairobi – a show of collective political will that succeeded in getting their cattle returned.

capital of Kenya according to some Akamba people). "Machakos" is really a corruption of Masaku's, after the headquarters of an Akamba chief of the time. The name is still seen all over town.

Distinctly friendly, and overwhelmingly Kamba, the town has a backdrop of green hills and a tree-shaded, relaxed atmosphere to its old buildings that is quickly endearing. The surrounding Mua Hills have lent their name to a brand of jam from the orchards which thrive on their slopes. The weaving of **sisal baskets** (*vyondo*) is a more visible industry, though, and a major occupation for many women, either full-time or behind the vegetable stand. Machakos effervesces and it's a great place to stay for a day or two, especially on Monday and Friday, market days, and above all if you are into buying some *vyondo* (baskets). Look for (though you can scarcely miss) the truly splendid and quite venerable **mosque**.

Practicalities

Apart from the many produce markets scattered about town, there are two **supermarkets**, Kutata and the Naivasha Self Service Store (both open

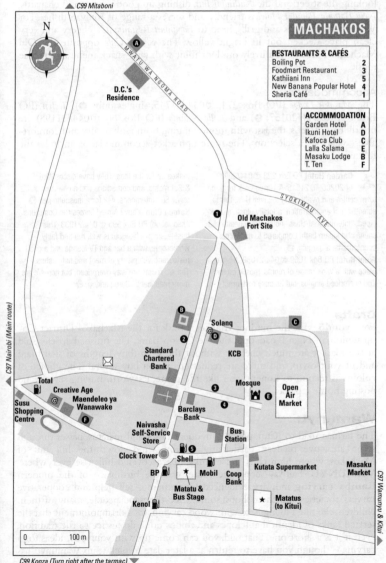

MACHAKOS

RESTAURANTS & CAFÉS
Boiling Pot	2
Foodmart Restaurant	3
Kathiiani Inn	5
New Banana Popular Hotel	4
Sheria Café	1

ACCOMMODATION
Garden Hotel	A
Ikuni Hotel	D
Kafoca Club	C
Lalla Salama	E
Masaku Lodge	B
T. Ten	F

▲ C99 Mitaboni

MWATU WA NGOMA ROAD

D.C.'s Residence

SYOKIMAU AVE

Old Machakos Fort Site

C97 Nairobi (Main route)

Solanq

Standard Chartered Bank

KCB

Total

Creative Age

Maendeleo ya Wanawake

Mosque

Open Air Market

Susu Shopping Centre

Barclays Bank

Naivasha Self-Service Store

Bus Station

Clock Tower

Shell

BP

Mobil

Coop Bank

Kutata Supermarket

Masaku Market

Matatu & Bus Stage

Matatus (to Kitui)

Kenol

0   100 m

C97 Wamunyu & Kitui

357

C99 Konza (Turn right after the tarmac) ▼

Mon–Sat 8am–8pm & Sun 9am–6pm). There's also the supermarket at the new Susu **shopping centre** on the way into town from Nairobi. The Barclays and Standard Chartered **banks** have ATMs. **Emails** can be sent from Creative Age or the Solanq cybercafés. For **buses and matatus** to Nairobi and Mombasa, head for the main stage in the centre of town. For services to Kitui (with connections there for Embu), the stage is just up on the Embu road, beside the noisy *jua kali* metal workers' area.

Machakos has the usual range of **eating places**, few of them gastronomically enticing. Two of the best are the enjoyable *Boiling Pot*, with its balcony overlooking the street; and the *Kathiiani Inn*, dishing up good curries and chapattis. *New Banana Popular Hotel* is friendly and serves a range of Kenyan dishes. For Western-style dishes and grills, head to *Foodmart Restaurant*, a cheery and very clean place decked out in bright yellow. The *Sheria Café* opposite the Old Machakos Fort Site is a lively outdoor joint with tasty snack menu and reggae music.

Accommodation

The *Masaku Lodge* (PO Box 274; ☎044/21745; singles only; ❶), *T. Ten* (PO Box 841; ☎044/20157; ❷) and *Lalla Salama* (PO Box 66; ☎044/21198) are utterly basic **B&Ls**, the last with rooms ranging from rank to airy and comfortable (ask to see a selection). The more upmarket accommodation includes the following:

Garden Hotel PO Box 223 ☎044/20037 or 20285, ℻21515. A 10min walk from the town centre and overlooking the Iveti Hills, this is something of an aberration, a totally plush, muzak-piped, "international-class" hotel with a health club, sauna and steam bath. Compared to its Nairobi counterparts, a bargain. ❺

Ikuni Hotel PO Box 1069 ☎044/21080. A large place with a wide range of rooms, mostly grotty and overpriced singles, but its busy restaurant makes up for it a little. They have discos Wed, Fri & Sat nights, and comedians and a one-man guitar show Sun afternoons. Ask for a mosquito net. ❷

Kafoca Club (Kenya Armed Forces Old Comrades Association) PO Box 595 ☎044/21933. This businessmen's hangout is well run and fairly wholesome, with a bar and TV lounge and a good restaurant with plenty of meat and fish dishes. The s/c rooms are way overpriced, but non-s/c are more reasonable. Safe parking. ❷

Crafts

For **vyondo**, visit the outdoor **market**, or ask for the Machakos District Co-op Union, in Ngei Road, opposite the Co-op Bank. The finished articles sold at the market are much cheaper without the strap (buy lengths of sisal braid and fit your own), and there are reductions if you buy several. The choice of colours is second to none; if you like the genre, it's worth buying several and posting home a parcel.

Wamunyu

The tarmac road to Kitui, plied by frequent buses and matatus, passes through some attractive scenery, particularly as you wind down the hill out of Machakos, where high cliffs and chunky, maize-covered hills rise everywhere. **WAMUNYU**, halfway along the route, was the birthplace of the modern **Kamba carving** industry, evidenced by numerous self-help and cooperative carvers' societies and their shops; some three thousand people, many of them children, eke out a living here with wood carving. It's a disappointment that the serried ranks of identical antelopes and rhinos don't do justice to the tradition, even if it is a short one. That said, you can come up with your own ideas for a carving – though you have to return at a later date to pick it up. Wamunyu has a number of basic **B&Ls**, the best of which is *Manisani Guest House* in Elimu Building (PO Box 171; ☎044/63291; **②**).

Kitui

Like Machakos 58km to the west, **KITUI**, 100km further esat, lies in an impoverished area and, from time to time, is badly hit by drought, with attendant malnutrition and occasional outbreaks of cholera. Despite its proximity to Nairobi, this region at the very edge of the Highlands is one of Kenya's least developed. The town is small and hasn't any outstanding features of interest, but there's a sizeable Swahili population, descendants of the traders and travellers who crisscrossed Ukambani in the nineteenth century. The town's mango trees were planted then, and the abundance of lodging houses is a reminder of the trading tradition. Kitui was the home village of **Kivoi**, the most celebrated Akamba trader. He commanded a large following which included slaves, and it was he who met the German missionary **Ludwig Krapf** in Mombasa and guided him up to Kitui in 1849, where he became the first european to set eyes on Mount Kenya.

Kitui is both a busy market and trading centre, the streets lined with arcaded shops. Despite the lack of sights (excepting perhaps Kauma Glass Mart, *the* place for drums and plastic religious icons), Kitui is an ideal place to get away from more mundane hassles for a few days. The town's atmosphere is the main draw: calm, relaxed and unhustly. The inhabitants are generally very friendly, and making genuine friends here seems easier than elsewhere.

Practicalities

There's nowhere to **stay** in Kitui above the budget category, and nothing much to choose between them, either. Hot water is invariably supplied in buckets. In the town centre, try: *Umau Guest House* (PO Box 202; no phone; **②**), which is friendly and has six large s/c rooms with nets and cold showers; the cleaner *Ark House* (PO Box 230; ☎044/22461; **②**), with seven s/c rooms around a courtyard; *Kithomboani Hotel*, under the same management, with cleanish s/c singles only (Ksh400) with nets; and *Kitui Tourist Hotel* (PO Box 869; ☎044/22254; **②**), also s/c, with nets and window screens, and breakfast thrown in. The best location is offered by the friendly if none-too-clean *Mumoni Hill Lodge* (PO Box 411; no phone; **②**), 2km from the centre down the Kibwezi road just before the

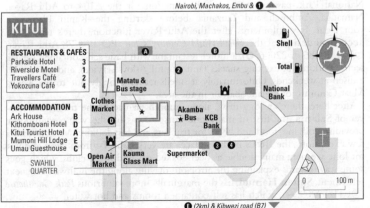

Nairobi, Machakos, Embu & ❶

KITUI

RESTAURANTS & CAFÉS
Parkside Hotel	3
Riverside Motel	1
Travellers Café	2
Yokozuna Café	4

ACCOMMODATION
Ark House	B
Kithomboani Hotel	D
Kitui Tourist Hotel	A
Mumoni Hill Lodge	E
Umau Guesthouse	C

Shell

Total

National Bank

Matatu & Bus stage

Clothes Market

Akamba Bus

KCB Bank

Open Air Market

Kauma Glass Mart

Supermarket

SWAHILI QUARTER

N

0   100 m

❺ (2km) & Kibwezi road (B7)

end of the tarmac. It's a peaceful retreat with four simple rooms with attached toilets (no showers), a relaxed and somnolent bar, and a lovely setting in large grounds planted with mango trees and plots of maize. They cook food to order, and you can **camp** here, too.

There's a row of cheap **eating** places backing on to the Swahili quarter. Other places to try include the *Parkside Hotel*; *Travellers Café*, which has good snacks and is frequented by NGO staff; the popular *Yokozuna Café*, a *nyama choma* joint; and the *Riverside Motel*, 1500m out of town on the Machakos road in Kalundu Market, serving especially good chicken and fish.

The Kitui–Kibwezi road, nearly all *murram*, is uneventful (apart from baobabs which sprout up sporadically on both sides) and isolated. To reach the coast, you're better off going back to Machakos and down the Mombasa Highway. Akamba **buses** (☎044/22052) have daily departures to Nairobi (8.30am) and Mombasa (7pm), both via Machakos. Some morning matatus leave for Embu, but catch them early unless you're happy to spend the day matatu-hopping. The road north to Embu is tarred to Kangonde, with fast tarmac and more public transport continuing to Embu from Kangonde (on the Thika–Garissa road) via Mwea National Reserve (see p.202).

The Mombasa Highway

If you travel south down the Mombasa Highway by **bus**, sit on the right of the vehicle for the best of the scenery, from which vantage you may, in exceptionally clear conditions, see **Kilimanjaro** (best in the morning or late afternoon), either on the stretch between the small settlements of Sultan Hamud and Kiboko, or to the west of Tsavo train station. **Driving at night** is best avoided, as dipped headlights are still something of a novelty, large animals on the road can be hard to see, and hold-ups and car hijacking are not unknown. If you have to travel after dark, make sure you have a spare tyre. Avoid driving alone, and be sure to drive with a full fuel tank.

This section does not cover the **Amboseli** or **Tsavo national parks**, for which see p.384 and p.374.

Around Emali: Kibiki and Nzaui

Heading southeast from Nairobi, the road runs along the east side of Nairobi National Park, passing at its end the junction for the A104 to Athi River, Namanga, Amboseli and Tanzania, before skirting the Kapiti Plains on your right. Five kilometres after the Athi River junction, there's reasonable **accommodation** at the *Small World Country Club* (PO Box 78 Athi River; ☎045/20486 or 22006; ❸), a motel-restaurant with basic self-contained *bandas*, secure parking, unexciting snacks (and painfully slow service), and a bar with a disco at weekends. Unfortunately, it smells rather strongly due to the Kenya Meat Commission's giant abattoir in the area.

After here, there's a long drive along smooth tarmac to the truckers' stopover of **Salama**, the first of many one-horse towns on the way to Mombasa, providing lodging, food and beers for truckers and lost-looking Maasai. With a few exceptions, the **B&Ls** in these places are very basic, far from clean and not for lone women; many double as beer-soaked day and night clubs, which goes some way towards explaining the atrocious driving along the highway. The next settlement, **Sultan Hamud**, has the marginally more salubrious *Park Guesthouse* (☎044/52209; ❷), which has self-contained rooms and hot water.

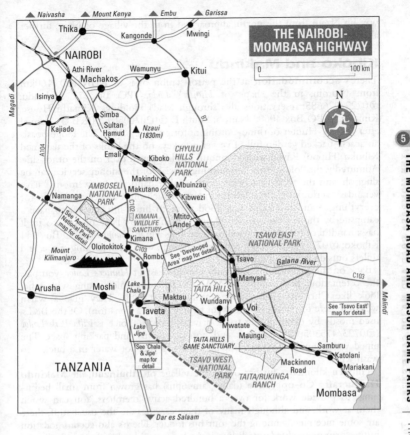

The first centre of any real significance is **EMALI**, which lies on the boundary of Maasai and Akamba territory. There's good accommodation here at the *Kindu Mall Bar* (PO Box 147; ☎044/22; ❷), which also has an unthreatening 24-hour bar and restaurant serving tasty *nyama choma*. The *Emali New Paris Hotel* (PO Box 187; no phone; ❷) has a disco every night which ends at 1am, a large tented bar, some self-contained rooms, and communal bathrooms and toilets which are rancid. Three kilometres beyond Emali, just after the railway flyover, a sharp turn to the right marks the start of the rough mud and *murram* C102, which heads off south to Amboseli's eastern gates. Just beyond here, the small centre of **Kibiki** is the regular Friday venue for a major **cattle market** which attracts hundreds of Maasai herders, as well as Akamba people and Kenya Meat Commission buyers. It's an animated scene and worth a pause if you coincide.

A north turn from Emali leads up into the Machakos Hills with the dramatic peak of **Nzaui** (1830m, 800m above the plain). Without your own transport, get a matatu from the Emali crossroads to Matiliku, some 15km from the main road; Nzaui rears up ahead. With luck, you'll find some schoolchildren to guide you up – it's a popular local trip. From the top of the 500-metre precipices on the south face there are sweeping views across the Kamba and Maasai plains to Mount Kilimanjaro. If you have a vehicle, there's also a lazy way up Nzaui from the north, approached from the village of Nziu, further along the same road.

Kiboko and Makindu

There's **accommodation** at the petrol-station oasis of **KIBOKO**, 160km from Nairobi, in the shape of *Hunter's Lodge* (PO Box 77 Makindu; ☎0722/926685; reservations also through Mada Holdings, Kimathi House, Kimathi St, PO Box 40683 Nairobi South B ☎020/605072; B&B ❺), named after the J.A. Hunter of rhino-potting notoriety (see p.383). The lodge boasts an acacia-backed garden full of vervet monkeys on the banks of the dammed Kiboko (Hippo) River, with a tranquil birdlife haven over on the other side. Admittedly, the "old rooms" are nothing special for the money, service can be sluggish, and the food isn't great; on the other hand, the "new rooms" have verandas overlooking the small reservoir – which more or less makes up for everything – and the lodge is a good place to hitch lifts. They also have a campsite by the reservoir (Ksh500 per person). The village of Kiboko itself has a handful of rudimentary lodgings, among which *Wamu Bar* (PO Box 144 Kiboko; ☎0721/465841; ❶), is decent enough, with nets, parking space, and toilets outside the compound.

Back on the main highway, twenty minutes east of *Hunter's Lodge*, you pass the ostentatious Sikh temple at **MAKINDU**, sometimes strung with what look like Christmas lights, and prettily unmistakable. They give a warm welcome here to travellers who want to stay (leave a donation). Of the B&Ls, used mostly by overnighting truck drivers, a good choice is *Villa Park Lodge* (☎0723/475505; ❶), with s/c and non-s/c rooms, and parking space. The piped water supply is erratic, but they'll bring you hot water in a bucket to wash with.

Thirteen kilometres further on, in the village of **Mbuinzau**, the **Makindu Handicrafts Co-operative** (daily 7am–6pm) has grown from small beginnings to provide work for over a hundred active members. You can watch them at work, and although many of their carvings are the usual stuff, there are some nice pieces among the tour-bus fodder. There's also accommodation in the form of s/c *bandas* with hurricane lamps and bucket showers in lieu of electricity and running water.

The road from here on to Mtito Andei is unusually scenic, with grand, sweeping views south over the Chyulu Hills and glimpses of lava flows and strange rock outcrops just to the north.

Kibwezi

KIBWEZI is a small Akamba trading centre off the main road at the B7 Kitui junction. There's good **accommodation** north of town at the *MSIP Guesthouse* (also called the *Danida Guesthouse*; PO Box 65; ☎044/3500098; ❷), in a shaded, tranquil location: follow the signposts from town for 2km. Formerly the headquarters of a Danish irrigation project, it's a friendly stopover, with hot water and four nice s/c rooms (it's wise to book ahead). Also to the north (signposted), and nice and homely, *Guenter's Guesthouse* (PO Box 387; ☎044/3500247; B&B ❸) has solar power, a generator and large storage tanks to keep the showers flowing, though hot water still comes in buckets. Thirty minutes drive southwest of town, towards The chyulu hills, is *Umani Springs Camp* (see p.392). In town, the *New Face Hotel* offers good food and interesting murals, while the Kenya Commerical Bank has an ATM and money-changing facilities. Kibwezi also boasts a small **market** where you can occasionally buy spiky green **soursops** – one of those fruits you either love or loathe (related to the custard apple, but larger and tarter, with a flavour reminiscent of pear drops). The town is known for its **honey**, which you'll be offered by countless sellers along the road. When it's good, it's delicious, but if there's a dry spell you may be treated instead to something approximating coloured syrup.

In and around **Kinyambu**, 16km from Kibwezi, you'll see thirty or so grass and brick huts, distinguishable from human dwellings by their lack of windows. Each hut contains up to ten hives, owned and tended by a number of local women's co-operatives, together called "The Kibwezi Honey Project". Along this stretch of the main highway you might also see Maasai cattle herders, here at the northernmost limits of their territory.

After Kibwezi, the altitude drops below 900m above sea level and large **baobabs** begin to appear along the highway, some, it is said, over 1000 years old. In the past, they were credited with all manner of spiritual powers and associations, and oral history has it that the Akamba were drawn to this area by the sponge-like centres of their trunks, which are a vital source of liquid during droughts. As to their strange, ungainly appearance, some legends tell that the baobabs used to be in the habit of walking around on their roots, until one day God got fed up with their peregrinations and resolved to keep them forever rooted to the soil, by replanting them upside down. In the low evening sunlight, the baobabs and the colourfully dressed Akamba women working the tiny plots of maize nestled between them are one of the highway's most beautiful sights.

Mtito Andei to Tsavo

A big sprawl of service stations and snackeries rising out of the dry country at the start of Tsavo National Park marks **MTITO ANDEI** (which means "Vulture Forest", sometimes softened to "Eagle Forest"). The *Tsavo Inn* (PO Box 20; ☏0720/379939; B&B ❺), by the Caltex garage, is a pleasant enough retreat if you don't mind the odd missing bath plug, with a tempting pool (Ksh200 for casual guests), but is well overpriced for non-residents. **Rooms** are large if a little frayed, but have nets and baths. **Camping** is possible at Kamboyo, 10km inside Tsavo West National Park (see p.375). If you want a cheap lodging in town, try the *Okay Bar and Restaurant* (PO Box 84; ☏0721/671897; ❶), with stuffy cell-like non-s/c rooms, and an adjoining bar that's good for a cold beer or three.

There are no fuel stations on the 97-kilometre stretch of highway between Mtito Andei and Voi, and the only place to get anything to **eat** is at **Manyani**, 2km past Manyani Gate for Tsavo East National Park. It has a number of very basic *dukas* and *hotelis* serving *githeri* and *ugali* to weary travellers. **Manyani prison**, on the west side of the road, opposite the village, was an infamous detention centre used by the British to hold suspected rebels during the Mau Mau uprising; hundreds were tortured and executed there, and few came out alive.

Manyani is close to the area where two **man-eating lions** played havoc with the building of the railway in 1898. The lions seem to have been preternaturally lucky, since they eluded Colonel Patterson's various weapons for nearly a year and ate 28 Indian labourers in that time, as well as the unfortunate Superintendent C.H. Ryall, whom they dragged off a train carriage during the hunt. The Field Museum in Chicago has the two stuffed man-eaters on display, and in 1998 organized an absurd research project to some nearby caves, where they had hoped to obtain the remains of Ryall himself; they found nothing. You won't see lions either, but along this section of the road through Tsavo park you may well come across **elephants**. Always a brick-red colour thanks to the soil, they used to be one of the commonest animals on the road, but increased traffic and the gradual erosion of their habitat (by herders, agriculture and the elephants themselves) means you have to be a little lucky to see them. Zebras on the other hand are frequently sighted grazing alongside the road.

Voi and the Sagala Hills

The only sizeable town between Machakos and Mombasa is **VOI**, which is 5km from the main gate to Tsavo East National Park, at the junction for the Taita Hills and Taveta. With new roads being built and lodgings and shops springing up everywhere, the place is fast becoming the best town for tourists to stop off. There are plenty of petrol stations, a couple of supermarkets, a Kenya Commercial Bank with an ATM, and lots of cheap *hotelis*.

The **train** to Mombasa (Ksh305 in second class) departs at 4am on Tuesdays, Thursdays and Saturdays, while the Nairobi-bound train (Ksh695) passes through town at 11pm on Tuesdays, Thursdays and Sundays. The station (☎043/30098) is ten minutes' walk south of the market. **Buses** come in all day en route between Nairobi and Mombasa, with some (operated by Malindi Bus) continuing on to Malindi. Mombasa–Taveta buses also stop here, and there are matatus to both Mombasa and Taveta. Wundanyi in the Taita Hills is likewise served by regular matatus, the last leaving around 5pm. For an account of Taveta and the Taita Hills, see pp.367–371.

Distarr Hotel is a good place for curries, with tasty chicken jeera and delicious fresh passion juice. *Silent Lodge* is slightly pricier, with more Western-style dishes such as pepper steak and chips, as well as Kenyan staples like beef stew and rice, and buffets (Ksh450). The *Tsavo Park* is pricier still, with European food and buffet lunches (Ksh450). For beer and music, the *Tsavorite*, on the same street as the post office, is a decent local nightspot.

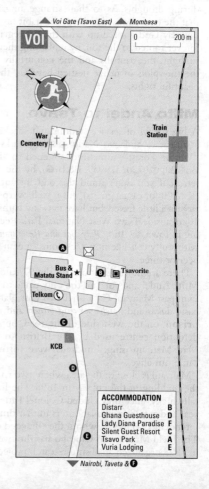

Accommodation

Voi has several excellent cheap **lodgings**.

Distarr Hotel PO Box 641 ☎043/30277. Best of
the cheapies, though not as cheap as the others,
with quite large s/c rooms, a good restaurant and a
laundry service. ❷
Ghana Guest House On the north-side slip road
500m from the centre; PO Box 492 ☎043/30291.
Clean (apart from the cockroaches) and peaceful
(no bar), with some s/c rooms, hot showers and
nets, and an *askari*. ❶

🏃 **Lady Diana Paradise** PO Box 368
☎0721/873099. Off the Nairobi road, 2.5km
north of town, this has breezy rooms (some s/c, with
hot water in buckets) with good views and nets, food
to order (including *nyama choma*), and the occasional
disco. Camping is also possible (price negotiable).
The *Ikanga Travellers Lodge*, on the main road 400m
north, is squalid but plays good music in its bar. ❶

Silent Guest Resort PO Box 143 Voi
☎043/30112, ✉silentguestresort@yahoo.com.
A well-run hotel with s/c and non-s/c singles,
doubles and triples. Every room has satellite TV, fan
and nets. B&B ❹
Tsavo Park Hotel PO Box 244
☎043/30050, ✉tsavoh@africaonline.co.ke.
Opposite the bus and matatu stage, this place
was once quite posh but has rather gone to seed,
though the rooms are still cool and spacious,
with a/c, as well as balconies, nets and phones.
B&B ❹
Vuria Lodging 600m down the north-side slip
road; PO Box 29 ☎0720/522819. Rough and ready
yet friendly, and the rooms aren't at all bad for the
price, s/c, with mosquito nets (but no hot water)
and a good bar out front. ❶

The Sagala Hills

An unusual day-trip from Voi – with some lovely walking country largely
unvisited by tourists – is the **Sagala Hills**, which rise just south of Voi. Regular
matatus run the 20km from town to **Sagala village**, a small rural centre with
little more than a store, a small *hoteli* serving nice *chai* and chicken, and a bar
opposite the football field. From Sagala, you'll need a local to guide you around
– children will be happy to oblige. A 45-minute walk takes you past a small
bridge to the even smaller settlement of **Talio**, which has wonderful views of
the Taita Hills, Mount Kasigau and the savanna below. From here, small paths
lead off through the green fields to the base of the hills (1–2hr) where there are
other little villages. Apart from some steep rocks which are used by climbers
from time to time, and occasional sightings of baboon or mongoose, the main
attraction here is the impression of a timeless rural existence. Visitors are rare, so
be tactful, especially with a camera, and generous with your time. In Talio itself,
you can either **stay** locally (someone should be happy to earn a few bob by
putting you up) or pitch a tent somewhere – ask at the school.

Ngutuni Game Sanctuary

Just southeast of Voi, and tucked into the space between the boundary of Tsavo
East and the road, lies the **Ngutuni Game Sanctuary** (free). Covering 30
square kilometres, this former ranch has a good network of drivable trails criss-
crossing the thorn bush. There's plenty of game here, too, including elephants,
lions and large numbers of buffalo. If you're in your own vehicle, you can
usually take a ranger for a game drive: alternatively, ask the lodge management
for a copy of their map of the sanctuary. While the sanctuary doesn't match
Tsavo East or West for spectacle or a sense of wilderness, it makes for a good
stopover between Nairobi and Mombasa, or an affordable base for exploring
the area.

There's great **accommodation** here in the form of the relatively new
🏃 *Ngutuni Lodge* (☎043/30747; reservations through Rex Resorts ⊛www
.rexresorts.com; FB $85 per person per night), popular with Nairobians and
mid-market tour groups. Rooms are a decent size and well equipped, with good
bathrooms, and each has a balcony facing the waterhole, which is flood-lit at
night. The lodge prides itself on good cooking, and staff are friendly and helpful.
It's certainly the best place to stay in the Voi area, outside the national park, and
real competition for the much pricier *Voi Safari Lodge*.

To the coast

After Voi, the road veers across the relentless **Maungu Plains**, also known as the Taru Desert, a plateau of "wait-a-bit" thorn and occasional baobabs which forms the migratory corridor for wildlife passing from Tsavo East to the foothills of Kilimanjaro. Scenically dreary for much of the year, the plains come alive with colour after heavy rains, and during May and June can be carpeted in convolvulus flowers. Before you get away from the Voi area completely, look out for Kenya's weirdest road sign, some 14km to the south on the left, erected by the local Round Table association: "The world 24 hours pram pushing record was set here 10th January 1972 – Distance 249.7 miles from start."

The roadstead of **MAUNGU**, roughly 25km from Voi, has a couple of B&Ls, top choice being the *Ruby Rock Highway Motel* (PO Box 458 Voi; ☎0722/692977; ❷). Rooms are bright, s/c (hot water in buckets) and set around a pleasant little courtyard, with secure parking, and there's a bar, restaurant and beer garden. Ten kilometres down a rough signposted track from Maungu is *Westermann's Safari Camp* (PO Box 80300 Voi; ☎043/30028, Ⓦwww.westermannssafaricamp.com; FB ❸), popular with German tourists. In the shadow of the imposing Kale 1 rock (which you can climb – it takes about an hour), it offers good food and a pool. It's worth paying a little extra here for one of the newer, bigger chalets with electric lighting (the older ones use hurricane lamps and are rather poky).

Taita and Rukinga wildlife conservancy

Twenty-five kilometres east of Maungu, a right (southward) turn opposite Tsavo East's Buchuma Gate (signposted "Taita Ranch") heads off a dusty 16km to **Satao Rock Camp** (PO Box 600 Voi; ☎0735/996699; reservations, which are compulsory, can be made with the camp or through Southern Cross in Mombasa, p.446; FB from $200; ❾), gorgeously sited on an exposed promontory scampered over by rock hyrax fearful of the eagles circling overhead. The views are spectacular, with a 360-degree panorama over Taita and Rukinga ranches, the Taita Hills and the distant foothills of Kilimanjaro. Though rather basic by "luxury tented camp" standards, it's comfortable enough, and the views, informal atmosphere, as well as the silence, make for a very relaxing stopover between Mombasa and Nairobi. If you're not driving, Southern Cross can arrange transport from Voi or Mombasa.

The camp is situated on Taita Ranch, which, along with neighbouring Rukinga Ranch, is part of a privately run venture to protect wildlife by giving local residents a stake in conservation projects. The combined area of 680 square kilometres is strategically placed on the migration route of plains game, elephant and lion, from the Galana River in Tsavo East to the foothills of Kilimanjaro in Tsavo West. Despite the thickness of the bush, spotting elephants is usually easy, and the nearby water hole – originally installed for a cattle corral – attracts baboon, buffalo, gazelle and occasional cheetah and lion. The staff are happy to guide you on walks or drives.

If you want to do more than just relax and go on safari however, the place to head is **Taita Discovery Centre (TDC)**, 16km west in Rukinga Ranch (PO Box 630 Voi; access also along 16km starting 6.7km east of dirt track from Maungu, signposted "Rukinga Ranch"), where you can stay in bunk-bedded *bandas* (FB ❼), and participate in a variety of well-thought-out ecological and cultural **activities** (lasting from an hour to several days), ranging from game drives and mountain biking to bush survival skills and village visits. You can even have a go at making paper from elephant dung (yes, honestly). If you want to get more seriously involved, there's also a volunteer programme (see p.95).

Past **Samburu** (no fuel supplies), the country is peopled mostly by members of the large **Mijikenda** ethnic group, their distinctive, droopy, thatched cottages often replaced nowadays by more formal square ones, increasingly also white-washed and tin-roofed in the coastal manner. The **Duruma** Mijikenda of this district herd cattle, make charcoal and grow some sisal – there's little else they can do in such a dry region. The small centres of **Maji ya Chumvi** ("salt water") and **Mariakani** ("place of the *mariaka*", *mariaka* being the Kamba arrows used in nineteenth-century wars against the Maasai) bring you closer to the coastal domain, with the coast really taking over at **Mazeras**, a largely Duruma town. The landscape here has a quite different cast, with its mango trees, bananas and cassava, and (encouragement for weary travellers) the sublime sight of endless stands of **coconut palms**. For details of Mazeras and the route along the ridge to the north, see p.464. The main road itself plunges on, lacking much of its tarmac, down the steep scarp to the Indian Ocean and Mombasa (see p.423).

If you're driving down to the northern coast (Kilifi, Watamu or Malindi) and the road from Mariakani to Mombasa is still in dire condition (as it had been for years at the time of writing), there is thankfully an alternative route, though only suitable for 4WD in wet conditions. This leads out of the centre of Mari-akani, heading more or less due east for 19km through the rolling Mijikenda back-country to **Kaloleni,** and then for a further 35km northeast through forest and farmland to rejoin the coastal highway a few kilometres south of Kilifi creek. Allow two hours.

The Taita Hills and the Taveta Road

Heading west from Voi to Taveta takes you into a very accessible but largely unvisited region. Apart from being a route into Tanzania, the **Taveta road** has some interesting possibilities to the north and south, while for much of the time the magnificent mass of Kilimanjaro looms on the horizon. West of the turning at Mwatate for Wundanyi and the Taita Hills, the A23 road to Taveta runs out of tarmac and you follow the railway line through the southern arm of Tsavo West (no fees to pay if you don't leave the road), mostly in a cloud of brilliant red dust. You're very likely to see some game, especially in the rainy season, but there's nowhere worth stopping at before Taveta.

To get a glimpse of the culture of this region, head up into the **Taita Hills**. From the junction at Mwatate, the road twists up 14km into amazingly precipitous and beautiful hills, striped with cliffs, waterfalls and dense cultivation, and highly populated; near the peaks are patches of thick forest. There's notable prosperity up here, and a strong sense of community. The **Taita people** are welcoming; most speak the Taita language, a member of the coastal Bantu family related to Swahili and Mijikenda.

Thrush under threat

Keen ornithologists head for the Taita Hills in search of *Turdus helleri*, the **Taita olive thrush**. This robin-like bird is olive brown on top, red-breasted and red-billed. The Taita olive thrush lives only in the Taita Hills and Mount Ngangai between 1200m and 1725m – which gives it a very small potential habitat. As it depends on virgin forest for its survival, the Taita olive thrush is very rare indeed, its total population estimated at little more than two hundred. It is noted for its bold, liquid warbling song. Good luck with the binoculars.

Wundanyi

Regular matatus from Voi pitch through the fertile chasms on the switchback road to the attractive little district capital of **WUNDANYI**. The conifer trees and a babbling brook running past Wundanyi's football field reinforce the feeling of departure from the thornbush and scrub below. This sense of suspended reality is accentuated by the **cave of skulls**, 1500m outside town, one of many ancestor shrines in the hills (there's one for each clan). The cave is on the Mbale road, 200m beyond *Hebron Christian Guesthouse*, and 500m before *Mwasungia Scenery Guesthouse*, hidden in a banana grove just below the road. In the niche rest the skulls of nineteen Taita ancestors, exhumed from their graves. Traditionally, the shrine was an advice centre where life's perplexities were resolved by consultation with the dead, and where sacrifices were made in times of drought. Beside the niche is a sacred *mvumo* tree, which always grows near water – a good omen. Christianity has eroded some of the reverence that the Taita once had for these shrines (and traditional dances and rituals have almost disappeared), but they are left undisturbed nonetheless.

Practicalities

The best **accommodation** option in town is the simple *Wundanyi Lodge*, just below the market (PO Box 1031; ☎043/42029; ❶). On the Mbale road, *Hebron Christian Guesthouse* (PO Box 1106; ☎043/42350; ❶, dorm beds Ksh200) has a peaceful location, single and double rooms, and dorms. A kilometre further down the road, and recommended for its helpful owners and lovely location rather than for its facilities, is the ramshackle *Mwasungia Scenery Guesthouse* (PO Box 1026; ☎043/30393; ❶). This is the best place to settle into if you're interested in finding out more about the Taita: the owner is knowledgeable, and can take you on walks around the hills to see waterfalls, skull caves and a cliff-top tree from which villains were once hurled to their fate. Rooms are basic, but you can camp (Ksh200 per person) in a beautiful orchard.

There aren't many **places to eat** in Wundanyi. Downhill from the matatu stage, *Paradise Hotel* is recommended for tasty meals and a lively atmosphere – especially emanating from the bar. Nearby, just up from the post office and KCB bank, and overlooking the football field (which is usually populated by grazing cattle), *Bistro 35 Cafeteria* is bright and cheerful. The big **market days** in Wundanyi are Tuesday and Friday. **Moving on** from Wundanyi, you'll find direct matatus to Voi and Mombasa, but for Taveta you'll have to change vehicles at Mwatate.

Taita Hills Wildlife Sanctuary

One place attracting tourist traffic in this district, particularly visitors on fleeting air safaris from the coast, is the 110-square kilometre **Taita Hills Wildlife Sanctuary** (day entry $50, including lunch), which isn't in the Taita Hills at all, but in the hillocky lowlands 15km beyond Mwatate on the Taveta road. It's run by the Hilton chain, with two lodges acting as bait (reservations ☎043/30243 or 30270, ✉saltlick@africaonline.co.ke; both ❾), though they're much more expensive than those at Tsavo or even Amboseli, and the setting isn't as good. *Taita Hills Hilton Safari Lodge* is just outside the reserve, a graceless concrete block half a kilometre from the road.

The sanctuary is well managed and, for most of the year, full of wildlife. Its small size means the rangers always have a good idea of where the animals are, and it's not uncommon to see two dozen species of mammals – among them large numbers of lions, elephants and grazers – in a morning game drive (included in the rate if you're lodging here). During the drier parts of the year, when the animals are not dispersed, *Salt Lick Lodge* on the southern side of the sanctuary provides water-hole game-viewing to rival the "tree hotels" of the Central Highlands. But it's for its bizarre **architecture** that *Salt Lick* is most famous: from a distance it looks like a clump of mushrooms sprouting from the swamp. Each of its rooms is a kind of turret on stilts, all of them linked by mock-suspension bridges – there's even a drawbridge at the lobby. This camp ensemble is supposedly in keeping with the area's **World War I** battle history – most of the important Anglo-German engagements in East Africa were fought on these plains.

Taveta and lakes Chala and Jipe

Connected to the rest of Kenya by appalling roads and a railway that rarely runs, **TAVETA** is situated on the Tanzania border at the end of the rural corridor running between the northern and southern sections of Tsavo West National Park. It's also a handy base for exploring lakes Chala and Jipe nearby. Gradually becoming part of metropolitan Kenya, Taveta has a mixed population of Taveta, Taita, Maasai, Akamba, Kikuyu and Luo, and even some Makonde (originally from Mozambique, they were brought in the 1930s to work the sisal estates). For a few moment's reflection, there's a **World War I cemetery** at the entrance to town.

The only paved street in Taveta crosses the railway line and heads straight for the border post, passing the KCB bank (no ATM) on its way. But the town's real main street runs north from the paved road immediately west of the level crossing. The best **accommodation** option is the excellent-value ⅍ *Challa Hotel* on the main street (PO Box 16; ☎043/5352240, ⓔchalla_ltd@yahoo.com; ❶), which has good s/c rooms around an internal courtyard, with hot water and nets. They serve good food, and have a relaxed TV bar. Two competitors, on the paved road to the border, are *Taveta Guesthouse* (☎043/5352429; ❶) and *Tripple J Paradise* (PO Box 450; ☎043/5352463; ❶), both pleasant enough, but their rooms are smaller than the *Challa's*, and they don't have electric sockets or secure parking. *Kuwako Bar*, 50m further up the main street from *Challa Hotel*, (PO Box 51; no phone; ❶), has magnificent, gaudy murals in its front restaurant, and dingy, rock-bottom rooms at matching prices.

The best place to **eat** in town is the *Challa*, but otherwise try the *Taveta Hotel*, on the other side of the main street, or a couple of restaurants on the street leading to the border post: the *New Golden Fish Hotel*, which of course offers fish in among the meat options, and the *Dar es Salaam Hotel* next door, which has very similar fare. The local *matoke* stew is popular, though you might baulk at eating eight green bananas in one sitting, even if they are smothered with gravy. For something completely different, try the *Taveta Prison Canteen* at the entrance to town, which has sodas and good food. The *Gate Way Pub*, just before the rail line, is a good place to sink a cold beer and chew on some *nyama choma*.

There are plenty of **matatus** from here to Voi, and **buses** daily to Mombasa. Matatus are most frequent on market days (Wed & Sat in Taveta; Tues & Fri at Chumvini – for the latter, you'll usually have to take a Voi-bound vehicle and change at the junction). On Tuesday and Saturday mornings, matatus continue to Oloitokitok (see p.391), near Amboseli National Park, to coincide with its

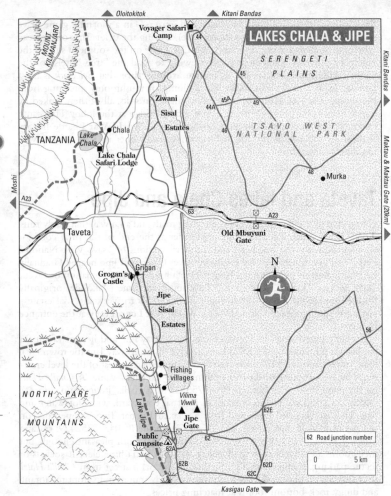

LAKES CHALA & JIPE

market. If you're driving, note that the **road to Oloitokitok** can be pretty rough going, and is often impassable in the rains.

The **Tanzanian border** post is 5km away, reached by *boda-boda* (Ksh40) or motorbike taxi (Ksh100). On the other side, there are regular matatus to Moshi, and thence to Arusha. Money-changers in Taveta's market sell Tanzanian shillings for Kenyan (at the time of writing, the rate was Tsh16 to Ksh1) but, as ever, beware of scams and rip-offs. The same people will also give Kenyan or Tanzanian shillings for US dollars, but not at a good rate (though, once you take commission into account, they still offer you a better deal than the bank, and without the queuing).

Lake Chala

A four-square-kilometre crater lake north of Taveta, Chala has one shore in Kenya and the other in Tanzania. It's right by the road to Amboseli, 8km from the junction outside Taveta and just a ten-minute walk up the slope. Transport isn't such a problem to **Lake Chala** – there are **buses** to Chumvini (beyond Chala) at least once a day. Four kilometres before Chala village is *Lake Challa Safari Lodge*, closed at the time of writing; it might be worth enquiring at *Challa Hotel* in Taveta, which has the same owner, for the latest news. If it doesn't reopen, the only way to stay near the lake is to camp rough around the rim.

Very deep and remarkably blue, Lake Chala is still paddled over by a few friendly fishermen in their dugouts and is spiritually significant; lake monster stories are part of the folklore. The lake is bilharzia-free and was believed to have no crocodile population. However, the death while swimming of a young British traveller in 2002, and the discovery of her body, missing an arm, points to a crocodile presence, and you're strongly advised not to swim here. Crocs and monsters aside, keep a lookout for the pinkish snakes that readers have reported seeing inside the crater wall – possibly a red-phase spitting cobra. You may also see green mambas, monitor lizards, large skinks, monkeys and baboons (be especially wary of the latter if you're camping).

Lake Jipe

Equally interesting, and totally different, is **Lake Jipe**, 35km south of Taveta. It's fed by Kilimanjaro's snowmelt at its northern end, passing via Lake Chala's underground outlet, as well as by streams flowing to the south from the Pare Mountains, across the border in Tanzania. Like Chala, Jipe straddles the Tanzanian border. The Kenyan shore is flat and thickly carpeted in reed beds; the northern end has several villages making a living from fishing, while Jipe's southeastern shore lies inside Tsavo West National Park.

There is no public transport to the lake, indeed very little transport at all. Short of finding a driver in Taveta to take you there, your only option, and by no means an unpleasant one, is to walk. The flat land between the Voi road and the lake is heavily planted under sisal, cotton fields and even coconuts. There are

Grogan's Castle

Seven kilometres from the Voi–Taveta road, **Grogan's Castle**, a white mansion on an isolated hill rising from the plain along the track to Lake Jipe, deserves a little detour. This extraordinary residence was built in the 1930s by Ewart Grogan, one of the most influential early colonists. His reputation was founded on a walk from the Cape to Cairo, which he undertook in 1898, on a notorious public flogging he carried out on three of his servants (nearly killing one of them), and on his wealth: his gilt-edged reputation was such that Grogan was able to dictate terms to the governor before he even arrived in Kenya. At the peak of his prosperity, he owned over 2500 square kilometres of land.

The "castle", evidently built as a kind of hacienda for the **sisal estates**, is totally run-down these days – the only residents of the house are a large colony of bats – but can be visited if you tip the *askari* (ask for him at the settlement of "Grigan" at the foot of the hill, a 1km walk). It's an enigmatic building, much of it stuck together with aircraft aluminium and tin roofs. There are two enormous circular living rooms with spectacular 360-degree views out towards Kilimanjaro and Lake Jipe. The huge bedrooms have mosquito-screened bed niches, whose steel mesh make them look more like animal cages. On one of the landings an ostentatious cash cupboard is suitably positioned, presumably for the casual display of wealth to passing guests. The Castle has been bought by the former local MP, but rumours of its impending transformation into a safari lodge have so far proved unfounded.

also wide areas of low bush. It's an unusual part of Kenya, rustling with bird and animal life. Driving or walking, head east from Taveta along the Voi road, turning right after 7.5km at the signpost for "Lake Jipe Safari Lodge", 1km beyond the turning for Ziwani Sisal Estate. From here, the track heads straight through the Jipe Sisal Estate to the lakeshore villages, 27km from the junction, passing the unmistakable Grogan's Castle on your right (see box, p.371).

The lakeshore and national park

At **Mukwajoni**, the fishing village 2km before the park gate, you'll find only the most basic provisions (apart from fish), so bring supplies from Taveta. There's nowhere to stay, though someone may be happy to put you up in their hut for a small fee. When exploring the bush around the lakeshore early in the morning, beware of **hippos**; you should keep a sharp eye out, especially between the park gate and the village. A feasible target for a couple of hours' **walk** are the two hills, Vilima Viwili, just outside the park boundary and about 2km east of the track. Once at the lake, the track becomes confused as it heads south towards Tsavo West's **Jipe Gate** (for details of park fees and regulations, see p.374) – keep as close to the lake as you can, as the gate is right on the shore. The rangers here are friendly and have little to do; they also have a **boat** ($5 per person) for a spot of crocodile and hippo-spotting. There's a **campsite** just inside the gate ($10 per person), with toilets and showers, and also simple *bandas* (book through the park warden, p.374; ❹), with nets. Despite the vicious attentions of mosquitoes, this is a peaceful and rewarding spot, and a paradise for ornithologists. *Lake Jipe Safari Lodge*, for which you may see signposts, has been closed for years.

Leaving the park, you've only really one option, which is a fifty-kilometre drive northeast to the gate at **Maktau**, a small settlement with another gate to Tsavo West's northern sector on the opposite side of the road (you won't need to buy another ticket unless staying another day), a war cemetery and a few *dukas*.

The parks

In these animal-rich national parks, the first realization of where you are – among real, uncaptured wildlife – is truly arresting. Which parks to visit can seem at first a pin-in-the-map decision: any of them can provide a store of amazing sight and sound impressions. The parks in this chapter are open all year round.

Amboseli and **Tsavo** are the two most accessible, with ever-busy game lodges, well-worn trails, large numbers of tourists in high season, and large, if brutally diminished, herds of elephant. Amboseli, with its picture-postcard backdrop of Mount Kilimanjaro and guaranteed **elephants**, is an instant draw, but the flat topography and lack of vegetation cover means you'll be sharing the stunning vistas with dozens of other safari vehicles. Tsavo, in contrast, is huge enough to escape company completely, except at **Mzima Springs**, for which it's worth being part of the crowd if necessary.

△ Balloon trip, Maasai Mara

Maasai Mara has the most fabled reputation, with horizons of wildlife on every side. Somewhat isolated in the west, it's well worth the effort (and perhaps the cost), especially during the yearly **wildebeest migration** that takes place sometime between July and November (at its most spectacular in August). The Mara is also *the* place to see **lions** – lots of them.

The **Samburu/Buffalo Springs/Shaba** complex and **Meru**, on the northeast side of Mount Kenya, have different varieties of animals, such as northern races and species of giraffe, zebra, antelope and ostrich. The Samburu complex – dry, thorny and split by the Ewaso Nyiro River – is increasingly popular and noted for its **crocodiles** and **leopards**, albeit baited ones. Meru, however, is perhaps the most beautiful Kenyan park, verdant and surprisingly unvisited.

For some idea of their current animal-viewing potential, the order of enthusiasm in recent travellers' accounts places Maasai Mara way out in front in terms of variety and numbers to be seen, then Samburu, Amboseli and Tsavo East, followed some way behind by Tsavo West, with Meru last of all. If you're interested in birds, you'll find favourable places to watch with your binoculars in all the parks, but it's worth pointing out that Maasai Mara (mostly open plains) is not, on the whole, good for birds, while by contrast Samburu (with its riverine environment) can be exceptionally rewarding.

The Tsavo national parks

Daily 6am–6pm; each park $27 per day/overnight, children $10; private vehicle Ksh200, camping $10 per person. Smartcard entry; nearest outlets at Mtito Andei main gate, Voi, Malindi Marine Park, Amboseli Namanga Gate. Wardens: Tsavo West, PO Box 71 Mtito Andei ☏ 045/622120 or 622483, ✉ adwildlife@kws.org; Tsavo East, PO Box 14 Voi ☏ 043/30049, ✉ tenp@africaonline.co.ke. No driving after 7pm. Speed limit 40kph. Maps: Tsavo West and Tsavo East (both KWS, 1:250,000).

Taken together, Tsavo West and Tsavo East make up by far the biggest of the Kenyan national parks, and one of the largest in the world, sprawling across 21,000 square kilometres of dry bush country, an area the size of Wales or Massachusetts. **Tsavo East** is the larger portion, though the sector north of the Galana River has only recently re-opened to tourists after decades of poaching and insecurity. South of the river, the great triangle of flat wilderness with Aruba Dam in the middle has become popular with coastal safari departures, since it offers a pretty sure chance of seeing plenty of animals, in a very open environment. The traditionally popular part of Tsavo is a mere one thousand square kilometres, the tall grass-and-woodland "**developed area**" of **Tsavo West**, located between the Tsavo River and the Mombasa Highway. Here, the combination of good access, excellent facilities and magnificent landscapes attracts tourists in large numbers, while the well-watered, volcanic soils support wooded grasslands and a great quantity and diversity of animal life – though it's not always easily observed.

With their numbered junctions and clearly defined **murram** roads and tracks, the Tsavo parks are easy to get around, so long as you have a map. To go from one part of the park to the other, make sure you are officially exited by going through one of the main gates, or you will be sent back. Don't forget the **distances** involved: if you set off somewhere, be sure you have time to get back to base by nightfall – both parks close their gates at 7pm, and it's illegal to drive around after then. Note also that Tsavo's **lions** have a reputation for ferocity. In the park, leave your vehicle at designated nature trails only, or where there's an obvious parking area. And even beyond the national park boundaries you should stay on your guard – the animals aren't fenced in.

KWS **maps** of both Tsavo parks show all park roads and numbered junctions, as well as lodges, features, elevation and terrain. They should be available at the main gates for Ksh450 each, as well as in shops in all the main lodges, and from KWS in Nairobi. Wild Visions produce a 1:78,000 map covering both parks, but it does not show all the roads, let alone junction numbers, and is next-to-useless for navigation.

Tsavo West

If you're looking for a visit outside an organized safari tour and don't have your own car, **TSAVO WEST** is probably the easiest as well as the cheapest of the big parks to explore. From Nairobi or Mombasa, take a bus to **Mtito Andei** (a service town for the lodges; see p.363). Barely 500m away is the park gate, one of the busiest in the country, so your chances of getting an onward ride are good. *Kilaguni Lodge*, 30km southwest, should be able to arrange onward transport, as they have regular evening vehicles for staff from the gate. If you get

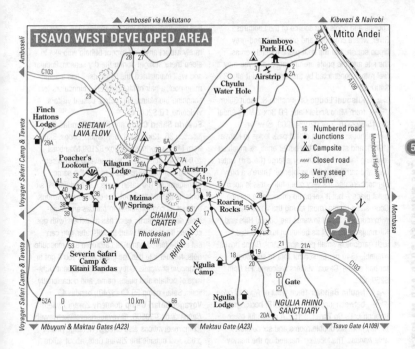

TSAVO WEST DEVELOPED AREA

Amboseli via Makutano ▲ ▲ *Kibwezi & Nairobi*

Mtito Andei

Kamboyo
Park H.Q.

Chyulu
Water Hole

Airstrip

Finch
Hattons
Lodge

SHETANI
LAVA FLOW

Poacher's
Lookout

Kilaguni
Lodge

Airstrip

Mzima
Springs

CHAIMU
CRATER

Rhodesian
Hill

Roaring
Rocks

RHINO VALLEY

Severin Safari
Camp &
Kitani Bandas

Ngulia
Camp

Gate

Ngulia
Lodge

NGULIA RHINO
SANCTUARY

16	Numbered road
•	Junctions
⛺	Campsite
////	Closed road
⟫⟫⟫	Very steep incline

0   10 km

Amboseli ◀ *Voyager Safari Camp & Taveta* ◀ *Voyager Safari Camp & Taveta* ◀

Mombasa Highway   *Mombasa* ▶

▼ *Mbuyuni & Maktau Gates (A23)*   ▼ *Maktau Gate (A23)*   ▼ *Tsavo Gate (A109)* ▼

stuck, the rangers are usually helpful and may allow you to camp just inside the park, though there's budget accommodation in Mtito Andei itself. It's also possible to reach the park by air from Nairobi's Wilson Airport, with SafariLink.

The **information centre** at *Kilaguni Lodge* (usually open during the high season) should have up-to-date locations of **lion prides** and **cheetahs**, and possibly **leopard sightings**, too. For information on the **southern part** of Tsavo West, read the sections on Lakes Chala and Jipe on pp.370–372.

Accommodation

A lack of budget **accommodation** is less of an obstacle in Tsavo West than in most of the other main parks. There are three **campsites** dotted around: one just outside Chyulu Gate, with shower and toilet, and conveniently close to *Kilaguni Lodge*; another, again with basic showers and toilets, a twenty-minute drive from the Mtito Andei Gate near the park headquarters at Kamboyo Hill; and one at Lake Jipe in the far south (p.372). In addition, there are two recommended and well-equipped **banda camps**, *Kitani* and *Ngulia*, which have a number of simple but comfortable chalets that can be taken on a self-catering basis (full board is also possible), and which are miles cheaper – as well as more charming – than the lodges. Bringing and cooking your own food can be an attractive proposition if you're sick of *ugali* and chips, or obsequious lodge service for that matter. Details for both are given below.

Finch Hattons Tented Lodge Kampi ya Simba, 15km northwest of junction 38, 65km from Mtito Andei Gate; PO Box 24423 Nairobi ☎ 020/553245, ⊛ www.finchhattons.com. Named after the aristocrat who introduced royalty to the bush, *Finch Hattons* must be the suavest of numerous luxury

tented camps around Kenya, with its fine bone china, cut crystal glasses and chandeliers, and impeccable service and food. The thirty tents are, of course, totally luxurious, with antique commodes, brass lamps and Afghan rugs (rooms 1–7 are best). The camp is sited around the springs and pools of a source of the Loolturesh River, where crocodile and great pink-and-grey hippo splash. Not the best place for children as the site and the pools are unfenced, and you may feel rather constricted by the formality of it all. FB $400; ⑨

Kilaguni Lodge Off junction 8, about 30km from Mtito Andei Gate; PO Box 2 Mtito Andei ☎045/622376–7 or 020/340000, ⓦwww .serenahotels.com. The oldest park lodge in Kenya (1962), and still one of the better ones, as much as anything for its prime site by a large (floodlit) water hole and terrific wildlife ambience. There's a busy atmosphere and it's very often full – this is not a quiet place – but it keeps up impeccable service. Good-sized rooms (most facing the wildlife action, with stunning views towards the Chyulu Hills and Kilimanjaro), as well as beautiful luxury suites, lush gardens, a small pool and petrol. Game drives available ($40 per person for four to six people for half a day). Casual visitors welcome. FB from $260; ⑨

Ngulia Bandas 18km west of *Ngulia Lodge* between junctions 17 and 18; bookings through Let's Go Travel, p.150. A delightful place to stay, with six double rooms and six comfortable *bandas*. The location, nestled up the heavily vegetated north slopes of Ngulia Hill, offers great views and even has its own water hole. The two- or three-bed *bandas* have bathrooms, showers and kitchens, and can be taken on a self-catering basis. FB ⑨ ($180), self-catering ❸

Ngulia Lodge 48km west from Tsavo Gate, off junction 18; PO Box 244 Voi ☎043/30050. Somewhat isolated in the more mountainous eastern side of the park, close to the rhino sanctuary, this is open-plan and offers tremendous views over the rhino sanctuary on the plains far below, but

has less immediate wildlife appeal than *Kilaguni*. There are two water holes by a terrace, but they rarely attract anything except buffalo who like to sleep there at night during the dry season. Popular and well maintained, the lodge itself has a swimming pool, a pair of high-powered binoculars for scanning the plains, and petrol. Casual visitors welcome. FB $200; ⑨

Severin Safari Camp and **Kitani Bandas** Off junction 36, 12km south of *Kilaguni Lodge*, 8km from Mzima Springs; PO Box 82169 Mombasa ☎041/548 5001–5, ⓦwww.severin-kenya.com. Two sites a kilometre apart, run by the same management. The safari camp has cool deluxe s/c tents, tastefully done out, not quite *Finch Hattons*, but just as comfortable. The *bandas* are pleasingly down-to-earth; each has a kitchen (with gas cooker; if you don't want to self-cater, you can eat at the tented camp), a bathroom and mosquito nets. Neither site has the great views you'd get at *Kilanguni* or *Ngulia*, but you do get frequent sightings of buffalo and plains game, and occasionally lions. Safari camp FB ⑨ ($240); bandas ❻

Voyager Safari Camp (formerly *Ziwani Tented Camp*) ☎043/30506, ⓔvoyagertsavo@kenyaweb .com; reservations also through Heritage Hotels, p.63. Just outside the Ziwani Gate, about 40km south of the "developed area", but most easily reached from the Taveta–Taita Hills road (see the Lake Chala map, p.370). On a glorious site by a small hippo and crocodile pool, and beside a dam in the Sante River, this has 25 full-size, permanent tents and excellent food. It's quite a distance from the park's main attractions, but free bonuses such as early-morning guided walks and night-time game drives (you provide the vehicle) – both possible because it is just outside the park boundaries – more than compensate. FB $250; ⑨

The "developed area"

The "developed area" is the hilliest sector of any of the parks covered in this chapter, and there's an unending succession of fantastic views across the plains, dotted with volcanic cones and streaked with forest at the water margins. When the animals are abundant, every turn in the track seems to bring you face to face with zebra, giraffe, huge herds of buffalo, casual prides of lions, or methodical, strolling elephants, almost orange from the dust. Among the more unusual animals to look for are the beautiful and shy **lesser kudu** antelope (always, it seems, running away).

In the 1960s, Tsavo had the biggest population of **black rhinos** in Africa – between 6000 and 9000 – and they were a common sight. By 1981, they had been poached to barely 100 individuals (the story is enlarged in the box on pp.382–383). The situation today has improved a little, though most rhinos have been removed to the safety of the **Ngulia Rhino Sanctuary** (daily 4–6pm; free, but if a ranger accompanies you, he'll expect a tip) where, if you drive around for any length of time, you're almost bound to see one (you can always visit the holding pen in the middle of the sanctuary and inspect the latest arrivals).

The trip further on, that takes you around the foot of **Rhodesian Hill**, is recommended too, and **Poacher's Lookout** (also called Ranger's Lookout), near *Severin* and *Kitani Bandas*, is a very promising place for a quiet scan with binoculars. There's a thatched shelter here where you can sit in the breeze.

Mzima Springs

The biggest attraction in Tsavo West is **Mzima Springs**, 48km from Mtito Andei and close to both *Kilaguni Lodge* and *Kitani Bandas*. This stream of crystal-clear water was made famous by Alan Root's 1983 film *Mzima: Portrait of a Spring*, which followed crocodiles and hippos in their underwater lives. Go very early to avoid the tour-bus atmosphere, and you won't be disappointed. With luck, some of the night's animal visitors may still be around, while the luxuriant growth around the water reverberates noisily with birds and monkeys.

There are two large pools, connected by a rush of rapids and shaded by stands of date and raffia palms. The upper (or long) pool is the favoured **hippo** wallow, while the **crocodiles** have retreated to the broader expanse of water lower down. It's worth walking around this lower pool to the right where, if you're stealthy, you have a good chance of seeing them – just make sure there's not one on the bank behind you. This word of caution applies equally to hippos, but they seem settled in their routine, content to snort and flounder just a little too far from the path for visitors' satisfaction. At the side of the top pool, a circular underwater **viewing chamber** has been built at the end of a short pier. Unless you're exceptionally lucky, all you'll see is a blue swirl of perpetually revolving fish.

The lava of the **Chyulu range** to the north filters the water to aquarium transparency prior to its arrival here: the porous rock absorbs the water like a sponge and gravity squeezes it into Mzima Springs. A direct pipeline from here to Mombasa, completed in 1966, is the source of most of the city's **drinking water**. Engineers summoned by the National Parks trustees devised a way of taking water from beneath the lava, *above* the spring; in so doing they sidelined an earlier proposal which would have raised the lower pool's level through the construction of a weir, and would probably have caused the hippos to stop breeding by ruining their "nursery". There are one or two signs of the pipeline in the area, but most are unobtrusive.

Mzima's two **nature trails** (really tree trails) aren't of great interest unless you happen to be a botanist, but it is easy nevertheless to spend a couple of hours in the area. Try to sit for a while completely alone on the bank and you'll begin to piece together the ecological miracle of the place, as the animals and birds forget about your presence. This is where those khaki safari outfits are actually practical.

Kilaguni Lodge

While *Kilaguni* is an expensive place to stay, sooner or later you're bound to turn up, and rightly so: a visit is rewarding enough just for the pleasure of sitting on the terrace with a cold beer and watching the enthralling circus going on a few yards away at the **water holes** (neither *Finch Hatton's* nor *Voyager Safari Camp* encourages day-trippers). Lunches here cost $20 per person. The main reception area is open to the panorama of the savanna and Chyulu Hills, and the views over the Ngulia rhino sanctuary on the plains far below (there's free use of high-powered binoculars) are amazing, but even in the lodge itself, wildlife abounds. Dazzling **birds** hop everywhere, **hyrax** scamper between the tables, and **agama lizards** skim along the walls (the miniature orange and blue dragons are the males in mating drag). In the grass below the terrace lives a colony of **dwarf mongooses**, while pompous **marabou storks** pace slowly up and down awaiting jettisoned bread from the dining room. Out by the water hole, **baboon troops**, **antelope**, **buffalo**, **zebra**, **giraffe** and **elephant** provide constant spectacle, with the occasional kill adding tension. At dusk, hundreds of **swallows** swoop back and forth to their nests in the roof and, later, **bats** swoop while **genets**, **jackals** and **hyenas** come for the meat scattered under the floodlights. You may get exceptional permission from the warden to drive here at night for this, most likely if you're camping, or staying at *Kitani bandas*.

Ngulia Lodge

Ngulia Lodge is a stopover on the annual southern migration of hundreds of thousands of European **birds**. It seems to be situated on a narrow migration corridor, but the reasons for its attraction for the birds – apart from its isolated lights – aren't really known. Ornithologists gather in November and early December to band the birds that are trapped in mist nets, and their occasional recapture in places as far afield as Malawi, Iran and Germany slowly helps to build a picture of where the birds are moving to. Perhaps not altogether surprisingly, few are ever caught at *Ngulia* again. Aside from bird-watching, visitors can take lunch ($15) or have a dip in the pool (Ksh300).

Lava flows

The lava that purifies Mzima's water can be seen in black outcrops all around this part of Tsavo. The **Shetani lava flow** is a spectacular example. Only 200 years old (the Chyulu Hills themselves are less than 500 years old), the eruption that spewed it out must have been a cataclysmic event for local people, and is still the focus of stories about fire and evil spirits (*shetani* means "devil" in Swahili). Legend has it that many people were buried by the hot lava flow, and their plaintive cries can be heard on certain nights. The local people appease the ghosts with offerings of food which, of course, are gone by daybreak. There are **caves** here that, despite one or two warnings, are worthy of investigation (you'll need a torch). One of them even has a ladder and a trail of identification plaques by the bones of luckless animal victims who stumbled down.

Chaimu crater is fun to walk over, but also dodgy. The lava is brittle, honeycombed and unstable, and very few plants have taken hold yet. It is possible to climb up to the volcano's crater rim, but this can be surprisingly hard work on the scree and shouldn't be attempted in the heat of the day. And when poking around Tsavo's caves and lava zones, you should be alert to the possibility of disturbing large **sleeping animals** as well as **snakes**.

Tsavo East National Park

Across the highway, the railway, and the apparent natural divide that separates Kenya's northern and southern environments, lies **TSAVO EAST**. Just a few hours' drive from the charter arrivals hall at Mombasa airport, the park finds itself very much the centre of tourist attention, especially for budget camping safaris.

Apart from some tumbled crags and scarps near Voi, Tsavo East is an uninterrupted plain of bush, dotted with the crazed shapes of baobab trees. It's a forbiddingly enormous reserve and at times over the last couple of decades has seemed an odd folly, especially since the whole of the sector north of the Galana River – almost two-thirds of the park's area – has been closed to the public due to the long war against elephant and rhino poachers (see the box on pp.382–383). Since the early 1990s, this has been more or less won and the elephants, if not the rhinos, are on the increase again, their numbers swelled by a major KWS translocation operation in 2005 to move 300 elephants from Shimba Hills (see p.470). With the northern sector secure and rangers in place, the whole of Tsavo East was opened for tourism in January 2006, though infrastructure is still basic.

Tsavo East has five **gates**, including **Mtito Andei Gate** in the northern sector. **Buchuma Gate** at the southeastern end is the one most used by safari vans from Mombasa, handy for Aruba Dam but far from the Galana River. To the east, **Sala Gate** is the one to use if you're starting from Malindi. It's 110km due west of Malindi along a seemingly endless dirt road, but there's no public transport further west than Kakoneni, 80km short of the gate, and safari vans are unlikely to offer you a lift without some form of payment. On the western side, **Manyani Gate**, near Mudanda Rock, is little used, but offers a choice of routes into the park. The main gate, and the one you should aim for if hitching, is about 7km from the town of **Voi** (see p.364). The rangers here are a helpful crowd, with sensible attitudes to lifts and hitching. There were no scheduled **flights** to the park at the time of writing.

Accommodation

There is only one public **campsite** in the park, *Ndololo* ($10 per person), which is 7km from Voi gate, at the western edge of Kanderi Swamp and off junction 173. This has showers and toilets, and firewood is available, but you'll need to bring your own food. The same firm that runs the *Tsavo Park Hotel* in Voi also have a tented camp right next door to *Ndololo*, and you may be able to find a lift from the hotel on their staff bus.

Lodges and luxury tented camps

Crocodile Camp 9km outside Sala Gate; PO Box 81443 Mombasa ☏043/30124, 🖷30123, 🖳www .africansafariclub.com. Like *Tsavo Buffalo Camp*, this is right on the river, but is larger and has a more formal, lodge-like feel, with landscaped gardens and imposing public areas. The tents are a/c, but not otherwise especially deluxe. One of the few African Safari Club places to admit drop-in visitors (for a nominal temporary membership fee). Lunch Ksh700. FB **7**

Epiya Chapeyu 5km east of junction 163, on south bank of the Galana River; reservations through Alphatauri Ltd; PO Box 14653 Nairobi ☏020/3749796 or 3750000, 🖂bigi@wananchi .com. Unstuffy, Italian-run camp in a lovely location, with apparently frequent visits by a group of immature male elephants, and hippo at night. The fourteen tents have bathrooms but are closely spaced, the better ones in the front row facing the river. The food is Italian, and they're happy to have unannounced guests, even for lunch (Ksh800), so long as they have room. Rates are per person, which makes it good value if you're on your own. Game drives and guided walks in the northern sector possible. FB **8**

Galdessa Camp 4km west of junction 111, south bank of the Galana River; reservations through Exclusive Classic Properties; PO Box 714, Village Market 00621 Nairobi ☏020/523156, 🖳www .galdessa.com. This Italian-run luxury camp organizes walking and fishing safaris along the river, plus camel safaris. Like *Epiya Chapeyu*, it's situated in one of the few areas of Tsavo East where you have a chance of spotting black rhino (the restaurant overlooks the river, where they sometimes drink), and elephants are often seen here. Rates, however, are extortionate. FB Ksh20,700; **9**

Patterson's Safari Camp 8km east of Mombasa Highway and Tsavo Gate; PO Box 49265 Nairobi ☏020/4450532, 🖂pattersons@wananchi.com. Situated on the banks of the Athi River, this is an ideal location if you want to visit both parks from one base. The eco-friendly architecture, white sand and spacious s/c tents, together with a helpful bunch of staff, give it the wild and yet intimate feel of a tropical island. As well as hippos, crocs and elephants, there's also plenty of birdlife thanks to its proximity to the Yatta Plateau. FB **8**

Satao Camp (Mukwajuni Camp) PO Box 90653 Mombasa ☏043/30415, 🖳www.sataocamp .com; bookings through Southern Cross Safaris, p.446. East of *Aruba Lodge*, off junction 144, this

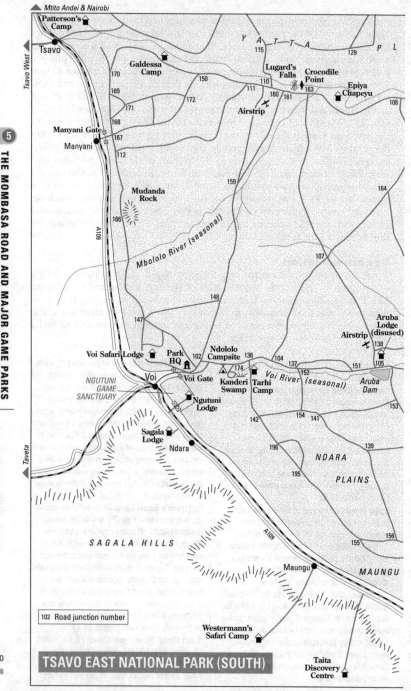

▲ Mtito Andei & Nairobi

Patterson's Camp

◄ Tsavo

◄ Tsavo West

Galdessa Camp

Y A T T A — P L
115
129

Lugard's Falls
Crocodile Point
110
111
160 161 163
108
Airstrip

Epiya Chapeyu

170
169
171
168
172
150

Manyani Gate
167
112
Manyani

166
Mudanda Rock

159

Mbololo River (seasonal)

164

107

148

147

Voi Safari Lodge
Park HQ
102
Ndololo Campsite
136
104
137
151
Aruba Lodge (disused)
Airstrip
138
105

Voi
NGUTUNI GAME SANCTUARY
Voi Gate
174
Kanderi Swamp
Tarhi Camp
152
Voi River (seasonal)
Aruba Dam

◄ Taveta

Ngutuni Lodge

Sagala Lodge
Ndara

142
154 141
196
195
NDARA PLAINS
153
139

156

SAGALA HILLS

A108

Maungu

MAUNGU
155

102 Road junction number

Westermann's Safari Camp

Taita Discovery Centre

TSAVO EAST NATIONAL PARK (SOUTH)

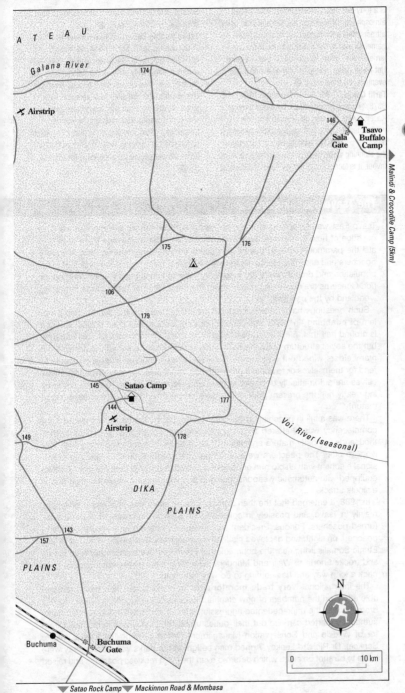

Galana River

174

✈ Airstrip

146
Sala
Gate

▲ Tsavo
Buffalo
Camp

► Malindi & Crocodile Camp (5km)

175

176

106

⚠

179

145   ■ Satao Camp

177

144
✈ Airstrip

149

178

Voi River (seasonal)

DIKA

PLAINS

157   143

PLAINS

Buchuma ●   ⚘ Buchuma
Gate

N

▼ Satao Rock Camp   ▼ Mackinnon Road & Mombasa

0   10 km

is a forty-bed luxury tented lodge, with a good atmosphere, game drives, and a water hole which attracts elephants, occasional lions and plains game. As well as the ordinary tents, there are larger "suite" tents, for around 30 percent more. Hot water (solar heated) is only available in the evenings. FB from $200; ⑨

Tarhi Camp PO Box 80733 Mombasa ☎041/548 6378, ⓦwww.camp-tarhi.de; bookings through Kedev, p.446. Situated off junction 136, this is a modest tented camp with reasonable facilities (all tents are s/c with hot running water), but lacking the stunning views of its pricier competitors. In its favour, it is located near the Voi River and Kanderi

Swamp, and receives occasional night visits from lions and even leopards. FB ⑥

Tsavo Buffalo Camp and **Tsavo River Hill** 200m outside Sala Gate; PO Box 556 Malindi ☎043/31192, ⓔcoralkey@africaonline.co.ke. Two camps in one, nicely sited on the Galana River. The "buffalo side" has eleven round *bandas*, small but comfortable. The "hill side" is more swish, with larger *bandas* done out with leopardskin-print sheets and drapes. Elephants and hippos are frequently sighted, and this is the park's cheapest option short of camping. Walk-in lunches Ksh750. Rates are per person (so good value for singles). HB ⑦

The Tsavo poaching wars

Tsavo East was for a long time the contentious focus for conservation issues. The question of how to manage the **elephants** – or whether to manage them at all – is still the paramount one, in theory. The policy for years has been to hunt the ivory poachers and allow the elephants to reach a natural balance, but the cycles of over-population and drought were too long for anyone to know if this was working out or not. Concerns are now being raised about the destruction of Tsavo East's remaining woodland by the pachyderms.

Such questions have been submerged for many years by the overbearing problem of **poaching**. In 1972, Tsavo's elephant population was over 17,000; today it is around half that. Elephants are intelligent animals with complex kinship patterns, but the social structure of the herds in many districts has been badly distorted, with many elders wiped out and too many inexperienced younger elephants unable to fend for themselves or to act in a properly mature, elephantine way. Orphaned infant calves are automatically doomed, while young elephants under 10 years, comprising nearly half the present population, have only a fifty–fifty chance of surviving to maturity.

There was a lull in poaching in the early 1980s, but by the end of the decade any complacency was shattered by an unprecedented slaughter of elephants in their thousands – mostly mature animals with large tusks, but including many with little ivory to offer. The poachers were no longer marginalized Akamba killing an occasional elephant with an old gun or poisoned arrows, but a new breed of ivory-hunters equipped with automatic weapons, going in and wiping out a whole family group in a single attack.

In 1988, it emerged that the then Somalian government was involved in poaching, mainly in Tsavo, and possibly in collusion with Kenyan Somalis and park-rangers-turned-poachers. Furious, President Moi personally ordered park rangers to shoot poachers on sight, and deployed his feared paramilitary General Service Unit (GSU). Ethnic Somalis living near the boundaries of Tsavo East were summarily rounded up and trucked north to Wajir and Mandera, rekindling a bitter resentment which goes back a long way and has nothing to do with poaching.

The international **ivory trade moratoriums**, in place from 1989, had a remarkable effect on the numbers of new elephant corpses being logged in Tsavo. Equally dramatic was the unprecedented aggression with which, in 1989, the Kenyan parks authorities started carrying out their duties under the bluntly pragmatic new Director of Wildlife and Conservation Management (which became the Kenya Wildlife Service), Dr Richard Leakey. Armed men caught in the parks without authority were liable to be shot on sight, which deterred even the most reckless poachers and raised

Voi Safari Lodge PO Box 565 Voi ☎ 043/30019, ⓦ voilodge.kenya-safari.co.ke; reservations through Kenya Safari Lodges & Hotels, p.63. This lodge, near Voi Gate, is almost as busy as its Tsavo West counterparts, with a magnificent savannas-cape plunging to the horizon and almost guaranteed game-viewing from the terrace, though the rooms aren't huge. The style is agreeable 1970s glam-kitsch: look out for the photo of Miss World 1972. FB $200; ⑨

Tracking through the park

With minibus safaris increasingly taking in Tsavo East, the emptiness of the park is no longer as overwhelming as it was, but the park's vastness means that for much of the time, you will still have the pleasure of exploring the wilderness completely alone. It's easy to get away off the two or three beaten tracks, and you may find something special – a **serval** perhaps, or a **striped hyena**. You're also very likely to see some of Tsavo's elephants which, attuned to the dangers

another human rights cloud over the country. Before the 1989 ban, three elephants a day were being killed by poachers; in 2004 the figure was 91 for the entire year which, given the rise in the Kenyan elephant population from 19,000 in 1989 to around 30,000 in 2005, is considered bearable. What poaching there is currently seems to centre around the northern sector of Tsavo East. Official figures and comment are notable by their absence, fuelling speculation that powerful figures may be involved. More worrying is the pressure from some countries to open up the ivory trade again, which in 1999 succeeded in allowing Zimbabwe, Botswana and Namibia to resume trading in ivory, leading to concerns that this may reopen the floodgates to poachers. Fortunately, this has not been the case and the elephant population continues to grow.

Rhinos

The black rhinos, of course, are even further down this vicious path to near-annihilation. Their number in Kenya is estimated at around 500 (compared to 330 in 1989, at the height of the poaching) – that is, somewhere around a quarter of the total population of the species, which remains under a serious threat of extinction. More than 95 percent of Kenya's rhino population (most of them in Tsavo) was destroyed in the 1970s, when the hunters began buying automatic weapons to slaughter what are essentially quite vulnerable animals. This escalation wasn't just the result of land pressure and human hardship in the countryside. More significant was a radical expansion of the market for rhino horns – not, as is popularly supposed, in China (where minute quantities of powdered rhino horn are used for tonics and aphrodisiacs), but in **Yemen**. Oil money put the rhino-horn dagger-handle, traditionally the prerogative of the rich, suddenly within reach of thousands of Yemeni men. Many tons of horns were smuggled out of Mombasa in dhows to meet demand.

Yet the savage groundwork was laid long before. After World War II, the Makueni area southeast of Machakos was designated as an Akamba resettlement area, and the colonial Kenya Game Department sent in one J.A. Hunter to clear it of unwelcoming rhinos. He lived up to his name, shooting 1088 black rhinos. (The Akamba didn't take to the scheme and it fizzled out.)

From the brink of disaster, there are now concentrations of breeding black rhinos in a number of ranches and sanctuaries – notably at Ngulia in Tsavo West, Nakuru, the Aberdares, Solio, and Lewa Downs and the neighboring Laikipia District. White rhinos have also been brought up from South Africa and there are an estimated 170 of this species now in Kenya, most of them located in conservation projects in Solio, Lewa and Nakuru. Saving the rhino has become a national cause.

they face from poachers, have taken to spending much of their time near the lodges and park roads where they are relatively safe. Large herds are not uncommon but the scarcity of really mature adults is noticable.

The Voi River's wooded margins often hide a profusion of wildlife: try the **Ndololo Campsite** at junction 173 and the pretty **Kanderi Swamp loop** at junction 174. Keep the windows up when driving through the tall grass and undergrowth, not only for security against large animals, but as a defence against the tsetse flies that may mistake your vehicle for a large animal. **Mudanda Rock** is particularly recommended at certain times of the year. Like a scaled-down version of Ayers Rock in Australia, it towers above a natural dam which, during the dry season, draws elephants in their hundreds. One of the ornithological wonders of the world is **Yatta plateau**, stretching from Mtito Andei towards the Galana River, along the eastern banks of the Athi River; among the world's largest lava flows, it is visited by birds migrating from Malawi, Oman, Iran, and even as far away as Germany and Russia.

Until its lodge closed, the obvious focus in Tsavo East was the beautiful **Aruba Dam**, the lake itself still an excellent spot for animal-watching. From here, most people head up towards the **Galana River**, unmistakable with its fringing cordon of branching doum palms. It's possible to cross the Galana at junction 160 in the dry season, but beware the smoothness of the rock bed, which belies the fact that many unwitting drivers all too easily get stuck in the attempt. Just to the east of here are the spectacular **Lugard's Falls**, where you can park and clamber around the bizarrely eroded rocks. Even in relatively dry seasons, the force of the falls, which progress from foaming rapids to narrow cascades gouged deep into the bedrock, is quite something. Some safari companies use the falls as a picnic site – apparently with KWS sanction – as evidenced by a litter of plastic wrappers and cigarette butts; please take your rubbish with you.

A kilometre east of the falls, another short diversion takes you to **Crocodile Point**, something of a let-down as the crocs are extraordinarily hard to see unless you get up close, which you're no longer allowed to do. Hippos are easier to spot, though.

Amboseli National Park and around

AMBOSELI is a small and very touristy park. It has suffered badly from off-road driving and its climate makes it a bleak, shimmering plain most of the year. Scenically, however, it is totally redeemed by the stunning spectacle of **Kilimanjaro** towering over it and (as in those clichéd safari photographs taken with telephoto lenses) appearing almost to fill the sky. Sunrise and sunset are the best times to see the mountain, especially during the rainy season when the air is much clearer, but for the most part it remains tantalizingly shrouded in a thick shawl of cloud. In the right light, the snowy massif, washed coral and orange, is devastatingly beautiful.

On the animal side, Amboseli, like Tsavo, is **elephant** country *par excellence*. You will see large herds, some with big tusks. Predators, apart from hyenas and jackals, are relatively scarce (lions are almost absent, thanks to the revenge wrought by the Maasai upon their expulsion from the park), but good numbers of herbivores are present. In the dry season, most of the animals crowd into the impenetrable marshy areas and patches of acacia woodland where food plants

What is now Amboseli was part of the Southern Maasai Reserve at the turn of the last century; tourism arrived in the 1940s and Amboseli Reserve was created as a wildlife sanctuary. Unlike Nairobi and Tsavo national parks, created at the same time and sparsely inhabited, Amboseli's swamps were used by the Maasai to water their herds and they saw no reason not to continue sharing the area with the wildlife and – if necessary – with the tourists. In 1961, the Maasai District Council at Kajiado was given control of the area. But the combined destructive capacities of cattle and tourists began to tell in the 1960s; a rising water table in the following decade brought poisonous alkali to the surface and decimated huge tracts of acacia woodland.

Kenyatta declared the 400-square-kilometre zone around the swamps (the present-day Amboseli) a **national park**, a status that utterly excluded the Maasai and their cattle. Infuriated, they all but exterminated the park's magnificent long-horned black rhinos over the next few years, seizing on Amboseli's tourist emblem with a vengeance (the survivors were moved out by the authorities). They also obliterated a good part of the lion population, which has still not recovered. Not until a piped water supply was set up for the cattle did the Maasai finally give up the portion of land within Amboseli's boundaries. They still, however, periodically pursue lion (which, of course, kill their cattle), although compromise appears to be the order of the day: in the dry seasons, you'll see numerous herds of cattle and their herders encroaching well into the park unhindered, as they always did.

The **erosion** of the Amboseli's grasslands by circling minibuses did much to destroy the park's purpose in the 1980s, turning it into a vehicle-clogged dustbowl that appealed little to animals or tourists. A concerted programme of environmental conservation, road-building and ditch-making was initiated, and this, combined with the toughest approach of any park to off-road driving (including fines and ejections), has improved the situation enormously. In 1992–93 heavy rains caused major **floods**, turning Amboseli into a swamp. The Kenya Wildlife Service responded with a $2million rehabilitation plan to rebuild park roads and culverts that had been destroyed, but the same thing happened again in 1997–98; these cycles of flood and subsequent drought were amplified by the El Niño effect, and seem to have become nature's way of culling the weakest and least adaptable animals. Unfortunately, this cycle also leaves the park more open to damage by vehicles: even at 10kph, the amount of dust thrown up is astounding.

In September 2005, Mwai Kibaki announced that **Amboseli's status** would be downgraded from national park to national reserve, thus passing from the KWS to Olkejiado County Council. The decision has unleashed a storm of controversy; in the eyes of many this was an attempt to gain the support of the Maasai in the constitutional referendum of November 2005, which the president lost. Opponents of a change in the park's status, including many conservation groups and the Kenya Tourist Federation, argue that the change will lead to bad management and a drop in revenue for the KWS which will, in turn, affect Kenya's other national parks. Supporters say the move will benefit the local Maasai community and encourage the involvement of local communities in wildlife conservation. At the time of writing the president's move was being challenged in the courts.

are available. But during and shortly after the rains the picture is different, the animals more dispersed and the landscape greener.

The **A104** road from Nairobi is tarmac all the way to Namanga on the Tanzanian border, from where it's a smooth 76-kilometre ride along recently improved *murram* to the park's centre, which can be reached in just under three hours nonstop from Nairobi. Driving from Nairobi, turn right off the Mombasa Highway on to the A104 after 23km, just after the dusty Bamburi Cement clinker grinding plant, at the southeastern extremity of Nairobi National Park. Public transport will only take you as far as Namanga (there are a few buses from Nairobi's Country Bus Station), from where you'll have to hitch; Namanga's petrol station, from where the *murram* road leads off east towards Amboseli, is probably the best place to start. As usual, the best chances are with Kenyan weekenders. Once in the park, you shouldn't have too much difficulty lining up lifts onwards. Routes to the **east of the park** are covered on pp.390–391. There are daily Airkenya and SafariLink **flights** from Nairobi's Wilson Airport (around $150 return in high season).

The route from Nairobi

The A104 through the Kapiti plains is unfortunately pretty dull, broken only by the **Maasai Ostrich Farm** (☎045/22505–6; Ksh100 including tour), signposted 7km off on the right 15km south of Athi River. Primarily a commercial farm providing meat to local butchers, they also have guided tours of the farm, a swimming pool, limited food and large picnic grounds. There's also the comical attraction of ostrich races, usually on Sundays.

At **Isinya**, there's a touristy **Maasai Leatherworking and Handicrafts Centre**, with some unusual work among the beaded key-rings and "marriage necklaces". Check out the handmade shoes and massive, heavy leather bags. If your stomach is strong, you can visit the tannery, and they're happy to see you in the workshops, too.

Further south, in the gentle hills where Maasai country really begins, is the district capital **KAJIADO**. Set among sisal spikes and acacia, it's a friendly market town, an ideal stopover after the hassle of Nairobi. Maasai in all their gear mix with other Kenyans in its busy streets and bars, and the daily **market**, part of which shelters in a modern breeze-block and corrugated-iron building near the mosque, is fascinating. The *Kaputiei B&L* (❷), opposite the Caltex petrol station, has the best cheap **rooms** in town. For **cheap eats**, try *Sizzlers* just down from the *Kaputiei*, or the *Central Hotel* opposite.

Namanga

The scenic interest picks up after Kajiado, as the road snakes into the hills, giving views of the conical Mount Meru in Tanzania (4565m), and your first glimpses of Kilimanjaro if the sky's clear. **NAMANGA** town sits square on the border, only 130km from Arusha in Tanzania.

Namanga River Lodge is the grandest **accommodation** option (PO Box 4; ❺). A colonial oddity composed of wooden cabins set amid pretty gardens, it was the halfway house on the old safari trail between Nairobi and Arusha. The place has a likeable, slightly cranky atmosphere, and has clearly seen better days but it's overpriced. Good snacks are served, and you can also happily camp in the garden (Ksh400 per person). Much better value are the s/c rooms (hot water in buckets) at the *Namanga Safari Lodge* next door (PO Box 5; ❶), with its pleasantly kitsch garden and bar, reasonable food, and cheaper camping, too (Ksh150 per person). Best of the two basic B&Ls is *Orock County B&L* (❷), at the start of the track to the *River Lodge*.

On the main road from Nairobi are several large **tourist emporiums**, including one not far north of Namanga and the other in the town itself, at the big petrol station. Both are packed to overflowing with Maasai bead- and leather-work, as well as Makonde ebony carvings from southern Tanzania and, of course, Kamba animals and Kisii soapstone. They're not especially cheap but you can strike reasonable bargains and the choice is huge. The glass beads used in the beadwork are actually from the Czech Republic, which exports them

△ Maasai gathering, Namanga area

to Peru and the Native American reservations as well as East Africa. And don't be misled by the expensive black-and-white marriage necklaces, which are not traditional Maasai ware; nor are the carved animal pendants. Among all the trinketry are genuine used articles which tend to attract high prices. For these, you might do better by making offers to people you meet on the road. Bartering clothes or food often works to the benefit of both parties.

The park

Daily 6am–6.30pm; $30 per day/overnight, children $10; private vehicle Ksh200, no camping. Smartcard entry; nearest outlet at Meshananai (Namanga) gate. Warden: PO Box 18 Namanga ☏ 0456/22250–1, ✉ amboseli.ngo@africaonline.co.ke. No driving after 7pm. Speed limit 30kph. Maps: Amboseli (Jacana Media, 2004), 1:50,000.

If you're **arriving**, as most people do, around midday in the dry seasons, Amboseli seems a parched, unattractive place, with Kilimanjaro disappointingly hazed into oblivion. Heading straight for the park's centre at Ol Tukai, with its lodges, workers, filling station, fences and barriers, doesn't improve first impressions. During the rains, however, it all looks far more impressive, with the lake partially filled, and a number of other seasonal lakes and ponds, the occasional home of small flocks of flamingos, pelicans, and other migratory species.

One road connects the park gate with "Ol Tukai" park centre; a second, which cuts right across Lake Amboseli on many maps, is rarely passable, and even in dry weather risks getting you bogged down in a treacherous version of quicksand – take care.

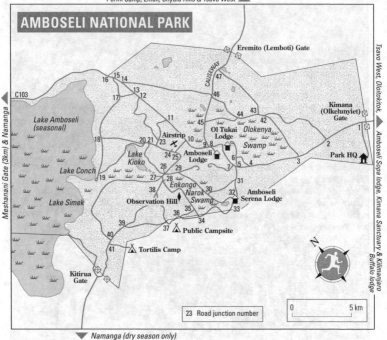

Porini Camp, Emali, Chyulu Hills & Tsavo West ▲

AMBOSELI NATIONAL PARK

Meshanani Gate (3km) & Namanga ◀

Tsavo West, Oloitokitok, ▶ Amboseli Sopa lodge, Kimana Sanctuary & Kilimanjaro / Kimana (Olkelunyiet) Buffalo lodge

▼ Namanga (dry season only)

23   Road junction number

0   5 km

Accommodation

The only budget accommodation is the **campsite** outside the park (Ksh500 per person), accessed from the signposted tracks leading west from *Amboseli Serena Lodge* or south from Observation Hill. It's a fine, wooded site, though no longer overrun with wildlife since it was partially fenced. Apart from warm sodas, a couple of toilets are the only facilities, and even water supplies are unreliable. You're also likely to be hassled by Maasai looking to pose for pictures, offering trinkets or visits to their *enkangs*, or simply demanding cash.

△ Accommodation at *Amboseli Lodge*

Besides the slick establishments listed below (most of which offer **game drives**, not restricted to residents, at around $40 per person), the closest **rooms** are at the B&L in Kimana (p.390), and in the Kimana Community Wildlife Sanctuary (p.390). Wherever you stay, be wary of semi-tame baboons and vervet monkeys, who will grab anything not tied down if it looks tempting, and can give a nasty bite if irritated.

Amboseli Lodge Ol Tukai area ⓣ & ⓕ045/622440; reservations also through Let's Go Travel (see p.150). Staff at this, the main package destination, are helpful and friendly, the food is good, and the cute chalet accommodation is comfortable. There are Maasai dancers in the evenings, and optional cultural talks. But the main draw is the fantastic full-on view of Kilimanjaro from all public areas and some of the rooms. A murky green pool, showers and meals (Ksh1000 per person) available to casual visitors. FB $160 low season, rising by a quarter in high season; ⑨

Amboseli Serena Lodge Southern park area ⓣ045/622361, ⓕ622430, ⓦwww.serenahotels.com. Located by the Enkongo Narok Swamps, which attract plenty of wildlife, the lodge has large, nicely decorated rooms adorned with animal murals. The pink sugarcube architecture is well hidden behind a jungle of tropical plants and creepers (you can plant trees, if you like, to save future visitors the sight), which encourages a kind of intimate, pseudo-bush feeling accentuated by touches like a stream running through the dining room. You can drop in for lunch (Ksh1100), but the pool is for resident guests only. Fuel available. FB $170 low season, $275 high; ⑨

Amboseli Sopa Lodge Just outside the eastern park gates ⓣ045/622361, ⓕ622430; reservations through Let's Go Travel (see p.150). Newly renovated lodge with charming animal-themed rooms, a rustic wooden bar/dining area and views out over to Kilimanjaro. There are a range of activities on offer, including Maasai village visits. FB $180 low season, $250 high; ⑨

Ol Tukai Lodge Ol Tukai area ⓣ045/622275, ⓕ622280; reservations ⓣ020/4445514, ⓦwww.oltukailodge.com. Stylish "rustic-safari" architecture, beautiful communal areas, and unspectacular wooden cottages, half of which look out beyond the fence towards the Amboseli plains, the other half towards Kilimanjaro. Two cottages are designed for disabled visitors, and there's good access throughout. There's a nice pool, and educational videos and Maasai dancers most evenings. The headquarters of Cynthia Moss's Amboseli Elephant Research project is nearby. FB $170 low season, $265 high; ⑨

Porini Camp In the Selenkay Conservation Area, north of Amboseli; reservations ⓣ020/7123129, ⓕ7120864, ⓦwww.porini.com. Small eco-camp with six comfortable en-suite tents in the middle of the bush, surrounded by acacias, and offering a variety of game drives and safari walks. At the time of writing a package is the only way to visit: a three-day, two-night trip by road from Nairobi starts at $500 per person.

🏃 **Tortilis Camp** Outside the southern park boundary at Kitirua; ⓦwww.tortilis.com; reservations through Cheli and Peacock (see p.152). Double and twin en-suite "tents", with beds on concrete floors under wicker roofs, with all the amenities you'd expect in a five-star city hotel. Set atop a low hill, it gives stunning views of Kilimanjaro and northern Tanzania as far as Mount Meru. The pool at sunset is quite something, and there's a feeling of intimacy with the wildlife. The camp is managed as a conservation project, which includes paying a proportion of your fee to local Maasai, and the possibility of (unduly expensive) visits to a Maasai *enkang*. $335 per person sharing in high season. FB $450 low season, $670 high; ⑨

Exploring the park

Small enough to cover easily in two or three game drives in a single day, Amboseli is mostly open country with good visibility. Because of this, you escape the nagging feeling you may get in other parks, that you may be in the wrong place and *that's* why you're not seeing any animals – here, you can look everywhere.

A good first stop is **Observation Hill**. Early in the morning, with Kilimanjaro a pervasive sky-filler to the south, the swamps of **Enkongo Narok**, replenished underground from the mountain top, are looped out in a brilliant emerald sash beneath. You can get out and walk around up here, and chat with the heavily armed wardens posted there.

There's always a concentration of animals along the swamps and the driveable tracks which closely follow their fringes. The swamps are permanent enough to keep **hippo** here all year and there are hundreds of **elephant** and **buffalo** plus, predictably, a raucous profusion of **birdlife**. **Lake Kioko**, between Lake Amboseli and Ol Tukai – most easily seen along the track between junctions 21 and 26, is a special oasis, and **Olokenya swamp** with its seasonal lakes north and east of Ol Tukai, is always worth slow exploration.

Lions are very rare, but **cheetahs** are seen fairly frequently in the woods a little further south, and there must be thousands of **giraffe** among the acacias. Look out, too, for the beautifully formed, rapier-horned **fringe-eared oryx** antelope, and **gerenuk** stretching up to forage in the trees.

The open plains are scoured by **zebra** and haphazard, solitary **wildebeest**. The two species are often seen together – a good deal from the zebras' point of view because in a surprise attack the predator usually ends up with the less fleet-footed wildebeest. There are tail-flicking **gazelle** out here, too: the open country provides good protection against lion or cheetah ambushes.

Opinions vary widely about the **Maasai cultural bomas** which are set up just outside the park west of *Amboseli Serena Lodge* (between junctions 33 and 34). After paying a fee (from Ksh300 up to $30 per person – it varies with your perceived ability to pay), you get the right to take as many pictures as you want, and may be treated to a display of traditional dancing, while the Maasai get the right to pitch their curios at you with practised persistence.

Kimana, Oloitokitok and points onwards

There are two routes **east out of Amboseli**. One heads through **Eremito Gate** (Iremito, or Lemboti) to meet the *murram* C102 Emali–Oloitokitok road at **Makutano**, a tiny, featureless Maasai trading centre. There's no problem with the C102 road in dry weather, but take care in the wet (4WD only), as it acquires some extremely tricky mud patches, and gets very slippery towards Oloitokitok. There's infrequent public transport along this road. The road from Eremito Gate continues beyond Makutano across the Chyulu Hills National Park (see p.392) and towards Kibwezi on A109 Nairobi–Mombasa Highway.

The second and more travelled road, the **C103** to Tsavo, is in a terrible condition. It leaves Amboseli in the southeast through **Kimana Gate** (also called Olkelunyiet), passing the roadstead of **KIMANA** at the junction with the C102. *Romunja B&L* here has basic rooms (❶). As a result of concerns about **security**, you still supposedly have to travel in convoy to Tsavo West with an official vehicle or armed guard, although there hasn't been an incident since the early 1990s. At the time of writing, there were daily departures in either direction (8.30am & 2.30pm from Ol Tukai and Tsavo's Chyulu Gate; 2–4hr). At other times you can pick up an escort at Ol Tukai, but he'll expect payment. It's possible to circumvent this arrangement if you're intending to turn off the C103 for Oloitokitok, Taveta or Emali.

The C102

If you turn left (north) at Kimana, a ten-kilometre drive along the C102 takes you to the signposted turning to the **Kimana Community Wildlife Sanctuary** (PO Box 362 Oloitokitok; daily 6.30am–7pm; $15). This is one of a growing number of Maasai group-ranch ventures setting aside land for wildlife conservation and tourism; self-imposed restrictions prohibit any livestock grazing or settlement except in times of severe drought. The 41-square-kilometre site, opened in 1996, includes plains, acacia woodland, and a wetland area which is watered by springs and frequented by lion, leopard, cheetah and hyena as well as antelope. There are three **campsites** in the sanctuary, the best signposted from the main road being *Kimana Leopard Camp*.

South of Kimana, the C102 climbs 15km up to the Maasai country town of **OLOITOKITOK** (pronounced "Loytoktok") right on the border with Tanzania, with Kilimanjaro's jagged satellite peak **Mawenzi** dead ahead. Oloitokitok is ignored by 99 percent of the tourist minibuses, and it's in a fabulous position, closer to Kilimanjaro than anywhere else in Kenya and high above the plains (altitude 1700m). It's also a **border crossing** for the Tanzanian town of Moshi a couple of hours away, nestled behind the mountain. Kilimanjaro's **Kibo Peak** is 25km away from Oloitokitok as the crow flies; you can arrange climbing tours in Oloitokitok at *Kibo Slopes Cottages*, and there are enough willing guides and porters, but don't get caught in Kilimanjaro National Park without having paid the park fee.

Oloitokitok is a relaxed place to settle into if you're interested in finding out more about the Maasai, as this is their easternmost major centre. On Tuesdays and Saturdays, when many Maasai are in Oloitokitok for the **weekly markets**, there's a fair amount of matatu traffic between here and Emali, as well as a service south to Taveta (some leave the day before to get to Oloitokitok). At other times, you will have to take pot luck with transport – start early. Oloitokitok has a petrol station, a post office and KCB bank (which takes ages to change money), as well as a few **B&Ls** at the top of the hill near the market. Best of these is the Christian-run *Safari's Lodge* (PO Box 291; ☎045/622088; ❷). Otherwise, *Hilltop Lodge* (PO Box 59; ☎045/622303; ❷) is reasonable. *Mwalimu Lodge* in the lower part of town is a serious watering hole. Superior to all is the modern *Kibo Slopes Cottages* (PO Box 218; ☎045/622091, ℱ622427, ⓦwww.kiboslopescottages.com; B&B ❻), 1km down a track to the left of the customs post, with good if overpriced s/c rooms (hot running water morning and evening), some with good views, and four-bed cottages costing the same as the double rooms.

Towards Taveta

On market days, you can catch a matatu to the town of **Taveta** (see p.369), almost 100km away near the southwestern tip of Tsavo West National Park. The journey, which skirts the border with Tanzania and the flanks of Kilimanjaro, is far off the beaten track, but scenically rewarding, as well as being on the shortest route from Amboseli to Voi on the Mombasa Road. Faster, and kinder to your vehicle if you're driving, is the tarmac road on the Tanzanian side, but it's expensive if you haven't got multiple-entry visas for both Tanzania and Kenya. On the Kenyan side, the road is unsurfaced except for the first 9km of soothing tarmac to Illasit (where the tarmac veers off right towards Tanzania: keep going straight), and often becomes impassable in the rains when the fine dust turns to mud.

As you leave Oloitokitok, the landscape changes from scrubby cattle pasture to neat – if dusty – plots of sisal and maize plantations, marking the end of Maasai territory. There are only a few settlements, acting as market centres for Maasai and Taveta agriculturers. The next accommodation is 58km away at **Chumvini** (Njukini), where the dogged *Gatanga Guest House* (PO Box 53 Taveta; ☎043/2639; ❶) has some basic non-s/c rooms, a down-at-heel bar with funny murals, a butchery and *nyama choma*. From here, you'll find more frequent transport on to Taveta (daily matatus, and buses on Tues, Wed, Fri & Sun). Further on, 10km short of Taveta, is the wonderful aberration of **Lake Chala** (see p.370).

Chyulu Hills National Park

Daily 6am–6pm; $15 per day/overnight, children $5; private vehicle Ksh200, camping $8 per person. Warden ☎ 0724/272019.

The **Chyulu Hills National Park**, which follows the spine of the Chyulu Hills lava ridge, is one of Kenya's least visited and least developed national parks. Aside from the scenery, and animals, including elephants, buffaloes, elands, forest hogs – even, in the park's northwestern corner, towards the Makedo Gate, the odd black rhino – the main attraction is **Leviathan Cave**, the world's second-longest lava tube. At present, you'd need to be a dedicated and well-equipped caver to explore Leviathan, but the park warden has plans to make at least part of the cave more easily accessible in the future. The park's Makedo Gate can be reached from Makutano on the C102 Emali–Oloitokitok road, while the Kibwezi Gate is reached from a junction 1km south of Kibwezi on the A109 Nairobi–Mombasa road; you'll need your own vehicle. The terrain inside the park is hard going and requires 4WD.

Accommodation in the park is limited to one **campsite** (bring your own tent and supplies) located by the park HQ, which is 1200m inside the Kibwezi Gate, but there are some excellent places to stay outside the park limits, any of which could make a good base for a visit. Like the park itself however, all are beyond the reach of public transport. A good choice, and certainly the best option for cavers, is *Umani Springs Camp* (PO Box 333 Kibwezi; ☎ 0721/317762; also bookable c/o PO Box 47363 Nairobi; ☎ 020/7120883; FB ❸), a relatively upmarket tented camp deep in the forest, with hot running water and its own generator. It can be reached along a twelve-kilometre track (very rough, but possible with care in an ordinary vehicle) that leaves the Mombasa road 2km north of Kibwezi, just where the railway crosses the road. The owner is a keen caver and, with advance notice, the camp may be able to help organize caving expeditions to Leviathan Cave. Even more upmarket, *Ol Donyo Wuas* (reservations through Bush Homes, p.63; $820 plus $20 per person in conservancy fee; ❾) is a deluxe eco-lodge on the other side of the park, 25km south of Makedo Gate. A few kilometres further southwest is the award-winning Campi Ya Kanzi (Ⓦ www.maasai.com; ❾), a Maasai-Italian collaboration, constructed without tree-felling and using solar panels.

Maasai Mara National Reserve

Daily 6.30am–7pm; $30 per day/overnight, children $10; private vehicle Ksh200, camping Ksh480 per person. Senior warden: PO Box 60 Narok ☎ 0305/22068 or 22268. No driving after 7pm. Speed limit 40kph. Maps: Tourist Maps of Kenya Maasai Mara National Reserve (2002) 1:50,000; and Maasai Mara National Reserve (Jacana Media, 2005) 1:100,000.

For a long list of reasons, **MAASAI MARA** is the best animal reserve in Kenya. The panorama sometimes resembles one of those wild animal wall charts, where groups of unlikely looking animal companions are forced into the artist's frame. You can see a dozen different species – or more – at one time: gazelle, zebra, giraffe, buffalo, topi, kongoni, wildebeest, eland, elephant, hyena, jackal, ostrich, and a pride of lions waiting for a chance. When the reserve was created, however, the scene looked very different. Traditionally, the **Maasai** lived in some harmony with the wildlife, hunting only lion and, in times of famine, eland and buffalo, the "wild cattle". Only the Okiek people (the "Dorobo in

Maa", meaning "people without cattle") hunted for a living. When the first European **hunting safaris** made the Mara world-famous in the early years of last century, they were ransacking a region recently deserted by the Maasai. Smallpox had ravaged the Maasai communities and rinderpest had torn through their cattle herds. By 1961, the white hunters had succeeded in bringing the Mara's lion population down to nine, and Maasai Mara was created as a game sanctuary – and a tourist attraction – to be administered by the Maasai District Council at Narok

Nearly 2000m above sea level, the reserve is a great wedge of undulating **grassland** in the remote, sparsely inhabited southwest part of the country, snuggled up against the border and, indeed, an extension of the even bigger **Serengeti plains** in Tanzania. This is a land of short grasses, where the wind plays with the thick, green mantle after the rains and, nine months later, whips up dust devils from the baked surface. Maasai Mara's climate is predictable, with ample rain, and the new grass supports an annual **wildebeest migration** of up to one and a half million animals from the dry plains of Tanzania. To travel through the reserve in August or September, while the wildebeest are in possession, is a staggering experience, like being caught up in the momentum of a phenomenal historic event. Whether you're watching this or a pride of lions hunting, a herd of elephants grazing in the marsh, or hyenas squabbling with vultures over the carcass of a buffalo, you are conscious all the time of being in a realm apart. There are few places on earth where animals hold such dazzling sway – it's as if you had found yourself in the New York of the natural world.

With its plentiful vegetation and wildlife, the reserve's **ecology** appears at first sight to be relatively resilient to the effect of the huge number of tourists who visit it every year. However, the Mara is the most visited park in Kenya (there are over two thousand beds in and around the reserve), and there are signs that the balance between tourist numbers and wildlife can't be maintained much longer. In parts, off-road driving, which kills the protective cover of vegetation, has created dust bowls which themselves begin to spread through the effects of natural wind and water erosion. During the rains, many roads become impassable, causing a welter of parallel tracks to appear, many of them knee-deep in mud by the time the rains move on, and which can take many years to heal.

On entering the reserve, you'll be handed a copy of the relevant **bylaws** and rules, which should be strictly adhered to, but which sadly in practice often aren't. The devolution in 2001 of the management of the western Mara Triangle part of the reserve to a non-profit company called Mara Conservancy has helped compliance, however, and though much remains to be done, there have been many improvements, such as drop in poaching, the restoration of roads and buildings, increased funding for local communities and the establishment of a more transparent means of revenue collection.

The vast majority of visitors come on prebooked safari packages, which invariably work out cheaper than going under your own steam. Travellers on a budget aren't well catered for in Maasai Mara. If you can't afford the more expensive lodges and luxury tented camps, there are very few alternatives to do-it-yourself **camping**.

Access is most straightforward, and most expensive (around $180 return), by the scheduled daily **air services** from Nairobi's Wilson Airport, as well as from Lewa Downs, Nanyuki and Samburu. The twelve-seater flights are thoroughly enjoyable, with elephants, warthog and wildebeest visible below, and the pilot announcing the lodges he would like to land at in his preferred order. Many of the lodges have their own **airstrips**; transfers from the airstrip to your lodge by jeep cost around $25 per person, with a minimum of four people usually required.

Road approaches to the Mara

If you decide to drive to the Mara, give yourself plenty of time – a good six to seven hours nonstop from Nairobi or Naivasha to the eastern end of the reserve, or, with an early start, nine or ten hours nonstop to the western end. And if you intend to do more than a tank's worth of driving, remember to stock up with cans of **petrol** at the last town you pass through (usually **Narok**). Although there are one or two new petrol stations on the new road between Narok and Bonet, and you may be able to buy petrol at some of the lodges (at a price), you cannot depend on either source. There's not much point visiting in anything other than a **4WD** car. Access routes via Talek, Musiara and Oloololo gates are all possible in dry weather (avoid them in wet), but even then can be exceedingly treacherous, with the main problem being frequent watery mud pits across the track. For details of driving on mud tracks, which may well have a bearing on your choice of approach, see p.58.

If you're heading here by road from Nairobi, there's the reward of the long drive across the Rift Valley, sweeping across dry, stupendous vistas of range lands – the heart of the Maasai country. Cattle are the economic mainstay, but extensive wheat fields are pushing south. While the land often looks empty, if you stop for five minutes, chances are that someone will appear – to request something or to offer a photo pose, or just to pass the time of day.

The easiest route to the Mara **from Nairobi** is via the A104 to Limuru, followed by the B3 all the way down to Narok. The latter is tarmac but is in variable condition, the section of road leading to Narok being particularly dodgy condition. Coming **from Naivasha**, you can join the B3 at **Mai Mahiu**. There's one **accommodation** option here: *Mount Longonot Transit Hotel* (PO

Over the Mau Escarpment to Narok

As a preliminary to Maasai Mara, the **Mau Escarpment** is a compelling alternative to the long rolling switchback of the main Mai Mahiu–Narok road. **From Lake Naivasha** (at the end of the lake road tarmac by Kongoni police station), and **from Nakuru** via **Njoro**, steep roads twist up over the escarpment. If you're starting out from further west, you can also get to Narok by the gradually improving Molo–Olenguerone road (see p.260), a route which allows the option of a more direct approach to the west end of the reserve. All these are for 4WD only. If you're using **matatus**, the Nakuru–Narok route is a little easier than the other two; the village of East Mau, near the peaks, is your first destination.

The **Mau range**, not as high but just as massive as the Aberdares, is rarely visited, enrapturing country, highly recommended for **hiking**. In the thin, clear air, Maasai and Nandi graze their cattle on luxuriant pastures, and large but steadily shrinking domains of thick, dark forest are still the home to **Okiek hunter-gatherers**, called Dorobo by the Maasai.

There's little **accommodation** in the Mau range. **Enangiperi**, for example, roughly the halfway point, has one, very basic "lodging" (more a bed in a barn) and you may find yourself asking, or being invited, to stay with people. This can arouse suspicions in the local authorities, who are sensitive about travellers in these parts because of ongoing friction between local people and immigrant farmers and landlords from other parts of Kenya.

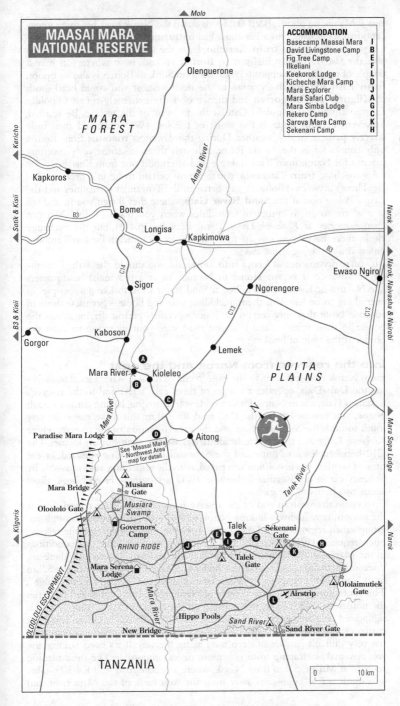

MAASAI MARA NATIONAL RESERVE

ACCOMMODATION	
Basecamp Maasai Mara	I
David Livingstone Camp	B
Fig Tree Camp	F
Ilkeliani	L
Keekorok Lodge	D
Kicheche Mara Camp	J
Mara Explorer	A
Mara Safari Club	G
Mara Simba Lodge	C
Rekero Camp	K
Sarova Mara Camp	H
Sekenani Camp	

Molo

MARA FOREST

Olenguerone

Kericho

Sotik & Kisii

Kapkoros

B3

Bomet

Longisa

Kapkimowa

B3 & Kisii

Sigor

C14

Amala River

Narok

Narok, Naivasha & Nairobi

Ewaso Ngiro

Ngorengore

C13

C12

Gorgor

Kaboson

Lemek

LOITA PLAINS

Mara River

Kioleleo

A

B

C

Aitong

N

Narok

Paradise Mara Lodge

D

See 'Maasai Mara - Northwest Area' map for detail

Talek River

Mara Sopa Lodge

Mara Bridge

Musiara Gate

Musiara Swamp

Talek

E I F G

Sékenani Gate

H

Narok

Olooolo Gate

Governors' Camp

RHINO RIDGE

J

Talek Gate

K

Kilgoris

Mara Serena Lodge

Mara River

Ololaimutiek Gate

OLOOLOLO ESCARPMENT

Hippo Pools

Sand River

L

Airstrip

New Bridge

Sand River Gate

TANZANIA

0   10 km

5

Box 9 Mahiu; no phone; B&B ❷), 500m down the Narok road, has some unexceptional s/c *bandas*, plus a bar and a bad restaurant.

If you're starting out **from Kericho**, leave the C23 just before **Sotik**, then take the fast B3 tarmac highway to **Bomet** (40km), from where you have a couple of options (see opposite). The B3 from Sotik to Bomet is also an option **from Kisii** and **South Nyanza** to the northwest, or you could head south to **Kilgoris** and **Lolgorien** and thence over the extremely rough Oloololo Escarpment to the Oloololo Gate at the far west of the reserve. Be warned, however, that this route is the worst of the lot, 4WD only, and then only scarcely passable in dry weather. During the day, most **matatus** from Bomet only run as far as the Amala River, although there are some early-morning matatus for Narok from Kisii and one mid-afternoon one from Kericho.

Approaching **from Tanzania**, you're almost certain to be in a private vehicle. There's a twelve-kilometre gap between the Tanzanian formalities and the Kenya Police post at the **Sand River Gate**, where they'll sign you in and tell you where to go to complete formalities when you reach Nairobi. You can change money at *Keekorok Lodge*, 10km away (see p.401), but the exchange clerks there have been known to limit this to an unhelpfully small amount unless you're staying at the lodge.

If you're driving out of Kenya **into Tanzania**, you should check the formalities in advance at Nyayo House in Nairobi, or at a provincial headquarters like Nakuru or Kisumu. The police at Sand River seem to like photocopies of everything to be left with them, including your log book – get these done in advance. Note that only certain car rental operators permit driving across the border in their vehicles, and that you must state your intention to cross the border at the time of booking.

Into the reserve from Narok and the east

From Narok (see opposite), to the eastern end of Maasai Mara, a local bus service, the **Dab–Dab,** operates a couple of times each afternoon to the reserve's Sekenani Gate; ask in Narok for details. If you're driving, having come through Narok, you branch left for the C12 road after 4km: this route makes its way south towards the Sekenani Gate and the eastern section of the reserve, where *Keekorok Lodge* and the reserve headquarters are the main human focuses. The C12 between Ewaso Ngiro and the Sekenani Gate is being surfaced; at the time of writing, the first 40km was paved, with the remaining 40km passable by ordinary car in dry weather (otherwise 4WD is required). From Narok, allow about two hours to the gate.

Access to the western end of the reserve is much faster since completion of the smooth new highway linking Narok with Bomet. Still, getting through the group ranch region of the Loita Plains, between the highway and the reserve, often requires 4WD, especially in wet weather (never assume dry conditions in the Mara region). West of the turnoff to the reserve's eastern end, there are three main turnings south off the highway. The first is at **Olulungu**, 32km from Narok, with signposts to "Mara Safari Camp" and "Voyager Safari Lodge". This route goes via the small centres of Ngorengore and Lemek and becomes the notorious **C13**. The second turning off the highway, 51km from Narok, is signposted "**Ngorengore**" and, likewise, joins with the C13. Unless you're an extremely experienced driver, the C13 is for dry weather only, and even then has very difficult patches of deep mud along the way. If it's been raining, the wet clay makes escaping from ruts more or less impossible. The third turning south is at **Mulot**, 53km from Narok, where a private road (toll Ksh500) takes you south, a few kilometres away from the west bank of the Mara river, and relatively fast towards *Mara Safari Club, Voyager Safari Lodge* and others outside the reserve, and ultimately to the Musiara Gate.

Into the reserve from Bomet and the west

Approaching the Maasai Mara from Kisumu, Kericho or Kisii, all routes converge on **BOMET**, an overblown village of just three streets running round the back of the Mobil station, and containing a small market, a few meagre *hotelis and dukas*, a KCB, post office, and some very basic lodgings. Past Bomet, the newly surfaced **B3** heads southeast for Narok, crossing the Amala River (which becomes the Mara River further downstream). The easiest route down to the reserve is via the toll road from the Mulot junction, mentioned above. A difficult alternative is the unpaved **C14** for Sigor and Kaboson, but though shorter than going via Mulot, this is very rough and difficult to navigate; stop regularly along the way to check with local people that you're on the right track. The first important (and unmarked) turning is about 5km south of Bomet. At Kaboson the C14 continues northwest, back towards Kilgoris and Kisii; turn off left in order to cross the Mara River and join the **C13**.

Narok

NAROK is the funnel through which almost all road transport enters the Mara. It's the last place to get fuel, a cold drink or almost anything for over 100km before you enter the reserve. First impressions aren't encouraging. *Afrikano*, on the left as you enter from the east, is a tourist trap of the first order, charging exorbitant prices for curios, food and drinks – though staff are on commission only. In the same vein, over the road, a brassy atmosphere pervades the Kobil service station and snack bar which, being the first petrol station on the way into town, waylays most of the minibuses with its big-game cut-outs, reticulated sunshades and cluster of souvenir shops selling very expensive Maasai paraphernalia. The Total station on the far side of town is cheaper and less hassly. If you're **hitching**, the Kobil station is probably the best point to wait, or try the bridge over the Engare Narok River on the west side of town.

Petrol rip-offs, tourist bazaars and touts aside, Narok is actually quite a lively little place, full of Maasai out shopping or doing business at the market. There's also the small but perfectly formed **Narok Maa Cultural Museum** (daily 9am–6pm; Ksh200), on the right as you come in, which is an excellent introduction to the Maasai (and Samburu) way of life. The walls have a fascinating collection of photographs taken by Maasai women, using disposable cameras given to them for the project, depicting important parts of their daily lives, such as water carrying, milking cattle, and raising children. Considering that it was the first time that any of the women had ever held a camera, the compositions are extraordinarily well judged.

Practicalities

If you're headed for the reserve but arrive in Narok after 4pm, you'll end up having to stay the night here, as you won't have time to get to the reserve by nightfall (gates close at 7pm). **Accommodation** is no problem as regards quantity, but quality and cost are another matter. You get reasonable value at the *Transit Hotel* (PO Box 384; ☎050/22288; ❸), opposite the Kobil station, with safe parking and so-so food. *Chambai Hotel* (PO Box 783; ☎050/22591; ❸), a tall building with a satellite dish near the mosque and opposite the market, is a better option; the spacious self-contained rooms with powerful hot showers are wonderful after a long bone-rattling drive to Narok from Nairobi. The best rooms are on the top two floors. Also decent is *Kanga Lodge* (❸) at the west end of town (turn right at the Agip station and matatu stage), with simple but acceptable rooms. You can **camp** at the *Members Club* (PO Box 4; ☎050/22383; Ksh200), 1km west of the Agip petrol station, which also has a few cheap and basic non-s/c *bandas* in a muddy site (①). Security is uncertain, as there's a rather rough bar here.

Catering for reputable safari groups, *Kenol Restaurant* (daily 6.45am–10.30pm), part of Kenol petrol station and supermarket, has good **food**, including marinated and deep-fried tilapia with rice, and fresh cold mango and passion-fruit juice. It's on the left-hand side of the main road if you're heading towards the Mara after leaving town. It's also the best place to stock up on provisions and cheap beer before you enter the reserve. *Hillside Cave Day & Night Club* on the main road does good chicken and *kienyeji*, and at night features a bizarre mix of traditionally-garbed Maasai and westernized Kenyans drinking and listening to reggae. Also on the main road, the *Three In One Bar & Restaurant* features live music at weekends.

National Bank of Kenya (Mon–Fri 9am–3pm, Sat 9–11am) and the **post office** are both on the main road. **Email** can be sent from Sky Apple Enterprises (Mon–Sat 8am–7pm) in Maa Towers, a building opposite the Commercial Bank of Kenya.

Reserve accommodation

Although there are about half a dozen **campsites** within the reserve itself, access to these is virtually impossible without a guide and your own, very sturdy 4WD transport (they're marked on most maps). However, the Mara extends far beyond the limits of the reserve, and game is usually in plentiful supply north of the boundaries, where most of the campsites are found.

If you're considering treating yourself, either on a safari package or independently, it's worth choosing where you stay carefully, although competition, and demanding clients, keep standards high in every price range. Pressure on the beds in and around the Mara can be intense, so **booking ahead** is essential if you want to be sure of your camp or lodge. Even if you can't afford to stay somewhere lavish, a taste of the high life can still be had if you splurge on food or drink at one of the lodges – though note that some don't open their doors to non-residents.

Be particularly wary of snatch-and-run **baboon raids** at the Mara campsites and lodges – baboons are prone to grab anything inviting-looking, whether edible or not, and dash off with it to examine it later. And avoid irritating these

---

Group Ranch tickets

Understandably unhappy at having been forced off the reserve lands, a number of Maasai Group Ranches adjacent to the reserve decided to create their own **wildlife trusts**, partially supported by KWS and other bodies, primarily to milk their own share of the tourist megabucks which hitherto flowed only into the local Transmara County Council's coffers. On paper, the aims are laudable: to promote the sustainable use of the natural and cultural resources found in the region; to ensure that environmental impacts from tourism are kept at a minimum; and to ensure a more equitable distribution of benefits derived from tourism. In practice, of course, corruption and local power-politics have already come into play.

All of the more upmarket tented camps and lodges situated outside the reserve now insist you buy Group Ranch tickets, whether you intend to enter the reserve proper or not. At least the tickets, which should have a silver hologram set across the central tear, are also valid for the reserve itself, and cost the same as the reserve tickets. Equally, reserve tickets bought at the gates are valid in the adjacent Group Ranch lands.

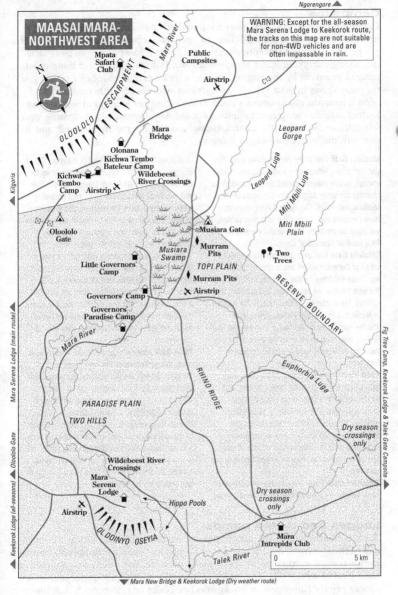

MAASAI MARA-NORTHWEST AREA

N

WARNING: Except for the all-season Mara Serena Lodge to Keekorok route, the tracks on this map are not suitable for non-4WD vehicles and are often impassable in rain.

Ngorengore

Mara River

Public Campsites

Airstrip

C13

OLOOLOLO ESCARPMENT

Mpata Safari Club

Mara Bridge

Olonana

Kichwa Tembo Bateleur Camp

Kichwa Tembo Camp

Wildebeest River Crossings

Airstrip

Leopard Gorge

Leopard Luga

Miti Mbili Luga

Musiara Gate

Miti Mbili Plain

Kilgoris

Oloololo Gate

Musiara Swamp

Murram Pits

TOPI PLAIN

Two Trees

Little Governors' Camp

Murram Pits

Airstrip

Governors' Camp

RESERVE BOUNDARY

Governors' Paradise Camp

Mara River

Euphorbia Luga

Mara Serena Lodge (main route)

RHINO RIDGE

Fig Tree Camp, Keekorok Lodge & Talek Gate Campsite

PARADISE PLAIN

Dry season crossings only

TWO HILLS

Oloololo Gate

Wildebeest River Crossings

Mara Serena Lodge

Dry season crossings only

Keekorok Lodge (all-seasons)

Airstrip

OL DOINYO OSEYIA

Hippo Pools

Mara Intrepids Club

0   5 km

Talek River

▼ Mara New Bridge & Keekorok Lodge (Dry weather route)

loveable simians, as they have been known to attack humans when provoked. Apparently, they have a particular fondness for toothpaste, but your camera bag is just as likely a target, if left within reach. You would be asking for trouble if you left your tent unguarded, either from robbery or wreckage by baboons (and probably both). Either pack up each morning or leave someone behind – perhaps a ranger if you can agree about his fee.

Campsites

Campsites outside the main gates are found at Oloololo, Musiara, Talek, Sekenani, Ololaimutiek and Sand River, and generally charge around Ksh200–400 per person per night (exceptions are noted below). Most lack even basic facilities, though drinking water may be available, and you can expect some good-natured pestering by the rangers, who will try to extract money by taking you on game drives in your vehicle – sometimes with success, other times not.

With tact, you can sometimes camp in the vicinity of lodges and tented camps located outside the reserve boundaries: a low-key approach (and stressing your self-sufficiency) helps. Be careful, though, as the reserve isn't fenced, and its denizens might get curious (or hungry).

Musiara Gate One of the most popular sites. You can camp by a little stream and, while you're safe enough, you're almost guaranteed to hear at close quarters the spine-tingling grunting roars of the Musiara lion prides. The rangers are quite happy to have campers and, if you have your own vehicle, will often be prepared to accompany you after dark for a meal at *Governors' Camp*.

Oloololo Gate The campsite here has wonderful views of the escarpment and is also very welcoming. There are three further sites (no facilities) on the east bank of the Mara River, just outside the reserve. These can be booked through the warden in Narok, but in practice you can just turn up. They're hard to locate but better than most of Talek River's, with deep shade from the trees and fewer flies. You're likely to have to pay Group Ranch fees here.

Sand River Perhaps the best of the campsites, with toilets and fresh water from a stream, and nicely located in a spot where animals come to drink at night. The attraction is its isolation: perhaps it's too isolated, as there have been robberies, and the site acquired an unsavoury reputation after the murder here of Julie Ward. The site is within the reserve, so you'll have to pay park fees.

Sekenani Gate There are a number of campsites here. *Sekenani Gate campsite* itself is pretty basic.

Just down the track to the east of the gate, *Olperr Elongo campsite* (see ⓦ www.biketreks.co.ke for details) is much better, with toilets, showers and security, tents and equipment for rent (including bikes for use outside the reserve), and the option of full-board camping. The fenced-in *Mara Springs Safari Camp* (reservations through Mountain Rock; PO Box 15796 Nairobi ☎ & ℻ 020/210051, ⓦ www.mountainrockkenya.com; $5 per person to camp, $15 per person in their tents, with beds, bedding and mosquito nets; FB available) is 2km from the gate. It's comfortable, with hot showers, spring water, kitchen and 24hr security, and the attraction of escorted "ecological and herbal medicine" hikes into the Naunaree Hills ($7–15 per person).

Talek Gate There is a large number of campsites along the north bank of the Talek River, east of the gate. Several are the more-or-less permanent territories of camping safari operators – fetch up when a group is in and you may be able to avail yourself of facilities, water and drinks, for a small charge. Note, however, that there have been a number of robberies here. A 5min walk west of Talek Gate and the bridge, *Riverside Campsite* is a public site with a kitchen, hot showers and flushing toilets. Nearby, the small centre of Talek has a few *dukas* and *hotelis* but no petrol.

Lodges and tented camps

With the exception of the very expensive *Mpata Safari Club* and, at the other end of the spectrum, the cheaper *David Livingstone Camp*, the **lodges** and **mid-range tented camps** are all about the same price, and offer pretty much the same level of service. There's nothing intrinsically cheaper about sleeping under canvas: private bathrooms in brick, wood or concrete tent-annexes, hot showers and some remarkably good food in the middle of the wilds naturally hoist prices sky-high. Incidentally, you'll rarely find baths, even in the most expensive places – water is scarce, despite what the state of the roads might tell you, so showers are the order of the day.

In the truly astronomical league, there are about half a dozen **luxury tented camps**, which are really little different from their mid-range cousins, with the exception of more pampering service and fewer guests, but even so you'll rarely have the place to yourself despite pretensions of exclusivity. Most of the guests arrive by air, so transfers from the nearest airstrip are also included.

One common additional cost is **game drives** in lodge or camp vehicles, which come to around $35 per drive per person. Establishments in the luxury tented camp listing below include game drives in their rates; the most luxurious places offer two or three game drives worked into their full-board price. If you fancy **night game drives** (with spotlights), you'll usually have to stay in one of the places outside the reserve, as driving inside is forbidden between 6.30pm and 6am without special permits.

Note that **low-season rates**, although fifty to sixty percent less than high-season rates, usually apply only to the long rains from mid-April to the end of June, when the grass is high and animals difficult to spot, and when road conditions make it sensible to pay for flights into the reserve. Where prices are given for places in price band ⑨, these are for double rooms unless otherwise stated.

Lodges

David Livingstone Camp ☎050/22546.
Upstream on the Mara, and miles from the reserve, near *Mara Safari Club*. There's good game-viewing in the vicinity, but the hippos seen from the bar don't quite compensate for few elephants, or predators (cattle are widely grazed here). Rooms are on the small side but they all have good views of the Mara River from their verandas, and rates are half those of the competition. ⑥ low season, ⑧ high.

Keekorok Lodge ☎050/22680; reservations also through Let's Go Travel (see p.150). A large and perennially busy hotel, *Keekorok* is the longest-established place to stay in the reserve, and still has high standards. It's situated in a rather open location, but is a good hour closer to Nairobi by road than *Mara Serena*, its main competitor, and handy during the rainy season for access to the plains. Rooms vary in size and style; there's a swimming pool, bougainvillea garden and a pleasant walkway round the back to a bar overlooking a small lake, where there are hippos and monkeys. Balloon flights, bush walks, bird walks and game drives are on offer. ⑨

Mara Serena Lodge ☎050/22253 or 22137, ⑩www.serenahotels.com. Located in a quiet area of the reserve, this lodge is beautifully designed (it's based on a re-creation of two Maasai *enkangs*, with smallish but appealing cave-like rooms) and blends nicely into the surroundings. Balloons again, and a pool. Incidentally, access to Oloololo Gate is atrocious; Sekenani Gate via *Keekorok Lodge* is the easiest option. FB $170 low season, $275 high; ⑨

Mara Simba Lodge ☎050/222590, ⑩www.marasimba.com; reservations also c/o PO Box 66601 Nairobi ☎020/4444401–2, ⑤4444403. From Sekenani Gate, head 5km south, then 7km west, to the lodge's location on the east bank of the Talek River. Closest of the lodges in style to a coastal resort hotel, with steep *makuti* roofs and wood-framed buildings. The rooms, in six two-storey wood and stone *bandas*, are large, have great showers, a/c and views from verandas over the river. There's excellent buffet-style food (and an impressive vegetarian menu by Kenyan standards). A resident naturalist conducts walking safaris (and night-time game drives) outside the reserve. FB low season $180, high $280; ⑨

Mpata Safari Club ☎ & ⑤0305/22538, ⑩www.mpata.com; reservations also through Mpata Investments Inc, twentieth floor, Anniversary Towers; PO Box 58402 Nairobi ☎020/244987, ⑤310859. Up on the northern spur of Oloololo Escarpment, about 25km from the Mara River Bridge along a pretty dreadful track, and thus most easily accessible by plane. The 21 stone-built *bandas*, including twelve suites, were designed by the architects of the *Safari Park Hotel* in Nairobi and are totally out of keeping with the area. Each *banda* has, among other comforts, a private veranda; the suites have outdoor Jacuzzis from which to watch the sunset. The restaurant serves French cuisine and there's a 20m pool. ⑨

Mid-range tented camps

The following **tented camps** ("mid-range" is purely a relative description; nearly all are luxurious) offer optional game drives and airstrip transfers. A "package" including three game drives a day adds $60–100 per person per day to the bill. The less accessible western-end places can arrange road transfers from *Keekorok Lodge* or Sekenani Gate for around $25 per person, usually for four people minimum.

Basecamp Maasai Mara Close to Talek Gate, outside the park boundary; reservations through Basecamp Travel, Ole Odume Rd; PO Box 43369 Nairobi ☎ 020/577490–2, ⓕ 577489, ⓦ www.basecampexplorer.com. The most eco-friendly lodge in the park: it runs on solar energy, uses compost toilets, recycles its waste, and is implementing a tree plantation project, among other initiatives. The simple and rustic design, blending perfectly with its surroundings, makes it all the more special. The tents are very comfortable, set on raised wooded platforms with verandas and en-suite bathrooms with open-air showers. There's a small observation platform with wonderful views out onto the Mara plains, a small open dining area and a fire around which guests congregate in the evenings. Activities include game drives, bush walks, and Maasai cultural evenings. You can also be put up at their *Dorobo Bush Camp*, with six basic tents, a small dining area and campfire, in a spectacular wilderness setting that truly feels miles away from civilization. ⑨

Fig Tree Camp Close to Talek Gate and just outside the boundary (but subject to park fees) ☎ 050/22131 or 22163, ⓕ 22131, ⓦ www .mada hotels.com. The location is lovely, overlooking a bend in the Talek River (tents 1–25 occasionally see animals coming to water), and it's unpretentious, which makes a welcome change from the bigger lodges. There are rooms as well as comfortable tents (the former in fragrant gardens, the latter overlooking the river), all rather closely spaced, and a small pool and fun treetop bar. Balloon flights ($385), game walks ($17) and moonlit dinners ($50) are also available, though the food is nothing special. The on-site balloon team can advise on the whereabouts of local wildlife. From around $220; ⑨

Kicheche Camp In the greater Mara area about 5km from Aitong; PO Box 15243 Nairobi; ☎ 020/891379, ⓦ www.kicheche.com. A small camp situated in a thickly wooded, animal-rich *lugga*, this is intimately hosted and great value, with a maximum of 22 guests in large tents (s/c with running water) with views across the plains. A favourite with photographers and naturalists, Kicheche has near-resident cheetahs and leopards.

Luxury tented camps

Governors' Camp ⓦ www.governorscamp.com. Located in the woods on a bend in the Mara River on the site of an old hunting camp, close to the fantastic game-viewing of the Musiara marsh (more or less impassable during the rains, as is the track up to Oloololo Gate; guests tend to fly

The adjoining *Kicheche Private Camp*, with seven slightly smaller tents (s/c, water supplied by staff) is ideal for a group or two families. Excellent meals; 24hr electricity. Game drives and walks extra. Closed April & May. $240; ⑨

Kichwa Tembo Camp ☎ 050/22465, ⓕ 22501, ⓦ www.kichwatembo.com; bookings also through Let's Go Travel (see p.150). Deep in the trees at the foot of the Oloololo Escarpment just outside the reserve, with excellent food and a pleasant pool, and famous for its black-tie dinners. Meryl Streep and Robert Redford stayed here while filming *Out of Africa*. Still, there's something strangely artificial about the place. Due to the liveliness of the local fauna, *Kichwa Tembo* (which means "elephant's head") is fenced in. FB with game drives $370 low, $520 high; ⑨

Rekero Camp ⓦ www.rekero.com; reservations also through Bush Homes of East Africa (see p.63). Although outside the reserve, this place has comfortable thatched, s/c cottages, which can house up to ten guests. On request, the Beatons – who run the place – can mobilize a traditional tented camp for three nights for four to ten people. As well as night and day game-viewing, activities include bush walks, picnics, and visits to Maasai and Dorobo communities. FB $550; ⑨

Sarova Mara Camp On the main C12 entrance road just inside the Sekenani Gate ☎ 050/22386 or 22194, ⓕ 22371, ⓦ www.sarovahotels.com. The most accessible of the Mara camps and lodges. There are over seventy well-furnished tents in jungly gardens, with lily ponds full of fish and families of mongoose populating the shrubberies. A vegetarian menu is available for every meal. Very popular and a little too touristy for some, but good value so long as you don't have kids (no reductions). FB $210; ⑨

Sekenani Camp ☎ 050/22454, ⓕ 22458, ⓦ www .sekenanicamp.com. On the reserve boundary 6km southeast of Sekenani Gate (which you have to pass through). Fifteen large, very private tents on stilts snuggled up to trees, with baths as well as showers, excellent food and a personal approach. The camp is run in collaboration with 26 Maasai families. There's no perimeter fence, so you get escorted to and from the dining area across a plank bridge by a spear-wielding Maasai. $250; ⑨

in). *Governors'* has retained its exclusive "bush" atmosphere despite the large number of tents (over 35), with no expense spared. Elephants trundle through at night; guards keep watch for more dangerous visitors and escort guests between their tents and the (excellent) restaurant. No pool. Tents

1–3 have no river views, and 25–30 can be noisy. Extremely pricey, and children's reductions are derisory. Doubles $550; ⑨

Kichwa Tembo Bateleur Camp Next door to the *Kichwa Tembo Camp* (see opposite) is the even more exclusive *Bateleur*, with nine super-luxurious "tents" complete with huge bathrooms, four-poster beds, antique furnishings and private butler service. There is also a lap pool. Activities are the same as at the main camp. Per person, per night: $350 low, $630 high; ⑨

Ilkeliani By the Talek River looking out onto the Mara plains ☎0733/258120, ⓦwww.ilkeliani. com; reservations through Africa Eco-Camps Ltd; PO Box 64196 Nairobi ☎020/3752889. Eco-friendly establishment with well-spaced tents and large verandas, so there is plenty of privacy. The maximum number of guests is 24. There are no set meal or game drive times – guests can be flexible and design their own itineraries. FB $450; ⑨

🏃 **Little Governors' Camp** ⓦwww .governorscamp.com. Reached by a 2km drive and then a rope-pulled boat across the Mara, this is the annexe from which the *Governors'* balloons fly. Hidden in the trees by its own water hole, with wonderful bird-watching, it's one of the reserve's smallest and most intimate setups, with 17 tents, and is always fully booked up in advance of the main camp. No pool, and difficult disabled access (steep steps). Same rates as *Governors' Camp*. ⑨

Mara Explorer ☎050/22321; reservations through Heritage Hotels (see p.63.) Situated along the Talek River, the tents are extremely lavish with fine carved mahogany furniture, oriental rugs with large verandas and a deck area complete with claw-foot Victorian tubs for open-air bathing. Guests are also provided with a personal butler on 24hr call. All the usual game drives and walks are on offer. From $400 per person per night; ⑨

Mara Intrepids Club ☎050/22321, ⓦwww. heritage-eastafrica.com. Thirty tents parked on a bluff overlooking the Talek River, just about accessible by road in the rains. The "tented suites" have four-poster beds. Baited leopards come daily, and there's a watchtower and swimming pool. $550; ⑨

Mara Safari Club ☎050/22172, Ⓕ22105, ⓦwww.lonrhohotels.com. Very modish tented camp, spaced out in a garden high up on a calm oxbow loop of the Mara River, but over 40km outside the reserve's Oloololo Gate, off the C14. There are fifty "tents", all the last word in luxury, with four-poster beds, huge marble bathrooms, and verandas with private views of the river. Hippos wallow and yawn in the chocolatey water below the camp (kept out of the camp by electric fences), while monkeys rampage through the trees on the opposite bank. Facilities include a heated swimming pool – at nearly 2000m, not such a bad idea. Balloon flights and visits to Maasai villages are available, but facilities are way overpriced (doubles are around $400 in high season) considering the camp's size and location. ⑨

Olonana ⓦwww.sanctuarylodges.com. Spacious permanent tents with mahogany furniture, plush en-suite bathrooms and verandas with spectacular views over the Mara River. The camp prides itself on its personalized attention, and game drives, meals and other activities can be taken at guests' leisure. FB from $210 per person per night in low season, at least $400 in high; ⑨

Around the reserve

This is the one part of Kenya where the concentrations of game that existed in the nineteenth century can still be seen. The most interesting areas, scenically and zoologically, are **westwards**, signalled by the long ridge of the Oloololo Escarpment. If you only have a day or two, you should spend most of your time here, near the **Mara River**.

It sometimes seems that wherever there are animals there are **people** – in minibuses, in land cruisers, in rented Suzukis, often parked in ravenous, zoom-lensed packs around understandably irritable lions, leopards and cheetahs (the official limit is five vehicles around an animal at any one time). This popularity is highly seasonal – it can be overbearing around Christmas – but it needn't spoil your visit. If you aren't driving yourself, encourage your tour driver to explore new areas (*not* off-road) and perhaps stress you'd rather experience the reserve in its totality than tick off animal species.

Fast **roads**, with improved, hard-core surfaces and theoretically uncrossable banks and ditches alongside, have been laid in various parts of the reserve, especially the east, and there is now a good all-weather route from Talek Gate to Sekenani Gate, inside the reserve. During the rains, however, and

The Maasai

After deep reflection on my people and culture, I have painfully come to accept that the Maasai must change to protect themselves, if not their culture. They must adapt to the realities of the modern world for the sake of their own survival. It is better to meet an enemy out in the open and to be prepared for him than for him to come upon you at home unawares.

Tepilit Ole Saitoti, Maasai (Elm Tree Books).

Of all Kenya's peoples, the **Maasai** have received the most attention. Often strikingly tall and slender, dressed in brilliant red cloth, with beads, metal jewellery, and – for young men – long, ochred hairstyles, they have a reputation for ferocity, pampered by an arch superiority complex. Traditionally, they lived off milk and blood (extracted, by a close shot with a stumpy arrow, from the jugular veins of their live cattle), and they loved their herds more than anything else, rarely slaughtering a beast. They maintained rotating armies of spartan warriors – the **morani** – who killed lions as a test of manhood. And they opposed all interference and invasion with swift, implacable violence. Their scorn of foreigners was absolute: they called the Europeans, who came swaddled in clothing, *iloridaa enjekat* or "those who confine their farts". They also derided African peoples who cultivated by digging the earth – the Maasai even left their dead unburied – while those who kept cattle were given grudging respect so long as they conceded that all the world's cattle were a gift from God to the Maasai, whose incessant cattle-raiding was thus righteous reclamation of stolen property. **Cattle** are still at the heart of Maasai society; there are dozens of names for different colours and patterns, and each animal among their three million is individually cherished.

Some of this noble savagery was undoubtedly exaggerated by slave- and ivory-traders, anxious to protect their routes from the Europeans. At the same time, something close to a cult of the Maasai has been around ever since Thomson walked *Through Maasailand* in 1883. In the early years of the colony, Delamere's obsession with the people and all things Maasai spawned a new term, "Maasai-itis", and with it a motley crop of romantic notions about their ancestors alluding to ancient Romans, Egyptians and even the lost tribes of Israel.

But the Maasai are assailed on all sides: by uplands farmers expanding from the north; to the south by eviction from the tourist/conservation areas within the Maasai Mara boundaries; and by a climate of opposition to the old lifestyle from all around. Sporadically urged to grow crops, go to school, build permanent houses, and generally settle down and stop being a nuisance, the Maasai face an additional dilemma in squaring these edicts with the fickle demands of the tourist industry for traditional authenticity. Maasai dancing is *the* entertainment, while necklaces, gourds, spears,

for some weeks after, the western parts of the reserve can be very wet and treacherous.

The only permanent route across the Mara River is the long haul via Mara New Bridge on the southern boundary to *Mara Serena*. Heading up from *Mara Serena* to Oloololo Gate, however, the main road skirts the western edge of Olpunyata Swamp, which is completely impassable in wet weather. Similarly dreadful is the shorter but ill-defined jumble of tracks known as the New Mara Serena Road, on the eastern edge of the swamp, for which you'd definitely need a guide in wet weather, and plenty of time in dry. Likewise, the crossings over the tributaries of the Talek are often impassable. In the rains, aim for the downstream one, 6km north from the *Mara Intrepids Club*, as the camp's Land Rovers may be able to tow you across if the water is high – an experience that's slightly more exciting than most people want.

shields, *rungus* (knobkerries), busts (carved by Akamba carvers) and even life-sized wooden *morani* (to be shipped home in a packing case) are the stock-in-trade of the curio and souvenir shops. For the Maasai themselves, the rewards are fairly scant. Few make much of a living selling souvenirs, but enterprising *morani* can do well by just posing for photos, and even better if they hawk themselves in Nairobi or down on the coast.

Many men persevere with the status of **warriorhood**, though modern Kenya makes few concessions to it. The *morani*, arrested for hunting lions and prevented from building *manyattas* for the *eunoto* transition in which they pass into elderhood, have kept most of the superficial marks of the warrior without being able to live the life fully. The ensemble of a cloth tied over one shoulder, together with spear, sword, club and braided hair, is still widely seen, and after circumcision, in their early days as warriors, young men can still be encountered out in the bush, hunting for birds to add to their elaborate, taxidermic headdresses. But there is considerable local frustration. When the pasture is poor, the *morani* have little compunction about driving their herds into the reserve to compete with the wildlife. All but a few of the Mara's black rhinos have been slaughtered for their horns in the last few decades (though a few more have now been brought in from elsewhere). And there have even been isolated attacks on tourist camps in and around the reserve.

Improved medicine and veterinary facilities having eased the old hardships of the traditional Maasai way of life, the Maasai have been expanding again, with **land** becoming the biggest issue. The Maasai have still not fully come to terms with the idea of individual ownership of it, although the recent introduction of wildlife reserves run by Maasai Group Ranches (see the box on p.398) seems at last to be providing a steady source of income from tourism. "Range schemes" – plans for growing wheat or rearing cattle – are also common now, though they are just as likely to benefit newcomers from other parts of Kenya as the local Maasai.

The lifestyle is changing: education, MPs and elections, new laws and new projects, jobs and cash, all impinge on the Maasai's lives – with mixed results. The traditional Maasai staple diet of curdled milk and cow's blood is rapidly being replaced by *ugali*. Many Maasai have taken work in the lodges and tented camps, while others end up as security guards in Nairobi. For the majority, who continue to live semi-nomadic lives among a welter of constraints, the future would seem to hold little promise. But that stubborn cultural pride – the kind of hauteur that keeps a cattle-owner thoroughly impoverished in cash terms, while he counts his 220 beasts – may yet insulate the Maasai against the social upheavals that seem certain to rock the lives of many Kenyans in the twenty-first century.

Visiting Maasai villages

One diversion you are likely to be offered, especially if travelling on an organized safari, is a visit to a **Maasai** *enkang* , usually called, incorrectly, a *manyatta* (an *enkang* is an ordinary homestead, a *manyatta* a ceremonial bush camp) Forget about the authenticity of tribal life: this is the real world. Many children are sick, many of the young men have fled to the fleshpots, and everyone wants your money. Unprepared and uncomfortable, most visitors find the experience a deeply depressing rip-off – $15–20 each in a group from a lodge or tented camp, or around Ksh400 per person if you arrange it yourself (don't expect the driver to hand over a decent share of the fee to your Maasai hosts). If you can forget any TV-documentary illusions, and actually sit down and talk to people, the experience can be transformed and full of laughter, as it will be if your own children are with you.

The animals

Big brunette **lions** are the best-known denizens of the reserve and there are usually several prides living around the **Musiara Swamps**, which are dry much of the year. It is sometimes possible to watch them hunt, as they take very little notice of vehicles. While lions seem to be lounging under every other bush, finding a **cheetah** is much harder (they can often be seen on the *murram* mounds alongside the Talek–Sekenani road). These are solitary cats – slender, unobtrusive and somewhat shy. When they move, their speed and agility are marvellous. If you are lucky enough to witness a kill (cynicism about such voyeurism is quickly dispelled when you find yourself on the spot), it's likely to take place in a cloud of dust, a kilometre from where the chase began. But cheetahs are vulnerable to too much harassment. Traditionally, they hunt at dawn and dusk (at the same times as tourists are hunting for photographs), but there is evidence that they are turning to a midday hunting pattern when the humans are shaded in the lodges – not a good time of day for the cheetah, which expends terrific energy in each chase and may have to give up if it goes on for more than thirty or forty seconds.

Leopards are rarely seen by visitors, though there are plenty of them. You can give yourself a serious case of risen hair when you come across their footprints down on the sandbanks at the edge of the Mara River outside the reserve boundary. But they are largely nocturnal and prefer to remain well out of sight. Their deep, grating roar at night – a grunt, repeated – is a sound which, once heard, you carry around with you.

Rangers are certain to know the current news about the **black rhinos** – every calf born is a victory – though finding them is often surprisingly difficult. Check out Rhino Ridge, where a handful of the reserve's surviving *faru* are sometimes obligingly positioned. There are also some **white rhinos** in the reserve, brought up from South Africa and closely guarded.

Maasai Mara's other heavyweights are about in abundance. The Mara River surges with **hippo**, while big families of **elephant** traipse along the forest margins and spread out into the Musiara marshes when the herbage is thick and juicy. The park is home to an estimated thousand or so elephants, with another five hundred living in the districts beyond its boundaries. **Buffalo** are seen all over and can be menacing when they surround a small jeep. It is the solitary old bulls that you need to watch out for – their reputation (and that of old rhinos) is not exaggerated. Tourists' vehicles get stoved in quite often, so always back off.

Among all these outstanding characters, the herds of humble grazers fade quickly into the background. It's easy to become blasé when one of the much-hyped "big five" (elephant, rhino, buffalo, lion, leopard) isn't eyeballing you at arm's length – but those are the hunter's trophies. **Warthog** families like rows of dismantled Russian dolls, **zebra** and **gazelle**, odd-looking **hartebeest** and slick, purple-flanked **topi** are all scattered with abandon across the scene. The topi are peculiarly characteristic of Maasai Mara, and there are always one or two in every herd standing sentry on a tussock or an old termite mound. Topi and **giraffe** – whose dream-like, slow-motion canter is one of the reserve's most beautiful and underrated sights – are often good pointers for predators in the vicinity. And the reserve has rare herds of **roan antelope** – swaggering, horse-sized animals with sweeping, curved horns, that you'll see elsewhere only in Ruma National Park near Kisii.

The wildebeest migration

It is the annual **wildebeest migration**, however, that plants Maasai Mara in the imagination. With a lemming-like instinct, the herds gather in their hundreds of thousands on the withering plains of Serengeti to begin the long, streaming journey northward following the scent of moisture and green grass in the Mara. They arrive in July and August, pouring over the Sand River and into the eastern side of the reserve around *Keekorok*, gradually munching their way westwards in a milling, unsettled mass and turning south again in October. Never the most graceful of animals, wildebeest play up to their appearance with unpredictable behaviour, bucking like wild horses, springing like jack-in-the-boxes, or suddenly sprinting off through the herd for no apparent reason.

The **Mara River** is the biggest obstacle they come up against. Heavy rains falling up on the Mau Range where the river rises can produce a sudden brown flood which claims thousands of animals as they try to cross. Like huge sheep (they are, in fact, most closely related to goats), the brainless masses swarm desperately to the banks and plunge in. Many are fatally injured on rocks and fallen branches; others are skewered by flailing legs and horns. With every surge, more bodies bob to the surface and float downstream. Heaps of bloated carcasses line the banks, injured and dying animals struggle in the mud, while vultures and marabou storks squat in glazed, post-prandial stupor.

The migration's full, cacophonous impact is awesomely melodramatic – both on the plains and at the deadly river crossings. This superabundance of meat accounts for the Mara's big lion population. Through it all, the **spotted hyenas** scamper and loiter like psychopathic sheep dogs. Half a million wildebeest **calves** are born in January and February before the migration; two out of three perish without returning to the Serengeti.

Balloon flights

At around $380 per person for the sixty- to ninety-minute flight plus breakfast with *vin mousseux* (or a Bloody Mary, depending on how you feel) **balloon "safaris"** are the ultimate in bush chic. Just watching the inflation and lift-off at dawn is a spectacular sight. From the air, the migration of the wildebeest resembles an ant's nest. In order to avoid frightening the animals unduly, however, there is a minimum height below which the balloons are not permitted to fly. Trips are run by several of the larger camps and lodges, including *Keekorok*, *Serena*, and *Fig Tree*. You don't have to be staying at the lodge they fly from: they'll come and pick you up at 5.30am. Operators include:

Adventures Aloft Reservations through Mada Hotels, Kapiti Rd; off Mombasa Rd; PO Box 40683 Nairobi ☎020/605328, ℻603597, ⊛www .madahotels.com. Flights from *Fig Tree Camp*.
Mara Balloon Safaris Ltd Reservations through Governors' Camps (see p.63). Flights from *Little Governors' Camp*, the most spectacular take-off

site, deep in the woods. They're the only people to cook your breakfast on the balloon's burners after you land.
Transworld Kenya Fifth floor, Corner House, Mama Ngina St/Kimathi St; PO Box 44690 Nairobi ☎020/333129, ℻333488, ℮transworld@form -net.com. Flights from *Mara Serena Lodge*.

Samburu, Buffalo Springs and Shaba national reserves

Daily 6.30am–6.30pm; $15 each reserve per day/overnight, children $10; private vehicle Ksh200, camping $8 ($10 in a "special" campsite). District Warden (Samburu): PO Box 53 Maralal ☎065/2053 or 2412. No driving after 7pm. Speed limit 30kph. Map: The Official Isiolo/Samburu County Council Map of Samburu, Buffalo Springs and Shaba National Reserves, 2004; 1:50,000, available at the park gates and Nairobi bookshops.

Up in the north of the country, in the hot, arid lowlands beneath Mount Kenya, **Samburu National Reserve** was set up in the late 1960s, a tract of country around the richest stretch of the Ewaso Ngiro (or Uaso Ngiro) River. In this region, the permanent water and the forest shade on the banks draw plentiful wildlife in the dry season and maintain many of the less peripatetic species year-round. While the wildlife spectacle doesn't always match that of the southern parks, the peace and scenic beauty of Samburu is unquestionable and, in the kind of mood swing which only an equatorial region can produce, the contrast with the fertile farming country of the Highlands just a few kilometres to the south couldn't be more striking. In the background, the sharp hill of **Koitogor** rises in the middle of Samburu Reserve, making a useful reference point. And on the horizon, 30km to the north, looms the gaunt red block of **Ol Olokwe** mountain. Head up into the scratchy bush in the south of **Buffalo Springs Reserve** and the whole region is spread out before you. Across the rutted surface of the Isiolo–Marsabit road lies the **Shaba National Reserve**, where Joy Adamson experimented with the release of hand-reared leopards. Highly recommended, Shaba is certainly much less visited than Samburu or Buffalo Springs.

On the fringes of what is still called the "NFD" (Northern Frontier District), the three national reserves were closed for many years after their creation, because of the war against Somali irredentists that flared over northern Kenya in the 1960s and early 1970s. Isolated incidents of banditry have recurred ever since, with major **security concerns** being raised during 1997–98, which saw a number of armed hold-ups of tourist vehicles as well as attacks on locals, some using guns that had apparently been rented out by home guards. Security has since been beefed up within the reserves, but the **road up from Isiolo** is still prone to occasional **banditry** – check the situation with a reputable travel agent in Nairobi, or with the police at the checkpoint just north of Isiolo.

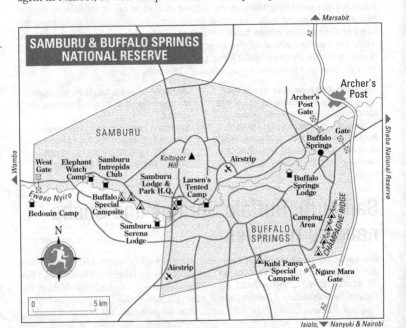

Although your chances of running into serious trouble are extremely slim, should you be unlucky enough to get on the wrong end of an AK–47, the usual rule applies: don't resist (though you might consider concealing valuables in the vehicle before leaving Isiolo).

Practicalities

If you're circling Mount Kenya, Samburu Reserve is close at hand, a couple of hours north of Nanyuki. Buses and matatus run down onto the hazy plain as far as Isiolo (p.588), as does the tarmac. Waiting at the Isiolo police barrier usually gets you a lift into the reserve itself in a few hours, although there are one or two matatus which daily venture across the jolting dirt track to Archer's Post.

If you're driving, you may be required to wait at the police checkpoint for a convoy to form for the short continuation to the reserve; you won't wait long, as there are plenty of safari vans which cover the stretch every day. Both Airkenya and SafariLink have **flights** from Nairobi to the Samburu lodges. Note that the daily/overnight **fees** chargeable in each reserve apply even if you're only in transit to the other: if you enter, you pay.

Lodges and tented camps

There are several lodges in Samburu/Buffalo Springs, and one in Shaba. They mostly offer very good low-season rates (April–July, except Easter). All rates are for **full board** and, as usual, are for doubles unless otherwise stated.

Bedouin Camp ☏0733/612996, ⓦwww
.bedouin-camp.com; bookings through Private
Wilderness; PO Box 6648, Nairobi ☏020/882028,
ⓕ882868. Set within a wilderness concession
adjoining the Samburu National Reserve are these
eight sumptuous tents furnished with four-poster
beds, oriental rugs and various safari relics. Dinner
is served in the candlelit mess tent and there is
also a 24hr butler service. A range of game-viewing activities are available, included in the $395 per
person per night rate; ⑨

Elephant Watch Camp Bookings through
Elephant Watch Safaris; PO Box 54667
Nairobi ☏020/891112, ⓕ809596, ⓦwww
.elephantwatchsafaris.com. A luxurious eco-
friendly camp nestled on the banks of the Ewaso
Nyiro River, in the Samburu National Reserve.
The proximity to the wildlife – especially the
elephants – is really something special. The
camp is a partner of an elephants charity, and
"elephant guides" look after guests, who are
limited to ten. $450/$500 per person per night,
low/high season; ⑨

Larsens Tented Camp Reservations through
Let's Go (see p.150). East of *Samburu Lodge*, this
is Samburu's smallest camp, very upmarket, with
seventeen en-suite tents facing the river. Game
drives are part of the deal, and the food is excellent. No children under 7 or children's rates, and
no pool (you can use the one at *Samburu Lodge*).
$520; ⑨

Samburu Intrepids Club ☏064/30811, ⓕ20022,
ⓦwww.heritage-eastafrica.com. Upstream of the
other lodges and camps on the north bank, an
impressive and very luxurious development, and a
good deal cheaper than *Larsens*. All 25 tents are
on stilts, furnished with unecological mahogany
furniture, four-poster beds and fans. Also offers
game drives, camel safaris and bird walks. $250
low season, $300 high; ⑨

Samburu Lodge ☏064/30762 or 30778,
ⓕ30781; reservations also through Let's Go (see
p.150). On the north bank, beautifully located on a
heavily wooded broad bend of the river as it passes
near the Samburu Reserve headquarters, this is the
oldest lodge in the reserves – with rooms of various standards, a pool and excellent food. Despite a
frenetically busy atmosphere around the riverside
terraces and crocodile-viewing bars, the glorious
setting is hard to fault. Good mechanics and fuel
available. Low season ⑧, high ⑨

Samburu Serena Lodge ☏064/30800, ⓦwww
.serenahotels.com. On the south bank, just outside
Buffalo Springs Reserve. Well managed, with a
good pool and great food, but not one of Serena's
best. $170 low season, $275 high; ⑨

Sarova Shaba Lodge Downriver in the Shaba
Reserve ☏064/30638 or 32030, ⓦwww
.sarovahotels.com. Very attractively landscaped,
with a superb swimming pool and streams running
through public areas (the thick vegetation obscures
views of big animals), but the fact that the

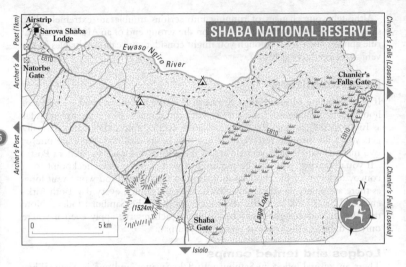

SHABA NATIONAL RESERVE

crystal-clear spring which feeds them was expropri-ated from the local population (a concrete well was dug for them instead) jars a little. Mosquito-netted

rooms with fans, and Samburu ceremonial marriages for those tying the knot around Christmas. Excellent naturalist. Fuel available. $235; **⑨**

Campsites

Initially, the best move for the wheelless is to get to the area of *Samburu Lodge* and camp near the park headquarters – not a wonderful site, with no toilets or running water (and the lodge may even make you pay for that commodity), but convenient and legal, if a little unhygienic. You can walk to the lodge's riverside bars and restaurant (get an escort after 6.30pm as there are animals everywhere), flop in the pool (occasionally restricted to guests), gloat over the crocodiles in the river below, and peer darkly through binoculars at the brief evening cabaret of leopards retrieving bait from a tree on the far bank. You can shell out $45 or so for a two-hour morning or evening game run in one of the lodge's land cruisers, or around $125 for the whole vehicle. Most people camping here without their own vehicles seem to manage to find the occasional ride around the reserve, if only because the opportunities exist to meet travellers with their own transport over a drink. Note that the **baboons** at the campsite here are beyond being an amusement; leave your tent and its contents under guard. The fact that baboons sometimes fall shrill victims to crocs at the water's edge seems less distressing after a day or two spent in the area.

Samburu has three other campsites on the north bank of the Ewaso Ngiro River, a few kilometres to the west of the bridge and park HQ. There are no facilities except at the farthest of these – *Buffalo Special* campsite, which has toilets and showers.

There are four public campsites in the Champagne Ridge area of **Buffalo Springs Reserve**, not far from the main gate, Ngare Mara. The camping area is a pretty one, among the acacias, and abounds with giraffe and other animals. There's also one "special" campsite in Buffalo Springs – *Kubi Panya*, on the Maji ya Chumvi stream.

There are two campsites in **Shaba**, though they can be closed if there's been much banditry or cattle raiding; the better one is on the banks of the Ewaso Ngiro some 9km from Natorbe Gate. Neither have any facilities.

△ Leopard at Samburu

Exploring the reserves

Except during and immediately after the rains, scrubby bush country takes up most of the reserve district, but there are some large acacia thickets, especially in the eastern part of **Buffalo Springs**. Here, the **springs** themselves are a welcome target; these are pools of clear if weedy water, one of which has been sanitized with concrete for the benefit of swimmers and (most of the time) the exclusion of crocodiles. If you have any doubts at all, do not swim. *Buffalo Springs Lodge*, a few kilometres away, is low-key and always welcoming for a drink. There's a fine jungly marsh reaching nearly to the terrace, where you'll often see animals.

If Samburu's **wildlife** is occasionally disappointing, it may be fairer to say that the dry country ecosystems are prone to large variations in animal populations as they move in search of water and pasture. Some visitors have tremendous luck and it can provide consistently excellent animal-watching. The best areas are along the south side of the river in Buffalo Springs Reserve, close to *Samburu Lodge*. Poaching has wiped out the rhino here, but lions are often seen – again, most often in Buffalo Springs.

Meanwhile, the locally burgeoning **elephant herds** have ruined some sections of the riverine forest. The range of rarer, and localized, races and species compensates, though. Common and conspicuous among these are the **reticulated giraffe** with its beautiful jigsaw marking; **Grevy's zebra**, the large, finely striped species that has a bushy mane and outsize ears; the **Somali ostrich**, which has blue rather than pink legs; and the **gerenuk** ("camel head" in Somali), the antelope species that stands on its hind legs to reach the foliage which it feeds upon. Samburu's **birdlife** is diverse and prolific and includes the marshal eagle, pygmy falcons, hornbills and Egyptian geese.

411

Samburu's **leopards** are a regular sight – at least from the terraces at *Samburu* and *Samburu Serena* lodges, both of which have taken to baiting the trees on the opposite banks with haunches of meat. Between drinks and dinner, guests get a floodlit view of the stealthy predator reduced to a giant pussycat. The stampede for cameras doesn't encourage the leopards to stay long, so efforts are made to attach the meat firmly to the tree. It's all pathetically contrived (and you can forget worthwhile pictures or videos at that distance without expensive equipment), but only with luck or dogged persistence will you see a wild leopard other than in such circumstances, and it's hard to blame the hotels for making the most of the local attractions. You should beware, at *Samburu Lodge*, of occasional excursions by the leopards across the river to the human zoo, hence the signs warning "Do not stray beyond the lit path".

Recent research has shown how little is really known about these cats. For the most part, they live off any small animals that come their way. The popular notion that they consume many baboons is apparently misled. Baboon troops will turn on an attacking leopard instantly and, unless surprised, usually manage to fend it off. Less organized monkeys of all kinds, however, are often caught, and in Samburu, the favourite hunting grounds are the stands of forest and clumps of strange, branching doum palms by the river which sometimes shake with monkeys. Black-faced vervet and blue monkeys are the commonest inhabitants.

Shaba

For **animals**, Shaba is rated the equal of its two neighbours, with lots of elephants, jackals and a few lions, and plains game including beautifully marked Grevy's zebra, reticulated giraffe and the gerenuk, which rarely if ever drinks, extracting water from morning dew on leaves. Unusually, you are permitted to walk in Shaba, in places (certainly from the airstrip to *Sarova Lodge*); the ranger at the gate can point out where.

If you've got wheels, you might consider venturing out of the reserve to the east to visit Chanler's Falls, 30km beyond Chanler's Falls Gate on the Ewaso Ngiro River, but double check the security situation first with the rangers – there's no one here except for Samburu herders and, if you're unlucky, heavily-armed raiders.

Meru National Park

Daily 6am–6.30pm; $20 per day/overnight, children $5; private vehicle Ksh200, camping $8 ($10 in a "special" campsite). Warden: PO Box 11 Maua ℡ 0164/20613, Ⓔadwildlife@kws.org. No driving after 7pm. Speed limit 40kph. Map: Tourist Maps of Kenya Meru National Park, 2004.

You don't see **Meru National Park** on many safari itineraries. Of the main parks covered in this chapter, it is the least visited – unspoiled and pristine. Abundantly traversed by **streams** flowing into the Tana River on its southern boundary, and luxuriantly rained upon, the rolling **jungle** of tall grass, riverine forest and swamp is lent a hypnotic, other-worldly quality by wonderful stands of prehistoric-looking **doum palms**; and with the high cover they provide, you can never be certain of what's going to be around the next corner.

True, the **animals** aren't always as much in evidence here as they can be in some other Kenyan wildlife parks, but the even more noticeable absence of

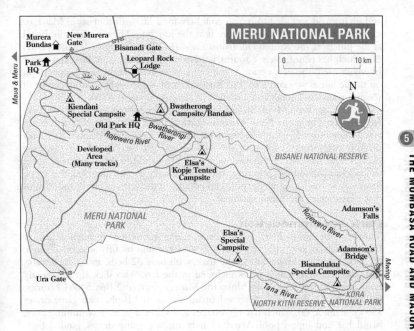

minibuses and land cruisers more than compensates. After visiting some of the less bushy parks, where the animals can be spotted from miles away, Meru's intimate, unusual landscape is quickly entrancing.

Meru is the area where the Adamsons released their most famous lioness **Elsa** back into the wild, and where their later series of experiments with orphaned cheetahs was cut short by the murder of Joy Adamson. The adjoining **Kora National Park** was the home of George Adamson, murdered by poachers or cattle-rustlers in August 1989 when he drove through their barricade. The reserve was promptly upgraded to national park status, but Adamson's grave was subsequently desecrated. Kora, and the three national reserves south and east of Meru – **Bisanadi**, **North Kitui** and **Rahole** – are all in the Land Rover expedition category, a total of 4500 square kilometres of scrub and semi-desert, and dense forest where they fringe the Tana River. Because of the history of bad security in the area, you need to check out the situation very carefully with KWS if you're considering entering the area.

Practicalities

Most visitors driving to Meru National Park come via Meru town (see p.196) towards the New Murera Gate. The alternative route, offering direct access from Embu (see p.200) through Ura Gate, can be hazardous in the rainy season, so check with locals before setting off.

Without your own vehicle, getting to the park isn't easy. From Meru town there are frequent buses and matatus to **MAUA**, one hour into the **Nyambeni Hills** on a pretty, paved road, with steep tea terraces and plantations of *miraa*. From Maua, other matatus run as far as Kiutini – a third of the way between Maua and the park gate. From there, however, you'll have to hitch the remaining 20km and, once there, you'll have to rely on the warden taking pity on you and giving you a guided tour. You could try for a lift with tourists in Maua, or rather about 3km up the hill before it at the junction. There's a friendly **hotel** at the junction, the *Kiringo Hill Tourist Lodge* (PO Box 300; ☎064/21081; B&B ❸), which has reasonable s/c rooms, better ones in cottages, but little hot water. In Maua itself, the best option is the calm *Maua Basin Hotel*, signposted 100m off to the left as you come in (PO Box 452; ☎064/21519; ❷), with a choice of s/c and non-s/c. There's also a branch of Barclays with an ATM.

On the route from Meru, the last fuel and supplies (there's no fuel in the park) are in Maua. The park's **New Murera Gate** is about 30km east of Maua, down a red *murram* road – the condition of which is sometimes diabolical – with magnificent scenery over your shoulder as you go: the Nyambenis towering above exotic *shambas* of bananas, sugar and corn, and the sky, as often as not, a gaudy cloud-mural of gathering storms. Gradually, as you descend, the scene gives way to the lank grass, termite cathedrals and the scattered trees and streams that characterize the park's savanna.

Park accommodation

The very beautiful *Elsa's Kopje Tented Camp* (bookings through Cheli & Peacock Safaris, see p.152; $600 in low season, rising by fifty percent in high; ❾) is the most exclusive unit in the park, with only 32 beds, and guided walks and day and night game drives included in the rate. Also slick is the recently renovated *Leopard Rock Lodge,* along the Murera river, (PO Box 34464 Nairobi; ☎020/600031, ☎862527, ⓦwww.leopardmico.com; FB plus two game drives $560 per night; ❾), which has 17 cottages and suites, a Jacuzzi, swimming pool, island bar and hippo pool. Activities here include game drives, guided bush walks, camel walks and bird-watching.

Right by the entrance to the park is *Murera Bandas*, comprising four units ($30 per *banda* per night), each with two bedrooms, a double and a single, plus a shared barbecue area. Large groups can be accommodated in a nearby dormitory which has bunk beds and a central kitchen. *Bwatherongi Bandas*, near the old park HQ, is a shady site with four en-suite *bandas*, each sleeping three ($30 per *banda* per night), but no cooking facilities.

The **public campsite** is 18km from the gate near the old park headquarters, on a stretch of open ground running down to a wooded stream. There are toilet and shower blocks, and firewood is plentiful, but bring your own bedding. The other option is to pick one of the "special" campsites dotted throughout the park (ask the rangers or the warden which are available, as they tend to open and close fairly regularly), none of which have any facilities except supplies of firewood. There are usually rivers nearby for water. Bookings for the *bandas*, public and "special" campsites are made through KWS (see p.64).

Exploring the park

Meru's many tracks are mostly sandy and firm; some of the junctions have signposts which are useful as long as you have the Survey of Kenya map, and the baboons haven't ripped them off again. It's easy to get lost in the vast wilderness; drivers have been known to find themselves in Tsavo East after a night of relentless searching for a lodge or a main gate. Though you're not required to take a ranger with you, if you intend exploring south of the "developed area" it's eminently advisable, more to provide radio backup in case of breakdown or getting lost than to combat bandits.

There are still plenty of enticing areas to investigate without going too far. The **Rojewero River**, the park's largest stream, is an interesting watercourse:

densely overgrown banks flash with birds and monkeys and dark waters ripple with turtles. Large and very visible herds of **elephant**, **buffalo** and **reticulated giraffe** are common, as are, in the more open areas, **gerenuk**, **Grevy's zebra** and **ostrich**. Several **white rhinos** have been reintroduced, and their numbers are up to around forty at the time of writing – a definite sign that the park is becoming a safer place. Predators seem scarce, though they may simply be hidden in the long grass – the smaller grazers must have a nerve-wracking time of it here. Large numbers of **leopards** captured in the stock-raising lands of Laikipia have been released in the park in recent years, but as usual you have little chance of seeing them.

Travel details

Road details for the main Nairobi–Mombasa route are given in chapters 1 and 6.

Trains

Voi to: Mombasa (3 weekly; 4hr); Nairobi (3 weekly; 9hr).

Buses

Kitui to: Machakos (4 daily; 1hr); Mombasa (daily; 9hr); Nairobi (3 daily; 2hr 30min).
Machakos to: Kitui (4 daily; 1hr); Mombasa (daily; 8hr); Nairobi (frequent; 1hr 30min); Voi (daily; 5hr).
Maua to: Embu (3 daily; 3hr); Meru (3 daily; 1hr); Nairobi (3 daily; 7hr).
Namanga to: Nairobi (daily; 3hr).
Narok to: Nairobi (2 daily; 4hr).
Taveta to: Arusha (1 daily; 4hr); Mombasa (4 daily; 5hr); Nairobi (2 weekly; 12hr); Voi (4 daily; 3hr).
Voi to: Malindi (daily; 4hr); Mombasa (frequent; 2hr 30min); Nairobi (frequent; 4–5hr); Taveta (4 daily; 2hr 30min).

Matatus

Frequencies are given only where there are relatively few departures.
Kitui to: Embu (infrequent; 3–4hr); Machakos

(45min).
Machakos to: Kitui (45min).
Namanga to: Nairobi (2hr 30min).
Narok to: Nairobi (3–4hr).
Oloitokitok to: Emali (infrequent; 2–3hr); Taveta (market days; 2hr 30min).
Taveta to: Oloitokitok (market days; 2hr 30min); Voi (3hr).
Voi to: Mombasa (2hr 30min); Taveta (3hr); Wundanyi (1hr).

Flights

Some flights to national parks operate in one direction only (hence there are no flights from Maasai Mara to Samburu).
Amboseli to: Nairobi (Airkenya and SafariLink; 2 daily; 1hr 15min).
Maasai Mara to: Nairobi (Airkenya and SafariLink; 4 daily; 45min).
Samburu to: Maasai Mara (Airkenya and SafariLink; 2 daily; 1hr 30min); Nairobi (Airkenya and SafariLink; 2 daily; 1hr 20min).
Tsavo West to: Nairobi (SafariLink; daily; 1hr).

The coast

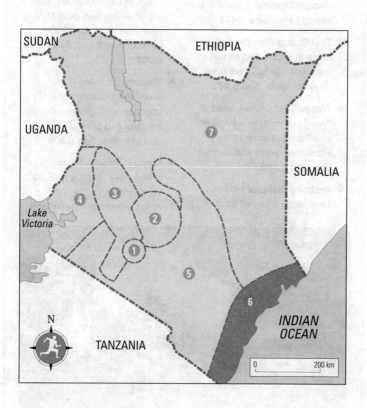

SUDAN · ETHIOPIA · UGANDA · SOMALIA · Lake Victoria · INDIAN OCEAN · TANZANIA · N · 0 200 km

CHAPTER 6 # Highlights

✳ **Fort Jesus** Seven centuries of coastal history are on show in this fascinating museum in Mombasa. See p.437

✳ **Mwaluganje Elephant Sanctuary** Almost guaranteed elephant-watching and a fine tented camp. See p.472

✳ **Tiwi Beach** With the reef close to shore, and some excellent low-key cottage developments. See p.473

✳ **Wasini** Tiny, undeveloped island community, a beachcomber's paradise with wonderful diving and snorkelling. See p.490

✳ **Arabuko-Sokoke Forest** East Africa's largest tract of indigenous coastal forest, offering excellent guided walks and the chance to see a range of monkeys, birds and butterflies. See p.499

✳ **Gedi** Try to visit this former town first thing in the morning or as the sun goes down, when the ruins are at their most atmospheric. See p.501

✳ **Watamu** Stunning bays, islets and casuarina-shaded beaches, with glorious coral gardens and good diving opportunities. See p.505

✳ **Lamu** Compelling, history-soaked city-state, a UNESCO World Heritage site, with no roads or vehicles. See p.528

△ Fort Jesus, Mombasa

6

The coast

Nearly everyone arrives on the coast at **Mombasa**, a much more enjoyable place to spend time than Nairobi. Kenya's second city is a tropical centre *par excellence*: steamy, lazy, at times unbelievably dilapidated, but genial. To the north and south there are superb **beaches** and a number of pockets of tourist development – of which the resort strip to the immediate north of the city is the busiest – but the coast is not yet highly developed in the Florida or Spanish *costa* sense. For many visitors (and this is one area where inexpensive package tourism has really taken off), the resort areas represent little more than sun, sea, sand and, even in the AIDS era, sex. You can, of course, have a wonderful time on the beaches doing nothing very much, but there's a lot more to this part of Kenya than some travel brochures might have you believe – and plenty to do if total lassitude drives you nuts after a few days.

Most obviously, the beaches are the launch pad for one of the most beautiful **coral reefs** in the world, rated in the top three by experienced divers, along with Australia's Barrier Reef and the Red Sea. With breathing apparatus you can do some spectacular dives, including night and wreck dives, but with even the most limited equipment – a snorkel and mask (or "goggles"), easily obtained almost anywhere – you can still enter what really is another world, either taking a boat or swimming out to discover sections of reef for yourself. The three most spectacular zones, enclosed in **marine national parks**, are far to the south off Wasini island, the area between Watamu and Malindi, and in the extreme north, off Kiwaiyu island.

The string of **islands** that runs up the coast – the main ones being Wasini, Funzi, Chale, Mombasa itself, Lamu, Manda, Pate, Kiwaiyu – are all worth visiting. Apart from their beach and ocean attractions, most of them have some archeological interest, which is also a constant theme on the mainland: the whole coast is littered with the **ruins** of forts, mosques, tombs and even whole towns. Some of these – including **Fort Jesus**, **Lamu** and the ruined town of **Gedi** – are already on the tourist circuit, but there are dozens that have hardly been cleared or investigated and they make for compelling exploration. Fort Jesus Museum in Mombasa has a map of locations.

Parts of the **far northeastern coastal region** are effectively out of bounds for casual visitors. Roaming Somali guerillas and other armed desperados make the area extremely dangerous, with attacks on vehicles and even local villages far from unknown.

Islam has long been a major influence on the coast, and the annual month of fasting – Ramadan (see p.71 for dates) – is widely observed. Visiting the coast during **Ramadan** might leave a slightly strange impression of a region where everyone is on night shift, but in practical terms it usually makes little difference.

419

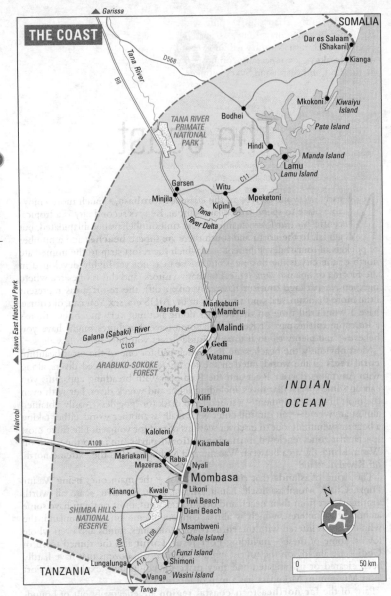

Nature and wildlife

The hundreds of kilometres of sandy beach that fringe the low-lying coastal strip are backed by dunes and coconut palms, traversed by scores of streams and rivers. Flowing off the plateaus through tumbling jungle, these waterways meander across a narrow, fertile plain to the sea. In sheltered creeks, forests of **mangrove** trees cover vast areas and create a distinctive ecological zone of tidal mud flats.

Wildlife on the coast is in keeping with the region's lush, intimate feel. The big game of upcountry Kenya is more or less absent (though Shimba Hills National Park near Mombasa is an exception), but smaller creatures are abundant. **Monkeys** are especially common, with troops of baboons regularly seen by the road, and vervet and Sykes' monkeys frequently at home in hotel gardens.

Responsible snorkelling, diving and fishing

Kenya's coral reefs are among the world's most beautiful, and fragile, ecosystems. A reef is a living entity: every branch or cluster of coral consists of thousands if not millions of individual living organisms called polyps, growing ever outwards as the older ones die and become covered in new growth. Coral grows extremely slowly, some species taking over a decade to expand a couple of centimetres.

Solid though it seems, coral is extremely sensitive, and even something as seemingly insignificant as a small change in sea temperature – such as happened in the 1997–98 El Niño event – can have disastrous effects. Even now, many sections of Kenya's reefs have barely begun to recover, and large sections appear grey and dead. Equally disastrous are human pressures, whether through accidental pollution or more deliberate activities. The damage caused by careless trawling and anchoring is obvious. Less obvious are the potentially damaging results of snorkelling and diving, so a few rules are worth bearing in mind.

If you haven't dived for a while, take a refresher course at one of the PADI schools at the beach hotels, and practise your buoyancy control in the safety of a swimming pool. Read the box on "Diving" on p.482.

When mooring a boat, ensure that you use established mooring points to avoid damaging the coral with anchors and chains. If there are no buoys, drop your anchor well away from the reef, and swim in.

Dive and swim carefully, never touching the corals, no matter how solid they appear. Even gentle abrasions can kill some polyps and all coral suffocates if covered with silt or sand thrown up by a careless swipe of fins (flippers) close to the sea floor. For this reason, some companies don't provide fins for snorkellers. If you do wear them, always be aware of where your feet are, and use only your hands to swim when you're close to anything. If you're an inexperienced diver, keep a good distance from the coral to avoid crashing into it.

Don't touch or feed anything, as your actions may cause stress to the animal, and interrupt behaviour. Although several companies encourage it, it's best not to feed fish. In some species, it encourages dependency, can change their behaviour (just like baboons on land, some fish can become aggressive), and it destabilizes the food chain.

Don't collect marine souvenirs. Souvenir collecting of shells, coral and starfish disrupts the ecosystem and is illegal in Kenya, and in most countries, as is all trade in sea-turtle products. Getting caught – whether in Kenya or at your airport of arrival – can land you in serious trouble. Similarly, although they are widely for sale, you shouldn't buy any of these items. With no market, people will stop collecting them. Note that the shellfish will have been killed to provide the shells you're offered.

Big game fishing takes a direct toll on the marine environment by reducing the population of natural predators, kicking off a potentially destructive chain reaction by increasing the populations of their prey, in turn increasing pressure on organisms further down the food chain. Among the game-fishing fraternity, steadily falling catch rates have spurred talk of introducing quotas. It seems likely that regulations will be imposed by law before the boat operators get around to it themselves. If you do go game fishing, you may prefer to tag and release your catch rather than killing and landing it.

Birdlife is prolific – if you harbour even a mild interest you should make a point of bringing binoculars. On the **reptile** front, snakes – brilliant disguise artists – are rarely seen, but lizards skitter everywhere, including upside down on the ceiling at night, and bug-eyed chameleons waver across the road, sometimes making it to the other side. So do giant millipedes, up to thirty centimetres long, harmless scavengers and known as Mombasa Expresses after the well-known slow train. **Insects**, including some fierce mosquitoes, are here in full force. But most, including the glorious butterflies of the Jadini and Arabuko-Sokoke forests, are attractive participants in the coast's gaudy show.

Transport to the coast

The **train journey** between Nairobi and Mombasa is, for many people, a highlight of Kenyan travel. While its unreliability makes it difficult to recommend unreservedly (hazards such as elephants on the line mean that trains are often hours late), all the research trips for this book have made frequent use of it. For more details see p.55 and pp.165–167. **Buses** from Nairobi to Mombasa go by day as well as night, and one firm even runs Nissan microbus matatus, or you could break the journey at places like Mtito Andei (jumping-off point for Tsavo West National Park) or Voi (for Tsavo East and the Taita Hills), but most of the road is dull. If you're driving, consider taking the route from Mariakani, to Kilifi to avoid the terrible road surface near Mombasa. For coverage of the whole route, see chapter 5, pp.360–367.

You can also **fly** to Mombasa, Malindi, Lamu and Kiwaiyu from Nairobi. Flying to Lamu from Nairobi makes sense if you have the cash (Ksh10,000 one way, Ksh17,000 return; see "Moving on from Nairobi" on pp.165–166) and not much time, as you avoid retracing your steps between Lamu and Mombasa, but it's not an interesting flight. The Malindi–Lamu hop (see "Travel details" on p.554) costs Ksh7000 round-trip Ksh3500 one-way, and gives stunning views over jungle and reef. For details on flying into Mombasa's Moi International Airport, see p.432.

Coast practicalities

There are four main **resort** areas – three to the north and one to the south. The suburban district north of Mombasa, consisting of **Nyali**, **Bamburi**, **Mtwapa** and almost merging into **Kikambala** over on the north side of Mtwapa Creek, is the first, often known as "North Coast"; further north comes **Watamu**, about two hours from Mombasa; and lastly **Malindi**, twenty minutes beyond Watamu. Along the "South Coast", south of Mombasa, **Diani Beach**, forty minutes' drive from the city, is the principal focus, with the lower-key **Tiwi Beach** to the north of it. However, most of these places have little that is recognizably Kenyan about them and, if you stay at an "all-inclusive" hotel, you won't see much of "real" Kenya. Apart from the odd small development, however, the rest of the coast is virtually untouched.

This part of Kenya is the most affected by the **seasons**. April, May and June are much less busy, and much cheaper, than the rest of the year. While the beaches tend to be damp and the weather muggy and overcast, you can make large savings on package holidays or, if you're travelling independently, reduce your hotel costs by as much as fifty percent.

As an alternative to hotels, you can stay in **self-catering villas**, **apartments** and **cottages**. There are various options along the beaches north of Mombasa, at Malindi and at Tiwi and Diani beaches, and it's a very sound financial proposition for families or groups.

One word of warning: tempting as it can be, **sleeping out**, except on the most deserted of beaches, is very unwise. Although the reputation of some areas for daylight theft and more grievous assaults is unfairly exaggerated, to sleep out anywhere near Mombasa or Malindi is asking for trouble – you'll have to find a room or pitch up at one of the handful of recognized campsites.

Mombasa and around

Arriving in **Mombasa** by plane or train in the morning, there's ample time, if the heat doesn't fell you, to head straight out to the beaches. But you should consider spending a day or two in Mombasa itself, tuning in to the coast (and to Kenya if you've just jetted in), catching the cadences of "Kiswahili *safi*" (pure Swahili) and looking around Kenya's most historic city. If you have time, there are two worthwhile trips you can make inland to areas that are much less known: **Shimba Hills National Park** to the southwest and, well off the beaten path to the northwest, the **Mijikenda country** between Mazeras and Kaloleni. If you would rather take this latter detour before reaching the coast proper – and it's a pleasant introduction to the region – buses from Nairobi can drop you at **Mazeras** (see p.464), a simple bus ride away from Mombasa.

Mombasa island has no proper beaches of its own. The nearest are **Shelly Beach**, covered in more detail on p.469, and **Nyali Beach**, covered on pp.450–454. Shelly Beach is relatively uninteresting and narrow, with the reef close to the shore, but fairly peaceful. Nyali is pretty good, crowded at weekends and

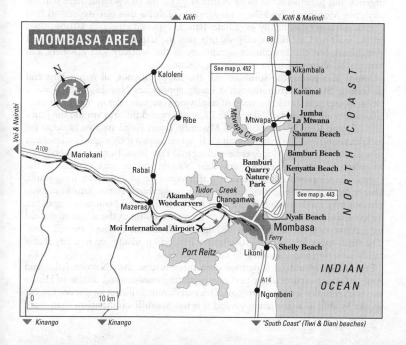

holidays, and the reef here is much further out. There are several public points of access to Nyali Beach, but the easiest is right by the entrance to the *Nyali Beach Hotel*. Most of the time, hotels don't mind if you use their own beaches, bars and restaurants. If it's simply a swim you're after, see "Swimming pools" on p.448.

Mombasa

Kenya's second city can come as a revelation. There's a depth of history here, and a sense of community Nairobi lacks. And, whereas Nairobi has very clear boundaries between rich and poor districts, things are less clearly defined in Mombasa. Sleazy, hot – you're always thirsty – and physically tropical in a way that could hardly be more different from the capital, **MOMBASA** is the slightly indolent hub of the coast – a faded, flaking, occasionally charming city that still feels, despite its gentle sprawl, like a small town that was once great.

Mombasa is actually an island, connected to the mainland by two causeways to the west, and by a bridge to the north, but still linked only by ferry to the south. The city is intricate and its streets wriggle deceptively. At its appealing heart is the **Old Town**, a lattice of lanes, mosques and cramped, old houses sloping gently down to the once-busy dhow harbour. **Fort Jesus**, an impressive reminder of Mombasa's complicated, bloody past, still overlooks the Old Town from where it once guarded the harbour entrance. It's now a national monument and museum.

Clustered all around you, within easy walking distance, is the whole expanse of downtown, modern Mombasa, with its wide streets and refreshing lack of high-rise buildings (though their number is steadily growing). While you won't doubt it's a chaotic city, the atmosphere, even in the commercial centre of one of Africa's busiest ports, is invariably relaxed and congenial. Rush hours, urgency and paranoia seem to be Nairobi's problems (as everyone here will tell you), not Mombasa's. And the gaping, marginal slums that one expects to find outside African cities hardly exist here. True, Likoni and especially Changamwe, on the mainland, are burgeoning suburbs that the municipality has more or less abandoned, but the brutalizing conditions of the Mathare Valley, Kibera and Korogocho shantytowns in Nairobi are absent.

Despite the palms, the sunshine and the happy languor, all is not bliss and perfection. **Street crime**, though it hardly approaches Nairobi's level, is still a problem, and you should be wary of displaying your valuables or accepting invitations to walk down dark alleys. The Likoni ferry and the area around the junction of Jomo Kenyatta Avenue with Mwembe Tayeri Road are two hotspots for pickpocketing and bag snatching, and it is not unknown for gangs of pickpockets to stalk tourists along Moi Avenue and around Fort Jesus. But, as a general rule, Mombasa is a far less neurotic city than Nairobi and, in stark contrast to the capital, there's nowhere in the centre that could be considered a no-go area. One indication of this is that the city stays awake much later. Climatic considerations may partly explain it but, at an hour when central Nairobi is empty but for taxis and *askaris*, Mombasans are to be seen strolling in the warm night, old men conversing on the benches in Digo Road, and many shops are still open. The small-town freedoms remain healthy here and it all adds up to a city that is richly satisfying and rewarding to stay in.

Ethnically, Mombasa is perhaps even more diverse than Nairobi. Asian and Arab influence is particularly pervasive, with fifty mosques and dozens of Hindu and Sikh temples lending a strongly Oriental flavour. Still, the largest contingent speaks Swahili as a first language and it is the **Swahili civilization** that, more than any other, accounts for Mombasa's distinctive character. You'll see women wearing head-to-foot *buibuis* or brilliant *kanga* outfits, men decked out in *kanzu* gowns and hip-slung *kikoi* wraps. The smaller community of white settlers and expatriates figures less prominently here than in Nairobi, but it continues to wield disproportionate economic and social clout.

As a tourist town, Mombasa doesn't go out of its way to please. Indeed, one of its best qualities is its utter lack of pretension. It is principally a port: **Kilindini** harbour takes up most of the western side of the island. Increasingly, too, Mombasa is an industrial city, boasting one of East Africa's major oil refineries (on your right as you arrive by train). In short, Mombasa is not a resort. Visiting sailors are as important to its tourist economy as bona fide tourists, and (a grievous shortcoming) the island has no real beaches. The vast majority of the obvious tourists that you'll see around the place are here only for the purpose of a shopping trip from their North or South coast beach hotels. You may not be able to resist the lure of the beaches for too long, but Mombasa deserves a little of your time unless you are in a big hurry; there are few places in the country with such a strong sense of identity.

Some history

Mombasa is one of East Africa's oldest settlements and, so long as you aren't anticipating spectacular historical sites, it's a fascinating place to wander. The island has had a town on it, located somewhere between the present Old Town and Nyali Bridge, for at least 700 years, and there are enough documentary snippets from earlier times to guess that some kind of settlement has existed here for at least 2000 years. Mombasa's own optimistic claim (frequently repeated in the tourist literature) to be 2500 years old, comes from Roman and Egyptian adventure stories.

Early tales

Precisely what was going on before the Portuguese arrived is still barely discernible. An armchair traveller, Al-Idrisi, wrote the following in the early twelfth century about a place called Manfasa that was in roughly the right location: "This is a small place and a dependency of the Zanj (coastal people). Its inhabitants work in the iron mines and hunt tigers. They have red-coloured dogs which fight every kind of wild beast and even lions." This sounds most unlikely, but then the history of Mombasa is a series of unlikely episodes. **Ibn Battuta**, the roving fourteenth-century Moroccan, spent a relatively quiet night here in 1332 and declared the people of the town "devout, chaste and virtuous . . . their mosques . . . strongly constructed of wood . . . the greater part of their diet . . . bananas and fish". But another Arab writer of a hundred years later found a less ordered society:

Monkeys have become the rulers of Mombasa since about 800 AH (1400 AD). They even come and take the food from the dishes, attack men in their own homes and take away what they can find. The master of the house chases the thieving monkey and does not cease cajoling him until the animal, having eaten the food, gives back the dish or vessel. When the monkeys enter a house and find a woman they hold congress with her. The monkeys divide into bands each with its own chief and march behind him in an orderly manner. The people have much to put up with.

Early Portuguese visitors

Mombasa had considerably worse depredations to put up with after **Vasco da Gama's** expedition, full of mercenary zeal, dropped anchor on Easter Saturday 1498. After courtesy gifts had been exchanged, relations suddenly soured and the fleet was prevented from entering the port. A few days later, richer by only

The coast is where East Africa meets the Classical World, and the influence of that world over many centuries is reflected in the local culture. One result is that **Islam** has long been the dominant religion here, and one thing you'll notice if coming from upcountry is the profusion of mosques and the correspondingly lower number of churches. Five times a day, towns and villages up and down the coast resound to the cry of the *muezzin*, Muslim festivals are big here, and during Ramadan you'll find many restaurants and cafés closed up, at least in the daytime (see the box on p.71). Nonetheless, Islam here takes rather a relaxed form, and you'll certainly have no difficulty finding a beer, for example, or a bar to drink it in.

Partly through the intermediary of Islam, with its direct and simple tenets, foreign ideas have shaped the society, language, literature and architecture of the coastal region. More than the pragmatic Portuguese, whose interests seem to have been entirely mercenary, immigrants and traders from Arabia, Iran and India – once or twice even China – have been a subtle and gradual influence on the coast. They would arrive each year in March or April on the northeast monsoon, the dry *kaskazi* wind, and return in September on the southerly monsoon or *kuzi*.

Some, by choice or mishap, would be left behind. Through intermarriage from the earliest times (even before Islam appeared on the scene in the seventh century), a distinct ancient civilization called **Swahili** emerged. Swahili, which is thought to derive from the same Arabic root as *sahel*, meaning edge or coast, is also a language, known to its speakers as **Kiswahili**. It is one of the more mainstream of the Bantu languages, which are spoken throughout much of Africa south of the equator. Like all old languages used by trading peoples, Swahili contains strong clues about who the people mixed with. Despite popular misconception, Swahili isn't based on Arabic any more than English is based on Latin, but it is full of words derived from Arabic and peppered with others of Indian, Portuguese and English origin.

The Swahili are not a "tribe" in any definable sense; no less than, say, Americans, they are the result of the mixed heritage reflected in their language. Questions of family background and status in the community have traditionally loomed large: families that trace their roots – not always very plausibly – to foreign shores in the distant past tend to claim superior social status. Nor, predictably, was skin colour ignored. Essentially Muslim, the Swahili interpretation of the religion varies from place to place and according to circumstance. Rigidity of form is an alien concept in Swahili culture. Essentially coastal, not all Swahili trade, nor do they all fish – some Swahili groups even avoid eating fish. Coconuts, mixed farming, cattle and goats are all vitally important.

The towns

Like the language, it was long thought that the towns of the coast began as implants, that is, as Arab, or even Persian, trading forts. It is now known that most were already in existence before any of the great post-Islamic wars and migrations took place in the Middle East. Mombasa, Malindi, Lamu and a host of lesser-known settlements are essentially ancient African towns that have always tolerated and even encouraged peaceful immigration from overseas. The Swahili style has always been to welcome the new and the sophisticated.

With few exceptions, however, any attempt to compromise the independence of these towns was met with violent resistance. The Portuguese were the least successful.

one sheep and "large quantities of oranges, lemons and sugar cane", da Gama went off to try his primitive diplomacy at Malindi, and found his first and lasting ally on the coast.

When they arrived at the end of the fifteenth century, cultural memories of the Moorish occupation of their own country were still fresh. Accommodation to Islam was not on their agenda and, despite a long acquaintance with the coast, they never established an enduring colonial presence, as they did in Goa on the southwestern Indian coast, further along the same trading route.

The slave inheritance

Slavery on the coast was originally less a black-and-white moral issue than is commonly assumed. In the past, it was not unusual for people in need to "lend" a member of the family to others in exchange for goods or services. The Mijikenda peoples (see p.466 for more background), for example, maintained close links with the coastal towns, trading their produce, providing armed forces when the towns were under threat, and being supplied in return with overseas trade goods, especially cloth and tools. As traders, the Swahili sometimes accumulated surpluses of grain on the coast at times of severe drought inland. In exchange for food supplies, Mijikenda children would be taken to the towns by their relatives and fostered with Swahili families with whom they had links – to become, in effect, slaves. Later, the children intermarried, or paid off the debt and returned, though a small number were probably sold overseas. But when slavery itself became a major aspect of commerce, and the available foreign goods irresistible (cloth, firearms and liquor from Holland, France, England and America), then any trace of trust in the old arrangement vanished. The weak and defenceless were captured and sold to slavers from the coast (or, in the case of the Akamba who live further inland, beyond the Mijikenda, they sold their own prisoners and insane), often to end up on Dutch or French plantations around the Indian Ocean or in Arabian households. And, with the domination of the Sultan of Oman on the coast in the early nineteenth century, and the large-scale emigration of Arabs to East Africa, slaves from the far interior were increasingly set to work on their colonial coastal farms and plantations. When the British formally freed the slaves in 1907, they became part of Swahili society.

Swahili proverbs and sayings

The Swahili are renowned for the imagery, rhythm and complexity of their **proverbs**. *Kangas* always have some kind of adage printed on one side and these are often traditionally Swahili. The first one listed below is the one most often heard. For more *kanga* aphorisms, see Ⓦwww.glcom.com/hassan/kanga.html.

Haraka, haraka: haina baraka – Haste, haste: there's no blessing in it.

Nyumba njema si mlango – A good house isn't (judged by) its door [ie, don't judge by appearances].

Mahaba ni haba, akili ni mali – Love counts for little, intelligence is wealth.

Faida yako ni hasara yangu – Your gain is my loss.

Haba na haba kujaza kibaba – Little by little fills the jug.

Kuku anakula sawa na mdomo wake – A chicken eats according to her beak [interpretations invited].

Mungu alihlolandika, haliwezi kufutika – What God has written cannot be erased.

Heri shuka isiyo kitushi, kama shali njema ya mauwa – Better an honest loincloth than a fancy cloak (of shame).

Mke ni nguo, mgomba kupalilia – A wife means clothes (like) a banana plant means weeding.

Mombasa was visited again in 1505 by a fourteen-strong fleet. This time, the king of Mombasa had enlisted 1500 archers from the mainland and stored arsenals of stone missiles on the rooftops in preparation for the expected **invasion** through the town's narrow alleys. The attack, pitching firearms against spears, poisoned arrows and stones, was decisive and brutal. The town was squeezed on all sides and the king's palace (of which no trace remains) was seized. The king and most of the survivors slipped out of town into the palm groves which then covered most of Mombasa island, but 1513 Mombasans had been killed – as against five Portuguese.

The king attempted to save Mombasa by offering to become a vassal of Portugal, but the request was turned down, the Portuguese unwilling to lose the chance to **loot** the abandoned town, picking over the bodies in the courtyards and breaking down the strongroom doors until the ships at anchor were almost overladen. Then, as a parting shot, they fired the town. The narrow streets and the cattle stalls between the thatched houses produced a conflagration that must have razed Mombasa to the ground.

Portuguese occupation

In 1528, the Portuguese returned once again to wreck and plunder the new city that had grown on the ashes of the old. In the 1580s, it happened twice more; on the last occasion, in 1589, there was a frenzied **massacre** at the hands of the Portuguese and – coincidentally – a marauding tribe of nomads from the interior called the Zimba (about whom little is known except their cannibalistic notoriety). The Zimba's unholy alliance with the Europeans came to a treacherous end at Malindi shortly afterwards, when the Portuguese, together with the townsfolk and 3000 Segeju archers, wiped them out.

Remarkably, only two years after this last catastrophe, Mombasa launched a major land expedition of its own against its old enemy, Malindi. It had finally met a decisive match. The party was ambushed on the way by Malindi's Segeju allies, who themselves stormed and took Mombasa, later handing over the town (in which they had little interest) to the Portuguese at Malindi. The Malindi corps transferred to Mombasa, the Malindi sheikh was grandly installed as sultan of the whole region, and the Portuguese set to work on **Fort Jesus**, dedicated in 1593.

Once completed, the fort became the focus of everything that mattered in Mombasa, changing hands a total of nine times between the early seventeenth century and 1875. The first takeover happened in 1631, in a **popular revolt** that resulted in the killing of every last Portuguese. But the Sultan, lacking support from any of the other towns under Portuguese domination, eventually had to desert the fort and the Portuguese, waiting in Zanzibar, reoccupied it. For the rest of the seventeenth century they continued to hold Mombasa, at first consolidating their control of the Indian Ocean trade.

Omani rule

Meanwhile, however, the **Omani Arabs** were becoming increasingly powerful. And as Dutch, English and French ships started to appear on the horizon, time was clearly running out for the Portuguese trading monopoly. Efforts to bring settlers to their East African possessions failed, and they retreated more and more behind the massive walls of Fort Jesus. Portugal's East African "empire" was under siege, and in 1696–98 Fort Jesus itself was isolated and besieged into submission by the Omanis who, with support from Pate and Lamu, had already taken the rest of the town. After 33 months almost all the defenders – the Portuguese corps and some 1500 Swahili loyalists – had died of starvation or plague.

Rapid disenchantment with the new Arab rulers spilled over in 1728 into a mutiny among the fort's African soldiers. The Portuguese were invited back

– for a year. Then the fort was again besieged, and this time the Portuguese gave up quickly. They were allowed their freedom, and a number were said to have married and stayed in the town. But Portuguese power on the coast was shattered for ever.

The new Omani rulers were the **Mazrui** family. Soon after the return of some kind of normality in Mombasa, they declared themselves independent of Oman, a direct challenge to the **Busaidi** family who had just seized power in the Arabian homeland. Civil war in Oman prevented the Busaidis from doing much about their wayward overseas agents; with the **Nabahani** family in Pate no longer paying much allegiance either, control of what were fast reverting to independent states was increasingly difficult. As usual, though, the lack of unity on the coast prevented any lasting independence.

British takeover

Intrigue in the Lamu Archipelago led to the Battle of Shela (p.530) and Lamu's unwittingly disastrous invitation to the **Sultan of Oman**, Seyyid Said, to occupy its own fort. From here, and by now with **British** backing, the Busaidis went on to attack Mazrui Mombasa repeatedly in the 1820s.

There was a hiccup in 1824 when a British officer, **Captain Owen**, fired with enthusiasm for defeating the slave trade, extended British protection to Mombasa on his own account, despite official British support for the slave-trading Busaidis. Owen's "Protectorate" was a diplomatic embarrassment and – not surprisingly – did not last long. The Busaidi government was only installed when the Swahili "twelve tribes" of Mombasa, the traditional inhabitants of the immediate hinterland, fell into a dispute over the Mazrui succession and called in Seyyid Said, the Busaidi leader. In 1840, he moved his capital from Oman to Zanzibar and, with Mombasa firmly garrisoned, most of the coast was soon in his domain.

Surviving members of the Mazrui family went to Takaungu near Malindi and Gazi, south of Mombasa. British influence was sharpened after their guns quelled the mutiny in 1875 of al-Akida, "an ambitious, unbalanced and not over-clever" commandant of the Fort. Once British hegemony was established, they leased the **coastal strip** from the Sultan of Zanzibar and Fort Jesus became Mombasa's prison, which it remained until 1958.

Since independence, Mombasa has seen a gradual decline, as air has taken over from sea for much freight transport, while the rise as a port of Dar es Salaam in Tanzania has provided Mombasa with competition. The New Nyali Bridge has been the city's only major construction project, with a bridge at Likoni much mooted but never built. 1993 saw violence on the streets between supporters and opponents of the fundamentalist Islamic Party of Kenya, led by charismatic preacher Sheikh Khalid Balala, and while the IPK does have a number of sympathizers in the city, its level of support is difficult to gauge as it has never been afforded legal status nor allowed to contest elections.

Arrival, city transport and information

Most people arrive in Mombasa by **plane** from Europe or Nairobi, or on the overnight **train**, a rather more civilized mode of transport, and one which leaves you pretty much in the middle of town. Alternatives are by **bus** and **matatu**, which will drop you off even more slap-bang in the centre of things.

If you've never been to Africa before, flying into Mombasa and merely driving through the suburbs to your hotel throws you into the place more quickly

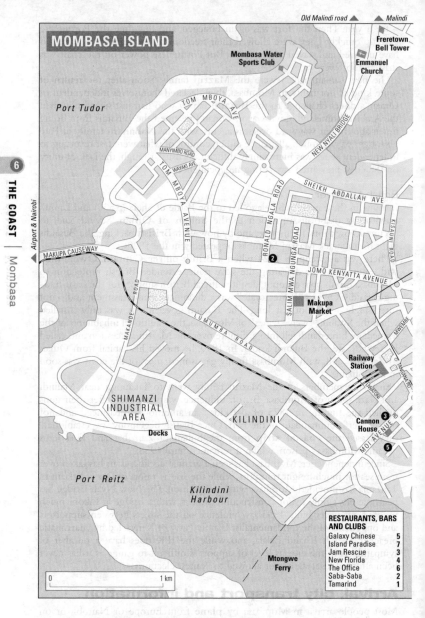

MOMBASA ISLAND

Old Malindi road ▲   ▲ *Malindi*

Freetown Bell Tower

Emmanuel Church

Mombasa Water Sports Club

Port Tudor

TOM MBOYA AVE

MANYIMBO ROAD

TOM WAYAKI AVE

NEW NYALI BRIDGE

SHEIKH ABDALLAH AVE

RONALD NGALA ROAD

SALIM MWA NGUNGA ROAD

KISAUNI ROAD

▲ *Airport & Nairobi*

MAKUPA CAUSEWAY

2

JOMO KENYATTA AVENUE

TOM MBOYA AVENUE

MAKANDE ROAD

LUMUMBA ROAD

Makupa Market

Railway Station

MWEMBE

TANGANA RD

LIWATONI

SHIMANZI INDUSTRIAL AREA

KILINDINI

Docks

Cannon House

3

MOI AVENUE

5

Port Reitz

Kilindini Harbour

Mtongwe Ferry

| 0 | 1 km |

RESTAURANTS, BARS AND CLUBS

Galaxy Chinese	5
Island Paradise	7
Jam Rescue	3
New Florida	4
The Office	6
Saba-Saba	2
Tamarind	1

than arriving in Nairobi's cosmopolitan embrace. You may even experience some level of **culture shock** from the poverty, the noise and the up-frontness of everything, but it's not a shock that will last long.

Getting around Mombasa is best, and easily done, on foot. With no bus services, **city transport** consists of matatus, which run from the GPO to Nyali

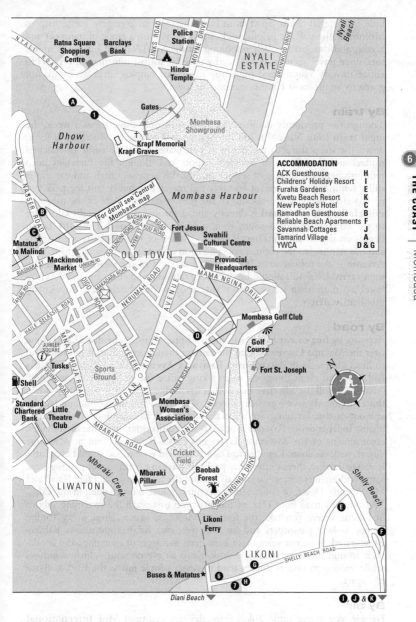

ACCOMMODATION

ACK Guesthouse	H
Childrens' Holiday Resort	I
Furaha Gardens	E
Kwetu Beach Resort	K
New People's Hotel	C
Ramadhan Guesthouse	B
Reliable Beach Apartments	F
Savannah Cottages	J
Tamarind Village	A
YWCA	D & G

Bridge, Tudor Docks and Likoni ferry, or taxis, a ride in which to anywhere in town shouldn't cost more than Ksh200.

The city's **tourist office**, operated by the Mombasa and Coast Tourist Association (MCTA), is on Moi Avenue, west of the Tusks near the BP petrol station (Mon–Fri 8am–4.30pm, Sat 8am–noon; ☎041/2225428). Although offering little in material terms (apart from brochures and an averagely useful map of Mombasa), the staff are helpful, and can advise you on a range of transport and accommodation matters. When looking for the MCTA office, beware of imitators, since travel agencies based nearby pose as "tourist information offices" to entice unwary visitors, and obviously firms that employ such tactics are not going to be the most honest operators in town.

By train

Though the previously daily service now runs only three times a week, the night **train** from Nairobi is still the best way of getting to Mombasa. It loops down the steep scarp to the ocean as you wake up to the rustle of starched waiters and the clatter of buckled teapots and, though the carriages need refurbishment, the quality of service on board is generally high and the trip is still a reminder of the era of leisurely rail travel. For full details see p.55 and pp.165–167. When you walk out of the station into the glare of the morning sun, **Haile Selassie Road** is directly ahead, leading in one straight kilometre to the city's main north–south thoroughfare, **Digo Road**. The **Old Town** begins on the far side of Digo Road. To the left of Haile Selassie are markets and bus stations; to the right, a concentration of hotels; then, parallel to it, **Moi Avenue** – the tourist strip. If you pick a taxi out of the swarm awaiting the train's arrival, Ksh150 should be the going rate to be taken to any town-centre hotel, no more than a five-minute ride, though you should have no security problems walking.

By road

Arriving by **bus** or **car** from Nairobi, first impressions can be dismal. You come over the Makupa Causeway with the railway, then diverge from it on the island to head 4km straight down **Jomo Kenyatta Avenue**. Although Mayor Balala had begun to clean things up since taking office (he resigned early in 1999), "shabby" is still the adjective that comes irresistibly to mind as you bump down this erstwhile showcase avenue: a scene of broken windows, crumbling facades and out-of-date hoardings smothers the street from its inception, via the triumphalist Independence Roundabout to its final disintegration in the diesel-laden environment of the Mwembe Tayari bus parks. If you get out at Mwembe Tayari, walk on down Kenyatta to Digo Road and your mood should lift a little. If you're driving, there's rarely any problem **parking**, with lots of parking bays, some with meters (charges nominal), around the intersection of Digo Road and Moi Avenue. Don't, of course, leave anything valuable unattended in the car.

Arriving by road from **Dar es Salaam**, you first reach the swarming suburb of Likoni, where you take the ferry to Mombasa island (5min; every 15min; hourly 1–4am; passengers and bicycles free, cars Ksh40, motorbikes Ksh20). Be **warned**: in recent years there have been incidents of muggings and sneak-theft around the ferry, usually at dusk. Keep an eye on your vehicle windows while waiting in line, as thieves tend to target people just as the ferry is about to depart.

By air

By air, you arrive some 10km from the city centre at **Moi International Airport** on the mainland near Port Reitz. Try to change into cool clothes before arrival – essential if you're being picked up from the airport and going straight on safari – as there's really nowhere to do it at the airport. Although the arrivals hall routinely swarms with the newly arrived and the soon-to-depart, the staff stay admirably cool and formalities are carried out with a minimum of fuss: passport checks take seconds. If you haven't got a **visa**, they are usually issued on the spot without delay ($50 or equivalent). The luggage carousels seem to work more often than not and reports of items going missing are rare, though pilfering from luggage does occur – take valuables in hand baggage. There are **bank booths** for exchanging money just outside the customs area, and the National Bank of Kenya has an ATM. Note that if you're flying directly on to Nairobi, you'll be clearing customs in Mombasa. And if you're going straight on safari, you won't touch Mombasa island at all. Vehicles pass through the back of Changamwe, a poor suburb, on their way out to the highway.

There is no airline bus service from the airport into town, nor currently any public bus, and the nearest matatu service is a kilometre away. Several of the **taxi** firms (such as Sacco Airport Taxis) have fixed rates which are posted, or which they will show you on request, and the hassle is generally not severe. The price to the centre of Mombasa is Ksh715, and fares are also fixed for the beach resorts, depending on which hotel you're headed for (Diani Beach around Ksh3700; Nyali Beach Ksh1300; Tiwi Beach Ksh3150; Shanzu Beach Ksh2200). You'll make a small saving but pay in lack of comfort by taking an unlicensed cab. You can call Sacco Airport Taxis on ☏041/433211–20 ext 2405.

You can also arrange to have a rented **car** waiting for you at the airport. Most rental companies that have offices or outlets in Mombasa will do this for you, though you'll usually need to go to their office in town to complete the paperwork and pay the deposit.

If you want to get into town the cheapest way possible, walk just under a kilometre from the airport to the first row of shack-like shops at the road junction for Magongo, where you can pick up a matatu to the GPO for Ksh20. On your way into town, on the left about 300m before you reach the Nairobi–Mombasa highway, is an enormous **Akamba woodcarvers' "village"**, where the art of woodcarving has been reduced to not much more than a human conveyor belt. It isn't a place you're likely to bother visiting unless you are out here anyway and there are no special reductions should you want to buy; it's just a good education in a lowly sector of the tourist industry and, that said, quite entertaining.

Accommodation

None of the well-known resort hotels is located on Mombasa island, and tour operators almost never offer city hotels, for obvious reasons: there's nothing that could be described as luxury. If real comfort is what you want, the closest option, the *Nyali Beach Hotel*, is a short drive or taxi ride from the centre, on the mainland to the north. This, and subsequent hotels along the North Coast, are covered in the section "North of Mombasa" (see p.450). At the other end of the scale, the city has a fair scattering of cheap lodgings, but none that really stands out as the obvious focus for budget travellers. There's a YWCA – good for long stays for men as well as women – but no youth hostel and no campsite. Note that **water supplies** in Mombasa are not a hundred percent reliable, and many cheap places feature the telltale buckets and plastic basins in bathrooms that indicate water sometimes has to be carried up. The tap water, when it runs, is usually safe to drink except in the rainy seasons, If in doubt, get bottled water.

Basic lodgings
You might reasonably expect to find a concentration of cheap **lodgings** in the Old Town. Curiously enough, this isn't the case, though most of them

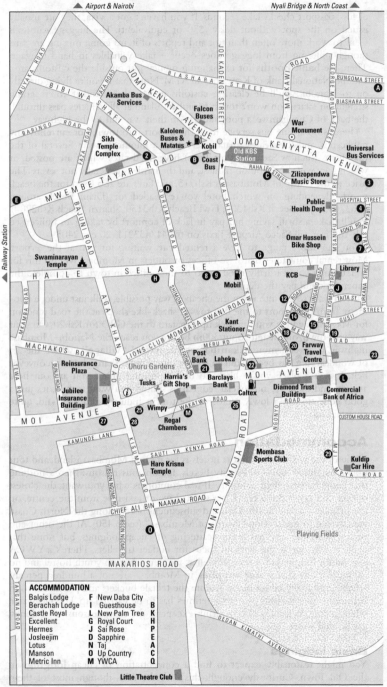

Airport & Nairobi ▲   **Nyali Bridge & North Coast** ▲

▲ Railway Station

Akamba Bus Services

Falcon Buses

BIASHARA STREET

JOE KADENGE STREET

MACKAWI ROAD

BUNGOMA STREET

BIASHARA STREET

A

MUYAKA ROAD

BIBI WA SHAFI ROAD

FAZA ROAD

JOMO KENYATTA AVENUE

Kaloleni Buses & Matatus ★ Kobil

War Monument

MORUBA STREET

Universal Bus Services

BARINGO ROAD

Sikh Temple Complex

2

B Coast Bus

JOMO KENYATTA AVENUE

Old KBS Station

RAHA LEO STREET

C

Zilizopendwa Music Store

HOSPITAL STREET

TURKANA STREET

3

MSANIFU KOMBO STREET

Public Health Dept

4

KONZI RD

6

MWEMBE TAYARI ROAD

JABA ROAD

BAJUNI ROAD

DURUMA ROAD

KWA SHIBU ROAD

D

E

Swaminarayan Temple

Omar Hussein Bike Shop

G

7

HAILE   SELASSIE   ROAD

Library

E

MKAMBA ROAD

AGA KHAN ROAD

SHIMONI STREET

H

8 9

Mobil

KCB

MAUNGANO ROAD

MSANIFU KOMBO STREET

TAITA ST.

J

12

MAUNGANO RD

13

14

15

GUSII STREET

TURKANA STREET

MACHAKOS ROAD

LIONS CLUB MOMBASA PWANI ROAD

WHITEFATHERS RD

Kant Stationer

MERU RD

CHEMBE ROAD

MERU   ROAD

18

20

19

Farway Travel Centre

23

TEWA ROAD

BUNJU ROAD

Reinsurance Plaza

Uhuru Gardens

Post Bank

Labeka

22

L

Commercial Bank of Africa

Jubilee Insurance Building

BP

Tusks

Harria's Gift Shop

Barclays Bank

Caltex

MOI   AVENUE

Diamond Trust Building

NGONYO ROAD

CUSTOM HOUSE ROAD

MOI   AVENUE

27

25

Wimpy

M

28

WAKATWA ROAD

Regal Chambers

26

MWANGO ROAD

29

Kuldip Car Hire

KAMUNDE LANE

KISUMU ROAD

SAUTI YA KENYA ROAD

Hare Krisna Temple

Mombasa Sports Club

MPYA ROAD

GIBSON NGOME RD

CHIEF ALI BIN NAAMAN ROAD

MNAZI MMOJA ROAD

O

Playing Fields

TANGANA ROAD

GIBSON NGOME RD

MAKARIOS ROAD

DEDAN KIMATHI AVENUE

ACCOMMODATION

Balgis Lodge	**F**	New Daba City	
Berachah Lodge	**I**	Guesthouse	**B**
Castle Royal	**L**	New Palm Tree	**K**
Excellent	**G**	Royal Court	**H**
Hermes	**J**	Sai Rose	**P**
Josleejim	**D**	Sapphire	**E**
Lotus	**N**	Taj	**A**
Manson	**O**	Up Country	**C**
Metric Inn	**M**	YWCA	**Q**

Little Theatre Club

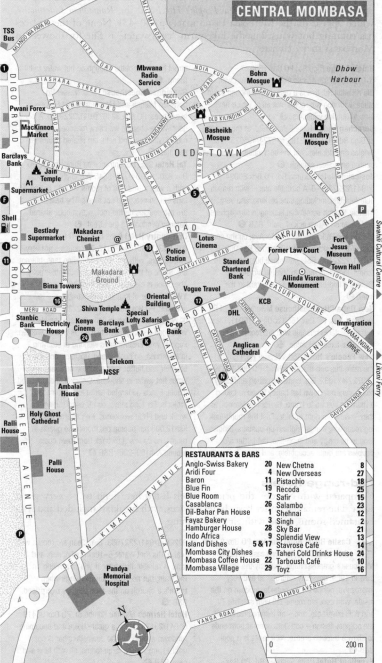

CENTRAL MOMBASA

TSS Bus

Dhow Harbour

Bohra Mosque

Mbwana Radio Service

Pwani Forex

MacKinnon Market

Basheikh Mosque

Mandhry Mosque

Barclays Bank

Jain Temple

A1 Supermarket

OLD TOWN

Shell

Bestlady Supermarket

Makadara Chemist

Lotus Cinema

Fort Jesus Museum

Former Law Court

Police Station

Standard Chartered Bank

Town Hall

Allinda Visram Monument

Bima Towers

Vogue Travel

Oriental Building

KCB

Stanbic Bank

Shiva Temple

Special Lofty Safaris

DHL

Immigration

Electricity House

Kenya Cinema

Barclays Bank

Co-op Bank

Telekom

Anglican Cathedral

NSSF

Ambalal House

Holy Ghost Cathedral

Ralli House

Palli House

Pandya Memorial Hospital

Swahili Cultural Centre

Likoni Ferry

6

THE COAST

RESTAURANTS & BARS

Anglo-Swiss Bakery	20	New Chetna	8
Aridi Four	4	New Overseas	27
Baron	11	Pistachio	18
Blue Fin	19	Recoda	25
Blue Room	7	Safir	15
Casablanca	26	Salambo	23
Dil-Bahar Pan House	1	Shehnai	12
Fayaz Bakery	3	Singh	2
Hamburger House	28	Sky Bar	21
Indo Africa	9	Splendid View	13
Island Dishes	5 & 17	Stavrose Café	14
Mombasa City Dishes	6	Taheri Cold Drinks House	24
Mombasa Coffee House	22	Tarboush Café	10
Mombasa Village	29	Toyz	16

0   200 m

435

▼ Likoni Ferry & South Coast

cluster in the streets just to the west. All are on the Central Mombasa map on pp.434–435, apart from the *New People's Hotel* and the *Ramadhan Guesthouse*, which appear on the Mombasa Island map, pp.430–431. None of these places has running hot water, but the lukewarm "cold water" is fine for showers in Mombasa's sticky climate.

Balgis Lodge Digo Rd; PO Box 1506 ⏏0721/693793. Across from the junction with Old Kilindini Rd, this is a respectable though basic place, with non-s/c rooms, not all of which have fans or outside windows. ❶

Berachah Lodge Haile Selassie Rd, at the corner of Digo Rd; PO Box 82192 ⏏0724/495025. S/c singles and doubles, not the best value in town, but central and clean enough. ❷

Josleejim Hotel Duruma Rd; PO Box 80094 ⏏041/2222867–8. A sizeable place, with reasonable facilities, including safe parking, and very friendly, though somewhat lacking in atmosphere, and could do with a lick of paint. B&B ❷

Metric Inn Wakatwa Rd, off Moi Ave, on the south side of the Tusks behind *Wimpy*; PO Box 98658 ⏏041/2222155. B&L with small but acceptable rooms, including more expensive s/c singles. There's a laid-back bar and restaurant at the front. ❷

New Daba City Guesthouse Mwembe Tayari Rd by Coast Bus; PO Box 1688 ⏏041/316041. Clean and respectable cheapie with s/c rooms, nets and hot water. Excellent value. ❷

New People's Hotel Abdel Nasser Rd, right by the main bus and matatu offices; PO Box 16639 ⏏0722/471032. Big, undistinguished and noisy block, very run-down but handy if you're taking a morning bus up to Lamu, Garissa or Malindi, as they leave from right outside. Past the rough-looking reception, things brighten up upstairs. Singles tend to be dingy and cube-like, but better s/c doubles are quite acceptable, and those facing the

street have real baths (though no hot water to fill them). ❷

Ramadhan Guesthouse Abdel Nasser Rd, between Malindi and Mombasa/Coast Express bus offices; PO Box 3248 ⏏041/2229965. A good-value cheapie with airy, reasonably clean rooms with fans and nets, but shared bathroom facilities. ❶

Taj Hotel Digo Rd, entrance on Bungoma St; PO Box 82021 ⏏041/2313545. A friendly welcome, with a very mixed bag of rooms, all with ceiling fans but no nets, and not all s/c. The best ones are the doubles on the roof, with a huge shared balcony overlooking the street. ❷

Up Country Hotel Raha Leo St; PO Box 40604 ⏏041/312659, ⏎495317. The doubles are very presentable, with big nets and ceiling fans, but not s/c. Some of the singles are s/c, but rather poky. The place is clean and well kept however. ❷

YWCA Corner of Kaunda and Kiambu avenues; PO Box 90214 ⏏041/2229856, ⏎ywcamsa@wananchi.com. Pleasant ambience with good security, open to men as well as women. Popular with East Africans working or studying in Mombasa, so book ahead. Upstairs rooms are breezier and better, with fans and nets, and sometimes hot water in showers. Cleanish, if dilapidated toilets. Funds generated assist local women's projects. For long stays, on HB basis during the week and FB at weekends, they charge just over Ksh12,000 per person per month. No guests in rooms, no curfew (taxi back from town costs around Ksh150–200). B&B ❸

Mid-range hotels

Compared with Nairobi, the pricier hotels listed here tend to be very good value. The remainder offer basic hotel services, with breakfast included and self-contained rooms, some with air conditioning.

Castle Royal Hotel Moi Ave; PO Box 82326 ⏏041/2220373, ⏎www.castlemsa.com. Mombasa's grandest hotel, formerly the *Palace*, built in 1909, now fully refurbished and very impressive, period on the outside, modern on the inside, with cool a/c rooms (all with satellite TV and WiFi coverage), and – an inspired feature of the original design – corridors open at both ends to allow a through breeze. All it lacks is a pool. B&B ❻

Excellent Hotel Haile Selassie Rd; PO Box

90228 ⏏041/2227683. Big, clean s/c rooms with real baths (hot water 6–10am only), nets and fans. A reliable first base if you're arriving on the train, but noisy on Sun mornings when there's a church on the roof. Slightly overpriced. B&B ❹

Hotel Hermes Msanifu Kombo St; PO Box 98419 ⏏041/2313599. Not a great choice and becoming rundown and boozy (the downstairs bar is open until 11pm). Mostly large rooms, all with fans and nets. B&B ❸

Lotus Hotel corner of Mvita and Cathedral roads; PO Box 90193 ☎041/2313207, ⓦwww.lotusmombasa.com. Overflowing with greenery, with plain but very neat and clean rooms, and located on a quiet corner not far from Fort Jesus, and often full. Every room has a/c and a phone, though the showers would benefit from higher water pressure. Visa cards accepted. B&B ⑤

Manson Hotel Kisumu Rd; PO Box 83565 ☎041/2222419–21, ⓦwww.mansonhotel.com. Large, clean rooms with balconies, some with fans, others a/c. TV lounge and bar-restaurant on the ground floor. The welcome isn't warm, but good value overall. B&B ④

New Palm Tree Hotel Nkrumah Rd; PO Box 90013 ☎041/315272 ext 17, ☎2222669. This must have been quite a grand place once upon a time, and it still has bags of charm, despite getting frayed around the edges. Rooms are spacious and clean, all s/c with fans but no nets. There's also a sunny first-floor courtyard with, bizarrely enough, sunbeds. Altogether much better than similarly priced competitors. B&B ④

Royal Court Hotel Haile Selassie Rd; PO Box 41247 ☎041/2220932–3, ⓦwww.royalcourtmom basa.co.ke. A very stylish hotel, with lift access, close to the railway station, with tasteful touches of Swahili decor in all the public areas. Twin rooms are a good size and face out over town, but singles are small and lack the views. All have spotless modern tiled bathrooms (with baths and hot water). Great breakfast buffets, and even a casino. Good value. B&B ⑥

Sai Rose Hotel Nyerere Ave; PO Box 83063 ☎041/2222897, ⓔhotelsairose@iconnect.co.ke. Just beyond the downtown hubbub, the standard rooms in the basement of this little place aren't much to write home about, but the deluxe rooms upstairs are bright and fresh, with a/c, TV and a mini-bar. B&B ④

Hotel Sapphire Mwembe Tayari Rd; PO Box 1254 ☎041/2494841, ☎hotelsapphire@africaonline. co.ke. Near the train station, a modern interconnecting five- and ten-storey block. The 110 rooms are all a/c, with satellite TV and phones, and the benefit of the only hotel pool in central Mombasa (8am–8pm; day guests pay Ksh200 adults, Ksh150 children). More expensive suites have kitchens. There's also a health club with gym, massage, Jacuzzi, steam bath and sauna. Three restaurants (including Chinese and Indian, but not always open). Good value. B&B ⑤

The City

Mombasa is not a city with a huge number of sights, but most visitors will want to check out its main one, Fort Jesus, in the shadow of which lies Mombasa's Old Town, still a charming hive of narrow lanes, mosques and carved Swahili doorways. In the modern town centre, the tusks that feature on so many postcards are not wildly exciting, though fans of 1930s architecture might appreciate one or two of the buildings from that era on Digo Road. Further afield, there's a baobab forest and a seventeenth-century pillar tomb which are worth a visit.

Fort Jesus

For all its turbulent past, today **Fort Jesus** (daily 8.30am–6pm; Ksh800, children Ksh400; ☎041/2312839) is a quietly studious museum-monument, surprisingly spacious and tree-shaded inside its giant walls, and retaining most of its original (over the centuries much repaired) character. The curious angular construction was the design of an Italian architect and ensured that assailants trying to scale the walls would always be under crossfire from one of the bastions. It is a classic European fortress of its age.

The best time to visit is probably first thing in the morning; the guidebook on sale is an interesting source of information. Look out especially for the restored **Omani House**, in the far right corner as you enter the fort. Avoiding head contact with the lintel, climb up to the flat roof for a wonderful view over Mombasa. Interesting in their own way, too, are the uncomfortable-looking, wall-mounted **latrines**, overhanging the ditch just south of the Omani House, which would presumably have been closed in with mats. It is immediately obvious that Fort Jesus was not so much a building as a small, resolutely fortified town in its own right. The ruins of a church, storerooms, and possibly even shops are up at this end and, to judge by some accounts, the main courtyard was at times a warren of simple dwellings. Captain Owen described it in 1824 as being: "... a mass of indiscriminate ruins, huts and hovels, many of them built wherever space could be found but generally formed from parts of the ruins, matted over for roofs."

Most of the archeological interest is at the seaward end of the fort, where you'll find the **Hall of the Mazrui** with its beautiful stone benches and eight-eenth-century inscription – and a sad quantity of more modern graffiti as well. A nearby room has been dedicated entirely to the display of a huge plaster panel of **wall paintings**, made with carbon and ochre by bored Portuguese sentries. Their subjects are fascinating: ships, figures in armour (including the captain of the fort wielding his baton), fish, and what seems to be a chameleon. Illiteracy precluded much writing but, oddly enough, there's nothing obscene either. The small **café** above the room with the wall paintings has been serving first-class lime juice for years (or, if you want something to eat, the museum **restaurant**, behind the ticket office, has a lunch dish each day and various snacks).

A **sound and light show** takes place daily except Tuesdays and Sundays at 7.30pm. This is organized by Jahazi Marine (℡041/5485001–5, ⓦwww .severin-kenya.com), as part of a dinner package including a hotel pick-up and dhow cruise for $75, or just the dinner and show at Fort Jesus for $55.

Fort Jesus Museum

The **museum**, on the eastern side of the fort where the main soldiers' barracks block used to be, is small, but still manages to convey a good idea of the age and breadth of Swahili civilization, and also has a decent display of Mijikenda ethnography (see p.466). Most of the displays are of pottery, indigenous or imported, some from as far afield as China and some of it over a thousand years old. A number of private collections have contributed pieces and there's probably still a wealth of material in private hands. Look out for the big carved door taken from the Mazrui house in Gazi (p.487) and also the extraordinary whale vertebra used as a stool. The museum has a good exhibit on the long-term project to recover as much as possible from the wreck of the *Santo Antonio de Tanna*, which sank in 1697 while trying to break the prolonged siege of the fort. Some 7000 objects have already been brought to the surface, but the bulk of the ship itself remains nine fathoms deep in the harbour.

The Old Town

From Fort Jesus, the **Old Town** is an easy objective. If you've got the time and the inclination for in-depth exploration, pick up a copy of the guidebook *The Old Town Mombasa*, published by the Friends of Fort Jesus and available there as well as in some bookshops (see "Listings", p.447). It has a good map, and loads of information on architecture, history and distinguished past residents.

First impressions – of a quarter entirely devoted to gift and **curio shops** – are none too encouraging. But this turns out to be purely the result of Fort Jesus' adjacent car park and tourist appeal, and the shops don't extend far into the Old Town. They are especially ostentatious down at the end of Ndia Kuu Road, where several emporiums are overwhelmingly luxuriant in their displays and multilingual enticements; one or two of them even provide free coffee. Many sell a lot of worthless junk and some deal in shells, including shell lamp stands, orna-ments and the like, a trade which operates on the fringes of the law in Kenya, and threatens marine wildlife. Further west, away from the fort, the stores are smaller, and correspondingly cheaper and less pretentious, with a couple of genuine antique shops along Kibokini Road. For more about buying crafts, see p.444.

The Old Town is not, in fact, that old. Most buildings date from the nineteenth century, and though there may be foundations and even walls that go back many centuries, you'll get a clearer guide to the age of the town from its twenty or so **mosques**.

The **Mandhry Mosque** on Bachawy Road, founded in 1570, is officially the oldest; rarely open to visitors, it has a striking minaret. The **Basheikh Mosque** on Old Kilindini Road, painted in green and white, is also acknowledged to be very old – "about 1300", they'll tell you, though this may be exaggerated. Entering the mosques – as long as they aren't locked – is usually all right for men if they are properly dressed (no shorts) and take their shoes off. Sometimes they may be expected to wash hands and feet. Women, however modestly dressed, will as often as not be politely refused.

Much of the other **architecture** in the Old Town is profoundly influenced by the Indian-style Zanzibari tastes of the Busaidi occupiers of the nineteenth century. This is particularly noticeable in the elegant fretwork balconies and shutters still maintained on a few houses, notably on Ndia Kuu. For older relics, you'll have to look further. There are a number of quite ancient tombs along the seafront, especially towards the northern end of the Old Town, some of which have pillars; this is the part of Mombasa considered to be "medieval", or in other words pre-Portuguese.

Returning south along the twisting **seafront road** ("seafront", although the harbour can only be glimpsed), you come to the gigantic mosque of the Bohra Muslims: "Burhani Masjid for Dawoodi Bohra Community", says the sign. In the unassuming setting of the Old Town, it is an imposingly massive edifice.

The dhow harbour

The **dhow harbour** is wildly overrated. There are usually a few boats in port but you can no longer expect to see dozens, let alone hundreds, of dhows, even at the end of the northeast monsoon in April, traditionally the peak time for arrivals. Seasonal variations are less important now that the big *jahazis* have engines. Nor are you likely to have the opportunity to go aboard one of these exotic vessels – a tourist tradition, with coffee and souvenirs, that has died out. Instead, try to imagine how it must once have looked, chat to the policemen standing around, and check with them before raising your camera (the harbour is sometimes considered a strategically sensitive subject). In fact, you might consider concealing it: muggings and other hassles are not uncommon. Attempting to travel by dhow from Mombasa is, regrettably, an equally discouraging story. Lamu holds more promise (see box on p.543).

The Jain temple

Heading up towards Digo Road, you might enjoy stopping by at the **Jain temple**, whose entrance is in Langoni Road (daily 10am–12.30pm; free; remove shoes and anything made of leather, and women are requested not to enter during their monthly period). This sublime creation – intricate icing sugar outside, scrupulously clean and scented within and decorated in dozens of pastel shades – was only built in 1963. Jainism is an Indian religion contemporary with Buddhism and commonest in Gujarat (home of the majority of Kenyan Asians), which holds all life to be sacred. The Jain faith prohibits the eating of any kind of animal – in its extreme form, even root vegetables are taboo – and aspires to release adherents from the physical universe and its eternal cycle of death and rebirth. The temple interior is ornamentally magnificent: the painted figurines of deities in their niches are each provided with a drain so they can be easily showered down, while around the ceiling, exquisitely stylized pictures portray scenes from a human life, including a familiar snake temptation in a garden.

Walks around Mombasa

For the most part, the rest of Mombasa's pleasures are simple. Strolling, with plenty of cold-drink stops, is a time-honoured Mombasan diversion. You will probably want to see that immortal pair of **elephant tusks** on Moi Avenue. To get to them, you have to run the gauntlet of curio booths that have almost hidden the cool hideaway of Uhuru Gardens on the right, with its Africa-shaped fountain. And when you get there, you may regret your determination to view the tusks close up: they are revealed as grubby aluminium.

More rewarding, if you have the time and inclination for a **long walk**, is the circuit that takes off around the breezy, seaward side of the island down **Mama Ngina Drive**: a fine morning's or evening's walk, when it seems to become the meeting place for half of Mombasa's Indian population. You can get back to town on a matatu from the market by Likoni ferry. There are lots of places to sit and watch the waves pounding the coral cliffs through the break in the reef. On the clifftop, protruding from the far side of the **golf course** (Mombasa Golf Club ☏041/2228531, @mombasagolf@wananchi.com; KGU affiliates Ksh1200, others Ksh1500), are the stumpy, insignificant remains of Fort St Joseph, built in 1826 to defend Mazrui Mombasa against the attacks of the Busaidi Omanis. Come down this clifftop promenade at weekends or in the early evening and you'll find plenty of other people doing the same – there are even food stalls in several places. At the end of Mama Ngina is an extensive and surprising forest of enormous **baobab trees**, frequently associated with ancient settlements on the coast.

Finally, to the west of the Likoni ferry roundabout is a huge pillar tomb, the **Mbaraki Pillar**. Supposedly the burial place of a seventeenth-century mainland sheikh, chief of one of the "twelve tribes", its eight-metre height is impressive enough, but it is nevertheless dwarfed by the towers of the nearby molasses refinery.

Eating

The city is full of places to eat, and **street food** is much better – and more available – than in Nairobi. During the day, you can get green coconuts (drink the coconut water, then scrape out and eat the jelly-like flesh); sugar-cane juice, freshly wrung from the cane; and cuplets of *kahawa thungu* (thick bitter coffee, usually flavoured with ginger).

By the bus stalls up Abdel Nasser Road and along Jomo Kenyatta Avenue and Mwembe Tayeri Road, you'll also find *miraa*. Street stalls farther afield, along Nyerere Avenue for example, sell freshly fried potato and cassava crisps. Many stalls (mostly open at night) offer what amount to full meals for under Ksh100, including *nyama choma* (roast meat), *muhogo wa nazi*, *samaki wa kupaka*, *chapatti*, *marondo*, and pilau. Try the spicy little kebabs (sometimes chicken, and called "chicken tikka" anyway). Some also sell cigarettes, sodas, and *miraa*. As well as around the bus termini on Abdel Nasser Road and along Jomo Kenyatta Avenue, you'll find them outside *Casablanca Day & Night Club*, nearby on Mnazi Moja Road, at the junction of Nkrumah, Digo and Moi Avenue at *Salambo Disco*, and further north on Digo Road outside the market.

Restaurants

Mombasa is well supplied with good, **cheap restaurants**. Especially if you're newly arrived from upcountry, they are one of the city's chief delights, as a discernible cuisine involving coconut, fish, chicken, rice and beans, incorporating spicy Asian flavours, begins to make an impression on your palate. Unfortunately, many Swahili restaurants have closed down, but you'll still find some excellent places stretched out along the north coast, and easily accessible by 24-hour matatus from outside the GPO: the best of these have been listed on p.453 (Nyali) and p.458 (Bamburi to Shanzu). The best seafood restaurant by a long way is *Tamarind* on the mainland side of Nyali Bridge (see p.453). Phone numbers are given in the reviews when it's usually a good idea to book. The places covered below appear on the Central Mombasa map except where noted.

Swahili food

Island Dishes Kibokoni St. Wonderful Swahili dishes, including vegetables with coconut, fish with coconut (often unavailable), *mkate wa kima* ("Swahili pizza"), and a selection of seasonal fruit juices, with mango and chilli sauce on the table to spice it up if you like it hot, and also sometimes tamarind in case you prefer it sweet and sour. There's a second branch about to open on Nkrumah Rd.

Recoda Moi Ave, near the Tusks. One of the oldest and most famous Swahili restaurants in Mombasa, now sadly stripped of everything that gave it any character, and revamped as a sterile generic diner. The food is good and cheap, but much the same as you can find anywhere else in town – *pilaus*, biriani, chicken tikka, plus a few special Swahili dishes if you're lucky. Daily 8.30am–midnight; closed Ramadan.

Tarboush Café Makadara Rd. Open-air eating and a great spot for grills, with shawarma, shish kebab, "chicken tikka" and curries plus good naan bread and gorgeous juices. If you like meat, this is an excellent place to check out the African-Indian-Arabic combination that makes up the local cuisine.

Fast food and hotelis

Aridi Four Hospital St. Bright and breezy cafeteria serving basic meals, snacks, all-day breakfast and good passionfruit juice.

Baron Digo Rd. Really more of a beer hall than a restaurant, though the beer isn't the cheapest in town, but there's decent food at moderate prices, with pizzas, grills and fish dishes (around Ksh300–400 a meal).

Blue Fin Meru Rd. Fish or chicken and chips, and other reasonably priced fry-ups, plus juices, and daily specials, but portions are small. Closed Sun.

Blue Room Haile Selassie Rd. Self-service with lots of spotless tiled tables, fans and a cool courtyard. Very Western, with a menu dominated by burgers and pizzas, plus a few vegetarian choices.

Lotus Hotel Corner of Mvita and Cathedral roads. Clean and efficient, with steaks, grills and curries;

the food is generally well cooked (though the goat can be a plateful of bones) and the chef is willing to do anything not already on the menu given a day's notice. Expect to pay around Ksh400 for a meal.

Mombasa City Dishes Turkana St. Cheap and cheerful diner, with lots of stews and basic Kenyan dishes in large servings at low prices.

Mombasa Village Mji Mpya Rd. Very popular open-air beer and barbecue spot, with live music and grilled meat by the kilo (minimum order half a kilo), including beef, lamb, pork chops and goat ribs, but you have to wait a while for them to cook it.

Indian cooking

Indo Africa Haile Selassie Rd. North Indian non-veg, and rather more expensive than the adjacent *New Chetna*. Decor notable for being absent, though the food is reliably good (and less fiercely spicy than *New Chetna's*). Try the prawn or fish masala, or *muttar paneer* (cooked, home-made cheese with peas) for vegetarians. Easily Ksh500 and up. Noon–2.30pm & 7–10.30pm, closed Tues evening.

New Chetna Haile Selassie Rd. A long-time favourite for tasty Gujarati vegetarian dishes at low prices. The eat-all-you-can vegetarian *thali* (Ksh270) is superb, and the lunchtime buffet (Ksh240) is also pretty good. If you don't like chilli, be aware that the food can be very hot, so treat with caution. Daily 8am–9.30pm for sweets and *pan*, noon–2.30pm & 6–9.30pm for meals.

Safir Maungano Rd. Indian and Swahili food in a small dining room or at one or two pavement tables. Curries, biriani and *pilau* for under Ksh200.

Shehnai Restaurant Fatemi House, Maungano Rd ☎ 041/2312492. Mughlai specialities with a good reputation, in a spacious and light interior with somewhat regal furniture. You're spoilt for choice (100 dishes): try *achar gosht* (tender mutton cooked in spices and flavoured with pickles), or *machi tandoorwalli* – rock cod marinated in spices and grilled in a clay oven. Vegetarian around Ksh450, non-veg Ksh650. Noon–2pm & 7–10.30pm, closed Mon.

Singh Restaurant Mwembe Tayari Rd ☎041/493283. A bit of a walk from the centre of town, but very tasty Punjabi curries when you get there. Noon–2.30pm & 7–10.30pm, closed Mon.

Splendid View Restaurant Maungano Rd. Fish and prawn dishes with butter or garlic are the speciality here, and very tasty they are too, at around Ksh300 a throw. Mon–Sat 11am–2pm & 4.30–10.30pm, Sun 5–10.30pm.

Stavrose Café Sheikh Jundani Rd/Maungano Rd. A small place that's been serving Indian snacks, tikka dishes and kebabs for years. Lunches around Ksh150–200. Mon–Fri 9am–7.30pm, Sat 9am–3pm.

Foreign cuisines

Galaxy Chinese Archbishop Makarios Rd, off the far end of Moi Ave (see Mombasa Island map) ☎041/2226132. Good Chinese food, though relatively pricey – if you want to be extravagant, try the pan-fried lobster with ginger and garlic. Branches on Diani Beach and Bamburi Beach. Daily 11am–2.30pm & 6–11pm.

Hamburger House Kisumu Rd, just past the Tusks off Moi Ave. Well above average, with an extensive menu.

New Overseas Moi Ave, 200m west of the Tusks ☎041/2230729–30. Excellent-value Cantonese and Korean cooking, focusing on seafood, with some more expensive specialities including steamed crab, tuna fish *sashimi*, and *kimchi* (spicy pickled cabbage) soup, all at around Ksh400–700. Daily 11am–3pm & 5.30–11pm.

Snacks and juice bars

For **snacking**, and the **drinks** you'll probably want to consume ceaselessly, there are corner cafés, hole-in-the-wall juice bars, and confectionery shops all over town.

Anglo-Swiss Bakery Chembe Rd. A good place for bread, cakes and pastries, but best in the morning, around 10am.

Dil-Bahar Pan House Digo Rd, at the corner of Bungoma Street. Indian snacks, *pan* (see below), excellent *chai* and good juices including melon and watermelon, occasionally even custard apple. A lovely calm refuge for a few hours, or a place to read the paper.

Fayaz Bakery Jomo Kenyatta Ave. A good range of cakes and biscuits, with a fair stab at Western

favourites like cheesecake and doughnuts as well as local specialities such as passion cake.

Mombasa Coffee House Moi Ave. The Kenya Coffee Board's elderly establishment does filter coffee, pineapple pie, and good breakfasts.

Pistachio Chembe Rd. It's hard to beat this snack bar for the quality of its ice cream and various kinds of coffee, but it isn't cheap.

Taheri Cold Drinks House Nkrumah Rd. Juices, samosas, sausages, meat pies and kebabs. Good for a snack, but closed weekends.

Pan shops

Highly characteristic of Mombasa are the Indian **pan shops**, often doubling as tobacconists and corner shops. Worth trying at least once, *pan* is a natural digestive and stimulant (not as strong as *miraa*), chewed and sucked but not swallowed. Its main ingredient is a chopped or shredded betel nut (from the areca palm), which is flavoured with your choice of sweet spices, chopped nuts and vegetable matter, syrup, and white lime, from a display of dishes, all wrapped in a hot-sweet, dark green leaf (which really does come from the betel vine). Tobacco is optional, but best avoided by novices. Pop the triangular parcel in your mouth and munch – it tastes as exotic and unlikely as it sounds – spitting out juice as you go. Two of the best *pan* counters in town are at the *Dil-Bahar* café (see above) and the *New Chetna* restaurant (see p.441).

Drinking and nightlife

Despite the city's overwhelmingly Muslim population, you won't go thirsty. There are several **nightclubs** too, though you might not guess as much during the day. Always check bills carefully as mistakes are increasingly common.

If you don't fancy joining the clubbing throng, then a stroll around the generally safe Old Town will uncover one or two **coffee-sellers** serving black *kahawa* from traditional high-spouted jugs. A perfect accompaniment to the coffee is perfumed almond *halwa*. This is a local speciality, not the sesame sweet of the Middle East, but more akin to the gelatinous Indian sweet of the same name, or to Turkish delight, though Kenyan *halwa* is superior to either; one of the best places to buy it is *Fatma Halwa Shop* at the corner of Langoni and Old Kilindini roads, which is open till 1am daily except Sunday.

Bars

Casablanca Mnazi Moja Rd, just off Moi Ave. This draws a big mixed crowd to a lively terrace, and the prostitutes gather here in force, especially upstairs. They can be a pain – or a laugh – depending on your mood. Cold beers, some (usually good) food, rooms by the hour, or even for the whole night. Food and drinks expensive by local standards.

Excellent Hotel Next door to the hotel, a large and cool old-timers' place, with food as well as beer. Unhustly, and no prostitutes.

Lotus Hotel One of the nicest places in town for a civilized beer, with a comfortable open-air bar as well as an air-conditioned one.

New Palm Tree A calm and cool, if somewhat dull, bar, where you can drink at some of the lowest prices in the town centre.

Sky Bar Moi Ave. Not exactly the place for a quiet drink: there's lots of action, gay as well as straight. You can't avoid company, as the prostitutes are out in force.

Nightclubs and live music

The major tourist hotels are situated outside town and, consequently, so are the flashiest **discos**, though the hotel discos themselves are generally pretty dull: for details of the best of the rest, read the "Nightlife" sections on p.453 (Nyali), and p.458 (Bamburi and Shanzu). This, unfortunately, leaves Mombasa itself depleted of hi-tech action, and few bands find it worthwhile to play on the island when the resorts pay more. Most of Mombasa's older-style nightclubs at the more disreputable, dock end of Moi Avenue have passed away. The recommendations given below are established and enjoyable. On busy nights (Wed, Fri & Sat), men are charged up to Ksh200 entry, while women are admitted half-price or free. The places below appear on the Central Mombasa map, except for *Jam Rescue Hotel*, *New Florida Nightclub* and *Saba-Saba*, which are shown on the Mombasa Island map.

Jam Rescue Hotel Moi Ave 400m west of the Tusks, at the corner with Liwatoni Rd. Traditional Kikuyu and Swahili music Wed, Fri and Sat nights.

New Florida Nightclub & Casino Mama Ngina Drive, overlooking the ocean. Attempts a slick scene, with a floor show and lots of glitter, but everyone knows what it's really for. While in the essentials it doesn't seem to differ noticeably from its Nairobi namesake – thumping disco, grinding hookers – it does benefit from the terrace by the sea, a pleasant little gaming room (free entry until 7.30pm; open from 6pm) and keg beer. It's 2km from the centre, so take a taxi here, or at least back.

Saba-Saba Corner of Jomo Kenyatta Ave and Ronald Ngala Rd. The bar at the front isn't very inspiring, but head out to the open terrace at the back, which is where the action is. There's often

live music, even in the day, and always a sweaty, local atmosphere.

Salambo Moi Ave. Open during the day as a dozy bar with very limited snacks, this comes to life at night as the city's only really local disco, with no panderings to tourists or to glitzy style (wonky hallway mirrors excepted). Mon to Sat there's a mix of Congolese sounds, soul and reggae, with midnight shows, acrobats, dancing and beauty contests. Open 24hr.

Toyz Baluchi St, behind the post office. Mixed feedback on this, central Mombasa's main club with professional DJs and a/c, plus drinks that become more expensive as the night wears on, and a good mix of sounds. Wed, Fri and Sat nights are packed, but other nights can be deserted. Generally hassle-free, and also gay-friendly.

Shopping

Mombasa is a good city for **shopping**, with a generally wide choice, and fewer hassles as you window-shop than in Nairobi. Once you know where to go for crafts, the business of buying souvenirs improves markedly. For cloth, Mombasa is blessed with Biashara Street.

The main tourist street, as you'll soon discover, is the stretch of Moi Avenue between the Tusks and Digo Road – a number of the retail businesses here are housed in premises going back to the early twentieth century. However, it's hard to take in the architecture when the pavement is lined with souvenir stalls. Sisal baskets, soapstone, beadwork and fake ebony carvings make up eighty percent of the wares. Those at the Digo Road end of Moi Avenue tend to be the most aggressive at touting their wares, and getting past without stopping is not easy while, if you do halt, making cool decisions can be fraught. The line of stalls on **Chembe Road** seems to be in something of a backwater, and they're more fun to deal with.

If you're **buying crafts** in Mombasa, whatever else you do, first go and have a look at ⚘ Harria's Gift Shop on Moi Avenue, near the Tusks (Mon–Sat 9am–6pm; credit cards accepted). It consistently offers good deals and you may even be able to get things here more cheaply than on the street. Its back room is also worth checking out. Labeka, also on Moi Avenue (Mon–Fri 8.30am–5.30pm, Sat 9am–5.30pm), is another good store for browsing, with sensible prices and a pleasant, hassle-free environment.

The usual rules apply when **bargaining** – don't start the ball rolling if you're not in the mood and never offer a price you're not prepared to pay. If you want quite a few items, it's worth browsing for a well-stocked stall and then, as you reach one near-agreement after another with the stallholder, add a new item to your collection. This way you should be able to buy well-finished *vyondo* (sisal

△ Shopping on Digo Road

baskets) in the range of Ksh600–1000, small soapstone items for Ksh150–500, and simple bracelets and necklaces for a similar price. It's impossible to estimate what you'll pay for carvings as the price depends as much on the workmanship as on the size of the piece. If you expressly *don't* want to purchase ebony (the wood is increasingly rare), you'll run into some amusing conversational one-way streets with stallholders who are a dab hand at "proving" their lumps of dyed acacia wood are ebony.

Markets

For a return to earth, visit Mombasa's municipal market, **Mackinnon Market**, which has a splendid abundance of tropical fruit, including such exotics as jackfruit (too big for most people at around 10 kilos, but you can buy it by the segment along Langoni Road) and soursops (like a bigger, tarter version of a custard apple). Behind the market is a row of stores devoted to spices, coffee and tea and several good sweet shops. Apart from the Mackinnon and the big street market off Mwembe Tayari, there's **Makupa market** in the heart of Majengo, the island's low-income housing district. A colourful, multipurpose market with a busy, rural atmosphere, it's well worth a visit. Go 1.5km up Jomo Kenyatta Avenue, then turn left at Salim Mwa Ngunga Road.

Cloth and hardware

Mombasa is also a cheap place to buy the **fabrics** the coast is famous for. Check out the latest *kanga* designs in **Biashara Street** (especially the section between George Morura Street and Digo Road), where they are usually available before anywhere else in Kenya. *Kangas* are distinguished from *kitenges* in that they also carry a printed message, whether "Jambo from Kenya" for the tourists, or more subtle proverbs and sayings in Swahili, still used as a means of communicating messages, either from a husband buying the cloth for his wife or mother-in-law, or by a wife to her husband. Some of the home-produced patterns are so good – unusual combinations of brilliant fast colours used to startling effect – they are beginning to make an impact abroad, though prices are usually higher than for imports (Ksh1200 for a pair of cotton *kitenge*, for example, as opposed to Ksh350 for an Indian or Pakistani version). Synthetic (nylon) cloth is much cheaper, around Ksh250 for *kangas*, Ksh300 for *kikois*, and Ksh500 for Maasai-style checkered wraps. You can also have clothes made to measure (around Ksh800 for a dress, for example). It's worth checking prices in several shops before buying, and perhaps going with company so you can bargain for several lots at once: they are always sold in pairs. In the high season, Biashara Street swarms with other tourists looking for "the real Mombasa", so you'll need all your haggling skills; it's actually quite difficult to budge prices more than a token Ksh40–50 for the sake of politeness, as business is just too good.

Beyond Mackawi Road, Biashara Street shifts from textiles to a less gaudy section of **household goods**, such as winnowing trays, coconut graters, palm bags, mats, spoons and furniture. It's more mundane, but just as interesting to browse. For genuine Indian **sarongs**, have a rummage through the Old Town.

Music

If you harbour even a passing interest in African **music**, Mombasa is as good a place as any to stock up on a few tapes or CDs. Prices are low: expect to pay between Ksh150 and Ksh180 for a cassette (for imported big names these are invariably low-quality pirates – copies of *Taarab* and traditional music are more likely to be legit), and anything from Ksh200 to Ksh1000 for a CD, depending on how kosher the copy is.

The best place for finding traditional Mijikenda music and Mombasan *taarab*, as well as traditional songs from the Wa-Bajuni of Lamu district, is Mbwana Radio Service (℡041/2221550), just off Pigott Place in the Old Town. You'll find popular African dance tunes from Kenya and the Congo as well as reggae and US soul divas in the street stalls all around town, especially in the streets between Biashara Street and Haile Selassie Road towards Digo Road – just follow your ears. Kikuyu and other Kenyan sounds, as well as ubiquitous gospel pop (sugary church hymns, basically) are available from the more permanent stuctures: try Zilizopendwa Music Store, a small shop just off Raha Leo Street behind the old market.

Safari operators

Mombasa is increasingly important as a **safari hub**, though for safaris further out, it's easier and cheaper to organize a trip from Nairobi (pp.149–152). **Renting a car** for an independent safari, prices tend to be a little cheaper in Mombasa than in Nairobi if you deal with a local company (Ksh3500–4500 per day for a small saloon rented over a week, including insurance and waivers), but the big multinationals remain expensive (Ksh4000–5000). See "Listings" opposite for details of companies.

There are various **safari** possibilities from Mombasa. You can visit Shimba Hills National Park (see p.470) on a day-trip (around $65), or overnight (around $160). Expect to pay $130 for a one-day safari (5am pick-up from your hotel) to Tsavo East, including lunch at *Voi Safari Lodge*, or $215 staying overnight. Air safaris, even to the Mara, are also quite feasible, though much more expensive (upwards of $500 for two days and one night), although only spending one night you run a higher risk of disappointing game drives. If you're going to **Lamu**, don't bother with inclusive arrangements: just take a flight there and sort out accommodation when you arrive. Many of the companies listed below also offer half-day **city tours** of Mombasa ($30–35). Things are much cheaper if you take public transport – full details are given throughout this chapter. The same applies to the much-touted overnight stays in Zanzibar: compare the $800 price for two nights all in with the regular $260 return airfare.

Abercrombie & Kent Fourth floor, Palli House, Nyerere Ave; PO Box 90747 ℡041/2222222, ✉info@akmombasa.co.ke. Impeccable reputation for luxurious tailor-made lodge tours. Expensive. KATO (Kenya Association of Tour Operators).

African Quest Safaris Mezzanine floor, Palli House, Nyerere Ave; PO Box 99265 ℡041/2227052, ⊛www.africanquest.co.ke. Large operator doing lodge safaris, from around $160 per day. KATO.

Farways Safaricentre Msanifu Kombo St; PO Box 87815 ℡041/2223307, ✉farways@africaonline.co.ke. Good value and personal service from a small, long-established company with an excellent network of operator contacts, including car rental, Zanzibar trips, accommodation bookings and safaris.

Kedev Off Links Rd, Nyali ℡041/5487356, ⊛www.kedev.de. Tailor-made safaris with a personal touch to Tsavo, Shimba Hills and beyond. Customers can also stay in Kedev's own guest-house in Nyali.

Pollman's Tours and Safaris Corner of Taveta Rd and Shimanzi Rd; PO Box 84198 ℡041/222 9082–4. City office on Moi Ave by *Mombasa Coffee House*. One of the biggest (you'll see its vehicles everywhere): reliable package-tour safaris. Lodge safaris from $160 per day.

Somak Holidays Somak House, Mombasa–Malindi Highway, Bamburi; PO Box 90738 ℡041/548 6197, ✉info@mombasa.somak-nairobi.com. Dependable upmarket operation. KATO.

Southern Cross Safaris Kanstan Centre, Nyali Bridge; PO Box 90653 ℡041/475074–6, ⊛www .southerncrosssafaris.com. Branch of the well-respected Nairobi company also agents for *Satao Camp* in Tsavo East. KATO.

Special Lofty Safaris First floor, Hassanali Building, Nkrumah Rd; PO Box 81933 ℡041/2220241, ⊛www.lofty-tours.de. Conscientious operator running its own safaris. Prefers you taking the more expensive but still well-priced "made to order" trips, though can run camping safaris from about $120 per day. The main draw is its experience and its land cruisers (a more personal way of travelling than by Nissan minibus, though it has these too). KATO.

UTC Moi Ave, corner of Bunju Rd; PO Box 84782

Listings

Airline companies Condor, c/o Atlantis Travel Services, Jubilee Insurance Building, Moi Ave ☎041/2221461, ✉service@atlantis.co.ke; Kenya Airways, Electricity House, Nkrumah Rd ☎041/2221251–9; Mombasa Air Safari, Moi Airport ☎041/3433061 or 3434265, ⊛www.mombasaairsafari.com.

American Express c/o Express Travel Group, Makena House, Nkrumah Rd, PO Box 90631 ☎041/2228081–3, ⊛www.etg-safaris.com.

Banks The best rates are at any of the numerous foreign exchange bureaux springing up around the city, but you will usually need your purchase receipt when changing traveller's cheques, and few accept Visa cards. Pwani Forex, Digo Rd opposite Mackinnon Market, is efficient and seems to give the best rates for traveller's cheques (Mon–Fri 8.30am–5pm, Sat 8.30am–1pm). Of the banks, the speediest is the Commercial Bank of Africa, Moi Ave (Mon–Fri 8.30am–2.30pm). Otherwise, you'll find branches of Barclays, most with ATM machines for Visa cards, throughout the city (Mon–Fri 9am–3pm, first and last Sat of the month 9–11am). Standard Chartered bank also has ATMs at its Maritime House (Moi Ave) and Treasury Square branches. Co-op Bank is on Nkrumah Rd; Postbank is east of the Tusks on Moi Ave. On Sundays you'll have to go to the airport to find a forex bureau open, unless you fancy your chances with the black market money changers hanging around the corner of Moi Ave and Digo Rd (usual rules apply: don't let them take you down a dark alley, in a shop is best, never hand over your bucks until you have the shillings in your hand and have counted them, and don't be put off checking by the old "quick, quick, the police are coming" ploy).

Bicycles Mombasa has no bike rental, but buying one is cheap enough: Omar Hussein on Haile Selassie Rd near Maungano Rd (Mon–Sat 8.30am–1pm & 2–6pm; ☎041/2225899) has a good selection. A one-speed Indian roadster costs Ksh3200, with mountain bikes upwards of Ksh5000.

Bookshops Mombasa has few compared with Nairobi, and most only stock schoolbooks and stationery. Kant Stationers, on Moi Ave, and Citizen's Bookshop, at the corner of Jomo Kenyatta Ave and Joe Kadenge St, are the best. There are

☎041/2229840, ⊛www.unitedtouring.com. This "ground operator" makes the bulk of its business in providing transport and drivers for other companies, but also offers a selection of reasonably priced, tried and tested itineraries. KATO.

also quite a few stalls around town selling used books. For maps, the best place is Harria's Gift Shop on Moi Ave.

Bus company booking offices Most are spread along Abdel Nasser Rd and Jomo Kenyatta Ave. The main ones are: Akamba Bus, Jomo Kenyatta Ave ☎041/3490269 or 3492696; Busscar, Abdel Nasser Rd ☎041/2222854; Coast Bus, Mwembe Tayari Rd opposite Kobil ☎041/2220158; Falcon, Jomo Kenyatta Ave, opposite Kobil ☎041/4900776; Le Coach, Abdel Nasser Rd opposite *New People's Hotel* ☎0722/981754; Linear, Jomo Kenyatta Ave ☎041/2311033; Ocean Line, Abdel Nasser Rd ☎0722/238503; Tawakal, Abdel Nasser Rd ☎0733/821218; TSS, Digo Rd, opposite *Dil-Bahar Pan House* (no phone).

Car rental Avenue Motors, Moi Ave ☎041/2225126, ✉avenue@africaonline.co.ke; Avis, Nkrumah Rd ☎041/2220465, ✉avismsa@wananchi.com, also at Moi Airport ☎041/243 5098; Budget, Kenyatta Ave ☎041/2221281, ☎2221282; Southern Cross Safaris, Kanstan Centre, Nyali Bridge, PO Box 90653 ☎041/475074–6, ⊛www.southerncrosafaris.com; Hertz, Moi Airport ☎041/3432405, ✉msa@hertz.co.ke; Kedev Car Hire, off Links Rd, Nyali ☎041/5487356, ✉kedev@africaonline.co.ke; Kuldip's Car Hire, Mji Mpya Rd ☎041/2223780, ✉Kuldipstr@form-net.com; National Car Rental, Harbour House, Moi Ave ☎041/2221358, ✉natcarma@africaonline.co.ke; Special Lofty Safaris, first floor, Hassanali Building, Nkrumah Rd ☎041/2220241, ⊛www.lofty-tours.de; Unik Car Hire and Safaris Fatemi Building, Maungano Rd ☎041/2314864, ☎2311384.

Cinemas The Kenya, Nkrumah Rd, is the most promising. Otherwise, try the Lotus on Makadara Rd. Both survive on a diet of Indian epics and love stories, with a few American films thrown in.

Consulates Canada c/o Mr N. Tejpar, Farways Safaris, Msanifu Kombo St ☎041/2223307 or 9, ✉farways@africaonline.co.ke; India c/o Mr D.S. Rana, Bank of India Building, Nkrumah Rd ☎041/2224433, ✉cimsa@swiftmombasa.com; Netherlands c/o Mrs B.R. Patalia, ABN-AMBRO Bank, Nkrumah Rd ☎041/2221291–2, ✉nedconsulate@wananchi.com; Seychelles c/o Mrs M. Sonon ☎041/2224923, ✉mason2001ke@yahoo.com; Tanzania twelfth floor, TSS Tower, Nkrumah Rd ☎041/2228595, ✉tancon@africaonline.co.ke (Mon–Fri 8am–3pm, visas for most nationalities issued while you wait, requiring $50 and two passport photos); UK c/o Mr James Knight, Seaforth Shipping, Cotts House, second floor, Moi Ave ☎2313776–7, ✉jknight@africaonline.co.ke; USA c/o Mr N.K. Mudukitsa, Moi Airport ☎041/3433943, ✉nmudukit@wananchi.com.

Courier services DHL, Ukumbusho House, Treasury Square, Nkrumah Rd ☎041/2223933, 📠2227837; FedEx, Diamond Trust Arcade, Moi Ave ☎041/2228631; UPS, New Nairobi Rd, Changamwe ☎041/2221703.

Dhow cruises Jahazi Marine Ltd (PO Box 89357 ☎041/548501–5, 🌐www.severin-kenya.com) does "cultural trips" ($50), sailing around Mombasa in the morning, with lunch at its otherwise expensive *Jahazi Restaurant* overlooking Tudor Creek, and the afternoon at the floating market, visiting a traditional herbalist and dhow builder. It also offers "Mombasa by Night" dhow cruises ($75 per person), including a son-et-lumière performance at Fort Jesus, and a French-style lobster dinner inside served by waiters dressed up as Portuguese, supposedly to remind you of the good old days when the only tourists were heavily armed raiders. Dining cruises are offered by the *Tamarind Dhow*, PO Box 99456 ☎041/474600, 🌐www.tamarind-dhow.com, run by the *Tamarind Restaurant* in Nyali (see p.453), with lunch and dinner sailings at $32 and $70 per person respectively.

Golf Mombasa Golf Club (see p.440); Nyali Golf and Country Club (see p.452).

Hospitals Pandya Memorial Hospital, Dedan Kimathi Ave (☎041/2313577 or 2313894), is hygienic and efficient, and has an ambulance service, as does St John's Ambulance Service (☎041/2490625). If you're planning to be out in the wilds a lot, Africa Air Rescue (AAR), Harbour House, Moi Ave (☎041/2226697 to join, 230035–7 in an emergency) offers short-term membership of its "flying doctors" scheme (see p.49).

Immigration You can get visitor's pass extensions at the immigration office near Provincial Headquarters on Mama Ngina Drive (☎041/2311745), but leave enough time, as you always have to wait.

Internet access Many places around town at generally low rates (much the same as Nairobi), including Makdara Cyber Net and JN Cyber Garden on Makadara Rd, *Blue Fin*, *Mombasa Coffee House*, and a couple of places in the Jubilee Insurance Building on Moi Ave. Plenty of others.

Libraries Kenya National Library, Msanifu Kombo Rd (Mon–Thurs 8am–6.30pm, Fri 8am–4pm, Sat 8am–5pm); Fort Jesus Museum (archeology; Mon–Fri 8am–12.30pm & 2–4.30pm); British Council, Jubilee Insurance Building, Moi Ave (Tues–Fri 9am–7pm, Sat 10am–1pm; ☎041/2223076) – has a small a/c library with recent editions of British papers and temporary membership available (Ksh200 per day), but you'll need a passport or similar ID to even get to the door.

Luggage storage Apart from hotels, the only place to leave bags is the railway station, but the rates (Ksh100 per piece per day) seem excessive, and it's only open sporadically (usually when trains are arriving or departing).

Maps The best map in print is *The Streets of Mombasa Island* map (Coast Map Agencies, 2004; Ksh250), which shows all the streets on the island. The same publisher also puts out a *Map of Mombasa District* (2003; Ksh250), which covers the north coast up as far as Mtwapa, and the area around Likoni on the south coast. If you want a map of the whole coast, plus Shimba Hills National Park, your best bet is *The Kenya Coast & Shimba Hills* (Mt Kenya Studies, 1992; Ksh450), which shows the whole coast from the border with Tanzania up to the border with Somalia. They can all be bought from Harria's Gift Shop on Moi Ave. The Survey of Kenya hasn't produced a map of Mombasa since 1977.

Motorbike rental Pedo Bikes, Kongoni Rd, near Mamba Village roundabout on mainland north of Nyali Bridge ☎041/471193.

Pharmacies The staff at Diamond Arcade Pharmacy, Diamond Arcade, Diamond Trust Building, Moi Ave (Mon–Fri 8am–6pm, Sat 9am–2pm; ☎041/231 6351), are pleasant and helpful. Island Chemist, by *Josleejim Hotel* in Duruma Rd, is open late (Mon–Sat 8.30am–8.30pm, Sun 9am–8.30pm). There's no longer any 24hr cover in Mombasa: hospital dispensaries can supply necessary drugs and medicaments out of hours.

Post office (see also "Courier services"). The post office for *poste restante* and main services is the General Post Office (GPO) in Digo Rd, entrance in Makadara Road (Mon–Fri 8am–6pm, Sat 9am–noon). There is a long row of call boxes alongside the entrance.

Supermarkets A1 Supermarket, corner of Hospital St and Digo Rd (Mon–Sat 9am–7pm, Sun 9am–1pm); Bestlady, Digo Rd, opposite Haile Selassie Rd (Mon–Sat 8.30am–8pm, Sun 9am–7pm).

Swimming pools The only one in the city centre is at *Hotel Sapphire* (8am–8pm; Ksh200 adults, Ksh150 children). Further out, the Mombasa Women's Association, Nyerere Ave, halfway to the Likoni ferry, has a pool (schooldays 5–7pm; Sat,

Sun & school holidays 7am–6.30pm; Ksh100).

Taxis Kenatco (Ambalal House, Nkrumah Rd ☎041/2227503) runs reliable 24hr taxis with fixed prices to the beach hotels.

Theatre The Little Theatre Club (PO Box 81143; ☎041/2229258) on Mnazi Moja Rd used mainly to be an outlet for amateur dramatics in the expat/settler community, but of late it has been hosting productions by drama groups from all over the coastal region. Seats usually cost around Ksh200.

Vaccinations For yellow fever, you have to go first to the town hall and pay (Ksh600), and then to the Public Health Department in Msanifu Kombo St, opposite the end of Hospital Rd (Mon–Fri 8am–4.30pm, closed lunchtime). For typhoid and cholera jabs, you need to go and buy the vaccine at Makandara Chemist in Makandara Rd, then take it to the Public Health Department, where they'll stick it in your arm for free.

Worship The Catholic Holy Ghost Cathedral is on Nyerere Ave. The Anglican Memorial Cathedral is off Nkrumah Rd, down on the right near Fort Jesus. The main Hindu temple is the new Shiva Temple by Jamhuri Park; there is also a Swaminarayan temple on Haile Selassie Rd at the corner of Bajuni Rd. The main Sikh temple is on Mwembe Tayari Rd. There are mosques all over town.

Moving on from Mombasa

Matatus to most destinations north and west of Mombasa, including Bamburi and Shanzu beaches and Mtwapa Creek, can be caught anywhere along Digo Road. Matatus to Malindi congregate at the south end of Abdel Nasser Road, near the junction with Mackawi Road by the mosque. For Kaloleni and Voi, they leave from the Kobil station at the junction of Mwembe Tayari Road with Jomo Kenyatta Avenue. Chania Travellers (☎0722/964726) runs matatus to Nairobi from a kiosk by the Caltex garage at the eastern end of Mwembe Tayari Road, generally departing mornings only. The only international matatu service is across the border to Tanga with TangaOne, which runs one matatu a day from its stand near Akamba on Jomo Kenyatta Avenue.

The overnight **train** for Nairobi leaves three times a week (Tues, Thurs & Sun) at 7pm, arriving at around 9am, and costs Ksh3160 in first class, Ksh2275 in second, and Ksh400 in third. Dinner, breakfast and a bed are included in first and second class.

Flights

The only scheduled flight from Mombasa to anywhere beyond Kenya and Tanzania is with the no-frills German airline Condor three times weekly to Frankfurt, currently $576 one way, $696 with onward connection to London. There are also sometimes charter flights to Britain, which you might be able to get a seat on. Airline bookings can either be made direct (see "Listings", p.447), or – often more cheaply – through a travel agent. Vogue Tours & Travel, opposite the Anglican Cathedral on Nkrumah Road (☎041/2223592, @vogue_travel@yahoo.com) is reliable, and can advise on cheap international flights out of Nairobi. Note also that if you're headed for Tanzania, including Zanzibar, you'll need to have had a yellow fever jab (and the yellow passport that comes with it). Within Kenya, your most useful flights are with Kenya Airways to Nairobi, and with Mombasa Air Safari to Lamu. See "Travel details" p.554 for frequencies and journey times.

Buses

There are services to **Lamu**, **via Malindi and Kilifi** with TSS, Tawakal and Falcon, and to **Malindi via Bamburi**, **Kikambala and Kilifi** with Busscar and others, from Abdel Nasser Road.

Heading for **Nairobi and the west**, competition is fierce, but some operators are more reputable than others. The safest bus company is Akamba. The usual fare is Ksh800–900. The night journey can be cold: take warm clothes. Falcon, Coast Bus and Linear run beyond Nairobi to Western Kenya.

Airport departures

When you're due to leave, before setting off for **Mombasa airport**, check and double-check the departure time with the airport or the ground agent. Note that if you're coming from a South Coast hotel, it can take a surprisingly long time to cross on the Likoni ferry, get through the city and out the other side to the airport. If you really want to avoid all that, it is possible to arrange an air transfer to Mombasa airport from Diani's Ukunda airstrip with Diani Air (☏0725/804611, ✉dianiair@iafrica.com) for two or more people at €70 a head. A taxi from town currently costs Ksh700 with Sacco Airport Taxis (☏041/433211–20 ext 2405), and roughly the same with Kenatco (☏041/2227503), both of which have fixed rates. There are no buses or matatus to the airport, but a matatu from Jomo Kenyatta Avenue to Magongo will drop you less than a kilometre short. Once in the terminal, if you're travelling independently, or suspect you may be in the wrong queue, repeat your destination airport to everyone you deal with. **Departure tax** ($20 on international flights, including Zanzibar; Ksh895 for domestic flights) should be included in the price of your ticket. If flying out of the country, avoid having any quantity of Kenya shillings left to re-exchange as the rates are poor and the commission swingeing, though you are allowed back to the forecourt bank booths from the departure lounge. Note that the duty-free shop does not accept shillings, and anything Kenyan will be cheaper in town.

Be aware that tourists on coastal bus services, especially Mombasa to Malindi or Nairobi, have been targeted by thieves using drugged food and drink to render their victims unconscious. Do not accept food or drink from strangers.

International services to Tanzania are operated by Falcon, a company not known for its high safety record, though in reality using its services is no more dangerous than using a matatu; its daily bus to Dar es Salaam via Tanga leaves from the corner of Mwembe Tayari Road with Jomo Kenyatta Avenue. For **Uganda**, Falcon runs a daily bus to the border at Malaba, and Busscar runs one to Busia, but your safest bet is with Akamba to Kampala, twice daily changing at Nairobi.

See "Travel details", p.554, for journey times and frequencies, "Listings", p.447, for bus company contact details.

North of Mombasa

It's easy to get out of Mombasa for the day to explore the nearby **North Coast**. If it's busier, brasher, and generally less pastoral than the **South Coast**, there are also more targets for a day-trip up here, with correspondingly less appeal if you simply want to stretch out on the beach. The resorts start just ten minutes' drive from the city centre. Alternatively, without your own vehicle, there is ample transport from the Abdel Nasser Road bus and matatu area near the *New People's Hotel*. Or simply walk over to the other side of Nyali Bridge and flag down transport. You won't wait long.

Nyali and Nyali Beach

Nyali, the comfortable suburb of Mombasa closest to the town, has a few minor items of interest of its own – apart from three of the North Coast's main hotels. It was the site of **Johan Ludwig Krapf**'s first missionary toehold on the east coast, four years before Livingstone arrived in Africa. Krapf reached Nyali with his wife and baby daughter in May 1844. His wife died of malaria on July 13, their baby the next day. The pathetic graves – now rather overgrown – are to be found at the end of the road leading past the *Tamarind Restaurant* (see p.453) and a couple of cement silos. Opposite, on a small knoll, is the stone **Krapf Memorial**.

There's another reminder of Mombasa's history in the site of the **Freretown Bell**, at the Nyali Road junction. The bell was erected by the Society of Freed Slaves in the 1880s to warn the people of Freretown (named after Sir Bartle Frere, who founded the freed slave community here) of any impending attack by Arab slavers. The district still has inhabitants who trace the roots of their freed-slave ancestors back to Malawi and Zambia. The bell hung silently under its small stone arch until the 1920s when it was removed for safekeeping to the nearby Emmanuel Church (Freretown's parish church, erected in 1889), where it is still in use. The bell you see at the Nyali Road junction is a plastic replica.

Behind Nyali Beach and the hotels, you can't miss **Mamba Village** on Links Road (daily 8am–6.30pm; Ksh650, children Ksh350). Nothing to do with poisonous snakes, this is the biggest crocodile (*mamba*) farm in Kenya, with hefty entry fees to the "crocodile trail" and film show. A series of semi-natural pools, created in a disused quarry, houses many thousands of crocodiles at all stages of growth (and a special freaks sideshow of congenitally deformed croc-lets – not a pleasant sight). The overall

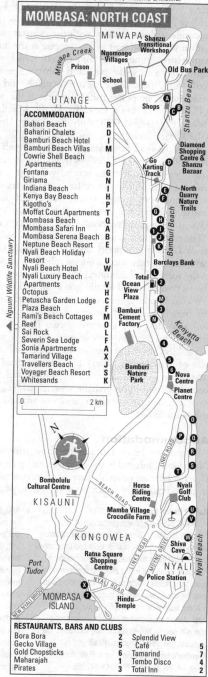

MOMBASA: NORTH COAST

Kikambala, Kilifi, Watamu & Malindi

MTWAPA

Shanzu Transitional Workshop

Ngomongo Villages

Prison

Old Bus Park

School

UTANGE

Shops

Shanzu Beach

Diamond Shopping Centre & Shanzu Bazaar

Go Karting Track

North Quarry Nature Trails

Bamburi Beach

Barclays Bank

Total

Ocean View Plaza

Bamburi Cement Factory

Kenyatta Beach

Bamburi Nature Park

Nova Centre

Planet Centre

Nguuni Wildlife Sanctuary

ACCOMMODATION

Bahari Beach	R
Baharini Chalets	D
Bamburi Beach Hotel	I
Bamburi Beach Villas	M
Cowrie Shell Beach Apartments	D
Fontana	G
Giriama	N
Indiana Beach	I
Kenya Bay Beach	H
Kigotho's	P
Moffat Court Apartments	T
Mombasa Beach	Q
Mombasa Safari Inn	A
Mombasa Serena Beach	B
Neptune Beach Resort	E
Nyali Beach Holiday Resort	U
Nyali Beach Hotel	W
Nyali Luxury Beach Apartments	V
Octopus	H
Petuscha Garden Lodge	C
Plaza Beach	F
Rami's Beach Cottages	M
Reef	O
Sai Rock	L
Severin Sea Lodge	F
Sonia Apartments	A
Tamarind Village	X
Travellers Beach	J
Voyager Beach Resort	S
Whitesands	K

0   2 km

Bombolulu Cultural Centre

KISAUNI

BEACH ROAD

Horse Riding Centre

Nyali Golf Club

Mamba Village Crocodile Farm

KONGOWEA

LINKS ROAD

Shiva Cave

Port Tudor

Ratna Square Shopping Centre

MOYNE DRIVE

NYALI

Nyali Beach

NYALI ROAD

Police Station

NEW NYALI BRIDGE

MOMBASA ISLAND

Hindu Temple

RESTAURANTS, BARS AND CLUBS

Bora Bora	2	Splendid View Café	5
Gecko Village	5	Tamarind	7
Gold Chopsticks	6	Tembo Disco	4
Maharajah	1	Total Inn	2
Pirates	3		

effect – with "croco-burgers" in the snack bar, the 5pm Pavlovian bell-ring feedings, and unlimited saurian souvenirs – is tacky in the extreme, and the crocodile trail sits uneasily with the skin-farming half of the "village", which is not on show. Also part of the empire is the adjacent **Botanical Garden and Aquarium** (same hours and ticket), which includes a thirty-minute guided walk around its snake park and gardens, specializing in the weirdest things it could find, including carnivorous plants and "fishes which blow up for not being eaten" (ie puffer fish). Also here is the *Mamba International Nightclub* (see p.453). Further down Links Road, the Mamba outfit now also offers **horse-riding** (℡041/3415778; daily 8am–5pm; 1hr beach trips Ksh950; lessons at Ksh200 for 30min).

Across the road from *Mamba Village* is **Nyali Golf and Country Club** (PO Box 95678; ℡041/471589, ℮nyaligolf@wananchi.com), a stuffy sort of place that doesn't go out of its way to welcome non-members. It maintains a dress code for men (shirts with collars, socks) in return for which it offers an ordinary swimming pool, squash, tennis (Ksh11,600 for a week's membership) and, of course, golf (free for members, Ksh2400–2600 for non-members, or Ksh1200–1300 if playing with a Nyali Club member; caddy Ksh200 for nine holes).

The main public access to the **beach** at Nyali is right by the entrance to *Nyali Beach Hotel*. It gets pretty busy at weekends. One oddity a little way south is a **cave** containing a natural *lingam* (phallic representation of the Hindu god Shiva) in the form of a stalacmite, plus a natural rock formation resembling Shiva's son, the elephant-headed Hindu god Ganesh. The area is maintained as a **temple** by the local Hindu Union, but visitors are welcome (remove shoes when entering the temple cave) and the site includes a pleasant ledge overlooking the ocean and a roofless cave containing two more Shiva *lingam* stalacmites. The story attached to the cave tells of a certain cow who was in the habit of rubbing her udders on the stalacmite to exude milk (pouring milk on the *lingam* is a way of worshipping Shiva). Her herder, afraid that the cow would damage her udders, hit her to get her to stop, upon which he was attacked by a swarm of bees. Admitted to hospital, he was treated by an Indian doctor who, hearing the story, decided to investigate, and was amazed to discover the Ganesh rock and the Shiva *lingam*.

Accommodation

All the larger hotels can arrange dhow trips, scuba and snorkelling, and trips to Nyali Golf Club, and in the evenings put on cheesy bands and other entertainment. Beaches here are generally narrow, often covered at high tide, and visitors are likely to be to pestered by beach boys. Taxis from Mombasa cost around Ksh600.

Bahari Beach Hotel PO Box 86693 ℡041/475456–62, ⓦwww.baharibeach.net. Formerly an African Safari Club place (still attracting mainly German clients), built in 1971 and refurbished in 1997, but lacks the character of more modern places, and can feel a little stuffy. In common with most Nyali hotels, rooms lack sea views (they overlook the manicured gardens instead) and the beach – at the bottom of a small cliff – is just a narrow strip of sand uncovered at low tide. Accommodation is in several two-storey blocks, and rooms are spacious and have balconies. HB ❽

Kigotho's Hotel (formerly *Roy's Pride Rock*), Links Rd; PO Box 86178 ℡041/472855,

℮kigothohotel@yahoo.com. A relatively cheap option set back from the coast (no view), this offers fourteen slightly tatty apartments (one-bedroom with double bed, two-bedroom with a double and two single beds) in separate blocks in the garden, all with fans, equipped with kitchenettes and fridges, and real baths as well as showers. There's also a small pool and a cheap bar-cum-*nyama choma* joint. ❹

Moffat Court Apartments Mt Kenya Rd; PO Box 34126 ℡041/473351, ⓦwww.africaonline. co.ke/moffatcourt. Turn right after Mamba Village. A dull modern three-storey block, but cheap, offering sixteen s/c suites, one- or two-bedroom (each bedroom with a double bed), and safe parking. Discounts for long stays, and negotiable low-season prices. ④

Mombasa Beach Hotel PO Box 90414 ☏041/471861–5, ℻472970, ⓦmombasabeach hotel.kenya-safari.co.ke; reservations through Kenya Safari Lodges & Hotels, p.63. Despite the clumsy 1970s architecture, there's a good atmosphere here – largely the result of its shady, clifftop location and the fact that it attracts many more African guests than its competitors. Facilities include tennis courts and two pools (one huge, the other down at the beach), plus the usual watersports. Lift access, but no specially designed disabled rooms. HB $200; ⑨

Nyali Beach Holiday Resort PO Box 1874 ☏041/472325, ⓔnbhr@wananachi.com. Terra-cotta-roofed Mediterranean-style development right on the beach, with two pools (one for children; Ksh400/Ksh200 for non-guests). Most of the sixteen rooms face both the pool and the beach, as do the self-catering apartments or "cottages" (two to six people; Ksh7500–15,000) equipped with kitchens. All rooms are large, s/c and clean, with a/c, nets and TVs. Much better views than *Nyali Beach* at a somewhat lower price. Restaurant and games room, safe parking. HB ⑥

🏃 **Nyali Beach Hotel** PO Box 90581 ☏041/471567–8, ⓔnyalisales@africaonline .co.ke; reservations through Block, p.63. Pleasant, bustling and well maintained, this is one of the coast's oldest (1946) and most reputable hotels. There are two good pools, five restaurants, an outdoor Jacuzzi and extensive gardens. Good disabled access (lifts and specially designed rooms), kids' paddling pool, PADI diving school, and wind-surfing. Standard rooms are very comfortable, but the only sea views are from the more expensive Palm Wing. Discos Wed, Fri and Sat. B&B ⑦

Nyali Luxury Beach Apartments PO Box 82843 ☏041/474125, ℻2223268. Next to *Holiday Resort*. Three-bedroom (six-person) self-catering apartments with a pool but no views for Ksh15,000 in principle, but try bargaining.

Reef Hotel Mwamba Drive; PO Box 82234 ☏041/471771–2 , ℻471349, ⓔreef@africaonline.co.ke. One of Nyali's best, a large and friendly 1972 resort (last renovated in 2004), and very much family oriented, with babysit-ters, day-long supervised kids' activities, and a playground and paddling pool to keep them busy. The Garden Wing is a little glum, but there are sea views from the Sea View wing (same price). Facili-ties include a disco, three pools (and pool games), massage, Jacuzzi, tennis courts, a PADI diving school and the usual watersports. HB ⑧

Tamarind Village Cement Silo Rd; PO Box 95805 ☏041/474600–2, ⓦwww.tamarind.co.ke. Next to the celebrated *Tamarind* restaurant, this is a luxurious self-service apartment complex with classy touches of Lamu architec-tural style. Apartments – all very spacious, a/c and en suite with large sitting rooms, kitchens and balconies – overlook Mombasa creek, and there's a gym, a squash court and two pools, but no beach. ⑧

Voyager Beach Resort ☏041/475114–5, ⓔinfo@VoyagerResorts.co.ke; reservations through Heritage Hotels, p.63. Impressive commu-nal areas, all meshwork *makuti* ceilings and marble floors, but the beach is a let-down: small and narrow, bounded by unsightly rubble and concrete defences, and covered at mid- and high-tides. Facilities include two tennis courts, three pools (and paddling pool, but nothing much else for chil-dren), and a PADI diving school. Lots of activities, including water aerobics every morning. All-inclu-sive $310; ⑨

Eating, drinking and nightlife

Kigotho's Hotel. Unfussy *nyama choma* served at the bar.

Mamba International Nightclub at Mamba Village ☏041/475180. Huge and popular *makuti*-roofed club, with an expensive sound system and laser light shows (Fri, Sat and Sun). There's a mixture of sounds (including jazz, bhangra, Congolese, reggae and cheesy disco), depending on the crowd. On Sun afternoons (3–10pm) there are family shows, acrobats and jugglers.

Maxim's Cellar at *Mombasa Beach Hotel*. French-style pretensions, with all the usual over-priced favourites (lobster thermidor and so on);

the bouillabaisse Marseillaise (seafood soup) is worth trying.

Tamarind Cement Silo Rd ☏041/474600–2, ⓦwww.tamarind.co.ke; reservations advisable. From Nyali Bridge, go right at the traffic lights by Freretown Bell Tower, then follow the signs. In a stupendous position, with Mombasa spread out across the creek, the *Tamarind* is one of the best eating houses in Kenya. Go for the seafood platter – a snip at Ksh5814 for two; otherwise, there's lobster Swahili, at around Ksh4000 for a medium-sized portion. A vegetarian menu is also available. At the jetty below, the same people run *The Tamarind Dhow*, a *jahazi* sailing dhow which has

For details of **dhow**-trip operators, read the box on p.483. Information on **scuba diving** is in the box on p.482.

been converted into Kenya's most expensive dining experience: the two-hour lunch session ($32) sails at 1pm, the four-hour evening bash, including a dance band, departs at 6.30pm ($70). If you've still got cash left over, the *Golden Key Casino* on the *Tamarind's* roof will relieve you of it.

From Nyali Bridge to Kenyatta Beach

Beyond the Freretown Bell and the junction for Nyali – always jostling with people trying to get transport to their shifts at the hotels – the main coast road ploughs through an area of burgeoning suburban growth. Ignored by the resort developers because it's too far from the sea, the primitive living conditions and milling activity here can come as a shock if you're fresh off the plane. Utange Camp (a Somali "intellectuals" refugee camp, full of writers, performers, musicians and their families) is not far away and its inhabitants have imposed an additional burden on the district. This is the Kenya coast that doesn't appear in the brochures. Matatus from Mombasa GPO or Abdel Nasser Road to Mtwapa come along this way, as far as Mtwapa town on the other side of Mtwapa Creek. Before you get back to the shore again, there are two very worthwhile objectives to be visited – **Bombolulu** and **Bamburi Quarry Nature Park** – both of them recommended outings whether you're travelling independently or on a package.

Bombolulu

Just off the main road 3km north of Nyali Bridge (matatu from Abdel Nasser Road or GPO in Mombasa), **Bombolulu** (workshops Mon–Fri 8am–12.45pm & 2–5pm; showroom Mon–Sat 8am–6pm; Cultural Centre Mon–Sat 8am–5pm; ⓦwww.apdkbombolulu.com) is a crafts training school and manufacturing centre that employs over 150 disabled people, mostly polio victims, in its five handicraft workshops (which you can visit). The **jewellery workshop** is the programme's biggest money-spinner, with hundreds of original designs in metal and local materials (old coins, seeds) exported to North America and Europe, where you'll come across them in charity gift catalogues. The shop is an excellent place to buy crafts, with somewhat lower prices than you'll find in run-of-the-mill tourist souvenir shops elsewhere. There's also a **cultural centre** (visitors Ksh450, including free transport from North Coast hotels), incorporating six traditional homesteads from several of Kenya's peoples, around a central restaurant and dance floor, where traditional crafts, cooking and farming are demonstrated while visitors can join in the dances of various tribes (lunchtimes).

Bamburi Quarry Nature Park

Five kilometres beyond Bombolulu, the **Bamburi Quarry Nature Park** (also called Haller Park; daily 8am–5pm; Ksh600, children Ksh300) is the result of an unusual attempt to rehabilitate a giant quarry. The Bamburi Cement Factory (whose giant kilns are visible from miles around) has been scouring the land for limestone here since 1954. In 1971, it began a concentrated programme of tree-planting in an effort to rescue the disfigured landscape, to put the small-is-beautiful principle into conservation practice – a modest contribution in a land of vast wildlife parks, but a terrific success. Later, as the project gained momentum, fish-breeding was established, and large numbers of animals and birds introduced, including several **hippos**. There are plenty of **crocodiles** in a setting devoid of Mamba Village's landscaped excesses and quite a comprehensive collection of snakes, including some dangerously unprotected poisonous ones. You'll have the opportunity to get close to a number of other, harmless, creatures, including pelicans, crowned cranes, various antelopes and some splendid giant tortoises. Feeding time is 11am for the giraffes, 4pm for the hippos and 5pm for the crocodiles.

The walking paths wind through dense groves of casuarina, a tree known for its ability to withstand a harsh environment, across ground which is mostly below sea level, permanently moist with salty water percolating through the coral limestone bedrock. The fish-farming side of the operation experiments with different types of **tilapia**, a freshwater fish highly tolerant of brackish conditions, many tons of which now reach shops and restaurants every year, including the park's own *Whistling Pine Restaurant* (daily 12.30–3pm & 7.30–10pm; ☎041/5487464), which dishes up croc and other game meat. There are two entrances: one on the main road opposite *Tembo* nightclub, and the main entrance opposite the cement factory itself. Mtwapa or Serena matatus from the GPO or Abdel Nasser Road will drop you at Bamburi Nature Trail bus stop by the first of these, but the main entrance is nearer the restaurant.

Other wildlife sites

On a similar theme and run by the same people as the Quarry Park, though not as impressive, are the newer **North Quarry Nature Trails** (daily 8am–6pm; Ksh200, children Ksh100), 4km further north (same buses and matatus: ask for "Bamburi Beach"), opposite the turning for *Bamburi Beach Hotel*. Intended mainly for joggers and cyclists (there are several looping tracks, and bicycles can be rented for use on the trails; (Ksh300 per hour), there's also a live Butterfly Exhibition Centre. Lastly, if the concept hasn't yet bored you, **Nguuni Wildlife Sanctuary** is the third of Bamburi Cement's sites (pre-booked visits only, through Forest Trails; PO Box 81995 Mombasa; ☎041/5485901–4, ⓦwww.lafargeecosystems.com), good for bird-spotting and for its herds of farmed **eland** and **oryx antelope**. There's also an ostrich farm.

Kenyatta and Bamburi beaches

These two contiguous stretches of beach, together with Shanzu just to the north (see p.458), are the heart of the "North Coast". If you're out for the day, there should, in most cases, be little difficulty in visiting a hotel and using its beachfront, especially if you buy some drinks or take a meal there. The exceptions are the "all-inclusive" places, which charge steep daily admission (anything up to Ksh3000). The beach itself is entirely public; it's the access to it which has been progressively restricted by the hotel developers. Either way, *Whitesands* and *Mombasa Serena Beach* are the nicest hotels along this stretch.

One beach that is unquestionably public is **Kenyatta Municipal Beach**, almost the only beach in the country where you'll see droves of ordinary Kenyans by the seaside. There's a great family atmosphere here – and consequently little or no hassle. The beach goes far out at low tide, exposing plenty of coral pools and miles of sand for undisturbed walks. There are sailing boats for rent and trips offered, and at the fringes under the low coconut trees, pedlars sell ice creams and sodas, snacks and drinking coconuts, while others rent out inflated car inner tubes. For many though, the main attraction is *Pirates* (daily, pools 9am–5pm, restaurant and bar 9am–midnight; ℡041/486020), a combination of waterslides, restaurant and breezy bar, with a similarly relaxed feel. The slides are a required outing for kids: they're as good as you'll find anywhere, certainly in Africa, consisting of one long, steep and fast one, with a big jump, and one curling and gentle. The slides cost Ksh300 per day, or Ksh100 for just the children's pools. The restaurant serves good if not amazingly cheap Mediterranean food. It's also the venue for popular nightly discos, with a mixed crowd and a variety of music.

If you'd like to try something different, there's a Swiss-run **go-karting** track at the northern end of Bamburi, just off the main road (daily except Mon 4–10pm; ℡0721/485247, Ⓦwww.mombasa-gokart.com; Ksh1000, children Ksh500).

Practicalities

There are three shopping centres along the main road from Nyali to Shanzu. The first and biggest consists of a development called The Planet Centre, on the corner of Links Road and the main highway, plus a larger one next door called the Nova Centre, which includes a large Nakumatt **supermarket**. Should you need a **doctor**, Dr Buran (℡041/5485238) has a surgery here. Further north, Ocean View Shopping Plaza, next to the hotel of the same name, has a branch of the efficient Commercial Bank of Africa (Mon–Fri 8.30am–4pm, with an ATM). And the shops just north of *Whitesands* include a small **post office** (Mon–Fri 8am–12.30pm & 2–5pm, Sat 9am–noon) and a branch of Barclays Bank (Mon–Fri 9am–3pm, Sat 9–11am), whose ATM invariably seems to be attended by youths trying on the old "sponsor me" scam (see p.90).

Accommodation

Nearly thirty **beach hotels** throng the six-kilometre shoreline that makes up Bamburi beach. If you're travelling on a tight budget, you'll find there's nowhere cheap to stay in the vicinity and – unless you're returning to Mombasa – you should forge on to the other side of Mtwapa Creek for some cheap hotels, or continue to the altogether more appealing beach and budget accommodation at Kikambala (see p.463).

Baharini Chalets Bamburi Beach; PO Box 90371 Mombasa ℡041/5485018. The cheapest of three adjacent apartment/chalet complexes tucked in behind a coral rag-rock headland, with a variety of large rooms, all with nets, fans and verandas. Some have sea views, others have cooking facilities. There's also a pool, and a beach restaurant and bar popular with prostitutes. If you're coming by public transport, get off at the *Severin Sea Lodge*. The off-note is the sometimes dodgy clientele. Prices negotiable. ❸

Bamburi Beach Hotel Bamburi Beach; PO Box 83966 Mombasa ℡041/5485611–7, Ⓦwww. bamburibeachkenya.com. Unexceptional mid-sized resort hotel with a nice pool, but slow service. On the plus side, most rooms have sea views. Facilities include PADI diving school, glass-bottomed boats, snorkelling, squash courts and a gym. HB ❽

Bamburi Beach Villas Kenyatta Beach next to *Pirates*; PO Box 82623 Mombasa ℡041/548

6161–2. Mediterranean-style terracotta-roofed self-catering development, with modern two-bedroom apartments (Ksh6000) in three-storey blocks, all with kitchens and verandas, but no view of the beach.

Cowrie Shell Beach Apartments next to *Baharini Chalets*; PO Box 10003 Bamburi ℡041/5485971, Ⓕ548 6580. Pleasantly weatherbeaten two-bedroom apartments sleeping four (Ksh3000 in high season), with kitchens, verandas and views of the sea through the coconut trees, better equipped than *Baharini*, somewhat more respectable, and run by a very friendly Greek lady. There's a pool and laundry, but no food (nearest supplies at Shanzu shops), and the beach is partially fenced to discourage beach boys. Discounts for longer stays.

Fontana Hotel PO Box 86291 Mombasa ℡041/5487554. Sixteen pleasant rooms with balconies overlooking a pool behind a restaurant on the main road with a very impressive *makuti* roof. Quiet, but 200m off the beach. B&B ❺

Giriama Hotel Kenyatta Beach, 100m south of the turn-off for *Pirates*; PO Box 86693 Mombasa ⓣ041/5486521, ⓔgiriama@africaonline.co.ke. A quiet, friendly and unpretentious little place, popular with Danish holidaymakers, with cool rooms, two pools and a beach bar. Also self-catering apartments at Ksh8300 for up to four people. HB 7

Indiana Beach Apartment Hotel Bamburi Beach; PO Box 82662 Mombasa ⓣ041/5485895, ⓦwww.indianabeachkenya.com. A block of s/c apartments (6) and a block of cool a/c rooms, not huge but nice and airy, with three pools and direct beach access, though no beach views. B&B 8

Kenya Bay Beach Hotel Bamburi Beach; PO Box 767 Mombasa ⓣ041/5487600, ⓦwww.kenyabay.com. One of the old generation, circa end-1960s, with the usual *makuti*-roofed reception resembling so many others. It's simpler and smaller than most, but friendly and attracts a mixture of nationalities. There's a watersports centre offering windsurfing, glass-bottomed boats, waterskiing and jet skis. HB 6

Neptune Beach Resort Bamburi Beach; PO Box 83125 Mombasa ⓣ041/5485701–3, ⓕ5485705, ⓦwww.neptunehotels.com. Slightly downmarket, but refreshingly lacking in pretension, this is a fun package destination with good staff, lots of activities and water sports, and a cheerful atmosphere. B&B 6

Octopus Hotel Bamburi Beach ⓣ041/5485395, reservations through Kahama Hotels; PO Box 33003 Nairobi 00600 ⓣ020/374 9870, ⓔinfo@klubhouse.co.ke. No-frills hotel, quiet and un-packagey, 100m off the beach, with plain rooms and hot water mornings only, though there are also bigger "executive rooms" with a/c, TV and a balcony. The nearest thing to a budget hotel on this stretch of coast. 4

Plaza Beach Hotel PO Box 88299 Mombasa ⓣ041/548 5321–4, ⓦwww.plazabeach.co.ke. Spotless with white tiles, cool a/c rooms and minimalist decor, but on a narrow plot. Specially adapted rooms are available for wheelchair users. HB 7

Rami's Beach Cottages Kenyatta Beach, next to *Bamburi Beach Villas*; PO Box 90223 ⓣ041/2223043, ⓕ2227221. Older and more characterful than its neighbour, but more expensive, slightly rundown and there's no pool. It has three four-bedroom family cottages, sleeping up to eight, at Ksh7500, with a lower rate if you rent by the month.

Sai Rock Hotel Bamburi Beach; PO Box 83063 Mombasa ⓣ041/5487644–5, ⓔsairock@iconnect.co.ke. A revamped hotel right on the beach, with an informal, friendly atmosphere, and lots of Kenyan guests, sunny decor in the rooms, two pools, a kids' club, and a distinct lack of walls in the public areas giving the whole place a relaxed, open feel. B&B 8

Severin Sea Lodge Bamburi Beach; PO Box 82169 Mombasa ⓣ041/5485001–5, ⓦwww.severin-kenya.com. Large, well-run resort hotel, with excellent sports and watersports, but no beach at high tide. Noted also for its *Imani Dhow* restaurant, which is a converted Zanzibari *jahazi* dhow, rather oddly placed in the gardens when really it should be in the water. Rooms, especially in "Comfort Class", are overpriced in high season (Dec–March), but very reasonable in low season (April–June). B&B $176; 9

Travellers Beach Hotel Bamburi Beach; PO Box 87649 Mombasa ⓣ041/5485121–6, ⓔtravhtls@africaonline.co.ke. Big, fun, package-tour setup with lots of shops and activities. You can swim into the lobby then slide out again, but you can't go on the beach at high tide, when it's submerged: four pools make up for that. Facilities include floodlit tennis and a/c squash courts, nightclub, kids' club, windsurfing, and a health club with sauna, Jacuzzi and steam bath. Dull gardens, and somewhat tenement-like blocks, though spacious and well-appointed rooms with a/c and TVs. Good Indian restaurant (*Sher-e-Punjab*, see p.458). HB 8

Whitesands Hotel Bamburi Beach; PO Box 90173 Mombasa ⓣ041/5485926–9, ⓕ5485652, ⓔwhitesands@form-net.com, reservations through Sarova, p.63. Large and established operation, with not a *makuti* roof in sight. Enormous public areas, with four interconnecting freeform pools (complete with fake beach and island) and busy restaurants. Standard rooms have sea views of sorts; larger executive rooms have satellite TV but no sea view. The hotel has the longest seafront on the Mombasa North Coast, offering jet skiing, scuba diving, windsurfing, pedalos, kayaks, and trips by "banana boat" and catamaran. However, the atmosphere may be too formal for some. HB $180; 9

Eating, drinking and nightlife

Apart from the multifarious attractions of *Pirates* on Kenyatta Beach (see p.455) and the expensive hotel restaurants, there are a good number of other **eating places**, most of which line the unpretty Mombasa–Malindi road. Matatus from Mombasa GPO or Abdel Nasser Road for Mtwapa run past most of the following, both day and night (fares around Ksh30); taxis from town cost around Ksh1000, depending on how far north you're going.

Bora Bora Ocean View Shopping Plaza. A pleasant bar, off the beach, with comfort food for homesick European package tourists, including German sausages, goulash, schnitzel, and sauerkraut with smoked pork. Also does some African dishes (such as *kuku paka*, chicken with coconut), and cold beers of course. The adjoining nightclub, famous in its day, has been closed for some time, but may yet reopen.

Gecko Village 200m north of Nova Centre. A 24hr bar and eatery with live music Wed and Sun from 6pm. There's an eclectic mix of food on offer, from *nyama choma* and T-bone steak to mulligatawny soup and guinea fowl in red wine sauce, with even a few attempts at Thai cuisine on the menu. Main courses go for around Ksh400–700. Drinks include a legit bottled version of palm wine, not quite the real thing, but close.

Gold Chopsticks 100m north of Nova Centre ☎041/5485496. Bamburi branch of Mombasa's posh Chinese eatery *Galaxy*, specializing in delectable seafood dishes such as pan-fried lobster with garlic and ginger. If the à la carte crustaceans are beyond your budget, you can always settle for the Sat night or Sun lunchtime buffet (including vegetarian options).

Maharajah In the *Indiana Beach Hotel*, Bamburi ☎041/5485895. North Indian tandoori with a seafood twist – dishes on offer include fish tikka or tandoori lobster, but there are plenty of chicken options too, mostly at around Ksh600. Free transport from North Coast hotels. Open from 7.30pm daily except Tues, also open Sun 12.30–3pm.

Pili Pili *Baharini Chalets*. The only bar/restaurant on the beach barring those in the big hotels, so

very popular, as well as a pick-up joint.

Sher-e-Punjab *Travellers Beach Hotel*. Unusual among hotel restaurants in that this one has acquired quite a reputation for style and quality. There are vegetarian dishes (paneer tikka, veg kebabs), chicken dishes (jalfrezi, korma), and mughlai dishes (rogan josh, mughlai biryani), and a Ksh847 veg or non-veg Sun lunchtime buffet.

Splendid View Café 100m north of *Gold Chopsticks*, next to *Gecko Village* ☎041/5487270. This Indian Mughlai is fibbing about the view, unless you count pink chairs and splendidly tacky fantasy paintings on the wall. The food's good though, with unusual daily specials like Baluchistani mutton *sajji* (whole roast leg of lamb), lots of chicken and seafood, and a daily tandoori BBQ. Shaded seating outside, and free transport from North Coast hotels. Under Ksh800 per person. Noon–2pm & 7–10pm, closed Mon.

Tembo Disco 100m north of the *Splendid View*, opposite Bamburi Quarry Nature Park ☎041/5485074, ⓦwww.tembo.net. Garden bar and restaurant open 24hr, with an underground disco (Mon–Thurs & Sun 9pm–5am, Fri & Sat 9pm–6am; women Ksh100, men Ksh150) playing a mixture of music (Congolese, Kenyan, hip-hop, soul, reggae), with occasional shows and body-building. Taxis wait outside.

Total Inn Ocean View Shopping Plaza, by Total garage. In case you were wondering where impecunious Kenyan hotel workers manage to eat up here on the coast, in amongst the expensive tourist joints, the answer is that they eat in places like this, with basic African dishes at honest African prices, nothing fancy, not a lobster in sight, and no item at more than Ksh100.

Shanzu

At the northern end of the piece of coast between Mombasa Harbour and Mtwapa Creek, Shanzu is dominated by exclusive holiday clubs, and is really too far from Mombasa to be a worthwhile day-trip for the beach, although it does have a couple of other attractions that may appeal to some.

The most unusual of these, 1km east of the Mombasa–Malindi road and copiously signposted, are the **Ngomongo Villages** (daily 9am–5pm; Ksh600, children Ksh300; ☎041/5487063; ⓦwww.ngomongo.com). Like Bamburi Nature Park, this is a reclaimed quarry, but one with a twist: as well as trees, it's been planted with a collection of ten mock rural homesteads, complete with permanent inhabitants in matching dress, representing the "most colourful tribes of Kenya". Don't expect authenticity, but do expect a fun half-day out in Kenya's only theme park. There are Akamba wood carvers, musicians, herbalists, and the unavoidable crocodile pit, with less common attractions of hands-on activities

Turtles

Several parts of Shanzu Beach, notably at *Mombasa Serena* hotel, are popular with **sea turtles** out for a spot of egg-laying. There are educational talks about this endangered species at *Serena* (Monday 7pm), where loud watersports are banned.

like archery, Luo-style hook fishing, Turkana-style harpoon fishing, grain pounding, and tree planting. There's also the *Kienyeji Bar & Restaurant*, which specializes in Kikuyu dishes.

Also worth a visit is the Shanzu Transitional Workshop for Disabled Young Women, 350m east of Ngomongo, run by the Mombasa Girl Guides (Mon–Sat 9am–6pm; c/o Mrs D.P. Shah; PO Box 80890 Mombasa; ☎041/2223078). Here, fourteen young women between 18 and 20 years old are currently being trained or employed in practical handicraft skills, turning out a small selection of well-made clothes (great Bermuda shorts), jewellery and leatherwork which is for sale. The idea is to graduate them with enough vocational training to enable them to become self-sufficient in the community. They don't get many visitors, so go and support the project if you can.

You'll find a large cluster of shops at Shanzu, by *Sonia Apartments*, with everything including the good Kelele Record Shop which sells African music CDs, and Internet access in the same enclosure.

Accommodation

There is precious little budget accommodation in Shanzu, and even most of the beach hotels are run by the Swiss-based African Safari Club company as resorts exclusively for their clients, and can only be booked through that company in Europe. Those listed here can be booked in the usual way.

Mombasa Safari Inn PO Box 87458 Mombasa ☎0725/698161. One of the few cheapies in Shanzu, friendly with modern s/c rooms, and a popular outdoor bar and restaurant (see below). **②**

🏃 **Mombasa Serena Beach Hotel** Shanzu Beach; PO Box 90352 Mombasa ☎041/5485721–4, ℱ5485453, ⓦwww .serenahotels.com, reservations through Serena Hotels, p.63. Beautifully put together in "high-Swahili" style, and very stylishly maintained, this is the most attractive proposition on this stretch of coast, and recently refurnished. There are loads of activities, most of them free: floodlit tennis and a/c squash courts, minigolf, windsurfing, PADI diving school, snorkelling, canoeing, and sailing, and they even take care of children. Great food (Ksh1200 for a drop-in evening meal).

The beachfront is popular with beach boys as well as the sea turtles. HB\$260; **⑨**

Petuscha Garden Lodge Shanzu; PO Box 88548 Mombasa ☎041/5485860, ⓔpetuschahotel@yahoo .com. Kenyan-German run, with seven spotless, modern and comfortable rooms with a/c or fans, two with real baths (others with showers), fronting onto a small pool and gardens. Use of split-level sitting room with plenty of books. **⑦**

Sonia Apartments and Beer Garden Diamond Shopping Centre, Shanzu; PO Box 84963 Mombasa ☎0722/427688. Spacious two-room apartments (Ksh2000 for up to four people) arranged around the courtyard restaurant and lively 24hr bar. All have their own cooking facilities and a/c. Fairly basic, but clean enough. Good value, so long as you don't mind the rather sleazy atmosphere.

Eating, drinking and nightlife

Shanzu is pretty tacky when it comes to eating places and watering holes, with most places catering purely for a captive market of package tourists. Don't expect to find any ordinary Kenyan eateries. One of the most laid-back places is the *Mombasa Safari Inn*, a cheery bar and restaurant with good grills, which is relatively cheap (main courses around Ksh350, and a full splash for around

Ksh500). The bar attracts prostitutes, but the outdoor atmosphere is mellow, and it's open daily from 8am until the last customer leaves. Another place worth trying is the *Cha Cha Bar*, next to the *Petuscha Hotel*, a pleasant and laid-back outdoor bar-restaurant under an octagonal *makuti* roof, where you'll pay around Ksh600 for a meal, Ksh1700 for seafood (food daily until 11pm, bar open later). The prostitutes are less of a hassle here than at other Shanzu venues, and there's occasional live music in the evenings.

Mtwapa Creek and north

Mtwapa Creek marks the edge of Greater Mombasa, and tropical suburbia – with its scattered villas, supermarkets, clubs and restaurants (and poverty) – is more or less left behind. From here on, the road heads more determinedly, with fewer distractions, up to Kilifi, Watamu and Malindi. Note: if you're **continuing north**, beyond Kikambala, skip to p.493.

Mtwapa

MTWAPA itself is in many ways the most pleasant of the main-road settlements, with a more established feel than Bombolulu, and a more ordinary Kenyan atmosphere. There are several fairly rudimentary **hotels** which are cheaper if you check in after 4pm and leave by 10am (you pay for the night only, as opposed to the day and night). The best is ☩ *Sweet Heart Lodge*, east of the main road, just north of the market (PO Box 835; ☎041/495598; B&B ❷). Also clean and well kept is the *Kamanjira Pub Restaurant*, on the east side of the main road about

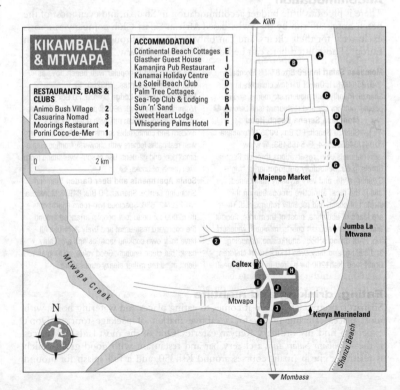

KIKAMBALA & MTWAPA

RESTAURANTS, BARS & CLUBS

Animo Bush Village	2
Casuarina Nomad	3
Moorings Restaurant	4
Porini Coco-de-Mer	1

ACCOMMODATION

Continental Beach Cottages	E
Glasther Guest House	I
Kamanjira Pub Restaurant	J
Kanamai Holiday Centre	G
Le Soleil Beach Club	D
Palm Tree Cottages	C
Sea-Top Club & Lodging	B
Sun 'n' Sand	A
Sweet Heart Lodge	H
Whispering Palms Hotel	F

0   2 km

▲ Kilifi

◆ Majengo Market

◆ Jumba La Mtwana

Mtwapa Creek

Caltex

Mtwapa

◆ Kenya Marineland

Shanzu Beach

N

▼ Mombasa

600m north of the bridge (PO Box 2120 Mombasa; ☏0733/824633; ❷). If you need something cheaper, the rather down-at-heel *Glasther Guesthouse* (❶) lies down a turning on the west side of the main road, directly opposite the one that leads to the *Sweet Heart*.

The main reasons to pause in Mtwapa are **boats** and **big fish**: the creek is fast becoming a focus for yachties and game fishermen. Day-long **dhow trips** (with snorkelling opportunities, and the $85 fee includes a trip up Mtwapa Creek and lunch at its *Aquamarine Restaurant*) are run most days (except Sun) by Kenya Marineland (PO Box 70 Mtwapa; ☏041/5485248 or 5485866, ⓦwww.kenyamarineland.com), leaving its jetty at around 9.30am; turn right at the signboard in Mtwapa 550m north of the bridge, and head along the dirt track for 1.5km, or ring ahead to get picked up from your hotel (free). There's also a 350,000-litre **aquarium** here (daily 8.30am–4.30pm; Ksh300, including entry to the obligatory reptile and snake park).

For **food**, the pleasant *makuti*-roofed *Casuarina Nomad*, 300m north of the bridge on the right, has delicious chargrilled meat and seafood, and is open 24 hours. *Muscat Dishes*, at the northern end of the village, serves tasty Swahili dishes, *nyama choma* and curries. For upmarket eats, the floating *Moorings Restaurant* is in a fine, breezy location on the north side of the creek, accessible down a track on the left 300m after the bridge, and has a mainly seafood menu (Tues–Sun 10am–11pm; ☏0722/411812; main courses Ksh550–1200) and reasonably priced drinks. It's a good place for talk and tales – and to hook up with others, either in person or via the notice board. *Aquamarine* at Kenya Marineland itself is overpriced, at getting on for Ksh2000 a meal. For **nightlife**, there's a large number of ever-changing disco and live-music venues, which rise and fall according to the fashion of the day: just ask around. More dependable are the discos at *Casuarina Nomad* (daily 6pm–6am), which usually feature "cocktails" of traditional dancers at weekends.

Further afield, *Animo Bush Village*, 3.3km north of Mtwapa Bridge and then 500m left (signposted; ☏0725/503133), is a former rural nightclub now revamped as a very laid-back *nyama choma* joint, with a goat-eaters' club and even guinea fowl on the menu, plus traditional bands and dancers (Sat & Sun afternoons 3–5pm), and dance music – especially reggae, or *bango* and other African sounds – on Friday, Saturday and Sunday nights (5pm–3am). It also provides cleanish s/c rooms with fans (❷).

Jumba la Mtwana

A totally different site worth pausing for (and worth a day out of town in its own right) is **Jumba la Mtwana** (daily 8am–6pm; Ksh500, children Ksh200). This national monument, one of three between Mombasa and Malindi, is the ruined centre of a wealthy fourteenth- or fifteenth-century Swahili community. The sign for the three-kilometre access road is 2km north of Mtwapa Creek bridge; if you're travelling by public transport and are dropped off at the junction, you have a good chance of getting a lift.

Jumba la Mtwana means "mansion of the slave", but it has been deserted for some 500 years and probably had a different name in the past. It's a small site in an enchanting setting among baobabs and lawns above the beach. This seems a strange place for a town, right on an open shore with no harbour, and it's possible the inhabitants were pushed here by raiding parties from inland groups, and relied on Mtwapa Creek as a safe anchorage for the overseas traders who visited yearly. Jumba is fortunate in having good water, but why it was deserted, and by whom, remains a mystery. A helpful little guidebook which costs Ksh100 is sometimes available at the ticket office – much of this account has been culled from it.

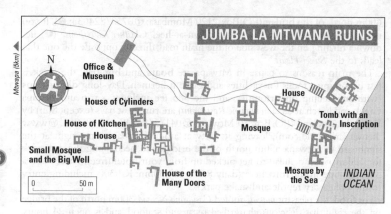

Compared with Gedi, further north (see p.501), Jumba's layout is simple. Though it lacks the eerie splendour of that much larger town, it must once have been a sizeable settlement; there were three mosques within the site and a fourth just outside. Most of the population would have lived in mud-and-thatch houses, which have long since disintegrated. In Swahili culture, building in stone (in fact, coral "rag" of different densities) has traditionally been the preserve of certain privileged people, principally the long-settled inhabitants of a town; newcomers would almost always build in less durable materials appropriate to their shorter-term stake in the community. It is believed that building in stone required legal sanction, as it was the material used for mosques.

The best of Jumba's mosques is the **Mosque by the Sea**, which shows evidence of there having been a separate room for women, something which is only nowadays becoming acceptable again in modern mosques. The cistern where worshippers washed is still intact, with coral foot-scrapers set nearby and a jumble of tombs behind the north wall facing Mecca. One of these has a Koranic inscription carved in coral on a panel facing the sea and must have been the grave of an important person:

Every soul shall taste death. You will simply be paid your wages in full on the Day of Resurrection. He who is removed from the fire and made to enter heaven, it is he who has won the victory. The earthly life is only delusion.

The **people of Jumba** seem to have been very religious and hygienic – virtues that are closely associated in Islam. Cisterns and water jars, or at least the remains of them, are found everywhere among the ruined houses, and in most cases there are coral blocks nearby which would have been used to squat on while washing. Latrines are all stone-lined with long-drops. Of course, it is possible that the poorer people of Jumba lived in squalor in their mud huts, yet even the **House of Many Doors**, which seems to have been a fifteenth-century "boarding and lodging", provided guests with private washing and toilet facilities.

Look out for the two **smaller mosques**, each with its well-preserved, carved coral *mihrab* (the arched niche that indicates the direction of Mecca), and for the strange chinks in several walls (in the House of the Cylinders and the Small Mosque), the purpose of which is unknown.

Jumba Beach is a good place to while away an afternoon – in fact, late afternoon, when the atmosphere hangs among the ruins like cobwebs, is probably the best time to come. Strange but attractive screw pines grow, aerial-rooted like mangroves, in the sand. You can take a **picnic** here, too; there are toilets and showers by the ticket office.

Kikambala

For a day-trip out of Mombasa without your own transport, **KIKAMBALA**, a few kilometres further up the coast, is about as far as you'd want to come (Kilifi-bound matatus and Malindi-bound matatus and buses from Abdel Nasser Road in Mombasa pass here regularly). Note that the topography here is very flat. The sea goes out for nearly a kilometre and it's largely impractical for bathing except at high tide, so if you're just coming for the day, consult a tide table before setting off (daily newspapers print this). Much of the coastal strip here is still thickly forested and the beach itself is a glorious white expanse, though it's 2–3km from the highway and there are no matatus. The only official **campsite** in the area is at the Kanamai Conference & Holiday Centre, or "Kanamai Youth Hostel". The first low-budget beach spot north of Mombasa, it makes a good stopover, and if you plan to stay more than a night you're not utterly marooned – there's often someone with a vehicle at the site who'll be going to the *dukas* on the main road to do some shopping and will let you tag along.

Accommodation

The Kikambala **hotels** are virtually the last on the coast north of Mombasa until you reach Kilifi. One downside of being this far out of town, if you haven't got a car, is that taxis into Mombasa cost over Ksh2000 each way. Vehicles normally approach the beach properties from the northern access road (other roads can get tricky in bad weather), 7.4km north of Mtwapa Bridge (signposted for "*Sun 'n' Sand*"). Coming from the south, it's often quicker to cut in 5.3km north of Mtwapa Bridge, which heads straight to *Kanamai*.

Continental Beach Cottages 3.6km along northern access road; PO Box 124 Mtwapa ☎041/32190. Not a great deal of atmosphere, but quiet and friendly, with a reasonable bar and restaurant and a pool, all set amid lots of tall, established coconut trees. The cottages ("singles" with one double bed, "doubles" with two twin-bed rooms) have a/c and nets, some with TV. Choice of self-catering or eating in the restaurant. **④**

🏃 **Kanamai Holiday Centre** 5.3km north of Mtwapa Bridge, then 3km along *murram*; PO Box 46 Matwapa ☎041/32101, ✉kanamai@iconnect.co.ke. Big, sprawling but pretty place under the coconuts, run by the National Christian Council of Kenya. Apart from double-room accommodation (roomy and well furnished, with good fans and nets), there are beds in dormitories (very basic, but spotlessly clean; Ksh350), or camping pretty much wherever you like (Ksh300 per person). *Kanamai* offers cheap meals in the dining room and has a shop with a few provisions, but there's no bar. A half-hour stroll north along the sandy lane through the woods brings you to the *Whispering Palms Hotel*, where you can join in all the usual holiday pursuits. B&B **⑤**

Le Soleil Beach Club 3.2km along northern access road; PO Box 84737 Mombasa ☎041/32195–6, ⊛www.lesoleilkenya.com. More like a tropical office block than a hotel, this is as tacky as it is popular, with a cosmopolitan variety of budget package tourists and tons of activities (and unlimited food and booze) covered if you opt for the all-inclusive deal (which is $14 a day more than half board). No day visits. HB **⑦**

Palm Tree Cottages 2.6km along northern access road; PO Box 82448 Mombasa ☎0722/343304. Four-bed houses with room for two in each. Not especially good value and a very uninspiring plot. **⑥**

🏃 **Sea-Top Club & Lodging** 1.7km along northern access road; PO Box 226 Kikambala ☎0723/651171. Family-run 24hr *nyama choma* bar and nightspot with nightly discos featuring Congolese sounds, soul, Caribbean and funk, and sometimes live bands. Simple but clean s/c rooms for weary clients, with fans and nets. The only place in Kikambala with a genuine African feel. **③**

Sun 'n' Sand 2.1km along northern access road; PO Box 2 Mtwapa ☎041/32621, ⊛www .sunnsand.co.ke. One of the oldest hotels on the Kenya coast, originally built in 1932 and most recently revamped in 2004 – it's among the biggest in the country, with 300 bright, functional rooms, furnished in some style. Four pools, with diving boards, an extended "river" and slides. Lots of activities, including a kids' club. There are several small shops and *dukas* near the gate if the club atmosphere begins to get claustrophobic. HB ➑

Whispering Palms Hotel 3.9km along northern

access road; PO Box 5 Kikambala ☎041/32028–9, ✉ whispers@africaonline.co.ke. Peaceful, isolated hideaway in palm-shaded grounds hosting a mix of package tourists from Britain and Europe. It's rather old-fashioned and would benefit from an overhaul, but is slightly cheaper than its equivalents closer to Mombasa. FB ➏

Eating and drinking

Outside of the hotels, there aren't many **restaurants** and **nightlife** options, though there are a couple of places along the main Mombasa–Malindi road. *Porini Le Coco-de-Mer*, 6.5km north of Mtwapa Bridge (☎0733/728435) is a long-established restaurant set in jungly gardens, and is friendly and laid-back, specializing in Seychelloise cuisine (lots of seafood and chicken, coconut milk and cassava), but was closed for renovations at our last check, so call to make sure it has reopened.

Inland from Mombasa

MAZERAS is just a short hop from Mombasa or, if you're coming from Nairobi, marks the end of the long vistas of scrub; it's perched right on the edge of the steep scarp, amid bananas and coconuts. If you're travelling by road, it isn't a bad idea to break your journey here and savour the new atmosphere. The *hotelis* serve good, flavourful, coastal *chai* and, for the travel-weary, Mazeras has a delightful **botanical garden** (daily 6am–6pm; free) – bamboo, ponds and green lawns for a snooze in the shade – just a couple of hundred metres back towards Mombasa. Across the road and up the hill a little way is a **mission** and its century-old church, signs of an evangelical presence in the hills behind Mombasa that goes back, remarkably, over 150 years. There are a couple of basic places to stay in Mazeras, among which *Weekend B&L* (PO Box 1; no phone; ➊), directly opposite the Kaloleni turn-off, with plain rooms and nets, should be adequate for a brief stopover.

For historians of Methodism and the Church Missionary Society or (more likely) connoisseurs of palm wine, the **road to Kaloleni**, 22km north of Mazeras is a required sidetrack; see the map on p.423. It's a beautiful trip in its own right: wonderfully scenic, looping through lush vales with a wide panorama down to the coast on the right and masses of **coconut trees** all around. There are frequent buses and matatus from Mombasa (the Kobil station at the junction of Jomo Kenyatta Avenue with Mwembe Tayari Road) to Kaloleni via Rabai, which makes this an easy day-trip away from the coast, especially appealing in the high season if your sense of adventure has become numbed by the influx of tropical paradise-seekers. If a round trip appeals, arrive in Kaloleni before mid-afternoon and you'll be able to catch a matatu further north to Kilifi, and from there back to Mombasa. If you're driving, note that there's no petrol at Mazeras, and only irregular supplies at Kaloleni, so fill up in Mombasa or Mariakani.

Rabai

RABAI, capital of the **Wa-Rabai** Mijikenda and site of the first Christian mission to be established in East Africa, is the first village you come to, 5km from Mazeras. It's also one of only two Mijikenda villages still occupying its original *kaya* (see p.466). A German pastor, the Reverend **Johan Ludwig Krapf**, came here in 1846 after losing his family at Nyali (see p.450), and left his mark on the community when, 41 years later, the imposing **St Paul's church**, now blue and white, was erected. The centre of the village and the church, surrounded by school rooms and sports fields, lie half a kilometre off the main road on the right as you come into Rabai from Mazeras. For the church and museum, fork left after 200m. Opposite the entrance to St Paul's, the first church to have been built (1846–48) now houses the modest **Krapf Memorial Museum** (daily 8am–6pm; Ksh500, children Ksh250). Not the most exciting place in Kenya, it contains a few well-presented photographs but little else. The ticket, however, includes a guided tour and explanation, with visits to a full-scale replica of the *kaya* (tourists are not allowed to wander through the real one), and the village's nearby viewpoint over the countryside. Next door to the museum is the house where Krapf used to live, and the adjacent cottage of Johann Rebmann, Krapf's proselytizing partner, is used as a school room. Between them, the two missionaries managed to explore a great deal of what is now Kenya without the demonstrations of firepower so many of their successors thought necessary. Krapf worked out the grammar of Swahili and produced a translation of the Bible. For all its significance, though, Rabai "centre" has, in all truth, hardly anything to offer, and there's nowhere in the village to stay, the nearest accommodation being in Mazeras (see opposite).

Ribe

RIBE (the Wa-Ribe village) is more substantial than Rabai, but harder to get to. Seven kilometres from Rabai, a road to the right snakes up from a deep valley floor: the village is 1.5km along it. Buses stop by the track. If you're driving, continue to a sign (on the right) for a lead mine. There are two bars and *hotelis* and a factory at the junction, which spews its dust over the neighbouring coconut and banana groves. Ribe itself is the second village along the track, about 4km from the main road. It consists of a few small shops and a basic bar-restaurant.

Fifteen minutes' walk away from Ribe, through the *shambas* and dense under-growth, is a tiny **cemetery**, regularly cleared of weeds and creepers, near the site of Ribe's Methodist mission, itself crumbled to its foundations and now completely overgrown. It isn't hard to find, and it's worth visiting if only to take a look at the pathetic graves of those few missionaries who struggled all the way here before succumbing in what must have been nearly impossible conditions. They were often very young: the Reverend Butterworth, whose carpentry skills ensured him a welcome arrival, died aged 23, just two months after getting there; they used his new tools to make the coffin. It isn't surprising that the cemetery faces out to sea, towards Mombasa, supplies, the mail and new settlers.

Kaloleni

The paved road comes to its end at **KALOLENI**. On the way, you pass through dense coconut groves where many of the trees have been initialled to avoid ownership disputes. The tapping of **palm wine** (*mnazi*), banned by the government, is still widely practised here, with the **Giriama** section of the Mijikenda leading the field. They call palm wine "the mother of the coconut", since tapping the trees for juice hinders formation of the nuts.

Tapping is done by cutting off the flower stem, binding it tightly and allowing the sap that would have produced new coconuts to collect in a container – usually a baobab pod – tied to the end. Here it ferments rapidly and has to be regularly collected. Variations in the local demand for *mnazi*, which is most often drunk at community gatherings like weddings and funerals, and in the coastal market for *copra* (the dried coconut flesh used in soap and oil manufacture), tend to influence the owners of trees in their decision whether to tap or to grow *copra*. You will see trees with the step-notches that enable the tappers

The Mijikenda peoples

The principal people of the coastal hinterland region are the **Mijikenda** ("Nine Tribes"), a loose grouping whose Bantu languages are to a large extent mutually intelligible, and closely related to Swahili. They are believed to have arrived in their present homelands in the sixteenth or seventeenth century from a quasi-historical state called Shungwaya, which had undergone a period of intense civil chaos. This centre was probably located somewhere in the Lamu hinterland or in the southwest corner of present-day Somalia. According to oral tradition, the people who left it were the Giriama, the Digo, the Rabai, the Ribe, the Duruma, the Chonyi, the Jibana, the Kauma and the Kambe (not to be confused with the Kamba of the interior).

All these tribes now live in the coastal hinterland, the **Giriama** to the north of Mombasa and **Digo** to the south being the largest and best-known. They share a degree of common cultural heritage. Each tribe has a traditional **kaya** central settlement, a fortified village in the forest, usually built on raised ground some kilometres from the coast, but sometimes right by the shore. Some Mijikenda peoples built only one *kaya*; others spawned secondary *kayas* or even whole clusters. The *kayas* still exist, although they are now sacred glades rather than fortified villages, and the dwelling place of ancestral spirits. In theory, they each contain a *fingo* – a charm said to derive from the ancestral home of Shungwaya – but these have nearly all been destroyed or, like the grave posts made from the *brachylinum* tree called *kigango* (*vigango* in the plural) that were also formerly a feature of each *kaya*, stolen for private collections of "primitive art" or loft-converters' ideas of interesting objets d'art.

Today, most *kayas* are rundown, but they are still remembered and visited by tribal elders. While their sacred aspect has ceased to have much relevance for most Mijikenda youth, their true significance comes out under pressure: when a German hotel developer took a fancy to Chale island (the whole of which is a gazetted *kaya*), he had to "buy" two Digo medicine men to appease the spirits – not best pleased with having their groves smothered in concrete. Nor is their human value the only reason to care about the *kayas*. Along with belief in their sacred qualities comes a local conservation tradition. In these forest tracts of between five hectares and three square kilometres nothing has ever been cultivated or disturbed. They represent a biological storehouse of immense diversity, unique along the East African coast. A WWF-backed botanical research programme run by the National Museums of Kenya has been under way for several years to map out the *kaya* ecosystems and to encourage the elders to reassert their authority over each one, something of an urgent matter as many are

to reach the top ending several metres below the crown, indicating that a tree has been left a number of years to develop coconuts.

Palm wine is locally available up and down the coast. Because it is illegal (and actually, its consumption is something of a social problem in some places), you won't find it openly on sale, but you should be able to locate a supply easily enough with a few discreet inquiries. It usually comes in plastic mineral-water bottles, and costs a lot less than beer – about Ksh50 a litre. It is best when cold, but rarely is, and you drink it (discreetly) through a reed straw with a coconut-fibre filter. As well as *mnazi*, tapped from the coconut palm, there is another variety of palm wine called *mukoma*, which comes from the doum palm, and is generally considered an inferior brew.

The only places to **stay** in Kaloleni are two basic guesthouses, the tin-roofed *Bububu Guesthouse* near the bus and matatu stand (T0734/794039; ●), which at least tries, with rooms available by the hour, day or night, and the cheaper but even more basic *makuti*-roofed *Kaloleni Guesthouse*, 700m up the old Kilifi road behind the post office and near St Luke's hospital (PO Box 105;

currently under threat from "land-grabbing" developers, usually well-connected and unscrupulous individuals or local politicians. More than twenty *kayas* have so far been gazetted in Kwale District, south of Mombasa, and the process has now started in the Kilifi area. There may be more than fifty altogether, though some could be so small they will disappear under the hoe or the caterpillar tractor before anyone remembers them. It may be possible to visit a *kaya*, but they are by no means tourist attractions. If you're genuinely interested, contact the Coastal Forest Conservation Unit (CFCU); PO Box 86 Ukunda; ☎040/3300071, ℮cfcu.kwale@swiftmombasa.com – the office is 3km south of Ukunda on the Lungalunga road, signposted to the right. The possibility that one or two of the old sacred groves might be opened to tourists to generate income still seems some way off. *The Kaya Complex* (Thomas T. Spear, Kenya Literature Bureau, Nairobi 1978) provides interesting reading on the subject.

Like so many other Kenyan peoples, the Mijikenda had age-set systems that helped cut across the divisive groupings of clan and subclan to bind communities together. Much of this tradition was lost during the last century; the installation of a new ruling elders' age-set, for example, required the killing and castration of a stranger.

Economically, the Mijikenda were, and still are, diverse. They were cultivators, herders (especially the Duruma and, at one time, the Giriama), long-distance traders with the interior, makers of palm wine (a Digo speciality now diffused all over Mijikenda-land), hunters and fishermen. They have local market cycles – four-day weeks in the case of the Giriama (days one and two for labour, day three for preparation, and day four, called *chipolata*, for market). They have successfully maintained their cultural identity, warring with the British in 1914 over the imposition of taxes and the demand for porters for World War I, and preserving a vigorous conservative tradition of adherence to their old beliefs in spirits and the power of their ancestors. This is most apparent in the relative ease with which you can pick up cassettes of **traditional music**, especially in Mombasa: wonderful rhythms and some very delicate *chivoti* flute melodies, with only a slight discernable Islamic influence, if at all. If you're really interested and have time to spare, even casual enquiries inland will elicit invitations to weddings or, less likely, funerals, where the old traditions – and music – are still very much centrepieces, despite the Christian veneer. Many Mijikenda, however, have found conversion to Islam a helpful religious switch in their dealings with coastal merchants and businessmen. This conversion seems to be the latest development in the growth of Swahili society.

no phone; ❶). Neither has electricity or running water, and washing is done with buckets.

Moving on, there are frequent buses and matatus back to Mombasa via Rabai and Mazeras, and less frequent matatus up to Kilifi, 40km away (catch these at the bottom of the hill by the Kilifi junction).

The South Coast

A continuous strip of beach runs between Likoni and Msambweni, backed by palms and broken once or twice by small rivers. Along the whole coast south from Mombasa to the Tanzanian border, there's just one highly

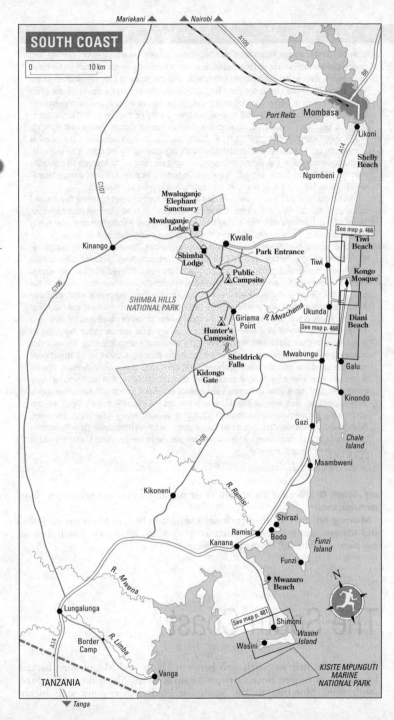

developed resort area, **Diani Beach**. South of Diani, the coast is little known and, in most tour operators' minds at least, nobody stops again until they reach **Shimoni**. This is great news if you have the time to go searching out untrodden beaches by car, bicycle or motorbike (all available to rent), or using the good local public transport. With your own transport, or with a safari company, you can also visit the **Shimba Hills National Park** and the neighbouring Mwaluganje Elephant Sanctuary, either overnight or on an easy day-trip excursion.

Most of the people who live along the coastal strip here are **Digo**, and their neat rectangular houses, made of dried mud and coral on a framework of wood, are a distinctive part of the lush roadside scene. Although they belong to the Mijikenda group of peoples, the Digo are unusual in being matrilineal: they traditionally traced descent through the female line, so that a man would, on his death, pass his property on to his sister's sons rather than his own. It is an unusual system with interesting implications for the state of the family and the position of women. However, the joint assault of Islamic and Western values over the last century has shifted the emphasis back towards the male line, and in many ways, women in modern Digo society have less freedom and autonomy than they had a hundred years ago.

Likoni and Shelly Beach

Taking the Likoni ferry (matatus from the post office on Digo Road) makes the sense of separation from Mombasa more immediate than crossing the bridges heading out of the city to the north. More pragmatically, the lack of a bridge has deterred developers and contributed to the South Coast's fairly late arrival in the tour brochures (though Diani is certainly making up for lost time). The ferries (free for foot passengers and bicycles, Ksh40 for cars, Ksh20 for motorbikes) operate around the clock (roughly every 15min, 4am–1am; every hour, 1am–4am). Beware of **pickpockets** here: keep your hands free, don't shake hands, and ensure money belts are secure and can't be cut off from behind.

LIKONI itself is a busy creekside suburb of Mombasa, straggling down the southbound road for a good 3km. A coast road runs off around the headland to the east (see Mombasa island map, pp.430–431), served by infrequent matatus, but Shelly Beach – named after its shells – is narrow and has large patches of exposed coral rag rock (bring rubber- or plastic-soled sandals), and tends to be strewn with seaweed, while the sea here is only feasible for swimming at high tide. Unless you're booked into a hotel already, hop on a bus or matatu and make for Tiwi or Diani. Apart from a host of very local (if rough-looking) eateries and good streetfood at Likoni ferry, the only real **restaurant** is the excellent *Island Paradise Bar & Restaurant*, next to *ACK Guesthouse*, whose tilapia, oddly enough (it's from Lake Victoria, not the Indian Ocean), is very good. For **nightlife**, there's *The Office* at the start of the road to Shelly Beach. Be warned, however, that it can be pretty rough after nightfall, with thefts common and stabbings not unknown.

Accommodation

The following addresses are all Mombasa PO boxes; distances are from the Likoni junction. Matatus from the junction run to just short of *Sea Breeze*. See Mombasa island map, pp.430–431.

ACK Guesthouse 300m; PO Box 96170
☎041/2451521, ⓔackmsaguesthouse@sw
iftmombasa.com. Even on a low budget, the Anglican Church of Kenya's coastal retreat might seem
an odd choice. But it's well run, the better rooms
are fine (showers and fans) and good value and,
while it's not on the beach, it's handy for Mombasa
and South Coast transport. There's a good swimming pool (Ksh100 for non-residents), and basic
food in the attractive patio dining room overlooking
the road, which is a popular meeting place for
locals. B&B ❹

Childrens' Holiday Resort 3.5km; PO Box 96048
☎0722/355442. A low-budget bungalow establishment from another age, the *Resort* is a non-profit
trust that goes way back, occupying a peaceful,
flat sandy site under the coconut palms, right on
the beach. Families are preferred, but couples and
singles aren't excluded. Self-catering only (utensils
provided, but cooker and fridge only in the larger
s/c cottages), all with electricity, some s/c but
most with outside showers and toilets. Bring your
own bed linen. Basic, but good value. Cottages for
two-plus. ❹

Furaha Gardens 1.3km; PO Box 96651 Mombasa
☎041/451015. A large modern development
consisting of clean and cool apartments (each at
Ksh4500 a night) in three-storey blocks around
a shared swimming pool. Each apartment has a
master bedroom with its own veranda, a second
bedroom, and a sitting room with a veranda and
kitchenette. It's designed for a couple with kids, but

two couples or four friends could take it, though
you'd then have to toss for the master bedroom.
All apartments have a/c, but it doesn't work in all
of them.

Kwetu Beach Resort 4km ☎0722/388035,
reservations through PO Box 42947 Nairobi
☎02/343828. A quiet, family-run place just
beyond the *Sea Breeze*, with clean, jolly s/c rooms
and a homely atmosphere despite the attached
bar-restaurant. You can also camp here (Ksh150
per person with your own tent, Ksh200 with tent
provided). B&B ❺

Reliable Beach Apartments 1.5km; PO Box
82630 ☎041/2451003. Good-sized apartments on
a plot of general ugliness, with no facilities apart
from a small pool. On a positive note, it's next to
the beach. Two-bedroom apartments (up to four
people) at Ksh4000.

Savannah Cottages 3.5km; PO Box 85965
☎0722/298222. Two-bedroom self-catering
cottages for four people at Ksh4500 a night, all a/c
with a kitchen, fridge and sitting room, spacious
and comfortable, and on the beach, but not on a
very nice stretch of it.

YWCA 350m; PO Box 96009 ☎041/2451403,
ⓔymcamsa@wananchi.com. Similar to the *ACK*
opposite, but not as nice, though it's peaceful,
and you don't have to be young, female or even
Christian. There's a choice of s/c or non-s/c
rooms, or a three-room cottage (Ksh4500), and
you can take bed and breakfast, half board, or full
board. B&B ❸

Shimba Hills National Park

Daily 6am–7pm. Entry $23, children $15. Warden: PO Box 30 Kwale;
☎ *040/2104259 or 2104266.*

Probably Kenya's most underrated wildlife refuge, **Shimba Hills National
Park** is under an hour from Mombasa, even less from Likoni and, at 500m
above sea level, wonderfully refreshing after the humidity down below. The hilly
park of scattered jungle and grassland is comparatively little visited, which is all
to the good, and has a quite wonderful game-viewing lodge and one of the
best-situated camping and *banda* sites anywhere.

Kwale and access to the park

The most straightforward option for visiting Shimba is on a **safari from
Mombasa** or from the coast. Trips from most coast hotels and travel agents cost
about $65 for a day-trip, $160 for an overnight at *Shimba Lodge*, and include
park entrance fees but not game drives or nature walks.

If you're **driving**, you'll probably need high-clearance 4WD in all but the
driest weather and, even so, the southern access road via Kindango Gate is
atrocious and often impassable. Note also that Kwale doesn't always have petrol.
There are fairly frequent **matatus** to **Kwale** from Likoni ferry bus park. The

park's **main gate** is inside the park, 3km beyond Kwale along an elephant-dunged *murram* road. Buses and matatus from Kwale will drop you here (it's illegal to walk, although there is no sign to tell you this). At the gate, you can try for **a lift** around the park. Since your best bet is with Mombasans, Sundays and public holidays are the easiest times. The last bus back to Mombasa from Kwale is at 8pm. In case of need, there are two **lodgings** in town. *Golden Guesthouse* (PO Box 272; ☎0722/605646; ❷) is the best, with pretty clean, s/c rooms and nets. Kwale has one of the world's biggest deposits of **titanium ore**, which Canadian company Tiomin Resources has now been given the go-ahead to mine, despite a campaign by environmentalists and local residents to stop it.

Moving on from Kwale, you could try a rarely used route away from the coast, heading northwest to Mariakani on the Nairobi highway, which is served by a few daily matatus. The first and only major town on the way is **Kinango**, where you might have to change vehicle. If you get stuck here, the only **hotel** is the basic *Kinango Silent Rest House* (❶). There are matatus from here to Mari-akani and Likoni.

Shimba Lodge

🏠 *Shimba Lodge* (PO Box 83 Kwale; ☎041/2229608, ⊛www.aberdaresafarihotels .com; HB $200; ❾) is a "tree hotel", a kind of coastal *Treetops*, though actually superior in all respects to the original. Check-in is from 3pm, but if you're driving and give advance notice, you can arrive early at the lodge for lunch ($15). It's all intensely atmospheric, as the building, apparently constructed entirely of pitch-dark timber (though it's actually mainly just cladding over the concrete), rises up through the trees and creepers, with aerial plantlife, birds, butterflies and humans all sharing the deep forest glade. The staff are instructed to speak in whispers, and remind guests to do so.

Given the rates, the standard rooms, with shared showers and toilets, might seem a disappointment at first, but when there are bushbabies on the branch outside, the possibility of a leopard, and a sweeping view of the dam and perhaps a fish eagle in the trees opposite, you don't spare too much thought for luxuries. From nearly all the rooms, on three floors, and from several bars and observation platforms, you have views across the small, dammed lake to thick forest. The best feature is the tree-level **walkway**, which runs for 100m or so from one end of the lodge to a platform high above the ground near a small clearing. Here you can watch elephants, warthogs, forest antelope and monkeys galore – if you're lucky. After dark, spotlights illuminate bushbabies, hundreds of bats and a whirling hailstorm of jungle insects. It's a memorable evening – and the food is good.

The early-evening "sundowner" **nature walk** (5pm; $20) is always enjoyable. The next morning there's the option of a proper **game drive** in the park (6am; $20), with the opportunity to see the sable antelope for which Shimba is famous. The nature walk and game drive also come included in a $148-per-person package deal, along with park fees and transport from Mombasa, which can be booked through the lodge.

Around the park

Predators are rare in Shimba Hills, but you may well see **elephant**, especially from the vantage of Elephant Hill or at the nearby **Sheldrick Falls**, particularly if you go early in the day. There are armed guards at Elephant Hill who will escort you to the falls; it's a very pretty walk down a steep hillside, atmospheric and partly wooded to the falls, but a long hike back up again – take water, and swimming gear if you want to splash in the pool, directly under the waterfall. Allow about three hours for the excursion. There were around 600 elephants in Shimba until the translocation of half of them to Tsavo North in 2005 (see p.379). The remaining 300 are still arguably more than Shimba can support: fortunately, the creation of the Mwaluganje Elephant Sanctuary (see below) has been a great success.

Look out also for the park's three **Maasai giraffe**, the product of a tentative experiment. Although Shimba had never had giraffe naturally, a small nucleus was introduced a decade ago after having been rescued from smugglers attempting to take them abroad. Unfortunately, one died in transit, another female died shortly after arrival, and the two males just disappeared, leaving only two females and distraught rangers. Two breeding males were then brought in, one more of the females died, but the other finally gave birth in December 1996, to the delight of everyone, though unfortunately she died soon after, and the group now consists of just three males. Spurred on by this modest success, **ostrich** have also been introduced. Shimba is best known, however, for its indigenous herds of **sable antelope**, magnificent-looking animals as big as horses, with great, sweeping horns. The park is their only habitat in Kenya (the similar but even bigger roan antelopes, which were relocated from western Kenya, died out, it's thought, through lack of necessary minerals). You may well see groups of chestnut-coloured sable females but the territorial, jet-black males are more solitary and harder to find. If you have a guide he'll know where to look, but they're most commonly seen in the area overlooking the ocean, between the public campsite and Giriama Point. Another good place to head for is **Makadara picnic site**: there are bats in the toilet and it's supposed to be a good place to see buffalo.

Camping in Shimba Hills

What Shimba Hills may lack in wildlife it more than makes up for with enchanting views in every direction, especially seawards. Haze tends to blot out Mombasa itself but the fringe of Diani Beach is usually visible. **Camping** is possible at two sites ($10 per person). The **public campsite** is located at one of the best vantage points in the park, about 3km from the main gate. The four *bandas* here (❸) are adequate (though the bedding, lamps, shower and nearby toilet can't be relied on, and the water needs purification), but the setting is sublime: a thickly forested bluff hundreds of metres above the coconut-crowded coastal plain. It's well worth spending the night up here just for the sunrise. If you do, you'll probably have the place to yourself. *Hunter's Camp* is preferred by Kenyans, but has no facilities whatsoever (book with the rangers).

Mwaluganje Elephant Sanctuary

To the northwest of Shimba and the area where the "sundowner walks" normally take place, just outside the national park, lies the **Mwaluganje Elephant Sanctuary** (PO Box 167 Kwale; ☎0722/343050, ✉mes@swiftmombasa.com; $15, children $2). Situated on the slopes of the privately owned Goloni Escarpment, it's a remarkable success story of a compromise solution. It was created in 1995 to defuse conflict between the local Duruma farmers and elephants, who had made a habit of trashing their crops and killing farmers attempting to defend their livelihoods. After consultation between the local people, Kenya Wildlife Service, and the Eden Wildlife Trust, 240 square kilometres were set aside for the sanctuary, separated along a third of its boundary from farmland with electric fencing, but left open elsewhere to keep the elephants' migration routes open.

The low-lying areas around the Manolo River are dominated by baobab, while thick brachystegia forest covers the escarpment's flanks, and harbours a surprising wealth of wildlife. You are "guaranteed" to see elephants here and, in time, it's hoped that threatened species can be relocated here from other parts of Kenya. Apart from the prolific birdlife, you might also see zebra, bushbuck, warthog, monkeys and (rarely) leopard.

The main gate is beyond the Shimba Hills park entrance, 14km west of Kwale, then 2km along a signposted track to the right (4WD only in the rains). There is another gate (Golini) along a track 5km northwest of Kwale. The only **accommodation** in the sanctuary is 🏕 *Travellers Mwaluganje Elephant Camp* (reservations through *Travellers Beach Hotel* in Bamburi; PO Box 87649 Mombasa; ☎ 041/5485121–6, ⓦ www.travellersbeach.com; ⑨). Most guests come on overnight packages from the coast ($155–165 per person), though day excursions are also available ($84–$94 per person including lunch, transport, park fee & game drive). Set along the shoulder of a low hill facing a well-established elephant trail, there are twenty twin-bedded tents under thatch roofs, each with veranda (watch the elephants walking past), bathrooms and electricity. You can also go on an escorted game drive through the sanctuary ($32 per person). The place still feels new and a little raw, but the setting along a water hole is delightful, and the staff extremely pleasant.

Tiwi Beach

Back on the coast, and south of Likoni, the first real magnet is **Tiwi Beach**. Popular among budget travellers having a bit of a splurge, Tiwi rates as genuine tropical paradise material and

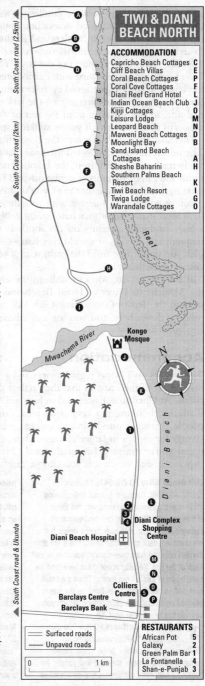

TIWI & DIANI BEACH NORTH

ACCOMMODATION

Capricho Beach Cottages	C
Cliff Beach Villas	E
Coral Beach Cottages	P
Coral Cove Cottages	F
Diani Reef Grand Hotel	L
Indian Ocean Beach Club	J
Kijiji Cottages	O
Leisure Lodge	M
Leopard Beach	N
Maweni Beach Cottages	D
Moonlight Bay	B
Sand Island Beach Cottages	A
Sheshe Baharini	H
Southern Palms Beach Resort	K
Tiwi Beach Resort	I
Twiga Lodge	G
Warandale Cottages	O

South Coast road (2.5km)

South Coast road (2km)

Tiwi Beaches

Reef

Mwachema River

Kongo Mosque

Diani Beach

South Coast road & Ukunda

Diani Beach Hospital

Diani Complex Shopping Centre

Colliers Centre

Barclays Centre
Barclays Bank

N

— Surfaced roads
— Unpaved roads

0   1 km

RESTAURANTS

African Pot	5
Galaxy	2
Green Palm Bar	1
La Fontanella	4
Shan-e-Punjab	3

attracts lots of Anglo-Kenyan families down from Nairobi. The reef lies just offshore, and there are good snorkelling opportunities at high tide, especially at the northern end. Beach hustlers and all the attendant hassles have mostly yet to arrive, especially in the northern section (fronted by *Sand Island* and *Maweni/ Capricho*). With the exception of the large *Tiwi Beach Resort* at its southern end, Tiwi is still cottage territory, with half a dozen or so plots vying with each other for business, some with low-key restaurants and bars. Tiwi's main drawbacks (some might say its advantages) are the lack of commercial bars, restaurants and nightlife, and its isolation from the rest of the coast. More serious are nagging concerns about security if you're walking anywhere: don't take any valuables.

There are two roads down to the beach from the main South Coast highway. The northernmost, signposted for *Sand Island*, *Capricho* and *Maweni*, is a narrow sandy track some 17km from the Likoni ferry; the second, about 1.5km further south, has a bigger clump of signboards and is much wider, and more reliable for driving in rain. Using either road, you're strongly advised not to walk, certainly if you've got all your luggage with you: these access roads through the cashews have seen many *panga* (machete)-point robberies. Waiting for a ride won't be a huge problem, certainly on the southern access road, where there's a fairly frequent taxi service (it should cost Ksh300–400), and most places will happily pick you up for free from the main road if you call ahead. Taxis from Mombasa cost about Ksh2000.

In the dry season, you can walk to the end of Tiwi Beach and wade across the Mwachema River to Diani Beach and the strange Kongo Mosque, right next to the *Indian Ocean Beach Club*. But again, there have been incidents of robbery down here, and you are not advised to go alone, certainly not with any valuables.

Accommodation

The seasons on Tiwi, as regards prices and availability, are slightly different from other parts of the coast in that they reflect the school holidays of their regular clients. At Christmas, Easter, and in July and August, it's hard to get in anywhere – advance booking is a very good idea. Price codes refer to the cost for two people sharing a one-bedroom cottage, where available; there are always big savings for groups in larger cottages. There isn't much in the real budget range unless you're camping (although *Coral Cove* has budget rooms), but the extra expense is well worth it if you choose carefully.

Cliff Beach Villas PO Box 24752 Nairobi Ⓣer0721/409068. Cottages, but not self-catering (fridges and cookers were removed, but there is a restaurant). The seven two-bedroom front cottages house four, with superb sea views, but are cramped, dark and rather basic. There are also thirteen one-bedroom (two-person) cottages at the back of the site. Security is not great here, and we have heard of thefts from rooms. There's a small pool, but no beach directly in front, as the site is perched on a coral rock promontory, though you can use the beach next door. ④

Coral Cove Cottages PO Box 200 Ukunda Ⓣ0722/732797, ⓌPwww.coralcove .tiwibeach.com. Excellent, large, stand-alone cottages (two-bedroom, sleeping four people, for Ksh5200) with good bathrooms and an attractive,

palm-shaded beach, all bathed in a laid-back atmosphere provided by low-key but consistently helpful management. Loads of dogs and cats, an aviary full of rescued parrots, and a troupe of vervet monkeys that regularly visit (the proprietor is keenly involved in animal conservation). The sea here is shallow (good for children), and favoured by turtles for laying eggs. Fruit, veg and fish vendors call daily. You can hire a cook/housekeeper for Ksh450 per day. As well as the two-bedroom cottages, there's a one-bedroom one (⑤), and a basic rondavel for budgeteers (③).

Maweni and Capricho Beach Cottages PO Box 277 Ukunda Ⓣ040/330041, ⓌPwww .mawenibeach.com. Two adjacent plots, now amalgamated under single management. *Maweni* has a variety of relatively simple self-catering cottages

Dhow trips and diving

For details of **dhow-trip operators**, read the box on p.483. Information on scuba diving is in the box on p.482.

in beautiful gardens with wild dik-diks and stunning sea views. *Capricho* is slightly pricier, with well-designed vault-roofed cottages, plenty of cool space, and a pool (which is open to *Maweni* guests too). Renovation is promised following amalgamation, and among other things, *Capricho* should get a poolside bar and restaurant. There's an *askari* on the beach to keep an eye on your things while you swim, and you can hire the services of a cook for Ksh300–500 per day. ⑤

Moonlight Bay PO Box 1778 Ukunda ☎040/330040, ⓦwww.moonlightbaycottages.net. A small place, with only four cottages, plus a bar and restaurant. You can self-cater (each cottage has a kitchen), or hire a cook (from Ksh250 per day), or eat at the restaurant. Vendors of fish, fruit and veg call by daily, and there are pretty gardens and easy beach access. ⑤

Sand Island Beach Cottages PO Box 5516 Diani ☎0733/660554, 040/3300043, ⓦwww.sandislandtiwi.com. Long established and well maintained, with fully equipped self-catering rustic cottages – all sea-facing – with new kitchen equipment and decent bathrooms. The old Kenya atmosphere is refreshingly informal, with charming family management, and the site is very attractive, with a shifting starfish-covered sand isle exposed with the tides just metres across the water, and safe swimming possible at all times. There's a coral garden nearby, and use of snorkelling equipment is free. The products of a working citrus orchard are available, and there are the ruins of old slave quarters in the grounds. Various cottages sleeping two to six people. ⑤

Sheshe Baharini Beach Hotel PO Box 63230 Nairobi ☎0735/511436, ⓔinfo@sheshebeach .com. One of Tiwi's most luxurious developments, and currently very good value, with comfortable a/c rooms in four categories, plus a pool, poolside bar, beach bar (serving wood-oven pizzas) and seafood restaurant, and watersports facilities nearby including glass-bottomed boats and windsurfing. B&B ⑤

Tiwi Beach Resort PO Box 1877 Ukunda ☎040/320801–3, ⓦwww.tiwibeachresort .com. The beach's only tourist hotel, a large and somewhat impersonal package affair. The main attraction is arguably the longest swimming pool in Kenya, actually a series of pools connected by canals and slides. The public areas are on one side, and rows of three-storey apartment blocks on the other. There's also a nightclub (*Diamonds*, from 10pm nightly), and a good Indian restaurant (*Sher-e-Punjab*; evenings only). Watersports include waterskiing, windsurfing, snorkelling and scuba diving. Free entry for day visitors. Wheelchair friendly, with adapted rooms. HB ⑥

Twiga Lodge PO Box 80820 Mombasa ☎040/320 5126. Hostel and campsite trading on a reputation established in the 1970s, and still popular with overlanders and budget travellers. The cheap rooms are rather barrack-like (no self-catering facilities, and some lack toilets), but the superior rooms, admittedly costing over twice as much, are big, bright and airy. You can also camp (Ksh200 per person). There's an adequately stocked provisions store and the bar-restaurant is lively and does reasonable food. ③

Diani Beach and around

Diani Beach ought to fulfil most dreams about the archetypal palm-fringed beach. The sand is soft and brilliantly white, the sea is crystal-clear turquoise, the reef is a safe thirty-minute swim or ten-minute boat ride away and, arching overhead, the coconut palms keep up a perpetual slow sway as the breeze rustles through the fronds. Competition for space, however, has begun to seriously mar Diani's paradisiacal qualities. Another drawback is that the beach tends to get covered at high tide, or leaves only a narrow strip of sand. As elsewhere in Kenya, all the beach is open to the public; it's only the access routes that are restricted by some hotels. On the positive side, the droves of hustlers – the "beach boys" who had become such a nuisance just a few years back that they

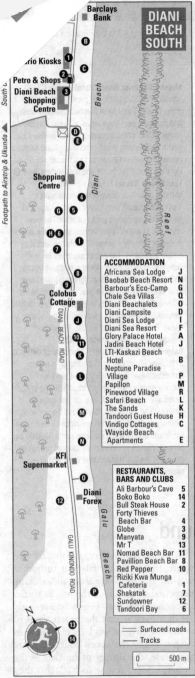

Footpath to Airstrip & Ukunda ◀

South Coast

Barclays Bank

DIANI BEACH SOUTH

Trio Kiosks ❶
Petro & Shops ❷
Diani Beach Shopping Centre ❸

Beach

Diani

Reef

Shopping Centre

❹

❺

❻

❼

❽

❾
Colobus Cottage

DIANI BEACH ROAD

❿
⓫

KFI Supermarket

Diani Forex

⓬

GALU KINONDO ROAD

Galu Beach

⓭
⓮

ACCOMMODATION

Africana Sea Lodge	J
Baobab Beach Resort	N
Barbour's Eco-Camp	G
Chale Sea Villas	Q
Diani Beachalets	O
Diani Campsite	D
Diani Sea Lodge	I
Diani Sea Resort	F
Glory Palace Hotel	A
Jadini Beach Hotel	J
LTI-Kaskazi Beach Hotel	B
Neptune Paradise Village	P
Papillon	M
Pinewood Village	R
Safari Beach	L
The Sands	K
Tandoori Guest House	H
Vindigo Cottages	C
Wayside Beach Apartments	E

RESTAURANTS, BARS AND CLUBS

Ali Barbour's Cave	5
Boko Boko	14
Bull Steak House	2
Forty Thieves Beach Bar	4
Globe	3
Manyata	9
Mr T	13
Nomad Beach Bar	11
Pavillion Beach Bar	8
Red Pepper	10
Riziki Kwa Munga Cafeteria	1
Shakatak	7
Sundowner	12
Tandoori Bay	6

N

══	Surfaced roads
—	Tracks

0   500 m

▼ **Q** (1.5km) & **R** (500m)

were beginning to drive tourists away – have now dwindled to a few relatively easily brushed-off diehards. Especially since the 2002 attacks on Israeli-connected targets (see p.622), security has been tightened up, with *askaris* posted all the way along the beach and the beach road, and much tighter security at hotel entrances, which has made life a lot harder for the hustlers.

If you're coming by public transport **from Mombasa**, first catch a matatu from Abdel Nasser Road, Jomo Kenyatta Avenue, or outside the GPO on Digo Road, to Likoni ferry (Ksh15) to make the crossing (free for foot passengers; Ksh40 for small cars). Once in Likoni, walk up with the crowd to the well-marked matatu stages on the left side, and catch one for "Diani" or "Beach" (Ksh50). If there are no direct ones, get one to Ukunda (Ksh50), and then make a connection down to the beach road (Ksh20) – you'll find plenty of transport both day and night. Don't walk, especially if you're burdened with luggage or valuables: the three-kilometre link road has a bad reputation – hard to tell how well founded – for muggings. Taxis from Mombasa cost around Ksh2000–2500. Alternatively, you could organize an air transfer from Mombasa to Ukunda airstrip, a couple of kilometres west of Diani post office – Diani Air (℡0725/804611, ℮ dianiair@iafrica.com) can arrange the flight at €70 per person for a minimum of two people.

There's an increasingly heavy scattering of proper shops along the strip, as well as a new post office. The main **shopping areas** on the north side are Diani Complex Shopping Centre (1.4km north of the junction) and Barclays Centre (almost opposite the junction). On the south side, the commerce kicks off with the Petro petrol station (900m) and Diani Beach Shopping Centre (1km), where vervet monkeys scamper across the designer *makuti*. There are more shops and businesses outside *Diani Sea Resort* and opposite *Diani Sea Lodge*.

Accommodation

Running 300m behind the beach, the Diani Beach road feels like Kenya's number-one strip in the high season. Fortunately, thick forest separates the road from the shore, though more of the **Jadini Forest** disappears every year as one new plot after another is cleared, usually not entirely legally. The **tourist hotels** that fill the plots are expensive by Kenyan standards and, if you've been travelling on a budget, the prices will come as a shock. If you're coming from abroad they seem more reasonably priced, and you'll find standards generally high. Most offer low-season reductions, which are generally good value.

The distances in the following listings are from the Ukunda junction on the Diani Beach road, by Barclays Bank.

Camping and budget rooms

Budget accommodation along the beach is sparse and none of the big hotels will entertain campers in their gardens. If you're a family or in a large group, renting a cottage (see below) is invariably better value than taking a room, and gives you the chance to cook up some local food in your own style. In addition to places listed here, *Diani Beachalets* (under "Cottages and apartments") has cheap two-person *bandas*.

Barbour's Eco-Camp 3km south, opposite *Ali Barbour's Cave* restaurant ☏0722/523278, ✉stilts@barboursafari.com. Just over the road from the beach, but right in the bush, with *bandas* on stilts, very well shaded pitches for camping ($5), a good bar-restaurant, and plenty of wildlife, including Sykes' and colobus monkeys, and bushbabies. ③

Chale Sea Villas 11km south, just before *Pine-wood*; PO Box 1766 Ukunda ☏0733/812246, ✉chaleseavilla@hotmail.com. A range of accommodation including one- or two-bedroom *bandas*, as well as camping (Ksh600 per person) way down on Galu Beach past the *Neptune*. There's a bar, and you can order breakfast and basic meals, though the *bandas* are equipped with kitchens. ⑤

Diani Campsite 1.4km south, next to the defunct *Trade Winds*; PO Box 5019 Diani Beach ☏0127/3136. Once something of an institution,

this site fell on hard times, but has now been revived, with small but well-maintained self-catering cottages, all with kitchens and mosquito nets, plus camping (Ksh300 per person – also with cooking facilities available), parking space, and a bar-restaurant. ⑤

Glory Palace Hotel 500m west on the way to Ukunda; PO Box 85527 Ukunda ☏040/3203392. More than adequate unit in this mini-chain of hotels, with a pool. Some rooms have a/c, others have a fan. Security appears sound, but caution would nonetheless be advised. B&B ③

Tandoori Guesthouse 3.5km south, behind *Tandoori Bay Restaurant* ☏040/3202020. The cheapest rooms in Diani (as opposed to Ukunda), and very reasonable for the price: clean, some of them pretty large, all with nets, three s/c, three not. The big disadvantage of this place is that it's off the beach, though you can walk there easily enough. ②

Cottages and apartments

As in the Tiwi Beach cottage listings, price codes refer to the cost of the whole cottage if double rooms are not available. As always, the larger cottages offer big savings for groups. Prices for most of these are negotiable, especially for poverty-stricken backpackers out of season. See maps on pp.473 and 476 for locations.

Coral Beach Cottages 300m north; PO Box 168 Ukunda ☏040/3203662, ✉munuthiafredi@hotmail.com. On a parched,

rundown site, this isn't an obvious first choice, with only three of its seventeen cottages plus five of its six apartments up for short-term rent. On the plus side, they face out over the sea, and prices are reasonable. ⑤

🏃 **Diani Beachalets** 6.5km south; PO Box 5076 ⊕040/3202180, ⓦwww .dianibeachalets.com. By far the best value on Diani, welcoming and homely, visited by duiker antelopes, bushbabies and colobus monkeys, this peaceful refuge is bang on the beach, with a variety of abodes, from simple two-bed *bandas* with fridge, electric light, communal showers and cooking area, to nice, s/c cottages with kitchen, sitting room and veranda. Fresh fish, fruit and veg from pedlars. There are also tennis courts, and the beach is pretty well deserted. *Bandas* ②, cottages ③

🏃 **Kijiji Cottages** 600m north; PO Box 5542 Diani Beach ⊕040/3300035, ⓦwww .kijijicottages.com. Formerly part of *Warandale*, these are the nicest cottages in Diani, extremely well kept, with a choice of different shapes and sizes, all spacious, comfortable and secluded. Sea-facing cottages cost slightly more (*Bonde* is the finest of the lot, with a superb terrace) but *Carudi*, away from the sea, is the most spacious. There's a pool, and regular visits by vervet, colobus and Sykes' monkeys as well as bushbabies. The staff clean for you, and you can hire a cook (Ksh1000 per day). ⑥

Vindigo Cottages 700m south; PO Box 77 Ukunda ⊕040/3202192, ⓔvindigocottages@hotgossip. co.ke. Seven vaguely down-at-heel self-catering cottages in woodland, with a pleasing rustic feel. The kitchens are fully equipped and the rooms are very private, with fans, electricity, running water in the showers and high-level toilets. Some have lovely views over the beach through the trees. The services of a cook can be hired for Ksh300 per day, fishermen and fruitsellers call daily and there are three night *askaris*. ⑤

Warandale Cottages 600m north; PO Box 11 Ukunda ⊕040/3202186, ⓦwww.warandale. freeservers.com. In the same group of cottages as *Kijiji*, and sharing the same grounds and pool, these are very similar, not quite as well kept, but still very clean, pleasant and spacious, some sea-facing, others (cheaper) set back among the trees, with the advantage of more likely bushbaby and monkey sightings. ⑥

Wayside Beach Apartments 1.4km south, follow signs to *Trade Winds*; PO Box 5398 Diani ⊕040/3203119, ⓔtmillia@yahoo.com. Stylish two- to six-bed self-catering apartments in a building around a good pool, set between the main road and defunct *Trade Winds* hotel, but not right on the beach. Has a sauna and jacuzzi, though neither gets much use. ⑤

Hotels north of the junction

Generally, the more interesting abodes worthy of major expenditure are to the south of the Ukunda junction – an area which also retains some flicker of pre-hotel times. To the north, the scene is brasher and more despoiled, and there's no forest either. Most hotels provide some sort of nightly entertainment, including uniformly cheesy bands at dinnertime. For locations of the hotels see Tiwi & Diani Beach North map, p.473.

Diani Reef Grand Hotel 1.6km; PO Box 35 Ukunda ⊕040/3202723, ⓦwww.dianireef. Originally put up in the 1970s, but completely revamped in 2005, this is one of the largest hotels on the coast, with three restaurants and five bars, plus regular and deluxe rooms in different wings, all cool and comfortable, with not much to distinguish them but the size of their balconies. Facilities include windsurfing, scuba-diving school, pedalos and inflatable canoes, the *Ace* casino and *Dunes Nightspot* (nightly 9pm–late), and there's a babysitting service. Wheelchair accessible, with adapted rooms. HB $270; ⑨

Indian Ocean Beach Club 3.6km; PO Box 73 Ukunda ⊕040/3203730, ⓔiobc@africaonline.co.ke; reservations through Jacaranda, Waiyaki Way; PO Box 14287, Nairobi ⊕020/4445818, ⓦwww .jacarandahotels.com. Opened in 1992, this is one of the best hotels on the coast. State-of-the-art rooms,

wonderful Lamu-style architecture and attentive management, with most watersports free and swimming possible at all tides in the creek. Fine groves of baobabs in the gardens, and oceanfront rooms don't cost much more. Wheelchair friendly, with one adapted room. B&B $188; ⑨

Leisure Lodge 1.2km; PO Box 84383 Mombasa ⊕040/3202011 or 3202014, ⓦwww.leisure lodgeresort.com. One of the earlier Diani hotels (1971) but revamped, in a striking location on low cliffs hollowed by bat-filled caves. The fine, tree-shaded beach is tucked beneath. There are several pools, an eighteen-hole par 72 golf course opposite the entrance, and a casino in the grounds (daily 9pm–3am, or later if there are still punters playing). Standard rooms lack sea views, but come with a/c, nets on request and satellite TV; club rooms are slightly more spacious, with two extra swimming pools for their exclusive use; "Oasis Villas" are even

Beach boys

Spending some peaceful time on the beach can sometimes appear virtually impossible because of the **hustlers** plying their wares, or their camel rides, or their boat trips, or just themselves. Fortunately, the problem has abated in recent years, but a few diehard beach-boy pesterers still hang on. People have different ways of dealing with them. Ignoring their greetings is considered rude, and may well not get rid of them in any case. One solution is to strike up a friendship of sorts with one beach boy, to buy at least something, or to go on a boat trip. Once you have a friend, and have done some business, you should find you can then use the beach with fewer hassles from the others. It's not so easy for single women, but the principle for most situations still applies – don't fight it. There is no need, incidentally, to feel physically threatened on the beach. Every hotel has its *askaris* (security guards) posted along the boundary between the plot and the beach, and they usually stay alert to the slightest sign of trouble – which is rare indeed.

more luxurious, with a private pool shared between each four villas. There's also a PADI diving school, windsurfing school and tennis courts. Popular with German and Swiss package tourists. HB $170; ⑨

Leopard Beach Hotel 800m; PO Box 34 Ukunda ☎040/3202110–2, ⓦwww .leopardbeachhotel.com. Sleek, modernized hotel set in lush gardens with ponds and waterfalls populated by lizards, friendly staff, a good atmosphere and decent food. Steps lead down to the beach. Superior rooms and cottages have sea views. Facilities include tennis, volleyball, canoeing, windsurfing,

snorkelling, glass-bottomed boats and PADI diving school. Wheelchair friendly with adapted rooms. HB €150; ⑨

Southern Palms Beach Resort 2.9km; PO Box 363 Ukunda ☎040/3203360–4, ⓦwww .southernpalms.com. Spacious and well-appointed package hotel with rooms in four-storey blocks with thatched roofs, two fabulous pools (one with Jacuzzi, both with water-level bars) that children as well as adults adore, friendly management and staff. PADI diving school, windsurfing, floodlit tennis courts, squash, gym. HB €140; ⑨

Hotels south of the junction

Tarmac continues another 4km beyond the end (6.5km south) of the good road, as far as the *Pinewood* on Galu Beach. Distances given are south from the junction.

Africana Sea Lodge 4.2km; PO Box 84616 Mombasa ☎040/3202622, ⓔahl@africaonline. co.ke; reservations through Alliance, p.63. On the same plot as *Jadini Beach*, and jointly owned with that and the *Safari Beach*, whose facilities guests can use, the *Africana* is sold as an all-inclusive fun hotel for couples, and is one of the few places which pulls off the balancing act between package tourism and personal service, with accommodation in comfortable but unembellished *bandas* (no sea views). All-inclusive €210; ⑨

Baobab Beach Resort 5.9km; PO Box 32 Ukunda ☎040/3202623, ⓦwww.baobab-beach-resort .com. An elegant and well-kept all-inclusive club (formerly *Robinson Club Baobab*, built in the 1970s), part of the German TUI chain, located at the end of Diani Beach proper on a coral rock promontory. Unfortunately, only the first row of bungalows have sea views. Day visits Ksh2500 half-day, Ksh3100 full-day. All-inclusive €150; ⑨

Diani Sea Lodge 3.5km; PO Box 37 Ukunda ☎040/3203081–3, ⓔdianisea@africaonline .co.ke. A large, slightly downmarket, Mediterranean-style all-inclusive version of the jointly owned *Resort*. The rooms are a let down: despite the good-sized double beds, a/c and frame-fitted nets, most are small, in bungalows set back in the gardens, and only ten are sea-facing. Pool and children's pool, gym, tennis court, crazy golf, windsurfing and PADI diving school. Mainly German clientele. Daily admission Ksh2160. Not the best all-inclusive, but relatively cheap. Wheelchair accessible. All-inclusive ⑧

Diani Sea Resort 2km; PO Box 37 Ukunda ☎040/3203081–3, ⓔdianisea@africaonline .co.ke. Built in 1991 and much more cheerful than its all-inclusive sister hotel, with consistently good service, nice staff and plenty of things to do. Most guests are German, many on long stays. Great pool (Ksh2160 for casual visitors), gym, tennis and squash courts, crazy golf, windsurfing and PADI diving school. All-inclusive ⑧

Jadini Beach Hotel 4.2km; PO Box 84616 Mombasa ⑦040/3202622, Ⓔahl@africaonline .co.ke; reservations through Alliance, p.63. Diani's longest-established resort hotel (1960s) with high standards and good atmosphere. Busy and cosmopolitan, and good for kids, with its daytime creche and activities. Besides the usual water sports, facilities include a PADI-accredited diving school, three tennis courts, the atmospheric *Jambo Village* restaurant, and St Stephen's Chapel for Sun morning repentance. Rooms are big and bright, most with sea views. Guests can also use the facilities at *Africana Sea Lodge* and *Safari Beach Hotel*. HB €162; ⑨

LTI-Kaskazi Beach Hotel 300m; PO Box 135 Ukunda ⑦040/3203170–9, Ⓔkaskazi@africaonline.co.ke. Well run and competitively priced, successfully balancing classy atmosphere with package-tour popularity. Heavy on the Arabic styling, with white-tiled floors, tinkling fountains and soaring *makuti* roofs. One of the few all-inclusive hotels to welcome day visitors (Ksh1650 including lunch and drinks), and the only place in Diani with drinking water in the taps. There's also the sad little ruined seventeenth-century "Diani mosque" in the garden, basically just an old wall. All-inclusive ⑧

Neptune Paradise Village 8.5km, on Galu Beach; PO Box 696 Ukunda ⑦040/3203061–4, Ⓦwww.neptunehotels.com. Decent rooms with pink cane furniture in tightly packed regular rows of two-storey *bandas* (no sea views), and a plot that requires lengthy, shadeless walks and has been extended seawards to the point where there is no beach left at high tide. Facilities include two full-size pools, two kids' pools, tennis courts, mini-golf, a bowling green, a scuba-diving school, windsurfing, and catamaran trips. All-inclusive, with mostly German clientele. Reasonably priced, but still overrated. Day visits Ksh1800. All-inclusive ⑧

🏃 **The Sands (Nomad)** 4.8km; PO Box 5066 ⑦040/3203643–8, Ⓦwww .thesandsatnomad.com. A former package hotel revamped as a "boutique resort" (a small deluxe establishment, in other words), very close to the beach, with only 37 rooms and suites, and personal service. There's a good Thai restaurant (see p.484), a pool, a dive school and a kitesurfing school, H20 Extreme. B&B €135; ⑨

Papillon Hotel 5.5km; PO Box 5292 ⑦040/3202213–5, Ⓦwww.rexresorts.com. Next door and superior to the snooty *Ocean Village Club*, and one of the few all-inclusives with a really cheerful holiday atmosphere. Staff are helpful and friendly, and there's loads for kids to do, with a playground, children's swimming pool and busy daily club. Most of the cool, pleasant rooms have sea views, too. Other activities include scuba diving, catamarans, pedalos and windsurfing, as well as glass-bottomed boats and snorkelling. Very good value. Day visits Ksh1500 till 6pm, Ksh1800 till midnight. All-inclusive ⑦

Pinewood Village 11km, on Galu Beach; PO Box 90521 Mombasa ⑦040/3203131–2, Ⓦwww. pinewood-village.com. An extremely stylish resort hotel on a nearly deserted stretch of beach far to the south of the main Diani strip. You can take an ordinary room and eat in the restaurant, or take a suite (choice of open-plan or separate sleeping and sitting rooms) and get the services of your own chef thrown in. Good value. HB ⑧

🏃 **Safari Beach Hotel** 5.1km; PO Box 90690 Mombasa ⑦040/3202726, Ⓔahl@africaonline.co.ke; reservations through Alliance, p.63. The best of the Alliance hotels, with good sports and watersports facilities (and PADI diving school), a disco, and a daily children's programme with full-time staff. Although not luxurious, the rooms are comfortable and spacious, set in two-room rondavels ranged up a gentle, wooded slope at the rear of the hotel. Guests can also use the facilities at *Africana Sea Lodge* and *Jadini Beach Hotel*. HB €174; ⑨

Around the resort

Enjoying yourself on Diani isn't difficult. You can rent snorkelling gear (about Ksh500) from just about anywhere, and float out across the lagoon to the **reef**. Remember how fiercely the sun is likely to burn and wear a T-shirt unless your complexion is sufficiently dark to protect you. You need to be a confident swimmer: there are no strong currents nor any real danger, but the reef is 600–1000m away and swimming back on the ebb tide can be tiring. Alternatively, a trip to the reef at low tide on one of the outrigger **canoes** is highly recommended. The crews know all the good (or at least the more reasonable) spots for snorkelling and it shouldn't cost you much more than Ksh1000 for an hour or three. One of the best areas is directly opposite *Baobab Beach Resort*,

△ Harvesting coconuts, Diani Beach

about 300m out towards the reef, where there is a cluster of coral heads. The sheltered lagoon behind the reef is also ideal for **windsurfing** (Ksh800 per hr) and you can also do **Kitesurfing** (courses from $70).

When you tire of the beach and the sea, or of just lying under the palm trees, you could **rent a bicycle** and go off exploring – from about Ksh600 per day. By matatu, Mombasa with its Old Town and shopping possibilities is an easy enough target for a day out. There's also the eighteen-hole par 72 **golf course** opposite the *Leisure Lodge* (which runs it) on the north side of the junction. For details of **dhow-trip** operators, see the box on p.483.

Kongo Mosque

For a short excursion with a goal, you could aim for the **Kongo Mosque** at the far north end of the beach, at the mouth of the Mwachema River, but it's not a place to visit on your own, and certainly not if carrying anything valuable, as the spot is known for muggings. It's most easily reached through the grounds of the *Indian Ocean Beach Club* – which gives you the opportunity to visit one of Diani's best-looking hotels. Beyond the boundary fence and inevitable *askari*, the Kongo Mosque is surrounded by venerable baobabs. Also known as Diani Persian Mosque, the building is enigmatic and disconcerting, with its five heavy wooden doors. There's an electric atmosphere here, the barrel-vaulted mosque brooding like a huge tomb under the trees. It is too complete to be considered a ruin, and has been fenced in by local Islamic leaders to encourage the community to start using it again in response to attempts by local politicians to appropriate the mosque and communal land for "development".

Although a sign suggests otherwise, you will, suitably attired and accompanied, be allowed to have a look around. Named after a forest, the mosque is thought to be either fourteenth or fifteenth century and the one remaining building – maybe the only stone one – of a Wa-shirazi settlement here (see p.488). The river mouth was the first safe anchorage south of Mombasa.

Jadini Forest

For a walk, or a jog, it's more interesting to head south along Diani road. Here there are more hotels, of course, but also, approaching the end of the paving, some wonderful patches of jungly forest comprising the dwindling **Jadini Forest** ("Jadini", disappointingly, turns out to be an embellished acronym made from the initials of members of a white settler family who once owned most of the land around here). There's the almost obligatory snake park, but if you'd like to search for some animals in the wild rather than support this venture, then any of the tracks leading off to the right will take you straight into magnificent stands of hardwood trees, alive with birds and butterflies, and rocking with vervet and **Angolan colobus monkeys**. The latter, whose population is estimated at around 1500, have come in for some special attention lately, as concern has mounted over land encroachment and deaths from speeding cars. The resultant campaign, spearheaded by the Wakuluzu Colobus Trust (at Colobus Cottage, 3.7km south; PO Box 5380 Diani Beach; ☎040/320 3519, ⊛www.colobustrust .org), has put up warning signs and speedbumps, and – most inventively – the wire, rope and wood "colobobridges" at known danger spots over the road, which the monkeys quickly learned to use. You can pick up more information at Colobus Cottage (Mon–Sat 8am–5pm), which also has a **forest nature trail** in its grounds (a guided half-hour walk costs Ksh500). Of the other monkeys,

---

Diving on the South Coast

Many South Coast hotels, and a good number along the North Coast, have **dive centres**, where you can do everything from a basic beginner lesson plus assisted dive (around $80) to a full course giving you an internationally recognized (usually PADI) qualification ($500 to "Open Water"; an additional $400 to "Advanced Open Water"). If you already have scuba certification, single dives cost around $50. You can nearly always take a free dip in the pool wearing diving equipment, to test your affinity – most people find breathing underwater curiously addictive.

Before choosing a centre, take time to compare the equipment of several companies, and ask them about their environmental policy, safety procedures and general experience. They should at the very least have up-to-date PADI ("Professional Association of Diving Instructors") or BSAC ("British Sub-Aqua Association") accreditation, and ideally be affiliated to Scuba Schools International (SSI). One of the oldest and best-established outfits, with an excellent reputation and good equipment, is Diving the Crab, on the beach between *Jadini* and *Africana* hotels on Diani (Blue Wave; PO Box 5011 Diani Beach; ☎040/3202003, ⊛www.divingthecrab.com). If you need more information, contact PADI directly in the United States at 30151 Tomas St, Rancho Santa Margarita, CA 92688–2125 (☎1-800/729-7234 or 949/858-7234, ⊛www.padi.com).

The Dive Sites of Kenya and Tanzania (see Contexts, p.671) is highly recommended reading for divers as well as snorkellers. See also the box on "Responsible snorkelling, diving and fishing" on p.421.

The following is a list of the main **dhow-trip operators**, all of which operate out of the South Coast. Unless stated, all will pick you up from your hotel (South Coast, and North Coast as far as Kikambala), either for free or for a nominal extra charge. For the most part, the dhows are not under sail but are powered by on-board or outboard motors. All can be booked direct, or though your hotel. If you're going to combine a dhow trip with snorkelling, see the box on p.421.

🏃 **Charlie Claw's** Wasini Island; PO Box 281 Ukunda ☏040/3202331 or 3203055, Ⓦwww.wasiniislandkenya.com. A choice of budget or all-inclusive deals (the latter gets you a more lavish lunch, with free drinks thrown in) on day-long dhow and snorkelling trips at Kisiti, with a seafood lunch at its restaurant on the north side of Wasini Island upon your hungry return. Costs $65 (budget) or $80 (all-inclusive) from Shimoni, $75/95 from South Coast hotels, $80/100 from the North Coast. Equipment and field guides are available on board. Scuba diving costs an additional $60 for two dives, or $35 for one.

Dolphin Dhow Barclays Centre, Diani Beach; PO Box 85636 Mombasa ☏040/320 2094, Ⓦwww.dolphindhow.com. Day-long dolphin-spotting trips combined with snorkelling (no flippers provided; bring your own). Early-morning pick-ups from North and South Coast hotels. Lunch on board. Dolphin sightings obviously not guaranteed. $100–105.

Funzi Island Club Just south of Colliers Centre, Diani Beach; PO Box 1108 Ukunda; ☏040/3202044, Ⓔfunzicamp@africaonline.co.ke. This expensive hotel (see p.488) also offers dolphin-spotting trips by dhow combined with crocodile spotting on the Ramisi River estuary. No snorkelling. Early-morning pick-ups from North and South Coast hotels. $100.

🏃 **Pilli-Pipa Dhow Safaris** Colliers Centre; PO Box 5185 Diani Beach; ☏040/3202401, Ⓦwww.pillipipa.com. Hugely enjoyable small-group dhow day-trips to Kisiti Marine National Park for outstanding snorkelling (field guides, masks, snorkels and fins provided), with a late lunch of crab claws, fine wine and Swahili food at a private house on Wasini Island. Departures most days at 8.30am from Shimoni jetty (collection can be arranged from both South and North Coast hotels). $100–105.

SSI East Africa (Blue Wave) By *Nomad Hotel*; PO Box 5011 Diani Beach; ☏040/3202003, Ⓔinfo@divingthecrab.com. Offers mangrove trips (by motorboat; 3–4hr) from next to *The Sands (Nomad) Hotel* in Diani south to mangrove channels in front of Chale Island, where you might see grey herons, fish eagles, cormorants and kingfishers. No pick-ups – you have to get yourself down to the office. $100.

baboons are most common, and are nasty-tempered pests: their nutritious diet of hotel leftovers means they've multiplied greatly, and are not afraid of humans. Keep your distance, as there have been many incidents of unwary tourists getting scratched and bitten. Overly tame **Sykes' monkeys** are also becoming a pest.

Snakes you are unlikely to come across. You'll be told the forest is the haunt of leopards, which is extremely unlikely. Come down here at night and you will see eyes in the dark, probably those of **bushbabies** – it's hard to believe that even leopards would put up with so violent a destruction of their habitat.

Eating, drinking and nightlife

Most of the hotels have snack menus, salad bars and all the rest. If you're on a budget, choose carefully and avoid the dubious temptation of Ksh300 fruit-juice cocktails, and you can still depart satisfied. The following listings, with distances given from the junction, include some of the best, and some of the best-value, places to eat and drink apart from the hotels.

Finding food for **self-catering** is straightforward enough, with ambulant fish and fruit sellers on the beach, various stalls along the beach road, and several supermarkets (see "Listings", p.486).

Restaurants

Ali Barbour's Cave 3km south ☎040/3202033, ⓦwww.georgebabour. com. Bizarrely built inside a deep coral cave: you enter at ground level and descend. The lavish French and seafood menu (lobster bisque, chilli crab, and duck in brandy sauce are among the highlights) runs to around Ksh5000 for two with wine – good food, well presented. Even if you're not eating, it's worth dropping in just to have a look. Don't wear shorts or a baseball cap. Open daily from 6pm.

Boko Boko 200m past *Club Neptune Village*, 9.3km south ☎040/3202344. Long-established Seychellois restaurant (slightly spicy, Creole cooking) set in a lush garden. Large *makuti*-cone hall with a few tables. Surprisingly reasonable, with main dishes from around Ksh400, but service is deathly slow.

Bull Steak House 600m south, behind Petro filling station. No bull, just very large slices of high-grade dead cattle (Angus to be precise), with T-bones at Ksh1350, or ribeyes for just over half that. In the way of sausages, it also serves one-metre bratwursts. Not recommended for vegetarians.

Galaxy Bazaar Complex Shopping Centre, 1.5km north ☎040/3300018. Classy Chinese restaurant with main dishes at around Ksh400–700. Free pick-up from hotels. Open daily 11.30am–2.30pm & 6–11pm.

Globe Diani Beach Shopping Centre, 1km south. Good and moderately priced home-style English cooking, with main courses at around Ksh400–500, and proper puddings for afters.

La Fontanella Colliers Centre, 300m north. Italian restaurant serving very decent pizzas and calzoni (Ksh450–600) as well as pasta, salads, seafood and decent espresso coffee.

Red Pepper 4.8km south, by *The Sands (Nomad)* hotel. Count on Ksh1000 per head at this stylish Thai restaurant with the accent on seafood. As you'd expect in Thai cuisine, some dishes are very spicy indeed (look out for the three pepper rating on the menu), so if you don't like chilli, choose carefully. Open evenings except Monday 7–10pm, plus Sat & Sun 12.30–3pm.

Shan-e-Punjab Diani Complex Shopping Centre, 1.4km north ☎040/320116. Indian restaurant and snack bar with an open-air garden, serving veg and non-veg Punjabi dishes. Around Ksh800 for a meal, Ksh1500 with seafood. Free transport from anywhere in Diani. Open daily 10am–11pm.

Cheaper food and bars

African Pot 300m north. By *Coral Beach Cottages*, a pleasant bar serving the usual Kenyan fare (tilapia, stew, *pilau*) at reasonable prices (Ksh200–300), with cold beer. Most of the food is good, but they're a bit heavy-handed with the salt on their *nyama choma* (you can tell them you want it without).

Forty Thieves Beach Bar & Restaurant 3km south. This budget beachside hangout is a good place for a daytime drink – a bit of a local watering hole – and perfect in the evening when its beach front is floodlit. Discos on Wed, Fri and Sat (and plenty of barefoot racing around the beach); live band and curry buffet on Sun, English premiership football matches live on TV, even a cybercafé.

Green Palm Bar 2.7km north. Opposite the closed *Golden Beach Hotel*, a popular place with cocktails under a *makuti* roof. The drinks are pricey but the food is reasonable, with main courses at Ksh350–400. They also have a pool, and even rooms.

Mr T Roof Garden Bar & Restaurant 9.2km south. A little overpriced for the standard menu of tourist, seafood and African dishes (main courses

Ksh300–500) but it's the breeze and the company that attract the clientele.

Nomad Beach Bar 4.8km south. At times wildly popular beach bar down at the water's edge, open 9am–6.30pm or later, with snacks, pizzas, seafood, plenty of booze, and famous Sun lunch curry buffet (Ksh900) – a real family affair, with regular live jazz or a one-man band.

Pavillion Beach Bar 3.8km south. A pleasantly laid-back drinking venue on lawns by the beach, reached through the disused buildings of the now-defunct *Two Fishes Lodge* hotel, and popular with residents and tourists alike. There's moderately priced food, and a live band (though somewhat middle-of-the-road) on Sat and Sun afternoons from 1pm. Open daily 10am–11pm.

Riziki Kwa Munga Cafeteria 700m south. A small shack in amongst the curio stalls just north of the Petro station, serving cheap and basic, but very good, Kenyan food. Good for breakfast (omelette and chapatti with tea) or lunch (beans in coconut sauce and pilau), and extremely cheap.

Sundowner 7km south. A very cheap restaurant and bar, completely unpretentious and not a hustler in sight, serving brilliant African food, seafood (crab, octopus or tuna and rice) plus some German dishes, even fish fingers and chips,

all freshly prepared, with a laid-back, relaxed atmosphere.
Tandoori Bay Opposite *Diani Sea Lodge*, 3.5km south. Down-to-earth Kenyan food at moderate prices, but no tandoori dishes despite the name.

Nightlife

To get around Diani Beach at night without your own vehicle, you'll have to rely on getting rides or walking. Hitching up and down the Diani road is generally safe and not too difficult and, while hotels issue warnings about walking on the beach at night (and there are *askaris* in number to underline them), under a full moon it's a pleasure that's hard to resist. In a group, minus your valuables, and not passing long stretches of bush, you're unlikely to have any problems.

Giriama dancing is one often-touted entertainment – probably not something to go out of your way to find (though the group "Drums of Africa" is exceptionally good), but fun if you happen upon it. A couple of professional troupes work the hotels, performing acrobatically to the accompaniment of superb drumming. You're also likely to happen across **Maasai dancers**, of varying degrees of authenticity. The guttural polyphonic singing is fascinating, though the performances usually end with a "Maasai market" where they flog you overpriced and not necessarily Maasai trinkets. Rarest of all are the **Taarab bands** (see p.649), who sometimes play in hotel dining rooms on special occasions or public holidays. Such entertainment is very seasonal and you won't find much going on when the crowds aren't in occupation. There are several **discos** along the road, each with its own idiosyncrasies. None of them even starts to warm up before 11pm. Drinks are priced at hotel rates or a little less.

Outside the cheesy hotel **discos**, Diani's main nightspot is 🎵 *Shakatak*, 3.5km south of the junction (daily 9pm–late; Ksh150), with a wooden dance floor and air conditioning. It's a bit of a dive, but it does play the heaviest mix on the strip. Lower-key places include the small dancefloor at *Tandoori Bay*, and another at a bar called *Manyata*, 4km south of the junction, though these won't carry on much past midnight.

Listings

Bakery The German *Bungoma Bakery*, by *Wayside Beach Apartments*, has a good range of fresh European breads and cakes.
Banks Barclays (Mon–Fri 9am–3pm, Sat 9am–11am), with ATM; the very efficient Commercial Bank of Africa at Diani Beach Shopping Centre (Mon–Fri 8.30am–4pm, Sat 9am–12.30pm, with an ATM next-door); Diani Forex opposite Galu Kinondo supermarket at the southern end of the strip (in theory Mon–Fri 9am–1pm & 2–5pm, Sat 9am–1pm, but not always open, even during those hours); Maritime Forex by Petro (Mon–Thurs 9am–4pm, Fri 9am–noon & 2–4pm, Sat 9am–1pm).
Bicycle and motor bike rental Bicycles for rent are surprisingly hard to come by. One place to try is Costarica, next to *Glory Palace Hotel* (☏040/320 2755, ✉costarica@swiftmombasa.com); if staff can find you a bike, they should rent it to you at a reasonable rate of around Ksh500 per day. Pitia

Tours in the Diani Complex Shopping Centre has bicycles for rent, but its asking price is a ridiculous Ksh1700 per day. Motorbikes are an easier proposition, available at Costarica and Pitia Tours, as well as from Fredlink at *Diani Sea Resort* shopping centre (☏040/320 2647, ✉fredlink@swiftmombasa.com), which also rents out scooters. Depending on the model and mileage deal, you'll pay around Ksh1500–3000 for a scooter, Ksh2000–4000 for a bike.
Car rental Glory Car Hire, c/o Seahorse Safaris, Diani Beach Shopping Centre ☏040/3203076; Costarica, next to *Glory Palace Hotel* ☏040/320 2755, ✉costarica@swiftmombasa.com; Pia's Rent a Car, Diani Beach Shopping Centre ☏040/320 2771, ✉piasrentacarltd@yahoo.co.uk.
Doctors Dr Rekhi, Diani Beach Hospital, is recommended (☏040/3202435–6); Dr Philip Varghese, *Diani Sea Resort* shopping centre (☏0733/602113; Mon–Fri 9am–12.30pm & 2.30–6pm, Sat

9am–1pm); Dr Lalit D. Kotak, opposite *Diani Sea Lodge* (☎040/320 2416; Mon–Fri 8.30am–12.30pm & 2.30–6pm, Sat 8.30am–12.30pm).

Hospital Diani Beach Hospital (☎040/3202435–6), next to Leisure Lodge Golf Club and Diani Complex Shopping Centre, is small and modern.

Internet access Relatively expensive compared to Mombasa or even Ukunda, but available at several places including *Forty Thieves Beach Bar*, Hot Gossip by *Legend* (just north of the post office) and Tellus at the Diani Complex Shopping Centre.

Notice boards Onjiko's Supermarket, behind Petro petrol station, has a reasonable board for buying and selling boats, vehicles and real estate.

Pharmacy South End Pharmacy, at Diani Beach Shopping Centre.

Post office opposite the junction for *Trade Winds* hotel, 1.4km north of the junction. Mon–Fri 8am–12.30pm & 2–5pm, Sat 9am–noon.

Supermarkets Muthaiga Mini Market, Diani Beach Shopping Centre (expensive; Mon–Sat 9am–6pm,

Sun 9am–1pm); Onjiko's, behind Petro (cheaper, with a deli counter; Mon–Sat 8am–7pm); KFI, just up from *Diani Beachalets* with a good range (Mon–Sat 9am–1.30pm & 3–6pm); and Shan-e-Punjab, Diani Complex Shopping Centre (daily 8.30am–6pm; best range of wines and spirits on the South Coast); Cabin at Colliers Centre (Mon–Sat 8am–6pm).

Taxis Most hotels have taxis in their forecourts, and there's also a stand opposite Barclays Bank. Otherwise try Call On Taxis by *Tandoori Bay* restaurant (☎040/3203163 or 3203459), or Malibu Taxis at Diani Beach Shopping Centre (☎0733/866746). *Tuk-tuks* can be found outside Barclays (☎0724/606060 or 0734/700700).

Travel agents There are various safari agents by the Petro garage and in the shopping centres along the strip, which open and close frequently enough. The less reputable ones try to pose as tourist information offices, and will hustle any passing tourist for business, but don't be taken in by the first one you visit: shop around.

Ukunda

Until a few years ago just a village on the highway, **UKUNDA** is now a scruffily burgeoning town and the main service centre for the resort hotels, strung out along the Likoni–Lungalunga road, with a post office (Mon–Fri 8am–12.30pm & 2–5pm, Sat 9am–noon), a KCB bank with ATM next door, a petrol station opposite, a couple of places with Internet access (BTS near *Casino Pub*, for example), which is cheaper than at Diani Beach, and hundreds of *dukas*. Only marginally touched by tourism, Ukunda has a life of its own, not all of it pleasant: the sprawl is an increasingly deprived area, and along with Likoni (p.469) was a centre of ethnic violence in the region prior to the 1997 elections, when some 100,000 "upcountry" people were forced to flee. Still, if your holiday isn't otherwise adventurous, it's worth a visit to see something of Kenya a little less unreal than the strip.

If you need accommodation in Ukunda (and if you're on a budget, you could consider staying here and simply catching matatus down to the part of the beach you want), there are several cheap **B&Ls**, the best of which is *Corner Guesthouse* (PO Box 855; ☎0724/173484; ❷), just north of the junction for the beach road. Quieter is the family-run *Gombato Lodge*, 2.5km north (no phone; ❷), with reasonable B&L-standard rooms, and a dozy bar.

For **nightlife**, almost anything here comes as a shock after Diani's more urbane delights. All the bars can seem (and sometimes are) pretty rough places, so go with a Kenyan friend if you can. Currently, the best are *New Dodoma Club*, 200m south of the beach road junction, the more mellow *Juhudi Club*, 400m further south of the junction, just before the filling station, and *Masai Club*, which is just north of the junction.

South to Shimoni

The Diani Beach road returns to gravel south of the *Pinewood*, although it continues in a driveable condition, through the little village of Kinondo, right down to Chale Point. Three hundred metres offshore, **Chale island**, once an uninhabited beauty spot, was acquired in the early 1990s by a German developer, with the help of two local MPs, despite its being public land and a gazetted Mijikenda *kaya* (see p.466). The resulting, ill-conceived *Chale Paradise Island* (PO Box 4 Ukunda; ☎040/3203535–6, ⓦ www.chaleislandparadise.com; FB $200; ⑨) angered local people and wiped out acres of natural vegetation. The owners nonetheless say that the development has been sensitive, that "only" a third of the island has been built upon and that the other part is a "nature reserve".

Gazi

Down the main coastal highway south of Ukunda, **GAZI** is next, a sleepy little village just off the road. It was once headquarters of the Mazrui leader **Sheikh Mbaruk ("Baruku") bin Rashid**, who acquired a reputation for torturing prisoners after half-suffocating them in the fumes of burning chillies. The story was perhaps intended to discredit him, as he was the principal figure behind the Mazrui Rebellion in 1895, an uprising against British authority that saw Mbaruk flying a German flag at his house and supplying his men with arms donated by the Germans. The British had to send for troops from India; even so, fighting continued for nine months before an Omani puppet regime was re-established and the rebels crushed. Mbaruk died in exile in German Tanganyika.

His mansion is now a primary school, which you can look around out of school hours. More than 150 years old, it was obviously a very grand place – the heavy ceiling timbers show that it once had an upper storey – but it is now sadly neglected. Fort Jesus Museum has plundered its fine front door and unfortunately left an ugly scar. To know where to stop for Gazi, you'll have to ask, as there isn't a sign on the highway. The village itself is on a deep, mangrove-filled bay and has no beach to speak of. "Gazi Beach", about 2km south of the village, is more promising.

Msambweni

Continuing down the road, **MSAMBWENI** is a sizeable village with a famous leprosarium. The road to the beach (there's often a police checkpoint at the junction) goes through the village, following the coast for several kilometres before turning back to the highway. The beach is lovely – low cliffs and less uniformity than Diani – and there are no beach hassles down here, but the tide goes out for miles, with lots of rock pools.

The only **accommodation** remaining at Msambweni beach is *Salima Club* (PO Box 9 Msambweni; ☎0734/781041, ⓔ aru_ch2005@yahoo.com; ⑥), a kilometre from the village. The architect did some original and beguiling work here on half a dozen self-catering beachfront cottages, now looking a bit weatherbeaten, but still charming and all with terraces overlooking the beach. There's also a beautiful pool beneath a baobab tree, but no restaurant. Accessibility can be a problem if you don't have your own transport – it's a kilometre from the village and a good half hour's walk from the main road, although the village is served by regular matatus from Likoni and Lungalunga.

Funzi island

If, instead of returning to the main road from Msambweni, you follow the coastline (either on the rough track or the beach), you will eventually reach **Funzi island**, separated from the mainland by a narrow channel that you can walk across at low tide. You can easily camp on the island if equipped for a fair amount of self-sufficiency. Funzi village is at the southern end, about 6km from the mainland, and there are beaches and sections of reef scattered close to the forested shore on both sides of the island. The exclusive *Funzi Island Club* – a tented camp in a grove of mango trees (PO Box 1108 Ukunda; ☎040/3202044, ✆funzicamp@africaonline.co.ke; FB ❾; sometimes closed May & June) – is a place to dream about.

Shirazi (Kifunzi)

The coast highway meanwhile passes through verdant regions of parkland, with borassus, doum and coconut palms (borassus are the ones with a bulge in the trunk) interspersed with swampy dells, before the landscape is firmly established as rolling fields of sugar cane, culminating in **Ramisi**, the coast's main sugar-producing area until the closure of its factory.

On the shore, just before you reach Ramisi, is the tiny and very old settlement of **SHIRAZI**, also known as Kifunzi (which means "little Funzi"). Any of the tracks through the sugar fields on the left of the road will take you to the hamlet – a scattering of houses in the jungle and a small harbour among mangroves. The people of Shirazi call themselves **Wa-shirazi** and are the descendants of a once-important group of the Swahili-speaking people. During the fifteenth and sixteenth centuries, they ruled the coast from Tiwi to Tanga (Tanzania) from their eight settlements on the shore. Around 1620, these towns were captured by the Wa-vumba, another Swahili group. The Wa-shirazi, now scattered in pockets along the coast, speak a distinctive dialect of Swahili. Historians used to think they originally emigrated from Shiraz, in Persia, but it now seems likely that very few of them have Persian ancestry and that the name was adopted for political reasons. Shirazi/Kifunzi, which may be one of the original eight villages, is an important Wa-shirazi centre.

Shirazi, like many villages on the coast, is a backwater in every sense. The people cut a small quantity of *boriti* (mangrove poles) – much less than they used to; they also fish and grow some produce in their garden plots, which are continually being raided by monkeys. But the setting is memorably exotic and worth the three-kilometre walk from the main road. They don't have sodas at Shirazi, but they do have coconuts and tranquillity.

The people who run Funzi Island Fishing Club have a camp on the shore at **Bodo**, just to the southwest of Shirazi. Bodo is a small cargo port, where you can sometimes pick up a ride to Pemba, Tanzania, a seven-hour voyage.

There are some unspectacular ruins of walls and a disused well amid tangled foliage just a 100m or so to the south of the village. On the north side is the more interesting hulk of a Friday mosque, its *mihrab* still standing. Elders here describe how earlier inhabitants were routed by the Maasai and fled to the Comoros Islands. They remember when the mosque was still intact, though by the beginning of the twentieth century it had already been abandoned.

Shimoni

In the 1980s, the Reagan administration had its eye on Wasini, the rocky sliver of an island just offshore from **SHIMONI**, as the site for a US naval base. Fortunately the idea was shelved, and Shimoni remains both idyllic and fascinating – a rare combination.

While you're here, you should visit the **caves** (daily 8.30–10.30am & 1.30–6pm; Ksh100) after which it was named (*shimo* in Swahili). Shimoni's caves have achieved fame in Kenya, if not much further afield, through the melodramatic warblings of Kenyan-born singer Roger Whittaker's song *Shimoni*, which was

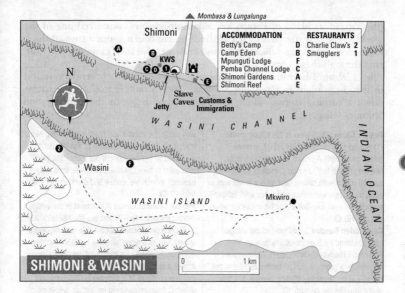

Map labels:

Mombasa & Lungalunga

Shimoni

ACCOMMODATION
Betty's Camp	D
Camp Eden	B
Mpunguti Lodge	F
Pemba Channel Lodge	C
Shimoni Gardens	A
Shimoni Reef	E

RESTAURANTS
Charlie Claw's	2
Smugglers	1

N

KWS

Slave Caves

Jetty

Customs & Immigration

WASINI CHANNEL

INDIAN OCEAN

Wasini

WASINI ISLAND

Mkwiro

SHIMONI & WASINI

0   1 km

actually recorded in the caves. A place of refuge from Maasai and other raiders, the caves are thought to have been used for storing slaves prior to shipment to Zanzibar. The evidence takes the form of metal rings attached to the rocks, to which it is supposed slaves were attached, and a now silted-up passage would have led them to boats waiting on the shore. National Museums of Kenya has agreed to investigate the caves for further evidence, and there are 5km of silted-up caves to excavate. Meanwhile, they have been opened to the public with an explanatory tour included in the price (proceeds to fund local development projects). Shafts of sunlight pierce through holes in the forest floor to illuminate the stalactites and dangling lianas quite beautifully. Six species of bat nest in the caves, of which you can see members of two on the tour (the insect-eating bats fly out en masse at dusk).

The ruined two-storey building opposite the cave was formerly the headquarters of the Imperial British East African Company, which was for a time based here. Nearby, the fish auction house by the jetty is also interesting – there's an auction every morning – though exciting exhibits like marlin and shark are rarely on the slab.

Practicalities

There are **matatus** from Likoni to Shimoni, but they can be sparse, and tend to run mostly early in the morning and after lunch. Vehicles for Lungalunga will drop you at the turn-off where you could wait for a lift, or a matatu, though through matatus will be packed to the gunwhales by the time they reach here.

Frequent **cargo dhows** sail from Shimoni to Tanzania, usually to Pemba (3hr; Ksh1000–2000) and sometimes direct to Zanzibar (6hr; Ksh2000–3000). Customs and immigration have offices in Shimoni. The journey is more difficult the other way, however, as many boats are smuggling goods from Tanzania into Kenya and do not want to complicate matters by carrying foreign passengers.

Although Shimoni is small, the demand for **accommodation** by big-spending game-fishermen has brought two good hotels. The Pemba Channel (the Tanzanian island of Pemba lies 50km offshore) is considered one of the world's very best stretches of sea for hunting big fish; it is impressive to think that marlin weighing a quarter of a ton and tiger sharks of close on half a ton race through these waters.

Since Wasini Island is an alluring ten-minute boat ride away, there's no reason to spend the night in town, but *Mwazaro Beach* is quite a magical alternative, down a turning halfway along the *murram* road between the highway and Shimoni village.

Betty's Camp 500m west of the village centre; PO Box 55 Ukunda ☎0722/434709, ⓦwww.bettys-camp.com. A choice of permanent tents, like the ones in tented safari camps, or small but tasteful rooms with ceiling fans, plus a small pool (Ksh750 for non-residents), and a bar, with fishing expeditions available, but a little bit pricey for what you get. HB ⑧

Camp Eden Bandas 300m west of the village centre, behind KWS (reservations through KWS; PO Box 55 Ukunda ☎040/52027). Wonderful for naturalists, a group of *makuti*-roofed *bandas* in the forest, run by the Kenya Wildlife Service. You can also camp ($8 per person). ③

🏃 **Mwazaro Beach** 1km off the Shimoni road, halfway between the highway and Shimoni; PO Box 1710 Ukunda ☎0722/711476, ⓦwww.keniabeach.com. "Where God makes holidays" is how the German owner describes this low-key resort at a sacred Digo *kaya* where, in contrast to Chale (see pp.486–487), approval from the ancestral spirits was sought and granted before development, conditional on conservation of the local culture and environment. It's on a lovely private beach, close to the delta of the Ramisi River, with mangrove swamps (eight of the nine species of mangrove native to Africa can be found here), excellent snorkelling at the nearby reef, plus creek and sea trips. There's solar and wind power only, drinkable spring water in the taps, and excellent Zanzibari set meals, with a choice of upmarket s/c coral-stone houses, or more basic but still comfortable palm and *makuti bandas*, all with good fitted nets. It's very idyllic, not easily accessible but well worth the effort if you really want to get away from it all. Camping is possible at Ksh300 per tent plus Ksh250 per person without meals, but you'll also want to take those (especially as fires are banned), though tea, coffee and drinking water are free. FB ⑧

Pemba Channel Lodge 800m west of the village centre; PO Box 84851 Mombasa ☎0722/205020–1, ⓦwww.pembachannel.com. For anglers, divers, snorkellers, or anyone else, the lodge's speciality is big game and fly-fishing, but it also has a diving school and offers week-long diving trips aboard the twenty-metre *M.Y. Kisiwani* (€1250; contact ⓔinfo@divingpemba.com for further details on this), plus snorkelling trips to Kisite-Mpunguti (in conjunction with Charlie Claw's, p.483), nice rooms and a pool. FB €220; ⑨

Shimoni Gardens Beach Holiday Resort 2km west of the village centre; PO Box 82037 Mombasa ☎0721/223412, ⓔkigless@swiftmombasa.com. Small but breezy rooms made of cane, reed and *makuti*, or sturdier stone-built cottages, not actually on the beach, but not too far away, with a bar and restaurant, plus a separate beach bar, and its own boats for snorkelling and fishing expeditions. B&B ⑥

Shimoni Reef Lodge 300m east of the village centre; PO Box 82234 Mombasa ☎040/52015, ⓔoes@africaonline.co.ke. Part of the Reef group of hotels, open all year, and aimed less at sport fishermen than at divers. Excellent accommodation in ten split-level cottages with separate bed and sitting areas, but rather average food. Sea-water swimming pool. B&B ⑦

Eating

Aside from a couple of basic *hotelis*, and popping across for lunch at *Mpunguti Lodge* or *Charlie Claw's* on Wasini (see p.483), your best bet is *Smuggler's*, an upcountry-style bar-restaurant just west of the slave caves, where you can usually get chicken, beef or goat, either stewed or roasted, accompanied by rice, *ugali* or chapatti. It also does good breakfasts.

Wasini island and offshore

WASINI is easily reached. *Charlie Claw's* (PO Box 281 Ukunda; ☎040/52410 or 3202331) will speed lunchers across the channel in its boat, but otherwise you'll have to hire a dhow (Ksh800–2000 depending on your bargaining skills). Local people use *jahazi*, sailing boat "matatus" which – notwithstanding the resentment of the diesel men – you should be able to use, too (Ksh200–300 each way in theory). This is certainly more fun, but you'll need to haggle determinedly.

Only 5km long and 1km across, Wasini has just a thousand inhabitants, and is totally adrift from the mainstream of coastal life. There are no cars, nor any need of them: you can walk all the way around the island in a couple of hours on the narrow footpaths through the bush, though few people do. With something of Lamu's cast about it, the island is completely undeveloped, and **Wasini village**, an old Wa-vumba settlement, is built in and around its own ruins. It's a fascinating place to wander and there's even a small pillar tomb which still has its complement of inset Chinese porcelain. The **beach** in front of the village is littered with shells, but don't assume anything: a lot of them have been collected from the reef and dumped here, and people will try to sell them to you, so it wouldn't be wise to treat them as legitimate beachcombings – and of course trade in seashells is illegal in Kenya. Nevertheless, the wealth of interesting items on the shores of Wasini – not just shells, but shards of pottery, pieces of glass, scrap metal – add up to a beachcomber's paradise you could explore for hours.

Behind the village is a bizarre area of long-dead **coral gardens** now raised out of the sea but still flooded by twice-monthly spring tides. You can stroll through this on a **boardwalk** (daily 9am–5pm; Ksh100), built by a local women's group, with funds going towards education and healthcare in the village. Walking through the coral grottoes with birds and butterflies in the air leaves a surreal impression of snorkelling on dry land. The ground is covered by a short swathe of sea grass – a tasty vegetable known locally as *mboga pwani* (sea vegetable) – among which small crabs dwarfed by their enormous right claws scuttle down holes they've excavated in the mud. Beyond the coral garden, the boardwalk continues into the mangrove swamp, an excellent chance to walk through an environment not usually easy to access. Exploring the rest of the island is also highly recommended – look out for monkeys in the mangroves and parrots in the palms.

Accommodation in Wasini is very limited (more by the island's total reliance on rainwater than by anything else), but you can stay at *Mpunguti Lodge*, commonly known as *Masood's* (PO Box 19 Ukunda; ☎0722/566623; FB ❺). It's very simple – no electricity, though flush toilets and showers have been installed, some rooms are s/c, and three rainwater tanks (with more under construction) mean that there is sufficient water for most of the year. The owner has quite a collection of old pottery and ceramics, for which he aims to eventually open a museum. Most beds are traditional Swahili. There's magnificent Swahili cooking and you can also **camp** here for Ksh200 per person, or sleep in a dorm for Ksh250. The owner can also arrange trips to the Marine National Park.

Rather more luxurious, but no less relaxing, is the house used by Pilli-Pipa dhow safaris (p.483) for lunching its day-tripping guests (on succulent crab claws, fried seaweed and other delights). If you contact staff in advance, they can pick you up. Full-board costs €70 per person (not s/c), and there's the opportunity of snorkelling trips and scuba diving, even PADI courses (PO Box 5185 Diani Beach; ☎ & ℻040/3202401,🌐www.pillipipa.com).

Kisite-Mpunguti Marine National Park

Daily 6am–6pm; $5, children $2. Warden: PO Box 55 Ukunda Shimoni ☎040/52027.

Wasini has ideal conditions for **snorkelling**, with limpid water all around. Both Pilli-Pipa and *Wasini Island Restaurant* (details for both above), a few minutes to the west of the village, run full-day trips in large dhows to the reefs around Kisite island, part of **Kisite-Mpunguti Marine National Park**, which usually has some of the best snorkelling in Kenya. Similar trips, on a more informal, ad hoc basis are run from *Mpunguti Lodge*.

The boats normally go out of the Wasini channel to the east, then turn south to pass the islets of **Mpunguti ya Chini** and **Mpunguti ya Juu** ("little" and "great") on the port side. Kisite islet, a coral-encircled rock about 100m long, 5km to the southwest, is the routine destination. The best parts of the Kisite anchoring area are towards the outer edge of the main "coral garden". There are fish and sea animals in abundance, including angel fish, moray eel, octopuses, rock cod and some spectacularly large (sixty-centimetre) sea cucumbers. At certain times of the year, however, the water is less clear, and it looks as if repeated anchorings have destroyed much of the coral in at least one small area, where the shallow sea bed is littered with broken ends and grey debris. Ask the crew if you'd like to try to find a better area: **Mako Koke Reef**, the other main part of the park, is about 4km to the west.

Vanga

Kenya's southernmost town, **VANGA** is also the largest of the coastal settlements to have been left alone by the tourist industry. Getting here involves travelling down one of the country's most beautiful, and usually deserted, roads, from the Shimoni junction to Lungalunga, on the Tanzanian border. The seventeen-kilometre *murram* road to Vanga begins, curiously, midway through the Kenyan border post at Lungalunga, where you have to explain your purpose to the officials. There are no lodgings, nor anywhere to eat, so take supplies. Turning left, the track skims the Tanzanian border through *shambas* and, as it nears the sea, tunnels through tall forest in deep shade. Vanga itself is in the **mangroves**, approached through the swamp down a causeway which is regularly flooded by spring tides.

The largish village has a main street, where men come in the evening to chew *miraa* and reflect on the community's isolation. "We have no employment", is a common complaint; the fishing co-operative is the only local provider of a cash income, but it isn't always able to buy the entire catch and members are not supposed to sell to anyone else. Many people sell garden produce in Mombasa, which explains the matatu departures through the night to ensure early arrival at the markets.

Most people are unlikely to come to Vanga as there isn't anywhere to stay in the town or anything much to do. The big old house on the seafront is a nineteenth-century British customs house, cared for, in theory, by the National Museums of Kenya but in practice falling down. Many of the houses in the village were constructed during World War I by German general Paul von Lettow-Vorbeck to billet troops he had recruited in German East Africa (modern Tanzania) to fight the British. It is said locally that a cache of gold he brought to pay them with remains buried under a baobab tree, but that it is cursed, and anyone who attempts to dig it up will immediately be struck dead. Allegedly, several people have defied the curse and not survived to tell the tale. For those who haven't come in search of buried treasure, dugout canoes can be rented very cheaply for wobbly punting trips through the mangroves, and you should be able to find someone in the village who'll put you up, and maybe even obtain a supply of *mnazi* (palm wine).

Coconut power and Climate Care

A local entrepreneur has developed a system to turn waste coconut husks into charcoal, which is then made into briquettes and sold on the local market. This source of renewable energy displaces traditional charcoal – one of the main causes of deforestation in Kenya. The organization Climate Care is providing money for more kilns, partly from air travellers' carbon emissions offsets (see p.39), to increase the output. Coconut charcoal will replace some of the coal used by Bamburi Cement Factory (see p.454), further reducing greenhouse gas emissions.

Onward to Tanzania

Lungalunga is the Kenyan border post if you're heading south to Tanzania, and easily reached by matatu from Likoni, or occasionally direct from Mombasa (Jomo Kenyatta Avenue at Mwembe Tayari Road). After completing border formalities on the Kenyan side, you can take a matatu or a taxi, or walk the 6km to Horohoro on the Tanzanian side. There are money changers at both border posts, who will change Kenyan shillings for Tanzanian shillings, or cash dollars, and no doubt euros, into either. Try to ascertain the current rate before entering into negotiations, and always check your change carefully. If buying Tanzanian shillings, you usually get the best rate on the Tanzanian side, and in fact you'll get them at a better rate for Kenyan shillings here than you will in Dar es Salaam or Tanga. Heading on, you can get a through bus to Dar es Salaam (try to get to Lungalunga by 9am to be sure of getting one), or take a *dala dala* (the Tanzanian expression for a matatu) to Tanga, and get onward transport from there. The journey to Tanga takes about two and a half hours, and a further five hours to Dar.

From Kilifi to Malindi

From Mtwapa Creek up to **Malindi**, the landscape is a diverse collage, from rolling baobab country and sisal plantations as you near **Kilifi** to groves of cashew trees after it; thick, jungly forest and swamp characterizes Mida Creek, and there's a more compact, populated zone of *shambas* and thicket as you approach Malindi. **Kilifi** and **Takaungu creeks** are stunning – the clash of blue water and green cliffs almost unnatural.

There is wide scope for **beach hunting** along this part of the coast. Malindi and, to some extent, Watamu have been developed, but Kilifi functions largely as a Giriama market-centre and district capital, while Takaungu seems virtually unknown, a throwback to pre-colonial days. There's also superb **snorkelling** at **Watamu** and **Malindi marine national parks**. And the ruined town of **Gedi**, deep in the forest near Watamu, is one of the most impressive archeological sites in East Africa.

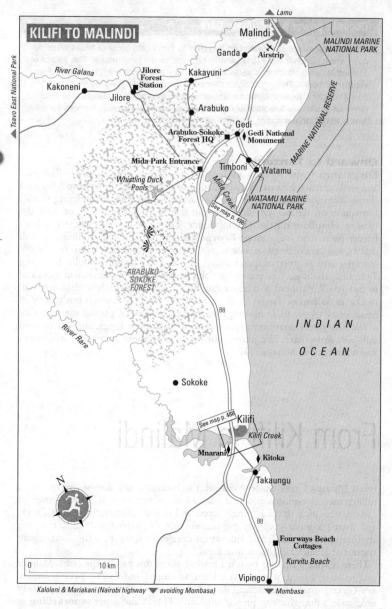

KILIFI TO MALINDI

Tsavo East National Park

Lamu

B8

Malindi

MALINDI MARINE NATIONAL PARK

Ganda

Airstrip

River Galana

Jilore Forest Station

Kakayuni

Kakoneni

Jilore

Arabuko

Gedi

Gedi National Monument

Arabuko-Sokoke Forest HQ

Mida Park Entrance

Timboni

Watamu

MARINE NATIONAL RESERVE

Whistling Duck Pools

Mida Creek

(See map p. 498)

WATAMU MARINE NATIONAL PARK

ARABUKO SOKOKE FOREST

INDIAN

OCEAN

River Rare

B8

Sokoke

See map p. 488

Kilifi

Kilifi Creek

Mnarani

Kitoka

Takaungu

N

B8

Fourways Beach Cottages

Kurvitu Beach

0   10 km

Vipingo

Kaloleni & Mariakani (Nairobi highway ▼ *avoiding Mombasa)*   ▼ *Mombasa*

Kilifi and around

Between Kikambala and Kilifi lies a major **sisal-growing** area, focused around
the small town of **Vipingo** (one or two *dukas* and *hotelis*, but not much else).
Across thousands of acres, plumb-straight rows of fleshy-leafed, cactus-like sisal
plants stretch in every direction, the surviving **baobab trees** standing out

Baobab stories

The **baobab**'s strange appearance has a number of explanations in mythology. The most common one relates how the first baobab planted by God was an ordinary-looking tree, but it refused to stay in one place and wandered round the countryside. As a punishment, God planted it back again – upside down – and immobilized it. Baobabs may live well over 2000 years, making them among the longest-living organisms. During a severe drought, their large green pods can be cracked open and the nuts made into a kind of flour. The resulting "hungry bread" is part of the common culture of the region. The tangy white pith of the baobab fruit is boiled with sugar to make a popular bright red sweet that you will see on sale at street stalls.

bizarrely (see box below). Towards Kilifi, the road bucks through a hilly area and the baobabs grow more profusely amid the scrub.

If you want **to stay** cheaply on this relatively undeveloped coastline, *Fourways Beach Cottages* is a good target (reservations: Happy Land Tours, third floor, Canon Tower New Wing; PO Box 83365 Mombasa; ☏041/2229405; ❺). An attractive modern complex of spacious self-catering tiled cottages and apartments, most with ocean views, there's also a restaurant and minimarket (both sometimes closed, so bring your own supplies), and a little pool next to an idyllic stretch of beach. Significantly, the reef is much closer to the shore in this area (Kurvitu Beach) than further south – a plus point for snorkellers. If you're travelling by public transport, ask the bus or matatu driver to drop you 1.6km north of Vipingo (18km north of Mtwapa), where you'll see a gravel track off to the right and a small rash of signboards including one for *Fourways* – it's about 3km along. **Be warned**, however, that this track has in the past been the scene of attacks and robberies on tourists – phone ahead to check the situation.

Takaungu

Ten kilometres before you reach Kilifi, there's a turn-off to the right to **TAKAUNGU**. Although there are a couple of matatus most days from Mombasa to Takaungu, the chances of a lift are relatively slim if you get dropped off at the turning, but the walk (5km) is not too long. Takaungu is enchanting – a quiet, composed village of whitewashed Swahili houses situated on a high bluff above **Takaungu Creek**. There are three mosques and one or two small shops and *hotelis*, but no formal lodgings except for the exceedingly expensive *Takaungu House* (☏0125/22479; ❾; bookings through Let's Go, p.150), which has a deep pool. If you want to stay in the village and you speak a little Swahili, people will put you up for a very reasonable price. Food supplies are variable; women will prepare food if you ask, and especially if you supply the ingredients. There's no produce market, but a small fish market by the creek – be there when the catch arrives to get the tasty ones. Takaungu is a place that repays time spent getting to know it. If you just want to sit back and relax, pass it by and head on to Lamu.

There's a small seaside **beach**, 1km east, through the secondary school. **Takaungu Creek** is startlingly beautiful, the colour of blue Curaçao, and absolutely transparent; the small swimming beach on the stream is covered at high tide, but you can still dive from the rocks. Upstream, the creek disappears between flanks of dense jungle. When you're ready to move on, the tiny, council-operated rowing boat provides a slow and almost free service across the creek to the Kilifi side; from there, it's a five-kilometre (90min) walk through the sisal fields to Kilifi bridge.

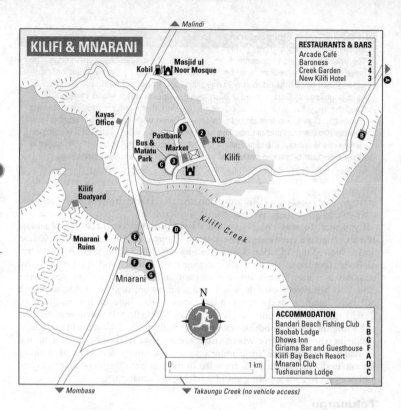

KILIFI & MNARANI

▲ Malindi

Kobil 🏛 Masjid ul
Noor Mosque

Kayas
Office

Postbank
Bus & Market
Matatu
Park
C 3

1 **2** KCB

Kilifi

Kilifi
Boatyard

Kilifi Creek

Mnarani
Ruins

E D

F 4
G

Mnarani

N

RESTAURANTS & BARS
Arcade Café 1
Baroness 2
Creek Garden 4
New Kilifi Hotel 3

ACCOMMODATION
Bandari Beach Fishing Club E
Baobab Lodge B
Dhows Inn G
Giriama Bar and Guesthouse F
Kilifi Bay Beach Resort A
Mnarani Club D
Tushauriane Lodge C

0   1 km

▼ Mombasa   ▼ Takaungu Creek (no vehicle access)

Kilifi, Mnarani and the creek

Kenya's coastline was submerged in the recent geological past, resulting in the
creation of the islands and drowned river valleys – the creeks – of today. **KILIFI**,
a small but animated place, is on such a creek. When the Portuguese knew it,
Kilifi's centre was on the south side of the creek and called **Mnarani** (still the
name of the village on that side). Together with Kitoka on the north side of
Takaungu Creek, and a settlement on the site of the present town of Kilifi, these
three constituted the "state" of Kilifi.

Kilifi town

With the building of the **bridge** in the 1980s, Kilifi's economy was dealt a hard
blow. All the creek-side trade made possible by the ferry's endless delays and
breakdowns ceased (the ferry itself is now a half-submerged wreck), and many
bars and *hotelis*, and half the town's lodgings, closed.

The town is draped along the north side of the creek to the east of the
bridge. If you're driving you'll probably pass it by; even most public transport travellers only see it from the inside of a bus while more fares are
being picked up. But staying the night is not an unpleasant prospect, and
while there's not a lot of choice it's certainly a better plan than arriving
late in Malindi.

There are two **banks** in town (KCB with an ATM, Postbank with Western
Union facilities), and a **post office** (Mon–Fri 8am–12.30pm & 2–5pm, Sat

9am–noon) down near the market. There's lots of **transport** to Mombasa or Malindi; most buses to Lamu and Garissa pass by around 8am.

Accommodation

Hotels are thin on the ground, especially if you want to stay in town. For beach accommodation, see the section under Kilifi Beach.

Bandari Beach Fishing Club Mnarani, on the south shore of the creek, 300m off the road from *Dhows Inn* to the Mnarani ruins; PO Box 508 ☏0733/724715. Small guesthouse that used to host parties of game fishermen, now getting a bit rundown but still has airy rooms with hot water and fans, food and beer. HB ❸

Dhows Inn Mnarani, at the south side of the bridge; PO Box 431 ☏ & ℻041/522028. Big, clean, good-value s/c rooms at this popular upmarket boozer and restaurant. ❷

Giriama Bar and Guesthouse Mnarani, on the road between *Dhows Inn* and Mnarani ruins; PO Box 1260 ☏0724/241937. Cheap and basic singles, plus a lively bar with pool tables. ❶

Mnarani Club South side of the creek, entrance near the bridge; PO Box 1008 Kilifi ☏041/522318–20, ℠www.mnaraniclub.com. A package resort with decent food and good service, and two categories of rooms (it's worth paying a bit extra for the more spacious Creek View rooms with bathtubs and parquet rather than lino-tile floors). The views over the creek from the hotel's pool are classic, and there's a private beach. ❼

Tushauriane Lodge By the bus and matatu stand; PO Box 259 ☏0733/379698. Ask at the hardware shop downstairs for the owner. The tallest and only option in the town centre, with basic and not terribly clean non-s/c rooms with mosquito nets but no fans – dingy, but very cheap. ❶

Eating

As for **eating** options, the **Oloitipitip Market** has a wide range of fruit and vegetables. The *New Kilifi Hotel* (closes 10pm) is a very busy local joint near the bus station, serving good cheap meals and snacks. *Arcade Café* does tasty meals in fresh, clean surroundings in the small arcade it shares with Postbank. More upmarket, try ⚘ *Baroness Restaurant* by KCB bank, where local dishes are joined by the likes of grilled snapper, pork chops, and pork fillet in pineapple sauce. **Nightlife** is concentrated on the main junction in Mnarani, south of the creek, where *makuti*-thatched *Creek Garden* bar and restaurant concentrates on *bango* and African beats, while the almost adjacent *Dhows Inn* has softer music.

Mnarani ruins

There's little of **sightseeing interest** in Kilifi itself. Its two main **mosques** – one a stumpy shed in the town centre, the other a new and attractively minareted blue, green and white temple, the Masjid ul Noor, at the north junction – more or less sum it up, but across the creek are the more interesting **Mnarani ruins**, which sit under the trees high above the water. To get to them, take the road west from the junction with the main highway at *Dhows Inn* and the *Creek Garden*, turn right at the end down towards the creek, and the site is signposted on your left near the old ferry landing – "follow the green posts" and then up a rather steep flight of stairs (7am–6pm; Ksh500, children Ksh250). The site is archeologically famous mainly for the large number of inscriptions found on its masonry, all in a difficult, and so far untranslated, form of monumental Arabic. They can be seen in several places, in particular in the well-preserved mihrab of the main mosque. Just behind this is a very tall octagonal white pillar tomb, which dominates the remains. In front of the mosque, a precipitous well plummets right down to creek level. A little way removed from the main mosque (signposted in front of the office), a smaller one is hidden away among the baobabs. As a whole, the site, though small, is pretty and photogenic, though for the non-buff its most memorable aspect is a superlative position and, after the visit, the opportunity to cool down in the creek along with the local kids.

In recent decades, as the **Giriama** section of the Mijikenda (see p.466) has expanded, Kilifi has become one of their most important towns. Giriama women are quickly noticed by everyone for their unusual **dress**, although it's gradually disappearing. Traditionally a kind of kilt of grass or leaves, it is now made of *kanga* cloth with hips and buttocks accentuated by a bustle of coir fibre stuffed underneath. Older women still occasionally go topless but younger women usually cover up, at least in town. The Mijikenda peoples, and the Giriama especially, are known as great sorcerers and practitioners of witchcraft, and Kilifi is still the frequent scene of accusations that sometimes reach the press. Kilifi is also now the site of an office of the coastal project working to conserve the Mijikenda's sacred groves, or *kayas* (the other office is at Ukunda – see p.486). The main work at present is to identify and gazette the *kayas* of the district but, in time, it's hoped that tourist visits will be feasible. If you're interested in finding out more about the project, call at the office just off the Mombasa–Malindi highway in Kilifi, or contact them in advance (PO Box 596 Kilifi; ☎042/522140, ✉cfcu.kilifi@swiftmombasa.com).

Kilifi Creek

Kilifi's seaside-settler/yachtie community tends to hover around the informal bar-restaurant at **Kilifi Boatyard** (☎041/525067, ⓦwww.kilifiboatyard.com), which is *the* place for making contacts if you have any ideas of Indian Ocean crewing in mind, and also a possible place to make contacts for sea-fishing excursions. There's no public transport here: if you don't have your own car you'll have to walk, unless you can get a lift. It's a little further up the south side of the creek from the old ferry landing, accessible via a dirt road from the old main road, 1km inland, then right 2km down a steep track to the waterfront. Easier access on foot is along the shore of the creek, but this is only easy at low tide. *Kilifi Boatyard* is a friendly place, with fine views of the creek and the dramatic new bridge. They turn out fresh and simple seafood dishes, including fish and chips, or crab samosas, and there's a notice board for yachties and fishermen to exchange news and trade kit.

Kilifi Beach

The real **beaches** around Kilifi are mostly accessible only through private property, and the best are up on the open coast to the northeast of the town. Along this ten-kilometre tarred road, however, there are several fairly recent developments. Distances for the following are given from the main Mombasa–Malindi road.

Baobab Lodge 3.2km; PO Box 537 ☎041/522570, ✉kilifibay@madahotels.com; reservations through Mada Holdings, Kimathi House, Kimathi St; PO Box 40683 Nairobi ☎020/603753, ⓦwww.madahotels.com. Attractively sited amid densely planted gardens and baobabs, in a pleasant position on a bluff above the shore. Tennis courts and a good pool with lots of shade (Ksh200 for non-residents), but little beach to speak of and no sea-swimming at low tide. The rooms, though, are spacious and well furnished, with a/c and fans, but lack sea views. FB ❽

Kilifi Bay Beach Resort 6.5km; PO Box 537 ☎041/522264 or 522511, ✉kilifibay@madahotels.com; reservations as for *Baobab Lodge*. The best of Kilifi's hotels, with a stunning location right on the beach (the best rooms have stupendous sea views; all have balconies), mature tropical gardens with coconut palms, a freeform pool for when the tide is out, great four-poster beds, spacious *makuti*-roofed communal areas, good service and decent breakfasts. Diving and water sports can be arranged. FB ❽

Arabuko-Sokoke Forest, Gedi and Kipepeo Butterfly Farm

Heading north from Kilifi to Watamu and Malindi, a number of interesting diversions en route provide a possible break from beach-related activities. Most of these centre around the **Arabuko-Sokoke Forest**, where you can walk, cycle or drive in search of the "small six" – the main stars in the forest's array of wildlife, in contrast to the "big five" of the savanna parks. Nearby, the ruins at **Gedi** provide by far the largest and most interesting of the coast's ancient stone ruins. If you're in a hurry, you can visit both forest and ruins together in a day, or alternatively, you can make excursions to either or both using Malindi, Watamu or even Kilifi as a base.

Arabuko-Sokoke Forest National Park

Daily 6am–6pm; $10, children $5; Forest Visitor Centre; PO Box 1 Gedi; ☏ 042/32462, ✉ sokoke@africaonline.co.ke.

The cashew trees lining both sides of the road north of Kilifi soon give way to tracts of jungle where monkeys scatter across the road and hornbills plunge into the cover of the trees as you approach. This is the **Arabuko-Sokoke Forest**, the largest patch of indigenous coastal forest left in East Africa. At one time it would have covered most of the coastal hinterland behind the shoreline settlements, part of an ancient forest belt which stretched from Mozambique to Somalia. If you have a car or a few days for some walking, there are some 400 square kilometres to explore, a tiny part of which in the far north (six square kilometres) was declared a national park in 1991.

The ban on cutting timber in the forest (often ignored), and on clearance of land for agriculture, has not endeared it to **local residents**, who have seen it as a useless waste of land, and are particularly not amused when elephants from the forest come out and decimate their crops. To combat this ill feeling, Kenya Wildlife Service, National Museums of Kenya and a forest support group, the Friends of Arabuko-Sokoke have pioneered a number of projects to make conservation of the forest useful to the local community. Among **initiatives** up and running are the Kipepeo Butterfly Project (see p.505), and a bee-keeping scheme in which people living around the forest are given beehives at low cost to produce honey from forest flowers; if you want to try some, it's sold at the Forest Visitor Centre and other outlets. Licences are also issued for the gathering of deadwood for fuel, and the harvesting of medicinal herbs, and an initiative is under way to contribute towards school fees for local children out of income generated from visits to the forest by tourists. The problem of incursions by elephants onto cultivated land is by no means confined to Arabuko-Sokoke, but electric fences are planned along parts of the forest boundary to prevent greedy pachyderms from having a jumbo munch-out on neighbouring *shambas*. If you would like to get involved in forest conservation projects, you can join the **Friends of Arabuko-Sokoke Forest** (Ksh1000 per year) at the Visitor Centre (PO Box 383 Watamu), or via its website at ⓦ www.watamu.net/foasf.htm.

Beside elephants (usually evidenced by their dung), Sykes' monkeys and yellow baboons, the forest shelters two rare mammal species: the 35-centimetre-high **Aders' (or Zanzibar) duiker** is a tiny, shy antelope, usually living in pairs, but which you're more likely to see around Gedi, where tourists no longer disturb them as much, and the extraordinary **golden-rumped elephant shrew**, which has been adopted as the symbol for the forest. The size of a small cat, this bizarre animal resembles a giant mouse with an elongated nose, running on stilts. In one of those mystifyingly evolved animal relationships, it consorts with a small bird, the **red-capped robin chat**, which warns it of danger and picks up insects disturbed by the shrew's snufflings. Your best chance of seeing a shrew is to look for its fluttering companion among the tangle of branches: the shrew will be close by. It can usually be seen (but not for long – it's very speedy) on the walk along the Nature Trail close to the Visitor Centre, or along the sandy tracks further inside the forest. You may also spot it darting across forest trails ahead of you. The exceedingly rare **Sokoke bush-tailed mongoose** is unlikely to put in an appearance – there have been no sightings since the mid-1980s. El Niño, which wreaked havoc over most of Kenya in 1997–98, was a boon for Arabuko, seeing an explosion in insect and frog populations, in turn providing a feast for their predators. The rains even attracted hippos into the park, though these have now gone, and the forest remains second in Africa only to the Okavango Delta in Botswana for the diversity of its frog population, a fact very much in evidence after a good rainfall. Those with a specific interest in amphibians can find photos and soundclips of the forest's frogs and toads on the Frogs of Arabuko-Sokoke Forest website at ⓦ www.calacademy.org/research/herpetology/frogs/kfrogs.html.

The forest is also home to a glorious variety of butterflies (see Kipepeo Butterfly Farm, p.505) and six globally threatened **bird species**, including the small **Sokoke scops owl**, which is found only in the red-soiled *cynometra* section of the forest, and the **Sokoke pipit** – both very hard to spot, although guides are on hand to help locate them. The other endangered birds are the Amani sunbird, Clark's weaver, East Coast akalat and spotted ground thrush.

Practicalities

Whether driving or walking, head first for the **Forest Visitor Centre**, 1.5km south of Gedi and the Watamu junction on the Malindi–Mombasa road, which provides an information pack of maps and fact sheets (Ksh120), and a Visitor's Guide detailing routes through the forest (Ksh300). The visitor centre is also the place to pick up a **guide** (see below). If you've got a tent, use it. **Camping** is permitted ($8 per person per night), but apart from the main site beside the Visitor Centre, you must be self-sufficient, and there are restrictions on the lighting of fires.

Walking is best done in the morning or late afternoon, and although this isn't the Amazon, a degree of preparation is wise if you plan on venturing far down any of the tracks leading off the main road. Survey of Kenya maps would be useful (the *Kenya Coast* tourist map at the very least), though the Visitor Centre maps are more than adequate for the main trails. A **compass** is also helpful. Official **ASF guides** are provided at the Visitor Centre (they can also be booked on ⓣ 0734/994931), and cost Ksh600 (per guide for up to four people) for three hours, Ksh1000 for up to six hours, Ksh1200 for up to twelve hours. All are professional and well versed in forest ecology. You can also use them for fantastic **night walks** (the chorus of frog calls is awesome), which would otherwise be impossible on your own. A specialist guide to locate birds costs Ksh200 more. An organized early-morning **birdwalk** (Ksh100) leaves the Visitor Centre on the first Saturday of every month at 6.30am.

Routes

A **nature trail** takes you from the Visitor Centre around the first part of the forest which, after rain, is spectacularly adorned with the nests of foam-nest tree frogs. It takes most of a morning, but is an easy walk and excellent introduction to the forest and its (medicinal) uses. Bring water and insect repellent. Another easy walk is to the **tree house**, a viewing platform atop a tree by a former sand quarry, from which you get superb vistas over the forest.

If you're short of time, there are several **driving routes**, more if you have 4WD, which are also suitable for bikes (see "Listings" on p.507 for details on bike rental in Watamu). The main route starts at the Mida entrance, 2km south of the Visitor Centre on the main Mombasa–Malindi road, and goes up to the View Point through brachystegia forest – look out for the rare Amani sunbird on the way. From the View Point, which looks east over the forest to Mida Creek and the Indian Ocean, a walking track continues for another 2km to a second viewing point which looks west onto cynometra forest and a large exposed escarpment. There are other paths along the western edge of the Whistling Duck Pools (at the junction between the brachystegia and cynometra forest on the main driving track between the Mida entrance and the viewpoints), which are a favourite haunt for white-faced whistling duck, little grebe and open-billed storks, as well as the odd elephant. Little used, but apparently excellent, is the "elephant track" (14km), which passes through both mixed and brachystegia forest; it starts at Gedi Forest Station, heading west for 8km before joining the driveable track to Jilore Forest Station. A left turn here takes you 5km down to the Mida entrance on the Mombasa–Malindi road. If you're going by taxi, haggle well, and before starting, drop in at the Visitor Centre, which has details of the routes.

Another approach to the forest from Malindi heads west on the road to Tsavo East, passing through Kikayuni and Jilore villages. Roads that can be driven or cycled – even walked if you can reach them early enough by matatu from Malindi – lead from both places down to the Mombasa–Malindi highway. **Kakayuni** is the larger of the two villages, and offers a forest road of 10km or so, leading via the small centre of **Arabuko** to the highway. Mostly, however, this path goes through marginal forest lands. A better bet is to continue to **Jilore**, whose location, high on a ridge overlooking a bend in the Sabaki/ Galana River, contrasts impressively with the deep forest all around.

The turning for Jilore Forest Station is to the left, just before you reach Jilore village, and the station about 3km down the track. At the first crossroads after the forest station's three huts, turn left: a good trail leads for 16km in a southerly direction to the Kilifi–Malindi highway. If you're doing this trip by car, the track is driveable (though 4WD helps over the deep sand), and it's also clear enough for walkers to follow without getting lost. The track is seldom used by motorists and you're not likely to see other people. Around its halfway mark, the soil changes from red *murram* to a light grey, soft coral sand, signalling the transition back to the coast proper. If you've been pootling along gently on a rented cycle from Malindi, this is pretty well the end of the relaxing bit, and you'll have to start getting off to push. Your eventual emergence onto the main highway, 5–6km south of Gedi, is sudden. Here, you could wait for a short time for a matatu straight back to Malindi or, if the day is still young and your energy not completely sapped, turn inland again a couple of kilometres north up the road, where the other track (described above) leads to Arabuko and Kakayuni.

Gedi

The Arabuko-Sokoke Forest may partly explain the enigma of **GEDI** (sometimes spelt Gede). This large, thirteenth- to seventeenth-century Swahili town was apparently unknown to the Portuguese, despite the fact that, for nearly a hundred years, they maintained a strong presence only 15km away in Malindi, at a time when Gedi is judged to have been at the peak of its prosperity. It is not mentioned (at least by the name of Gedi) in any Arabic or Swahili writings

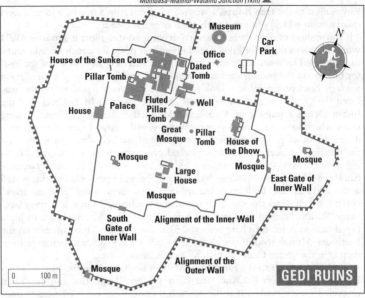

either and, bafflingly, it has to be assumed that, set back from the sea and deep in the forest, it was never noticed.

The **ruins** (daily 7am–6pm; Ksh500, children Ksh250) are confusing, eerie and, in the late afternoon, hauntingly beautiful. Even if you are resolutely uninterested in seeing any of the other sites on the coast, don't miss this one. Forest has invaded the town over the three centuries since it was deserted, and baobabs and magnificent buttress-rooted trees tower over the dimly lit walls and arches. Gedi has a sinister reputation and local people have always been uneasy about it; it has collected an unhealthy share of ghost stories and tales of inexplicable happenings since 1948, when it was opened as a national park and tourists started to visit. Some of this cultural memory may derive from the supposed occupation of the ruins in the eighteenth century by **Oromo**-speaking people (probably ancestors of the Orma, whose present-day territory starts just north of Malindi), a tribe of irrepressible expansionists whose violent and unsettled lifestyle was long a major threat to the coastal communities. This part explains how they got to be known, until recently, as *Galla*, an offensive term which was applied to them by the native Amhara and Mijikenda. The Oromo, it's believed, were the original cause of Gedi's desertion by its inhabitants.

The longer you stay here, the further you seem from an answer to Gedi's anomalies. The display of pottery shards from all over the world in the small **museum** shows that the town must have been actively trading with overseas merchants, yet it is 5km from the sea and 2km from Mida Creek; the coastline has probably moved inland over the centuries, so it might previously have been further away still. Then, at times of supposed Oromo aggression, sailing into Mida Creek would have been like entering a lobster pot. The reasons for Gedi's location remain thoroughly obscure and its absence from historical records grows more inexplicable the more you think about it.

Gedi tingles spines easily, even today, particularly if you are on your own. James Kirkman, the archeologist who first worked at the site, remembers: "when I first started to work at Gedi I had the feeling that something or somebody was looking out from behind the walls, neither hostile nor friendly but waiting for what he knew was going to happen." Kirkman's booklet, usually available at the entrance gate (Ksh100), has a lot of interesting details as well as a plan of the site, which we've reproduced here. Its directions, however, tend to lead you in circles; it's better just to follow your nose.

Any bus or matatu travelling between Malindi and Watamu or Kilifi can drop you off at Gedi junction, where the B8 Malindi–Mombasa road meets the turn-off for Watamu. The junction is a ten-minute walk from the site, which is clearly signposted.

The site
The town seems fairly typical of medieval Swahili settlements. It was walled, and originally covered about a quarter of a square kilometre – some 45 acres. The majority of its estimated 2500 citizens, or at least inhabitants, probably lived in mud-and-thatch huts, long overwhelmed and dissolved by jungle, on the southern, poorer side of town, the side away from Mecca. The palace and the "Stone Town" were in the north. When the site was reoccupied at the end of the sixteenth century, after a hiatus of fifty or so years, a new inner wall was built, enclosing just this prestigious zone.

The **Palace**, with its striking entrance porch, sunken courts and honeycomb of little rooms, is the most impressive single building. The concentration of

△ Ruins at Gedi

houses to its right is where most of Gedi's interesting finds were made and they are named accordingly: House of the Scissors, House of the Ivory Box, House of the Dhow (with a picture of a dhow on the wall). If you have already been to Lamu, the tight layout of buildings and streets will be familiar, although in Gedi all the houses were single storey. As usual, sanitary arrangements are much in evidence. Gedi's toilets are all of identical design, and superior to the long-drops you find in Kenya today. While many of the houses have been modified over the centuries, these bathrooms seem original, almost as if the town was purpose-built, like a housing estate. Look out for the **House of the Sunken Court**, one of the most elaborate, with its self-conscious emulation of the Palace's courtyards.

Gedi's **Great Mosque**, one of seven on the site, was its Friday mosque, the mosque of the whole town. Compared with other ruined mosques on the coast, this one is very large and had a *minbar*, or pulpit, of three steps in stone, rather than the usual wooden construction. Perhaps an inkling of the kind of people who worshipped here – and they were both men and women – and their form of Islam, comes from the carving of a broad-bladed **spearhead** above the arch of the mosque's northeast doorway. Whoever they were, they were clearly not the "colonial Arabs" long believed by European classical scholars to have been the people of Gedi: it's hard to believe that Arabs would have made use of the spear symbol of East African pastoralists.

Nearby is a good example of a **pillar tomb**. These are found all along the coast and are associated with men of importance – chiefs, sheikhs and senior community elders. The fact that this kind of grave is utterly alien to the rest of the Islamic world is further indication that coastal Islam was distinctly African for a long time. Such tombs aren't constructed any more, though there's a nineteenth-century one in Malindi. It looks as if the more recent waves of Arab immigration to the coast have tended to discourage what must have seemed to them an eccentric, even barbaric, style. The **Dated Tomb** next door to the office gives an idea of Gedi's age. Its epitaph reads 802 AH – or AD 1399. Also by the office, the new **museum** exhibits finds from the site including imported artefacts such as Chinese Ming vases and Spanish scissors, evidence of trade with lands very far afield. There are also exhibits of Swahili cultural artefacts, and temporary exhibitions in the adjoining salon.

Gedi wildlife

It's easy to spend hours here, and rewarding to walk down some of the well-swept paths through the thick jungle away from the main ruins. In the under-growth, you catch spooky glimpses of other buildings still unexcavated. And with patience you'll see a **golden-rumped elephant shrew** (see p.499). Gedi also has monkeys, bushbabies, tiny duiker antelope and, according to local belief, a huge, mournful, sheep-like animal that follows you like a shadow down the paths.

Watch out, incidentally, for the *siafu* **ants** that have colonized many of the ruins. They form thick brown columns massing from one hole to another and sometimes gather in enormous clumps. Be careful where you put your feet when stepping over walls. And try not to stand on the walls themselves: they are fragile, and the freedom to walk around Kenya's ruins without restriction isn't likely to continue if they suffer as a result. Incidentally, the **snake farm** near the entrance isn't the best of its kind; just a guide/tout who takes you to a *shamba* (farm) in the forest where a couple of snakes are produced and paraded around the guide's neck.

Kipepeo Project Butterfly Farm

By the entrance to Gedi ruins is Kenya's first working butterfly farm, **Kipepeo** ("butterfly" in Swahili; daily 8am–5pm; Ksh100, children Ksh50). This is the base for a project which helps local residents benefit from the proximity of the forest by exploiting the overseas market for exotic butterflies – for preserved collections and walk-through butterfly "farms". People catch adult butterflies with a net, and place the females on plants of the species eaten by their caterpillars, encouraging them to lay eggs. When hatched, the caterpillars are looked after and kept in food until they pupate, at which point the chrysalises are taken to the butterfly farm, where they are shipped to foreign customers and the breeders paid for their trouble. Some pupae are also kept for the farm itself, while those which are not sold simply return to the wild. Vistors to the farm can see the butterflies at various stages of development, from larva (caterpillar) through pupa (chrysalis) to adult (butterfly). The project's visitor centre provides information on the project and Arabuko-Sokoke Forest in general, and also has local handicrafts on display, as well as locally produced honey. Morning is the best time to visit, when the butterflies are most active and you have a chance of seeing them emerging from their pupae.

Watamu

After Gedi, **WATAMU** seems fairly superficial. It consists simply of a small agglomeration of hotels, a strip of beachfront private homes, a compact coconut village of *hotelis* and curio stands, and the **beach**. It tends to cater for package holidaymakers staying in the large hotels along it, but there's still plenty for the backpacker – beautiful beaches, a superb marine park and lively young nightlife. Watamu is well used to tourists: making friends is easy, and you can look around the village without being too badly pestered. As the beach is part of the marine park, KWS regulations have recently been enforced to clear beach boys and hawkers off the beach.

Although one or two of the hotels are very pleasant, the beach and the coral offshore are the main justification for visiting Watamu. Fortunately, they are justification enough. This is an exceptional shoreline, with three stunning **bays** – Watamu Bay, the Blue Lagoon and Turtle Bay – separated by raised coral cliffs and dotted with tiny, sculpted coral islets scuttled over by crabs. If you like beach walks, bring a pair of rubber- or plastic-soled sandals – the coral rock is sharp. Out in the **Watamu Marine National Park**, the submerged crags of living coral gardens are – despite all the visits in glass-bottom boats – as vivid and magically perfect as they must have been for millennia. And, despite the high profile of tourism here, there's an easier-going atmosphere than at, say, Diani or Malindi, with fewer security problems than at Malindi and the coastline north and south of Mombasa. Watamu is a good place to go **diving** – or to learn the skill, with at least three diving schools offering one-off dives or approved courses at standard rates (p.511). It's worth knowing, however, that from June to October **seaweed** is often swept onto the beach and the sea can be murky, while in July it's often too rough to snorkel or dive anyway.

Among environmental intiatives, one that many hotels participate in, and individual tourists can contribute to, is **Watamu Turtle Watch** (PO Box 125; ☎042/32118, ⓦwww.watamuturtles.com), a project to protect the eggs of threatened marine turtles from poaching (in both senses) by paying local people to guard nests. The same group also pays fishermen to hand in turtles that have become ensnared in fishing nets for rerelease into the sea, and individuals can

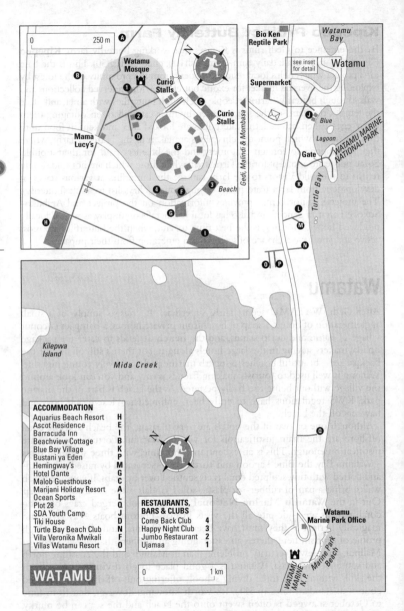

sponsor a nest for guarding or a turtle for release. Turtle Watch is informed when nests they are guarding hatch, so if you contact them, you may be able to go and see the baby turtles scuttling down the sand from their nest into the sea.

Getting to Watamu is easy, with frequent matatus making the run from Malindi. Buses and matatus between Mombasa or Kilifi and Malindi will drop you at the Gedi junction, leaving you to walk, hitch, wait for a matatu, or take a taxi for the last 6km. The road from Gedi and the junction is dead straight. Just before Watamu, it passes the settlement of **Timboni**, with three speed humps; just down an alley to the left (east) of the road by the third hump, the Women's Health Centre sells excellent handmade neem soap, using coconut oil and extracts derived from the neem tree. Introduced into this part of Kenya from India, the neem has numerous medicinal properties and its leaves are used as a natural mosquito repellent.

Coming into Watamu itself, the road from Gedi passes the **post office** (Mon–Fri 8am–12.30pm & 2–5pm, Sat 9am–noon) before it hits the beach road, which matatus scud up and down all the time. Just north of the junction, behind the post office is a **supermarket** with, next door, a very pricey internet office. If you continue up the beach road a little way past the turning for the supermarket, a road off to the right takes you into **Watamu village**. Just under a kilometre beyond that, on the left, a superb little **reptile park**, Bio-Ken (daily 10am–noon & 2–5pm; Ksh700), breeds green and black mambas for anti-venom, and houses a large collection of snakes, plus a few tortoises and a token croc, and you'll be guided round by someone who actually knows a bit about reptiles.

A right turn at the beach road junction brings you to four main resort hotels – *Blue Bay Village*, *Ocean Sports*, *Hemingways* and *Turtle Bay* – twenty or thirty private homes and, at the end of the narrow bar along which the road runs, the marine park ticket office. And that's Watamu.

Watamu village

Watamu village is a weird mixture of unhurried fishing community and frenzied europhile souvenir centre. The traditional rubs elbows with the pseudo-hip; Samburu and Maasai *morani* in full ochred splendour stand around waiting for photographers (and potential female customers); the Jamia Mosque has a notice which reads "All Muslims are Well Come for Prayers. No Trespass. By Management."

The centre of the village is a small **square** at the end of the tarmac road, with a couple of curio shops. The square's main purpose seems to be to allow the curio-stand owners to size up the latest punters as they arrive (German and Swiss tourists on their way to the *Watamu Beach Hotel* pass this way). But the pressure to buy is relatively subdued and after a couple of visits down here your face, and dress, become known and you can go about your business with a nod and a smile. Not that there's anything much to be done; apart from a few bars and restaurants, there's little to keep you from the beach. There's also no bank in town – if you need to change money, the safari operators will usually oblige. Mama Lucy's supermarket sells, among other things, honey from Arabuko-Sokoke Forest.

There are a couple of good **restaurants** on the road into the village. *Ascot Hotel* caters mainly to Italians, and has a superb wood-fired pizza oven, and wine at moderate pices; the *Dante* is usually very enjoyable, reasonably priced, and has cheap beer. For **bars and nightlife**, try the *Happy Night Club* and the *Come Back Club*, both popular and open till late. More dubious is *Ujamaa Bar & Restaurant*, essentially a pick-up joint posing as a pub. *Jumbo Restaurant* is a lively bar with mostly inexpensive food, unless you go for the mixed seafood grill, which will set you back a cool Ksh1800.

Bicycle rental is offered by a number of outlets, especially in high season when it gets quite competitive (Ksh300–600 per day, depending on season and number of days). Bikes are a great way of getting to know Watamu, with the Gedi ruins and anywhere on the beach road easily reachable in thirty minutes or so.

Village accommodation

There's a wide variety of **accommodation** in the village itself – everything from humble and uninviting B&Ls to a pleasant holiday hotel. Bear in mind that some establishments either close or just tick over out of season, remaining open with a skeleton staff. As ever, the tour places are much cheaper if you book them as part of a package. The very central places risk being loud at night, thanks to nearby nightclubs.

THE COAST | Watamu

Ascot Residence Hotel PO Box 348 ☏ 042/32326, ⓦ www.ascotresidence.com. Seems to occupy most of the middle of what you feel should be Watamu village. Looks like a very expensive hotel but is very good value, catering mainly for Italians: well-designed rooms with massive beds, fans and patios, and a large dolphin-shaped pool. Good breakfasts. It can become fairly lively in high season. B&B ❻

🏃 **Beachview Cottage** PO Box 483 ☏ 042/32383, ⓔ watamubeachview@yahoo. com. Clean and friendly, with a nice pool, a roof terrace with views of the beach, and spotless s/c rooms. Double rooms each have a kitchen, single rooms share one. ❹

Hotel Dante PO Box 183 ☏ 042/32243. Small, but homely s/c rooms with fan, with a good restaurant, though it doesn't have the *Veronika*'s shady garden or breakfasts. ❷

Malob Guesthouse PO Box 105 ☏ 042/32260. A clean and quiet B&L, with fans and nets in the rooms, which are all s/c. A better-value alternative to the *Dante* or *Villa Veronica*. ❷

Marijani Holiday Resort PO Box 282 ☏ 042/32448, ⓦ www.marjani-holiday-resort.com. A very pleasant surprise: friendly, welcoming, and informal German-run place, with superb rooms in two stylish houses. The rooms are very comfortable and exceptionally good value, with huge four-poster beds and spacious nets, fans, and spotless bathrooms (showers). All have fridges, some have kitchens or (oddly) sunbeds, and separate kitchens are available. There's even a three-bedroom family house in case you have a big enough family to fill it. Safe parking; bicycle rental (Ksh200 per hour); surfboards (Ksh500 per hour). Not on the beach, nonetheless highly recommended. ❹

Tiki House PO Box 227 ☏ 0734/703622. A small family-run place hidden away inside the village (the entrance is painted in zebra stripes), with three different-sized clean s/c rooms and a two-room apartment, plus use of shared kitchen facilities. ❷

Villa Veronika Mwikali PO Box 57 ☏ 042/32083. More or less a B&L, run by a Kikamba–Swiss couple, with fairly ordinary rooms with nets, some s/c, around a courtyard. Has a shady, intimate, almost Mediterranean feel. ❷

Beach hotels and other accommodation

Several of these establishments focus on watersports, with diving and game fishing on offer. The big fishing competition in the first or second week of March can make accommodation scarce. But in May and June the hotels usually have excellent low-season rates, sometimes available only in packages of seven nights. The following listings are arranged from north to south. Matatus from Watamu, and some from Malindi, only go as far as *Turtle Bay Beach Club*, where *boda-bodas* can be engaged to take you further south.

Barracuda Inn PO Box 59 ☏ 042/32509, ⓦ www. barracudainn.com. Unusual hotel with impressive *makuti*-vaulted reception on the shore of the Blue Lagoon, populated mainly by Italians, and well worth considering for an excellent-value getaway break (though note that the second-floor open-air dining terrace is inaccessible to wheelchairs). The beach outlook is only matched by the *Watamu Beach* and here the scene is more intimate. Ground-floor rooms are more spacious – all have telephones and a/c, and there are tennis courts and pool. FB ❽

SDA Youth Camp PO Box 222 ☏ 042/52265. Run by the Seventh Day Adventists mainly as a lecture place for schoolkids. For those on a really low budget, it should be possible to camp here, if you can find the caretaker to get permission. Dubious water and toilet facilities, but lots of camping space, all set in the dunes under coconuts and casuarinas with a great view of the Blue Lagoon.

Aquarius Beach Resort PO Box 96 ☏ 042/32069, ⓦ www.aquariuswatamu.com. Very pleasant if misleadingly named hotel, far from the beach.

Comfy if slightly sombre rooms have a/c plus ceiling fans. Closed off season. HB ⑥

Blue Bay Village PO Box 162 ☎042/32626, ⓔbluebay@africaonline.co.ke. Mostly Italian-patronized package-holiday complex, with beautiful, palmy gardens and a good pool. If you're going to stay, don't compromise – only the deluxe rooms are worth the money (standard rooms lack a/c). FB ⑧

🏃 **Ocean Sports** PO Box 100 ☎042/32008, ⓦwww.oceansports.net. Slightly macho place, whose reputation ("Open Shorts") has sailed before it for years. During holiday times it swarms with young "Kenya Cowboys" (white Kenyans) doing very much their own thing, but it's right on the beach, and allows camping. Blue marlin trophies gawp from the walls but the rooms are nice (fans and a/c), the staff pleasant and the food good. HB $160 ⑨

Hemingway's PO Box 267 ☎042/32624, ⓕ32256, ⓦwww.hemingways.co.ke; reservations through Express Travel Group; PO Box 40433 Nairobi ☎02/334722–7, ⓕ334825. Sharing a plot with *Ocean Sports*, the contrast is great. From Oct to April, landing sharks and marlin is still high on the agenda, but this is a really top-class hotel where the atmosphere tends towards formal and there's nothing much for children. Rooms in the new wing are wonderful, large with huge beds; all rooms have a/c and sea views. Lovely beach with a number of coral outcrops within swimming distance. Food is variable. Snorkelling, dhow cruises, creek fishing and day-trips. Prices are in sterling. HB £123 ⑨

Turtle Bay Beach Club PO Box ☎042/32003, ⓦwww.turtlebay.co.ke. Expertly run, all-inclusive holiday club, full of happy holidaymakers (mainly British, some German). Lots to do, lots to eat, and plenty to drink. Cramped gardens. Facilities include PADI diving and windsurfing schools, tennis, and a giant chessboard. Participates in community and environmental initiatives. You can have a one-day sample of club life (either up to 5pm, or from 5pm onwards) for Ksh2000. All-inclusive ⑧

Bustani ya Eden PO Box 276 ☎042/32262. Plain, comfortable chalet-style rooms, all s/c (hot and cold water) with fans, attached to a locally renowned bar-restaurant, with reasonably priced seafood and African dishes. No beach. B&B ④

Villas Watamu Resort PO Box 150 ☎042/32487. Some 400m from the road, a German-run Mediterranean-style self-catering villa development (not a *makuti* roof in sight) with a dramatic line in verandas and a huge pool, as well as a restaurant. Not overly exciting, and no beach (15min walk), but security is good and the rates, for spacious a/c accommodation with fully equipped kitchens, are very reasonable. Clean and proper. ④

🏃 **Plot 28** (formerly *Mrs Simpson's*) PO Box 33 ☎042/32023, ⓔmwamba@arocha.org. The late Barbara Simpson used to host guests at her home here, now a field studies centre run by Christian conservationist group A Rocha, who are keeping up Mrs Simpson's tradition. You don't need to be a Christian or a conservationist to stay here, and there are six good rooms for rent, all s/c with fans and nets, some with solar-powered electricity and hot water. You can also camp (Ksh750 per person). The beach here is deserted, with no beach boys for miles. Snorkelling trips can be arranged, although you can simply rent a mask and snorkel (Ksh100) and swim out 300m to the nearest reefs. There are also bird-watching trips to Arabuko-Sokoke Forest, the Galana (Sabaki) River and Mida Creek, and even turtle-watching expeditions. FB ③

Watamu Marine National Park and other excursions

The **Watamu Marine National Park** (daily 6am–6pm; $5, children $2; Warden PO Box 333 Watamu ☎042/32393) stretches along the coast from the Blue Lagoon to Mida Creek. Its **total exclusion zone** for fishermen has not been greeted with rhapsody all round. On the other hand, tourists come in larger numbers every year and Watamu evidently hasn't gone far wrong in identifying their needs. This is prime **snorkelling** and **diving** territory, highly rated even by professionals, as the reef is in excellent condition and the water usually totally clear. Harmless **whale sharks** visit the area regularly, a highlight for any diver.

If you've never taken a swim before in a shoal of coral fish, the spectacle can be breathtaking: every conceivable combination of colour and shape – and a few inconceivable ones – is represented. It seems impossible that fish should take such forms. The ostentatious dazzle of some of them, especially the absurd parrot fish, can be simply hilarious. The most common destination is the "**coral gardens**", a kilometre or two offshore, where the boat drifts, suspended in 5–6m of scintillatingly clear water. Here, over a group of giant coral heads, where fish naturally congregate and where offerings of bread have obviously further encouraged them, you enter the unusual park. If you can get hold of a copy, an out-of-print booklet called *The Watamu Snorkeller's Guide* by Richard Bennett has a map of the coral off Watamu, articles on the main types of fish, and suggested snorkelling routes.

If you can **dive to the sea floor**, you'll get an intense experience of sharing the undersea world with the fish and the coral. Watch out for the small, harmless octopuses that stay motionless until disturbed and then jet themselves across the sea bed – they're brilliant masters of disguise, altering their form, texture and colour to fit their surroundings. Above, the boat's hull creates a deep shadow which, associated with food from the passengers, attracts thousands of fish. As you return to the surface, they move out of the way in mysterious unison, each one avoiding all the others in a kind of natural light show of fantastic beauty. If such adventures aren't your forte, the glass bottoms of the boats provide an alternative view – but it's often a rather obscure and narrow one.

For **visits to the park**, *Ocean Sports* and *Hemingway's* both run glass-bottom boat snorkelling trips (Ksh800, including park fee). Otherwise, you'll have to haggle with the boatmen along the beach, or outside the park headquarters and ticket office down at the south end of the Watamu road at Temple Point. Expect to pay Ksh600–800 per person (including park fees) for a two-hour trip in a glass-bottomed boat combining the coral gardens with a trip along Mida Creek. Masks, snorkels and sometimes fins are provided, but remember to take plenty of sun cream and a T-shirt. Boats wait until everyone has had enough of swimming, so will stay as long as you want to. A four-hour snorkelling trip for two should cost under Ksh2000, including park fees. From the park HQ, a track leads 500m or so to a pretty little beach at Temple Point, with some sunshades and small boats, by the entrance to Mida Creek.

Grouper and dolphin spotting – and Sudi island

At the entrance to Mida Creek is a famous group of caves. Known as the "**Big Three Caves**", these are the meeting place of a school of **giant groupers**, or rock cod, that once numbered only three but are now many more. Up to 2m long and weighing over 300 kilos, these are placid, stationary monsters – thankfully for anyone intrepid enough to dive down 3–4m for a closer look. The site is a good kilometre offshore and there are some moderate currents; boat trips normally only take place at the turn of neap high tides, when visibility, depth and currents give the optimum conditions. You need a permit from the park warden to visit the Big Three Caves – this is usually given freely.

Less predictable sea excursions are also arranged in quest of **dolphins**. These are fairly frequently seen offshore, but it's become accepted practice to pay only a nominal charge for the trip if you're unsuccessful. Check it out before committing yourself. A new excursion, offered by most hotels, is to **Sudi island** in Mida Creek, where a boardwalk takes you right through the mangrove swamps.

Diving and game fishing

From September to April, the **diving** possibilities are extensive at Watamu and you don't need to go far; most of the best dive sites are within thirty minutes of the beach. There are three dive centres, and if you're an experienced diver the best plan is probably to visit all of them and make your own assessment of their competence and suitability. Scuba Diving Kenya offers the lowest prices, but Aqua Ventures caters better for absolute beginners.

The sort of **money** involved, if you're a qualified diver, is something around €30–40 per dive including equipment, less (around €20 per dive) with your own equipment (excluding tanks and weights). There are reductions if you book a series of dives, and small supplements for night- and wreck-dives. If you haven't dived for a while, you should be asked to do a check-out dive (usually free) or a one-day refresher. Lastly, if you're a beginner, you can do either a one-day, one-dive course (around €70), or opt for the proper PADI course of four dives over five days – leading to certification and your log book – for around €300 inclusive (to "Open Water" level).

Aqua Ventures *Ocean Sports;* PO Box 275 ☎ & ☏ 042/32420, ⊛ www.diveinkenya.com.
Scuba Diving Kenya Next to *Blue Bay Village;* PO Box 160 ☎ 042/32099, ⊛ www.scuba-diving-kenya.com.
Turtle Bay Beach Club PO Box 457 Malindi ☎ 042/32003, ⊛ www.turtlebay.co.ke.

Hemingway's Fishing Centre organizes sea-fishing trips (shark, marlin, sailfish and swordfish are among the game) at €280 a day for up to four people, or €400–450 (depending on season) for up to six – individuals may be able to tag along with a group.

Malindi and around

When Vasco da Gama's fleet arrived at **MALINDI** in 1498, it met an unexpectedly warm welcome. The king of Malindi had presumably heard of Mombasa's attempts to sabotage the fleet a few days earlier and, no friend of Mombasa himself, he was swift to ally himself with the powerful – and dangerous – Portuguese. Until they finally subdued Mombasa nearly one hundred years later, Malindi was centre of operations for the Portuguese on the East African coast. Once Fort Jesus was built, Malindi's ruling family was invited to transfer their power base there, which they did, and for many years Malindi was virtually a ghost town as its aristocrats lived it up in Mombasa under Portuguese protection.

Malindi's reputation for hospitality to strangers has stuck, and so has the suggestion of sell-out. As a steadily growing development area for the cultivation of German and Italian euros the town is slipping towards cultural anonymity: it can't seem to make up its mind whether it wants to be a Mombasa or a Lamu. While retaining a Swahili atmosphere, which Mombasa has partly lost in urban development, it utterly lacks Lamu's self-contained tranquillity. Heavily dependent on tourism, the town has gone into decline economically as holiday-makers have turned their sights elsewhere. It's now making great efforts to reverse that trend, starting with a clear-out of the beach boys and hawkers that were such a nuisance to tourists in the past, and aiming to abandon its former dependence on the Italian package-tour market. Nonetheless, although Malindi makes an excellent base for visits to places like Gedi ruins and Arabuko-Sokoke Forest, it remains a town unashamedly geared towards beach tourism.

Consequently, whether you enjoy Malindi or not depends, at least in part, on how highly you rate the unsophisticated parts of Kenya, and whether you appreciate a fully fledged resort town for its facilities or loathe it for its tackiness. And of course it depends on when you're here. During the summer-holiday season (Malindi's best month, sea- and weather-wise, is August), as well as in

December and January, the town can sometimes be a bit nightmarish. In a busy high season (and it's a while since Malindi has seen one) everything African seems to recede behind the swarms of window-shopping tourists and Suzuki jeeps. Even so, Malindi at its worst is still relatively placid compared with, say, Spain or the Greek islands, and off season (reduced here to the long rains only – April to June) can seem positively subdued, as if exhausted. At this time of year, when it is often damp and grey, with piles of seaweed washed ashore, Malindi has the air of a south of England beach resort: the faded muddle of an ageing seaside town – garnished with tropical plants.

Fortunately, Malindi has some important saving graces. Number one is the **coral reef**. The combined Malindi/Watamu Marine National Park and Reserve encloses some of the best stretches on the coast. Kisite-Mpunguti, on the south coast, and Kiunga, further north, are reckoned by some connoisseurs to be even better, but the Malindi fish have seen many more strange faces in masks and have become so used to humans that they swarm in front of you like a kaleidoscopic snowstorm. Malindi is also a **game-fishing** centre with regular competitions, and a bit of a **surfing** resort, too. Good-sized rollers steam into the bay through the long break in the reef during July and August and in early September, whipped up by the southerly monsoon winds which are likely to get you sand-blasted on the beach.

Despite the heavy reliance on tourism, Malindi still has some interest as a Kenyan town with an ancient history and a few places of interest other than its beach and reef. An interesting old Swahili quarter, one or two "ruins", a busy market, shops, *hotelis* and plenty of lodgings all compensate for the tourist boutiques, beauty salons and real estate agencies. The fact that Malindi has a broad range of places to stay within walking distance of the beach – and a broad range of places to eat and spend money within walking distance of the hotels – gives it a clear advantage over Watamu, Diani or the places more immediately north of Mombasa. As for the Italian package tourists, they have left the town with something that nowhere else in Kenya can boast: some of the best pizzas, pasta and ice cream in the whole of Africa.

The best way to get around Malindi and its environs is **by bicycle** (several places rent bikes. The flat countryside around Malindi is ideal and Gedi (90min) or Watamu (2hr) are easy objectives, with the guarantee that you'll be blown either there or back by the wind, depending on the time of year. The northern reaches of the wonderful Arabuko-Sokoke Forest are within easy reach too (see p.499).

Arrival, orientation and information

If you're arriving from the south, you'll end up at the main **bus station** and matatu area, about ten minutes' walk south of town along the Mombasa road; a taxi or *tuk-tuk* to the centre shouldn't cost more than Ksh200, or Ksh300–400 to the beach hotels. Coming from Lamu or Garissa, you'll be dropped by the companies' booking offices in the town centre between the market and the messy, noisy high street where the cheapest of the B&Ls are found. The main focus of town is from here up to the misleadingly named Uhuru Gardens (a dusty patch of shade) and then north along the commercial Lamu Road.

Malindi **airport** is barely 3km south of the town centre and you can walk into Malindi in half an hour. Matatus heading to the main stage (which is about halfway between the airport and the town centre) will pick you up on the main road just outside the airport; otherwise, taxis charge around Ksh800 to beach hotels, or Ksh500 into town.

Pokot girl, northern Rift

Traditional dress

Kenya's indigenous peoples belong to more than forty distinct ethnic groups, commonly known as tribes. Though these are most clearly differentiated by their mother tongue, traditional tribal dress also used to be a good indicator of ethnic affiliation, and in the early colonial period travellers were made aware of their location by the clothing of people in the villages they passed. With the arrival of the cash economy during the colonial era, clothing became more a question of personal taste – though for the majority of people that means one set of clothes, selected from the piles of secondhand garments exported by Western charities and sold at roadside markets. Traditional dress is, however, still significant as an identifier in a number of communities, especially along the coast, among the pastoral tribes of the Rift Valley and throughout the north. For other tribes, traditional garb is worn on ceremonial occasions or sometimes by those who make a living on the fringes of the tourist industry.

Swahili women in buibuis and kanga

Swahili

Coastal dress styles are some of the most distinctive and influential in Kenya. The Swahili (see p.426), a loosely defined ethnic group that itself consists of a number of distinct tribes and sections, are almost exclusively Muslim and have adopted several variations of traditional Islamic dress from the Middle East, in particular from the southern Arabian Peninsula. The basic garment for men is the kikoi, a colourfully woven sarong that reaches from waist to shins, often in brilliantly contrasting colours. They are not to be confused with the less expensive kangas, wraps of printed cotton worn exclusively by women and usually featuring Swahili proverbs and epithets. Unless fishing or doing heavy labour, men always wear a shirt or vest, but formal wear consists of topping the shirt and *kikoi* with a long cotton kanzu – a gown, usually white and usually worn with a neatly embroidered skull cap or *kofia*.

The formal attire of most Swahili women, especially those of high status, outside the house is the buibui, a black cloak and shawl that completely conceals the woman's identity, leaving only a tiny gap, or a gauze veil, to see through.

Maasai and Samburu

Of all Kenya's peoples, the Maasai (see p.404), particularly their men, decked in brilliant red cloth, with beads, metal jewellery, and – for young men – long, ochred hairstyles, have received perhaps the most attention from outsiders. Although the wearing of red cloth is very widespread and is as close to a "national costume" as any in Kenya, it does not much predate the colonial period: throughout most of their three- to four-hundred-year history in Kenya, the Maasai wore skins and had no use for cotton cloth. Only with the availability of brilliantly dyed imports did the use of powerfully symbolic blood-red clothing become widespread. Today, the warrior ensemble of a cloth tied over one shoulder, together with weapons and braided hair, is still widely seen, while, after circumcision, in their early days as warriors, young men can be encountered out in the bush, hunting for birds to add to their elaborate, taxidermic headdresses. The Samburu (see p.578), who split from their Maasai-speaking cousins around the seventeenth century, wear similar attire – though men often

Maasai man with beads and ochre

go bare-chested. Like other pastoralists, they tend to appear in shirts and trousers only for rare visits to town, where traditional dress is normally considered unacceptable. Maasai and Samburu women invariably wear *kangas* these days, the designs chosen according to personal taste, and most women cover their breasts, an innovation of the late twentieth century. Long earrings and stacks of bead necklaces are, however, still the norm.

Kikuyu

Among the mixed farming and trading people of the Mount Kenya region, traditional costume was in many respects similar to that of the Maasai. The Kikuyu (see p.173) dressed exclusively in animal skins, tanned, softened and sewn together. Goatskin was the preferred material, but sheepskins were also used. The Kikuyu have a long history of smelting and iron-working, so volumes of heavy metal jewellery, often composed largely of wire, were also worn, especially by women. By the middle of the twentieth century, most Kikuyu men had adopted European clothes and blankets, but women tended to be more traditional. Today, however, Kikuyu fashions for both sexes are entirely cosmopolitan. "Traditional" costume as worn today, for dances or cultural events, invariably includes goatskins, worn over cloth wraps for modesty, and plenty of ornamentation, as well as white face and body paint, or *karia andus*, made of lime.

Turkana man wearing *aberait* (wrist-knife)

Turkana

You'll still see older Turkana (see p.564) people in more remote parts wearing very few clothes or, in some cases, animal skins. Stacks of heavy jewellery, ostrich egg necklaces and beadwork are also very common, and men usually sport lethal wrist-knives – bracelet-like blades sheathed with strips of leather.

The traditional **colour symbolism** of Kenya's peoples focused around black or dark blue, white and red, the three "primary" colours for which non-derived terms exist in nearly all Kenyan languages. Black was usually seen as a propitious colour, indicating rain clouds, fecundity and wealth; white a colour with spiritual significance alluding to bones, death and ancestors as well as semen, milk and vital potential; and red the colour of war and triumph. Headdresses made of colobus monkey skins (as worn by the Kikuyu dancer pictured, left) were widely used in ceremony and ritual. Cloth, when it became available in the interior from about the early nineteenth century – dyed black or indigo, red or bleached white – became a convenient way of expressing these symbolic meanings through ritual, and more casually in everyday wear.

Giriama

Living along the coast between Kilifi and Malindi, but traditionally not in the towns or along the shore, the Giriama (see p.498) are part of the Mijikenda ("nine tribes") ethnic group, whose ancestry they trace back to a mythical state or cultural heartland called Shungwaya, in present-day southern Somalia.

The most distinctive Giriama dress form, the rinda, is a kind of kilt worn by women. In pre-colonial times it was made of grass or leaves but, as high-status cloth became available, women started making their *rindas* out of pleated *kanga* material, emulating the grass skirt, and stuffing a bustle of coconut fibre under the waistband at the back to accentuate the buttocks as the old-style rinda had done. By the turn of the century, many Giriama women had adopted Swahili-style two-piece *kanga* dress, but on the backcountry roads you will still see stooped old ladies with the traditional padded backside.

Luo

For the cattle-herding-turned-fishing Luo (see p.285), traditional dress consisted of very little and, until World War I, many people typically went naked or wore scanty loincloths of skin or sisal. Today, the Luo, who live around Kisumu and on the shores of Lake Victoria, are one of the most Westernized of all Kenya's tribes, and you'll find Luos working in the civil service, the tourist industry or in business, throughout the country. Traditional dress is history, and you'll only see it for special ceremonies, when senior elders may don huge plumes of feathers, embellished with tusks and metal ornamentation.

Luo men at public ceremony

From the main **bus and matatu park**, there are frequent services to Gedi, Watamu, Kilifi and Mombasa, and infrequent local matatus and buses for points inland. In addition, some matatus for Watamu leave from the town centre by the market in Mama Ngina Road.

Flying to **Lamu** (Ksh3500 one way, Ksh7000 return) is an experience not to be missed, but **buses** are much cheaper. Services start off from Mombasa, and pass by their Malindi booking offices in the centre of town by the market (marked on our map) at around 8.30am each day. The companies serving Lamu are Tawakal (☎042/31832), with three daily services, and TSS (no office) and Falcon (☎042/30850), with one each. It's advisable to buy your ticket for Lamu the day before – otherwise you may have an exceedingly uncomfortable standing-up experience to look forward to. In the 1990s, buses were subject to occasional **bandit raids**, but improved security on the road has seen an end to such attacks, and there is no longer any need to travel by armed escort, though it may still be worth confirming the current situation before buying your bus ticket. Whether travelling by bus or **driving** your own vehicle to Lamu, you'll have to change onto a **boat** at Mokowe (Ksh50).

The **tourist office** is on the first floor of the Malindi complex on Lamu Road (Mon–Fri 8am–12.30pm & 2–4.30pm; ☎042/20747, ✉malindi@swiftglobal .com). Staff don't have much in the way of information, but are the people to contact if you have a serious complaint about a hotel, safari operator or restaurant. A good online source of information is the Magical Malindi website, Ⓦwww.malindikenya.com.

Accommodation

As for **accommodation**, there's plenty of it: a couple of dozen beach hotels and all-inclusive "club resorts", and cottage and villa complexes providing for the crowds of high-season visitors, though over Christmas, room availability may be restricted. The cheap town lodgings, too, tend to fill up in high season, and also during Maulidi and at the end of Ramadan. Establishments catering essentially for tourists generally vary their prices seasonally, by up to fifty percent, though as usual the cheapest places keep the same low prices all year round.

Budget rooms and camping

There are lots of cheap choices among the town lodgings, with some good travel-ler-oriented guesthouses as well as standard **B&Ls**, and one or two more unusual offerings. With the permanent closure, however, of *Silversands Campsite*, 2km south of the town centre on the beach of the same name, the only **campsite** in Malindi is now at the KWS headquarters at Casuarina Point, 5km from town (see p.519). If you're on your own and walking down this way, especially between the town centre and the *Coral Key/Driftwood* area, just past Silversands beach, it's worth knowing that there have been instances of muggings in the past, so avoid walking on this road after dark.

Blue Lodge PO Box 209 ☎042/30246. The tall blue building near *Fondu Wehu* is a standard B&L popular with locals, and the best of the ultra-cheap options. Most rooms with nets, some s/c. ❶

Dagama's Inn PO Box 5073 ☎042/31942. A variety of rooms, some s/c, simple but clean, with nets. Best are the two front rooms overlooking the beach, with fans and a balcony. ❷

Fondo Wehu Guesthouse PO Box 5805; no phone. Charming family-run guesthouse, far from the beach but popular with budget travellers. Seven good rooms with nets and fans, but not s/c. Very laid-back. ❶

Gilani Hotel PO Box 380 ☎042/20307. Above the restaurant, and overpriced. The four big and breezy upstairs rooms at the front with balconies are the best and only reasons to stay here. B&B ❸

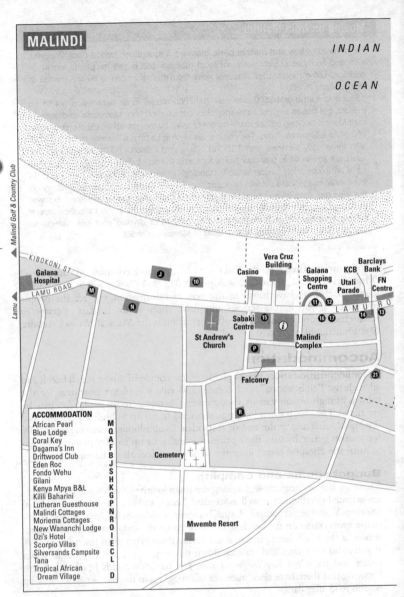

MALINDI

INDIAN

OCEAN

Malindi Golf & Country Club

Lamu

KIBOKONI ST.

Galana
Hospital

LAMU ROAD

M

N

J

10

Casino

Vera Cruz
Building

Galana
Shopping
Centre

KCB

Barclays
Bank

Utali
Parade

FN
Centre

LAMU RO

11 12

16 17

14 13

Sabaki
Centre

15

i

St Andrew's
Church

P

Malindi
Complex

Falconry

R

21

ACCOMMODATION

African Pearl	M
Blue Lodge	Q
Coral Key	A
Dagama's Inn	F
Driftwood Club	B
Eden Roc	J
Fondo Wehu	S
Gilani	H
Kenya Mpya B&L	K
Kilili Baharini	G
Lutheran Guesthouse	P
Malindi Cottages	N
Moriema Cottages	R
New Wananchi Lodge	O
Ozi's Hotel	I
Scorpio Villas	E
Silversands Campsite	C
Tana	L
Tropical African	
Dream Village	D

Cemetery

Mwembe Resort

Kenya Mpya B&L Mama Ngina St; PO Box 209 ☏042/30461. Big enough rooms in a four-storey block, not all s/c or with fans, with cleanish sheets. ②

Lutheran Guesthouse PO Box 409 ☏042/30098. Set in a large garden, with double rooms only

(clean and mosquito-netted with fans, two s/c), plus two self-catering bungalows, each for four people (Ksh1500 per day, Ksh7500 per week, Ksh22,500 per month). There's a no-alcohol policy. B&B ②
New Wananchi Lodge PO Box 209; no phone. Basic flophouse above the Wananchi day and

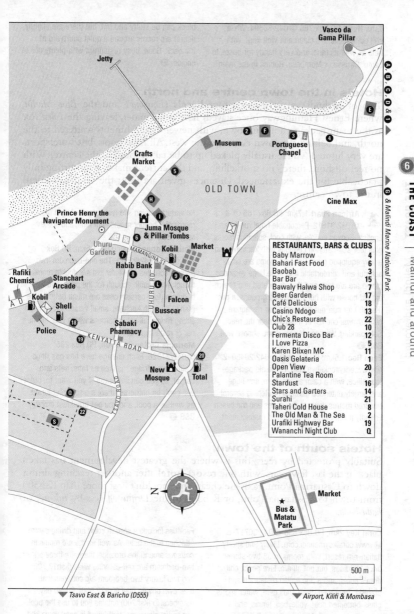

RESTAURANTS, BARS & CLUBS

Baby Marrow	4
Bahari Fast Food	6
Baobab	3
Bar Bar	15
Bawaly Halwa Shop	7
Beer Garden	17
Café Delicious	18
Casino Ndogo	13
Chic's Restaurant	22
Club 28	10
Fermenta Disco Bar	12
I Love Pizza	5
Karen Blixen MC	11
Oasis Gelateria	1
Open View	20
Palantine Tea Room	9
Stardust	16
Stars and Garters	14
Surahi	21
Taheri Cold House	8
The Old Man & The Sea	2
Urafiki Highway Bar	19
Wananchi Night Club	Q

▼ *Tsavo East & Baricho (D555)*

▼ *Airport, Kilifi & Mombasa*

night club, so you can draw your own conclusions about how it is largely used, but for all that it is friendly, reasonably clean, and good value, especially if you want to be right in the centre of town, and it is also, of course, handy for the bar downstairs. **1**

Ozi's Hotel PO Box 60 ☎042/20218, ℮ozi@swiftmalindi.com. Very secure and friendly, popular with travellers, but none of the rooms are s/c, though all have ceiling fans. Next to mosque. Free laundry (five items a day). B&B **3**

Tana Hotel PO Box 766 ⓣ 042/30594. While still quite basic, it's clean and well kept, with nets as well as fans, and very handy for buses to Lamu, Garissa or Mombasa. Rooms in the main block can be stuffy and hot, but there are slightly dearer s/c rooms around a quiet courtyard at the back. Good, busy restaurant with plenty of choice. 2

Hotels in the town centre and north

Two of Malindi's main package-tour **hotels** (*Lawford's*, and the *Blue Marlin*, where Ernest Hemingway once stayed) have gone under, leaving the *Eden Roc* as the main package hotel in town, with newer establishments scattered to the north, and behind the town centre to the west. All have pools, but watersports are very limited (you're usually picked up to be taken south of the centre). With no reef offshore, there's no snorkelling, and the current makes windsurfing only practicable for the experienced. Distances given are from the Uhuru Gardens in the town centre.

African Pearl 1.7km; PO Box 165 ⓣ & ⓕ 042/31612. Personable hotel run by an English–Kenyan couple, with cool, spacious rooms, plus four self-catering cottages with kitchens, and a fully equipped gym. The best rooms are characterful and comfortable and have large verandas (some are a/c too), and they're located in a charming old house with hot water, nice grounds, a pool (Ksh300 for non-guests), and a bar-restaurant (with *nyama choma*) at the front near the road. Safe parking. Very good value if you choose well. B&B 5

Eden Roc 1.5km; PO Box 350 ⓣ 042/20480–2, ⓦ www.edenrockenya.com. Large old package-tour place, with a calm atmosphere, and huge and largely untended gardens stretching several hundred metres down to the dunes and the beach. Friendly if somewhat disorganized management. No watersports on site (you're collected in the morning). Cheaper rooms with fans, and some suites. B&B 6

Malindi Cottages Lamu Rd, 1.5km; PO Box 992 ⓣ & ⓕ 042/21071. The one-bedroom (two-person) cottages are really just s/c double rooms, though reasonable enough for the price. The two-bedroom (four-person) ones are much better value (Ksh3000), with kitchens, small verandas and huge sitting rooms, all set in gardens with a pool but no bar or restaurant. 3

Moriema Cottages 1.5km; PO Box 235 ⓣ 042/31326. Each cottage here has gas rings, a sink and a fridge, as well as fans, nets and carpet, so you can self-cater if you want to, but if you can't be bothered, there's also a restaurant, as well as a pool, and you get breakfast anyway. B&B 5

Hotels south of the town

Suitably protected by reefs, this is where the greatest development has taken place in the last few years, with one **resort hotel** after another reaching almost down to Casuarina Point. Taxis are cheap, and shouldn't cost more than Ksh500 from town to Casuarina Point, or Ksh300 to the *Driftwood*, less by *tuk-tuk* or *boda-boda*.

Coral Key 2km; PO Box 556 ⓣ 042/30717–8, ⓦ www.coralkeymalindi.com. Lively and sporty Italian-run resort, with rooms in 38 two-storey brick buildings, but not all a/c. Five pools, children's pools, and a fine Italian restaurant and pizzeria. Trendy Fri disco, plus gym, water sports, glass-bottomed boat, volleyball, tennis, and a rock-climbing wall. Also run *Tsavo Buffalo Camp*, just outside Tsavo East (p.382). B&B 8

Driftwood Club 2.2km; PO Box 63 ⓣ 042/20155, ⓦ www.driftwoodclub.com. Trading on its good food and established reputation among the Anglo–Kenyan community, this is an informal setup, friendly and excellent value. Facilities include a squash court and diving centre attached to the hotel. As well as the a/c rooms in *cottages* around the grounds, there are three pricier two-bedroom a/c self-catering villas (Ksh17,700), and two luxury two-bedroom a/c cottages with their own private pool (Ksh22,500). Cheap day membership (Ksh200) entitles you to use the pool, bar and sunloungers. Half board is good value and buffet dinners are highly recommended-the cooking is excellent. B&B 8

Kilili Baharini 4km; PO Box 93 ⓣ 042/20169, ⓦ www.kililibaharini.com. Rather a classy setup on the road to Casuarina Point. Rooms are organized in small enclaves, each set around its own pool, so

you never have to venture more than a few metres outside your door for a swim. There's also a bigger main pool. All rooms are nice and fresh with a/c and tasteful Swahili-style furniture, and a veranda, where breakfast is served, and there's even a beauty centre where they'll rub you all over with their own Kilili brand of gooey cosmetics. B&B €156; ⑨
Scorpio Villas 1km; PO Box 368 ☏042/20194, ⓦwww.scorpiovillas.co.ke. A well-conceived "village", with pool and restaurant, small-scale, friendly and dense with tropical vegetation. The rooms are charmingly furnished, not hugely deluxe, but characterful, with Swahili-style four-poster beds. B&B ⑦

Tropical African Dream Village 2.7km; PO Box 939 ☏042/31879, ⓦwww.planhotel.com. The result of a merger of two adjacent hotels, this is a huge all-inclusive *makuti* and tropical garden complex – an Italian-slanted holiday resort with a wide range of water sports available. Rooms are classed as "African", "British colonial" and "Swahili–Lamu", and are all spacious and pretty deluxe, with a nod to the styles suggested by the names. Security guards keep out anyone with no specific business at the hotel. Wheelchair friendly with specially designed rooms for guests with disabilities. All-inclusive €180; ⑨

The Town

Other than the beach and the sea, strolling around town is the occupation of most of Malindi's temporary residents, and is not without its idiosyncratic rewards. The old part of Malindi is a half-hour diversion: interesting enough,

△ Juma Mosque, with pillar tomb

even though there's nothing specific to see and few of the buildings date from before the second half of the nineteenth century. But the juxtaposition of the earnest and ordinary business of the old town with the near-hysterical *mzungu*-mania only a couple of minutes' walk away on Lamu Road produces a bizarre, schizophrenic atmosphere that epitomizes Malindi.

The town has an amazingly salacious reputation which is not entirely home-grown. Some European tour operators have in the past been quite inventive in their every-comfort-provided marketing strategies. In the immediate aftermath of the first AIDS-awareness crisis in the late 1980s, there was a massive slump in German tourism to Malindi, but memories are short, it seems; a quick glance at some of the town's bars at night is enough to convince you that the sex safari is back in full swing. Though Germans still come, in recent years Italians have dominated.

Archeologically, Malindi's offerings are scant. The two **pillar tombs** in front of the Juma (Friday) Mosque on the waterfront are fine upstanding examples of the genre, though the shorter one is only nineteenth century. This being Malindi, its appearance is sometimes described as "circumcized", though Islamic scholars on the coast do not of course accept the automatic phallic label applied by foreigners.

Malindi's other monuments are Portuguese. **Vasco da Gama Pillar** (1499), down on the point of the same name, makes a good target for a stroll. The **Portuguese Chapel** is a tiny whitewashed cube of a church now covered with *makuti*, whose foundations were laid in the sixteenth century on the site of a Portuguese burial. The most recent Portuguese bequest is the ugly 1959 **Monument to Prince Henry the Navigator** on the seaward side of Uhuru Gardens. These monuments however contrast uncomfortably with the "Vasco da Gama = Killer" and "Da Gama traitor" graffiti which appeared around town in 1998, on the 500th anniversary of da Gama's arrival in Malindi and which are still visible in some places.

Malindi also has a little zoo called the **Falconry** (daily 9am–5.30pm; Ksh300), with various birds, snakes, crocodiles and a giant tortoise. A nineteenth-century trader's shop on the waterfront has been made into a town **museum** (daily 9am–6pm; Ksh500), with a coelacanth fish downstairs, and some photographs of archeological sites on the coast upstairs, plus temporary exhibitions, but absolutely nothing to justify the rather steep entry fee.

Crafts and shopping

There are two main outdoor areas to head for when you're in the buying mood. Most obvious is the **crafts market** on the seashore below the old town. Naturally, if you stray down here you'll be pounced upon, and leaving without buying anything isn't easy. On the other hand, you can also leave with all sorts of little free gifts if you strike the right bargain. The other area is the **Malindi Handicraft Co-operative**, 2.5km west of the new market and matatu stage (daily 8am–6.30pm; ⓦwww.malindi-handicrafts.org), where you can see and freely photograph the woodcarvers at work. There's no bargaining at the shop, but you can discuss prices direct with the carvers and place specific orders.

Alternatively, for more expensive crafts and the possibility of browsing unhur-riedly, try one of the **upmarket shops** along Lamu Road, just to the north of Uhuru Gardens. Prices are naturally very high, but visits are useful for checking comparative values and gauging top prices. At Malindi Arcade, for example, they have lots of top-quality crafts and objets d'art, including old Lamu silver and jewellery as well as more familiar items available on the street. Our Shop nearby has pricier but finer pieces from all over Africa.

Snorkelling and watersports

Not unexpectedly, **snorkelling** ("goggling") and other **watersports** are Malindi's touristic *raison d'être*. Windsurfing, water-skiing, diving and deep-sea game fishing are all cheaper here than at the resorts around Mombasa. Malindi Bay is the main wave-surfing stretch and surfboards are available from all the tourist hotels in town. Unfortunately, all watery activities are marred somewhat by the Galana (Sabaki) River's annual outpouring of thousands of tons of prime red topsoil from the upcountry plateaus. The cloudy water prevents the growth of coral north of Vasco da Gama Point and, ironically, Malindi Bay and the tour-group hotels dotted along it face out across dun-coloured sands to a muddy-brown seascape from November to January when the upcountry short rains that carry the mud (exacerbated by deforestation along the riverbanks) coincide with the southerly currents of the *kaskazi* monsoon. Murky as it is, this water is not unpleasant to swim in. Note that the shore can get very windy around September, and in June–July and November the beach becomes covered in seaweed – many hotels clear their beachfronts daily, though the seaweed is clean and perfectly harmless, and in fact prevents erosion of the beach (clearing it is prohibited within the limits of the marine park).

Beach **access** is not a big problem, though the easiest place – and closest to the road – is on the south side of town at Silversands beach. The beach at the town centre and to the north is a good five to ten minutes' walk from the road. There are several public access points (see our map), and some hotels will allow use of their beach access for a small fee, which means you can use their pool and leave your towel and clothes on their guarded premises. *Driftwood*, for example, allows use of their pool and premises for Ksh200 per day (and it's also a good place to eat). The all-inclusive hotels charge much more (*African Dream* levies €30), but this does include lunch and free drinks.

Malindi Marine National Park

Trips out to the **marine park** (daily 6am–6pm; $5, children $2) can be arranged with the boat-trip salesmen who make their rounds of *the* beaches and hotels most mornings. Alternatively, make your own way down to the park office and very pretty beach at **Casuarina Point**, 5km from town, where you can choose your boat, captain and all. You should find a little room for discussion but won't be able to knock down prices much below the current going rate of Ksh3000 (excluding park fees) for two hours, especially at peak seasons. Note that your outing may be curtailed if you bargain too ruthlessly. Try to check out the condition of masks and snorkels, and insist on a set for each member of the party. Flippers aren't likely to be up to much (assuming they fit you). The six square kilometres of the national park take in the loveliest areas of coral garden, a couple of kilometres offshore, and the trip is worth every shilling you finally agree on. Unless you have a mortal fear of snorkelling or getting wet, don't bother with the **glass-bottomed boats** (about Ksh3000–5000 for two hours), which generally have saucepan-sized windows. The **snorkelling** itself is sublime and, especially if you've never done it before, an experience which will stay with you forever. It's possible to **camp** ($8 per person) at a site by the park office (PO Box 109; ☏042/20845), where there are also a couple of *bandas* (❷), which cost less to use than pitching a tent.

With your own or rented gear, of course, you could swim to the reef outside the boundaries of the marine park. All the beachfront hotels from Vasco da Gama Point south as far as *White Elephant Sea Lodge* (3.6km from the town centre) are to the north of the marine park, but the reef is anything from 300–800m offshore.

There are three **dive centres** with diving schools: Aqua Ventures, based at the *Driftwood* (☎042/20155, ⓦwww.diveinkenya.com), which is the cheapest of the three, and promises "special rates for backpackers"; Blue-Fin, based at *Tropical African Dream Village* (☎0722/261242, ⓦwww.bluefindiving.com), and Upinde, based at *Kilili Baharini* (☎0723/962123, ⓔupinde@katamail .com). All offer one-day introduction courses and five-day PADI Open Water qualification courses. Good diving zones to ask about include Shark Point, Tewa, Barracuda Point and Fargialla. The diving season in Malindi is from July to October only – diving isn't generally possible during the rains (April–May), as they roughen up the sea beyond the reefs, and at other times, silt makes the water too murky. Between October and April, you'll probably be taken down to Watamu to dive. For general advice and information about diving, see the Watamu account (p.509) and the boxes on p.482 and p.483.

The Marafa Depression: Hell's Kitchen

Northwest of Malindi, the **Marafa Depression** is the remains of a large sandstone ridge, now reduced by wind, rain and floodwater to a series of gorges, where steep gullies and narrow arêtes alternately eat into or jut from the main ridge wall. The colours of the exposed sandstone range from off-white through pale pinks and oranges to deep crimson, all capped by the rich tawny topsoil. It's particularly dramatic at sunset.

"Hell's Kitchen" is the common nickname for this pretty spectacle, though the locals call it *Nyari* – "the place broken by itself" – and tell numerous moralizing **stories** about its dark origins. The village that once stood here was favoured with the news of a forthcoming miracle, and the villagers were commanded to move on. All did so, except one old woman who refused to believe such nonsense. The village (and the old lady) disappeared soon after, leaving *Nyari*. Whether that was the miracle is not reported, but it's interesting to note how the story varies according to the teller – in Islamic circles "God talked through an angel" to deliver the message, while among traditionalists, "the gods informed a wise woman".

To get there, fork right at the end of Marafa village, and the canyon is about 500m along on the left, invisible until you're right at its edge. At the lip of the gorge, the first signs of commercialism – a small car park and a couple of seasonal souvenir stands – don't detract much from the site. It's easy to descend the steep path to the bottom and you can count on spending an hour or two exploring the natural architecture of what looks like an early *Star Trek* set. There's a scattering of *dukas* and *hotelis* among Marafa village's whitewashed, thatched houses, and one basic but very welcoming **hotel**, *Marafa Hell's Kitchen Guesthouse* (PO Box 6 Madina via Malindi; B&B ❷), at the end of the village, on the right facing the depression, with clean rooms, beds with mosquito nets, shared toilet and shower, and a pleasant garden. They can also arrange guided walks to Hell's Kitchen, and provide food given some notice. There is also a **campsite**.

With a vehicle, you might sensibly combine a visit to the Marafa Depression with the Arabuko-Sokoke Forest (see p.499) by crossing the Galana/Sabaki River – if the bridge across the river at Jilore (marked on some maps) actually existed. In its absence, take the road out of Malindi heading north (which involves a left turn on the other side of the Sabaki bridge) and from there go via **Marikebuni** and **Magarini**. You're looking at a round trip of about 80km, one which would be hard by **public transport** (buses run in both directions every hour or so from around 6am until around 3pm), but much easier if you have your own vehicle.

Eating, drinking and nightlife

You're presented with two basic options for **eating** in Malindi. The first is ordinary *hoteli* fare supplemented by a scattering of seriously cheap Indian-style juice and samosa bars in the ramshackle eateries dotted about the **market** by the Lamu and Garissa bus company offices. The second is a much higher-price bracket that includes the big hotels and a small number of more lavish restaurants catering mainly for tourists. It's worth remembering that the main package market here is Italian, and some of the Italian-run places do make very fine Italian food, which can be a nice change if you've been living on a diet of *nyama choma* and pilau for weeks.

If you're buying your own food, **Malindi Market** is celebrated for fruit and vegetables – second, on the coast, only to Mombasa's. In the way of **delicatessen**, Malindi's speciality is smoked sailfish, absolutely delicious and available as a starter at several restaurants, including the *Driftwood* and *The Old Man and the Sea*. It can also be bought in packets from Kingfisher, by the *Metro* hotel, but only frozen in packets of a half or quarter kilo. Kingfisher also sells honey from Arabuko-Sokoke Forest. Cheese is available from The Cheese Shop in Utali Parade on Lamu Road, and from the Italian supermarket at the Sabaki Centre.

Basic eateries and bar-restaurants

Bahari Fast Food Town centre near Juma Mosque. Good, tasty, cheap food, but despite the name, often rather slow in coming.

🏃 **Bawaly and Sons Halwa Shop** Town centre near Uhuru Gardens. Highly deserving of a mention, a long-established spot famous for its excellent fragrant version of the gooey jelly, sold as far afield as Australia and the UK. The minimum order is a quarter kilo, but you can eat a small amount on the spot and have the rest wrapped up to take away. Tiny cups of spiced *kahawa* come free. Daily 8.30am–12.15pm & 3–5.45pm.

Café Delicious Kenyatta Rd. A small diner serving breakfasts, snacks and basic cheap meals.

Oasis Gelateria South side of Malindi, on the beach 2km from the centre. This big snack bar is very good – as much for its delicious omelettes and espresso as for the forty flavours of ice cream. Sadly, it's part of a huge and hideous time-share complex which has occupied what remained of

Silversands public beach. Open daily 8am–midnight in high season, 3–11pm in low.

Open View By Total roundabout on the outskirts of town. Good Kikuyu food including meat stews and *githeri*, and plenty of cold beer.

Palantine Tea Room Mama Ngina St, next to *Kenya Mpya B&L*. Large and busy local eatery; *ugali* or chips with everything. Cheap, and open round the clock.

Stars and Garters Lamu Rd, next to Barclays Bank. Brash and busy *makuti*-roofed complex, especially popular for the English football screened on its satellite TVs in the bars. Good range of snacks, and fuller meals too, including pasta, seafood and grills, with a disco every evening.

🏃 **Taheri Cold House** Fakhri Complex, Tsavo Rd. A good spot for juices, snacks and cheap meals. The "Zanzibari mix" is worth a try – a mix of snacks in a sauce, served up like a breakfast cereal. Tues–Thurs 7.30am–8.30pm, Fri–Sun 7.30am–11pm, closed Mon.

Upmarket restaurants

🏃 **Baby Marrow**, Silversands Rd, near the Portuguese Chapel ☎0733/542584. Expensive but very good Mediterranean-style food, including grilled tuna steaks or snapper, lobster or prawns *à la Catalana*, or – in case you fancy a change from fish – pepper steak. Mains around Ksh500–900. Daily 11am–2pm & 6–11pm.

Baobab, next to the Portuguese Chapel on the seafront. Moderately priced curries, Italian and African dishes (Ksh250–500), and pricey seafood (Ksh500–1600). Worth patronizing for cheap, cold beer and its sweeping views over the beach and fishing boats. Open daily 8am–11pm.

Bar Bar Sabaki Centre, Lamu Rd. A little piece of Italy in Kenya, with authentic and wonderful pizzas and pasta (Ksh300–550), and excellent espresso coffee, as well as pricier meat and seafood dishes.

Driftwood Club South of Silversands beach ☏042/30569. Always a good place to eat, but the Ksh520 Sun curry buffet is worth planning your day around, and prices in general are far from unreasonable. Starters include smoked sailfish and oyster bisque, and the salads and chocolate cake are good, too.

I Love Pizza ☏042/20672. Upmarket, and the pizzas and pasta dishes (Ksh250–700) are really not bad. They push their seafood, though, which is also good. Recommended. Open daily noon–3pm & 7–10pm.

Karen Blixen MC Galana Shopping Centre, Lamu Rd. Italian-style tourist trap, with pleasant tables under shade outside. Attractions include American

breakfast (Ksh300), and some rather pricey pizzas, pasta and other light lunches (*prosciutto* with melon, even).

The Old Man & The Sea ☏042/31106. High-class, slightly quirky restaurant with an international menu (starters include smoked sailfish, sashimi and gazpacho), specializing in seafood and steaks, with some vegetarian dishes. Not outrageously expensive either, with main dishes mostly in the Ksh350–650 range. Daily noon–2.30pm & 7–11pm.

Surahi ☏042/30452. A good North Indian restaurant (rated one of Malindi's best) with a limited range of moderately priced dishes and an uncluttered, cool dining room. Mutton dishes include rogan josh and mutton chilli masala, and there are also fish dishes, and vegetarian dishes, mostly featuring paneer. Tues–Sun 11am–3pm & 6–10pm.

Drinking

After dark, especially in high season, Malindi throbs with action. For **live music**, international African music stars sometimes perform at *Market Village*, inside the Malindi Showground off the airport/Mombasa road. It's always more fun to go with someone from Malindi, but you should have no worries about taking a taxi and going on your own.

Beer Garden Lamu Rd, next to *Stars and Garters*. Quite German – come for a beer and bratwurst to start the evening. Burgers and steaks available too. Open daily from 9am till the last customer leaves.
Casino Ndogo Lamu Rd. A bar popular with both local residents and tourists, with *nyama choma* daily, and live music on Fri, Sat and Sun.
Chic's Restaurant Little food despite the name. A popular beer garden, at its liveliest on Sat nights

with local bands playing 7pm–midnight.
Urafiki Highway Bar Kenyatta Rd. Cheerful and unpretentious bar with tables inside and out.
Wananchi Night Club Cheap and friendly local hangout, actually a "day and night club" rather than a nightclub, open 24hr, with lots of blue fluorescent lights and slighly garish decor. It ought to be horribly sleazy, but it's actually quite laid-back.

Nightlife

Casino Malindi Lamu Rd. Free entry to anyone playing (daily 9am–5am). It's almost worth playing a few hands or spins just to watch the grim-looking Italian bosses tending their novice Kenyan croupiers.
Club 28 Lamu Rd, adjacent to *Eden Roc Hotel*. Originally exclusively for under-28s, this small nightclub has its ups and downs, but it's good when it hits the mood.
Fermenta Disco Bar Galana Shopping Centre from 8pm. Expensive Italian "piano bar" which plays Euro-trash when not inflicting karaoke.

Hotel discos A speciality of the south side of Malindi, usually in a different hotel each night through the week, but rather insipid affairs out of season, and the music's pure cheese.

Stardust Lamu Rd, opposite Galana Shopping Centre. The happening club, especially in season, when half the people in the resort – Italians and Kenyans alike – seem to be here waggling their bums to disco hits of the 1980s, and occasionally something more recent.

Listings

Airlines Kenya Airways (Utali Parade; PO Box 634 ☏042/20237) flies daily to Lamu and Nairobi's Kenyatta Airport. East African Safari Air (c/o Alamanda

Safaris, Stanchart Arcade ☏042/31193) also flies daily to Nairobi. Airkenya (c/o Eltome Travels, Galana Shopping Centre; PO Box 548 ☏042/20411) flies to

Nairobi's Wilson airport. You can book flights at the airlines' offices, or at any travel agency, though the less reputable of these will charge you more.

Banks Barclays, KCB and Standard Chartered (all Mon–Fri 9am–3pm, Sat 9–11am) have 24hr ATMs. Postbank is in the Malindi Complex on Lamu Rd. The casino changes money at any time, but at bad rates. Dollar forex bureau in the FN Center on Lamu Rd (Mon–Thurs 9am–5pm, Fri 9am–12.15pm & 2–5pm, Sat 9am–1pm) charges no commission and involves less messing about.

Books Sabaki Pharmacy on Kenyatta Rd sells or swaps used novels, mainly trashy pulps.

Car rental No car rental firms exist in Malindi, but Southern Sky Safaris in the Malindi Complex (☎042/20493, ⓦwww.southernskysafaris.com) should be able to organize something.

Golf Malindi Golf and Country Club; PO Box 320 Malindi ☎042/20404, an unusual eleven-hole (fifteen-tee) course.

Horse riding Try the Kibokoni Riding Centre, 4km north of town off the Lamu road. You'll pay around Ksh800 an hour, including a guide, for short bush rides in the vicinity. Beginners can go on a leading rein.

Hospitals The Galana Hospital on Lamu Rd (at the north end of town on the road to Lamu, just past *Sultan Villas*; ☎042/ 30575) is the best in an emergency. Alternatively, Malindi District Hospital in Hospital Rd (☎042/20490–1) is pretty decent.

Immigration On the second floor of a decrepit-looking building on the waterfront road by the Juma Mosque (☎042/20149).

Internet access Malindi Connections, Malindi Complex; Y Net, Stanchart Arcade; Bling Net, Lamu Rd, opposite *Stars and Garters*; Intercommunications, FN Centre.

Pharmacy Sabaki Pharmacy, Kenyatta Rd, at the corner of Tsavo Rd (daily 8am–9pm); Rafiki Chemist, Noorani Arcade, Lamu Rd.

Post and telephone office The main post office is just off Lamu Rd opposite the police station (Mon–Fri 8am–5pm, Sat 9am–noon), and has a good *poste-restante* service.

Supermarkets There are several small places in the shopping arcades up Lamu Rd in the town centre, the best – with the widest range – being Sona at Galana Shopping Centre. Try also the Indian Supermarket at the Sabaki Centre.

Taxis Baobab Taxis (☎042/30499) has fixed rates posted opposite the Portuguese Chapel on the baobab tree that serves as its HQ. *Tuk-tuks* are cheaper, *boda-bodas* cheaper still.

Travel agents A good scattering along Lamu Rd and the seafront all offer similar services, including train bookings. As well as the companies listed under "Airlines" opposite, try North Coast Travel on Lamu Rd near Barclays Bank (☎042/30312, ⓔncts@swiftmalindi.com).

Malindi to Lamu

Installed by a window on the bus, you can fully appreciate the flat, gentle, dull landscape, sometimes brown and arid, but more usually grey-green and swampy with plenty of large birdlife, which opens out as Malindi's low hills are left behind.

When the scenery palls, the bus trip is enlivened by the other passengers and by stops at the Tana River Delta area towns of **Witu** (see p.526), Mkunumbi and sometimes Mpeketoni for *chai* and a bite to eat. Occasional flashes of colour – the sky-blue cloaks of **Orma** herders or the red, black and white of shawled **Somali** women – break up the journey, along with wonderful **birdlife** and **wild animals** too: giraffe and antelope, notably waterbuck, even the odd elephant if you look hard enough. If you're driving yourself, you could also make a diversion to the **Tana River National Primate Reserve**.

The road is fast tarmac from Malindi to Garsen. Beyond Minjila – 7km south of Garsen at the junction for the Garissa and Lamu roads (the old road to Lamu from Garsen itself was washed away by floods in 1998) – the tarmac is rough and continues for only 20km, before trundling along the mud-and-*murram* New Garsen Causeway, hurriedly rebuilt in the aftermath of the 1997–99 El Niño floods. This was scheduled to be surfaced, too (which would vastly reduce the risk of hold-ups), but the Chinese pulled out, complaining of inadequate security provided for them after a spate of *shifta* attacks.

Garsen itself isn't anyone's favourite place, and something of a dead-end now that the Lamu road bypasses it. There's no electricity or bank, but there is petrol, a post office and police station. There are a couple of lodgings and no shortage of *hotelis*. In season, Garsen's mangoes are reckoned to be some of the best and cheapest in Kenya.

Tana River National Primate Reserve

Daily 6am–6pm; $15 per day/overnight, children $5; private vehicle Ksh200, camping $8 per person. Warden: PO Box 4 Hola; ☎046/2035.

Inland, north of Garsen, is the **Tana River National Primate Reserve** – main refuge of two of Kenya's rarest and most beautiful monkeys. It isn't easy to get to without your own vehicle, but buses heading for Garissa occasionally stop in Mnazini village; otherwise it's a six-kilometre walk from the main road (so long as the area isn't flooded). If the district is flooded, you'll almost certainly find yourself being taken by poled canoe from just down the Mnazini track all the way to the village itself; it takes about an hour. Regarding **security**, the reserve itself appears relatively secure, and is guarded by a special team of armed KWS rangers. However, the village of **Wenje**, just to the north, has acquired local notoriety as the base for a gang of bandits which operates in the area – take local advice if you're driving.

Mnazini is a fine, coastal-style village beneath mango trees. There are no lodgings but *hotelis* will take you in for the night once you've cleared it with the sub-chief and the headman. One of the village shops also has most of what you're likely to need for a few days' stay in the reserve. Beyond Mnazini, there's nothing in the way of food but occasional fruit and garden vegetables.

Nobody in the area knows the Tana River National Primate Reserve by that name. Locals all refer to **Mchelelo**, the site of the primate research headquarters. The twelve-kilometre walk to get there involves two river crossings over the Tana's meanders, and there's no way you'd find the route through the **bush** and **gallery forest** unguided. Pokomo **guides** are happy to help and not hustling.

Depending on water levels, you may find you can wade across. If you need a boat, it shouldn't normally cost anything. You enter the forest at Kitere and walking thereafter becomes much more pleasant in the cool shade.

Reserve practicalities

The easiest way to visit the reserve is on an organized tour from Malindi. These are run by the safari desk at *Mwembe Resort*, which is on the edge of town, about 1km west of *Eden Roc Hotel* (PO Box 1072; ☎042/45111, ✉mwembe lodge@mwemberesort.com). For €250, you can go on a two-day excursion, staying in bungalows at the upmarket *Tana River Lodge*. Even if you'd rather go to the reserve under your own steam, contact the safari desk if you want to stay at the lodge.

The only other accommodation in the reserve is **Mchelelo Campsite**, which is small, secluded, and ravishingly pretty, with a shower and long-drop. However, it's the site of a National Museums of Kenya research camp and the primatologists here are not used to visitors. If you don't have a letter from the NMK (and preferably an introduction and advance warning sent ahead) you may not be able to stay.

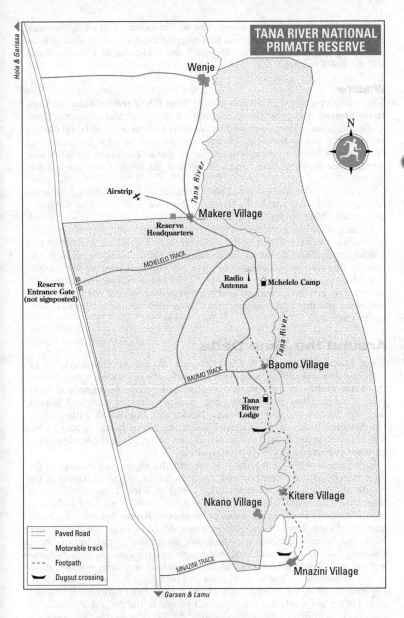

TANA RIVER NATIONAL PRIMATE RESERVE

Wenje

Tana River

Airstrip

Makere Village

Reserve
Headquarters

MCHELELO TRACK

Radio
Antenna

Mchelelo Camp

Reserve
Entrance Gate
(not signposted)

Tana River

BAOMO TRACK

Baomo Village

Tana
River
Lodge

Nkano Village

Kitere Village

Mnazini Village

MNAZINI TRACK

Garsen & Lamu

Paved Road
Motorable track
Footpath
Dugout crossing

If you're **driving**, the Baomo or Mchelelo tracks to the river are the ones to use, though the latter doesn't seem to be signposted from the road. The track to Baomo is indicated on the road.

If you're lucky, you'll be made reasonably welcome at Makere, or at least allowed to camp. It has to be reiterated, however, that they don't have organized facilities for visitors – and you may even be given a section of fully armed rangers on the anti-poaching force to accompany you, in military fashion, as you walk the paths looking for monkeys and watching the area's superb birdlife. One or two young guides from Makere village will also help to locate the primates, as will the KWS rangers.

Wildlife

The reserve's protected inhabitants include **Tana River red colobus** and **Tana River crested mangabey** monkeys, both extremely rare and vulnerable. These species occur more commonly in the rainforests of western Uganda and Congo, and are indicative of the time, centuries ago, when these great forests covered the whole of Africa – west to east. In the meantime, continued encroachment on the forest threatens both species of monkey; the colobus very rarely leaves the trees.

Your chances of seeing groups of both monkeys are good. The forest areas are fairly restricted, even within the reserve, and it's not difficult to find them in a day or two. Other wildlife in the area includes blue monkeys, baboons, Grevy's and Burchell's zebra, oryx, lesser kudu, various squirrels and even lions, giraffe and buffalo. On the east side of the park you can see elephants, and there's also a small seasonal population of the endangered Hunter's hartebeest, or hirola, here. At one time it was possible to make raft and boat trips on the sluggish river, dodging large numbers of hippos and crocodiles, but such adventures haven't operated as commercial safaris for years (see overleaf for details about something like this further downstream). You're likely to find local people willing to take you.

Around the Tana Delta

If you have a 4WD vehicle or a little patience, the trip north to Lamu can be stretched over several days, with time to explore the fascinating region around the **Tana Delta**: on the west side, the Pokomo village of **Ngao** and other villages on the river itself; on the east, a dune-shrouded coast and **Kipini**, with the Swahili ruins of **Ungwana**, **Shaka** and **Mwana** all within 12km. Do, however, make careful enquiries about any recent bandit attacks in the region before going. If you're genuinely interested, try to see the warden of the museum at Fort Jesus for further information.

As yet almost wholly untouched by tourism, the region to the north of the Tana River Delta – centred around the little fishing village of **Kipini** at the mouth of the Tana and the larger market centre of **Witu**, 21km inland – more than repays the slight hassle of finding a room. Though it's hard to believe, with its lack of electricity, tap water or telephones, **Kipini** was once the headquarters of Tana River District, before it was shifted to Hola at Independence. Nowadays, its erstwhile role is evident only in a mixed population of Orma, Pokomo, Bajuni, Somali and Swahili, who get by on fishing, small-scale farming and some herding. Unfortunately, things look set to change – somebody is selling off communal land to developers, and prime beach front is going cheap. Big-time investors are moving in, and have also tried vast agricultural schemes, most failing, but displacing many pastoral people in the process. The villagers have been examining proposals to protect the Tana's ecosystem by putting it under the Ramsar Treaty (which obliges governments and others to protect wetlands of ecological importance), as well as to combat illegal trawlers off the coast, which damage corals, kill turtles and have already caused the disappearance of swordfish. To get a closer look, you can organize local boat rides up the Tana from Kipini – passing crocodiles, and hundreds of birds, such as malachite and pied kingfishers, African fish eagles, and goliath herons. Further upstream is the Ozi Forest.

To get to Kipini, leave the Lamu bus at Witu, where there's a connecting matatu to the village. There are no formal **lodgings**, but you should be able to stay with a local family for the price of a B&L; plenty of cheap, wholesome Swahili *hotelis* serve delicious *dalasini* cinnamon tea. Alternatively, you could stay in **Witu** (again, no formal lodgings, though the German NGO, GASP, has an excellent guesthouse which it may let you use), and rent a **bicycle** locally for getting around. From Witu, most **buses** heading for Malindi pass through at around 10am, with Lamu-bound services arriving a little earlier. There are few if any vehicles along the road after 2pm.

You can **stay** near the delta mouth at the expensive *Tana River Delta Camp* in the dunes near the ocean (ⓦwww.tanadelta.org, ⓔtanadelta@africaonline. co.ke; ⑨), with six *bandas* made from driftwood, mangrove poles and *makuti*. The place comes highly recommended: there are boat trips and excellent guided walks available (including mud baths if you're in the mood), though at a steep $240–320 per person per night.

The Lamu Archipelago

A cluster of hot, low-lying desert islands tucked into the coast near the Somalian border, **Lamu** and its neighbours have a special appeal that many find irresistible. While each town or village has its own distinct character, together they epitomize a separate spectrum of Swahili culture. For although the whole coast is – broadly – "Swahili", there's a world of difference between these islands and the coconut beaches of Mombasa and Malindi.

To a great extent the islands are anachronisms. Electricity arrived here only a few decades ago, there are still almost no motor vehicles, and life moves at the pace of a donkey or a dhow. Yet there have been considerable internal changes over the centuries and Lamu itself is now changing faster than ever. Because of its special position in the Islamic world as a much-respected religious teaching centre, Saudi Arabian aid has poured into the island: the hospital, schools and religious centres are all supported by it. At the same time, there have been efforts to open up Lamu beyond its present tourist market, which so far has encompassed only budget travellers and short-stay air safaris. Foreign sponsors are eagerly sought and several lodging houses have been set up with what is bluntly called "white-girl money". Islanders are ambivalent about the future. A string of hotels along the beach, a bridge to the mainland – all seems possible, and all would contribute to the destruction of Lamu's timeless character. Some upcountry officials working here might not disapprove – with only a couple of bars, the town is not a popular posting.

But the damage that would be done goes further than spoiling the tranquillity. The Lamu archipelago is one of the most important sources for knowledge about pre-colonial Africa. **Archeological sites** indicate that towns have existed on these islands for at least 1200 years. The dunes behind Lamu beach, for example, are said to conceal the remains of long-deserted settlements.

And somewhere close by on the mainland, perhaps just over the border in Somalia, archeologists expect one day to uncover the ruins of Shungwaya, the town which the nine tribes that comprise the Mijikenda people claim as their ancestral home. The whole region is an academic's delight, a source of endless confusion and controversy, and a place where there is still real continuity between history and modern life.

Lamu island itself, most people's single destination, still has plenty to recommend it, despite a serious fire in 1993 and the inevitable sprouting of satellite dishes. **Manda**, directly opposite, is little visited except for the lifeline it provides with the outside world – the local airstrip. **Pate island**, accessible by dhow or motorboat, makes a fascinating excursion if you have a week or more in the area. **Kiwaiyu**, not quite within the archipelago, but exotic and alluring enough to be worth the effort, is a wisp of a beach island 9km long and less than 1km across, lying to the northeast of the other islands. Those who visit Kiwaiyu normally arrive by air, but you can also reach it by grouping together to charter a dhow in Lamu.

Lamu

Perhaps best left until the end of your stay in Kenya, **LAMU** may otherwise precipitate a change in your plans as you're gently lulled into a slow rhythm in which days and weeks can pass by unheeded and objectives easily forgotten. For many people, Lamu's deliciously lazy atmosphere is the best worst-kept secret on the coast. Eyes, ears, tongue and nose get a comprehensive work-out here, so that actually *doing* anything is sometimes a problem. Hours can be blissfully spent on a roof or a veranda just watching the town go by, its mood swinging effortlessly from one of the day's five prayer calls to the next, from tide to tide, and from dawn to dusk.

If this doesn't hit the right note for you, you may actually rather hate Lamu. Hot, dirty and boring are adjectives that have been applied by perfectly sane, pleasant people, and you can certainly improve your chances of liking the place by not coming here at the tail end of the dry season, when the town's gutters are blocked with dried refuse, the gardens in the houses wilt under the sun and the heat is sapping.

Lamu is something of a **myth** factory. Conventionally labelled "an old Arab trading town", it is actually one of the last viable remnants of the **Swahili civilization** that was the dominant cultural force all along the coast until the arrival of the British. In the late 1960s and early 1970s, Lamu's unique blend of beaches, gentle Islamic ambience, funky old town, and host population well used to strangers, was a recipe which took over where Marrakesh left off. It acquired a reputation as Kenya's Kathmandu: the end of the (African) hippie trail and a stopover on the way to India. Shaggy foreigners were only allowed to visit on condition they stayed in lodgings and didn't camp on the beach.

Not many people want to camp out these days. The proliferation of good, reasonably priced lodgings in the heart of **Lamu town** encourages an ethos more interactive than hippie-escapist. Every other traveller you've met along the way seems to end up here. Happily, travellers and locals cross paths enough to avoid any tedium – though for women travelling without men, this can itself become tedious (see p.545). Having said that, there can hardly be another town in the world as utterly unthreatening as Lamu. Leave your room at midnight for a breath of air and you can stroll up a hushed Harambee Avenue, or tread up the darkest of alleys, where you need fear absolutely nothing. This is an exhilarating experience.

If you seriously want to spend all your time on the **beach**, staying in **Shela** village seems the obvious solution, and there are several quite stylish possibilities here, though hardly anywhere really inexpensive.

Some history

The undeniably **Arab** flavour of Lamu is not nearly as old as the town itself. It derives from the later nineteenth century when the **Omanis**, and to some extent the **Hadhramis** from what is now Yemen, held political and cultural sway in the town. The first British representatives in Lamu found themselves among pale-skinned slave-owning Arab rulers. The cultural and racial stereotypes that were subsequently propagated have never completely disappeared.

Lamu was established on its present site by the fourteenth century, but there have been people living on the island for much longer than that. The freshwater supplies beneath Shela made the island very attractive to refugees from the mainland and people have been escaping here for two thousand years or more – most recently in the 1960s, when Somali secessionists and cattle-raiders caused havoc. It was also one of the earliest places on the coast to attract settlers from the Persian Gulf; there were probably people from Arabia and southwest Asia living and intermarrying here even before the foundation of Islam.

In 1505, Lamu was visited by a heavily armed **Portuguese** man-of-war and the king of the town quickly agreed to pay the first of many cash tributes as protection money. For the next 180 years Lamu was nominally under Portuguese rule, though the Portuguese favoured Pate as a place to live. In the 1580s, the **Turkish** fleet of Amir Ali Bey temporarily threatened Portuguese dominance, but superior firepower and relentless savagery kept them out, and Lamu, with little in the way of an arsenal, had no choice but to bend with the wind – losing a king now and then to the Portuguese executioners – until the Omanis arrived on the scene with fast ships and a serious bid for lasting control.

By the end of the seventeenth century, Lamu's Portuguese predators were vanquished and for nearly a century and a half it had a revitalizing breathing space. This was its **Golden Age**. Lamu became a republic ruled over by the *Yumbe*, a council of elders who deliberated in the palace (now a ruined plot in the centre of town), with only the loosest control imposed by their Omani overlords. This was the period when most of the big houses were built and when Lamu's classic architectural style found its greatest expression. Arts and crafts flourished and business along the waterfront made the town a magnet throughout the Indian Ocean. Huge ocean-going dhows rested half the year in the harbour, taking on ivory, rhino horn, mangrove poles and cereals. There was time to compose long poems and argue about language, the Koran and local politics. Lamu became the northern coast's **literary and scholastic focus**, a distinction inherited from Pate.

For a brief time, Lamu's star was in the ascendant in all fields. There was even a famous victory at the **Battle of Shela** in 1812. A combined Pate–Mazrui force landed at Shela with the simple plan of capturing Lamu – not known for its resolve in battle – and finishing the construction of the fort which the Nabahanis from Pate had begun a few years earlier. To everyone's surprise, particularly the Lamu defenders, the tide had gone out and the invaders were massacred as they tried to push their boats off the beach. Appalled at the overkill and expecting a swift response from the Mazruis in Mombasa, Lamu sent to Oman itself for Busaidi protection and threw away independence forever. Had the eventual outcome of this panicky request been foreseen, the Lamu Yumbe might have reconsidered. Seyyid Said, Sultan of Oman, was more than happy to send a garrison to complete and occupy Lamu's fort – and from this toehold in Africa, he went on to smash the Mazrui rebels in Mombasa (see p.429), taking the entire coast and moving his own sultanate to Zanzibar.

Lamu gradually sank into economic collapse towards the end of the nineteenth century as Zanzibar and Mombasa grew in importance. In a sense, it has been stagnating ever since. The building of the Uganda railway from Mombasa and the banning of slavery did nothing to improve matters for Lamu in economic terms, and it seems that decline has kept up with the shrinking population. However, the **resettlement programme** on the mainland at Lake Kenyatta (Mpeketoni) is already spinning off new faces to Lamu, and a revived commercialism from upcountry has taken root around the market square.

Lamu Town

Perhaps surprisingly for so laid-back a corner of Kenya, there's no shortage of things to do in **LAMU TOWN**. A UNESCO World Heritage site, it's unendingly fascinating to stroll through, with few monuments but hundreds of ancient houses, arresting street scenes and cool corners to sit and rest. And the **museum** outshines all others in Kenya bar the National Museum in Nairobi.

Maulidi, a week-long celebration of Muhammad's birth, sees the entire town involved in processions and dances, and draws in pilgrims from all over East Africa and the Indian Ocean. For faithful participants, the Lamu Maulidi is so laden with *baraka* (blessings) that some say two trips to Lamu are worth one to Mecca in the eyes of God. If you can possibly arrange it, this is the occasion to be in Lamu, but unless you make bookings, you'll need to arrive at least a week in advance to have any hope of getting a room. For the starting dates of Maulidi, see p.71. The other principal festival of the year is the recently established **Lamu Cultural Festival** held in November to promote Swahili culture and heritage. With donkey and dhow racing, swimming and dancing, traditional craft displays, including carving, dhow-building, embroidery and henna decoration – all of it fairly competitive – the festival engages the town for the best part of a week.

Arrival, orientation and information

The **bus trip** here ends at **Mokowe** on the mainland, where a chugging *mtaboti* (motorboat bus; Ksh50) takes you out around the creek for the thirty-minute ride to the town. The *mtabotis* are timed to coincide with the buses, though there are other less frequent services throughout the day. Grab your luggage, ignore the touts pulling you every which way, and jump on the boat which seems fullest – all the boats go to Lamu. If you're **driving**, leave your vehicle in the car park where it will, by all accounts, be safe; tipping the *askari* beforehand may improve security further. Don't be misled by boys who try to sell you a *mtaboti* charter; just wait for the next public *mtaboti* with everyone else.

Planes land on Manda island, across the harbour directly opposite the town. If you're staying a few days only and then flying out, it's a very good idea to go straight to the appropriate airline office on arrival to **reconfirm** your return seat. The short boat trip from the airstrip (Ksh100 to Lamu Town on boats run by the airlines, or to Shela on boats run by *Peponi Hotel*, in principle for customers only) gives a wonderful panorama of Lamu's nineteenth-century waterfront.

Once at the harbour, you'll inevitably be met by a bevy of **beach boy hustlers** offering to take your baggage and guide you to a hotel. If you go with them, they'll claim at least a third of your room rent from the hotelier, which will mean a fifty percent mark-up on your bill. Unfortunately, it's very difficult to avoid the "services" of these characters; they'll certainly not allow you to stand around on the quayside looking at your map, so it's best to know in advance how to get to your preferred hotel from the jetty. You can also tell them firmly but politely that you do not want their help; if they follow you anyway, tell the receptionist on arrival that they have followed you against your wishes and that you will not stay if the hotel intends to add their commission to your bill. The beach boys also sell *bangi* (marijuana) – though you'd be very ill-advised to buy it from them (setups are common) – and will be keen to offer their services as **guides**. If you need a guide in Lamu, your best bet is to ask

Moving on from Lamu

Bus companies running daily to Mombasa via Malindi and Kilifi are TSS, Falcon Coach, Tawakal Minibuses, and Zam Zam Coach. All leave Mokowe jetty on the mainland between 7am and 7.30am; the ferries leave Lamu Town at 6–6.30am to connect. The buses are supposed to travel in convoy but rarely do unless there's been a recent incident. Buy tickets (about Ksh600 to Mombasa) the day before or earlier to be sure of a seat (booking offices hours generally daily 8.30am–12.30pm, 2.30–4.30pm & 7–8.30pm). Tawakal is the fastest, and costs Ksh50 more then the others; it also fills up quickly so should be booked as far in advance as possible.

Kenya Airways, under *Casuarina Guesthouse* (☎042/632040–1); SafariLink, next to the *Sunsail Hotel*; and AirKenya on Harambee Avenue in Langoni (☎042/633445), have daily **flights** to Nairobi. Tickets should be booked or reconfirmed as early as possible. Cancelling tickets you've already got from Mombasa, Malindi or Nairobi is a pain, as refunds are usually only available from the issuing agent.

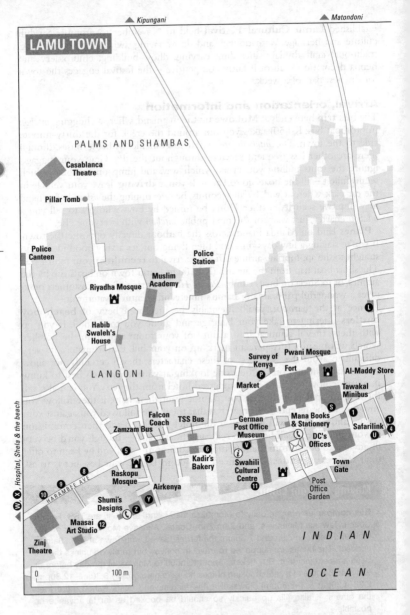

LAMU TOWN

▲ Kipungani   ▲ Matondoni

PALMS AND SHAMBAS

Casablanca
Theatre

● Pillar Tomb

Police
Canteen

Riyadha Mosque

Muslim
Academy

Police
Station

Habib
Swaleh's
House

LANGONI

Survey of
Kenya

Pwani Mosque

Fort

Al-Maddy Store

Market

Tawakal
Minibus

Falcon
Coach

TSS Bus

Zamzam Bus

German
Post Office
Museum

Mana Books
& Stationery

DC's
Offices

Safarilink

Kadir's
Bakery

Town
Gate

Raskopu
Mosque

Airkenya

Swahili
Cultural
Centre

Post
Office
Garden

Shumi's
Designs

Maasai
Art Studio

Zinj
Theatre

HARAMBEE AVE

▶ W, X, Hospital, Shela & the beach

INDIAN

OCEAN

0   100 m

other travellers to recommend one, or visit the **Lamu Tour Guides Association**, whose members carry small white laminated ID cards. You'll need to tell
any guide you engage which places you would like to visit and agree a fee:
Ksh300–400 per day would be an acceptable wage.

Initially confusing, Lamu town is not the random clutter of houses and alleys it
appears. The town is divided into two main parts – **Mkomani** is the northern end

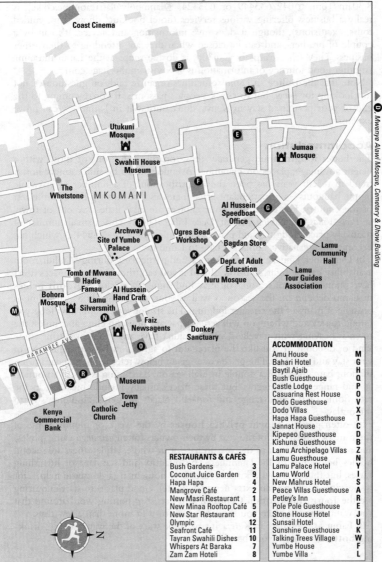

Coast Cinema

Ⓑ

Ⓒ

Ⓔ

Utukuni Mosque

Jumaa Mosque

Swahili House Museum

Ⓕ

The Whetstone MKOMANI

Al Hussein Speedboat Office

Ⓖ

Ⓗ

Ⓘ

Archway Site of Yumbe Palace

Ⓙ

Ogres Bead Workshop

Bagdan Store

Lamu Community Hall

Ⓚ

Dept. of Adult Education

Tomb of Mwana Hadie Famau

Nuru Mosque

Lamu Tour Guides Association

Bohora Mosque

Al Hussein Hand Craft

Lamu Silversmith

Ⓜ

Ⓝ

Faiz Newsagents

Ⓞ

Donkey Sanctuary

HARAMBEE AVE.

Ⓠ

Museum

Ⓡ

❷

Town Jetty

❸

Catholic Church

Kenya Commercial Bank

RESTAURANTS & CAFÉS	
Bush Gardens	3
Coconut Juice Garden	9
Hapa Hapa	4
Mangrove Café	2
New Masri Restaurant	1
New Minaa Rooftop Café	5
New Star Restaurant	6
Olympic	12
Seafront Café	11
Tayran Swahili Dishes	10
Whispers At Baraka	7
Zam Zam Hoteli	8

ACCOMMODATION	
Amu House	M
Bahari Hotel	G
Baytil Ajaib	H
Bush Guesthouse	Q
Castle Lodge	P
Casuarina Rest House	O
Dodo Guesthouse	V
Dodo Villas	X
Hapa Hapa Guesthouse	T
Jannat House	C
Kipepeo Guesthouse	D
Kishuna Guesthouse	B
Lamu Archipelago Villas	Z
Lamu Guesthouse	N
Lamu Palace Hotel	Y
Lamu World	I
New Mahrus Hotel	S
Peace Villas Guesthouse	A
Petley's Inn	R
Pole Pole Guesthouse	E
Stone House Hotel	J
Sunsail Hotel	U
Sunshine Guesthouse	K
Talking Trees Village	W
Yumbe House	F
Yumbe Villa	L

N

and **Langoni** the southern. When discovering Lamu for yourself, you shouldn't get lost too easily if you remember that **Harambee Avenue** – the Usita wa Mui or Njia Kuu – runs parallel to and 50m behind the waterfront, and that streets leading into town all run slightly uphill.

Lamu's **Tourist Information Centre**, at the southern end of town and just off Harambee Avenue (officially Mon–Fri 8.30am–noon & 2–4.30pm, Sat

8.30am–1pm; ☏042/633449 or 633324, ✉lamupoly@africaonline.co.ke), is really a business offering various services (hotel booking, dhow trips, guided tours, excursions), though it does give information and advice. It's run by a couple of brothers, and can be closed when they are attending to their other business. They sell a **map** for Ksh300, as do the shops at the Lamu museum. Another good journey of information is ⓦwww.lamuheritage.com.

Note that the **police** in Lamu sometimes organize raids on guesthouses, not just looking for *bangi*, but to check people's passports. If you're coming to the end of your permitted stay in Kenya, don't outstay it in Lamu – it can prove expensive.

Accommodation

The better **lodgings** are generally those on the waterfront or those with a height advantage; places on Harambee Avenue tend to be suffocatingly hot. A trend in recent years has been the "gentrification" of a number of erstwhile hippie hangouts – with attendant price increases that outstrip those in the rest of the country. For **camping**, your choices are all a little way out of town, at *Peace Villas*, or *Talking Trees* at *Dodo Villas*. There's also a small number of relatively pricey lodgings and private houses in **Shela** (see p.544) – which has become an alternative, upmarket base to Lamu town.

In December, January, July and August, and particularly during Maulidi, room availability can be tight, so **book ahead** if you can (though several places don't have phones). Out of season, you may find some places closed. **Room prices** in Lamu depend on the season as well as your bargaining skills – haggling is possible at many of the cheaper lodgings. The size of your group, how long you intend to stay and when you will actually pay are all useful chips and, unless the town is heaving with travellers, you shouldn't have any problem getting some kind of discount. If you like the place, aim to agree a rate for the duration of your stay and pay daily. The price codes given below refer to the standard price, without bargaining, for a double in high season. Bargaining is less of an option at mid-range establishments, but these places usually include breakfast in the rate. Some of the mid-range and top-end places are gems, absolutely worth the outlay.

It's often possible to rent **private houses** by the week or month. Some of these are occupied part of the year by their owners (often *wazungu* Lamu-philes) and rented out the rest of the year in part or in whole, while others are second homes belonging to local families. The quantity and standard of furnishing varies, but there's always a kitchen, usually a houseman (a domestic help – for his services you'll pay an extra negotiated rate). Good places to start enquiring are the Tourist Information Centre; if you persist in putting word around that you want to rent a place you shouldn't have to wait more than a few days.

In Lamu, as elsewhere in Kenya, it pays to be wary of the water supply; drinking **bottled water** is your best bet.

Budget and mid-range

Amu House PO Box 230 ☏ & ℗042/633420. Extremely attractive and welcoming, this is a restored, American-owned stone house with additional rooms on top, built in the same style. The doubles and triples are airy, with large bathrooms. Dinner available upon request. Good value. B&B ⑤

Bahari Hotel Harambee Ave near the Lamu Community Hall; PO Box 298 ☏042/633172,

℗633231. Twenty basic but spacious s/c rooms on several floors, around a cool, plant-filled court-yard. Features include amusing four-poster beds, nets and fans, and most rooms have a fridge. The rooftop terrace is excellent, and a good place to meet other travellers. Haggle hard for a good deal. B&B ❸

Bush Guesthouse PO Box 22; no phone. Rooms in a tall building accessed from an alley between

Harambee Ave and the sea. Only two rooms are s/c, but they're all secure and have mosquito nets and fans. There's also a small kitchen and communal lounge overlooking the sea, and a roof where you can sunbathe. The starting price is over the odds but can be bargained down in low season. B&B ❸

Castle Lodge Beside the fort; PO Box 10; no phone. Eight simple rooms, some with fans, all with nets, none s/c. Rooms 1 and 2 are the best, overlooking the market; 8 and 9 on the roof have good views. ❸

Casuarina Rest House PO Box 10 ☎ & ℱ 042/633123; no touts. Over the old police station (now Kenya Airways), with a whole variety of rooms from very basic to quite comfortable (the best are the two at the front and the two on top). It's a bit rundown these days, however. Only two rooms are s/c; most have fans. There's a kitchen and an excellent waterfront roof terrace. Rate is room-only. ❸

Dodo Guesthouse Harambee Ave; PO Box 210 ☎ 042/633408. Three rooms, one s/c, in a small unsigned house just round the corner from the Tourist Information Centre, which runs it, and where enquiries can be made. Another *Dodo* house, near the Swahili House Museum, has more rooms, the best of which is the one on the roof. ❸

Dodo Villas Halfway between Lamu and Shela along the main footpath, 100m from the beach; PO Box 260 ☎ 042/632257. A large house with airy guest rooms and several small cottages. There's a good restaurant too, and the friendly owner is a mine of information. ❹

Hapa Hapa Guesthouse PO Box 213 ☎ 042/633145. Behind the popular eating place of the same name, with two big double rooms at the front. Only one room has a fan — top-floor rooms are open to the *makuti* roof, which keeps a breeze blowing. ❷

Jannat House PO Box 195 ☎ 042/633414, ⓦ www.jannathouse.com. Hugely atmospheric place, owned by a Swedish family and arranged around a jungly courtyard with much of its original decoration (stuccowork niches and furniture) still intact. There's a wide array of terraces with comfy chairs and lovely views over the town. The rooms are s/c with nets and fans, but are nothing special. There is an excellent swimming pool, and a restaurant/bar serving excellent seafood. They also offer a range of courses, such as in Swahili and Kenyan drumming, to name two. B&B ❺

🏃 **Kipepeo Guesthouse** PO Box 14 ☎ 042/633569 or 0722/559436, ⓔ aarumii@yahoo.com or dagmar-obo@web.de. Run by a charming German woman and her Kenyan husband, this small new guesthouse has airy, comfortable double rooms opening onto a huge balcony, and some of the best seafront views in town. ❹

Lamu Archipelago Villas Langoni waterfront; PO Box 339 ☎ 042/633247, ℱ 633111. The s/c rooms here aren't that great but the position, right on the waterfront, is a plus. Avoid the back rooms, which could bring on claustrophobia. B&B ❹

Lamu Guesthouse Next to the Lamu silversmith on Harambee Ave; PO Box 240 ☎ 042/633338. A well-maintained old house right in the heart of things, which has been owned by the same Indian family for seven generations. It's inevitably somewhat hot and stuffy given its location, but the ceilings are high and there are nets and fans; a few of the rooms are s/c. Good value. ❸

New Mahrus Hotel Harambee Ave, opposite the Tawakal Minibus office; PO Box 25 ☎ & ℱ 042/633001. Rambling old place in a good location, though not on the waterfront. It has its own creaking if rundown charm. Rooms and rates vary widely. The top floor is "first-class" and nothing special (rooms 1 and 2, overlooking the fort, are the best), the second floor is "second-class" and just ordinary B&L standard. ❹

Peace Villas Guesthouse PO Box 160 ☎ 042/633020. This is the one of two places to camp in Lamu town — if you really want to. Most people use the dorms or double rooms (s/c, with fans), but management is slack. It's a good 10min walk from the town centre, out in the sand and palm trees; follow the phone lines out of town until you reach a clearing and it's over to your right, painted white, red and black. ❷

Pole Pole Guesthouse PO Box 195 ☎ 042/633344. Getting a bit rundown, but still pleasant, and very good value, especially if you're used to B&Ls. It has a fantastic roof terrace with a bird's-eye view from the roof, one of the highest up in town. Nets and fans in most rooms. ❸

Stone House Hotel PO Box 193 ☎ 042/633544, ℱ 633149. An overly modified eighteenth-century house with orange coral ragrock stuck on most walls, the rooms furnished in a mixture of Swahili and upcountry styles. The thirteen rooms (three not s/c) have phones, but none are as classy as the brochures suggest. Rooftop restaurant. B&B ❻

Sunsail Hotel In the old stone "Mackenzie" trader's house on the waterfront; PO Box 400 ☎ 042/632065–6, ℱ 632666. Rooms have high ceilings and smart tiled bathrooms, but this doesn't compensate for the fact that they're a bit on the small side, and only the two at the front have sea views. It does have a nice waterfront terrace, but you can do better elsewhere. B&B ❺

Sunshine Guesthouse PO Box 224 ☎042/633087. A pleasant, slightly mouldering place with a good terrace. Use of kitchen (with cooker and fridge) is a bonus. Five of the ten rooms are s/c, and all rooms have fans and nets over the beds. Bathrooms are a bit grubby, but it remains good value, especially if you haggle. ❸

Talking Trees Village Sharing a location with *Dodo Villas* (see p.535), through whom bookings should be made. A peaceful and beautiful campsite (putting aside the barbed-wire fence), but a 20min trudge from either Lamu or Shela. Ksh300 per tent.

Yumbe House PO Box 81 ☎ & ⓕ042/633101. A lovely conversion, professionally managed, and a positive alternative to *Petley's* if you want some real comfort and style. The top room is definitely the best. Singles are good value. You may be put up at *Yumbe Villa*, their annexe, a few minutes' walk away. B&B ❺

Expensive

Baytil Ajaib PO Box 328 ☎042/632033, ⓦwww .baytilajaib.com. A recently restored Lamu town house with two impeccably decorated apartments and two suites centred around a large courtyard. The house can also be rented in its entirety. HB: apartments from $255 a night; suites $305 a night; ❾

Lamu Palace Hotel Langoni waterfront, PO Box 421 ☎042/633272, ⓕ633104. The biggest thing to hit Lamu's waterfront; in years, a three-storey construction incorporating a restaurant terrace and bar. Only four of the two dozen or so s/c, a/c rooms face the sea. The seamless tourist-class style appeals to many, but puts off those looking for something more real; look elsewhere and you'll get a better deal for half the price. ❼

Lamu World On the seafront by the Lamu Community Hall; PO Box 471 ☎042/633491, ⓕ633492, ⓦwww.lamuworld .com. A stunning new place consisting of two traditional houses, Salama and Azania, each with five s/c bedrooms with a dressing area, private terrace and fantastic deep stone bath. There's also a wonderfully cool, white courtyard complete with plunge pool. The houses can be rented in their entirety, including use of dhow and the services of a cook and house stewards, for $1350 a night; otherwise doubles cost $270. ❾

Petley's Inn Close to the town jetty; PO Box 4 ☎ & ⓕ042/633107. Under the same ownership as *Lamu Palace Hotel*, for which it seems to function as a kind of annexe, periodically closed depending on business. Rooms have fans and nets (the best two face the sea); some have a/c and have been done up in "upmarket-rustic" style. There's a small roof-level swimming pool, a great courtyard, and a rooftop bar that's a lively evening hangout. Overpriced, but they take credit cards. B&B ❼

The Town

Very few towns in sub-Saharan Africa have kept their original **town plan** so intact (Timbuktu in West Africa is another), and Lamu's history is sufficiently documented, and its architecture well enough preserved, to give you a good idea of how the town developed. The main division is between the **waterfront** buildings and the town behind, separated by **Usita wa Mui**, now Harambee Avenue (actually a narrow alley for the most part). Until around 1830, this was the waterfront, but the pile of accumulated rubbish in the harbour had become large enough by the time the fort was finished to consider reclaiming it; gradually, those who could afford to, built on it. The **fort** lost its pre-eminent position and Lamu, from the sea, took on a different aspect, which included Indian styles such as arches, verandas and shuttered windows.

Behind the waterfront, the **old town** retained a second division between **Mkomani** district, to the north of the fort, and **Langoni** to the south. These locations are important as they distinguish long-established (Mkomani) from the still-expanding (Langoni). This north–south division is found in most Swahili towns and reflects the importance of Mecca, which is due north.

Lamu is divided further into over forty *mitaa* or "**wards**", corresponding to blocks. The names of these suggest a great deal about how the town once looked and they're all listed in *Lamu Town: A Guide* by James Allen (out of print; copies in Lamu Fort Library). Kinooni ("whetstone corner") ward boasts to this day a heavy block of stone on the corner for sharpening swords, reputedly imported from Oman. And Utakuni ("main market") ward still has a row of shops, even though most of this north side of town is now purely residential.

It is difficult to construct a guided tour of Lamu – serendipity comes to everyone here, and in any event, you're better off exploring whenever you have a spare hour or two – but the following are worth pursuing whenever you lack the energy for the beach.

Stone architecture

Lamu's **stone houses** are unique, perfect examples of architecture appropriate to its setting. The basic design is a topless box enclosing a large courtyard, around which are set inward-facing rooms on two or three floors. These rooms are thus long and narrow, their ceilings supported by close-set timbers or mangrove poles (*boriti*). Most had exquisite carved doors at one time, though in all but a few dozen homes these have been sold off to pay for upkeep. Many also had *zidaka*, plasterwork niches in the walls to give an illusion of extended space, which are now just as rare. Bathroom arrangements are ingenious, with fish kept in the large water storage cisterns to eat mosquito larvae. On the top floor, a *makuti* roof shades one side. In parts of Lamu these old houses are built so close together you could step across the street from one roof to another.

The private space inside Lamu's houses is barely distinguishable from the public space outside. The noises of the town percolate into the interiors, encouraged by the constant flow of air created by the narrow coolness of the dark streets and the heat which accumulates on upper surfaces exposed to the sun. You can find out more in Usam Ghaidan's book *Lamu: A Study in Conservation*, which has reams of architectural and technical information; unfortunately, it is out of print, but can be consulted in the town library.

Lamu Museum

The one place you should definitely count on devoting an hour or so to is **Lamu Museum** (daily 8am–6pm; Ksh200, children Ksh100; Ⓦ www.museums .or.ke/reglm.html), built in 1891 on the ocean front, and serving as the

Tradition and morality in Lamu

A number of **old photographs** on display in the museum belie pronouncements about "unchanging Lamu". The women's cover-all black **buibui**, for example, turns out to be a fashion innovation introduced comparatively recently from southern Arabia. It wasn't worn in Lamu much before the 1930s when, ironically, a degree of emancipation encouraged women of all classes to adopt the high-status styles of purdah. In earlier times, high-born women would appear in public entirely hidden inside a tent-like canopy called a **shiraa**, which had to be supported by slaves; the abolition of slavery at the beginning of the twentieth century marked the demise of this odd fashion.

Outsiders have tended to get the wrong end of the stick about Swahili seclusion. While women are undoubtedly heavily restricted in their public lives, in private they have considerable freedom. The notion of **romantic love** runs deep in Swahili culture. Love affairs, divorces and remarriage are the norm, and the *buibui* is perhaps as useful to women in disguising their liaisons as it is to their husbands in preventing them. This gives a slightly different timbre to the attentions shown by Lamu men to unattached *wazungu* women – frustration isn't always the reason, money usually is.

All this comes into focus a little when walking the backstreets. You may even bump into some of Lamu's **transvestite** community – cross-dressing men whose community is accepted and long established and derives from Oman. In fact, the more you explore, the more you realize that the town's conventional image is like the walls of its houses – a severe facade concealing an unrestrained interior.

residence of the British colonial governors before independence. Of Kenya's regional museums, this is the one that best lives up to its name. There's no need to fill spare rooms here with game trophies and trivia; the region's history provides more than enough material.

As you enter, there's a large aerial photo of the town for a fascinating bird's-eye insight. Elsewhere, exhibitions of **Swahili culture** – architecture, boats and boat-building, domestic life – are displayed. There are also rooms devoted to the non-Swahili peoples of the mainland: farmers like the **Pokomo**, **Orma** cattle herdsmen and **Boni** hunters. Two magnificent ceremonial **siwa horns**, one in ivory from Pate, the other from Lamu itself in brass, are the prize exhibits – probably the oldest surviving musical instruments in black Africa. The Pate *siwa*, slightly more ancient, dates from between 1690 and 1700. Wooden imitations are on sale all around town.

The museum can arrange guided tours to archeological and historical sites on Manda and Pate islands; contact the senior curator at ©lamuse@hotmail.com.

Lamu Fort Environment Museum

The **fort**, which was begun in 1809 and completed in 1821, seems oddly stranded in its modern-day position, deprived of its role as defender of the waterfront. It served as a prison until 1984, but it's now a national monument and open as the **Lamu Fort Environment Museum** (same times and prices as Lamu Museum), as well as housing the town's **library**. The "temporary exhibition" first installed in 1993 is still there, unrefreshed. It's an enthusiastic display of information about the environment and evolution, incorporating local sea-life in tanks, but it looks more like an elaborate school project than anything you'd expect to find in a public building. Look out for the very interesting set of colour photos of archeological sites in the Lamu Archipelago. It's fun to walk round the ramparts, getting bird's-eye views of the town.

Mosques

When you start checking out some of Lamu's 23 **mosques**, you'll find that any tone of rigid conformity you might expect is lacking. Most are simple,

△ Minaret of the Jumaa Mosque, Lamu Town

spacious buildings, as much refuge/men's clubs as places of prayer. There's no special reason to enter them; their doors are always open and there's little to see. Male visitors, suitably dressed, are normally allowed inside, women generally excluded. Unfortunately, the **Mwenye Alawi Mosque** at the north end of town, once Lamu's only exclusively female mosque, has been taken over by the men, leaving the women to pray at home.

The oldest-known mosque is the **Pwani Mosque**, by the fort, parts of which date back to the fourteenth century. Lamu's present Friday mosque is the **Jumaa**, the big one in Pangahari ("sword-sharpening place") ward.

The star of Lamu's mosques, as well as being one of the youngest, is the sumptuous **Riyadha Mosque** well to the back of town in Langoni. It was built at the beginning of the twentieth century and has brought about a radical shift in Lamu's style of Islam, and indeed in the status of Lamu in the Islamic world. It was founded by a descendant of the prophet, or sharif, called **Habib Swaleh**, who came from the Hadramaut (Yemen) to settle in Lamu in the mid-nineteenth century (his house, close by the mosque, is acknowledged with a plaque but is a more or less empty wattle-and-daub structure, containing a caretaker's bed and a few old papers). Habib Swaleh and his group introduced a new freedom to the five-times-daily prayers with singing, tambourines and spontaneous readings from the Koran. They attracted a large following, particularly from the slave and ex-slave community, but gradually from all social spheres, even the aristocratic families with long Lamu pedigrees. Some of the other mosques adopted the style but the Riyadha, apart from being Lamu's largest, is still the one most closely associated with this kind of inspirational worship. Non-Muslim men who visit while worship is in session are likely to be invited in and encouraged to sit cross-legged with the rest of the assembly. Any sense of stale ritual is far removed: the atmosphere is light, the music infectious. The Riyadha is also famous as the spiritual home of Lamu's annual **Maulidi** celebration

Next to the Riyadha is the big, square **Muslim Academy** – like the Riyadha itself, and so much else in Lamu, heavily under Saudi patronage. Both men and women are allowed to have a look around, but there's very little to see.

Other sights

After the fort, the only other national monument in Lamu (though you may not believe it when you see it) is the fluted **pillar tomb** behind Riyadha Mosque. This may date from as far back as the fourteenth century, and the occasional visit by a tourist might persuade the families in the neighbourhood that it's worth preserving; it can only be a matter of time before it leans too far and collapses on a passing child. In the middle of town, by a betel plot, is another tomb, that of **Mwana Hadie Famau**, a local woman of the fifteenth or sixteenth century. This has been walled up and lost the porcelain-embedded pillars which would have stood at each corner.

The **Swahili House Museum** in Mkomani (daily 8am–6pm; Ksh200, children Ksh100) is an eighteenth-century house that's been restored to an approximation of its original appearance. Unfortunately, the house is very small, consisting only of a small courtyard, two sleeping galleries, two toilets and an upstairs kitchen and roof, and the guided tour (included in the entrance fee) is extremely brief and poor value. Indeed, there are plenty of private houses, and even a number of guesthouses, with superior architectural interest.

Heading north out of town, through Tundani ("fruit-picking place") and Weyoni ("donkey racetrack") wards, you reach the **cemetery**, goal of many religious processions and an interesting short walk. Past suburbs, you come out by the slaughterhouse and rubbish dumps, populated by marabou storks. In the inlet behind them, several large **dhows** and smaller boats are moored. Many are rotting, but one or two are quite new, even unfitted. Tradition notwithstanding, Lamu, rather than Matondoni (see p.546), seems to be the island's main boat-building centre. If you have dreams of owning a dhow (they make great houseboats), you'll need several thousand dollars handy, $6500 for a forty-foot hull, say. The price depends largely on the time required to build it – two years isn't unusual.

Eating and drinking

There are enough **restaurants** and passable *hotelis* in Lamu to enable you to eat out twice a day for a week without going back to your first port of call. And nowhere else in Kenya is there such a concentration of eating places with an overwhelmingly budget-traveller clientele, though at the same time there are waterfront eating houses charging ten times as much, with prices really rocketing in the peak seasons.

A fine balance has been achieved between what is demanded and what can be supplied: yoghurt, fruit salad, pancakes, muesli, milkshakes and puréed fruit juices have become Lamu specialities. Superb lobster (actually crawfish, so no claws) and crab dishes, oysters, snapper and delicious steaks of swordfish, barracuda and shark are also on many menus – it's a nice change to find a fishing town where you can actually eat seafood relatively cheaply. Upcountry staples – beans, curries, pilau, steak, chicken, chips, eggs, even *ugali* – are available from a number of ordinary **hotelis** crowded along Harambee Avenue, particularly in Langoni. Also along Harambee Avenue, around the corner from the *Casuarina*, you'll find tiny mutton kebabs (wrapped in a chapatti) and cakes on sale at night; they cost next to nothing and are usually delicious. Local meat is notoriously stringy; several of the tourist-oriented places thus order regular supplies from Malindi by plane.

If you spend any time in Lamu, you'll probably run into someone offering you a "genuine" Swahili **dinner at home**. At its best, this is a great way of seeing how the majority of Lamu's inhabitants live, and the food can be delicious. On the other hand, the price demanded at the end (which, like everything in Lamu, depends mainly on your perceived ability to pay) might not necessarily be any cheaper than having eaten in a decent restaurant. As in a restaurant, pay after your meal, not before.

If you enjoy doing your own **cooking** (several lodgings have kitchens you can use), a whole new world starts to open up. The **produce market** in front of the fort – run for the most part by upcountry women – has everything you'll need, with separate sections for meat, fish, and fruit and veg; for fresh fish or shellfish, get there very early. By 9am all the interesting ones have been sold. Check out also the "**crab and lobster market**", little more than a pair of weighing scales over a ditch in an alley, south along the shore just in from the last building. Lamu has wonderful **fruit** and is famous for its enormous, aromatic mangoes, but you should also try the unusually sweet and juicy grapefruit. While you're here, you might also find one of Lamu's traditional exports, **betel**, the green vine you see trailing out of all the empty plots in town. The sweet hot-tasting leaves are wrapped around other ingredients, including white lime and betel nut, which stains the teeth red, to make *pan* for chewing. Rather sweeter, the *halwa* shop is on Harambee Avenue in Langoni, and there's a good bakery facing the right side of the fort. **Supermarkets** are listed on p.542.

Although you can always get a **drink** (bottles of rot-gut Safari "whisky", totally colourless, as well as expensive bottles of wine, appear out of nowhere if you spread the word), only *Petley's* (daily 5pm–midnight) or the *Lamu Palace* (all day) have alcohol licences. At other places, you can sometimes order "ice-cold tea". It's also worth trying the police canteen in Langoni, which offers the cheapest beer in town.

Hotelis and snack bars

Mangrove Café Next to *Petley's Inn*. Popular traveller's café serving up freshly squeezed juices and snacks.

New Masri Restaurant Harambee Ave, across from the *New Mahrus Hotel*. Serves Swahili curries and fish dishes to an assortment of locals and tourists.

New Minaa Rooftop Café Just off Harambee Ave, Langoni. A pleasant roof terrace restaurant that's also a good place to mingle with the locals. Serves good fried fish, beans in coconut and chapattis.

New Star Restaurant Harambee Ave, Langoni. In a large and tatty *makuti*-roofed shelter, this is one of the few restaurants catering equally to travellers and locals, and one of the cheapest in town. It's especially good for breakfast before an early-morning walk to the beach. Daily 5.30am–10.30pm.

Olympic Popular beachfront place for fresh juices, snacks and meals.

Seafront Café Next to the Swahili Cultural Centre, and open till midnight, this travellers' restaurant offers coconut fish or beans, rice, pilau and *karanga*, though standards are variable.

Tayran Swahili Dishes Harambee Ave, Langoni. Locals squeeze together at shared tables in this tiny little place to eat fried fish, beans, samosas and *mandaazi*.

Zam Zam Hoteli Harambee Ave, Langoni. Cheap *hoteli* for curries, coconut beans and samosas, with hardly a *mzungu* to be seen.

Restaurants and cafés

Bush Gardens On the waterfront, competing for the same business as *Hapa Hapa* but more upmarket, this seafood and kebab place has a popular following and a charming proprietor. The food varies from very average to first-rate (the grilled garlic fish is magnificent); prices aren't as costly as you might expect. Daily 7am–10pm.

Coconut Juice Garden Harambee Ave. Good juices and shakes, which you order blended as you wish – combinations include orgasmic coconut and banana, or passion fruit and pawpaw. They also do food.

Hapa Hapa A popular, friendly, very central seafront rendezvous – the food is inexpensive, generally good (occasionally excellent), and then there are its famous pint jugs of freshly pressed juices, milk shakes and banana pancakes. More down-to-earth than *Bush Gardens*, and a good place to while away the hours.

Lamu Palace Restaurant *Lamu Palace Hotel*. This impressive restaurant is quite reliable and does realistically priced all-you-can eat seafood buffets, grills and a nice line in Italian and pasta dishes.

Stone House Rooftop Restaurant *Stone House Hotel*. Upmarket eats, mainly seafood and pasta, and great views over Lamu.

Whispers At Baraka Harambee Ave, Langoni ☏ 042/633355. Pretentious it may be (it comes with a *parfumerie*, "Baraka Gallery" gift shop and invitation-only "artistes' colony"), but it's not easy to resist real espresso and wonderful cakes, pastries, and breakfasts, unless you're really counting the pennies. Expensive. Daily 9am–8.30pm, closed 2–4pm low season and throughout May & June.

Listings

Bank KCB, on the waterfront, is the only bank in Lamu (Mon–Fri 9am–3pm, Sat 9–11am), and has an ATM.

Books Try the museum for a small selection of new souvenir books, or Mana Books and Stationery for a small and rather dusty selection of magazines and novels. The Maasai Art Studio on the beachfront has a stall of secondhand novels.

Cinemas The Zinj Theatre on Harambee Ave in Langoni screens American or Indian films. It also occasionally screens live English Premiership or European Champions League football matches. The Coast Cinema and the Casablanca Cinema show films and videos.

Clothes and tailors A number of shops along Harambee Ave will run up clothes very cheaply in a day or so. The easiest way to end up with something that fits is to provide a model garment. Shumi's Design, on the waterfront in Langoni, is recommended. Langoni is the place to hunt out *kangas* and *kikois*. The Swahili Cultural Centre (daily 9am–12.30pm & 2–4pm) has a small selection of not terribly inspiring dresses and bags made by trainee girls working above the German Post Office, and a few other curios.

Crafts and souvenirs Woodcarving shops are mostly found along Harambee Ave in Mkomani. Model dhows, chests, furniture and *siwa* horns are all attractive but bulky. Beautifully hand-carved safari chairs are also a hassle to carry, but the prices make them worth acquiring. Some of the shops selling jewellery and trinkets have genuinely old and interesting pieces. Look out for tiny lime caskets in silver, earlobe plugs in buffalo horn or silver, and old coins. A recommended silversmith is *Lamu Silversmith* on Harambee Ave just up from the *Lamu Guesthouse*. *Ogres Bead Workshop*, run by two brothers from Nairobi has wonderful handmade jewellery. Both these firms can make custom pieces.

Discos There's usually a disco on Fri & Sat at the *Civil Servants' Club*, about 1km south of the GPO (entrance on the waterfront). Full Moon parties happen regularly on Manda Island or Coconut Beach; they're unadvertised but locals are usually in the know.

Film Camera film and processing for negatives and prints of 36 exposures in three days) are available from Bagdam Store at the northern end of Harambee Ave.

Henna painting A number of women around town offer this for hands and feet, for which you can expect to pay around Ksh200 for both hands or both feet. The best women have portfolios of designs to choose from. If done properly, your hands or feet will be bound in cloth for twelve hours and the design should stay for up to six months. Try Urembo beauty center at the *Hapa Hapa* café.

Hospital The hospital, out in the direction of Shela (☎042/633012), attracts patients from a huge part of northeastern Kenya, but it's better to seek treatment elsewhere (Malindi, for example) if possible. There are also several private clinics – ask around.

Immigration In the District Commissioner's (DC's) offices on the waterfront.

Internet access There is an Internet café at the post office; you buy a scratch card downstairs for Ksh200, which allows for 1hr 30min of surfing. Simply type in your pin code and log off when finished.

Library The town library is on the top floor of the fort (Mon–Fri 8am–12.30pm & 2–5.30pm,

Sat 10am–noon; ☎0121/33201; five-visit pass Ksh100). It has a surprisingly good collection, with lots on Lamu, as well as a sixteenth-century Koranic manuscript.

Music cassettes Al-Hussein Hand Craft, on Harambee Ave, has tapes of *taarab* and traditional Wa-Bajuni and Mijikenda music.

Newspapers and magazines These arrive about 11am, and are available from Faiz Newsagents, at the northern end of Harambee Ave. They also sell tide tables. Newspapers get snapped up quickly in Lamu and the supply is limited.

Post and telephone office The post office is directly between the fort and the waterfront. *Poste restante* is available, and there are cardphones outside the building, but they don't always have phone cards for sale. The new telephone exchange on the Langoni waterfront is a better bet for calls.

Speedboat charter Not exactly in keeping with the spirit of Lamu's lifestyle, it certainly gets you from A to B effectively, but drinks diesel fuel and is thus expensive. A company called Al Hussein have a boat which can comfortably seat four, plus captain and "small captain"; their office is on Harambee Ave in Mkomani (PO Box 156; ☎042/633509), and they also can be contacted through Al-Hussein Hand Craft. Rates are currently around Ksh5000 for Pate, Ksh12,000 to Kiwaiyu, and Ksh8000 to Faza. In Shela, *Peponi Hotel* offers a similar service at similar prices.

Supermarkets Al Maddy Store (daily 9am–12.30pm & 5–10pm in theory, but often shuts earlier), and Bagdan Store (Mon–Sat 8.15am–12.30pm & 4–10pm, Sun 8.15am–12.30pm), both on Harambee Avenue.

Swahili lessons Being suffused in Swahili culture, Lamu is a good place to learn the language – the Tourist Information Centre can put you in touch with a teacher. Alternatively, ask at the Department of Adult Education on Harambee Ave or at Lamu Museum.

Travel agents Tawasal Tours (PO Box 248; ☎ & ☎042/633533, ✉ tawasal@africaonline.co.ke), at *Milimani Guesthouse*, a 10min walk inland from the fort (ask), specializes in ecological and educational trips for college groups.

Windsurfing Try Satan at *Talking Trees* or Baka Windsurfing at *Peponi* in Shela; both charge around Ksh650/hr.

Around the island

The one place everyone goes on Lamu is, of course, the **beach**, which more than repays the slight effort of getting there. The walk is enlivened by the village of **Shela**, at the start of the beach 3km south of Lamu town. Don't take any valuables if you walk here – there have been muggings in the past. It's also possible to catch a **boat** from Lamu to Shela, for Ksh100 per person. Fewer

Dhow trips

Where the hotel hustlers left off after you settled in, the dhow-ride men take up the challenge. You'll be persistently hassled until you agree to go on a trip and then, as if the word's gone out, you'll be left alone. The truth is that your face quickly becomes familiar to anyone whose livelihood depends upon tourists. In fact, the dhow trips are usually a lot of fun and, all things considered, very good value. The simplicity of Swahili sailing is delightful, using a single lateen sail that can be set in virtually any position and never seems to obstruct the view. Sloping past the mangroves, with their primeval-looking tangle of roots at eye level, hearing any number of squeaks and splashes from the small animals and birds that live among them, is quite a serene pleasure.

There are limitless possibilities for dhow trips, though only a short "menu" is usually offered. The cheapest trip is a slow sail across Lamu harbour and up Takwa "river", fishing as you go, followed by a barbecue on the beach at **Manda island**, then back to town. This might commence with some squelching around in the mud under the mangroves, digging for huge bait-worms. If the trip is timed properly against the tides, you can include a visit to **Takwa ruins** or, for rather more money, you can stay the night on the beach behind the ruins and come back the next day. This is usually done around full moon. Few sailors are prepared to venture out into the ocean, so Takwa has to be approached from the landward side up the creek, and this can only be done at high tide – and if misjudged can mean a long wait at Takwa before you can set off again.

A further variation has you sailing south down Lamu harbour, past the headland at Shela and out towards the ocean for some **snorkelling** over the reefs on the southwest corner of Manda around **Kinyika rock**. Snorkel and mask are normally provided, but bringing your own is obviously much better. Though the snorkelling is excellent, it is difficult for beginners as there are strong currents at all but neap tides. One variation which is not especially recommended is a dhow trip to Matondoni – these tend to end up being over-organized when you get there.

Dhows from Lamu to **Mombasa** are relatively straightforward (though the other direction is virtually impossible), assuming it's the right time of year (roughly once a week from December–March).

Practicalities

The **price** you pay will depend on where you want to go, for how long, and how much hard work it's going to be for the crew. Agree on the price beforehand (a full day with lunch costs around Ksh800), then gather as large a group as is practicable and pay up afterwards, although some captains may ask you for a small deposit to secure your place. Try also to agree on who's supplying food and drink apart from any fish you might catch. Whatever you pay, chances are it'll be much cheaper than any equivalent trip taken in Malindi or Watamu.

Cameras are easily damaged on dhow trips, so wrap them up well in a plastic bag. And take the clothes and drinks you'd need for a 24-hour spell in the Sahara – you'll burn up and dry out otherwise.

It's possible to head to Mombasa by dhow. Having found an agreeable captain, you'll need to visit the District Commissioner's secretary's office (see p.542) for a form absolving the captain and the government of all responsibility in the case of mishap. Take one copy to the captain, which he'll present to customs, on the first floor across the courtyard, when he files his crew and passenger manifest. They'll tell you it's a 36-hour trip to Mombasa, but count on some doldrums and allow up to three or even four days. Bring fruit and anything else you anticipate needing to break the monotony of unvarying fish and *ugali* meals. You should get a passage for less than Ksh2000.

people see the **interior** of Lamu island itself, which is a pity, as it's a pretty, if rather inhospitable, reminder of how remarkable it is that a town exists here at all. Much of it is patched into *shambas* with the herds of cattle, coconut palms, mango and citrus trees that still provide the bulk of Lamu's wealth. The two villages you might head for here are **Matondoni** and **Kipungani**.

Shela

SHELA, once a thriving settlement, is now in limbo, midway between rural decline and upmarket tourist boom. Its people, who trace their ancestry back to Manda island and speak a dialect of Swahili quite distinct from Lamu town's, are gradually leaving the village, many of them going to Malindi. A number of fine old houses have been bought by foreigners and converted into ravishing holiday homes, decked in bougainvillea and empty most of the year. Shela's only sight is the strange, much-photographed **Friday Mosque**, built in 1829, which stands out for its rocket-shaped minaret, unusual in East Africa. If you're suitably dressed, you can ask politely to go up to the top.

The gaggle of beach boys playing football at low tide, or loafing around sizing up the latest speedboat tourist arrivals from Manda airstrip, are part of the limited **gay scene**; *Peponi* ("Heaven"), its only international-class hotel, is the natural venue.

Accommodation

While Shela is an utterly hedonistic place to lounge away a few days, it doesn't offer the thrill of staying among the mosques and street life of Lamu town itself, and there are virtually no **restaurants** here aside from those in the hotels. From time to time there are a dozen or more private **houses** available to rent, usually on a weekly basis; most of these are renovated townhouses which will cost you a fortune unless you're in a big group and can share the cost. Much cheaper houses (Ksh3000–5000) are available if you ask around. The ones reviewed below are upmarket options. **Lamu Homes** in Nairobi (T & F 020/4446384, W www.lamuhomes.com) has various properties to rent on its books.

Hotels

Bahari Guesthouse 100m north of *Peponi*, PO Box 59 T 042/632046. You pay a premium for the location, right next to the water (according to the manager, at high tide you can jump from the balcony straight into the sea). The five rooms, all s/c, are simple but nicely done and just about give good value in low season. There is an excellent restaurant downstairs. B&B ⑥

Bongo House PO Box 284 T 042/633479. A small but good-value place near the Friday Mosque, with four large s/c rooms. ④

Island Hotel PO Box 179 T 042/633290, F 633568; reservations through Lamu Homes. Spacious, attractively furnished rooms, and a restful atmosphere. The penthouse is especially appealing – almost open-air, like sleeping on the roof but in privacy and comfort. All rooms have fans and nets on frames. The rooftop restaurant is good and reasonably priced, candlelit at night, and serves mild but tasty Swahili curries, grilled fish, and vegetarian dishes, plus juices and snacks, but

doesn't have an alcohol licence. Sometimes closed May to mid-June. B&B ⑥

Kijani House PO Box 266 T 042/633235–7, F 633374, W www.kijani-house.com. Pretty and comfortable French-owned hotel, well run but not as luxurious as you might imagine from their brochure – and prices are steep. The superior rooms are excellent (1, 3, 4 and 5 are best), but the standard ones are overpriced. Besides a restaurant and bar, it has two small freshwater pools set in a tropical garden leading directly to the sea. Closed May & June. B&B ⑧

Peponi Hotel PO Box 24 T 042/633421–3, F 633029, W www.peponi-lamu.com. Shela's main beachfront focus, where everyone stops in for a cold drink (or a good single malt). It's fabulously situated, and offers superb food and service. It's best to pay the extra for rooms in the main house; the standard rooms (in the four undistinguished block-like structures across from the main building), are a bit mundane. Non-seasonal rates. Closed May & June. B&B $250; ⑨

Pwani Guesthouse PO Box 59 ☎ 042/633540. Stylish, roomy house, co-owned with the *Bahari*, overlooking *Peponi*. The three doubles and two singles (all s/c) offer various options, but all, by Shela standards, are a good deal, with their old furniture, antique stuccowork and soft light. Breakfast and dinner are taken on the rooftop terrace, which has beautiful sea views. B&B ⑥

Shella Rest House PO Box 305
☎ 042/633091, ℻ 633542. Up past *Island Hotel*, turn first right and then left. Belonging to the firm that runs the much pricier *Shella Royal House*, this has eight rooms, all very different (two are s/c), including a funny one on a converted balcony with only curtains for privacy (and security). Even without haggling, these are the cheapest rooms in Shela. ④

Shella Royal House PO Box 305 ☎ 042/633091 or 0722/698059, ℻ 633542, ⓦ www.shellaroyal house.com. A bright and breezy place, with bright yellow floors and stairs. The rooms, all with mahogany four-posters, are of varying standards. There's a great swing bed on the roof terrace, perfect for lounging, and a fabulous "honeymoon room" on the top floor. B&B ⑦

Shela White House At the top of the alley leading past *Shela Pwani*, PO Box 305 ☎ 042/633091, ℻ 633542. Three s/c rooms in a stand-alone three-storey house, of which two are sea-facing and s/c. They can cook food to order, or you can use the kitchen. Roof terrace. B&B ⑥

The Stopover Bookings through Lamu Homes. Five s/c rooms directly on the seafront near the dhow harbour, and all opening out on to balconies with sea views. There's also a restaurant overlooking the sea, serving great fish curries. The three first-floor rooms can be rented out as a self-catering apartment with kitchen facilities. ⑦

Houses for rent

Beach House, Shela House and Palm House Reservations c/o PO Box 39486 Nairobi, ☎ 020/4442171, ℻ 4445010, ⓦ www.shelahouse .com, or through ⓦ www.scottdunn.com in the UK. Three luxury houses near the Friday Mosque. *Beach House* is right on the waterfront, sleeping twelve, and costs from $4200 per week in low season; *Shela House* sleeps ten (from $2100) and *Palm House* eight (from $2100). All come with house staff. *Beach House* was purpose built, the other two converted, and none of the interiors owe much to traditional Swahili style.

Jasmine House Reservations through Lamu Homes. Small house with three en-suite doubles, and a garden with different-leveled seating areas and a Jacuzzi-style pool.

Kisimani House Reservations through Let's Go Travel (see p.150). Ostensibly the oldest house in Lamu, with beautiful decor (downstairs mostly original) and terraces; it sleeps eight and has house staff. *Jihari House*, next door, is linked by a communicating walkway, so by renting both you can even accommodate a group of sixteen. From $1050 per week.

Mnarani House Reservations c/o Lamu Homes. Three doubles and two singles in a large airy house, with a charming walled garden, and five separate terraces. From $1500 a week for the house.

The beach

A usually deserted twelve-kilometre sickle of white sand, backed by empty **sand dunes**, Lamu's **beach** is the real thing; you half-expect Robinson Crusoe to come striding out of the heat haze. Unprotected by a reef, the sea here has some motion to it for once, and it is one of the few places on the coast where, at certain times of the year, you can body-surf (August is probably best). Unfortunately, women may find that wanderers along the beach can be a nuisance, muggings are not unheard of, and there were two rapes a few years ago, so stay in shouting distance of other sunbathers and preferably go to the beach in company. There is a Kenya Navy security post in the dunes.

That said, the **sun** is a more likely assailant. There's absolutely no cover and you'll find that the wind is too strong for erecting a sunshade. Ordinary sunscreen cream is available in town; coconut oil, sold in town, is used by some to avoid drying out, but you need a deep tan to begin with, otherwise your skin fries.

You can either walk the pleasant shoreline from Lamu's harbour down to Shela village (30min at low tide; 40min at high tide, when you take the track that veers inland after the last of the dhows) and then head as far down the sands as you like, or you can get a dhow to take you (Ksh300–500, negotiable), or try to find a motorboat taking a bunch of local people down (Ksh50 per person). The third option you might be tempted to try – striking out across the *shambas* behind town and heading direct for the middle of the beach, is actually a time-consuming and exhausting short cut that involves wading through deep sand. On arrival at Shela, if you've walked along the shore, you can reward your limited exertions at the *Bahari Restaurant* with a drink or a bite to eat, or head straight for the cold beers at *Peponi*. Bear in mind that if you walk for miles along the beach in the early morning, you'll have to do it back again in the heat of the day.

Matondoni and Kipungani

MATONDONI is the most talked-about destination on Lamu apart from Shela and the beach, but in truth, it's not wildly exciting and its fame as the district's principal dhow-building centre seems misplaced. However, the walk there is a fine one if you start early (the soft sand track isn't fun in blazing sunshine). A sane, enjoyable alternative is to go by **donkey**: fix up a beast through your guesthouse reception, or you can take one of the sand dhows on its trip from Lamu jetty to Matondoni, get some lunch and walk back along the line of the telephone wires.

If you really want to look around the whole island, proceed from Matondoni to **KIPUNGANI**, one hour's walk from the end of the beach (4hr from Shela village). This is the halfway mark on the round-the-island walk; the whole trip takes eight or nine hours at least. It is useful to know the state of the tides for the stretch from Matondoni to Kipungani, as you can take a direct route through the mangroves at low tide (but don't get caught out). Kipungani has an upmarket **hotel**, 1500m before the village, in the shape of *Kipungani Explorer* (reservations through Heritage Hotels, p.63; closed after Easter to early July; ❾; FB $300), a delightful "desert island" complex of fourteen simple mat-and-*makuti* thatch *bandas* up on the beach, with bar and restaurant decorated with driftwood and the products of beachcombings. The food is superb, the views over the sands and channel are exceptional, and the welcome, service, and sense of blissful isolation are everything you could ask for. Excursions, windsurfing and snorkelling trips are all on offer, and there's a pool, too. You can get there direct from Lamu town by speedboat (30min), or more slowly by dhow.

Nearby is ⚜ *Kizingo*, a new, secluded eco-lodge, created in partnership with nearby Kipungani village (PO Box 138 Lamu, ☎0733/954770 or 0722/901544, ⊛www.kizingo.com; $145 per person per night; ❾). There are six thatched *bandas* nestled among the sand dunes, each with perfect sea views, and the food served up at the restaurant is wonderfully fresh. From November to April you can swim with wild bottlenose dolphins and between November and June turtles lay eggs on the beach; the friendly owners will take guests to watch the newborn turtles make their way into the ocean.

Manda island

Practically within shouting distance of Lamu town, **Manda** – with next to no fresh water – is almost uninhabited and, apart from being the site of the main airstrip on the islands, and the location of the old ruined town of **Takwa** (favourite destination of the dhow-trip operators) is not much visited either. Significant archeologically for the ruins of Takwa and Manda, the north side of the island is also the location of the very exclusive *Blue Safari Club* (⊛www.bluesafariclub.com)

Elephants ahoy!

One of the strangest wildlife spectacles in Kenya – which you're most unlikely to see unless you organize an expedition especially and have plenty of time to wait – is the sight of **elephants swimming** between the mainland and Manda Island, with only their trunks and flapping ears above the water. Some forty to fifty members of the much larger mainland Dodora herd have a traditional migratory route which takes them, just before the onset of the long rains (usually one day in March), across the narrow Mkanda Channel to Manda island. The mangrove leaves amply supply their food and salt requirements, and though there's no fresh water, amazingly, the elephants have somehow learned that by rolling in the ground, they can make troughs which catch the rain.

a more or less private establishment catering for heads of state and similar clients (it charges over $1000 in high season). Altogether different is the *Manda Beach Club*, run by the same people as Chale Island (p.486), which has already managed to offend Shela's inhabitants with its loud disco music, floodlights at night, and by the purchase of a plot of land at Shela for the sole purpose of piping water over to Manda. Much more in keeping with local sensibilities is *Diamond Beach Village* (ⓦwww.diamondbeachvillage.com; B&B; closed April–July; ❹–❺) on the southern arm of Manda. Simple s/c bandas (and a rather wacky treehouse in a baobab) ecological principles and a superb beachfront location add up to a very fine place to stay. They have evening electricity and pride themselves on great food.

The island is crisscrossed with paths through the jungle, should you be taken by the urge to spend a day there. Rumours have been flying around the archipelago that either an American naval facility, or a new seaport for northeast Kenya, or a gas terminal for the finds around Garissa, is going to be built on Manda. The hoteliers and farmers were given notice to leave a few years back and the dredgers started clearing the channels. For the moment, though, it's all quietened down again. **Motorboats** run by the airlines make the crossing from Lamu town to the Manda **airstrip jetty** – where they sell "duty-free mangoes" in the "departure lounge" – and you can use them if you want to visit the island, though airline passengers get priority.

Takwa ruins

Whether you make a flying visit to **Takwa** (daily 8am–6pm; Ksh200), a thirty-minute boat ride from Lamu, or sleep out on the beach behind it (there are some shelters), the site is well worth seeing. A flourishing town in the sixteenth and seventeenth centuries, it was deserted (as usual, no one knows why), and is in many respects reminiscent of Gedi (see p.501). As at other sites, toilets and bathrooms figure prominently in the architecture. In Islam, cleanliness is so close to godliness as to almost signify it – the Takwans must have been a devout community. The doors of all the houses face north towards Mecca, as does the main street with the **mosque** at the end of it. The mosque is interesting for the pillar at one end, which suggests it was built on a tomb site (that of a founder of the town perhaps), and for the simple lines of its *mihrab*, so different from the ornate curlicues of later designs. Another impressive **pillar tomb** stands alone, just outside the town walls, its date translating to about 1683, and it still occasionally attracts pilgrims from Shela (some of whom claim their ancestry lies in Takwa), who come to pray for rain.

Takwa has been thoroughly cleared but, in order to preserve it for the future, hardly excavated at all. What has been found, however, suggests an industrious and healthy community, living in an easily defensible position with a wall all around the town, the ocean on one side behind the dunes and mangroves on the other. Despite this, they appear to have left in a panic and, as usual, there's ample room for conjecture about why. Part of the great appeal of Kenya's ruined towns lies in the open debate that still continues about who, precisely, their builders and citizens were, and why they so often left in such evident haste. And there's always the fascinating possibility that old Swahili manuscripts will turn up to explain it all.

There's a simple dormitory-style *banda* available at the ruins, where you can **stay** for around Ksh1000 per person. Facilities are minimal (take food and water), but the setting is magnificent.

Pate island

Only two hours by ferryboat from Lamu, totally unaffected by tourism and rarely visited, **Pate island** has some of the most impressive ruins anywhere on the coast and a clutch of old Swahili settlements which, at different times, have been as important as Lamu or more so. There are few places on the coast as memorable.

Pate is mostly low-lying and almost surrounded by mangrove swamps; no two maps of it ever agree (ours on p.528 shows only the permanent dry land, not the ever-changing mangrove forests that surround it in the shallow sea), so getting on and off the island requires deft awareness of the tides. This apparent remoteness coupled with a lack of information deters travellers but, in truth, Pate is not a difficult destination, and is an easier island to walk around than Lamu, with none of that island's exhausting soft sand.

A **water taxi** (one of three plying the route; roughly Ksh70 to Mtangawanda, Ksh100 to Faza, Ksh150 to Kisingitini) leaves daily except Friday, about one hour before high tide (which can be very early in the morning), from the municipal jetty at Lamu. On reaching the **Mkanda Channel**, you pass the ferry making the return trip; the Mkanda is navigable only at high tide, and even then it can be a close call when the boat is overloaded, as it usually is. The boat, sometimes accompanied by dolphins, then calls at a deserted spot called **Mtangawanda** (the dock for Pate town, which takes 2–3hr from Lamu), followed by **Faza** at the northern end of the island, which is up to four hours away from Lamu, finally docking at Kijinitini (Kisingitini), thirty minutes further on.

The obvious plan, having walked to Pate town from Mtangawanda dock (1hr, though you'll need directions after 45min for the minor side track; it gets slippery in the rains, so watch out), is to walk through **Siyu** to Faza, returning to Lamu by ferry from there. You could also do this in reverse, of course, but there is a major drawback in that the boat might not pick you up at Mtangawanda on its return if, as often happens, it's full. The walk itself can be done in a day if the tides force an early start, but you may well find yourself wanting to stay longer and breaking for at least a night in Siyu.

Two other possibilities include catching a dhow from Mtangawanda to Pate town instead of walking, though arriving at low tide means you'll need to wade through shallow waters which are favoured by stingrays – or you can catch a connecting *mtaboti* ferry at Mtangawanda for Siyu (1hr).

Some history

According to its own **history**, the *Pate Chronicle*, the town was founded in the early years of Islam with the arrival of Arabian immigrants. This statelet is supposed to have lasted until the thirteenth century, when another group of dispossessed Arab rulers – the **Nabahani** – arrived. The story may have been embellished by time but archeological evidence does support the existence of a flourishing port on the present site of Pate as early as the ninth century; probably by the fifteenth century the town exerted a considerable influence on most of the quasi-autonomous settlements along the coast, including Lamu. As usual, the claims of the royal line to be of overseas extraction were by now more political than biological.

The first **Portuguese** visitors were friendly, trading with the Pateans for the multicoloured silk cloth for which the town had become famous, and they also introduced gunpowder, which enabled wells to be easily excavated, a fact which must have played a part in Pate's rising fortunes. During the sixteenth century, a number of Portuguese merchants settled and married in the town, but as Portugal tightened its grip and imposed taxes, relations quickly deteriorated. There were repeated uprisings and reprisals until, by the mid-seventeenth century, the Portuguese had withdrawn to the security of Fort Jesus in Mombasa. Even today, though, several families in Pate are said to be Wa-reno (from the Portuguese *reino*, "kingdom"), meaning of Portuguese or part-Portuguese descent.

During the late seventeenth and eighteenth centuries, having thrown out the old rulers and avoided domination by new invaders like the Omani Arabs, Pate underwent a **cultural rebirth** and experienced a flood of creative activity similar to Lamu's. The two towns had a lively relationship, and were frequently in a state of war. At some time during the Portuguese period, Pate's harbour had started to silt up and the town began to use Lamu's, which must have caused great difficulties. In addition, Pate was ruled by a Nabahani king who considered Lamu part of his realm. The disastrous Battle of Shela of 1812 (see p.530) marked the end of Lamu's political allegiance to Pate and the end of Pate as a city-state.

Practicalities

Apart from the motorboat (see above), you can, of course, choose to take a dhow to Pate, and even up to Kiwaiyu. If you have the time, and some companions, it's a fine trip, for which you should allow a good four to five days in all. Alternatively, if you have less time but can afford to spend a lot more, you might look into taking a speedboat (see "Listings", p.542) which would enable you to reach Pate town direct, from the south, at high tide, in less than half an hour. But you'd have to wait until the next high tide to get out of Pate creek, unless the speedboat went round to Mtangawanda or Siyu, leaving you to walk. There are many possible permutations.

Accommodation on Pate island is rarely a problem but, with no proper lodgings, a **tent** is a useful back-up. Normally, you'll be invited to stay by someone almost as soon as you arrive in a village; before setting off from Lamu, it may help to ask the museum staff for recommendations. It's wise to take **water** with you (five litres if possible) as Pate's supplies are unpredictable and often very briny. Most islanders live on home-produced **food** and staples brought from Lamu and, although there are a few small shops on the island, it's a good idea to have some emergency provisions. These make useful gifts as well. **Mosquitoes** and flies (especially in May and June) are a serious menace on Pate. The shops sell mosquito coils but, during the day, you may be glad to have some repellent.

If you plan on spending several days on Pate, and you're interested in the archeology of the region, you should ask for **advice** and **contact names** from Lamu Museum and Lamu Fort, and don't forget to have a good look at the photo display at the latter.

Pate town

From the dock at Mtangawanda (which has the only **beach** in the vicinity – watch out for sharks), a narrow **footpath** leads to Pate through thick bush; ask for the *ndia ya Pate*, the path to Pate. Once on the trail it's easy to follow. You cross a broad, tidal "desert", pockmarked with fiddler crab holes, then climb a slight rise to drop through thicker bush, and arrive after an hour on the edge of town.

Despite its small size, **PATE** could hardly be described as a village. Yet, reduced to the status of sub-location, its only link with government an assistant chief, its sole provision a primary school, the town is today a mere shadow of its former self. But at least its inhabitants are said to remain the richest on the island, thanks to their cash crop, **tobacco**, possibly introduced by the Portuguese and certainly grown here longer than anywhere else on the coast.

There's no electricity, no alcohol and obviously no cars. After Lamu it comes as a series of surprises. The town plan is pretty much the same – a maze of narrow streets and high-walled houses – but here the streets are made of earth, and the houses are built of coral and dried mud, unplastered and somehow forbidding. The overall layout is confusing, with little slope, as in Lamu, to help direction. Pateans do, in fact, refer to the "upper" and "lower" parts of town – Kitokwe and Mitaaguu respectively. The lower part is down near the town dock, which is only briefly underwater at high tide. If you arrive from Mtangawanda in the "upper" part of town – reputedly poorer and less friendly – you're likely to be struck immediately by the *Wapate* – the **people**, and notably the women. Brilliant, determined ladies, with short, bushy hair and rows of gold earrings, stare out directly, unhidden by *buibuis*. Some wear nineteenth-century American gold dollars or half-dollars, though these reminders of the great Yankee trading expeditions have become so valuable that many have been sold. Big **earlobe plugs** made of silver, gold or buffalo horn can also be seen, as well as nose-rings. If you speak any Swahili, you're likely to find the dialect here unrecognizable. *Wazungu* are rare and, after Lamu's studied repose, Pate is arrestingly upfront in its dealings with foreigners.

At night, the town resounds with the chimes of dozens of big old **wall clocks**, further reminders of American trade here in the nineteenth century, which, juxtaposed with the muezzins' calls to prayer, sound thoroughly bizarre.

The Nabahani ruins

More layers are peeled off Pate's enigmatic exterior when you start to explore the ruins of the **Nabahani** town just outside the modern one. The acres of walls, roofless buildings, tombs, mosques and unidentifiable structures are fascinating, the more so perhaps because this isn't an "archeological site" in the commonly expected mould. Tobacco farmers work in the stony fields between the walls.

Boys will guide you around the ruins for a small payment, but don't expect anyone to take you at night; although it's very beautiful in a full moon, you'll have to go alone because the locals are afraid of the *djinn* and ghosts living there. Most impressive are the **Mosque with Two Mihrabs**, a nearby house that still has a facing of beautiful *zidaka* (niches) on one wall, and the remains of a sizeable mansion. This last building, you'll be told, is a **Portuguese house**. Certainly, the worn-down stumps of bottle glass projecting from the top of one of its walls do lend it a curiously European flavour, and in the plaster on another wall are scratched two very obvious galleons. Its ceiling slots are square for timbers rather than round for *boriti*, as elsewhere in the ruins.

Shards of pottery and household objects lie in the rubble everywhere, but many of the interiors of the buildings are so clogged with tangled roots and vegetation that getting in is almost impossible. It is worth persevering, however: the sense of personal discovery is exciting and immensely satisfying (if you can ignore the mosquitoes).

Many of the walls and buildings have already been demolished to obtain lime for tobacco cultivation. Without weighty financial backing, it's hard to see how the National Museums of Kenya could preserve the remains of old Pate as well as compensate the farmers. Gradually, tragically, it is all returning to the soil.

Siyu

The path from Pate to Siyu is a slightly tricky eight kilometres. Having set off in the right direction, you will find the first half-hour fairly straightforward; if in doubt, bear right. You come to a crossroads (easily missed unless you look backwards) and turn right. This narrow red dirt path soon broadens into a track known as the *barabara ya gari* (the "motor highway" – there was once a car); it takes you to a normally dry tidal inlet where you veer left a little before continuing straight on through thick bush for another hour to reach Siyu. Wherever the bush on either side is high enough you may come across gigantic spiders' webs strung across the path. The spiders are brightly coloured, non-hairy, and merely waiting for insects, but they are nevertheless intimidating. Fortunately, they have the sense to build their webs high up and well out of the way.

Siyu is even less well documented than Pate. Still access by sea, the town was a flourishing and unsuspected centre of Islamic scholarship from the seventeenth to the nineteenth century and apparently something of a **sanctuary** for Muslim intellectuals and craftsmen. While Lamu, Pate and other trading towns were engaged in political rivalry and physical skirmishing, Siyu never had its heart in commerce or maritime activities, and never attracted much Portuguese attention. Instead, there was enormous devotion to **Korancopying**, **book-making**, **text illumination**, and cottage industries like the **woodcarving** and **leatherwork** for which it's still famous locally. Siyu **sandals** are said to be absolutely the best (though plastic flip-flops have forced almost all the makers out of business), and Siyu **carved doors** are among the most beautiful of all Swahili doors, with distinctive guilloche patterns and inlays of ground shell.

The sources of wealth and stability for Siyu's flowering are a little mysterious, but the town's agricultural base obviously supported it well and it was probably the largest settlement on the island in the early nineteenth century, with up to thirty thousand inhabitants. In 1873, the British vice consul in Zanzibar could still describe it as "the pulse of the whole district".

These days you wouldn't know it. Less than four thousand people live here, and signs of the old brilliance are hard to find. Siyu lost its independence and presumably much of its artistic flair when the sultan of Zanzibar's Omani troops first occupied the fort in 1847 – though it was twenty years before the Omanis were able to hold it for more than a brief spell.

The Town

Built in the early nineteenth century (no one knows for sure by whom), **Siyu Fort** is the town's most striking building and indeed, in purely monumental terms, the most imposing building on the whole island. Substantially renovated, it is one of the few surviving traces of the glory days. It's freely accessible, though watch out for dangers like the well and the unstable walls. Around the outskirts of Siyu on the south side are a number of quite impressive **tombs**. The big domed tomb with porcelain niches dates from 1853.

Most of Siyu's houses today conform to the "open-box" plan typical of the Kenyan coast: yellowish mud with a ridged *makuti* roof, open at each end. These houses stand, each on its own, with no real streets to connect them so, although it's larger than Pate, Siyu feels far more like a village. The cultural isolation of these communities from each other, a separateness which continues to this day, is easily appreciated after arriving in Siyu from Pate. There are still few *buibuis* here, but there's much less jewellery in evidence and the atmosphere is altogether less severe.

Shanga ruins

You'll need the help of a qualified guide if you hope to visit the ruins of **SHANGA**, a large Swahili town at least 1000 years old, which would be almost impossible to find unaided. Expect to pay around a couple of hundred shillings for a guide. Shanga is on the south coast of the island, about an hour's walk from Siyu. You have to fight your way, literally, through the undergrowth when you arrive at the site. The most impressive sight is the white pillar tomb, eminently phallic, which you come to first. The very large Friday mosque nearby and a second mosque nearer the sea are only the most obvious of innumerable other remains in every direction.

Excavations at Shanga have revealed a walled site of thirteen acres, with five access gates and a cemetery outside the walls containing 340 stone tombs. There was even a sea wall. Inside the town, 130 houses were surveyed, together with what looks to have been a palace similar in some respects to the one at Gedi. Shanga is believed to have been occupied from the ninth to the fourteenth centuries and no very convincing reasons have been found for its abandonment, nor why it was never mentioned by travellers and traders of the time.

Limited work has been done to restore some of the plaster in a set of wall niches and on the fluted pillar tomb, but on the whole the clearing and excavating only seems to have encouraged the jungle. Getting from one ruin to the next isn't easy. Dangerously camouflaged **wells** and **snakes**, both common, add further to the Shanga experience. If you walk on down to the sea – and assuming you have a certain capacity for hardship in paradise – there's a beautiful **beach** and some ideal camping spots.

Faza

Siyu to **FAZA** is a shorter walk than from Pate to Siyu and more interesting, through waist-high grass, fertile *shambas* and sections of bush. It takes about two hours, but you'll need guidance, at least as far as the airstrip inherited from a 1980s oil-prospecting venture. From there it's straightforward. An hour or so out of Siyu, you reach the first *shambas*. Faza suffered a serious fire in 1990, which razed many houses to the ground and caused devastation. Today, you would hardly know.

Archeologically, Faza has less to offer than its neighbours. It was one of the most defiant Swahili towns over any attempts to usurp its independence. It was razed by the Pate army after a dispute over water rights in the fifteenth century, and again by the Portuguese in 1586 after collaborating with the Turkish fleet of Amir Ali Bey. On this occasion, the entire population was massacred and the head of Faza's king was taken to Goa in a barrel of salt to be paraded triumphantly in the streets. Faza's unfortunate history may partly account for its relative lack of ruins, but one success is commemorated in the **tomb** of Seyyid Hamed bin Ahmed al-Busaidy (also known as Amir Hamad), commander-in-chief of the sultan of Zanzibar's forces, who met his death in 1844 under a hail of arrows. He was on an expedition against Siyu and Pate, and retreating to the relative safety of Faza when he was ambushed by a party of Siyu bowmen. His grave (*kaburi*), with a long epitaph, lies just outside Faza.

On a coast of islands, it's not surprising that Faza itself is almost an island, surrounded by tidal flats and mangroves. A secondary school, health centre, police station (with nothing to do) and even a post office and telephone exchange have made Faza the most important settlement on Pate island. There's even a Land Rover ambulance donated by Saudi Arabia, the only vehicle on the island. Every few years a lodging house opens, but the lack of visitors forces them to close sooner or later. Fishing is the commonest occupation, with much of the catch going to a cold room at Kisingitini, from where it's shipped to Mombasa.

As a contemporary Kenyan rural centre, Faza makes an interesting place to walk around and you're almost certain to have plenty of time to fill before the boat leaves. A fine evening stroll takes you across the mud on a new concrete causeway to the thickets on the "mainland", where the island's expanding secondary school is located. From Faza you could, if you wanted, walk on to the other villages on the island, all fairly modern and bunched together within forty minutes of Faza: Kisingitini, Bajumwali, Tundwa (Chundwa), and the closest, Nyambogi.

There are several ruined mosques around Faza, including the very crumbled Kunjanja Mosque. The ruins of the eighteenth-century **Mbwarashally Mosque** (also known as the Shala Fatani Mosque) merit a visit, however. Now theoretically protected by the National Museums of Kenya, the mosque – barring its *mihrab* – is just a pile of rubble; the *mihrab*, however, turns out to incorporate exquisite and unusual heart motifs, including the *shahada* (the Islamic creed) inscribed within an inverted heart shape.

Kiwaiyu

From Faza you're within striking distance of the desert island retreat of **Kiwaiyu** (also spelt Kiwayu), about an hour by *mtaboti*, if you can find one. A group **dhow charter** in Lamu is probably cheaper: for Ksh4000–5000 a day, you can charter a small dhow for four or five days, including breakfast and dinner, snorkelling and fishing gear, and plenty of fresh water. You can expect to spend at least 24 hours on the journey in each direction, depending on wind, tides and the skill of the crew. The snorkelling around the **Kiunga Marine National Reserve** is nice enough, though not as consistently good as at Malindi/Watamu, but the experience of sailing, the nights under the stars, and the acquaintance of the Swahili crew are altogether highly recommended. Kiwaiyu also has Airkenya and SafariLink **flights** from Nairobi.

Budget travellers stay at the reasonable *Kasim's* camping and *banda* site, near the beach on the inshore coast of the island just a few hundred metres north of **Kiwaiyu village**. *Kasim's* has several palm-mat *bandas*, plus a couple of unusual tree houses (camping Ksh200; ②). Most people just drag one of the cane beds down onto the beach and sleep under the stars. The village has limited provisions in a couple of shops, but most guests eat what is prepared each day and served in the little "dining room".

Five minutes south of *Kasim's* is the village, quiet, rural and friendly enough. A further ten minutes south, you come to the "Italian cold store" – a stalled shellfish export project with attached accommodation. Ten minutes' walk further still, you reach a house on the high southern tip of the island. This is a fishing camp (the plane you may have seen parked near the village belongs to the owner), but it's strictly private and does not provide accommodation to walk-in visitors. From here, the superb, ocean-facing beach, with the reef close offshore, is just a scramble down the sandy hillside. There are one or two first-class **snorkelling** spots off this southern tip of the island, with huge coral heads and a multitude of fish. Ask for precise directions as it's possible to spend hours looking and still miss them. You'll need good footwear to survive the dead coral reef.

Luxury lodges

There are two **luxury lodges** at Kiwaiyu. *Munira Island Camp*, about 2km north of Kiwaiyu village, is a group of seven spacious *bandas* planted on the crest of the island to catch the breeze (bookings through PO Box 40088 Nairobi; ⓣ020/512213, ⓕ512543; FB $175 per person per night; ⑨). "Mike's Bandas", as the establishment is also known, is very laid-back and civilized, and there's plentiful birdlife in the vicinity. It's a favourite with Anglo-Kenyans and those who find even *Peponi* too busy. Transfers from Lamu Island come to around $35 per person. **Kiwayu Safari Village** (ⓣ020/600107, ⓕ606990, ⓦwww.kiwayu .com; all-in packages $600 per day for two; ⑨) is nestled on a pristine, palm-shaded beach across the channel from the northern end of Kiwaiyu, within the Kiunga National Marine Reserve. The combination of exclusive, palm- and grass-thatch cottages (all s/c) and excellent food and watersports makes for a romantic getaway at a very high price.

Travel details

Trains

Mombasa to: Nairobi (3 weekly; 14hr).

Buses

Mombasa to: Busia (2 daily; 15hr); Dar es Salaam (3 daily; 14–16hr), via Tanga (7hr); Garissa via Kilifi, Malindi, Garsen and Hola (2 daily; 8–10hr); Kisumu (5 daily; 14hr); Lamu via Kilifi and Malindi (5 daily; 7–8hr); Malaba (1 daily; 15hr); Malindi via Kilifi (aproximately hourly; 90min); Nairobi (frequent, but especially around 7am and 7pm; 7–9hr).

Matatus

Frequencies are given only where there are relatively few services.
Likoni to: Diani Beach (occasional; 45min); Kinango via Kwale (1hr); Kwale (40min); Lungalunga (2hr); Msambweni (1hr); Shelly Beach (15min); Shimoni (1hr 30min); Ukunda (change here for Diani Beach; 30min).

Mombasa to: Bamburi (15min); Kaloleni (1hr 30min); Kinango (occasional, via Mazeras; 1hr 30min); Malindi (1hr 30min); Mtwapa (30min); Nairobi (mornings only; 7hr); Tanga (daily; 4hr); Voi (2hr 30min).

Flights

Kiwaiyu to: Nairobi Wilson (1–2 daily; Airkenya and SafariLink; 2hr).
Lamu to: Malindi (Kenya Airways and Mombasa Air Safari; 1–2 daily; 30min); Nairobi Wilson (1–2 daily; Airkenya and SafariLink; 1hr 30min).
Malindi to: Lamu (Kenya Airways and Mombasa Air Safari; 1–2 daily; 30min); Nairobi Kenyatta (Kenya Airways and East African Safari Air; 2 daily; 1hr 15min); Nairobi Wilson (Airkenya; 3–6 weekly; 1hr 30min).
Mombasa to: Dar es Salaam (Precision Air; 1–2 daily; 1hr 30min) via Zanzibar (50min); Lamu (Mombasa Air Safari; 2 weekly; 1hr 15min); Nairobi (Kenya Airways 6–7 daily; 1hr).

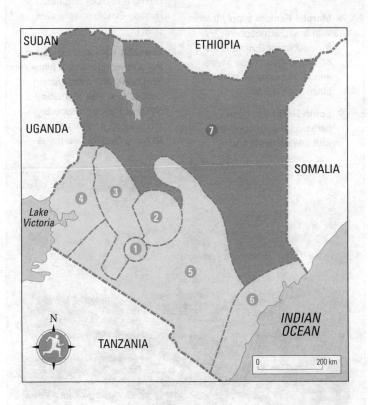

7

The North

CHAPTER 7

Highlights

❋ **Central Island National Park**
Totally untouched volcanic
sanctuary in the middle of
Lake Turkana, where Nile
crocodiles breed. A memorable boat trip from the lake's
western shore. See p.568

❋ **Maralal** Remote supply town
with a wild atmosphere. Try
the exuberant Buffalo Hotel
or Yare Safaris' base where
annual camel races take
place. See p.572

❋ **South Horr** Lush oasis
hemmed in by mountains,
with fine camping and

great opportunities to meet
Samburu people. See p.580

❋ **Loiyangalani** End-of-the-
world kind of place on the
eastern shore of shimmering
Lake Turkana, home of the
fishing and croc- and hippo-
hunting Elmolo people. See
p.581

❋ **Marsabit** Remotely located in
the northern deserts, a highland oasis with a fascinating
cultural mix. Visit Marsabit
National Park with superb
crater lakes, elephants and
amazing birdlife. See p.593

△ Turkana overland trip

The North

There is one half of Kenya about which the other half knows nothing and seems to care even less.

Negley Farson, Last Chance in Africa

Kenya is rarely thought of in terms of desert, but **the North** – over half the country in area – is exclusively arid land, burned out for more than ten months of the year. Unfortunately, it's also renowned as the most **dangerous** area in Kenya, with cattle-rustling, tribal feuding and armed banditry making a large swathe of the north, east of the Isiolo–Marsabit–Moyale road, too risky to visit. See the box on p.587 for further advice and precautions. Apart from these trouble spots, the old Northern Frontier District (still called NFD by many) remains one of the most exciting and adventurous parts of Africa for travel: a vast tract of territory, crisscrossed by ancient migration routes, and still tramped by the nomadic Samburu, Boran, Rendille, Gabbra, Turkana, and Somali herders.

The target for most travellers is the wonderful jade splash of **Lake Turkana**, very remote in feel and highly unpredictable in nature (when British sailors first ventured on it, they reckoned it could turn "rougher than the North Sea"). To get there, you have the option of organized camping safaris, as well as matatus and lorries up from the hub of highlands Kenya; few visitors drive themselves. Elsewhere in the north, travelling can be harder going, usually by gut-shaking lorries, with heat and dust constant, the water often briny and useless for washing. But the **desert towns** have their own rewards, not least in the bewilderment of arriving and finding places so little known yet so important to an enormous compass of countryside and population.

Because of the layout of the **roads** and **tracks** that radiate north from the Central Highlands, you'll need to make a decision about which "spokes" to cover; there are few east–west routes. Don't be over-ambitious. Bus and matatu services are patchy at best, whilst lorries and hitching can work out, but are exhausting. If you're driving, water, enough fuel and mechanical know-how should be your priorities since you'll need to be almost self-sufficient. Most people on business, and relief workers, now fly to the North, and cannot conceive why a tourist would even want to go there, let alone by land transport. In practical terms, the current situation limits you to the two main routes up to Lake Turkana, the Mathews Range and, with caution, the route to Marsabit, which then doubles back to Turkana via North Horr.

Though the landscape is parched for most of the year, when the **rains** do come (usually around May) they can have dramatic effect, bringing torrents

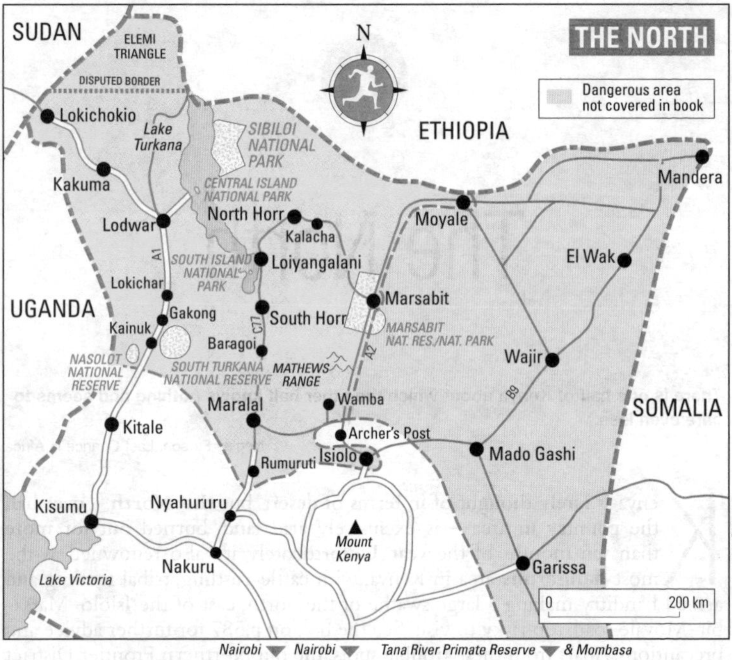
THE NORTH
SUDAN
ELEMI TRIANGLE
DISPUTED BORDER
N
Dangerous area not covered in book
Torit & Juba
Lokichokio
Lake Turkana
SIBILOI NATIONAL PARK
ETHIOPIA
Mandera
Kakuma
CENTRAL ISLAND NATIONAL PARK
North Horr
Moyale
Lodwar
Kalacha
A1
SOUTH ISLAND NATIONAL PARK
Loiyangalani
El Wak
Lokichar
Marsabit
UGANDA
Gakong
South Horr
C77
Kainuk
MARSABIT NAT. RES./NAT. PARK
Baragoi
A2
Wajir
NASOLOT NATIONAL RESERVE
SOUTH TURKANA NATIONAL RESERVE
MATHEWS RANGE
B9
Maralal
Wamba
SOMALIA
Kitale
Archer's Post
Isiolo
Mado Gashi
Rumuruti
Kisumu
Nyahururu
Mount Kenya
Mogadishu
Nakuru
Garissa
Lake Victoria
0
200 km
Nairobi
Nairobi
Tana River Primate Reserve
& Mombasa

of water along the ravines, tearing away fords and bridges, and sweeping over the plains to leave an ooze of mud and new shoots. In these conditions, you can easily be stranded – even along the paved road up to Lodwar. However, if your plans are flexible, it's an exciting time to explore. Driving your own vehicle during the rainy season is not recommended unless you've got 4WD and experience.

Turkana

Lake Turkana stretches south for 250km from the Ethiopian border, down through Kenya's arid lands, bisecting the rocky deserts like a turquoise sickle. It's hemmed in by sandy wastes and black-and-brown volcanic ranges, and the lake scene changes constantly. The water, glassy, milky blue one minute, can become slate-grey and choppy or a glaring emerald green, sometimes even jade, the next.

The lake was discovered for the rest of the world only in 1888 by the Austrians **Teleki** and **von Hohnel**, who named it "Rudolf" after their archduke and patron. Later, it became eulogized as the "Jade Sea" in John Hillaby's book about his camel trek. The name "Turkana" only came into being during the wholesale Kenyanization of place names in the 1970s. By then, it had also been dubbed the "Cradle of Mankind", the site of revelatory fossil discoveries in the field of human evolution. And it was becoming something of a spiritual mecca for atavists, an excuse for a week of riotous assembly in a safari lorry or a dignified weekend in a Cessna and a lakeshore lodge.

But to depict Lake Turkana as "Kenya's latest touristic discovery", as one or two glossies would have you believe, is, thankfully, a monstrous piece of hype:

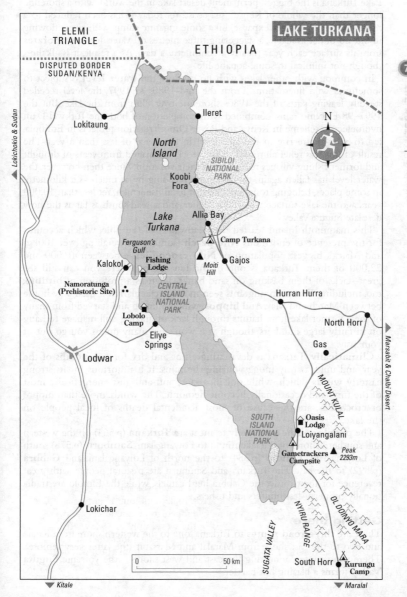

there are two lodges, one on each shore, catering for perhaps a dozen people between them at any one time. Otherwise, there are a few B&Ls, one or two windy campsites and that's it. As yet, the only **asphalt** – that certain sign of imminent change – is the crooked finger that reaches north from **Kitale** to **Lodwar** and on to **Kalokol** on the western shore.

Ecology and climate

Lake Turkana is the biggest permanent desert lake in the world, with a shoreline longer than the whole of Kenya's sea coast. Yet today it has been reduced to a mere sliver of its former expanse. Like some gigantic sump, with rivers flowing in but no outlet available, a staggering three metres of water depth **evaporates** from its surface each year (nearly a centimetre a day). As a result, it is alkaline, though not inimical to some aquatic life.

In common with other lakes with no outflow, the **water level** is subject to sometimes wild fluctuations. From the mid-1980s to 1997, the level receded steadily, leaving parts of the 1980s shoreline over 8km from the lake. But the 1997–98 El Niño rains, combined with completion of both the Turkwel Dam hydroelectric scheme in Kenya and River Omo irrigation projects in Ethiopia, led to a six-metre rise in the lake level in the space of less than a year. The result of this was relief all round, as fish stocks recovered from years of drought and former fishing villages rediscovered their vocation. Since then however, the water level has fallen again, the lakeshore receding by as much as a kilometre in some places, bringing tougher times for local fishermen. Yet less than 10,000 years ago the lake surface was 150m higher, and spread south as far as the now desolate Suguta Valley.

This mammoth inland sea fed the headwaters of the Nile, which accounts for the presence of enormous **Nile perch** (sometimes weighing over 100kg) and Africa's biggest population of **Nile crocodiles** – between 10,000 and 22,000 of them. Turkana is one of the few places where you can still see great stacks of them basking on sand banks. There is a profusion of **birdlife**, too, including European migrants seen most spectacularly on their way home between March and May. And **hippos**, widely hunted and starved from many of their former lakeshore haunts through lack of grazing, still manage to hang on in fairly large numbers, though you won't see many unless you go out of your way.

Climatically, Turkana is devastatingly hot and dry for ten months of the year, and unpleasantly muggy during the rains. It is notorious for its strong easterly **winds** which, while not incessant, puff and gust energetically most of the time and occasionally become demonic. The winds, more than hippos or crocodiles, are the cause of most accidental deaths of local people on the lake.

The **people** you are most likely to meet are **Turkana** (p.564) on the western and southern shores of the lake round to Loiyangalani, **Samburu** (p.578) south of Loiyangalani, **Elmolo** (p.584) to the north of Loiyangalani, and **Gabbra** (p.592) to the east. The Turkana and Samburu are pastoral people with great reverence for their cattle, the Gabbra herd camels, while the Elmolo are traditionally property-less hunters and fishers.

Getting there

There are **three road routes** to Turkana: one to the western shore from Kitale and two to the east shore from Maralal and Marsabit (the latter very remote). There is no route connecting the east and west shores – the volcanic **Suguta Valley** forms a blazing hot barrier.

The western approach, from **Kitale to Lodwar**, is the one used by most independent travellers without their own vehicles. For **transport**, there's a choice of buses or lorries, but the road is diabolical and takes several hours to traverse.

On the east, the **Maralal–Loiyangalani route** is the one used by nearly all of the Turkana **camping safari** lorries (the main operators are Gametrackers, see p.149). If you can afford $500–600 or so for a week-long trip, it has definite advantages: magnificent scenery and a great sense of adventure.

The third route, from **Isiolo to Loiyangalani** via **Marsabit** and **North Horr**, is feasible if you are prepared to wait around for days for lifts, first from Isiolo to Marsabit, and then on to North Horr. But it's not much used and is not advised if you are driving in your own vehicle. The safari company Gametrackers uses this route for its longer Turkana Bus trips via the Chalbi Desert, and may be prepared to give you a lift if a bus is passing (route details are given on p.597).

A last option is **flying**. There are no scheduled flights, but flights to Lake Turkana are usually included as part of weekend packages, costing $500–700 per person, with accommodation at either Ferguson's Gulf (*Fishing Lodge*) or Loiyangalani (*Oasis Lodge*). Otherwise, ask around at Nairobi's Wilson Airport, or try one of the companies listed on pp.149–150, or an air charter company (p.152); the cost will amount to over $2000 to hire even a small plane. Although flying here destroys much of the sense of the lake's isolation, and the usual brief visit doesn't give enough time to explore, the flight itself – low down between the Aberdares and Mount Kenya – is sublime.

North to Lodwar and the western lakeshore

From Kitale, a number of **buses** leave for Lodwar in the early morning (the first at around 6am), with the last stragglers leaving just after midday, taking about seven hours. Alternatively, you might try **hitching** – there are plenty of trucks and jeeps bound for the aid centre at Lokichokio, northwest of Lodwar near the Sudanese border, and stopping a vehicle is not too difficult, though it's advisable to find out the going rate in advance (it was around Ksh600 at time of writing). Make sure you take plenty of water for this trip, as unexplained delays, breakdowns and the like are all too common. During Moi's time, the road was plagued by bandits, mostly marauding Turkana and Pokot youth, and vehicles had to travel in convoy; since Moi's departure however, the new administration has tightened up security, and the road is now safe for vehicles to travel routinely.

The best part of the journey is the beginning, covered in chapter 4 (p.329). The last bank before Lodwar is at **Makutano** (see p.329), where it is also a good idea to fill up with fuel, though you should be able to find that further north at **Ortum**, and you *may* find diesel (but not petrol) at Lokichar.

After the Marich Pass, you come out of the Cherangani Hills and onto the plain, passing from Pokot into Turkana territory when you cross the Turkwel River just before **Kainuk**. The change of scenery is dramatic, but from the thorny wilderness of the **Turkana Plains** beyond, it's hard to extract much of scenic interest unless you're a desert aficionado, though the regular stops to pick up increasingly wild-looking passengers maintain gently heightening expectations about the far north you're heading into.

North of Sebit (which is just before Ortum and the Marich pass; see map p.272), the tarmac begins to break up, and by the time you get down onto the plain, its condition is so bad that the road might just as well not be surfaced at all. Plans to resurface it have been held up by disputes over funding. Meantime, it can just about be negotiated in a 2WD car, but very carefully, and at a snail's pace.

At Kainuk, there is a possible detour to the **Nasalot National Reserve** ($15, children $5; access by car only – Ksh200 extra), which bounds the northern slopes of the mountains and the southern fringes of the south Turkana plains. From the gate, 6km off the Lodwar road (signposted on the left), the winding paved route drops several hundred metres into the heat, with plunging precipices and spectacular views all round, to the **Turkwel Gorge** and **hydroelectric dam**.

As the reserve is mostly covered with thick bush, **spotting animals** isn't all that easy: the elephants here, though larger than their southern cousins, hide themselves pretty well, and your best chance of seeing them is on the paved road at dawn or dusk. You'd be unusually fortunate to see any of the reserve's lions and leopards. Otherwise, the diminutive dik-dik antelopes are plentiful, if shy – you'll see them bounding into the bushes ahead of you, and there are also buffalo and warthogs. Camping is not allowed, but there are some extremely good value **bandas** by the dam (Ksh300 per three-bed room).

Beyond Nasalot back on the main A1 Lodwar road, another detour to the right takes you to the **South Turkana National Reserve** (free entry, though there are plans to extract charges as for Nasalot), which lacks Nasalot's scenic grandeur, but is where the elephants migrate to between March and July.

Lodwar

For most Kenyans, mention of **LODWAR** conjures up remote and outlandish images of the badlands, an aberrant place where anything could befall you. And the Turkana District capital is, to put it mildly, a wild town – unformed and incongruous in this searing wilderness. During the 1980s it became Kenya's desert boom town, the lake's fishing, the possibility of oil discoveries and the new road from Kitale all encouraging inward migration. While **Turkana people** have always predominated, **Luo** and **Luhya** also arrived in search of opportunities. With the exhaustion of farming country in the south, Lodwar and the area around it became increasingly attractive to pioneers and cowboys of all sorts. But this expansion has now fizzled out and Lodwar has returned to being a sleepy frontier town. Newspapers arrive with the first matatu each afternoon, hours after the rest of the country have received theirs, and men sit reading them, discussing the daily stories, trying to reduce the **isolation** felt here.

Apart from just hanging around and taking in the scene, there's not a lot to do in Lodwar. If you have the time and some spare energy, you can **hike** up one of the hills behind the town (the guides from *Nawoitorong Guesthouse* are best). Lodwar's canopy of acacias makes it surprisingly invisible below, but the view stretches for miles. For **handicrafts**, you'll find good woven baskets on sale at the *Nawoitorong Guesthouse*. If you plan any walking, you might want to pick up a pair of **5000-mile shoes** (flip-flops made from old truck tyres), which are comfortable and virtually unbreakable, and can be found in the streets behind *New Salama Hotel*.

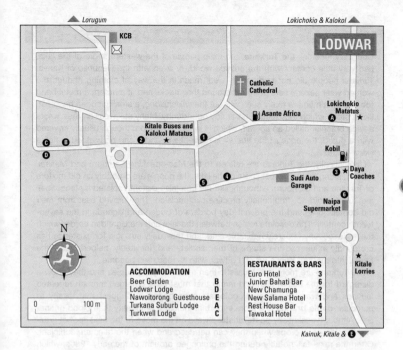

KCB

LODWAR

Catholic
Cathedral

Lokichokio
Matatus
A

Asante Africa

Kitale Buses and
Kalokol Matatus
1

Kobil

C **B**

D

2

3 **Daya
Coaches**

Sudi Auto
Garage

5 **4**

6

Naipa
Supermarket

N

Kitale
Lorries

ACCOMMODATION	
Beer Garden	B
Lodwar Lodge	D
Nawoitorong Guesthouse	E
Turkana Suburb Lodge	A
Turkwell Lodge	C

RESTAURANTS & BARS	
Euro Hotel	3
Junior Bahati Bar	6
New Chamunga	2
New Salama Hotel	1
Rest House Bar	4
Tawakal Hotel	5

0   100 m

Practicalities

Lodwar is an incredibly hot, dusty town most of the year, but for a day or two you may find the rough, frontier atmosphere exhilarating, especially after the faintly parochial air of the Highlands. There's a KCB **bank** with an ATM, a **post office** (Mon–Fri 8am–5pm, Sat 9am–noon) and a number of places to stay. If you're using a mobile phone, note that Lodwar is covered by Celtel, but not by Safaricom. If your vehicle needs looking at after braving the road from Kitale, Sumi Auto Garage comes highly recommended, and is the one used by NGOs.

Buses to Kitale gather in the main street around *New Salama Hotel*, and almost always leave in the evening, around 7–8pm, travelling by night. The one daily bus to Nairobi, run by Daya Coaches, leaves from its office next to the *Euro Hotel* (which is owned by the same proprietor). If you want to travel to Kitale by day, head down in the morning to the roundabout at the eastern end of the main street, where you can flag down a **lorry** heading south. Local lads may also offer to help you find a vehicle for a small tip. **Matatus** for Kalokol, and an occasional one to Kitale, leave from the main stage in the centre of town, near the buses, but Peugeots for Lokichokio have their own stage on the east side of town, opposite the Kobil filling station.

Accommodation

None of the following has hot water as such, but the supply is invariably tepid rather than cold, especially by evening time.

Beer Garden PO Box 19, no phone. Primarily a bar, and at weekends a disco, but has some of the cheapest rooms in town, singles only (will sleep a couple), equipped with mosquito nets and ceiling fans, but non-s/c and with rather grotty bathrooms. Don't bother to stay here on Fri or Sat nights if you

Until very recently, **the Turkana**, the main people of the western shore of the lake, had very little contact with the outside world, or even with the Republic of Kenya. Turkana people did not traditionally wear much in the way of clothing, though the women wear several tiers of beads around their necks and, if married, a metal band too. Turkana men are rarely seen without their *akichalong*, a small wooden headrest, like a stool, which they recline on at any opportunity. Many still wear on their wrists a wide bracelet called an *aberait*, which is in fact a weapon: though usually covered with a guard, the edge of the *aberait* is razor-sharp, and it can be wielded in fights like a blade.

Linguistically, the Turkana are related to the Maa-speaking Samburu and Maasai. Indeed, along the northwest shore of the lake, the people are probably an old mixture of Turkana and Samburu, although, like the Luo (also distantly related by language), the Turkana did not traditionally practise circumcision. They moved east from their old homeland around the present-day borders of Sudan and Uganda in the seventeenth century. The desolate region between the lake and the Ugandan border which they now occupy is barely habitable land, and their daily struggle for existence has profoundly influenced the shape of their society and, inevitably, helped create the funnel into modern Kenya which Lodwar, with its road, has become.

The Turkana are more individualistic than most Kenyan peoples and they show a disregard for the ties of clan and family that must have emerged through repeated famines and wars. Some anthropologists have begun to suggest that loyalty to particular **cattle brands** is a more important indicator of identity than blood or lineage. Although essentially **pastoralists**, always on the move to the next spot of grazing, they do grow crops when they can get seed and when the rains are sufficient. Often the rains fail, notably during the prolonged drought of the early 1980s, which took a terrible toll on children. The situation has eased since then, but life is still very much a matter of day-to-day survival, aided here and there by hand-outs from the UN and other agencies. With characteristic pragmatism, the Turkana have scorned the taboo against fish so prevalent among herders, and **fishing** is a viable option that is increasingly popular.

Turkana **bellicosity** is infamous in Kenya (Turkana migrants to the towns of the south are frequently employed as *askaris*). Relations with their neighbours – especially the Merille to the north of the lake, the Samburu to the south, and the Pokot to the southwest – have often been openly aggressive. British forces were engaged in the gradual conquest of the Turkana – the usual killings, livestock raids and property destruction – and they succeeded, at some cost, in eventually disarming them of their guns in the 1920s. But the Merille, meanwhile, were obtaining arms from Abyssinia's imperial government, and they took advantage of the Turkana's defenceless position. When war was declared by Italian-held Abyssinia in 1940, the British rearmed the Turkana, who swiftly exacted their savage revenge on the Merille. They were later disarmed again. Now, it is the Turkana who are the victims once again: in the far north, heavily armed Toposa raiders from Sudan are thought to have killed almost ten thousand Turkana in recent years.

Violence is no longer in the air down at **Ferguson's Gulf** – though you might see older Turkana men with scars on their arms and chests to indicate who they've killed: females on the left upper arm and chest, males on the right. Turkana directness is unmistakable in all their dealings with *wazungu*. They are, for example, resolute and stubborn bargainers, while offers of relatively large sums for photos often leave them stone cold – not necessarily from any mystical fear of the camera, but because of a shrewd estimation of what the market will stand, and hence, presumably, of their own reputation. Unlike the Maa-speaking warriors, the Turkana rarely pose for photos for a living, although the exceptions are increasing in number.

can't sleep with music, as the rooms adjoin the dancefloor. ❶

Lodwar Lodge PO Box 74 ☎0721/339094. Formerly *Nature Lodge*, and owned by a local politician, this place burnt down but has now risen phoenix-like, revamped with a restaurant, outdoor bar and *bandas*, these last still under construction at time of writing, but due to open soon. ❷

🏃 **Nawoitorong Guesthouse** PO Box 192 ☎054/21208, ✉edfrhp@imul.com. Part of the Turkana Women's Conference Centre, a cooperative set up in 1984 by four women who began baking bread together, it is made of local materials, partly solar-powered, and uses profits to help Turkana women educate themselves and each other. It still bakes its own bread, and serves occasionally excellent food. There are good showers, the non-s/c rooms in the main compound are spotless

and have great mosquito nets, but lack privacy and can be noisy; the three s/c cottages (Ksh1400) are better but more expensive. This is by far the best accommodation in Lodwar (it's open to both sexes), but has the disadvantage of being some way out of town (1km south over the Turkwel bridge, then 1.5km east). B&B; rooms ❶ cottages ❷

Turkana Suburb Lodge PO Box 266 ☎054/21218. Basic, but it's got what you need: decent enough s/c and non-s/c rooms, with ceiling fans and mosquito nets. It's also handy for the Lokichokio stage; the adjoining *hoteli* isn't up to much, however. ❶

Turkwel Lodge PO Box 14 ☎054/21099. The most presentable of the town-centre lodgings, clean s/c rooms with nets and ceiling fans, plus a good bar and restaurant out front. The rooms are reasonably quiet, and there's secure parking. ❷

Eating and drinking

For **food**, *New Salama Hotel*, by the main bus, taxi and matatu stage, serves tasty meat and fish stews, and is a good place to try Lake Turkana tilapia, reputedly the sweetest fish in East Africa. *Turkwel Lodge* also cooks up some good, solid grub, mainly in the form of chicken. Not far from the main stage, *Tawakal Hotel* is new and popular and offers "federation" (a combo of pilau, mince, spaghetti and chapatti) or *aleso* (boiled goat meat with broth). *Euro Hotel*, opposite the Kobil filling station, near the Loki stage, is open round the clock and provides tea, chapattis, *mandaazi* and all the usual staples. For *nyama choma*, try the *Beer Garden*. For bread, or even a meal, you could pop over to *Nawoitorong*, and for general provisions, Naipa **supermarket** stocks a reasonable range. If you need something to keep you awake on an all-night bus journey, *Top Ranking Miraa Base* is right by the stage, a few doors from the *New Salama*.

Drinking in Lodwar is usually done outdoors – *Lodwar Lodge* and the *Beer Garden*, for example, both have bars with open-air seating. *Turkwel Lodge* has seats outdoors but under cover, while *Junior Bahati Bar*, near the Loki stage, has a pool table inside, and drinking *bandas* outside. If you still want to drink indoors, check out the lurid seats and jungly murals at *New Chamunga*, or the *Rest House Bar*, which has comfy chairs, and old and new Kenyan tunes on its sound system. The *Beer Garden* is Lodwar's only **disco**, operating Friday and Saturday nights, with a mixture consisting mainly of Kenyan music and reggae.

Kalokol

Though Ferguson's Gulf (see p.567) is the only easily accessible place to head for on the lakeshore, the village you want initially is called **KALOKOL** (formerly known as Lokwar Kangole). There are several matatus making the trip daily from Lodwar; if you're hitching, try the Kobil station or wait further up along the road.

There's little point in visiting Kalokol for its own sake. It has a surprising amount of hassle for such a small place (600 or so permanent inhabitants), and only one basic **lodging**, *Kalokol Tours Lodge & Hotel* (PO Box 3; ☎0735/467251; ❶), which is very cheap but extremely rundown, with stuffy shacks for rooms, and none too clean. It does, however, have space to pitch a tent (Ksh70) and can also arrange boat trips, though it is perhaps better to enquire with the fishermen on the lakeshore proper, 4km to the east.

△ Turkana men, near Kalokol

While **food** supplies have improved a little with the opening of a few *dukas*, Kalokol doesn't have a lot in this line and it's not a bad idea to bring at least some fruit with you from Kitale or Lodwar. Water supplies, too, are erratic, and iodine or purifying tablets are essential if you intend to drink it. *Kalokol Tours Lodge & Hotel* should be able to rustle up a basic meal for you, or you can try the Somali-run *Loima Hotel*, but don't expect gourmet cuisine.

The dancing stones of Namoratunga

During the one- to two-hour journey to Kalokol, look out for the **standing stones of Namoratunga**, 15km before Kalokol on the right, some 50m off the road. They're easy to miss, being only a small cluster of metre-high cylindrical stones similar to the sacks of foraging sold by the Turkana, with the curious oddity that the Turkana have the habit of balancing small rocks on top of the large stones. Like a miniature Stonehenge, the pillars are a spiritual focus and, usually in December, they're the scene of a major gathering of Turkana clans. The stones pre-date the arrival of the Turkana, but little is known about them, even by the Turkana (the name "namoratunga" is used by them to describe any standing stone site). One theory, that the stones were aligned with the positions of important stars in Eastern Cushitic astronomy and were therefore used to determine the dates of ritual ceremonies, appears to have been discounted. Some people call them "dancing stones", following a legend which had a small tribe of people dancing on the site. When strangers arrived (possibly the Turkana), the dancers pleaded with the visitors not to laugh at them, a plea which they ignored, with the result that the dancers were turned to stone. More plausible reasons for their existence might be the concentration of haematite and copper ore around the site, the smelting of which (for making weapons) may have acquired ritual significance in the past. Uphill from the stones you'll find several raised rock cairns covering ancient graves, some perfectly delineated with larger regular stones. It's fascinating, and all rather mysterious.

A fishy story

In the late 1970s, **Kalokol** acquired a big Norwegian-aided fish-filleting and freezing plant and many Turkana came to the cooperative there looking for a livelihood. Altogether, around 20,000 had homed in on the lake's fishing opportunities by the early 1980s. Many were persuaded to give up their herds, but thousands of animals were driven down to the lakeshore while their owners looked for work, bringing ecological disaster to the area around Kalokol and Lodwar. Firewood gathering and over-grazing were the main causes, coupled with the prolonged drought that afflicted much of sub-Saharan Africa at that time. The fish project was a failure almost from the beginning. The plant's electricity requirements could not possibly be met by the local supply; it ran the cold rooms for just two days. Then the trawler sank. And as these major setbacks were being contemplated, the diversion for irrigation of water from the Omo River in Ethiopia, and the construction of the Turkwel Dam in south Turkana, began to decrease the lake's supply, leaving the Norwegian jetty high and dry several kilometres from the shore. Compounded by plummeting fish stocks, the project was finally abandoned amidst bitter recriminations and accusations of corruption and mismanagement. The joke, if there is one – and a lesson to all NGOs – is that the Norwegians had only considered freezing the fish: as soon as the project was jettisoned, the locals moved in, broke the factory's windows, and embarked on the glaringly obvious solution that had eluded the Europeans – inside the shaded, breezy hulk of the factory, they simply laid out their fish to dry.

The village is especially good for buying **Turkana crafts** and souvenirs: wonderful (and far too big) baskets, rich-smelling, oiled head stools (*akichalong*), ostrich shell necklaces, and a whole array of snuff and tobacco horns made of cowhorn (traditionally) or pieces of plastic piping. When you've had enough, there are matatus back to Lodwar, but don't leave it till too late in the afternoon. Otherwise, you can try your luck hitching – traffic is sparse so a lift is far from guaranteed, though there are sometimes trucks in the mornings and evenings that go all the way through to Kitale.

Ferguson's Gulf

To visit the lake, you might want to pay one of the children in Kalokol to be your guide, though it's easy to find your own way there. Having been dry for much of a decade, the El Niño rains of 1997–98 once again filled **Ferguson's Gulf** though the years since have again seen a decline in the lake's level.

Simply being by the lake fills the time here, with the constantly mutating background of the western shore across the bay, as well as the closer prospect of Turkana fishermen, hundreds of species of birds, and the occasional glimpse of crocodile or hippo on the water surface. From a distance, the activity at the water's edge seems silent since the wind whips the sound away westwards, lending the whole scene a bizarre, dream-like quality. Down on the shore you can talk with the children who follow you everywhere, and who often speak good English. If you make friends, you can be taken looking for snakes (be careful), to see *tembo* brewing (always by women) or, if you're lucky, to a dance. Ordinary teenagers' and children's dances happen several times a week, but are best when there's a full moon: the boys tie cans of stones to their ankles and pretend to ignore the girls' flirting.

Although guests often **swim** in the lake, which is pleasantly warm, the threat of a crocodile attack, while remote, is ever-present and you are advised to stay out of the water. You should also be wary of hippos and, equally, of the dangers of sunstroke and heatstroke in the lake's extreme climate.

The lodge and Longech

It's about 6km through scrub and palm groves from Kalokol to the *Lake Turkana Fishing Lodge* (PO Box 509 Lodwar; no phone; ⑤); after 1km, turn left at the (defunct) Italian fishing project sign and continue for another 3km. From the jetty at the end, you can get a boat to the lodge (Ksh1000–2000 return). It is also possible to walk the last 2km round the bay, though that may change if the water level rises again.

The lodge has been opening and closing sporadically for many years now, and has had several different owners. Perched at the end of a sandy spit, it offers shade, shelter from the fan-heater wind and a beautiful view across the lake, but it caters mostly to weekend visitors who arrive by air, and midweek it's invariably empty. Its **campsite** has moved down to the mainland by the former Italian fishing project (a rotten Ksh500 per person), though with the amount of hassle you can expect from local kids this isn't likely to appeal for very long in any case. Alternatively, people may give you bed space in **LONGECH**, the village that stretches a couple of kilometres down the former shoreline, for a small fee or for a trade of some of your belongings. Fresh or dried fish is usually available, but the only other food is the lodge's expensive set menu.

When you're tired of wandering around Longech, being mobbed by toddlers, watching the fishermen paddling out on their waterlogged rafts, and the pied kingfishers hovering and plunging over the shallows, there are a few active things to do. If you're feeling rich and macho, you can rent **fishing** rods and the lodge's boat and, with luck, land several hundred pounds of Nile perch. By all accounts, though, the perch don't play properly and almost line up to be landed. Fishermen rate the tiger fish as more of a fighter. The lodge will cook your catch for you and you can add your mark to the fishermen's tales on the walls of the bar.

Central Island National Park

Daily 6am–7pm; $15, children $5. Warden: PO Box 9 Lodwar.

A trip to **Central Island National Park** is highly recommended. This is one of two island national parks in the lake (the other is the less accessible South Island). Central Island is a unique triple volcano poking gauntly out of the water. The island covers just five square kilometres, most of which is taken up by two crater lakes (a third has dried up) hidden behind its rocky shores. One of the lakes is the only known habitat of an ancient species of tilapia, a reminder of the time when Lake Turkana was connected to the Nile. The island is the nesting ground for big colonies of water birds but, like some African Galapagos, it really belongs to the reptiles. Crocodiles breed here in the largest concentration in Africa, and at the right time of year (usually April–May) you can witness the newly hatched croc-lets breaking out of the nests and sprinting with loud squeaks down to the crater lake where they'll pass their first season. The vegetation is scant, but some of the sheltered lees are overgrown with thick grass and bushes for a short period each year, and the nests are dug beneath this foliage.

Boat trips are expensive: expect to pay Ksh7000–10,000 for the round trip, depending on your bargaining skills. The *Lake Turkana Fishing Lodge* charges Ksh8000 for a six- to eight-passenger boat, but you may be able to get a better price from the lakeshore fishermen. The park warden or one of his rangers normally accompanies you on each visit. If you find a boat, the best plan is to go immediately rather than make arrangements in advance. Do be sure, however, that it is thoroughly lake-worthy and that the crew know what they are doing; vicious squalls can blow up fast and it's at least 10km to the island. Taking your own compass might be a good idea.

Boats across the lake

You may also be able to **rent a boat** with a helmsman at Ferguson's Gulf or Eliye Springs (see below) for a trip to the remote archeological sites of **Koobi Fora** and **Sibiloi National Park** (see p.585), 48km across the lake. Prices start at Ksh15,000–20,000; bargain hard, and check the state of the boat before you go

Eliye Springs

Eliye Springs, 66km south of Lodwar, used to be *the* place for travellers on the lakeshore and still attracts the occasional overland truck and self-sufficient 4WD weekenders. **Getting there** and back is the main problem. Failing a lift in Lodwar (where you can wait for days), you might **rent a vehicle** for the round trip, at around Ksh5000 with driver (4WD advisable as the trail gets very sandy towards the end). However, if you'll be staying overnight or longer at Eliye Springs, don't count on the vehicle returning to pick you up, and it's a long walk back.

Alternatively, you could **walk** from Ferguson's Gulf or Kalokol: just follow the coast for 55 or so sweltering kilometres, and take plenty of drinking water. There are crocodiles along the shore for much of the way, which makes a night walk ill-advised. Another possible route from Kalokol is a little shorter (45–50km); it cuts across the desert inland and this *is* really only feasible overnight, preferably by moonlight, due to the heat. A guide will cost around Ksh2000, and it's quite an adventure – bring plenty of water. The only other possibility is to **rent a boat** from Ferguson's Gulf for up to Ksh2000 per hour; the boat seats four, and the trip takes four to six hours. If you're only going one way, you will still have to pay for the return leg regardless.

Eliye Springs itself readily compensates for the hassles of the journey – a paradisal place with rustling doum palms watered by hot springs, with gorgeous views, and nothing to do except lounge about and swat flies. *Eliye Springs Bandas* (PO Box 15 Lodwar; no phone), has rooms and *bandas*, all completely bare and unfurnished. You can sleep in them or pitch a tent for Ksh250 per person. There is water, but you'll need to bring your own food.

On the lakeshore north of Eliye Springs, the very upmarket *Lobolo Camp* (reservations through Bush Homes, p.63; ◉) organizes excursions up the Omo River, and across to Koobi Fora. These, and indeed the camp, are often booked up, so reserve well in advance if you want to stay here. Most guests fly in by private charter.

Onwards from Lodwar

A good paved road allows fast travel from Lodwar up to Lokichokio, passing the refugee centre at **Kakuma**, 144km northwest of Lodwar. This was set up for people fleeing the civil war in southern Sudan, but with the end of that conflict, refugees are now beginning to trickle back, even before machinery has been set up to facilitate their return. Kakuma has food, basic lodging and (usually) fuel, but nothing to warrant a stopover.

Lokichokio and Sudan

The border town of **Lokichokio** (Lokichoggio, often called just **Loki**) is an unremittingly dry and rocky place, and even more of a cowboy town than Lodwar, with an eclectic mix of rough international types, businessmen, tribal Turkana, haggard relief workers, doctors, pilots, nurses and missionaries. During the civil war in southern Sudan, it was the main UN aid centre for that region, and remains the major supply centre for NGOs within Sudan, with hundreds of personnel, Kenya's busiest airfield, and numerous bars for tired relief workers.

Loki sprawls along two main roads: the Juba road, which heads north towards Sudan, and the Lopiding road, which heads east. The **matatu stage** is at the junction where these two roads meet the Lodwar road, with the **airport** on the west side of town (accessed on a road branching off the Lodwar road 200m south of the matatu stage). Other than by plane – there are three daily flights between Loki and Nairobi, operated by ALS and East African Safari Air – the best way to and from Lokichokio is by Peugeot or shared taxi; these do the run from Lodwar in two and a half hours, compared with four or five hours by Nissan or by bus. **Getting around** Loki is best accomplished by taxi.

Things tend to be expensive in Lokichokio. The cheapest **accommodation** is at *Link Hotel*, on the Juba road at the northern end of town (☎0724/916232; ②). Favoured by Sudanese (and a good place to buy or sell Sudanese dinars), it has rather poky non-s/c *bandas* on offer. Slightly better, the *Sunbird Guesthouse* (☎0735/199217; ②), also on the Juba road, but not so far up, has clean and quite large non-s/c rooms with nets and ceiling fans. *ACHA Camp* is run by the African Centre for Human Advocacy, and located off the Lopiding road, turning left at a camp, while *748*, run by the air service (PO Box 62448 Nairobi 00200; ☎0720/675704, ⑩www.achacentre.org; FB ⑤) has both s/c and non-s/c rooms, and throws in three meals a day. Also offering meals with their accommodation, as well as swimming pools and free laundry are two places favoured by NGO workers and pilots, and full of well-fed *wazungu*: *Kate Camp*, on the Lopiding road (PO Box 16; ☎054/32077; FB ⑤), where the ordinary *tukuls* (huts) aren't that great, but the round *tukuls*, for Ksh700 bucks more, are bright and spacious with ceiling fans; and *Trackmark*, behind *Kate Camp* (follow the road round at *748*; PO Box 44077 Nairobi 00100; ☎054/32245, ⑥lokicamp@yahoo.com; FB ⑤), with s/c and non-s/c tents, which are better than they sound, and s/c *tukuls*, some with a/c.

For **food**, *Makuti Bar*, opposite *Sunbird Guesthouse*, is a great spot for chicken and *nyama choma*, not to mention cold beer. *Links Hotel* has Sudanese and Ethiopian dishes. Alternatives include the *Sunbird* itself, and *Prajos Pub*, directly opposite, a few doors north of *Makuti Bar*. *Kate Club* offers Ksh550 buffets, or a "special" dinner for Ksh700, and also has a bar, as does *Trackmark*. For nightlife, your best bet is *Webbs Nightclub*, just south of *Makuti Bar* on the Juba road.

The **post office** is north of town, off the Juba road and opposite immigration. There's a KCB **bank** with ATM in the UN (Afex A) compound off the Lopiding road, and a forex bureau at *Kate Camp* (Mon–Fri 8am–6.30pm, Sat & Sun 8.30am–6.30pm), which buys and sells dollars, sterling and euros, as well as Sudanese dinars, Ugandan shillings and South African rand, but not cheques travellers'. **Internet access** is available at *Trackmark*, but the offices of the **airlines** – East African Safari Air (c/o Bunson Travel) and ALS – are at *Kate Camp*.

If you're **flying to Nairobi**, it may be possible to get a place on a UN or NGO flight (they usually fly in full and leave empty) – talk to the Kenya Airports Authority people at the airport to enquire about this. It may also be possible, if you have the relevant paperwork, to get on a UN flight to **Juba**; enquire about this with the UN coordinators at their compound. The Sudan Relief and Rehabilitation Council (SRRC), next to *Link Hotel* on the Juba road, will not issue visas to enter New Sudan, and will direct you to its office in Nairobi, but this may change, and you *may* be able to get an entry permit for New Sudan at the Sudanese border post at **Nadafal**. If you enter or leave Kenya at Nadafal, you must go and get stamped in or out at the immigration office in

Lokichokio, which is west of the Juba road at the northern end of town (daily 6am–6.30pm). If you are coming from Sudan without a Kenyan visa, it can issue you with one. The road to **Juba** is currently being graded with *murram*, but at the time of writing, there was regular transport only as far as **Torit**, beyond which the road is still being de-mined.

Maralal, the Mathews and East Turkana

From Nairobi, the journey up to **Loiyangalani** en route to Turkana is a good deal shorter than to the west shore, but even full tilt on the rough roads it's a full two-day **drive**. The roads are incredibly rough for most of the way and to be sure of arriving you'll need 4WD (a long-wheel-base Suzuki jeep is ideal) and spare petrol. Even then, if you go during the rainy season, you could be held up for 24 hours or more at several points.

The obvious solution is a **camping safari**, though, as with any group travel, this has its limitations. Still, a week isn't long enough for irritations to detract from the experience and most people thoroughly enjoy these trips, coming back loaded with amazing souvenirs and photographs, and stories of weird and wonderful encounters. A major drawback is the brevity of organized trips and the fact that they therefore run to a rough timetable. The best company is Gametrackers, which uses Bedford Lorries (or land cruisers if the group size is small). Its weekly round trips (departing Fridays) via the Chalbi Desert are unique and highly recommended.

If your budget is tight, but you have time and a flexible attitude and don't want a spoon-fed adventure, the maximum exposure to Turkana and the north comes from travelling completely independently and *without* your own vehicle. This may require some patience, as there is little **public transport**, and you will probably have to hitch a ride up from **Maralal**.

The routes to Maralal

Three roads lead to **Maralal**, the Samburu district town at the end of the first stage of the trip north.

Nyahururu to Maralal: C77

The easiest route, the **C77**, rolls up from Nyahururu via Rumuruti: tarmac to Rumuruti, and then poor-quality *murram* to Maralal (it's feasible without 4WD, but not if you value the health of your car). Each morning at least one **bus** and three or four *matatus* leave Nyahururu. **Rumuruti** (onomatopoeic Maa for "mosquito") is hardly noticeable any more and merely marks the end of the paved road, but this former Maasai stronghold of western Laikipia was settled by British soldiers after World War I and many of their ranches still exist (see p.202 for a full account of Laikipia). However, there's some very good game country in the vicinity, so you might want to **stay**. In Rumuruti itself, the *Jojas Hotel* and the *Laikipia Club* have low-priced s/c rooms (●), while there are good, cheap eats at the *Buffalo Village Inn*. Alternatively, head 20km north to *Bobong Campsite* (see below), or, if money's no object, *Loisaba Wilderness* on the Colcheccio ranch at the edge of the Laikipia Plateau (PO Box 1348 Nanyuki; ☎062/31072, ⊛www.loisaba.com; FB from $780; ●). It comprises a lodge with seven luxurious en-suite rooms, two self-contained houses (each with its own set of staff) and, best of all, two sets of "star beds" for a night out in the open. Activities include camel rides, mountain biking, river rafting and a spa.

The road follows the **Ewaso Ng'iro River** (see the Laikipia map on p.203) for some way beyond Rumuruti into Samburu-land proper, where the two other routes described below join it. Passing *Bobong Campsite* on a bluff to the left (Ol Maisor cattle ranch; PO Box 5, Rumuruti; ☎062/32718; camping Ksh250 per person, *bandas* ❷), which boasts fantastic views over the Ewaso Ng'iro plains, a small pool and a range of activities from tubing to bird walks, the road climbs, broad and stony, towards Maralal's plateau. At **Suguta Marmar** (the boundary between Central Province and the Rift Valley), 20km south of Maralal, there's little more than a livestock auction yard, and a basic checkpoint, plus a few cheap *hotelis*.

Lake Baringo to Maralal: C77

The second route is the lonely but well-constructed *murram* road from the **Rift Valley**, which in its earlier stages has breathtaking views back over Lake Baringo and some fascinating Pokot villages on the way. It's only a D road, but don't be discouraged for that reason from driving it (though there have been occasional hold-ups at gunpoint along the way). There are no buses, and you'd be lucky to find a *matatu*. For the best chances of **hitching** success, ask at *Lake Baringo Club* or wait at the Kampi ya Samaki junction (see p.268).

Isiolo to Maralal: A2 and C79/C78

The maddeningly corrugated **A2** comes up from **Isiolo** past Archer's Post (p.591), then heads off left as the **C79** past the turn for Wamba, where it becomes the **C78**. Despite a continuation of the A2's washboard surface, the C79/78 has everything to recommend it scenically, including some magnificent desert buttes and sweeping views over the valley of the Ewaso Ng'iro River, which flows on through Samburu. The garishly decorated "Babie Coach" runs this route (Isiolo–Maralal), leaving one or the other town every other day, usually packed full of Samburu warriors. Matatus run daily in both directions. Your best chances of **hitching** a ride are at the Samburu lodges inside the national reserve (see p.407), or at the Isiolo police barrier.

Maralal

Some of the Laikipia settlers would have dearly liked to set themselves up around the cool, conifer-draped highlands of **MARALAL**. But even before British administrators made this the district capital, Maralal had been a spiritual focus for the **Samburu people** and, despite some dithering, the colonial administrators didn't accede to the settlers' demands.

Maralal is a peculiar town, spread with exaggerated spaciousness around a depression in the hills. Samburu people crowd its dusty streets, with a brilliant

Maralal International Camel Derby

The Maralal International **Camel Derby** provides for a strange weekend during the second week of August. Anyone may enter, or just spectate, as dozens of competitors from East Africa, Europe, China, Australia and South Africa battle it out over 12-kilometre amateur and 42-kilometre semi-professional stages. Entry fees are very reasonable: amateur class, including camel and handler, is Ksh3000; professional Ksh2500. There is also a tie-in with the Kenya Amateur Cycling Association which organizes mountain-bike and amateur cycling races. The event is based at the *Yare Safari Club* (see p.575), where you can get more details.

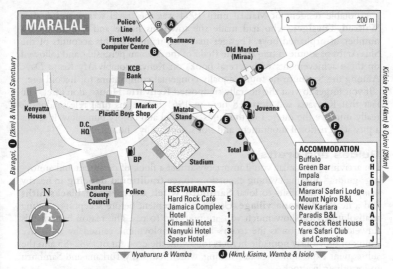

MARALAL

- Police Line
- @ **A**
- First World Computer Centre **B**
- Pharmacy
- Old Market (Miraa) **C**
- KCB Bank
- **D**
- Market
- Plastic Boys Shop
- Matatu Stand
- **1**
- Jovenna
- **2**
- **4**
- **F**
- **G**
- Kenyatta House
- D.C. HQ
- **3**
- **E**
- **5**
- Total **H**
- BP
- Stadium
- Samburu County Council
- Police

0   200 m

Baragoi, (2km) & National Sanctuary

Kirisia Forest (4km) & Opiroi (35km)

N

ACCOMMODATION

Buffalo	C
Green Bar	H
Impala	E
Jamaru	D
Mararal Safari Lodge	I
Mount Ngiro B&L	F
New Kariara	G
Paradis B&L	A
Peacock Rest House	B
Yare Safari Club and Campsite	J

RESTAURANTS

Hard Rock Café	5
Jamaica Complex Hotel	1
Kimaniki Hotel	4
Nanyuki Hotel	3
Spear Hotel	2

Nyahururu & Wamba   **J** (4km), Kisima, Wamba & Isiolo

collage of skins, blankets, beads, brass, and iron, and a special smell, too – of sour milk, fat, and cattle. The main hotel is called *Buffalo Hotel*. The place sets itself up for Wild West comparisons and the climate is appropriate – unbelievably dusty, almost always windy and, at 2220m, sharp enough at night for log fires and braziers. All it needs is wolves – and even there hyenas fill the role.

Of course, the regular arrival of safari lorries means that Maralal has plenty of persistent souvenir salesmen. Yet despite this, it's a good place to get to know the Samburu and especially worthwhile on Christian holidays. Many Samburu around the town have become Catholics and the colourful procession on Palm Sunday – mostly thousands of women, waving branches and leaves – is riveting.

△ Camels lined up for the Derby, Maralal

A notable resident of Maralal until 1994 was the travel writer and Arabist **Wilfred Thesiger**, who had made the town his home and had adopted a number of orphaned boys. Thesiger made his name with his accounts of the Shia Arabs of southern Iraq and the Bedu of the Arabian peninsula, and followed up these achievements with several books on Kenya, notably *My Kenya Days*. Among the Samburu he found equally congenial companions for his old age.

If you forget to visit the liberally signposted **Kenyatta House**, don't fret. The fact that Kenyatta was detained here in 1961 before his final release doesn't really improve the interest of this unexceptional and empty bungalow. It seems a pity it's a national monument and not some family's home.

Guides and crafts

On arriving in Maralal, you'll invariably attract a flock of persistent and annoying "guides" offering evening excursions to see **traditional dancing** in nearby *manyattas*, or else visits to local **Samburu witch doctors** and **blacksmiths** and a nearby **Turkana village**. Use your judgement before accepting, making it absolutely clear how much you are prepared to pay. The reason behind this unwelcome attention is the town's high unemployment, caused by a massive influx of previously nomadic herders following the drought of 1982–85 and the subsequent explosion in cattle-rustling, which led many Turkana and Samburu to lose their livestock.

An attempt to tame the guides by organizing them into disciplined groups is the **Plastic Boys' Co-operative Self-Help Group**, so named after the street children who used to make dolls and trinkets using plastic bags and cartons. They have now progressed, under the guidance of the Kenya Wildlife Service and various NGOs, to carving and selling woodcrafts, spears and other touristy items. Their shop is in the market, and they should be able to sort you out with a guide, should you need one. A rival set-up is the **Home Boys' Co-operative**, a self-styled group of unemployed, local young men selling jewellery and other handicrafts, also with its own shop in the market.

Maralal National Sanctuary and Safari Lodge

Maralal Safari Lodge (PO Box 70, ☎065/62060; bookings second floor, Windsor House, Muindi Mbingu St, PO Box 15020 Nairobi, ☎020/211124, ℱ211125), signposted 2–3km out of town on the Lake Turkana road, is comfortable, under-subscribed and very attractive with its huge wooden chalet-style rooms (❼). Your patronage is welcome in the bar and restaurant, and you can sit on the terrace to watch the animals from the surrounding **Maralal National Sanctuary** and Yamo Forest (zebra, baboon, impala, eland, warthog, buffalo and hyena) filing up the hill to the concrete water hole a few metres away.

Practicalities

If you're **continuing north**, note that Maralal is the last place where you can rely on supplies of **petrol**, and **change money** – at the smart KCB (Mon–Fri 8.30–2.30am, Sat 8.30–10.30am), at *Yare Safari Club* (also the representative for KATO and KTF for the area and able to offer up-to-date information on security), or at the *Maralal Safari Lodge* (where they don't have much cash). If **beer** is important to you (and it can assume great importance up in the desert), then stock up on that too before heading off. **Internet** access is available at the First World Computer Centre next door to the pharmacy.

If you don't have your own vehicle, you may find a source of **rides onward** at *Yare* safari club(see opposite) or the lodge, but you're more likely to catch vehicles by staying in town and spreading the word at the petrol stations. Let it be known you are willing to travel in the back of a lorry – many people will assume you're not. Supply lorries do go up to Loiyangalani and your chances of scoring a lift – eventually, even if it takes you a week – are good. Irregular rides, again with transport vehicles, is the way to get to Baragoi, and to Nyahururu and Isiolo. Nakuru is served daily by Nyayo Bus. There are early morning matatus for Nairobi, otherwise catch one to Rumuruti or Nyahururu, and change there. There are also twice-daily buses to Nairobi via Nyahururu.

Accommodation

Setting aside the excellent lodge, Maralal has a large number of **cheap lodgings**, the more acceptable of which are listed here; the mid-range *Yare Safari Club* also has **camping** facilities.

Buffalo Hotel PO Box 28 ☎065/62028. The main travellers' haunt, decent, but more expensive than usual and not for light sleepers. ❶

Green Bar PO Box 7. Friendly with a decent restaurant. ❶

Impala Hotel PO Box 142 ☎065/63292. Clean, friendly and basic. Rooms have shared bathroom (with hot showers) . ❶

Jamaru Hotel PO Box 245 ☎065/62215. Maralal's largest; rather spartan but with a good, busy restaurant, and some s/c rooms too. ❷

Mt Ngiro B&L PO Box 11 ☎065/62289. Decent (if a little grubby) rooms with shared bathrooms. ❶

New Kariara Hotel PO Box 68. The cheapest and best in town, this is also Maralal's only two-storey hotel. It has basic but clean rooms, festooned with bougainvillea, all with mosquito nets; bring your own padlock. Get a room on top – on a good morning you can see Mount Kenya. ❶

Paradis B&L PO Box 193 ☎065/62297. Another local joint, its bar is open till midnight and frequented by Samburu and Turkana tribesmen. Cheap and reasonable. ❶

Peacock Rest House PO Box 76 ☎065/62068. Its singles and doubles are not s/c, but the place is clean and has hot water. ❶

Yare Safari Club and Campsite PO Box 281 Maralal ☎065/62295; in Nairobi ☎ & ☎020/214099, ✉yare@africaonline.co.ke. Just over 4km down the Isiolo road, beyond Wilfred Thesiger's old home, *Yare* is Maralal's main tourist centre, with some beautiful thatched *bandas*, a pleasant campsite (Ksh200 per person; under Ksh100 for tent rental), a well-stocked bar, and a restaurant (order well in advance, as it can take the kitchen up to two hours to prepare a dish). There's a resident Samburu blacksmith who plays superb Samburu guitar and has a small crafts stall selling jewellery, fertility dolls and handmade spears. Activities on offer include camel rides ($3 per hour including handler), guided walks ($25 per day), and mountain-biking treks to Lake Turkana or other parts of Samburu District. It also runs seven-day camel safaris from Nairobi (from $510 per person). B&B ❸

Eating, drinking and entertainment

Maralal boasts a surprising number of good **restaurants** as well as the usual run of cheap and filling eating houses. The popular *Spear Hotel* is one of the best, with a great atmosphere, widescreen TV, breakfasts, curries and samosas. *Maralal Safari Hotel* serves *githeri* to Samburu warriors with lolloping reggae in the background. *Jamaica Complex Hotel* is big on *nyama choma*, whilst the *Nanyuki Hotel*, by the matatu stand, has huge portions of Swahili food (*mchele* stew a speciality) at very low prices. *Kimaniki Hotel* is a busy bar and disco, and the excellent *Hard Rock Café* (no relation to the international chain) is a great little place with cheap snacks and friendly owners with plenty of advice on travel in the region.

A night spent in Maralal's numerous **bars** can be exhilarating, infuriating, dangerous or just plain daft. *Buffalo Hotel* used to be the best of the lot, but most of the colourful ex-pats in the area have gone, and you are now more likely to encounter wheedling con merchants and a host of bizarre local nutcases. There's a **cinema** opposite the *Starlight Bar* which usually gets in some genuine celluloid on Saturdays. The bar itself is a straightforward drinking den full of broken stools and fallen pride.

Wamba and the Mathews Range (Lenkiyio Hills)

In terms of the vastness of the north, the **Mathews Range** is virtually on Maralal's doorstep. The range, most of which is a forest reserve, is impressively wild hill country, with Mathew Peak (Ol Doinyo Lenkiyio) rising to 2375m. Lower down, the mountains are heavily cloaked in forest and thick bush; unusual vegetation includes "living fossil" cycad plants, giant cedars and podocarpus. Among the animal life, you can look out for (but shouldn't expect to meet) small numbers of black rhinos – every one of them known and tracked, for its own safety, by forest guards and their Samburu staff – and really outstanding butterflies. This is first-rate walking and exploring country for hardy travellers, but you need to be fully self-sufficient, which includes having all your food requirements.

First target is **WAMBA**, a one-street town 5km off the C78/79 highway, roughly midway between Maralal and Isiolo. You can get the odd matatu here from Maralal, or use the Babie Coach which passes by the Wamba turning just after midday (heading out from Maralal one day, coming back from Isiolo the next). Wamba's main focus is its large, modern Catholic hospital outside town. *Saudia Lodge* (●), in town, is pretty well the only **B&L**, with clean, pleasant and very cheap rooms. There are a few *dukas*, though they have no fuel and little in the way of fresh food, only basic fruit or veg. You might try *Imani Bar & Restaurant,* which serves the usual limited range of stews and a reasonable *githeri.*

The big mountain you can see outside town (9km to the peak as the crow flies) is **Warges**. Guides from Wamba will take you up there, though they'll stress how full of wild animals it is and how much their lives (not yours of course) are at risk. If you have a serious interest in witchcraft, one of Kenya's most respected **witch doctors** lives in the shadow of the mountain. Forget the town guide – he is resolutely *not* a tourist attraction. Instead, make discreet enquiries with the Kenya Wildlife Service rangers who regularly pass through Wamba, or else, if your Maa is good enough, with one of the young Samburu *morani*, but make sure you are accompanied by someone who really knows the place.

Kitich Camp and campsite

The main route from Wamba is towards the expensive bush-luxury *Kitich Camp* and the nearby KWS station campsite. If you're four-wheel-driving, you basically set off towards Barsaloi (Parsaloi) along a rough road that commences just half a kilometre along the Wamba access road. From here you drive 15km, then turn right and do a further 17km to **Ngilai** (follow the yellow stones). Some 6km further, you fork left to ford the **Ngeng River**. With the mountains looming all around, this is the way into the heart of the Mathews; the campsite is a couple of kilometres up the track on the other side, and *Kitich Camp* some 4km further north. Note that there's no fuel along the way and normally none for sale at Kitich.

If you're on foot, find a guide in Wamba and set off cross-country, direct to Ngilai, crossing several *luggas*, and seeing almost nobody on the way. The distance is about 30km and an exhausting day's walk; double-check in Wamba whether the site is still open. Ngilai has a Lutheran mission (2km out of the centre to the north) and a single shop, which may put you up for the night if you can't make the final 8km to the campsite before nightfall.

Once there, the **KWS campsite** is pleasant and shady, with showers and toilet, and water available from the nearby pools. Note that there is no food available at the campsite and, while you can go angling in the river, there's a limit to how much catfish a person can stand. Unfortunately, **Kitich Camp** (bookings through Bush Homes of East Africa; p.63), nestled unobtrusively on the river bank beneath towering giant figs, doesn't go out of its way to welcome travellers, and a night here – at around $600 – is exceptionally expensive.

If you want to walk any distance, you're strongly advised to take a guide, either from the camp or from the campsite (where they'll seek you out if you're camping). There are some fine **excursions**, including short walks up the valley to wonderful, deep, rock pools where you can swim. The area around the Ngeng Valley is thick with wildlife. There are elephants everywhere, buffaloes, hyenas, leopards and plenty of more innocuous game. You really have to watch yourself, especially if you go down near the river. It's a lot of fun, but take care.

North from Maralal: into Samburu-land

The first stretch of the road **north from Maralal** climbs higher into the **podocarpus forests** of the national sanctuary, before dropping down across the Lopet Plateau to the Elbarta Plains, 15km east of the scorching Suguta Valley. The northern boundary of the sanctuary has been scarred by climatic changes and the wholesale burning of much of its valley sides, presumably to make way for cattle pasture. Other theories posit the local administration police ("Home Guard"), or Kenya Police Reserves (heavily armed Samburu herders) as responsible, suggesting that they remove the natural cover which facilitates the **cattle-rustling** raids that have become endemic between the Samburu and their northern Turkana neighbours. The raids come to a head at the end of the year and during the dry months of January and February, as Samburu herders take their livestock up north towards Baragoi on the Samburu–Turkana border. Once in the Suguta Valley, stolen cattle are difficult to retrieve due to the valley's exceptionally high temperatures (up to 60°C), lack of water and the rough terrain.

Twenty kilometres from Maralal, a detour to the left takes you through the village of **Poror**, past a large wheat-farming project and, after 6km, to the dramatic scimitar edge of the **Losiolo Escarpment**. There is a charge of Ksh100 per person to enter the area; Ksh200–400, depending on your bargaining skills, to camp. The Rift Valley is, by its nature, bordered from end to end by vertiginous escarpments and each one seems more impressive than the last. But Losiolo is not just an escarpment, it's a colossal amphitheatre dropping down to Suguta Valley, 2000m below. Try to get here very early in the morning. From Poror, the road north is increasingly rough and hot as it drops down through the Samburu Hills on to the Lopet plateau. Settlements from here on are few but evenly scattered. The first is **Morijo**, which has some basic *chai* kiosks, one or two Somali-run *dukas*, a mission and a police station. **Marti**, 20km further north, is much the same.

Baragoi

Sitting 37km north of Marti is **BARAGOI**, in the heart of the barren Elbarta Plains, watered only occasionally by run-off from the Samburu Hills and Ndoto Mountains. The river which skirts the town is dry for much of the year, and in times of drought the pits which are dug into it by women fetching water can reach depths of over 6m. It's a blistering, dusty and unforgiving land, dotted here and there with sun-bleached bones and populated only by red-robed semi-nomadic herders armed with spears or bows and arrows to protect their cattle, goats and camels against the endemic rustlers (*ngorokos*).

First settled in the 1930s, Baragoi retains its original function as the region's major livestock market, attracting both Samburu and Turkana for whom the

The Samburu

The **Samburu** are historically close to the Maasai. Their languages are nearly the same (both Maa) and culturally they are virtually indistinguishable to an outsider. Both came from the region around present-day northwest Turkana in the seventeenth century. The Samburu turned east, establishing themselves in the mountain pastures and spreading across to the plains; the Maasai continued south.

Improvements in health and in veterinary care over the last century have swelled the Samburu population and the size of their herds. Many in the driest areas of their range in the northeast have turned to camel herding as a better insurance against drought than cattle. Since livestock is the basis of relations between in-laws (through the giving of "bridewealth" from the husband to his wife's family), having camel herds has disrupted patterns of marriage and initiation into new generations because camel herds increase more slowly than cattle herds. Memories, recording every transaction over successive generations, are phenomenal (the Samburu have only just begun to acquire writing).

The Samburu age-set system, like many others in Africa, is a complicated arrangement to which a number of anthropologists have devoted lifetimes of investigation. Essentially it's a gerontocracy (rule by old men) and the elders are assured, by the system they manipulate, of having the first choice of young women to marry. The promiscuous and jingoistic – but, by Samburu reckoning, still juvenile – warriors are forced to wait, usually until their thirties, before initiation into elderhood, marriage and children bring them a measure of real respect. In turn, they perpetuate the system on their own sons, who have everything to gain by falling in line and much to lose if they withdraw their stake in the tradition, perhaps by going to Nairobi or the coast to look for work. And the reality on the ground is all about twice as confusing as it sounds on paper.

For women the situation is very different. They are married at 15 or 16, immediately after their clitoridectomy and before they have much chance to rebel. But they may continue affairs with their *morani* boyfriends, the unmarried juniors of their new, much older husbands. This polygamy in itself seems to be an important motivating force for the whole generation system. For the warriors and their girlfriends, there's a special young people's language – a vocabulary of conspiratorial songs and idioms – which has to be modified with the initiation of every age-set, so that it's kept secret from the elders.

This highly intricate system is now beginning to collapse in many areas, with a widespread disruption of pre-colonial ways; even the circumcision initiation of boys to warriorhood is less of a mass ceremony. While herds are still the principal criterion of wealth, people in some areas are turning to agriculture. After the rains you can see planting holes at the roadside in certain places, with corn the main crop. There are enormous problems for such initiatives, especially when there's no aid or government support, but they do show that the standard stereotypes don't always fit. As for the *morani* warriors, opportunities for cattle-raiding and lion-killing have diminished with more efficient policing of their territories, although there are still frequent clashes with the Turkana in the north of Samburu-land. For some, tourist hunting has taken over. You can even see *morani* in full rig striding past the hotels on the Indian Ocean beaches.

town also marks the invisible boundary between their respective grazing lands. Yet, things have changed a lot over the last few years. A construction boom has spawned dozens of one-storey cinder-block buildings in which half a dozen new hotels, numerous bars and restaurants have taken root. A clue to this sudden expansion lies in the name of a bar at the north end of the village – *Bosnia Wines & Spirits*. Shortly after the UN resolved to send peacekeepers to former Yugoslavia, a 900-strong Kenyan battalion was despatched to help patrol a ceasefire line around the self-proclaimed (now defunct) Serbian Republic of Krajina. News of the detachment spread quickly, particularly of the astronomical sums to be made serving in UNPROFOR (soldiers were paid up to $1200 a month, compared with the average Kenyan monthly wage of around $70). Samburu warriors from around Baragoi and Lesriken, 25km east, were quick to enlist for the second and third missions to Bosnia, the last of which returned in 1994.

The Bosnian experience has not been without its problems. For some, sudden wealth has led to alcoholism as hard spirits have become affordable, and even cocaine abuse, and on arriving in Baragoi you may be assailed by various madmen and "guides" who missed out on their brothers' good fortunes. Unpleasant though the reception can be, weather the storm (the locals will help you out of any serious trouble) and you'll find that Baragoi is a fascinating place, well worth a day or two of anyone's time.

The livestock market

Down off Bosnia Street to the northwest of town is the **livestock market**. It's a gentle, unhurried affair where old men with gnarled hands and ostrich plumes in their hair play *ngiles* (*mbau*) with stones and seeds on "boards" carved out of the bone-dry earth as they wait for business to arrive. Here, Samburu deal with Rendille and Turkana, some of whom may have spent up to seven days walking their livestock south from the lake. In turn the Samburu, and sometimes Turkana, trek southeastward for five or six days to reach Isiolo where, with luck, they resell their animals at a profit.

If the herder is of **courting** age (Samburu *moran*; Turkana *lmoli*), Isiolo is also where he buys the beads, necklaces and bangles with which to woo his bride. Once back home, he will not only present her with these gifts, but mime and sing the attributes of the animals which will provide him and his family with their means of survival. For these semi-nomads, animals are the source of all wealth, and the young herder must represent them favourably to attract the attention and confidence of a bride. To this end, he selects a single castrated bull, camel or goat which he then mimics, indicating with his hands and gestures its size, colour, the shape of its horns, even its temperament. There's a comical side to all this, too, for even the poorest herder, whose beast may only be a goat with lopsided horns, must dance to attract a spouse and does this by raising a few smiles with a self-deprecating parody of his goat. Dances are held almost nightly in the *manyattas* on the outskirts of town, wild and hugely enjoyable events at which you are bound to be made welcome. Cameras, of course, are generally not acceptable. Ask around at the market or else try one of the *manyattas* behind the primary school.

Practicalities

There are no official **money-changing** facilities in town, but there is a **post office** (Mon–Fri 8am–5pm) and decent **car mechanic** (Dalfer Welders, opposite the post office). Emergency **petrol supplies** can be had, at a price, from Mount Ngiro Supplies. There's been talk for years of a new Bosnia-financed petrol station at the head of Bosnia Street, but nothing substantial as yet.

As at Maralal, you have to line up a lift with supply lorries, mission jeeps and the like if you want to head on, either north or south. The police station on the north side of town is helpful, but be prepared to wait for several days.

The basic but clean *New Highbury Pub and Lodging* (PO Box 37; ●) is the best place to **stay**. It has a decent **restaurant** and bar, but better is *Joy Cafe* at the south end of the main drag, a cheerful place, with good snacks and cold beers.

South Horr and Kurungu Camp

Baragoi marks the end of the forbidding Elbarta plains, as the road now climbs into ravine and mountain country, fantastically green if there's been rain. Some 30km from Baragoi, a track to the left towards Nyiru, signed by a red gas cylinder, leads to Desert Rose Camel Safaris (p.151), which organizes luxury camel treks of six days or more in the surrounding *luggas* and hills and up to Lake Turkana, with vehicle back-up and two nights at its *Desert Rose Lodge* (FB ●).

There's a positive jungle all year round at the oasis village of **SOUTH HORR** (*horr* means "flowing water"), wedged tightly between the Nyiru and Ol Doinyo Mara mountains. With its pleasantly somnolent atmosphere, ample shade and relaxed herders lounging under the trees, it's a great place to bunk down for a night or three, and making friends is easy despite the language barrier. There are a few cheap *hotelis* and cold drinks at *Arsenal Inn*, but only rarely beer. If you stay the night, you've a choice of half a dozen basic **B&Ls** (all ●). There's good, dirt-cheap **camping** at the *Forest Department Campsite*, located up a rough trail to the left of the road a kilometre before South Horr. Facilities consist of long-drops, an *askari*, and a river for drinking water, bathing and washing the dust out of your clothes. This site, just a short walk from South Horr village where most vehicles stop, is a good base for meeting up with supply or mission vehicles in hopes of a lift north.

Well worth a visit in the village itself is SALTLICK (Semi-Arid Lands Training and Livestock Improvement Centres Kenya), which concerns itself with supporting the local pastoralist Samburu communities via honey-production projects and cash-crop experiments involving the Senegalese acacia gum tree; it's a mine of information on Samburu culture. For a more intimate experience, you might try asking about the **camel market** which is held on occasions a few kilometres south of the village at a roadside well.

Kurungu Camp

Kurungu Camp, 6km north of South Horr along the sandy, vegetation-festooned track, is a good place to bump into other motorized tourists. The **campsite** (bookings on Nairobi ☎020/330130; Ksh200 per person) is slightly rundown these days but the setting is fabulous, surrounded by flowering bushes and shaded by distinguished old trees. It's worth spending a couple of nights at Kurungu and exploring the **mountain forest** around you – it hides lots of wildlife and bursts with birds and butterflies. Unfortunately, nearly all the elephants and buffaloes have been poached. You can be guided by Samburu *morani* up the lower slopes or, more ambitiously, on the stiff hike up to **Nyiru peak**, which has stunning views over Lake Turkana. If you entertain thoughts of any more daring expeditions in the region, **camel hire** should cost in the region of Ksh600–1000 per beast per day. Be careful if you're embarking on anything way off the beaten track. Many men who will sell themselves as **guides** have led surprisingly sheltered lives; they don't know the desert like the backs of their hands any more than you do. Real knowledge and experience are sought after and more expensive.

At Kurungu, you are also likely to have the (mixed) pleasure of **Samburu dancing**, especially if on an organized safari. For about Ksh300–500, you are allowed into the arena to take as many pictures of the dancers as you want, although they do not mask their displeasure. Scepticism is briefly swamped by the hour-long jamboree that follows. A troupe of *morani* goes through an informal dance programme, flirtatiously threatening the audience with whoops and pounces. Young women and girls join in – sometimes with the evident disapproval of older Samburu onlookers – to be propositioned with whisks of the men's ochred hair-dos. Meanwhile, there's the constant offering of necklaces, trinkets, spears, pouches and more photo poses, to be negotiated individually with those who are too old or too young to dance.

Down to the lake

After South Horr, the track winds down between the Nyiru Range to your left and the **Ol Doinyo Mara** mountains to the right, before opening onto featureless plains of black lava with the massif of Kulal dominating the northern horizon. The lava is hard and jagged – a vicious test for tyres – and the track itself, pummelled to a fine dust, can become a quagmire after a rainstorm. This is Turkana territory. The numerous **stone circles** and **cairns** around here are the remains of settlements and burial sites, which, with a keen eye, you'll learn to recognize all over the region. Most distinctive are the low semicircular constructions, which you'll see in use as you approach the lake: these serve as shelters against the viciously hot wind that blows almost incessantly off the flanks of Kulal. The burial cairns are by no means as ancient as they appear, as traditionally neither the Turkana nor Samburu (who migrated from this area a few hundred years ago) buried their dead, but instead simply left the bodies out in the open for wild animals to eat. The more important members of the community, such as blacksmiths and respected elders, were sometimes buried under cairns, or were left in a hut whose door would be walled up. The site would be abandoned and thereafter never again be used for human habitation. Since independence and the rise in the power of Christian missions, however, both Turkana and Samburu are now obliged to bury their dead.

Just when you were beginning to wonder, **Lake Turkana** appears as the road drops away in front: a stunning vista of shot blues and greens, with the black, castellate silhouette of South Island hanging as if suspended between lake and sky. Descending a little further along a viciously rocky stretch of road known to drivers as The Staircase, you come to several bays where people have swum in the past (this isn't advised because of crocodiles), a few tiny temporary fishing settlements and, an hour or so later, Loiyangalani.

Loiyangalani and around

LOIYANGALANI – "the place of the trees" – is a small community far from metropolitan Kenya, a vague agglomeration of grass huts, mud huts, tin shacks, a police station, a school, a few campsites, and a luxury lodge. The land around is mostly barren and stony, scattered with the carcasses of livestock, with palm trees and acacias clustered around the settlement's life source, a **hot spring** of fresh water. This empties into two pools near the police station, one for men, the other for women.

The village came into being in the early 1960s with the *Oasis Lodge* and its airstrip, and the Italian mission to the **Elmolo** people, a small group who live by hunting and fishing on the southeastern lakeshore. Somali raiders ransacked both establishments in 1965, but since then the two institutions have been left alone. The mission is now starting to thrive and its net of influence has reached most of Loiyangalani's more permanent inhabitants, especially the children who come to the school.

For all its apparent drabness, the village isn't dull. When you've had enough of haggling for artefacts and fantastic quartz, onyx, amethyst and other semi-precious stones collected from Kulal – as well as the odd fossil – you can wander over to the springs and the school. You'll inevitably pick up a cluster of teenagers – Turkana, Elmolo, Samburu, Rendille – eager to practise their English. Swahili has never made much impact up here and English is the usual teaching medium. Education is perhaps the most positive of the major influences – which otherwise include state interference, Christianity and tourist money – bringing pressure to bear on local customs and traditions.

The **mission**, while changing the structure of traditional society (through conversions to Catholicism, which have been particularly effective among the Elmolo), is at the same time helping to make local people sufficiently independent to resist unwanted change and to make choices about their future, by helping to set up income-generating schemes such as the shops, some of the boats and a new service station. Some of the Italian missionaries are extremely open and informative and, although you can't be assured they'll have any time to meet you, the chance to talk to them about Loiyangalani may well arise if you're around for a few days. For non-Christians, however, the whole concept of missionaries and their work can be difficult to swallow. For all their schools and clinics, it's difficult to escape the feeling that these people – for so long "untouched" by the outside world – managed very well with their original beliefs and traditions, which formed the basis of their society, cosmology and human relations. With Christianity now ascendant, the old structures are breaking down fast and some risk being lost completely (the Elmolo lost their language in March 1998 following the death of its last speaker, for example). By preferring to convert children, rather than their more obstinate parents, the deeper morality of the well-meaning missionaries is questionable at best. More positively, there's a small library at the mission, which you're free to use.

Loiyangalani's "**beach**" is a grubby strip a couple of kilometres down the road. Many of the loose stones on the shore shelter scorpions (not serious) and carpet vipers (very serious). In the evenings, **dances** often take place around Loiyangalani – informal, energetic, pogo-ing performances for fun, always worth checking out. Track them down by the booming sound of collective larynxes. It's the girls who ask the boys to dance, and you're welcome to join in (no cameras or torches unless permission is expressly given and paid for, usually Ksh500 per person).

Practicalities

The German-run *Oasis Lodge* (PO Box 14829 Nairobi; ☏020/600470; FB $240; ❾; closed mid-May to mid-June) tries to be exclusive, and certainly charges as if it were. There's a Ksh300 daily entrance fee to casual visitors to discourage them from drinking the entire stock of beer; the fee at least entitles you to swim in its two, jealously guarded pools and soak up the great views from the dining/bar area. The **accommodation**, however, in small and run-down "chalets", is certainly not worth the expense. More useful is the lodge's **car-rental service**, ideal for visiting Sibiloi National Park (see p.585), but the prices are very high (upwards of $180 per day including driver). Similarly expensive are its hiking trips up Kulal and around (around $140 per person per day) and its tours to the Elmolo village ($75 per person per day). Fishing boats can be rented for $35 per hour, with fishing licences for an additional Ksh400, and you can charter a five-seater Cessna 206 from Nairobi to the lodge for

$1300. You're advised to bargain hard for all the lodge's services, and to double-check on any price before taking anything on.

Much more down to earth is the **B&L** run by Mama Changa, who, apart from supplying much of the Turkana's beadwork necklaces and bracelets, has eighteen cleanish but perfectly adequate rooms round the back of the misnamed *Cold Drink Hotel* (its fridge seems to be in a permanent state of disrepair), each with a kerosene lamp and free drinking water (❶). This is the place to meet up with other travellers and drivers, should there be any. Totally different in style, but equally pleasant and recommended, is *Mosaretu Camp*, adjacent to *Oasis Lodge*, which is run by the local branch of the women's Maendeleo ya Wanawake movement. Apart from camping (Ksh150–200 per tent; watch out for snakes and scorpions), there are five traditional *bandas* (❶) under the palm trees, with mosquito nets and mattresses; other facilities include toilets, showers, a curio shop and a kitchen. The same people also own the *Rhino Camp* on the other side of town. The *Palm Shade Camp*, behind the *Cold Drink Hotel*, is a clean new site with cool *bandas* (❸) with mosquito nets, filtered water and a kitchen, and camping (Ksh400 per person). Last, but not least, 7km to the south of Loiyangalani on the lakeshore (a long hot walk) is probably Lake Turkana's most perfect campsite, operated by Gametrackers for its Turkana safaris, with thatched *bandas* facing out over the lake. There's little shade, and the *bandas* are small and cramped, but the views are unparalleled. Gametrackers uses it for only two or three days a week, so you may be able to do a deal with the caretaker.

Food is more difficult. The *Cold Drink Hotel* claims to give "best service, no matter how long it takes" but is nothing special, and has a propensity to charge tourist rates. The *New Salaama Hotel*, just off the main drag, serves good spicy Somali food, while *Mpasso Bar* is a pleasant thatched-roof, open-air compound with snacks, cold beers, and a games area with pool table and darts.

South Island National Park
Daily 6.30am–6.30pm; $15, children $5.

If you want to visit **South Island National Park**, you should ask about a trip at the lodge first, but spread the word and you may find a much cheaper means of getting there. It's a thirty-kilometre round trip, so the weather needs to be fair. By all accounts, it's one of the weirdest places to stay a night, in the unlikely event of the warden allowing you to do so; its volcanic vents, rising some 300m above sea level, give out a ghostly luminous glow that has long put off local fishermen from venturing there.

Mount Kulal
On dry land, you could make a stab at climbing **Mount Kulal**, if you have the energy. There are two summits, joined by a narrow and dicey ridge. The climb itself, once you're on the right track, is straightforward enough, but talk to some gem-hunters who may guide you up. And note that, although Kulal seems to tower over Loiyangalani, two days is barely enough to walk to the base and back; you really will need transport unless you're very determined and suitably equipped. The views from the top are fabulous, with the lake on one side and the searing Chalbi Desert on the other, and bird-watchers have the added incentive of a rare species of **white-eye** peculiar to the mountain. Bring all the **water** you will need, as there are no supplies on the mountain.

Elmolo Bay
At **Elmolo Bay**, 8km north of Loiyangalani, lives the last viable community of **Elmolo people**. To visit them, you pay a fixed fee per person (currently

The Elmolo

The people of Loiyangalani with the best claim to be the original inhabitants are the **Elmolo**. In Kenya, they're famous for being famous. Dubbed "the smallest tribe in the world" (in number, not size, and even smaller after a rival tribe, the Boran, raided the community, killing men of fighting age) the Elmolo call themselves *el-Des*, but their usual name comes from the Samburu *loo molo onsikirri*, "the people who eat fish". They once inhabited South Island, but now occupy a couple of islands in Elmolo Bay, and a few gatherings of grass huts on the torrid shores 8km north of Loiyangalani. Most of the 600-strong community live here, partly by **fishing** and the occasional heroic crocodile or hippo hunt (officially banned), partly by **cash receipts** from tourist visitors (see opposite).

The Elmolo are enigmatic. At the time of Teleki's discovery of the lake, they spoke a **Cushitic** language, the family of languages to which Somali and Rendille belong. Recent linguistic research on historical migrations points to their having arrived on the shores of Lake Turkana at a very early time – perhaps over 2000 years ago. They seem to have no tradition of livestock-herding, which might have been kept up if they had turned, like the Turkana, to fishing as a supplement. Today they speak **Samburu** (the last Elmolo-speaker died in March 1998) and have started to intermarry with them. This, as well as the mission's influence, has been quite significant in raising their numbers (from less than 200 twenty-odd years ago) and also in diluting their cultural identity. Once strictly monogamous, polygamy isn't uncommon now and they also send many children to the school in Loiyangalani as weekly boarders. On the slope, right behind the village, a new Catholic church looms.

All this signals the final curtain for a culture and history that has been largely ignored or denied. The conventional wisdom about hunter-gatherers in Kenya is that they are often the descendants of pastoralists who lost their herds. But if the Elmolo are, as some say, pastoral Rendille who took to fishing in order to survive, then it's strange that they have never tried to replace their herds. For without herds, they could never hope to pay bridewealth for wives from their non-fishing neighbours in the traditional way. A better explanation, and one favoured by the Elmolo themselves, is that their people have always been fishermen and hunters and, until very recently, pressures from other tribes, particularly the Turkana, had pushed them almost to the point of annihilation.

By the the end of the twentieth century, the Elmolo fishing culture was beginning to rub off on other ethnic groups and even the Samburu have started to eat fish. As long ago as 1972, Peter Matthiessen wrote in *The Tree Where Man was Born*:

The Samburu and Turkana may linger for weeks at a time as guests of the Llo-molo, who have plenty of fish and cannot bear to eat with all these strangers hanging around looking so hungry. Other tribes, the Llo-molo say, know how to eat fish better than they know how to catch them . . . "We have to feed them," one Llo-molo says, "so that they will feel strong enough to go away."

The Elmolo are a charming and hospitable people, and how they survive in their chosen environment is almost beyond belief. Outwardly similar in dress and appearance to the other people of the area, they are slightly smaller, but the bowed legs which are supposed to be the characteristic result of their diet seem to be confined to the older people – you might have thought all that fish would give them strong bones.

Incidentally, don't get worried when a mother hands you her child, then asks for money; she's not selling her offspring, but simply wants you to sponsor the child's education with a large wad of cash.

Ksh700) to the headman, for freedom to roam the village, including the right to take photos and a trip to the island opposite the bay to look for crocodiles. During the week, many children are at school in Loiyangalani; they come home at the weekend, which is the best time to visit. Impromptu dances start, little hands are slipped engagingly into yours for a walk around the low, grass huts. If you have a digital camera you'll be extremely popular with the village children, eager to look at their image on screen. You will also be shown the "market", a circular stall in the centre of the village with beadwork, belts, fertility dolls and gourds. It's a novel, disturbing experience which contrives to be stage-managed and voyeuristic at the same time. Because of their friendliness, their small number and the increased interest shown in them, the Elmolo risk being taken advantage of by tourists. However, the usual rules apply: ask before you take pictures and be generous with your time and your wallet.

Over on the island – which, because of Lake Turkana's lowering, you can now reach by a causeway – you should see **crocodiles** if you walk softly and approach the far shore cautiously. On the island's stern, rocky beaches, the remains of Elmolo fish picnics and old camps can be found everywhere; one find was a nearly fossilized hippo tusk from some long-ago feast. Today, a hippo hunt has to be organized discreetly (strictly speaking, hunting hippos is illegal) and usually takes place further north on the marshier shores below Moiti Hill. Hippos have gone from Loiyangalani.

Sibiloi National Park

Daily 6.30am–6pm; $15, children $5, vehicle entry Ksh200. Warden: PO Box 219 Lodwar.

Sibiloi National Park provides a powerful temptation to go further north – even for jumping ship if you came up to Turkana by safari tour. **Access** is the main problem, as vehicles heading there from Loiyangalani are extremely rare (a two-week wait might be considered lucky). If you have enough money (upwards of $180 per day), the easiest way is to hire one of *Oasis Lodge*'s battered Land Rovers (with driver). With your own vehicle (high clearance 4WD essential for the first section along the northern flanks of Mount Kulal), a full day's drive might get you there, but be sure to get precise directions from as many people as you can beforehand in Loiyangalani, as most maps are useless. From the Loiyangalani–North Horr road, turn left after some 45km, after the road begins to drop down from Mount Kulal's rocky shoulder. From here, a completely desolate track heads due north for 40km to the settlement of Hurran Hurra, where a left should get you to the camel watering-point and settlement of Gajos, another 40km northwest. Another left here (heading west, then northwest) begins to drop down towards the lake and the national park itself. **Camp Turkana**, near the shore just south of Alia Bay, marks the park's southern boundary, with the National Museums' base of Koobi Fora another 10km further up. Getting back down without your own transport is a matter of waiting (a potentially long time) for any southbound transport: the museums people are obviously the best bet for this.

Apart from **flying in** (around $1000 return from Nairobi's Wilson Airport – you have to negotiate with the pilots), an alternative way of getting there is by boat from Ferguson's Gulf on the lake's western shore, near Kalokol (p.565). Prices vary according to your bargaining skills and perceived ability to pay, though around $200–300 for a return crossing is probably normal (you may have to pay more, however, to convince your boatman to wait longer than one night for the return leg if you're into an extended stay, and he'll expect you to arrange all his food and accommodation requirements, too). There's also an infrequent National Museums supply boat from here.

Discoveries in human prehistory

Sibiloi was created to protect the sites of numerous remarkable **hominid fossil** finds that have been made since 1968 by Richard Leakey's, and latterly Kamoya Kimeu's, team from the University of Nairobi. The park, more than 1600 square kilometres of rock desert and arid bush, is an exceptional source because many of the fossils are found on the surface, blown clean by the never-ending wind. The finds set back the dates of intelligent, co-operative, tool-making behaviour among hominids further and further all the time, but most of the species concerned are assumed to have died out. The crucial discoveries that will link humankind to our prehuman ancestors have yet to be made. One striking find made at Sibiloi in 1972 was "1470", the skull of a *Homo habilis* over two million years old, believed to be a direct ancestor of modern *Homo sapiens*. Sibiloi was declared a national park a year later. As more and more discoveries are made here (currently nearing 200), on the other side of the lake (where excavations have yielded the earliest *australopithecine* known, *Australopithecus anamensis*, dated between 4.2 and 3.9 million years), in southern Ethiopia and at Olduvai in northern Tanzania, evolutionary theories are beginning to flesh out.

The so-called **museum** at the "expedition" headquarters in Alia Bay, where some of the fossils (including part of a one-and-a-half-million-year-old elephant) are supposedly displayed *in situ*, isn't easily traced; all that was found on a last attempt were empty ranger buildings and unhelpful staff. There are camping facilities bookable through the National Museums of Kenya Headquarters in Nairobi (see p.128).

Animal life

At times, Sibiloi has a surprising wealth of **wildlife**. Indeed, until the 1930s, there were large numbers of elephant living here. Rainless years, ivory hunters, and especially the increase in the herds of livestock, contributed to their demise. But lion, cheetah, hyena, both kinds of zebra (the ordinary Grant's and the finer-striped, taller Grevy's), giraffe, ostrich, Grant's gazelle, topi, kudu and gerenuk all occur here, though there's no guarantee you'll see much. Because of the protection from hunters, hippos and crocodiles are numerous. The tree cover is minimal. The closest you're likely to come to finding trees is the petrified forest of stone trunks, reminders of the lush vegetation of the lakeshore in prehistoric times.

The Koobi Fora field schools

Possibly the best way of visiting the archeological sites is by coinciding your trip with one of two six-week **field schools** organized by the National Museums of Kenya in tandem with Rutgers University in the USA (Ⓦwww.koobifora.rutgers.edu). Approximate dates are from June to mid-August, and from mid-August to September. The first two weeks involve "ecological tours" around Nairobi and other national parks, followed by four weeks of rooting around at Koobi Fora with the experts where you're taught excavation methods and fossil analysis. Some places are awarded as bursaries, but unless you're an especially deserving case, the fees are upward of $1000: enquiries to the Director of Koobi Fora Field School, PO Box 40658 Nairobi; Ⓣation020/742131, Ⓕ741424.

The northeast

Northeastern Kenya has a single and limited travel circuit: up through **Isiolo** to **Marsabit Mountain and National Park**. It's well worth doing, especially as it's the only route in the northeast currently considered relatively safe. Beyond,

Travel in the northeast – a warning

The **northeast** of Kenya has long been known for lawlessness, but what was sometimes dismissed as only the exaggerated fear and ignorance of "downcountry" Kenyans acquired a more brutal reality in the 1990s which continues today.

Since the flight of Somali dictator Siad Barre in 1991, and that country's anarchic disintegration into warring fiefdoms, northeastern Kenya has borne the full brunt of Somalia's desperate refugee crisis. Recurring armed clashes have caused Somali families in central and southern regions to flee their homes and because the border is largely an uncontrolled one, the war itself occasionally spills over too. There's also the largely unknown quantity of the "Oromo Liberation Front", which claims parts of Kenya and Ethiopia as the Oromo-speaking peoples' homeland, and which has been blamed for a number of civilian massacres, and increasingly cold-blooded bandits, who primarily target commercial vehicles, foreign aid workers and refugee camps.

The northeast is also home to tribes whose main means of subsistence is livestock. Inter-tribal rivalry has led to cattle rustling and there have been violent clashes over grazing areas and water. All this has been made more volatile by prolonged drought in the region. Whatever the complicated situation on the ground, you can be sure of one thing: there are more people than before with guns, ammunition and little else. Armed attacks on remote villages and convoys have become commonplace.

The military presence in the northeast is pervasive: roadblocks, vehicle searches and armed escorts are part of everyday life, yet for all this the military presence is also almost entirely ineffective. Very seldom do incidents reported result in arrests. Indeed, some accuse the police of being complicit in the crimes.

We've endeavoured to note the current security situation for all parts of this chapter, but you're strongly advised to seek advice on the ground before travelling anywhere covered in the following pages as the situation can change quickly. For example, the area between Isiolo and Archer's Post, including Samburu and Buffalo Springs National Reserves, was considered safe for several years before 1997, after which it suffered repeated attacks on villages and tourists. Though the situation in the parks is now controlled by the KWS, things could easily change again.

In summary, the main no-go area at the time of writing is the entire region east of the A2, meaning everything east of the Isiolo–Marsabit–Moyale road, including Wajir, Habeswein, El Wak, and Mandera. Areas where extreme caution are advised are the roads from Mwingi to Garissa, and Garsen to Garissa. Safer, but better visited with organized safari groups (if not on an organized trip, it is necessary to travel in convoy and/or have a security escort), include the Isiolo–Marsabit–Moyale road itself, Archer's Post to Maralal, and the road from Malindi to Garsen and Lamu. At the time of writing caution was also advised in the Marsabit area as there had been several violent incidents including, in July 2005, the massacre by armed raiders of more than seventy people in villages in the region; and armed-bandit attacks in the Songa forest. If visiting the regions mentioned, use your judgement, and ask advice everywhere you go, but bear in mind that the region has never been declared a safe zone by the government, even since before independence. Driving at night, incidentally, is not only the height of folly, but is also illegal.

or east of Marsabit, the remote administrative outposts of Mandera, Wajir and Garissa are too dangerous to visit (see box, p.587).

Travel throughout the northeast has a special quality. The normal stimuli of passing scenery, animals, people and events fleetingly witnessed is replaced with a massive open sky, shimmering greenish-brown earth, and just occasionally a speck of movement – some camels, a pair of ostriches, a family moving on with their donkeys. It's a sparse, absorbingly simple landscape. And not the least of its attractions is the restful absence of hassle and shove, and a solitude hardly found anywhere else.

A visit to **Moyale** offers the possibility of a brief trip to **Ethiopia**, and is the only recognized crossing into that country and beyond. Incidentally, the road up from Moyale to Addis Ababa is entirely surfaced. There are generally no special conditions attached to crossing for a few hours to wander around.

Isiolo

ISIOLO is the northeast's most important town and the hub for travel to Marsabit and Moyale. Southernmost of the "Northern Frontier" towns, Isiolo is on the border between two different worlds – the fertile highlands and the desert. A measure of the untamed badlands beyond is given by the three military training schools based here: Infantry, Combat Engineering and Artillery, as well as a tank regiment. Isiolo is a frontier in every respect. The **Somali influence** here is something noticeable everywhere in the northeast, and Isiolo is one of their most important towns in Kenya because

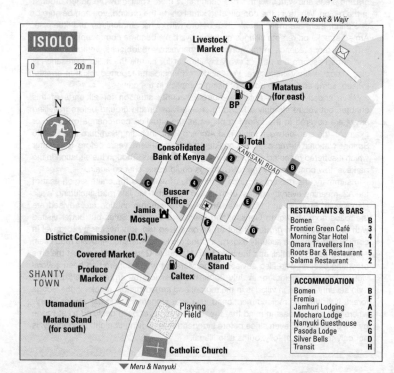

▲ Samburu, Marsabit & Wajir

ISIOLO

0   200 m

N

Livestock Market

Matatus (for east)

BP

Total

KANISANI ROAD

Consolidated Bank of Kenya

Buscar Office

Jamia Mosque

District Commissioner (D.C.)

Covered Market

SHANTY TOWN

Produce Market

Utamaduni

Matatu Stand (for south)

Caltex

Matatu Stand

Playing Field

Catholic Church

RESTAURANTS & BARS

Bomen	B
Frontier Green Café	3
Morning Star Hotel	4
Omara Travellers Inn	1
Roots Bar & Restaurant	5
Salama Restaurant	2

ACCOMMODATION

Bomen	B
Fremia	F
Jamhuri Lodging	A
Mocharo Lodge	E
Nanyuki Guesthouse	C
Pasoda Lodge	G
Silver Bells	D
Transit	H

▼ Meru & Nanyuki

it was here that many veteran Somali soldiers from World War I were settled. Recruited in Aden and Kismayu, they gave up their nomadic lifestyle to become livestock and retail traders.

But **the town** is lively and welcoming, relatively safe and hassle free (although travel north of here is not; see box, p.587). It's also a cultural kaleidoscope, with Boran, Meru, Samburu and some Turkana inhabitants as well as the Somalis. To someone newly arrived from Nanyuki or Meru, the upland towns seem ordinary in comparison. Women from the irrigated *shambas* around Isiolo sell cabbages, tomatoes and carrots in the busy market. Cattle owners, nomadic camel traders and merchants exchange greetings and the latest news from Nairobi and Moyale. In the livestock market, goats scamper through the alleys. Hawkers stroll along the road raising their Somali swords and strings of bangles to the minibuses heading up to Samburu National Reserve (see p.407). And, in the shade, energetic *miraa*-chewing and hanging around are the major occupations. *Miraa* has a long history in Somali culture, and the Nyambeni Hills, where most of the Kenyan crop is grown, are just 30km away (p.413).

Practicalities

If you get a late **bus** from Nairobi you'll arrive in the middle of the night, and the town can be seen glittering out on the plain far below for an hour or more beforehand. During Ramadan, lanterns glow along the pavements for the *miraa* sellers and most of the shops are still open. You can find a B&L or sleep on the bus until dawn – probably a safer bet. There is a Consolidated **bank** and a **post office** (both Mon–Fri 8.30am–1pm & 2–5pm).

Accommodation

Isiolo boasts one reasonable, mid-range **hotel**. Of the more humble **lodgings**, all are cheap, and several surprisingly good value. There's also a good place 10km south of town in the form of the shaded *Rangeland Hotel* (☎064/2340; ❸), which also has a small playground for children.

Bomen Hotel PO Box 67 Isiolo ☎064/2389, ℉2225. The best and most expensive in town: clean, polite and serving good lunchtime buffets. Rooms lack fans, but are s/c and have nets, and hot water mornings and evenings. ❸
Fremia Hotel PO Box 402 ☎064/2307. Basic B&L with non s/c rooms and shared bathrooms with hot showers. ❶
Jamhuri Lodging PO Box 88 ☎064/2065. Newly renovated, clean, courteous and mellow – currently the most popular cheap place. Laundry facilities. Not s/c. ❶
Mocharo Lodge PO Box 106 ☎064/2385. Good value and safe parking. Recommended. ❶

Nanyuki Guesthouse PO Box 451 ☎064/2168. Reasonable and dirt cheap, with spartan rooms, nets, fresh cold milk, dry-cleaning facilities and safe parking. ❶
Pasoda Lodge PO Box 62 ☎064/2162. Quiet and clean, with inexpensive meals. All rooms s/c with nets. Safe parking. ❷
Silver Bells Hotel Between the *Bomen* and *Pasoda*; PO Box 247 ☎064/2251. Clean, quiet and mid-priced, with a grubby cocktail bar which sells only beer and soda. ❶
Transit Hotel PO Box ☎064/2148. On the same street as the *Roots Bar & Restaurant*. Simple, clean rooms with mosquito nets. ❷

Eating and drinking

Somali *hotelis* provide excellent **food**, day and night. Now that you're in the northeast, you'll see pasta (usually spaghetti) appearing quite prominently on menus – one of the better Italian bequests to the Somalis.

Bomen Hotel The *nyama choma* at the patio bar is worthwhile for meat-eaters.

Frontier Green Café A brilliant, tree-filled garden-restaurant with disco (Wed, Fri & Sat), fluorescent spider's webs and UV tubes – in outlandish contrast with the rest of the town. Long popular for its good spiced *chai* for next to nothing a glass.

Morning Star Hotel Pretty good – especially noted for its samosas – and it has some ultra-cheap accommodation.

Omara Travellers Inn A bar and *nyama choma* joint better for its food than its cheap rooms.

Roots Bar & Restaurant The best place in Isiolo; a clean, lively and popular bar and restaurant with a reggae soundtrack and great *nyama choma*.

Salama Restaurant Recommended for an early breakfast or the very good spaghetti.

Shopping and guides

Isiolo is one of the best places to buy **bracelets** of copper, brass and aluminium. Prices are generally around Ksh50 for the simple ones, up to Ksh200 for the heavier, more complicated designs, if you can bargain effectively (starting prices are much higher). Short "Somali swords" in red leather scabbards are also much in evidence. The "sharp boys" who mob you near the markets will invariably offer to guide you to one of the few blacksmiths in town to watch the fascinating process of twisting the wires for the bangles. Profits come from buying rough bangles, then polishing and selling them. If you go, you're generally expected to make a purchase and tip a few shillings to the boys. While the bangle and knife salesmen throng as soon as you sit down for a *chai*, their approach is rarely aggressive. Women offer small wooden dolls with woven hair, which in the past were given to young girls as both toys and fertility charms. Some of the former "sharp boys" have recently teamed up to start the **Utamaduni Self-Help Group** (PO Box 16; office in the market opens Mon–Fri 3–5.30pm), which aims to organize and rehabilitate homeless and orphaned youth in community-based projects (for example, by building small bridges over sewage ditches). Though some of their members are still a little rough around the edges, it's a laudable venture, and the best place to get a **guide** for visiting local *manyattas* (they must have an ID card; you should pay Ksh500–800 for a full day). For trips further afield, test the guide first on a one-day trip in the environs of Isiolo before trusting him on a longer journey.

Moving on from Isiolo

When heading north, waiting in Isiolo is a predictable part of the trip. The only public transport onwards from Isiolo is to Wamba (see p.576) and Maralal via Archer's Post, details for which are given overleaf. Otherwise, there are no buses and only limited matatu services north or east from Isiolo, so your only options for travel to Marsabit and Moyale are either **self-drive**, which is ill-advised for all but the most experienced, well-equipped and mechanically skilled driver, or **hitching a ride** with a truck in convoy. If you're lucky, you might get a lift with one of the mission or aid vehicles. Note if you're driving that Isiolo is the last **fuel** stop until Maralal or Marsabit.

To Nairobi via the Central Highlands

There is one daily **bus** service to Nairobi via Nanyuki, leaving around 7.30am. For matatus you have to be at the market stage before sunrise – last departures at 6am are not unheard of.

North to Marsabit and Moyale

For many years this route has been considered highly dangerous due to attacks by **bandits** and it is advised to travel in convoy and with security escorts. Though the situation changes from year to year, the main trouble spots at the time of writing were the area around Marsabit, and the approach to Moyale, which is subject to more frequent raids from neighbouring Ethiopia. **Matatus** go as far as Archer's Post, which is only helpful if you're visiting Samburu or Shaba national reserves (see p.407 & p.412). Otherwise, try for trucks at the **police roadblock** 3km north of Isiolo at the **end of the tarmac**, by the junction for Wajir, where drivers sign their vehicles out of town. There are usually a few heading up to Moyale daily, and most take passengers (for a fee). You'll have to stand on top of the load along with the other, usually male, passengers, although given the state of the roads, this is actually more comfortable than sitting down. Alternatively, Gametrack-ers' Turkana Bus passes through Archer's Post early in the morning every Saturday, which – if the driver's amenable – can take you as far as Marsabit, probably for a fee. If you do get a lift, the 262km to Marsabit takes seven to ten hours, with the next leg to Moyale (245km) anything from ten hours to two days, depending on the state of the road and the frequency of hold-ups, natural or otherwise. Trucks charge upwards of Ksh1000.

West to Maralal

The **Isiolo–Archer's Post–Maralal** run is served by the wacky Babie Coach, a converted Bedford lorry which makes the journey every day between Isiolo and Maralal (or vice versa), leaving one town at around 9am to reach the other five to six hours later – though you could stop off in Wamba (p.576) to explore the grandly mysterious Mathews Range. On the days that Babie Coach is on its homebound run to Isiolo, you may find the odd matatu going to Maralal. If you're **driving** the route yourself, bring enough fuel for the whole journey – there are no supplies at Wamba.

To Marsabit and North Horr

No matter the speed, this is a fantastically uncomfortable trip, with rocks, ruts and corrugations that shake smaller vehicles to breaking point. Somewhat unbelievably, the road is said to have been surfaced at least three times in the past, all the way to Moyale – not a trace of which remains.

Passing over the occasionally dry Ewaso Ngiro River and a police barrier, you hit the agglomeration of shiny-roofed shacks and rows of *dukas* which is **ARCHER'S POST**. This is as far north as you'll get by matatu, although lifts into Samburu and Shaba national reserves (see p.407 & p.412) may be forthcoming from Kenya Wildlife Service personnel, who frequent a number of particularly good bars. There are some **rooms** here, too, should you fail: try *Accacia Shade Inns* (①) which also has a **campsite** (with no guarantee of security). There's no **petrol** available; the nearest is an expensive trip to either *Samburu Lodge* or *Sarova Shaba Lodge* in the reserves. Finally, advertising "hard and pertinent facts about the Samburu people", **Samburu Cultural Centre** (daily 10am–4pm; PO Box 548 Isiolo), half a kilometre from Archer's Post market along the Samburu National Reserve road, has a small **ethnographic museum** and *manyatta*, complete with ironmongery, woodwork and beadwork for sale, displays of dancing, and more.

North of Archer's Post, the road veers northwest and for thirty minutes the great mesa – over 2000m – of **Ol Olokwe Mountain** (or Ol Doinyo Sabache) spreads massively across the horizon in front of you. If you're travel-ling independently with a vehicle, it can be climbed. If you fancy something

Peoples of the Marsabit area

Identities in the northeast can be confusing. The largest group are the **Boran**, part of the **Oromo peoples** (formerly called Galla, an Amhara term of abuse), whose homeland was near the Bale Mountains in Ethiopia, from where they suddenly exploded out, in all directions, in the sixteenth century. The pastoral Boran developed and flourished in what is now southern Ethiopia, but Menelik's conquest of the area and the oppressive Amhara regime caused some of them to move down to the lowlands (much less suitable for their cattle) of northern Kenya; the first Boran arrived in Marsabit only in 1921. Similarly recent Ethiopian immigrants to the region between Marsabit and Moyale are the **Burji**, an agricultural people who were called down by colonial administrators in the 1930s who wanted crops grown to feed themselves. The Burji took quickly to Western education and trade, and as a result dominated Marsabit politically in the first decade after independence. There's little love lost between the nomadic Boran and the settled Burji.

At around the time of the Oromo expansion, another group of people - the forefathers of the Gabbra - arrived in northern Kenya, causing havoc in the region, only to be themselves pressured by the ensuing expansion of **Muslim Somalis** from the east. The ancestors of the **Gabbra** became "Boranized" to the extent that they changed their language and adopted Boran customs. Although most Boran and Gabbra, especially those who adopted a more sedentary life, have adopted Somali styles in dress and culture, they eschew Islam, in preference for their own religions. The **Rendille**, to the northwest of Marsabit, look and act like Samburu, with whom they are frequently allied; they speak a language close to Somali but have non-Muslim religious beliefs. They normally herd camels rather than cattle and, to a great extent, continue to roam the deserts, facing the prospect of settling down without any enthusiasm at all and visiting Marsabit only for vital needs or a brief holiday.

In Marsabit itself, distinctions other than superficial ones are increasingly hard to apply as people intermarry, more children are sent to school, and downcountry ideas – and Christian missionaries – percolate up the road. Still, language and religious beliefs remain significant in deciding who does what and with whom, and outside the town, individual tribal identities are as strong – and potentially bloody – as they have ever been.

more organized and worthy, **Namunyak Wildlife Conservation Trust** (PO Box 88 Wamba; information and bookings from Let's Go Travel in Nairobi, p.150) is a community-wildlife venture set up in 1995 to preserve some 300 square kilometres of land around the mountain for the benefit of local Samburu. They offer walking safaris up the mountain led by Samburu *morani*, rich pickings for bird-spotters with frequent sightings of Gambaga flycatcher, shining sunbird, the tiny cisticola, stone partridge, and Kenya's largest nesting colony of Ruppell's vultures. You might also see dik-dik, klipspringer, Chandler's mountain reedbuck, rock hyrax, vervet monkey, olive baboon, and (very rarely) leopard and elephant.

For several hours beyond Ol Olokwe you roar across the flat **Kaisut Desert**. **Laisamis** isn't much of a break – a low windblown cluster of tin-roofed huts and Samburu, offering sodas and toothbrush sticks to passers-by – and the Losai National Reserve isn't any different from the rest of the scenery. The **approach to Marsabit**, though, is unmistakable. The road begins to climb and suddenly you're on a hilly island in the desert, a region of volcanic craters, lush meadows and forest. The branches of the trees on the steep slopes are disguised by swathes of Spanish moss, looking at first glance like algae-covered rocks in shades of grey and green.

Marsabit town

MARSABIT is a surprise. It's hard to prepare yourself, after the flat dustlands, for this fascinating hill oasis, in the desert but not of it. Rising a thousand metres above the surrounding plains, *Saku*, as the mountain is known by locals, is permanently green, well watered by the clouds which form and disperse over it in a daily cycle. The high forest is usually mist-covered until late morning, the trees a characteristic tangle of foliage and lianas.

The town is capital of the largest administrative district in the country, as well as a major meat- and livestock-trading centre. Small and intimate in feel, the lively cultural mix (see box) in the main market area is the biggest buzz: transient **Gabbra** herdsmen and **Boran** with their prized short-horn cattle, women in the printed shawls and chiffon wraps of **Somali** costume rubbing elbows with ochred **Rendille** wearing skins, high stacks of beads and wire, and fantastic braided hairstyles. There are government workers here, too, from other parts of Kenya, and a scattering of **Ethiopian immigrants** (mainly Burji) and refugees. For some Marsabit background, try Mude Dae Mude's novel *The Hills are Falling* (Transafrica, Nairobi 1979), now out of print but you might still find a copy in Nairobi. If you're interested in **traditional music**, ask for George's Music Store.

Walks out of town

There are a number of trips you can make on foot from Marsabit in a few hours or less – particularly good restoratives if you haven't got your own vehicle and failed to get into the national park (see p.595). The easiest, with rewarding views, is the short walk up to the big wind-powered **generator** on a hill just west of the town. Turn left just before the police barrier and simply follow the path.

A longer excursion takes you up to the **VOK transmitter** behind the town, an excellent morning or afternoon hike through lush forest with magnificent panoramas of the whole district from the top. There are wells up here, too (see below). During the rainy season, everything is tremendously green and you walk over flowering meadows through clouds of butterflies.

From there, you should be able to see the closest sizeable crater, **Gof Redo**, about 5km north of the town in the fork of the roads to Moyale and North Horr. Follow either road from the fork for 3km, then turn left or right accordingly for a one-kilometre cross-country walk. The crater is quite a favoured hideout for greater kudu, and there's a population of cheetah around here too, not infrequently

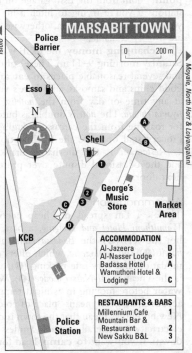

MARSABIT TOWN

0   200 m

Police Barrier

◄ Isiolo

Esso

N

Shell

A

B

George's Music Store

1

2

3

C

D

Market Area

KCB

► Moyale, North Horr & Loiyangalani

Police Station

ACCOMMODATION
Al-Jazeera	D
Al-Nasser Lodge	B
Badassa Hotel	A
Wamuthoni Hotel & Lodging	C

RESTAURANTS & BARS
Millennium Cafe	1
Mountain Bar & Restaurant	2
New Sakku B&L	3

▼ *Marsabit National Park*

seen from a vehicle (but likely to flee if you're on foot). You can scramble down the crater wall. Gof Redo can't really be missed, but a friend from town would be reassuring.

Even easier is a walk to the "**singing wells**" at Ulanula (called Hulahula by some). These are less exotic than they sound, but they're still a good excuse to explore. Ulanula is a conical peak to the right of the Isiolo road, about 6km from town. Leaving Marsabit, you cross two bridges, then turn left and climb 200–300m up a narrow, tangled ravine. A concrete holding-tank, visible from the road, gives the place away. Behind it are two natural wells, the first with a wooden trough in front, the second longer and apparently deeper, containing a fluctuating depth of brown, frog-filled water. A silent pumphouse stands by.

The **singing** is done not by the wells but by the Boran herders who use them. When the water is low, human chains are formed to get it out with luxuriantly leaking leather buckets; singing helps the work. At the driest times of the year you may be lucky and witness this, but try to get here early. Animals are usually driven to the wells after dawn, and it's a brisk 75-minute walk from town. Go out there in the late afternoon, though, and you should get a lift back with one of the day's vehicles up from Isiolo.

Practicalities

Moving on from Marsabit, you'll find that one or two trucks do occasionally spend the night in Marsabit, heading to or from Moyale or Isiolo. Otherwise, the convoy to Moyale usually passes in the afternoon, and that towards Isiolo anytime between 5 and 11pm. The best place to wait is at the **police checkpoint**, 300m from the Esso garage on the Isiolo road. Ask around the petrol stations if you're trying to hitch a lift to Loiyangalani; with your own tent, your first target is Kalacha, otherwise aim for North Horr. Supplies of **fuel** are usually available.

For **changing money**, the KCB is open Monday to Friday 9am–1pm and Saturday morning 9–11am. There's also a **post office** (Mon–Fri 8am–5pm), and several reasonable places to **eat and drink**. The *Millennium Cafe* serves good chips and samosas, and there's very cheap food in a lively atmosphere at any time of day from the *hotelis*: hefty pancakes, *githeri*, *mandaazi* and *nyama choma*. The *hotelis* double as butchers so you can select your own slab for roasting from the carcasses hanging up. There's a well-stocked shop and grocery stall opposite the Shell station. If you're thirsty, the *Mountain Bar & Restaurant* is the die-hards' drinking den, with a mix of characters and the occasional dispute over prostitutes – or try the *New Sakuu B&L* next door.

Accommodation

There's a fair spread of cheap accommodation in town, including the *Wamuthoni Hotel and Lodging*, a basic hotel with clean rooms and shared hot showers (❶); the *Badassa Hotel*, an unexceptional B&L with a decent *hoteli* (❶); the *Al-Jazeera*, which offers extremely cheap and peaceful accommodation and very safe parking (❶); and a little further out, by the market, is the cheaper *Al-Nasser Lodge* (❶). Whichever you choose, ask about **hot water** before moving in as night temperatures can drop very low (by some accounts, *Marsabit* means "place of cold") and lukewarm showers are no fun. New boreholes mean that the town is currently well supplied with water, and electricity is generally reliable (unless the diesel-powered generator breaks down). If you want **to camp**, head for the national park's main gate.

Marsabit National Park

Daily 6.30am–6pm; $15, children $5, vehicles Ksh200, camping $10, "special"
campsites $15. Warden: PO Box 42 Marsabit; ☎ 069/2028; Map: Tourist Maps of
Kenya/KWS Marsabit National Park and Reserve at 1cm:1km.

Having made the long journey to Marsabit, you'll certainly want to get into
the **park**. The forest is wild and dense, its two crater lakes idyllically beautiful.
Except during the long rains (March–June), there's a good chance you'll see
some of the long-tusked Marsabit **elephants**, relatives of the famous Ahmed
– a big tusker to whom Kenyatta gave "presidential protection", with elephant
guards tracking him day and night (now replicated in fibreglass in the National
Museum in Nairobi). His replacement, Mohammed, whose tusks were estimated
at a cool 45kg each side, has also gone to the elephant's graveyard. The park is
also renowned for its **greater kudu** antelope and there's a very wide range of
other wildlife. Between the nearly impenetrable forests of the peaks and the
stony scrub desert at the base of the mountain, however, you'll need a little luck
for sightings. This is a rewarding park, but one where you have to look hard.

Practicalities

The park's **main gate** is at the edge of town, past the bank and the District
Commissioner's office. It's not often visited and you may be in for a long wait
if you want a lift around its forest tracks. In addition, government officers and
soldiers garrisoned in town drive up to the **lodge** (see below) fairly frequently.
This short trip, with the view over the first lake – Gof Sokorte Dika – and its
forested rim, is a lot better than nothing. You might also be able to convince an
armed ranger to escort you to the first lake (say Ksh500) – it's a wonderful walk
through the forest, with clouds of butterflies and the occasional mouth-drying
encounter with buffalo or elephant.

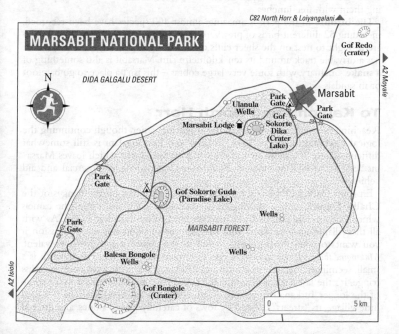

Do not attempt to **drive in the park** without 4WD, as many of the roads are steep and tend to be ridiculously muddy.

There's a **campsite** near the main gate (100m down the hairpin to the left of the ranger's house) which is free in theory, although the rangers may request a small fee, especially if you wish to use the new toilet and shower block. It's a wonderfully shaded place overrun with baboons swinging on the lianas.

There are several other places to camp in the park. Gof Sokorte Guda (Lake Paradise), a stunning, dark pool a kilometre across for much of the year, has wonderful sites on its crater rim, where a night would be chilly and thrillingly spent – lion, leopard and the rare and shaggy striped hyena are all seen and heard from time to time. This *Lake Paradise Special Campsite* costs $15 per person (plus park entry fee), but does not include the Ksh500 or so "guiding fee" for the obligatory accompanying ranger.

🏕 *Marsabit Lodge* (PO Box 488; ☎069/2411, 🖷2416; FB ❼) sits on the shore of Gof Sokorte Dika, its outstanding views and the exquisite beauty of its location compensating for the shabby rooms and slightly spooky emptiness. Elephants are no longer common visitors, since the salt that lured them is no longer laid out but you can see buffalo and other wildlife converging at the lake below.

Marsabit's fauna

Your animal count in the park will very much depend on the season of your visit. Good rains can encourage the grazers off the mountain and out into the temporarily lush desert, and the predators (always far fewer) will follow. **Elephants** especially are tremendous wanderers, sometimes strolling into town, causing pandemonium. More problematically, the people of Marsabit have been encouraged to cultivate around the base of the mountain, at the same time creating a barrier to the elephants' free movement and unintentionally providing them with free lunches.

The **birdlife** in the park is amazing: almost 400 species have been recorded, including 52 different birds of prey. Very rare **lammergeiers** (bearded vultures) are thought to nest on the sheer cliffs of Gof Bongole, the largest crater, which has a drivable track around its ten-kilometre rim. Marsabit is also something of a **snake** sanctuary, with some very large cobras – this isn't a place to go barefoot or in sandals.

To Kalacha and North Horr

Reaching North Horr from Marsabit is getting easier, though continuing the logical next step down to Lake Turkana and Loiyangalani is still somewhat difficult. There is a more or less regular passenger lorry which leaves Marsabit "often", as well as mission, Education Department, commercial and aid vehicles.

En route, **MAIKONA** is a friendly Gabbra settlement on the fringes of the **Chalbi Desert**, with a thriving daily market for goats and cattle (the camels which become ubiquitous from here on tend to be traded at Isiolo). As with all the villages up here, keep your camera out of sight, and ask permission if you want to take **photographs**: belief in the camera's evil eye is prevalent. *Mazingira Tourist Lodge* may have one or two rooms (❶). Some 5km north is a small, seemingly miraculous oasis pond of blue water with a sweet green grass fringe. It's the last fresh water until **KALACHA**, a regular night stop for some of the longer Turkana expeditions (Gametrackers stays here). Kalacha is a neat little village, its "streets" defined by rows of carefully placed stones, and litter, if there were any, quickly blown away by the furnace wind. There are two very basic *dukas*, a bar that sells very hot beer, and the humble but friendly *Bismillahi Hotel* which has rooms (**①**). Also worth a look is the Catholic church, whose interior walls are covered with beautiful Ethiopian paintings. But the real treat is the remarkably good mission-run 🏕 **campsite** – dusty and barren yet with decent showers and even a rather inventive swimming pool/water tank, that subsequently feeds an irrigation system. The water, pumped up by a windmill, is sporadically chlorinated. Local Gabbra cluster to sell their wares and to pick up what useful items they can.

From Kalacha to North Horr, the track streaks out over blinding white salt pans and shifting quicksands, ducks behind straggly oasis clusters of half-dead palm trees, and finally loses itself in a vast orange expanse rimmed only by the floating hulks of very distant mountains. The exact path of the road varies annually, and in April is often impassable when the rains bring with them a circus of flamingoes. **NORTH HORR**, when you finally reach it, is a welcome haven, with a handful of *dukas*, the Somali *Mandeleo Hotel* (**①**), opposite the mosque, for traditional fare, rooms at the *Mandera Tourist Hotel* (**①**), and a bright yellow phone box. From here on down to Loiyangalani, the terrain becomes even tougher as the road painfully climbs the volcanic foothills of Mount Kulal, but the view from the top, looking down over the lake far away, can be spellbinding.

To Moyale and beyond

From Marsabit, the **journey to Moyale** takes between five and nine hours depending on the vehicle. For the first three of these you descend from the mountain's greenery past spectacular craters – **Gof Choba** is the whopper on the left – to the forbidding black moonscape of the **Dida Galgalu Desert**. Dida Galgalu means "plains of darkness", according to one Boran story. Another account derives it from Galgalu, a woman buried here after she died of thirst trying to cross it. The road arrows north for endless miles, then cuts east across watercourses and through bushier country beneath high crags on the Ethiopian frontier. En route, you pass a new refugee centre at Lugga Walde (or Walda), 80km before Moyale (a UN and American IRC charity camp), and the turning to the small village of **Sololo** on the Ethiopian border, arrestingly sited between soaring peaks, which can be climbed for stunning views over the northern plains and Ethiopian highlands. Sololo has a mission, which may let you camp in their grounds, and a single lodging/brothel (the *Treetop*). Note that the road to Sololo, and the last stretch into Moyale, sees occasional **armed hold-ups**, though nothing as vicious as those further south and east. Again, the usual rule applies – travel in convoy, and don't resist.

There are some magnificent, towering **termite mounds** along the northern part of the route. They're a sight that seems quintessentially African, yet one which can be quickly taken for granted as the 250km from Marsabit to Moyale roll by with a few slight bends, a couple of scenery changes and the occasional lone herder with his livestock. Over distances that would take days to cover on foot you can see where you have been and where you are going – as if the pastoralists' conservatism were reflected in the landscape.

The road doubles north again and winds up through the settlements of Burji farmers – an agricultural people who emigrated from Ethiopia early in the twentieth century – past their beautifully sculpted houses and sparse fields, to Moyale.

Moyale

Straddling the Ethiopian border, **MOYALE** makes Marsabit look like a metropolis. Though the town is growing rapidly, and was recently supplied with electricity, the centre is small enough to walk around in fifteen minutes. You'll find several sandy streets, a pretty mosque, a few *dukas*, a bar, a camel-tethering ground, two petrol stations (one of which occasionally belies its defunct appearance), a big police station, a fairly large market area, a new KCB bank and an incredibly slow post office – five weeks to Europe. Moyale is not much to write home about in fact, and there's not a lot to do except wander around, perhaps try some camel milk (very rich and creamy) and pass the time of day with everyone else, with or without the aid of *miraa*. Note that there is the odd shooting in town involving "Ethiopian bandits", with the local population as victims. It's a regular enough occurrence, it seems, judging by the practised haste of the shopkeepers in sealing up their businesses on hearing even distant gunfire.

The most interesting aspect of Moyale is its **architecture** – at least, the good number of traditionally built houses which are still standing (the rest were bombed and shelled during World War II, after which the good citizens of Moyale clubbed together for "less fortunate people", contributing £80 to the colony's "Food for Britain Fund"). The Boran build in several styles, including circular mud-and-thatch huts, but in town the houses are rectangular, of mud and dung on a wood frame, with a flat or slightly tilted roof projecting 1–2m to form a porch, supported by sturdy posts and tree trunks. The roof is up to 50cm thick, a fantastic accretion of dried mud, sticks, scrap, and vegetation. Chickens and goats get up there, improving the roof's fertility, and every time it rains another layer of insulating herbage springs up. As a result, the houses are cool while the outside temperature hovers above 30°C for most of the year (July and August are cooler).

Practicalities

Accommodation is very limited and all firmly in the budget category. The most established B&L is *Barissah Hotel* (❶), which shares frontage with the bar. It has a dozen dark cubes around an earth compound, and, while it's hardly clean, it's friendly enough. The **restaurant** has *karanga* and chapattis every evening, 24-hour *malayas*, and a permanent supply of warm tea. You need to bring a padlock, and "showers" (a basin of water) have to be ordered.

A second lodging, where family and guests share the same roof, is *Bismillahi B&L* (❶), across the way from the *Barissah* behind the Esso pumps. It's slightly more expensive, and facilities here don't match the *Barissah*'s, but the food is good. *Silent Lodge* (❶), just outside town near the police barrier, has clean, three-bedded rooms and is perhaps the most promising place. There are other B&Ls on the main street, past the mosque.

The water in Moyale can be briny at times and it's worth bringing a few litres of drinking water up from Marsabit. You can obtain **clean water** in Moyale from the Ministry of Water.

Into Ethiopia

The most interesting prospect in Moyale is to cross the valley into **Ethiopia** and spend a few hours, or even a night, there. For Kenyans and Ethiopians, the border is an open one. For foreigners there are just a few formalities on the Kenyan side, none on the Ethiopian side, and crossing is easy. Doubtless the situation depends much on the latest directives from Nairobi and Addis, and on relations between the two governments, which have generally been good, although local tensions are currently high between competing clans in the district, exacerbated by Ethiopian pastoralists who have encroached on the Kenyan side.

You can increase your chances by ensuring your Kenyan visa is a multiple-entry type, thus allowing you back in again. Naturally, an Ethiopian visa wouldn't hinder your progress either, though the embassy in Nairobi is not likely to concede that entry through Moyale would be permitted (by the rule book, tourists go into Ethiopia only by air through Addis Ababa). As temptation, however, the Ethiopians have trumped the Kenyans and have built a smooth tarmac road from the border all the way to Addis.

Ethiopian Moyale is larger than its Kenyan counterpart and noticeably more prosperous with some piped water, and a long-established electricity supply. There are several bars, a hotel that wouldn't look out of place in a small town in Greece, lots of simple stores, and plenty of eating places. You can pay for everything in Kenyan shillings. The market buzzes colourfully with camels and goats, piles of spices, flour and vegetables. Otherwise, life here seems much the same as over the border, but easier. As a back-door view of Ethiopia, however, it is no more representative than the other side of town is of Kenya.

Travel details

On the main axes – Kitale–Lodwar, Nyahururu–Baragoi and Isiolo–Moyale – you will rarely be stuck for a ride too long. Least frequented is the route up to Loiyangalani and this, together with Isiolo–Moyale, has no bus service. Particulars of road transport are given throughout the chapter.

Buses

This indicates the minimum service you can expect in the north.

Isiolo to: Maralal (every 2 days; 6–8hr); Nairobi (1 daily; 5–6hr).

Lodwar to: Nairobi (1 daily; 15hr); Kitale (6 daily; 8hr); Lokichokio (1 daily; 4hr).

Maralal to: Nairobi (2 daily; 7hr); Nyahururu (2 daily; 3–4hr).

Matatus

Isiolo to: Maralal (daily 6hr); Nairobi (2–3 daily; 5hr); Nanyuki (1–2 daily; 2hr), Meru (2–3 daily; 1hr).

Lodwar to: Lokichokio (4hr by Nissan, 2hr 30min by Peugeot); Kalokol (1hr).

Maralal to: Nairobi (daily; 6hr); Nyahururu (daily; 3hr).

Flights

Lokichokio to: Nairobi (ALS and East African Safari Air; 3 daily; 1hr 45min).

Contexts

Contexts

History

Kenya's precolonial past is still the subject of endless conjecture, and it can be difficult for the traveller to keep much sense of it – especially since the physical record in ancient architecture is virtually nonexistent upcountry. On the coast, settlement ruins, old documents and the Islamic tradition help considerably to retain the feeling of a long past. What follows, up to the colonial period, is a much condensed overview, intended to pull together the historical accounts of individual peoples that are given throughout the guide. More emphasis is given here to the history of the last hundred years or so.

The cradle of humankind

Kenya may be the place where human beings first evolved. Some of the oldest remains apparently belonging to **ancestral hominids** have been found in the Tugen Hills, and the remains of what are thought to be our later ancestors have been found on the shores of Lake Turkana and at Koobi Fora. Even so, concrete evidence of the origins of humanity remains scant, and new finds could easily turn the latest theories upside down.

The East African **Rift Valley** is ideal territory for the search for human origins: volcanic eruptions have repeatedly showered thick layers of ash and cinders over fossil beds, building up strata that can be reliably used to compare ages. The **Leakey** family has been instrumental in much of the work that has been done. Olduvai Gorge in Tanzania was the first major site to disclose evidence of human prehistory, and Louis Leakey and his wife, Mary, worked there from the 1930s. Their son, Richard, went on to explore the Turkana region and found even older fossils, putting Kenya in the spotlight of scientific attention. A suggestion in support of the "cradle of humankind" idea is that the Rift Valley's very formation – a major event on the earth's crust, which began some twenty million years ago – could have been the environmental spark that was the catalyst for human evolution.

In 2000, the Tugen Hills yielded finds from around six million years ago, of a hitherto unknown species named *Orrorin tugenensis*. It was possibly the **first hominid** – that is to say, the first known specimen of a creature on our side of the evolutionary divide between humans and the modern-day great apes – though *Sahelanthropus tchadensis*, discovered in Chad in 2002, is another possible contender. The *O. tugenensis* remains were of a creature that was still an ape but that, crucially, walked upright on two legs. Specimens have also been found in Kenya of the hominids known as **australopithecines**, who seem to have appeared around 4.2 million years ago. Samples of *Australopithecus anamensis*, the earliest known australopithecine, were unearthed on the east side of Lake Turkana in 1965. Examples of later australopithecines have also been found in Kenya, but it is no longer thought that these were our direct ancestors. Evidence that they were not comes in the form of **fossil skull 1470** (its catalogue number), discovered by Bernard Ngeneo in 1972 and now in the National Museum in Nairobi. Between two and three million years old, it's an example of *Homo habilis*, "handy man", the first known member of our own genus, *Homo*. Ngeneo's discovery showed that the earliest members of our genus had co-existed with the later australopithecines.

Almost as important was the discovery in 1984 of the nearly complete 1.6-million-year-old skeleton of 12-year-old **"Turkana Boy"**, a member of the later species *Homo erectus* ("upright" man – though the australopithecines probably spent most of their time upright too), our immediate ancestor, found at Nariokotome on the western shore of Lake Turkana. It was probably *H. erectus* who developed **speech** and discovered how to make **fire**, while improving enormously on the **tool-making** efforts of *H. habilis*. **Olorgasailie** and **Kariandusi** are two "hand axe" sites, probably belonging to *H. erectus*, which have been used within the last five hundred thousand years. And it was *H. erectus* who, if the "cradle" theory is right, spread the humanoid gene pool to Asia, Europe and the rest of Africa, where, over the next few hundred thousand years, *Homo sapiens* emerged on the scene.

Early inhabitants

Real history begins with the **hunter-gatherers**. Numbering probably fewer than a hundred thousand, living in small units of several families, and either staying in one place for generations or moving through the country according to the dictates of the seasons, these earliest human inhabitants may have been related to the ancestors of present-day Pygmy and Khoisan (Bushmen) peoples, and probably spoke "click" languages similar to those of the Khoisan peoples of southern Africa and Tanzania today. Remnant hunter-gatherer groups still live in remote parts of Kenya – the **Boni** on the mainland north of Lamu, the **Sanye** along the Tana River and the **Okiek** and **Dorobo** in parts of the highlands – but their languages have mostly been adopted from neighbouring peoples. The hunting and gathering way of life is one that has persisted in the cultural memories of most Kenyan peoples, and some of the groups who still practise it may have veered away from farming or herding societies in times of hardship.

The earliest distinct migration to Kenya was of **Cushitic**-speaking people from the Ethiopian Highlands. Occasional hunters and gatherers themselves, they were also livestock herders and farmers; over the centuries, they filled the areas that were too dry for a purely subsistence way of life. They also absorbed many of the previous inhabitants through intermarriage. Having herds and cultivating land brought up questions of ownership, inheritance and water rights, and an elaboration of social institutions and customs to deal with them. The Cushites had a strong material culture, using stone, particularly obsidian, to produce beautiful arrowheads, knives and axes, and they made a whole range of pottery utensils. They left evidence of their settlements in burial cairns and living sites at places like Hyrax Hill, near Nakuru. The same people may have built the irrigation works still used today along the Elgeyo Escarpment, west of Lake Baringo. For the most part, the earliest Cushites were absorbed by peoples who came later and they adopted new languages and customs. The changes were not all one-sided, however: **circumcision** and **clitoridectomy** (female circumcision), practised by the early Cushites, became important cultural rituals for many of the peoples who succeeded and absorbed them.

The **Somali** and **Rendille** of the northeast are the main groups still speaking Cushitic languages, though their arrival in Kenya was more recent. Today, only the Boni speak a language related to the Southern Cushitic of the first farmers and herders, although the Boni themselves are hunter-gatherers.

For present-day Kenya, the most important arrivals began to reach the country in the first few centuries AD. From the northwest and the headwaters of the Nile came the **Nilotic**-speaking ancestors of the so-called **Kalenjin** peoples; from the west and south came speakers of **Bantu** languages, forebears of today's **Kikuyu**, **Gusii**, **Akamba** and **Mijikenda**, among others. (Bantu, a word coined by twentieth-century linguists, derives from the common stem for "person" – *ntu* – and the plural prefix *ba*. The word is not found in any of the six hundred contemporary Bantu languages spread across the continent, but it may have been the one used for "people" in the proto-language before it diversified.)

Along with their languages, the new arrivals brought new technologies, including iron-working. **Iron** had enabled the Bantu to spread from the Nigeria/Cameroon area across central Africa, clearing the virgin forests and hoeing the ground for their crops. Eastwards, they encountered new Asian food crops – bananas, yams and rice – some of which arrived in East Africa by way of the Indonesian colonization of Madagascar. This new diversity of foods helped people to settle permanently in chosen regions. The Kalenjin peoples consolidated in the Western Highlands. The Bantu were particularly successful and, as their broad economic base took hold across the southern half of Kenya, their languages quickly spread. Herding, hunting, fishing and gathering were important supplements to the agricultural mainstay, while trade conducted with their exclusively pastoral or hunter-gatherer neighbours, especially in iron tools, carried their influence further. By about 1000 AD, Kenya's Stone-Age technology had been largely replaced by an Iron-Age one and, as human domination of the country increased, the beginnings of real specialization in agriculture and herding set in among the peoples.

Down on the **coast**, Bantu immigrants mixed, over several hundred years, with the Cushitic-speaking inhabitants and with a continuous trickle of settlers from Arabia and the Persian Gulf. With the advent of Islam, this melange gradually gave rise to a distinct culture and civilization – **Swahili** – speaking a Bantu language laced with foreign vocabulary. The Swahili were Kenya's link with the rest of the world, trading animal skins, ivory, agricultural produce and slaves, for cloth, metals, ceramics, grain, ghee and sugar, with ships from the Middle East, India and even China. The Swahili were the first Kenyans to acquire firearms. They were also the first to write their language (in the Arabic script) and the first to develop complex, stratified communities based on town and countryside. Swahili history is covered in more depth in chapter 6.

Later arrivals

New **American crops** – corn, cassava and tobacco – spread through Kenya after the Portuguese arrived in the early sixteenth century. They undoubtedly increased the country's population capacity, while enabling a greater degree of permanent settlement and providing new trade goods.

At about this time, a pastoral **Nilotic**-speaking people, distantly related to the earlier Kalenjin arrivals, began a migration from the northwest. These were the first **Luo**-speakers who, some generations earlier, had left their homeland (around Wau in southern Sudan) for reasons that were probably largely economic. In the alternately flooded and parched flatlands around the Nile, unusual conditions could be catastrophic. The Luo ancestors were always on the move, herding, planting, hunting or fishing. Politically, they had a fairly complex organization as, for months on end, while the Nile flooded, communities would be stranded in concentration along the low ridges. Several good years might be followed by drought, and population pressure then forced less dominant groups to go off in search of water and pasture. The overall trend was southwards. Groups of migrants picked up other, non-Luo-speakers on the way, gradually assimilating them through intermarriage and language change, always drawing attention with the impressive regalia and social standing of their *ruoth* – the Luo kings.

On the shores of Lake Victoria, where the Luo finally settled, sleeping sickness is thought to have wiped out many of their herds. But they were pragmatic, resourceful people, whose background of mixed farming and herding during the era of migration supported them. They turned to agriculture and, increasingly, to fishing.

Towards the end of the seventeenth century, another Nilotic, pastoral people, the **Turkana**, appeared in Kenya. Linguistically closer to the Maasai Nilotes, they seem to have shared the Luo resilience to economic hardship and they, too, have (recently) turned to fishing. Also like the Luo, and almost unique among Kenyan peoples, they have never practised circumcision.

The Maa-speakers – **Maasai** and **Samburu** – were the last group to arrive in Kenya, and their rise and fall had far-reaching effects on neighbouring peoples. Moving southwards from the beginning of the seventeenth century, they expanded swiftly thanks to their nomadic pastoral lifestyle, and in a few generations they were transformed from an obscure group into a dominant force in the region. Culturally, they borrowed extensively from their neighbours, especially the **Kalenjin** peoples, who spoke **Nandi**. Nandi words and Kalenjin cultural values were adopted, including circumcision, the age-set system and some ancient (originally probably Cushitic) taboos against eating fish and certain wild animals. It's likely that much of the "traditional" Maasai appearance also owes something to these contacts. The Maasai migration was no slow spread. Their cattle were periodically herded south and other peoples were raided en route to enlarge the herds; by 1800, they were widely established in the Rift Valley and on the plains, everywhere between Lake Turkana and Kilimanjaro. In response to Maasai dominance, many of the Bantu peoples adopted their styles and customs. Initiation by genital mutilation, probably already practised by most Bantu-speakers, was imbued with a new significance – especially for the Kikuyu – by intermarriage and close, if not always peaceable, relations with the Maasai.

Severe **droughts** in the nineteenth century pushed the Maasai further and further afield in search of new pastures, bringing them into conflict, and trade, with other peoples. Drought, disease and rinderpest epidemics (which killed off their cattle) were also responsible for a series of civil wars between different Maasai sections in the second half of the nineteenth century. These **Maasai civil wars** disrupted the **trading networks** which had been set up between the coast and the interior, mainly by Swahili, Mijikenda, Akamba and Kikuyu. Dutch, English and French goods were finding their way upcountry, and American interests were already being served nearly two centuries ago, as white calico cloth (still called *amerikani* today) became a major item of profit. In the last throes of the slave trade's existence, **slaves** were being exported from western Kenya and Uganda.

Largely in response to slavery and widespread fighting, the first **missionaries** installed themselves upcountry (the earliest went inland from Mombasa in 1846). Throughout this period, the Maasai disrupted movements through their territories and attacked Swahili slavers, Bantu traders and explorer-missionaries alike. The Maasai *morani* were specifically trained for raiding – a kind of guerrilla warfare – but, while their reputation lived on, they were bitterly divided among themselves and not organized on anything like a tribal scale.

By the time Europe had partitioned the map of Africa, the Maasai, who could have been the imperialists' most intractable enemies, were unable to retaliate effectively. The **Nandi** of the Western Highlands, the main people of the Kalenjin group, had begun to take the Maasai's place as Kenya's most feared adversaries, and put up the stiffest resistance. They were organized to the extent of having a single spiritual leader, the *orkoiyot*, who ruled what was in effect a theocracy. Their war of attrition against the British delayed advances for a number of years. But the Nandi did not have the territorial advantage that would have helped the Maasai, and the murder of their *orkoiyot*, **Koitalel**, by the British, destroyed their military organization.

On the coast, the **Sultanate of Oman**, which had ousted the Portuguese from Mombasa in 1698, ruled all the way from Lamu down to Mozambique, making Zanzibar its capital in 1840. Oman was already under British influence, and officially a British protectorate, when it split in 1856; Zanzibar, including what is now the coast of Kenya, became a sultanate in its own right.

The scramble for Africa

All Kenya's peoples resisted colonial domination to some degree. In the first twenty years of British attempts to rule, tens of thousands were killed in ugly massacres and manhunts, and many more were made homeless. Administrators – whose memoirs (see "Books", p.680) are the most revealing background for that period – all differed in their ideas of the ultimate purpose of their work and the best means of imposing British authority.

British interests in East Africa at the close of the nineteenth century had sprung from the European power struggle and the "scramble for Africa". The 1885 Berlin Conference chopped the continent into arbitrary spheres of influence. Germany was awarded what was to become Tanganyika; Britain got Kenya and Uganda. In 1886, formal agreements were drawn up and Kilimanjaro was ceded to Victoria's grandson, the Kaiser, giving each monarch a snowcapped equatorial mountain.

Uganda was the focus of British interest, since Kenya – decimated by drought, locusts, rinderpest and civil war – seemed largely a deserted wasteland. And Uganda was strategically important for **control of the Nile** – which had long been a British preoccupation. But rivalry wasn't far beneath the seemingly amicable surface and Germany clearly had Uganda earmarked too. Britain's claim was in danger of lapsing if Uganda could not be properly garrisoned and supplied, and Kenya was the necessary base from which to do that.

In 1888, the British government granted permission for commercial operations in Uganda to the **Imperial British East Africa Company** (IBEAC), which, for sea access, leased a wide swath of southern Kenya from the Sultan of Zanzibar. The British also authorized the IBEAC to administer Uganda and that section of Kenya on their behalf. The company officers – mostly young and totally inexperienced English clerks – established a series of trading forts at fifty-mile intervals in a line connected by a rough ox-track leading from Mombasa into Uganda. Machakos, Murang'a and Mumias all began as IBEAC stations.

The IBEAC eventually went bankrupt, having failed to establish any kind of administration. The British government stepped into the breach in 1895, declaring a **protectorate** over Uganda and Kenya. Having thus acquired the region, the British decided to build a **railway**. This classic, valedictory piece of Victorian engineering took six years to complete and cost the lives of hundreds of Indian labourers. Financially, it was a commitment which grew out of all proportion to the likely returns and continued to grow long after the last rail was laid. But its completion transformed the future of East Africa. From now on, the supply lines were secure and the interior only a month's journey from Europe by ship and rail. Suddenly, the prospects for developing the cool, fertile Kenya highlands looked much more attractive than the distant unknowns of Uganda and its powerful kingdoms.

More immediately, the railway physically divided the **Maasai** at a time when they were already disunified and moving into alliances with the British. Their grazing lands, together with the regions of the **Kalenjin** peoples and the **Kikuyu** on the lower slopes of the highlands, were to become the heartland of white settlerdom.

The Kenya colony

Many in Edwardian Britain saw Kenya as a land of opportunity: a new New Zealand, or even a Jewish homeland (a party of Zionists was actually escorted around Kenya but declined the offer). It was Sir Charles Eliot, the Protectorate's second governor, who was the main mover behind the **settlement scheme**. While some colonialists urged consideration for the "rights of natives", the growing clamour of voices claiming the support of British taxpayers – who had met the bill for the railway – outweighed any altruism. Eliot's extrava-gant reports on the potential of BEA (British East Africa) were published and government policy was directed towards getting the settlers in and making the railway pay. Landless aristocrats, middle-class adventurers, big-game hunters, ex-servicemen and Afrikaners (the farming land was also advertised in South Africa) began to trickle up the line. Using ox-wagons to get to the tracts of bush they had leased, they started their farms from scratch. Lord Delamere, governor himself for a time, was their biggest champion. In the years leading up to World War I, the trickle of settlers became a flood and by 1916 the area "alienated" to **European settlers** had risen to 15,000 square kilometres of the best land. Imported livestock was hybridized with hardy, local breeds; coffee, tea, sisal and pineapples were introduced and thrived; European crops flour-ished and cereals soon covered vast areas.

Nearly half the land worth farming was now in the hands of settlers, but it had rapidly become clear that it was far from empty of local inhabitants. Colonial invasion had occurred at a low point in the fortunes of Kenya's peoples and, unprepared for the scale of the incursion, they were swiftly pushed aside into "native reserves" or became squatters without rights. As populations recovered, serious land shortages set in. The British appointment of "chiefs" – whose main task was to collect a tax on every hut – had the effect of diverting grievances against colonial policy onto these early collaborators and laying the foundations of a class structure in Kenyan society. Without a money economy, employment was the only means available to pay taxes and, effectively, a system of forced labour had been created. The whole apparatus quickly became entrenched in a series of **land and labour laws**. A poll tax was added to the hut tax; all African men were compelled to register to facilitate labour recruitment; squatters on alienated land were required to pay rent, through labour; and cash cropping on African plots was discouraged or banned (coffee licences, for example, were restricted to white farmers). The highlands were strictly reserved for white settlement, while land not owned by Europeans became Crown Land, its African occupants "tenants at will" of the Crown and liable to summary eviction.

Asians, too, were excluded from the highlands. While the leader of Kenya's Indians, **A.M. Jeevanjee**, had called for the transformation of Kenya into the "America of the Hindu", the proposal never came near consideration by the British. Barred from farming on any scale – except in the far west, where they developed sugar cane as an important crop – Indians concentrated on the middle ground, setting up general stores (*dukas*) across the country, investing in small industries and handling services.

World War I

World War I had a number of profound effects, although there were comparatively few battles in Kenya itself. Some 200,000 African porters and soldiers were conscripted and sent to Tanganyika (German East Africa), where one in four of them died. Those who returned were deeply influenced by the experience. They had seen European tribes at war with each other, they had experienced European fallibility, and witnessed the kind of organization used to overcome it.

General von Lettow Vorbeck, the German commander, waged a dogged campaign against British forces despite the fact that his own were vastly outnumbered, with the aim of engaging as much manpower as possible and taking the heat off German forces in Europe. Nevertheless, the Germans lost the war – and Tanganyika – to the British, whose commitments in East Africa were suddenly multiplied.

Sir Edward Northey, governor of Kenya at the time of armistice, pushed his **Soldier Settlement Scheme** through without difficulty. Its aim, to double the settler population in Kenya to nine thousand and increase revenue, seemed promising enough to a government sapped by war. But the Soldier Settlement Scheme was bitterly resented by Africans, particularly those who had fought alongside the soldiers and were now excluded from their gains.

Early nationalism and reaction

Political associations sprang up among those with a mission-school education and ex-servicemen: the Kikuyu Association, the Young Kikuyu Association and the Young Kavirondo Association. **Harry Thuku,** secretary of the Young Kikuyu Association, realized its potential and re-formed it as the East Africa Association in order to recruit on a nationwide basis. The hated registration law by which every African was obliged to carry a pass – the *kipande* – was a prime grievance, but tax reduction, introduction of land title deeds and wage increases were demanded as well. Alliances were built up with embittered Indian associations and 1921 saw a year of protests and rallies. These culminated in Thuku's detention and the shooting by police of 25 demonstrators at a mass rally calling for Thuku's release. He remained in detention for eleven years.

The Indian constituency eventually secured two nominated seats (not elected) on the Legislative Council. Africans, meanwhile, remained voiceless, landless, disenfranchised and segregated by the **colour bar**.

As the settlers became established, they began to contribute appreciably to the income of the colony (which Kenya had officially become in 1920). Most of them seem to have believed that they were in at the beginning of a long and glorious pageant of white dominion. Indeed, settler self-government, along Canadian or South African lines, was a declared aim. African demands were hardly heeded by the authorities, but the Colonial Office was in a difficult position over the **Indians**, who were already British subjects and whose demands for equal rights they had trouble in refuting. Tentative proposals to give them voting rights, allow unrestricted immigration from India and abolish segregation caused alarm and indignation among the settlers. Their **Convention of Associations**, already arguing the case for white home rule, formed a "Vigilance Committee", which worked out detailed military plans for rebellion, including the kidnapping of the governor and the deportation of the Indians. Sensing a crisis, the Colonial Office drew up a white paper and a grudging settlement was reached that allowed five Indians and one Arab to be elected to the Legislative Council (the colony's local government), as opposed to eleven Europeans.

The primacy of African "interests", admirably reiterated yet again in the Devonshire Declaration of 1923, was still denied any real expression. A system of **de facto apartheid** was being practised. It was in this climate in the 1920s and 1930s that, floating above their economic troubles, the settlers had their heyday – the **Happy Valley life** so appallingly and fascinatingly depicted in *White Mischief* (see p.668) and other books.

Education, Kenyatta and the Kikuyu

The opportunities available to Africans came almost entirely through **mission schools** at first. Again, there was conflict between government and settlers on the question of **education**. The Colonial Office was committed, on paper at least, to the general development of the country for all its inhabitants, while the white farmers were on the whole adamant that raising educational standards could only lead to trouble. A crude form of Swahili had become the language of communication between Africans and Europeans. But the teaching of English was a controversial issue that hard-liners foresaw eventually rebounding on government and settlers alike. In frustration, the Kikuyu set up self-help **independent schools** in the 1930s, primarily in order to teach their own children English.

Whether barring access to English education would ultimately have made any difference is debatable, but by the late 1930s there were already enough educated Africans to pose the beginnings of a serious challenge to white supremacy. One of these was **Jomo Kenyatta**. Born some time between 1889 and 1895 near Kiambu, just north of Nairobi, and educated at the Scottish Mission Center in nearby Thogoto, Kenyatta adopted his name from the traditional beaded belt (*kenyatta*) he always wore.

After Thuku's imprisonment and the bloodshed at Nairobi in 1921, the East African Association was dissolved and was succeeded by the **Kikuyu Central Association** (**KCA**), which Kenyatta joined in 1928. The KCA was the spearhead of nationalism and lobbied hard for a return of alienated land, the lowering of taxes and for elected African representatives on the Legislative Council. It also protested against missionary efforts to outlaw **female circumcision**, on the grounds that the church was attempting to undermine Kikuyu culture. This last conflict led to a leadership crisis in the KCA and for a number of years threatened to swamp other issues.

Kenya survived the 1929 stock market crash and the resulting world **trade slump** as the colonial government became increasingly committed to the struggling settlers it was now bailing out. Exports fell catastrophically; coffee-planting by non-whites was still prohibited and the tax burden continued to be placed squarely on Africans. Faced with this crisis, even some of the settlers began to accept that large-scale changes were in order. Just as awareness was growing that the economy could not survive indefinitely unless Africans were given more of a chance to participate in it, Kenya was thrown into World War II.

World War II – and Mau Mau

Perhaps not surprisingly, soldiers were easily recruited into the **King's African Rifles** when Italian-held Ethiopia (then Abyssinia) declared war on Kenya. Volunteers wanted money, education and a chance to see the world; conscripts, filling the quotas assigned to their chiefs, faced a life at home or on the native reserve that was no better. Propaganda immediately succeeded in casting Hitler's image as the embodiment of all racist evil. Some Africans thought the war, once won, would improve their position in Kenya. They were partly right. Military campaigns in Ethiopia and Burma owed much of their success to African troops and during the war their efforts were glowingly praised by Allied commanders.

On the soldiers' return, a new awareness, more profound than that felt by those returning from World War I, came upon them. The white tribes of Europe had fought the war on the issue of self-determination; the message wasn't lost on Africans. Yet still, in almost every other sphere of life, they were demeaned and humiliated. The KCA had been banned at the outbreak of war, allegedly for supporting the Italian fascists, and African political life was subdued. Real change, for 99 percent of the population, was still a dream.

Kenya's food-exporting economy had done well out of the war and it was clear the colony could make a major contribution to Britain's recovery. The postwar Labour government encouraged economic expansion without going far enough to include Africans among the beneficiaries of the investment. Industrialization gathered momentum and there was a rapid growth of towns. There was also further promotion of **white immigration** – a new influx of European settlers arrived soon after the war – and greater power was given to the settlers on the Legislative and Executive Councils. Population growth and intense **pressure on land** in the rural areas were leading to severe disruptions of traditional community life as people were shunted into the reserves or else left their villages to search for work in the towns. On the political front, militant **trade unionism**, dominated by ex-servicemen, gradually usurped the positions of those African leaders who had been prepared to work with the government.

Postwar African politics

A single African member, Eliud Mathu, was appointed to the Legislative Council in 1944. More significant, however, was the formation of the **Kenya African Union (KAU)**, a consultative group of leaders and spokesmen set up with the governor's approval to liaise with Mathu. The KAU's first president was Harry Thuku.

Kenyatta had spent most of the period between 1931 and 1946 in Britain, campaigning for the KCA, studying anthropology under Malinowski at the London School of Economics and writing his homage to the Kikuyu people,

Facing Mount Kenya. His **return** in 1946, to an unexpectedly tumultuous welcome, signalled a real departure for African political rights and the birth of a new current of nationalism. The KAU was transformed into an active political party – and ran straight into conflict with itself. The **radicals** within the party wanted sweeping changes in land ownership, equal voting rights and abolition of the **pass law**, under which all black Kenyans were restricted in their movements and forced to carry an internal passport. The **moderates** were for negotiation, educational improvement, multiracial progress and a gradual shift of power. They were not convinced that their best interests lay in confronting the British head-on; they had all achieved considerable ambitions within the settler economy. Kenyatta, elected KAU president in 1947, was ambitious himself, but the Europeans mistrusted his intentions and rumour-mongered about his communist connections, his visit to Russia during his time abroad and his personal life.

Despite Kenyatta's efforts to steer a middle course, the KAU became increasingly radical and Kikuyu-dominated. While he angled to give the party a multitribal profile to appease the settlers, he also managed to sacrifice some moderates in the leadership for the sake of party unity. There were defections as well. Several radicals joined an underground movement and took oaths of allegiance against the British. Oath-taking groups emerged secretly all around the Central Highlands and, by 1951, a Central Committee was organized to coordinate activities.

The Mau Mau Rebellion

The Central Committee began murdering its opponents and attacking white-owned property in what was to become known as the **Mau Mau Rebellion**. The origin of the name Mau Mau is obscure (it may derive from *muma*, a traditional Kikuyu oath), but the insurgents never used it, calling themselves the **Land and Freedom Army** (**LFA**). The British accused the KAU leadership of involvement, but this seems unlikely, though the insurgents used Kenyatta's name in their propaganda. The LFA consisted largely of young men from the rural periphery of towns like Nyeri, Fort Hall (Murang'a) and Nairobi, and membership was overwhelmingly Kikuyu. One of the main factors prompting them into violent action was that land seizure by the settlers meant they no longer had enough land to feed themselves. Many insurgents had taken part in strikes during the late 1940s, and others were ex-soldiers who had fought for the British and learned guerrilla warfare in places like Burma.

In August 1952, following arson attacks on the homes of people who had refused to take the Mau Mau oath, the government imposed a curfew on three districts of Nairobi where support for the insurgents was strong. But in October, **Chief Waruhiu wa Kungu**, the government's most senior African official, was murdered in Nairobi in broad daylight after making a speech condemning the Mau Mau. The British reacted by declaring a **State of Emergency**, and arresting any suspected insurgents. Within ten days, they had detained nearly four thousand people.

Kenyatta had played a delicate political game, condemning strikes and even oath-taking but ready to seize on any chance to exploit the situation. Now he and other KAU leaders were arrested and interned for their supposed part in the uprising. Thousands of **British troops** were sent to Kenya, and a **Kikuyu Home Guard** was formed to combat the Mau Mau, but the hardcore guerrillas fled into and lived off the jungle for months on end, launching surprise attacks at night. They relied on considerable support from the Kikuyu homesteads for supplies, intelligence reports and stolen weapons.

By early 1953, the rebels were becoming more daring. In January they murdered a settler family, the Rucks, including their 6-year-old son, and in March, a party of 83 insurgents raided **Naivasha police station**, releasing 173 detainees and seizing a large quantity of weaponry. Almost simultaneously, a force of some one thousand insurgents attacked the village of **Lari**, northwest of Nairobi, whose residents were Kikuyus loyal to the colonial regime, many of them Home Guard members. The insurgents burned down their homes and hacked to death around 84 people; only 31 survived.

The British now declared "**Special Areas**" in which anyone who failed to stop when challenged would be shot, and "**Prohibited Areas**" – including the Aberdares and Mount Kenya – in which all black people would be shot on sight. In April 1954 they put Nairobi under military control, rounding up all the city's Kikuyu residents and detaining 17,000 of them, before extending the operation to other Kikuyu areas. By the end of the year, there were 77,000 prisoners in British **concentration camps**, where they were subject to arbitrary acts of brutality and murder at the hands of British troops. At one point, a third of the entire male Kikuyu population was being held in detention.

Under emergency powers, a policy of "**villagization**" was also enforced: by the end of 1955, over a million people – almost the entire Kikuyu population – had been forcibly resettled in villages policed by guards and fenced with barbed wire. It was during this period that the cluster of closely related small tribes known today as the **Kalenjin**, acquired their name, which means "I tell you" in their common language, Nandi. Forging together the Nandi, Pokot, Elgeyo, Marakwet, Tugen and others under a single umbrella, it was largely the creation of the colonial authorities, seeking to recruit and reinforce support against the Kikuyu-dominated Mau Mau.

At its height in 1953, the insurgency consisted of some fifteen thousand guerrillas, but little by little the British hunted them down. By September 1956, only around five thousand remained. The **end of the revolt** came in October that year with the capture and execution of **Dedan Kimathi**, the LFA's commander-in-chief. The State of Emergency nonetheless continued until 1960, when it was abandoned after news that British troops had bludgeoned detainees at **Hola** detention camp, killing eleven and injuring sixty, escaped into the press and caused a scandal in Britain.

During the uprising, insurgents had murdered 32 white settlers and around 2000 African civilians. Fifty British troops lost their lives. The British had hanged 1090 rebels – more than in any other colonial uprising – and claimed to have killed around 11,000 guerrillas, destroying much of the documentation about the detention camps before independence. New evidence however, collected by Caroline Elkins of Harvard University (see "Books", p.669), suggests that British forces killed more than 50,000 people, perhaps even 100,000. Many of these, uncommitted to Mau Mau, yet living in key locations as far as the British were concerned, were caught, sometimes literally, in the crossfire. No British officials were ever prosecuted for atrocities committed during the Emergency, nor has Britain ever apologized to Kenya for it.

Independence – uhuru

With the Emergency over, the KAU leaders still at liberty set about exploiting the European fear of a repeat episode. Anything that now delayed the fulfilment of African nationalist aspirations could be seen as fuel for another revolt. There was no longer any question of a South African-style, white-dominated independence. Settlers, mindful of the preparations for independence taking place in other African countries, began rallying to the cry of multiracialism in a vain attempt to secure what looked like a very shaky future.

At the 1960 Lancaster House Conference in London, called to discuss Kenya's future, African representatives won a convincing victory by pushing through measures to give them majorities in the Legislative Council and the Council of Ministers. The members of these bodies, all nominated by the colonial authorities, included **Tom Mboya**, the prominent and charismatic Luo trade unionist, and the radical politician **Oginga Odinga** (another Luo), as well as **Daniel Arap Moi** and the Mijikenda leader **Ronald Ngala**. A new constitution was drawn up and eventual access to the White Highlands was accepted. The declaration promised that "Kenya was to be an African country": the path to independence was guaranteed; British Prime Minister Harold Macmillan said as much in a speech to the South African parliament at the time the Lancaster House Conference was meeting. The settlers perceived a "calamitous betrayal", with universal franchise and African-dominated independence expected within ten years. (In fact, it happened earlier than anticipated.)

Minority tribal associations, meanwhile, foresaw troubles ahead if the Kikuyu/Luo elite achieved independence for Kenya at the cost of the smaller constituencies. In 1960, the Kenya African National Union (**KANU**) was formed, dominated by the Kikuyu and Luo politicians who had campaigned most prominently against British colonial rule. Soon after, a second, more moderate party, the Kenya African Democratic Union (**KADU**), was created, with Britain's help, to federate the minority, largely rural-based, political associations in a broad defensive alliance against Kikuyu/Luo domination. One of KADU's leading members was **Daniel Arap Moi**.

Elections were held in 1961, KANU emerging with nineteen seats against KADU's eleven. But KANU refused to form a government until Kenyatta was released. A temporary coalition government was formed, composed of KADU, European and Asian members. Kenyatta was duly released and, six months later, a member resigned his seat, making room for him on the Legislative Council. In 1962, Kenyatta became Minister for Constitutional Affairs and Economic Planning – a wide portfolio – in a new coalition government formed out of the KADU alliance and KANU. Despite a second London conference to try to reach an agreement about the federal constitution demanded by KADU, the question was left in the air. Independence elections the following year seemed to answer the constitutional question: KANU emerged with an even greater lead and a mandate for a non-federal structure. On June 1 – **Madaraka Day** – Kenyatta became Kenya's first prime minister. And on December 12, 1963, control of foreign affairs was handed over and Kenya became formally **independent**.

The Kenyatta years – *harambee*

It was barely sixty years since the pioneer settlers had arrived. Many of them had panicked, sold up and left before independence, but others decided to stay under an **African government**. Despite his years in detention, Kenyatta turned out to have more consideration for their interests than could have been foreseen. He held successful meetings with settlers in his home village; his bearded, genial image and conciliatory speeches assuring them of their rights and security quickly earned him wide international support and the respected title Mzee (Elder). Many Europeans retained important positions in administration and the judiciary.

Milton Obote and Julius Nyerere, leaders of newly independent Uganda and Tanzania, held talks with Kenyatta on setting up an **East African Community** to share railways, aviation, postal services and telecommunications, and customs and excise. This was formally inaugurated in 1967. There was a mood of optimism: it looked very much as if Kenya had succeeded against all the odds.

But there were urgent issues to contend with. **Land reform** and the rehabilitation of freedom fighters and detainees were the most pressing. Large tracts of European land were bought up and a programme to provide small plots to landless peasants was rapidly instigated. Political questions loomed large as well. On December 12, 1964, Kenya became a republic, its head of state no longer the Queen, but rather President Kenyatta. KADU was dissolved "in the interests of national unity", its leaders absorbed into the ruling KANU party, making Kenya a de facto one-party state. For the sake of "national security", British troops were kept on, initially to quell a revolt of ethnic Somalis in the northeast and an army mutiny in Nairobi. A defence treaty has kept a British force at Nanyuki ever since.

There was heavy emphasis on **harambee** (pulling together), endorsed by Kenyatta at all his public appearances. *Harambee* meetings became a unique national institution, fund-raising events at which – in a not untraditional way – donations were made by local notables and politicians towards self-help healthcare and educational programmes. During the 1960s and 1970s, hundreds of *harambee* schools were built and equipped in this way. But the ostentatious gifts, and particularly the guaranteed press coverage the next day with donors listed in order of value, sometimes reduced the *harambee* vision of community development to an exercise in patronage and competitive status-seeking.

On the **economic front**, the first decade of independence saw remarkable changes and rapid growth. The settlers' fairly broad-based crop-exporting economy was a powerful springboard for development, and not difficult to transfer to African control. While many large landholdings were sold *en bloc* to African investors, smaller farmers did begin to contribute significantly to export earnings through coffee, tea, pyrethrum and fruit. Industrialization proceeded at a slower pace. Kenya's mineral resources are very limited and the country relies heavily on oil imports. **Foreign investment** wasn't especially beneficial, as investors were given wide freedoms to import equipment and technical skills and to re-export much of the profit.

The resettlement programme was abandoned in 1966, its objectives "largely attained". But many peasants, having been squatters on European farms, were now "illegal squatters" on private African land. Thousands migrated to the towns where unemployment was already a serious problem. Kenya was becoming a class-divided society. **Growth**, rather than a radical redistribution of wealth, was the government's main concern. Although by 1970 more than two-thirds of the European mixed farming lands were occupied by some 50,000 Africans, and the overall standard of living had improved considerably, income disparities were greater than ever. **Kikuyu-Luo domination** – particularly Kikuyu – was strongly resented by other groups, though it was perhaps inevitable that the people who had lost most and suffered most under British rule should expect to receive the most benefits from independence.

Political opposition

It was in this climate that KANU's leadership split. **Oginga Odinga**, the party vice-president, resigned in 1966 to form the socialist **Kenya People's Union**

(**KPU**) and 29 MPs joined him. The ex-guerrilla Bildad Kaggia became deputy head of the KPU and a vocal agitator for poorer Kikuyu. Kenyatta and Mboya closed ranks in KANU and prepared for political conflict. KPU was anti-capitalist and pro-non-alignment. KANU – led in this respect by Tom Mboya – stressed the need for close ties with the West, and for economic conditions that would attract foreign investment. The KPU's stand was denounced as divisive, and the party was barely tolerated for three years, its members harassed and detained by the security forces, its activities obstructed by new legislation and constitutional amendments.

In KANU, Odinga's post of vice-president was taken, briefly, by Joseph Murumbi and then, with behind-the-scenes encouragement from the British (keen to avoid a radical in the job), by Daniel Arap Moi. Odinga had strong, grassroots support in the Luo and Gusii districts of western Kenya. But **Tom Mboya**'s supporters came from an even broader base, including many poor Kikuyu. By the end of the 1960s, speculation was mounting about whether he would be able to take over the presidency on Kenyatta's death. As the Mzee's right-hand man he was widely tipped to succeed – a possibility that alarmed Kenyatta's Kikuyu supporters. In July 1969, Mboya was gunned down by a Kikuyu assassin in central Nairobi. No high-level complicity in the murder was ever brought to light, but Mboya's death was a devastating blow to Kenya's fragile stability, setting off shock waves along both class and tribal divisions. There was widespread fighting and rioting between Kikuyu and Luo, fuelled by years of rivalry and growing feelings of Luo exclusion from government. During a visit by Kenyatta to Kisumu – where he attended a public meeting at which Odinga and his supporters were present – hostility against his entourage was so great that police opened fire, killing at least ten demonstrators.

The KPU was immediately banned and Odinga detained without trial. Although the constitution continued to guarantee the right to form opposition parties, non-KANU nominations to parliament were, in practice, forbidden. There was a resurgence of oath-taking among Kikuyu, Meru and Embu, pledging to maintain the Kikuyu hold on power. The Kikuyu contingent in the army was strengthened and a new force of shock troops, the **General Service Unit** (**GSU**), was recruited under Kikuyu officers; independent of police and army, it was to act as an internal security force. In the early 1970s, Kikuyu control – of the government, the administration, business interests and land – gripped tighter and tighter.

Internationally, however, Kenya was seen as one of the safest **African investments** – a model of stability only too happy to allow the multinational corporations access to its resources and markets. The development of the tourist industry helped give the country a positive profile. And, in comparison with most other African countries, some still fighting for independence and others beset by civil war or paralysed by drought, Kenya's future looked healthy enough. But in achieving record economic growth, foreign interests often seemed to crush indigenous ones. An elite of profiteers – nicknamed **wabenzi** after the Mercedes Benzes they favoured – extracted enormous gains out of transactions with foreign companies. Nepotism was blatant and Kenyatta himself was rumoured to be one of the richest men in the world. For the mass of Kenyan people, life was hardly any better than before independence. Students poured out of the secondary schools with few prospects of using their qualifications; population increase was the highest in the world; and, most damaging of all, land distribution was still grossly unfair in a society where land was the basic means of making a living.

In 1975, in the first ever explicit public attack on the Kikuyu monopoly of power, the radical populist MP **J.M. Kariuki** warned that Kenya could become a country of "ten millionaires and ten million beggars". He was arrested for his pains then, some weeks later, was found murdered in the Ngong Hills. A massive turnout at his funeral was followed by angry **student demonstrations**. "Kariuki's death", wrote the then outspoken *Weekly Review*, "instils in the minds of the public the fear of dissidence, the fear to criticize, the fear to stand out and take an unconventional public stance." In the following years, a number of other MPs were detained, and the issue of landlessness ceased to be one that many people were prepared to shout about.

Kenyatta retreated into dictatorial seclusion, propped up by close Kikuyu cronies. As parliament, and even the cabinet, took an increasingly passive role in decision-making, the pronouncements from the Mzee's "court" began to be accompanied by vague suggestions of threats to his government from unspecified foreign powers. By 1977, the **East African Community** had ceased to function. Hostility towards socialist policies in Tanzania, delayed elections, further detentions and growing allegations of corruption formed the sullen backdrop to **Kenyatta's death**, in bed, on August 28, 1978.

Kenya under Moi

The passing of the Mzee took Kenya by surprise. There was a nationwide outpouring of grief and shock, but for many, also a sense of relief, and anticipation that the future might better reflect the ideals of twenty years earlier. Vice-president **Daniel Arap Moi** smoothly assumed power and quickly gathered popular support with moves against corruption in the civil service (where the mass of Kenyans felt it most), his stand against tribal nepotism (he himself was from the minority Kalenjin), and the release of all Kenyatta's political prisoners.

But the honeymoon was short. Odinga and other ex-KPU MPs were prevented from standing in the 1979 elections. Student protests began again; the closing of the university became an annual event. On the international scene, the whole Indian Ocean region became strategically important with the fall of the Shah of Iran and the Soviet invasion of Afghanistan. Kenya developed closer ties with the United States, extending military facilities to American vessels in exchange for gifts of grain after a failure of the harvest in 1983.

In the first year or two of his presidency, Moi's **nyayo** (footsteps) philosophy of "peace, love and unity" in the wake of Kenyatta found wide appeal, and his apparent honesty and outspoken attacks against tribalism impressed many, making him friends abroad. But the failure to make any adjustments in economic policy in favour of the rural and urban poor caused growing resentment at home.

On Sunday August 1, 1982 – three months after constitutional amendments were pushed through to make Kenya officially a one-party state (to prevent Oginga Odinga registering a new political party, the Kenya Socialist Alliance) – sections of the Kenya Air Force attempted a **military coup**. Without support in the other armed forces however, the coup was easily put down by the army and the GSU, who killed scores of perceived coup supporters, heralding a new clampdown on students (the university was dissolved) and dissident voices, such as Oginga Odinga, who was placed under house arrest.

In May 1983, the country was distracted by the "**Njonjo affair**", when Moi supporters accused Attorney General Charles Njonjo of being groomed by an unnamed foreign power to take over as president. Njonjo, a member of the Kikuyu elite who had shored up Kenyatta, was the main rival of **Mwai Kibaki**, the sober and respected vice-president in the line-up to succeed Moi. He was eventually granted a pardon, but his political life was over. The Njonjo affair filled the papers for over a year, and succeeded in distracting the public and easing the volatility engendered by the coup attempt. Oginga Odinga and a number of other political detainees were released.

Despite Moi's efforts to throttle all dissent, the groundswell of resentment continued to grow. An opposition group, **Mwakenya** (a Swahili acronym for Union of Nationalists to Liberate Kenya), attracted attention through its pamphlets calling for the replacement of the Moi government, new democratic freedoms and an end to corruption and Western influence. Hundreds of people were arrested, and their defence lawyers tended in turn to get arrested themselves. In 1987, an **Amnesty International** report roundly condemned Kenya's human rights record, as detainees died in custody and prisoners were routinely tortured and kept in waterlogged cells beneath Nyayo House in Nairobi. Public meetings of more than five people were only permitted with police approval (rarely granted), and all dissent, even within KANU, was crushed.

The path to multiparty democracy

In February 1990 **Robert Ouko**, the Luo foreign minister favoured by the West and widely viewed as a potential successor to the presidency, was murdered, sparking off a week of **rioting** nationwide, most violent in Ouko's home town of Kisumu. July of that year saw Central Highlands towns in violent tumult as public opposition to the government mounted, and a Nairobi pro-democracy rally on July 7 (**Saba Saba** – Swahili for 7/7, as the event came to be known) degenerated into a riot, leading to dozens of deaths in street battles with armed police.

Moi blamed "hooligans and drug addicts" for the Saba Saba riots, and the government came down hard on journalists, virtually stifling local newspapers and accusing the foreign press, and particularly the BBC, of mischief-making. Relations with the international community plummeted – against prevailing trends in Africa, Moi's stubborn resistance to adopting a multiparty system riled his overseas backers. He seemed barely aware of the end of the Cold War and the hard reassessment of aid distribution taking place among the rich countries.

Ouko's murder and the Saba Saba riots were followed by the suspicious and gravely embarrassing death in a road accident near Naivasha of the outspoken **Bishop Alexander Muge** on his return from a visit to western Kenya. Muge's car collided head-on with a lorry which veered onto the wrong side of the road. The Archbishop, who had spoken out forcefully against the Muoroto evictions, had been warned against his visit to Luo-land in the most menacing terms by the Minister for Labour, who subsequently resigned from the cabinet. (Another Catholic priest, the influential American cleric, John Kaiser, was found dead in suspicious circumstances in the same area in 2000.)

In 1991, the steady build-up of an opposition lobby became so powerful it could no longer be dismantled and jailed member by member. Oginga Odinga – effectively Kenya's elder statesman – set up the **Forum for the Restoration of Democracy** (**FORD**) in association with his son **Raila Odinga** and the influential Law Society chairman, **Paul Muite**. FORD quickly attracted government opponents from all quarters. Moi called them "rats" that would be "crushed", but by the end of 1991, Kenya's immediate future was increasingly out of Moi's control. John Troon, the ex-Scotland Yard man hired by Moi to investigate Ouko's murder, revealed that the greatest suspicion fell on the president's closest advisor Nicholas

Biwott, and his internal security chief, Hezekiah Oyugi, both of whom were sacked, arrested and later released "for lack of evidence", but not reinstated.

In the wake of this, the **Paris group** of donor nations suspended balance-of-payment support to Kenya for six months, pending economic and political reforms. Moi got the message. Within days he announced there would be multiparty elections for the next parliament and a free vote for the presidency at the end of 1992.

The 1992 elections

FORD found the transformation from opposition lobby group to **political party** very hard to manage. As a party it was promiscuous in the welcome it extended to every ex-KANU minister who made the leap, and with elections approaching, it promptly split into three factions, each with its own presidential candidate. The split revealed the **ethnic divisions** of multiparty politics, and

Richard Leakey

Although now internationally renowned as a wildlife conservationist, Richard Leakey rose to prominence as a palaeontologist from the shadows of his eminent parents Mary and Louis Leakey. He published several books and eventually became head of the National Museums of Kenya in Nairobi.

In 1989, facing an international outcry over the poaching of elephants and the serious impact that was already having on the tourist industry, President Moi hired Leakey to take charge of the **Kenya Wildlife Service** (KWS). Leakey's first move was a characteristically bold one: he invited the world's press to watch Moi ignite Kenya's US$3million stockpile of confiscated **ivory** – producing the most memorable photo opportunity of the Moi presidency. He went on, with Moi's support, to create anti-poaching units and briefed them to shoot to kill any poachers in the parks, transforming the KWS from a demoralized sector of the civil service into what one staff member called "the most radical institution in Africa". The World Bank and other donors were so impressed they gave over US$140million in grants. The poaching stopped, the elephants and rhinos were saved from the brink of extinction, and Kenya's international image was partially restored.

But Leakey's success went too far for some local politicians, particularly in Maasai-land. His confrontational approach to the balance of human and animal needs in the parks – all humans out – infuriated many. And he seemed incorruptible: the KWS had dried up completely as a source of patronage.

In June 1993, on a routine flight at the controls of his Cessna plane, Leakey crashed, losing both legs in the accident. Foul play was suspected, but not proven. Within months he was walking on artificial limbs, anxious to get back to work. But there had been a mood change in his employers. Noah Ngala, tourism minister at the time, announced that evidence of corruption and mismanagement had been unearthed at the KWS. No more bitter irony could be imagined. In January 1994, Leakey resigned from the KWS and was replaced by the less trenchant David Western, an advocate of human-animal coexistence. Leakey, meanwhile, entered politics, applying with a group of intellectuals to register their new party, **Safina**. He now found himself being denounced as a racist colonial by Moi, accused of plotting against Kenya with foreign backers.

Remarkably, after his political ambitions were curtailed, Leakey briefly took on the KWS role for a second time, after Western was sacked in 1998 for failing to attract the international limelight that comes so easily to Leakey. In 1999, Moi appointed Leakey cabinet secretary and head of the civil service, with particular responsibility for **fighting corruption**, but he was forced to resign less than two years later.

it became impossible to enter the political arena without constant reference to the language groups of the politicians and their supporters.

Using a combination of fraud, ballot-stuffing, manipulation of electoral rules, physical prevention of opposition candidates from presenting nomination papers, printing money to buy off the voters, and changing the polling date at the last minute, Moi made sure that he and his party won the **1992 election**. But for the first time in years, there was also an elected multiparty opposition, including the three FORD factions, and the Democratic Party under former Vice-President Mwai Kibaki, who came third in the presidential poll behind Moi and Odinga. KANU had almost no MPs from Kikuyu or Luo areas. One party not allowed to fight the poll was the fundamentalist Islamic Party of Kenya, active in the coastal area, whose leader Khalid Salim Ahmed Balala spent most of the campaign in detention on a trumped-up charge of "imagining" the death of President Moi.

Despite dubious practices in the elections, the international community was unimpressed with the fractious opposition, and the **IMF** and **World Bank** decided that there had, in the end, been much support for the incumbents. After a row in which Moi called their economic demands "suicidal and dictatorial", donor nations agreed to pick up the aid programme, two years after it had ceased, although this did little to refill the coffers pilfered since the end of the 1980s. The aid was contingent on stringent conditions, foremost among them a dramatic raft of privatizations of nationalized industries, including post and telecommunications, the railways and the national produce and cereals board. Part of the justification for privatization was that it would reduce the cash available for siphoning off as political patronage.

In 1994 the **Goldenberg Scandal** broke when a Kenya Central Bank employee, David Munyakei, blew the whistle on a series of fraudulent tax rebates on exports by a firm called Goldenberg International, which claimed to be exporting gold and diamonds. These would have to have been illegally imported from the Congo, then in a state of civil war. A commission convened to investigate the scandal in 2003 has claimed that as much as US$850million – a fifth of Kenya's GDP – was thus stolen from the Central Bank. Judges and politicians were implicated in the scam, allegedly including Moi and members of his family.

Early in 1995, the white ex-Kenya Wildlife Service chief, **Richard Leakey** (recently sacked from his conservation post by Moi), joined Paul Muite to form a new political party, **Safina** ("Ark"), with the intention of binding together the fragmented opposition. Moi's reaction was unsubtle: "What do I say to Leakey? I say no, no and no to any white man who wants to lead Kenya". Safina's application to register as a legal party was turned down and, at a meeting in Nakuru, Leakey and party leaders were beaten up.

The 1997 elections

Two years of economic slowdown followed, with strikes by teachers and nurses, mass demonstrations for constitutional reform and the breakdown of relations with the IMF (which led to a run on the Kenyan shilling). Senior figures in the main opposition parties (FORD-K, FORD-A and the Democratic Party) agreed to work together, with a single presidential candidate for the **1997 elections**, Mwai Kibaki. Richard Leakey coordinated the alliance and raised funds. Moi unbanned Safina, but only when it was too late for the party to organize a presidential candidate.

The run-up to the elections was dominated by debate between KANU hard-liners and the **National Convention Executive Committee (NCEC)** – a coalition of religious leaders, unionists and student activists. By June 1997, the opposition, and particularly students, were howling for reforms in advance of the elections. Police stormed Nairobi University to stop a rally commemorating the 1990 Saba Saba demonstrations, and left more than a dozen dead while brutally putting down protests that had broken out around the country.

Repression alternated with promises of reform through the rest of year, accompanied by a series of national strikes until, in November 1997, the Constitutional (Amendment) Act removed some of the legislation restricting freedom of movement and speech. Despite this, Mombasa erupted in violence in August 1997, when two police stations were attacked, six policemen killed, weapons stolen and dozens of upcountry people later killed and thousands more expelled by armed gangs who terrorized the district of **Likoni**. Notices circulated "reclaiming" the coast for its indigenous inhabitants, and demanding the largely Kikuyu newcomers return to their home districts.

Elections were held in December, and the vote, predictably, split along ethnic lines. The Kalenjin constituencies of the Rift Valley, along with the Maasai and Samburu, the Somali, Turkana, coastal and many Luhya and Kisii constituencies, largely voted for Moi and KANU. Mwai Kibaki's Democratic Party did well in the Kikuyu areas, in whose heartland, not even Jomo Kenyatta's son, **Uhuru Kenyatta**, could win a seat for KANU. Raila Odinga, with his National Development Party (NDP), was well supported, but only locally, in Luo-land. Moi won the presidential election with 2.4 million votes; Kibaki came second with 1.9 million.

Ethnic violence

For years, any reference to **multiparty politics** by KANU leaders was accompanied by dire warnings of the bloody consequences for tribal harmony of such a system. Once the government was forced into a corner on the issue by foreign aid donors, the prophecy was quickly realized. Ethnic allegiance swamped the new political order before it had even consolidated, so that the opposition parties were unable to formulate policies and election strategies that were free of ethnic considerations.

For decades, the Rift Valley and other normally unproductive areas had been the destination for emigrating Kikuyu, Luo and Luhya, who bought marginal farmlands in the areas where they settled, and tried to apply their farming techniques among the local Kalenjin and Maa-speakers while benefiting from local aid and subsistence initiatives. Victims of the early attacks in Rift Valley Province described organized gangs of youths terrorizing non-Kalenjin homesteads and villages, while local police arrived too late to do anything or just stood by.

As KANU politicians warned that the Kalenjin should watch their backs for attacks by "outsiders", so their predictions were soon coming true. Kikuyu vigilante groups began to retaliate and, in turn, provided spurious justification for Kalenjin fears. The violence was not so much the "clashes" or "fighting" (certainly not "tribal war") of newspaper headlines, as the looting of property, theft of livestock, burning of houses, and the beating up or killing of anyone who got in the way of the perpetrators. Their message was, "Get off our land", and thousands of victims moved to refugee camps outside Eldoret, Nanyuki and other towns. At least 3000 people were killed in violence between different language groups in the Rift Valley, western Kenya and on the coast during the 1990s, and at least 300,000 people were displaced, nearly all of them non-Kalenjin, in **ethnic cleansing**.

The violence proved counterproductive in electioneering terms, as the government lost more votes from disgust with their inaction than it gained from forcing opposition voters out of marginal KANU constituencies. Probably the aim was simply to demonstrate to the world at large that multipartyism in Africa leads to tribal violence. In this – to the Moi government's lasting shame – it succeeded.

Moi's final term

The aftermath of the elections saw inter-ethnic violence flare up again in the Rift Valley, mostly between Kikuyu and Kalenjin. Discussion on constitutional reform got under way in April 1998, with a consultative forum set up, but Moi attempted to hijack constitutional review by having it shifted to parliament. In December, parliament duly voted to appoint a select committee on constitutional reform under Raila Odinga (who was increasingly cosying up to Moi), prompting opposition politicians and religious leaders to set up a rival commission called **Ufungamano**.

The horrific August 1998 **bombing** of the American Embassy (see p.123) led to a suspension of faction fighting. Charles Njonjo, a figure in the political wasteland for fifteen years, took up the chair of the disaster fund. But the lull was short-lived. As the dust settled, business as usual was quickly resumed. The judicial inquiry into ethnic clashes resumed its grindingly slow process, while there were more than a hundred further killings, mostly of Kikuyu, in Laikipia and Nakuru districts, in January 1999. Police made no arrests.

Following a rapprochement with Raila Odinga, Moi continued trying to bring opposition figures on side, and made Richard Leakey cabinet secretary with special responsibility for combating corruption. In June 2001, KANU and Odinga's NDP joined together in a formal coalition, Odinga joining the cabinet as energy minister. Professor Yash Pal Ghani, an academic appointed to head a parliamentary commission on the constitution, managed to achieve a merger with Ufungamano. The resulting Constitutional Review Commission had twelve Ufungamano members and fifteen parliamentarians, though members were still subject to vetting by Moi.

With elections approaching in 2002, Odinga dissolved the NDP, which merged into KANU, a move that Moi hoped would bring Luo voters over to the party. The opposition also did some merging, when twelve groups, including FORD-K and the Democratic Party, joined to form the National Alliance Party of Kenya (**NAK**). Meanwhile Moi decided in August to back Uhuru Kenyatta as KANU's presidential candidate. Kenyatta was widely seen as a figurehead who would front a new regime on Moi's behalf, and Moi's backing of him particularly annoyed Raila Odinga, who had hoped to be the party's candidate. He and a number of other KANU bigwigs resigned their ministerial posts and set up a "Rainbow Alliance" within the party, opposed to Kenyatta's candidacy. In October they left KANU and formed a Liberal Democratic Party (LDP), which joined with the NAK to form a **National Rainbow Coalition** (**NARC**), with a single presidential candidate, Mwai Kibaki. NARC won the December **2002 elections**, and KANU was turfed out of government for the first time since independence, though it remains the largest opposition party.

Just before the elections, Kenya's tourist industry was shaken by a **bomb attack** on an Israeli-owned tourist hotel near Mombasa which killed thirteen people, simultaneous with an attempt using surface-to-air missiles to shoot down an Israel-bound charter flight leaving Mombasa. Details remain unclear, but there seem to be connections between these attacks and the 1998 US embassy bombing; the perpetrators also seem to have had international connections with the al-Qaeda network.

All in all, **Moi's legacy** was not great: living standards had fallen under his rule (a drought in 1999 and 2000 exacerbated the situation), and most Kenyans were living below the poverty line. Ethnic strife had worsened, largely thanks to Moi's divide-and-rule politics, and so had the human rights situation. With Moi and KANU out, both Kenyans and the country's financial backers were now hoping for better.

The new regime

Kibaki took up the presidency with a promise of **constitutional reform** within one hundred days. One thousand days later, Kenya was still waiting. The biggest wrangle involved the proposed post of prime minister, which Odinga saw as his, apparently following a secret deal with Kibaki. The post as originally conceived would have taken much executive power away from the president, but Kibaki was keen for this not to happen. Part of the problem was that NARC was really only a loose alliance of political wannabes and ethnic blocs, which soon began to fragment without Moi as a common opponent to unite it. A constitutional convention was set up at the **Bomas** conference centre near Nairobi in April 2003, but in a **draft constitution** passed in June 2005, the Bomas proposals were shot through with amendments tabled in parliament, most notable among them the provision that the post of prime minister be in the president's gift. However, the amendments also included a radical shake-up of Kenya's **land laws**, including proposals that women should have the right to inherit land, that foreigners should not be able to own land and that foreign 1000-year leases be reduced to 99 years, and there were long-overdue measures to return the victims of ethnic cleansing to their rightful locations in the country. Odinga and several other cabinet ministers came out in opposition to the proposed constitution, which went to the country in a **referendum** in November 2005. The ballot-paper symbol for a "yes" vote was a banana, for the "no" vote an orange, and politicians who favoured the original Bomas proposals joined forces with those who wanted no change at all in an Orange Team to campaign for a "no" vote.

The poll was peaceful and there was no attempt at vote-fixing (despite many predictions to the contrary), resulting in a rejection of the proposed constitution by a 2:1 margin. Kibaki subsequently dismissed his cabinet, appointing a new set of ministers without Odinga and other supporters of the Orange Team, who thus joined KANU in opposition, marking in effect the end of the NARC coalition. Constitutional reform was left in the air, but supporters of the Bomas proposals still hope for a new constitution based on a separation of powers between the president and a prime minister.

In other fields, Kibaki has done better at reform. In January 2003, his administration introduced **free primary education** for all, bringing schooling to one and a half million more children, though the move has been beset by logistical problems, teacher shortages, and a fall in schools' performance, with private schools dominating exam result leagues. The **press** is largely freer post-Moi; however, in March 2006, in a now infamous raid, masked police stormed the offices of the Standard media group (which includes KTN TV, owned by the Moi family), burning papers, smashing equipment and seizing tapes. The Kibaki faction had been infuriated by negative press and allegedly fabricated stories, but neither president nor ex-president had anything to say about the raid.

One of Kibaki's more inspired ministerial appointments was of **Wangari Maathai**, a staunch campaigner for debt cancellation and land reform, and founder of Kenya's remarkable grassroots environmental lobby, the **Green Belt Movement** (@www.greenbeltmovement.org), for which she was awarded the 2004 Nobel Peace Prize. Started in 1977, the Movement promotes education, community empowerment and environmental awareness; it has set up over six hundred community networks and over six thousand tree nurseries, and has planted more than thirty million trees around the country. Professor Maathai became Assistant Minister for the Environment and Natural Resources.

The IMF and the World Bank resumed lending to Kenya in 2003 after the new government set up a five-year **Economic Recovery Strategy**, with a commitment to **fighting corruption** while opening up to **privatization**. An Anti-Corruption and Economic Crimes Act and a Public Officers Ethics Act were passed during 2003, and anti-graft campaigner John Githongo appointed as anti-corruption czar. Many public officials suspected of taking bribes were also purged.

Unfortunately, allegations of **corruption** involving senior government figures have continued unabated. In February 2005, the then British High Commissioner Sir Edward Clay accused officials in the new administration of what he called a "looting spree" of corruption, which had cost Kenya hundreds of millions since NARC took over. The scandal, largely focused on the security industry, came to be known as **Anglo-Leasing** (the name of one of the companies involved) – a web of scams in which government money was paid to non-existent companies or for bogus or massively inflated contracts. Foreign Minister Chirau Mwakwere was furious with Clay, and summoned him to "give facts and figures and to name names", but John Githongo appeared to agree with Clay when he resigned a few days later saying he could no longer serve the government, and fled into exile in the UK. In January 2006, he produced a dossier accusing four ministers of corruption and implying knowledge of this on the part of the president. Two of the ministers were subsequently dropped by the president like hot potatoes. The allegations led to several aid donors suspending contributions, while at the same time the country was being hammered by a second year of **drought** and the northeast was in the grip of a serious famine. Playing one crisis off against another, in February 2006 Kibaki released part of the report into the Goldenberg scandal, hoping to divert attention onto the misdeeds of the Moi era.

Public support for the NARC administration has fallen back since the post-election honeymoon, and there has been much dissatisfaction at the disappointing efforts towards constitutional reform, especially in Luo areas, which even saw rioting when parliament approved the amended draft constitution. There has also been criticism of President Kibaki's laid-back style, partly the result of injuries sustained in a car accident during the 2002 election campaign, which have forced him to take it easy.

Meanwhile, there is a feeling among smaller ethnic groups that a unitary Kenyan government means Kikuyu rule, and the ascendancy of a "Mount Kenya Mafia" composed of the related Kikuyu, Meru and Embu. This view has fuelled calls for greater decentralization, even federalism – or **majimboism** as it's known in Kenya. Mount Kenya people, for their part, point to the uncomfortable lining up of ethnicity and religion in the largely Islamic northeast and coastal provinces, where a federal system has the greatest appeal.

The future may look brighter now than it did under Moi, but the old spectres of corruption and tribalism remain to be vanquished, and the problems of landlessness, unemployment and poverty loom as large as they ever did. Nonetheless, after years of decline, Kenya at least seems to have started moving in the right direction.

Wildlife and the environment

D espite the tremendous losses of the twentieth century, Kenya teems with wildlife. In one place or another, not just inside the protective boundaries of the forty-odd parks and reserves, it's possible to see almost all of the country's big animals. Even outside the parks, if you travel fairly widely, you're almost certain to note various gazelles and antelopes, zebra and giraffe – even hippo, buffalo, crocodile and elephant. Monkeys and baboons can be seen almost anywhere and are a regular menace.

If this impression of abundant wild animals slightly alarms you, rest assured that any danger is minimal. Outside the park boundaries the big cats are hardly ever seen, and man-eating lions and enraged elephants are no more a realistic cause for concern than the few remaining rhinos, which live entirely within the parks; buffaloes, though plentiful, are only really dangerous when solitary. Perhaps the one animal to be a little wary of is the hippo, especially on land. For lonely hikes – on Mount Kenya, Mount Elgon and the Aberdares, for example – hiring a guide is sometimes a good idea. Statistically, however, your chances of being attacked by a wild animal in Kenya are very small.

The country's **birdlife** is even more noticeable than its mammals, and astonishingly diverse, attracting ornithologists from all over the world and converting many others as well. There are over a thousand species in all, ranging from the thumb-sized red-cheeked cordon bleu to the ostrich.

This introduction to Kenya's habitats, mammals, birds, reptiles and amphibians complements our colour guide at the front of the book, which should be useful in identifying the main species of mammals likely to be seen on safari. For more detailed coverage, a good, full-length field guide is very valuable – some recommended **books** are listed on p.662.

Forest and woodland habitats

Several forest types are present in Kenya, including mountain, coastal and lowland dry forests.

Highland forests

The highlands support rich forests, which give way to agricultural lands as you approach Nairobi. The characteristic landscape in the highlands is patches of evergreen trees separated by vast meadows of grasses – often wire grass and Kikuyu grass.

The highland forest is quite limited in extent in Kenya; it's typically found above 1500m, and also on isolated massifs. It bears some resemblance to lowland forest, but contains different tree species and does not normally grow as tall or dense. Typical trees of this forest include **camphor**, *Juniperus procera* (the "cedar" tree of East Africa) and **podocarpus**. The better-developed forests are found on the wetter, western slopes of the massifs. Above the forest line, stands of giant bamboo are found at altitudes of over 2500m. Along the lower, drier edge of the highlands, trees grow less high and are dotted in fields of tall grass; various species of olive tree are commonly found here.

The **main highland forest areas** are to be found on Mount Kenya, Mount Elgon, the Mau Escarpment, the Aberdares and Mount Marsabit. **Mount Kenya** displays a mountain summit plant community (known as **Afro-Alpine**), which bears a strong similarity to that found on other high East African mountains (there's more on Mount Kenya's high-altitude flora on p.180). The highest part of the montane forest belt, at altitudes over 2900m, is characterized by a giant form of St John's wort. Above this, giant heather and Proteus trees form a heather belt, while at even higher altitudes, open marshy moorland is found, dominated by tussock grasses, giant groundsel and giant lobelia. Higher still, the tree groundsel comes into its own (this has an upper limit of 4460m).

Several species of **near-endemic birds** are associated with the highland forest habitat. These are Jackson's francolin (a game bird of high-altitude forest undergrowth), the dazzling golden-winged sunbird (golden-yellow wings and long, yellow tail streamers) and Hartlaub's turaco. Other typical birds of these forests and streams include African black duck, mountain buzzard, bar-tailed trogon, white-starred robin, mountain warbler and mountain wagtail.

The Kakamega Forest

West of the Rift Valley, the 240 square kilometres of Kakamega Forest, and a few adjacent outliers, are examples of the Guineo-Congolian **equatorial forest**, which is more typically a feature of central and west Africa and is now very restricted within Kenya. For this reason, many bird and plant species not encountered elsewhere in Kenya are found here – it's a memorable experience to be in the forest at first light when the shafts of morning sun spear their way through the tallest boughs of the semi-evergreen trees.

Lowland and coastal forest and woodlands

Very few areas of **lowland rain forest** are left in Kenya, mainly restricted to the coastal strip, and the banks of the lower Athi and Tana rivers. The soils of these forests quickly lose their fertility when cleared for agriculture, and many of the areas that remain are degraded.

Lowland woodland areas are found inland of the coastal forest strip and away from the rivers. Woodlands are defined as more open forest areas with the ground flora dominated by grasses and the forest canopy covering as little as twenty percent of the area. Trees in such woodlands may average only 4–5m high.

The rain forests, all threatened by human incursions, include **Witu Forest** near Lamu, the **Mida-Gedi forest**, the **Sabaki River Forest** near Malindi, forest fragments in the **Shimba Hills** and the **Ramisi River Forest** on the southern coast.

The most important area of natural forest is the **Arabuko-Sokoke Forest**, which lies slightly inland along the western side of the main coast road, south of Malindi and north of Kilifi. Arabuko-Sokoke is unique in that it comprises a largely unbroken block of 420 square kilometres of coastal forest, consisting of brachystegia woodland (containing a huge variety of birdlife), dense cynometra forest, and zones of mixed lowland rain forest that are very rich in plants, mammals and insects.

Large areas of the coastal plain are covered in moist, tree-scattered grasslands. On the beach itself, tall **coconut palms** and the rather weedy-looking **casuarina** (known as whistling pine) dominate the high-tide line.

Grassland

Grassland with scattered trees (wooded savanna) covers vast areas in Kenya, both in the **Lake Victoria basin** (which includes the Mara), and **south and east of Mount Kenya** at elevations of 1000–1800m. This type of ecosystem prevails because of regular fires. Many of the trees that persist are broad-leaved and deciduous, protected from fire damage by their corky bark. In areas with a similar altitude, but with more erratic rainfall, a thin scattering of tall, flat-topped acacia trees, along with shorter acacias, occurs amongst the grassland, producing the archetypal imagery of the East African landscape.

Desert and semi-desert

Typical desert and semi-desert flora comprises **thornbush and thicket**. Thirty kilometres inland from the Indian Ocean, beyond the fringes of the Arabuko-Sokoke Forest and others, is the eastern edge of the **Nyika wilderness**, which stretches west to the edge of the highlands. Nyika is characterized by an often impenetrably thick growth of stunted, thorny trees, which are grey for most of the year, but become green during the rainy season. Scaly-barked species such as acacia and euphorbia species occur in this plant community.

Desert grass-bush and the drier **desert scrub** communities cover nearly seventy percent of the land area of Kenya, mainly in the east, north and northeast. These areas are at low altitude (below 600m) and have unreliable rainfall, suffering long droughts, a lack of regular flowing water and strong wind exposure. Vegetation is sparse and scrubby, with bushes and occasional, widely scattered tall trees, mainly baobab, mwangi and mgunga (acacia) trees. Much of the ground free of bushes is covered by dispersed bunches of grass and other low shrubs. However, much of the soil surface here is bare.

The true desert habitat is drier still and plant life is very limited in some areas. Many of the trees and bushes (if present at all) are dwarf. Large areas are bare, stony desert with a thin and patchy growth of desert grasses and perhaps a few bushes along dry river margins or dry water courses.

Wet habitats

The Kenyan coast is dominated by two major habitat types, sandy beach and mangrove forest. There are also some offshore rocky islands and coral reefs along the coast, which provide refuge for birds, but there are no breeding sites of pelagic seabirds (birds of the open ocean) in the country. Many species of shore birds (waders) are found in tidal creeks and estuaries, for example at Mida Creek, on the Sabaki estuary, and also on the Lamu Archipelago. One unique wader species, the **crab plover** – a pied wader which runs to catch crabs for food – overwinters at Mida Creek.

Lakes

The savanna of the **Great Rift Valley** is dotted with bird-rich lakes, ranging from the two freshwater lakes – Naivasha and Baringo – to intensely saline ones like Magadi and Bogoria. The Rift Valley acts as a magnet to passage and wintering birds.

The vast expanse of **Lake Victoria** is an example of an oligotrophic lake – fed mainly by rainwater falling on to the lake's surface, rather than being fed by rivers and streams. As a result, it has a relatively low nutrient concentration. A feature of the lake is its papyrus beds and marshlands which harbour birds not found elsewhere in Kenya.

Rivers

There are very few permanent riverine habitats in Kenya, because the country is so dry, but those river systems which exist are extremely attractive to birds and mammals. The best examples of such rivers are the **Tana** and **Athi-Galana-Sabaki** systems.

Mangrove forest

Marine mangrove swamps are found in many parts of the coast. The largest tracts, and the areas from which most mangrove poles (boriti) are cut for the building trade, are in the Lamu Archipelago, but all the coastal creeks are more or less bordered by mangroves (mkoko in Swahili). There are also areas of saline grassland on the landward side of some of the mangrove thickets. Although fun to travel through by boat, mangrove forests are not noted for their faunal diversity. One unusual animal you're bound to see is the **mudskipper**, a fish on the evolutionary road to becoming an amphibian.

Mammals

Kenya has more than a hundred species of large native mammals. The majority of species are vegetarian grazers, browsers and foragers at the lower end of the food chain – animals such as monkeys, rodents and antelopes. The big predators are fewer in species and tend to be the dominant topic of conversation at game lodges. Everyone remembers seeing lions or cheetahs for the first time. To see a leopard is often a personal goal, and a highlight. Once you get the bug, you'll be looking out for a lone striped hyena, rather than the common and gregarious spotted version, or for a serval cat rather than a cheetah. But don't ignore the less glamorous animals. There can be just as much satisfaction in spotting a shy, uncommon antelope, or in noting rarely observed behaviour, as in ticking off one of the more obvious predatory status symbols.

Primates

There are twelve species of primates in Kenya, excluding Homo sapiens. They range from the pint-sized, slow-motion, lemur-like potto, found in Kakamega Forest, to the baboon. Kenya no longer has any great apes (the family to which the gorilla and the chimpanzee belong), although they probably only became extinct in the western forests, of which Kakamega is a relic, in the last five hundred years, during which time the region was widely settled by humans. The legend of the Nandi Bear (see p.318) is probably connected with those passed-down memories. A new **chimpanzee sanctuary** has recently been established at Sweetwaters in Laikipia, "stocked" with chimps from Jane Goodall's famous Gombe Stream reserve in Tanzania. Today, the primate you are certain to see almost anywhere in Kenya, given a few trees, is the **vervet** (p.19), a small, lightweight monkey that has no difficulty adjusting to the presence of humans and, if possible, their food. The vervet is one of the guenons – typical African monkeys, with distinctive facial markings and hairstyles, all wonderfully adapted to a life on the prowl for fruits, leaves, insects and just about anything else small and tasty. Almost as common in certain areas, notably on the coast, is **Sykes' monkey** (p.19). At Diani Beach, a number of Sykes' troops have become notoriously accustomed to stealing food from hotel dining tables, and large males will even raid bedrooms. Upcountry populations of Sykes' (or blue) monkey appear to be more timid.

It's upcountry where you are most likely to see the beautiful, leaf-eating **black and white colobus monkeys** (p.18) although they can also be spotted in the Diani forest. They are usually found high in the tree canopy; look out for the pure white young. The related **Tana River red colobus** (p.18) is only found in the remote Tana River National Primate Reserve, which also shelters the dwindling population of Tana River crested mangabeys, a partly ground-dwelling monkey with a characteristic Mohican-style crest of hair. Other rare or more localized monkeys include: the red-tailed guenon of the far west; the stocky but distinguished looking De Brazza's monkey, with its white goatee, found almost exclusively in Saiwa Swamp National Park; and the **Patas monkey** (p.18), a moustachioed plains runner of the dry northwest and Laikipia.

If you stay in a game lodge, you are quite likely to see **bushbabies** at night (see p.19), as they frequently visit dining rooms and verandas. There's a large, cat-sized species (the greater galago) and a small bushbaby not much bigger than a kitten (the lesser galago). Both are engaging animals, with sensitive, inquisitive fingers and large eyes and ears to aid them in their hunt for insects and other small animals.

On safari you'll have plenty of opportunities to watch **baboon troops** (p.18) up close. Large males can be somewhat intimidating in size and manner, disconcertingly so towards women. Troops, averaging forty to fifty individuals, spend their lives, like all monkeys, in clear, but mutable social relationships. Rank and precedence, physical strength and kin ties all determine an individual's position in this mini-society led by a dominant male. The days revolve around the need to forage and hunt for food (baboons will consume almost anything, from a fig tree's entire crop to a baby antelope found in the grass). Grooming is a fundamental part of

▼ Black-and-white colobus

the social glue during times of relaxation. When baboons and other monkeys perform this massage-like activity on each other, the specks which they pop into their mouths are sometimes parasites – notably ticks – and sometimes flakes of skin.

Rodents and hyraxes

Rodents aren't likely to make a strong impression on safari, unless you're lucky enough to do some night game drives – or preferably walks. In that case you may see the bristling back end of a **crested porcupine** (p.20) or the frenzied leaps of a **spring hare** (p.20), dazzled by headlights or a torch. In rural areas off the beaten track you may occasionally see hunters taking home **giant rats** or **cane rats** – shy, vegetarian animals, which make good eating. Kenya has several species of **squirrel**, the most spectacular of which is the giant forest squirrel, with its splendid bush of a tail, and the nocturnal flying squirrel – which actually glides, rather than flies, from tree to tree, on membranes between its outstretched limbs. Both are most likely to be seen in Kakamega Forest. Very widespread, however, are the two species of **ground squirrel** – striped and unstriped – which are often seen, dashing along the track in front of the vehicle, in Tsavo National Park and the Samburu reserves.

Rock hyraxes (p.24), which you are certain to see at Hell's Gate National Park and on Mount Kenya, look like they should be rodents. In fact the rock hyrax and closely related tree hyrax are technically ungulates (hoofed mammals) and form a classificatory level entirely their own. Their closest living relatives are elephants, with which they share distant common ancestry. Present-day hyraxes are pygmies compared with some of their prehistoric ancestors, which were as big as a bear in some cases. Rock hyraxes live in busy, vocal colonies of twenty or thirty females and young, plus a male. In a few places they are extremely tame and wait to be fed by passing hikers. Usually, however, they are timid in the extreme – not surprising in view of the wide range of predators that will eat them.

Carnivores

Kenya's carnivores are some of the most exciting and easily recognizable animals you'll see. Although often portrayed as fearsome hunters, pulling down plains game after a chase, many species do a fair bit of scavenging and all are content to eat smaller fry when conditions dictate or the opportunity arises.

Of the large cats, **lions** (p.23) are the easiest species to find. Lazy, gregarious and physically large – up to 1.8m in length, not counting the tail, and up to a metre high at the shoulder – they rarely make much effort to hide or to move away, except on occasions when a large number of tourist vehicles intrude. They can be seen in nearly all the parks and reserves, and their presence is generally the main consideration in determining whether you're allowed out of your vehicle or not. Popular parks where lions are normally absent are Hell's Gate and Lake Bogoria (you can hike in both); parks which are inhabited by lions, but in which you can generally hike, include the Aberdares and Mount Kenya. "Man-eating" lions appear from time to time but seem to be one-off feline misfits. Normally, lions hunt cooperatively, preferring to kill very young, old or sick animals, and making a kill roughly once in every two attacks. When they don't kill their own prey, they will steal the kills of cheetahs or hyenas.

Leopards (p.23) may be the most feared animals in Kenya. Intensely secretive, alert and wary, they live all across the country except in the most treeless zones. Their unmistakable call, likened to a big saw being pulled back and forth, is unforgettable. Although often diurnal in the parks, they are strictly nocturnal wherever human pressures impinge, and sometimes survive on the outskirts of towns and villages, carefully preying on different herds of domestic animals to avoid a routine. They tolerate nearby human habitation and rarely kill people unprovoked. Accidents do occur, however, and disturbed individuals occasionally take to human-hunting – or are forced to become "man-eaters" through infirmity. For the most part, leopards live off any small

△ Lioness

animals that come their way, pouncing from an ambush and dragging the prey up into a tree where it may be consumed over several days. Monkeys, especially the relatively less organized species such as colobus and vervet, are frequent prey. Baboons, unless very unlucky, are usually able to mob a leopard to defend the troop. The spots on a leopard vary from individual to individual, but they always appear in the form of rosettes. Melanistic (black) leopards are known as panthers or black panthers, and seem to be more common in some areas (Mount Kenya and the Aberdares, for example) than others.

In the flesh, the **cheetah** (p.23) is so different from the leopard, it's hard to see how there could ever be any confusion. Cheetahs are lightly built, finely spotted, with small heads and very long legs. Unlike leopards, which are highly arboreal, cheetahs never climb trees. They live alone, or sometimes briefly form a pair during mating, and hunting too is normally a solitary activity, down to eyesight and an incredible burst of speed that can take the animal up to 100kph (70mph) for a few seconds. Cheetahs can be seen in any of the large, upcountry parks, though Nairobi National Park is as easy a place to find them as any.

Other large Kenyan cats include the beautiful part-spotted, part-striped **serval** (p.23), found in most of the parks, though somewhat uncommon; and the aggressive, tuft-eared **caracal** (p.22), a kind of lynx, which is seen even less often than the serval, favouring drier zones like Tsavo East and the Samburu complex.

The biggest carnivore after the lion is the **spotted hyena** (p.22); it is also, apart from the lion, the meat-eater you will most often see. Although considered a scavenger par excellence, the spotted hyena is a formidable hunter, most often found where antelopes and zebras are present. Exceptionally efficient consumers, with immensely strong teeth and jaws, spotted hyenas eat virtually every part of their prey, including bones and hide and, where habituated to humans, often steal shoes, unwashed pans and trash from tents and villages. Although they can be seen by day, they are most often active at night – when they issue their unnerving, whooping cries. Clans of twenty or so animals are dominated by females, which are larger than the males and compete with each other for rank. Curiously, female hyenas' genitalia are hard to distinguish from males', leading to a popular misconception that they are hermaphroditic. Not surprisingly, in view of all their attributes, the hyena is a key figure in local mythology and folklore.

In comparison with the spotted hyena, you are not very likely to see a **striped hyena**. A usually solitary animal, it's slighter and much rarer than its spotted relative, though occasionally glimpsed very early in the morning.

The commonest members of the dog family in Kenya are the **jackals**. The black-backed or silver-backed jackal (p.21) and the similar side-striped jackal, can be seen just about anywhere, both species usually in pairs. The golden jackal is most likely to be seen in the Mara. **Bat-eared foxes** (p.20) are also not uncommon, and unmistakable in appearance. However, the unusual and rather magnificent **hunting dog** (p.21) is now extremely rare in Kenya, having been present in reasonable numbers forty years ago. Canine distemper has played a big role in their decline, as have human predation and habitat disruption. There are a number of packs in the country, and if the opportunity exists to see them – in Laikipia, for example – you will hear about it.

Among smaller predators, the unusual **honey badger** or **ratel** (p.21) is related to the European badger and has a reputation for defending itself extremely fiercely. Primarily an omnivorous forager, it will tear open bees' nests (to which it is led by a small bird, the honey guide), its thick, loose hide rendering it impervious to their stings. **Genets** (p.22) are reminiscent of slender, elongated cats (they were once domesticated around the Mediterranean, but cats proved better mouse-hunters). In fact they are viverrids, related to mongooses. and are frequently seen after dark around national park lodges, where they live a semi-domesticated existence.

Most species of **mongoose** (p.22) are also tolerant of humans and, even when disturbed out in the bush, can usually be observed for some time before disappearing. Their snake-fighting reputation is greatly overplayed: in practice they are mostly social foragers, fanning out through the bush like beaters on a shoot, rooting for anything edible – mostly invertebrates, eggs, lizards and frogs.

The **civet** (p.21) is a stocky animal, resembling a large, terrestrial genet. It was formerly kept in captivity for its musk (once a part of the raw material for perfume), which is secreted from glands near the tail. Civets aren't often seen, but they are predictable creatures that wend their way along the same paths at the same time night after night, so if there's one nearby, you'll see it.

Elephants

Elephants (p.24) are found throughout Kenya. Almost all the big plains and mountain parks have their populations. These are the most engaging of animals to watch, perhaps because their interactions, behaviour patterns and personality have so many human parallels. Like people, they lead complex, interdependent social lives, growing from helpless infancy, through self-conscious adolescence, to adulthood. Babies are born with their cows in close attendance, after a 22-month gestation. The calves suckle for two to three years, from the mother's two breasts between her front legs.

Elephants' basic **family units** are composed of a group of related females, tightly protecting their babies and young and led by a venerable matriarch. It's the matriarch that's most likely to bluff a charge – though occasionally she may get carried away and actually tusk a vehicle or person. Bush mythology has it that elephants become embarrassed and ashamed after killing a human, covering the body with sticks and grass. They certainly pay much attention to the disposal of their own dead relatives, often dispersing the bones and spending time near the remains. Old animals die in their seventies or eighties, when their last set of teeth wears out and they can no longer feed.

Seen in the flesh, elephants seem even bigger than you would imagine – you'll need little persuasion from those flapping, warning ears to back off if you're too close – but they are at the same time surprisingly graceful, silent animals on their padded, carefully placed feet. In a matter of moments, a large herd can merge into the trees and disappear, their presence betrayed only by the noisy cracking of branches as they strip trees and uproot saplings.

Managing the elephant population (see the "Poaching Wars" box on p.382) leads to arcane ecological puzzles in which new factors keep emerging; current wisdom suggests that elephants are in a way "architects" of their environment. Overpopulation is usually the result of old migration routes being cut off, forcing the animals into unnatural reserves – like the Mara – where their massive appetites can appear to be destructive. Adults may consume up to 170kg of plant material daily – that works out at well over 3000 tons of foliage through the Mara's collective elephant gut each month. However, this foliage destruction by crowded herds also puts new life into the soil. Acacia seeds sprout much better after being eaten and dunged by elephants than if they simply fall to the ground. Dung beetles gratefully tackle the football-sized elephant droppings, break them into pellets and pull them into their burrows where the seeds germinate. Elephants also dig up dried-out water holes with their tusks (they're either right- or left-tusked, in the same way as humans favour one hand or the other), providing moisture for other animals.

Rhinos

There are two species of **rhinoceros** (p.24) found in Africa – the hook-lipped or black rhino, and the much heavier wide-lipped or white rhino. Both are on the brink of extinction in the wild. The shape of their lips is far more significant than any alleged colour difference, as it indicates their respective diets (browsing for the black rhino, grazing for the white) and favoured habitats (thick bush and open grassland respectively).

Rhinos give birth to a single calf, after a gestation period of fifteen to eighteen months, and then the baby is not weaned until it is at least a year, sometimes two years, old. Their population growth rate is slow compared with most animals – another factor contributing to their predicament.

Native white rhinos have been extinct for several hundred years in Kenya, but reintroduced animals (principally from South Africa) have always done well – when allowed the chance to do so out of the sights of poachers.

The smaller black rhinos were, until the mid-1970s, a fairly common sight in most of the parks. In the 1960s, Amboseli, for example, had hundreds of magnificent black rhinos, some with graceful, long upper horns over a metre in length. The facts behind their rapid and depressing decimation are given in some detail on p.383.

Today, there are around 500 black rhinos in Kenya, and just a few dozen white rhinos. You can see black rhinos in Maasai Mara, Lake Nakuru, Nairobi, Aberdares and Mount Kenya national parks and Ngulia Rhino Sanctuary in Tsavo West. White rhinos can be seen in Maasai Mara and Lake Nakuru. Small numbers of both species can also be encountered at private ranches in northern Kenya, especially in Laikipia, north of Mount Kenya. Such is the threat to their survival, the exact location of rhino groups is not always made widely known.

Hippos

Hippopotamuses (p.26) are highly adaptable, and found throughout Kenya wherever rivers or freshwater lakes are deep enough for them to submerge and have a surrounding of suitable grazing grass. By day they need to spend most of their time in water to protect their thin, hairless skin from dehydration.

Hippos can be found everywhere from the humid estuary of the Tana River to the chilly mountain district of Nyahururu, including the briny Lake Nakuru in the central Rift Valley and Lake Turkana in the semi-desert of the northwest. After dark, hippos leave the water to spend the whole night grazing, often walking up to 10km in one session. In the Maasai Mara, they wander across the savanna; at Lake Naivasha they plod through farms and gardens; and everywhere they are rightly feared.

Hippos are reckoned to be responsible for more human deaths in Africa than any other animal. These occur mostly on the water, when boats accidentally steer into hippo pods, but they can be aggressive on dry land, too, charging and slashing with their fearsomely long incisors. They can run at 30kph if necessary and have a small turning circle. Although uncertain on land (hence their aggression when cornered), they are supremely adapted to long periods in water. Their nostrils, eyes and ears are in exactly the right places and their clumsy feet become supple paddles – as can be seen, if you're very lucky, from the underwater observatory at Mzima Springs in Tsavo West National Park, for example.

Zebras

Zebras (p.25) are closely related to horses and, together with wild asses, form the equid family. Of the three species of zebra, two live in Kenya. Burchell's has thick stripes and small ears and is found in suitable habitats in most parts of the country, while Grevy's is a large animal with very fine stripes and big, saucer-like ears, restricted to Tsavo East and the northern parks and reserves.

Burchell's zebras found in Kenya are mostly the granti subspecies and often called Grant's zebras. In the far north, they tend to have a very short mane, or even none at all. In Tsavo West and other parts of southern Kenya, they tend to exhibit the "shadow striping" typical of the species in southern Africa (fawn stripes between the black ones). In Amboseli and the Mara, Burchell's zebras gather in migrating herds up to several thousand strong, along with wildebeest and other grazers. In contrast, Grevy's zebras live in small territorial herds.

△ Burchell's zebra

Pigs

The commonest wild pig in Kenya is the **warthog** (p.25), regularly sighted throughout Kenya up to altitudes of over 2000m. Quick of movement and nervous, warthogs are notoriously hard to photograph as they're generally on the run through the bush, often with the young in single file, tails erect. They shelter in holes in the ground, usually old aardvark burrows, and live in family groups, usually a mother and her litter of two to four piglets, or occasionally two or three females and their young. Boars join the group only to mate, and are distinguishable from sows by their prominent face warts, which are thought to be defensive pads protecting their heads during often violent fights.

Although a favourite prey animal of large cats – and humans – the warthog's survival doesn't appear to be threatened, although its rooting and wallowing behaviour brings it into conflict with farmers.

Two other much rarer pigs, both nocturnal, live in Kenya: the huge, dark-coloured **giant forest hog**, a bristly, big-tusked pig which lives in the highlands and is most likely to be seen from a tree hotel on Mount Kenya or in the Aberdares; and the **red river hog** or **bush pig** which is very rarely seen, though not uncommon in dense forest, close to agriculture and river margins.

Giraffes

The tallest mammals on earth, **giraffes** (p.26) are common and unmistakable. Non-territorial, they gather in loose leaderless herds and spend the day browsing on the leaves of trees too high for other species (acacias and combretums are favourites), while at night they lie down and ruminate. Bulls test their strength while in bachelor herds. When a female is in heat, which can happen at any time of year, the dominant male mates with her. She will give birth after a gestation of approximately fourteen months. Over half of all young, however, fall prey to lions or hyenas in their early years.

Kenya has three types of giraffe, differentiated from each other by their pattern and the configuration of their short horns. Most often seen is the **Maasai giraffe**, with two horns and a very broken pattern of dark blotches on a buff or fawn background. This is the giraffe you'll see in Maasai Mara, Amboseli and Tsavo West. Roughly north of the Nairobi–Mombasa road (coincidentally a natural dividing line) lives the dramatically patterned **reticulated giraffe**, which normally has three or five horns and boldly defined chestnut patches on a very pale background. The more solidly built **Rothschild's giraffe**, which has a pattern more like crazy paving (also with well-defined blotches) and usually two horns, is found only in parts of western Kenya (and over the border in Uganda). There's disagreement among zoologists over whether any of the giraffe's subspecies should be accorded the status of separate species – particularly concerning the reticulated giraffe – but they all interbreed.

Hollow-horned ruminants

This category of mammals includes buffalo and all the antelopes – exemplified by the two-toed cud-chewers illustrated on pp.26–32 of our colour wildlife guide. The **buffalo** itself (p.26) is a very common and much-photographed safari animal, closely related to the domestic milk- and meat-producing cow. Buffaloes live in herds of 100 to 300 and rarely make much effort to move when vehicles approach. Indeed, they aren't troubled by close contact with humans, and you don't have to read the papers in Kenya long before finding an example of buffaloes trampling crops or goring a farmer.

The rather ungainly **hartebeest** family (p.27) includes one of the rarest antelopes in Kenya, Hunter's hartebeest of the lower Tana River. The Coke's hartebeest or kongoni, however, is found widely in southern Kenya, and **topi** (p.27) are practically emblematic of the Maasai Mara, their main habitat. The **blue wildebeest** (p.27) is also particularly associated with the Mara. Their spectacular annual migration through the reserve is described on p.406.

Of the **gazelles**, the most obvious are **Thomson's** and **Grant's** (both p.28), easily seen at the roadside in many parts of southern Kenya. The range of Grant's gazelle extends further north to encompass the northern parks (Samburu, Meru) where "Thommies" are absent. The **gerenuk** (p.27) is an unusual browsing gazelle able to nibble from bushes standing on its hind legs (its name is Somali for "giraffe-necked"). Although considered an arid land specialist, its range encompasses most of Kenya east of the Rift Valley. The **impala** (p.28), although not a gazelle, is closely related and very common throughout much of Kenya.

The **reedbuck** (p.28) and **waterbuck** (p.29) are related to each other, both spending much time in or near water. The common or Bohor reedbuck has a patchy distribution in southern Kenya, whereas the waterbuck is common in many central and southern areas.

Some of the smallest antelopes in the world are quite easily seen in Kenya. Found all over the country, **Kirk's dikdik** (p.29) is a common miniature antelope, measuring no more than 40cm in height, which usually pairs for life. The **suni**, which is uncommon, but can be encountered almost anywhere in forest cover, is even smaller (32cm). Other small Kenyan antelopes – all fairly widespread but nowhere common – include the surprisingly aggressive **steinbok** (p.32) which, despite a height of only 50cm, defends itself furiously against attackers; the **oribi** (p.32), with its rather charming foreplay (when the female is in heat, the male pushes his head under her hindquarters and pushes her along on her forelegs like a wheelbarrow race); and the **klipspringer** (p.32), which has hooves wonderfully adapted for scaling near-vertical cliffs.

The duikers (from the Dutch for "diver", referring to their plunging into the bush) are larger – the **common duiker** (p.29) is around 60cm high – though they appear smaller because of their hunched posture. The common duiker is found throughout the country in many habitats, but most duikers are more choosy and prefer plenty of dense cover and thicket. These include the tiny Zanzibar duiker (whose range in Kenya is restricted to the Arabuko-Sokoke Forest), the widespread red duiker and blue duiker, and the more localized black-fronted duiker (Mount Kenya and Mount Elgon) and yellow-backed duiker (Mau forest).

Kenya's big antelopes are the Tragelaphinae – twisted-horn bushbuck types – and the Hippotraginae – horse-like antelopes. The **bushbuck** itself (p.30) is notoriously shy – a loud crashing through the undergrowth and a flash of a chestnut rump are all most people witness. The **bongo** is a particularly impressive member of this group, now confined to the highlands of Mount Kenya, the Aberdares (where it's sometimes seen at tree hotels), and possibly the Cheranganis and Mau Escarpment. The **sitatunga** (p.30) is a smaller relative, semi-aquatic by nature, found in Kenya only in remote corners of the Lake Victoria shoreline, at the very accessible Saiwa Swamp National Park, where they are easy to see, and in Lewa Conservancy in Laikipia. Also easily spotted, almost anywhere in the country, is the huge, cow-like **eland** (p.30), with its distinctive dewlap. The two species of kudu are not uncommon where they exist at all, but they are very localized. Both are browsers. You're most likely to see **greater kudu** (p.30) at Lake Bogoria or Marsabit and **lesser kudu** (p.31) in Tsavo West or East, but neither species in the Mara.

The horse-like antelopes include the very fine **fringe-eared oryx** (p.31), which is found almost everywhere except the Mara; the massive **roan antelope** (p.31), restricted to the Mara and the Lambwe valley in western Kenya (after an abortive relocation attempt to Shimba Hills, southwest of Mombasa); and the handsome **sable antelope** (p.31) which lives, and thrives, only in the Shimba Hills.

Other mammals

Of Kenya's other mammals, you're not likely to see more than a glimpse. Rarest of all is the **dugong**, the marine mermaid-prototype, of which there are believed to be a handful of individuals remaining, drifting in the shallows around the Lamu Archipelago.

△ Dugong

The insectivorous **elephant shrews** are worth looking out for, simply because they are so weird. Your best chance of a sighting is of the golden-rumped elephant shrew, at Gedi on the coast (see p.499).

The **aardvark** (p.19) is one of Africa's – indeed the world's – strangest mammals, a solitary termite-eater weighing up to 70kg. Its name, Afrikaans for "earth pig", is an apt description, as it holes up during the day in large burrows – excavated with remarkable speed and energy – and emerges at night to visit termite mounds within a radius of up to 5km, to dig for its main diet. It is most likely to be common in bush country well scattered with tall termite spires.

Pangolins are equally unusual – nocturnal, scale-covered mammals, resembling armadillos and feeding on ants and termites. Under attack, they roll themselves into a ball. The ground pangolin, the only species found in Kenya (most pangolins are arboreal), lives mainly in savanna districts.

Kenya's many **bats** will usually be a mere flicker over a water hole at twilight, or sometimes a flash across the headlights at night. The only bats you can normally observe in any meaningful way are fruit bats hanging from their roosting sites by day. The hammer-headed fruit bat, sometimes seen in Kakamega Forest, has a huge head and a wingspan of more than a metre.

Birds

Kenya boasts the second-highest country bird list – after the Congo – in Africa, at over 1070 species (this compares with no more than 300 for Britain and around 600 for North America). Nearly eighty percent of Kenya's birds are thought to breed in the country, with the remainder breeding during the northern summer in the Palaearctic region (Europe, north Africa and Asia north of the Himalayas) but wintering in tropical Africa. Many of these are familiar British summer visitors, such as swallows, nightingales and whitethroats, which have to negotiate or skirt the inhospitable Sahara on their migration. In winter, the migrant terns and waders can seem to dominate Kenya's shorelines, and the Palaearctic swallows and warblers may comprise a large proportion of the birds in bushland habitats.

If you're a novice **bird-watcher**, Kenya is an excellent place to start. No amount of wildlife documentaries can do justice to the thrill of glimpsing your first colourful bee-eaters overhead (twelve species have been recorded in Kenya, three or four of which you might expect to encounter), watching rollers and shrikes swoop from perches to hunt insects, or seeing groups of vultures wheeling and dipping in the skies overhead as they prepare to arrive at a kill. The wide variety and accessibility of habitats makes bird-watching in Kenya highly rewarding. The keenest independent bird-watchers might expect to encounter over 600 species in a four-week period, whereas some of the organized bird-watching tour groups, living and breathing birds for a three-week period, might record over 700 species in that time; one tour group holds the African record of 797 species in 25 days. However, even for those just dipping into the hobby or with limited time and choice of itineraries, Kenya offers some wonderful surprises.

Interesting bird records from the country can be submitted to the **Bird Committee** at Nature Kenya, PO Box 44486, Nairobi (einfo@naturekenya. org). Another useful contact is the **African Bird Club** (c/o BirdLife International, Wellbrook Court, Girton Rd, Cambridge CB3 0NA, UK), which produces an excellent regular bulletin and occasional well-produced monographs and itineraries. See also "Bird-watching in Nairobi" on p.129.

Distribution

Only a few species of birds are found throughout Kenya. Three which will become familiar to sharp-eyed visitors are the **laughing dove**, the **African drongo** (an all-black crow-like bird with a forked tail) and the **grey-headed sparrow**. Most other species have well-defined distributions dependent on habitat type, itself a reflection of altitude and rainfall patterns.

Part of Kenya's bird diversity can be explained by the large numbers of species reaching the edge of their known ranges inside its borders. These include birds originating in the Horn of Africa but having their western or southwestern limits in Kenya (for example, the Somali bee-eater), species widespread in southern Africa which reach their northern limits here (such as the rufous-bellied heron), coastal species which are confined to the east (for example, the mangrove kingfisher), species from west African equatorial forests whose ranges just overlap the forest patches in west Kenya (for example, the grey parrot), and species occurring along the southern edge of the Sahel which reach the extreme southeast of their range in Kenya (for example, the Abyssinian roller).

Many Kenyan birds display two more or less separate populations, one on the coast, the other in the highlands. This is determined by habitat: the coastal areas tend to have much less rain than the highlands, and are much hotter with a more severe dry season. In some species, such as the widespread speckled mousebird, two distinct races are evolving.

Endemic and near-endemic species

Of over a thousand species of bird found in Kenya, there are only six **endemic species** (that is, species found only in Kenya). Although these species are unlikely to be encountered by the novice and can be difficult to identify, their existence serves to emphasize Kenya's remarkable birdlife. They comprise two species of cisticola (small, skulking species, found in dense vegetation), a species of lark found only in the Marsabit and Isiolo areas, Sharpe's pipit (found in high grasslands in western and central Kenya), Clarke's weaver (found only in and around the Arabuko-Sokoke Forest), and Hinde's pied babbler (found in the vicinity of Kianyaga near Embu).

Many bird-watchers are attracted to Kenya by the large number of **near-endemic species**, confined to northeast Africa, for which Kenya offers a reasonably accessible chance of a sighting. These include Heuglin's bustard, the Somali bee-eater (a very pale, open-country bee-eater found in the north and often noted at Samburu), Hartlaub's turaco (a green species of turaco, only found in highland forests in East Africa), and the small Sokoke Scops owl found most easily around the Arabuko-Sokoke Forest.

Large walking birds

Several species of large, terrestrial (or partly terrestrial) birds are regularly seen on safari. Their size and common form of locomotion (though the secretary bird and marabou stork can both fly perfectly well, and the ground hornbill is not flightless) makes them the birds most frequently spotted by non-ornithologists.

The locally common, distinctive **ostrich** is found in dry, open plains and semi-desert. The world's biggest bird, at up to 2.5m high, it is virtually absent from the coastal strip, but can readily be seen in Nairobi National Park and most other parks.

◀ Secretary bird

The **secretary bird** is a large, long-tailed, long-legged bird, grey-white in colour with a scraggy crest (the quills of which gave it its name), black on the wings and with black "stockings". A bird of dry, open bush and wooded country, often seen in pairs, it is most commonly noticed stalking prey items which it has disturbed from grassland. Prey includes beetles, grasshoppers, reptiles and rodents, sometimes up to the size of a hare. Secretary birds are scarce in west Kenya and at the coast, but can be seen easily in Nairobi National Park.

The **marabou** is a large, ugly stork, up to 1.2m in height, with a bald head and a dangling, pink throat pouch. Most specimens look as if they're in an advanced state of decomposition. The marabou flies with its head and neck retracted (unlike other storks) and is often seen in dry areas, including towns, where it feeds on small animals, carrion and refuse. A large population of marabous is usually considered a sign that waste management is a problem in the area.

Another reasonably common walking bird is the **ground hornbill**. This impressive creature lives in open country and is the largest hornbill by far. Black, with red face and wattles, it bears a distinct resemblance to a turkey. It's not uncommon to come across pairs, or sometimes groups, of ground hornbills, especially in the Mara, trailing through the scrub on the lookout for small animals. They nest among rocks or in tree stumps.

Flamingos and ibises

Many visitors to Kenya are astounded by their first sight of **flamingos** – a sea of pink on a soda-encrusted lake, which, together with the salt-rich smell of the lake and the stench of the birds' guano, powerfully evokes East Africa. Two species are found in Kenya, the greater flamingo and the lesser flamingo. Both are birds of the Rift Valley lakes and adjacent areas, and both are colonial nesters.

Much the commoner of the two is the **lesser flamingo**, which is smaller, pinker and with a darker bill than its greater relative. The Rift Valley population of lesser flamingos, with over a million birds gathering at one time at lakes Bogoria and Nakuru, is one of only three populations in Africa. This species is nomadic, moving in relation to fluctuating food supplies, water levels and alkalinity, and flocks can leave or arrive at an area in a very short period of time – an estimated 400,000 birds have been recorded leaving Lake Bogoria over a seven-day period. Lesser flamingos feed by filtering suspended aquatic food, mainly blue-green algae that occurs in huge concentrations on the shallow soda lakes of the Rift.

Greater flamingos may occur in their thousands but are considerably fewer in number than the lessers. They are bottom feeders, filtering small invertebrates as well as algae. Although greaters tend to be less frequently nomadic than their relatives, they are more likely to move away from the Rift Valley lakes to smaller water bodies and even the coast.

The most widely distributed **ibis** species (stork-like birds with downcurved bills) is the **sacred ibis**, which is found near water and human settlements. It has a white body with black head and neck, and black tips to the wings. Also frequently encountered is the **Hadada ibis**, a brown bird with a green-bronze sheen to the wings and noisy call in flight, found near wooded streams, cultivated areas and parks in southern Kenya.

Water birds

Most large water bodies, apart from the extremely saline lakes, support several species of **ducks and geese**, many of which breed in Europe, but overwinter in Africa.

Several species of **herons, storks and egrets** occur in areas with water, or can be observed overflying on migration. The commonest large heron is the black-headed heron, which can sometimes be found far from water. Mainly grey with a black head and legs, the black heron can be seen "umbrella-fishing" along coastal creeks and marsh shores: it cloaks its head with its wings whilst fishing, which is thought to cut down surface reflection from the water, allowing the bird to see its prey more easily.

The **hamerkop** is a brown, heron-like bird with a sturdy bill and mane of brown feathers, which gives it a top-heavy, slightly prehistoric appearance in flight, like a miniature pterodactyl. Hamerkops are widespread near water and build large, conspicuous nests that are often taken over by other animals, including owls, geese, ducks, monitor lizards or snakes.

Guineafowl

Four species of these large, grey game birds are found in Kenya. The **vulturine guineafowl** is a bird of very arid areas, recognized by the long tapered feathers hanging from the base of the neck over a royal-blue chest. The well-known **helmeted guineafowl**, a bird of moister areas, has a bony yellow skull protrusion (hence its name). The crested and the Kenya crested guineafowl are both birds of thickets.

Birds of prey

Kenya abounds with birds of prey – kites, vultures, eagles, harriers, hawks and falcons. Altogether, over 75 species have been recorded in the country, several of which are difficult to miss.

Six species of **vulture** range over the plains and bushlands of Kenya and are often seen soaring in search of a carcass. All the species can occur together, and birds may travel vast distances to feed. The main differences are in feeding behaviour: the lappet-faced vulture, for example, pulls open carcasses; the African white-backed feeds mainly on internal organs; the hooded vulture mainly picks from bones.

Two other birds of prey that are firmly associated with East Africa are the **bateleur**, an eagle that is readily identified by its silver wings, black, stumpy body shape and chestnut-red, wedge-shaped tail; and the **fish eagle**, whose haunting calls render a sense of emptiness and space to many a wildlife television documentary. Fish eagles are generally found in pairs near water, often along lake shores.

Cranes and bustards

Kenya's national bird, the **crowned crane**, is found in the south and west of the country. It is a distinctive, elegant bird, the head crowned with an array of yellow plumes. Crowned cranes are often seen feeding on cultivated fields or in marshy areas.

Some nine species of **bustard** occur in the plains and grasslands of Kenya. These large, open-country species are long-legged and long-necked and are very well camouflaged among the browns and yellows of their African backdrop. The heaviest flying bird in the world, the Kori bustard, is commonest in the Rift Valley highlands. Bustards are affected by intensive, small-scale agricultural and human presence, and several species have undergone a decline in Kenya.

◄ Crowned crane

Parrots and lovebirds

Eight species of Psittacidae have been recorded in Kenya, three of which are introduced. The parrot species that you're most likely to see is the **brown parrot**, which occurs in wooded areas in the west of the country. Lovebirds are small, green, hole-nesting birds (like small parrots) and are readily seen in the acacias around Lake Naivasha, where a feral breeding population of **yellow-collared lovebirds** has become established. This species has been introduced to Kenya from Tanzania, and hybridizes with the introduced and very similar **Fischer's lovebird**.

Go-away birds and turacos

These distinctive, related families are found only in Africa. Medium-sized and with long tails, most **go-away birds** (named after their call) and **turacos** have short rounded wings. They are not excellent fliers, but are very agile in their movements along branches and through vegetation. Many species are colourful and display a crest. The largest, the magnificent **great blue turaco** (blue above, and green and brown below) is found only in the western forests in Kenya –

notably at Kakamega, where it is one of the largest species in the forest. Other turacos are generally green or violet in colour, and all are confined to thickly wooded and forest areas. Open-country species, such as the widely distributed and common **white-bellied go-away bird**, are white or grey in colour.

Mousebirds

Three species of mousebird are found in Kenya. Their name derives from their rapid scampering through thick tangles of branches using unusually adapted claws. They can be identified by their slight crests and their long, tapering tails. Generally grey or brown in colour, they're noisy and feed actively in quite open vegetation. The **speckled mousebird** is a very common species throughout southern Kenya, often found in small groups at forest margins and in suburban gardens.

Rollers, shrikes and kingfishers

A family of very colourful and noticeable birds of the African bush, **rollers** perch on exposed bushes and telephone wires and chase flying insects. They take their name from their impressive courtship flights – a fast dive with a rolling and rocking motion, accompanied by raucous calls. Many have a sky-blue underbody and sandy-coloured back, and long tail streamers are a distinctive feature of several Kenyan species. The **lilac-breasted roller** is a common and conspicuous species.

Shrikes are found throughout Kenya. Fierce hunters with sharply hooked bills, they habitually sit on prominent perches, and eat insects, reptiles and small birds.

Kingfishers are some of Kenya's most colourful and noticeable birds, with eleven species found here. They range in size from the tiny **pygmy kingfisher**, which feeds on insects and is generally found near water, to the **giant kingfisher**, a shy fish-eating species of wooded streams in the west of the country. Several kingfishers eat insects rather than fish and they can often be seen perched high in trees or on open posts in the bush where they wait to pounce on passing prey. A common and widespread insectivorous species is the **chestnut-bellied kingfisher**.

Hornbills

Named for their long, heavy bills, surmounted by a casque or bony helmet, hornbills generally have black and white plumage. Their flight consists of a series of alternate flaps and glides. When in flight, hornbills may be heard before they are seen, the beaten wings making a "whooshing" noise as air rushes through the flight feathers. Many species have bare areas of skin on the face and throat and around the eyes, with the bill and the casque often brightly coloured, their colours changing with the age of the bird. Thirteen species have been recorded in Kenya, most of them omnivorous, but tending largely to eat fruit. Several species are common open-country birds; **silvery-cheeked hornbills** are sometimes seen in Nairobi. Hornbills have interesting breeding habits: the male generally incarcerates the female in a hollow tree, leaving a hole through which he feeds her while she incubates the eggs and rears the young.

Woodpeckers

The abundance of trees within such a variety of habitats in Kenya means that many species of woodpecker (up to fourteen) are present. One species you're almost certain to encounter is the sparrow-sized **cardinal wood-pecker**.

Sunbirds

Sunbirds are bright, active birds, feeding on nectar from flowering plants, and distributed throughout Kenya, wherever there are flowers, flowering trees and bushes. Over 35 species have been recorded in the country, with many confined to discrete types of habitat. Common species in the Nairobi area are **variable** and **scarlet-chested sunbirds**. Males are brightly coloured and usually identifiable, but many of the drabber females require very careful observation to identify them.

Starlings

The glorious orange and blue starlings which are a common feature of bush-land habitats – usually seen feeding on the ground – belong to one of three species. The **superb starling** is the most widespread of these, found every-where from remote national parks to gardens in Nairobi. It can be identified by the white band above its orange breast. Similar starlings are the larger **golden-breasted**, often seen in Tsavo National Park, and **Hildebrand's** (also orange-breasted), which is commonest around Machakos but can be encountered all over southern Kenya.

Weavers and whydahs

These small birds are some of the commonest and most widespread of all Kenyan birds. Most male **weavers** have some yellow in the plumage, whereas the females are rather dull and sparrow-like. In fact, many species appear superficially very similar; distinctions are based on their range and preferred type of habitat. Weavers nest in colonies and weave their nests into elongated shapes, which can be used to help in the identification of the species. Many nests are situated close to water or human habitation and sometimes hang suspended. The **golden palm weaver** is the species you'll commonly see on the coast, often in hotel gardens.

Whydahs are also known as widow birds. The **paradise whydah** has extremely ornate tail feathers, with the central pair of tail feathers flattened and twisted into the vertical. Male paradise whydahs are mainly black in colour, and perform a strange bouncing display flight to attract females.

Reptiles and amphibians

There is only one species of crocodile in Kenya – the big **Nile crocodile** which, left to grow, can reach 6m or more in length and is considered a cunning and dangerous animal. You'll see them in the Mara River, in the Tana, at Mzima Springs in Tsavo West, in great numbers in Lake Turkana and, if you take the trouble to look, in many other rivers and large bodies of water.

Kenya has many species of **snake**, some of them quite common, but your chances of seeing a wild specimen here are more remote than in Australia or the USA, or even certain parts of Europe. In Kenya, as all over Africa, snakes are both revered and reviled and, while they frequently have symbolic significance for local people, that is quite often forgotten in the rush to hack them to bits with a panga upon their discovery. All in all, snakes have a very hard time surviving in Kenya.

Common **non-poisonous species** of snake include the rock python (a constrictor growing up to 5m or more in length), the egg-eating snake and the sand boa. Common **poisonous species** include the green and black mambas (fast, agile, arboreal snakes), the boomslang, the spitting cobra and the dangerous puff adder, which is probably responsible for more bites than any other, on account of its sluggish disposition. Most snakes flee on detecting the vibrations of human footsteps.

Tortoises are quite frequently encountered on park roads in the morning or late afternoon. Some, like the leopard tortoise, can be quite large, up to 50cm in length, while the hinged tortoise (which not only retreats inside its shell but shuts the door, too) is much smaller – up to 30cm. In rocky areas, look out for the unusual pancake tortoise, a flexible-shelled species that can put on quite a turn of speed but, when cornered in its fissure in the rocks, will inflate to wedge itself inextricably, thus avoiding capture. Terrapins or turtles of several species are common in ponds and slow-flowing streams. On the coast, sea turtles breed and it's not unusual to see them from boats during snorkelling trips.

Lizards are common everywhere, harmless and often colourful. The commonest are **rock agamas**, the males often seen in courting "plumage", with brilliant orange heads and blue bodies, ducking and bobbing at each other. They live in loose colonies often near human habitation; one hotel may have hundreds, its neighbours none. The biggest lizards, **Nile monitors**, grow to nearly 2m in length and are often seen near water. From a distance, as they race off, they look like speeding baby crocodiles. The other common monitor, the smaller savanna monitor, is less handsomely marked.

◀ Jackson's chameleon

A large, docile lizard you may come across is the **plated lizard**. Growing to 40cm, this intelligent, mild-mannered reptile is often found around coastal hotels, looking for scraps from the kitchen or pool terrace. At night, on the coast, the translucent little aliens on the ceiling are **geckos**, catching moths and other insects, and worth encouraging. By day, their minuscule relatives, the day geckos (velvet grey and yellow), patrol coastal walls. In the highlands you may come across prehistoric-looking three-horned **Jackson's chameleons** creeping through the foliage – and there are several other species of chameleon, living in most parts of the country, which, owing to their excessive slowness, you are most likely to see squashed flat on the road.

In the **amphibian** world, you tend to hear examples long before you see them. You may come across the odd toad, sitting under a footpath light, waiting for insects to drop on to the ground. There are, however, dozens of species of frogs and tree frogs, ranging from the common squeaker to the red and black rubber frog.

Music

A lthough the music of Kenya is less well known abroad than that of a number of other African countries, its home-grown vitality is there if you listen, and Nairobi's audiences and recording facilities have long been a draw for musicians from all over east and central Africa, bringing to the city a pan-African musical flavour.

All the people of Kenya have **traditional musical cultures**, some of which have survived more intact than others, for with the majority of Kenyans being Christian nowadays, gospel music has all but obliterated traditional music in many areas. Among the Kikuyu and the Kalenjin, for example, traditional music is almost extinct, and elsewhere, to hear anything at all, you need time, patience and local people's trust before being allowed to witness what can still be very sacred events. Kenyan **gospel** itself is sadly not the uplifting version of African American churches in the United States, but a tinny, synthesized and homogenous form.

As for **popular music**, there is no single identifiable genre of "Kenyan pop", but rather a number of styles that borrow freely from and cross-fertilize with one another. Within Kenya's extremely widespread **benga** style, many musicians perform most of their songs in one of the local indigenous languages. Other musicians, especially those playing rumba styles, aim at a broad national audience and thus perform in **Swahili**; the big-name bands can usually muster sufficiently large audiences in sprawling, ethnically diverse towns like Nairobi, Nakuru or Mombasa. Yet others offer a local variant of the **Congolese** sound, with lyrics in **Lingala** (a Congolese tongue, understood by almost no one in Kenya).

A useful complement to this music overview can be found at ⊛www .eastafricanmusic.com, put together by the author of this article, and featuring biographies of several musicians, articles on the Kenyan scene over the years and lists of recommended albums.

Traditional music

Music has traditionally been used to accompany ceremonies, events and **rites of passage**, from celebrations at a baby's birth to songs of adolescence and warriorhood, and from marriage, harvests and solar and lunar cycles to festivities, religious events and death. The oldest of Kenya's musical traditions is **ngoma**, a term which, in most Bantu languages of Kenya, refers to a specific kind of drum and a related dance; *ngoma* is nowadays used generally to describe all the facets of a musical performance, including the accompanying dances.

Although an inter-ethnic *ngoma* called *beni* ("band") emerged on the coast at the beginning of the twentieth century and spread inland (you can still witness this anachronistic, marching-band form on special occasions in Lamu), *ngoma* music today is essentially ethnic, related to a specific language group and using the respective vernacular and local dance rhythms. *Ngoma* also provides most of the music used during the life-cycle festivities (birth, initiation and circumcision, marriage and death), whether in the town or the country. Look out for recordings by Luhya *sukuti* groups, the *sukuti* being the central drum of these ensembles.

The following is a brief tribe-by-tribe run-down of more easily encountered traditional music and instruments. Obviously, there's much more available if

you know where to search and what to ask for: essential **reading** for this
is George Senoga-Zake's *Folk Music of Kenya* (Uzima Press, Nairobi). Other
works on music are thin on the ground, though most bookshops stock a
reasonable selection of school textbooks, some of which provide a handy
introduction to the subject. You can usually find cassettes and a few CDs of
traditional music locally, though it may take a little perseverance. Another
source of background on traditional music, with audio clips, is ⓦwww
.bluegecko.org.

Akamba and Chuka

The **Akamba** are best known for their skill at drumming, but this tradition has
sadly now all but disappeared. To find any musicians, you'll have to go well off the
beaten track in Ukambani. Like that of the Akamba, **Chuka** music from the east
side of Mount Kenya is drumming genius, and is likewise almost extinct. Your
only hope is to catch the one remaining band (which currently plays at the *Mount
Kenya Safari Club* near Nanyuki), or pale imitations in coastal holiday resorts.

Bajuni

The **Bajuni** are a small ethnic group living in the Lamu Archipelago and
on the nearby mainland, and are known musically for a recording of an epic
women's work song called *Mashindano Ni Matezo*. One of only very few
easily available recordings of women singing traditionally in Kenya, it features
counterpoint singing that gradually becomes hypnotic, punctuated by metal-
lic rattles and supported by subdued drumming. You can find it in Lamu,
Kilifi or Mombasa.

Boran

The **Boran**, who live between Marsabit and the Ethiopian border, have a rich
musical tradition. The Arab influence is readily discernible, as are more typically
Saharan rhythms; most distinctive is their use of the *chamonge*, nowadays a large
cooking pot loosely strung with metal wires. Recordings are difficult to obtain;
ask in either Isiolo or Marsabit.

Gusii

Gusii music is certainly Kenya's oddest. The favoured instrument is the *obokano*,
an enormous version of the Luo *nyatiti* lyre which is pitched at least an octave
below the human voice, and which at times can sound like roaring thunder.
They also use the ground bow, essentially a large hole dug in the ground over
which an animal skin is tightly pegged. The skin has a small hole cut in the
centre, into which a single-stringed bow is placed and plucked: the sound defies
description. Ask around in Kisii and you should be able to pick up recordings
easily enough.

Luhya

Luhya music has a clear Bantu flavour, easily discernible in the pre-
eminence of drums. Of these, the *sukuti* is best known, sometimes played in
ensembles, and still used in rites of passage such as circumcision. Recordings
are easily available in Kakamega and Kitale, and in some River Road shops
in Nairobi.

Luo

The **Luo** are best known as the originators of *benga* (see p.650). Their most distinctive musical instrument is the *nyatiti*, a double-necked eight-string lyre with a skin resonator which is also struck on one neck with a metal ring tied to the toe. It produces a tight, resonant sound, and is used to generate sometimes remarkably complex, hypnotic rhythms. The instrument was used in the fields to relieve workers' tiredness, the music typically beginning at a moderate pace and quickening progressively, the musician singing over the sound. The lyrics cover all manner of subjects, from politics and change since the *wazungu* arrived, to moral fables and age-old legends. Look out also for recordings of *onand* (accordion) and *orutu* (a single-stringed fiddle).

Maasai

The nomadic lifestyle of the **Maasai** tends to preclude the carrying of large instruments, and as a result their music is one of the most distinctive in Kenya, characterized by a total lack of instruments and by some astonishing polyphonous multi-part singing. This can be call-and-response: sometimes women are included in the chorus, but the most famous form is the songs of the *morani*, where each man sings part of a rhythm, more often than not from his throat (rather like a grunt), which together with the calls of his companions creates a pattern of rhythms. The songs are usually competitive (expressed through the singers alternately leaping as high as they can) or bragging – about how the singer killed a lion, or rustled cattle from a neighbouring community. The Maasai have retained much of their traditional culture, so singing is still very much used in traditional ceremonies, most spectacularly in the *eunoto* circumcision ceremony in which boys are initiated into manhood to begin their ten- to fifteen-year stint as *morani*.

Most tourists staying in big coastal hotels or in game park lodges in Amboseli and Maasai Mara will have a chance to sample Maasai music in the form of groups of *morani* playing at the behest of hotel management. Recordings can be difficult to find, though there is an excellent US website on Maasai music, @www.laleyio.com, with audio clips, and a CD available to order.

Mijikenda

The **Mijikenda** of the coast have a prolific musical tradition which has survived Christian conversion, and is readily available on tape throughout the coastal region. Performances can occasionally be seen in the larger hotels. Most of the music available is from the Giriama section of the Mijikenda, who live inland of Malindi. Like the Akamba, the Mijikenda are superb drummers and athletic dancers. The music is generally light and overlaid with complex rhythms, impossible not to dance to. Look out also for the *kiringongo* music of the Chonyi people, which features the xylophone (an instrument otherwise unknown in Kenya).

Samburu

Despite its having been discovered by tourists and authors of coffee-table books, the only recordings of **Samburu** music are tracks on occasional compilations. Like their Maasai cousins, whose singing it closely resembles, Samburu musicians make a point of not playing instruments – at least in theory. In practice, they do play small pipes, and also a kind of guitar with a box resonator and loose metal strings – which seems to be related to the *chamonge* of the Borana. But these are played purely for pleasure, or to soothe a crying baby, and are thus not deemed "music" by Samburu. Listen out also for the sinuously erotic rain songs sung by women in times of drought. For recordings, ask around at the lodges and campsites in Samburu/Buffalo Springs National Reserves, or – better still – in Maralal.

Turkana

Until the 1970s, the **Turkana** were one of Kenya's remotest tribes, and in large part are still untouched by Christian missionaries. Their traditional music is based loosely on a call-and-response pattern. The main instrument is a kudu antelope horn with or without finger holes, but most of their music is entirely vocal. A rarity to look out for are the women's rain songs, sung to the god Akuj during times of drought. As traditional music is still played on ceremonial occasions (and being nomadic, the Turkana have no electricity or tape recorders), finding cassettes is extremely difficult; it's a question of asking around in Loiyangalani. You're usually welcome to join performances in Loiyangalani for a small fee.

Popular music

Until the mid-1990s, the defining elements of Kenyan popular music had always been the interplay of guitars, with prominent solos, and the **cavacha** rhythm – a kind of clavé beat, popularized in the mid-1970s by Congolese groups such as Zaiko Langa Langa and Orchestra Shama Shama. While rapid-fire percussion, usually on the snare or high hat, continues to underlie a great sweep of Kenyan music, it's worth noting that the scene is very different to that of only ten or fifteen years ago; the ranks of the elder generation of pop musicians have thinned all too quickly in recent years, with a startling number of experienced younger musicians having also died. Suspicions that HIV/AIDS may be a factor in many of these cases are rarely confirmed. Whatever the causes, the effects have been devastating not only in the loss of creative talent, but also because with these musicians goes the living memory of the historical context and evolution of Kenyan music. Partly as a result of this changing of the guard, a new generation of musicians and producers with quite different backgrounds, training and experience is beginning to make its mark.

The arrival of the guitar

From the early 1950s on, with the coming of recording and broadcasting, the introduction of new instruments and the more widespread use of the **guitar**, an acoustic guitar-based music developed as accompaniment to songs sung in **Swahili**. A basis for Swahili-language popular music had already been laid by the *beni* groups flourishing in East African towns during the first half of the century. *Beni* songs, as well as the new guitar songs, featured the strong and critical social commentary so beloved of Kenyans. The songs were usually in the form of a short story and may comment on an actual political or social topic, or perhaps recount a personal experience of the musician. Romantic lyrics are almost non-existent, even in songs dealing with men and women.

The guitar styles themselves developed out of different instrumental techniques and musical perceptions, but they were influenced by the records available at

Taarab music

Taarab (or *tarab/tarabu*), the main popular music of the coastal Swahili people, deserves special mention. It has a long tradition in the festive life of the Swahili, especially at weddings, and is also the general music of entertainment of the coastal communities. Many of the lead singers and bandleaders of *taarab* groups are women, almost unique in Kenyan traditional music. Furthermore, the music has strong Arabic/Islamic overtones in instrumentation, especially in the haunting vocals. Earlier *taarab* groups used the full Arabic orchestra, including the lute-like *oud* and violins. Today, the main instruments are mandolin or guitar and either an Indian harmonium or a small electronic organ/piano, plus a variety of local, Arabic or Indian drums. Indian movies, with their strong musical component, are very popular among the coastal people and this has led to many features of Indian music being absorbed into *taarab*.

On Lamu island, the old centre of Swahili culture, most weddings today are served by a few amateur *taarab* groups, with professional groups bussed up from Mombasa only for more well-to-do marriages. The **Zein Musical Party**, now based in Mombasa, is the heir of Lamu's *taarab* tradition. Zein l'Abdin was born in Lamu and hails from a family in which the Swahili arts were highly valued. Together with the Swahili poet Sheikh Nabhany, Zein has unearthed a number of poems, dating back to the nineteenth century, which he has included in his repertoire. But Zein isn't just a fabulous singer and composer; he also ranks as the finest *oud* player in East Africa and is well known throughout the Islamic world.

Maulidi Musical Party, **Zuhura & Party** and **Malika** have, for the past three decades, been Mombasa's main wedding favourites. Singer Maulidi Juma and group are at ease both with traditional Swahili wedding songs and the Hindi-style songs so characteristic of Mombasa *taarab*, with Swahili words set to tunes from the latest Bollywood movie. Maulidi Musical Party can stand as the prototype Mombasa ensemble, its sound being based on a keyboard, with fills by accordion, guitar, bass and percussion. Many rhythms are rooted in local *ngoma* traditions, and bandmaster Mohamed Shigoo's keyboard work stands out as especially original, with a strong flavour of harmonium (which he used to play earlier in his career) and *nzumari* (a local double-reed horn). Shigoo and the Maulidi Musical Party used to back Malika (Asha Abdo Suleiman) when she was visiting from Somalia, where she lived for a while in the 1970s and 1980s. Following the outbreak of civil war she has been based in Mombasa once again, and hers is still the female voice most in demand here; few can rival her stage aura. Mombasa's other female star is the enchanting **Zuhura Swaleh**, whose energetic songs have a firm base in the local *chakacha* rhythms and lyrics. The *taishokoto* is a prominent sound in her group.

With Malika, Maulidi and Zuhura in their 50s now, and their voices having suffered from the strain of singing for six hours in a row at weddings, the audience is look-ing for new stars. **Sitara**, second voice in Maulidi Musical Party for some years, emerged with her own group Diamond Star, taking half of Maulidi's band with her. She is popular with the young wedding audience for her Swahili covers of some of the latest Western and Indian pop songs. A more recent appearance on the scene is **Yusuf Mohamed "Tenge"**, following in the steps of Maulidi and Juma Bhalo, who used to be the hero of Indian-style *taarab*.

the time, mainly from other parts of Africa. Kenyan musicians of the period cite the finger-picking style of **Jean Bosco Mwenda** and **Losta Abelo**, both from Katanga (today, Shaba Province in the Congo), and **George Sibanda**, from Bulawayo in Zimbabwe, as important inspirations. From this period, the notables of Kenya's acoustic guitar styles were **John Mwale**, **George Mukabi** (directly out of the Luhya *sukuti* tradition) and **Isaya Mwinamo**.

The 1960s saw the introduction of **electric guitars** as well as larger groups (of three to four guitars). Finger-picking guitarists from western Kenya and the smoother, driving, electric-guitar sound of groups like **Equator Sound Band** (Equator was a leading record label of the time), featuring the songs of **Daudi Kabaka**, **Fadhili William**, **Nashil Pichen** and **Peter Tsotsi**, dominated the airwaves and the record stores. Daudi Kabaka reigned as the "King of Twist", the twist being essentially a fast version of the South African rhythm found in songs such as "The Lion Sleeps Tonight". Into the 1970s, while Kabaka's African Eagles and others continued to play their brands of Swahili music, many top Kenyan groups, such as the Ashantis, Air Fiesta and the Hodi Boys, were playing Congolese covers and international pop, especially soul music, in the Nairobi clubs.

Benga and other modern styles

In the 1970s, a number of musicians began to define the direction of an emerging form, **benga**, which more than any other Kenyan music became Kenya's most characteristic pop sound. Although it originated with the Luo people of western Kenya, practically all the Kenyan guitar bands play variants of it, and today most of the regional or ethnic pop groups refer generally to their music as *benga*.

As a pop style, *benga* actually dates back to the 1950s, when musicians began adapting traditional dance rhythms and the sounds of the *nyatiti* and *orutu* to the acoustic guitar and later to electric instruments. During its heyday in the 1970s and into the 1980s, *benga* music dominated Kenya's recording industry and was very popular even in west and southern Africa.

By any measure, the most famous *benga* group is **Shirati Jazz**, led by D.O. (Daniel Owino) Misiani. Born in Shirati, Tanzania, just south of the Kenyan border, he has been playing *benga* since the mid-1960s and is still going strong. His style is characterized by soft, flowing and melodic two-part vocal harmonies, a very active, pulsating bass line that derives at least in part from traditional *nyatiti* and drum rhythms, and stacks of invigorating guitar work, the lead alternating with the vocal.

Other important *benga* artists include the pioneering **Colella Mazee** and **Ochieng Nelly** – either together or separately in various incarnations of **Victoria Jazz** and the **Victoria Kings** – as well as **George Ramogi** and his Continental Luo Sweet Band. The mid-1990s also saw the emergence of **Okatch Biggy** (Elly Otieno Okatch) **and Heka Heka** and **Prince Jully** (Julius Okumu) with the **Jolly Boys Band**. Today Heka Heka (and various offshoots of it) and the Jolly Boys have continued to flourish, moving into new, more risqué territory. After Prince Jully's death in 1997, Jully's wife, Lillian Auma, began fronting the Jolly Boys as Princess Jully, and the response has been nothing short of phenomenal. She draws enthusiastic crowds wherever she performs.

One Luo name which doesn't fit neatly under the *benga* banner is **Ochieng Kabaselleh** and the Luna Kidi Band. His songs were mostly in Luo, but sometimes with a liberal seasoning of Swahili and English. Likewise, the melodies and harmonies are from the *benga* realm but the rhythm, guitar work, and horns suggest influences from the Congolese/Swahili-dominated sound. Kabaselleh, who languished in prison for several years for "subversion" in the 1980s, returned to the music world with a flood of new releases in the 1990s. He died in 1998, a victim of complications related to diabetes.

A related group that Kabaselleh started in the late 1970s with several of his brothers continues today as **Bana Kadori**. Originally brought together as a recording group, they are now an active performing band, their music running from Kabaselleh's hybrid *benga*-rumba style to mainstream *benga*.

Luhya

Many of Kenya's famous guitarists and vocalists come from the Luhya highlands just to the north of Lake Victoria and Luo-land. This was the ancestral home of early finger-picking guitarists like **John Mwale** and **George Mukabi**, as well as the late **Daudi Kabaka**, and another twist proponent still active in the music business, **John Nzenze**. While these musicians fostered broad appeal through Swahili language, other Luhya musicians stayed closer to their home areas both musically and linguistically. In *benga* style, **Sukuma bin Ongaro** is famous for his humorous social commentaries. Even if you can't understand the language, his music is great to dance to and, of course, has some super guitar licks.

Shem Tube is a Luhya vocalist/guitarist whose music straddles both past and present – though it's his past which has given him a following in Europe, thanks to a vintage compilation in the *omutibo* style featuring his group **Abana ba Nasery** (the Nursery Boys). Coming together as a trio in the early 1960s, Abana ba Nasery used traditional Luhya rhythms and melody lines, but their two-guitar line-up and three-part vocal harmonies, with rhythms scraped from the neck ridges of the old Fanta bottle, presaged elements of modern Kenyan pop. Although they've never earned enough money to buy their own electric guitars and amps, Abana ba Nasery have had a string of local hits as an electric band under the stage names Mwilonje Jazz and Super Bunyore Band.

Kikuyu

As Kenya's largest ethnic group, the Kikuyu-speaking people of Central Province and Nairobi are a major market force in Kenya's music industry. Perhaps because of this large "built-in" audience, few Kikuyu musicians have tried to cross over into the national Swahili or English-language markets.

Kikuyu pop has a traditional melodic structure, quite distinct from those of the Luo and Luhya of western Kenya. Most often the songs incorporate elements of *benga* and *cavacha*, but it's not unusual for there to be a dose of country and western, reggae or Congolese soukous. From the 1970s into the 1990s, the king of Kikuyu pop was indisputably **Joseph Kamaru**, who over the course of his career carved out something of his own musical empire, including a large performing band and dancers, two music stores and a recording studio. Still going strong in 1993, Kamaru shocked his fans by announcing that he had been "born again" and retired from music performance to devote his efforts to evangelism and gospel music promotion.

At least a part of the void left by Kamaru has been filled by Jane Nyambura, one of very few female headliners in Kikuyu pop. Known these days simply as **Queen Jane**, she's a staunch advocate of the inclusion of traditional folk forms and local languages within contemporary pop, an approach which has limited her radio exposure, but hasn't prevented her and four of her brothers and sisters from make their living from her band.

Akamba

Kamba pop music is firmly entrenched in the *benga/cavacha* camp, though it has distinctive features of its own. One is the delicate, flowing rhythm guitar, the flow often reminiscent of the old carousel calliope, that underlies many arrangements. While the primary guitar plays chords in the lower range, the second guitar, often in a high register, plays a fast pattern of fills. This is discernible in many of the recordings of the three most famous Kamba groups; the **Kalambya Boys** and **Kalambya Sisters**, **Peter Mwambi and his Kyanganga Boys**, and **Les Kilimambogo Brothers Band**. With socially relevant lyrics, intricate guitar weaves and a solid dance-beat backing, Les Kili-mambogo Brothers Band began recording in Swahili and achieved widespread popularity in Kenya, though their career was brought to an end by the death of leader **Kakai Kilonzo** in 1987. These days, a new generation of musicians is drawing the limelight away from the old guard, with the **Katitu Boys Band** dominating the Kamba market.

Congolese

Congolese musicians have been making musical waves in Kenya since the late 1950s, but it wasn't until the mid-1970s, after the passing of the American soul craze, that music from Congo began to dominate the city nightclubs. One of the first Congolese musicians to settle in Kenya during this period was **Baba Gaston**, who had already been in the business for twenty years when he arrived in Nairobi with his group Baba National in 1975. A prolific musician, he stole the scene until his retirement as a performer and recording artist in 1989. Following Gaston, such groups as **Super Mazembe**, **Les Mangelepa** (some of Gaston's own musicians), as well as **Samba Mapangala** and an early version of his **Orchestra Virunga** took hold in the city. This period is still regarded as the golden age of Lingala music in Kenya and it flourishes locally with plenty of CD reissues in the shops.

Congolese music remains popular in various clubs in Nairobi and the larger Kenyan towns. In fact, some of the musicians of this golden period can be found performing today in successor bands to Mazembe and Mangelepa. Veteran Congolese star **Lessa Lassan** continues with his group **Popolipo**, and there are plenty of young aspiring Congolese émigrés waiting in the wings for their turn to shine.

In both Congolese and Swahili popular music, **rumba** has always been a major ingredient. Songs typically open with a slow-to-medium rumba that ambles through the verses, backed by a light percussion of gentle congas, snare and high hat. Then, three or four minutes into the song there's a transition – or more often a hiatus. It's goodbye to verses and rolling rumba as a much faster rhythm, highlighting the instrumental parts, especially solo guitar and brass, takes over with a vengeance. Swahili music over the last thirty years has been particularly faithful to this two-part structure, although today, both Swahili and Congolese musicians often dispense with the slow portion altogether.

Swahili bands: the Tanzanian influence

Kenya's own brand of **Swahili pop** music has its origin in the Tanzanian pop styles of the 1970s, though the Kenyan variety has followed a separate evolu-tionary path from the Tanzanian mainstream. In addition to the stylistic features it shares with the Congolese sound (light, high-hat-and-conga percussion and a delicate two/three-guitar interweave), the Kenyan Swahili sound is instrumen-tally sparse, allowing the bass to fill in gaps, often in syncopated rhythms. While the Congolese musicians are famous for their vocals and their intricate harmo-nies, Swahili groups are renowned for their demon guitarists and crisp, clear guitar interplay. Trumpets and saxes are common in recorded arrangements but usually omitted in club performances because of the extra expense.

One of the first Tanzanian groups to migrate to Kenya was **Arusha Jazz**, the predecessor of what is now the legendary **Simba Wanyika Original** ("Simba Wanyika" means "Lion of the Savanna"). Founded by Wilson Peter Kinyonga and

These are two songs you're almost certain to hear, sooner of later, regardless of where you stay or how you travel.

Jambo Bwana
by Teddy Kalanda Harrison

Jambo, jambo Bwana	Greetings, greetings Bwana
Habari gani?	How are you doing?
Nzuri sana	Very well
Wageni, mwakaribishwa	Visitors, you are all welcomed
Kenya yetu	In our Kenya
Hakuna matata	There are no problems
Kenya ni nchi nzuri	Kenya's a beautiful country
Hakuna matata	There are no problems
Nchi ya kupendeza	A pleasing country
Hakuna matata	There are no problems
Nchi ya maajabu	A country of wonders
Hakuna matata	There are no problems
Nchi yenye amani	A country of peace
Hakuna matata	There are no problems

Malaika
Authorship disputed, first popularized by Fadhili William

Malaika, nakupenda malaika	Angel, I love you angel
Malaika, nakupenda malaika	Angel, I love you angel
Nami nifanyeje, kijana mwenzio?	And me, what shall I, your boyfriend, do?
Nashindwa na mali sina wee	If I weren't struggling for money
Ningekuoa malaika	I would marry you angel
Nashindwa na mali sina wee	If I weren't struggling for money
Ningekuoa malaika	I would marry you angel
Pesa zasumbuwa roho yangu	Money is the source of my heartache
Pesa zasumbuwa roho yangu	Money is the source of my heartache
Nami nifanyeje, kijana mwenzio?	And me, what shall I, your boyfriend, do?
Nashindwa na mali sina wee	If I weren't struggling for money
Ningekuoa malaika	I would marry you angel
Nashindwa na mali sina wee	If I weren't struggling for money
Ningekuoa malaika	I would marry you angel
Kidege, hukuwaza kidege	Little bird, I'm always dreaming of you, little bird
Kidege, hukuwaza kidege	Little bird, I'm always dreaming of you, little bird
Nami nifanyeje, kijana mwenzio?	And me, what shall I, your boyfriend, do?
Nashindwa na mali sina wee	If I weren't struggling for money
Ningekuoa malaika	I would marry you angel
Nashindwa na mali sina wee	If I weren't struggling for money
Ningekuoa malaika	I would marry you angel

CONTEXTS | Music

his brothers George and William, the group began performing in Mombasa in 1971. In 1975, with Tanzanian recruit Omar Shabani on rhythm and Kenyan Tom Malanga on bass, the brothers shifted to Nairobi where, over a twenty-year period, they were favourites of the city's club scene and made scores of recordings. They broke up in the 1990s after the deaths of George and Wilson Kinyonga.

The **Wanyika** name is also famous in East Africa for several bands that emerged from Simba Wanyika Original. The group's first big split occurred in 1978 when the core of supporting musicians around the Kinyonga brothers left to form **Les Wanyika**. Under the leadership of Tanzanian lead guitarist John Ngereza, they remained one of Nairobi's top bands right up to his death in 2000. Their rumba music was distinguished by imaginative compositions and arrangements, a typically lean, clean sound and the delicious blend of Professor Omari's rhythm guitar mastery with John Ngereza's lead guitar and Tom Malanga's bass. The vocals, too, were great, handled by Ngereza, whose inclusion as a guest artist on Orchestre Virunga's 1997 US tour finally brought him some international exposure. Sadly, 1998 saw the death of Professor Omari, who had composed many of the group's early hits, and following the death of John Ngereza, the Les Wanyika name lasted only a few months before the group broke up.

Another important figure in the Wanyika story is Tanzania-born **Issa Juma**, who quickly established a name for himself in Kenya as a premier vocalist in the early days of Les Wanyika. Issa formed Super Wanyika in 1981 and over the next few years had a series of hits featuring half a dozen other variations on the Wanyika names. One of the most prolific artists of the 1980s, he was perhaps the most versatile and creative of the Swahili artists in his willingness to take his music in different directions. His recorded output features many numbers that were a kind of fusion of Swahili rumba and *benga,* but isn't limited to this.

Foremost among other Tanzanians and Kenyans performing in the Swahili style are the **Maroon Commandos**. Members of the Kenyan Army, the Commandos are one of the oldest performing groups in the country. They first came together in 1970 and were initially mainly a covers band playing Congolese hits, but by 1977 they had become a strong force in the Swahili style with the huge Taita-language hit "Charonyi Ni Wasi." The Commandos have proven themselves quite experimental at times, mingling Swahili and *benga* styles and occasionally adding a keyboard and innovative guitar effects. Currently, the only serious proponents of the Swahili rumba sound after the Maroon Commandos are **Abdul Muyonga and Everest Kings**. Perhaps the last of Kenya's great Swahili rumba bands was the late Twahir Mohamed's **Golden Sounds Band**, whose songs adhered to the complex evolutionary structure of the genre, but also featured a much denser vocal and instrumental sound.

Tourist and international pop

Where Kenyan pop meets the tourist industry, at the coastal resorts around Mombasa, bands can make a living just playing hotel gigs. These bands typically feature highly competent musicians, relatively good equipment and a fairly polished sound. The best of them are worth catching, typically playing an eclectic selection of old Congolese rumba tunes as warm-ups, popular international covers, a few Congolese favourites of the day, greatest hits from Kenya's past, and some original material that leans heavily towards the American/Euro pop sound, but with lyrics relating to local topics.

The most successful Kenyan group in this field has been the oddly named **Them Mushrooms**, now renamed **Uyoga** (Swahili for "mushroom"). The band managed to graduate from the coastal hotel circuit when they moved to Nairobi in 1987, but their music lives on at the coast, in particular their crowning achievement, the tourist anthem "Jambo Bwana". While Uyoga are proud to take credit for this insidiously infectious bit of fluff, they have shown over their long career that they have serious musical intentions, having been involved in a series of highly successful and diverse collaborations, including with one of the earliest of Kenyan guitar pioneers, **Fundi Konde**, *taarab* star Malika and the Kikuyu singer Queen Jane. Since 1993, the band have returned to their reggae roots.

Them Mushrooms' long-time counterpart in the hotel circuit, **Safari Sound**, have the distinction of having made Kenya's best selling album ever in *The Best of African Songs*, a veritable greatest hits of hotel classics with songs such as "Malaika", a beautiful composition about ill-starred love (see box, p.653).

The evolving scene

In the early 1990s, the Kenyan music business was at a low point. Piracy and diminishing sales meant that, as a business, recorded music was hardly worth the effort – and the music that was being produced at the time hardly seemed worth buying anyway. By the mid-1990s, however, a number of factors would set the stage for a radical departure from the styles of previous generations of Kenyan pop musicians. For one thing, Kenya experienced the rise of **commercial FM radio**, which helped acquaint Kenyans with current reggae, ragga, house, dancehall, hip-hop and R&B from abroad. Also around this time, **new technology** made recording much more affordable, and a new breed of independent Kenyan producers began to emerge.

New groups were formed, performing in styles inspired largely by music from abroad, but adding local elements in language, subject matter and sometimes melody and instrumentation. **Tedd Josiah**, **Bruce Odhiambo** and **Suzanne and Gido Kibukosya** were among the producers who were instrumental in shepherding along these new artists, often with quite different musical intentions, from hip-hop covers of African pop classics to gospel balladry. Some of the best material of the time was showcased on two CDs put together by Josiah, *Kenyan: The First Chapter* and *Kenyan: The Second Chapter*. Notable from the first of these is **Kalamashaka**'s "Tafsiri Hii", the trio's trendsetting Swahili hip-hop song addressing the reality of street life. *The Second Chapter* introduced the duo **Gidigidi Majimaji**, who went on to release a superb album, *Ismarwa*, a rare example of the successful fusion of local African sounds with hip-hop. In 2002, Gidigidi Majimaji made a major imprint on the cultural fabric of the nation with their hard-hitting number "Who Can Bwogo Me?" The word *bwogo* means "to scare" in Luo, and the song expresses the notion of defiance as they answer their own question with "I am unbwogable." The song was not written as a political statement but, released in a general election year, it was unofficially adopted as the theme of the opposition to President Moi and his party and played constantly. The word "unbwogable" has now entered the Kenyan lexicon.

In much the same way that Josiah's *Chapters* CDs introduced a host of new artists to radio and the public, the production house known as **Ogopa Deejays** have, at the time of writing, released three compilations featuring acts who would go on to become fixtures of the Kenyan pop charts: the late **E-Sir**, **Redsan**, **Kleptomaniaks**, **Wahu**, **Big Pin** and **Mr Lenny** are just a few of many successful Ogopa artists. Much of the Ogopa sound is encompassed by the style known as **kapuka**, built on a mixture of Kenyan hip-hop, ragga and house. Kapuka gets plenty of airplay and *kapuka* artists are often featured at corporate-sponsored events and festivals.

Kenyan hip-hop artists draw a distinction between their music and *kapuka*, criticizing the latter for its shallowness and lack of meaningful social content. They point out that a great many *kapuka* practitioners have never experienced the hardships of the poor in the urban slums; instead, their love songs and party music represent the African middle class. And indeed, one of the biggest stars at the time of writing is the wealthy rapper **CMB Prezzo**, who actually brags about his fortunate circumstances in his music. Always the showman, at his concerts Prezzo makes it a point to be seen arriving with his well-dressed entourage in the finest automobiles. He actually hired a helicopter to airdrop him at a music awards ceremony, scoring points for style, but no awards. In contrast, most of the "true" hip-hop scene in Kenya centres around the youth of urban housing estates and slums; their music gets little exposure on radio and not much press. One of the finest representations of this is the *Kilio cha Haki* compilation, featuring the talents of musicians and rappers from Nairobi's slums, recorded in a makeshift studio with Dutch producers.

Another segment of Kenya's new music scene comprises musicians looking to their traditions for elements they can reshape into contemporary pop music. **Yunasi**, **Kayamba Afrika** and USA-based **Jabali Afrika** emphasize rich vocal harmonies blended with traditional African percussion and stringed instruments along with guitar, bass and keyboards. **Nairobi City Ensemble** takes a slightly different approach in their album *Kalapapla*. The group begins with what they term "authentic melodies" from traditional roots but makes the sound completely contemporary with modern instruments, guest rappers, and the thoughtful use of traditional string instruments like the Luo *nyatiti* and *orutu*. Finally, singer-songwriter and guitarist **Suzzana Owiyo** deserves special mention for her innovative way of bringing the melodies and instruments of her traditional Luo culture into a modern pop context. All these efforts are attracting a lot of critical interest, and despite being largely ignored by Kenyan radio and by the under-30s, have resulted in financial support being offered by organizations such as Nairobi's Alliance Française, and plenty of invitations to the artists concerned to perform in major music festivals in other parts of Africa and further afield.

Discography

The following recordings are all available on CD.

Abana Ba Nasery *Classic Acoustic Recordings from Western Kenya* (GlobeStyle, UK). A charming collection of finger-picking acoustic guitar music. The central position of the solo guitar in Kenya's electric groups is anticipated here in Shem Tube's solos.

Abana Ba Nasery *!Nursery Boys Go Ahead! The Guitar and Bottle Kings of Kenya* (GlobeStyle, UK/Xenophile, US). This CD captures the crisp ABN sound in recordings made on their 1991 UK tour. It also involves the trio in some interesting collaborations with European artists, some of which really get rocking.

H.N. Ochieng Kabaselleh & the Lunna Kidi Band *Sanduku ya Mapendo and Achi Maria* (Equator Heritage Sounds, US). From the area around Lake Victoria, Kabaselleh was one Kenyan bandleader whose music always stood apart – an interesting mix of Luo *benga*, Swahili rumba and Congolese influences, exemplified by these two collections of Kabaselleh's double-A-sided singles from the 1980s.

🎵 **Kakai Kilonzo** *Best of Kakai Vol 1* (Shava Musik, Germany). From the mid-1970s until his death in 1987, Kakai was at the top of the Kamba music scene in Kenya, and with catchy Swahili lyrics and a very together *benga* sound, he had fans from all parts of the country and beyond. This is a fine compilation of Kakai's singles from the 1980s which usually featured a song split between the A- and B-sides, but which here have been neatly stitched back together.

Fundi Konde *Fundi Konde Retrospective Vol 1 (1947–56)* (RetroAfric, UK). Full of enticing, vintage Kenyan pop: imagine a vocal line like a mellow, two-part "Chattanooga Choo Choo", add a smooth, jazzy electric guitar, bass and clarinet, and you have the ingredients for the typical Konde track. One of Kenya's most renowned early guitarists and the creator of many of what Kenyans consider the classics. His heyday was the 1950s, but he was rediscovered by Kenyans in the 1990s through his collaboration with Them Mushrooms.

🎵 **Gidigidi Majimaji** *Ismarwa* (A'mish, US). The duo of Joseph Ogidi and Julius Owino burst on the scene with "Ting' Badi Malo" (found on the *Rough Guide to Kenyan Music*), and are perhaps the most innovative and successful of Kenya's new breed of music stars, blending clever lyrics, African rhythms and instruments and contemporary hip-hop sounds. This was a gem of a debut, beautifully combining all those elements with a strong rhythmic component and tantalizingly fresh acoustic sounds. The alternative take on *Ting Badi Malo* found here, with its foghorn bass (mimicking a traditional horn),

light acoustic guitar, and tight Luo rap, is much rootsier than the version on the Rough Guide CD.

Gidigidi Majimaji *Many Faces* (Gallo, South Africa). Recorded with a number of South African guest artists, and thus featuring *kwaito* and other South African styles.

🎵 **Golden Sounds Band** *Swahili Rumba* (Naxos World, US). Led by the brilliant saxophonist/arranger Twahir Mohamed, Golden Sounds played rumba music in the tradition of the Wanyika bands and Maroon Commandos. Repeated listens are required before you really begin to appreciate all that this album offers, in the evolutionary development of musical motifs over tracks lasting around eight minutes apiece.

🎵 **Les Wanyika** *Paulina: The Best of Professor Omari Shabani and John Ngereza* (Tamasha, Kenya). Les Wanyika were the last of the great Swahili rumba bands in the "Wanyika" lineage, dating back to the early 1970s, and this album is an absolute gem, bringing together some of Les Wanyika's finest material. The eloquent interplay of the guitars of John Ngereza and Professor Omari is stunning.

🎵 **Samba Mapangala & Orchestra Virunga** *Virunga Volcano* (Earthworks/Stern's, UK). From the mid-1970s to the early 1990s, Orchestra Virunga were one of Kenya's most exciting groups and the Congolese vocalist, Samba Mapangala, was one of Kenya's most gifted talents. He has since relocated to the USA but is still a favourite in East Africa. *Virunga Volcano* is in a class all of its own, each song like a story that develops over a ten-minute period, exploring different combinations of rhythm, melody and harmony right through to the finish. As fresh and enticing today as it was when released back in the early 1980s.

Samba Mapangala & Orchestra Virunga *Virunga Roots Volume 1* (Virunga, USA). Made in 1989 in Nairobi and Paris; the four Nairobi numbers have luscious horns and that great East Africa feel, while the Paris tracks are suitably slick, having been laid down with some of the great Congolese session men of the day.

Collela Mazee and Victoria B Kings Band *Jessica* (Equator Heritage Sounds). Classic Luo *benga* music of the late 1970s and early 1980s: a pounding beat, pulsing bass, and brilliant guitars, each track ending with a luscious guitar solo.

D.O. Misiani & Shirati Band *Benga Blast!* (Earthworks/Stern's, UK) and *Piny Ose Mer/The World Upside Down* (GlobeStyle, UK). One of the founding fathers of *benga* music, Daniel Owino Misiani is still playing after more than thirty years. These are both fine collections of his work, the former in glorious mono, being the rough, unpolished sound of the old Pioneer House studios.

John Amutabi Nzenze & Friends *Angelike Twist* (Equator Heritage Sounds). John Nzenze is a pioneering figure in Kenyan music who started his recording career as a teen back in the 1950s. This compilation beautifully highlights his contribution to the acoustic finger-picking guitar styles of the 1950s and the electric "twist" style that followed in the 1960s.

🏃 **Ayub Ogada** *En Mana Kuoyo* (Real World, UK). Based in the UK, Ayub Ogada is a Luo who has been exploring and bridging cultural boundaries over the last two decades. This low-key, largely acoustic album enthralls with beautiful melodies and captivating rhythms, and features elements of the Luo tradition.

🏃 **Orchestra Super Mazembe** *Giants of East Africa* (Earthworks/Stern's, UK). Congolese group

Super Mazembe played the dance halls and bars of Kenya for nearly thirty years before their recent (possibly temporary) demise. In songs such as "Kasongo" and "Shauri Yako", they exemplify the definitive sound of Congolese rumba in East Africa. Mazembe's early 1980s LP, *Kaivaska*, kindled much of the enthusiasm of the time for Afropop in the UK and Europe. This collection includes five of the best songs off *Kaivaska*, including "Kasongo", plus "Shauri Yako".

Suzzana Owiyo *Mama Africa* (ARC Music, UK). This debut from a talented singer-songwriter is a delightful mix of traditional instruments, Owiya's acoustic guitar and electric sounds with a few rough edges.

Suzzana Owiyo *Yamo Kudho* (Blu Zebra, Kenya). Picking up where *Mama Africa* left off, *Yamo Kudho* is more polished and a tighter package, delivering sublime melodies with a bright acoustic sound (even with electric guitar and bass) and mixing in traditional Luo *orutu*, *oporo* (horn), and percussion.

Simba Wanyika Original *Pepea* (Stern's, UK). Their only European CD release, and superbly produced, allowing the band to shine on new recordings of some of their biggest hits of the previous twenty years.

Them Mushrooms (Uyoga) *Them Mushrooms* (Rags Music, UK). Successful graduates of the coastal hotel circuit, Them Mushrooms have had an illustrious thirty-year career, and now own and operate one of the best studios in the country. Apart from the first two songs, this CD comprises their remakes of classic Kenyan tunes from the 1950s and 1960s.

Victoria Kings *The Mighty Kings of Benga* (GlobeStyle, UK). A different perspective on *benga* (ie not Shirati Jazz) and a very good compilation, at that. The Victoria Kings started in the early 1970s with Ochieng Nelly as bandleader, soon joined by long-time musical partner Collela Mazee, and went on to become one of the top-selling recording groups of the golden age of *benga* in the late 1970s and early 1980s.

Eric Wainaina *Sawa Sawa* (Wainaina/Kaufmann Prod, USA/Kenya). Originally part of the Five Alive singing group of the mid-1990s, Wainaina went off to the USA to study at the Berklee College of Music. Bringing together an innova-tive mix of Kenyan pop sounds with American soft-rock influences, he's one of the stars of the new genera-tion of Kenyan musicians, though this is his only CD release to date. The album spans a broad range of styles, from uptempo African dance rhythms to ballads and smooth jazz. Kenyans really connected with the song "Nchi ya Kitu Kidogo" (Nation of Kickbacks), decrying, albeit with great humour, the way bribery has permeated Kenyan society. And for Swahili speakers, there are comedic interludes from the Kenyan troupe Redykyulass.

Compilations

Guitar Paradise of East Africa and **Kenya Dance Mania** (Earthworks/Stern's, UK). An excellent introduction to Kenya's various styles, although the material is not always the most representative of the artists. Highlights on *Guitar Paradise* include the classic hit "Shauri Yako" by Super Mazembe as well as Ochieng Kabaselleh's "Achi Maria". *Kenya Dance Mania* includes some classics of the 1970s and 1980s, such as Les Wanyika's "Sina Makosa" and Maroon Commandos' evergreen hit "Charonyi Ni Wasi".

Kilio cha Haki (UpToYouToo, Netherlands). Its title translating as "A cry for justice", this album was the outcome of a month-long recording project initiated by a Dutch foundation, bringing together 38 talents from Nairobi's Eastlands slum area, who together created some truly innovative hip-hop. The excellent notes transcribe and translate the poignant Swahili lyrics dealing with the harsh realities of the slums. Proceeds go towards the development of a studio in Eastlands.

Luo Roots: Musical Currents from Western Kenya (GlobeStyle, UK). Performances of traditional Luo music, suggesting the foundations of the *benga* style.

The Nairobi Beat: Kenyan Pop Music Today (Rounder, USA). A cross-section of mid-1980s Kenyan pop put together by the author of this article. It showcases some of the best examples of regional *benga* styles: Luo, Kikuyu, Kamba and Luhya, plus a couple of Swahili and Congolese dance tunes for good measure.

The Rough Guide to the Music of Kenya (World Music Network, UK). A sampling of the many Kenyan styles of popular music, including the guitar-centric *benga* and Swahili rumba styles, *taarab* from the coastal region, current day "traditional" sounds, and the shifting sounds of the younger generation (including Gidi-gidi Majimaji's "Ting Badi Malo").

Zanzibara 2: 1965–1975 (Buda Musique, France). A delightful collection of *taarab* music recorded by Mombasa's Mzuri Records. Features songs by the likes of Zuhura Swaleh, Zein l'Abdin and Maulidi Juma.

Doug Paterson with contributions from Jens Finke and Werner Graebner; "Malaika" translated by Farouk Abdillah.

Books

There is a substantial volume of reading matter on Kenya, though much of the European output has been fairly lightweight and some of the more scholarly works tend to be indigestible.

For predeparture reading, the growing body of **Kenyan literature** provides a good foretaste. Some of the following titles may be most easily available in Kenya (for imports in the UK, try the Africa Book Centre in Brighton, ®www.africabookcentre.com). You can buy Kenyan books online from Nairobi's Legacy Bookshop at ®www.Legacybookshop.com.

Although a number of authors have written in the older languages of Kenya, **English** still predominates as the medium for artistic expression, a situation which creates dilemmas for writers struggling both to reach a readership at home and to find viable channels for publication. If you want to explore, visit the excellent *Kwani?* website ®www.kwani.org edited by Binyavanga Wainaina. Titles marked 🏃 are particularly recommended.

Travel and general accounts

🏃 **David Bennum** *Tick Bite Fever.* Memoir about growing up in an expat household in the 1970s from a British newspaper journalist. Full of acid wit, this is an amusingly dry alternative to more cloying accounts.

Bill Bryson *Bill Bryson's Africa Diary.* A brief but typically engaging book, recounting Bryson's travels around Kenya learning about the work of Care International. All profits go to Care.

Bartle Bull *Safari: A Chronicle of Adventure.* A great, macho slab of a book, jammed with photos. It's grotesque but utterly compelling – even if the cruelty and foolish waste of the hunting era, so recently past, is emotionally wearing.

Negley Farson *Behind God's Back.* An American journalist's account of his long overland journey across Africa on the eve of World War II. A lively book if you can stomach the alarming shifts between criticism of the colonial world and participation in its worst prejudices.

Dick Hedges *Tilda's Angel.* If you want to know all about the man

behind Safari Camp Services and the Turkana Bus, this is for you. Good on what makes Anglo-Kenyans tick.

John Hillaby *Journey to the Jade Sea.* An obvious one to read before a trip to Lake Turkana. Hillaby's account of his walk in the early 1960s is dated and not always informative – an adventure, as he writes, "for the hell of it", with sprinklings of tall stories and descriptions of loony incompetence.

🏃 **Corinne Hoffmann** *The White Masai.* Extraordinary account, effectively a journal, of a Swiss woman's extended love affair with a Samburu man, and her life in Barsaloi, from the late 1980s to the early 1990s.

J. Ludwig Krapf *Travel and Missionary Labors in Africa.* The account of the first missionary at Mombasa, and the first European to set eyes on Mount Kenya.

David Lamb *The Africans.* There's really no contest between Lamb, a Los Angeles Times hack, and Marnham (see below) for a contemporary view of the continent. *The Africans* has been something of a best seller, but Lamb's fly-in, fly-out technique is a muddled, statistical rant, couched in Cold War rhetoric; even when ostensibly uncovering a pearl of wisdom, he can be unpleasantly offensive.

Patrick Marnham *Fantastic Invasion: Dispatches from Africa.* Although written in the 1970s, nothing since has matched this withering and devastatingly sharp collection, which includes several essays on Kenya. An excellent book, which tunnels beneath the mountain of dross written about Africa.

Peter Matthiessen *The Tree Where Man Was Born.* Wanderings and musings of the Zen-thinking polymath in Kenya and northern Tanzania, first published in 1972. Enthralling for its detail on nature, society, culture and prehistory, and beautifully written, this is a gentle, appetizing introduction to the land and its people.

George Monbiot *No Man's Land.* A journey through Kenya and Tanzania, providing a shocking exposé of Maasai dispossession and a major criticism of the wildlife conservation movement.

Dervla Murphy *The Ukimwi Road.* Murphy's bike ride from Kenya to Zimbabwe becomes – for her – a trip through lands lost to AIDS and neo-colonialism.

Shiva Naipaul *North of South.* A fine but caustic account of the late Naipaul's life and travels in Kenya, Tanganyika and Zambia in the 1970s. Always readable and sometimes hilarious, the insights make up for the occasionally angst-ridden social commentary and some passages that widely miss the mark.

Craig Packer *Into Africa.* A professor of ecology, evolution and behaviour, Packer puts it all to good use in day-by-day reflections during an eight-week field trip.

Joyce Poole *Coming of Age with Elephants.* Deeply sympathetic account of studying the social and sexual behaviour of elephants in Amboseli.

Keith B. Richburg *Out of America; a Black Man Confronts Africa.* Nairobi bureau chief for the Washington Times from 1991–94, Richburg discovered that he was American, not African, and preferred it that way. A rather depressing read – and partial by the nature of its author: journalists need stories, and that usually means bad news – and unfortunately likely to stoke the flames of moral relativism.

Rick Ridgeway *The Shadow of Kilimanjaro.* The American adventurer and filmmaker took a walk in 1997 through the bush from Kilimanjaro to Mombasa – mostly through Tsavo West and East, along the Tsavo-Galana River. Robust, readable and full of passionate enthusiasm for the wild country and the wildlife.

Oona Strathern (ed) *Traveller's Literary Companion: Africa.* Brief selections of literature from or about virtually every African country, including a good raft of Kenyan pieces.

Louis Taussig *Resource Guide to Travel in Sub-Saharan Africa: Vol 1 East and West Africa.* Extraordinarily detailed country-by-country coverage of every published source of interest to travellers or expatriates, as well as bookstores, libraries, mapping institutes, children's resources and conservation societies, to list just a few.

Wilfred Thesiger *My Kenya Days.* The account of thirty-odd years in northern Kenya by a very strange man indeed – an old Etonian noble savage with no interest in modern Africa, wedded to his own ego and a reactionary, glamour-laden view of his tribal companions.

Joseph Thomson *Through Maasailand: To the central African Lakes and Back*. First published in 1885, these two volumes detail Thomson's African journeys of exploration.

Daisy Waugh *A Small Town in Africa*. A year in the life of Isiolo.

Essays

Wahome Mutahi *How to be a Kenyan*. A satirical view of Kenyan life by one of the country's most popular newspaper columnists. Painfully funny, and rather close to the bone, the book takes a humorous look at Kenya's very worst side – it won't put you off the country, but it will certainly give you a chuckle at Kenya's expense. Mutahi followed it up with a sideswipe at Kenyan

Evelyn Waugh *A Tourist in Africa*. First published in 1960, Waugh's diary of a short trip to Kenya, Tanganyika and Rhodesia is determinedly arrogant and uninformed, but funny, too – and brief enough to consume at a single sitting.

women entitled *How to be a Kenyan Lady*.

Renato Kizito Sesana *Father Kizito's Notebook*. Kenyan life from the Catholic (as opposed to catholic) perspective of Fr Kizitos weekly columns in the Sunday Nation. Full of insights into the struggle to survive that most people here call life, infused with humour and compassion.

Wildlife

Having a field guide makes a huge difference to travelling on safari. Many of the following are not published in the US but are easily found in Kenya itself.

Mohamed Amin, Duncan Willets and Brian Tetley *The Beautiful Animals of Kenya*. Lavish photos but sparing text, an easy, lightweight book, but more a tourist souvenir than a serious guide to Kenyan wildlife.

Michael Blundell *Wild Flowers of East Africa*. Botanical companion in the series.

Jean Dorst and Pierre Dandelot *Larger Mammals of Africa*. Readable and accessible with lively illustrations, though it tends to favour classifying many races as separate species.

Richard E. Estes *The Safari Companion*. This book aims to explain not only what animals you're looking at, but also what they're doing, and its illustrated explanations make fascinating reading.

T. Haltenorth and H. Diller *Mammals of Africa*. A rival for Dorst and Dandelot, which tends to find fewer species in the variety of mammals out there. With its superabundance of detail, this might look like first choice, but the somewhat stylized paintings are less meaningful than Dorst and Dandelot's when you're thumping through the bush, and much of the text is superfluous for all but the professional zoologist.

John Karmali *The Beautiful Birds of Kenya*. Like its companion volume, *Beautiful Animals*, a tourist souvenir of Kenyan birds with lots of colour photos.

Jonathan Kingdon *The Kingdon Field Guide to African Mammals*. A detailed and comprehensive catalogue of African land mammals, illustrated with photographs and distribution maps for each species.

Ray Moore *Where to Watch Birds in Kenya*. Invaluable tips and background for the devoted bird-watcher.

Ber van Perlo *Birds of Eastern Africa*. An essential pocket guide, providing clear colour illustrations and distribution maps for every species known to occur in East Africa, though little by way of descriptive text.

Dave Richards *Photographic Guide to the Birds of East Africa*. Over three hundred colour photos.

Chris Stuart and Tilde Stuart *Field Guide to the Larger Mammals of Africa*. Good field guide published in the late 1990s.

Nigel Wheatley *Where to Watch Birds in Africa*. Tight structure and plenty

of useful detail make this a must-have for serious bird-watchers in Africa; 25 pages on Kenya.

John Williams *Birds of East Africa*, *Field Guide to the Butterflies of Africa*, *National Parks of East Africa*. *Birds* is the standard spotter's tome. *Butterflies* is exotic and useful – if you can get hold of a copy. *National Parks* covers parks, reserves, mammals and birds, but there's too much space devoted to long lists of fauna, and the practical details for the parks are too dated to be of any use.

Zimmerman, Turner and Pearson *A Field Guide to the Birds of Kenya and Northern Tanzania*. Comprehensive coverage in a brand new paperback edition.

Colonial writers

🏃 Isak Dinesen (Karen Blixen) *Out of Africa*. This has become something of a cult book, particularly in the wake of the movie. First published in 1937, it describes Blixen's life (Dinesen was a nom de plume) on her Ngong Hills coffee farm between the wars. Read today, it seems to hover uncertainly between contemporary literature and historical document. It's an intense read – lyrical, introspective, sometimes obnoxiously and intricately racist, but worth pursuing and never superficial, unlike the film. Karen Blixen's own *Letters from Africa 1914–1931* (trans. Anne Born) gives posthumous insights.

Harry Hook *The Kitchen Toto*. By way of an antidote to a surfeit of settlers' yarns, this screenplay tells the story of Mwangi, a Kikuyu houseboy caught up in the early stages of the Mau Mau rebellion. Writer-director Hook's movie is as keen as a country *panga* and draws masterful performances from a largely unknown cast.

Elspeth Huxley *The Flame Trees of Thika*, *The Mottled Lizard*. Based on

her own childhood, from a prolific author who also wrote numerous works on colonial history and society, including *White Man's Country*, a biography of the settlers' doyen, *Lord Delamere*, and *Out in the Midday Sun: My Kenya*, both as readable, if also predictable, as any. Her last book, *Nine Faces of Kenya* is a somewhat dewy-eyed anthology of colonial East African ephemera. More interesting is the collection of her mother's letters, *Nellie's Story*, which includes some compelling coverage of the Mau Mau years from the pen of a likeably eccentric settler.

Beryl Markham *West with the Night*. Markham made the first east–west solo flight across the Atlantic. This is her only book about her life in the interwar Kenya colony, drawing together adventures, landscapes and contemporary figures. Not great literature, but highly evocative.

🏃 Richard Meinertzhagen *Kenya Diary 1902–1906*. The haunting day-to-day narrative of a young British officer in the protectorate. Meinertzhagen's brutal descriptions of "punitive expeditions" are chillingly matter-of-fact and make the endless tally of his wildlife slaughter pale inoffensively in comparison. As a reminder of the savagery that accompanied the British intrusion, and a stark insight into the complex mind of one of its perpetrators, this is disturbing, highly recommended reading. Good photos, too.

Judith Thurman *Isak Dinesen: The Life of a Story Teller.* A biography that sets the record straighter and was the source of much of the material for the *Out of Africa* film.

Errol Trzebinski *The Lives of Beryl Markham.* In which, among much else, it is suggested that Markham did not, and could not, have written *West with the Night.*

Kenyan fiction in English

Chinua Achebe and C.L. Innes (eds) *African Short Stories.* A collection which treats its material geographically, including Kenyan stories from Jomo Kenyatta, Grace Ogot, Ngugi and a spooky offering (*The Spider's Web*) from Leonard Kibera, brother of Sam Kahiga (a short story by whom appears on p.679).

Thomas Akare *The Slums.* A bleaker read than Mwangi, but also more humane. Without quotation marks, the dialogue melds seamlessly into the narrative; no doubts about the authentic rhythms of Kenyan English here. But much is assumed to be understood and there's much that won't be, unless you're sitting under a 25-watt light bulb in a River Road B&L.

Lalage Bown (ed) *Two Centuries of African English.* Includes non-fiction extracts from the work of J.M. Kariuki (Mau Mau detainee – see p.669), Ali Mazrui on intellectuals and revolution, Githende Mockerie and R. Mugo Gatheru recounting their childhoods, and Tom Mboya on Julius Nyerere, first president of Tanzania.

Charlotte H. Bruner (ed) *Unwinding Threads: Writing by Women in Africa.* Also geographical, with succinct introductions to each region. East Africa features Kenyan writers Charity Waciuma and the excellent Grace

Ogot, whose *The Rain Came* is a bewitching mystery myth, combining traditional Luo tales with her own fiction in a perplexingly "Western" form. There's a new collection edited by Bruner, entitled *African Women's Writing.*

Sam Kahiga *Flight to Juba – Short Stories, The Girl from Abroad.* Vital, exasperating, obnoxious and plain crazy – a writer to love to hate (see excerpted story, p.679).

John Kiriamiti *My Life in Crime.* This racy autobiographical account, penned in prison by a professional robber, was so successful that the author went on to write two novels (*Son of Fate* and *The Sinister Trophy*) plus an account of his time as a villain told from his fiancée's point of view (*My Life with a Criminal: Millie's Story*).

J. Roger Kurtz *Urban Obsessions, Urban Fears: the postcolonial Kenyan novel.* Explores the relationship between Kenyan fiction in English and the city of Nairobi. Includes a comprehensive bibliography of all the Kenyan novels in English since Ngugi's *Weep Not, Child* was first published in 1964.

Bramwell Lusweti *The Way to the Town Hall.* Enjoyable satire aimed at small-town politicians and businessmen. A Swahili dictionary (to translate the characters' names) is a help.

Ngugi wa Thiong'o, the dominant figure of modern Kenyan literature, currently lives in the USA: although his books in English are not banned in Kenya, his political sympathies are not welcome.

Ngugi's work is art serving the revolution – didactic, brusque, graphic and unsentimental. His novels, especially the later ones, are unforgiving: the touch of humour that would leaven the polemic rarely comes to the rescue. Powerful themes – exploitation, betrayal, cultural oppression, the imposition of Christianity, loss of and search for identity – drive the stories along urgently. Characters deal with real events and the changes of their time, struggling to come to terms with the influences at work on their lives.

Ngugi's style is heady, idealistic and undaunted, never teasing or capricious. Disillusioned with English, his first work in Kikuyu, in collaboration with Ngugi wa Mirii, was the play *Ngahiika Ndeenda* (*I Will Marry When I Want*), and its public performance by illiterate peasants at the Kamiriithu Cultural Centre in Limuru got him detained for a year. Ngugi's work in the Kikuyu language is now banned, or rarely available, in Kenya.

Most of Ngugi's writings in English are published in the paperback Heinemann African Writers series. Try *Secret Lives* for short stories, *Weep Not, Child* for a brief but glowing early novel, or, for the mature Ngugi, *Petals of Blood* – a richly satisfying detective story that is at the same time a saga of wretchedness and struggle (see p.675 for an excerpt). Others include *The River Between*, on the old Kikuyu society and the coming of the Europeans; *A Grain of Wheat*, about the eve of independence; *Devil on the Cross* (written in detention on scraps of toilet paper); and *Matigari* (The Patriots). *Matigari*, first published in Kikuyu by Heinemann in 1986 (published in the USA by Africa World Press), had a remarkable effect in the Central Highlands. Rumours circulated that a man, Matigari, was spreading militant propaganda against the government. The police even tried to track him down, before realizing their mistake and confiscating all copies of the book.

Apart from *I Will Marry When I Want*, Ngugi has written two other plays, *The Black Hermit* and *The Trial of Dedon Kimathi* (with Micere Mugo). Academic works include *Moving the Centre*, a collection of essays. Ngugi's contribution to Kenyan literature is enormous, and delving in is rewarding, if not always easy.

M.G. Vassanji *The In-between World of Vikram Lall*. Remarkable epic – winner of the 2003 Giller Prize for Canadian fiction – of multiple alienations and the power of corruption in a world of competing moralities. Lall is the chief protagonist, a Ugandan Asian exiled to Canada having been named Kenya's most corrupt man.

Binyavanga Wainaina and others *Discovering Home*. A collection of short stories, including the final shortlist for the 2002 Caine Prize for African Writing, this includes the eponymous winning piece by the Nakuru-born editor of the @www.kwani.org website. Wainaina is a wonderful new talent, crisply setting Kenyan humour and tragedy, and especially the meaning of home for diaspora Kenyans, in a beautiful frame.

Marjorie Oludhe Macgoye *Victoria* and *Murder in Majengo*. Two novels – available in one volume – giving a Luo woman's view on life in Kenya, from one of the country's few published women writers.

Charles Mangua *Son of Woman*. Less down and out, but a lot more "street" than Meja Mwangi, Mangua tells the tale of a son of a prostitute and his misadventures: hard-bitten and cynical, but engaging nonetheless. In a very different style, his second novel, *A Tail in the Mouth*, looks at the Mau Mau rebellion through the eyes of a young man caught up in it and swept along by events.

Ali Mazrui *The Trial of Christopher Okigbo*. A clever "novel of ideas" from the US-based political scientist, who always succeeds in infuriating both critics of Kenya and its supporters. His *Cultural Forces in World Politics* is a survey of cultural and political ideas which also addresses the issues surrounding Salman Rushdie's *Satanic Verses*.

David Mulwa *Master and Servant*. Growing up in colonial Kenya: a funny and affecting string of episodes.

Mude Dae Mude *The Hills are Falling*. Life from Marsabit to Nairobi.

Meja Mwangi *Going Down River Road*; *Carcase for Hounds*;

Kill Me Quick. Mwangi is lighter and more accessible than Ngugi, his fiction infused with the absurdities of urban Nairobi slum life. *Going Down River Road* is the best known: convincing scenes, chaotic action and sharp dialogue (though it's never clear whether the English/American street cool is meant to be real, or an effort to render the Swahili-Kikuyu "Sheng" slang of the slums). Great in situ reading. Mwangi was shortlisted for the Commonwealth Writers' Prize, with *Striving for the Wind* (1992), set in a rural rather than urban location.

Ngugi wa Thiong'o *Decolonising the Mind: The Politics of Language in African Literature*. Ngugi has long been closely associated with attempts to move Kenyan literature and African literature in general towards expression in the readers' mother tongues (see box p.665).

Kenneth Watene *Sunset on the Manyatta*. A Maasai man in Germany.

Kenyan poetry

The oldest form of written poetry in Kenya is from the coast. **Swahili poetry** reads beautifully even if you don't understand the words. Written for at least 300 years, and sung for a good deal longer, it's one of Kenya's most enduring art forms. An *Anthology of Swahili Poetry* has been compiled and rather woodenly translated by **Ali A Jahadmy**, but some of Swahili's best-known classical compositions from the Lamu Archipelago are included, with pertinent background. There's a more enjoyable anthology of romantic and erotic verse, *A Choice of Flowers*, with **Jan Knappert**'s idiosyncratic translations and interpretations, and the same linguist's *Four Centuries of Swahili Verse*, which expounds and creatively interprets at much greater length. A translation of an exquisite poem from the latter is included on p.683.

Upcountry poetry in the sense of written verse is a recent form. But oral folk literature was often relayed in the context of music, rhythm and dance.

Wole Soyinka (ed) *Poems of Black Africa*. A hefty and catholic selection. Its Kenyan component includes the work of Abangira, Jared Angira, Jonathan Kariara and Amin Kassam.

Heinemann Book of African Poetry. Includes the work of Kenyan poet Marjorie Oludhe Macgoye.

Kenya in modern western fiction

🏃 **Justin Cartwright** *Masai Dreaming*. A compelling novel juxtaposing a film-maker's vision of Maasai-land with the barbarities of the Holocaust, linked by the tapes of a Jewish anthropologist.

Jeremy Gavron *Moon* Vivid short novel about a white boy growing up on a farm during the Emergency.

Martha Gellhorn *The Weather in Africa*. Three absorbing novellas, each dealing with aspects of the Europe–Africa relationship, set on the slopes of Kilimanjaro, in the "White Highlands" of Kenya and on the tourist coast north of Mombasa.

David Lambkin *The Hanging Tree* (Penguin, UK/Counterpoint, USA). A human-nature-through-the-ages

saga which makes a good yarn – in fact, several yarns.

🏃 **John Le Carré** *The Constant Gardener*. The spymaster turns his hand to a whodunnit, in which a campaigner against the misdeeds of Western drug companies in Kenya is raped and murdered. Her husband, a British diplomat in Nairobi, fails to believe official explanations and starts his own investigation. A brilliantly crafted story, recently made into a movie, though not always convincing in its portrayal of today's expat society.

Barbara Wood *Green City in the Sun*. A white settler family come into conflict with a Kikuyu medicine woman in one of the few credible novels about the realities of colonial Kenya by a *mzungu* writer.

History and peoples

Kenya in African history

Basil Davidson *Let Freedom Come: Africa in Modern History*. Lucidly argued and very readable summary of nineteenth- and twentieth-century events.

Christopher Hibbert *Africa Explored: Europeans in the Dark Continent 1769–1889*. Entertaining read, devoted in large part to the "discovery" of east and central Africa.

Alan Moorehead *The White Nile*. A riveting account of the search for the source and European rivalries for control in the region.

Roland Oliver and J.D. Fage *A Short History of Africa*. Dated, but still the standard paperback introduction.

Thomas Pakenham *The Scramble for Africa*. The story of how the European powers rushed to conquer and exploit Africa in the name of commerce, Christianity and civilization, in the last two decades of the nineteenth century. Not specifically about Kenya, but extremely relevant to Kenyan history.

Kenya in general

Jeffrey A. Fadiman *When We Began There Were Witchmen*. Recounts the story of the Meru people from their mythical origins in Shungwaya in

northeastern Kenya to the decimation of Meru culture by a tiny handful of missionaries and colonial administrators.

Fedders and Salvadori *People and Cultures of Kenya*. A useful tribe-by-tribe introduction.

Terry Hirst *The Struggle for Nairobi*. Sort of large-format "Nairobi for Beginners" that manages to make town planning (or the lack of it) fascinating, bringing together a mass of otherwise hard-to-get information about the city's growth.

Kenya's People. A series of ten pamphlets providing a simple and reliable background on ten of Kenya's peoples. Aimed at Kenyan secondary schools, they're pitched just right for culturally uninitiated visitors.

Jomo Kenyatta *Facing Mount Kenya*. A traditional, functionalist, anthropological monograph, but written by a member of the society in question – in this case, the Kikuyu – under the supervision of Bronislaw Malinowski at the London School of Economics, shortly before World War II. One of the few scholarly works ever written on traditional Kikuyu culture, this is as interesting for the insights it offers

on its author as for its quite readable content. Good Kikuyu glossary.

Maxon and Ofcansky *Historical Dictionary of Kenya*. From a reliable series that covers nearly every African country, this is an A to Z of Kenya's history. Includes an extensive bibliography.

William R. Ochieng *A History of Kenya*. Somewhat pedestrian but the best general overview from prehistory to 1980, with useful maps and photos to show the way. *A Modern History of Kenya 1895–1980* covers the twentieth century in eight chapters – solid enough up to the middle of Kenyatta's reign.

William R. Ochieng (ed) *Themes in Kenyan History*. A new collection of writings by historians and other academics, all teaching in Kenyan universities.

Thomas Spear and Richard Waller (eds) *Being Maasai*. Articles about Maasai identity – a subtle and interesting field, and vital reading for anyone concerned with the ethnic politics of modern Kenya.

Coastal history

G.S.P. Freeman-Grenville *The east African Coast*. If you're heading for the coast, this is fascinating – a series of accounts from the first century to the nineteenth – vivid and often extraordinary.

Sarah Mirza and Margaret Strobel *Three Swahili Women*. Three histories of ritual, three women's lives. Born between 1890 and 1920

into different social backgrounds, these biographies document enormous changes from the most important of neglected viewpoints.

James de Vere Allen *Swahili Origins: Swahili Culture and the Shungwaya Phenomenon*. The life work of a challenging and readable scholar, bound to raise a fascinating field of study to new prominence.

Protectorate and colonial Kenya

James Fox *White Mischief*. Investigative romp through the events surrounding the notorious unsolved murder of Lord Erroll, one of Kenya's most aristocratic settlers, at Karen in 1941. Well told

and highly revealing of British Kenyan society of the time. Michael Radford's 1987 film version is equally enjoyable, and a good deal more stimulating than the *Out of Africa* movie.

Charles Miller *The Lunatic Express*. The story of *that* railway. Miller narrates the drama of one of the great feats of Victorian engineering – as bizarre and as madly magnificent as any Wild West epic – adding weight with a broad historical background of East Africa from the year dot. The same author's The Battle for the Bundu follows a little-known corner of World War I, as fought out on the plains of Tsavo between British Kenya and German Tanganyika – immensely readable.

Errol Trzebinski *The Kenya Pioneers*. Despite academic pretensions, this is something of a paean to the early settlers.

The Mau Mau rebellion

David Anderson *Histories of the Hanged: Testimonies from the Mau Mau Rebellion in Kenya*. Previously published as Britain's Dirty War in Kenya, this adds further weight to Elkins' case, published in the same year (see below), that the British response to Mau Mau was unnecessarily harsh and of doubtful legality.

Bruce Berman *Control and Crisis in Modern Kenya*. A study of the growth of state control, from the 1890s through to interwar crisis and post-war disintegration.

Donald L. Barnett and Karari Njama *Mau Mau from Within: Autobiography and Analysis of Kenya's Peasant Revolt*. An account based on personal recollections.

Robert B. Edgerton *Mau Mau: An African Crucible*. An account of the revolt based on guerrillas' testimonies. Includes explorations of the role of women and class formation in modern Kenya.

Caroline Elkins *Britain's Gulag: The Brutal End of Empire in Kenya*. Published in 2005, this Pulitzer prize-winning study of the reality of Britain's colonial war in Kenya, brings bleak context to the legal cases that have been lodged by survivors. As ever, the truth, towards which this feels like the nearest approach so far, is far worse than was ever imagined at the time.

Tabitha Kanogo *Squatters and the Roots of Mau Mau 1905–63*. Delves into the early years of the "White Highlands" to show how resistance, and the conditions for revolt, were built into the relations between the settler land-grabbers and the peasant farmers and herders ("squatters") they usurped. Strong on the role of women in the Mau Mau movement.

J.M. Kariuki *Mau Mau Detainee: The Account by a Kenya African of His Experience in Detention Camps*. A remarkably forbearing account of life and death in the detention camps. Kariuki's vision for the future of Kenya and his loyalty to Kenyatta have a special irony after his assassination in 1975.

David Throup *Economic and Social Origins of Mau Mau*. An examination of the story from the end of World War II, covering the colonial mentality and differences in efficiency between peasant cash-cropping and more wasteful plantation agriculture.

Post Independence

Jean Davison *Voices from Mutira: Change in the Lives of Rural Gikuyu Women 1910–1995*. Rich, unself-consciously moving and particularly interesting for the attitudes it documents on brideprice and genital mutilation.

Anthony Howarth *Kenyatta: A Photographic Biography.* A roughly hewn biography composed of an amalgam of black-and-white photographs, news clippings and quotations. It doesn't pretend to be exhaustive, but manages to capture the spirit of the leader and the struggle for Independence.

Kenneth King *Jua Kali Kenya.* First serious study of Kenya's important informal sector – the self-employed fixers and manufacturers who work under the "hot sun" (the jua kali). Great photos.

Tom Mboya *The Challenge of Nationhood.* The vision of Kenya's best-loved statesman – and a Luo – assassinated in 1969 for looking like a clear successor to Kenyatta.

Andrew Morton *Moi: the Making of an African Statesman.* Strange subject for the author of *Diana: Her True Story* and a strangely compelling book is the result. While it would be impossible to deny this is a sycophantic biography – Morton's reported conversations with Moi usually dry up just as the reader formulates the critical question – simply getting access to the notoriously defensive president was remarkable in itself. The research is here; there are insights, but also too many factual inaccuracies not to cast a shadow of doubt over the whole account.

Jeremy Murray-Brown *Kenyatta,* and **David Goldsworthy** *Tom Mboya: The Man Who Kenya Wanted to Forget,* are the two big biographies: both weighty and deeply researched.

Arts

Jane Barbour and Simiyu Wandibba *Kenyan Pots and Potters.* This comprehensive description of pot-making communities includes techniques, training, marketing and sociological perspectives.

Ngugi wa Thiong'o *Detained – A Writer's Prison Diary.* A retrospective of Kenya's history up to 1978, woven into the daily routine of political detention during Kenyatta's last year. Ngugi discourses widely and, while his reflections are occasionally pedantic or obscure and sometimes written with almost religious fervour, he hits home often. *His Barrel of a Pen: Resistance to Repression in Neo-Colonial Kenya* (Africa World Press, USA) hones some of his points sharply (see also the box on p.665).

Oginga Odinga *Not Yet Uhuru.* The classic critique of Kenya's direction at the time it was written.

Bethuel Ogot and William Ochieng (eds) *Decolonization and Independence in Africa 1940–93.* The standard work on these years, asking how much Kenya's – and other countries' – difficulties are linked to the colonial past and the process of growing away from it.

Geoff Sayer *Kenya: Promised Land?.* Concise, readable essays – newspaper-article length with good photography, properly captioned – that get right to the point about the issues that make Kenya the fascinatingly problematic place it is.

WorldFocus Kenya. Children's introduction to the country – one of a series for the seven-plus age group – written with style and intelligence, and incorporating good photos and case studies of real people.

Roy Braverman *Islam and Tribal Art.* A useful paperback text for the dedicated.

Susan Denyer *African Traditional Architecture.* Useful and interesting, with hundreds of photos (most of them old) and detailed line drawings.

Frank Willett *African Art*. An accessible volume; good value, with a generous illustrations–text ratio.

Geoffrey Williams *African Designs from Traditional Sources*. A designer's and enthusiast's sourcebook, from the copyright-free publishers.

Mountain, hiking and diving guides

Paul Clarke *Mountains of Kenya*. A detailed and practical guide, comprehensively updated since its earlier incarnation and well worth buying if you plan to do any Kenyan hiking.

Guide Book to Mount Kenya and Kilimanjaro. For fully equipped alpinism, this is indispensable.

Anton Koornhof *The Dive Sites of East Africa*. Highly recommended if you're at all taken by snorkelling or diving, with detailed text on each and every major site in Kenya, Tanzania and Zanzibar, beautifully illustrated and with thoughtful sections on environmental matters. One to make you dream.

Coffee-table books

Mohamed Amin *Cradle of Mankind and Portrait of Kenya*. Stunning photographs of the Lake Turkana region, by the award-winning maverick photo-journalist Amin, killed in the Comoros plane hijack in 1997.

Anne Arthus–Bertrand and Anne Spoerry, photos by Yann Arthus-Bertrand *Kenya from the Air*. Superb images of the country from the eagle's viewpoint.

Paul Goldstein and Roger Hooper *Dotted Plains, Spotted Game*. Photographed entirely in the Mara, an impressive new collection, concentrating on the big cats.

Mitsuaki Iwago *Serengeti*. Stunning scenes and portraits from Serengeti (the Tanzanian continuation of the Maasai Mara) from a master photographer. Simply the best volume of wildlife photography ever assembled, this makes most glossies look feeble. If you're trying to persuade someone to visit East Africa – or if any aesthetic argument

were needed to preserve the parks and animals – this is the book to use.

David Keith Jones *Shepherds of the Desert*. Brilliant photos (many in black and white), with a text more lucid and less superficial than most glossies; this book concerns itself only with northern Kenya.

Brian Jackman and Jonathan Scott *The Marsh Lions*. Beautifully produced and painstakingly researched study of the lions and other animals around the Musiara Marsh in Maasai Mara.

Tepilit Ole Saitoti and Carol Beckwith *Maasai*. The Maasai coffee-table book; some photos are too much to take at reading distance. Exquisite but largely staged portraits of Maasai culture (and even Beckwith's camera can't disguise the tourist souvenirs in the background). Variably interesting, chauvinistic text, which plays the cult value of the Maasai for all it's worth.

Writing from Kenya

Very little Kenyan literature appeared in print before World War II. But while East Africa has tended to lag behind the rest of the continent in modern forms – the novel, short stories, drama and modern poetry – there's a rich tradition of oral literature and a specifically coastal Swahili verse culture that put African stories into writing as long as three hundred years ago.

The oral tradition in print

With the exception of the coast, precolonial Kenyan literature was entirely oral, and stories were passed – and modified – from generation to generation. These **folk tales**, commonly told by the leaders of the community to the children, were very often "trickster" tales about animals. While they frequently contained a moral, their main purpose was to entertain.

The hare's practical joke

A long, long time ago, there were two people who were very good friends. One was Mr. Hare and the other Mr. Hyena. They used to visit each other and on each of these visits, the Hare used to carry in his bag some honey and sweetened meat. He used to put his little finger in the bag and give his friend to lick. Said the Hare: "Brother, I have something very, very sweet in my bag here. Take it and see for yourself." The Hyena liked it very much.

"Hi, Hi, Brother Hare, give me some more, more I say. It is very, very . . ."

"No, no, this is a sweetness that you must have a little at a time."

And the same thing happened day after day for many days. One day, the Hare came on as usual and said:

"Brother Hyena, may I give you something very, very sweet, sweeter than sweetness itself?"

"Yes, my good friend, I'd love some very, very much." And the Hare gave his sweetened finger to the Hyena to lick.

"Oh, Hare, my very good friend do give me more."

"No, no, old man, you cannot eat much of this sweetness. It is a sweetness that must be eaten sparingly."

"But brother, where do you get much much sweetness?"

"I get it from those mountains you see above our heads," pointing at the white clouds. "Once you eat this sweetness you should never pass piss or shit because then the sweetness gets lost."

"Then what do people do so that they do not pass out piss or shit after they have eaten this sweetness?"

"Ah, Mr. Hyena, that is very simple, they have their bottoms sewn up and if you want, I can do the sewing up for you."

"Yes, yes, do sew it up for me." And the Hare sewed the Hyena's bottom.

They took three bags each and the Hare led the way to the sweetness that never passes. Now the Hyena ate the honey, the honeycombs and the dead bees. Then the Hare said: "Now that we have filled our stomachs and our bags let us go home." Now when they were on the way, the Hyena went down to the stream to drink some water. And when he drank he just dropped down like a stump of a tree. He stayed and stayed and stayed there; his eyes popping out like sweet potatoes. He stayed there for so many days, until he thought he was going to die.

One day he saw the Eagle coming down to drink some water – said he:

"Good Brother Eagle, help me."

"Hi, brother, how shall I help you?"

"Come round behind me at my bottom end. You will see a string going right through it, prick it and pull carefully because I feel pain. I was sewn up by the Hare and he did a very bad thing."

Now as soon as the Eagle touched this string a flood of piss and shit rushed out and covered the Eagle and the piss was like a mountain with the Eagle as the core.

One day there was a heavy rain which washed away the piss and shit, slowly by slowly until the Eagle emerged with a scratch on the neck. He flew away swearing revenge on the Hyena. For many days he and the Hyena played hide and seek until one day the Hyena, being the foolish person, forgot that he was the sworn enemy of the Eagle. The Eagle being clever did not want a physical contact with the Hyena. He knew very well that the Hyena was stronger than him. Now he started to show the Hyena the choice pieces of meat that he carried in his bag and every day he gave a little to the Hyena saying: "Brother, I carry this kind of meat, have a bite" and the Hyena said: "Brother Eagle, these delicacies, this choice meat you give me, where does it come from?"

"Now, Brother Hyena, these delicacies, the choice meats are very, very many. If you like, I can take you where they come from. But," continued the Eagle, "it is impossible to get that meat alone. You must come too. Now go and collect all your people. Let them bring bags, tins and drums. Then we shall bring as much meat as will last for three years."

The Hyena was very happy and he ran to collect all his people. Panting: "Do you see all that meat above? My friend brings it to me every day. Now this friend has told me to collect all my people so that we can go and fetch this meat. Let each one of you bring tins, bags or drums and I, with your permission, will ask the Eagle to mention the day on which we can go."

Said all Hyenas: "Hi, we also would like to eat the white choice meat."

All the Hyenas of that country had gathered together and when they saw the Eagle coming towards them they said: "Now, Brother Eagle, let us go to get this meat. Tell us when we can go".

The Eagle said, "We shall go on the third day from today. Be ready."

On that day the Hyena gathered and the Eagle arranged them in a line according to age, the smallest one being put at the back. The Eagle was right in front. He said to the Hyena behind him: "Now, Brother, hold tight to the feathers of my tail," and the Hyena held tight. "Everybody hold each other's tail," he shouted and then he flew up, up, up, and heading to the choice meats in the sky. Now when they had gone very high, the Eagle asked:

"Are you all clear off the ground?"

"No, no, some are still touching the ground." He flew, flew and flew.

"Can you see the earth?"

"Yes, yes, we can see it." The Eagle was waiting to hear that all the Hyenas could no longer see the earth.

"Can you see the earth?"

"We see it dimly now." The Eagle flew and flew.

"Do you still see the earth?"

"We see only black, black darkness, we cannot tell where the earth is."

The Eagle knew then that the distance from the earth was very, very great. Then he said to the Hyena behind him:

"Hi, hi, my friend, a scratch, a scratch on my back wing," and the Hyena behind let go the tail feathers of the Eagle. Suddenly the whole line of Hyenas went tumbling down. Kuru Kuru Kuru like the sound of thunder. Some Hyenas crushed their limbs, their bones and died instantly. Some died before they reached the earth. Only the last Hyena was left, but she acquired a limp in the leg which she carries to this day.

Reprinted from *Kikuyu Folktales*, edited and translated by Rose Gecau. By permission of Kenya Literature Bureau.

Hare and Hornbill

Hare and hornbill were great friends. One day Hare said: "My friend, we have looked for girls all over this land, and there are none that are good enough for you and me. Let us go up to Skyland, perhaps we will find some suitable ones."

Hornbill replied: "I know it is getting a bit late for us to get married, but you know my problem, you know I have this terrible thing!"

"You mean your chronic diarrhoea? But that is nothing to worry about." Hare produced a cork of the right size and blocked up Hornbill's anus.

The two friends made preparations for the journey, and after saying good-bye to their families, Hare got on Hornbill's back and they flew up through the clouds into Skyland. There was a big marriage dance. Hare and Hornbill put on their dancing costumes and went straight into the arena. Hornbill danced gracefully, touching the ground lightly and moving his wings up and down to the rhythm of the drums. His neck swayed this way and that way, and his eyes sparkled with love. Hare danced as best he could, but he could not follow the rhythm of the dance, and sang out of tune; moreover, his big ears looked funny. Beautiful girls fought to dance before Hornbill, but none came anywhere near Hare; and when he approached the girls they ran away from him. That night Hornbill slept with a very pretty girl. Hare slept cold.

The next day Hornbill won two girls; Hare again slept cold. The next night when Hornbill was asleep, resting beside his fourth lover, Hare tip-toed into the house and unhooked the cork. Three days' accumulation of diarrhoea spewed out and flooded the entire house. The stench rose like smoke and the dancers fled from the arena, and Hornbill woke up, and in great shame flew down through the clouds, leaving Hare behind.

There was much commotion as the Skylanders tried to find out what had happened. Hare denied all knowledge of the cause of the trouble.

"But where is your handsome friend?" they asked.

"I am also looking for him," said Hare, adding, "I must find him otherwise it will be a bit difficult to return to earth."

When they failed to find Hornbill the Skylanders decided to get rid of Hare by lowering him down to earth on a rope of plaited grass. The girls cut many heaps of grass. They made the rope and tied one end around Hare's waist and continued to plait the other end as Hare was lowered downwards. The Skylanders gave Hare a drum and told him, "As soon as you reach the earth beat this drum very hard so that the girls may stop plaiting the rope." Hare thanked the Skylanders, said good-bye and began his homeward journey.

Hare descended slowly through the clouds, but on seeing the faint tips of the highest mountain he hit the drum very hard. The skylanders stopped plaiting and dropped the rope. Hare came hurtling down like a falling stone. But just before hitting the ground he cried to the smallest black ants, "Collect me! Collect me! Collect . . ."

Hare hit the ground and broke up into many many very small pieces. The smallest black ants collected the pieces and put them together again, and Hare became alive. But today when Hare is running you hear his chest making crackling sounds, because the bones of his chest were not put together properly.

Reprinted from *Hare and Hornbill*, a collection of folk tales edited and translated by Okot p'Bitek. By permission of Heinemann Educational Books.

Petals of Blood

Ngugi wa Thiong'o is Kenya's best-known writer and one of the country's most consistently outspoken critics. The following extract from the satirical *Petals of Blood* has been taken from the middle of the book. The people of Ilmorog, a village in the Rift Valley, are beginning to appreciate the power and influence of the New Kenya.

Changes come to Ilmorog

Munira folded the newspaper and went to Wanja's place to break the news. He felt for her and Nyakinyua. He did not expect favours. He just wanted to take her the news. And to find out more about it. She was not at her Theng'eta premises. Abdulla told him that she had gone to Nyakinyua's hut. Munira walked there and found other people. News of the threatened sale must have reached them too. They had come to commiserate with her and others similarly affected, to weep with one another. They looked baffled: how could a bank sell their land? A bank was not a government: from whence then, its powers? Or maybe it was the government, an invisible government, some others suggested. They turned to Munira. But he could not answer their question. He only talked about a piece of paper, they had surrendered to the bank. But he could not answer, put to sleep, the bitter scepticism in their voices and looks. What kind of monster was this bank that was a power unto itself, that could uproot lives of a thousand years?

He went back and tried to drink Theng'eta, but it did not have the taste. He remembered that recently he had seen Wambui carting stones to earn bread for the day and he wondered what would happen to the old woman. She was too old to sell her labour and sweat in a market.

"The old woman? Nyakinyua?" Munira echoed Karega's question, slowly. "She died! She is dead!" he added quickly, almost aggressively, waking up from his memories.

Karega's face seemed to move.

Nyakinyua, the old woman, tried to fight back. She tramped from hut to hut calling upon the peasants of Ilmorog to get together and fight it out. They looked at her and they shook their heads: whom would they fight now? The Government? The Banks? KCO? The Party Nderi? Yes who would they really fight? But she tried to convince them that all these were one and that she would fight them. Her land would never be settled by strangers. There was something grand, and defiant, in the woman's action – she with her failing health and flesh trying to organise the dispossessed of Ilmorog into a protest. But there was pathos in the exercise. Those whose land had not yet been taken looked nervously aloof and distant. One or two even made disparaging remarks about an old woman not quite right in the head. Others genuinely not seeing the point of a march to Ruwaini or to the big City restrained her. She could not walk all the way, they told her. But she said: "I'll go alone . . . my man fought the white man. He paid for it with his blood . . . I'll struggle against these black oppressors . . . alone . . . alone . . ."

What would happen to her, Munira wondered.

He need not have worried about her. Nyakinyua died peacefully in her sleep a few days after the news of the bank threat. Rumour went that she had told

Wanja about the impending journey: she had said that she could not even think of being buried in somebody else's land: for what would her man say to her when she met him on the other side? People waited for the bank to come and sell her land. But on the day of the sale Wanja redeemed the land and became the heroine of the new and the old Ilmorog.

Later Munira was to know.

But at that time only Abdulla really knew the cost: Wanja had offered to sell him her rights to their jointly owned New Building. He did not have the money and it was he who suggested that they sell the whole building to a third person and divide the income between them.

So Wanja was back to her beginnings.

And Mzigo was the new proud owner of the business premises in Ilmorog.

Wanja was not quite the same after her recent loss. For a time, she continued the proud proprietor of the old Theng'eta place. Her place still remained the meat-roasting centre. Dance steps in the hall could still raise dust to the roof, especially when people were moving to their favourite tunes:

How beautiful you are, my love!
How soft your round eyes are, my honey!
What a pleasant thing you are,
Lying here
Shaded by this cedar bush!
But oh, darling,
What poison you carry between your legs!

But Wanja's heart was not in it. She started building a huge wooden bungalow at the lower end of her shamba, some distance from the shanty town that was growing up around Abdulla's shop, the lodgings and the meat-roasting centre, almost as a natural growth complement to the more elegant new Ilmorog. People said that she was wise to invest in a building the money remaining after redeeming her grandmother's shamba: but what was it for? She already had a hut further up the shamba, hidden from the noise and inquisitive eyes of the New Ilmorog by a thick natural hedge. She went about her work without taking anybody into her confidence. But it was obvious that it was built in the style of a living house with several spacious rooms. Later she moved in: she planted flower gardens all around and had electric lights fixed there. It was beautiful: it was a brave effort so soon after her double loss, people said.

One night the band struck up a song they had composed on their first arrival. As they played, the tune and the words seemed to grow fresher and fresher and the audience clapped and whistled and shouted encouragement. The band added innovations and their voices seemed possessed of a wicked carefree devil.

This shamba girl
Was my darling
Told me she loved my sight.
I broke bank vaults for her,
I went to jail for her,
But when I came back
I found her a lady,
Kept by a wealthy roundbelly daddy,
And she told me,
This shamba-lady girl told me,
No, Gosh!
Sikujui
Serikali imebadilishwa
Coup d'état!

They stopped to thunderous handclaps and feet pounding on the floor. Wanja suddenly stood up and asked them to play it again. She started dancing to it, alone, in the arena. People were surprised. They watched the gyrations of her body, speaking pleasure and pain, memories and hopes, loss and gain, unfulfilled longing and desire. The band, responding to the many beating hearts, played with sad maddening intensity as if it were reaching out to her loneliness and solitary struggle. She danced slowly and deliberately toward Munira and he was remembering that time he had seen her dancing to a juke-box at Safari Bar in Kamiritho. As suddenly as she had started, she stopped. She walked to the stage at the bandstand. The "house" was hushed. The customers knew that something big was in the air.

"I am sorry, dear customers, to have to announce the end of the old Ilmorog Bar and meat-roasting centres, and the end of Ilmorog Bar's own Sunshine Band. Chiri County Council says we have to close."

She would not say more. And now they watched her as she walked across the dusty floor toward where Munira was sitting. She stopped, whirled back, and screamed at the band. "Play! Play! Play on. Everybody dance – Daaance!" And she sat down beside Munira.

"Munira, wouldn't you like to come and see my new place tomorrow night?"

Munira could hardly contain himself. So at long last. So the years of waiting were over. It was just like the old days before Karega and the roads and the changes had come to disturb the steamy peaceful rhythm in Ilmorog, when he was the teacher.

The next day he could not teach. He could not talk. He could hardly sit or stand still in one place. And when the time came, he walked to her place with tremulous hands and beating heart. He had not been inside the new house and he felt it an honour that she had chosen him out of all those faces.

He knocked at the door. She was in. She stood in the middle of the room lit by a blue light. For a second he thought himself in the wrong place with the wrong person.

She had on a miniskirt which revealed just about everything, and he felt his manhood rise of itself. On her lips was smudgy red lipstick: her eyebrows were pencilled and painted a luminous blue. What was the game, he wondered? He thought of one of the many advertisements he had earlier collected: Be a platinum blonde: be a whole new you in 100% imported hand-made human hair. Wanja was a really new her.

"You look surprised, Mwalimu. I thought you always wanted me," she said, with a false seductive blur in her voice. Then in a slightly changed voice, more natural, which he could recognise, she added: "That's why you had him dismissed, not so? Look now. They have even taken away my right, well, our right to brew. The County Council says our licence was sold away with the New Building. They also say our present premises are in any case unhygienic! There's going to be a tourist centre and such places might drive visitors away. Do you know the new owner of our Theng'eta breweries? Do you know the owner of the New Ilmorog Utamaduni Centre? Never mind!" She had, once again, changed her voice: "But come: what are you waiting for?" She walked backwards: he followed her and they went into another room – with a double bed and a reddish light. He was hypnotized. He was angry with himself for being tongue-tied and yet he was propelled toward her by the engine-power of his risen body and the drums in the heart. Yet below it all, deep inside, he felt a sensation of shame and disgust at his helplessness.

She removed everything, systematically, piece by piece, and then jumped into bed.

"Come, come, my darling!" she cooed from inside the sheets.

He was about to jump into bed beside her and clasp her to himself, when she suddenly turned cold and chilly, and her voice was menacing.

"No, Mwalimu. No free things in Kenya. A hundred shillings on the table if you want high-class treatment."

He thought she was joking, but as he was about to touch her she added more coldly:

"This is New Kenya. You want it, you pay for it, for the bed and the light and my time and the drink that I shall later give you and the breakfast tomorrow. And all for a hundred shillings. For you. Because of old times. For others it will be more expensive."

He was taken aback, felt the wound of this unexpected humiliation. But now he could not retreat. Her thighs called out to him.

He took out a hundred shillings and handed it to her. He watched her count it and put the money under the mattress. Now panic seized him. His thing had shrivelled. He stood there and tried to fix his mind on the old Wanja, on the one who had danced pain and ecstasy, on the one who had once cried under watchful moonbeams stealing into a hut. She watched him, coldly, with menace, and then suddenly she broke out in her put-on, blurred, seductive voice.

"Come, darling. I'll keep you warm. You are tonight a guest at *Sunshine Lodge*."

There was something pathetic, sad, painful in the tone. But Munira's thing obeyed her voice. Slowly he removed his clothes and joined her in bed. Even as the fire and thirst and hunger in his body were being quenched, the pathetic strain in her voice lingered in the air, in him, in the room everywhere.

It was New Kenya. It was New Ilmorog. Nothing was free. But for a long time, for years to come, he was not to forget the shock and the humiliation of the hour. It was almost like that first time, long ago, when he was only a boy.

Indeed, changes did come to Ilmorog, changes that drove the old one away and ushered a new era in our lives. And nobody could tell, really tell, how it had happened, except that it had happened. With a year or so of the new Ilmorog shopping centre being completed, wheatfields and ranches had sprung up all around the plains: the herdsmen had died or had been driven further afield into the drier parts, but a few had become workers on the wheatfields and ranches on the earth upon which they once roamed freely. The new owners, master-servants of bank power, money and cunning came over at weekends and drove in Landrovers or Range Rovers, depending on the current car fashion, around the farms whose running they had otherwise entrusted to paid managers. The peasants of Ilmorog had also changed. Some had somehow survived the onslaught. They could employ one or two hands on their small farms. Most of the others had joined the army of workers who had added to the growing population of the New Ilmorog. But which New Ilmorog?

There were several Ilmorogs. One was the residential area of the farm managers, County Council officials, public service officers, the managers of Barclays, Standard and African Economic Banks, and other servants of state and money power. This was called Cape Town. The other – called New Jerusalem – was a shanty town of migrant and floating workers, the unemployed, the prostitutes and small traders in tin and scrap metal. Between the New Jerusalem and Cape Town, not far from where Mwathi had once lived guarding the secrets of iron works and native medicine, was All Saints church, now led by Rev. Jerrod Brown. Also somewhere between the two areas was Wanja's *Sunshine Lodge*, almost as famous as the church.

The shopping and business centre was dominated by two features. Just outside it was a tourist cultural (Utamaduni) village owned by Nderi wa Riera and a

West German concern, appropriately called Ilmorog African Diamond Cultural and Educational Tours. Many tourists came for a cultural fiesta. A few hippies also came to look for the Theng'eta Breweries which, starting on the premises owned by Mzingo, had now grown into a huge factory employing six hundred workers with a number of research scientists and chemical engineers. The factory also owned an estate in the plains where they experimented with different types of Theng'eta plants and wheat. They brewed a variety of Theng'eta drinks: from the pure gin for export to cheap but potent drinks for workers and the unemployed. They put some in small plastic bags in different measures of one, two and five shillings' worth so that these bagfuls of poison could easily be carried in people's pockets. Most of the containers, whether plastic or glass bottles, carried the famous ad, now popularized in most parts of the country through their sales vans, newspapers and handbills: POTENCY – Theng'a Theng'a with Theng'eta. P=3T.

The breweries were owned by an Anglo-American international combine but of course with African directors and even shareholders. Three of the four leading local personalities were Mzigo, Chui and Kimeria.

Long live New Ilmorog! Long live Partnership in Trade and Progress!

Reprinted from *Petals of Blood*. By permission of Heinemann Educational Books.

Short story – Sam Kahiga

Short stories are immensely popular in Kenya and you'll find stacks of well-thumbed, short romantic novels at any second-hand bookstall. **Sam Kahiga**'s energetic, exasperatingly racy style, sprinkled with a combination of British and American idioms, is strange at first, but his stories are revealing about the values of modern, urban Kenya.

A high voltage affair

At school I was afflicted by that chronic laziness that is often the lot of young students who think they are especially clever and can pass any exam through sheer genius. After getting my "O" levels with nine points and no sweat at all, I went to Strathmore College for "A" levels. I remember my goal then – to be a nuclear physicist. And if that was too advanced for the Third World then I'd compromise gracefully, step down, and just be a bloody good research scientist. The Third World could do with some of those.

Well my "A" levels were a disaster. What could I blame it on? Girls, booze or drugs? I blame it on the lot – plus the sort of risky confidence that comes after you've been top of the class too many times. Of my days in Strathmore I remember the movies and the parties rather than what happened in the labs. Except for jokingly trying to invent a drug that could give one a trip I hardly applied myself. And when the final results came out I realized that I was on a bad trip that just wouldn't end up in the university. It was bad, shocking, in fact.

Guys whose IQs were nowhere near as high as mine got called up to the university. As for me I was bad news in academic circles. Trying to save face I applied feverishly to foreign universities. My daddy could afford to send me to one. But no foreign university seemed interested. I kept trying until my daddy casually let me know that if I was intending to go abroad I would have to get the dough myself. That's what is known as fatherly affection.

Let me explain his attitude, for I understood it perfectly. My daddy (his friends and enemies call him GM) was no kid-spoiler. Although he could afford to send me round the world seven times he wasn't going to help because I had proved I was a failure. If I had failed at home I would not succeed abroad. I realized from his acid comments that he knew about the kind of life I had led at Strathmore – girls, booze, drugs. Could he then seriously think of sending me to America, that modern Babylon and hippy headquarters.

"Go on your own," said GM. He had turned a blind eye to my mischief until I let him down and failed to make it to the university. And GM is not the kind of man you let down and get away with it. He himself had never failed. Where he couldn't work his way out smoothly he bulldozed. If the front door was closed he tried the back door. That was the way he made his millions in the construction business.

Sons of poor men were going to university, so why not GM's first-born? He felt betrayed. What was it that he had not done for me? My pocket money had been two hundred and fifty bob a month. And he had told me to buy any book that I wanted. So why had I not gone to university?

GM had never even been to high school because he had been born too many years before the fruit of independence ripened. When independence came he was just a mason grade three. We lived at Shauri Moyo. GM grabbed his share of the fruit and we moved off to Lavington where I had my own motor-cycle and a couple of rooms to myself which were a mess of wires, novels and beat music that made my mother ill. The smell of my strange "cigarettes" made her ill too, but mothers are like that. You have to be patient with them.

I agree that GM spoilt me. But all the money and stuff he showered on me was on the understanding that I would live up to his expectations, which I did until those hazy "A" levels. In fact I did more. For instance at seventeen I was the maintenance man around the place, the little genie who knew what was wrong with the TV, the fridge or even his car. GM couldn't even change his own spark plugs. He trusted me to tune and service his car and considered me the last word in wiring. Now you can begin to understand about the two hundred and fifty bob pocket money. I spent most of it on cocaine.

After I had failed GM didn't want to see me again. He is a very unforgiving man. He had dug up my Strathmore background and it had shocked him so much that he didn't want me to even touch his car.

What finally broke up our relationship was when the disciplinarian daddy in him came to the surface and he thought he could teach me a physical lesson just because my room smelt of something strange. He sniffed and realized that it was grass.

The rest is embarrassing. Let's just say that there was yet another side of me that he hadn't known. I had a panther's reflexes that had come from picking up all that one needs to know about judo and karate. I didn't hurt him at all but he stared at me from the floor with great surprise. Through his gaping mouth I saw a little film of blood on his small white teeth – nothing serious.

After that there was nothing else to do except pack. The mansion at Lavington was a bit too small for both of us.

Somehow I feel that this background is important before I tell the story that follows. When I went to the Power Institute to train as a technician for the Power Company I went on my own ticket. The exams accompanying the interview were tough and gruelling to most of the boys but I sailed through, although I was half-starving. They accepted me at the Power Institute on my own merit, not a millionaire's influential word. It is important that this is understood.

Every young boy carries in his heart the soft-focus image of a woman he could love, serve and die for. I'm still not sure whether she eventually turns up, this ever youthful, totally compliant dream girl whom you want to set on a pedestal and worship. She is mutable, changing with your fancy and experience, but something remains constant about her, whether you are twelve or forty.

This constancy I guess is the subservience to your ego. She will love you no matter what happens, no matter who else is there. She loves you when you are vomiting into the toilet bowl and sticks by your side as you piss into a dark alley. She will be petite and cuddlesome when you are in a gentle mood and you want her to be like that. She will have an Afro hairdo if that's what you want. She's a virgin, nobody ever touched her before. Sometimes her breasts are small, sometimes her breasts are large. Sometimes she's innocent, sometimes she's master of the Kama Sutra, a deep well of erotic knowledge.

The first time she came to me in the flesh (or was it her more mundane twin sister?) was at the Power Institute at the beginning of the second year. My thoughts were hardly on love but on electro-magnetic forces, watts, ohms and coulombs. Instead of breasts I was thinking of turbines and transformers and the only kick I ever got during those sober, sombre months was the flow of electrons through me whenever I was fool enough to step on a live wire. In short, I was immersed in electricity, my biggest love since childhood. I hadn't seen anybody for a year – nobody mattered. For companions I had watts, coils and ohm's law. If I needed a drink, coke was enough, thanks. The hostel supplied the grub. There wasn't much else I felt I needed.

Then during Easter we had a dance at the hostel and this chick came along with one of the boys. I remember I was pretty lonesome hanging around the stuffy room with my coke and yet expecting nothing from all the bull-shit. To make things worse it was raining badly outside and I couldn't walk back to the hostel even if I had wanted to.

What is dancing? I asked myself. Some hangover from some primitive era. Some sort of savage convolution totally outside the realm of scientific discipline. I wanted to go home but the damn rain was falling. When I looked out of the window the world was suddenly lit up by the taut gnarled roots of a devilish lightning flash. "Jupiter's thunder-bolt." "God's footstep." To scientists: atmospheric electric phenomena. I wanted to go to bed.

She was very pretty but couldn't have been with a worse man. Mbote was rude, coarse and argumentative. He was a slum child and he was proud of the fact. No efforts at all to be a gentleman. The girl he was with was a lady from the toe up to the rich mass of black hair. And if I wasn't wrong she was trying to catch my eye.

I put my ginger ale on the ledge of a window (tired of cokes by now). I singled her out from the rest of the clumsy humanity, forgave her for imperfections and dared with her to a slow number.

"What's your label?" I asked.

"I beg your pardon?"

"The name. What's your name?"

"Esther."

"Esther what?"

"Mbacia."

Esther Mbacia. I was a bit annoyed with her for looking like my dream girl while going around with a guy like Mbote. My dream girls are supposed to be my own. They shouldn't be wandering around among crude wolves. They might get eaten. I wouldn't have been surprised if she ended up in Mbote's cubicle.

"You didn't tell me your name, but I know you," she said. "You are GM's son, aren't you?"

"So?" I asked coldly.

"I used to see you when you were in Strathmore. I was then in Kenya High.

You know, when you had that motor-cycle." I couldn't help grinning.

"Your girl-friend was my classmate, Edith." Edith, a grass addict.

"Mbacia," I said. "Is your father the Mbacia? Mbacia Enterprises?"

"Happens to be," she said.

"Oh."

"Oh, what?"

"Nothing."

We laughed together. And then I saw the livid angry eyes of Mbote staring at me over the rim of his glass of alcoholic poison. He was mixing everything, the only way he could get drunk cheaply. He had drunk changaa ever since he was a small boy in Majengo slums, so beer to him was mere water.

"Your boyfriend looks angry and dangerous," I said.

"He's not my boyfriend," said Mbacia's daughter.

There might have been a fight that night had I been just any other boy. But my reputation was good. They knew my reflexes. Mbote was a dreaded street fighter who bullied almost everybody else but he knew I could paralyse him by just touching a nerve. Neatly, with no glasses being broken. He didn't want that. I didn't want to be unfair so I gave her a date and went to bed.

So that's how the tragic triangle started. Poor slum boy grabs a rich girl, wants to make her happy in his own rude way. Rich boy comes along with polished karate and his father's millions behind him and poor boy has no chance. The fact that I was broke most of the time didn't worry her one bit. In fact it seemed to add to my attraction. GM's son, but always broke. How funny!

I liked serious movies but also liked seeing Chinese movies to improve on my karate. She liked ice-cream, chewing gum and I'm not quite sure what else. I liked her. A girl doesn't have to have a line of interest to be liked. I still don't know her line of interest. She doesn't share my passion for turbines and trans-formers but so what? So nothing. She was high voltage. There were electrostatic forces in her breasts. When she smiled at me the electrons flowed. She was my cathode and I was her anode.

She was Mbote's heartbreak. Poor slum boy, son of a Majengo prostitute, he had never had any love in his life. He thought he had found it in Esther. Esther thought she had found it in me. The eternal triangle.

He came to me one night when I was reading and knocked on the door of my cubicle. He was totally drunk. I threw him out. I threw him out because he called me a hybrid.

"Just because you are a hybrid and she's a hybrid you feel you must cross-breed. To keep the millions in one family."

"Get the hell out," I said. But I had to remove him physically.

What I think shattered him was my bringing Esther to the end of term dance. At first he was vulgar and insulting, though not talking to us directly. I heard the words "hybrid" and "cross-breeding" and tried to take no notice. Then I saw that he was staring at us silently, no longer speaking. The jilted lover: why not just find a girl? Why let this thing play on his complexes? I wished I could give him the girl but I was already in love with her. Or maybe there was this vacuum in my soul that she very conveniently filled. Sometimes it's difficult to distinguish love from the flight from loneliness.

The following morning was Sunday and that was when the nightmare began. Most of the boys had already gone home and the hostel was almost deserted.

With a towel around my loins I went into the shower room. Mbote who was waiting for that move came and locked the door with a key. Standing outside the door he told me a lot of things. How he had loved and how I had ruined his chances.

Swahili poetry

Swahili poetry is Kenya's oldest written literature, recorded in Arabic script since the seventeenth century and in the Roman alphabet since the beginning of the twentieth century. The oldest poems are praise and wedding songs from the oral tradition and narrative epics relating the early years of Islam. There's a wide variety of forms, but the rhythms and rhymes are not too unfamiliar to Western ears. Swahili, with its infinite capacity for allusion and imagery, has produced some beautiful verse. **Shaaban Robert**, who died in 1962, is probably the greatest twentieth-century Swahili poet. This lament for his wife was written in the shairi metre of sixteen syllables to the line.

AMINA

Amina unmejitenga, kufa umetangulia,	Amina, you have withdrawn yourself, you led the way in dying,
Kama ua umefunga, baada ya kuchanua,	Like a flower you have closed, after having opened first,
Nukuombea mwanga, peponi kukubaliwa.	I pray for you, my light, that you may be welcomed in paradise.
Mapenzi tuliyofunga, hapana wa kufungua.	The love we made between us, no one ever will undo it.
Nilitaka unyanyuke, kwa kukuombea dua,	I had hoped that you would rise again, and I prayed for you,
Sikupenda ushindike, maradhi kukuchukua,	I did not want you to be defeated, and be carried away by the disease,
Ila kwa rehema yake, Mungu amekuchagua.	But by His mercy, God has chosen you.
Mapenzi tuliyofunga, hapana wa kufungua.	The love we made between us, no one ever will undo it.
Majonzi hayananeki, kila nikikumbukia,	My grief is indescribable, every moment I remember,
Nawaza kile na hiki, naona kama ruia,	I keep thinking this and yonder I see things as if I were dreaming,
Mauti siyasadiki kuwa, mwisho wa dunia.	I did not believe in death first, that it was the end of the world, this life.
Mapenzi tuliyofunga, hapana wa kufungua.	The love we made between us, no one ever will undo it.
Nasadiki hazizi, roho hazitapotea,	I believe that souls don't perish, they cannot be lost forever,
Twafuata wokozi, kwa mauti kutujia,	We pursue salvation's pathway, when death's angel comes to meet us,
Nawe wangu mpenzi, Peponi utaingia.	And you, my beloved partner, you will enter heaven's gateway.
Mapenzi tuliyofunga, hapana wa kufungua.	The love we made between us, no one ever will undo it.
Jambo moja nakumbuka, sahihi ninalijua,	Just one thing I do remember, one I know for sure and truly,
Kuwa sasa umefika, ta'bu isikosumbua,	That you have now reached the place where no suffering can plague you,
Kwayo nimefurahika, nyuma nilikobakia.	Therefore do I still feel gladdened, here where I am left behind.
Mapenzi tuliyofunga, hapana wa kufungua.	The love we made between us, no one ever will undo it.
Ninamaliza kutunga, kwa kukuombea dua,	I have finished my composing, while for you I pray,
Vumbi tena likiunga, roho likirudishiwa,	When dust is rejoined together, when the soul returns into it,
Mauti yakijitenga, mapenzi yatarejea.	While the power of death retires, then our love will be returning.
Mapenzi tuliyofunga, hapana wa kufungua.	The love we made between us, no one ever will undo it.

Translated by Jan Knappert, 1979. Reprinted from *Four Centuries of Swahili Verse*, by permission of the translator.

"What's the point of locking the door?"

"I want to kill you."

The shower was running, the warm water caressing my skin. He was going to kill me. He must be joking. And yet I knew how reckless he was, the kind of strange practical jokes he used to play on people. Better watch out.

"Look Mbote, Esther is mine," I said, wearily.

"You snatched her. You rich people think you can snatch everything. You think you are smart. You'll pay for it."

"How?"

"I want to make you dance. You like dancing I'll make you dance."

"Look, open the door and stop being stupid. What are you up to?"

"When you come out of there you won't be alive."

"Why?"

"The shower room is wired. I'm just about to give you a thousand volts." I got the idea. I broke into a sweat. I stared at the wet floor of my death cell. The water would conduct the electricity from wherever the terminals were.

"Open the door and don't be stupid," I cried and that was the last thing I said before the current shot up through my bare feet and shot me up to the ceiling. I screamed, then hit the floor unconscious.

Hospital. The first week was a blank. The next one I began to recognise people – chaps from the Power Institute, GM, Esther.

The third week I was fine and that was when they told me that Mbote had electrocuted himself when I was in a coma. The cops had come for him and rather than face the law he had taped electric wires to his head. He had turned on the switch, died instantly and made headlines for the first and last time.

I try to look on it all to see why and how it happened but I'm still not strong enough to sort out little psychological details. Or perhaps my mind just refuses to work. I saw a picture of Mbote's mother in the papers and she was wailing, saying he was a good boy. I take my own refuge behind public opinion for that's all I can do. Public opinion has it that Mbote was crazy to try and electrocute GM's son. He was quite right to electrocute himself, though. But he shouldn't go round trying to electrocute heirs to millions. (GM wants to know if I need bodyguards.)

It all depresses me. When my heart is really low I call up Esther on the phone.

"Doctor says I need lots of therapy, girl, and only you can give it to me. So come over quick."

She always does. I told you she's high voltage – if you see what I mean. Maybe she really *is* hybrid.

Reprinted from the collection *Flight to Juba*. By permission of Longman Kenya.

Language

Language

Language

urprisingly, perhaps, **Swahili** is one of the easiest languages to learn. It's pronounced exactly as it's written, with the stress nearly always on the penultimate syllable. And it's satisfyingly regular, so even with limited knowledge you can make yourself understood and construct simple sentences.

In Kenya, you'd rarely be stuck without Swahili, but it makes a huge difference to your perceptions if you try to speak it. People are delighted if you make the effort (though they'll also tend to assume you understand more than you do). Don't forget that for many Kenyans Swahili is another foreign language they get by in, like English. For travels further afield in East Africa, and especially in Tanzania, some knowledge of Swahili is a very useful backup.

The language has spread widely from its coastal origins to become the lingua franca of east Africa and it has tended to lose its richness and complexity as a result. Upcountry, it is often spoken as a second language with a minimum of grammar. On the coast, you'll hear it spoken with tremendous panache: oratorial skills and punning (to which it lends itself with great facility) are much appreciated. Swahili is a Bantu language (in fact one of the more mainstream of the family), but it has incorporated thousands of foreign words, the majority of them Arabic, but including Portuguese and English. Far more of this Arabic inheritance and borrowing is preserved on the coast. The "standard" dialect is derived from Zanzibar Swahili, which the early missionaries learned and first transcribed into the Roman alphabet. **Written Swahili** is still not completely uniform, and you'll come across slight variations in spelling, particularly on menus.

Books and courses

There are several published language **courses** around. *Teach Yourself Swahili* by Joan Russel (Teach Yourself Books, 1995) is an excellent book, with practical everyday Swahili that you can use from the beginning. *Kiswahili kwa Kitendo* ("Swahili by Action", US only, Africa World Press, 1988) is the best bet if you find ordinary grammars indigestible. The course by Joan Maw, *Swahili for Starters* (Oxford University Press, 1999), is good. As for phrasebooks, try the *Rough Guide Swahili Dictionary Phrasebook* which includes links to MP3 files to practice your pronunciation at Ⓦwww.roughguides.com.

Pronunciation

Once you get the hang of voicing every syllable, **pronunciation** is easy. Each vowel is syllabic. However, odd-looking combinations of consonants are often pronounced as one syllable. **Mzee**, for example, is pronounced "mz-ay-ay" (rhyming with "hey") and **shauri** (troubles, problem) is pronounced "sha-oo-ri" while **mgonjwa** ("ill") has just two syllables – "mgo-njwa". Nothing is silent.

You'll often come across an "**m**" where it looks out of place: this letter can precede any other. That is because it's a noun prefix (usually replaced in the plural with "wa-" or "mi-"), as in **mtoto** – child (plural: **watoto**) or **mti** – tree (plural: **miti**). Just add a bit of an "m" sound at the beginning; "mm-toto". Don't say "um-toto" or "ma-toto"– you'll be misunderstood. In one or two nouns beginning with "mb" or "mv" (with no change in the plural), the "m" merges into the "b" or "v", as in **mbuzi** – goat or goats. The letter "n" can precede a number of others and gives a nasal quality. "Ng" followed by an apostrophe makes a sound like the "ng" in banger (try saying it without the "ba", and then use it in a word like **ng'ombe** – cow or beef); without the apostrophe, it's like two separate letters as in "finger" (or as in **nguo** – garment, clothes).

For memorizing, it often helps to ignore the first letter or syllable. Thousands of nouns, for example, start with "ki" (singular) and "vi" (plural), and they're all in the same noun class.

A as in Arthur	**M** as in Martian
B as in bed	**N** as in nonsense
C doesn't exist on its own	**NG** as in finger or hunger, with a clear "g" sound
CH as in church, but often sounds like a "t", a "dj", or a "ky"	**NG'** as in wrong or banger, with no "g" sound
D as in donkey	**O** as in orange, never as in "open" or "do"
DJ like the "j" in pyjamas	**P** as in penguin
DH like a cross between dhow and thou	**Q** doesn't exist (except in early Romanized texts; now "k")
E between the "e" in Edward and "ai" in ailing	**R** as in rapid
F as in fan	**S** as in Samson
G as in good	**T** as in tiny
GH at the back of the throat, like a gargle or a French "r"	**TH** as in thanks, never as in them
H as in harmless	**U** as in lute
I like the "e" in evil	**V** as in victory
J as in jug	**W** as in wobble
K as in kiosk, sometimes like soft "t" or "ch"	**X** doesn't exist
KH like the "ch" in loch	**Y** as in you
L as in lullaby, but often pronounced like an "r"	**Z** as in zero

Elementary grammar

Noun classes put people off Swahili. They are something like the genders in French or Latin in that you alter each adjective according to the class of noun. In Swahili you add a **prefix** to the word. Each class covers certain areas of meaning and usually has a **prefix** letter associated with most of its nouns. For example, words beginning "m" in the singular and "wa" in the plural are almost always people (eg mtu/watu – person/people; mtalii/watalii – tourist/tourists). Words beginning "ki" or "ch" (singular), and "vi" or "vy" (plural) are in the general class of "things", notably smallish things (eg kitabu/vitabu – book/books; chumba/vyumba – room/rooms). Words beginning "m" (singular) and "mi" (plural) are often trees and plants (eg mti/miti – tree/trees), or have connections with life. One of the biggest classes of nouns (the "N class") has no prefix, though nouns in it often begin with "n", "mb" or "mv"; they do not change in the plural (eg ndizi – banana/bananas, njui – road/roads, mbu – mosquito/mosquitoes). Most abstract nouns begin with "u" (eg uhuru – freedom, utoto – childhood). There are seven classes altogether, with singular and plural versions of each.

Prefixes get added to **adjectives**, so you get **kiti kizuri** – a good chair; **mtu mzuri** – a good person; **miti mizuri** – good trees. Really correct Swahili, with everything agreeing, isn't much spoken except on the coast, and you can get away with murder. But once you've grasped the essential building blocks – the root meanings and the prefixes, suffixes and infixes of one or two letters which turn them into words – it becomes a very creative language to learn. Swahili nouns don't have articles, either definite ("the") or indefinite ("a"or "an"), which makes the language a little easier, while losing nothing in richness.

Although Swahili nouns are relatively complicated compared to other languages, the **verb** system is reasonably simple. You begin with a prefix for the person, then a marker for the tense (or just "ku-" for the infinitive; we've added hyphens for clarification), and then the verb root. So from the verb **ku-taka** – to want, you get **ni-na-taka** – I want, **u-li-taka** – you wanted, and **wa-ta-taka** – they will want. The present marker "na" isn't really a tense marker but a little connective the best translation of which is really "with". Negatives are a bit more difficult: in principle, you add "ha-" at the beginning, but in the present you take away the tense marker and change the last letter to "i", so the negative of **tu-na-jua** (we know) is **ha-tu-ju-i** (we don't know); also, the "ha-" gets merged into the singular person prefixes, as shown below.

Personal prefixes

I – **ni-** (sometimes omitted in the present; negative si-). Eg: **najua** I know, **sijui** I don't know

you (sing.) – **u-** (negative hu-)

he or she – **a-** (negative ha-)

we – **tu-** (negative hatu-)

you (pl) – **m-** (negative ham-)

they (people or animals) – **wa-** (negative hawa-)

Third person prefixes for inanimate objects are usually the same as their noun prefixes, but are i- (singular) and zi- (plural) for the common nouns in the N-class. However, for people and animals, regardless of the class, they are always a- and wa-

Pronouns

I, me – **mimi**

you (sing.) – **wewe**

he, she, him, her – **yeye**

we, us – **sisi**

you (pl) – **ninyi**

they, them – **wao**

Tense markers

past (did) – **-li-** (**-ku-** in negative)

perfect (has done) – - **-me-** (negative –ja-, with the implication not yet)

present (does or is doing) – - **-na-** (omitted in negative)

future (will do) – - **-ta-**

infinitive (to do) – **ku-**

One or two very common short verbs keep the "ku-" of the infinitive when making tenses (except negatives), for example **kuja** - to come, **kula** - to eat

Verbs

to be able (can) - **kuweza** (**mnaweza kusema Kiswahili** - you (plural) can speak Swahili)

to bring - **kuleta** (**tumeleta** - we've brought)

to buy - **kununua** (**walinunua** - they bought)

to come - **kuja** (keeps "ku-"; **walikuja** - they came)

to come from - **kutoka** (**unatoka wapi?** - where do you come from?)

to drink - **kunywa** (keeps "ku-"; **atakunywa** - s/he will drink)

to eat - **kula** (keeps "ku-"; **tumekula** - we have eaten)

to give - **kupa** (keeps "ku"; **alikupa** - s/he gave)

to go - **kwenda** (ie ku-enda; **unaenda** or **unaenda** - you are going)

to hear - **kusikia** (**hajasikia** - s/he hasn't heard yet)

to like/love - **kupenda** (**anapenda kulala** - s/he likes to sleep)

to look - **kutazama** (**utatazama** - you looked)

to meet - **kuonana** (**tutaonana** - we will meet, ie "see you")

to say, speak - **kusema** (**alisema** - s/he said)

to see - **kuona** (**niliona** - I saw)

to sleep - **kulala** (**hatukulala** - we didn't sleep)

to stay - **kukaa** (**mtakaa?** - will you (plural) stay?)

to think - **kufikiri** (**ninafikiri** or **nafikiri** - I think)

to be tired - **kuchoka** (**sichoki** - I'm not tired)

to understand - **kuelewa** (**sielewi** - I don't understand)

to want - **kutaka** (**ninataka** or **nataka** - I want)

To be and to have: two special cases

To be - **kuwa** - is not used in the present. It keeps "ku-"; **watakuwa** - they will be. In the present, "to be" in the sense of "am" "are" or "is" is simply **ni** or, in the negative ("am not", "isn't", "aren't"), **si**. These very common constructions are often used with a personal pronoun as listed on p.689. For example: **Mimi si Mkenya, ni mtalii** - I'm not Kenyan, I'm a tourist, or **Yeye ni mbaya** - S/he's bad.

To have - **kuwa na** - is literally "to be with", as in **nilikuwa na mbwa** - "I had a dog",

with a personal verb prefix in front. In the present it's simpler still: **nina, una, ana** - I have, you have s/he has; **tuna, mna, wana** - we have, you (plural) have, they have. Thus: **nina gari** (literally "I with car"- I have a car).

Also useful is the suffix **-ko**, which means to be in a place, and takes the same prefixes except that the prefix for "he" or "she" is **yu-** instead of a-. Hence **niko wapi?** - where am I? **John yuko wapi?** - where's John? **posta iko wapi?** - where's the post office?

Words and phrases

The words and phrases listed here are all in common usage, but Swahili (like English) is far from being a homogeneous language, so don't be surprised if you sometimes get some funny looks. And, for lack of space for explanation, there are a number of apparent inconsistencies; just ignore them unless you intend to learn the language seriously. These phrases should make you understood at least.

Useful greetings, exchanges and etiquette

Jambo - Hello, good day, how are you? (multipurpose greeting, means "Problems?")

Jambo - (the response) No problems

Hujambo? - (gramatically correct) Hello, good day, how are you?

Sijambo - (gramatically correct) No problems

Habari? - How are things? (literally "News?")

Mambo? - (informal, colloquial, literally "things?/issues?") How goes?/Hi!

Sasa? - (literally "now?") How goes?

Vipi? – (informal, colloquial, no literal translation) What's up?

Safi – (informal, colloquial, literally "pure") Cool, sweet

Fiti – (informal, colloquial, literally "fit") Cool, excellent

Hodi! – Hello? Anyone in? (said on knocking or entering)

Karibu – Come in, enter, welcome (also said on offering something)

Kwaheri/ni – Goodbye to one/many

Asante/ni – Thank you to one/many

sana – very (a common emphasis)

Bwana – Mister, the equivalent of Monsieur in French (**mabwana** is the plural)

Mama – like the French Madame or Mademoiselle, for adult women

kjana – youth, teenager (pl. **vijana**)

mtoto – child, kid (pl. **watoto**)

Jina lako nani? – What's your name?/What are you called?

-zungu – white, European (eg **mzungu** – white person; **wazungu**, white people)

Basics

My name is/I am called – **Jina langu/Nina itwa**

Where are you from? – **Unatoka wapi?**

Where are you staying? – **Unakaa wapi?**

I am from – **Ninatoka**

I am staying (at/in) – **Ninakaa**

See you! – **Tutaonana!** (lit. "We shall meet")

yes, that's right – **ndiyo** (denoting agreement, even with a negative)

no – **hapana**; **siyo**; **la** (Arabic heard mostly on the coast)

I don't understand – **Sifahamu/Sielewi**

I don't speak Swahili, but... – **Sisemi kiswahili, lakini...**

How do you say...in Swahili – **Unasemaje kwa kiswahili...?**

Could you repeat that? – **Sema tena** (lit. "speak again")

Speak slowly – **Sema pole pole**

I don't know – **Sijui**

where (is)? – **wapi?**

here – **hapa**

when? – **lini?**

now – **sasa**

soon – **sasa hivi**

Signs

Hatari! – Danger

Angalia!/Onyo! – Warning

Mbwa mkali! – Fierce dog!

Hakuna njia! – No entry!

why? – **kwa nini?**

because. . . – **kwa sababu. . .**

but – **lakini**

who? – **nani?**

what? – **nini?**

which? – **gani?**

true – **kweli**

and/with – **na**

or – **au**

isn't it? – **siyo?** (equivalent of French n'est-ce pas?)

I'm English (or British)/Scottish/Welsh/Irish/American/Canadian/Australian/a New Zealander/Kenyan

– **Mimi ni mwingereza/mskochi/mwelsh/muairish/mwamerika/mkanada/mwaustralia/mnyuziland/mkenya**

The plural for nationalities will begin with "**Wa-**" instead of "**M-**". Scottish and Welsh readers will no doubt not be pleased to know that **Mwingereza** is used to mean "British" rather than just "English", and that Britain or the UK are usually referred to as **Uingereza**, which strictly speaking should mean England.

And two phrases you're more likely to hear than to ever say

Piga picha mimi! – Take a picture of me!

Saidia maskini! – Help the poor!

Adjectives and idioms

good - -zuri (with a prefix at the front)
bad - -baya (ditto)
big - -kubwa
small - -dogo
a lot of - -ingi
other/another - -ingine
not bad - si mbaya
OK, right, fine - sawa
fine, cool - safi
completely - kabisa
just, only - tu (kitanda kimoja tu - just one bed)
thing(s) - kitu (vitu)

No problem - Hakuna wasiwasi/Hakuna matata
problems, hassles - wasiwasi, matata
friend - rafiki
sorry, pardon - samahani
It's nothing - Si kitu
Excuse me, let me through - Hebu
What's up? - Namna gani?
If God wills it - Inshallah (heard often on the coast)
please - tafadhali (rare upcountry and not heard much on the coast either)

Daily needs

Naweza kulala wapi? - Where can I sleep?
Naweza kulala hapa? - Can I stay here?
chumba (vyumba) - room(s)
kitanda (vitanda) - bed(s)
kiti (viti) - chair(s)
meza - table(s)
choo, bafu - toilet, bathroom
wanaume, wanawakea - men, women
maji ya kuosha - washing water
maji moto/baridi - hot/cold water
Nina njaa - I'm hungry
Nina kiu - I'm thirsty
Iko...? or Kuna...? - Is there any...?
Iko..., or Kuna... - Yes there is...
Haiko..., or Hakuna... - No there isn't any
Ngapi? - How much?
pesa - money
Bei gani...? - What price...?
Pesa ngapi...? - How much is...?
Nataka... - I want...

Sitaki... - I don't want...
Nipe/Niletee - Give me/Bring me (can I have?)
tena - again/more
tosha/basi - enough
ghali sana - expensive
rahisi - cheap (also "easy")
sumni - fifty cents
Punguza kidogo! - Reduce the price, come down a little!
duka - shop
benki - bank
posta - post office
hoteli - café, restaurant
simu - telephone
sigara - cigarettes
Mimi mgonjwa - I'm ill
daktari - doctor
hospitali - hospital
police - polisi
chai - tip, bribe

Travel and directions

kusafiri - travel
safari - journey
bas, basi/mabasi - bus(es)
gari (magari) - car(s), vehicle/s
teksi - taxi
baiskeli - bicycle
treni - train

ndege - plane
chombo/meli - boat/ship
petroli - petrol
njia/ndia - road, path
barabara - highway
kwa miguu (literally "by feet") - on foot/ walking

Inaondoka lini? - When does it leave?

Tutafika lini? - When will we arrive?

pole pole - slowly

haraka - fast, quickly

Ngoja!/Ngoja kidogo! - Wait!/Hang on a moment!

Simama! - Stop!

Unaenda wapi? - Where are you going?

Mpaka wapi? - To where?

Kutoka wapi? - From where?

Kilometa ngapi? - How many kilometres?

Nenda... - I'm going to...

Songa!/Songa kidogo - Move along, squeeze up a little

Twende, endelea - Let's go, carry on

moja kwa moja - straight ahead

kulia - right

kushoto - left

juu - up

chini - down

Nataka kushuka hapa - I want to get off here

Gari imevunjika - The car has broken down

Time, calendar and numbers

What time is it? - Saa ngapi?

four o'clock - saa nne (ie 4 hours past dawn or dusk, in other words 10am or 10pm; see p.96)

quarter past - na robo

half past - na nusu

quarter to - kasa robo

minutes - dakika

daytime - mchana

night time - usiku

dawn - alfajiri

morning - asubuhi

early - mapema

yesterday - jana

today - leo

tomorrow - kesho

last week/this week/next week - wiki iliopita/ wiki hii/wiki ijayo

this year - mwaka huu

this month (lit. "moon") - mwezi huu

Monday - jumatatu

Tuesday - jumanne

Wednesday - jumatano

Thursday - alhamisi

Friday - ijumaa

Saturday - jumamosi

Sunday - jumapili

1 - moja

2 - mbili

3 - tatu

4 - nne

5 - tano

6 - sita

7 - saba

8 - nane

9 - tisa

10 - kumi

11 - kumi na moja

12 - kumi na mbili

20 - ishirini

21 - ishirini na moja

30 - thelathini

40 - arobaini

50 - hamsini

60 - sitini

70 - sabini

80 - themanini

90 - tisini

100 - mia moja

121 - mia moja na ishirini na moja

1000 - elfu

Menu and food terms

The lists below should be adequate for translating most Swahili menus and explaining what you want, though bear in mind that spelling may vary.

Basics

food – **chakula**
water, juice – **maji**
ice – **barafu**
table – **meza**
plate – **sahani**
spoon – **kijiko**
knife – **kisu**
fork – **uma**
bottle – **chupa**
bill – **hesabu**
salt – **chumvi**
pepper – **piripiri**
bread – **mkate**
butter, margarine – **siagi**
sugar – **sukari**

milk – **maziwa**
egg(s) – **yai (mayai)**
fish – **samaki**
meat – **nyama**
vegetables – **mboga**
sauce – **mchuzi**
fruit – **matunda**
more, another – **ingine**
half – **nusu**
roast – **choma (nyama choma** – roast meat, is the food for parties and celebrations)
boiled – **chemka**
fried – **kaanga**
hot – **moto**
cold – **baridi**

Snacks

chapa – unleavened, flat wheat bread, baked on a hot plate or in an oven (tandoor)
halwa – gelatinous sweetmeat, like Turkish delight
keki – cake
kitumbuo – deep-fried rice bread
mandaazi – deep-fried sweet dough, sometimes flavoured with spices, known as mahamri on the coast

maziwalala – yoghurt (literally: "milk asleep")
mkate mayai – "egg-bread": soft thin dough wrapped around fried egg and minced meat
samosa – deep-fried triangular case of chopped meat and vegetables
tosti/slice – slice of bread

Dishes

frigisi – chicken giblets
githeri – kikuyu dish of beans and corn, sometimes with meat
irio/kienyeji – potato, cabbage and beans mashed together (Mount Kenya region)
kima – mince
matoke – green banana, usually boiled and mashed
mboga – vegetables: usually potatoes, carrots and onions in meaty gravy
mchele – plain white rice
michicha – spinach cooked with onions and tomatoes

pilau – rice with spices and meat
sukuma wiki – boiled green leaves, usually a kind of spinach
ugali/sima – cornmeal boiled to a solid porridge with water, occasionally milk; yellow ugali is considered inferior to white but is more nutritious
uji – porridge or gruel made of millet; good for chilly mornings
wali – rice with added fat and spices; almost pilau

Meat

kondo – lamb
kuku – chicken
mbuzi – goat
mushkaki – kebab – small pieces of grilled, marinated meat on or off the skewer

ng'ombe – beef
nguruwe – pork
steki – steak, grilled meat

Fruit

limau – lime
machungwa – oranges
madafu – green coconuts
maembe – mangos
mastafeli – soursops
matopetope – custard apples
nanasi – pineapple

nazi – coconuts
ndimu – lemon
ndizi – bananas
papai – papaya/pawpaw
parachichi – avocado
pera – guava
sandara – mandarins

Vegetables

maharagwe – red kidney beans, often cooked with coconut
mahindi – corn
mbaazi – pigeon peas, small beans
mtama – millet (made into a gruel for breakfast)
muhogo – cassava

ndizi – bananas or plantains (often served with meat dishes)
nyanya – tomatoes (also means grandmother)
sukuma wiki – greens, usually kale or collard greens
viazi – potatoes
vitunguu – onions

Drinks

busaa – maize beer
chai, chai kavu, chai strungi – tea, black tea, strongly spiced tea
changa'a – hootch, illegal spirits
mnazi – coconut palm wine
muratina – porridgey kikuyu honey and millet beer

mabziwalala – fermented milk/almost yoghurt (literally "sleeping milk")
kahawa – coffee
bia, tembo – beer
pombe – booze

Swahili animal names

Animal is **mnyama** (plural **wanyama**) but most species' names are the same in singular and plural.

Bweha – Jackal
Bweha masigio – Bat-eared fox
Choroa – Oryx
Chui – Leopard
Dondoo – Steinbok, grysbok
Duma – Cheetah

Faru – Rhinoceros
Fisi – Hyena
Fisi maji – Otter
Fungo – Civet
Kakukuona– Pangolin
Kalasinga – De Brazza's monkey

Kalunguyeye – Hedgehog
Kamandegere – Springhare
Kanu – Genet
Kiboko – Hippopotamus
Kima – Monkey (usually Sykes' monkey)
Kindi – Ground squirrel
Kobe – Tortoise
Komba – Bushbaby
Kongoni – Hartebeest
Korongo – Roan antelope
Kuru – Waterbuck
Mamba – Crocodile
Mbega – Colobus monkey
Mbuni – Ostrich
Mbuzi mawe – Klipspringer
Mbwa – Dog
Mbwa mwitu – Hunting dog
Mdudu – Insect, bug
Mjusi – Lizard
Mondo – Serval
Muhanga – Aardvark
Ndege – Bird (also means plane)
Ndeze – Cane rat
Ndovu – Elephant
Ngiri – Warthog
Nguchiro – Mongoose
Nguruwe – Pig, hog
Nsya – Duiker
Nungu – Porcupine
Nyamera – Topi

Nyani – Baboon
Nyati – Buffalo
Nyegere – Ratel
Nyoka – Snake
Nyumbu – Wildebeest
Paa – Suni antelope
Paka – Cat
Paka pori – Wild cat
Pala hala – Sable antelope
Papa –Shark
Pembere –Tree hyrax
Pimbi – Rock hyrax
Pofu – Eland
Punda – Horse, ass
Punda milia – Zebra
Sange – Elephant shrew
Simba – Lion
Simbamangu – Caracal
Soko – Chimpanzee
Sunguru – Hare, rabbit
Swala granti – Grant's gazelle
Swala pala – Impala
Swala tomi – Thomson's gazelle
Swala twiga – Gerenuk
Tandala – Kudu
Taya – Oribi
Tohe – Reedbuck
Tumbili – Vervet monkey
Twiga – Giraffe

Other languages

The following brief lists are intended only for introductions and as a springboard for communication. If you'll be spending time in a particular linguistic region, you may be surprised at how difficult it is to track down usable primers and phrasebooks for these languages. Very little material exists for non-native speakers of African languages, though you can make some progress if you're prepared to struggle (with a dictionary) with short novels or the Bible and the like. However, even the prodigiously stocked library of London University's School of African and Oriental Studies is rather bereft of user-friendly material.

Luo (Lake Victoria)

How do you do? – **Iriyo nade?**
Response: – **Ariyo maber!**
Thank you – **Erokamano**

1 – **Achiel**
2 – **Ariyo**
3 – **Adek**

4 – Angwen

5 – Abich

6 – Auchiely

7 – Abiriyo

8 – Aboro

9 – Ochiko

10 – Apar

Maa (Maasai)

Greetings to a man: – **Lo murrani! Supa!**

Response: – **Ipa!**

Greetings to a woman: – **Na kitok! Takuenya!**

Response: – **Iko!**

Thank you (very much!) – **Ashe (naleng!)**

Goodbye! – **Sere!**

1 – **Obo**

2 – **Aare**

3 – **Okuni**

4 – **Oonguan**

5 – **Imiet**

6 – **Ile**

7 – **Oopishana**

8 – **Isiet**

9 – **Ooudo**

10 – **Tomon**

Kikuyu (Central Highlands)

How are things? – **Kweruo atia?**

Fine! – **Ni kwega!**

How are you? – **Waigua atia?**

Are you well? (pl.) – **Wi mwega/Muri ega?**

Response: ("Nothing wrong") – **Asha, ndi mwega**

Goodbye (when you're leaving) – **Tigwo na wega**

Goodbye (when you're staying) – **Thii na wega**

1 – **Imwe**

2 – **Igiri**

3 – **Ithatu**

4 – **Inya**

5 – **Ithano**

6 – **Ithathatu**

7 – **Mugwanja**

8 – **Inyanya**

9 – **Kenda**

10 – **Ikumi**

Glossary

These words are all in common usage. Remember, however, that plural forms often have different beginnings.

AFCO – Armed Forces Catering Ordnance

Age set/age grade – Generation who have passed through rites of passage together, often including people of widely differing chronological ages

ASK – Agricultural Society of Kenya

Askari – Policeman, security guard

Banda – Any kind of hut, usually round and thatched

Bangi, Bhang – Marijuana

Baobab – Species of tree whose trunk retains water

Barabara – Main road

Bau – Traditional calculation game of pebbles and holes

Boda-boda – Bicycle taxi

Boma – A fort or defensive stockade, often used to mean a small village or cluster of huts

Boriti – Mangrove poles, used on the coast for building and exported to the Gulf states for the same purpose

Buibui – The black cover-all cloak and scarf of Swahili women

Bwana – Mister, a polite form of address

Chai – Not just tea, but also the common term for a tip, or more often a small bribe or persuasion

Choo – Toilet (pronounced cho)

Duka – Shop, store

Duka la dawa – Chemist

Enkang – Maasai village

FORD – Forum for the Restoration of Democracy, opposition political party

Fundi – Mechanic, craftsman, expert

Gari – Car

Gema – The ethnic grouping of Gikuyu (Kikuyu), Embu and Meru

GK – Government of Kenya

Group ranch – Community owned grazing area with title deeds, rather than traditional rights

Harambee – "Pull together" – the ideology of peaceable community development

espoused by Jomo Kenyatta. Harambee meetings are local fund-raising gatherings – for schools, clinics, etc – but they've come in for some criticism in recent years as politicians vie to contribute the most money.

Hoteli – Small restaurant, chai shop, café, rarely with accommodation

Jiko – Kitchen or cooker

Jua kali – "Hot sun" – open-air car repairer's yard or small workshop

Kanga – Printed cotton sheet used as a wrap, often incorporating a motto

Kanisa – Church

KANU – Kenya African National Union, Kenya's ruling political party

KBC – Kenya Broadcasting Corporation

Kikoi – Brightly coloured woven cloth

Laibon – Maasai spiritual leader, with the status of regional headman

Lugga/Laga Dry river valley (usually in the north)

Maendeleo – Progress, development

Magendo – Corruption, bribery, abuse of power

Majimboism – The creation of federal blocks in formerly heterogeneous regions – these days associated with ethnic cleansing

Makonde – Beautifully worked Tanzanian wood carving, typically in ebony and representing entwined spirit families – much copied in the tourist markets

Makuti – Palm-leaf roof common on the coast

Malaika – Angel

Malaya – Prostitute

Mama – Common term of address for married women

Manamba – Matatu tout, "turnboy"

Manyatta – Temporary cattle camp, often loosely used for a village (Maasai)

Maskini – The poor, beggars (Saidia maskini! – "Help the poor!")

Matatu – Pick-up taxi, usually full to overflowing

Mbenzi – Member of the rich elite (presumed to have a Mercedes; plural wabenzi)

Miraa – Qat, a natural stimulant (see p.197)

Mkenya – Kenyan (pl. wakenya)

Moran – Man in the warrior age group of Maasai or Samburu (pl. morani)

Msikiti – Mosque

Mtalii – Tourist (pl. watalii)

Mtoto – Child (pl. watoto)

Mungiki – Anti-establishment Kikuyu youth cult that violently rejects western values

Mungu – God

Murram – Red or black clay soil, usually referring to a road

Mwananchi – Person, peasant, worker (pl. wananchi, "the people")

Mzee – Old man: "the Mzee" is Kenyatta

Mzungu – White person (pl. wazungu)

NCCK – National Christian Council of Kenya

NDP – National Development Party, mainly Luo

Ngai – Supreme god of the Kikuyu and other groups

NGO – Non-governmental organization

Ngoma – Dancing, drumming, party, celebration

Njia – Road, path

Nyayo – "Footsteps" – the follow-in-his-footsteps philosophy of post-Kenyatta Kenya propounded by President Moi

Panga – Multi-purpose short machete carried everywhere in the countryside

Pesa – Money, cash (lit. "silver")

Pombe – Booze

Safari – Journey of any kind

Shamba – Small farm, plot

Soda – Fizzy drink, but also a euphemism for a tip

Stage – Matatu stand

Uhuru – Freedom, independence

Ukimwi – AIDS

Ulaya – Europe

Wananchi – See *mwananchi*

Watu – Literally "people", but often used slightly disparagingly by expats and anglo-Kenyans, especially when referring to their staff

Wazungu – See *mzungu*

Travel store

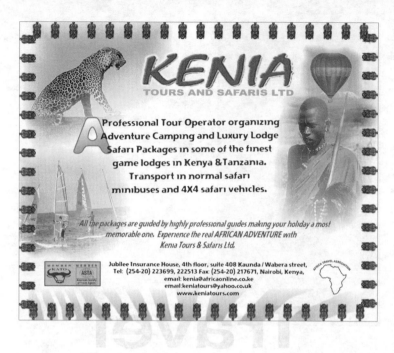

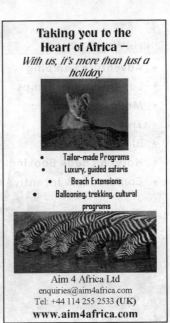

The Driftwood Beach Club

informality at its best.

Something to write home about.

Dear Sharon,

I'm having a wonderful time here! There's so much to do! Between snorkeling, beach volleyball, deep sea fishing, tennis, windsurfing, diving (need I go on?) I couldn't have dreamed of a better holiday. And at the end of the day I get to pamper myself at the health club.

Charles can't believe his luck. What with 10 restaurants to choose from and goodness only knows how many bars! (We're free to use any of the facilities in all three hotels – just as long as we're staying in one of them!) …

Alliance Africana
SEA LODGE

Alliance Jadini
BEACH HOTEL

Alliance Safari
BEACH HOTEL

Alliance Naro Moru
RIVER LODGE

… But really, we've been boating twice already. And he seems to have taken an interest in the aerobics class (!!)

And the kids – bless the Adventures Club, always keeps them busy with something.

You must join us next hols. We'll be going to Alliance Naro Moru River Lodge. It has the most breath-taking view of Mt Kenya and we can go camping and mountain climbing.

Wish you were here. Love lots, Jenny.

Small print and Index

A Rough Guide to Rough Guides

Published in 1982, the first Rough Guide – to Greece – was a student scheme that became a publishing phenomenon. Mark Ellingham, a recent graduate in English from Bristol University, had been travelling in Greece the previous summer and couldn't find the right guidebook. With a small group of friends he wrote his own guide, combining a highly contemporary, journalistic style with a thoroughly practical approach to travellers' needs.

The immediate success of the book spawned a series that rapidly covered dozens of destinations. And, in addition to impecunious backpackers, Rough Guides soon acquired a much broader and older readership that relished the guides' wit and inquisitiveness as much as their enthusiastic, critical approach and value-for-money ethos.

These days, Rough Guides include recommendations from shoestring to luxury and cover more than 200 destinations around the globe, including almost every country in the Americas and Europe, more than half of Africa and most of Asia and Australasia. Our ever-growing team of authors and photographers is spread all over the world, particularly in Europe, the USA and Australia.

SMALL PRINT

In the early 1990s, Rough Guides branched out of travel, with the publication of Rough Guides to World Music, Classical Music and the Internet. All three have become benchmark titles in their fields, spearheading the publication of a wide range of books under the Rough Guide name.

Including the travel series, Rough Guides now number more than 350 titles, covering: phrasebooks, waterproof maps, music guides from Opera to Heavy Metal, reference works as diverse as Conspiracy Theories and Shakespeare, and popular culture books from iPods to Poker. Rough Guides also produce a series of more than 120 World Music CDs in partnership with World Music Network.

Visit www.roughguides.com to see our latest publications.

Rough Guide travel images are available for commercial licensing at www.roughguidespictures.com

Rough Guide credits

Text editors: Richard Lim & Ann-Marie Shaw
Layout: Amit Verma and Pradeep Thapliyal
Cartography: Ashutosh Bharti
Picture editor: Sarah Smithies
Production: Katherine Owers
Proofreader: Helen Castell
Cover design: Chloë Roberts
Editorial: **London** Kate Berens, Claire Saunders, Geoff Howard, Ruth Blackmore, Polly Thomas, Clifton Wilkinson, Alison Murchie, Karoline Densley, Andy Turner, Keith Drew, Edward Aves, Nikki Birrell, Helen Marsden, Alice Park, Sarah Eno, Joe Staines, Duncan Clark, Peter Buckley, Matthew Milton, Tracy Hopkins, David Paul, Lucy White, Ruth Tidball; **New York** Andrew Rosenberg, Steven Horak, AnneLise Sorensen, Amy Hegarty, Hunter Slaton, April Isaacs, Sean Mahoney, Ella Steim
Design & Pictures: **London** Simon Bracken, Dan May, Diana Jarvis, Mark Thomas, Jj Luck, Harriet Mills; **Delhi** Madhulita Mohapatra, Umesh Aggarwal, Ajay Verma, Jessica

Subramanian, Ankur Guha, Sachin Tanwar
Production: Sophie Hewat, Aimee Hampson
Cartography: **London** Maxine Repath, Ed Wright, Katie Lloyd-Jones; **Delhi** Manish Chandra, Rajesh Chhibber, Jai Prakash Mishra, Rajesh Mishra, Animesh Pathak, Jasbir Sandhu, Karobi Gogoi
Online: **New York** Jennifer Gold, Suzanne Welles, Kristin Mingrone; **Delhi** Manik Chauhan, Narender Kumar, Manish Shekhar Jha, Rakesh Kumar, Chhandita Chakravarty
Marketing & Publicity: **London** Richard Trillo, Niki Hanmer, David Wearn, Demelza Dallow, Louise Maher, Jess Carter; **New York** Geoff Colquitt, Megan Kennedy, Katy Ball; **Delhi** Reem Khokhar
Custom publishing and foreign rights: Philippa Hopkins
Manager India: Punita Singh
Series editor: Mark Ellingham
Reference Director: Andrew Lockett
PA to Publishing Director: Megan McIntyre
Publishing Director: Martin Dunford

Publishing information

This 8th edition published September 2006 by
Rough Guides Ltd,
80 Strand, London WC2R 0RL
345 Hudson St, 4th Floor,
New York, NY 10014, USA
14 Local Shopping Centre, Panchsheel Park,
New Delhi 110017, India
Distributed by the Penguin Group
Penguin Books Ltd,
80 Strand, London WC2R 0RL
Penguin Putnam, Inc.
375 Hudson Street, NY 10014, USA
Penguin Group (Australia)
250 Camberwell Road, Camberwell,
Victoria 3124, Australia
Penguin Books Canada Ltd,
10 Alcorn Avenue, Toronto, Ontario,
Canada M4V 1E4
Penguin Group (New Zealand)
Cnr Rosedale and Airborne Roads
Albany, Auckland, New Zealand
Cover design by Peter Dyer.

Typeset in Bembo and Helvetica to an original design by Henry Iles.

Printed and bound in China

© Richard Trillo 2006

No part of this book may be reproduced in any form without permission from the publisher except for the quotation of brief passages in reviews.

736pp includes index

A catalogue record for this book is available from the British Library

ISBN 978-1-84353-651-2

Help us update

We've gone to a lot of effort to ensure that the 8th edition of **The Rough Guide to Kenya** is accurate and up to date. However, things change – places get "discovered", opening hours are notoriously fickle, restaurants and rooms raise prices or lower standards. If you feel we've got it wrong or left something out, we'd like to know, and if you can remember the address, the price, the time, the phone number, so much the better.

We'll credit all contributions, and send a copy of the next edition (or any other Rough Guide

if you prefer) for the best letters. Everyone who writes to us and isn't already a subscriber will receive a copy of our full-colour thrice-yearly newsletter. Please mark letters: **"Rough Guide to Kenya Update"** and send to:

Rough Guides, 80 Strand, London WC2R 0RL, or Rough Guides, 4th Floor, 345 Hudson St, New York, NY 10014. Or send an email to **mail@roughguides.com**

Have your questions answered and tell others about your trip at
www.roughguides.atinfopop.com

Acknowledgements

Richard Trillo thanks everyone who worked on this guide, especially Daniel Jacobs and Nana Luckham for so tirelessly and enthusiastically hitting the road in Kenya; Doug Paterson for another fine musical revamp; and Jens Finke for his enlightening input. For generous aid, ideas and encouragement on previous editions, continuing indebtedness is owed to Jeremy Torr for the amazing English Cycles mountain bike that got me round Kenya in the first place; Bruce Buckland and Michelle Cox in Malindi; Mark Dubin; David Else; Emma Gregg; Okigbo Ojukwu; Rosie Mercer; Tony Stones; Jackie Switzer; Tony Zurbrugg; the Khans in Kisii and Robert Gordon and family. For memorable times in Kenya, my love and thanks to the Weissbart family – who could have mutinied, but kindly chose not to – and to Teresa, Alex, David and Phoebe – for whom mutiny is a way of life.

The author also thanks the following people who helped out so generously on the ground in Kenya: Alan Dixson (Let's Go Travel) and family for kind assistance and hospitality; Kerin Larby at the Driftwood in Malindi; Raymond Matiba and Joseph Ng'ang'a of Alliance Hotels; David Parkinson and Gustavo D Romano Oliveira at Lewa; Patrick Smith and team at *Africa Confidential*; Greg Monson and Richard Yoga at Kicheche, Paul Goldstein at Exodus, Morisson and Mosses at Concorde; Nishit Lakani at Suntrek; Chris, Milli and all at Malewa; Kenneth Nyangena, Nimesh Patel, Melba Correia and Ian Taplin of Rex Resorts; and for useful emails and input: Madhav Bhalla; Michael Dyer; Karen Anne Falconer; Jake Grieves-Cook; Kerstin Handelman; Melanie McGrath; Amanda Mitchell; Pierre E Oberson; Kiri Olsen; and Lina Sideras at the Sheldrick Trust.

From **Daniel Jacobs**, thanks to: Alan Dixson (Let's Go Travel), Nishit Lakhani (Suntrek Safaris), Nelson S. Kakayi, John Wachiaya, Murray Levet, Odd Bredu and Loice, Jack Obonyo, Jane and Julia Barnley (Sirikwa Safaris), David Roden (Marich Pass Field Studies Centre), Tony Kimeri and Peninhah Nderi, Kyongo Kimeri, Solomon Gatilif, Robin Osrin, Richard Griffin, Richard Mwakavi, Joshua Mwariri.

Nana Luckham would like to thank: Joyce Wangui, Rosemary Mugambi and Jackie Sasai at Serena Hotels; Claire Roadley at Ethos Marketing; Tony Sawe at the Palacina Residence & Suites; Joseph Muya at Lake Nakuru Lodges; David Chianda at Gametrackers; Jolly Esmail at Central Rent-a-car; Klas Wallin and Godfrey Mwirigi at Basecamp Explorer; Ken and Lars at Nairobi Backpackers; Susan Linnée; Michael Ngige; Harun Mwangi; Patrick Smith; Binyavanga Wainaina; Ben Swift; Andia Kisia; Michael Chege; Vincent D. Naidu at Timeless African Safaris; James Gituanja and Amos Miriti at the Stanley Hotel, and Alan Dixson at Let's Go Travel.

Readers' letters

Many thanks to the following readers and correspondents, whose letters and emails about the seventh edition have been indispensable in guiding us on our research trips.

Alnavaz Amlani, Kara Babrowski, Agoritsa Baka, Andrew Ball, Catherine Bell, Madhav Bhalla, Gillian Birch, Teresa Borelli, Jeroen Bouman, Sue Britton, Vincent Cahill, Ruth and Joseph Cerere Mulandi, Brian Clark, Riccardo Cocchi, Chloe Day, Dixie Dean, André Dienske, Janet Dobson, Aart Dubbeldam, Mark Fairweather, Chris F, Peter Feys, Chris Frean, Nick Gale, Javier Gómez-García, Hans Goossens, Marimu Goundar, Rory and Susie Graham, David and Sally Griffin, Bruce Havelock, Brian Heeter, Sharon Holmes, Neil Jones, Guido Kerpestein, James Killick, Steffen Juul Krahn, Tania Kurland, Brad Lang, Bruce Leimsidor, Jim Lindsay and Pamela Collett, Monika Luetke-Entrup, Lynn from Vancouver, Sue Macey, Rosie MacGregor, Frances Marr and George Tidmarsh, Tom Martin, Fiona Mackay, Jonathan Moss, Jullie Muteithia, Moire O'Sullivan, Bertha Owuor, Helga Pfeiffer, Naomi Pinkerton, Dennis Pinto, Joonatan Portman, Margaret Powell, Tim Raemaekers, Ben Randell, Liisa Riihimaki, Isaac John Roang, Danielle Rodgers, Craig Rogers, Steve Rogers, Rainie Samuels, Jane Sandham, Hank Selke, Carrie Seltzer, Robert Shaw, Roger Sherrin, Andrew Shufflebotham, Barbara Simons, Steve Smith, Mary Stephen, Paula Stone, Louis L. Straney, Neil & Dee Stratton, Andrew Szefler, Nicole Tami, Rebecca Threlfall, Lesley Thompson, Dagmar Timmer, Jim & Tara Tindal, Andrew Towne, Barbara van Male, Sarah Venn, Erika Voiss, Gavin Wakefield, Natalie Weber, Tilo Wechselberger, Chris Williams, Barbara and Eric Wolstenholme, Sophy Wong, Alice L. Wood, Lee and Colleen Wood, Naomi Wood, Nick Wouters, Edward Wright, and Jeff and Lola.

Photo credits

All photography © Rough Guides except the following:

Title page
Giraffes silhouetted against sunrise, Maasai Mara Kenya © Mike Hill/Alamy

Full page
Elephants, Tsavo East National Park © Giampiccolo Angelo/4Corners Images/SIME

Introduction
Kikuyu man wearing face paint © Images of Africa
Matatu, Nairobi © Daniel Jacobs
On safari © Richard Trillo
Maasai woman wearing traditional bead necklaces and ear ornaments © Images of Africa
Kisumu © Daniel Jacobs

Things not to miss
01 Hut Tarn, 4500m, Mount Kenya © Richard Trillo
02 Turkana overland safaris and flash flood © Richard Trillo
03 Kakamega Forest © Friedrich von Horsten/ Images of Africa
04 Rhino © Richard Trillo
05 Balcony at Shompole © Frans Lanting/Corbis
06 Balloon at Little Governor's Camp, Maasai Mara © Richard Trillo
07 Cave of Skulls, Wundanyi © Richard Trillo
08 Dhow © David Keith Jones/Alamy/Images of Africa Photobank
09 Tea pickers near Kericho © David Keith Jones/ Images of Africa
10 Narrow streets of Lamu town © Nigel Pavitt/ John Warburton-Lee
11 Hornbill in Laikipia ©Richard Trillo
12 Wood carver, Mombasa © Khanh Doh/Eye Ubiquitous
13 Diver © Stephen Frink/Corbis
14 Wildebeest migration, Mara River © David Keith Jones/Images of Africa
15 *Nyama choma* © Richard Trillo
16 Twahir Mohamed and Golden Sounds Band © Twahir Mohamed
17 Elephant and keeper, David Sheldrick Trust © Richard Trillo
18 Bush walk © Richard Trillo
19 Fort Jesus, Mombasa © David Keith Jones/ Images of Africa
20 Gedi Ruins, near Watamu © David Keith Jones/Images of Africa
21 Tiwi beach © Zute Lightfoot/Alamy
22 Hippopotamuses, Mzima Springs © David Keith Jones/Images of Africa

23 Lamu men in traditional dress celebrating Maulidi © Nigel Pavitt/John Warbuton-Lee

Mammals of East Africa colour insert
All images © Bruce Coleman Picture Library except:
Red colobus monkey © Peter Blackwell/Images of Africa
Lesser bushbaby © Peter Davey/Bruce Coleman/ Alamy
Pangolin © Ian Michler/Images of Africa
Lion and lioness © Peter & Beverley Pickford/ Images of Africa
White rhino © Peter & Beverley Pickford/Images of Africa
Bushpig © Nigel J. Dennis/Images of Africa
Maasai giraffe © Geoffrey Morgan/Alamy
Reticulated giraffe © Martin Harvey/Images of Africa
Sharpe's grysbok © Stu Porter/Alamy
Suni antelope © David Keith Jones/Images of Africa/Alamy
Fringe-eared oryx © David Keith Jones/Images of Africa/Alamy

Crafts and shopping colour insert
Crafts shop, Diani © Richard Trillo
Woodcarver, Machakos © Jenny Matthews/Alamy
Women with baskets © Carl & Ann Purcell/Corbis
Turkana wrist-knives © Richard Trillo
Maasai beads © J Marshall/Alamy/Tribaleye Images
Boys making wireframe toys ©Jenny Matthews/ Alamy

Traditional dress colour insert
Pokot woman with traditional brass earrings © Images of Africa
Swahili women, Lamu © Nigel Pavitt/John Warburton-Lee
Samburu warrior © David Keith Jones/Images of Africa
Kikuyu traditional dress © Richard Trillo
Turkana map sharpening *aberait* © Daniel Jacobs
Kikuyu Dancer © Carl & Ann Purcell/Corbis
Luo elder with traditional dress and headdress of ostrich feathers and hippo tusks Kisumu © David Keith Jones/Alamy/Images of Africa/ Photobank

Black and white pictures
p.102 David Sheldrick Trust © Richard Trillo
p.105 Nairobi London-style taxi © Jenny Matthews/Alamy
p.117 *Norfolk Hotel* © Images of Africa
p.127 Matatu © Daniel Jacobs

ROUGH GUIDES

SMALL PRINT

ROUGH GUIDES

SMALL PRINT

Index

Map entries are in colour.

INDEX

725

Map symbols

maps are listed in the full index using coloured text

Regional Maps

— Minor roads (mostly unpaved)
= Main roads (mostly paved)
----- Footpath
—•— Railway
— — Ferry route
— River
—••— International border
—•—• Chapter division boundary
⌃⌃ Mountain range
▲ Mountain peak
〰 Escarpment
〰 Cliff
〰 Hill
〰 Viewpoint
☼ Crater
◠ Cave
⚸ Waterfall
〰 Marshland
〰 Spring
♦ General point of interest
🕯 Lighthouse
⊼ Picnic area
⛳ Golf course
⊠—⊠ Gate
⌂ Lodge
⌂ Park HQ
⚠ Campsite
⊙ Monument
✕ Airport

✕ Airstrip
▨ Park/reserve
🗀 Forest
▨ Beach
▨ Glacier

Town Maps

= Roads
---- Unpaved roads
∴ Ruin
◉ Accommodation
▣ Restaurant
★ Bus stop
🛢 Petrol station
⊞ Hospital
@ Internet access
ⓘ Information office
© Telephone
⊠ Post office
🅿 Parking
⛪ Monastery
✡ Synagogue
☪ Mosque
▲ Temple
⊞ Church
▨ Building
◯ Stadium
⊞ Cemetery
▨ Park

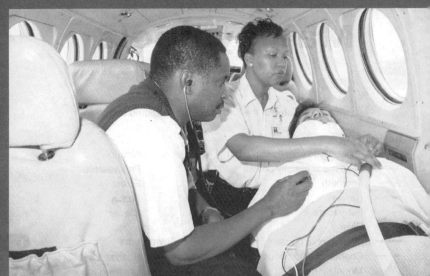

US$15*could save a life. Yours

Just once, can we persuade you to give selfishly

If you find yourself within 1,000kms of Nairobi and in need o emergency medical treatment, look to the heavens

The Flying Doctors is an Air Ambulance service for East Africa and beyond, including world wi repatriation. We have our own fleet of fully equipped aircraft and ground ambulances that car for the needs of our patients ranging from routine transfers to intensive care transports.

The Flying Doctors provides membership for free evacuation and transfer flights to Nairobi fo members in Kenya, Uganda, Tanzania and Burundi.

As a visitor to any of the countries mentioned, you would benefit from our service in case of a emergency but also help us reach out to millions of local people in need of vital medical servi

We have very affordable rates for visitors coming to above mentioned countries and annual ra

All unutilised membership subscriptions go towards support of AMREF's outreach programm and charity evacuations.

To become a member, or for more details, call Nairobi +254 20 601594/602495 or email flyingdocs@amrefke.org. You may also apply online via www.amref.org